POETRY IN ...
An Anthl...

POETRY IN ENGLISH
An Anthology

General Editor
M.L. ROSENTHAL

The Middle Ages
BERYL ROWLAND
York University

The Sixteenth and Seventeenth Centuries
A. KENT HIEATT
University of Western Ontario

The Restoration and Eighteenth Century
HOWARD WEINBROT
University of Wisconsin

The Nineteenth Century
V.A. DE LUCA
University of Toronto

The Twentieth Century
The Early Moderns
M.L. ROSENTHAL
New York University

The Late Moderns
ROSEMARY SULLIVAN
University of Toronto

Versification
SALLY M. GALL
Editor, *EIDOS/The International
Prosody Bulletin*

New York   Oxford

OXFORD UNIVERSITY PRESS
1987

Oxford University Press

Oxford   New York   Toronto
Delhi   Bombay   Calcutta   Madras   Karachi
Petaling Jaya   Singapore   Hong Kong   Tokyo
Nairobi   Dar es Salaam   Cape Town
Melbourne   Auckland

and associated companies in
Beirut   Berlin   Ibadan   Nicosia

Published by Oxford University Press, Inc.
198 Madison Avenue, New York, New York 10016-4314

Oxford is a registered trademark of Oxford University Press

Library of Congress Cataloging-in-Publication Data
Poetry in English.
Includes index.
1. English poetry
I. Rosenthal, M.L. (Macha Louis), 1917–
PR1175.P657   1987   821'.008   87-14059
ISBN 0-19-520539-1

6 8 9 7

Printed in the United States of America

ACKNOWLEDGMENTS

A.R. AMMONS. "Corsons Inlet" and "He Held Radical Light" are reprinted from *The Selected Poems, 1951-1977*, of A.R. Ammons, by permission of W.W. Norton & Company, Inc. Copyright © 1977, 1975, 1974, 1972, 1971, 1970, 1966, 1965, 1964, 1955 by A.R. Ammons.

ANONYMOUS. From "Layamon's Brut 'The Passing of Arthur' " and "The Proverbs of Alfred" from *Middle English Literature* by Charles W. Dunn and Edward T. Byrnes, copyright © 1973 by Harcourt Brace Jovanovich, Inc. Reprinted by permission of the publisher. "Wife's Lament," "Seafarer," and "Brunanburg" from *10 Old English Poems* by K. Mallone. Reprinted by permission of The Johns Hopkins University Press. "Noah" from *The Wakefield Pageants* edited by A.C. Cawley. Reprinted by permission of Manchester University Press. "Beowulf" from *Beowulf*, translated by Burton Raffel. Copyright © 1963 by Burton Raffel. Reprinted by arrangement with New American Library, New York, New York. "Adam Lay Y-bounden," "Canute at Ely," "I Sing of a Maiden," "Jolly Jankin," "Judas," "Now Springs the Spray," "Of Jesu Christ I Sing," "Piers Plowman," and "Ubi Sunt" from *The Oxford Book of Medieval English Verse* by C. & K. Sisam (1970). Reprinted by permission of Oxford University Press. "The Three Ravens" from *The Oxford Book of Ballads* edited by James Kinsley (1969). Reprinted by permission of Oxford University Press. "Sir Gawain and the Green Knight" from *Sir Gawain and the Green Knight* edited by R.A. Waldron (1970). Reprinted by permission of R.A. Waldron and Northwestern University Press.

JOHN ASHBERY. Reprinted by permission of Viking Penguin, Inc.: "My Erotic Double" from *As We Know* by John Ashbery. Copyright © John Ashbery 1979. "At North Farm" from *A Wave* by John Ashbery. Copyright © 1981, 1982, 1983, 1984 by John Ashbery. "Crazy Weather" from *Houseboat Days* by John Ashbery. Copyright © 1977 by John Ashbery.

MARGARET ATWOOD. "Disembarking at Quebec" from *Journals of Susanna Moodie* © Oxford University Press 1970. "Torture" and "Earth" from *True Stories* © Margaret Atwood 1981. Used by permission of Oxford University Press Canada.

W.H. AUDEN. Reprinted from *W.H. Auden: Collected Poems* edited by Edward Mendelson, by permission of Random House, Inc., and Faber and Faber Ltd.: "The Decoys" copyright 1934 and renewed 1962 by W.H. Auden; "O What Is That Sound," "On This Island" copyright 1937 and renewed 1965 by W.H. Auden; "Sonnets from China, X" copyright 1945 by W.H. Auden; "Lullaby" copyright © 1973 by the Estate of W.H. Auden; "Musée des Beaux Arts," "In Memory of W.B. Yeats" copyright 1940 and renewed 1968 by W.H. Auden; "September 1, 1939" copyright 1940 by W.H. Auden; From "Horae Canonicae 1. Prime" copyright 1951 by W.H. Auden; "The Shield of Achilles" copyright 1952 by W.H. Auden.

IMAMU AMIRI BARAKA (LE ROI JONES). "I Substitute for the Dead Lecturer" from *The Dead Lecturer*. Reprinted by permission of The Sterling Lord Agency, Inc. Copyright © 1964 by Le Roi Jones. "The Turncoat" and "An Agony, As Now" from *Selected Poetry of Amiri Baraka/Le Roi Jones*. Copyright © 1979 by Amiri Baraka. Reprinted by permission of William Morrow & Co.

JOHN BERRYMAN. Reprinted by permission of Farrar, Straus and Giroux, Inc. and Faber and Faber Ltd.: "Sonnet #7" from *Berryman's Sonnets* by John Berryman. Copyright © 1952, 1967 by John Berryman. "Scholar at the Orchid Pavilion" from *Delusions, Etc.* by John Berryman. Copyright © 1969, 1971 by John Berryman. Copyright © 1972 by the Estate of John Berryman. "Dream Songs #1, 29, 53, 76" from *Seventy-Seven Dream Songs by John Berryman*. Copyright © 1959, 1962, 1963, 1964 by John Berryman.

ELIZABETH BISHOP. "The Fish," "Sestina," "In the Waiting Room," and "One Art" from *The Complete Poems 1927-1979* by Elizabeth Bishop, copyright © 1979, 1983 by Alice Helen Methfessel. Reprinted by permission of Farrar, Straus and Giroux Inc.

GWENDOLYN BROOKS. All poems are reprinted from *The World of Gwendolyn Brooks* by permission of the author.

BASIL BUNTING. "Briggflatts: An Autobiography I" © Basil Bunting 1978. Reprinted from Basil Bunting's *Collected Poems* (1978) by permission of Oxford University Press.

GEOFFREY CHAUCER. From "The Canterbury Tales 'The General Prologue,' 'The Friar's Prologue and Tale,' 'The Pardoners' Prologue and Tale,' '' from "Troylus and Criseyde 'Book III' 'Book V''' and "To Rosemounde" from *The Complete Poetry and Prose of Geoffrey Chaucer*, edited by John H. Fisher. Copyright © 1977 by Holt, Rinehart & Winston. Reprinted by permission of CBS College Publishing.

AUSTIN CLARKE. From "Mnemosyne Lay in Dust, I, V" from *Collected Poems*. Used by permission of The Dolmen Press and Wake Forest University Press.

ROBERT CREELEY. "The Whip," "Kore," and "The Rain" from *For Love Poems 1950–1960*, copyright © 1962 Robert Creeley, reprinted with the permission of Charles Scribner's Sons, and *Poems 1950-1965* by Robert Creeley, reprinted by permission of Marion Boyars Publishers Ltd.

E.E. CUMMINGS. Reprinted by permission of Liveright Publishing Corporation: "Buffalo Bill's," "goodbye Betty, don't remember me," "ladies and gentle this little girl," "who's most afraid of death?" from *Tulips and Chimneys* by E.E. Cummings. Copyright © 1923, 1925 and renewed 1951, 1953 by E.E. Cummings, copyright © 1973, 1976 by The Trustees for the E.E. Cummings Trust. Copyright © 1973, 1976 by George James Firmage. "r-p-o-p-h-e-s-s-a-g-r" reprinted from *No Thanks* by E.E. Cummings. Copyright © 1935 by E.E. Cummings, copyright © 1968 by Marion Morehouse Cummings, copyright © 1973, 1978 by The Trustees for the E.E. Cummings Trust, copyright © 1973, 1978 by George James Firmage, "ponder, darling, these busted statues" reprinted from *IS 5* by E.E. Cummings. Copyright © 1926 by Horace Liveright, copyright © 1954 by E.E. Cummings, copyright © 1985 by the E.E. Cummings Trust, copyright © 1985 by George James Firmage. Reprinted by permission of Harcourt Brace Jovanovich, Inc. from *Complete Poems 1913–1962* by E.E. Cummings: "plato told," copyright 1944 by E.E. Cummings, renewed 1972 by Nancy T. Andrews; "silence," copyright 1958 by E.E. Cummings. All poems also reprinted by permission of Grafton Books, A Division of the Collins Publishing Group, from *The Complete Poems 1913–1962* by e.e. cummings.

JAMES DICKEY. Reprinted by permission of Wesleyan University Press: "The Performance," copyright © 1960 by James Dickey, from *Into the Stone*; "The Heaven of Animals," copyright © 1961 by James Dickey, from *Drowning with Others*. "The Heaven of Animals" first appeared in *The New Yorker*.

H.D. (HILDA DOOLITTLE). "Pear Tree" from *H.D., Collected Poems: 1912–1914*. Copyright © 1982 by the Estate of Hilda Doolittle. "Heat" and "Oread" from *H.D., Selected Poems*. Copyright © 1925, 1953, 1957 by Norman Holmes Pearson. Reprinted by permission of New Directions Publishing Corporation and Cancarnet Press Limited.

WILLIAM DUNBAR. "The Dance of the Seven Deadly Sins" from *Middle English Literature* by Charles W. Dunn and Edward T. Byrnes, copyright © 1973 by Harcourt Brace Jovanovich, Inc. Reprinted by permission of the publisher.

ROBERT DUNCAN. "Ingmar Bergman's Seventh Seal" from *The Opening of the Field* by Robert Duncan. Copyright © 1960 by Robert Duncan. "Strains of Sight" and "After a Passage in Baudelaire" from Robert Duncan *Roots and Branches*. © 1964 by Robert Duncan. Reprinted by permission of New Directions Publishing Corporation.

T.S. ELIOT. Reprinted by permission of Harcourt Brace Jovanovich, Inc.: "The Love Song of J. Alfred Prufrock," "The Waste Land," "Marina," "Journey of the Magi," "Rhapsody on a Windy Night" from *Collected Poems 1909–1962* by T.S. Eliot, copyright 1936 by Harcourt Brace Jovanovich, Inc., copyright © 1963, 1964 by T.S. Eliot; "Burnt Norton" from *Four Quartets* by T.S. Eliot, copyright 1943 by T.S. Eliot, renewed 1972 by Esme Valerie Eliot. All poems also reprinted by permission of Faber and Faber Ltd. from *Collected Poems 1909–1962* by T.S. Eliot.

WILLIAM EMPSON. All poems reprinted from *Collected Poems of William Empson*, copyright 1949, 1977 by William Empson by permission of Harcourt Brace Jovanovich, Inc., Lady Empson and Chatto & Windus.

KENNETH FEARING. All poems reprinted from *Collected Poems* by Kenneth Fearing by permission of Indiana University Press.

ROBERT FROST. All poems from *The Poetry of Robert Frost* edited by Edward Connery Lathem. Copyright 1923, 1928, 1930, 1939, 1947, © 1969 by Holt, Rinehart and Winston. Copyright 1936, 1942, 1951, © 1956, 1958, 1962 by Robert Frost. Copyright © 1964, 1967, 1970, 1975 by Lesley Frost Ballantine. Reprinted by permission of Henry Holt and Company, the Estate of Robert Frost and Jan Cape Ltd.

GINSBERG. From *The Collected Poems* by Allen Ginsberg "To Aunt Rose" and "Back on Times

Square, Dreaming of Times Square". Copyright © 1958 by Allen Ginsberg. "America" copyright © 1956, 1959 by Allen Ginsberg. Reprinted by permission of Harper & Row, Publishers, Inc. All poems also from Allen Ginsberg *Collected Poems 1947–1980* (Viking Books, 1985), copyright © Allen Ginsberg, 1984. Reproduced by permission of Penguin Books Ltd.

ROBERT GRAVES. "Down, Wanton, Down" and "To Juan at the Winter Solstice" from *Collected Poems 1975* by Robert Graves. Used by permission of A.P. Watt Ltd. on behalf of The Executors of the Estate of Robert Graves.

THOM GUNN. Reprinted by permission of Faber and Faber Ltd.: "On the Move" from *The Sense of Movement* by Thom Gunn, "In Santa Maria del Popolo" and "A Map of the City" from *My Sad Captains* by Thom Gunn, and "For Signs" from *Moly* by Thom Gunn. All poems also reprinted by permission of Farrar, Straus and Giroux, Inc., from *Selected Poems 1950–1975* by Thom Gunn. Copyright © 1957, 1958, 1961, 1967, 1971, 1973, 1974, 1975, 1976, 1979 by Thom Gunn.

RAMON GUTHRIE. All poems from *Maximum Security Ward and Other Poems* by Ramon Guthrie. Copyright © 1984 by Sally M. Gall. Reprinted by permission of Persea Books, Inc. 225 Lafayette Street, New York, N.Y. 10012.

MICHAEL HARPER. All poems from *Images of Kin: New and Selected Poems* © 1970, 1971, 1972, 1973, 1974, 1975, 1976, 1977 by Michael S. Harper. Reprinted by permission of University of Illinois Press.

ROBERT HAYDEN. Selections are reprinted from *Angle of Ascent, New and Selected Poems* by Robert Hayden, by permission of Liveright Publishing Corporation. Copyright © 1975, 1972, 1970, 1966 by Robert Hayden.

SEAMUS HEANEY. "Casualty" and "The Skunk" from *Fieldwork* by Seamus Heaney. Copyright © 1976, 1979 by Seamus Heaney. Reprinted by permission of Farrar, Straus and Giroux, Inc. and Faber and Faber Ltd.

ROBERT HENRYSON. "The Testament of Cresseid" from *Middle English Literature* by Charles W. Dunn and Edward T. Byrnes, copyright © 1973 by Harcourt Brace Jovanovich, Inc. Reprinted by permission of the publisher.

GEOFFREY HILL. Reprinted by permission of Andre Deutsch Ltd.: "Mercian Hymns, VI, IX, XII, XXV" from *Mercian Hymns* and "An Apology for the Revival of Christian Architecture in England" from *Tenebrae*. All poems also reprinted from *Collected Poems* by Geoffrey Hill. Copyright © 1985 by Geoffrey Hill by permission of Oxford University Press, Inc.

LANGSTON HUGHES. "50-50" and "Down and Out" copyright 1942 by Alfred A. Knopf, Inc. Copyright © 1959 by Langston Hughes. Reprinted from *Selected Poems of Langston Hughes* by permission of Alfred A. Knopf, Inc. "Letter" from *Montage of a Dream*, copyright © 1951 by Langston Hughes, copyright © renewed 1979 by George Houston Bass. Reprinted by permission of Harold Ober Associates Incorporated.

TED HUGHES. Reprinted by permission of Faber and Faber Ltd.: "Pike" from *Lupercal* by Ted Hughes; "Two Legends," "That Moment," "Dawn's Rose," and "Littleblood" from *Crow* by Ted Hughes. Reprinted by permission of Harper & Row, Publishers, Inc.: "Two Legends" from *Crow* by Ted Hughes. Copyright © 1971 by Ted Hughes; "Pike" copyright © 1959 by Ted Hughes, "That Moment," "Dawn's Rose," "Littleblood" copyright © 1971 by Ted Hughes from *New Selected Poems* by Ted Hughes.

RANDALL JARRELL. Reprinted by permission of Farrar, Straus and Giroux, Inc.: "The Black Swan," "The Orient Express," "The Death of the Ball Turret Gunner" from *The Complete Poems* by Randall Jarrell. "The Elementary Scene" from *The Woman at the Washington Zoo*. Copyright © 1960 by Randall Jarrell. Reprinted with permission of Atheneum Publishers, Inc. All poems also reprinted by permission of Faber and Faber Ltd. from *The Complete Poems* by Randall Jarrell.

DAVID JONES. Reprinted by permission of Faber and Faber Ltd. from *In Parenthesis* by David Jones.

PATRICK KAVANAGH. "Father Mat" from *Collected Poems*. Reprinted by permission of Devin-Adair Publishing Company, and by kind permission of Katherine B. Kavanagh, c/o Peter Fallon, 19 Oakdown Road, Dublin 14, Ireland.

GALWAY KINNELL. "The Dead Shall Be Raised Incorruptible" from *The Book of Nightmares* by Galway Kinnell. Copyright © 1971 by Galway Kinnell. Reprinted by permission of Houghton Mifflin Company.

THOMAS KINSELLA. "His Father's Hands" from *One and Other Poems*. Used by permission of The Dolmen Press Ltd. "First Light" and "Ancestor" used by permission of the author.

PHILIP LARKIN. "Toads" and "Poetry of Departures" by Philip Larkin are reprinted from *The Less Deceived* by permission of The Marvell Press, England. "Here" and "Mr. Bleaney" are reprinted from *The Whitsun Weddings* by Philip Larkin by permission of Faber and Faber Ltd.

DENISE LEVERTOV. Reprinted by permission of New Directions Publishing Corporation: "Pleasures" and "Terror" from Denise Levertov, *Collected Earlier Poems 1940–1960*. Copyright © 1959 by Denise Levertov Goodman. "Losing Track" from Denise Levertov, *Poems 1960–1967*. Copyright © 1963 by Denise Levertov Goodman. First published in *Poetry*.

ROBERT LOWELL. Reprinted by permission of Farrar, Straus and Giroux, Inc.: "Memories of West Street and Lepke," "Skunk Hour," "For the Union Dead," and "Water," from *Selected Poems* by Robert Lowell. Copyright © 1976 by Robert Lowell. "Suicide" from *Day By Day* by Robert Lowell. Copyright © 1975, 1976, 1977 by Robert Lowell. Reprinted by permission of Faber and Faber Ltd.: "Memories of West Street and Lepke" and "Skunk Hour" from *Life Studies* by Robert Lowell, "For the Union Dead" and "Water" from *For the Union Dead* by Robet Lowell, and "Suicide" from *Day By Day* by Robert Lowell.

HUGH MACDIARMID (CHRISTOPHER GRIEVE). "Love," "O Wha's the Bride?" and "Old Wife in High Spirits" are reprinted with permission of Macmillan Publishing Company from *Collected Poems* by Hugh MacDiarmid. © Christopher Murray Grieve 1948, 1962. Copyright © 1967 by Macmillan Publishing Company.

ROBERT MANNYNG OF BOURNE. "The Dancers of Colbek" from *The Oxford Book of Medieval English Verse* by C. & K. Sisam (1970). Reprinted by permission of Oxford University Press.

JAMES MERRILL. "Between Us," "The Mad Scene," and "Days of 1964" from *Nights and Days* (1966) in *From the First Nine Poems 1946–1976*. Copyright © 1982 by James Merrill. Reprinted with the permission of Atheneum Publishers, Inc.

W.S. MERWIN. Reprinted with the permission of Atheneum Publishers, Inc. and David Higham Associates Limited: "The Bathers" from *Green With Beasts* (1956) and "The Drunk in the Furnace" from *The Drunk in the Furnace* (1960) in *The First Four Book of Poems*. Copyright © 1975 W.S. Merwin. "For a Coming Extinction" from *The Lice*. Copyright © 1967 W.S. Merwin.

JOHN MONTAGUE. All poems from *Selected Poems*, Exile Editions (Canada) and Wake Forest University Press (U.S.). Reprinted by permission of the author.

MARIANNE MOORE. Reprinted with permission of Macmillan Publishing Company: "Poetry" and "A Grave" from *Collected Poems* by Marianne Moore. Copyright 1935 by Marianne Moore, renewed 1963 by Marianne Moore and T.S. Eliot. "The Mind Is an Enchanting Thing" from *Collected Poems* by Marianne Moore. Copyright 1944 by Marianne Moore, renewed 1972 by Marianne Moore. All poems also reprinted by permission of Faber and Faber Ltd. from *The Complete Poems of Marianne Moore*.

EDWIN MUIR. All poems from *Collected Poems* by Edwin Muir. Copyright © 1960 by Willa Muir. Reprinted by permission of Oxford University Press, Inc., and Faber and Faber Ltd.

HOWARD NEMEROV. "History of a Literary Movement" and "The Goose Fish" from *The Collected Poems of Howard Nemerov* are reprinted by permission of the author.

FRANK O'HARA. "The Day Lady Died" from *Lunch Poems* by Frank O'Hara. Copyright © 1964 by Frank O'Hara. Reprinted by permission of City Lights Books. "Chez Jane" copyright © 1954 by Maureen Granville-Smith, Administratix of the Estate of Frank O'Hara and "Why I Am Not a Painter" copyright © 1958 by Maureen Granville-Smith, Administratrix of the Estate of Frank O'Hara are reprinted from *The Collected Poems of Frank O'Hara*, by permission of Alfred A. Knopf, Inc.

CHARLES OLSON. "Maximus to Himself," "Song 3" and "Maximus to Gloucester, Letter 27" from *The Maximus Poems* by Charles Olson. © 1983 The Regents of the University of California. Reprinted by permission of the University of California Press.

P.K. PAGE. All poems from *The Glass Air: Selected Poems*, reprinted by permission of the author.

SYLVIA PLATH. Reprinted by permission of Harper & Row, Publishers, Inc. from *The Collected Poems of Sylvia Plath* edited by Ted Hughes: "Daddy," "Balloons" and "Edge" copyright © 1963 by Ted

Hughes, "Ariel" and "Words" copyright © 1965 by The Estate of Sylvia Plath. All poems also reprinted by permission of Olwyn Hughes from *Collected Poems* by Sylvia Plath, published by Faber and Faber, London, copyright Ted Hughes 1965 and 1981.

EZRA POUND. "The Return," "The Coming of War: Actaeon," "In a Station of the Metro," "Hugh Selwyn Mauberley, Part I: I, II, IV, V," reprinted by permission of New Directions Publishing Corporation from Ezra Pound, *Personae*, copyright 1926 by Ezra Pound, and Faber and Faber Ltd. from *Collected Shorter Poems of Ezra Pound*. "Canto I, XIII, XLV, XLVII, LXXIV, LXXXI" from Ezra Pound, *The Cantos of Ezra Pound*. Copyright 1934, 1940, 1948 by Ezra Pound © 1972 by the Estate of Ezra Pound. Reprinted by permission of New Directions Publishing Corporation and Faber and Faber Ltd.

JOHN CROWE RANSOM. "Bells for John Whiteside's Daughter," "Janet Waking," and "Dead Boy" copyright 1924 by Alfred A. Knopf, Inc. and renewed 1952 by John Crowe Ransom. Copyright 1927 by Alfred A. Knopf, Inc. and renewed 1955 by John Crowe Ransom. Reprinted from *Selected Poems Third Edition, Revised and Enlarged* by John Crowe Ransom, by permission of Alfred A. Knopf, Inc. All poems also from *Selected Poems* by John Crowe Ransom (Methuen London, Ltd.), used by permission of Laurence Pollinger Limited.

PETER REDGROVE. "For No Good Reason" and "Required of You this Night" from *Sons of My Skin: Selected Poems 1954-74*. "Light Hotel" from *The Weddings at Nether Powers and Other New Poems*. Reprinted by permission of Routledge & Kegan Paul Ltd.

ADRIENNE RICH. Reprinted by permission of W.W. Norton & Company, Inc.: "The Phenomenology of Anger" from *Poems Selected and New, 1950-1974*, by Adrienne Rich. Copyright © 1974, 1973, 1971, 1969, 1966 by W.W. Norton & Company, Inc. Copyright © 1967, 1963, 1962, 1961, 1960, 1959, 1958, 1957, 1956, 1955, 1954, 1953, 1952, 1951 by Adrienne Rich. "Your small hands, precisely equal to my own" from "Twenty-One Love Poems" from *The Dream of a Common Language, Poems 1974-1977*, by Adrienne Rich. Copyright © 1974 by W.W. Norton & Company, Inc.

EDWIN ARLINGTON ROBINSON. Reprinted by permission of Macmillan Publishing Company from *Collected Poems* by Edwin Arlington Robinson: "Eros Turannos" copyright 1916 by Edwin Arlington Robinson, renewed 1944 by Ruth Nivison; "Mr. Flood's Party" copyright 1921 by Edwin Arlington Robinson, renewed 1949 by Ruth Nivison.

THEODORE ROETHE. Reprinted by permission of Doubleday & Company, Inc., and Faber and Faber Ltd. from *The Collected Poems of Theodore Roethke* "My Papa's Waltz" copyright 1942 by The Hearst Corporation, "Elegy for Jane" and "The Visitant" copyright 1950 by Theodore Roethke, "I Knew a Woman" copyright 1954 by Theodore Roethke, "In a Dark Time" copyright © 1960 by Beatrice Roethke as Administratrix of the Estate of Theodore Roethke.

CARL SANDBURG. Reprinted by permission of Harcourt Brace Jovanovich, Inc.: "The Lawyers Know Too Much" and "Balloon Faces" from *Smoke and Steel* by Carl Sandburg, copyright 1930 by Harcourt Brace Jovanovich, Inc.; renewed 1948 by Carl Sandburg. "When I asked for fish . . ." from "Whiffs of the Ohio River at Cincinnati" in *Good Morning, America*, copyright 1928, 1956 by Carl Sandburg.

SIEGFRIED SASSOON. "The General" and "Repression of War Experience" from *Collected Poems* by Siegfried Sassoon. Copyright 1918, 1920 by E.P. Dutton & Co. Copyright 1936, 1946, 1947, 1948 by Siegfried Sassoon. Reprinted by permission of Viking Penguin Inc., and George Sassoon.

ANNE SEXTON. Reprinted by permission of Houghton Mifflin Company and The Sterling Lord Agency, Inc.: "Ringing the Bells" from *To Bedlam and Partway Back* by Anne Sexton. Copyright © 1960 by the Nation Associates, Inc. Copyright © 1969 by Anne Sexton. "The Starry Night" from *All My Pretty Ones* by Anne Sexton. Copyright © 1961, 1962 by Anne Sexton. "End, Middle, Beginning" from *45 Mercy Street* by Anne Sexton. Copyright © 1976 by Linda Grey Sexton and Loring Conant, Jr., Executors of the Estate of Anne Sexton.

LOUIS SIMPSON. Reprinted by permission of Wesleyan University Press: "Carentan O Carentan" copyright © 1949 by Louis Simpson from *A Dream of Governors*; "A Story about Chicken Soup" copyright © 1963 by Louis Simpson from *At the End of the Open Road*.

STEVIE SMITH. All poems from Stevie Smith, *Collected Poems*, copyright © 1972 by Stevie Smith, reprinted by permission of New Directions Publishing Corporation and *The Collected Poems of Stevie Smith* (Penguin Modern Classics) by permission of James MacGibbon.

GARY SNYDER. All poems from Gary Snyder, *Turtle Island*. Copyright © 1972 by Gary Snyder. Reprinted by permission of New Directions Publishing Corporation.

WALLACE STEVENS. Reprinted from *The Collected Poems of Wallace Stevens*, by permission of Alfred A. Knopf, Inc. and Faber and Faber Ltd.: "Peter Quince at the Clavier," "The Emperor of Ice-Cream," "Sunday Morning," "Thirteen Ways of Looking at a Blackbird," and "The Snow Man" copyright 1923 and renewed 1951 by Wallace Stevens; "The Idea of Order at Key West" copyright 1936 by Wallace Stevens and renewed 1964 by Holly Stevens; from "The Auroras of Autumn" copyright 1948 by Wallace Stevens.

DYLAN THOMAS. All poems from Dylan Thomas, *Poems of Dylan Thomas*. Copyright 1939, 1946 by New Directions Publishing Corporation, 1945 by the Trustees for the copyrights of Dylan Thomas, 1952 by Dylan Thomas. Reprinted by permission of New Directions Publishing Corporation and David Higham Associates Limited

CHARLES TOMLINSON. "Paring the Apple," "Farewell to Van Gogh," and "On the Hall at Stowey" © Charles Tomlinson 1985. Reprinted from Charles Tomlinson's *Collected Poems* (1985) by permission of Oxford University Press.

ROBERT PENN WARREN. "Little Girl Wakes Early" copyright © 1985 by Robert Penn Warren. "Bearded Oaks" copyright © 1942 and renewed 1970 by Robert Penn Warren. Reprinted from *New and Selected Poems, 1923-1985* by Robert Penn Warren, by permission of Random House, Inc.

RICHARD WILBUR. Reprinted by permission of Harcourt Brace Jovanovich, Inc.: "The Beautiful Changes" from *The Beautiful Changes and Other Poems*, copyright 1947, 1975 by Richard Wilbur; "Love Calls Us to the Things of This World" from *Things of This World*, copyright © 1956 by Richard Wilbur; "Advice to a Prophet," copyright © 1959 by Richard Wilbur, reprinted from his volume *Advice to A Prophet and Other Poems*. First published in *The New Yorker*. Reprinted by permission of Faber and Faber Ltd.: "The Beautiful Changes" and "Love Calls Us to the Things of This World" from *Poems 1943-1956* by Richard Wilbur; "Advice to a Prophet" from *Advice to a Prophet* by Richard Wilbur.

WILLIAM CARLOS WILLIAMS. Reprinted by permission of New Directions Publishing Corporation: "Danse Russe," "The Widow's Lament in Springtime," "Spring and All," "To Elsie," "The Red Wheelbarrow," "At the Ball Game," "The Yachts" from William Carlos Williams' *Collected Earlier Poems*. Copyright 1939 by New Directions Publishing Corporation. "The Dance" from William Carlos Williams' *Collected Later Poems*. Copyright 1944 by William Carlos Williams. "Patterson, Book V, ii" from William Carlos Williams' *Paterson*. Copyright © 1949, 1958 by William Carlos Williams.

JAMES WRIGHT. Reprinted by permission of Wesleyan University Press: "A Blessing" copyright © 1961 by James Wright from *The Branch Will Not Break*, first appeared in *Poetry*; "Willy Lyons" copyright © 1962 by James Wright from *Shall We Gather at the River*. Reprinted by permission of Random House, Inc.: "The Journey" from *This Journey* by James Wright. Copyright © 1982 by Anne Wright, Executrix of the Estate of James Wright.

W.B. YEATS. Reprinted with permission of Macmillan Publishing Company, A.P. Watt Ltd on behalf of Michael B. Yeats and Macmillan London, from *The Poems* by W.B. Yeats, edited by Richard J. Finneran: "The Magi," "The Dolls," "Memory," copyright 1916 by Macmillan Publishing Company, renewed 1944 by Bertha Georgie Yeats; "A Deep-Sworn Vow," copyright 1919 by Macmillan Publishing Company, renewed 1947 by Bertha Georgie Yeats; "Easter 1916," "The Second Coming," copyright 1924 by Macmillan Publishing Company, renewed 1952 by Bertha Georgie Yeats; "Sailing to Byzantium," "The Tower," "The Road at My Door," "Nineteen Hundred and Nineteen, Parts I & II," "Two Songs from a Play," "Leda and the Swan," "Among School Children," copyright 1928 by Macmillan Publishing Company, renewed 1956 by Georgie Yeats; "A Dialogue of Self and Soul," "Byzantium," "Crazy Jane Talks with the Bishop," copyright 1933 by Macmillan Publishing Company, renewed 1961 by Bertha Georgie Yeats; "Long-Legged Fly," "Politics," copyright 1940 by Georgie Yeats, renewed 1968 by Bertha Georgie Yeats, Michael Butler Yeats and Anne Yeats.

LOUIS ZUKOFSKY. From "29 Poems, 2,27" and "The Ways" from *ALL, The Collected Short Poems of Louis Zukofsky*. Copyright © 1971, 1966, 1965 by Louis Zukofsky. Reprinted by permission of W.W. Norton & Company Inc., the Estate of Louis Zukofsky and Jonathan Cape Ltd.

There are a few poems whose copyright owners have not been located after diligent inquiry. The publishers would be grateful for information enabling them to make suitable acknowledgments in future printings.

CONTENTS

*AN ASTERISK DENOTES SELECTIONS THAT ARE NOT COMPLETE WORKS.

The Sixteenth Century

The Seventeenth Century

The Restoration and Eighteenth Century

The Twentieth Century

Versification

INTRODUCTION

English poetry began over a thousand years ago, in a language as foreign to us now as German or Swedish: the language of the Anglo-Saxon invaders who overran the Celtic inhabitants of Britain. The rough power and heavy alliteration of their verse still find echoes in modern poetry. Partly under the influence of later invaders from France, Middle English evolved. Geoffrey Chaucer, the first great English poet known to us by name, adapted many verse forms borrowed from other European traditions to this very flexible phase of English speech. By the fifteenth century, modern English more or less as we know it had emerged, although its free-wheeling spelling and its vocabulary, some of which has become archaic or obsolete, can often make it look rather strange to us today.

In our own time, five centuries later, our sense of "English" keeps changing. The language has spread, by conquest and colonization, first to nearby Scotland, Wales, and Ireland, then to North America, and finally to far-off Australia and New Zealand and as a second language in many other countries. In the process, it has absorbed elements of various native languages and cultures. It is a far cry from the primitive beat and lament of the Anglo-Saxon "Seafarer" to the courtly sixteenth-century sonnets of Sir Philip Sidney, and it is an even farther cry, perhaps, to the blues-based rhythms of the American black poet Langston Hughes. The stream of verse in English is broad, deep, and intricately winding.

This volume offers a thoughtful sampling from ten centuries of the unpredictable evolution of lyrical, narrative, meditative, and dramatic poems in all their incidental sub-varieties, ranging from ballad to epic, from satire to prayer, and from pure song, giddily irrational but lovely, to inspired intellectual pyrotechnics. By far the greater number of poems here printed are from the last four hundred years, with the highest proportion of these allotted to the periods since 1800. But a generous representation of earlier work is also desirable — and should remind us that we are neither cleverer nor more talented than our ancestors near or distant.

In fact, we shall grasp the import of poetry best if we hear it as the living voice of memory: the immortal part of human experience. The more poetry we come to know, the more intimately close the past becomes, and the more we realize how much of it has persisted into the present. In good poems we can feel the pulse of other lives, of whatever time-period, as if they were our own.

Three examples mentioned earlier show vividly how this happens. The Anglo-Saxon "Seafarer" expresses the loneliness, hardships, and bitter nostalgia of a northern vassal in exile, and the fatalistic piety he summons up in his misery. Sidney's "With how sad steps, Oh Moon, thou climb'st the skies" is the elegantly stylized complaint of a lover whose constant devotion has met with scorn. A reader familiar with sophisticated love poetry of the English Renaissance will recognize the grieving tone and the symbolic address to the moon (seen as another sad lover) as typically "Petrarchan." That is, they represent an attitude, a turn of phrase and rhetoric, and a verse pattern made fashionable by the fourteenth-century Italian poet Petrarch. Hughes's "Down and Out" is as stylized in its way as Sidney's Petrarchan sonnet. It is so close to the wailing realism of a modern blues-song that it might actually be one. All these pieces, far apart though they are in time and culture, speak convincingly out of their different worlds of experience. All of them, too, will seem alien to most modern readers: the first because of the relatively primitive tribal life and elemental physical hardship it reflects; the second because of the ritualized and aristocratic conventions, with a philosophical ingredient ultimately derived from Plato, surrounding its view of love; and the third because of its atmosphere of abject and squalid poverty. Despite these alien aspects, however, the poems do connect with any willing reader, for the inner humanity of their feelings of loss and need must strike responsive chords. Their whole art lies precisely in the way their phrasing, rhythms, sound, and movement create this effect.

Clearly, then, poets are artists shaping what they make out of all these elements of language. Therefore they are often drawn to systematic study of what other poets before them have accomplished. Just as composers and other musicians usually have their heads full of melodies and technical discoveries of their predecessors, so do poets as well, and so do all people who grow to love poetry and to expand their curiosity about it: its origins, its chief works and their creators, its varied tendencies and how they grow.

The selections that follow have been made by a team of experienced teachers and scholars, each chosen as a specialist in his or her literary period. Each has had primary responsibility for the selections, headnotes, and annotations for that period: Professor Beryl Rowland for Old and Middle English, Professor A. Kent Hieatt for the sixteenth and seventeenth centuries, Professor Howard Weinbrot for the Restoration and eighteenth century, Professor V.A. DeLuca for the nineteenth, the undersigned for the earlier twentieth century, and Professor Rosemary Sullivan for the period after Dylan Thomas. Our aim has been to gather, in a volume of reasonable size, as much as we can of the best poetry in the best available versions — that is, the latest texts approved by the poets themselves or by competent scholars.

A related purpose is to print work especially characteristic of individual poets, major tendencies, and periods. Most of the famous poems of the tradition will be found here, but we also take into account new kinds of information (and recent critical thinking) about poems and texts. Thus, we include a complete sequence by Emily Dickinson, chosen from the many she stitched together in the little homemade notebooks known as her "fascicles." To see the poems of this sequence in the order she herself arranged them in — ignored until very recently by all her editors — is to rediscover her genius in an entirely new light. Our sense of poetry of the past is not a constant. It may hold fairly firm for a quarter-century or so, but critical consensus shifts. It was not so long ago that Shelley was being discounted by leading critics, John Clare's name was rarely mentioned, and the writing of Ireland's leading poets after Yeats was virtually unknown outside of Dublin.

Still, certain landmarks, from Chaucer's tales to Shakespeare's sonnets to Keats's odes to modern masterpieces like Yeats's "Leda and the Swan" and Eliot's *The Waste Land*, have held firmly enough — miracles of imagination that one returns to at intervals throughout a lifetime and finds somehow different each time. Sometimes, it is true, an "established" touchstone may lose its glow over the years while still commanding respectful attention. Or a poet's work, though uneven or "controversial" as to quality, may yet remain truly memorable as in the case of Poe. Thoughts such as these are bound to arise concerning the poems in an anthology representing such a sweep of centuries; and they become all the more challenging as one approaches the most recent poetry, for obvious reasons.

In any case, certain fundamental questions need to be raised concerning *any* poem, apart from the plain matters of what it's all "about" and what the literal meaning of words and allusions may be. What is the dominant tone or level of feeling, and how does it develop in coloration and intensity between the beginning and end of the poem? How does the form used—blank verse, say, or rhyming couplets, or some variety of free verse—reinforce these qualities? Where the style and preoccupations of a poem seem more or less unfamiliar to the modern reader, it is especially important to get at the human feeling imbedded in the language: the sting of intellectual wit, or the pleasure in well-turned expressions of sentiment or wisdom in the tones of cultivated conversation in seventeenth- and eighteenth-century verse, for instance; or the saturation in Christian faith, sometimes felt as the simplest sort of piety, sometimes as an aspect of realistic presentation of the lives and speech of ordinary folk, and sometimes expressed tortuously and with sophisticated questioning, in earlier centuries.

Because poetry is much more an art than is generally recognized, it is important to bear in mind that true poems do not exist simply to convey certain ideas or attitudes, or to illustrate historical tendencies. Almost inevitably they will certainly do these things, by implication if not by direct statement, as all human creations must. Nevertheless, argument and discussion belong primarily to the realm of prose. The reverberations of sensuous images, emotional evocation, and patterns of sound are far more subliminal and psychologically expressive in poetry — so much so that the best poems are organic structures of subjective feeling and awareness rather than reasoned proofs or explanations. The bulk of the poems here have been chosen with this principle in mind, since philosophy, though often beloved of poets, is not our province. On the other hand, we have taken some thought to make sure that the most persistently employed metrical and other formal techniques of poets writing in English are well represented. To assist students in recognizing these techniques and their significance, we include an essay on prosody — the art of versification — by Dr. Sally M. Gall. This essay is at some pains not only to make clear the function and primary elements of prosody but also to suggest ways in which the anthologized poems illustrate them.

Ideally, poems should be read in tranquil privacy or shared companionably by like-minded friends who read aloud to one another, shouting "Bravo!" or "Thumbs down!" at appropriate points. Ideally, too, all one would ordinarily need by way of help when reading would be a good dictionary and perhaps an atlas and a handbook of mythology. The most important part of one's education is the part one undertakes on one's own — looking up a book and reading it if an author refers to it in an interesting way; checking on historical events a poem seems to take for granted the reader knows about; or talking over a provocative but somewhat ambiguous passage with some knowledgeable friend. We have tried to avoid over-explaining poems in our headnotes on authors and in our annotations to individual poems. But for one reason or another, we have unapologetically given aid where it would seem to do the most good, as when a poem has a particularly elusive or intricate line of association that might well put off an inexperienced reader. We have kept the pleasure principle in the foreground of this anthology; pleasure, after all, is a considerable inducement to the study of an art.

The full extent of a good poem's artistry and its emotional nuances — which of course account for the pleasure it affords — becomes clearer when we read it aloud. Poems need to be *heard*, and shared with others if possible, just as do musical compositions. While experienced readers have the knack of hearing silently, as it were, they also know how revealing an actual *performance* of a poem can be. (In the same way, people who are sufficiently musical can "hear" scores simply by reading them, but are hardly contented with that limited experience.) Also, reading aloud prevents our getting bogged down in a single phrase or line and losing touch with the poem's whole movement.

Finally, "getting" a poem's whole movement helps us see that poetry is more than arbitrary "self-expression." Like other arts, it intensifies normal experience and perception by its concentrated focus; and it normalizes unusual subjective states by enabling us to share them.

The editors are, first and foremost, grateful to Dr. Richard Teleky of the Canadian branch of the Oxford University Press, who originally envisioned this anthology and who has been instrumental in overseeing it through every phase. We also want to thank Sally Livingston, Patricia Sillers, and Phyllis Wilson of Oxford Canada for their assistance in various stages of production, as well as Margaret Kaufhold, for her handsome cover design.

M.L.R.

A NOTE ON TEXTS AND ORGANIZATION

The editors of this anthology have selected the latest texts approved either by the authors or — when such texts are not definitely known — by their best editors. Although a few minor alterations have been made for the sake of clarity or consistency within a given poem, in the interest of authenticity no attempt has been made at overall standardization of spelling or numbering style. Dates of publication appear on the right at the end of each poem or sequence; a second date in italics indicates significant alterations. Dates of composition, when known, appear on the left; in cases where the manuscript itself includes the date or place of composition, this information is italicized. The editors' annotations appear at the bottom of each page (or, when a second poem begins on the same page, following the poem in question). They are indicated by superscript numbers within the poems except in the Middle Ages section, where the glosses accompanying the source texts are tagged by line numbers only.

The Middle Ages

OLD ENGLISH POETRY

When did English poetry begin? Why is Chaucer who was writing in the late fourteenth century called "the Father of English poetry"? The answers are not far to seek. The earliest English poetry took its language and its literary form from North West Germany, from whence came the tribes that settled in Britain in the fifth century A.D. That it was written down at all was due to the scribes in the monasteries. Christianity in Britain, which owed its impetus to Augustine's little band coming from Rome to Kent in A.D. 597 and Aidan's coming from Ionia to Northumbria in 634–35, was responsible for the survival of Old English poetry as we know it.

Today Old English looks like a foreign language. Even by the eleventh century Christianity and the Viking invasions had drastically affected its vocabulary. With the catastrophic Norman conquest of 1066, the continuity of the language itself was broken. For the next two hundred years the languages used by the educated and powerful were French and Latin. The language of the new royal court was a French dialect. By the time English came to be used once more as a literary language, it had changed: a large number of words had been introduced from France, many older native words had disappeared, the elaborate system of declensions of nouns, pronouns, and adjectives had broken down, vowel sounds and the conjugation of verbs had been modified, and the syntax was different. After the Conquest, some literature, especially that of a popular kind such as the lyric, was no doubt transmitted orally, and didactic prose, historical records, and even some poetry continued to be written down in the vernacular. Nevertheless, most poetry after the Conquest was in Latin and French. When Chaucer chose to write in English, he had to forge a new vocabulary for poetry, adapting inherited native verbal traditions to the poetics of the more sophisticated European cultures of his day.

There are two major kinds of Old English poetry: one reflects biblical themes, the other the Germanic heroic tradition. The works are anonymous, apart from a technically sophisticated hymn of praise attributed by Bede to Caedmon, an illiterate lay brother in a Northumbrian monastery in the seventh century, and some poems signed by Cynewulf who probably lived early in the ninth century. Since all the material was written down in the monasteries, not surprisingly, Christian poems predominate, many of them based on Latin sources. These include biblical paraphrase, stories based on Genesis, Exodus, Daniel, and the apocryphal book of Judas, scenes from the life of Christ and the lives of the saints, homilies, metrical paternosters, and psalms.

Much Old English secular poetry has a pagan background although it was given a Christian coloring when written down. The original *scop* or bard, a poet very highly regarded at the Germanic court, was accustomed to chanting traditional poems and composing new ones at feasts and on ceremonial occasions. Such poems present an ancient heathen culture and extol the old way of life. They are permeated with what has been termed "Anglo-Saxon melancholy," nostalgia, grim awareness of past or imminent misfortunes, the inevitability of fate, and a sense of stoical resignation alleviated solely by exultation in the courage and prowess of heroes. Only heroes achieved a kind of immortality: by dying gloriously, they earned enduring fame when their stories were commemorated in the songs of the *scop*. Such is the ethos not only of the great epic *Beowulf*, but of battle pieces such as the tenth-century "Brunanburg" which describes how Athelstan, King of England, and his brother Edmund vanquished an invading force of Scots and Vikings.

The two other Old English poems in this anthology are seemingly subjective and personal. "Wife's Lament" is an enigmatic monologue. The speaker's husband has gone overseas, leaving her to be harassed by relatives and forced to live in a lonely hut in the woods. While the simplicity of diction movingly conveys a specific picture of the wife's plight, the poem treats of the husband's motives and reactions with tantalizing ambiguity. "Seafarer" is also a monologue. The first part presents a speaker who describes his hardships and loneliness at sea. A sense of personal alienation is coupled with a nostalgia for the past seafaring life, and the poet vividly conveys sounds and sights of nature in language drawn from the traditional stock of poetic phrases. Yet

this description is also symbolic. The second part consists of direct homiletic exhortation. The call of the sea is a call to the Christian path of self-denial and suffering; the landlubber is the unbeliever, delighting in the easy life.

Because Old English is in effect a foreign language to most readers, we here present modern translations in the hope that they will suggest the elemental energy of the originals and lead interested readers to seek them out.

BEOWULF

Beowulf, a poem of 3,182 lines, is the chief literary monument of Old English poetry. Although not comparable in structure or design to the *Iliad* or the *Aeneid*, it is an epic that nevertheless possesses a genuine unity of its own. The manuscript containing the poem, Cotton Vitellius A XV, was written about the year A.D. 1000, but the original was probably set down in the first half of the eighth century, when the old pagan story was retold by a Christian poet. The plot, part folk tale, part heroic legend, originated in northern Europe and reflects tribal life and its ideals. Beowulf is the first hero to have the characteristics of a Christian knight, and his story is told in high style, with a dignity fitting the subject—which is no less than the exaltation of the Germanic courtly culture.

The poem is skillfully constructed around two widely separated episodes. In the first Beowulf, a youthful prince of the Geats, goes to Denmark and kills two monsters, one in the king's hall, the other in an underwater lair. In the second Beowulf becomes king and is killed in his old age while slaying a dragon that is ravaging his kingdom. In the first two passages selected, the evil monster Grendel comes from the mere (lake) and despoils Herot, the royal hall of the Danes. He continues his slaughter year after year until he is mortally wounded in combat with the hero, Beowulf. In the third passage

a firebreathing dragon, enraged when a runaway slave steals a jeweled cup from his treasure-hoard, lays waste the land and burns the royal hall. Despite his advanced age, Beowulf, now king, prepares for a fight to the death.

It is not the story element that makes *Beowulf* a great poem but the dramatic speeches, visual descriptions, history, and folklore concerning three Scandinavian kingdoms, analyses of reactions and motivations, and philosophical digressions, all presented with the utmost sophistication in a rich, highly stylized, poetic language.

Characteristic of this poem and also of other Old English poems is a nostalgic recapitulation of the glorious achievements of the past and of the virtues of the heroic age. The most important relationship was that between the warrior and his lord, which was readily Christianized in the religious poetry of the same period. The warrior loyally served his king as a companion rather than as a servant and was rewarded by goods and lifelong friendship. The bond was also strong between kinsmen: if a relative was killed, either revenge or "wergild" (manprice) had to be exacted from the murderer. Tribal society was thus an arena for innumerable blood feuds. Stability was deceptive, and a sense of doom, even a cosmic irony, hung over every enterprise. Fate was inextricably linked with the supreme virtue—

personal courage. Heroes fought their way to glory. They gloried in battle while the ravens circled over the battlefield, eager for carrion. But the predominant tone was elegiac: courage might influence fate, yet for all the testing, fate was fixed ("wyrd biδ ful araed").

Old English poetry is accentual and alliterative. Its meter is defined by stress patterns, not by vowel length or number of syllables. Each line normally contains a varying number of unaccented and unalliterated syllables; three accented syllables in the line, two in the first part and one in the second, all begin with the same consonant, or with vowels, and take the chief emphasis in the line, as these lines from Beowulf, 102–03, indicate:

$$x \quad x \quad / \quad x \quad /$$
waes se grimma gaēst Grendel hāten,

$$/ \; x \quad / \quad / \; x$$
māere mearcstapa se þe mōras hēold

(The grim spirit was called Grendel, a well-known patroller of the marches, who held the moors, the fen, and the fastness.)

From Beowulf

100 So Hrothgar's men lived happy in his hall
Till the monster stirred, that demon, that fiend,
Grendel, who haunted the moors, the wild
Marshes, and made his home in a hell
Not hell but earth. He was spawned in that slime,
Conceived by a pair of those monsters born
Of Cain, murderous creatures banished
By God, punished forever for the crime
Of Abel's death. The Almighty drove
Those demons out, and their exile was bitter,
110 Shut away from men; they split
Into a thousand forms of evil—spirits
And fiends, goblins, monsters, giants,
A brood forever opposing the Lord's
Will, and again and again defeated.
    Then, when darkness had dropped, Grendel
Went up to Herot, wondering what the warriors
Would do in that hall when their drinking was done.
He found them sprawled in sleep, suspecting
Nothing, their dreams undisturbed. The monster's
120 Thoughts were as quick as his greed or his claws:
He slipped through the door and there in the silence
Snatched up thirty men, smashed them
Unknowing in their beds and ran out with their bodies,
The blood dripping behind him, back
To his lair, delighted with his night's slaughter.

            . . .

710   Out from the marsh, from the foot of misty
Hills and bogs, bearing God's hatred,
Grendel came, hoping to kill
Anyone he could trap on this trip to high Herot.

He moved quickly through the cloudy night,
Up from his swampland, sliding silently
Toward that gold-shining hall. He had visited Hrothgar's
Home before, knew the way—
But never, before nor after that night,
Found Herot defended so firmly, his reception
720 So harsh. He journeyed, forever joyless,
Straight to the door, then snapped it open,
Tore its iron fasteners with a touch
And rushed angrily over the threshold.
He strode quickly across the inlaid
Floor, snarling and fierce: his eyes
Gleamed in the darkness, burned with a gruesome
Light. Then he stopped, seeing the hall
Crowded with sleeping warriors, stuffed
With rows of young soldiers resting together.
730 And his heart laughed, he relished the sight,
Intended to tear the life from those bodies
By morning; the monster's mind was hot
With the thought of food and the feasting his belly
Would soon know. But fate, that night, intended
Grendel to gnaw the broken bones
Of his last human supper. Human
Eyes were watching his evil steps,
Waiting to see his swift hard claws.
Grendel snatched at the first Geat
740 He came to, ripped him apart, cut
His body to bits with powerful jaws,
Drank the blood from his veins and bolted
Him down, hands and feet; death
And Grendel's great teeth came together,
Snapping life shut. Then he stepped to another
Still body, clutched at Beowulf with his claws,
Grasped at a strong-hearted wakeful sleeper
—And was instantly seized himself, claws
Bent back as Beowulf leaned up on one arm.
750   That shepherd of evil, guardian of crime,
Knew at once that nowhere on earth
Had he met a man whose hands were harder;
His mind was flooded with fear—but nothing
Could take his talons and himself from that tight
Hard grip. Grendel's one thought was to run
From Beowulf, flee back to his marsh and hide there:
This was a different Herot than the hall he had emptied.
But Higlac's follower remembered his final
Boast and, standing erect, stopped
760 The monster's flight, fastened those claws
In his fists till they cracked, clutched Grendel
Closer. The infamous killer fought
For his freedom, wanting no flesh but retreat,

Desiring nothing but escape; his claws
Had been caught, he was trapped. That trip to Herot
Was a miserable journey for the writhing monster!
The high hall rang, its roof boards swayed,
And Danes shook with terror. Down
The aisles the battle swept, angry
770 And wild. Herot trembled, wonderfully
Built to withstand the blows, the struggling
Great bodies beating at its beautiful walls;
Shaped and fastened with iron, inside
And out, artfully worked, the building
Stood firm. Its benches rattled, fell
To the floor, gold-covered boards grating
As Grendel and Beowulf battled across them.
Hrothgar's wise men had fashioned Herot
To stand forever; only fire,
780 They had planned, could shatter what such skill had put
Together, swallow in hot flames such splendor
Of ivory and iron and wood. Suddenly
The sounds changed, the Danes started
In new terror, cowering in their beds as the terrible
Screams of the Almighty's enemy sang
In the darkness, the horrible shrieks of pain
And defeat, the tears torn out of Grendel's
Taut throat, hell's captive caught in the arms
Of him who of all the men on earth
790 Was the strongest.
That mighty protector of men
Meant to hold the monster till its life
Leaped out, knowing the fiend was no use
To anyone in Denmark. All of Beowulf's
Band had jumped from their beds, ancestral
Swords raised and ready, determined
To protect their prince if they could. Their courage
Was great but all wasted: they could hack at Grendel
From every side, trying to open
800 A path for his evil soul, but their points
Could not hurt him, the sharpest and hardest iron
Could not scratch at his skin, for that sin-stained demon
Had bewitched all men's weapons, laid spells
That blunted every mortal man's blade.
And yet his time had come, his days
Were over, his death near; down
To hell he would go, swept groaning and helpless
To the waiting hands of still worse fiends.
Now he discovered—once the afflictor
810 Of men, tormentor of their days—what it meant
To feud with Almighty God: Grendel
Saw that his strength was deserting him, his claws
Bound fast, Higlac's brave follower tearing at

His hands. The monster's hatred rose higher,
But his power had gone. He twisted in pain,
And the bleeding sinews deep in his shoulder
Snapped, muscle and bone split
And broke. The battle was over, Beowulf
Had been granted new glory: Grendel escaped,
820   But wounded as he was could flee to his den,
His miserable hole at the bottom of the marsh,
Only to die, to wait for the end
Of all his days. And after that bloody
Combat the Danes laughed with delight.
He who had come to them from across the sea,
Bold and strong-minded, had driven affliction
Off, purged Herot clean. He was happy,
Now, with that night's fierce work; the Danes
Had been served as he'd boasted he'd serve them; Beowulf,
830   A prince of the Geats, had killed Grendel,
Ended the grief, the sorrow, the suffering
Forced on Hrothgar's helpless people
By a bloodthirsty fiend. No Dane doubted
The victory, for the proof, hanging high
From the rafters where Beowulf had hung it, was the monster's
Arm, claw and shoulder and all.

· · ·

. . . Beowulf ruled in Geatland,
Took the throne he'd refused, once,
And held it long and well. He was old
With years and wisdom, fifty winters
2210   A king, when a dragon awoke from its darkness
And dreams and brought terror to his people. The beast
Had slept in a huge stone tower, with a hidden
Path beneath; a man stumbled on
The entrance, went in, discovered the ancient
Treasure, the pagan jewels and gold
The dragon had been guarding, and dazzled and greedy
Stole a gem-studded cup, and fled.
But now the dragon hid nothing, neither
The theft nor itself; it swept through the darkness,
2220   And all Geatland knew its anger.

But the thief had not come to steal; he stole,
And roused the dragon, not from desire
But need. He was someone's slave, had been beaten
By his masters, had run from all men's sight,
But with no place to hide; then he found the hidden
Path, and used it. And once inside,
Seeing the sleeping beast, staring as it
Yawned and stretched, not wanting to wake it,
Terror-struck, he turned and ran for his life,

2230   Taking the jeweled cup.
                       That tower
    Was heaped high with hidden treasure, stored there
    Years before by the last survivor
    Of a noble race, ancient riches
    Left in the darkness as the end of a dynasty
    Came. Death had taken them, one
    By one, and the warrior who watched over all
    That remained mourned their fate, expecting,
    Soon, the same for himself, knowing
2240   The gold and jewels he had guarded so long
    Could not bring him pleasure much longer. He brought
    The precious cups, the armor and the ancient
    Swords, to a stone tower built
    Near the sea, below a cliff, a sealed
    Fortress with no windows, no doors, waves
    In front of it, rocks behind. Then he spoke:
      "Take these treasures, earth, now that no one
    Living can enjoy them. They were yours, in the beginning;
    Allow them to return. War and terror
2250   Have swept away my people, shut
    Their eyes to delight and to living, closed
    The door to all gladness. No one is left
    To lift these swords, polish these jeweled
    Cups: no one leads, no one follows. These hammered
    Helmets, worked with gold, will tarnish
    And crack; the hands that should clean and polish them
    Are still forever. And these mail shirts, worn
    In battle, once, while swords crashed
    And blades bit into shields and men,
2260   Will rust away like the warriors who owned them.
    None of these treasures will travel to distant
    Lands, following their lords. The harp's
    Bright song, the hawk crossing through the hall
    On its swift wings, the stallion tramping
    In the courtyard—all gone, creatures of every
    Kind, and their masters, hurled to the grave!"
      And so he spoke, sadly, of those
    Long dead, and lived from day to day,
    Joyless, until, at last, death touched
2270   His heart and took him too. And a stalker
    In the night, a flaming dragon, found
    The treasure unguarded; he whom men fear
    Came flying through the darkness, wrapped in fire,
    Seeking caves and stone-split ruins
    But finding gold. Then it stayed, buried
    Itself with heathen silver and jewels
    It could neither use nor ever abandon.
      So mankind's enemy, the mighty beast,
    Slept in those stone walls for hundreds

2280 Of years; a runaway slave roused it,
Stole a jeweled cup and bought
His master's forgiveness, begged for mercy
And was pardoned when his delighted lord took the present
He bore, turned it in his hands and stared
At the ancient carvings. The cup brought peace
To a slave, pleased his master, but stirred
A dragon's anger. It turned, hunting
The thief's tracks, and found them, saw
Where its visitor had come and gone. He'd survived,
2290 Had come close enough to touch its scaly
Head and yet lived, as it lifted its cavernous
Jaws, through the grace of almighty God
And a pair of quiet, quick-moving feet.
The dragon followed his steps, anxious
To find the man who had robbed it of silver
And sleep; it circled around and around
The tower, determined to catch him, but could not,
He had run too fast, the wilderness was empty.
The beast went back to its treasure, planning
2300 A bloody revenge, and found what was missing,
Saw what thieving hands had stolen.
Then it crouched on the stones, counting off
The hours till the Almighty's candle went out,
And evening came, and wild with anger
It could fly burning across the land, killing
And destroying with its breath. Then the sun was gone,
And its heart was glad: glowing with rage
It left the tower, impatient to repay
Its enemies. The people suffered, everyone
2310 Lived in terror, but when Beowulf had learned
Of their trouble his fate was worse, and came quickly.

    Vomiting fire and smoke, the dragon
Burned down their homes. They watched in horror
As the flames rose up: the angry monster
Meant to leave nothing alive. And the signs
Of its anger flickered and glowed in the darkness,
Visible for miles, tokens of its hate
And its cruelty, spread like a warning to the Geats
Who had broken its rest. Then it hurried back
2320 To its tower, to its hidden treasure, before dawn
Could come. It had wrapped its flames around
The Geats, now it trusted in stone
Walls, and its strength, to protect it. But they would not.
    Then they came to Beowulf, their king, and announced
That his hall, his throne, the best of buildings,
Had melted away in the dragon's burning
Breath. Their words brought misery, Beowulf's
Sorrow beat at his heart: he accused

Himself of breaking God's law, of bringing
2330 The Almighty's anger down on his people.
Reproach pounded in his breast, gloomy
And dark, and the world seemed a different place.
But the hall was gone, the dragon's molten
Breath had licked across it, burned it
To ashes, near the shore it had guarded. The Geats
Deserved revenge; Beowulf, their leader
And lord, began to plan it, ordered
A battle-shield shaped of iron, knowing that
Wood would be useless, that no linden shield
2340 Could help him, protect him, in the flaming heat
Of the beast's breath. That noble prince
Would end his days on earth, soon,
Would leave this brief life, but would take the dragon
With him, tear it from the heaped-up treasure
It had guarded so long. And he'd go to it alone . . . .

8th century

Wife's Lament

I sing of myself, a sorrowful woman,
of my own unhap. All I have felt,
since I grew up, of ill let me say,
be it new or old—never more than now:
I have borne the cross of my cares, always.

First my friend went far from home,
over the waves; I was awake at dawn,
I wondered where he was, day and night.
Then I went out, unhappy wife,
10 lonely and wretched, looking for fellowship.

The man's kindred, with minds of darkness,
began to plot to part us two,
that we might lead a life most hateful,
live most aloof, and I longed for him.

My lord bade me lodge in this hut
Little I know of love-making here,
of sweet friendship. My soul is mournful
to find my man, my friend, my mate
heavy-hearted, happy not at all,
20 hiding his mood, harboring ill
under a blithe bearing. We both made vow
that death alone should drive us asunder,
naught else in the world; that was, but is no more;

it is now as if it had never been,
that friendship of ours. Far and nigh now
I must bear the hate of my best beloved.

They drove me out to dwell in the woods
under an oak tree, in that old stone-heap.
Fallen is this house; I am filled with yearning.
30   The dales are dim, the downs are high,
the bitter yards with briars are grown,
the seats are sorrowful. I am sick at heart,
he is so far from me. There are friends on earth,
lovers living that lie together,
while I, early and all alone,
walk under the oak tree, wander through these halls.
There I must sit the summerlong day,
there I can rue my wretchedness,
bewail my many woes, my hardships
40   for I cannot rest from my cares ever,
nor from all the longing that in this life befell me.

It is the way of a young man to be woeful in mood,
hard in his heart's thought; to have, besides,
a blithe bearing and a breast full of care,
a throng of woes alike when his worldly bliss
belongs all to him and when he lives an outcast
in a far country. My friend is sitting,
a cliff for shelter, cold in the storm,
a friend weary in mood, flooded with water
50   in his dismal dwelling, doomed to sorrow.

That man, my friend, is mindful too often
of a happier house. Hard is the lot
of one that longs for love in vain.

30 downs   hills

Seafarer

I will tell a true tale of myself,
say my farings, how I far and oft
toil-days underwent and times of hardship.
Breast-cares I have borne, bitter enough,
care-seats many in keel I have known,
fearful roll of waves. There fell to me oft
hard night-watches at head or stern
when the ship lurches along the cliffs.
My feet were bound with frost, were bitten
10   with cold fetters; my cares moaned there

hot about the heart; hunger broke the mood
of the sea-weary soul from within.
The man that fares fairest on land
can never know how, numb with care,
I sailed the ice-cold sea all winter,
the road of the wretched, bereft of kinsmen,
hung with icicles. Hail flew in showers.
There I heard only the ice-cold wave,
the sea, make song; the swan at times.
20   I took my glee in the gannet's voice,
had lay of whilp for laughter of men,
and mew-music for mead-drinking.
There tempests beat stone cliffs: there the tern gave answer,
the icy-feathered; full oft the eagle screamed there,
the wet-feathered. Not one of my kinsmen
could help my hapless heart in that faring.

    The great of earth, the glad with wine,
who lead in towns a life of bliss,
little they mind how, many a time and oft,
30   I was doomed to bide on the deep, weary.
The night darkened, from the north came snow,
frost bound the fields, there was fall of hail,
coldest of seeds. They overcome me now,
the thoughts of my heart, till I think to try
high seas, the play of salt billows.
Deep goes the mood that drives my soul
to fare from home, that, far away,
I may find the stead where strangers dwell.

    Not a man on earth is so mood-lofty
40   nor so good of his gifts, nor so glowing in youth,
nor in his deeds so daring, nor with so dear a lord
that he never has fear of his faring to sea,
what the Lord may list to lay upon him.
He recks not of the harp, nor of ring-taking,
nor of lust for women, nor of worldly hopes,
he recks of naught but roll of waves;
but ever he feels longing who fares out to sea.
Blossoms take the woods, the towns grow fair,
the fields are in flower, fast goes the world:
50   all those move the man whose mood is bent,
whose thought is ready, who thinks even so
to fare afar, on the flood to ride.
And the cuckoo warns with woeful voice,
summer's ward sings, sorrow he heralds,
bitter, in breast-hoard. The blissful, the lucky,
can never know what need some bear
who widest wander the way of outlaws.
So, now, my soul soars from my bosom,

the mood of my mind moves with the sea-flood,
60   over the home of the whale, high flies and wide
to the ends of the earth; after, back to me
comes the lonely flier, lustful and greedy,
whets me to the whale-way, whelms with his bidding
over deep waters. Dearer, then, to me
the boons of the Lord than this life that is dead
in a land that passes; I believe no whit
that earthly weal is everlasting.

    One woe of three ever awaits each man,
dooms him to doubt ere his day is come:
70   illness or eld or the edge of the sword
fails not to fell the fey and the dying.
Therefore for each man after he is dead
that laud in the speech of the living is best
that he worked with a will, ere away he must,
to bring it about, braving his foes
in doughty deeds to the devil's hurt,
that the children of men should choose to praise him,
and his laud, after, should live with the angels
always, for aye, in everlasting bliss
80   with the heavenly host. Gone hence are the days,
all the high mood of the earth's kingdom;
there is not a king nor a kaiser now,
nor a gold-giver like the great of old,
when most they matched them in mighty deeds
and lived with fame in lordliest wise.
Gone is this glory, all; glee is departed.
The weaker walk this world and hold it,
spend it in hardship; splendor is stricken,
earthly honor ages and withers,
90   so now each of men through middle earth:
eld fares on him, his face turns pale,
the greybeard grieves; his good friends of yore,
begotten of athelings, he knows given to earth.

    When the soul flees it then the flesh no whit
can swallow sweetness, nor soreness feel,
nor move a hand, nor with the mind take thought.
Though brother bury by his brothers dead
sundry hoardings, though he sow full wide
the grave with gold, it will not go with them.
100 The sinful soul can seek no help
in gold the wrath of God to face,
if he hides it away while here he lives.
Great is the fear of God, thereby goes the earth.
He fixed, made fast the firm bottoms,
the ends of the earth and the upper heavens.
Dull is he who dreads not his Lord; to him comes death unwarned.

Happy is he who humble lives; to him comes heaven's favor;
the Lord makes fast his mood, for he believes in its might.
The mood must steer a strong spirit, hold it steadfast and true
110   and worthy of man's trust, in its ways full clean.
Aright each man should rule evil,
to loved and loathed alike do no wrong,
though folded in fire he fain would have
(or burnt on bale to bone and ashes)
the friend he found! Fate is stronger,
God is greater than the grasp of a man.
Of the home we have, heedful let us be,
and care let us give how we come thither,
and try we must, too, to take our way
120   to the everlasting, endless bliss of heaven.
In the love of the Lord life, there, is set,
hope, in the heavens. To the Holy One be thanks
that he lifted us up, the Lord of hosts,
world without end, everlasting God. Amen.

Brunanburg

Athelstan the king, captain of earls,
bounteous lord of men, and his brother too,
Edmund the prince, won everlasting glory
in the onslaught of war, by the edge of the sword
at Bruna's borough; the board-wall they clove,
they hewed shields low with hammers' leavings,
the heirs of Edward; it was inborn, handed down
from their forefathers, that in fight they oft
against each foe should defend their land,
10   their hoards and homes. Their haters perished,
the people of the Scots and the pirate host;
the fey fell to earth. The field grew dark
with soldiers' blood after the sun rose up
in morningtide, the marvelous star,
glided across the sky, the bright candle of the Lord,
of God eternal, till the glorious creature
sank at eve, set. Many a soldier lay there,
many a man of the North, marred by the spear,
shot over the shield, many a shipman and Scot too,
20   weary, tired of war. The West-Saxons
pressed on in force all the day long,
pushed ahead after the hostile army,
hewed the fleeing down from behind fiercely,
with mill-sharp swords. The Mercians withheld
the hard handplay no whit from a man
of those that with Anlaf came over the waves,
by ship invaded our shores from abroad,

6 hammers' leavings swords.

warriors doomed to die in war-play.
On that field of battle lay five young kings,
30   put to sleep by the sword, and seven over that,
earls of Anlaf, endless numbers
of pirates and Scots. There was put to flight
the Northmen's prince, by need compelled
to seek his ship with a small band of men.
The keel pushed off, the king went out
on the fallow flood, he was fated to live.
So there Constantinus came by flight too,
the cunning old king, to his kith in the north,
the grey-haired kemp; he had no cause to be glad
40   of the crossing of swords; of his kin he was robbed,
of friends bereft on the field of battle,
he lost them in war, and he left his son
on the slaughter-ground, left him slain by wounds
in fight, the youth. The father had no cause
to boast about the battle-play of swords,
the evil old man, nor had Anlaf more;
with their loot they had no cause to laugh and say
they were better in strife, in battle-work
on the combat-ground, in the clash of banners,
50   the meeting of spears, the men's encounter,
the weapon-crossing, the war game they played
with the sons of Edward on the slaughter-field.
Then the Northmen went with the nail-studded ships,
dreary darts' leavings, on Dingesmere,
over deep water for Dublin bound,
back to Ireland, beaten, put to shame.

    Likewise the brothers, both together,
the king and the prince, sought kith and home,
the land of Wessex, elate with the war.
60   The host of corpses behind them they left
to the black raven, the beak-faced one,
the dark-clothed one, and to the dun eagle,
the white-tailed erne, hungry war-bird,
and to the greedy wolf, grey beast of the woods,
to devour and relish. So vast a slaughter
of men never yet was made before this
on this island of ours with the edge of the sword
(if we take for true what is told us in books
or by the old and wise), since from the east hither
70   the Angles and Saxons came up, to these shores,
over broad waters sought Britain out,
the keen war-smiths, overcame the Welshmen,
the worshipful kemps, and won the land.

    A.D. 937

33 prince Anlaf. **54 leavings** survivors.

MIDDLE ENGLISH POETRY

English poetry immediately following the Norman Conquest reflects the instability of the period. Some of it has been lost, and although much that remains is didactic and seems to convey the customary monastic, theocentric view of life, the continuum was broken. The change was not simply linguistic; the native traditions were too insular, too backward-looking to be assimilated into the continental tastes of the new ruling class. A new vernacular poetry had to be fashioned to accommodate the dynamic culture, but it did not fully emerge until the fourteenth century, when English came to be spoken by those who had hitherto customarily used French. In the search for the beginnings of Middle English poetry, a few pieces assume importance because of their age. No lyric poetry before the thirteenth century has survived, but the comments of an early-twelfth-century chronicler at Ely suggest that it may have flourished much earlier. According to him, King Cnut composed poetry. While journeying by water to Ely, the king heard the chanting of the monks and immediately composed verses on the subject. We have only the first verse, which is reproduced here, but the chronicler stated that there were other verses "which even to the present time are still sung publicly in dances and remembered in the sayings of the wise."

"The sayings of the wise" included the "Proverbs of Alfred," probably not written by the famous king who ruled Wessex from 871 to 899 but so named in tribute to him as a great patron of letters. The proverbs contain popular everyday sayings, but the overall intention is religious. Similarly, most of the poetry and prose of the Middle English period is religious, reflecting a world dominated by God and his church. Frequently, doctrinal lessons were expressed through the allegorizing of God's two great books: the Book of Nature, in which God revealed his love for man and his awesome power; and the Bible, in which every event had a spiritual meaning, with direct correspondences (such as Noah's Ark prefiguring Christ's

church) between the Old Testament and the New. Dramatized biblical stories designed to teach the way to salvation were the basis of the Mystery plays. Written in verse and in colloquial language, these plays were performed in cycles by the craft guilds (*mysteres* in Middle English) for more than two centuries and were associated with religious festivals. Even poems that seem to have secular themes are religious. For example, "The Owl and the Nightingale," written early in the twelfth century in the genre of the scholarly debate, is clerkly and, in the view of some critics, allegorical, despite its lively dialogue and personal observation of nature.

Secular stories—fictions purporting to be dramatic experiences in the lives of women and men—were undoubtedly as popular as they have always been. To the public of this period, romances and shorter pieces such as the lyric and the ballad must have been what the novel became to the reader in the nineteenth century and television to the viewer in the mid-twentieth century. Most of the romances were translated from French; they were courtly and sophisticated in tone and interest, some consisting largely of embellishments to the historical careers of founding members of great houses. In England many such romances experienced unskillful revisions and alterations. The result was a narrative verse far removed from its originals and even farther removed from the stylized heroic verse of the Anglo-Saxon scop or bard, even though the obligations of heroism were its major concerns. It became, to use the words of Chaucer's Harry Bailey, "rym dogerel."

Yet it was possible for a poet writing in early post-Conquest English and possessing a knowledge of the techniques of Old English poetry to take the story of Arthur, create a poem of high literary quality, and present it as a historical memorial of his own race. Layamon's *Brut*, translated from the Anglo-Norman, conveys a most dignified and dynamic sense of the past. It uses the alliterative style and traditional language to evoke the same nostalgic sense of past glories as that reflected in the oral compositions of earlier times. In the passage quoted here, King Arthur, having vanquished the traitor Modred, is himself mortally wounded. He consigns his kingdom to a young relative and declares that he will go to Avalon to be healed by the Fairy Queen Argante and then return to his kingdom. At this point, a boat appears with two women in it. They place Arthur gently in the boat and carry him away. Different as this quasi-heroic poem is from the late fourteenth-century *Sir Gawain and the Green Knight*, also based on an Arthurian theme, its style, language, and epic treatment merit its inclusion with the finest example of this popular genre.

The popularity of the romance was no doubt due partly to a belief that it had some historical foundation. History made fiction respectable and permitted attention to be diverted to it from the didactic works of piety and religious zeal that dominated throughout the period. Chaucer conceives of *Troylus and Criseyde* as history; he presents the *Canterbury Tales* as an event that actually happened. Similarly, the dream vision, a popular form of the late thirteenth and fourteenth centuries, was important because the dream was an event; it had happened in the mind of the narrator. It is therefore not surprising that poets such as William Langland, Robert Henryson, and William Dunbar all used traditional devices to present their fictions as having some basis in actuality.

Verse narratives were not necessarily romances, of course. Some of the most dramatic were saints' lives, and these often included *exempla* within the tale. The *exemplum*, a short story with a moral, was popular with the homilists and also appeared in verse sermons and manuals of religious instruction. The lively tale of the sacrilegious dancers, embedded in a long didactic poem by Robert Mannyng of Bourne, belongs to this genre.

While the range of literature in the late thirteenth and the fourteenth centuries became more diverse, the Christian life continued to be the paramount concern. There were numerous religious lyrics, manuals of piety, and versified compositions such as "A Love Rune" which, in a characteristically medieval fashion, turned the language of secular love into the language of religion. There were also allegories as diverse as "The Parlement of the Thre Ages" and "Piers Plowman," which presented the problem of man's salvation, amply illustrating it with natural description and observations of the past and the contemporary world.

It was at the time when Langland was writing that Middle English poetry reached its peak. Chaucer's work dominates the period, of course, but attention must be paid to Langland's great poem, to the works of the *Gawain*-poet and, however briefly, to those of Chaucer's untalented but industrious friend, John Gower. Their poetry reflects diverse backgrounds—popular, courtly, or learned—and appears to have been destined for a variety of audiences. Gower's poetry seems pitched to the courtly and the well educated; Langland's to the laity, to the "lewed" rather than to the learned; the works of the *Gawain*-poet to the sophisticated courtier or cleric. But what of Chaucer? His great romance *Troylus* is addressed to lovers, and we would assume, as did the early fifteenth-century illustrator who depicted the poet reciting to elegant lords and ladies, that the immediate audience was courtly. But was the immediate audience of the *Canterbury Tales* the same—or did it include the mixed stratum of the middle classes, whose characters, language, cultural interests, and livelihoods are so vividly depicted?

There was an increase of literary patronage among the well-to-do at this time. Chaucer was a court poet and so, presumably, was the writer of *Sir Gawain and the Green Knight*; Gower, a wealthy Kentish landowner, dedicated his *Confessio Amantis* to Richard II. Langland, writing for a mixed audience of clerics and the newly prosperous middle class, may have been an exception. Yet he was a priest, learned in theology and knowledgeable about contemporary life in general, especially the corruption of the church, and may well have had some financial support while writing the three versions of his great work.

The fifteenth century was a period when prose made the chief contribution to English literature. The lyric, the ballad, and drama flourished, but the courtly writer, hailing Chaucer as "the flower of eloquence," felt that success was to be achieved by concentrating on his language and form. Poems such as Hoccleve's *The Regimen of Princes* and John Lydgate's *The Fall of Princes* are derivative, lengthy, and uninspiring. The most vital poetry was composed in Scotland by men who wrote for an educated audience in and around the court of James IV. With the possible exception of John Skelton (see next section), there was no equal in England to Robert Henryson and William Dunbar. Like the English poets, they were admirers of Chaucer as the great rhetorician and inherited his modes and themes. While they were technically brilliant with an extraor-

dinary command of language, they were also innovators in many of their works. Henryson's sequel to Chaucer's *Troylus* is dramatic and profound, yet totally different in spirit: it provides one of the unforgettable moments in literature when, toward the end of the poem, the hero rides past a group of lepers, among whom is his former love. In Dunbar we see the culmination of an immense variety of medieval poetic practices. He can write conventional allegory in ornate diction, or he can distort the traditions with extraordinary originality. But despite their sensitivity, technical sophistication, and skillful exploitation of all the varied resources of native speech and style, these poets were still medieval, looking back to a poet who had died almost a century earlier. In England, the fact that Stephen Hawes, famous in 1505 but now too minor to be included here, imitated Lydgate, an imitator of Chaucer, rather than Chaucer himself, is further confirmation of the exhaustion of poetic inspiration and the need for new ideas and fresh approaches.

From Canute at Ely

Cnut's Song

Merie sungen the munėchės binnen Ely
Tha Knut king rew ther-by.
"Roweth, knightės, neer the land
And herė we thes munėchės sang."

TRANSLATION
Sweetly sang the monks in Ely when King Canute rowed by. "Row, men, nearer the land and let us hear this song of the monks."

From The Proverbs of Alfred

XIII

Thus queth Alvred:
"If thu havest seorewe, ne seye thu hit than arewe.
Seye hit thine sadelbowe, and ryd thee singinde forth.
Thenne wile wene thet thine wise ne con
That thee thine wise wel thee lyke.

Serewe if thu havest, and the erewe hit wot,
Byfore, he thee meneth; byhynde, he thee teleth.
Thu hit myht segge swych mon that hit thee ful wel on;
Wythute echere ore he on thee muchele more.
10   Byhüd hit on thire heorte, that thee eft ne smeorte;
Ne let thu hyne wite al that thin heorte bywite.''

TRANSLATION

   Thus said Alfred: "If you have a sorrow, do not tell it to one who is a betrayer.
Tell it to your saddlebow, and ride forth singing. Then anyone who does not know
your state of affairs will suppose that your state pleases you well. If you have a
sorrow and the betrayer knows about it, in your presence he will commiserate with
you; behind your back he will mock you. You might tell your sorrow to the very
person who would heartily wish it on you; without any pity he will wish so much
more on you. Conceal it in your heart, so that it may not bring you pain again; and
do not let him know all that your heart may care about."

       XIV

     Thus queth Alvred:
"Ne schaltu nevere thi wif by hire wlyte cheose,
For never none thinge that heo to thee bryngeth.
Ac leorne hire cüste—heo cutheth hi wel sone!
For mony mon for ayhte üvele i-auhteth,
And ofte mon of fayre, frakele i-cheoseth.
Wo is him that üvel wif bryngeth to his cotlif;
So him is alyve that üvele y-wyveth,
For he schal uppon eorthe dreori i-würthe.
10   Mony mon singeth that wif hom bryngeth;
Wiste he hwat he brouhte, wepen he myhte."

TRANSLATION

   Thus said Alfred: "You must never choose your wife by her looks, and never for
anything that she brings to you. But learn to know her behavior— she will show that
very quickly! For many a man because of wealth calculates amiss, and often a man
chooses as one who is beautiful one who is vile. Woeful is he who brings an evil
wife to his dwelling; so too is it for him in his life who marries badly, for he shall be
miserable on the earth. Many a man sings who brings home a wife; if he knew what
he brought, he might well weep."

       XV

     Thus queth Alvred:
"Ne würth thu never so wod ne so wyn-drunke
That evere segge thine wife alle thine wille.
For if heo i-seye thee bivore thine i-vo alle,
And thu hi myd worde i-wreththed hevedest,
Ne schulde heo hit lete, for thing lyvyinde,
That heo ne scholde thee forth upbreyde of thine baleu-sythes.
   "Wymmon is word-wod and haveth tunge too swift.
Theyh heo wel wolde, ne may heo hi nowiht welde."

TRANSLATION

Thus said Alfred: "Never be so foolish or so drunk with wine that you ever tell all your counsel to your wife. For if she were to see all your enemies in front of you, and you had angered her with some word, she wouldn't be able to stop herself, for any living thing, from scolding you right then for your misfortunes.

"Woman is word-crazy and has too swift a tongue. Even though she might well wish to, she can't control it at all."

XVI

Thus queth Alvred:
"Idelschipe and overprute, that lereth yong wif üvele thewes,
And ofte that heo wolde do that heo ne scholde.
Thene unthew lihte leten heo myhte
If heo oft a swote forswunke were.
Theyh hit is üvel to buwe that beo nüle treowe,
For ofte museth the kat after hire moder.
"The mon that let wymmon his mayster i-würthe
Ne schal he never beon i-hürd his wordes loverd,
10   Ac heo hine schal steorne totrayen and toteone,
And selde würth he blythe and gled, the mon that is his wives qued.
"Mony appel is bryht withute and bitter withinne;
So is mony wymmon on hyre fader bure
Schene under schete, and theyh heo is schendful.
So is mony gedelyng godlyche on horse
And is, theyh, lütel wurth—
Wlonk bi the glede and üvel at thare neode."

TRANSLATION

Thus said Alfred: "Idleness and conceit teach a young wife evil habits and often make her want to do what she should not. Vice she might easily avoid if often she were exhausted in sweat. Yet it is hard to bend that which does not wish to be straight, for often the kitten will chase mice in the same way as her mother.

"The man that lets a woman become his master will never be listened to as the lord of his own word, but she will severely torment and harass him, and seldom will he be contented and happy, the man who is his wife's victim.

"Many an apple is outwardly shiny and bitter within; so too many a woman in her father's bower is fair under the sheet and yet is disgraceful. So, too, many a companion is handsome on horse and is yet worth little—brave at the fireside and useless at need."

XVII

Thus queth Alvred:
"Nevre thu, bi thine lyve, the word of thine wyve
Too swithe thu ne arede.
If heo beo i-wreththed myd worde other myd dede,
Wymmon wepeth for mod oftere than for eny god,
And ofte, lude and stille, for to vordrye hire wille.

Heo wepeth otherhwile for to do thee gyle.
"Salomon hit haveth i-sed that wymmon can wel üvelne red.
The hire red foleweth, heo bryngeth hine to seorewe,
10   For hit seyth in the Leoth as cuenes forteoth.
Hit is ifürn i-seyd that cold red is quene red;
Hu he is unlede that foleweth hire rede.
"Ich hit ne segge nouht forthan that god thing nys god wymmon
The mon the hi may i-cheose and i-covere over othre."

TRANSLATION

Thus said Alfred: "Never in your life accept the word of your wife too soon. If she is enraged by word or by deed, a woman will weep for anger more often than for any good reason, and often, loud or soft, to get her own way. At other times she will weep to cheat you.

"Solomon has said that woman well knows evil counsel. He who follows her counsel, she will bring him to sorrow, for it says in the Song[1] that women deceive. It is said of old that woman's counsel is cold counsel, that he is wretched who follows her counsel.

"I do not therefore say that a good woman is not a good thing for the man who can choose her and select her from among the others."

[1] presumably in reference to Proverbs (attributed to Solomon) 7:5: ". . . keep thee from the strange woman, from the stranger which flattereth with her words."

From Layamon's Brut

The Passing of Arthur

Arthur wes forwunded, wunder ane swithe.
Ther to him com a cnave the wes of his cünne.
He wes Cadores sune, the eorles of Cornwaile.
Constantin hehte the cnave; he wes than kinge deore.
Arthur him lokede on, ther he lai on folden,
And thas word seide mid sorhfulle heorte:
"Constantin, thu art wilcume. Thu weore Cadores sone.
Ich thee bitache here mine kineriche.
And wite mine Brüttes a to thines lifs;
10   And hald heom alle tha laghen tha habbeoth i-stonden a mine daghen,
And alle tha laghen gode tha bi Utheres daghen stode.
"And Ich wülle varen to Avalun to vairest alre maidene,
To Argante, there quene, alven swithe sceone;
And heo scal mine wunden makien alle i-sunde,
Al hal me makien mid haleweighe drenchen.
And seothe Ich cumen wülle to mine kineriche
And wunien mid Brütten mid müchelere wünne."

Aefne than worden ther com of se wenden
That wes an sceort bat lithen, sceoven mid üthen;
20 And two wimmen therinne, wunderliche i-dihte;
And heo nomen Arthur anan and a-neouste hine vereden
And softe hine a-dun leiden, and forth gunnen hine lithen.
   Tha wes hit i-wurthen that Merlin seide whilen,
That weore unimete care of Arthures forthfare.
Brüttes i-leveth yete that he bön on live
And wunnien in Avalun mid fairest alre alven,
And lokieth evere Brüttes yete whan Arthur cumen lithe.
Nis naver the mon i-boren of naver nane bürde i-coren
The cunne of than sothe of Arthure sügen mare.
30 But while wes an witeghe, Merlin i-hate;
He bodede mid worde—his quithes weoren sothe—
That an Arthur sculde yete cum Anglen to fülste.

c. 1200

TRANSLATION

Arthur was mortally wounded, grievously and severely. To him there came a youth who was of his kin. He was the son of Cador, the earl of Cornwall. Constantine the youth was called; he was dear to the king. From where he lay on the ground, Arthur looked upon him and spoke these words with sorrowful heart:

"You are welcome, Constantine. You were Cador's son. I here entrust my kingdom to you. And guard my Britons ever in your lifetime; and on their behalf keep all the laws that existed in my days and all the good laws that in Uther's days existed.

"And I will go to Avalon to the fairest of all maidens, to Argant the queen, an elf most beautiful; and she will make my wounds all sound, make me all whole with healing potions. And then I shall come back to my kingdom and dwell with the Britons in great bliss."

Even at these words, there came travelling from the sea a short boat, moving, driven by the waves, and two women in it, wondrously clad; and they took Arthur into it and went in beside him and laid him down gently, and they journeyed away.

Then was fulfilled what Merlin had previously said, that there would be unbounded sorrow at the departure of Arthur. The Britons still believe that he is alive and dwells in Avalon with the fairest of all elves, and the Britons ever look for the time, even yet, when Arthur will come back. Never has the man been born of any chosen woman that can tell more of the truth concerning Arthur. But once there was a wizard called Merlin; he announced by word— his sayings were true—that an Arthur was still to come as an aid to the Angles.

THE BALLAD

Of all the literary genres, the ballad is perhaps the one with the most universal appeal. The reason for its popularity is not hard to explain: it is a song that tells a story and deals with a dramatic, even sensational, situation simply and objectively, allowing the action to unfold in narrative and dialogue. Usually composed in couplets or quatrains, a ballad may have a refrain, but, unlike the refrain of a carol, it is not necessarily relevant to the story or even meaningful. Ballad themes reflect a folk culture that is often primitive and violent. The stories have to do with cruel stepmothers, fairies, revenants, jealousy of a brother, sister, or lover, infidelity or betrayal, parricide, and incest. Usually the ballad plunges immediately into the climactic event and proceeds rapidly, naturally, and impersonally toward an outcome that almost invariably contains elements of tragedy. The impact of the story is heightened by simple, concrete language, the use of set phrases such as "lily white hand" or "milk white hynde," and by "incremental repetition," which advances the story by making small changes in repeated phrases.

The origin and early history of ballads remain in dispute. Who wrote them? Do they have their genesis with an individual poet or are they the product of communal creation? Bishop Thomas Percy, in the preface to his *Influential Reliques of Ancient English Poetry* (1765), ascribed the ballads to medieval minstrels. The Romantics thought ballads the spontaneous compositions of the folk. While it is not improbable for groups to extemporize simple narrative songs in the course of group activities, an individual singer must have been responsible for creating the song. Once it was sung it may have become the property of all who heard it and may even have been recomposed many times. Ballads exist in many versions, and the process of variation obviously went on from generation to generation.

The dates of the ballad texts are also in dispute. One group of scholars considers that the date of a given text is no indication of how long the ballad may have been in oral circulation. Many think ballads stretch back to a primitive antiquity, while others hold that the dates prove the ballads to be a late medieval phenomenon. Few ballads in their present form are older than the fifteenth century.

"Sir Patrick Spens" is presented with a fine sense of dramatic contrast and ironic overtones. With the greatest possible economy, the action moves swiftly from the comfort of the court to the hazards of the sea life, back to high society again, and then to the bottom of the sea. Both the king and Sir Patrick ask questions, but Sir Patrick's are cheerfully rhetorical, suggesting that he is amused that his fine reputation has placed his life in jeopardy. The elderly knight's proposal, which will cause the tragedy, contrasts with the boy's ominous warning, and both court and sailors finally come together with the drowned nobles—already portrayed as somewhat ludicrous in their elaborate garb, lying at the feet of the dauntless sea-captain.

"Thomas Rymer," a lively account of a mortal's union with a fairy, uses a common Celtic motif: the otherworld queen, visiting this world on a hunt, abducts the hero, who then acquires special powers as a result of the association. The hero here is actually a historic person of the thirteenth century, Thomas Rymor of Earlston, who gained a reputation for prophecy. Dramatic dialogue and brief narrative convey the story effectively, despite the conventional imagery. In "Lord Randal" dramatic dialogue alone is the vehicle for the story: the mother asks the questions, the son answers. The focus is on the stark, sensational events, and their impact is intensified by incremental repetition. The concluding stanzas make use of the ballad device known as the Testament and achieve a startling climax when the dying man bequeathes "hell and fire" to the mistress who has poisoned him.

Sir Patrick Spens

The king sits in Dumferling toune,
    Drinking the blude-reid wine:
"O whar will I get guid sailor,
    To sail this schip of mine?"

Up and spak an eldern knicht,
    Sat at the kings richt kne:
"Sir Patrick Spens is the best sailor
    That sails upon the se."

The king has written a braid letter,
10   And signd it wi his hand,
And sent it to Sir Patrick Spens,
    Was walking on the sand.

The first line that Sir Patrick red,
    A loud lauch lauched he;
The next line that Sir Patrick red,
    The teir blinded his ee.

"O wha is this has don this deid,
    This ill deid don to me,
To send me out this time o' the yeir,
20   To sail upon the se!

"Mak haste, mak haste, my mirry men all,
    Our guid schip sails the morne":
"O say na sae, my master deir,
    For I feir a deadlie storme.

"Late late yestreen I saw the new moone,
    Wi the auld moone in her arme,
And I feir, I feir, my deir master,
    That we will cum to harme."

O our Scots nobles wer richt laith
30   To weet their cork-heild schoone;
Bot lang owre a' the play wer playd,
    Thair hats they swam aboone.

O lang, lang may their ladies sit,
    Wi thair fans into their hand,
Or eir they se Sir Patrick Spens
    Cum sailing to the land.

9 braid broad. **14 lauch** laugh. **16 ee** eye. **29 laith** loath. **30 cork-heild schoone** cork-heeled shoes. **31 owre** ere, before. **32 aboone** above. **35 Or eir** ere ever.

O lang, lang may the ladies stand,
   Wi thair gold kems in their hair,
Waiting for thair ain deir lords,
40   For they'll se thame na mair.

Haf owre, haf owre to Aberdour,
   It's fiftie fadom deip,
And thair lies guid Sir Patrick Spens,
   Wi the Scots lords at his feit.

38 kems combs. **41 haf owre** halfway over,
i.e., halfway home.

Thomas Rymer

True Thomas lay oer yond grassy bank,
   And he beheld a ladie gay,
A ladie that was brisk and bold,
   Come riding oer the fernie brae.

Her skirt was of the grass-green silk,
   Her mantel of the velvet fine,
At ilka tett of her horse's mane
   Hung fifty silver bells and nine.

True Thomas he took off his hat,
10   And bowed him low down till his knee:
"All hail, thou mighty Queen of Heaven!
   For your peer on earth I never did see."

"O no, O no, True Thomas," she says,
   "That name does not belong to me;
I am but the queen of fair Elfland,
   And I'm come here for to visit thee.

"But ye maun go wi me now, Thomas,
   True Thomas, ye maun go wi me,
For ye maun serve me seven years,
20   Thro weel or wae as may chance to be."

She turned about her milk-white steed,
   And took True Thomas up behind,
And aye wheneer her bridle rang,
   The steed flew swifter than the wind.

For forty days and forty nights
   He wade thro red blude to the knee,
And he saw neither sun nor moon,
   But heard the roaring of the sea.

4 brae hillside. **7 ilka tett** each lock. **17 maun** must.

O they rade on, and further on,
30   Until they came to a garden green:
"Light down, light down, ye ladie free,
    Some of that fruit let me pull to thee."

"O no, O no, True Thomas," she says,
    "That fruit maun not be touched by thee,
For a' the plagues that are in hell
    Light on the fruit of this countrie.

"But I have a loaf here in my lap,
    Likewise a bottle of claret wine,
And now ere we go farther on,
40   We'll rest a while, and ye may dine."

When he had eaten and drunk his fill,
    "Lay down your head upon my knee,"
The lady sayd, "ere we climb yon hill,
    And I will show you fairlies three.

"O see not ye yon narrow road,
    So thick beset wi thorns and briers?
That is the path of righteousness,
    Tho after it but few enquires.

"And see not ye that braid braid road,
50   That lies across yon lillie leven?
That is the path of wickedness,
    Tho some call it the road to heaven.

"And see not ye that bonny road,
    Which winds about the fernie brae?
That is the road to fair Elfland,
    Where you and I this night maun gae.

"But Thomas, ye maun hold your tongue,
    Whatever you may hear or see,
For gin ae word you should chance to speak,
60   You will neer get back to your ain countrie,"

He has gotten a coat of the even cloth,
    And a pair of shoes of velvet green,
And till seven years were past and gone
    True Thomas on earth was never seen.

44 **fairlies** wonders. 49 **braid** broad. 50 **lil-**
lie leven charming glade. 59 **gin ae** if one.
61 **even** uniform in quality.

Lord Randal

"O where ha you been, Lord Randal, my son?
And where ha you been, my handsome young man?"
"I ha been at the greenwood; mother, mak my bed soon,
For I'm wearied wi huntin, and fain wad lie down."

"And wha met ye there, Lord Randal, my son?
And wha met you there, my handsome young man?"
"O I met wi my true-love; mother, mak my bed soon,
For I'm wearied wi huntin, and fain wad lie down."

10 "And what did she give you, Lord Randal, my son?
And what did she give you, my handsome young man?"
"Eels fried in a pan; mother, mak my bed soon,
For I'm wearied wi huntin, and fain wad lie down."

"And wha gat your leavins, Lord Randal, my son?
And wha gat your leavins, my handsome young man?"
"My hawks and my hounds; mother, mak my bed soon,
For I'm wearied wi huntin, and fain wad lie down."

"And what becam of them, Lord Randal, my son?
And what becam of them, my handsome young man?"
"They stretched their legs out an died; mother, mak my bed soon,
20 For I'm wearied wi huntin, and fain wad lie down."

"O I fear you are poisoned, Lord Randal, my son!
I fear you are poisoned, my handsome young man!"
"O yes, I am poisoned; mother, mak my bed soon,
For I'm sick at the heart, and I fain wad lie down."

"What d' ye leave to your mother, Lord Randal, my son?
What d' ye leave to your mother, my handsome young man?"
"Four and twenty milk kye; mother, mak my bed soon,
For I'm sick at the heart, and I fain wad lie down."

"What d' ye leave to your sister, Lord Randal, my son?
30 What d' ye leave to your sister, my handsome young man?"
"My gold and my silver; mother, mak my bed soon,
For I'm sick at the heart, and I fain wad lie down."

"What d' ye leave to your brother, Lord Randal, my son?
What d' ye leave to your brother, my handsome young man?"
"My houses and my lands; mother, mak my bed soon,
For I'm sick at the heart, and I fain wad lie down."

"What d' ye leave to your true-love, Lord Randal, my son?
What d' ye leave to your true-love, my handsome young man?"
"I leave her hell and fire; mother, mak my bed soon,
40 For I'm sick at the heart, and I fain wad lie down."

27 kye cows

Binnorie

There were twa sisters sat in a bour;
  Binnorie, O Binnorie!
There cam a knight to be their wooer,
  By the bonnie milldams o' Binnorie.

He courted the eldest with glove and ring,
But he lo'ed the youngest abune a' thing.

The eldest she was vexèd sair,
And sair envìed her sister fair.

Upon a morning fair and clear,
10 She cried upon her sister dear:

"O sister, sister, tak my hand,
And let's go down to the river-strand."

She's ta'en her by the lily hand,
And led her down to the river-strand.

The youngest stood upon a stane,
The eldest cam and push'd her in.

"O sister, sister, reach your hand!
And ye sall be heir o' half my land:

"O sister, reach me but your glove!
20 And sweet William sall be your love."

Sometimes she sank, sometimes she swam,
Until she cam to the miller's dam.

Out then cam the miller's son,
And saw the fair maid soummin' in.

"O father, father, draw your dam!
There's either a mermaid or a milk-white swan."

The miller hasted and drew his dam,
And there he found a drown'd womàn.

You couldna see her middle sma',
30 You gowden girdle was sae braw.

You couldna see her lily feet,
Her gowden fringes were sae deep.

24 soummin swimming.

All amang her yellow hair
A string o' pearls was twisted rare.

You couldna see her fingers sma',
Wi' diamond rings they were cover'd a'.

And by there cam a harper fine,
That harpit to the king at dine.

And when he look'd that lady on,
40 He sigh'd and made a heavy moan.

He's made a harp of her breast-bane,
Whose sound wad melt a heart of stane.

He's ta'en three locks o' her yellow hair,
And wi' them strung his harp sae rare.

He went into her father's hall,
And there was the court assembled all.

He laid his harp upon a stane,
And straight it began to play by lane.

"O yonder sits my father, the King,
50 And yonder sits my mother, the Queen;

"And yonder stands my brother Hugh,
But by him my William, sweet and true."

But the last tune that the harp play'd then—
    Binnorie, O Binnorie!
Was, "Woe to my sister, false Helèn!"
    By the bonnie milldams o' Binnorie.

48 by lane alone, of itself.

The Three Ravens

There were three ravens sat on a tree,
    Down a downe, hay down, hay downe,
There were three ravens sat on a tree,
    With a downe;

There were three ravens sat on a tree,
They were as blacke as they might be,
    With a downe derrie, derrie, derrie, downe, downe.

The one of them said to his make,
Where shall we our breakfast take?

10   Downe in yonder greené field
There lies a knight slain under his shield.

His hounds they lie downe at his feete,
So well they can their master keepe.

His hawkes they flie so eagerly
There's no fowle dare him come nie.

Downe there comes a fallow doe
As great with yong as she might goe.

She lift up his bloody hed
And kist his wounds that were so red.

20   She got him up upon her back
And carried him to earthen lake.

She buried him before the prime,
She was dead her selfe ere even-song time.

God send every gentleman
Such hawkes, such hounds, and such a leman.

8 make mate. **13 can** do. **14 eagerly** fiercely. **15 fowle** bird. **nie** near. **16 doe** The fallow deer was yellowish-brown in color and smaller than the red deer. Like the white doe of other ballads and of folklore, perhaps this creature is the knight's lover changed into a doe. Or she may be the Christian soul come for Christ, her bridegroom; or the knight may be the wounded Keeper of the Grail, the Maimed King of the Grail legend. There is surely some allusion to the daily sacrifice of Christ in the Mass. **17 yong** young. **21 earthen lake** pit, cavity in the earth, i.e., grave. **22 prime** the first liturgical hour (6 a.m.), or any time between that and 9 a.m. (great prime). **23 even-song** vespers, the evening office (6 p.m.), or dusk. **25 leman** lover.

ROBERT MANNYNG
OF BOURNE

Mannyng (born c. 1283) was educated at Cambridge and lived for fifteen years as a canon at Sempringham Priory, six miles from Bourne. Using a French penitential manual as his source, he produced *Handling Sin*, a didactic poem of some twelve thousand lines. Although he emphasizes the moral lesson to be learned, his lively treatment of the well-known tale of the sacrilegious carolers evinces more sympathy for the unfortunate dancers than for the priest who cursed them.

From Handling Sin

The Dancers of Colbek

It was upon a Cristemesse night
That twelve fooles a carolle dight,
In wodehed, as it were in cuntek;
They come to a town men calle Colbek.
The cherche of the town that they to come
Is of Saint Magne, that suffred martyrdome;
Of Saint Bukcestre it is alsò,
Saint Magnes sister, that they come to.
Here names of alle thus fond I write,
10   And as I wot now shul ye wite:
Here lodèsman, that made hem glew,
Thus is write, he hight Gerlèw.
Twey maidens were in here covìne,
Maiden Merswinde and Wibèssine.
Alle these come thider for that ènchesoun
Of the preestès doughter of the toun.
    The preest hight Robert, as I can ame;
Azone hight his sone by name;
His doughter, that these men wulde have,
20   Thus is write, that she hight Ave.
Echone consented to o wil
Who shuld go Ave out to til;
They graunted echone out to sende
Bothe Wibèssine and Merswinde.
    These wommen yede and tolled her out
With hem to carolle the cherche about.
Bevune ordeined here carolling;
Gerlew endited what they shuld sing.
This is the carolle that they sunge,
30   As telleth the Latin tunge:
"Equitabat Bevo per silvam frondosam,
Ducebat secum Merswindam formosam.
Quid stamus? cur non imus?"
"By the levèd wode rode Bevoline,
With him he leddè fair Merswine.
Why standè we? why go we nought?"
This is the carolle that Grisly wrought.
This song sunge they in the cherchèyerd—
Of foly were they nothing afèrd—

1 **night** eve. **2 carolle** dance accompanied with song; **dight** made. **3 wodehed** madness; **cuntek** lawlessness. **4 come** came; **Colbek** Kolbigk (Saxony). **5 to come** came to. **6 Magne** Magnus. **8 that** (the church) which. **9 –11** the names of all of them I found written thus, and you shall now know them as I do: their leader, who directed their singing. **12 hight** was called. **13 Twey** two; **covìne** band. **15–16 for . . . town** on account of the daughter of the priest of the town. **17 can ame** think. **21** everyone agreed unanimously. **22 til** entice. **25 yede** went; **tolled** lured. **26 hem** them. **34 levèd** leafy. **37 Grisly** Gerlew. **39 nothing afèrd** in no way afraid.

40   Unto the matines were allé done,
     And the messé shuld biginné sone.
       The preest him revèst to beginné messe,
     And they ne left ther-fore never the lesse,
     But daunséd forth as they bigan—
     For all the messé they ne blan.
       The preest, that stood at the autère
     And herd here noise and heré bere,
     Fro the auter down he nam
     And to the cherché porche he cam
50   And said: "On Goddes behalve, I you forbede
     That ye no lenger do swich dede;
     But cometh in on fair manère
     Goddés servise for to here,
     And doth at Cristin mennés lawe:
     Carolleth no more, for Cristés awe!
     Worshippeth Him with alle your might
     That of the Virgine was bore this night."
       For alle his bidding lefte they nought,
     But daunséd forth as they thought.
60   The preest there-for was sore agreved:
     He prayd God, that he on beleved,
     And for Saint Magne, that He wulde so werche—
     In whos worship sette was the cherche—
     That swich a venjaunce were on hem sent,
     Ar they out of that stede were went,
     That they might ever right so wende
     Unto that timé twelvemonth ende
     (In the Latine that I fond thore
     He saith not "twelvemonth" but "evermore");
70   He curséd hem there allé same
     As they caroléd on here game.
       As soone as the preest hadde so spoke
     Every hand in other so fast was loke
     That no man might with no wunder
     That twelvemonthe parte hem asunder.
       The preest yede in when this was done
     And commaunded his sone Azòne
     That he shulde go swithe after Ave,
     Oute of that carolle algate to have.
80   But al to late that word was said,

40 Unto until. **41 messé** mass. **42 him revèst** robed himself. **43** and they did not desist on that account at all. **45 blan** stopped. **46 autère** altar. **47 bere** uproar. **48 nam** went. **51 lenger** longer; **swich** such. **52 cometh** come. **54 doth at** behave according to. **55 for . . . awe** out of reverence for Christ. **58 lefte** desisted. **59 thought** intended. **60 there-for** at that; **agreved** incensed. **61–3** he prayed God, in whom he trusted, and for the sake of St. Magnus —in whose honor the church was built—that He (God) would bring it about. **65 Ar** before; **stede** place. **66 right so wende** go on like that. **67** i.e., for twelve months time; **68 fond thore** found there. **70 same** together. **71 on here game** for their amusement. **73 loke** locked. **74 wunder** miraculous power. **78 swithe** quickly. **79 algate to have** to get (her) by any means.

For on hem alle was the venjaunce laid.
Azone wende wel for to spede;
Unto the carolle as swithe he yede;
His sister by the arm he hente,
And the arm fro the body wente;
Men wundred allé that there wore,
And merveile mowe ye heré more,
For sethen he had the arm in hand,
The body yede forth caroland,
90   And nother the body ne the arm
Bledde never bloode, cold ne warm,
But was as drye, with al the haunche,
As of a stok were rive a braunche.
Azone to his fader went
And brought him a sory presènt:
"Looke, fader," he said, "and have it here,
The arm of thy doughter dere
That was myn owné sister Ave,
That I wende I might a save.
100   Thy cursing now sene it es
With venjaunce on thy owné fles.
Felliche thou cursedest, and over-soone;
Thou askedest venjaunce: thou hast thy boone!"
You thar not aske if there was wo
With the preest and with many mo.
The preest that cursèd for that daunce,
On some of his fil harde chaunce.
He tooke his doughter arm forlorn
And biried it on the morn;
110   The nexté day the arm of Ave
He fond it ligging above the grave.
He biried it another day,
And eft above the grave it lay.
The thriddé time he biried it,
And eft was it cast out of the pit.
The preest wulde birie it no more:
He dredde the venjaunce ferly sore.
Into the cherche he bare the arme
For drede and doute of moré harme;
120   He ordeined it for to be
That every man might with eye it see.
These men that yede so carolland
Alle that yeré, hand in hand,

82 Azo expected to succeed. 83 as swithe at once. 84 hente seized. 86 that there wore who were there. 87 and you may hear a greater marvel. 88 sethen after. 89 caroland dancing. 90 nother neither; ne nor. 92 haunche shoulder. 93 as if a branch were torn from a trunk. 99 a save have saved. 100 es is.

101 fles flesh. 102 Felliche savagely. 103 boone request. 104 You thar you need. 105 mo more. 107 some one; fil fell. 108 he took his daughter's torn-off arm. 109 morn morrow. 111 ligging lying. 113 eft again. 117 ferly extremely. 119 doute fear.

They never out of that stedė yede,
Ne none might hem thennė lede.
There the cursing first bigan,
In that place aboute they ran,
That never ne felt they no werynes—
As many bodyes for going dos—
130   Ne mete ete, ne drank drinke,
Ne slepte onely alėpy winke.
Night ne day they wist of none,
When it was come, when it was gone;
Frost ne snow, hail ne raine,
Of colde ne hete, felte they no paine;
Heer ne nailės never grewe,
Ne solowed clothes, ne turnėd hewe;
Thunder ne lightning did hem no dere—
Goddes mercy did it fro hem were—
140   But sunge that song that the wo wrought:
"Why standė we? why go we nought?"
    What man shuld ther be in this live
That ne wulde it see and thider drive?
The Emperoure Henry come fro Rome
For to see this hardė dome.
When he hem say, he weptė sore
For the mischefe that he say thore.
He did come wrightės for to make
Covering over hem, for tempest sake.
150   But that they wrought it was in vain,
For it come to no certàin;
For that they sette on o day,
On the tother down it lay.
Ones, twyes, thryės, thus they wrought,
And all here making was for nought.
Might no covering hile hem fro colde
Til time of mercy that Crist it wolde.
    Time of grace fil thurgh His might
At the twelvemonth ende, on the Yolė night.
160   The same houre that the preest hem band,
The same houre atwinne they wand;
That houre that he cursed hem inne,
The same houre they yede atwinne,
And as in twinkeling of an eye

---

125 **thennė** thence. 126 **There** where. 128 there. 148 **did** caused to. 149 **for tempest**
without feeling any weariness. 129 **for going** **sake** for bad weather. 150 **that** what. 151 for
dos do from activity. 131 nor slept even a sin- it came to nothing. 152–53 for what they built
gle wink. 132 They were unaware of night or one day was lying flat the next day. 155 and all
day. 136 **Heer** hair. 137 nor did (their) clothes their work was in vain. 156 **hile** protect. 157
grow dirty, nor (their) complexion change. 138 till the time of mercy which Christ willed. 158
dere harm. 139 **were** ward off. 142 **in this** **fil** fell, came. 159 **Yolė night** Christmas Eve.
live living. 143 who would not want to see it 160 **band** bound. 161 **atwinne** apart; **wand**
and hasten there? 145 **dome** punishment. 146 went.
say saw. 147 **mischefe** misfortune; **thore**

Into the cherché gun they flye,
And on the pavement they fil alle downe
As they had be dede, or fal in a swoune.
   Three days stil they lay echone,
That none stered other flesh or bone;
170   And at the three dayés ende
To life God graunted hem to wende.
They sette hem up and spak apert
To the parishe preest, sire Robèrt:
"Thou art ensample and ènchesoun
Of oure long confusioun;
Thou maker art of oure travàile,
That is to many grete mervàile;
And thy travàile shalt thou soone ende,
For to thy long home soone shalt thou wende."
180   Alle they rise that iché tide
But Avé: she lay dede beside.
Grete sorowe had her fader, her brother;
Merveile and drede had alle other:
I trow no drede of soulé dede,
But with pine was brought the body dede.
The first man was the fader, the prest,
That deyd after the doughter nest.
This iche arme that was of Ave,
That none mighté leye in grave,
190   The Emperoure did a vessel werche
To do it in and hange in the cherche,
That alle men might see it and knawe,
And thenk on the chaunce when men it sawe.
   These men that hadde go thus carolland
Alle the yere, fast hand in hand,
Though that they were then asunder,
Yet alle the worlde spake of hem wunder.
That same hopping that they first yede,
That daunce yede they thurgh land and lede;
200   And, as they ne might first be unbounde,
So eft togeder might they never be founde,
Ne might they never come ayain
Togeder to o stede, certàin.
   Foure yedé to the court of Rome,
And ever hopping about they nome;
Sunderlepés come they theder,

---

165 **gun they flye** they fled. 167 **As** as if; **fal** fallen. 169 **stered** stirred; **other** either. 171 **wende** return. 172 they stood up and spoke plainly. 174–75 you are the occasion and cause of our long humiliation. 179 **long** eternal. 180 they all rose that very hour. 181 **beside** beside them. 184–85 not, I am sure, fear for the death of her soul, but because her body died in great pain. 187 **nest** next. 190 **did . . . werche** had a vessel made. 191 **do** put. 193 and remember what had happened when they saw it. 199 **lede** nation. 201 **eft** afterwards. 203 **o stede, certàin** one place, indeed. 205 **nome** went. 206 they came there separately.

But they come never eft togeder.
Here clothes ne roted, ne nailès grewe,
Ne heer ne wax, ne solowed hewe,
210 Ne never hadde they amendèment,
That we herde, at any corseint,
But at the virgine Saint Edight,
There was he botened, Teodright,
On oure Lady day, in lenten tide,
As he slepte her toumbe beside:
There he had his medicine
At Saint Edight, the holy virgìne.
   Bruning the bishop of Saint Tolous
Wrote this tale so merveilous;
220 Sethe was his name of more renoun—
Men callèd him the pope Leoun.
This at the court of Rome they wite,
And in the kronikeles it is write
In many stedes beyond the see,
More than is in this cuntré.
Therfor men saye—and wel is trod—
"The nerè the cherche, the firther frɔ God."

early 14th century

209 **wax** grew. 211 **corseint** saint's shrine.
212 Edith of Wilton. **botened** cured; Theo-
dric. 214 **Lady** Lady's; **lenten** spring. 218
i.e., Bruno bishop of Toul. 220 **Sethe** after-
wards. 221 Leo IX. 226 **trod** believed. 227
nere nearer.

THE LYRIC

The Middle English lyric did not spring from anything to be found in Old English litera-ture. One of the most important contributions to its development was probably the carole, a song-dance in which stanzas were sung by a leader and the refrain by the whole company. The carole was popular on the Continent long before the Norman Conquest, and in England the survival of refrains suggests that it may have been the earliest kind of lyric of the common people. The courtly lyric, after making its way from the south to northern France, also influenced English poetry together with the medieval hymn in accentual Latin verse. Secular and religious lyrics in England were written in Latin and French as well as English—and, in one fourteenth-century poem, in all three!

Many lyrics reflect the learned and courtly tradition of poetry. Others inject the tradi-tion with simpler expressions and direct sentiment, or even discard it altogether. It is not always easy to determine whether a lyric is sophisticated or artless. "Western Wind," a poem preserved in an early sixteenth-century songbook, has been termed popular because of its use of natural imagery and direct passion, but it may well have been the work of a learned poet skillfully manipu-lating the style and effects of traditional folk poetry.

The sacred or secular love lyric is usually in the form of a dramatic address, set in a context more complex than a mere lover's appeal to his mistress would suggest. The basic secular models are French. In the *chanson d'aventure*, the chance meeting, the speaker riding in the woods meets a young woman whom he engages in love talk; in the *reverdie*, or spring song, the speaker, either explicitly or implicitly, compares his own sad love longings with the joyous sounds, sights, and movements of returning spring; in the *chanson mal mariée* an unhappy wife relates the miseries of being married to an old man; in the *pastourelle* a man and a woman in a rural setting play the verbal game of love with urbanity and sophistication.

Sometimes an English adaptation may defy convention. In "Now Springs the Spray," the poet rides into the woods and meets a young woman who is grieving over her past love. A typical French sequence would depict her consoling herself with a new lover —the poet himself. Instead, this woman remains unpacified, declaring that she will take her revenge on the man who has jilted her.

Lyrics were preserved only in monasteries. Bishops, such as Richard de Ledrede, who held the see of Ossory from about 1316 to 1360, seem to have found some of the secular ones offensive and to have urged the clergy to compose sacred songs. There are more religious lyrics than secular ones, yet a surprising number of secular lyrics have survived. Three of the four religious lyrics given here are in the high style—works of considerable complexity by skillful poets. "I Sing of a Maiden," for example, seemingly so artless, celebrates the Incarnation with images from nature that are also liturgical symbols. It is learned, written in a style whose art lies in the total concealment of art. The secular lyrics offered here show a similar sophistication. The striking poem "Judas" (c. 1250) is one of the earliest. Because it uses the ballad meter, dialogue, stark narrative, and incremental repetition, it is sometimes referred to as the first English ballad. With its narrative drawn partly from the New Testament and partly from the medieval traditions associated with Judas, the poem may have been composed as a processional hymn for an ecclesiastical festival.

Ubi Sunt?

Where beeth they biforen us weren,
Houndès ladden and havekès beren,
   And hadden feeld and wode?
The richè levedies in here bour,
That werèden gold in here tressour,
   With here brightè rode,

Eten and drunken and maden hem glad;
Here lif was al with gamen y-lad;
   Men k nelèden hem biforen.
10   They beren hem wel swithè heye,
And in a twinkling of an eye
   Here soulès weren forloren.

Where is that lawing and that song,
That trailing and that proudè yong,
   Tho havekes and tho houndes?

1 they they (who). **2** who led hounds and carried hawks. **4 levedies** ladies; **here** their. **5 werèden** wore; **tressour** head-dress. **6 rode** complexion. **7 hem** them(selves). **8 gamen** pleasure; **y-lad** led. **10 wel swithè heye** very proudly. **12 forloren** lost. **13 lawing** laughing. **14 trailing** trailing of robes; **yong** gait. **15 Tho** those.

Al that joy is went away;
That wele is comen to waylaway,
To manye hardė stoundes.

Here paradis hy nomen here,
20 And now they lien in helle y-fere;
That fire it brennės evere.
Long is ay and long is o,
Long is way and long is wo;
Thennes ne cometh they nevere.

Dreghy here, man, then, if thou wilt,
A litel pine that me thee bit;
Withdraw thine eises ofte.
Thegh thy pinė be unrede,
And thou thenke on thy mede,
30 It shal thee thinken softe.

If that feend, that foulė thing,
Through wikkė roun, through fals egging,
Nethere thee haveth y-cast,
Up! and be good chaunpioun;
Stand, ne fall na more adown
For a litel blast.

Thou tak the roodė to thy staf,
And thenk on Him that there-on yaf
His lif that was so leef.
40 He it yaf for thee; thou yeeld it Him;
Ayein His fo that staf thou nim,
And wrek Him of that theef. . . .

Maiden moder, hevene-queen,
Thou might and canst and owest to been
Oure sheeld ayein the fende.
Help us sinnė for to fleen,
That we moten thy Sone y-seen
In joye withouten ende.

---

16 **went** gone. 17 **wele** happiness; **waylaway**
lamentation. 18 **stoundes** times of trial. 19 **hy**
nomen they took. 20 **y-fere** together. 21 **bren-**
nės burns. 22 **ay** always; oever. 23 **way**
misery. 24 **Thennes** thence. 25 **Dreghy** en-
dure. 26 a little suffering that is imposed on you.
27 forgo your comforts often. 28 though your
pains be severe. 29 **And** if. 30 it shall seem
mild to you. 32 **roun** counsel; **egging** incite-
ment. 33 **Nethere** down. 37 **to** as. 38 **yaf**
gave. 39 **leef** dear. 40 **yeeld** repay. 41 **Ayein**
against; **nim** take. 42 **wrek Him of** avenge
himself on. 44 **might** have the power; **owest**
ought. 46 **fleen** shun. 47 **moten** may.

Now Springs the Spray

Now springés the spray,
   All for love ich am so seek
That slepen I ne may.

As I me rode this endré day
   O my playinge,
Seigh ich wher a litel may
   Bigan to singe:
     "The clot him clinge!
     Wai is him i love-longinge
10   Shal libben ay!"
       Now springés, *etc.*

Soon ich herde that mirie note
   Thider I drough;
I fonde hire in an erber swote
   Under a bough,
   With joy enough.
     Soon I asked: "Thou mirie may,
     Why singest thou ay?"
     Now springés, *etc.*

20   Then answérde that maiden swote
   Mid wordés fewe:
"My lemmàn me haves bihote
   Of lové trewe:
   He chaunges anewe.
     If I may, it shal him rewe,
     By this day!"
     Now springés, *etc.*

1 now that the spray comes into leaf. **2 ich** I; **seek** sick. **4–5** as I was riding the other day for pleasure. **6 Seigh** saw; **may** maid. **8** may the clod (of the grave) shrivel him. **9–10** wretched is he who must always live in love-longing. **12–14** as soon as I heard that delightful song I went there; I found her in a lovely arbor. **17 Soon** at once. **21 Mid** with. **22** my sweetheart has made me a vow. **25** I shall make him rue it, if I can. **26** i.e., indeed.

Judas

It was upon a Shere Thorsday that oure Loverd aras;
Ful mildé were the wordés He spak to Judàs:

"Judas, thou most to Jurselem, oure meté for to bugge;
Thritty platen of selver thou bere upo thy rugge.
Thou comest fer i the brode strete, fer i the brode strete;
Some of thiné kinésmen ther thou meight y-mete."

1 **Shere . . . aras** Maundy Thursday that our Lord arose. **3 most** must (go); **bugge** buy. 4 thirty pieces of silver you are to carry on your back. **5 fer** far. **6 meight** may.

Y-mettė with his sister, the swikelė wimòn:
"Judas, thou were wurthė me stendė thee with ston,
Judas, thou were wurthė me stendė thee with ston,
10   For the falsė prophetė that thou bilevest upon."

"Be stillė, levė sister, thyn hertė thee tobreke!
Wistė myn Loverd Crist, ful wel He wolde be wreke."

"Judas, go thou on the rok, high upon the ston,
Lay thyn hevėd i my barm, sleep thou thee anon."

Soonė so Judas of slepė was awake,
Thritty platen of selver from him weren y-take.

He drow himselvė by the top, that al it lavede a bloode;
The Jewės out of Jurselem awenden he were woode.

Forth him com the richė Jew that heightė Pilatus:
20   "Wilte thou sell thy Loverd, that heightė Jesus?"

"I n'il selle my Loverd for nonės cur_ės eighte,
Bute it be for the thritty platen that He me biteighte."

"Wilt thou selle thy Lord Crist for enės cunnės golde?"
"Nay, bute it be for the platen that He habben wolde."

In Him com our Lord gon, as His postles seten at mete:
"How sittė ye, postles, and why n'illė ye ete?
How sittė ye, postles, and why n'illė ye ete?
Ich am y-bought and y-sold today for ourė mete."

Up stood him Judas: "Lord, am I that?
30   I n'as never o the stude ther me thee evel spak."

Up him stood Peter, and spak with al his mighte:
"Though Pilatus him come with ten hundred knighte,
Though Pilatus him come with ten hundred knighte,
Yet ich woldė, Loverd, for thy lovė fighte."

"Stille thou be, Peter! Wel I thee y-knowe;
Thou wilt forsake me thriėn ar the cok him crowe."

7 **Y-mettė** (He) met; **swikelė** treacherous.
8 were . . . thee deserve to be stoned. **11–12**
be quiet, dear sister, may your heart break within
you! If my Lord Christ knew, he would be prop-
erly avenged. **14** lay your head in my lap, go
to sleep directly. **15 Soonė so** as soon as.
17 he tore his hair, so that it all streamed with
blood. **18 awenden** supposed; **woode** mad.
19 him com came; **heightė** was called.
21 I will not sell my Lord for riches of any
kind. **22 Bute** unless; **biteighte** entrusted.
23 enės . . . golde gold of any kind. **24 habben**
have. **25** our Lord came walking in as his
apostles were sitting at their meal. **26 How**
why. **28 Ich** I. **29–30 am . . . spak** is it me?
I was never in the place where evil was spoken
of you. **32 him come** should come. **34 for
thy love** for love of you. **35 Stille** quiet.
36 thrien . . . crowe thrice before the cock
crows.

Of Jesu Christ I Sing

Now ich see blostmė springe,
  Ich herde a fugheles song,
A swetė longinge
  Myn herte thurghout sprong,
That is of luvė newe,
That is so swete and trewe
  It gladieth al my song.
Ich wot mid y-wisse
My lif and eke my blisse
10   Is al theron y-long.

Of Jesu Crist I singe
  That is so fair and fre,
Swetest of allė thinge;
  His owe ich owe wel be.
Ful fer He me soghte,
Mid hard He me boghte,
  With woundė two and three;
Wel sore He was y-swunge
And for me mid spere y-stunge,
20   Y-nailėd to the tree.

When ich myselfė stande
  And mid herte y-see
Y-therlėd feet and hande
  With gretė nailės three—
Bloody was His heved;
Of Him n'as noght by-leved
  That of pine were free—
Wel oghtė myn herte
Al for His luvė smerte,
30   Sic and sory be.

A way! that I ne can
  To Him turne al my thoght
And makien Him my lefman
  That thus me hath y-boght
With pine and sorewe longe,
With woundė depe and stronge:
  Of luve ne can I noght.
His blood fel to the grounde
Out of His swetė wounde,
40   That of pine us hath y-broght.

1–2 now that I see blossom coming out (and) I have heard a bird's song. 4 sprong has sprung up. 7 gladieth makes joyful. 8 mid y-wisse with certainty. 10 y-long dependent. 12 fre noble. 14 ought indeed to be his own. 15 fer far. 16 Mid hard with suffering. 18 y-swunge scourged. 23 Y-therlėd pierced. 25 heved head. 26 no part was left of him. 27 pine pain. 29 smerte to feel pain. 31 A way alas. 33 lefman beloved. 37 I am incapable of love. 40 of out of.

Jesu, lefman softe
  Thou yif me strengthe and might,
Longinge sore and ofte
  To servy thee aright;
And leve me pinė drye
Al for thee, swete Marìe,
  That art so fair and bright.
Maiden and moder milde,
For love of thinė childe
50   Ernde us hevene light.

Jesu, lefman swete,
  Ich sendė thee this song,
And wel ofte ich thee grete
  And biddė thee among.
Yif me soonė lete
And minė sinnės bete,
  That ich have do thee wrong.
At minė livės ende,
When ich shal hennė wende,
60   Jesu, me underfong! Amen.

41 softe kind. 42 yif give. 45 and grant that I
may endure pain. 50 win heaven's light for us by
your intercession. 54 and pray to you cons-
tantly. 55–7 grant that I may straightway renounce
and atone for my sins, for what I have done to
wrong you. 59 shal must; henne hence. 60
underfong receive.

I Sing of a Maiden

I sing of a maiden
  That is makėles;
King of alle kingės
  To her son she ches.
He cam also stillė
  Ther His moder was,
As dew in Aprìlle
  That falleth on the gras.
He cam also stillė
10   To His moderes bowr,
As dew in Aprìlle
  That falleth on the flowr.
He cam also stillė
  Ther His moder lay,
As dew in Aprìlle
  That falleth on the spray.
Moder and maiden
  Was never none but she;
Wel may swich a lady
20   Godės moder be.

2 makėles matchless, mateless. 4 she took as
her son. 5 also stillė as silently. 6 Ther where.

Adam Lay Y-bounden

Adam lay y-bounden,
  Bounden in a bond;
Four thousand winter
  Thought he not to long;
And al was for an appel,
  An appel that he took,
As clerkès finden writen
  In herè book.

Ne hadde the appel takè been,
10 The appel take been,
Ne hadde never our Lady
  A been hevene-queen.
Blessèd be the time
  That appel takè was!
Therefore we moun singen
  "*Deo Gracias!*"

4 to too. **7 clerkès** learned men. **8 herè** their. **9** had not the apple been taken. **11–12** our Lady would never have been queen of heaven. **15 moun** may.

Jolly Jankin

"*Kyriè,*" so "*kyriè,*"
  Jankin singeth miriè,
With "aleyson."

As I went on Yole day
  In oure prosession,
Knew I joly Jankin
  By his mery tone—
Kyrièleyson.

Jankin began the offis
10 On the Yolè day,
And yet me thinketh it dos me good,
  So mery gan he say
"*Kyrièleyson.*"

Jankin red the pistil
  Ful faire and ful wel,
And yet me thinketh it dos me good,
  As ever have I sel.
Kyrièleyson.

Jankin at the *Sanctus*
20 Craketh a mery note,

1 "*Kyriè*" *Kyrie eleyson*—"Lord have mercy" —used at the beginning of the Mass. **2 miriè** sweetly. **3 "aleyson"** pun on name "Alison." **12 gan** did. **14 pistil** Epistle. **17** as I hope always to be happy. **20, 24 Craketh** sings in very short notes.

And yet me thinketh it dos me good—
I payėd for his cote.
Kyrièleyson.

Jankin craketh notės
An hunderid on a knot
And yet he hakketh hem smállere
Than wortės to the pot.
Kyrièleyson.

30   Jankin at the *Angnus*
Bereth the pax-brede;
He twinkelėd, but said nought,
And on myn foot he trede.
    Kyrièleyson.

Benedicamus Domino,
Crist fro shame me shilde!
Deo gracias therto—
Alas, I go with childe!
Kyrièleyson.

25 knot cluster. **26 hem** them. **27 wortės** herbs. **29 Angnus** Agnus. **30 pax-brede** pax, osculatory. **31 twinkelėd** winked. **35** may Christ shield me from shame.

Western Wind

Westron winde, when will thou blow,
The smalle raine downe can raine?
Christ if my love were in my armes,
And I in my bed againe.

MEDIEVAL RELIGIOUS DRAMA

The performance of mystery plays—a series of pageants dealing with the Biblical history of man from the fall of the angels and the creation to judgment day—was an annual event in many parts of England from the fourteenth to the mid-sixteenth century. Only four relatively complete cycles of such plays survive, those of York, Chester, Lincoln, and Wakefield, but evidence indicates that many other cities had their cycles, and at least one hundred others produced individual pageants. Performed on stages in the streets, the drama was favored by the church as a means of bringing the story of redemption to the masses. The monks probably composed the plays, and the craft guilds were responsible for performing them and for discharging the often very heavy expenses involved in connection with costumes and stage machinery. The plays—of which there might be some fifty in one cycle—were allotted to the craft considered appropriate to the subject. The flood might be enacted by the shipwrights, master mariners, or watermen; the crucifixion, by the butchers or carpenters. In York, to celebrate Corpus Christi day, such plays were performed at a number of different stations in the city, beginning at 4:30 a.m. and ending at dusk. Slick staging and rapid transfer apparently enabled the entire cycle to be performed at each stage in turn.

The play of Noah appears in all the cycles and was an indispensable part of the repertory. Not only did the traditional quarrels of Noah and his wife provide scope for primitive comedy, but the story was thematically important: Noah's wife was the recalcitrant Eve; Noah was Christ; the flood, judgment day. This version is the work of a dramatic genius from Wakefield, a town some forty miles from York. The hand of the Wakefield Master, as he is called, is notable in other redactions in the Towneley Cycle, especially in the artistry of the comic scenes and the creation of dramatic suspense. The play of the flood was elaborately staged on three levels: heaven, the hill on which Noah's wife spins, and the ark that Noah builds in full view of the audience (from prefabricated parts). The anti-feminist portrayal of Noah's wife as a shrew is a folk-tale motif used extensively in Europe, in literature and in art throughout the Middle Ages.

From Noah

Noe. I thank the, Lord so dere, that wold vowchsayf
  Thus low to appere to a symple knafe.
  Blis vs, Lord, here, for charité I hit crafe;
  The better may we stere the ship that we shall hafe,
  Certayn.
Deus. Noe, to the and to thi fry
  My blyssyng graunt I;
  Ye shall wax and multiply
180 And fill the erth agane,
  When all thise floodys ar past, and fully gone away.
                    [Exit Deus.
Noe. Lord, homward will I hast as fast as that I may;
  My wife will I frast what she will say,
  And I am agast that we get som fray
  Betwixt vs both,

2. PROCESSUS NOE CUM FILIIS

  For she is full tethee,
  For litill oft angré;
  If any thyng wrang be,
  Soyne is she wroth.
              [Tunc perget ad vxorem]
190 God spede, dere wife! How fayre ye?
Vxor. Now, as euer myght I thryfe, the wars I the see.
  Do tell me belife, where has thou thus long be?
  To dede may we dryfe, or lif, for the,
  For want.
  For when we swete or swynk,
  Thou dos what thou thynk,
  Yit of mete and of drynk
  Haue we veray skant.

Noe. Wife, we ar hard sted with tythyngys new.
200   *Vxor*. Bot thou were worthi be cled in Stafford blew,
    For thou art alway adred, be it fals or trew.
    Bot God knowes I am led—and that may I rew—
    Full ill;
    For I dar be thi borow,
    From euen vnto morow
    Thou spekys euer of sorow;
    God send the onys thi fill!

                        [To the women in the audience:
    We women may wary all ill husbandys;
    I haue oone, bi Mary that lowsyd me of my bandys!
210   If he teyn, I must tary, howsoeuer it standys,
    With seymland full sory, wryngand both my handys
    For drede;
    Bot yit otherwhile,
    What with gam and with gyle,
    I shall smyte and smyle,
    And qwite him his mede.

    Noe. We! hold thi tong, ram-skyt, or I shall the still.
    Vxor. By my thryft, if thou smyte, I shal turne the vntill.
    Noe. We shall assay as tyte. Haue at the, Gill!
220   Apon the bone shal it byte.   *[Strikes her.*
    Vxor.   A, so! Mary, thou smytys ill!
    Bot I suppose
    I shal not in thi det
    Flyt of this flett:
    Take the ther a langett
    To tye vp thi hose!   *[Strikes him.*

GEOFFREY CHAUCER

1340?–1400

Geoffrey Chaucer was born about 1340 into a prosperous merchant family living on London's Thames Street, close to the barges that brought wine and sherry from France and Spain. His grandfather and father both served as deputy to the king's butler, and Chaucer's own royal connection was established when, in 1357, he apparently became a page in the household of Elizabeth, wife of Lionel, the third son of Edward III. In 1359 he fought in France, and in March 1360, after being taken prisoner near Rheims, he was evidently regarded sufficiently highly to be ransomed by the king. Thereafter he held various important offices until his death in 1400.

His activities caused him to be named in almost five hundred contemporary documents, and he would have had some place in the history of his time had he never written a line of poetry. He was a diplomat, intermittently engaged in royal affairs in France, Spain, and Italy, and a high-level civil servant, occupying such powerful posts as controller of customs and subsidies on wool for the port of London (1374–86), controller of the petty customs on wines and other merchandise (1382–86), clerk of the King's Works (1389–91), and sub-forester of the royal forest of North Petherton (1390–1400[?]). He was also justice of the peace for Kent (1385, 1386) and member of Parliament (1386).

Such activities brought him into personal acquaintance with the leading men and women of his time, whether they were in the royal households, business and civic life, or the worlds of learning, literature, art, and religion. He was on friendly terms with three successive reigning monarchs, all of whom gave him pensions, and he married into society. As an esquire he wedded a court *damoiselle*, Philippa, daughter of Sir Paon de Roet and sister of John of Gaunt's third wife. Both Chaucer and Philippa received pensions from John of Gaunt, and Chaucer was associated with this powerful fourth son of Edward III for much of his lifetime.

What we know of Chaucer's personal life is limited. He says little about himself in his writings. The "I" in his poetry is not the historical fourteenth-century courtier and man of affairs or even the man of letters, but a fictional character humorously presented as incompetent both as a poet and as a lover. We do know, however, that from 1374 to 1386 he lived at Aldgate in a house on the city wall, later in Kent and in Greenwich, and, for the last year of his life, in a house in the garden of St. Mary's Chapel, within the sanctuary of Westminster Abbey, where he was subsequently buried. Of his family life we can only conjecture. He appears to have had two sons, Thomas, who became a wealthy landowner, and "little Lewis," for whom Chaucer wrote the *Treatise on the Astrolabe* (1391). An Elizabeth Chaucy became a nun in Barking in 1381, and since John of Gaunt paid her expenses, the conjecture has been made that Philippa may have been John's mistress and that Elizabeth, and, indeed, Thomas also, may have been his children.

The world in which the poet lived was one of political, economic, and cultural instability. It was an age of anxiety, of disintegration accelerated by frequent wars, famine, repressive legislation, general lawlessness, and the widespread and virulent bubonic plague, or Black Death. Chaucer's own career seems to have been a troubled one despite his various lucrative positions and his obvious success as man of affairs, royal servant, and poet. He was frequently engaged in litigation, mainly for nonpayment of his debts, and at one time even took out letters of protection granting him immunity from legal suits for two years. Two incidents appear to put him in an unfavorable light and suggest that Chaucer, far from being an ivory-tower poet, competed on society's own terms. In 1380, a London baker's daughter called Cecilia Chaumpaigne gave up her right to legal action against Chaucer concerning her *raptus*. *Raptus* could mean either rape or abduction, and we know nothing further of the nature of Chaucer's involvement. The second incident concerns his posts at the Customs. A petition in Parliament in 1386 demanded that the king remove all customs controllers appointed for life—"because of their extortions." As far as we know, Chaucer's posts were not for life, but he had held them longer than anyone else. Less than two months later he was replaced in both offices.

Yet, despite the problems of his busy and often dramatic life and the precariousness of his position in a society in which death came swiftly and violently to the politically unskilled or unfortunate, Chaucer all this time was writing the magnificent, sophisticated poems that have engaged readers' attention ever since. Perhaps the most distinctive quality in his work comes from his confronting the jarring elements of his age with tolerance, even amusement, resolving the tensions by a subtle but pervasive use of irony. His early major poems show the influence of the elaborate French school, and we surmise that he wrote all those untraced love lyrics and ditties which, according to his friend John Gower, he composed in his youth, in French, the common language of the court. *The Book of the Duchess* (an elegy for John of Gaunt's first wife, who died in 1369), *The House of Fame*, *The Parliament of Fowls*, and *The Legend of Good Women* are cast in the form of dream allegory and employ numerous conventions prescribed by the French rhetoricians. In *Troylus and Criseyde* and *The Canterbury Tales*, two works that are not only Chaucer's finest achievement but are among the greatest in English literature, Chaucer scrapped the dream allegory form in the interests of dramatic narrative. But he retained the best in rhetorical techniques while forging his own form and style. Even the language had

to be found, and he created from his reading and from the contemporary vernacular the appropriate styles to treat different subjects, whether high, middle, or low. The result is that his presentation of the manners, rituals, speech and morals of his age seems to be tellingly authentic and to offer profound and timeless insights into human nature. His poetry contains that quality characteristic of all great poetry: that of being open to reinterpretation. It continues to provide new meanings for successive generations who, however much they may disagree with one another even on most important matters of literary criticism, nevertheless share the complex and deeply moving experience that the poetry offers.

From The Canterbury Tales

The General Prologue

HERE BIGYNNETH THE BOOK OF THE TALES OF CAUNTERBURY.

Whan that Aprill with his shoures soote
The droghte of March hath perced to the roote,
And bathed every veyne in swich licour
Of which vertu engendred is the flour;
Whan Zephirus eek with his sweete breeth
Inspired hath in every holt and heeth
The tendre croppes, and the yonge sonne
Hath in the Ram his halfe cours yronne,
And smale foweles maken melodye,
10   That slepen al the nyght with open eye—

1 Aprill accent on the first syllable. Note that the first two measures of the poem begin with accented beats. **his** its. "It" did not have a separate possessive until the seventeenth century. **shoures soote** gentle showers. The unmutated form of "swete," "swote," or "soote" was generally used to translate Latin *suavis*; "swete" was used to translate *dulcis*. **2 droghte of March** dryness of March. Early spring is a relatively dry season in southern England. **3 veyne** veins in the plants; **swich licour** such liquid. **4 vertu** potency, from Latin *virtus*. **5 Zephirus** the west wind; in classical mythology husband of Flora, goddess of flowers, and father of Carpus, god of fruit. **eek** also. **6 Inspired** breathed into; **holt and heeth** woodland and plain. **7 croppes** new foliage; **yonge sonne** just beginning its annual

journey after the vernal equinox. In Chaucer's time the English legal year began on March 25. **8** The zodiacal house of Aries (the Ram) in Chaucer's time extended from March 12 to April 11. Halfway through this would place the date c. 27 March—but see *Man of Law's Tale* l. 5. Hence, it has been concluded that Chaucer meant "has completed the half of the Ram's course [that occurs in April—the other half having occurred in March]," i.e., was entering the house of Taurus which began April 12. If April 18 in *Man of Law's Tale* refers to the second day of the pilgrimage, the first day would be April 17. Skeat argued that April 17, 1387, in the week after Easter, was the most probable date. **halfe** Some manuscripts read "half his."

So priketh hem nature in hir corages—
Thanne longen folk to goon on pilgrimages,
And palmeres for to seken straunge strondes
To ferne halwes, kowthe in sondry londes;
And specially from every shires ende
Of Engelond to Caunterbury they wende
The hooly blisful martir for to seke
That hem hath holpen whan that they were seeke.
   Bifil that in that seson on a day
20 In Southwerk at the Tabard as I lay
Redy to wenden on my pilgrymage
·To Caunterbury with ful devout corage,
At nyght was come into that hostelrye
Wel nyne and twenty in a compaignye
Of sondry folk, by aventure yfalle
In felaweship, and pilgrimes were they alle,
That toward Caunterbury wolden ryde.
The chambres and the stables weren wyde,
And wel we weren esed atte beste.
30 And shortly, whan the sonne was to reste,
So hadde I spoken with hem everichon
That I was of hir felaweship anon,
And made forward erly for to ryse,
To take oure wey ther as I yow devyse.
   But nathelees, whil I have tyme and space,
Er that I ferther in this tale pace,
Me thynketh it acordaunt to resoun
To telle yow al the condicioun
Of ech of hem, so as it semed me,
40 And whiche they weren, and of what degree,
And eek in what array that they were inne,
And at a knyght than wol I first bigynne.

   A KNYGHT ther was, and that a worthy man,
That fro the tyme that he first bigan
To riden out, he loved chivalrie,
Trouthe and honour, fredom and curteisie.
Ful worthy was he in his lordes werre,
And therto hadde he riden, no man ferre,

11 **corages** hearts. 13 **palmeres** professional pilgrims whose emblem was a palm frond; **strondes** lands. 14 **ferne halwes, kowthe** faraway saints (or shrines), known; **sondry** various. 17 **blisful martir** blessed St. Thomas à Becket, martyred in Canterbury Cathedral in 1170. 18 **holpen** helped; **seeke** sick. 20 **Southwerk** (Southwark) the borough south of London Bridge. **Tabard** inn identified by a sign shaped like a smock. 24 **Wel nyne and twenty** Evidently Chaucer intended thirty story tellers (including himself), but the number cannot be made to fit the text. 25 **aventure** chance. 28 **wyde** spacious. 29 **esed atte beste** accommodated in the best manner. 30 **shortly** to be brief about it. 32 **anon** immediately. 33 **made forward** (we) made an agreement. 34 **devyse** (will) relate. 36 **pace** pass (go). 38 **condicioun** circumstances. 40 **whiche** what; **degree** status (rank). 45 **chivalrie** the ethical code of chivalry; also feats of arms. 46 **Trouthe** integrity; **fredom** generosity. 47 **lordes werre** feudal lord's war. 48 **ferre** further.

As wel in cristendom as in hethenesse,
50   And evere honoured for his worthynesse.
     At Alisaundre he was whan it was wonne.
Ful ofte tyme he hadde the bord bigonne
Aboven alle nacions in Pruce.
In Lettow hadde he reysed and in Ruce,
No Cristen man so ofte of his degree.
In Gernade at the seege eek hadde he be
Of Algezir, and riden in Belmarye.
At Lyeys was he and at Satalye,
Whan they were wonne, and in the Grete See
60   At many a noble armee hadde he be.
At mortal batailles hadde he been fiftene,
And foughten for oure feith at Tramyssene
In lystes thries, and ay slayn his foo.
This ilke worthy knyght hadde been also
Somtyme with the lord of Palatye
Agayn another hethen in Turkye,
And everemoore he hadde a sovereyn prys.
And though that he were worthy, he was wys,
And of his port as meeke as is a mayde.
70   He nevere yet no vileynye ne sayde
In al his lyf unto no maner wight.
He was a verray, parfit, gentil knyght.
But for to tellen yow of his array,
His hors weren goode, but he was nat gay.
Of fustian he wered a gypoun
Al bismotered with his habergeoun,
For he was late ycome from his viage,
And wente for to doon his pilgrymage.

     With hym ther was his sone, a yong SQUIER,
80   A lovyere and a lusty bacheler,

49 hethenesse heathen lands. **51 Alisaundre** Alexandria, captured 1365. The Knight's campaigns range from 1344 to 1386—unlikely for one man; all are against pagans at war with Christian Europe. **52 bord bigonne** sat in the place of honor at banquets. **53 nacions in Pruce** The Knights of the Teutonic Order, fighting in Prussia against the invaders from central Asia, were organized by nationality, like the students in medieval universities. **54 Lettow . . . Ruce** Lithuania and Russia, areas of warfare for the Teutonic Order; **reysed** campaigned. **56, 57, 62 Gernade** Granada; **Algezir** a city in Granada, captured in 1344; **Belmarye, Tramyssene** Moorish kingdoms in North Africa. All these names are associated with the struggles of the Christians against the Moors in Spain and North Africa throughout the fourteenth century. **58 Lyeys . . . Satalye** Saracen cities in Asia Minor, won in 1361 and 1367. These two and the capture of Alexandria (l. 51 above) were campaigns of Pierre de Lusignan, Christian king of Cyprus. **59 Grete See** Mediterranean. **60 armee** armed invasion. **62–63 foughten . . . In lystes** single combat by champions to decide the outcome of a battle. **65 Palatye** another city in Asia Minor, in 1365 bound by treaty to Cyprus. **67 sovereyn prys** high reputation. **68 worthy . . . wys** "Fortitudo et sapientia" were the most valued qualities of the hero from classical times onward. **69 port . . . meeke as is a mayde** behavior. In *Republic* Bk. II, Plato wrote, "Where shall we find (in a soldier) at once a meek and magnanimous temperament?" **71 wight** person. **72 verray, parfit, gentil** true, perfect, courteous. **74 hors** horses; **gay** gaily dressed. **75 fustian . . . gypoun** coarse cloth tunic. **76 bismotered . . . habergeoun** soiled by his coat of mail. **77 late** recently; **viage** journey. **80 lovyere** lover (southern, perhaps deprecatory, dialect form); **bacheler** Bachelors in arms aspired to be knights, just as bachelors of arts strived to be masters.

With lokkes crulle as they were leyd in presse.
Of twenty yeer of age he was, I gesse.
Of his stature he was of evene lengthe,
And wonderly delyvere, and of greet strengthe.
And he hadde been somtyme in chyvachie
In Flaundres, in Artoys, and Pycardie,
And born hym weel, as of so litel space,
In hope to stonden in his lady grace.
Embrouded was he, as it were a meede
90 Al ful of fresshe floures, whyte and reede.
Syngynge he was or floytynge al the day.
He was as fressh as is the monthe of May.
Short was his gowne, with sleves longe and wyde.
Wel koude he sitte on hors and faire ryde.
He koude songes make and wel endite,
Juste and eek daunce, and weel purtreye and write.
So hoote he lovede that by nyghtertale
He slepte namoore than dooth a nyghtyngale.
Curteis he was, lowely, and servysable,
100 And carf biforn his fader at the table.

A YEMAN hadde he and servantz namo
At that tyme, for hym liste ride so,
And he was clad in cote and hood of grene.
A sheef of pecok arwes, bright and kene,
Under his belt he bar ful thriftily—
Wel koude he dresse his takel yemanly;
His arwes drouped noght with fetheres lowe—
And in his hand he baar a myghty bowe.
A not-heed hadde he, with a broun visage.
110 Of wodecraft wel koude he al the usage.
Upon his arm he baar a gay bracer,
And by his syde a swerd and a bokeler,
And on that oother syde a gay daggere
Harneised wel and sharp as point of spere;

81 **crulle . . . presse** curly, as if they had been artificially dressed. **83 evene lengthe** average, i.e., not odd. **84 delyvere** agile. **85 chyvachie** cavalry action. **86 Flaundres . . . Artoys . . . Pycardie** In 1383 the English engaged in a "crusade" in Flanders and neighboring districts in support of Pope Urban VI of Rome against the French supporters of Pope Clement VII of Avignon. This was merely another episode in the Hundred Years War. **88 lady** lady's. **89 Embrouded** embroidered; **meede** meadow. **91 floytynge** fluting (or whistling). **93 Short . . . wyde** i.e., very fashionable dress. **95** compose the music, compose the lyric. **96 purtreye** draw. The Squire possessed all the genteel accomplishments.

99 **lowely** humble. **100 carf** carved, another gentlemanly accomplishment. **101 hadde he** i.e., the Knight. **102 hym liste** he chose. **103 grene** Lincoln green was the traditional color of foresters' clothes. **104 pecock arwes** Like the Squire and several of the subsequent pilgrims, the Yeoman is decked out in his festive finery for the pilgrimage. **108 myghty bowe** Longbowmen had proved to be England's most effective weapon against France in the Hundred Years War. **109 not-heed** closely cut hair; cf. the long curls of the Squire, and the Cavaliers and Roundheads of 1642. **111 gay bracer** ornamented leather wristguard. **112 bokeler** small shield. **114 Harneised wel** with a good sheath and belt.

A Cristophre on his brest of silver sheene.
An horn he bar, the bawdryk was of grene;
A forster was he, soothly, as I gesse.

There was also a Nonne, a PRIORESSE,
That of hir smylyng was ful symple and coy;
120 Hire gretteste ooth was but by Seint Loy.
And she was cleped madame Eglentyne.
Ful weel she soong the service dyvyne,
Entuned in hir nose ful semely,
And Frenssh she spak ful faire and fetisly,
After the scole of Stratford atte Bowe,
For Frenssh of Parys was to hire unknowe.
At mete wel ytaught was she with-alle:
She leet no morsel from hir lippes falle,
Ne wette hir fyngres in hir sauce depe.
130 Wel koude she carie a morsel and wel kepe
That no drope ne fille upon hire brest.
In curteisie was set ful muchel hir lest.
Hir over-lippe wyped she so clene
That in hir coppe ther was no ferthyng sene
Of grece, whan she dronken hadde hir draughte.
Ful semely after hir mete she raughte.
And sikerly she was of greet desport,
And ful plesaunt, and amyable of port,
And peyned hire to countrefete cheere
140 Of court, and to been estatlich of manere,
And to ben holden digne of reverence.
But, for to speken of hire conscience,
She was so charitable and so pitous
She wolde wepe, if that she saugh a mous
Kaught in a trappe, if it were deed or bledde.
Of smale houndes hadde she that she fedde
With rosted flessh, or milk and wastel-breed.
But soore wepte she if oon of hem were deed,
Or if men smoot it with a yerde smerte—

115 A Cristophre a Christopher medal. St. Christopher is the patron saint of travelers. 116 bawdryk baldric. 119 coy reserved (Latin *quietus*), or affecting reserve. 120 Seint Loy St. Eligius, a particularly handsome, genteel French saint of the sixth century. 121 Eglentyne a typical romance heroine's name, but there was a Madam Argentyn in St. Leonard's nunnery near Stratford-at-Bow (just outside London) which Chaucer had visited as a youth. She was not prioress. 123 Entuned in hir nose Authorities point out that this is the correct way to sing Gregorian chant. 124 fetisly elegantly. 125 scole of Stratford atte Bowe i.e., she spoke provincial (Anglo-Norman) French. 127 mete dining. The description of the Prioress's table manners resembles some of the Duenna's satirical comments on women in *Roman de la Rose* 13, 374 ff. 132 curteisie . . . lest elegant manners, pleasure. 134 coppe . . . ferthyng cup, spot the size of a farthing (dime). 136 semely politely; raughte reached. 137 sikerly certainly; desport geniality. 138 port bearing. 139 countrefete cheere imitate the behavior. 141 digne worthy. 145 Kaught in a trappe This was, by way of contrast, a period of such hardship for poor human beings that it had led to the Peasants' Revolt (1381). 146–47 Church law forbade nuns to have dogs. wastel-breed white bread, made with bolted flour (French, *gâteau*). At this time peasants ate black bread, and meat only on the rarest occasions. 149 men smoot the Germanic impersonal used for the passive; yerde smerte yardstick smartly.

150 And al was conscience and tendre herte.
Ful semyly hir wympul pynched was,
Hir nose tretys, hir eyen greye as glas,
Hir mouth ful smal, and therto softe and reed.
But sikerly she hadde a fair forheed;
It was almoost a spanne brood, I trowe,
For, hardily, she was not undergrowe.
Ful fetys was hir cloke, as I was war.
Of smal coral aboute hire arm she bar
A peire of bedes, gauded al with grene,
160 And theron heng a brooch of gold ful sheene
On which ther was first write a crowned A,
And after *Amor vincit omnia*.

Another NONNE with hir hadde she,
That was hir chapeleyne, and preestes thre.

A MONK ther was, a fair for the maistrie,
An outridere, that lovede venerie,
A manly man, to been an abbot able.
Ful many a deyntee hors hadde he in stable.
And whan he rood, men myghte his brydel heere
170 Gynglen in a whistlynge wynd als cleere
And eek as loude as dooth the chapel belle
Ther as this lord was kepere of the celle.
The reule of Seint Maure or of Seint Beneit,
By cause that it was old and somdel streit,
This ilke Monk leet olde thynges pace,
And heeld after the newe world the space.
He yaf nat of that text a pulled hen

151 **semyly** correctly; **wympul** nun's head-dress. **152 tretys** well-shaped (aristocratic). The description—up to the forehead—is that of a romance heroine. **greye** blue(?)—a favorite color for medieval aristocratic eyes, male or female. **154 fair forheed** A high forehead was admired. There is some evidence that for nuns it should not have been so exposed; and coupled with the next two lines it suggests fleshiness. **156 hardily** certainly; **nat undergrowe** In medieval England, where food was scarce, fatness connoted wealth. **157 fetys** elegant; **war** aware. **158–59 smal coral . . . peire of bedes** set (peire) of small coral beads, a rosary; **gauded** divided by green beads; e.g., the modern rosary known as Our Lady's Psalter consists of fifteen decades of beads commemorating the 150 Psalms. **162 *Amor vincit omnia*** Virgil, *Eclogue* X.69 and proverbial. **164 chapeleyne** an official in a nunnery, secretary and assistant to the prioress. **preestes thre** This brings the number of pilgrims in the Prologue to thirty-two, and only one priest appears later. Perhaps it should read "and the prest is thre," or else Chaucer left the line incomplete and someone filled in the phrase for rhyme (it appears in all manuscripts). **165 maistrie** better than all others (French *pour la maistrie*, a medical term meaning "of special efficacy"). **166 outridere** an official who rode about overseeing the monastery's farms and manors; **venerie** hunting (double entendre on venery, "sexual pleasure"?). **168 deyntee** superior (Latin *dignitatem*). **170 Gynglen** Small bells were fashionable harness decorations; the flowers called Canterbury Bells take their name from clusters of small bells often worn by pilgrims' horses. **172 celle** a dependent priory (to the supervision of which the Monk, it is implied, devoted little time). **173 Seint Maure . . . Seint Beneit** St. Benedict, founder of the Benedictine order in 529 at Monte Cassino, Italy, and author of the most famous monastic rule. St. Maurus, according to legend a pupil of St. Benedict, introduced the Benedictine Rule into France c. 550. **174 streit** strict. **175 ilke** same; **pace** pass. **176 space** course. **177 pulled** plucked.

That seith that hunters been nat hooly men,
Ne that a monk, whan he is recchelees,
180 Is likned til a fissh that is waterlees—
This is to seyn, a monk out of his cloystre.
But thilke text heeld he nat worth an oystre.
And I seyde his opinioun was good.
What, sholde he studie and make hymselven wood,
Upon a book in cloystre alwey to poure,
Or swynken with his handes, and laboure,
As Austyn bit? How shal the world be served?
Lat Austyn have his swynk to hym reserved!
Therfore he was a prikasour aright.
190 Grehoundes he hadde as swift as fowel in flight.
Of prikyng and of huntyng for the hare
Was al his lust; for no cost wolde he spare.
I seigh his sleves ypurfiled at the hond
With grys, and that the fyneste of a lond.
And, for to festne his hood under his chyn,
He hadde of gold ywroght a ful curious pyn,
A love-knotte in the gretter ende ther was.
His heed was balled, that shoon as any glas,
And eek his face, as he hadde been enoynt.
200 He was a lord ful fat and in good poynt;
His eyen stepe and rollynge in his heed,
That stemed as a forneys of a leed;
His bootes souple; his hors in greet estaat.
Now certeinly he was a fair prelaat.
He nas nat pale as a forpyned goost.
A fat swan loved he best of any roost.
His palfrey was as broun as is a berye.

A FRERE ther was, a wantowne and a merye,
A lymytour, a ful solempne man.
210 In alle the ordres foure is noon that kan
So muchel of daliaunce and fair langage.
He hadde maad ful many a mariage

---

178 hunters . . . hooly Nimrod, Genesis 10:9,
or St. Jerome on Psalm 90, but a medieval com-
monplace. 179 recchelees reckless, disobedient.
180 fissh . . . waterlees *Vitae Patrum, PL*
73.858, but another commonplace. 184 What
why; wood crazy. 186 swynken work. 187
Austin bit St. Augustine commands. In *De
Opere Monachorum, PL* 40.547, St. Augustine
instructed monks to avoid idleness through regular
manual labor, but this is another commonplace of
monastic rules. 189, 191–92 prikasour . . .
pryking . . . hare . . . lust hard riding, track-
ing, rabbit, pleasure; but all these terms could
have sexual double entendre. 193 ypurfiled fur-
trimmed. 194 grys fine gray fur. 196 curious
intricate. 199 enoynt anointed (with oil). 200

in good poynt stout (French *embonpoint*). 201
stepe bright, flashing. 202 stemed . . . a leed
glowed like the fire under a pot (ancient utensils
were made of lead or lead alloys). 203 greet
estaat fine condition. 205 forpyned distressed.
207 palfrey riding horse. 208 wantowne live-
ly; but many of the terms describing the Friar
have sexual double entendre: here "morally lax."
209 lymytour a friar who paid a fee for an
exclusive territory in which to bet (see ll. 252bc
below); solempne important. 210 ordres foure
Dominican, Franciscan, Carmelite, Augustinian;
kan knows. 211 daliaunce blandishment. 212
maad . . . mariage presumably because the
women had been his mistresses.

Of yonge wommen at his owene cost.
Unto his ordre he was a noble post.
Ful wel biloved and famulier was he
With frankeleyns over al in his contree,
And eek with worthy wommen of the toun,
For he hadde power of confessioun,
As seyde hymself, moore than a curat,
220   For of his ordre he was licenciat.
Ful swetely herde he confessioun,
And plesaunt was his absolucioun—
He was an esy man to yeve penaunce
Ther as he wiste to have a good pitaunce.
For unto a poure ordre for to yive
Is signe that a man is wel yshryve,
For if he yaf, he dorste make avaunt,
He wiste that a man was repentaunt;
For many a man so hard is of his herte,
230   He may nat wepe, althogh hym soore smerte.
Therfore in stede of wepynge and preyeres
Men moote yeve silver to the poure freres.
His typet was ay farsed ful of knyves
And pynnes for to yeven faire wyves.
And certeinly he hadde a murye note:
Wel koude he synge and pleyen on a rote;
Of yeddynges he baar outrely the pris.
His nekke whit was as the flour delys;
Therto he strong was as a champioun.
240   He knew the tavernes wel in every toun,
And everich hostiler and tappestere
Bet than a lazar or a beggestere,
For unto swich a worthy man as he
Acorded nat, as by his facultee,
To have with sike lazars aqueyntaunce.
It is nat honeste, it may nat avaunce,
For to deelen with no swich poraille,
But al with riche and selleres of vitaille.
And over al ther as profit sholde arise

214 post support. **216–17 frankeleyns . . . wommen** The mendicant orders had originally been founded to minister to the poor; see ll. 240-50 below. **218–20 confessioun . . . licenciat** One of the principal tensions of the church in the Middle Ages was the conflicting authority of the friars and parish priests to hear confession and grant absolution for sins. The fact that pardoners could also provide forgiveness for sins further confused the situation. **curat** the assistant priest who did the work in a parish, often in the absence of the vicar (see l. 509 below). **224 pitaunce** gift. **226 yshryve** shriven, absolved. **227 avaunt** boast. **233 typet . . . farsed** hood, stuffed. As the men-dicant orders degenerated, the friars took on functions of peddlers, quack doctors, etc. **236 rote** fiddle. **237 yeddynges** ballads; **pris** prize. **238, 264 nekke whit . . . lipsed** A white neck and lisping were regarded as indications of sensuality. **flour delys** lily. **239 champioun** champion brawler. **241 hostiler** innkeeper; **tappestere** barmaid (the "-stere" is the Old English feminine suffix). **242 lazar** leper (or merely sick person); **beggestere** beggarmaid. **244 Acorded nat** it was not suit able **facultee** ability. **247 deelen** deal; **poraille** poor trash. **248 vitaille** food.

250   Curteis he was and lowely of servyse.
      There nas no man nowher so vertuous.
      He was the beste beggere in his hous,
252b   And yaf a certeyn ferme for the graunt—
252c   Noon of his bretheren cam ther in his haunt—
      For thogh a wydwe hadde noght a sho,
      So plesaunt was his "In principio,"
      Yet wolde he have a ferthyng er he wente.
      His purchas was wel bettre than his rente.
      And rage he koude, as it were right a whelpe.
      In love-dayes ther koude he muchel helpe,
      For ther he was nat lyk a cloysterer
260   With a thredbare cope, as is a poure scoler,
      But he was lyk a maister or a pope.
      Of double worstede was his semycope,
      That rounded as a belle out of the presse.
      Somwhat he lipsed for his wantownesse
      To make his Englissh sweete upon his tonge.
      And in his harpyng, whan that he hadde songe,
      His eyen twynkled in his heed aryght,
      As doon the sterres in the frosty nyght.
      This worthy lymytour was cleped Huberd.

270   A MARCHANT was ther with a forked berd,
      In mottelee, and hye on horse he sat,
      Upon his heed a Flaundryssh bevere hat,
      His bootes clasped faire and fetisly.
      His resons he spak ful solempnely,
      Sownynge alwey th'encrees of his wynnyng.
      He wolde the see were kept for any thyng
      Bitwixe Middelburgh and Orewelle.
      Wel koude he in eschaunge sheeldes selle.
      This worthy man ful wel his wit bisette—
280   Ther wiste no wight that he was in dette,

---

250 lowely humbly. **252b ferme** rent. See "lymytour," l. 209 above. **252c haunt** territory. **253 sho** shoe. **254 "In principio"** The fourteen opening verses of the Gospel of St. John were the friars' habitual salutation, used as a sort of magical incantation. **256 purchas** income. **257 rage . . . whelpe** usually interpreted "romp like a puppy," but equally possibly "be nasty as a dog" to anyone who did not make a donation. **258 love-dayes** days set apart for settlement of differences by arbitration, in which the clergy often acted as arbiters. Eventually the "day" came to denote simply the practice of conciliation rather than legal proceeding. **259 cloysterer** recluse. **260 cope** cloak. **263 presse** bell mold. **268 frosty nyght** See the Monk's eyes above (l. 201). Dante associated sins of passion with heat, sins of malice with cold. **269 Huberd** not a common name in the fourteenth century, but in *Roman de Renart* the kite is named Hubert. **270 forked berd** high fashion for the time. **271 mottelee** cloth of mixed color; **hye on horse** i.e., in order to be imposing. **272 Flaundryssh bevere hat** beaverskin hat made in Flanders. **273 fetisly** elegantly. **274 resons** opinions. **275 Sownynge** implying; **wynnyng** profit. **276 wolde** wanted; **kept for any thyng** protected at any cost. **277 Middelburgh** Middleburgh, Dutch port licensed (stapled) to import English wool 1384–88 (which helps date the composition of the General Prologue); **Orewelle** Orwell, the river by Ipswich, one of the English staple ports. **278 eschaunge sheeldes selle** make money exchanging currencies. "Sheeldes" were French gold *florins d'escu*. **279 bisette** employed.

So estatly was he of his governaunce
With his bargaynes and with his chevyssaunce.
For sothe he was a worthy man withalle,
But, sooth to seyn, I noot how men hym calle.

A CLERK ther was of Oxenford also
That unto logyk hadde longe ygo.
As leene was his hors as is a rake,
And he nas nat right fat, I undertake,
But looked holwe, and therto sobrely.
290 Ful thredbare was his overeste courtepy,
For he hadde geten hym yet no benefice,
Ne was so worldly for to have office.
For hym was levere have at his beddes heed
Twenty bookes, clad in blak or reed,
Of Aristotle and his philosophie,
Than robes riche, or fithele, or gay sautrie.
But al be that he was a philosophre,
Yet hadde he but litel gold in cofre.
But al that he myghte of his freendes hente,
300 On bookes and on lernynge he it spente,
And bisily gan for the soules preye
Of hem that yaf hym wherwith to scoleye.
Of studie took he moost cure and moost heede.
Noght o word spak he moore than was neede,
And that was seyd in forme and reverence,
And short and quyk and ful of hy sentence.
Sownynge in moral vertu was his speche,
And gladly wolde he lerne and gladly teche.

A SERGEANT OF THE LAWE, war and wys,
310 That often hadde been at the Parvys,
Ther was also, ful riche of excellence.
Discreet he was and of greet reverence—
He semed swich, his wordes weren so wise.

281 **estatly** dignified; **governaunce** management. 282 **chevyssaunce** buying and selling on credit for interest. 284 **noot how** don't know what. 285 **clerk** student (all university students then were ostensibly studying for the clergy). 286 **logyk** the top of the bachelor of arts "trivium" (grammar, rhetoric, logic), before proceeding to the master of arts "quadrivium" (arithmetic, geometry, astronomy, music). Perhaps mild humor is intended. 290 **overeste courtepy** overcoat. 291 **benefice** ecclesiastical appointment. 292 **office** secular appointment as clerk in government or for a rich lord. 294 **Twenty bookes** A single large codex, handwritten on enough vellum to make, for example, fifty pairs of shoes, might be worth as much as one-sixth the price of a town house. 296 **fithele** fiddle; **sautrie** psaltery (harp). 297–98 **philosophre . . . gold** double entendre on philosophers as alchemists, whose chief preoccupation was thought to be trying to turn base metals to gold, often with the help of the "philosopher's stone." 299 **hente** get. In a period of patronage, most students in the university were aided by wealthy patrons. 302 **scoleye** study, attend school. 303 **cure** attention. 305 **in forme and reverence** formally and respectfully. 306 **sentence** implication. 307 **Sownynge** resounding, reflecting. 309 SERGEANT OF THE LAWE one of about twenty justices especially appointed by the king to act as judges and barons of the exchequer; **war** wary. 310 **Parvys** paradise, the court in front of a church; in this instance, the porch of St. Paul's Cathedral, where lawyers met their clients.

Justice he was ful often in assise,
By patente and by pleyn commissioun.
For his science and for his heigh renoun,
Of fees and robes hadde he many oon.
So greet a purchasour was nowher noon:
Al was fee symple to hym in effect,
320 His purchasyng myghte nat been infect.
Nowher so bisy a man as he ther nas,
And yet he semed bisier than he was.
In termes hadde he caas and doomes alle
That from the tyme of Kyng William were yfalle.
Therto he koude endite and make a thyng,
Ther koude no wight pynche at his writyng;
And every statut koude he pleyn by rote.
He rood but hoomly in a medlee cote,
Girt with a ceint of silk, with barres smale—
330 Of his array telle I no lenger tale.

A FRANKELEYN was in his compaignye.
Whit was his berd as is the dayesye;
Of his complexioun he was sangwyn.
We loved he by the morwe a sop in wyn.
To lyven in delit was evere his wone,
For he was Epicurus owene sone,
That heeld opinioun that pleyn delit
Was verray felicitee parfit.
An housholdere, and that a greet, was he;
340 Seint Julian he was in his contree.
His breed, his ale, was alweys after oon.
A bettre envyned man was nowher noon.
Withoute bake mete was nevere his hous,
Of fissh and flessh, and that so plenteuous,
It snewed in his hous of mete and drynke,
Of alle deyntees that men koude thynke.
After the sondry sesons of the yeer,

314 Justice judge; **assise** county court. **315 patente** royal warrant; **pleyn commissioun** full commission. **316 science** knowledge; **renoun** reputation. **317 robes** Payment was frequently in the form of clothing, jewelry, etc. **318 purchasour** Skillful operators were beginning to be able to purchase feudally entailed properties. **319 fee symple** owned outright, without legal restrictions. **320 infect** invalidated. **323 In termes . . . caas . . . doomes** in negotiating, cases, decisions (i.e., the precedents of common law). **324 William** William the Conqueror. **325 endite and make a thyng** compose and draw up a legal document. **326 wight pynche** person protest; again possibly double entendre, since there was a contemporary sergeant of the law named Thomas Pynchbek. **327 koude he pleyn by rote** knew he fully by heart. **328 hoomly** informally; **medlee** cloth of mixed color. **329 ceint** belt; **barres** metal ornaments. **331 FRANKELEYN** a wealthy landowner. **333 sangwyn** The four medieval temperaments (humors) were choleric, phlegmatic, melancholic, and sanguine, the last being characterized by excess of blood and a ruddy complexion. **334 morwe** morning; **sop in wyn** bread soaked in wine. **335 delit** sensual pleasure; **wone** habit. **336 Epicurus** The popular view equates Epicureanism with hedonism. **337 pleyn delit** total pleasure; **338 verray felicitee** true bliss. **340 Seint Julian** patron saint of hospitality. **341 after oon** uniformly good. **342 envyned** provided with wine. **347–48 sesons . . . chaunged** menu in

So chaunged he his mete and his soper.
Ful many a fat partrich hadde he in muwe,
350 And many a breem and many a luce in stuwe.
Wo was his cook but if his sauce were
Poynaunt and sharp, and redy al his geere.
His table dormant in his halle alway
Stood redy covered al the longe day.
At sessiouns ther was he lord and sire.
Ful ofte tyme he was knyght of the shire.
An anlaas and a gipser al of silk
Heeng at his girdel, whit as morne milk.
A shirreve hadde he been, and a contour.
360 Was nowher swich a worthy vavasour.

An HABERDASSHERE and a CARPENTER,
A WEBBE, a DYERE, and a TAPYCER,
And they were clothed alle in o lyveree
Of a solempne and a greet fraternitee.
Ful fressh and newe hir geere apiked was:
Hir knyves were chaped noght with bras
But al with silver; wroght ful clene and weel
Hire girdles and hir pouches everydeel.
Wel semed ech of hem a fair burgeys
370 To sitten in a yeldehalle on a deys.
Everich, for the wisdowm that he kan,
Was shaply for to been an alderman.
For catel hadde they ynogh and rente,
And eek hir wyves wolde it wel assente;
And elles certeyn were they to blame.
It is ful fair to been ycleped "madame,"
And goon to vigilies al bifore,
And have a mantel roialliche ybore.

A COOK they hadde with hem for the nones
380 To boille the chiknes with the marybones,
And poudre-marchant tart and galyngale.

accordance with the seasons, such as hot or cold, feast day or fast day. **349 muwe** coop. **350 breem** bream; **luce in stuwe** pike in fish pond. **352 Poynaunt** piquant. **353 dormant** laid out; trestle tables were ordinarily removed between meals. **355 sessiouns . . . lord and sire** At county courts the lord of the manor presided. **356 knyght of the shire** representative to Parliament. **357 anlaas** dagger; **gipser** purse. **359 A shirreve** a sheriff; **a contour** a tax collector. **360 vavasour** holder of land by subinfeudation. **361 HABERDASSHERE** dealer in men's clothes and sewing notions. **362 WEBBE** weaver; **TAPYCER** tapestry weaver. **363–64 o lyveree . . . fraternitee** same uniform. The guildsmen belonged to a liveried parish fraternity having both religious and social functions, perhaps the Guild of St. Fabian and St. Sebastian of St. Botolph's Church in Aldersgate Ward, which was a center of the cloth trade. **365 apiked** furbished. **366 chaped** mounted. **369 burgeys** prosperous citizen. **370 yeldehalle** guildhall; **deys** platform. **371 kan** knew. **372 shaply** suitable; **alderman** elected official. **373 catel** chattels (property); **rente** income. Only prosperous people could afford the entertaining and other expenses attendant upon civic office. **377 vigilies** services before guild festivals at which aldermen's wives would enjoy precedence. **379 nones** occasion. **380 marybones** marrowbones. **381 poudre-marchant tart** tart spice; **galyngale** sweet spice.

Wel koude he knowe a draughte of Londoun ale,
He koude rooste and sethe and broille and frye,
Maken mortreux, and wel bake a pye.
But greet harm was it, as it thoughte me,
That on his shyne a mormal hadde he.
For blankmanger, that made he with the beste.

A SHIPMAN was ther, wonynge fer by weste.
For aught I woot, he was of Dertemouthe.
390 He rood upon a rouncy, as he kouthe,
In a gowne of faldyng to the knee.
A daggere hangynge on a laas hadde he
Aboute his nekke, under his arm adoun.
The hoote somer hadde maad his hewe al broun.
And certeinly he was a good felawe.
Ful many a draughte of wyn had he ydrawe
Fro Burdeux-ward, whil that the chapman sleepe.
Of nyce conscience took he no keepe.
If that he faught, and hadde the hyer hond,
400 By water he sente hem hoom to every lond.
But of his craft to rekene wel his tydes,
His stremes, and his daungers hym bisides,
His herberwe, and his moone, his lodemenage,
Ther nas noon swich from Hulle to Cartage.
Hardy he was and wys to undertake.
With many a tempest hadde his berd been shake.
He knew alle the havenes, as they were,
Fro Gootlond to the cape of Fynystere,
And every cryke in Britaigne and in Spayne.
410 His barge ycleped was the Maudelayne.

With us ther was a DOCTOUR OF PHISIK;
In al this world ne was ther noon hym lik,
To speke of phisik and of surgerye,
For he was grounded in astronomye.
He kepte his pacient a ful greet deel
In houres by his magyk natureel.

382 knowe recognize; **Londoun ale** London ale was particularly good. **383 sethe** boil. **384 mortreux** stews. **386 mormal** a pustulous sore. **387 blankmanger** a white pudding of milk, rice, and condiments. **388 wonynge** living. **389 Dertemouthe** a port in Devonshire notorious for smugglers and pirates. **390 rouncy** a pack horse; **kouthe** He rode like a sailor. **391 faldyng** coarse wool. **392 laas** lace, strap. **397 Burdeux-ward** coming from Bordeaux; **chapman** merchant. **398 nyce** scrupulous; **keepe** heed. **399 hyer hond** victory. **400 By water** He threw his victims overboard. **401 craft to rekene** skill to calculate. **402 stremes** currents. **403 herberwe** anchorage; **moone** moon (most legitimate seamen navigate during the day by the sun); **lodemenage** piloting. **404 Hulle** Hull in northern England; **Cartage** Carthage in North Africa or Cartagena in Spain. **408 Gootlond** Gotland in the Baltic; **Fynystere** "land's end" in Spain. **409 cryke** creek (smuggler's haven); **Britaigne** Brittany. **410 Maudelayne** In 1391 Peter Risshenden was recorded as the master of a ship named the *Maudeleyne* out of Dartmouth. **414 astronomye** astrology; the effects of medicines and treatments (natural magic) were thought to depend upon a person's horoscope. **416 houres** the favorable hours of the horoscope.

Wel koude he fortunen the ascendent
Of his ymages for his pacient.
He knew the cause of everich maladye,
420 Were it of hoot, or coold, or moyste, or drye,
And where engendred, and of what humour.
He was a verray, parfit praktisour.
The cause yknowe, and of his harm the roote,
Anon he yaf the sike man his boote.
Ful redy hadde he his apothecaries
To sende hym drogges and his letuaries,
For ech of hem made oother for to wynne—
Hir frendshipe nas nat newe to bigynne.
Wel knew he the olde Esculapius,
430 And Deyscorides, and eek Rufus,
Olde Ypocras, Haly, and Galyen,
Serapion, Razis, and Avycen,
Averrois, Damascien, and Constantyn,
Bernard, and Gatesden, and Gilbertyn.
Of his diete mesurable was he,
For it was of no superfluitee,
But of greet norissyng and digestible.
His studie was but litel on the Bible.
In sangwyn and in pers he clad was al,
440 Lyned with taffata and with sendal,
And yet he was but esy of dispence.
He kepte that he wan in pestilence,
For gold in phisik is a cordial;
Therefore he lovede gold in special.

A good WIF was ther OF biside BATHE,
But she was somdel deef, and that was scathe.
Of clooth makyng she hadde swich an haunt,
She passed hem of Ypres and of Gaunt.
In al the parisshe wif ne was ther noon
450 That to the offrynge bifore hire sholde goon;
And if ther dide, certeyn so wrooth was she

417–18 ascendent . . . ymages presumably astrological representations related to the patient's horoscope. 420 the four humors. 422 verray true; parfit perfect. 424 boote remedy. 426 letuaries electuaries (drugs in syrups). 427 wynne profit. 429–34 Aesculapius, Dioscorides, Rufus, Hippocrates, and Galen were famous Greek physicians. Serapion, Hali (Ali ben el-Abbas), Rhazes, Avicenna, and Averroes were Persian and Arabic physicians. Damascien and Constantinus Africanus were early Christian physicians. Bernard Gordon, John Gaddesden, and Gilbertus Anglicus were famous British physicians. Gaddesden was an instructor at Merton College and court physician. 435 mesurable moderate. 439 sangwyn red; pers blue. 440 taffata . . . sendal varieties of silk. 441 esy of dispence moderate of expenditure. 442 wan acquired; pestilence plague. 443 double entendre: aurum potibile was a certified medieval medicine. 445 biside BATHE St. Michael's juxta Bathon was a parish just north of Bath given over to weaving. 446 scathe unfortunate. 447 haunt skill. 448 passed . . . Ypres . . . Gaunt surpassed; perhaps humorous, since weavers of the west of England were known to be inferior to those of the Low Countries (Ypres and Ghent are both in modern Belgium). 450 offrynge bifore Precedence in church was evidently important; see l. 377 above and Parson's Tale, l. 407.

That she was out of alle charitee.
Hir coverchiefs ful fyne weren of ground.
I dorste swere they weyeden ten pound
That on a Sonday weren upon hir heed.
Hir hosen weren of fyn scarlet reed,
Ful streite yteyd, and shoes ful moyste and newe.
Boold was hir face, and fair, and reed of hewe.
She was a worthy womman al hir lyve.
460 Housbondes at chirche dore she hadde fyve,
Withouten oother compaignye in youthe—
But therof nedeth nat to speke as nowthe.
And thries hadde she been at Jerusalem.
She hadde passed many a straunge strem.
At Rome she hadde been, and at Boloigne,
In Galice at Seint-Jame, and at Coloigne.
She koude muchel of wandrynge by the weye.
Gat-tothed was she, soothly for to seye.
Upon an amblere esily she sat,
470 Ywympled wel, and on hir heed an hat
As brood as is a bokeler or a targe,
A foot-mantel aboute hir hipes large,
And on hir feet a paire of spores sharpe.
In felaweshipe wel koude she laughe and carpe.
Of remedies of love she knew per chaunce,
For she koude of that art the olde daunce.

A good man was ther of religioun,
And was a poure PERSOUN of a toun,
But riche he was of hooly thoght and werk.
480 He was also a lerned man, a clerk,
That Cristes gospel trewely wolde preche.
His parisshens devoutly wolde he teche.
Benygne he was, and wonder diligent,
And in adversitee ful pacient,
And swich he was preved ofte sithes.
Ful looth were hym to cursen for his tithes,
But rather wolde he yeven, out of doute,
Unto his poure parisshens aboute
Of his offrying and eek of his substaunce.

453 coverchiefs kerchiefs; **ground** texture. **454 ten pound** again humorous exaggeration. **456 hosen** tight, laced leggings. **457 streite** straitly (closely). **460 chirche door** The marriage was performed at the door, after which the couple entered the church for Mass. **461 Withouten** without counting. **465 Boloigne** Boulogne (France). **466 Seint-Jame** St. James of Compostella in Galicia (Spain); **Coloigne** Cologne (Germany). **467 koude** knew. **468 Gat-tothed** gaptoothed, by physiognomists supposed to indicate a bold, lascivious nature. **469 amblere** easy-gaited saddle horse. **470 Ywympled** swathed in a headdress that covered all but the face. **471 bokeler . . . targe** terms for shields. **472 footmantel** a protective outer skirt. **474 carpe** joke. **475 remedies** One of Ovid's erotic books is the *Remedia amoris*. **478 PERSOUN** Parson. **482 parisshens** parishioners. **485 swich** such; **sithes** times. **486 cursen** excommunicate; **tithes** one-tenth of one's income owed to the church. **489 offryng** voluntary offering to the priest; **substaunce** income from property belonging to the church.

490 He koude in litel thyng have suffisaunce.
Wyd was his parisshe and houses fer asonder,
But he ne lefte nat, for reyn ne thonder,
In siknesse nor in meschief to visite
The ferreste in his parisshe, muche and lite,
Upon his feet, and in his hand a staf.
This noble ensample to his sheep he yaf,
That first he wroghte, and afterward he taughte.
Out of the gospel he tho wordes caughte,
And this figure he added eek therto,
500 That if gold ruste, what shal iren do?
For if a preest be foul, on whom we truste,
No wonder is a lewed man to ruste.
And shame it is, if a preest take keep,
A shiten shepherde and a clene sheep.
Wel oghte a preest ensample for to yive,
By his clennesse, how that his sheep sholde lyve.
He sette nat his benefice to hyre
And leet his sheep encombred in the myre
And ran to Londoun unto Seinte Poules
510 To seken hym a chaunterie for soules,
Or with a bretherhed to been withholde,
But dwelte at hoom, and kepte wel his folde
So that the wolf ne made it nat myscarie.
He was a shepherde and noght a mercenarie.
And though he hooly were and vertuous,
He was nat to synful men despitous,
Ne of his speche daungerous ne digne,
But in his techyng discreet and benygne.
To drawen folk to hevene by fairnesse,
520 By good ensample, this was his bisynesse.
But it were any persone obstinat,
What so he were, of heigh or lough estat,
Hym wolde he snybben sharply for the nonys.
A bettre preest I trowe that nowher noon ys.
He waited after no pompe and reverence
Ne maked hym a spiced conscience,
But Cristes loore and his apostles twelve
He taughte, but first he folwed it hymselve.

With hym ther was a PLOWMAN, was his brother,
530 That hadde ylad of dong ful many a fother.

490 **suffisaunce** sufficiency. 494 **ferreste** farthest; **muche and lite** great and small. 495 **staf** emblem of the good shepherd. 497 **wroghte** performed. 502 **lewed** ignorant. 503 **keep** heed. 504 **shiten** befouled with excrement. 507–09 **hyre . . . ran to Londoun** hire someone to care for his parish and himself take another job in London (see l. 219 above). 510 **chaunterie** cathedral chapel endowed for a priest to say daily masses for the souls of the endowers. 511 **bretherhed** guild; **withholde** to be supported. 516 **despitous** contemptuous. 517 **daungerous ne digne** disdainful nor haughty. 521 **But it** but if any person. 523 **snybben** scold; **nonys** promptly (without hesitation). 525 **waited after** expected. 526 **spiced** overfastidious, affected. 530 **fother** cart load.

A trewe swynkere and a good was he,
Lyvynge in pees and parfit charitee.
God loved he best with al his hoole herte
At alle tymes, thogh him gamed or smerte,
And thanne his neighebore right as hymselve.
He wolde thresshe, and therto dyke and delve,
For Cristes sake, for every poure wight,
Withouten hire, if it lay in his myght.
His tithes payde he ful faire and wel,
540 Bothe of his propre swynk and his catel.
In a tabard he rood upon a mere.

Ther was also a REVE, and a MILLERE,
A SOMNOUR, and a PARDONER also,
A MAUNCIPLE, and myself—ther were namo.

The MILLERE was a stout carl for the nones;
Ful byg he was of brawn, and eek of bones.
That proved wel, for over al ther he cam,
At wrastlynge he wolde have alwey the ram.
He was short-sholdred, brood, a thikke knarre;
550 Ther was no dore that he nolde heve of harre,
Or breke it at a rennyng with his heed.
His berd as any sowe or fox was reed,
And therto brood, as though it were a spade.
Upon the cop right of his nose he hade
A werte, and theron stood a toft of herys
Reed as the brustles of a sowes erys.
His nosethirles blake were and wyde.
A swerd and bokeler bar he by his syde.
His mouth as greet was as a greet forneys.
560 He was a janglere and a goliardeys,
And that was moost of synne and harlotries.
Wel koude he stelen corn and tollen thries.
And yet he hadde a thombe of gold, pardee.
A whit cote and a blew hood wered he.

531 swynkere laborer. 534 gamed or smerte pleasant or unpleasant. 535 neighebore Medieval Christian doctrine was summed up in Matthew 22:37–39: "Thou shalt love the Lord thy God with all thy heart, and with all thy soul, and with all thy mind. This is the first and great commandment. And the second is like unto it, Thou shalt love thy neighbour as thyself." 536 dyke and delve ditch and dig. 537 wight person. 540 propre swynk own labor; catel property. 541 tabard workingman's smock, and the name of the Southwark inn at which Chaucer's Canterbury pilgrimage begins; mere a gentle mount traditionally ridden by priests and women. 545 carl Danish form of churl, fellow. This description should be compared with that in

Reeve's Tale ll. 3925 ff. 548 ram a prize at country contests. 549 knarre knot (as in wood). 550 dore . . . of harre door off its hinges. 551 rennyng running (at), butting — such heaving and butting were evidently the Miller's ideas of sport. 554 cop ridge. 557 nosethirles nostrils. 558 bokeler shield. 559 forneys furnace; suggesting medieval representations of the gaping mouth of hell. 560 janglere windbag; goliardeys teller of dirty stories. By Chaucer's day "goliard" meant a vagabond cleric. 562 tollen thries take his toll or percentage thrice. 563 thombe of gold double entendre: a thumb skilled in testing grain and flour, but there was also a proverb, "An honest miller has a golden thumb," meaning there is no such thing as an honest miller.

A baggepipe wel koude he blowe and sowne,
And therwithal he broghte us out of towne.

A gentil MAUNCIPLE was ther of a temple,
Of which achatours myghte take exemple
For to be wise in byynge of vitaille.
570 For wheither that he payde or took by taille,
Algate he wayted so in his achaat
That he was ay biforn and in good staat.
Now is nat that of God a ful fair grace
That swich a lewed mannes wit shal pace
The wisdom of an heep of lerned men?
Of maistres hadde he mo than thries ten
That weren of lawe expert and curious,
Of which there were a duszeyne in that hous
Worthy to been stywardes of rente and lond
580 Of any lord that is in Engelond,
To maken hym lyve by his propre good
In honour dettelees, but if he were wood,
Or lyve as scarsly as hym list desire;
And able for to helpen al a shire
In any caas that myghte falle or happe—
And yet this Manciple sette hir aller cappe.

The REVE was a sclendre colerik man.
His berd was shave as ny as ever he kan.
His heer was by his erys ful round yshorn.
590 His top was dokked lyk a preest biforn.
Ful longe were his legges and ful lene,
Ylyk a staf: ther was no calf ysene.
Wel koude he kepe a gerner and a bynne.
Ther was noon auditour koude on him wynne.
Wel wiste he by the droghte and by the reyn
The yeldynge of his seed and of his greyn.
His lordes sheep, his neet, his dayerye,
His swyn, his hors, his stoor, and his pultrye
Was hoolly in this Reves governynge,
600 And by his covenant yaf the rekenynge,
Syn that his lord was twenty yeer of age.

---

567 MAUNCIPLE . . . temple business agent for a college, in this case for one of the Inns of Court, two of which occupied buildings confiscated when the order of Knights Templars was suppressed in 1312. Chaucer may have attended such an institution and observed such a clever servant. 568 achatours purchasers. 570 taille talley, i.e., on credit. 571 wayted attended; achaat buying. 574 swich a lewed such an unlearned; pace surpass. 577 curious cunning. 579 stywardes stewards (managers); rente income. 581 lyve by . . . good live within his own means. 582 wood crazy. 583 scarsly econom-ically. 585 caas situation; falle or happe befall or happen. 586 sette hir aller cappe deceived them all. 587 REVE reeve, manager of a farm; colerik of bilious humor, peevish. 588 shave Being shaved in a full-bearded age was unnatu-ral, sinister. In illustrations, Satan is never bearded vs. the full-bearded Lord. 590 dokked cut short, see the Yeoman, l. 109 above. 593 kepe a gerner protect a granary. 594 auditour the lord's ac-countant who audited the Reeve's receipts and expenditures. 597 neet cattle. 598 stoor live-stock. 600 covenant contract.

Ther koude no man brynge hym in arrerage.
Ther nas baillif, ne hierde, nor oother hyne
That he ne knew his sleighte and his covyne;
They were adrad of hym as of the deeth.
His wonyng was ful faire upon an heeth;
With grene trees shadwed was his place.
He koude bettre than his lord purchace;
Ful riche he was astored pryvely.
610   His lord wel koude he plesen subtilly,
To yeve and lene hym of his owene good,
And have a thank, and yet a cote and hood.
In youthe he hadde lerned a good myster,
He was a wel good wrighte, a carpenter.
This Reve sat upon a ful good stot,
That was al pomely grey and highte Scot.
A long surcote of pers upon he hade,
And by his syde he baar a rusty blade.
Of Northfolk was this Reve of which I telle,
620   Biside a toun men clepen Baldeswelle.
Tukked he was as is a frere aboute,
And evere he rood the hyndreste of oure route.

    A SOMONOUR was ther with us in that place
That hadde a fyr-reed cherubynnes face,
For sawcefleem he was, with eyen narwe.
As hoot he was and lecherous as a sparwe,
With scalled browes blake and piled berd.
Of his visage children were aferd.
Ther nas quyksilver, lytarge, ne brymstoon,
630   Boras, ceruce, ne oille of tartre noon,
Ne oynement that wolde clense and byte,
That hym myghte helpen of his whelkes white,
Nor of the knobbes sittynge on his chekes.

---

603 baillif farm boss; **hierde** herdsman; **hyne** farm laborer. **604 sleighte** trick; **covyne** dishonesty. **606 wonyng** home. **608 bettre . . . purchace** had more money with which to buy. **609 astored** In Chaucer's time wealth would be reckoned more in food and equipment stored away than in money in the bank. **611 lene** lend. **612 cote and hood** Payment was frequently in clothing; see l. 317 above. **613 myster** mystery, craft. **615 stot** farm horse. **616 pomely** dappled; **highte** was called. **617 surcote of pers** blue overcoat. **619–20 Northfolk . . . Baldeswelle** Chaucer was indirectly concerned with the management of some of the Norfolk estates (although not this one) of the young Earl of Pembroke. Perhaps he had had dealings there with someone

like this reeve. **622 hyndreste . . . route** last in our company. Since the Miller evidently rode at the head of the procession (l. 566 above), it appears that Chaucer was already preparing for their quarrel. **623 SOMONOUR** a process-server for the ecclesiastical courts, which were charged with regulating morals and domestic life, and were, by Chaucer's time, in very low repute. **624–25 fyr-reed . . . sawcefleem . . . narwe** suffering from a skin disease that caused facial swelling and narrowing of the eyes. **626 hoot** hot, lascivious. **627 scalled** scabby; **piled** bald in spots. **629–30 quyksilver** mercury; **lytarge** white lead; **brymstoon** sulfur; **Boras** borax; **ceruce** again white lead; **oille of tartre** cream of tartar. **632 whelkes** pustules.

Wel loved he garleek, oynons, and eek lekes,
And for to drynken strong wyn, reed as blood.
Thanne wolde he speke and crie as he were wood,
And whan that he wel dronken hadde the wyn,
Thanne wolde he speke no word but Latyn.
A fewe termes hadde he, two or thre,
640 That he had lerned out of som decree—
No wonder is, he herde it al the day,
And eek ye knowen wel how that a jay
Kan clepen "Watte" as wel as kan the pope.
But whoso koude in oother thyng hym grope,
Thanne hadde he spent al his philosophie.
Ay "Questio quid iuris" wolde he crie.
He was a gentil harlot and a kynde;
A bettre felawe sholde men noght fynde.
He wolde suffre for a quart of wyn
650 A good felawe to have his concubyn
A twelf-monthe, and excuse hym atte fulle.
Ful prively a fynch eek koude he pulle.
And if he foond owher a good felawe,
He wolde techen hym to have noon awe
In swich caas of the ercedekenes curs,
But if a mannes soule were in his purs,
For in his purs he sholde ypunysshed be.
"Purs is the ercedekenes helle," seyde he.
But wel I woot he lyed right in dede.
660 Of cursyng oghte ech gilty man him drede,
For curs wol slee right as assoillyng savith,
And also war hym of a *Significavit*.
In daunger hadde he at his owene gise
The yonge girles of the diocise,
And knew hir conseil, and was al hir reed.
A gerland hadde he set upon his heed
As greet as it were for an alestake.
A bokeleer hadde he maad hym of a cake.

634 garleek, onyons, and eek leeks foods thought in the Middle Ages to inflame sexual desire and cause skin disease. The Israelites hungered after these pungent Egyptian foods in contrast to manna (Numbers 11:5). **636 wood** demented. **643 clepen "Watte"** say "Wat" (Walter). **644 grope** test. **646 "Questio quid iuris"** the question is, what point of law applies? —a familiar tag in legal proceedings. **647 harlot** rascal. **652 fynch . . . pulle** perhaps double entendre, pluck a bird (blackmail), but with sexual or even homosexual overtones. **653 owher** anywhere; **good felawe** boon companion. **655 ercedekenes curs** archdeacon's excommunication. The archdeacon presided over ecclesiastical courts, whose punishments were supposed to be penance and excommunication rather than prison and execution. **656 But if** unless. **661 assoillyng** absolution. **662 war** beware; *Significavit* "Be it known" (the opening of a writ of excommunication). **663 daunger** power; **gise** pleasure. **664 girles** double entendre: young person (of either sex), but beginning to be restricted to young females, and Chaucer so uses it at *Miller's Tale* l. 3769. **665 reed** counselor. **667 greet . . . alestake** The sign of a tavern was a horizontal stake projecting into the street, adorned by a wreath or bush. **668 bokeleer** shield; **cake** round loaf.

With hym ther rood a gentil PARDONER
670 Of Rouncivale, his freend and his compeer,
That streight was comen fro the court of Rome.
Ful loude he soong "Com hider, love, to me!"
This Somonour bar to hym a stif burdoun.
Was nevere trompe of half so greet a soun.
This Pardoner hadde heer as yelow as wex,
But smothe it heeng as dooth a strike of flex.
By ounces henge his lokkes that he hadde,
And therwith he his shuldres overspradde,
But thynne it lay, by colpons oon and oon.
680 But hood, for jolitee, wered he noon,
For it was trussed up in his walet.
Hym thoughte he rood al of the newe jet;
Dischevelee, save his cappe, he rood al bare.
Swiche glarynge eyen hadde he as an hare.
A vernycle hadde he sowed upon his cappe.
His walet lay biforn hym in his lappe,
Bretful of pardoun, comen from Rome al hoot.
A voys he hadde as smal as hath a goot.
No berd hadde he, ne nevere sholde ꞏave.
690 As smothe it was as it were late shave.
I trowe he were a geldyng or a mare.
But of his craft, fro Berwyk into Ware,
Ne was ther swich another pardoner.
For in his male he hadde a pilwe-beer,
Which that he seyde was Oure Lady veyl.
He seyde he hadde a gobet of the seyl
That Seint Peter hadde, whan that he wente
Upon the see, til Jhesu Crist hym hente.
He hadde a croys of latoun ful of stones,

669–70 PARDONER of Rouncivale . . . compeer
Pardoners were employed by religious and chari-
table institutions (like the dependent house of the
Spanish order of Our Lady of Roncevaux which
maintained a hospital at Charing Cross, just out-
side London) to sell indulgences, or commutations
of penances imposed for sins. By the fourteenth
century sale of indulgences was a major source of
revenue for all branches of the church, and very
serious abuses had arisen. The Summoner should
have been protecting people against these abuses.
672 "Com hider . . ." line from a popular love
song. **673 stif burdoun** strong bass. **676 strike
of flex** hank of flax. **677 ounces** small bits.
679 colpons oon strands one. **680 jolitee** plea-
sure, affectation. **682 newe jet** new fashion. **683
Dischevelee . . . bare** with hair loose, bare-
headed. Until recently going bareheaded in public
had been considered immodest. **684 Swiche gla-**

rynge such staring. **685 vernycle** a small ver-
onica. St. Veronica was reputed to have lent Jesus
her kerchief to wipe his face when he was carrying
the cross to Calvary. When he returned it to her,
his features were miraculously imprinted on it.
Copies of this "vera icon" (true likeness) were
sold in Rome as Pilgrims' mementos. **687 Bretful**
brimful. **691 geldyng** The signs lead to the
conclusion that the Pardoner was impotent. His
impotence intimates the impotence of his par-
dons as the Summoner's disease intimates the cor-
ruption of the ecclesiastical courts. **692 Berwyk
into Ware** from Berwick-on-Tweed, south of
Edinburgh, to Ware, north of London — i.e.,
from one end of England to the other. **694 pilwe-
beer** pillowcase. **696 gobet** big piece. **698
hente** grasped, when he tried to walk on the
water (Matthew 14:31). **699 latoun ful of stones**
fake gold (copper alloy), set with fake jewels.

700 And in a glas he hadde pigges bones.
But with thise relikes, whan that he fond
A poure person dwellynge upon lond,
Upon a day he gat hym moore moneye
Than that the person gat in monthes tweye.
And thus, with feyned flaterye and japes,
He made the person and the peple his apes.
But trewely to tellen atte laste,
He was in chirche a noble ecclesiaste.
Wel koude he rede a lessoun or a storie,
710 But alderbest he song an offertorie,
For wel he wiste, whan that song was songe,
He moste preche and wel affile his tonge
To wynne silver, as he ful wel koude;
Therefore he song the murierly and loude.

Now have I toold you shortly, in a clause,
Th'estaat, th'array, the nombre, and eek the cause
Why that assembled was this compaignye
In Southwerk at this gentil hostelrye
That highte the Tabard, faste by the Belle.
720 But now is tyme to yow for to telle
How that we baren us that ilke nyght,
Whan we were in that hostelrie alyght.
And after wol I telle of oure viage
And al the remenaunt of oure pilgrimage.
But first I pray yow, of youre curteisye,
That ye n'arette it nat my vileynye
Thogh that I pleynly speke in this mateere,
To telle yow hir wordes and hir cheere,
Ne thogh I speke hir wordes proprely.
730 For this ye knowen al so wel as I,
Whoso shal telle a tale after a man,
He moot reherce as ny as evere he kan
Everich a word, if it be in his charge,
Al speke he never so rudeliche and large,
Or ellis he moot telle his tale untrewe,
Or feyne thyng, or fynde wordes newe.
He may nat spare, althogh he were his brother;
He moot as wel seye o word as another.
Crist spak hymself ful brode in hooly writ,

700–01 bones . . . relikes fake religious relics.
702 upon lond in the country. 705 feyned pretended; japes tricks. 706 apes made monkeys of them. 710 alderbest best of all. 711 wiste knew. 712 affile file, sharpen. 719 Belle No inn named the Bell has been identified near the Southwark Tabard. Bell was the name of one of the licensed houses of prostitution in Southwark in

the sixteenth century, and perhaps in the fourteenth. 721 baren conducted; ilke same. 726 arette attribute; vileynye vulgarity. 728 cheere attitude(s). 729 proprely exactly. 733 charge power. 734 large broadly, indecorously. 736 feyne pretend. 737 he were the protagonist of the tale. 738 o word one word.

740 And wel ye woot no vileynye is it.
Eek Plato seith, whoso kan hym rede,
The wordes moote be cosyn to the dede.
Also I prey yow to foryeve it me,
Al have I nat set folk in hir degree
Heere in this tale, as that they sholde stonde.
My wit is short, ye may wel understonde.
    Greet chiere made our Hoost us everichon,
And to the soper sette he us anon.
He served us with vitaille at the beste.

750 Strong was the wyn, and wel to drynke us leste.
A semely man oure HOOSTE was withalle
For to been a marchal in an halle.
A large man he was with eyen stepe—
A fairer burgeys was ther noon in Chepe—
Boold of his speche, and wys, and wel ytaught,
And of manhod hym lakked right naught.
Eek therto he was right a myrie man,
And after soper pleyen he bigan,
And spak of myrthe amonges othere thynges,

760 Whan that we hadde maad our reken‚nges,
And seyde thus: "Now, lordynges, trewely,
Ye been to me right welcome, hertely;
For by my trouthe, if that I shal nat lye,
I saugh nat this yeer so myrie a compaignye
Atones in this herberwe as is now.
Fayn wolde I doon yow myrthe, wiste I how.
And of a myrthe I am right now bythoght,
To doon yow ese, and it shal coste noght.
    "Ye goon to Caunterbury—God yow speede!

770 The blisful martir quite yow youre meede!
And wel I woot, as ye goon by the weye,
Ye shapen yow to talen and to pleye.
For trewely, confort ne myrthe is noon
To ride by the weye doumb as a stoon.
And therfore wol I maken yow disport,
As I seyde erst, and doon yow som confort.
And if yow liketh alle by oon assent
For to stonden at my juggement,
And for to werken as I shal yow seye,

780 To-morwe, whan ye riden by the weye,

---

740 woot know. **741 Plato** *Timaeus* 29, but Chaucer took it from Boethius, cf. III prosa 12, 1. 207 in his translation. **744 nat set** In a court poem, the author might be expected to observe precedence in the order of the tales. **751 semely** appropriate, impressive; **HOOSTE** final e lacking here and elsewhere in manuscripts, but meter always calls for disyllabic pronunciation. **752 marchal** marshal, major-domo. **753 stepe** bright, prominent. **754 burgeys** citizen; **Chepe** Cheapside, the main business street of London. **758 pleyen** to be sociable. **760 maad our rekenynges** paid our bills. **765 Atones** at one time; **herberwe** hostel. **766 Fayn** gladly; **wiste** if I knew. **767 myrthe** an entertainment. **770 quite** repay; **meede** reward. **771 woot** know. **772 talen** tell tales; **pleye** enjoy yourselves. **775 disport** diversion. **778 stondent at my juggement** accept my direction or idea.

Now, by my fader soule that is deed,
But ye be myrie, I wol yeve yow myn heed!
Hoold up youre hondes, withouten moore speche."
    Oure conseil was nat longe for to seche.
Us thoughte it was noght worth to make it wys,
And graunted hym withouten moore avys,
And bad him seye his voirdit as hym leste.
    "Lordynges," quod he, "now herkneth for the beste,
But taak it nought, I prey yow, in desdeyn.
790 This is the poynt, to speken short and pleyn,
That ech of yow, to shorte with oure weye,
In this viage shal telle tales tweye
To Caunterbury-ward, I mene it so,
And homward he shal tellen othere two,
Of aventures that whilom han bifalle.
And which of yow that bereth hym best of alle,
That is to seyn, that telleth in this caas
Tales of best sentence and moost solaas,
Shal have a soper at oure aller cost
800 Heere in this place, sittynge by this post,
Whan that we come agayn fro Caunterbury.
And for to make yow the moore mury,
I wol myselven goodly with yow ryde,
Right at myn owene cost, and be youre gyde.
And whoso wole my juggement withseye
Shal paye al that we spenden by the weye.
And if ye vouchesauf that it be so,
Tel me anon withouten wordes mo,
And I wol erly shape me therfore."
810   This thyng was graunted, and oure othes swore
With ful glad herte, and preyden hym also
That he wolde vouchesauf for to do so,
And that he wolde been oure governour,
And of our tales juge and reportour,
And sette a soper at a certeyn pris,
And we wol reuled been at his devys
In heigh and lough. And thus by oon assent
We been acorded to his juggement.
And therupon the wyn was fet anon.
820 We dronken, and to reste wente echon
Withouten any lenger taryynge.
Amorwe, whan that day gan for to sprynge,
Up roos oure Hoost, and was oure aller cok,
And gadrede us togidre alle in a flok,

784 **conseil** deliberation; **seche** seek. 785 **make it wys** make an issue of it. 786 **avys** deliberation. 787 **voirdit** verdict (idea); **leste** desired. 791 **shorte with** make shorter. 795 **whilom** once upon a time. 796 **bereth hym** conducts himself. 798 **sentence** wisdom; **solaas** delight. 799 **at oure aller cost** at the expense of all of us. 805 **withseye** contradict. 807 **vouchesauf** agree. 809 **shape** prepare. 814 **reportour** accountant. 816 **devys** will. 817 **heigh and lough** in all respects. 823 **aller** of all.

And forth we riden a litel moore than paas
Unto the wateryng of Seint Thomas.

    And there oure Hoost bigan his hors areste
And seyde, "Lordynges, herkneth, if yow leste.
Ye woot youre foreward, and it yow recorde.
830   If even-song and morwe-song accorde,
Lat se now who shal telle the firste tale.
As evere mote I drynke wyn or ale,
Whoso be rebel to my juggement
Shal paye for al that by the wey is spent.
Now draweth cut, er that we ferrer twynne;
He which that hath the shorteste shal bigynne.
Sire Knyght," quod he, "my mayster and my lord,
Now draweth cut, for that is myn accord.
Cometh neer," quod he, "my lady Prioresse.
840   And ye, sire Clerk, lat be youre shamefastnesse,
Ne studieth noght; ley hond to, every man!"
    Anon to drawen every wight bigan,
And shortly for to tellen as it was,
Were it by aventure, or sort, or cas,
The sothe is this, the cut fil to the Knyght,
Of which ful blithe and glad was every wyght,
And telle he moste his tale, as was resoun,
By foreward and by composicioun,
As ye han herd. What nedeth wordes mo?
850   And whan this goode man saugh that it was so,
As he that wys was and obedient
To keepe his foreward by his free assent,
He seyde, "Syn I shal bigynne the game,
What, welcome be the cut, a Goddes name!
Now lat us ryde, and herkneth what I seye."
And with that word we ryden forth oure weye,
And he bigan with right a myrie cheere
His tale anon, and seyde in this manere.

---

825 litel . . . paas leisurely, at little more than a footpace. **826 wateryng of Seint Thomas** a place for watering horses about a mile and a half on from the Tabard. **829 foreward** agreement. **835 draweth cut** draw straws; **ferrer** farther. **841 studieth** don't daydream. **842 wight** person. **844 aventure, or sort, or cas** All mean "by chance." **845 sothe** truth. **847 resoun** reasonable. **848 foreward** agreement; **composicioun** arrangement.

The Friar's Prologue and Tale

THE PROLOGE OF THE FRERES TALE

This worthy lymytour, this noble Frere,
He made alwey a maner louryng chiere
Upon the Somonour, but for honestee
No vileyns word as yet to hym spak he.
But atte laste he seyde unto the wyf,
1270 "Dame," quod he, "God yeve yow right good lyf.
Ye han heer touched, also moot I thee,
In scole-matere greet difficultee.
Ye han seyd muche thyng right wel, I seye.
But dame, heere as we ryde by the weye
Us nedeth nat to speken but of game,
And lete auctoritees, on Goddes name,
To prechyng and to scole of clergye.
But if it lyke to this compaignye,
I wol yow of a somonour telle a game.
1280 Pardee, ye may wel knowe by the name
That of a somonour may no good be sayd;
I praye that noon of you be yvele apayd.
A somonour is a rennere up and doun
With mandementz for fornicacioun,
And is ybet at every townes ende."
    Oure Hoost tho spak, "A, sire, ye sholde be hende
And curteys, as a man of youre estaat;
In compaignye we wol have no debaat.
Telleth youre tale and lat the Somonour be."
1290   "Nay," quod the Somonour, "lat hym seye to me
Whatso hym list. Whan it comth to my lot,
By God, I shall hym quiten every grot.
I shal hym tellen which a greet honour
It is to be a flaterynge lymytour,
And of many another manere cryme
Which nedeth nat rehercen for this tyme.
And his office I shal hym telle, ywis."
Oure Hoost answerde, "Pees, namoore of this."
And after this he seyde unto the Frere,
1300 "Tel forth youre tale, leeve maister deere."

1265 **lymytour . . . Frere** a begging friar with an assigned territory. "Friar" is an anglicization of French *frère*, brother. 1266 **louryng chiere** lowering (sullen) expression (manner). 1267 **honestee** propriety. 1268 **vileyns** rude. 1271 **thee** prosper. 1272 **scole-matere . . . difficultee** i.e., on difficult scholastic questions. 1275 **game** entertainment. 1276 **lete** leave. 1280 **name** i.e., from the term itself. 1282 **yvele apayd** be displeased. 1284 **mandementz** summonses, literally to come before the ecclesiastical court, but with the suggestion of coming to fornication itself. 1285 **ybet** beaten. 1286 **hende** gracious. 1288 **debaat** quarrel. 1292 **quiten** repay; **grot** groat (silver fourpence). 1297 **office** function.

HEERE BIGYNNETH THE FRERES TALE.

Whilom ther was dwellynge in my contree
An erchedekene, a man of heigh degree,
That boldely dide execucioun
In punysshynge of fornicacioun,
Of wicchecraft, and eek of bawderye,
Of diffamacioun, and avowtrye,
Of chirche reves, and of testamentz,
Of contractes, and of lakke of sacramentz,
Of usure, and of symonye also.
1310 But certes, lecchours dide he grettest wo—
They sholde syngen if that they were hent—
And smale tytheres weren foule yshent
If any persone wolde upon hem pleyne.
Ther myghte asterte hym no pecunyal peyne.
For smale tithes and for smal offrynge
He made the peple pitously to synge,
For er the bisshop caughte hem with his hook,
They were in the erchedeknes book.
And thanne hadde he, thurgh his jurisdiccioun,
1320 Power to doon on hem correccioun.
He hadde a somonour redy to his hond—
A slyer boye nas noon in Engelond,
For subtilly he hadde his espiaille
That taughte hym wher that hym myghte availle.
He koude spare of lecchours oon or two
To techen hym to foure and twenty mo.
For thogh this somonour wood was as an hare,
To telle his harlotrye I wol nat spare,
For we been out of his correccioun.
1330 They han of us no jurisdiccioun,
Ne nevere shullen, terme of alle hir lyves.
    "Peter, so been wommen of the styves,"
Quod the Somonour, "yput out of my cure!"

1302 **erchedekene** archdeacon, the disciplin- ary officer of a diocese, who administered its ecclesiastical court, charged with overseeing the moral health of the community as summarized in ll. 1304–10. 1305 **bawderye** procuring. 1306 **diffamacioun** slander; **avowtrye** adultery. 1307 **chirche reves** church wardens (i.e., their behavior), or possibly church robberies. 1307–08 **testamentz . . . contractes** i.e., abuses in con- nection with wills, marriage contracts, etc. 1308 **lakke of sacramentz** failure to observe any of the seven sacraments; baptism, confirmation, communion, marriage, ordination, penance, and extreme unction. 1309 **usure** Loaning money for interest was prohibited by canon law. **symonye** the buying and selling of church offices. 1311 **syngen . . . hent** i.e., wail, caught. 1312 **smale tytheres** The tithe was officially a tax of 10 percent of one's income. **foule yshent** treated harshly. 1313 **persone** i.e., parson (priest). 1314 **asterte hym . . .** i.e., the tithe cheater could in no way escape financial punishment (a fine). 1315 **offrynge** voluntary contribution (in addition to the tithe). 1317 **hook** The bishop's pastoral crook here assumes a sinister aspect. 1323 **subtilly** se- cretly; **espiaille** network of spies. 1324 **availle** profit. 1326 **techen** lead. 1327 **wood** crazy. 1328 **harlotrye** wickedness; however, the mod- ern sense of sexual immorality was already deve- loping. 1329 **we** we (i.e., friars); **correccioun** authority. 1332 **styves** brothels (stews). 1333 **cure** responsibility.

"Pees, with myschance and with mysaventure,"
Thus seyde oure Hoost, "and lat hym telle his tale.
Now telleth forth, thogh that the Somonour gale,
Ne spareth nat, myn owene maister deere."
    This false theef, this somonour, quod the Frere,
Hadde alwey bawdes redy to his hond,

1340   As any hauk to lure in Engelond,
That tolde hym al the secree that they knewe,
For hire acqueyntance was nat come of newe.
They weren his approwours prively.
He took hymself a greet profit therby;
His maister knew nat alwey what he wan.
Withouten mandement a lewed man
He koude somne, on peyne of Cristes curs,
And they were glade for to fille his purs
And make hym grete feestes atte nale.

1350   And right as Judas hadde purses smale,
And was a theef, right swich a theef was he;
His maister hadde but half his duetee.
He was, if I shal yeven hym his laude,
A theef and eek a somnour and a baude.
He hadde eek wenches at his retenue
That wheither that Sir Robert or Sir Huwe,
Or Jakke, or Rauf, or whoso that it were
That lay by hem, they tolde it in his ere.
Thus was the wenche and he of oon assent;

1360   And he wolde fecche a feyned mandement
And somne hem to chapitre bothe two,
And pile the man and lete the wenche go.
    Thanne wolde he seye, "Freend, I shal for thy sake
Do striken hire out of oure lettres blake.
Thee thar namoore, as in this cas, travaille;
I am thy freend ther I thee may availle."
Certeyn he knew of briberyes mo
Than possible is to telle in yeres two.
For in this world nys dogge for the bowe

1370   That kan an hurt deer from an hool knowe
Bet than this somnour knew a sly lecchour
Or an avowtier or a paramour.

1334 myschance . . . mysaventure and bad luck to you. **1336 gale** makes a commotion. **1339 bawdes** procurers. **1340 lure** the feathers at the end of a thong by which a falcon was recalled to its master. **1343 approwours** profit makers (from Old French *prou*, profit). **1346 mandement** official document; **lewed** ignorant. **1347 curs** excommunication. **1349 atte nale** at the ale (house) (from Old English *et tham*). **1350 purses** Judas carried the purse for the disciples; cf. John 12:6. **1352 duetee** amount due him. **1353 laude** praise (deserts). **1354 baude** procurer. **1359 oon assent** in a collusion. **1360 feyned mandement** spurious summons. **1361 chapitre** the chapter (ecclesiastical) court. **1362 pile** pluck (despoil). **1364 striken hire** erase her name. **1365 thar** about it; **travaille** trouble (yourself). **1366 availe** help. **1369 dogge . . . bowe** dog trained to hunt with a bowman. **1372 avowtier** adulterer; **paramour** lover (with sexual implication).

And for that was the fruyt of al his rente,
Therfore on it he sette al his entente.
　　And so bifel that ones on a day
This somnour evere waityng on his pray
Rood for to somne an old wydwe, a ribibe,
Feynynge a cause, for he wolde brybe.
And happed that he saugh bifore hym ryde
1380　A gay yeman under a forest syde.
A bowe he bar and arwes brighte and kene;
He hadde upon a courtepy of grene;
An hat upon his heed with frenges blake.
　　"Sire," quod this somnour, "hayl, and wel atake."
　　"Welcome," quod he, "and every good felawe.
Wher rydestow, under this grenewode shawe?"
Seyde this yeman, "Wiltow fer to day?"
　　This somnour hym answerde and seyde, "Nay.
Heere faste by," quod he, "is myn entente
1390　To ryden for to reysen up a rente
That longeth to my lordes duetee."
　　"Artow thanne a bailly?" "Ye," quod he.
He dorste nat, for verray filthe and shame
Seye that he was a somonour, for the name.
　　"Depardieux," quod this yeman, "deere broother,
Thou art a bailly, and I am another.
I am unknowen as in this contree;
Of thyn aqueyntance I wolde praye thee
And eek of bretherhede, if that yow leste.
1400　I have gold and silver in my cheste;
If that thee happe to comen in oure shire,
Al shal be thyn, right as thou wolt desire."
　　"Grantmercy," quod this somonour, "by my feith!"
Everych in ootheres hand his trouthe leith,
For to be sworne bretheren til they deye.
In daliance they ryden forth hir weye.
　　This somonour, that was as ful of jangles
As ful of venym been thise waryangles
And evere enqueryng upon everythyng,
1410　"Brother," quod he, "where is now youre dwellyng
Another day if that I sholde yow seche?"
　　This yeman hym answerde in softe speche,

1373 fruyt . . . rente the best part of his income.
1376 pray prey (victim). 1377 ribibe fiddle;
cf. l. 1573. Halliwell suggested that this slang
term for an old woman may have come from a
confusion of Latin *vetula*, old woman, and *vitula*,
viol. 1382 courtepy of grene short coat; cf. the
yeoman, *General Prologue* l. 103, but it has been
observed that the devil is also a hunter (after
souls) and wears green. 1383 frenges fringes
(or bindings). 1384 wel atake well met (over-
taken). 1386 shawe grove. 1390 reysen
collect. 1391 longeth . . . duetee belongs to
what is owed. 1392 bailly bailiff (farm super-
visor). 1395 Depardieux in God's name—an
interesting oath from a devil; cf. ll. 1483 ff. 1399
leste are agreeable. 1404 trouthe troth; i.e.,
they shook hands on it. 1406 daliance merri-
ment. 1407 jangles idle chatter. 1408 venym . . .
waryangles poison, shrikes or butcher birds
who impaled their prey on thorns which were
thereafter considered poisonous.

"Brother," quod he, "fer in the north contree,
Where as I hope som tyme I shal thee see.
Er we departe I shal thee so wel wisse
That of myn hous ne shaltow nevere mysse."
    "Now, brother," quod this somonour, "I yow preye,
Teche me whil that we ryden by the weye—
Syn that ye been a baillif as am I—
1420 Som subtiltee, and tel me feithfully
In myn office how that I may moost wynne;
And spareth nat for conscience ne synne,
But as my brother tel me how do ye."
    "Now by my trouthe, brother deere," seyde he,
"As I shal tellen thee a feithful tale:
My wages been ful streite and ful smale.
My lord is hard to me and daungerous,
And myn office is ful laborous,
And therfore by extorcions I lyve.
1430 For sothe, I take al that men wol me yeve.
Algate, by sleyghte or by violence
Fro yeer to yeer I wynne al my dispence.
I kan no bettre telle, feithfully."
    "Now certes," quod this somonour, "so fare I.
I spare nat to taken, God it woot,
But if it be to hevy or to hoot.
What I may gete in conseil prively,
No maner conscience of that have I.
Nere myn extorcioun, I myghte nat lyven,
1440 Nor of swiche japes wol I nat be shryven.
Stomak ne conscience ne knowe I noon;
I shrewe thise shrifte-fadres everychoon.
Wel be we met, by God and by Seint Jame!
But, leeve brother, tel me thanne thy name,"
Quod this somonour. In this meene while
This yeman gan a litel for to smyle.
    "Brother," quod he, "wiltow that I thee telle?
I am a feend; my dwellyng is in helle.
And heere I ryde about my purchasyng
1450 To wite where men wold me yeven anythyng.
My purchas is th'effect of al my rente.
Looke how thou rydest for the same entente —
To wynne good, thou rekkest nevere how.
Right so fare I, for ryde I wold right now
Unto the worldes ende for a preye."
    "A," quod this somonour, "benedicite, what sey ye?

1413 north contree Hell was considered to be in the north. **1415 wisse** inform. **1420 subtiltee** trick. **1426 streite** strait (narrow). **1427 daungerous** demanding. **1431 Algate** always. **1432 wynne** earn; **dispence** expenditure. **1437 conseil** secret. **1439 Nere** were it not for.

1440 japes tricks; **shryven** absolved (cured). **1442 shrewe** curse; **shrifte-fadres** confessors. **1444 leeve** dear. **1449 purchasyng** acquiring. **1450 wite where** know whether. **1451 purchas is th'effect . . . rente** acquisition is the sum total of my income.

I wende ye were a yeman trewely.
Ye han a mannes shap as well as I.
Han ye a figure thanne determinat
1460   In helle, ther ye been in youre estat?''
        "Nay, certeinly," quod he, "ther have we noon;
But whan us liketh we kan take us oon,
Or elles make yow seme we been shape.
Somtyme lyk a man, or lyk an ape,
Or lyk an angel kan I ryde or go.
It is no wonder thyng thogh it be so;
A lowsy jogelour kan deceyve thee,
And pardee, yet kan I moore craft than he.''
        "Why," quod this somonour, "ryde ye thanne or goon
1470   In sondry shap and nat alwey in oon?''
        "For we," quod he, "wol us swiche formes make
As moost able is oure preyes for to take.''
        "What maketh yow to han al this labour?''
        "Ful many a cause, leeve sire somonour,''
Seyde this feend, "but alle thyng hath tyme.
The day is short and it is passed pryme,
And yet ne wan I nothyng in this day.
I wol entende to wynnen, if I may,
And nat entende oure wittes to declare.
1480   For, brother myn, thy wit is al to bare
To understonde althogh I tolde hem thee.
But, for thou axest why labouren we,
For somtyme we been Goddes instrumentz
And meenes to doon his comandementz,
Whan that hym list, upon his creatures,
In divers art and in diverse figures.
Withouten hym we have no myght, certayn,
If that hym list to stonden ther-agayn.
And somtyme, at oure prayere, han we leve
1490   Oonly the body and nat the soule greve:
Witnesse on Job, whom that we diden wo.
And somtyme han we myght of bothe two,
This is to seyn, of soule and body eke.
And somtyme be we suffred for to seke
Upon a man and doon his soule unreste,
And nat his body, and al is for the beste.
Whan he withstandeth oure temptacioun,
It is a cause of his savacioun,

1457 wende thought. 1459 determinat Since devils could assume any shape, theologians debated about their natural form in hell. 1463 make yow seme make it seem to you. 1468 kan know; craft skill. 1470 sondry different shape(s). 1475 The devil quotes Ecclesiastes 3:1. 1476 pryme 9 a.m. 1478 entende to wynnen i.e., attend to business (capturing souls).

1479 wittes to declare intellect to display. 1485 hym list it pleases him. 1486 art method(s); figures shapes. 1488 list . . . agayn it pleases him to oppose (what we do). 1489 prayere entreaty; leve permission. 1490 greve to punish. 1491 Job Job 1:12, 2:6. 1492 myght of power over.

Al be it that it was nat oure entente
1500 He sholde be sauf but that we wolde hym hente.
And somtyme be we servant unto man,
As to the erchebisshop Seint Dunstan,
And to the apostles servant eek was I."
"Yet tel me," quod the somonour, "feithfully,
Make ye yow newe bodies thus alway
Of elementz?" The feend answerde, "Nay.
Somtyme we feyne, and somtyme we aryse
With dede bodyes in ful sondry wyse,
And speke as renably and faire and wel
1510 As to the Phitonissa dide Samuel—
And yet wol som men seye it was nat he;
I do no fors of youre dyvynytee.
But o thyng warne I thee, I wol nat jape:
Thou wolt algates wite how we been shape;
Thou shalt herafterwardes, my brother deere,
Come there thee nedeth nat of me to leere,
For thou shalt by thyn owene experience
Konne in a chayer rede of this sentence
Bet than Virgile while he was on lyve,
1520 Or Dant also. Now lat us ryde blyve,
For I wole holde compaignye with thee
Til it be so that thou forsake me."
"Nay," quod this somonour, "that shal nat bityde.
I am a yeman knowen is ful wyde;
My trouthe wol I holde, as in this cas.
For though thou were the devel Sathanas,
My trouthe wol I holde to thee my brother,
As I am sworn—and ech of us til oother—
For to be trewe brother in this cas.
1530 And bothe we goon abouten oure purchas.
Taak thou thy part, what that men wol thee yeve,
And I shal myn; thus may we bothe lyve.
And if that any of us have moore than oother,
Lat hym be trewe and parte it with his brother."
"I graunte," quod the devel, "by my fey."
And with that word they ryden forth hir wey.
And right at the entryng of the townes ende,

1500 sauf saved; **hente** get. **1502 Dunstan** St. Dunstan, archbishop of Canterbury (961–88), was reputed to have subjected demons. **1503 apostles** In saints' legends, the apostles subject demons to their service. **1506 elementz** i.e., are your temporal shapes created of substance (or merely illusions)? **1507 feyne** pretend (create illusion). **1508 dede bodyes** enter into corpses. **1509 renably** reasonably. **1510 Phitonissa . . . Samuel** In the Vulgate the Witch of Endor is called "pythonissam" (Paralipomenon. 10:13).

The spirit called up in 1 Samuel 28:11 ff. (Vulgate I Kings) was reputed to be not Samuel but a fiend. **1512 no fors** no regard; **dyvynytee** study of theology. **1513 jape** joke. **1514 wolt . . . wite** i.e., always want to know. **1516 leere** learn. **1518 Konne . . . chayer rede** will know how to deliver lectures on the subject. **1519–20 Virgile . . . Dant** Both Virgil's *Aeneid* and Dante's *Inferno* describe the underworld. **1520 blyve** briskly. **1523 bityde** happen. **1525 trouthe** troth (promise). **1534 parte** share.

To which this somonour shoop hym for to wende,
They saugh a cart that charged was with hey,
1540 Which that a cartere droof forth in his wey.
Deep was the wey, for which the carte stood.
The cartere smoot and cryde as he were wood,
"Hayt, Brok! Hayt, Scot! What, spare ye for the stones?
The feend," quod he, "yow fecche, body and bones,
As ferforthly as evere were ye foled,
So muche wo as I have with yow tholed!
The devel have al, bothe hors and cart and hey."
    This somonour seyde, "Heere shal we have a pley."
And neer the feend he drough, as noght ne were,
1550 Ful prively, and rowned in his ere,
"Herkne, my brother, herkne, by thy feith!
Herestow nat how that the cartere seith?
Hent it anon, for he hath yeve it thee,
Bothe hey and cart, and eek his caples thre."
    "Nay," quod the devel, "God woot, never a deel.
It is nat his entente, trust thou me weel.
Axe hym thyself, if thou nat trowest me;
Or elles stynt a while, and thou shalt see."
    This cartere thakketh his hors upon the croupe,
1560 And they bigonne drawen and to stoupe.
"Heyt now," quod he, "ther Jhesu Crist yow blesse,
And al his handwerk, bothe moore and lesse!
That was wel twight, myn owene lyard boy.
I pray God save thee, and Seinte Loy!
Now is my cart out of the slow, pardee."
    "Lo, brother," quod the feend, "what tolde I thee?
Heere may ye se, myn owene deere brother,
The carl spak oon, but he thoghte another.
Lat us go forth abouten oure viage;
1570 Heere wynne I nothyng upon cariage."
    Whan that they coomen somwhat out of towne,
This somonour to his brother gan to rowne:
"Brother," quod he, "heere woneth an old rebekke
That hadde almoost as lief to lese hire nekke
As for to yeve a peny of hir good.
I wole han twelf pens, though that she be wood,

1538 shoop . . . wende planned to go. 1539
charged loaded. 1541 Deep deep with mud;
stood stuck. 1543 spare ye i.e., do you spare
yourselves (*OED*, "refrain from action because
of difficulty")? 1545 ferforthly . . . foled i.e.,
sure as you were born. 1546 tholed suffered.
1548 a pley some fun. 1549 noght ne were
i.e., casually. 1550 rowned whispered. 1553
Hent take; anon at once. 1554 caples cart
horses. 1555 woot, never a deel knows, not at
all. 1557 trowest believe. 1558 stynt stop (be
quiet). 1559 thakketh pats; croupe rump.

1562 handwerk creations. 1563 twight pulled;
lyard gray. 1564 Loy the patron saint of car-
ters; but see the Prioress, *General Prologue* l.
120 note. 1565 slow slough (mud). 1570 car-
iage technical term for a feudal lord's claim on
the use of his tenant's horses and carts, which
could be commuted by money payment called
"cariage"; i.e., the devil will make no profit on
this cart and these horses. 1572 rowne whisper.
1573 woneth . . . rebekke lives, fiddle (cf. note
to l. 1377 above). 1576 wood mad.

Or I wol sompne hire unto oure office;
And yet, God woot, of hire knowe I no vice.
But for thou kanst nat, as in this contree,
1580 Wynne thy cost, taak heer ensample of me.''
   This somonour clappeth at the wydwes gate.
"Com out," quod he, "thou olde virytrate!
I trowe thou hast som frere or preest with thee.''
   "Who clappeth?" seyde this wyf, "Benedicitee,
God save you, sire; what is youre sweete wille?''
   "I have," quod he, "of somonce here a bille.
Upon peyne of cursyng, looke that thou be
Tomorn bifore the erchedeknes knee
T'answere to the court of certeyn thynges.''
1590   "Now, Lord," quod she, "Crist Jhesu, kyng of kynges,
So wisly helps me, as I ne may.
I have been syk, and that ful many a day.
I may nat go so fer," quod she, "ne ryde,
But I be deed, so priketh it in my syde.
May I nat axe a libel, sire somonour,
And answere there by my procuratour
To swich thyng as men wole opposen me?''
   "Yis," quod this somonour, "pay anon—lat se—
Twelf pens to me, and I wol thee acquite.
1600 I shal no profit han therby but lite;
My maister hath the profit and nat I.
Com of, and lat me ryden hastily;
Yif me twelf pens; I may no lenger tarye.''
   "Twelf pens!" quod she, "Now, lady Seinte Marie
So wisly help me out of care and synne,
This wyde world thogh that I sholde wynne,
Ne have I nat twelf pens withinne myn hoold.
Ye knowen wel that I am poure and oold;
Kithe youre almesse on me, poure wrecche.''
1610   "Nay thanne," quod he, "the foule feend me fecche
If I th'excuse, though thou shul be spilt!''
   "Allas!" quod she, "God woot, I have no gilt.''
   "Pay me," quod he, "or by the sweete Seinte Anne,
As I wol bere awey thy newe panne
For dette which that thou owest me of old.
Whan that thou madest thyn housbonde cokewold,
I payde at hoom for thy correccioun.''
   "Thou lixt," quod she, "by my savacioun,
Ne was I nevere er now, wydwe ne wyf,
1620 Somoned unto youre court in al my lyf;
Ne nevere I nas but of my body trewe.

1577 sompne summon; **office** court. **1580**
Wynne earn; **cost** expenses. **1582 virytrate**
hag. **1586 bille** document. **1587 cursyng** ex-
communication. **1591 ne may** cannot. **1595**
libel written copy of the accusation. **1596 pro-** curatour proxy. **1597 opposen** bring against.
1598 anon now. **1607 hoold** possession. **1609**
Kithe show; **almesse** charity. **1611 spilt**
ruined. **1617 correccioun** fine. **1618 lixt** lie.

Unto the devel, blak and rough of hewe,
Yeve I thy body and my panne also!''
    And whan the devel herde hire cursen so
Upon hir knees, he seyde in this manere,
"Now Mabely, myn owene moder deere,
Is this youre wyl in ernest that ye seye?''
    "The devel,'' quod she, "so fecche hym er he deye,
And panne and al, but he wol hym repente!''
1630   "Nay, olde stot, that is nat myn entente,''
Quod this somonour, "for to repente me
For any thyng that I have had of thee.
I wolde I hadde thy smok and every clooth.''
    "Now brother,'' quod the devel, "be nat wrooth;
Thy body and this panne been myne by right.
Thou shalt with me to helle yet tonyght,
Where thou shalt knowen of oure privetee
Moore than a maister of dyvynytee.''
And with that word this foule feend hym hente;
1640 Body and soule he with the devel wente
Where as that somonours han hir heritage.
And God, that maked after his ymage
Mankynde, save and gyde us alle and some,
And leve thise somonours goode men bicome!

    Lordynges, I koude han toold yow, quod this Frere,
Hadde I had leyser for this Somnour heere,
After the text of Crist, Poul, and John,
And of oure othere doctours many oon,
Swiche peynes that youre hertes myghte agryse,
1650 Al be it so no tonge may it devyse,
Thogh that I myghte a thousand wynter telle,
The peynes of thilke cursed hous of helle.
But for to kepe us fro that cursed place,
Waketh and preyeth Jhesu for his grace
So kepe us fro the temptour Sathanas.
Herketh this word, beth war as in this cas:
The leoun sit in his awayt alway
To sle the innocent, if that he may.
Disposeth ay youre hertes to withstonde
1660 The feend that yow wolde make thral and bonde.
He may nat tempte yow over youre myght,
For Crist wol be youre champion and knyght.
And prayeth that thise somonours hem repente
Of hir mysdedes er that the feend hem hente!

HEERE ENDETH THE FRERES TALE.

1630 stot cow. **1633 smok . . . clooth** i.e., underclothes and every rag. **1636 with me** Cf. Luke 23:43. **1639 hente** grabbed. **1644 leve** let. **1646 leyser for** permission of. **1649 agryse** terrify. **1650 Al be it so** nevertheless. **1657 leoun sit . . . awayt** lies in wait, Psalm 10:9. **1660 thral** slave.

The Pardoner's Prologue and Tale

THE WORDES OF THE HOOST TO THE PHISICIEN AND THE PARDONER

Oure Hooste gan to swere as he were wood,
"Harrow," quod he, "by nayles and by blood!
This was a fals cherl and a fals justise.

290 As shameful deeth as herte may devyse
Come to thise false juges and hire advocatz.
Algate this sely mayde is slayn, allas!
Allas, to deere boughte she beautee!
Wherfore I seye al day as men may see
That yiftes of Fortune and of Nature
Been cause of deeth to many a creature.
Of bothe yiftes that I speke of now

300 Men han ful ofte moore for harm than prow.
"But trewely, myn owene maister deere,
This is a pitous tale for to heere.
But nathelees, passe over, is no fors.
I pray to God so save thy gentil cors,
And eek thyne urynals and thy jurdones,
Thyn ypocras, and eek thy galiones,
And every boyste ful of thy letuarie;
God blesse hem, and oure lady Seinte Marie.
"So moot I theen, thou art a propre man,

310 And lyk a prelat, by Seint Ronyan!
Seyde I nat wel? I kan nat speke in terme;
But wel I woot thou doost myn herte to erme
That I almoost have caught a cardynacle.
By corpus bones, but I have triacle,
Or elles a draughte of moyste and corny ale,
Or but I heere anon a myrie tale,
Myn herte is lost for pitee of this mayde.
Thou beel amy, thou Pardoner," he sayde,
"Telle us som myrthe or japes right anon."

320 "It shal be doon," quod he, "by Seint Ronyon.

287 wood crazy. **288 Harrow** exclamation from an ancient Norman warning cry. **nayles . . . blood** The strongest oaths were for centuries those related to Christ's crucifixion. **291 advocatz** attorneys. **292 Algate** at any rate; **sely** innocent (blessed). **297–98** Many editions insert here a couplet from the early version: "Hir beaute was hir deth, I dar wel sayn./ Allas, so pitously she was slain!" The early version of the link ends with l. 298, but there are a number of variations in its readings through 329. **300 prow** profit. **303 fors** matter. **304 cors** body. **305 jurdones** chamber pots. **306 ypocras . . . galiones** medicines named for the famous physicians Hippoc-

rates and Galen; the former was a recognized term; the latter is evidently Herry Bailley's invention. **307 boyste** box; **letuarie** electuary (medicine in syrup). **309 theen** prosper. **310 Ronyan** a Scottish saint, Ronan, but taken to be double entendre of "runnion," kidney, sexual organ. **311 in terme** in learned terms. **312 erme** grieve. **313 cardynacle** evidently the Host's error, which many manuscripts correct to "cardiacle," heart attack. **314 corpus bones** an ignorant mistake for Corpus Dei; **triacle** medicine. **315 moyste and corny** fresh. **316 anon** immediately. **318 beel amy** French feminine, *belle amie*, sweetheart. **319 japes** jokes.

But first," quod he, "heere at this ale stake
I wol bothe drynke and eten of a cake."
   And right anon thise gentils gonne to crye,
"Nay, lat hym telle us of no ribaudye!
Telle us som moral thyng that we may leere
Som wit, and thanne wol we gladly heere."
   "I graunte, ywis," quod he, "but I moot thynke
Upon som honest thyng while that I drynke."

HEERE FOLWETH THE PROLOGE OF THE PARDONERS TALE.

    Lordynges, quod he, in chirches whan I preche,
330 I peyne me to han an hauteyn speche
And rynge it out as round as gooth a belle,
For I kan al by rote that I telle.
My theme is alwey oon, and evere was:
Radix malorum est cupiditas.
    First I pronounce whennes that I come,
And thanne my bulles shewe I, alle and some.
Oure lige lordes seel on my patente,
That shewe I first my body to warente,
That no man be so boold, ne preest ne clerk,
340 Me to destourbe of Cristes hooly werk.
And after that thanne telle I forth my tales.
Bulles of popes and of cardynales,
Of patriarkes and bisshopes I shewe,
And in Latyn I speke a wordes fewe,
To saffron with my predicacioun,
And for to stire hem to devocioun.
Thanne shewe I forth my longe cristal stones,
Ycrammed ful of cloutes and of bones—
Relikes been they, as wenen they echoon.
350 Thanne have I in latoun a sholder-boon
Which that was of an hooly Jewes sheep.
"Goode men," I seye, "taak of my wordes keep;
If that this boon be wasshe in any welle,
If cow, or calf, or sheep, or oxe swelle
That any worm hath ete or worm ystonge,
Taak water of that welle and wassh his tonge,
And it is hool anon; and forthermoor,
Of pokkes and of scabbe and every soor
Shal every sheep be hool that of this welle

---

321 **ale stake** projecting pole hung with a garland or bush as the sign of an alehouse. 323 **gentils** gentlefolk. 324 **ribaudye** ribaldry (coarse humor). 325 **leere** learn. 328 **Upon** about; **honest** moral. 330 **peyne me** take pains; **hauteyn** dignified. 332 **kan** know; **by rote** by heart. 333 **oon** one (the same). 335 **pronounce whennes** tell whence (i.e., Rome). 336 **bulles** official documents (from Latin *bulla*, seal). 337

lige lordes seel . . . patente pope's seal, licence (short for "letters patent," i.e., to be shown publicly). 338 **my body to warente** to protect myself. 339 **ne . . . ne** neither, nor. 345 **saffron** yellow condiment used to spice and adorn food; **predicacioun** preaching. 347 **cristal** Cf. *General Prologue* l. 700. 348 **cloutes** rags. 349 **wenen** believe. 350 **latoun** brass. 352 **keep** heed. 355 **worm** snake. 358 **pokkes** pox.

360 Drynketh a draughte. Taak kepe eek what I telle:
  If that the goode man that the beestes oweth
  Wol every wyke, er that the cok hym croweth,
  Fastynge, drynken of this welle a draughte,
  As thilke hooly Jew oure eldres taughte,
  His beestes and and his stoor shal multiplie.
    "And, sires, also it heeleth jalousie;
  For though a man be falle in jalous rage,
  Lat maken with this water his potage,
  And nevere shal he moore his wyf mystriste,
370 Though he the soothe of hir defaute wiste,
  Al had she taken preestes two or thre.
    "Heere is a miteyn eek, that ye may se.
  He that his hand wol putte in this mityan,
  He shal have multipliyng of his grayn,
  Whan he hath sowen, be it whete or otes—
  So that he offre pens, or elles grotes.
    "Goode men and wommen, o thyng warne I yow:
  If any wight be in this chirche now
  That hath doon synne horrible, that he
380 Dar nat for shame of it yshryven be,
  Or any womman, be she yong or old,
  That hath ymaked hir housbonde cokewold,
  Swich folk shal have no power ne no grace
  To offren to my relikes in this place.
  And whoso fyndeth hym out of swich blame,
  They wol come up and offre in Goddes name,
  And I assoille hem by the auctoritee
  Which that by bulle ygraunted was to me."
    By this gaude have I wonne, yeer by yeer,
390 An hundred mark sith I was pardoner.
  I stonde lyk a clerk in my pulpet,
  And whan the lewed peple is doun yset,
  I preche so as ye han herd bifoore,
  And telle an hundred false japes moore.
  Thanne peyne I me to strecche forth the nekke,
  And est and west upon the peple I bekke,
  As dooth a dowve sittynge on a berne.
  Myne handes and my tonge goon so yerne
  That it is joye to se my bisynesse.
400 Of avarice and of swich cursednesse
  Is al my prechyng, for to make hem free
  To yeven hir pens, and namely unto me,

361 oweth owns. 362 wyke week. 364 thilke
the same. 365 stoor livestock. 368 potage soup.
370 soothe truth; defaute fault. 371 Al al-
though. 373 mitayn mitten. 376 pens pence;
grotes groats (silver coins worth fourpence).
380 yshryven absolved. 382 cokewold cuck-
old. 384 offren make offering. 385 fyndeth
hym out i.e., is not guilty. 387 assoille (will)
absolve. 389 gaude trick. 390 mark formerly
worth two-thirds of a pound. 392 lewed ignorant
(lay). 394 japes tricks. 395 peyne I I am careful.
396 bekke nod. 397 berne barn. 398 yerne
eagerly. 399 bisynesse gesticulation (as in "stage
business"). 401 free open-handed. 402 namely
especially.

For myn entente is nat but for to wynne,
And nothyng for correccioun of synne.
I rekke nevere, whan that they been beryed,
Though that hir souls goon a-blakeberyed!
For certes, many a predicacioun
Comth ofte tyme of yvel entencioun;
Som for plesance of folk and flaterye,
410   To been avaunced by ypocrisye,
And som for veyne glorie, and som for hate.
For whan I dar noon oother weyes debate,
Thanne wol I stynge hym with my tonge smerte
In prechyng, so that he shal nat asterte
To been defamed falsly, if that he
Hath trespased to my bretheren or to me.
For though I telle noght his propre name,
Men shal wel knowe that it is the same
By signes and by othere circumstances.
420   Thus quyte I folk that doon us displesances;
Thus spitte I out my venym under hewe
Of hoolynesse, to semen hooly and trewe.
   But shortly myn entente I wol devyse:
I preche of nothyng but for coveityse.
Therfore my theme is yet, and evere was,
Radix malorum est cupiditas.
Thus kan I preche agayn that same vice
Which that I use, and that is avarice.
But though myself be gilty in that synne,
430   Yet kan I maken oother folk to twynne
From avarice, and soore to repente.
But that is nat my principal entente—
I preche nothyng but for coveitise.
Of this mateere it oghte ynogh suffise.
   Thanne telle I hem ensamples many oon
Of olde stories longe tyme agoon.
For lewed peple loven tales olde;
Swiche thynges kan they wel reporte and holde.
What, trowe ye the whiles I may preche,
440   And wynne gold and silver for I teche,
That I wol lyve in poverte wilfully?
Nay, nay, I thoghte it nevere, trewely,
For I wol preche and begge in sondry landes;
I wol nat do no labour with myne handes,

403 wynne accumulate. **405 rekke** care; **beryed** buried. **406 a-blakeberyed** a-blackberrying. **407 predicacioun** sermon (preaching). **409 plesance** pleasing. **412 debate** fight. **414 asterte** escape. **416 trespased** injured. **420 quyte** requite (repay). **423 devyse** reveal. **426** The root of evil is cupidity—the love of money (I Timothy 6:10). **430 twynne** separate. **437 lewed** ignorant. **438 reporte** repeat; **holde** remember. **439 trowe** believe. **441 wilfully** voluntarily. Voluntary poverty had become a major issue in the church by the fourteenth century; see *Wife of Bath's Tale* ll. 1179 ff. **444 labour with . . . handes** Like voluntary poverty, manual labor had been one of the ideals of original monastic Christianity; see *General Prologue* l. 187 and note.

Ne make baskettes and lyve therby,
By cause I wol nat beggen ydelly.
I wol noon of the apostles countrefete;
I wol have moneie, wolle, chese, and whete,
Al were it yeven of the povereste page,
450   Or of the povereste wydwe in a village,
Al sholde hir children sterve for famyne.
Nay, I wol drynke licour of the vyne
And have a joly wenche in every toun.
   But herkneth, lordynges, in conclusioun:
Youre likyng is that I shal telle a tale.
Now have I dronke a draughte of corny ale,
By God, I hope I shal yow telle a thyng
That shal by reson been at youre likyng.
For though myself be a ful vicious man,
460   A moral tale yet I yow telle kan,
Which I am wont to preche for to wynne.
Now hoold youre pees; my tale I wol bigynne.

HEERE BIGYNNETH THE PARDONERS TALE.

   In Flaundres whilom was a compaignye
Of yonge folk that haunteden folye,
As riot, hasard, stywes, and tavernes,
Where as with harpes, lutes, and gyternes
They daunce and pleyen at dees bothe day and nyght,
And eten also and drynken over hir myght,
Thurgh which they doon the devel sacrifise
470   Withinne that develes temple in cursed wise
By superfluytee abhomynable.
Hir othes been so grete and so dampnable
That it is grisly for to heere hem swere.
Oure blissed Lordes body they totere—
Hem thoughte that Jewes rente hym noght ynough—
And ech of hem at otheres synne lough.
And right anon thanne comen tombesteres
Fetys and smale, and yonge frutesteres,
Syngeres with harpes, baudes, wafereres,
480   Whiche been the verray develes officeres
To kyndle and blowe the fyr of lecherye
That is annexed unto glotonye.

447 countrefete imitate. 449 of by; page servant. 451 Al even though; sterve die. 452 vyne Wine was much more expensive than beer. 463 Flaundres Flanders, in present Belgium; whilom once (formerly). 464 haunteden haunted, practiced. 465 riot, hasard, stywes wild parties, gambling, brothels. 466 gyternes guitars. 468 over hir myght beyond their strength. 471 superfluytee overindulgence. 474 totere tear. Oaths were traditionally thought to tear Christ's body to pieces; this idea was related to the fact that oaths were so often upon aspects of his crucifixion. 476 lough laughed. 477–78 tombesteres . . . frutesteres female tumblers and fruit peddlers ("ster" is a feminine suffix, cf. "tappster," "spinster," "Baxter"); Fetys shapely. 479 baudes procurers; wafereres cake peddlers.

The hooly writ take I to my witnesse
That luxurie is in wyn and dronkenesse.
Lo, how that dronken Looth, unkyndely,
Lay by his doghtres two, unwityngly;
So dronke he was, he nyste what he wroghte.
Herodes, whoso wel the stories soghte,
Whan he of wyn was repleet at his feeste,
490   Right at his owene table he yaf his heeste
To sleen the Baptist John, ful giltelees.
Senec seith a good word doutelees;
He seith he kan no difference fynde
Bitwix a man that is out of his mynde
And a man which that is dronkelewe
But that woodnesse, fallen in a shrewe,
Persevereth lenger than dooth dronkenesse.
O glotonye, ful of cursednesse!
O cause first of oure confusioun!
500   O original of oure dampnacioun,
Til Crist hadde boght us with his blood agayn!
Lo, how deere, shortly for to sayn,
Aboght was thilke cursed vileynye!
Corrupt was al this world for glotonye.
Adam oure fader and his wyf also
Fro Paradys to labour and to wo
Were dryven for that vice, it is no drede.
For whil that Adam fasted, as I rede,
He was in Paradys; and whan that he
510   Eet of the fruyt deffended on the tree,
Anon he was out cast to wo and peyne.
O glotonye, on thee wel oghte us pleyne!
O, wiste a man how manye maladyes
Folwen of excesse and of glotonyes,
He wolde been the moore mesurable
Of his diete, sittynge at his table.
Allas, the shorte throte, the tendre mouth,
Maketh that est and west and north and south,
In erthe, in eir, in water, men to swynke
520   To gete a glotoun deyntee mete and drynke.
Of this matiere, O Paul, wel kanstow trete:
"Mete unto wombe, and wombe eek unto mete,
Shal God destroyen bothe," as Paulus seith.
Allas, a foul thyng is it, by my feith,
To seye this word, and fouler is the dede,
Whan man so drynketh of the white and rede

484 luxurie lechery. **485 Looth, unkyndely** Lot, unnaturally (Genesis 19:30–38). **488 whoso . . . soghte** i.e., whoever might seek out his story. **490 heeste** command (Matthew 14:1–12). **492 Senec** Seneca (in his *Letters*, no. 83). **495 dronkelewe** habitually drunk. **496 shrewe** twisted personality. **499 cause first** i.e., Adam, Eve, and the apple. **501 boght** redeemed. **510 deffended** forbidden. **513 wiste** if a person knew. **515 mesurable** moderate. **519 swynke** work. **522 wombe** stomach; cf. Paul, 1 Corinthians 6:13. **526 white and rede** wine.

That of his throte he maketh his pryvee
Thurgh thilke cursed superfluitee.
    The apostel wepyng seith ful pitously,
530 "Ther walken manye of whiche yow toold have I—
I seye it now wepyng, with pitous voys —
They been enemys of Cristes croys,
Of whiche the ende is deeth; wombe is hir god!"
O wombe, O bely, O stynkyng cod,
Fulfilled of donge and of corrupcioun!
At either ende of thee foul is the soun.
How greet labour and cost is thee to fynde!
Thise cookes, how they stampe and streyne and grynde
And turnen substaunce into accident
540 To fulfille al thy likerous talent.
Out of the harde bones knokke they
The mary, for they caste noght awey
That may go thurgh the golet softe and swoote.
Of spicerie of leef and bark and roote
Shal been his sauce ymaked by delit,
To make hym yet a newer appetit.
But certes, he that haunteth swiche delices
Is deed whil that he lyveth in tho vices.
    A lecherous thyng is wyn, and dronkenesse
550 Is ful of stryvyng and of wrecchednesse.
O dronke man, disfigured is thy face,
Sour is thy breeth, foul artow to embrace,
And thurgh thy dronke nose semeth the soun
As though thou seydest ay "Sampsoun, Sampsoun."
And yet, God woot, Sampsoun drank nevere no wyn.
Thou fallest as it were a styked swyn;
Thy tonge is lost, and al thyn honeste cure;
For dronkenesse is verray sepulture
Of mannes wit and his discrecioun.
560 In whom that drynke hath dominacioun
He kan no conseil kepe, it is no drede.
Now kepe yow fro the white and fro the rede,
And namely fro the white wyn of Lepe,
That is to selle in Fysshstrete or in Chepe.
This wyn of Spaigne crepeth subtilly
In othere wynes, growynge faste by,
    Of which ther ryseth swich fumositee

527 pryvee privy (by vomiting). **534 cod** bag (here stomach). **536 soun** sound. **537 fynde** provide for. **539 substaunce . . . accident** a philosophical joke: in scholastic terminology "substance" is the ideal Platonic reality, and "accident" the imperfect material manifestation of that ideal. **540 likerous talent** greedy (lecherous) nature. **542 mary** marrow; **noght** nothing. **543 swoote** blandly (sweetly); cf. *General Prologue* l. 1 note. **545 by** for. **547 swiche** delices such delicacies. **550 stryvyng** quarreling. **555 woot** knows. **556 styked swyn** stuck pig. **557 honeste cure** seemly behavior (self-control). **558 verray sepulture** really (the) burial. **561 conseil** confidence. **563 Lepe** in Spain. **564 Fysshstrete . . . Chepe** London streets. **565 crepeth subtilly** The practice of adulterating expensive French wines with cheaper wines from Spain and elsewhere is evidently very old.

That whan a man hath dronken draughtes thre,
And weneth that he be at hoom in Chepe,
570 He is in Spaigne right at the toune of Lepe—
Nat at the Rochele, ne at Burdeux toun —
And thanne wol he seye "Sampsoun, Sampsoun!"
     But herkneth, lordynges, o word I yow preye,
That alle the sovereyn actes, dar I seye,
Of victories in the Olde Testament,
Thurgh verray God that is omnipotent,
Were doon in abstinence and in preyere.
Looketh the Bible and ther ye may it leere.
     Looke Attilla, the grete conquerour,
580 Deyde in his sleep with shame and dishonour,
Bledynge ay at his nose in dronkenesse.
A capitayn sholde lyve in sobrenesse.
And over al this, avyseth yow right wel
What was comaunded unto Lamwel—
Nat Samuel, but Lamwel, seye I—
Redeth the Bible, and fynde it expresly
Of wyn-yevyng to hem that han justise.
Namoore of this, for it may wel suffise.
     And now that I have spoken of glotonye,
590 Now wol I yow deffenden hasardrye.
Hasard is verray mooder of lesynges,
And of deceite, and cursed forswerynges,
Blaspheme of Crist, manslaughtre, and wast also
Of catel and of tyme; and forthermo,
It is repreeve and contrarie of honour
For to ben holde a commune hasardour.
And ever the hyer he is of estaat,
The moore is he yholden desolaat.
If that a prynce useth hasardrye,
600 In alle governaunce and policye
He is, as by commune opinioun,
Yholde the lasse in reputacioun.
     Stilboun, that was a wys embassadour,
Was sent to Corynthe in ful greet honour
Fro Lacidomye to make hire alliaunce.
And whan he cam, hym happede par chaunce
That alle the gretteste that were of that lond
Pleyynge atte hasard he hem fond.

---

569 weneth thinks. **571 Rochele . . . Burdeux** homes of the expensive French wines. **578 leere** learn. **584 Lamwel** See Proverbs 31:4–5, "It is not for kings, O Lemuel, it is not for kings to drink wine; not for princes strong drink; / Lest they drink, and forget the law, and pervert the judgment of any of the afflicted." **590 deffenden hasardrye** censure gambling. **591 lesynges** lyings. **592 forswerynges** perjuries. **593 Blas-** **pheme of** blasphemy against; **wast** waste. **594 catel** chattels (property). **595 repreeve** shame. **598 yholden** considered. **603 Stilboun** This and the following exemplum are from John of Salisbury's *Policraticus* via John of Wales's *Communiloquium*. In *Policraticus*, the ambassador is called "Chilon." **605 Lacidomye** Sparta (famous for its "Spartan" life style).

610 For which as soone as it myghte be
He stal hym hoom agayn to his contree
And seyde, "Ther wol I nat lese my name,
Ne I wol nat take on me so greet defame
Yow for to allie unto none hasardours.
Sendeth othere wise embassadours,
For by my trouthe me were levere dye
Than I yow sholde to hasardours allye.
For ye that been so glorious in honours
Shul nat allyen yow with hasardours
As by my wyl, ne as by my tretee."
620 This wise philosophre, thus seyde hee.
    Looke eek that to the kyng Demetrius
The kyng of Parthes, as the book seith us,
Sente him a paire of dees of gold in scorn,
For he hadde used hasard ther-biforn,
For which he heeld his glorie or his renoun
At no value or reputacioun.
Lordes may fynden oother maner pley
Honeste ynough to dryve the day awey.
    Now wol I speke of othes false and grete
630 A word or two, as olde bookes trete.
Gret sweryng is a thyng abhominable,
And fals sweryng is yet moore reprevable.
The heighe God forbad sweryng at al,
Witnesse on Mathew, but in special
Of sweryng seith the hooly Jeremye,
"Thou shalt swere sooth thyne othes and nat lye,
And swere in doom and eek in rightwisnesse,
But ydel sweryng is a cursednesse."
Bihoold and se that in the firste table
640 Of heighe Goddes heestes honurable
Hou that the seconde heeste of hym is this,
"Take nat my name in ydel or amys."
Lo, rather he forbedeth swich sweryng
Than homycide or many a cursed thyng—
I seye that as by ordre thus it stondeth,
This knoweth that his heestes understondeth
How that the seconde heeste of God is that.
And fortherover I wol thee telle al plat
That vengeance shal nat parten from his hous
650 That of his othes is to outrageous.
    "By Goddes precious herte and by his nayles,"

611 **lese** lose. **621 Demetrius** His identity is unknown; Skeat suggests Demetrius Nikator, king of Syria. **622 Parthes** Parthians (Persians); **book** formerly taken to mean *Policraticus*, but R.A. Pratt now argues for *Communiloquium*. **634 Mathew** Cf. Matthew 5:34. **636 sooth** true. **637 in doom** with judgment. **639 firste table** the stone tablet containing the first five of the Ten Commandments. **640 heestes** commandments. **641 seconde** second in Vulgate; third in King James. **645 by ordre** in order (i.e., second from the beginning). **646 knoweth** (He) knows. **648 plat** plainly (flat). **649 parten** depart. **651 Goddes . . . herte** On oaths see l. 474 above.

And "By the blood of Crist that is in Hayles,
Sevene is my chaunce and thyn is cynk and treye,"
"By Goddes armes, if thou falsly pleye
This daggere shal thurghout thyn herte go,"
This fruyt cometh of the bicched bones two —
Forsweryng, ire, falsnesse, homycide.
Now for the love of Crist, that for us dyde,
Lete youre othes bothe grete and smale.
660   But, sires, now wol I telle forth my tale.
        Thise riotoures thre of whiche I telle,
Longe erst er prime rong of any belle,
Were set hem in a taverne for to drynke,
And as they sat they herde a belle clynke
Biforn a cors was caried to his grave.
That oon of hem gan callen to his knave,
"Go bet," quod he, "and axe redily
What cors is this that passeth heer forby,
And looke that thou reporte his name weel."
670   "Sire," quod this boy, "it nedeth never-a-deel;
It was me toold er ye cam here two houres.
He was, pardee, an old felawe of youres,
And sodeynly he was yslayn tonyght,
Fordronke as he sat on his bench upright.
Ther cam a privee theef men clepeth Deeth
That in this contree al the peple sleeth,
And with his spere he smoot his herte atwo
And wente his wey withouten wordes mo.
He hath a thousand slayn this pestilence.
680   And, maister, er ye come in his presence,
My thynketh that it were necessarie
For to be war of swich an adversarie.
Beth redy for to meete hym everemoore—
Thus taughte me my dame. I sey namoore."
        "By Seinte Marie," seyde this taverner,
"The child seith sooth, for he hath slayn this yeer
Henne over a mile withinne a greet village
Bothe man and womman, child, and hyne, and page.
I trowe his habitacioun be there.
690   To been avysed greet wysdom it were
Er that he dide a man a dishonour."
        "Ye, Goddes armes," quod this riotour,

652 **Hayles** Hayles Abbey in Gloucestershire which claimed to have a vial of Christ's blood. 653 **cynk . . . treye** five, three; combinations in dice (craps). 565 **bicched bones** bitched (i.e., cursed) dice. 657 **Forsweryng** perjury; **ire** anger. 662 **prime** 9 a.m. 664 **belle** hand-bell carried before the corpse at a funeral. 665 **cors** corpse. 666 **knave** servant boy. 667 **Go bet** go at once; **redily** quickly. 674 **Fordronke** "For" is an intensifier. 675 **clepeth** call. 679 **pestilence** The frantic escapism of the rioters in this tale and the ritual quality of their search for death are associated with the frenzy of despair that swept Europe during the plague years. 686 **sooth** truth. 687 **Henne** hence. 688 **hyne** farm laborer; **page** court attendant. 689 **trowe** believe. 690 **avysed** prepared.

"Is it swich peril with hym for to meete?
I shal hym seke by wey and eek by strete,
I make avow to Goddes digne bones!
Herkneth, felawes, we thre been al ones;
Lat ech of us holde up his hand til oother,
And ech of us bicomen otheres brother,
And we wol sleen this false traytour Deeth.
700   He shal be slayn, he that so manye sleeth,
By Goddes dignitee, er it be nyght."
    Togidres han thise thre hir trouthes plight
To lyve and dyen ech of hem for oother
As though he were his owene ybore brother.
And up they stirte, al dronken in this rage,
And forth they goon towardes that village
Of which the taverner hadde spoke biforn.
And many a grisly ooth thanne han they sworn,
And Cristes blessed body they torente—
710   Deeth shal be deed, if that they may hym hente!
    Whan they han goon nat fully half a mile,
Right as they wolde han troden over a stile,
An oold man and a poure with hem mette.
This olde man ful mekely hem grette,
And seyde thus, "Now, lordes, God yow see!"
    The proudeste of thise riotoures three
Answerde agayn, "What, carl with sory grace,
Why artow al forwrapped save thy face?
Why lyvestow so longe in so greet age?"
720   This olde man gan looke in his visage,
And seyde thus: "For I ne kan nat fynde
A man, though that I walked into Ynde,
Neither in citee ne in no village,
That wolde chaunge his youthe for myn age;
And therfore moot I han myn age stille
As longe tyme as it is Goddes wille.
Ne Deeth, allas, ne wol nat han my lyf.
Thus walke I lyk a restelees kaityf,
And on the ground, which is my moodres gate,
730   I knokke with my staf bothe erly and late,
And seye, "Leeve mooder, leet me in!
Lo, how I vanysshe, flessh and blood and skyn.
Allas, whan shul my bones been at reste?
Mooder, with yow wolde I chaunge my cheste
That in my chambre longe tyme hath be,

---

694 wey byway; **strete** highway. **695 digne** honored. **696 al ones** all of one mind. **697 holde up . . . til** hold up to (as a sign of swearing fidelity). **702 trouthes plight** made their promises (plighted their troth). **704 ybore** born. **709 torente** Cf. 1. 474 above and note. **710 hente** take, grasp. **712 troden . . . stile** climbed, stile to get over a fence. **715 yow see** i.e., see to you (care for you). **717 carl** fellow (churl, a disparaging reference). **718 forwrapped** completely wrapped ("for" is an intensifier). **724 chaunge** exchange. **728 kaityf** wretch. **731 Leeve** dear. **734 chaunge my cheste** exchange my chest (of worldly property).

Ye, for an heyre clowt to wrappe me.''
But yet to me she wol nat do that grace,
For which ful pale and welked is my face.
"But, sires, to yow it is no curteisye
740 To speken to an old man vileynye
But he trespasse in word or elles in dede.
In Hooly Writ ye may yourself wel rede,
'Agayns an oold man, hoor upon his heed,
Ye sholde arise.'' Wherfore I yeve yow reed,
Ne dooth unto an oold man noon harm now
Namoore than that ye wolde men did to yow
In age, if that ye so longe abyde.
And God be with yow, where ye go or ryde.
I moot go thider as I have to go.''
750   "Nay, olde cherl, by God thou shalt nat so,''
Seyde this oother hasardour anon.
"Thou partest nat so lightly, by Seint John!
Thou spak right now of thilke traytour Deeth,
That in this contree alle oure freendes sleeth.
Have heer my trouthe, as thou art his espye,
Telle where he is or thou shalt it abye,
By God and by the hooly sacrement!
For soothly thou art oon of his assent
To sleen us yonge folk, thou false theef!''
760   "Now, sires,'' quod he, "if that ye be so leef
To fynde Deeth, turne up this croked wey,
For in that grove I lafte hym, by my fey,
Under a tree and there he wole abyde.
Noght for youre boost he wole him nothyng hyde.
Se ye that ook? Right there ye shal hym fynde.
God save yow, that boghte agayn mankynde
And yow amende.'' Thus seyde this olde man.
And everich of thise riotoures ran
Til he cam to that tree, and ther they founde
770 Of floryns fyne of gold ycoyned rounde
Wel ny an eighte busshels as hem thoughte.
No lenger thanne after Deeth they soughte,
But ech of hem so glad was of that sighte,
For that the floryns been so faire and brighte,
That doun they sette hem by this precious hoord.
The worste of hem he spak the firste word.
"Bretheren,'' quod he, "taak kepe what I seye;
My wit is greet, though that I bourde and pleye.

---

736 heyre clowt haircloth burial sheet. 738
welked withered. 741 But unless. 743 Agayns
in the presence of; Leviticus 19:32. 744 reed
advice. 748 where ye go whither you walk. 751
hasardour gambler. 752 partest . . . lightly
depart (get away), so easily. 755 trouthe word

(troth); espye spy. 756 abye pay for. 758 assent
i.e., in agreement with. 762 fey faith. 764
nothyng not at all. 765 ook oak. 766 boghte
agayn redeemed. 767 amende correct. 770
floryns gold coins worth six or more silver shil-
lings. 778 bourde joke.

This tresor hath Fortune unto us yeven
780   In myrthe and joliftee oure lyf to lyven,
And lightly as it comth so wol we spende.
Ey, Goddes precious dignitee, who wende
Today that we sholde han so fair a grace?
But myghte this gold be caried fro this place
Hoom to myn house—or elles unto youres—
For wel ye woot that al this gold is oures,
Thanne were we in heigh felicitee.
But trewely, by daye it may nat bee.
Men wolde seyn that we were theves stronge,
790   And for oure owene tresor doon us honge.
This tresor moste ycaried be by nyghte
As wisely and as slyly as it myghte.
Wherfore I rede that cut among us alle
Be drawe, and lat se wher the cut wol falle;
And he that hath the cut with herte blithe
Shal renne to towne, and that ful swithe,
And brynge us breed and wyn ful prively.
And two of us shul kepen subtilly
This tresor wel. And if he wol nat tarie,
800   Whan it is nyght we wol this tresor carie
By oon assent where as us thynketh best."
That oon of hem the cut broghte in his fest
And bad hem drawe and looke where it wol falle,
And it fil on the yongeste of hem alle,
And forth toward the toun he wente anon.
    And also soone as that he was gon
That oon of hem spak thus unto that oother,
"Thow knowest wel thou art my sworn brother;
Thy profit wol I telle thee anon.
810   Thou woost wel that oure felawe is agon.
And heere is gold, and that full greet plentee,
That shal departed been among us thre.
But nathelees, if I kan shape it so
That it departed were among us two,
Hadde I nat doon a freendes torn to thee?"
    That oother answerde, "I noot hou that may be.
He woot wel that the gold is with us tweye.
What shal we doon? What shal we to hym seye?"
    "Shal it be conseil?" seyde the firste shrewe,
820   "And I shal tellen in a wordes fewe
What we shal doon, and brynge it wel aboute."
    "I graunte," quod that oother, "out of doute,

779 **Fortune** According to the Boethian world view, Fortune grants only mutable, temporal felicity; God alone grants eternal felicity. 781 **lightly** easily. 782 **wende** thought. 786 **woot** know. 790 **honge** hanged. 793 **rede** advise; **cut** draw straws. 798 **kepen subtilly** protect secretly. 801 **oon assent** common agreement. 812 **departed** divided. 816 **noot** don't know. 819 **conseil** confidential; **shrewe** wretch (bad-tempered animal). 822 **graunte** agree (promise); **doute** without a reservation.

That by my trouthe I shal thee nat biwreye."
"Now," quod the firste, "thou woost wel we be tweye,
And two of us shul strenger be than oon.
Looke whan that he is set that right anoon
Arys as though thou woldest with hym pleye,
And I shal ryve hym thurgh the sydes tweye
Whil that thou strogelest with hym as in game,
830 And with thy daggere looke thou do the same.
And thanne shal al this gold departed be,
My deere freend, bitwixen me and thee.
Thanne may we bothe oure lustes all fulfille,
And pleye at dees right at oure owene wille."
And thus acorded been thise shrewes tweye
To sleen the thridde, as ye han herd me seye.
    This yongeste, which that wente unto the toun,
Ful ofte in herte he rolleth up and doun
The beautee of thise floryns newe and brighte.
840 "O Lord," quod he, "if so were that I myghte
Have al this tresor to myself allone
There is no man that lyveth under the trone
Of God that sholde lyve so murye as I."
And atte laste the feend, oure enemy,
Putte in his thought that he sholde poyson beye
With which he myghte sleen his felawes tweye—
Forwhy the feend foond hym in swich lyvynge
That he hadde leve hem to sorwe brynge.
For this was outrely his fulle entente,
850 To sleen hem bothe and nevere to repente.
And forth he gooth, no lenger wolde he tarie,
Into the toun unto a pothecarie,
And preyde hym that he hym wolde selle
Som poyson that he myghte his rattes quelle,
And eek ther was a polcat in his hawe
That, as he seyde, his capouns hadde yslawe,
And fayn he wolde wreke hym, if he myghte,
On vermyn that destroyed hym by nyghte.
    The pothecarie answerde, "And thou shalt have
860 A thyng that, also God my soule save,
In al this world ther is no creature
That eten or dronken hath of this confiture
Noght but the montance of a corn of whete
That he ne shal his lif anon forlete—
Ye, sterve he shal and that in lasse while
Than thou wold goon a paas nat but a mile,

---

823 **trouthe** word (troth); **biwreye** betray. 828 **ryve** stab. 833 **lustes** pleasures. 843 **murye** merry. 847 **lyvynge** condition of life. 848 **leve** permission (leave). 852 **a pothecarie** an apothecary (druggist). 854 **quelle** kill. 855 **polcat** weasel (Old French *poule*, fowl + cat); **hawe** yard. 857 **wreke** revenge. 862 **confiture** concoction. 863 **montance** amount; **corn** grain 864 **anon forlete** immediately give up. 865 **sterve** die. 866 **goon a paas** walk at a footpace.

The poysoun is so strong and violent.''
   This cursed man hath in his hond yhent
This poysoun in a box, and sith he ran
870   Into the nexte strete unto a man
And borwed of hym large botels thre,
And in the two his poyson poured he.
The thridde he kepte clene for his owene drynke
For al the nyght he shoop hym for to swynke
In cariynge of the gold out of that place.
And whan this riotour, with sory grace,
Hadde filled with wyn his grete botels thre,
To his felawes agayn repaireth he.
   What nedeth it to sermone of it moore?
880   For right as they hadde cast his deeth bifoore,
Right so they han hym slayn, and that anon.
And whan that this was doon, thus spak that oon,
''Now lat us sitte and drynke and make us merie,
And afterward we wol his body berie.''
And with that word it happed hym par cas
To take the botel ther the poyson was,
And drank, and yaf his felawe drynke also,
For which anon they storven bothe two.
   But certes, I suppose that Avycen
890   Wroote nevere in no canon ne in no fen
Mo wonder signes of empoisonyng
Than hadde thise wrecches two er hir endyng.
Thus ended been thise homycides two
And eek the false empoysonere also.
   O cursed synne of alle cursednesse!
O traytours homycide, O wikkednesse!
O glotonye, luxurie, and hasardrye!
Thou blasphemour of Crist with vileynye
And othes grete of usage and of pride!
900   Allas, mankynde, how may it bitide
That to thy creatour, which that the wroghte
And with his precious herte-blood thee boghte,
Thou art so fals and so unkynde, allas?
   Now goode men, God foryeve yow youre trespas,
And ware yow fro the synne of avarice.
Myn hooly pardoun may yow alle warice—
So that ye offre nobles or sterlynges
Or elles silver broches, spoones, rynges.
Boweth youre heed under this hooly bulle!

---

868 yhent taken. **869 sith** then. **874 shoop hym** planned; **swynke** work. **880 cast** planned. **881 anon** at once. **885 par cas** French, by chance. **888 storven** died. **889 Avycen** Avicenna, famous ancient Persian physician. **890 canon . . . fen** Avicenna's most famous treatise, *Liber canonis medicinae*, was divided into fens (Arabic *fann*, a unit of technical exposition). Lib. IV, fen vi, treats of poisons. **891 wonder** wonderful (awesome). **897 luxurie** lechery; **hasardrye** gambling. **899 usage** habit. **905 ware** beware. **906 warice** save. **907 So that . . . nobles . . . sterlynges** if, gold coins, silver coins.

910   Com up, ye wyves, offreth of youre wolle!
       Youre names I entre heer in my rolle anon;
       Into the blisse of hevene shul ye gon.
       I yow assoille by myn heigh power,
       Yow that wol offre, as clene and eek as cleer
       As ye were born.—And lo, sires, thus I preche.
       And Jhesu Crist, that is oure soules leche,
       So graunte yow his pardoun to receyve,
       For that is best—I wol yow nat deceyve.
         But, sires, o word forgat I in my tale:
920   I have relikes and pardoun in my male
       As faire as any man in Engelond,
       Whiche were me yeven by the popes hond.
       If any of yow wole of devocioun
       Offren, and han myn absolucioun,
       Com forth anon and kneleth heere adoun
       And mekely receyveth my pardoun,
       Or elles taketh pardoun as ye wende
       Al newe and fressh at every miles ende—
       So that ye offren, alwey newe and newe,
930   Nobles or pens whiche that be goode and trewe.
       It is an honour to everich that is heer
       That ye mowe have a suffisant pardoneer
       T'assoille yow in contree as ye ryde
       For aventures whiche that may bityde.
       Paraventure ther may fallen oon or two
       Doun of his hors and breke his nekke atwo.
       Looke which a seuretee is it to yow alle
       That I am in youre felaweship yfalle,
       That may assoille yow bothe moore and lasse
940   Whan that the soule shal fro the body passe.
       I rede that oure Hoost heere shal bigynne,
       For he is moost envoluped in synne.
       Com forth, sire Hoost, and offre first anon,
       And thou shalt kisse my relikes everychon—
       Ye, for a grote: unbokele anon thy purs."
         "Nay, nay," quod he, "thanne have I Cristes curs.
       Lat be," quod he, "it shal nat be, so theech!
       Thou woldest make me kisse thyn olde breech
       And swere it were a relyk of a seint,

---

910 wolle wool. The Pardoner will take any sort of offering. **913 assoille** absolve of sin. **916 leche** physician. **920 male** bag. **923 of devocioun** out of (through). **927 taketh** take (receive); **wende** ride along. **929 So that** i.e., as long as. **932 mowe** can; **suffisant** capable. **934 aventures** experiences. This could allude to the sort of picaresque adventures that are made so much of in novels like *Don Quixote* and *Tom Jones*. **937 seuretee** assurance. **940 body passe**

Extreme unction, like baptism, absolution, and marriage, was one of the sacraments of the church reserved to ordained clergy like the Parson. Chaucer is voicing his criticism of the system of pardons and pardoners by having the Pardoner claim this vital privilege. **941 rede** advise. **942 envoluped** enveloped (involved). **945 grote** silver coin worth fourpence. **946 have I** i.e., I would have. **947 theech** may I prosper. **948 breech** underpants.

950 Though it were with thy fundement depeint.
But by the croys which that Seint Eleyne fond
I wolde I hadde thy coillons in myn hond
Instide of relikes or of seintuarie.
Lat kutte hem of, I wol thee helpe hem carie.
They shul be shryned in an hogges toord.''
   This Pardoner answerde nat a word.
So wrooth he was, no word ne wolde he seye.
   ''Now,'' quod oure Hoost, ''I wol no lenger pleye
With thee ne with noon oother angry man.''
960 But right anon the worthy Knyght bigan,
Whan that he saugh that al the peple lough,
''Namoore of this, for it is right ynough.
Sire Pardoner, be glad and myrie of cheere;
And ye, sire Hoost, that been to me so deere,
I prey yow that ye kisse the Pardoner.
And Pardoner, I prey thee drawe thee neer,
And as we diden lat us laughe and pleye.''
Anon they kiste and ryden forth hir weye.

HEERE IS ENDED THE PARDONERS TALE.

c. 1390

950 fundement depeint bottom (anus), stained (painted). **951 Eleyne** St. Helena, Mother of the Emperor Constantine, was believed to have found the true cross. **952 coillons** testicles, but cf. *General Prologue* l. 691. **953 seintuarie** box for relics (sanctuary). **954 Lat kutt hem** let them be. **955 shryned** enshrined; **toord** turd. **961 lough** laughed.

From Troylus and Criseyde

From Book III

This Troylus, with blysse of that supprised,
Put al in Goddes hand, as he that mente
Nothyng but wel, and sodcynly avysed
He hire in armes faste to hym hente.
And Pandarus with a ful good entente
Leyd hym to slepe, and seyde, ''If ye ben wyse,
1190 Swowneth not now, lest more folk aryse!''

What myght or may the sely larke seye
Whan that the sperhauk hath it in his fot?
I kan no more, but of thise ilke tweye,
To whom this tale sucre be or sot,
Though that I tarye a yer, somtyme I mot

1184 supprised seized. **1186 avysed** fully conscious. **1191 sely** innocent. **1194 sucre** sugar (sweet); **sot** soot (bitter). **1195 tarye a yer** Chaucer was aware of the agonizing protraction of the foreplay in his poem (which is not over yet). This was a deliberate device in troubadour poetry, which saw anticipation as a more effective impulse for poetry than consummation—as Keats likewise recognized in ''Ode on a Grecian Urn.''

After myn auctour tellen hire gladnesse,
As wel as I have told hire hevynesse.

Criseyde, which that felte hire thus itake,
As writen clerkes in hire bokes olde,
1200 Right as an aspes lef she gan to quake
Whan she hym felte hire in his armes folde.
But Troylus, al hool of cares colde,
Gan thanken tho the blysful goddes sevene.
Thus sondry peynes bryngen folk to hevene.

This Troylus yn armes gan hire streyne,
And seyde, "O swete, as evere mot I gon,
Now be ye kaught, now is ther but we tweyne.
Now yeldeth yow, for other bote is non."
To that Criseyde answerde thus anon,
1210 "Ne hadde I er now, my swete herte dere,
Ben yold, ywys, I were now not here!"

O soth is seyd, that heled for to be
As of a fevre or other gret syknesse,
Men moste drynke, as men may ofte se,
Ful bittre drynke; and for to han gladnesse,
Men drynken ofte peyne and gret distresse—
I mene it here, as for this aventure,
That thorugh a peyne hath founden al his cure.

And now swetnesse semeth more swete
1220 That bitternesse assayed was byforn,
For out of wo in blysse now they flete—
Non swych they felten sith that they were born.
Now is this bet than bothe two be lorn.
For love of God, take every womman hede
To werken thus, yf it come to the nede.

Criseyde, al quyt from every drede and tene,
As she that just cause hadde hym to tryste,
Made hym swych feste it joye was to sene,
Whan she his trowthe and clene entente wyste;
1230 And as abowte a tre, with many a twyste,
Bytrent and wryth the soote wodebynde,
Gan eche of hem in armes other wynde.

And as the newe abayssed nyghtyngale,
That stynteth first whan she gynneth to synge,
Whan that she hereth any herde tale,

1203 **sevene** the seven planets that control man's destiny. 1208 **bote** alternative. 1211 **yold** yielded. 1220 **assayed** experienced. 1221 **flete** float. 1223 **lorn** lost. 1226 **tene** grief.

1231 **Bytrent** encircles; **wryth** twines; **soote** sweet. 1233 **abayssed** startled. 1234 **stynteth** stops. 1235 **herde tale** shepherd talk.

Or in the hegges ony wight sterynge,
And after siker doth hire voys out rynge,
Right so Criseyde, whan hire drede stente,
Opened hire herte and tolde hym hire entente.

1240 And right as he that seth his deth yshapen,
And deye mot, in ought that he may gesse,
And sodeynly rescous doth hym escapen
And from his deth is brought in sykernesse,
For al this world, yn swych present gladnesse
Was Troylus, and hath his lady swete.
With worse hap God lat us nevere mete!

Hire armes smale, hire streyghte bak and softe,
Hire sydes longe, flesshly, smothe, and white,
He gan to stroke, and good thryft bad ful ofte
1250 Hire snowysshe throte, hire brestes rounde and lyte.
Thus in this hevene he gan hym to delyte,
And therwithal a thowsand tyme hire kyste,
That what to don for joye unnethe he wyste.

Than seyde he thus, "O Love, O Charite,
Thi moder ek, Citherea the swete,
After thiself next heried be she—
Venus mene I, the wel-willy planete—
And next the, Imeneus, I the grete,
For nevere man was to yow goddes holde
1260 As I, which ye han brought fro cares colde.

"Benygne Love, thow holy bond of thynges,
Whoso wol grace and lyst the nought honouren,
Lo, his desir wol fle withouten wynges.
For noldestow of bounte hem socouren
That serven best and most alwey labouren,
Yet were al lost, that dar I wel seyn certes,
But yf thi grace passed oure desertes.

"And for thow me, that lest kowde deserve
Of hem that noumbred ben unto thi grace,
1270 Hast holpen, ther I lykly was to sterve,
And me bistowed in so heygh a place
That thilke boundes may no blysse pace,
I kan namore but laude and reverence
Be to thy bounte and thyn excellence!"

1237 **siker** reassured (secure). 1238 **stente**
stopped. 1240 **yshapen** planned out. 1241 **is**
certain to die for all that he can tell. 1242 **doth
hym** causes him. 1243 **sykernesse** safety. 1246
hap luck. 1249 **thryft bad** blessing invoked.
1253 **unnethe** hardly; **wyste** knew. 1255
Citherea Venus. 1256 **heried** praised. 1256 **wel-**

willy well-willing (benevolent—to lovers). 1258
Imeneus Hymen, god of marriage. 1259 **holde**
indebted (beholden). 1262 **wol grace** desires
favor. 1263 **his desir** what he desires; **fle** fly.
1267 **passed** surpassed. 1268 **for thow** because
you. 1270 **sterve** die. 1272 **thilke boundes** the
bounds of it; **pace** surpass. 1273 **laude** praise.

And therwithal Criseyde anoon he kyste,
Of which, certeyn, she felte no dishese.
And thus seyde he, "Now wolde God I wyste,
Myn herte swete, how I yow myght plese.
What man," wuod he, "was evere thus at ese
1280 As I, on which the faireste and the beste
That evere I say deyneth hire herte reste?

"Here may men se that mercy passeth ryght;
The experience of that is felt in me,
That am unworthi to so swete a wyght.
But herte myn, of youre benyngnite,
So thynketh, thowgh that I unworthi be,
Yet mot I nede amenden in som wyse,
Right thorugh the vertu of yowre heygh servyse.

"And for the love of God, my lady dere,
1290 Syn God hath wrought me for I shal yow serve—
As thus I mene, that ye wol be my stere,
To do me lyve, if that yow lyste, or sterve—
So techeth me how that I may deserv̄
Youre thank so that I thorugh myn ignoraunce
Ne do nothing that yow be displesaunce.

"For certes, fresshe wommanliche wyf,
This dar I seye, that trouthe and diligence,
That shal ye fynden in me al my lyf;
Ne I wol nat, certeyn, breken youre defence;
1300 And if I do, present or in absence,
For love of God, lat sle me with the dede,
If that it lyke unto youre wommanhede."

1282 passeth surpasses. 1287 amenden im-   die. 1299 breken transgress; defence prohi-
prove. 1291 stere guide. 1292 do   make; sterve   bition. 1301 lat sle me let me be slain.

From Book V

Whan they unto the paleys were yeomen
Of Troylus, thei down of hors alighte,
And to the chambre hire wey than han they nomen,
And into tyme that it gan to nyghte,
They spaken of Criseyde the brighte.
And after this, whan that hem bothe leste,
Thei spedde hem fro the soper unto reste.

O morwe as soone as day bygan to clere,
520 This Troylus gan of his slep t'abreyde,
And to Pandare, his owen brother dere,
"For love of God," ful pitously he seyde,

514 nomen taken. 520 abreyde wake up.

"As go we seen the paleys of Criseyde;
For syn we yet may have no more feste,
So lat us seen hire paleys atte leste."

And therwithal, his meyne for to blende,
A cause he fond in towne for to go,
And to Criseyde hous thei gonnen wende.
But Lord, this sely Troylus was wo!
530   Hym thoughte his sorwful herte braste a-two.
For whan he saugh hire dorres sperid alle,
Wel neigh for sorwe adown he gan to falle.

Therwith whan he was ware and gan byholde
How shet was every wyndowe of the place,
As frost hym thoughte his herte gan to colde,
For which with chaunged deedlych pale face,
Withouten word, he forthby gan to pace,
And, as God wolde, he gan so faste ryde
That no wight of his contenaunce aspide.

540   Than seyde he thus, "O paleys desolat,
O hous of houses whilom best yhight,
O paleys empty and disconsolat,
O thou lanterne of which queynt is the light,
O paleys whilom day that now art nyght,
Wel oughtestow to falle, and I to dye,
Syn she is went that wont was us to gye.

"O paleys whilom crowne of houses alle,
Enlumyned with the sonne of alle blysse,
O ryng fro which the ruby is out falle,
550   O cause of wo that cause hast ben of lisse,
Yet syn I may no bet, fayn wolde I kysse
Thy colde dores, dorste I for this route;
And farewel shryne, of which the seynt is oute!"

Therwith he caste on Pandarus his eye,
With chaunged face, and pitous to byholde;
And whan he myght his tyme aright aspye,
Ay as he rod, to Pandarus he tolde
His newe sorwe and ek his joyes olde,
So pitously and with so dede an hewe
560   That every wight myghte on his sorwe rewe.

Fro thennesforth he rideth up and down,
And everything cam hym to remembraunce
As he rod forby places of the toun

---

526 **meyne** household; **blende** deceive (blind). **529 sely** the usual spectrum of meaning: silly, innocent, blessed. **530 braste** would break (burst). **531 sperid** barred. **537 forthby ... pace** pass by. **541 whilom** formerly; **yhight** called. **543 queynt** quenched. **546 gye** guide. **550 lisse** joy. **551 fayn** happily. **552 route** crowd. **560 rewe** have pity. **563 forby** by.

In whiche he whilom hadde al his plesaunce.
"Lo, yende saugh I myn owene lady daunce,
And in that temple, with hire eyen clere,
Me kaughte first my righte lady dere.

"And yender have I herd ful lustily
Me dere herte laugh; and yender pleye
570 Saugh ich hire ones ek ful blysfully;
And yender ones to me gan she seye,
'Now goode swete, love me wel, I preye.'
And yond so goodly gan she me byholde
That to the deth myn herte is to hire holde.

"And at that corner in the yonder hous
Herde I myn alderlevest lady dere,
So wommanly with vois melodious,
Syngen so wel, so goodly, and so clere,
That in my soule yet me thenketh ich here
580 The blisful sown. And in that yonder place
My lady first me tok unto hire grace."

This Diomede, of whom yow telle I gan,
Gooth now withinne hymself ay arguynge,
With al the sleighte and al that evere he kan,
How he may best, with shortest taryinge,
Into his net Criseydes herte brynge.
To this entent he koude nevere fyne;
To fysshen hire he leyde out hook and lyne.

But natheles, wel in his herte he thoughte
That she nas nat withoute a love in Troye.
780 For nevere sythen he hire thennes broughte,
Ne koude he sen hire laughen or maken joie.
He nyst how best hire herte for t'acoye.
"But for to assaye," he seyde, "it nought ne greveth,
For he that nought n'assayeth, nought n'acheveth."

Yet seide he to hymself upon a nyght,
"Now am I not a fool that wot wel how
Hire wo for love is of another wight,
And hereupon to gon assaye hire now?
I may wel wite, it nyl nat ben my prow.
790 For wyse folk in bokes it expresse,
'Men shal nat wowe a wight in hevynesse.'

"But whoso myghte wynnen swych a flour
From hym for whom she morneth nyght and day,

566 **clere** bright. 567 **kaughte** caught sight of.
568 **lustily** gaily. 574 **holde** bound. 575 **yonder**
more distant. 576 **alderlevest** dearest of all. 580
yonder place i.e, Diephebus' house. 773
sleighte guile. 776 **fyne** cease. 780 **sythen** since.
782 **nyst** didn't know; **acoye** tame (quiet). 789
prow profit. 791 **hevynesse** i.e., who is sad.

He myghte seyn he were a conquerour.''
And right anoon, as he that bold was ay,
Thoughte in his herte, "Happe how happe may.
Al sholde I deye, I wole hire herte seche.
I shal no more lesen but my speche.''

This Diomede, as bokes us declare,
800 Was in his nedes prest and corageous,
With sterne voys and myghty lymes square,
Hardy, testyf, strong, and chevalrous
Of dedes, lyk his fader Tideus;
And som men seyn he was of tunge large.
And heyr he was of Calydoyne and Arge.

Criseyde mene was of hire stature;
Therto of shap, of face, and ek of chere,
Ther myghte ben no fayrer creature.
And ofte tyme this was hire manere,
810 To gon ytressed with hire heerys clere
Doun by hire coler at hire bak byhynde,
Which with a thred of gold she wolde bynde.

And save hire browes joyneden yfere,
Ther nas no lak in ought I kan espyen.
But for to speken of hire eyen clere,
Lo, trewely, thei writen that hire syen
That Paradys stood formed in hire eyen.
And with hire riche beaute everemore
Strof love in hire ay which of hem was more.

820 She sobre was, ek symple, and wys withal,
The beste ynorisshed ek that myghte be,
And goodly of hire speche in general;
Charitable, estatlych, lusty, and fre,
Ne nevere mo ne lakkede hire pyte;
Tendre-herted, slydynge of corage;
But trewely, I kan nat telle hire age.

799–840 The portraits of Diomede, Criseyde, and Troylus represent a conventional rhetorical type of which the portraits of the pilgrims in *Canterbury Tales* are supreme examples. The convention dates back to the "characters" of Theophrastas and leads on to the character writers of the seventeenth century, the character sketches in the *Spectator Papers*, etc. The ultimate source for this addition is Joseph of Exeter, *Frigii Daretis Ylias*, combined with details from Benoit and other parts of the *Filestrato*: but the portraits circulated independently, and what intermediaries Chaucer may have used has not been ascertained. **802 Hardy** brave; **testyf** impetuous; **chevalrous** loving chivalric combat. **804 tunge large** tongue lax. **805 Calydoyne** Calydon; **Arge** Argos. **806 mene** average height. **807 chere** expression. **810–811 ytressed/Doun . . . byhynde** i.e., hanging in braids down her back. 813 **browes joyneden** her brows met—a defect in beauty to Europeans, but a special mark of beauty in Greece and the Near East. **816 syen** saw. **821 ynorisshed** brought up. **823 estatlych** dignified; **lusty** gay; **fre** generous. **825 slydynge of corage** unstable of will; C.S. Lewis takes this to be the essential characteristic of Criseyde, which explains all of her behavior—irresolution resulting from fear.

And Troylus wel woxen was in highte,
And complet formed by proporcion
So wel that kynde it not amenden myghte;
830　Yong, fresch, strong, and hardy as lyon;
Trewe as stel in ech condicion;
On of the beste enteched creature
That is or shal whil that the world may dure.

And certeynly in storye it is founde
That Troylus was nevere unto no wight,
As in his tyme, in no degre secounde
In dorryng don that longeth to a knyght.
Al myghte a geaunt passen hym of myght,
His herte ay with the ferste and with the beste
840　Stod paregal, to dorre don that hym leste.

1382–85

829 **kynde** nature. **830 hardy** brave. **831**
condicion situation. **832 enteched** endowed.
834 storye history. **837 dorryng don** daring
to do (Spenser's "derring-do"); **longeth** be-
longs. **838 passen** surpass. **840 paregal** equal
(French); **dorre** dare.

To Rosemounde

Madame, ye ben of alle beaute shryne
As fer as cercled is the mapamounde,
For as the cristall glorious ye shyne,
And lyke ruby ben your chekes rounde.
Therwyth ye ben so mery and so jocounde
That at a revell whan that I se you daunce,
It is an oynement unto my wounde,
Thogh ye to me ne do no daliaunce.

For thogh I wepe of teres ful a tyne,
10　Yet may that wo myn herte nat confounde.
Your semy voys, that ye so small out twyne,
Maketh my thoght in joy and blys habounde.
So curtaysly I go, with love bounde,
That to myself I sey, in my penaunce,
"Suffyseth me to love you, Rosemounde,
Thogh ye to me ne do no daliaunace."

Nas never pyk walwed in galauntyne
As I in love am walwed and iwounde,
For whych ful ofte I of myself devyne
20　That I am trewe Tristam the secounde.

2 mapamounde map of the world. Medieval
maps of the world enclosed in frames were often
so designated, or by the Latin *mappa mundi*. **9**
tyne tub. **11 semy** thin (small); **twyne** twist
out. **17 walwed** wallowed; **galauntyne** a pi-
quant wine sauce. **19 devyne** divine (under-
stand). **20 Tristam** lover of Iseult, who drank
the magic love potion.

My love may not refreyde nor affounde;
I brenne ay in an amorouse plesaunce.
Do what you lyst; I wyl your thral be founde,
Thogh ye to me ne do no daliaunce.

TREGENTIL   CHAUCER

21 refreyde grow cold; affound founder   ship of the poem. It is in imitation of the colo-
(sink). TREGENTIL.—CHAUCER. The colophon, phon of the *Troylus* on the preceding verso of
in a later hand, offers no evidence of the author- the manuscript.

PIERS PLOWMAN

Little is known about the author of *Piers Plowman*, one of the greatest and most complex poems of the Middle Ages. Evidence suggests that he was William Langland (c. 1332- c. 1400), "Long Will" as he is called in the text. He trained as a Benedictine priest at the priory of Great Malvern and took minor orders but did not secure a benefice. He married and lived with his wife, Kitte, and daughter, Calote, in Cornhill, London, where he sang the paternoster, the psalter, and the seven penitential psalms for the souls of those who contributed to his support. Three different versions (1362, 1377, 1392) of his poem exist, all written in the distinctive unrhymed alliterative long line. His work is not courtly in its vocabulary and seems to have been intended for "lewed" folk as well as for the learned. It presents in powerful language a panorama of society— the king, nobility, clergy, and workers. The observation is acute and unsparing and provides the most vivid and contemporary picture we have of medieval life. But Langland's aims were not sociological or political. Conservative and uncompromisingly idealistic, his solution to contemporary evils was for man to model his life on the gospels. His major concern was how to achieve the perfect life within the scheme of God's grace.

The poem is a multiplication of the customary allegorical dream form. Instead of one dream, there are ten, two of which are dreams within dreams, all contained within some twenty sections or *passus*. In the first part, the *Visio*, the narrator falls asleep and sees a field "ful of folk," a scene that enables him to make a critical commentary on society and to seek a solution through individual responsibility and conscience. In the passage cited here, everyone is engaged in some occupation that attracts the attention of the moralist. In the second and longer part, called the *Vita*, which concerns the life of Dowel, Dobet, and Dobest, the poet falls asleep again and sees Conscience preaching. This is where the vigorous portraits of the Seven Deadly Sins appear, one of which is reproduced here. The sinners are brought to repentance and sent out in search of Truth. But no one knows the way until Piers the Plowman explains it in allegorical terms. The dreamer is the central figure, symbolizing the ideal servant of God. A climax is reached with a vision of the crucifixion and redemption in which Christ assumes the nature of Piers. The last passus again depicts the decadence of the world, with the church attacked by anti-Christ. Truth is overturned, Castle Unity is besieged, and the search begins again for Piers Plowman and the Christian life.

Any summary is misleading because it suggests a coherent linear development that the work does not possess. The dreams, interspersed with short waiting periods, are presented from many different angles, and the unity must be sought in certain patterns, images, redefinitions, parallel situations, and combinations, and in the multiple significances of the allegory, rather than in an overall structure. Yet the subject itself possesses the unity. It is a quest for truth and understanding by a narrator who is a personification of all men, of the errant individual will, and of Langland himself.

From Piers Plowman

The Field Full of Folk

In a somer seson whenne softe was the sunne
I shop me into a shroud as I a shep were,
In habite as an hermite unholy of werkes,
Wente wide in this world wondres to here.
But on a May morwening upon Malverne hilles
Me befel a ferly, of fairye me thoughte;
I was wery ofwandred and wente me to reste
Under a brod bank by a bournes side;
And as I lay and lenede and lookede on the watres,
10   I slomerede into a sleeping, it swyede so merye.
Thenne gan I mete a merveillous swevene:
That I was in a wildernesse, wiste I nevere where;
Ac as I beheld into the Est on high to the sunne
I saw a towr on a toft tryely y-maked;
A deep dale benethe, a dungeoun thereinne
With deepe dikes and derke and dredful of sight.
   A fair feeld ful of folk fand I there-betwene,
Of alle maner of men, the mene and the riche,
Worching and wandringe as the world asketh.
20   Some putte hem to plow, playede ful selde,
In setting and sowing swunke ful harde,
Wonne that these wastours with glotonye destroyeth.
And some putte hem to pride, aparailede hem thereafter,
In countenaunce of clothing comen disgised.
In prayers and penaunce putten hem manye,
Al for love of oure Lord livede wel straite,
In hope for to have hevene-riche blisse,
As ancres and hermites that holden hem in celles,
Coveite not in cuntré to cairen aboute
30   For no likerous liflode here likam to plese.
And some chosen to chaffare, they chevede the betere,
As it seemeth to oure sight that suche men thriven.
And some merthes to make, as minstrales cunne,
And gete gold with here glee giltles, I trowe.

1 **softe** warm. 2 I dressed myself in a garment as if I were a shepherd. 3 **In habite as** clothed like. 6 a marvelous thing befell me, by magic as it seemed to me. 7 **wery ofwandred** weary from wandering. 8 **by side** by the side of a stream. 9 **lenede** rested. 10 I dozed to sleep, it sounded so pleasant. 11 then I dreamed a wonderful dream. 12 **wiste** knew. 13 **Ac** but. 14 **toft** hill; **tryely** excellently. 16 **dredful of sight** of terrifying aspect. 17 **fand** found. 18 **the mene and the riche** the lowly and the great. 19 **Worching** working; **asketh** requires. 20 **putte . . . plow** devoted themselves to ploughing; **selde** seldom. 21 **setting** planting; **swunke** toiled. 22 **Wonne that** gained what; **destroyeth** consume. 23-24 and some devoted themselves to pride, dressed themselves up accordingly, went about in fantastic guises to show off their clothes. 26 **wel straite** very austerely. 27 trusting to have the bliss of the kingdom of heaven. 28 **As ancres** such as anchorites; **holden him** keep themselves. 29 **Coveite** desire; **cairen** go. 30 for the sake of any delightful way of life to gratify their bodies. 31 and some took to trading, they prospered the better. 32 **As** for. 33 and some took to entertaining, as minstrels know how to. 34 **with . . . giltles** for their music without sin.

Glutton in the Tavern

Now biginneth Glotoun for to go to shrifte,
And caires him to kirke-ward his conpte to shewe.
Fasting on a Friday forth gan he wende
By Betene hous the brewestere, that bad him good morwen,
And whiderward he wolde the brew-wif him askede.
"To holy churche," quod he, "for to here masse,
And sennes sitte and be shrive, and sinege no more."
    "I have good ale, gossip. Glotoun, wilt thou assaye?"
    "Hast thou," quod he, "any hote spices?"
10 "I have peper and pionie and a pound of garleke,
A ferthing-worth fenkel-sedes, for fasting-dayes I boughte it."
    Thenne goth Glotoun in, and grete othes after.
Sesse the souteress sat on the benche,
Watte the warnere and his wif drunke,
Timme the tinkere and twaine of his knaves,
Hicke the hackenayman and Hewe the nedlere,
Clarice of Cockes Lane, and the clerk of the churche,
Sire Peres of Prydie and Purnele of Flaundres,
An hayward, an heremite, the hangeman of Tybourne,
20 Dawe the dikere with a doseine harlotes
Of portours and of pike-purses and of pilede tooth-draweres,
A ribibour and a ratoner, a rakere and his knave,
A ropere and a redingkinge, and Rose the dishere,
Godefray the garlek-monger and Griffith the Walshe,
And of upholderes an heep, erly by the morwe
Geven Glotoun with glad chere good ale to hanselle.
    Clement the coblere cast off his cloke,
And to the newe faire nempnede forth to selle;
Hicke the hackenayman hit his hood after,
30 And bade Bitte the bochere been on his side.
There were chapmen y-chose this chaffare to praise,
That who so hadde the hood sholde not have the cloke,

4 By . . . brewestere past the house of Beten, the ale-wife. 5 And . . . wolde and where he was going. 6 quod said. 7 and afterwards sit and make confession, and sin no more. 8 gossip friend; assaye try (it). 10 pione peony-seeds. 11 fenkel fennel. 12 grete othes after coarse oaths follow. 13 souteress cobbler-woman. 14 warnere gamekeeper; drunke were drinking. 15 knaves servants. 16 hackenayman keeper of horses for hire; nedlere needle-maker. 17 Cockes Lane Cock Lane (where women of ill fame were lodged); clerc i.e., clerk in minor orders. 18 Sire Peres Sir Piers (i.e., a priest) of ?Priddy (Somerset) and Petronella (i.e., a wanton woman) of Flanders. 19 hayward hedge-keeper. 20 dikere ditcher; harlotes scoundrels. 21 pilede bald-headed. 22 ribibour a rebeck-player; ratoner a rat-catcher; rakere a scavenger; his knave his boy. 23 ropere ropemaker; redingkinge (unexplained); dishere dish-seller. 24 Walshe Welshman. 25 and a great number of dealers in secondhand goods, early in the morning. 26 Geven . . . to hanselle gave as a token of good will. 28 and proffered it for sale at the New Fair (? i.e., by barter). 29 hit his hood then tapped his hood. 30 bochere butcher. 31 Bargainers were chosen there to value these articles. 33–39 and that (whoever got) the better thing, assessed by arbitrators, should compensate (him who got) the worse. They (the bargainers) hastily got up and whispered together and valued these bargains apart by themselves, and there were plenty of oaths because one was getting the worse bargain. They could not honestly agree, indeed, till they asked Robin the ropemaker to stand up and nominated him as an umpire, so that there should be no wrangling.

And that the bettere thing, by arbitreres, bote sholde the worse.
Tho risen up rape and rouned togideres,
And praisede this penyworthes apart by hem selve,
And there were othes an heep for on sholde have the worse.
They couthe not, by here consience, acorden for treuthe,
Til Robin the Ropere arise they bisoughte
And nempned him for an oumper, that no debat were.
40   Hicke the hostiler hadde the cloke,
In covenaunt that Clement sholde the cuppe fille,
And have Hickes hood the hostiler, and holde him y-served;
And who so repentede him rathest sholde arise after
And grete Sire Glotoun with a galoun of ale.
    There was laughing and lowring and "Let go the cuppe!"
Bargaines and bevereges bigan tho to awake;
And seten so til evensong, and sungen umbywhile,
Til Glotoun hadde y-globbed a galoun and a gille.

c. 1375

40 **hostiler** ostler. **41-43** on condition that Clement should fill his cup at Hick's expense and have Hick the ostler's hood and consider himself satisfied; and the first person to repudiate the bargain should stand up afterwards. **44 grete** reward. **45** there was laughing and scowling and "Pass round the cup!" **46 tho to awake** to flow then. **47 seten so** so they went on; **umbywhile** at times. **48 y-globbed** gulped down.

SIR GAWAIN AND THE GREEN KNIGHT

Mystery surrounds *Sir Gawain and the Green Knight*. The work is universally admired as the finest of the Middle English romances; yet it exists only in a single copy, the product of a commercial scriptorium in the latter part of the fourteenth century. The author, evidently highly educated, steeped in European literary and theological traditions, and personally familiar with all aspects of aristocratic life and culture, is unknown. The speculation is that he was attached to some baronial court in the northwest Midlands, the locale of the reputed dialect of the poem. But although his enormous vocabulary was enriched with many archaic words suited to the native alliterative style that he adopted and transformed with such remarkable effect, he was obviously sophisticated and utterly unprovincial in his perspectives and interests.

For his Arthurian romance he combined two ancient motifs of Celtic folklore: the *Beheading Game* and the *Temptation*, the one occurring in the Middle Irish *Bricriu's Feast* and the other in a bardic tale in the Welsh *Mabinogion* and elsewhere. In the first, the hero accepts a challenge to strike a stranger with an axe on condition that he will receive a return blow one year later; in the second the hero is subjected to the temptations of the wife of his host who is seeking to test him.

In *Sir Gawain and the Green Knight*, unknown to the hero, both stranger and host are the same person. The test of courage and the test of honor are ironically interdependent. The outcome of the second situation determines the outcome of the first and is responsible for the life or death of the hero. The structure is, indeed, admirably suited to a theme that explores the nature and limitations of personal integrity and culminates in the hero's acquisition of self-knowledge.

The story is developed with great artistry. There is a remarkable and curiously satisfying symmetry of structure; the descriptive language possesses the color and minute particularization of the early miniatures in the Duke of Berry's *Book of Hours*; the characters are presented perceptively and convincingly, and the story progresses with a finesse enhanced by the poet's urbanity and witty appreciation of the irony of the human situation.

In the passage below, the poet describes the festivities at King Arthur's court at Camelot at Christmas, the scene of jousts, parades, song dances, chanting of Mass, and the giving of gifts, climaxed by a splendid feast. As was customary on such occasions, King Arthur will not eat until he has either heard or seen some dramatic event. At this point a huge knight enters and stuns the company to silence by his appearance. Both he and his horse are brilliant green in color.

From Sir Gawain and the Green Knight

This kyng lay at Camylot upon Krystmase
With mony luflych lorde, ledes of the bet—
Rekenly of the Rounde Table alle tho rich brether—
40 With rych revel oryght and rechles merthes.
Ther tournayed tulkes by tymes ful mony,
Justed ful jolilé thise gentyle knightes,
Sythen kayred to the court, caroles to make;
For ther the fest was ilyche ful fiften dayes,
With alle the mete and the mirthe that men couthe avyse:
Such glaum ande gle glorious to here,
Dere dyn upon day, daunsyng on nyghtes—
Al was hap upon heghe in halles and chambres
With lordes and ladies, as levest him thoght.
50 With all the wele of the worlde thay woned ther samen,
The most kyd knyghtes under Krystes selven
And the lovelokkest ladies that ever lif haden,
And he the comlokest kyng, that the court haldes;
For al was this fayre folk in her first age,
On sille,
The hapnest under heven,
Kyng hyghest mon of wylle—
Hit were now gret nye to neven
So hardy a here on hille.

37 According to French romance, Arthur held court five times a year, on the great Christian festivals, Easter, Ascension, Whitsun, All Saints', and Christmas. In the *Livre de Carados*, possibly the poet's source for the story of the Beheading Game, the challenger enters Arthur's court at Carduel at the Whitsuntide feast. **43 caroles** courtly ring dances with singing; cf. the description in Chaucer's translation of the *Roman de la Rose* ll. 743 ff. **51 under Kyrstes selven** except Christ himself. **54** Arthur and his courtiers were all in their youth (first age); by implication this was also the golden age of Arthur's court and reign, before the appearance of the treachery that brought about the downfall of the Round Table; the theme of the first stanza (the rise and fall of kingdoms) is heard faintly in the background.

60 Wyle New Yer was so yep that hit was newe cummen,
That day doubble on the dece was the douth served.
Fro the kyng was cummen with knyghtes into the halle,
The chauntré of the chapel cheved to an ende,
Loude crye was ther kest of clerkes and other,
Nowel nayted onewe, nevened ful ofte.
And sythen riche forth runnen to reche hondeselle,
Yeyed "Yeres yiftes!" on high, yelde hem bi hond,
Debated busyly aboute tho giftes;
Ladies laghed ful loude thogh thay lost haden
70 And he that wan was not wrothe—that may ye wel trawe.
Alle this mirthe thay maden to the mete tyme.
When thay had waschen worthyly, thay wenten to sete,
The best burne ay abof, as hit best semed;
Quene Guenore ful gay graythed in the myddes,
Dressed on the dere des, dubbed al aboute:
Smal sendal bisides, a selure hir over
Of tryed tolouse, of tars tapites innoghe
That were enbrawded and beten wyth the best gemmes
That myght be preved of prys wyth penyes to bye
80   In daye.
      The comlokest to discrye
      Ther glent with yen gray;
      A semloker that ever he sye
      Soth moght no mon say.

Bot Arthure wolde not ete til al were served;
He was so joly of his joyfnes, and sumwhat childgered,
His lif liked hym lyght; he lovied the lasse
Auther to longe lye or to longe sitte,
So bisied him his yonge blod and his brayn wylde.
90 And also another maner meved him eke,
That he thurgh nobelay had nomen: he wolde never ete

Upon such a dere day, er hym devised were
Of sum aventurus thyng, an uncouthe tale
Of sum mayn mervayle that he myght trawe,
Of alderes, of armes, of other aventurus;
Other sum segg hym bisoght of sum siker knyght
To joyne wyth hym in justyng, in jopardé to lay,
Lede, lif for lyf, leve uchon other,
As fortune wolde fulsun hom, the fayrer to have.
100 This was kynges countenaunce where he in court were,
At uch farand fest among his fre meny
     In halle.
     Therfore of face so fere
     He stightles stif in stalle;
     Full yep in that New Yere,
     Much mirthe he mas with alle.

Thus ther stondes in stale the stif kyng hisselven,
Talkkande bifore the hyghe table of trifles ful hende.
There gode Gawan was graythed Gwenore bisyde,
110 And Agravayn a la Dure Mayn on that other syde sittes—
Bothe the kynges sister-sunes and ful siker knightes;
Bischop Bawdewyn abof bigines the table,
And Ywan, Uryn son, ette with hymselven.
Thise were dight on the des and derworthly served,
And sithen mony siker segge at the sidbordes.
Then the first cors come with crakkyng of trumpes
Wyth mony baner ful bryght, that therbi henged;

92–94 er . . . mervayle until he had been told of some daring enterprise, a strange tale of some great wonder. **95 alderes** either princes (Old English *aldor*) or ancestors (Old English *ældra*); the two are, indeed, confused in Middle English in some contexts. *Morte Arthure* 13: "Off elders of alde tyme and of theire awke dedys" appears to support the meaning "elders, ancestors" here; however, the phrase "elders of alde tyme" may be redundant and probably an adaptation or a scribal corruption of a poorly understood "alderes (princes) of alde tyme." **96–99** or else some man entreated him for a true knight to engage in jousting with him, for a man ("lede") to lay life against life in jeopardy, either one to concede victory to the other, as fortune saw fit to help ("fulsun") them. Ll. 97–99 summarize the terms of honorable combat. **109–13** Agravain and Gawain were sons of Lot, king of Orkney; their mother was Arthur's half-sister, Anna (sometimes known as Belisent). Guenevere sits on Arthur's left, at the center of the table; Gawain and Agravain are to the left of her. On Arthur's right are Bishop Baldwin and Iwain. **110 a la Dure Mayn**

of the hard hand; **on that other syde** i.e., Gawain's. **112 abof bigines the table** sits in the place of honor (at the right of the host). When the host sat at the end of the table the guest of honor would occupy the first place on his right at the "top" of the long side. The poet does not introduce the Round Table, though he uses the phrase for the abstract "Arthur's court"; in general the background details of the romance are drawn from contemporary aristocratic life. **113 ette with hymselven** shared dishes with him (i.e., with Baldwin), cf. l. 128. At the end of a line, "hymselven" is frequently used for "him," with no special emphasis. **116 cors** A course comprised a variety of dishes (enough to constitute a complete meal by any modern standard). A medieval banquet consisted of a number of these courses. For instance, at the marriage of Henry IV in 1403, there were three meat courses and three fish courses, each course consisting of between seven and fourteen separate dishes and ending in its own *soltelé* (sweetmeat). Cf. l. 128. **117 Wyth . . . bryght** resplendent with many a banner.

Newe nakryn noyse with the noble pipes,
Wylde werbles and wyght wakned lote,
120 That mony hert ful highe hef at her towches.
Dayntés dryven therwyth of ful dere metes,
Foysoun of the fresche, and on so fele disches
That pine to fynde the place the peple biforne
For to sette the sylveren that sere sewes halden
      On clothe.
Iche lede as he loved hymselve
Ther laght withouten lothe;
Ay two had disches twelve,
Good ber and bryght wyn bothe.

130 Now wyl I of hor servise say yow no more,
For uch wye may wel wit no wont that ther were.
Another noyse ful newe neghed bilive,
That the lude myght haf leve liflode to cach;
For unethe was the noyce not a whyle sesed,
And the fyrst cource in the court kyndely served,
Ther hales in at the halle dor an aghlich mayster,
On the most on the molde on mesure hyghe;
Fro the swyre to the swange so sware and so thik,
And his lyndes and his lymes so longe and so grete,
140 Half-etayn in erde I hope that he were,
Bot mon most I algate mynn hym to bene,
And that the myriest in his muckel that myght ride;
For of bak and of brest al were his bodi sturne,
Both his wombe and his wast were worthily smale,
And alle his fetures folwande in forme, that he hade,
      Ful clene.
For wonder of his hue men hade,
Set in his semblaunt sene;
He ferde as freke were fade,
150 And overal enker grene.

    c. 1390

119 spirited, piercing trills roused echoes.
126 as . . . hymselve as he himself liked.
132–33 another, quite new, noise drew near suddenly, so that the prince might have leave to take food; cf. ll. 90. ff. **134** for scarcely a moment after the music had finished (cf. ll. 116 ff.). The double negative is merely emphatic. **135 served** "Was" is understood from the previous line. **137** the very biggest man on earth in height. **141–42** (that) I think he was half-giant on earth, but at any rate I suppose (declare?) him to be the

biggest man (on earth) and moreover the most elegant for his size who could ride a horse. **145–46** and every part of him agreeing in proportion completely. Possibly, however, "folwande in forme" is an oblique reference to his color (l. 148): matching in outward appearance (color). This would enable us to understand "for" (l. 147) in its usual sense. In either case, "that he hade" qualifies "fetures," repeating the force of "his" rather than "forme."

THE SCOTTISH POETS: HENRYSON AND DUNBAR

Robert Henryson and William Dunbar used to be regarded principally as admirers, developers, and modifiers of Chaucer's poetical art; they are now valued as brilliant poets in their own right. Writing in Scotland in the late fifteenth and early sixteenth centuries, they were sophisticated poets, well aware of both courtly and popular traditions. The work that they produced is of astonishing variety, technically skillful, and often imaginative in language and presentation. Dominated as they were by the Christian ethic, these poets were nevertheless daringly innovative at times in their adaptation of conventional forms and concepts.

All that is known about Robert Henryson (c. 1425–c. 1505) is that he lived in Dunfermline and may have taught at the Benedictine Abbey grammar school. Since the town was a favorite royal seat, he may have been familiar with the courts of James III and James IV. His poetry indicates that he was an uncompromising moralist, humorist, ironist, and a sharp though not always unkindly observer of contemporary life. In his well-known *Moral Fables*, his achievement lies in the skill with which he transforms stock Aesopian and Reynardian incidents into well-organized verse tales, outstanding for careful presentation of plot, climax, and moral conflict and for vigorous portrayal of characters in description and in a dramatic dialogue that suggests the language and rhythms of everyday speech. While the basically pagan genre is contained in a Christian world of allegory and symbol, the action is set in a milieu that provides insights simultaneously into timeless aspects of human nature and into specific features of contemporary life.

The Moral Fables imply criticism of corruption in church and state and sympathy for the oppressed. Many other poems by Henryson are also profoundly moralistic. In *Orpheus and Eurydice*, Orpheus' inability to resist a backward glance at his wife is the triumph of sensuality over the rational part of man's nature; in *The Testament of Cresseid*, the heroine is afflicted with leprosy as a terrible punishment for her profligacy and impiety; in *The Thre Deid Pollis*, the conventional theme of *memento mori* is brought home to "sinful man" by means of a dramatic confrontation with three skulls; even the humorous adaptation of the French *pastourelle* in *Robene and Makyne*, tells of unsatisfied love and the importance of expediency—"The man that will nocht quhen he may/Sall haif nocht quhen he wald."

Despite the variety of his poetry and the attitudes that we may detect in it, we know little of Henryson the man. Especially interesting, therefore, is the passage from *The Testament of Cresseid* below. In place of the conventional spring setting, the poet presents northern winds, hailstorms, and himself as a weary old man, chilled in heart and body, huddled over a fire.

Slightly more is known about William Dunbar (c. 1460–c. 1521). He apparently graduated from the University of St. Andrew's with a B.A. in 1477 and an M.A. in 1479, and, though intended for the priesthood, he served for some years at the court of a genial patron of the arts, James IV.

Court life is reflected in much of his occasional verse. His large and extraordinarily varied collection of poems—religious and secular lyrics, debates, visions, moral meditations, prayers, sardonic petitions, bawdy songs, invectives, satires, burlesques, and other works less easy to classify—contains public poems commemorating such events as the marriage of James IV to Princess Margaret of England in 1503. In these poems he uses elaborate "aureate diction," experimenting with decorative European rhetorical conventions and with Chaucer's "high" style.

Mercurial, dynamic, subtle, dazzlingly versatile, and emotionally intense are commendatory terms justly applied to Dunbar's poetry. Probably all these qualities and more are evinced in one of his best-known works,

Two Married Women and a Widow, in which the poet overhears the intimate confessions of three richly dressed matrons celebrating Midsummer's Eve in an exotic garden. Although the women are spiritual heirs to the Wife of Bath, the tone is misogynistic and coarser than Chaucer's. Yet as a piece of psychological and social drama and as a literary tour de force it is brilliant. The language is crammed with ironic echoes from lyric, proverbial expression, and romance, and with exaggerations of rhetorical formulae.

Dunbar is a master of the high, middle, and low styles, of the heavily decorative, of the macaronic (combining several languages), of the alliterative, and of a crude vernacular. He augmented the language of northern England with the resources of a sophisticated international culture, with rich imagery drawn from the visual arts, the lapidary, bestiary, heraldry, the Bible, and the liturgy, as well as from everyday objects or activities, such as tar-barrels, chamber-pots, bull-baiting, and the hanging of felons. But for all his wit, the prevailing mood is sombre and reflects an obsession with death and decay. In contrast to Henryson's, his parody on the *pastourelle*, "In secreit place this hyndir nycht," presents a dialogue between two lovers derisively, in terms that are too savage and obscene to be amusing. Dunbar's fiercely solemn spirit is, however, well-suited to *The Dance of the Seven Deadly Sins*, a poem in which he gives a new perspective to a traditional theme.

ROBERT HENRYSON

From The Testament of Cresseid

VI

I mend the fyre and beikit me about,
Than tuik ane drink my spreitis to comfort,
And armit me weill fra the cauld thair-out.
To cut the winter nicht and mak it schort,
40   I tuik ane quair—and left all uther sport—
Writtin be worthie Chaucer glorious
Of fair Creisseid and worthie Troylus.

VII

And thair I fand, efter that Diomeid
Ressavit had that lady bricht of hew,
How Troilus neir out of wit abraid
And weipit soir with visage paill of hew;
For quhilk wanhope his teiris can renew
Quhill Esperus rejoisit him agane.
Thus quhyle in joy he levit, quhyle in pane.

VIII

50   Of hir behest he had greit comforting,
Traisting to Troy that scho suld mak retour,

36 **beikit** warmed. 37 **ane** a; **spreitis** spirits. 38 **fra** from. 40 **quair** book. 41 **be** by. 43 **fand** found. 44 **Ressavit** received; **hew** hue. 45 **abraid** jumped. 46 **soir** sorrowfully; **visage** face. 47 **quhilk wanhope** which despair; **can renew** flowed. 48 **Quhill** until; **rejoisit** gladdened. 49 **quhyle** for a while; **levit** lived; **pane** torment. 50 **behest** promise. 51 **Traisting** trusting; **scho suld** she should; **retour** return.

Quhilk he desyrit maist of eirdly thing,
For-quhy scho was his only paramour.
But quhen he saw passit baith day and hour
Of hir ganecome, than sorrow can oppres
His wofull hart in cair and hevines.

IX

Of his distres me neidis nocht reheirs,
For worthie Chauceir in the samin buik,
In gudelie termis and in joly veirs,
60   Compylit hes his cairis, quha will luik.
To brek my sleip ane uther quair I tuik
In quhilk I fand the fatall destenie
Of fair Cresseid, that endit wretchitlie.

X

Quha wait gif all that Chauceir wrait was trew?
Nor I wait nocht gif this narratioun
Be authoreist or fenyeit of the new
Be sum Poeit, throw his inventioun,
Maid to report the lamentatioun
And wofull end of this lustie Creisseid,
70   And quhat distres scho thoillit, and quhat deid.

XI

Quhen Diomeid had all his appetyte
And mair fulfillit of this fair ladie,
Upon ane uther he set his haill delyte
And send to hir ane lybell of repudie
And hir excludit fra his companie.
Than desolait scho walkit up and doun,
And sum men sayis into the court commoun.

XII

O fair Cresseid, the flour and A per se
Of Troy and Grece, how was thow fortunait
80   To change in filth all thy feminitie,
And be with fleschelie lust sa maculait,
And go amang the Greikis air and lait,
Sa giglotlike takand thy foull plesance?
I have pietie thow suld fall sic mischance.

c. 1470

52 **eirdly** earthly. 53 **For-quhy** because. 54 **quhen** when. 55 **ganecome** return; **can oppres** oppressed. 56 **cair and hevines** sorrow and grief. 57 **me . . . reheirs** I need not relate. 58 **samin** same. 59 **joly veirs** pleasant verse. 60 **hes** has; **quha** whoever. 61 **quair** book. 62 **quhilk** which. 64 **Quha wait gif** who knows if. 66 **authoreist or fenyeit** authorized or feigned. 67 **Be** by; **throw** through. 70 **quhat** what; **scho** thoillit she suffered; **deid** did. 71 **Quhen** when. 72 **mair** more. 73 **haill** whole. 74 **lybell** bill; **repudie** divorce. 75 **fra** from. 76 **scho** she. 77 **court commoun** streets. 78 **A per se** matchless one. 79 **fortunait** destined. 81 **sa maculait** so stained. 82 **air and lait** early and late. 83 like a harlot taking your foul pleasure? 84 **pietie** pity; **sic** such.

Robene and Makyne

Robene sat on gud grene hill,
Kepand a flok of fe.
Mirry Makyne said him till,
"Robene, thow rew on me!
I haif the luvit lowd and still,
Thir yeiris two or thre;
My dule in dern bot gif thow dill,
Dowtles but dreid I de."

Robene ansert: "Be the rude,
10   Nathing of lufe I knaw,
Bot keipis my scheip undir yone wid,
Lo, quhair thay raik on raw!
Quhat hes marrit the in thy mude,
Makyne, to me thow schaw;
Or quhat is lufe, or to be lude?
Fane wald I leir that law."

"At luvis lair gife thow will leir,
Tak thair ane A B C:
Be heynd, courtass, and fair of feir,
20   Wyse, hardy and fre,
So that no denger do the deir
Quhat dule in dern thow dre.
Preiss the with pane at all poweir,
Be patient and previe."

Robene anserit hir agane,
"I wait nocht quhat is luve.
Bot I haif mervell incertane
Quhat makis the this wanrufe:
The weddir is fair, and I am fane,
30   My scheip gois haill aboif;
And we wald play us in this plane,
They wald us bayth reproif."

"Robene, tak tent unto my taill,
And wirk all as I reid,
And thow sall haif my hairt all haill,
Eik and my madinheid.
Sen God sendis bute for baill,
And for murning remeid,
I dern with the, bot gif I daill,

---

2 fe sheep. 2 Makyne a popular girl's name, diminutive of Mary, Maud, Margaret, etc. 4 rew have pity. 5 the luvit loved you. 7 dule misery; dill sooth. 9 Be the rude by the cross. 12 raik on raw wander in the fields. 13 marrit upset. 17 lair learning. 21 denger power; deir harm. 22 dre endure. 23 Preiss strive. 24 previe secret. 28 wanrufe restlessness. 39 I dern in secret; bot gif I daill unless I deal with you.

40   Dowtless I am bot deid."
"Makyne, tomorne this ilk a tyde,
And ye will meit me heir,
Peraventure my scheip ma gang besyd,
Quhill we haif liggit full neir;
Bot mawgre haif I and I byd,
Fra thay begin to steir;
Quhat lyis on hairt I will nocht hyd;
Makyn, than mak gud cheir."

"Robene, thow reivis me roif and rest:
50   I luve bot the allone."
"Makyne, adew; the sone gois west,
The day is neir hand gone."
"Robene, in dule I am so drest,
That lufe wilbe my bone."
"Ga lufe, Makyne, quhairevir thow list,
For lemman I lue none."

"Robene, I stand in sic a styll;
I sicht, and that full sair."
"Makyne, I haif bene heir this quhyle;
60   At hame god gif I wair."
"My huny, Robene, talk ane quhill,
Gif thow will do na mair."
"Makyne, sum uthir man begyle,
For hamewart I will fair."

Robene on his wayis went,
Als licht as leif of tre;
Mawkin murnit in hir intent,
And trowd him nevir to se.
Robene brayd attour the bent;
70   Than Mawkyne cryit on hie,
"Now ma thow sing, for I am schent!
Quhat alis lufe at me?"

Mawkyne went home withowttin faill,
Full wery eftir cowth weip.
Than Robene in a ful fair daill
Assemblit all his scheip.
Be that sum pairte of Mawkynis aill
Outthrow his hairt cowd creip;
He fallowit hir fast thair till assaill,
80   And till hir tuke gude keip.

49 reivis me roif and rest deprive me of peace
of mind. **56 lue** love. **69 attour the bent** over
the grass.

"Abyd, abyd, thow fair Makyne!
A word for ony thing!
For all my luve it sal be thyne,
Withowttin depairting.
All haill thy harte for till haif myne
Is all my cuvating;
My scheip tomorne quhill houris nyne
Will neid of no keping."

"Robene, thow hes hard soung and say,
90 In gestis and storeis auld,
The man that will nocht quhen he may
Sall haif nocht quhen he wald.
I pray to Jesu every day
Mot eik thair cairis cauld,
That first preissis with the to play,
Be firth, forrest or fawld."

"Makyne, the nicht is soft and dry,
The wedder is warme and fair,
And the grene woid rycht neir us by
100 To walk attour allquhair;
Thair ma na janglour us espy,
That is to lufe contrair;
Thairin, Makyne, bath ye and I
Unsene we ma repair."

"Robene, that warld is all away
And quyt brocht till ane end,
And nevir agane theirto perfay
Sall it be as thow wend.
For of my pane thow maid it play,
110 And all in vane I spend:
As thow hes done, sa sall I say,
Murne on! I think to mend."

"Mawkyne, the howp of all my heill,
My hairt on the is sett,
And evirmair to the be leill,
Quhill I may leif but lett;
Nevir to faill, as utheris feill,
Quhat grace that evir I gett."
"Robene, with the I will nocht deill:
120 Adew, for thus we mett."

---

86 cuvating desire. **89 hard** heard. **95 preissis**
strives. **113 howp** hope; **heill** health. **116 but**
lett without hindrance.

Malkyne went hame blyth annewche,
Attour the holttis hair.
Robene murnit, and Malkyne lewche;
Scho sang, he sichit sair.
And so left him, bayth wo and wrewche,
In dolour and in cair,
Kepand his hird under a huche,
Amang the holtis hair.

1724

122 **holttis hair**   gray woods. 127 **huche** cliff.

WILLIAM DUNBAR

The Dance of the Seven Deadly Sins

    Off Februar the fyiftene nycht,
Full lang befoir the dayis lycht,
I lay intill a trance;
And then I saw baith hevin and hell.
Me thocht, amangis the feyndis fell
Mahoun gart cry ane dance
Off schrewis that wer nevir schrevin
Aganis the feist of Fasternis Evin
To mak thair observance.
10 He bad gallandis ga graith a gyis
And kast up gamountis in the skyis
That last came out of France.

    "Lat se," quod he, "now quha begynnis."
With that, the fowll Sevin Deidly Synnis
Begowth to leip at anis.
And first of all in dance wes Pryd
With hair wyld bak and bonet on syd,
Lyk to mak waistie wanis.
And round abowt him as a quheill
20 Hang all in rumpillis to the heill
His kethat for the nanis.
Mony prowd trumpour with him trippit;
Throw skaldand fyre ay as thay skippit,
Thay gyrnd with hiddous granis.

1 **off** of; **fyiftene** fifteenth. 2 **lang** long. 3 **intill** in. 4 **baith** both. 5 **Me thocht** it seemed to me; **feyndis fell** fell fiends. 6 **Mahoun . . . ane** Mohammed called out a. 7 **Off schrewis** of wretches; **schrevin** absolved. 8 **Aganis** for; **Fasternis Evin** Shrove Tuesday. 10 **gallandis . . . graith** gallants go prepare; **gyis** masquerade. 11 **gamountis** gambols 12 **last** just. 13 **quha** who. 15 **Begowth** began; **anis** once. 17 **wyld** dressed. 18 **Lyk** likely; **waistie wanis** homes impoverished. 19 **quheill** wheel. 20 **Hang** hung. 21 **kethat** clothing; **nanis** occasion. 22 **trumpour** cheater; **trippit** danced. 23 **skaldand** scalding; **ay** ever; **skippit** skipped. 24 **gyrnd** grimaced; **granis** groans.

Heilie harlottis on hawtane wyis
Come in with mony sindrie gyis,
Bot yit luche nevir Mahoun.
Quhill preistis come in with bair-schevin nekkis,
Than all the feyndis lewche and maid gekkis,
30   Blak Belly and Bawsy Brown.

Than Yre come in with sturt and stryfe.
His hand wes ay upoun his knyfe;
He brandeist lyk a beir.
Bostaris, braggaris, and barganeris
Eftir him passit into pairis,
All bodin in feir of weir,
In jakkis and stryppis and bonettis of steill;
Thair leggis wer chenyeit to the heill.
Frawart wes thair affeir.
40   Sum upoun udir with brandis beft;
Sum jaggit uthiris to the heft
With knyvis that scherp cowd scheir.

Nixt in the dance followit Invy,
Fild full of feid and fellony,
Hid malyce and dispyte.
For pryvie hatrent that tratour trymlit.
Him followit mony freik dissymlit
With fenyeit wirdis quhyte,
And flattereris into menis facis,
50   And bakbyttaris in secreit places
To ley that had delyte,
And rownaris of fals lesingis.
Allace that courtis of noble kingis
Of thame can nevir be quyte!

Nixt him in dans come Cuvatyce,
Rute of all evill and grund of vyce,
That nevir cowd be content.
Catyvis, wrechis, and ockeraris,
Hud-pykis, hurdaris, and gadderaris
60   All with that warlo went.

25 Heilie scornful; **on . . . wyis** in disdainful manner. **26 sindrie gyis** varied style. **27 luche** laughed; **28 Quhill** when. **29 lewche** laughed; **gekkis** faces. **31 sturt** disturbance. **32 ay** ever. **33 brandeist** menaced; **beir** boar. **34 barganeris** wranglers. **35 into** in. **36 bodin** ready; **feir** equipment; **weir** war. **37 jakkis and stryppis** padded jackets and bands. **38 chenyeit** chainmailed. **39 Frawart** aggressive; **affeir** behavior. **40 udir** others; **brandis beft** swords beat. **41 jaggit** stabbed; **heft** hilt. **42 cowd** scheir could cut. **44 feid** feud. **45 Hid** hidden; **dispyte** spite. **46 pryvie hatrent** secret hatred; **trymlit** trembled. **47 mony . . . dissymlit** many a dissembling man. **48 fenyeit . . . quhyte** feigned fair words. **49 into** to. **51 ley** lie. **52 rownaris** whisperers; **lesingis** lies. **54 quyte** quit. **56 grund** source. **58 Catyvis** scoundrels; **ockeraris** usurers. **59 Hud-pykis . . . gadderaris** misers, hoarders, and gatherers. **60 warlo** deceiver.

Out of thair throttis thay schot on udder
Hett moltin gold, me thocht a fudder,
As fyreflawcht maist fervent.
Ay as thay tomit thame of schot,
Feyndis fild thame new up to the thrott
With gold of allkin prent.

    Syne Sweirnes, at the secound bidding,
Come lyk a sow out of a midding;
Full slepy wes his grunyie.
70 Mony sweir, bumbard belly-huddroun,
Mony slute daw and slepy duddroun
Him servit ay with sounyie.
He drew thame furth intill a chenyie,
And Belliall with a brydill renyie
Evir lascht thame on the lunyie.
In dance thay war so slaw of feit,
Thay gaif thame in the fyre a heit
And maid tham quicker of counyie.

    Than Lichery, that lathly cors,
80 Come berand lyk a bagit hors,
And Ydilnes did him leid.
Thair wes with him ane ugly sort
And mony stynkand, fowll tramort
That had in syn bene deid.
Quhen thay wer entrit in the dance,
Thay wer full strenge of countenance
Lyk turkas birnand reid.
All led thay uthir by the tersis,
Suppois thay fyllt with thair ersis,
90 It mycht be na remeid.

    Than the fowll monstir Glutteny
Off wame unsasiable and gredy
To dance he did him dres.
Him followit mony fowll drunckart
With can and collep, cop and quart,

---

61 udder others. **62 Hett** hot; **me thocht** it
seemed to me; **fudder** mass. **63 As fyreflawcht**
like lightning. **64 Ay** ever; **tomit thame** emp-
tied themselves. **65 Feyndis** fiends. **66 allkin
prent** every kind of impression. **67 Syne
Sweirnes** then Sloth. **68 midding** dung heap.
69 grunyie snout. **70** many a slothful, oafish
fat hulk. **71 slute daw** a sluttish slattern; **dud-
droun** sloven. **72 ay** ever; **sounyie** attention.
73 intill in; **chenyie** chain. **74 renyie** rein.
75 lunyie hindquarters. **76 of** on their. **77
Thay** they (the fiends); **heit** heating. **78
counyie** response (?). **79 lathly cors** loath

some body. **80 berand** neighing; **bagit** gelded.
82 sort group. **83 mony stynkand** many a
stinking; **tramort** corpse. **85 Quhen** when;
entrit entered. **86 full strenge** very strange.
87 turkas . . . reid tongs glowing red. **88
All** though; **uthir** others; **tersis** penises. **89
Suppois** which though; **with . . . ersis** their
bottoms with. **90 It mycht** there could; **na
remeid** no remedy. **92 Off . . . unsasiable** of
belly insatiable. **93 him dres** prepare himself.
94 drunckart drunkard. **95 collep, cop**
flagon, cup.

In surffet and exces.
Full mony a waistles wallydrag
With wamis unweildable did furth wag
In creische that did incres.
100 "Drynk!" ay thay cryit with mony a gaip.
The feyndis gaif thame hait leid to laip;
Thair lovery wes na les!

Na menstrallis playit to thame, but dowt,
For glemen thair wer haldin owt
Be day and eik by nycht,
Except a menstral that slew a man;
Swa till his heretage he wan
And entirt be breif of richt.

Than cryd Mahoun for a Heleand padyane;
110 Syne ran a feynd to feche MakFadyane
Far northwart in a nuke.
Be he the correnoch had done schout,
Erschemen so gadderit him abowt
In Hell grit rowme thay tuke.
Thae tarmegantis with tag and tatter
Full lowd in Ersche begowth to clatter
And rowp lyk revin and ruke.
The devill sa devit wes with thair yell
That in the depest pot of hell
120 He smorit thame with smuke.

c. 1500

97 **Full** very; **wallydrag** wastrel. 98 **wamis
unweildable** bellies unwieldy. 99 **creische** blubber. 100 **ay** ever; **gaip** gasp. 101 **feyndis**
fiends; **hait leid** hot lead; **laip** lap up. 102
lovery allowance; **na** no. 103 **but** without. 104 **haldin owt** kept out. 105 **Be** by; **eik**
also. 107 **Swa till** so to; **wan** won. 108 **entirt**
entered; **breif** writ; **richt** right. 109 **Heleand
padyane** Highland pageant. 110 **Syne** then;
feynd fiend; **MacFadyane** MacFadyan, some typical Highland Scot, or perhaps the traitor Mac-Fadyan, who, according to Henry the Minstrel's
Wallace, was slain by Wallace. 112 **Be** when;
correnoch lament. 113 **Erschemen** Ersemen
(Highlanders). 114 **grit rowme** great space.
115 **Thae tarmegantis** those savages. 116 **Full**
very; **Ersche begowth** Erse (Gaelic) began. 117
rowp croaked; **revin and ruke** raven and rook.
118 **sa devit** so dazed. 120 **smorit** smothered.

The Sixteenth Century

JOHN SKELTON
1460?–1529

Skelton is an untypical poet of his period—bouncy, comical, and winning even when satirical. His way of thinking is very much of the Middle Ages, yet he was learned enough in typical Renaissance subject-matter to tutor the future Henry VIII and was touched by the high Renaissance regard for poetry. In one sense he was a professional poet: he was given the degree of "laureate" (certifying his ability to write Latin poetry) by three universities. He was associated with the English court, although for a time he was rector of the parish of Diss in Norfolk. His satire on Henry VIII's minister Wolsey gained him a short imprisonment. Partly because of the special quality of his poetry, his character became a magnet for comical, disreputable stories, which were accumulated in "jest-books" after his death.

His sardonic "Tunning of Elinor Rumming" is a harsh, unsentimental joke, written in his characteristically short, two-stress,

rhyming lines that became so attractive to modern poets—Auden, for example. It projects a fierce physical delight in grotesque opposites to the conventional ideal of feminine beauty and purity. Elinor herself, an incredible hag, sells ale from a huge, filthy tub (chickens roost above it) to avid, blowsy women. They scurry in with whatever they can beg, borrow, or steal to pay for quantities of this ale and get whoopingly and vomitingly drunk.

"To Mistress Margaret Hussey," in contrast, is in the medieval ballade form, with a haunting refrain suited to the lyric praise of a refined lady. Here, Skelton creates a far different effect—that of worshiped artifice—with his short lines (used, apparently, by no other ballade maker).

Spelling is modernized, but the residual extra syllable at the ends of some words is indicated.

From The Tunning of Elinor Rumming[1]

        Then Marjorie Milk-Duck
        Her kirtle she did uptuck
420   An inch above her knee,
        Her legges that ye might see;
        But they were sturdy and stubbèd,
        Mighty pestles and clubbèd,
        As fair and as white
        As the foot of a kite.[2]
        She was somewhat foul,
        Crook-nebbèd[3] like an owl,
        And yet she brought her fees,
        A cantle[4] of Essex cheese,
430   Was well a foot thick,
        Full of maggottès quick;[5]
        It was huge and great
        And mighty strong meat
        For the devil to eat;
        It was tart and punyèt.[6]

[1]**Tunning** brewing
[2]**kite** a rapacious bird of prey
[3]**Crook-nebbèd** crook-nosed

[4]**cantle** slice
[5]**quick** live
[6]**punyet** pungent

Another sort of sluttès—
Some brought walnuttès,
Some apples, some pears,
Some brought their clipping shears,
440   Some brought this and that,
Some brought I wot nere[7] what,
Some brought their husband's hat,
Some puddings and linkès,[8]
Some tripès that stinkès.
    But of all this throng
One came them among—
She seemed half a leech—[9]
And began to preach
Of the Tuesday in the week
450   When the mare doth keek,[10]
Of the virtue of an unset leek
And of her husband's breek.[11]
With the feathers of a quail
She could to Bordeaux sail;
And with good ale barm[12]
She could make a charm
To help withal[13] a stitch:
She seemed to be a witch.

1517   c. 1521

[7]**nere** know not
[8]**linkès** linked sausages
[9]**leech** doctor
[10]**keek** kick
[11]Like a quack doctor dispensing ridiculous lore

she preaches of unlucky days and the curative properties of a seedling leek and her husband's breeches (or rump).
[12]**barm** frothy yeast floating on brewing ale
[13]**withal** therewith

To Mistress Margaret Hussey

Merry Margaret
As midsummer flower,
Gentle as falcon
Or hawk of the tower;[1]
    With solace and gladness,
Much mirth and no madness,[2]
All good and no badness,
So joyously,
So maidenly,
10   So womanly
Her demeaning[3]
In every thing,

[1] Mistress Margaret is a refined ("gentle") member of the upper class. Falconry was a sport for that class, which had much personal feeling for the treasured birds. A hawk of the tower is the best kind, skilled in rising to a great height and then swooping.
[2]**madness** foolishness
[3]**demeaning** behavior

Far, far passing
That I can indite[4]
Or suffice to write
Of merry Margaret
As midsummer flower,
Gentle as falcon
Or hawk of the tower;
20   As patient and as still
And as full of good will
As fair Isaphil;[5]
Coliander,[6]
Sweet pomander,[7]
Good Cassander;
Steadfast of thought,
Well made, well wrought;
Far may be sought
Erst[8] that ye can find
30 So cortays,[9] so kind
As merry Margaret,
This midsummer flower,
Gentle as falcon
Or hawk of the tower.

c. 1495   1523

[4] **indite** compose
[5] **Isaphil** Hipsipyle was a noble, beautiful princess of Greek mythology. Such references (see also the one to the Trojan princess Cassandra below) in late medieval lyrics are likely to be vaguely, picturesquely evocative without much

specific meaning.
[6] **Coliander** coriander
[7] **pomander** perfume ball
[8] **Erst** before
[9] **cortays** courtly, courteous

SIR THOMAS WYATT

1503–1542

The most important English poet of his time, Wyatt was a university-educated courtier and diplomat who had traveled to France and Italy. Although he composed poems (often to be sung to the lute) in the native courtly tradition, he also adapted some of Petrarch's sonnets of frustrated love into English with great success and influence. Metrically, these experimental pieces fall between the seemingly disorganized fifteenth-century verse-line (caused, it is thought, by the disappearance of the separately sounded final "e" in English in Chaucer's time) and the metrical regularity of Wyatt's younger contemporary Surrey and the poets later in the century. The occa-

sional deliberate roughness of the line in Wyatt's own English poems, where his control seems sure, suits the no-nonsense quality in much of what he has to say.

Today's readers enjoy the way Wyatt deflates his own evocations of picturesque love-melancholy with uninhibited male bravado. While his poems in the English tradition do not use the figurative intricacy of the Petrarchan sonnet or of the later part of the century, his less self-conscious images achieve great immediacy through plain-speaking directness (most notably in the deer-mistress metaphor of "They Flee from Me").

My Galley Chargèd with Forgetfulness[1]

My galley chargèd with forgetfulness
Thorough sharp seas in winter nights doth pass[2]
'Tween rock and rock; and eke mine enemy, alas,
That is my lord, steereth with cruelness;
And every oar a thought in readiness
As though that death were light in such a case.
An endless wind doth tear the sail apace
Of forcèd sighs and trusty fearfulness.[3]
A rain of tears, a cloud of dark disdain
Hath done the wearied cords great hindrance,
Wreathed with error and eke with ignorance.
The stars be hid that led me to this pain.
Drowned is reason that should me comfort
And I remain despairing of the port.

10

1557

---

[1] The original of this, Petrarch's *Rime* 189, follows:

Passa la nave mia colma d'oblio
per aspro mare, a mezza notte, il verno,
enfra Scilla e Caribdi; et al governo
siede 'l signore, anzi 'l nimico mio;
a ciascun remo un penser pronto e rio
che la tempesta e 'l fin par ch'abbi a scherno;
la vela rompe un vento umido, eterno

di sospir, di speranze e di desio;
pioggia di lagrimar, nebbia di sdegni
bagna e rallenta le già stanche sarte,
che son d'error con ignoranzia attorto.
Celansi i duo mei dolci usati segni;
morta fra l'onde è la ragion e l'arte:
tal ch'i' 'ncomincio a desperar del porto.

[2] **thorough** through
[3] **trusty** confident

They Flee from Me

They flee from me that sometime did me seek
With naked foot stalking in my chamber.
I have seen them gentle, tame, and meek
That now are wild and do not remember
That sometime they put themself in danger
To take bread at my hand; and now they range
Busily seeking with a continual change.

Thanked be fortune it hath been otherwise
Twenty times better, but once in special,
In thin array after a pleasant guise,
When her loose gown from her shoulders did fall
And she me caught in her arms long and small,[1]
Therewithal sweetly did me kiss
And softly said, "Dear heart, how like you this?"

10

It was no dream: I lay broad waking.
But all is turned thorough[2] my gentleness

---

[1] **small** slender
[2] **thorough** through

Into a strange fashion of forsaking.
And I have leave to go of her goodness
And she also to use newfangleness.³
20   But since that I so kindely⁴ am served
I would fain know what she hath deserved.

1557

³ **newfangleness** fickleness
⁴ **kindely** intended sarcastically, like "goodness"

above, but also according to her nature, kind

The Long Love That in My Thought Doth Harbour¹

The long love that in my thought doth harbour
And in mine heart doth keep his residence
Into my face presseth with bold pretence
And therein campeth, spreading his banner.
She that me learneth to love and suffer
And will that my trust and lust's negligence²
Be reined by reason, shame, and reverence,
With his hardiness taketh displeasure.
Wherewithal unto the heart's forest he fleeth,
10   Leaving his enterprise with pain and cry,
And there him hideth and not appeareth.
What may I do when my master feareth,
But in the field³ with him to live and die?
For good is the life ending faithfully.

1557

¹ Compare Surrey's "Love That Doth Reign"
(p. 133 below) which, like this, translates
Petrarch's *Rime* 140. The original follows:

Amor, che nel penser mio vive e regna
E 'l suo seggio maggior nel mio cor tène,
Talor armato ne la fronte vène,
Ivi si loca, et ivi pon sua insegna.

Quella ch'amare e sofferir ne 'nsegna
E vòl che 'l gran desio, l'accesa spene,
Ragion, vergogna e reverenza affrene,
Di nostro ardir fra se stessa si sdegna.

Onde Amor paventoso fugge al core,
Lasciando ogni sua impresa, e piange, e trema;
Ivi s'asconde, e non appar piú fòre.

Che poss'io far, temendo il mio signore,
Se non star seco in fin a l'ora estrema?
Ché bel fin fa chi ben amando more.

² l. 6 Wyatt's attempt to get Petrarch's mean-
ing into the line forces the sense; probably:
reckless trust in my love's success and reckless
desire.
³ **field** field of battle

Like to These Unmeasurable Mountains

Like to these unmeasurable mountains
Is my painful life, the burden of ire:
For of great height be they and high is my desire,
And I of tears and they be full of fountains.
Under craggy rocks they have full barren plains;
Hard thoughts in me my woeful mind doth tire.
Small fruit and many leaves their tops do attire;

Small effect with great trust¹ in me remains.
The boist'rous winds oft their high boughs do blast;
10 Hot sighs from me continually be shed.
Cattle in them and in me love is fed.
Immovable am I and they are full steadfast.
Of the restless birds they have the tune and note,
And I always plaints² that pass thorough³ my throat.

1557

¹ **trust** hope, confidence   ³ **thorough** through
² **plaints** laments

Blame Not My Lute¹

Blame not my lute for he must sound
Of this or that as liketh² me.
For lack of wit the lute is bound
To give such tunes as pleaseth me.
Though my songs be somewhat strange³
And speaks such words as touch thy change⁴
    Blame not my lute.

My lute, alas, doth not offend
Though that perforce he must agree
10 To sound such tunes as I intend
To sing to them that heareth me.
Then though my songs be somewhat plain
And toucheth some that use to feign⁵
    Blame not my lute.

My lute and strings may not deny
But as I strike they must obey.
Break not them then so wrongfully
But wreak⁶ thyself some wiser way.
And though the songs which I indite⁷
20 Do quit⁸ thy change with rightful spite
    Blame not my lute.

Spite askèth spite and changing change
And falsèd faith must needs be known.
The faults so great, the case so strange
Of right it must abroad be blown.
Then since that by thine own desèrt⁹
My songs do tell how true thou art
    Blame not my lute.

¹ The lute is a synecdoche for poetic compo-   ⁵ **use to feign** are accustomed to dissemble
  sition.   ⁶ **wreak** avenge
² **liketh** appeals to   ⁷ **indite** compose
³ **strange** estranged   ⁸ **quit** repay
⁴ **change** fickleness   ⁹ **desèrt** deserving

Blame but thyself that hast misdone
30 And well deservèd to have blame.
Change thou thy way so evil begun
And then my lute shall sound that same.
But if till then my fingers play
By thy desèrt their wonted way
      Blame not my lute.

Farewell, unknown, for though thou break
My strings in spite with great disdain
Yet have I found out for thy sake
Strings for to string my lute again.
40 And if perchance this foolish rhyme
Do make thee blush at any time
      Blame not my lute.

from ms., 1913

The Furious Gun

The furious gun in his raging ire,
When that the ball is rammèd in too sore[1]
And that the flame cannot part from the fire,
Cracketh in sunder, and in the air doth roar
The shivered[2] pieces. Right so doth my desire
Whose flame increaseth from more to more;
Which to let out I dare not look nor speak,
So inward force my heart doth all to-break.

1557

[1] **sore** hard   [2] **shivered** shattered

Whoso List To Hunt[1]

Whoso list to hunt, I know where is an hind,[2]
But as for me, helas,[3] I may no more.
The vain travail hath wearied me so sore,
I am of them that farthest cometh behind.
Yet may I by no means my wearied mind
Draw from the deer, but as she fleeth afore
Fainting I follow. I leave off therefore
Since in a net I seek to hold the wind.
Who list her hunt, I put him out of doubt,
10 As well as I may spend his time in vain.
And graven with diamonds in letters plain
There is written her fair neck round about:
"*Noli me tangere*[4] for Caesar's I am,
And wild for to hold though I seem tame."

from ms., 1913

[1] adapted from Petrarch, *Rime* 190; **list** wishes
[2] **hind** female deer
[3] **helas** alas
[4] *Noli me tangere* Touch me not (John 20:17).

These words from the Vulgate are traditionall
supposed to point here to Anne Boleyn as pre-
empted by Henry VIII.

HENRY HOWARD, EARL OF SURREY
1517–1547

Firmly attached to the older Wyatt, Surrey was, like him and like the later Sir Philip Sidney, a courtier and soldier as well as a poet. He had a reputation for unruly behavior. He fought and was once wounded in campaigns in Britain and on the Continent. His powerful family (generally inclined toward reconciliation with the Catholics) lost influence when Howard's cousin Catherine, fifth wife of Henry VIII, was executed in 1542 on grounds of unchastity and adultery. Although he was commander of the English garrison at Boulogne in 1545–46, he was executed on trumped-up charges just before Henry died.

His poetic power, and his acquaintance with the new learning and Italian influences in the Renaissance, are evidenced in his sonnets, the most smoothly managed ones before Sidney's (but in the form that Shakespeare was later to use), and in his translations from Virgil's *Aeneid*. His independence of spirit in choosing unrhymed iambic pentameter—blank verse—for these translations is astonishing and in a way momentous. Although he may have been led to it by a similar Italian form, English blank verse was as good as unknown before him but thereafter came to seem the most natural English measure, as though wedded to the genius of the language. Not surprisingly, he was unable to counterpoint this newly invented prosodic form as variously with the natural rhythms of speech as Shakespeare was to do in his maturity, yet Surrey's *Aeneid* often reads very well aloud. Above all, the meter seems a natural choice for a poet trying to reproduce in English Virgil's enormously skillful, classically restrained effects. Gavin Douglas's earlier stanzaic *Aeneid* incorporates more of Virgil's meaning by using many more words, but sounds less like the real *Aeneid* than Surrey's rendition does.

Love That Doth Reign[1]

Love that doth reign and live within my thought,
And built his seat[2] within my captive breast,
Clad in the arms wherein with me he fought,
Oft in my face he doth his banner rest.
But she that taught me love, and suffer pain,
My doubtful hope and eke[3] my hot desire
With shamefast[4] look to shadow and refrain,[5]
Her smiling grace converteth straight to ire.
And coward Love then to the heart apace
10 Taketh his flight, where he doth lurk and plain[6]
His purpose lost,[7] and dare not show his face.
For my lord's guilt thus faultless bide[8] I pain.
Yet from my lord shall not my foot remove.
Sweet is the death that taketh end by love.

1557

[1] Compare this translation of Petrarch's *Rime* 140 with Wyatt's "The Long Love," p. 130 above.
[2] **seat** chief residence
[3] **eke** also
[4] **shamefast** modest
[5] **refrain** restrain
[6] **plain** lament
[7] **purpose lost** frustrated intention
[8] **bide** endure

From The Aeneid, Book II[1]

. . . Whom when I saw assembled in such wise,
So desperately the battle to desire,
Then furthermore thus said I unto them:
"O ye young men of courage stout, in vain,
For nought, ye strive to save the burning town.
What cruel fortune hath betid, ye see.
The gods out of the temples all are fled,
450   Through whose might long this empire was maintained.
Their altars eke[2] are left both waste and void.
But if your will be bent with me to prove
That uttermost that now may us befall,
Then let us die, and run amid our foes.
To vanquished folk despair is only hope."
With this the young men's courage did increase,
And through the dark, like to the ravening wolves
Whom raging fury of their empty maws
Drives from their den, leaving with hungry throats
460   Their whelps behind, among our foes we ran
Upon their swords unto apparent death,
Holding[3] alway the chief street of the town,
Cover'd with the close shadows of the night.
   Who can express the slaughter of that night,
Or tell the number of the corpses slain,
Or can in tears bewail them worthily?
The ancient famous city falleth down
That many years did hold such seignory.
With senseless bodies every street is spread,
      . . .

   Coroebus then, encouraged by his chance,
Rejoicing said, "Hold forth the way of health,[4]
My feres,[5] that hap and manhood hath us taught:
Change we our shields; the Greek arms do[6] we on;
500   Craft or manhood, with foes what recks[7] it which?
The slain to us their armor they shall yield."
And with that word Androgeus'[8] crested helm
And the rich arms of his shield did he on;
A Greekish sword he girded by his side;
Like[9] gladly Dimas and Riphaeus did;

---

[1] Surrey here translates Virgil's *Aeneid*, II.346–
420. Aeneas, the Trojan hero of the epic and the
later founder of Rome, awakes during the night
to find that the Greeks, having besieged Troy for
ten years, have now entered the city. Some had
hidden in the hollow horse-idol that the Trojans
had been tricked into dragging within their walls,
and these have now emerged to open the gates.
In the passage here, Aeneas leads a group of
young Trojan warriors in a hopeless, outnum-
bered rally against the Greeks who are destroy-
ing Troy.
[2] **eke** also
[3] **holding** keeping to
[4] **health** preservation
[5] **feres** companions
[6] **do** put
[7] **recks** matters
[8] **Androgeus** Androgeos, an otherwise ur-
known Greek warrior
[9] **like** likewise

The whole youth gan them clad in the new spoils.
Mingled with Greeks for no good luck to us
We went, and gave many onsets that night,
And many a Greek we sent to Pluto's court;[10]
510 Other there fled and hasted to their ships
And to their coasts[11] of safeguard ran again;
And some there were, for shameful cowardice
Clamb up again unto the hugy horse
And did them hide in his wellknowen womb.

Ay me, bootless it is for any wight
To hope on aught, against will of the gods.
Lo where Cassandra, Priam's[12] daughter dear,
From Pallas' church was drawn with sparkled tress,
Lifting in vain her flaming eyen to heaven—
520 Her eyen, for fast her tender wrists were bound.
Which sight Coroebus raging could not bear,
Reckless of death, but thrust amid the throng,
And after we through thickest of the swords.

Here were we first y-battered with the darts
Of our own feres from the high temple's top,
Whereby of us great slaughter did ensue,
Mistaken by our Greekish arms and crests.
Then flocked the Greeks, moved with wrath and ire
Of the virgin from them so rescuèd—
530 The fell Ajax and either Atrides
And the great band cleped the Dolopes.[13]
As wrastling winds out of dispersed whirl
Befight themselves, the west with southern blast,
And gladsome east proud of Aurora's horse;[14]
The woods do whiz;[15] and foamy Nereus,[16]
Raging in fury with threeforked mace,
From bottom's depth doth welter up the seas:
So came the Greeks. . . .

c. 1540   1557

---

[10]**Pluto's court** the underworld of the dead
[11]**coasts** areas
[12]**Priam** king of Troy. His daughter Cassandra
was a prophetess; here she is dragged from the
temple of the goddess of wisdom. The young
Trojan warrior Coroebus (1.521) is devoted to
her.
[13]ll. 530–31 Ajax was a great leader among the
Greeks. The Atrides were Agamemnon and

Menelaus, sons of Atreus. The Dolopians were
a band of Greeks having a special loyalty to
Pyrrhus, son of Achilles.
[14]**Aurora's horse** the horse of the sun's chariot,
rising out of the east, where the goddess Aurora
dwells
[15]**whiz** rustle
[16]**Nereus** a sea god

ANONYMOUS

Jerusalem, My Happy Home

Jerusalem, my happy home,
When shall I come to thee?
When shall my sorrows have an end,
Thy joys when shall I see?

O happy harbor of the saints,
O sweet and pleasant soil,
In thee no sorrow may be found,
No grief, no care, no toil.

10   There lust and lucre cannot dwell,
There envy bears no sway;
There is no hunger, heat, nor cold,
But pleasure every way.

Thy walls are made of precious stones,
Thy bulwarks diamonds square;
Thy gates are of right¹ orient pearl,
Exceeding rich and rare.

Thy turrets and thy pinnacles
With carbuncles² do shine;
Thy very streets are paved with gold,
20   Surpassing clear and fine.

Ah, my sweet home, Jerusalem,
Would God I were in thee!
Would God my woes were at an end,
Thy joys that I might see!

Thy gardens and thy gallant walks
Continually are green;
There grows such sweet and pleasant flowers
As nowhere else are seen.

Quite through the streets, with silver sound,
30   The flood of life³ doth flow;
Upon whose banks on every side
The wood of life doth grow.

There trees forevermore bear fruit,
And evermore do spring;
There evermore the angels sit,
And evermore do sing.

¹ **right** real
² **carbuncles** red gems
³ **flood of life** the river of the water of life,
bordered (ll. 31–32) by the trees of life (Revelation 22:1–2)

Our Lady sings *Magnificat*[4]
With tune surpassing sweet;
And all the virgins bear their part,
40   Sitting about her feet.

Jerusalem, my happy home,
Would God I were in thee!
Would God my woes were at an end,
Thy joys that I might see!

1601

[4] *Magnificat* canticle of the Virgin Mary begin-
ning "My soul doth magnify the Lord" (Luke
1:46–55)

Weep You No More, Sad Fountains[1]

Weep you no more, sad fountains;
    What need you flow so fast?
Look how the snowy mountains
    Heaven's sun doth gently waste.
    But my sun's heavenly eyes
        View not your weeping,
        That now lie sleeping
    Softly, now softly lies
        Sleeping.

10   Sleep is a reconciling,
    A rest that peace begets.
Doth not the sun rise smiling
    When fair at even he sets?
    Rest you then, rest, sad eyes,
        Melt not in weeping
        While she lies sleeping
    Softly, now softly lies
        Sleeping.

1603

[1] put to music in John Dowland's "Third . . .
Book of Songs or Airs," 1603

SIR PHILIP SIDNEY
1554–1587

Sidney stands with Shakespeare and Spenser as one of the most important and innovative figures of the sixteenth-century Renaissance in England. He differs radically from them and from almost all other remarkable poets in having been born and bred in the highest power-structure of his nation. His father had governed Ireland. His mother, belonging to the highly placed Dudley family, had been an intimate of Queen Elizabeth's from their childhood. His marriage and his many other connections qualified him further for high place. The difficulty in his position, which finally created time in his career for literature, was that he was an intellectually convinced Protestant activist while Queen Elizabeth was a pragmatic procrastinator.

Belonging historically and by native gifts to the first generation of humanistically educated Englishmen—those whom humanism tried to make intellectually and rhetorically suitable leaders of a commonwealth — Sidney had attended a distinguished grammar school and Oxford. He then undertook a long, educative tour in France, Germany, Austria, Hungary, Italy, and Poland. In that period, more than any other Englishman of his time, he gained respect and friends in Continental ruling and humanist circles through his personal attractiveness, knowledgeable sincerity, and wide-ranging intellect.

Two widely separated periods of power followed. Elizabeth made him the head of an extremely important embassy to the Holy Roman Emperor and the Elector Palatine in 1576. He distinguished himself in this charge (on Sidney's way home, the Dutch ruler William of Orange even proposed that his sister marry Sidney), but he also exceeded Elizabeth's wishes by attempting to promote a Protestant League of northern states against Catholic Spain. Subsequently he angered her further with a letter protesting against the project of her marriage to a French prince. Elizabeth then lost trust in him; for years he had almost no duties except ornamental or poetic ones. Finally she relented and made him her governor of Flushing, one of the two ports which the Netherlands had granted her in connection with her support in the struggle against their Spanish rulers, in the years just before the Armada. He probably would have been advanced higher if he had not been fatally wounded in a minor engagement before Zutphen. A sequel to his death was an unprecedented flood of eulogies and condolences from all over Europe.

It was only in 1577–84, when Sidney was largely thrown back on his own resources between these two times of favor, that it occurred to him to apply his remarkable powers to the problems of creating a new kind of literature. His *Defence of Poesy* is the great critical document of the age, identifying the potential of divinely inspired poetry to create golden worlds above the brazen one of our fallen nature. The combined version of the two forms of his pastoral narrative *Arcadia*, interspersed with poems, profoundly influenced Shakespeare, Spenser, and other poets of his time and centuries after. His approach to the problem of a new English poetry was so fundamental, and so engaged in using any tradition that might enrich the English one, that he briefly led a movement to abandon English accentual prosody itself and follow quantitative rules of the Greek and Latin classical kind, in which length of utterance rather than stress would establish patterns never previously heard in English. "Fortune, Nature, Love," below, is one of the products (see Thomas Campion's similar later effort); but Sidney, developing at enormous speed, soon abandoned this ambitious program in favor of what turned out to be his enduring contribution to English versification: the marvelously sensitive compromise by which the natural stresses of a passionate speaker's voice are distributed tellingly over the regular iambic pentameter line.

This is the poetic achievement of his sonnet sequence *Astrophel and Stella* ("star-lover" and "star"), the first significant amatory sequence in English, standing with Shakespeare's and Spenser's and influencing both of them. For an equally passionate, resourceful projection of frustrated love one has to go back to Petrarch himself. The historical circumstances which are so often recited as underlying this sequence are surely at some distance from Sidney's actual creation: on his deathbed the great Earl of Essex had urged his daughter, Penelope Devereux, as a fitting wife for Sidney, but Sidney's father opposed the match. Later she married Lord Rich. Sidney apparently began writing these sonnets some months after the engagement; several sonnets allude to Rich's name as despicable.

It is through *Astrophel* that Sidney is generally known. Such a directly passionate communication, at the beginning of a literary movement that had so sophisticated a later development, is sometimes thought to embody a succession of simple-minded, rather heavy poses. Actually, however, ironical complexity, so vigorous as sometimes to seem a little gratuitous, is a frequent note in Sidney's poetry. How far this irony

could go is suggested by "What Length of Verse?" (below), in praise of a girl named Mopsa, in the first, very funny version (the *Old Arcadia*) of his prose pastoral romance. The reigning duke in it employs Mopsa's father as adviser, thinking this countryman embodies the pastoral virtue of straightforward honesty. In fact this standard pastoral assumption is turned on its head: the father is coarse, stupid, and dishonest. Mopsa is all three and also ugly and ill-natured; she is no sweet, pastoral beauty. Having fourteen lines, the poem looks like a sonnet, but it runs a truck through the sonnet's habitual complex rhyme schemes by restricting itself to simple couplet rhymes. The lines are written in the old-fashioned, déclassé poulter's measure (six feet alternating with seven in each couplet). Sidney derides this long-winded, jogging measure in line 1 by associating the length of the line with the "good" of Mopsa, which is nonexistent. Her qualities are detailed in the popular device of a sonneteering "blazon," a standard enumeration often ending with the parts covered by clothing. The similes here seem Petrarchanly sumptuous but in fact turn the tradition upside down. The speaker in the *Old Arcadia* attributes the poem to one "Alethes," signifying "sincerity" in Greek.

What Length of Verse?[1]

What length of verse can serve brave[2] Mopsa's good to show,
Whose virtues strange, and beauties such, as no man them may know?
Thus shrewdly burdened, then, how can my Muse escape?
The gods must help, and precious things must serve to show her shape.

Like great god Saturn, fair, and like fair Venus, chaste;[3]
As smooth as Pan, as Juno mild, like goddess Iris faced.
With Cupid she foresees, and goes god Vulcan's pace;
And for a taste of all these gifts, she borrows Momus' grace.

[1] See headnote to Sidney.
[2] **brave** splendid
[3] ll. 5–8 Saturn is actually old and ugly. Following this, Venus is unchaste, Pan is hairy and rough, Juno is severe, Iris is the rainbow, Cupid is blind, Vulcan is lame, and Momus is disagreeable.

Her forehead jacinth-like,[4] her cheeks of opal hue,
10   Her twinkling eyes bedecked with pearl, her lips of sapphire blue,
Her hair pure crapall stone,[5] her mouth, O heavenly wide,
Her skin like burnished gold, her hands like silver ore untried.

As for those parts unknown, which hidden sure are best,
Happy be they which will believe, and never seek the rest.

c. 1580   1590

[4] **jacinth** reddish-orange
[5] **crapall stone** supposed to grow in a toad's head

Fortune, Nature, Love

   — — — — ◡◡ — — ◡◡ — —
   — — — ◡◡ — — ◡◡ — ◡◡ — [1]

Fortune, Nature, Love, long have contended about me,
    Which should most miseries, cast on a worm that I am.
Fortune thus gan say: "Misery and misfortune is all one,
    And of misfortune, fortune hath only the gift.[2]
With strong foes on land, on seas with contrary tempests
    Still do I cross this wretch, what so he taketh in hand."
"Tush, tush," said Nature, "this is all but a trifle, a man's self
    Gives haps or mishaps, ev'n as he ord'reth his heart.
But so his humor I frame, in a mould of choler adjusted,[3]
10   That the delights of life shall be to him dolorous."

Love smiled, and thus said: "Want join'd to desire is unhappy.
    But if he nought do desire, what can Heraclitus ail?[4]
None but I, works by desire; by desire have I kindled in his soul
    Infernal agonies unto a beauty divine,
Where thou poor Nature left all thy due glory, to Fortune
    Her virtue is sovereign, Fortune a vassal of hers."
Nature abash'd went back; Fortune blush'd; yet she replied thus:
    "And ev'n in that love, shall I reserve him a spite."
Thus, thus, alas! woeful in Nature, unhappy by Fortune,
20   But most wretched I am, now Love awakes my desire.

c. 1580   1593

[1] See headnote to Sidney. Here the supposed pattern of long and short syllables is given as it appeared in the *Old Arcadia* at the head of this poem (which, because Sidney considered it fine, was assigned to an aristocratic speaker). Actually it reads, with a little forcing of the stress, like the dactylic hexameter (often beginning with a single stress) of nineteenth-century, similarly classicizing figures, principally Goethe in German and Longfellow, whose *Evangeline*, for instance, opens: "This is the forest primeval.

The murmuring pines and the hemlocks, / Bearded with moss and in garments green, indistinct in the twilight . . ."
[2] l. 4 Only Fortune has the gift of dispensing misfortune.
[3] **a mould of choler adjusted** a body parched by the dry, hot humor associated with being atrabilious and gloomy
[4] **what can Heraclitus ail?** what could bother even Heraclitus, a pessimistic Greek philosopher?

My True Love Hath My Heart[1]

My true love hath my heart, and I have his
By just exchange, one for the other given;
I hold his dear, and mine he cannot miss,[2]
There never was a better bargain driven.
His heart in me, keeps me and him in one;
My heart in him his thoughts and senses guides;
He loves my heart, for once it was his own;
I cherish his, because in me it bides.
His heart his wound receivèd from my sight;
My heart was wounded with his wounded heart,
For as from me on him his hurt did light,
So still methought in me his hurt did smart;
    Both equal[3] hurt, in this change[4] sought our bliss:
    My true love hath my heart, and I have his.

10

c. 1580   1593

[1] a sonnet from the *Old Arcadia*, in the Shakespearean form and with a return of the first line in the last, as in a song (and with a reminder of the second line in the next-to-last one)

[2] **miss** live without
[3] **equal** equally
[4] **change** exchange

Leave Me, O Love[1]

Leave me, O Love, which reachest but to dust,
And thou, my mind, aspire to higher things.
Grow rich in that which never taketh rust.
Whatever fades but fading pleasure brings.
Draw in thy beams and humble all thy might
To that sweet yoke where lasting freedoms be,
Which breaks the clouds and opens forth the light
That doth both shine and give us sight to see.
O take fast hold; let that light be thy guide
In this small course which birth draws out to death,
And think how evil becometh him to slide
Who seeketh heav'n and comes of heav'nly breath.
    Then farewell, world! Thy uttermost I see!
    Eternal Love, maintain thy life in me.

10

c. 1581   1598

[1] from *Certain Sonnets*

From Astrophel and Stella

I

Loving in truth, and fain[1] in verse my love to show,
That the dear she might take some pleasure of my pain,
Pleasure might cause her read, reading might make her know,

[1] **fain** desirous

Knowledge might pity win, and pity grace obtain,
I sought fit words to paint the blackest face of woe:
Studying inventions[2] fine, her wits to entertain,
Oft turning others' leaves, to see if thence would flow
Some fresh and fruitful showers upon my sunburned brain.
But words came halting forth, wanting Invention's stay;
10   Invention, Nature's child, fled stepdame Study's blows;
And others' feet still seemed but strangers in my way.
Thus, great with child to speak, and helpless in my throes,
    Biting my truant pen, beating myself for spite:
"Fool," said my Muse to me, "look in thy heart, and write."

[2] **inventions** close to our meaning, but also a technical term of rhetoric, meaning discoveries of new matter

XI

In truth O Love, with what a boyish kind
Thou dost proceed in thy most serious ways,
That when the heaven to thee his best displays,
Yet of that best thou leav'st the best behind!
For, like a child that some fair book doth find,
With gilded leaves or color'd vellum plays,
Or, at the most, on some fine picture stays,
But never heeds the fruit of writer's mind;
So when thou saw'st, in Nature's cabinet,
10   Stella, thou straight look'st babies in her eyes,[1]
In her cheeks' pit thou didst thy pitfold[2] set,
In her breast bo-peep or couching[3] lies,
    Playing and shining in each outward part;
    But, fool, seek'st not to get into her heart.

[1] **thou . . . eyes** saw reflections of yourself — Cupid — in each of her pupils   [2] **pitfold** net   [3] **couching** playing hide-and-seek

XXI

Your words, my friend, right healthful caustics,[1] blame
My young mind marred, whom love doth windlass[2] so
That mine own writings, like bad servants, show
My wits quick in vain thoughts, in virtue lame;
That Plato[3] I read for naught but if he tame
Such coltish years; that to my birth I owe
Nobler desires, lest else that friendly foe,
Great expectation, wear a train of shame;
For since mad March great promise made of me,
10   If now the May of my years much decline,

[1] **caustics** corrosives to burn away diseased tissue   [2] **windlass** ensnare   [3] **Plato** He best taught the love of what is above the world of the senses.

What can be hoped my harvest-time will be?
Sure, you say well: "Your wisdom's golden mine
   Dig deep with learning's spade." Now tell me this—
Hath this world aught so fair as Stella is?

XXX

Whether the Turkish new-moon minded be[1]
To fill his horns this year on Christian coast;
How Poles' right king means without leave of host
To warm with ill-made fire cold Muscovy;
If French can yet three parts in one agree;
What now the Dutch in their full diets boast;
How Holland hearts, now so good towns be lost,
Trust in the shade of pleasing Orange-tree;
How Ulster likes of that same golden bit
10   Wherewith my father once made it half tame;
If in the Scotch Court be no welt'ring[2] yet:
These questions busy wits to me do frame.
   I, cumbered with good manners, answer do,
   But know not how, for still I think of you.

[1] ll. 1–11 allusions to the news of the day. The Turks may continue their incursions into Christendom (cf. the new moon on the Turkish flag). The king of Poland attacks the Dukedom of Muscovy in 1580–81. The Catholics, Huguenots, and moderates in France may still fight each other. The Dutch (i.e., the Germans, proverbial big eaters) are boasting in the Diet of the Holy Roman Empire, 1576–82. Trust in the Dutch leader, William of Orange, may decline because of his loss of towns to the Spaniards. The Irish, on whom Sir Henry Sidney had imposed taxation, may or may not be stirring against it.

[2] welt'ring unrest

XXXI

With how sad steps, Oh Moon, thou climb'st the skies,
How silently, and with how wan a face!
What, may it be that even in heav'nly place
That busy archer[1] his sharp arrows tries?
Sure, if that long-with-love-acquainted eyes
Can judge of love, thou feel'st a lover's case;
I read it in thy looks: thy languished grace,
To me that feel the like, thy state descries.
Then even of fellowship, Oh Moon, tell me,
10   Is constant love deemed there but want of wit?
Are beauties there as proud as here they be?
Do they above love to be loved, and yet
   Those lovers scorn whom that love doth possess?
   Do they call virtue there ungratefulness?[2]

[1] busy archer Cupid
[2] l. 14 Do the ladies there give the name of virtue to their ungratefulness?

XXXIX

Come sleep, Oh sleep, the certain knot of peace,
The baiting[1] place of wit, the balm of woe,
The poor man's wealth, the prisoner's release,
Th'indifferent[2] judge between the high and low;
With shield of proof[3] shield me from out the prease[4]
Of those fierce darts Despair at me doth throw;
Oh make in me those civil wars to cease;
I will good tribute pay, if thou do so.
Take thou of me smooth pillows, sweetest bed,
10   A chamber deaf to noise and blind to light,
A rosy garland and a weary head;
And if these things, as being thine by right,
    Move not thy heavy grace, thou shalt in me,
    Livelier than elsewhere, Stella's image see.

[1] **baiting** resting
[2] **indifferent** unprejudiced
[3] **of proof** of proven strength
[4] **prease** crowd

XLI

Having this day my horse, my hand, my lance
Guided so well that I obtained the prize,
Both by the judgment of the English eyes
And of some sent from that sweet enemy, France,
Horsemen my skill in horsemanship advance,
Town-folks my strength; a daintier[1] judge applies
His praise to sleight[2] which from good use[3] doth rise;
Some lucky wits impute it but to chance;
Others, because of both sides I do take
10   My blood from them who did excel in this,
Think nature me a man of arms did make.
How far they shoot awry! The true cause is,
    Stella looked on, and from her heavenly face
    Sent forth the beams which made so fair my race.

[1] **daintier** finer
[2] **sleight** dexterity
[3] **use** practice

XLV

Stella oft sees the very face of woe
Painted in my beclouded, stormy face,
But cannot skill[1] to pity my disgrace,
Not though thereof the cause herself she know,[2]
Yet, hearing late a fable which did show,
Of lovers never known, a grievous case,

[1] **skill** find how
[2] l. 4 even though she knows herself to be the cause

Pity thereof got in her breast such place
That, from that sea derived, tears' springs did flow.
Alas! If fancy, drawn by imaged things,
10   Though false, yet with free scope more grace doth breed
Than servant's wrack,[3] where new doubts honor brings,[4]
Then think, my dear, that you in me do read
    Of lover's ruin some sad tragedy.
    I am not I; pity the tale of me.

[3] wrack wreck
[4] where . . . brings In the case of her own lover's desperation, her chastity (her "honor") still inspires doubts about his actual feelings and general propriety.

XLIX

I on my horse, and Love on me, doth try
Our horsemanships, while by strange work I prove
A horseman to my horse, a horse to Love,
And now man's wrongs in me, poor beast, descry.[1]
The reins wherewith my rider doth me tie
Are humbled thoughts, which bit of reverence move,
Curbed in with fear, but with gilt boss[2] above
Of hope, which makes it seem fair to the eye.
The wand[3] is will; thou, fancy, saddle art,
10   Girt fast by memory; and while I spur
My horse, he[4] spurs with sharp desire my heart;
    He sits me fast, however I do stir;
    And now hath made me to his hand so right
    That in the manage[5] myself takes delight.

[1] l. 4 Like a poor horse I see human cruelties to myself.
[2] gilt boss gold stud on the bit
[3] wand whip
[4] he love
[5] manage horseman's art

LXXI

Who will in fairest book of Nature know
How virtue may best lodged in beauty be,
Let him but learn of love to read in thee,
Stella, those fair lines which true goodness show.
There shall he find all vices' overthrow,
Not by rude force, but sweetest sovereignty
Of reason, from whose light those night birds[1] fly,
That inward sun in thine eyes shineth so.
And, not content to be perfection's heir
10   Thyself, dost strive all minds that way to move,
Who mark in thee what is in thee most fair.
    So while thy beauty draws the heart to love,
    As fast thy virtue bends that love to good.
    "But ah," Desire still cries, "give me some food."

[1] night birds emblems of vice

LXXXII

Nymph of the garden where all beauties be,
Beauties which do in excellency pass
His who till death look'd in a wat'ry glass,[1]
Or hers whom naked the Trojan boy did see;[2]
Sweet garden-nymph, which keeps the cherry-tree[3]
Whose fruit doth far the Hesperian taste[4] surpass,
Most sweet-fair, most fair-sweet, do not, alas,
From coming near those cherries banish me.
For though, full of desire, empty of wit,
10   Admitted late by your best-graced grace,
I caught at one of them, and hungry bit,
Pardon that fault; once more grant me the place,
    And I do swear, even by the same delight,
    I will but kiss; I never more will bite.

[1] 1. 3 Narcissus pined away looking at his own reflection in water.
[2] 1. 4 Paris judged Venus, naked, to be the most beautiful of three contending goddesses.
[3] **cherry-tree** her lips
[4] **Hesperian taste** taste of mythic apples of the Gardens of the Hesperides

XCI

Stella, while now by honor's cruel might
I am from you (light of my life) misled,[1]
And that fair you, my sun, thus overspread
With absence' veil, I live in sorrow's night,
If this dark place yet show, like candle-light,
Some beauty's piece (as amber-color'd head,
Milk hands, rose cheeks, or lips more sweet, more red
Or seeing jets, black[2] but in blackness bright),
They please, I do confess, they please mine eyes.
10   But why? Because of you they models be,
Models such be wood-globes[3] of glist'ring skies.
Dear, therefore be not jealous over me,
    If you hear that they seem my heart to move;
    Not them, O no, but you in them I love.

[1] ll. 1–2 Honorable duty compels the speaker to travel elsewhere (where he sees other women).
[2] **jets, black** jet-black eyes, like Stella's
[3] **wood-globes** wooden models of the real celestial regions

XCIX

When far-spent night persuades each mortal eye
(To whom nor Art[1] nor Nature granteth light)
To lay his then mark-wanting shafts[2] of sight,
Clos'd with their quivers, in sleep's armory,
With windows ope then most my mind doth lie,

[1] **Art** artificial means, like a candle
[2] **mark-wanting shafts** arrows lacking a target

Viewing the shape of darkness, and delight
Takes in that sad hue which with the inward night
Of his maz'd powers[3] keeps perfect harmony.
But when birds charm and that sweet air which is
10 Morn's messenger, with rose-enamel'd skies
Calls each wight to salute the flower of bliss,
In tomb of lids then buried are mine eyes,
   Forc'd by their lord, who is asham'd to find
   Such light in sense, with such a darken'd mind.

[3] **maz'd powers** the mind's confused faculties

CIV

Envious wits, what hath been mine offense,
That with such poisonous care my looks you mark,
That to each word, nay sigh of mine, you hark,
As grudging me my sorrow's eloquence?
Ah, is it not enough that I am thence,
Thence, so far thence, that scarcely any spark
Of comfort dare come to this dungeon dark,
Where rigorous exile locks up all my sense?
But if I by a happy[1] window pass,
10 If I but stars upon mine armor bear—
Sick, thirsty, glad (though but of empty glass),[2]
Your moral notes straight my hid meaning tear
   From out my ribs, and puffing, prove that I
   Do Stella love; fools, who doth it deny?

[1] **happy** happy, even though Stella no longer looks through the window (see "empty glass" below)

[2] **empty glass** the glass of the window, but also an empty glass vessel, containing nothing to relieve his sickness and thirst

Eleventh Song

"Who is it that this dark night
Underneath my window plaineth?"[1]
It is one who from thy sight
Being, ah, exiled, disdaineth
Every other vulgar light.

"Why, alas, and are you he?
Be not yet those fancies changèd?"
Dear, when you find change in me,
Though from me you be estrangèd,
10 Let my change to ruin be.

[1] Stella's words are in quotation marks; the speaker-lover's follow hers in each stanza.

"Well, in absence this will die;
Leave to see and leave to wonder."
Absence sure will help, if I
Can learn how myself to sunder
From what in my heart doth lie.

"But time will these thoughts remove;
Time doth work what no man knoweth."
Time doth as the subject prove;[2]
With time still[3] th'affection groweth
20   In the faithful turtle dove.

"What if you new beauties see,
Will not they stir new affection?"
I will think they pictures be,
Image-like, of saint's perfection,
Poorly counterfeiting thee.

"But your reason's purest light
Bids you leave such minds[4] to nourish."
Dear, do reason no such spite;
Never doth thy beauty flourish
30   More than in my reason's sight.

"But the wrongs love bears will make
Love at length leave undertaking."
No, the more fools it do shake,
In a ground of so firm making,
Deeper still they drive the stake.

"Peace, I think that some give ear;
Come no more, lest I get anger."[5]
Bliss, I will my bliss forbear;
Fearing, sweet, you to endanger;
40   But my soul shall harbor there.

"Well, begone, begone, I say,
Lest that Argus' eyes[6] perceive you."
Oh, unjustest fortune's sway,
Which can make me thus to leave you,
And from louts to run away.

c. 1582   1591

[2] l. 18 Time's effect depends on who is being affected.
[3] **still** always
[4] **minds** feelings

[5] **lest I get anger** am the object of angry jealousy
[6] **Argus' eyes** Argus had a hundred eyes to guard Io, whom Juno wished to keep from Jupiter.

EDMUND SPENSER
1552–1599

Spenser was the greatest English poet of the sixteenth century. Although his poetic style is sometimes criticized as overly decorative, formal, long-winded, repetitious, and cloyed by Petrarchan sweetness, he needs to be read on his own terms. For most of his career he worked to combine the best techniques of earlier native English poetry with those of the classical, Italian, and French poetry in the humanist Renaissance tradition. Thus, his figurative devices are "Petrarchan" while his vocabulary partly derives from Chaucer and Langland (occasionally archaic in his day) and he uses such native English effects as profuse alliteration. Similarly, his complex stanzaic rhyme schemes develop from both English and foreign traditions. Uninterested in the kind of startling immediacy achieved by Shakespeare and Donne, he uses strongly parallel effects, elaborately constructed, as in *Amoretti* XLIV, below, where Orpheus' poetry reconciles quarreling heroes and the lover's poetry fails to harmonize his own tempestuous feelings. Such effects, inconspicuous and slowly cumulative, demand a reader's careful attention.

A commoner who attended an excellent London grammar school and Cambridge University, he was much attached to Sidney (partly as a patron). Spenser realized more fully than any other Englishman the humanist, Sidneyan ideal of the poet as a divinely inspired moral educator and the poem as a world that should disclose moral truth more clearly than the fallen world of personal experience and history. Like Italian and French Renaissance poets, he wrote chiefly in an epideictic mode: that is, he praised and idealized the central symbols of national power—the queen and her court—in order to portray the human embodiments of heroic

secular achievement as they ought to be. He spent much of his life as a colonial official and landholder in southern Ireland.

The morality and psychology of human relations and the extraordinary symbolic systems used to express them are what interest today's reader of *The Faerie Queene*. Most of the poetry in this selection is concerned with relations between man and woman, on which Spenser manages to be both traditional and highly original. His sonnet sequence *Amoretti* uses many Petrarchan devices but departs from all other English sequences in being prompted by a successful (although difficult and long) courtship —historically Spenser's own, when he was about forty and the woman in her twenties. The sequence culminates in the great marriage-ode "Epithalamion." Here, the festive, time-honored marriage themes (the bride's beauty and chastity, the groom's ardor, the sexual humor, the community's paradoxically orgiastic but decorous participation, the joys of the wedding night, the invocation of fertility and many notable descendants) occur within a frame of marriage viewed as the high point of the human cycle, in harmony with the other cycles of the universe. According to this view, God sought to create, through those cycles, the best possible likeness of eternity in the world of time, by making an image of eternity, forever joyously and lovingly circling back upon itself. Spenser used a numerological ordering to portray this. Among its many refinements is the number of "long lines" (pentameters plus hexameters) in the poem, which corresponds to the number of days in the year, and the number of stanzas, which corresponds to the hours of the day.

From Ruins of Rome[1]

XXXII

Hope ye, my verses, that posterity
Of age ensuing shall you ever read?
Hope ye, that ever immortality
So mean harp's work may challenge for her meed?
If under heaven any endurance were,
These monuments, which not in paper writ,
But in porphỳre and marble do appear,
Might well have hoped to have obtainèd it.
Nath'less my lute, whom Phoebus deigned to give,[2]
10   Cease not to sound these old antiquities;
For if that Time do let thy glory live,
Well may'st thou boast, however base thou be,
    That thou art first, which of thy nation sung
    Th' old honour of the people gownèd long.[3]

1591

[1] a non-amatory sonnet sequence translated from Joachim Du Bellay's *Antiquitez de Rome*. Having lived four years in Rome, this great French Renaissance poet expressed in his sequence a sense of the physical ruins of the city, destroyed by time and its own moral weakness, but also a sense of an eternal Rome, surviving in the classical literature that it had inspired. A recent discovery shows that similar themes in relation to the beloved friend in Shakespeare's sonnets recall Spenser's *Ruins of Rome*. Cf. Sonnet LV, which contradicts the fear that the poem will not immortalize its subject, repeats "posterity," "marble," "monuments," and "time," and substitutes "living" record for "let thy glory live" from *Ruins* XXXII. Spenser also contradicts this fear in his No. XXXIII.
[2] **Phoebus** god of poetry
[3] **gownèd long** clad in togas, a reminiscence of Virgil's *Aeneid* I.282.

From Amoretti

I

Happy ye leaves, whenas those lily hands,
Which hold my life in their dead-doing might,
Shall handle you, and hold in love's soft bands,
Like captives trembling at the victor's sight.
And happy lines, on which, with starry light,
Those lamping eyes will deign sometimes to look,
And read the sorrows of my dying sprite,[1]
Written with tears in heart's close-bleeding[2] book.
And happy rhymes, bathed in the sacred brook
10   Of Helicon,[3] whence she derivèd is;
When ye behold that angel's blessed look;
My soul's long-lackèd food, my heaven's bliss;
    Leaves, lines, and rhymes, seek her to please alone,
    Whom if ye please, I care for other none.

[1] **sprite** spirit
[2] **close-bleeding** secretly bleeding
[3] **the sacred brook of Helicon** stream flowing from Mt. Helicon, which is sacred to the muses — source of poetic inspiration and of heavenly exaltation

VIII

More than most fair, full of the living fire,
Kindled above unto the Maker near;
No eyes but joys, in which all powers conspire,[1]
That to the world nought else be counted dear;
Through your bright beams doth not the blinded guest
Shoot out his darts to base affections wound;
But angels come to lead frail minds to rest
In chaste desires, on heavenly beauty bound.
You frame my thoughts, and fashion me within;
10   You stop my tongue, and teach my heart to speak;
You calm the storm that passion did begin,
Strong through your cause, but by your virtue weak.
    Dark is the world, where your light shinèd never;
    Well is he born, that may behold you ever.

[1] ll. 3, 5–6 A commonplace of love poetry was that the beams seeming to come from the beloved's eyes were darts propelled by blind Cupid (the "guest" in the eyes below), but Platonically they were imagined to inspire a higher love, directed to exalted ends.

XXII

This holy season, fit to fast and pray,[1]
Men to devotion ought to be inclined:
Therefore, I likewise, on so holy day,
For my sweet saint some service fit will find.
Her temple fair is built within my mind,
In which her glorious image placèd is;
On which my thoughts do day and night attend,
Like sacred priests that never think amiss.
There I to her, as th' author of my bliss,
10   Will build an altar to appease her ire;
And on the same my heart will sacrifice,
Burning in flames of pure and chaste desire:
    The which vouchsafe, O goddess, to accept,
    Amongst thy dearest relics to be kept.

[1] Lent, the forty days of the Christian year before Christ's rising from the tomb on Easter (see the Easter sonnet, LXVIII, below). Fasting (like Christ's forty-day fast in the wilderness) and putting away fleshly sin (to atone for man's sin of killing Christ) were Lenten requirements.

Spenser's use of Christian motifs in love sonnets is unique in the English Renaissance. The number of days in Lent, plus intervening Sundays, correspond to the number of sonnets from this one to the Easter one. At the end of the fasting period, the speaker wins his beloved.

XXXIV

Like as a ship,[1] that through the ocean wide,
By conduct of some star, doth make her way,
Whenas a storm hath dimmed her trusty guide,
Out of her course doth wander far astray:
So I, whose star, that wont[2] with her bright ray
Me to direct, with clouds is overcast,
Do wander now, in darkness and dismay,
Through hidden perils round about me placed;
Yet hope I well that, when this storm is past,
10   My Helice,[3] the loadstar[4] of my life,
Will shine again, and look on me at last,
With lovely light to clear my cloudy grief.
   Till then I wander careful, comfortless,
   In secret sorrow, and sad pensiveness.

[1] **Like as a ship** commonplace metaphor for a despairing lover (cf. Wyatt's "My galley charged with forgetfulness") or for anyone deprived of hope. A contemporary emblem (a symbolic picture with explanatory verse) of a ship in storm with two stars appearing represents a beleaguered country that may yet be saved.
[2] **wont** was used
[3] **Helice** the constellation of the Great Bear, circling the pole star
[4] **loadstar** pole star

XLIV

When those renownèd noble peers of Greece,[1]
Through stubborn pride, amongst themselves did jar,[2]
Forgetful of the famous golden fleece;
Then Orpheus[3] with his harp their strife did bar.
But this continual, cruel, civil war,
The which myself against myself do make;
Whilst my weak powers of passions warreyed[4] are;
No skill can stint, nor reason can aslake.[5]
But, when in hand my tuneless harp I take,
10   Then do I more augment my foes' despite;
And grief renew, and passions do awake
To battle, fresh against myself to fight.
   'Mongst whom the more I seek to settle peace,
   The more I find their malice to increase.

[1] ll. 1–3 The Argonauts, led by Jason, undertook a long, perilous voyage to win a supreme prize, the Golden Fleece.
[2] **jar** quarrel
[3] **Orpheus** supposed the prototype of all poets, moving stones, trees, and beasts with his song
[4] **warreyed** in contention
[5] **aslake** assuage

LXVII

Like as a huntsman after weary chase,[1]
Seeing the game from him escaped away,
Sits down to rest him in some shady place,
With panting hounds beguilèd of their prey:
So, after long pursuit and vain assay,[2]
When I all weary had the chase forsook,
The gentle deer returned the self-same way,
Thinking to quench her thirst at the next[3] brook:
There she, beholding me with milder look,
10   Sought not to fly, but fearless still did bide;
Till I in hand her yet half trembling took,
And with her own good-will her firmly tied.
   Strange thing, meseemed,[4] to see a beast so wild,
   So goodly won, with her own will beguiled.

[1] l. 1 the hunt as another traditional metaphor of the lover's pursuit of his beloved
[2] **assay** attempt
[3] **next** nearby
[4] **meseemed** it seemed to me

LXVIII

Most glorious Lord of life, that on this day[1]
Didst make Thy triumph over death and sin,
And, having harrowed hell,[2] didst bring away
Captivity thence captive, us to win:
This joyous day, dear Lord, with joy begin;
And grant that we, for whom Thou diddest die,
Being with Thy dear blood clean washed from sin,
May live for ever in felicity!
And that Thy love we weighing worthily,
10   May likewise love Thee for the same again;
And for Thy sake, that all like dear[3] didst buy,
With love may one another entertain.[4]
   So let us love, dear love, like as we ought:
   Love is the lesson which the Lord us taught.

[1] **this day** Easter
[2] **harrowed hell** Between his death on Good Friday and his resurrection on Easter Sunday, Christ was said to have descended to hell and harrowed (plundered) it by rescuing the right-eous.
[3] **like dear** at an equally high price (his death)
[4] **entertain** Christ's two commandments are to love him entirely and to love our neighbors as ourselves.

LXX

Fresh spring, the herald of love's mighty king,
In whose coat-armour richly are displayed[1]
All sorts of flowers, the which on earth do spring,
In goodly colours gloriously arrayed;
Go to my love, where she is careless[2] laid,
Yet in her winter's bower[3] not well awake;
Tell her the joyous time will not be stayed,
Unless she do him by the forelock take;[4]
Bid her therefore herself soon ready make,
10   To wait on Love amongst his lovely crew;
Where every one, that misseth then her make,[5]
Shall be by him amerced[6] with penance due.
    Make haste, therefore, sweet love, whilst it is prime;[7]
    For none can call again the passèd time.

[1] ll. 1–2   A herald wore a sleeveless covering, like a gown, on which the coat of arms of his master was represented.
[2] careless   heedless
[3] bower   bedchamber
[4] ll. 7–8   Opportunity was imagined as having hair on the front of his head by which he could be seized. After he had passed by he could not be grasped, because the back of his head was bald.
[5] make   mate
[6] amerced   punished
[7] prime   the first part of the day, but also of the year. The sonnet is a classical instance of *carpe diem* ("seize the day"). Cf. Herrick's "Corinna's Going A-Maying," p. 246 below.

LXXI

I joy to see how, in your drawen work,[1]
Yourself unto the bee ye do compare;
And me unto the spider, that doth lurk[2]
In close await, to catch her unaware:
Right so yourself were caught in cunning snare
Of a dear foe, and thrallèd to his love;
In whose strait bands ye now captivèd are
So firmly, that ye never may remove.
But as your work is woven all above
10   With woodbind flowers and fragrant eglantine,
So sweet your prison you in time shall prove,
With many dear delights bedeckèd fine.
    And all thenceforth eternal peace shall see
    Between the spider and the gentle bee.

[1] drawen work   embroidery
[2] ll. 2–3   "Spider" and "bee" preserve the initials of Spenser and Elizabeth Boyle, to whom the sequence is directed and whom he marries in "Epithalamion."

LXXV

One day I wrote her name upon the strand;
But came the waves, and washèd it away:
Again, I wrote it with a second hand;
But came the tide, and made my pains his prey.
Vain man, said she, that dost in vain assay
A mortal thing so to immortalize;
For I myself shall like to this decay,
And eke[1] my name be wipèd out likewise.
Not so, quoth I; let baser things devise
10 To die in dust, but you shall live by fame:
My verse your virtues rare shall eternize,
And in the heavens write your glorious name.[2]
  Where, whenas death shall all the world subdue,
  Our love shall live, and later life renew.

[1] **eke** also
[2] l. 12 Transformation into a constellation is often the eternal reward of figures in classical myth, but here Spenser may refer to the astronomical number pattern in "Epithalamion."

LXXXVIII

Like as the culver,[1] on the barèd[2] bough,
Sits mourning for the absence of her mate;
And, in her songs, sends many a wishful vow
For his return that seems to linger late:
So I alone, now left disconsolate,
Mourn to myself the absence of my love;
And, wand'ring here and there all desolate,
Seek with my plaints to match that mournful dove.
Ne[3] joy of aught that under heaven doth hove[4]
10 Can comfort me, but her own joyous sight:
Whose sweet aspect both God and man can move,
In her unspotted pleasance to delight.[5]
  Dark is my day, whiles her fair light I miss,
  And dead my life that wants such lively bliss.

c. 1594   1595

[1] **culver** dove
[2] **barèd** leafless
[3] **Ne** nor
[4] **hove** dwell
[5] l. 12 chaste pleasure caused by her beauty

Epithalamion

Ye learnèd sisters,[1] which have oftentimes
Been to me aiding, others to adorn,
Whom ye thought worthy of your graceful rhymes,
That even the greatest did not greatly scorn
To hear their names sung in your simple lays,
But joyèd in their praise;
And when ye list your own mishaps to mourn,
Which death, or love, or fortune's wreck did raise,
Your string could soon to sadder tenor turn,
10   And teach the woods and waters to lament
Your doleful dreariment.
Now lay those sorrowful complaints aside;
And having all your heads with girlands crowned,
Help me mine own love's praises to resound;
Ne[2] let the same of any be envì'd:
So Orpheus did for his own bride,
So I unto myself alone will sing;
The woods shall to me answer, and my echo ring.

Early, before the world's light-giving lamp
20   His golden beam upon the hills doth spread,
Having dispersed the night's uncheerful damp,
Do ye awake; and with fresh lustihead
Go to the bower of my belovèd love,
My truest turtle-dove,
Bid her awake; for Hymen[3] is awake,
And long since ready forth his masque to move,
With his bright tead that flames with many a flake,[4]
And many a bachelor to wait on him,
In their fresh garments trim.
30   Bid her awake therefore, and soon her dight,[5]
For lo the wishèd day is come at last,
That shall, for all the pains and sorrows past,
Pay to her usury of long delight:
And whilst she doth her dight,
Do ye to her of joy and solace sing,
That all the woods may answer, and your echo ring.

Bring with you all the nymphs that you can hear[6]
Both of the rivers and the forests green,

---

[1] **learnèd sisters** the muses, patrons of the arts (and thus of learning). In the following lines they have already aided Spenser to write poems in praise of others and to mourn misfortune (in his *Complaints*) so powerfully as to cause insensible objects like trees and waters to lament. (The songs of Orpheus, the prototypical poet, mentioned in l. 16, had influenced nature in this way; his poetry had persuaded the Underworld to release his wife from death.)
[2] **Ne** nor
[3] **Hymen** god of marriage and the wedding feast, carrying a torch ("tead") and leading a procession ("masque")
[4] **flake** spark
[5] **dight** dress
[6] **that you can hear** that can hear you

And of the sea that neighbours to her near:
40 All with gay girlands goodly well beseen.
And let them also with them bring in hand
Another gay girland,
For my fair love, of lilies and of roses,
Bound true-love wise,[7] with a blue silk riband.
And let them make great store of bridal poses,[8]
And let them eke[9] bring store of other flowers,
To deck the bridal bowers.
And let the ground whereas her foot shall tread,
For fear the stones her tender foot should wrong,
50 Be strewed with fragrant flowers all along,
And diap'red like the discoloured mead.[10]
Which done, do at her chamber door await,
For she will waken straight;
The whiles do ye this song unto her sing,
The woods shall to you answer, and your echo ring.

Ye nymphs of Mulla,[11] which with careful heed
The silver scaly trouts do tend full well,
And greedy pikes which use therein to feed
(Those trouts and pikes all others do excel);
60 And ye likewise, which keep the rushy lake,
Where none do fishes take:
Bind up the locks the which hang scattered light,
And in his waters, which your mirror make,
Behold your faces as the crystal bright,
That when you come whereas my love doth lie,
No blemish she may spy.
And eke ye lightfoot maids, which keep the deer,
That on the hoary mountain use to tower;[12]
And the wild wolves, which seek them to devour,
70 With your steel darts do chase from coming near;
Be also present here,
To help to deck her, and to help to sing,
That all the woods may answer, and your echo ring.

Wake now, my love, awake, for it is time;
The rosy Morn long since left Tithone's[13] bed,
All ready to her silver coach to climb;
And Phoebus gins to shew his glorious head.
Hark how the cheerful birds do chant their lays
And carol of Love's praise.
80 The merry lark her matins sings aloft;

---

[7]**Bound . . . wise** in a love knot
[8]**poses** nosegays
[9]**eke** also
[10]l. 51 variegated like a many-colored meadow
[11]**Mulla** Spenser's name for the River Awbeg,
near his Irish estate
[12]**tower** (a hawking term) rise to a great height
[13]**Tithone** Tithonus was the husband of Aurora,
the morn.

The thrush replies; the mavis descant[14] plays:
The ouzel shrills; the ruddock warbles soft;[15]
So goodly all agree, with sweet consent,[16]
To this day's merriment.
Ah my dear love, why do ye sleep thus long,
When meeter[17] were that ye should now awake,
T' await the coming of your joyous make,[18]
And hearken to the birds' love-learnèd song,
The dewy leaves among.
90   For they of joy and pleasance to you sing,
That all the woods them answer, and their echo ring.

My love is now awake out of her dreams,
And her fair eyes, like stars that dimmèd were
With darksome cloud, now shew their goodly beams
More bright than Hesperus[19] his head doth rear.
Come now, ye damsels, daughters of delight,
Help quickly her to dight:
But first come ye fair hours,[20] which were begot
In Jove's sweet paradise of Day and Night;
100   Which do the seasons of the year allot,
And all, that ever in this world is fair,
Do make and still[21] repair:
And ye three handmaids of the Cyprian Queen,
The which do still adorn her beauty's pride,
Help to adorn my beautifullest bride:
And, as ye her array, still throw between
Some graces to be seen;
And, as ye use to Venus, to her sing,
The whiles the woods shall answer, and your echo ring.

110   Now is my love all ready forth to come:
Let all the virgins therefore well await:
And ye fresh boys, that tend upon her groom,
Prepare yourselves, for he is coming straight.
Set all your things in seemly good array,
Fit for so joyful day:
The joyfull'st day that ever sun did see.
Fair sun! shew forth thy favourable ray,
And let they lifeful heat not fervent be,
For fear of burning her sunshiny face,
120   Her beauty to disgrace.
O fairest Phoebus, father of the Muse,

[14]**descant** melodic counterpart
[15]ll. 81–82 **mavis** a thrush; **ouzel** a blackbird; **ruddock** a European robin
[16]**consent** agreement, but also musical concord
[17]**meeter** more suitable
[18]**make** mate
[19]**Hesperus** evening star, Venus
[20]**hours** The Hours were classical goddesses of both the seasons and the hours of the day (hence children of Day and Night), who brought all good things related to the daily and annual cycles. They relate here to the astronomical pattern of numbers in the poem (see headnote). The handmaids of Venus at 1. 103 are the three Graces.
[21]**still** continually

If ever I did honour thee aright,
Or sing the thing that mote[22] thy mind delight,
Do not thy servant's simple boon refuse;
But let this day, let this one day, be mine;[23]
Let all the rest be thine.
Then I thy sovereign praises loud will sing,
That all the woods shall answer, and their echo ring.

Hark how the minstrels gin to shrill aloud
130   Their merry music that resounds from far,
The pipe, the tabor,[24] and the trembling croud,[25]
That well agree withouten breach or jar.
But, most of all, the damsels do delight
When they their timbrels[26] smite,
And thereunto do dance and carol sweet,
That all the senses they do ravish quite;
The whiles the boys run up and down the street,
Crying aloud with strong confusèd noise,
As if it were one voice.
140   *Hymen, iö*[27] *Hymen, Hymen*, they do shout;
That even to the heavens their shouting shrill
Doth reach, and all the firmament doth fill;
To which the people standing all about,
As in approvance, do thereto applaud,
And loud advance her laud;
And evermore they *Hymen, Hymen* sing,
That all the woods them answer, and their echo ring.

Lo! where she comes along with portly pace,
Like Phoebe,[28] from her chamber of the east,
150   Arising forth to run her mighty race,
Clad all in white, that 'seems[29] a virgin best.
So well it her beseems, that ye would ween[30]
Some angel she had been.
Her long loose yellow locks like golden wire,
Sprinkled with pearl, and purling flowers atween,[31]
Do like a golden mantle her attire;
And, being crownèd with a girland green,
Seem like some maiden queen.
Her modest eyes, abashèd to behold

[22]**mote** might
[23]Spenser appeals to Phoebus, god of poetry and of the sun, to let this one day, of all the days made by the sun, belong to the groom. This line is also the 105th "long line" (see headnote) in the poem, and the wedding day (June 13 — see l. 266) is the 105th day from March 1. March was the first month in the Elizabethan calendar, although the official year began on March 25. Perhaps Spenser began his series of days on March 1 because he wanted each two stanzas of the total of twenty-four to correspond to a month.
[24]**tabor** drum
[25]**croud** viol
[26]**timbrels** tambourines
[27]*iö* (Greek) a shout of joy or triumph
[28]**Phoebe** Diana, the moon
[29]**'seems** suits
[30]**ween** guess
[31]**purling flowers atween** flowers flowing between the pearls, like a brook flowing around stones

160   So many gazers as on her do stare,
       Upon the lowly ground affixèd are;
       Ne dare lift up her countenance too bold,
       But blush to hear her praises sung so loud,
       So far from being proud.
       Nathless[32] do ye still loud her praises sing,
       That all the woods may answer, and your echo ring.

       Tell me, ye merchants' daughters,[33] did ye see
       So fair a creature in your town before;
       So sweet, so lovely, and so mild as she,
170   Adorned with beauty's grace and virtue's store?
       Her goodly eyes like sapphires shining bright,
       Her forehead ivory white,
       Her cheeks like apples which the sun hath rudded,
       Her lips like cherries charming men to bite,
       Her breast like to a bowl of cream uncrudded,
       Her paps like lilies budded,
       Her snowy neck like to a marble tower;
       And all her body like a palace fair,
       Ascending up, with many a stately stair,
180   To honour's seat and chastity's sweet bower.
       Why stand ye still, ye virgins, in amaze,
       Upon her so to gaze,
       Whiles ye forget your former lay to sing,
       To which the woods did answer, and your echo ring?

       But if ye saw that which no eyes can see,
       The inward beauty of her lively sprite,[34]
       Garnisht with heavenly gifts of high degree,
       Much more then would ye wonder at that sight,
       And stand astonisht like to those which red[35]
190   Medusa's mazeful head.[36]
       There dwells sweet love, and constant chastity,
       Unspotted faith, and comely womanhood,
       Regard of honour, and mild modesty;
       There virtue reigns as queen in royal throne,
       And giveth laws alone,
       The which the base affections[37] do obey,
       And yield their services unto her will;
       Ne thought of thing uncomely ever may
       Thereto approach to tempt her mind to ill.
200   Had ye once seen these her celestial treasures.
       And unrevealèd pleasures,
       Then would ye wonder, and her praises sing,
       That all the woods should answer, and your echo ring.

[32]**Nathless** nevertheless
[33]**merchants' daughters** The merchants' daughters (like the merchants of *Amoretti* XV) are well acquainted through trade with good examples of sapphires, ivory, apples, and cream.
[34]**sprite** spirit
[35]**red** perceived
[36]l. 190 Medusa had serpents for hair. Twisting about, they made patterns like a maze; also, people who saw the head were turned into stone in their amazement.
[37]**affections** emotions

Open the temple gates unto my love,
Open them wide that she may enter in,
And all the posts adorn as doth behove,[38]
And all the pillars deck with girlands trim,
For to receive this saint with honour due,
That cometh in to you.
210   With trembling steps, and humble reverence,
She cometh in, before th' Almighty's view;
Of her ye virgins learn obedience,
Whenso ye come into those holy places,
To humble your proud faces:
Bring her up to th' high altar, that she may
The sacred ceremonies there partake
The which do endless matrimony make;
And let the roaring organs loudly play
The praises of the Lord in lively notes;
220   The whiles with hollow throats
The choristers the joyous anthem sing,
That all the woods may answer, and their echo ring.

Behold whiles she before the altar stands,
Hearing the holy priest that to her speaks,
And blesseth her with his two happy hands,
How the red roses flush up in her cheeks,
And the pure snow, with goodly vermeil stain
Like crimson dyed in grain:
That even th' angels, which continually
230   About the sacred altar do remain,
Forget their service and about her fly,
Oft peeping in her face that seems more fair
The more they on it stare.
But her sad[39] eyes, still fastened on the ground,
Are governèd with goodly modesty,
That suffers not one look to glance awry,
Which may let in a little thought unsound.
Why blush ye, love, to give to me your hand,
The pledge of all our band!
240   Sing, ye sweet angels, Alleluia sing,
That all the woods may answer, and your echo ring.

Now all is done: bring home the bride again;
Bring home the triumph of our victory:
Bring home with you the glory of her gain,[40]
With joyance bring her and with jollity.
Never had man more joyful day than this,
Whom heaven would heap with bliss.
Make feast therefore now all this livelong day;

[38]l. 206 Adorning the pillars and sprinkling
them with wine (l. 253) were Roman wedding
customs that Spenser preserves from classical
epithalamia.
[39]**sad** sober
[40]**of her gain** of gaining her

This day for ever to me holy is.
250 Pour out the wine without restraint or stay,
Pour not by cups, but by the bellyful,
Pour out to all that wull,[41]
And sprinkle all the posts and walls with wine,
That they may sweat, and drunken be withal.
Crown ye God Bacchus with a coronal,[42]
And Hymen also crown with wreaths of vine;
And let the Graces dance unto[43] the rest,
For they can do it best:
The whiles the maidens do their carol sing,
260 To which the woods shall answer, and their echo ring.

Ring ye the bells, ye young men of the town,
And leave your wonted[44] labours for this day:
This day is holy; do ye write it down,
That ye for ever it remember may.
This day the sun is in his chiefest height,
With Barnaby the bright,[45]
From whence declining daily by degrees,
He somewhat loseth of his heat and light,
When once the Crab[46] behind his back he sees.
270 But for this time it ill ordainèd was,
To choose the longest day in all the year,
And shortest night, when longest fitter were:[47]
Yet never day so long, but late[48] would pass.
Ring ye the bells, to make it wear away,
And bonfires make all day;[49]
And dance about them, and about them sing,
That all the woods may answer, and your echo ring.

Ah when will this long weary day have end,
And lend me leave to come unto my love?
280 How slowly do the hours their numbers spend,[50]
How slowly does sad Time his feathers[51] move.
Haste thee, O fairest planet, to thy home,
Within the western foam:
Thy tired steeds[52] long since have need of rest.
Long though it be, at last I see it gloom,
And the bright evening-star with golden crest

---

[41]**wull** want it
[42]**coronal** garland
[43]**unto** for
[44]**wonted** usual
[45]**Barnaby the bright** St. Barnabas day, June 11, the summer solstice in Spenser's time
[46]**Crab** Cancer, the zodiacal constellation through which the sun passed in early July; **back** probably influenced by the customary backward movement of crabs
[47]l. 272 This kind of humor was traditional in epithalamia.

[48]**late** finally
[49]l. 275 a surviving pagan custom at Midsummer
[50]l. 280 a clear allusion to the relation between the measure of the verses ("numbers") of the poem and the hours (personified Hours) of the day
[51]**feathers** wings
[52]**steeds** the horses drawing the chariot of the sun

Appear out of the east.[53]
Fair child of beauty, glorious lamp of love
That all the host of heaven in ranks dost lead,
290 And guidest lovers through the nightes dread,
How cheerfully thou lookest from above,
And seem'st to laugh atween thy twinkling light,
As joying in the sight
Of these glad many which for joy do sing,
That all the woods them answer, and their echo ring.

Now cease ye damsels your delights forepast,
Enough it is that all the day was yours:
Now day is done, and night is nighing fast,
Now bring the bride into the bridal bowers.
300 Now night is come, now soon her disarray,
And in her bed her lay;
Lay her in lilies and in violets,
And silken curtains over her display,
And odoured sheets, and arras[54] coverlets.
Behold how goodly my fair love does lie,
In proud humility,
Like unto Maia, whenas Jove her took
In Tempe, lying on the flow'ry grass,
'Twixt sleep and wake, after she weary was,
310 With bathing in the Acidalian brook.[55]
Now it is night, ye damsels may be gone,
And leave my love alone,
And leave likewise your former lay to sing:
The woods no more shall answer, nor your echo ring.

Now welcome night, thou night so long expected,
That long day's labour dost at last defray,[56]
And all my cares, which cruel Love collected,
Hast summed in one, and cancellèd for aye:[57]
Spread thy broad wing over my love and me,
320 That no man may us see;
And in thy sable mantle us enwrap,
From fear of peril and foul horror free.
Let no false treason seek us to entrap,
Nor any dread disquiet once annoy
The safety of our joy;
But let the night be calm and quietsome,
Without tempestuous storms or sad affray:
Like as when Jove with fair Alcmena lay,

[53]ll. 286–87 a curious mistake. When appearing
at sundown Venus is always in the west.
[54]**arras** tapestry
[55]**Maia . . . Tempe . . . Acidalian brook** Maia,
most beautiful of the Pleiades, bore Jove's son
Hermes, god of learning. Tempe, a vale in

Thessaly, and the Acidalian brook, sacred to
Venus, are Spenser's additions.
[56]**defray** requite
[57]l. 318 financial metaphors (like "defray")
of numerous liabilities combined into one and
then canceled

When he begot the great Tirynthian groom:[58]
330 Or like as when he with thyself[59] did lie
And begot Majesty.
And let the maids and young men cease to sing,
Ne let the woods them answer, nor their echo ring.

Let no lamenting cries, nor doleful tears,
Be heard all night within, nor yet without:
Ne let false whispers, breeding hidden fears,
Break gentle sleep with misconceivèd doubt.
Let no deluding dreams, nor dreadful sights,
Make sudden sad affrights;
340 Ne let house-fires, nor lightning's helpless[60] harms,
Ne let the Puck, nor other evil sprites,
Ne let mischievous witches with their charms,
Ne let hobgoblins, names whose sense we see not,
Fray us with things that be not:
Let not the screech-owl nor the stork be heard,
Nor the night-raven, that still[61] deadly yells;
Nor damnèd ghosts, called up with mighty spells,
Nor grisly vultures, make us once afeard:
Ne let th' unpleasant quire of frogs still croaking
350 Make us to wish their choking.
Let none of these their dreary accents sing;
Ne let the woods them answer, nor their echo ring.

But let still silence true night-watches keep,
That sacred peace may in assurance reign,
And timely sleep, when it is time to sleep,
May pour his limbs forth on your[62] pleasant plain;
The whiles an hundred little wingèd loves,[63]
Like divers-feathered doves,
Shall fly and flutter round about your bed,
360 And in the secret dark, that none reproves,
Their pretty stealths shall work, and snares shall spread
To filch away sweet snatches of delight,
Concealed through covert night.
Ye sons of Venus, play your sports at will!
For greedy pleasure, careless of your toys,
Thinks more upon her paradise of joys,
Than what ye do, albeit good or ill.
All night therefore attend your merry play,
For it will soon be day:
370 Now none doth hinder you, that say or sing;
Ne will the woods now answer, nor your echo ring.

---

[58] ll. 328–31 Jove stretched one night into three when he lay with Queen Alcmena and begot the great hero Hercules, born in Tiryns and servant (groom) to its king for a time.
[59] with thyself with Night (Spenser's invented myth)

[60] helpless beyond help
[61] still ever
[62] your Night's
[63] wingèd loves cupids

Who is the same, which at my window peeps?
Or whose is that fair face that shines so bright?
Is it not Cynthia,[64] she that never sleeps,
But walks about high heaven all the night?
O fairest goddess, do thou not envy
My love with me to spy:
For thou likewise didst love, though now unthought,[65]
And for a fleece of wool, which privily
380   The Latmian shepherd once unto thee brought,
His pleasures with thee wrought.
Therefore to us be favourable now;
And sith[66] of women's labours thou hast charge,
And generation goodly dost enlarge,
Incline thy will t' effect our wishful vow,
And the chaste womb inform with timely seed,
That may our comfort breed:
Till which we cease our hopeful hap to sing;
Ne let the woods us answer, nor our echo ring.

390   And thou, great Juno, which with awful[67] might
The laws of wedlock still dost patronize;
And the religion[68] of the faith first plight
With sacred rites hast taught to solemnize;
And eke for comfort often callèd art
Of women in their smart,[69]
Eternally bind thou this lovely band,
And all thy blessings unto us impart.
And thou, glad Genius,[70] in whose gentle hand
The bridal bower and genial bed remain,
400   Without blemish or stain,
And the sweet pleasures of their love's delight
With secret aid dost succour and supply,
Till they bring forth the fruitful progeny:
Send us the timely fruit of this same night.
And thou, fair Hebe,[71] and thou, Hymen free,
Grant that it may be so.
Till which we cease your further praise to sing;
Ne any woods shall answer, nor your echo ring.

And ye high heavens, the temple of the gods,
410   In which a thousand torches flaming bright
Do burn, that to us wretched earthly clods
In dreadful darkness lend desirèd light;
And all ye powers which in the same remain,
More than we men can feign,
Pour out your blessing on us plenteously,

---

[64]**Cynthia** the moon goddess, generally regarded as virginal but also as presiding (as Lucina) over childbirth (l. 383). She loved a shepherd of Latmos and was won by Pan dressed as a sheep. Spenser blends these myths.
[65]**unthought** unremembered

[66]**sith** since
[67]**awful** awesome
[68]**religion** sanctity
[69]**smart** labor pains
[70]**Genius** spirit presiding over generation
[71]**Hebe** Juno's daughter, goddess of youth

And happy influence[72] upon us rain,
That we may raise a large posterity,
Which from the earth, which they may long possess
With lasting happiness,
420 Up to your haughty palaces may mount;
And, for the guerdon[73] of their glorious merit,
May heavenly tabernacles there inherit,
Of blessed saints for to increase the count.
So let us rest, sweet love, in hope of this,
And cease till then our timely joys to sing;
The woods no more us answer, nor our echo ring!

Song made in lieu of many ornaments,
With which my love should duly have been deckt,
Which cutting off through hasty accidents,
430 Ye would not stay your due time to expect,
But promised both to recompense:
Be unto her a goodly ornament,
And for short time an endless monument.

c. 1594   1595

[72]**happy influence**   astrological good fortune
[73]**guerdon**   reward

From The Faerie Queene

From Book IV (*Friendship*), canto x
(*Scudamor in the Temple of Venus*)[1]

35
By her the heaven is in his course contained,
And all the world in state unmovèd stands,
As their almighty maker first ordained,
And bound them with inviolable bands;
Else would the waters overflow the lands,
And fire devour the air, and hell[2] them quite,
But that she holds them with her blessèd hands.
She is the nurse of pleasure and delight,
And unto Venus' grace the gate doth open right.

[1]The knight Scudamor ("shield of love") has told of his pugnacious approach to the Isle of Venus, defeating twenty other suitors and gaining a shield picturing a remorseless god of love, which enables him to impose his will on the reluctant Amoret. The competitive, thrusting spirit, which is part of Venus's domain on the approaches to the island (and in the animals in the song below), brings Scudamor through obstacles and over the water (like the bulls below) to the island, where the other aspect of Venus's power appears: harmonious friendship and sexual union to which the masterful Cupid is probably antipathetic. The passage opens with a reference to the goddess Concord, guardian of the temple entrance, making an accordant universe out of attraction and repulsion (Love and Hatred). Scudamor's probably unwise domination of Amoret, with dire consequences, can be compared with the mutual harmony between male and female in *Amoretti* and *Epithalamion* (see notes below).

[2]**hell**   destroy

36

By her I entering half dismayèd was,
But she in gentle wise me entertained,
And twixt herself and Love did let me pass;
But Hatred would my entrance have restrained,
And with his club me threatened to have brained,
Had not the lady with her powerful speech
Him from his wicked will uneath[3] refrained;
And th'other eke[4] his[5] malice did impeach,
Till I was throughly past the peril of his reach.

37

Into the inmost temple thus I came,
Which fuming all with frankincense I found,
And odors rising from the altars' flame.
Upon an hundred marble pillars round
The roof up high was rearèd from the ground,
All decked with crowns, and chains, and garlands gay,
And thousand precious gifts worth many a pound,
The which sad lovers for their vows did pay;
And all the ground was strowed with flowers, as fresh as May.

38

An hundred altars round about were set,
All flaming with their sacrifices' fire,
That with the steam thereof the temple sweat,
Which rolled in clouds to heaven did aspire,
And in them bore true lovers' vows entire:
And eke an hundred brazen cauldrons bright,
To bathe in joy and amorous desire,
Every of which was to a damsel hight;
For all the priests were damsels, in soft linen dight.

39

Right in the midst the goddess self did stand
Upon an altar of some costly mass,
Whose substance was uneath to understand:
For neither precious stone nor dureful brass
Nor shining gold nor moldering clay it was;
But much more rare and precious to esteem,
Pure in aspect, and like to crystal glass,
Yet glass was not, if one did rightly deem,
But being fair and brickle,[6] likest glass did seem.

40

But it in shape and beauty did excel
All other idols which the heathen adore,
Far passing that which by surpassing skill
Phidias did make in Paphos isle of yore,

---

[3] **uneath** with difficulty
[4] **eke** also

[5] **his** Hatred's
[6] **brickle** brittle

With which that wretched Greek, that life forlore,[7]
Did fall in love:[8] yet this much fairer shined,
But covered with a slender veil afore;
And both her feet and legs together twined
Were with a snake, whose head and tail were fast combined.[9]

41

The cause why she was covered with a veil
Was hard to know, for that her priests the same
From people's knowledge labored to conceal.
But sooth it was not sure for womanish shame,
Nor any blemish which the work mote blame,
But for, they say, she hath both kinds in one,
Both male and female, both under one name:
She sire and mother is herself alone—
Begets and eke conceives, ne[10] needeth other none.[11]

42

And all about her neck and shoulders flew
A flock of little loves[12] and sports and joys,
With nimble wings of gold and purple hew,
Whose shapes seemed not like to terrestrial boys,
But like to angels playing heavenly toys,
The whilst their eldest brother was away,
Cupid their eldest brother: he enjoys
The wide kingdom of love with lordly sway,
And to his law compels all creatures to obey.[13]

43

And all about her altar scattered lay
Great sorts of lovers piteously complaining:
Some of their loss, some of their loves' delay,
Some of their pride, some paragons[14] disdaining,
Some fearing fraud, some fraudulently feigning,
As every one had cause of good or ill.
Amongst the rest some one through love's constraining
Tormented sore, could not contain it still,
But thus brake forth that all the temple it did fill.

44

Great Venus, queen of beauty and of grace,
The joy of gods and men, that under sky
Dost fairest shine, and most adorn thy place,

---

[7] **forelore** lost
[8] **Phidias . . . in love** A Greek youth was said to have fallen in love with a statue of Venus by Praxiteles (not Phidias). Paphos was sacred to Venus.
[9] **a snake. . . combined** A symbol of completeness is the ouroboros, a serpent bending in a circle, its tail in its mouth.
[10] **ne** nor
[11] **she hath both kinds. . . none** The hermaphrodite described in ll. 366–69 was frequently used as a symbol of completeness and harmony in the Renaissance.
[12] **loves** cupids
[13] **The whilst . . . obey** This masterful Cupid, resembling the one on Scudamor's shield, is significantly absent from this harmonious scene.
[14] **paragons** fellow suitors

That with thy smiling look dost pacify
The raging seas, and mak'st the storms to fly:
Thee, goddess, thee the winds and clouds do fear,
And when thou spread'st thy mantle forth on high,
The waters play and pleasant lands appear,
And heavens laugh and all the world shows joyous cheer.

45

Then doth the daedal[15] earth throw forth to thee
Out of her fruitful lap abundant flowers,
And then all living wights,[16] soon as they see
The spring break forth out of his lusty bowers,[17]
They all do learn to play the paramours:
First do the merry birds, thy pretty pages
Privily prickèd with thy lustful powers,
Chirp loud to thee out of their leavy cages,
And thee their mother call to cool their kindly[18] rages.

46

Then do the savage beasts begin to play
Their pleasant frisks, and loathe their wonted[19] food;
The lions roar, the tigers loudly bray,
The raging bulls rebellow through the wood,
And breaking forth dare tempt the deepest flood
To come where thou dost draw them with desire:
So all things else that nourish vital blood,
Soon as with fury thou dost them inspire,
In generation seek to quench their inward fire.

47

So all the world by thee at first was made,
And daily yet thou dost the same repair,
Ne aught on earth that lovely is and fair
But thou the same for pleasure didst prepare.
Thou art the root of all that joyous is,
Great god of men and women, queen of th'air,
Mother of laughter, and wellspring of bliss,
O grant that of my love at last I may not miss.

48

So did he say, but I with murmur soft,
That none might hear the sorrow of my heart,
Yet inly groaning deep and sighing oft,
Besought her to grant ease unto my smart,

---

[15]**daedal** artfully creating
[16]**wights** beings
[17]**Then doth . . . lusty bowers** Note similar language and context of *Amoretti* LXX ("Fresh spring").
[18]**kindly** nature–inspired
[19]**wonted** habitual

And to my wound her gracious help impart.
Whilst thus I spake, behold with happy eye
I spied where at the idol's feet apart
A bevy of fair damsels close did lie,
Waiting whenas the anthem should be sung on high.

49

The first of them did seem of riper years
And graver countenance than all the rest,
Yet all the rest were eke her equal peers,
Yet unto her obeyèd all the best.
Her name was Womanhood, that she expressed
By her sad[20] semblant and demeanor wise,
For steadfast still her eyes did fixèd rest,
Ne roved at random after gazer's guise,
Whose luring baits ofttimes do heedless hearts entice.

50

And next to her sat goodly Shamefastness,[21]
Ne ever durst her eyes from ground uprear,
Ne ever once did look up from her dais,
As if some blame of evil she did fear,
That in her cheeks made roses oft appear.
And her against[22] sweet Cheerfulness was placed,
Whose eyes like twinkling stars in evening clear
Were decked with smiles that all sad humors chased,
And darted forth delights, the which her goodly graced.

51

And next to her sat sober Modesty,
Holding her hand upon her gentle heart,
And her against sat comely Courtesy,
That unto every person knew her part,
And her before was seated overthwart[23]
Soft Silence, and submiss Obedience,
Both linked together never to dispart,
Both gifts of God not gotten but from thence,
Both garlands of his saints against their foes' offence.

52

Thus sat they all around in seemly rate,[24]
And in the midst of them a goodly maid
Even in the lap of Womanhood there sat,
The which was all in lily white arrayed,
With silver streams amongst the linen strayed,
Like to the morn when first her shining face

---

[20]**sad** sober
[21]**Shamefastness** virtuous propriety
[22]**against** opposite

[23]**overthwart** opposite
[24]**rate** manner

Hath to the gloomy world itself bewrayed,[25]
That same was fairest Amoret[26] in place,
Shining with beauty's light and heavenly virtue's grace.

53

Whom soon as I beheld my heart gan throb,
And wade in doubt what best were to be done,
For sacrilege meseemed the church to rob,
And folly seemed to leave the thing undone
Which with so strong attempt I had begun.
Tho shaking off all doubt and shamefast fear,
Which ladies' love I heard had never won
Mongst men of worth, I to her steppèd near
And by the lily hand her labored up to rear.

54

Thereat the foremost matron me did blame,
And sharp rebuke for being overbold,[27]
Saying it was to knight unseemly shame
Upon a recluse virgin to lay hold
That unto Venus' services was sold.[28]
To whom I thus: Nay, but it fitteth best
For Cupid's man with Venus' maid to hold,
For ill your goddess' services are dressed
By virgins, and her sacrifices let to rest.

55

With that my shield I forth to her did show,
Which all that while I closely had concealed,
On which when Cupid with his killing bow
And cruel shafts emblazoned she beheld,
At sight thereof she was with terror quelled
And said no more; but I which all that while
The pledge of faith, her hand, engagèd held,
Like wary hind[29] within the weedy soil,[30]
For no entreaty would forgo so glorious spoil.

---

[25]**bewrayed** revealed
[26]**Amoret** Note presence of "amor" in both "Scudamor" and "Amoret." Amoret had been raised by Venus's command in the Garden of Adonis, where natural sexual pleasure ruled (for generation's sake), and is now in the Temple of Venus, presumably for an association with the cultivated virtues (from art, not nature) associated with friendship, as in harmonious marriage.
[27]**for being overbold** After the marriage of Scudamor and Amoret described earlier, Amoret is cruelly imprisoned in the House of Busirane in *The Faerie Queene* III. The final chamber of

this house, containing the idol of cruel Cupid, is inscribed "Be not too bold," although the two earlier ones carry the inscription "Be bold." Scudamor's fiery boldness has apparently succeeded in mastering Amoret erotically but has not found the larger basis of harmony in voluntary friendship.
[28]**sold** dedicated
[29]**hind** female deer
[30]**Like . . . soil** Compare this hunting imagery with *Amoretti* LXVII ("Like as a huntsman), although there the deer surrenders herself willingly.

56

And evermore upon the goddess' face
Mine eye was fixed for fear of her offence,
Whom when I saw with amiable grace
To laugh at me[31] and favor my pretence,
I was emboldened with more confidence,
And nought for niceness nor for envy sparing,
In presence of them all forth led her thence,
All looking on and like astonished staring,
Yet to lay hand on her not one of all them daring.

57

She often prayed and often me besought,
Sometime with tender tears to let her go,
Sometime with witching smiles, but yet for nought
That ever she to me could say or do
Could she her wishèd freedom[32] fro[33] me woo,
But forth I led her through the temple gate,
By which I hardly[34] passed with much ado,
But that same lady which me friended late
In entrance did me also friend in my retrate.[35]

58

No less did Danger[36] threaten me with dread
Whenas he saw me, maugre[37] all his power,
That glorious spoil of beauty with me lead,
Than Cerberus, when Orpheus did recov'r
His leman from the Stygian prince's bower.[38]
But evermore my shield did me defend
Against the storm of every dreadful stour:[39]
Thus safely with my love I thence did wend.
So ended he his tale where I this canto end.

1596

[31]**To laugh at me** Perhaps Venus favors Scudamor laughingly because she promotes male enterprise as much as sexual harmony.

[32]**wished freedom** Compare the deer's being tied with her own good will in *Amoretti* LXVII.

[33]**fro** from

[34]**hardly** with difficulty

[35]**retrate** retreat; **But that same . . . retrate** Concord probably helps Scudamor out of the temple, as well as into it, in accordance with her function of reconciling attraction and repulsion. The female knight Britomart (see next selection from *The Faerie Queene*) rescues Amoret from the erotic compulsion of the House of Busirane and becomes her friend, and a final friendship between Scudamor and Amoret seems part of Spenser's intention in his first-edition conclusion to the Busirane episode.

[36]**Danger** This traditional figure had tried to block Scudamor on the bridge leading to the island. His original meaning, the beloved's haughty sense of herself, was sometimes enlarged to include danger from family and rival suitors.

[37]**maugre** in spite of

[38]**That glorious . . . bower** Cerberus, the watchdog of the underworld, objected when Orpheus won the right to remove his wife from there. Orpheus' loss of his wife before he reached the upper regions does not bode well for Scudamor's achievement. **leman** lover

[39]**stour** disturbance

From Book V (*Justice*), canto vii
(*Britomart at Isis' Church*)[1]

9

For other beds the priests there usèd none,
But on their mother Earth's dear lap did lie,
And bake[2] their sides upon the cold hard stone,
T'inure themselves to sufferance thereby
And proud rebellious flesh to mortify.
For by the vow of their religion
They tièd were to steadfast chastity
And continence of life, that, all forgone,
They mote[3] the better tend to their devotion.

10

Therefore they mote not taste of fleshly food,
Ne[4] feed on aught, the which doth blood contain,
Ne drink of wine, for wine they say is blood,
Even the blood of giants which were slain
By thundering Jove in the Phlegrean plain.[5]
For which the earth (as they the story tell),
Wroth with the gods, which to perpetual pain
Had damned her sons, which 'gainst them did rebel,
With inward grief and malice did against them swell.

11

And of their[6] vital blood, the which was shed
Into her pregnant bosom, forth she brought
The fruitful vine, whose liquor bloody red
Having the minds of men with fury fraught,
Mote in them stir up old rebellious thought,
To make new war against the gods again:

[1] Britomart, the female knight of this poem, in the tradition of many female epic warriors (related indirectly to the Amazons), is an ideal human, androgynous in her combined virtues associated with males and females. Unlike her friend Amoret, she finds happiness in her love for the knight Artegal, who first fights with her, envying her martial accomplishment, and then learns to woo her to gain her voluntary love. The scene in the temple of Isis duplicates these events allegorically, but it is also one of Spenser's most elegant pieces of symbolism because of the multiplicity of its reference. The Egyptian divine couple Isis and Osiris were familiar but historically exotic for the Renaissance. Spenser's Osiris denotes the law-giver, like Artegal, whose harsh justice needs to be tempered by the equitable mercy of Isis. At the same time the association with another law-giver, Bacchus, allows Spenser to give the crocodile (Osiris) and Artegal the orgiastic, wine-associated tendencies resisted by the ascetic priests of Isis' temple, and to associate these tendencies with the male, passionate mastery of Artegal that is finally quelled by Isis and Britomart in the harmony of love.

[2] bake harden. Note resemblance of these priests to those in *Amoretti* XXII ("This holy season"), Spenser's self-denying Lenten sonnet.

[3] mote might

[4] Ne nor

[5] Even the blood . . . plain The battle between the gods and the giants (whose mother was earth, lowest of the four elements) was often allegorized as a conflict between reason and passion.

[6] their the giants'

Such is the power of that same fruit that nought
The fell contagion may thereof restrain,
Ne within reason's rule her madding mood contain.

12

There did the warlike maid herself repose,
Under the wings of Isis all that night,
And with sweet rest her heavy eyes did close
After that long day's toil and weary plight.
Where whilst her earthly parts with soft delight
Of senseless sleep did deeply drownèd lie,
There did appear unto her heavenly sprite[7]
A wondrous vision, which did close imply
The course of all her fortune and posterity.

13

Her seemed, as she was doing sacrifice
To Isis, decked with miter on her head
And linen stole after those priestes' guise,
All suddenly she saw transfigurèd
Her linen stole to robe of scarlet red,
And moon-like miter to a crown of gold,
That even she herself much wonderèd
At such a change, and joyèd to behold
Herself adorned with gems and jewels manifold.[8]

14

And in the midst of her felicity
An hideous tempest seemèd from below
To rise through all the temple suddenly,
That from the altar all about did blow
The holy fire, and all the embers strow
Upon the ground, which, kindled privily,
Into outrageous flames unwares did grow,
That all the temple put in jeopardy
Of flaming, and herself in great perplexity.[9]

---

[7]**sprite** spirit

[8]stanza 13 The priests of Isis wear her crescent moon in their headdresses (miters), and white linen robes (stoles) signifying purity. Britomart's garments now change to royal ones, but they are also associated with Isis' golden crown and her occasional red robe (the idol of her in the temple is silver, robed in white linen). As with Amoret in the preceding selection, white and silver often signify virginity or the female principle in *The Faerie Queene*; red often signifies relation with a male, passionate principle: when the face of the symbolically androgynous Britomart is revealed in her battle with Artegal, it is ruddy and bears silver drops of sweat (IV.vi.19).

[9]stanza 14 The tempest "from below" is apparently the passionate force from the earth that chaste priests had feared. The crocodile of the next stanza, who has up to now lain at the feet of the idol of Isis, represents Osiris but also Artegal. It now ingests this passionate, earthly force of the rebellious giants and seeks to do violence to Britomart. Either Isis, or Britomart as Isis, quells him with the goddess's wand (as Britomart had formerly unhorsed Artegal in battle with her magic lance). The crocodile then uses gentle persuasion (as Artegal, but not Scudamor, had done) and gains Britomart's willing love, in something like a Freudian dream.

15

With that the crocodile, which sleeping lay
Under the idol's feet in fearless bower,
Seemed to awake in horrible dismay,
As being troubled with that stormy stour,[10]
And gaping greedy wide did straight devour
Both flames and tempest, with which grown great
And swollen with pride of his own peerless power,
He gan to threaten her likewise to eat,
But that the goddess with her rod him back did beat.

16

Tho[11] turning all his pride to humblesse meek,
Himself before her feet he lowly threw
And gan for grace and love of her to seek,
Which she accepting he so near her drew
That of his game she soon enwombèd grew,
And forth did bring a lion of great might,
That shortly did all other beasts subdue.[12]
With that she wakèd, full of fearful fright,
And doubtfully dismayed through that so uncouth[13] sight.

1596

[10]**stour** tumult
[11]**Tho** then
[12]**And forth . . . subdue** In the myth of *The*

Faerie Queene the progeny of Britomart and
Artegal are the English royal line.
[13]**uncouth** strange

SIR WALTER RALEGH
1552-1618

A tempestuous, proud, and passionate man, the relatively low-born Ralegh somehow gained Elizabeth I's favor after brief episodes at Oxford University, in soldiering on the continent, and in the Middle Temple in London, where lawyers were trained. He became conspicuous, powerful, and rich through her patronage, hatching plans against Spain and for colonizing the New World, but fell from the queen's favor when he married one of her attendants. Under James I he was unjustly accused of treason and imprisoned for thirteen years. He was freed to lead his last romantically conceived expedition to Virginia, but beheaded on his return. His speculative philosophizing and experimentation and his history-writing further indicate his wide intellectual interests.

Like Sidney, Ralegh would not publish his poetry during his lifetime in books for sale to the general public. The best of the poetry attributed to him often combines Elizabethan sensuousness with a sense of transitoriness, death, and the afterlife that can be called Metaphysical. Compare, for instance, "Nature, that washed her hands in milk" with Marvell's "To His Coy Mistress" in the next section.

The Nymph's Reply to the Shepherd[1]

If all the world and love were young,
And truth in every shepherd's tongue,
These pretty pleasures might me move
To live with thee and be thy love.

Time drives the flocks from field to fold
When rivers rage and rocks grow cold,
And Philomel[2] becometh dumb;
The rest complains of cares to come.

The flowers do fade, and wanton fields
10   To wayward winter reckoning yields;
A honey tongue, a heart of gall,
Is fancy's spring, but sorrow's fall.

Thy gowns, thy shoes, thy beds of roses,
Thy cap, thy kirtle, and thy posies
Soon break, soon wither, soon forgotten,
In folly ripe, in reason rotten.

Thy belt of straw and ivy buds,
Thy coral clasps and amber studs,
All these in me no means can move,
20   To come to thee and be thy love.

But could youth last, and love still breed,
Had joys no date,[3] nor age no need,
Then these delights my mind might move,
To live with thee and be thy love.

1600

[1] This lyric replies to Marlowe's "Passionate
Shepherd to His Love," p. 194 below.

[2] **Philomel** nightingale
[3] **date** terminal date

Nature, That Washed Her Hands in Milk

Nature, that washed her hands in milk,
  And had forgot to dry them,
Instead of earth took snow and silk,
  At Love's request to try them,
If she a mistress could compose
To please Love's fancy out of those.

Her eyes he would should be of light,
  A violet breath, and lips of jelly;
Her hair not black, nor overbright,
10   And of the softest down her belly;
As for her inside he 'ld have it
Only of wantonness and wit.

At Love's entreaty such a one
  Nature made, but with her beauty
She hath framed a heart of stone,
  So as Love, by ill destiny,
Must die for her whom Nature gave him
Because her darling would not save him.

But Time, which Nature doth despise
20   And rudely gives her love the lie,
Makes Hope a fool, and Sorrow wise,
  His hands do neither wash nor dry;
But being made of steel and rust,
Turns snow and silk and milk to dust.

The light, the belly, lips, and breath,
  He dims, discolors, and destroys;
With those he feeds but fills not Death,
  Which sometimes were the food of joys.
Yea, Time doth dull each lively wit,
30 And dries all wantonness with it.

Oh, cruel Time! which takes in trust
  Our youth, our joys, and all we have,
And pays us but with age and dust;
  Who in the dark and silent grave
When we have wandered all our ways
Shuts up the story of our days.

c. 1610

The Passionate Man's Pilgrimage[1]

Give me my scallop-shell[2] of quiet,
My staff of faith to walk upon,
My scrip[3] of joy, immortal diet,
My bottle of salvation,
My gown of glory, hope's true gage,[4]
And thus I'll take my pilgrimage.

Blood must be my body'd balmer,[5]
No other balm will there be given,
Whilst my soul like a white palmer[6]
10 Travels to the land of heaven,
Over the silver mountains,
Where spring the nectar fountains;
And there I'll kiss
The bowl of bliss,
And drink my eternal fill

[1] quite possibly written when Ralegh was sentenced to death in 1603, although the sentence was commuted to life imprisonment
[2] **scallop-shell** traditional badge of pilgrims
[3] **scrip** satchel
[4] **gage** pledge
[5] **balmer** embalmer
[6] **palmer** pilgrim

On every milken hill.
My soul will be a-dry before,
But after it will ne'er thirst more.

And by the happy blissful way
20   More peaceful pilgrims I shall see,
That have shook off their gowns of clay
And go appareled fresh like me.
I'll bring them first
To slake their thirst
And then to taste those nectar suckets,[7]
At the clear wells
Where sweetness dwells,
Drawn up by saints in crystal buckets.

And when our bottles and all we
30   Are filled with immortality,
Then the holy paths we'll travel,
Strewed with rubies thick as gravel,
Ceilings of diamonds, sapphire floors,
High walls of coral, and pearl bowers.

From thence to heaven's bribeless hall
Where no corrupted voices brawl,
No conscience molten into gold,
Nor forged accusers bought and sold,
No cause[8] deferred, nor vain-spent journey,
40   For there Christ is the king's attorney,
Who pleads for all without degrees,[9]
And He hath angels,[10] but no fees.

When the grand twelve million jury
Of our sins and sinful fury
'Gainst our souls black verdicts give,
Christ pleads His death, and then we live.
Be thou my speaker, taintless pleader,
Unblotted lawyer, true proceeder,
Thou movest salvation ever for alms,
50   Not with a bribèd lawyer's palms.

And this is my eternal plea
To Him that made heaven, earth, and sea,
Seeing my flesh must die so soon,
And want a head to dine next noon,
Just at the stroke when my veins start and spread,
Set on my soul an everlasting head.
Then am I ready, like a palmer fit,
To tread those blest paths which before I writ.

1604

[7]**suckets** sweets
[8]**cause** legal case
[9]**degrees** distinction

[10]**angels** punning on gold coins so-called (and bearing the image of an angel)

SAMUEL DANIEL
1562–1619

Among the numerous works of this pleas-
ing minor Elizabethan poet is this dialogue
that wittily defends the heroic life by building
on an episode in the *Odyssey* of Homer.

Ulysses and the Siren[1]

SIREN

Come worthy Greek, Ulysses come,
Possess these shores with me:
The winds and seas are troublesome,
And here we may be free.
   Here may we sit, and view their toil
That travail[2] on the deep,
And joy the day in mirth the while,
And spend the night in sleep.

ULYSSES

Fair nymph, if fame or honor were
10   To be attained with ease,
Then would I come and rest with thee,
And leave such toils as these.
   But here it dwells, and here must I
With danger seek it forth:
To spend the time luxuriously
Becomes not men of worth.

SIREN

Ulysses, O be not deceived
With that unreal name:
This honor is a thing conceived,[3]
20   And rests on others' fame.[4]
   Begotten only to molest
Our peace, and to beguile
(The best thing of our life) our rest,
And give us up to toil.

ULYSSES

Delicious nymph, suppose there were
Nor honor, nor report,
Yet manliness would scorn to wear[5]
The time in idle sport.

---

[1] A debate between honorable action and pleasure
is here attached to the story in *Odyssey* XII of
the beautiful sirens who by their singing lure
mariners to wreck their ships: Ulysses stopped
his men's ears with wax and had himself bound
to the mast so that he alone could hear them.
[2] **travail** punning on "travel"
[3] **conceived** imagined
[4] **fame** rumor
[5] **wear** wear out

For toil doth give a better touch
30   To make us feel our joy:
And ease finds tediousness as much
As labor yields annoy.[6]

SIREN
Then pleasure likewise seems the shore
Whereto tends all your toil,
Which you forgo to make it more,
And perish oft the while.[7]
    Who may disport them diversly
Find never tedious day,[8]
And ease may have variety
40   As well as action may.

ULYSSES
But natures of the noblest frame[9]
These toils and dangers please,
And they take comfort in the same,
As much as you in ease,
    And with the thoughts of actions passed
Are recreated still,
When pleasure leaves a touch at last,
To show that it was ill.

SIREN
That doth opinion only cause,
50   That's out of custom bred,
Which makes us many other laws
Than ever Nature did.[10]
    No widows wail for our delights,
Our sports are without blood;
The world, we see, by warlike wights[11]
Receives more hurt than good.

ULYSSES
But yet the state of things require
These motions of unrest,
And these great sports of high desire
60   Seem born to turn them best,
    To purge the mischiefs that increase
And all good order mar:
For oft we see a wicked peace
To be well changed for war.

---

[6]**annoy** trouble
[7]ll. 35–36 You forgo pleasure now for a future goal supposed to yield greater pleasure, but you often destroy yourselves in the process.
[8]ll. 37–38 Those who can find different kinds of pleasures are never bored.

[9]**frame** making
[10]ll. 49–52 Manmade custom makes us think ill of pleasure, but the true nature of things knows nothing of such manmade laws.
[11]**wights** men

SIREN
Well, well Ulysses then I see
I shall not have thee here,
And therefore I will come to thee,
And take my fortunes there.
70   I must be won that cannot win,
Yet lost were I not won:
For beauty hath created been,
T' undo, or be undone.[12]

1605

[12]l. 72   to defeat and seduce, or to be defeated and seduced. Daniel's final conversion of the siren, a mythical creature inhabiting rocks, into a woman to be won is an original stroke.

MICHAEL DRAYTON
1563–1631

Like other Elizabethan poets, Drayton was concerned with love and heroism. He was brought up as a page in a noble house and depended on patronage. His work was strongly influenced by Spenser and Shakespeare, but the one poem included from his sonnet sequence *Idea* is notably original.

The title of his very nationalistic ode "His Ballad of Agincourt" and its ballad-like swing support the notion, already expressed by Sidney, that longer English ballads of warlike deeds were the native English answer to the imported tradition of the heroic poem.

From Idea

Since There's No Help

Since there's no help, come let us kiss and part:
Nay, I have done; you get no more of me,
And I am glad, yea, glad with all my heart,
That thus so cleanly I myself can free;
Shake hands for ever, cancel all our vows,
And when we meet at any time again,
Be it not seen in either of our brows
That we one jot of former love retain.
Now at the last gasp of love's latest breath,
10   When, his pulse failing, passion speechless lies,
When faith is kneeling by his bed of death,
And innocence is closing up his eyes,
Now, if thou wouldst, when all have given him over,
From death to life thou mightst him yet recover.

1619

His Ballad of Agincourt[1]

Fair stood the wind for France,
When we our sails advance,
Nor now to prove our chance
Longer will tarry;
But putting to the main,
At Caux, the mouth of Seine,
With all his martial train,
Landed King Harry.

And taking many a fort,
10 Furnished in warlike sort,
Marcheth towards Agincourt
In happy hour;
Skirmishing day by day
With those that stopped his way
Where the French general lay,
With all his power.

Which in his height of pride,
King Henry to deride,
His ransom to provide
20 To the king sending;
Which he neglects the while,
As from a nation vile,
Yet with an angry smile
Their fall portending.

And turning to his men,
Quoth our brave Henry then,
"Though they to one be ten,
Be not amazèd.
Yet have we well begun;
30 Battles so bravely won
Have ever to the sun
By fame been raisèd.

"And for myself," quoth he,
"This my full rest shall be;
England ne'er mourn for me,
Nor more esteem me.
Victor I will remain,
Or on this earth lie slain;
Never shall she sustain
40 Loss to redeem me.[2]

[1] Henry V's astonishing victory in 1415, against great odds, was, like those of Poitiers and Crécy (l. 41), a rallying point for English nationalism and had already been celebrated in Elizabethan times in Shakespeare's *Henry V*. Drayton's poem, published in 1619, came roughly sixty years after the English had lost their last foothold in France.
[2] ll. 39–40 Feudal nobility, unlike common soldiers, were generally ransomed when captured.

"Poitiers and Crécy tell
When most their pride did swell,
Under our swords they fell;
No less our skill is,
Than when our grandsire great,[3]
Claiming the regal seat,
By many a warlike feat
Lopped the French lilies."

The Duke of York so dread
50 The eager vaward[4] led;
With the main Henry sped
Amongst his henchmen.
Exeter had the rear,
A braver man not there;
O Lord, how hot they were
On the false Frenchmen!

They now to fight are gone,
Armour on armour shone,
Drum now to drum did groan,
60 To hear was wonder;
That with the cries they make
The very earth did shake;
Trumpet to trumpet spake,
Thunder to thunder.

Well it thine age became,
O noble Erpingham,[5]
Which didst the signal aim
To our hid forces;
When from a meadow by,
70 Like a storm suddenly,
The English archery
Struck the French horses.

With Spanish yew so strong,
Arrows a cloth-yard long
That like to serpents stung,
Piercing the weather,
None from his fellow starts,
But playing manly parts,
And like true English hearts,
80 Stuck close together.

---

[3] ll. 45–48 Edward III, great-grandfather of Henry V, had humbled the fleur-de-lis (the French royal arms of lilies) at Crécy in 1346.

[4] **vaward** vanguard
[5] **Erpingham** an old knight, supposed to have been given the honor of beginning the battle

When down their bows they threw,
And forth their bilboes[6] drew,
And on the French they flew,
Not one was tardy;
Arms were from shoulders sent,
Scalps to the teeth were rent,
Down the French peasants went;
Our men were hardy.

This while our noble king,
90 His broad sword brandishing,
Down the French host did ding,
As to o'erwhelm it;
And many a deep wound lent,
His arms with blood besprent,
And many a cruel dent
Bruisèd his helmet.

Gloucester, that duke so good,
Next of the royal blood,
For famous England stood,
100 With his brave brother;
Clarence, in steel so bright,
Though but a maiden knight,
Yet in that furious fight
Scarce such another.

Warwick in blood did wade,
Oxford the foe invade,
And cruel slaughter made
Still as they ran up;
Suffolk his axe did ply,
110 Beaumont and Willoughby
Bare them right doughtily,
Ferrers and Fanhope.

Upon Saint Crispin's day[7]
Fought was this noble fray,
Which fame did not delay
To England to carry;
O, when shall English men
With such acts fill a pen,
Or England breed again
120 Such a King Harry?

1606, 1619

---

[6] **bilboes** swords
[7] **Saint Crispin's day** October 25

CHRISTOPHER MARLOWE
1564–1593

Son of a thriving shoe-manufacturer, Marlowe was a brilliant if unruly scholarship student at Cambridge University, apparently doing secret government service as well. In the theater he was a precocious success and early influence on Shakespeare, his exact contemporary. His *The Tragical History of Dr. Faustus* remains a powerful poetic drama, reflecting also Marlowe's freethinking intellectualism. His virtuosity is represented here by the uncompleted but richly sensuous *Hero and Leander*, written partly in imitation of the Latin poet Ovid's erotic tales. Marlowe manages the form ingeniously, using lighthearted, faintly ironic, voluptuously charged hyperbole and Petrarchan conceits. Ben Jonson praised his "mighty line"; he is a clear forerunner of Keats.

From Hero and Leander

From First Sestiad

On Hellespont, guilty of true-loves' blood,
In view and opposite two cities stood,
Sea-borderers, disjoin'd by Neptune's might:
The one Abydos, the other Sestos hight.[1]
At Sestos Hero dwelt: Hero the fair,
Whom young Apollo courted for her hair,
And off'red as a dower his burning throne,
Where she should sit for men to gaze upon.[2]
The outside of her garments were of lawn,[3]
10   The lining purple silk, with gilt stars drawn;
Her wide sleeves green, and bordered with a grove,
Where Venus in her naked glory strove
To please the careless and disdainful eyes
Of proud Adonis that before her lies.
Her kirtle[4] blue, whereon was many a stain
Made with the blood of wretched lovers slain.
Upon her head she ware[5] a myrtle wreath,
From whence her veil reach'd to the ground beneath.
Her veil was artificial flowers and leaves
20   Whose workmanship both man and beast deceives.
Many would praise the sweet smell as she pass'd,
When 'twas the odour which her breath forth cast;
And there for honey bees have sought in vain,

[1] **hight** was called
[2] **Hero the fair . . . upon** This imagined act of Apollo begins a concentrated metaphorical and symbolic evocation of beauty and seductiveness, in which Ovidian and Petrarchan imagery turns Hero into a walking conceit, as in a court masque or a symbolic painting. The lightheartedly ironical effect of overstatement is part of the character of this miniature epic and does not relate to Hero's later displayed sexual innocence: the blood-stained skirt, the veil with vegetation made by art so skilled as to seem natural, the bees around her head, the pebbles turned to diamonds by her beauty, the buskins (classical boots) decorated with jeweled birds, perched on coral branches, chirping when fed sugar-water by an attendant, Cupid's proverbial blindness attributed to the brightness of her beauty, and night portrayed as Nature's mourning for having lost a large supply of her beauty to Hero.
[3] **lawn** fine, thin linen
[4] **kirtle** skirt
[5] **ware** wore

And, beat from thence, have lighted there again.
About her neck hung chains of pebble-stone,
Which, light'ned by her neck, like diamonds shone.
She ware no gloves, for neither sun nor wind
Would burn or parch her hands, but to her mind[6]
Or warm or cool them, for they took delight
30   To play upon those hands, they were so white.
Buskins of shells all silvered used she,
And branch'd with blushing coral to the knee,
Where sparrows perch'd, of hollow pearl and gold,
Such as the world would wonder to behold.
Those with sweet water oft her handmaid fills,
Which as she went would chirrup through the bills.
Some say for her the fairest Cupid pin'd,
And looking in her face, was strooken blind.
But this is true, so like was one the other,
40   As he imagin'd Hero was his mother,[7]
And oftentimes into her bosom flew,
About her naked neck his bare arms threw,
And laid his childish head upon her breast,
And, with still panting rock'd, there took his rest.
So lovely fair was Hero, Venus' nun,[8]
As Nature wept, thinking she was undone,
Because she took more from her than she left,
And of such wondrous beauty her bereft;
Therefore, in sign her treasure suff'red wrack,
50   Since Hero's time hath half the world been black.
Amorous Leander, beautiful and young
(Whose tragedy divine Musaeus[9] sung)
Dwelt at Abydos; since him dwelt there none
For whom succeeding times make greater moan.
His dangling tresses that were never shorn,
Had they been cut, and unto Colchos borne,
Would have allur'd the vent'rous youth of Greece
To hazard more than for the Golden Fleece.[10]
Fair Cynthia[11] wish'd his arms might be her sphere;
60   Grief makes her pale because she moves not there.
His body was as straight as Circe's[12] wand;

[6]**but to her mind**   as she wished
[7]**mother**   Venus
[8]l. 45   The medieval theme of a nun of Venus
reverses Christian values. Perhaps Marlowe
associated it with the ritual temple prostitutes
of some ancient Near Eastern religion.
[9]**Musaeus**   His fifth-century poem created the
story of Hero and Leander.
[10]ll. 57–58   Here and later, note allusions to
the concurrent homosexuality and heterosex-
uality that were features of upper-class Greek
and Roman life as depicted in classical poetry.
Colchos was the resting place of the fleece of a
golden, winged ram from whose back Helle

had fallen, giving her name to the Hellespont,
where Hero and Leander now live. Later Jason
and his Argonauts had ventured to gain the
Golden Fleece in Colchos; Jason also began his
fatal love-affair with Medea, whom he took
from there.
[11]**Cynthia**   moon goddess. The moon's sphere
was imagined as crystalline, the first of the
concentric planetary spheres centered on the
earth.
[12]**Circe's**   Circe was a witch-figure who seduc-
tively enthralled men and turned them into
beasts.

Jove might have sipp'd out nectar from his hand.[13]
Even as delicious meat is to the taste,
So was his neck in touching, and surpass'd
The white of Pelops' shoulder.[14] I could tell ye
How smooth his breast was, and how white his belly,
And whose immortal fingers did imprint
That heavenly path with many a curious dint
That runs along his back, but my rude pen
70   Can hardly blazon forth the loves of men,
Much less of powerful gods; let it suffice
That my slack muse sings of Leander's eyes,
Those orient[15] cheeks and lips, exceeding his[16]
That leapt into the water for a kiss
Of his own shadow, and despising many,
Died ere he could enjoy the love of any.
Had wild Hippolytus[17] Leander seen,
Enamoured of his beauty had he been;
His presence made the rudest peasant melt,
80   That in the vast uplandish country dwelt.
The barbarous Thracian soldier, mov'd with nought,
Was mov'd with him, and for his favour sought.
Some swore he was a maid in man's attire,
For in his looks were all that men desire,
A pleasant smiling cheek, a speaking eye,
A brow for love to banquet royally;
And such as knew he was a man would say,
"Leander, thou art made for amorous play:
Why art thou not in love, and lov'd of all?
90   Though thou be fair, yet be not thine own thrall."
    The men of wealthy Sestos, every year,
For his sake whom their goddess held so dear,
Rose-cheek'd Adonis,[18] kept a solemn feast.
Thither resorted many a wand'ring guest
To meet their loves; such as had none at all
Came lovers home from this great festival.
For every street like to a firmament
Glistered with breathing stars, who where they went
Frighted the melancholy earth, which deem'd
100   Eternal heaven to burn, for so it seem'd
As if another Phaethon had got
The guidance of the sun's rich chariot.[19]
But far above the loveliest Hero shin'd,
And stole away th'enchanted gazer's mind;

[13] l. 62 Jove became enamored of Ganymede,
a beautiful youth (l. 148), and carried him off
to be both cupbearer and beloved. The analogy
with Leander is clear.
[14] **Pelops' shoulder** made of ivory
[15] **orient** glowing;
[16] **his** Narcissus'
[17] **Hippolytus** son of Theseus, who emulated

Diana in hunting and chastity
[18] **Adonis** beloved of Venus, but killed by a boar:
another tragic love
[19] ll. 99–102 Earth (melancholy because lowest
of the four elements) thinks of Phaethon, son of
Apollo, who lost control of the chariot of the
sun (another star) and allowed it to descend too
low.

For like sea-nymphs' inveigling harmony,[20]
So was her beauty to the standers by.
Nor that night-wand'ring, pale and wat'ry star,[21]
When yawning dragons draw her thirling[22] car
From Latmus mount up to the gloomy sky,
110   Where crown'd with blazing light and majesty
She proudly sits, more overrules the flood
Than she the hearts of those that near her stood.
Even as, when gaudy nymphs pursue the chase,
Wretched Ixion's shaggy-footed race,[23]
Incens'd with savage heat, gallop amain
From steep pine-bearing mountains to the plain,
So ran the people forth to gaze upon her,
And all that view'd her were enamour'd on her.
And as in fury of a dreadful fight,
120   Their fellows being slain or put to flight,
Poor soldiers stand with fear of death dead-strooken,
So at her presence all surpris'd and tooken
Await the sentence of her scornful eyes;
He whom she favours lives, the other dies.
There might you see one sigh, another rage,
And some (their violent passions to assuage)
Compile sharp satires, but alas too late,
For faithful love will never turn to hate.
And many, seeing great princes were denied,
130   Pin'd as they went, and thinking on her died.
On this feast day, O cursed day and hour,
Went Hero thorough[24] Sestos, from her tower
To Venus' temple, where unhappily,
As after chanc'd, they did each other spy.
So fair a church as this had Venus none;
The walls were of discoloured[25] jasper stone,
Wherein was Proteus carved, and o'erhead
A lively vine of green sea-agate spread;
Where by one hand light-headed Bacchus hung,
140   And with the other, wine from grapes outwrung.
Of crystal shining fair the pavement was;
The town of Sestos call'd it Venus' glass.[26]
There might you see the gods in sundry shapes,
Committing heady riots, incest, rapes:[27]

[20]**sea-nymphs' . . . harmony** like the Sirens, who drew ships onto rocks by their singing
[21]**night-wand'ring . . . star** the moon
[22]**thirling** piercing, like a flying arrow
[23]**Ixion's . . . race** centaurs, proverbially libidinous. Ixion, their progenitor, was chained to a revolving wheel because he had mated with Juno.
[24]**thorough** through
[25]**discoloured** varicolored
[26]**glass** mirror
[27]The power of love in classical mythology was a resource for erotic poetry. Jove's marriage to Juno was incestuous. He seduced Danae by descending in a shower of gold, even though she was imprisoned at the top of a tower. For Ganymede, see note 13. Jove is imagined bellowing because in the form of a bull he carried off Europa. Iris is the goddess of the rainbow. Mars, god of war, was trapped with Venus in an iron net made by her husband, the artificer-god, and his helpers. The war that destroyed Troy resulted from Paris' carrying off Helen. The forest god Silvanus mourns Cyparissus, turned into a cypress by Apollo.

For know that underneath this radiant floor
Was Danae's statue in a brazen tower,
Jove slyly stealing from his sister's bed,
To dally with Idalian Ganymede,
Or for his love Europa bellowing loud,
150 Or tumbling with the Rainbow in a cloud;
Blood-quaffing Mars, heaving the iron net
Which limping Vulcan and his Cyclops set;
Love kindling fire, to burn such towns as Troy;
Silvanus weeping for the lovely boy
That now is turn'd into a cypress tree,
Under whose shade the wood-gods love to be.
And in the midst a silver altar stood;
There Hero sacrificing turtles'[28] blood,
Veil'd to the ground, veiling her eyelids close,
160 And modestly they opened as she rose.
Thence flew Love's arrow with the golden head,[29]
And thus Leander was enamoured.
Stone still he stood, and evermore he gazed,
Till with the fire that from his count'nance blazed
Relenting Hero's gentle heart was strook:
Such force and virtue hath an amorous look.

. . .

[28]**turtles'** turtledoves'
[29]**arrow . . . head** Cupid's gold-headed arrows
inspired love; the leaden ones inspired hate or
lust.

From Second Sestiad

10 So on she goes, and in her idle flight
Her painted fan of curled plumes let fall,
Thinking to train[1] Leander therewithal.
He being a novice, knew not what she meant,
But stay'd, and after her a letter sent,
Which joyful Hero answer'd in such sort
As he had hope to scale the beauteous fort
Wherein the liberal Graces lock'd their wealth,
And therefore to her tower he got by stealth.
Wide open stood the door, he need not climb,
20 And she herself before the 'pointed time
Had spread the board, with roses strew'd the room,
And oft look'd out, and mus'd he did not come.
At last he came; O who can tell the greeting

[1] **train** draw

These greedy lovers had at their first meeting?
He ask'd, she gave, and nothing was denied;
Both to each other quickly were affied.[2]
Look how their hands, so were their hearts united,
And what he did she willingly requited.
(Sweet are the kisses, the embracements sweet,
30   When like desires and affections meet,
For from the earth to heaven is Cupid rais'd,
Where fancy is in equal balance peis'd.)[3]
Yet she this rashness suddenly repented,
And turn'd aside, and to herself lamented,
As if her name and honour had been wrong'd
By being possess'd of him for whom she long'd;
Ay, and she wish'd, albeit not from her heart,
That he would leave her turret and depart.
The mirthful god of amorous pleasure smil'd
40   To see how he this captive nymph beguil'd;
For hitherto he did but fan the fire,
And kept it down that it might mount the higher.
Now wax'd she jealous, lest his love abated,
Fearing her own thoughts made her to be hated.
Therefore unto him hastily she goes,
And, like light Salmacis, her body throws
Upon his bosom,[4] where with yielding eyes
She offers up herself a sacrifice
To slake his anger, if he were displeas'd.
50   O what god would not therewith be appeas'd?
Like Aesop's cock, this jewel he enjoyed,[5]
And as a brother with his sister toyed,
Supposing nothing else was to be done,
Now he her favour and good will had won.
But know you not that creatures wanting sense
By nature have a mutual appetence,
And wanting organs to advance a step,
Mov'd by love's force, unto each other leap?[6]
Much more in subjects having intellect
60   Some hidden influence breeds like effect.
Albeit Leander, rude[7] in love, and raw,
Long dallying with Hero, nothing saw
That might delight him more, yet he suspected
Some amorous rites or other were neglected.
Therefore unto his body hers he clung;
She, fearing on the rushes to be flung,
Striv'd with redoubled strength; the more she strived,

---

[2] **affied** mutually trusting
[3] **peis'd** weighted
[4] **And, like . . . bosom** She threw herself on Hermaphroditus; the gods turned the two into one, a hermaphrodite.
[5] l. 51 In Aesop's fable he found a jewel but was ready to exchange it for a seed-grain.
[6] l. 58 Inanimate objects drawn by magnetism (a kind of love) leap together.
[7] **rude** untaught

The more a gentle pleasing heat revived,
Which taught him all that elder lovers know.
70   And now the same 'gan so to scorch and glow,
As in plain terms (yet cunningly) he crav'd it;
Love always makes those eloquent that have it.
She, with a kind of granting, put him by it,[8]
And ever as he thought himself most nigh it,
Like to the tree of Tantalus[9] she fled,
And, seeming lavish, sav'd her maidenhead.
Ne'er king more sought to keep his diadem,
Than Hero this inestimable gem.
Above our life we love a steadfast friend,
80   Yet when a token of great worth we send,
We often kiss it, often look thereon,
And stay the messenger that would be gone:
No marvel, then, though Hero would not yield
So soon to part from that she dearly held.
Jewels being lost are found again, this never;
'Tis lost but once, and once lost, lost for ever.
    Now had the Morn espied her lover's steeds,
Whereat she starts, puts on her purple weeds,
And red for anger that he stay'd so long,
90   All headlong throws herself the clouds among.
And now Leander, fearing to be miss'd,
Embrac'd her suddenly, took leave, and kiss'd.
Long was he taking leave, and loath to go,
And kiss'd again, as lovers use to do.

· · ·

His secret flame apparently[10] was seen,
Leander's father knew where he had been,
And for the same mildly rebuk'd his son,
Thinking to quench the sparkles new begun.
But love, resisted once, grows passionate,
140   And nothing more than counsel lovers hate.
For as a hot proud horse highly disdains
To have his head controll'd, but breaks the reins,
Spits forth the ringled[11] bit, and with his hooves
Checks[12] the submissive ground, so he that loves,
The more he is restrain'd, the worse he fares.
What is it now but mad Leander dares?
"O Hero, Hero!" thus he cried full oft,
And then he got him to a rock aloft,
Where having spied her tower, long stared he on't,
150   And prayed the narrow toiling Hellespont

---

[8]**put him by it** deflected him
[9]**Tantalus** Part of his punishment in Hades was
that the branch bearing fruit withdrew when-
ever he reached for it.

[10]**apparently** clearly
[11]**ringled** ringed
[12]**checks** stamps

To part in twain, that he might come and go,
But still the rising billows answered "No."
With that he stripp'd him to the ivory skin,
And crying, "Love, I come," leapt lively in.

   . . .

   By this, Leander, being near the land,
Cast down his weary feet, and felt the sand.
Breathless albeit he were, he rested not
230 Till to the solitary tower he got,
And knock'd and call'd, at which celestial noise
The longing heart of Hero much more joys
Than nymphs and shepherds when the timbrel[13] rings,
Or crooked[14] dolphin when the sailor sings.
She stay'd not for her robes, but straight arose,
And drunk with gladness to the door she goes,
Where seeing a naked man she screech'd for fear—
Such sights as this to tender maids are rare—
And ran into the dark herself to hide;
240 Rich jewels in the dark are soonest spied.
Unto her was he led, or rather drawn,
By those white limbs, which sparkled through the lawn.[15]
The nearer that he came, the more she fled,
And seeking refuge, slipp'd into her bed.
Whereon Leander sitting thus began,
Through numbing cold all feeble, faint and wan:
"If not for love, yet, love, for pity sake,
Me in thy bed and maiden bosom take;
At least vouchsafe these arms some little room,
250 Who, hoping to embrace thee, cheerly[16] swum.
This head was beat with many a churlish billow,
And therefore let it rest upon thy pillow."
Herewith affrighted Hero shrunk away,
And in her lukewarm place Leander lay,
Whose lively[17] heat, like fire from heaven fet,[18]
Would animate gross clay, and higher set
The drooping thoughts of base-declining souls
Than dreary[19] Mars carousing nectar bowls.
His hands he cast upon her like a snare;
260 She, overcome with shame and sallow fear,
Like chaste Diana when Actaeon[20] spied her,
Being suddenly betray'd, div'd down to hide her.
And as her silver body downward went,
With both her hands she made the bed a tent,
And in her own mind thought herself secure,
O'ercast with dim and darksome coverture.

---

[13]**timbrel** tambourine
[14]**crooked** curving
[15]**lawn** diaphanous cloth
[16]**cheerly** gladly
[17]**lively** life-giving

[18]**fet** fetched
[19]**dreary** gory
[20]**Actaeon** This hunter happened on Diana when
    she was bathing in a stream.

And now she lets him whisper in her ear,
Flatter, entreat, promise, protest and swear;
Yet ever as he greedily assay'd
270 To touch those dainties, she the harpy[21] play'd,
And every limb did as a soldier stout
Defend the fort, and keep the foeman out.
For though the rising iv'ry mount he scal'd,
Which is with azure circling lines empal'd,
Much like a globe (a globe may I term this,
By which love sails to regions full of bliss),
Yet there with Sisyphus[22] he toil'd in vain,
Till gentle parley did the truce obtain.
Wherein Leander on her quivering breast.
280 Breathless spoke something, and sigh'd out the rest;
Which so prevail'd as he with small ado
Enclos'd her in his arms and kiss'd her too.
And every kiss to her was as a charm,
And to Leander as a fresh alarm,[23]
So that the truce was broke, and she alas
(Poor silly maiden) at his mercy was.
Love is not full of pity (as men say)
But deaf and cruel where he means to prey.
Even as a bird, which in our hands we wring,
290 Forth plungeth, and oft flutters with her wing,
She trembling strove; this strife of hers, like that
Which made the world, another world begat[24]
Of unknown joy. Treason was in her thought,
And cunningly to yield herself she sought.
Seeming not won, yet won she was at length;
In such wars women use but half their strength.
Leander now, like Theban Hercules,
Ent'red the orchard of th'Hesperides,[25]
Whose fruit none rightly can describe but he
300 That pulls or shakes it from the golden tree.
And now she wish'd this night were never done,
And sigh'd to think upon th'approaching sun,
For much it griev'd her that the bright daylight
Should know the pleasure of this blessed night,
And them like Mars and Erycine[26] display'd,
Both in each other's arms chain'd as they laid.

1598

[21]**harpy** Harpies were female monsters who ruined banquets about to be eaten.
[22]**Sisyphus** He was condemned to roll a stone uphill without ever reaching the top.
[23]**alarm** summons to action
[24]ll. 291-92 Strife and Love controlled the making of the world from chaos, according to one myth.
[25]**Hesperides** custodians of a garden where golden apples grew
[26]**Erycine** Venus. See note 27 to the First Sestiad, p. 188 above.

The Passionate Shepherd to His Love[1]

Come live with me, and be my love,
And we will all the pleasures prove[2]
That valleys, groves, hills and fields,
Woods, or steepy mountain yields.

And we will sit upon the rocks,
Seeing the shepherds feed their flocks
By shallow rivers, to whose falls
Melodious birds sing madrigals.

And I will make thee beds of roses,
10   And a thousand fragrant posies,
A cap of flowers, and a kirtle,[3]
Embroid'red all with leaves of myrtle,

A gown made of the finest wool
Which from our pretty lambs we pull,
Fair-lined slippers for the cold,
With buckles of the purest gold,

A belt of straw and ivy-buds,
With coral clasps and amber studs,
And if these pleasures may thee move,
20   Come live with me, and be my love.

The shepherd swains shall dance and sing
For thy delight each May morning.
If these delights thy mind may move,
Then live with me, and be my love.

1599, 1600

[1]See Sir Walter Ralegh's answering lyric, "The Nymph's Reply to the Shepherd," p. 176 above.
[2]**prove** try out
[3]**kirtle** a skirt or dress

WILLIAM SHAKESPEARE
1564–1616

The son of a merchant in Stratford-on-Avon, Shakespeare did not attend university but made his way in his twenties into the risky, irregular life of professional acting and playwriting in London. He gradually won recognition as the best and financially most successful dramatist of his time.

Shakespeare's sonnets, although they are sensuously rich and laden with conceits, escape the Petrarchan model and achieve a marvelous emotional immediacy. The fourteen lines of the Shakespearean sonnet fall (like Surrey's; see p. 133) into three quatrains and a couplet rhyming abab cdcd efef gg. The Petrarchan model (as in Wyatt, p. 129) is constructed as an octet rhyming abbaabba, followed by a sestet rhyming variously.

The sequence in Shakespeare's collection of sonnets is not chronological, but the sonnets do hint at a connected story. The speaker in the sonnets is in love with a young friend who is socially superior, perhaps a patron, of surpassing beauty and apparent constancy in his love for the speaker. In Elizabethan thinking, friendship was an attachment as important and potentially as emotional as heterosexual love—a view in keeping with the example of male friendships in Plato's Socratic dialogues, dating from an Athenian culture in which the line between such friendship and homosexual love was fluctuating and indefinite. The friend's constancy turns out not to be complete—he becomes sexually entangled with a beautiful, provocative brunette who was, and continues to be, sexually enthralling to the speaker himself. The speaker's jealousy, reproaches, sacrificial self-torture, and continuing love for his friend generate some of the most telling sonnets in the sequence.

Some of these sonnets deal with the sense of loss, ruin, and death that Time, personified as a malevolent being, imposes on created things. The friend's inevitable future loss of beauty and life is seen against a background of change in nature and the ruination of antique monuments and glory. The only sure defense against Time is the eternity of the poem itself, inspired by the excellence and beauty of the friend. Shakespeare's use in the sonnets for Spenser's *Ruins of Rome* (p. 150; the translation of the French Renaissance poet Joachim Du Bellay's sonnet sequence *Les Antiquitez de Rome*) shows that his thinking here derives from the familiar idea of the eternity of ancient Latin literature, inspired by Roman excellence. Living in Rome, Du Bellay had contrasted the ghostly ruins of the physical city, destroyed by Time, with the survival—through a secular eternity of 1,500 years or more—in its Latin poetry of the idea of Rome.

Songs from Elizabethan plays, particularly Shakespeare's, are among the loveliest of lyrics. They not only illuminate the play's action at the point where they are sung, but deepen and embellish it emotionally.

Passages from two plays by Shakespeare, one early and one late, illustrate both the character and development of his poetry and the evolution of some of his dramatic methods. Blank verse, beginning in English with Surrey's translation of Virgil's *Aeneid*, descends in *Richard III* (the early play here) from Shakespeare's older contemporaries: the regular pentameter and end-stop lines are as powerfully and regularly accentuated as the character of Richard—the embodiment of villainy—is grippingly melodramatic. With maturity Shakespeare relaxed his handling of the iambic pentameter line. The beat became less obtrusive and less regular, the natural voice continuing without pause from one line to the next. This development was part of his growing ability to make a single dramatic scene carry many meanings beyond mere action. In the late *A Winter's Tale*, the speech is so natural that one needs to look twice to see how exquisitely the verse is handled.

From Sonnets

XVIII

Shall I compare thee to a summer's day?
Thou art more lovely and more temperate.
Rough winds do shake the darling buds of May,
And summer's lease hath all too short a date.[1]
Sometime too hot the eye of heaven shines,
And often is his gold complexion dimmed;
And every fair from fair sometime declines,

---

[1] **date** duration

By chance or nature's changing course untrimmed.²
But thy eternal summer shall not fade
10   Nor lose possession of that fair thou ow'st;³
Nor shall Death brag thou wand'rest in his shade,
When in eternal lines to time thou grow'st.
    So long as men can breathe or eyes can see,
    So long lives this and this gives life to thee.

²**untrimmed**   stripped of beauty   ³**ow'st**   ownest

XIX

Devouring Time, blunt thou the lion's paws,¹
And make the earth devour her own sweet brood;
Pluck the keen teeth from the fierce tiger's jaws,
And burn the long-lived phoenix² in her blood;
Make glad and sorry seasons as thou fleets,
And do whate'er thou wilt, swift-footed Time,
To the wide world and all her fading sweets.
But I forbid thee one most heinous crime:
O, carve not with thy hours my love's fair brow,
10   Nor draw no lines there with thine antique³ pen;
Him in thy course untainted⁴ do allow
For beauty's pattern to succeeding men.
    Yet, do thy worst, old Time. Despite thy wrong,
    My love shall in my verse ever live young.

¹**blunt . . . paws**   blunt the claws of even this
keenly devouring predator
²**phoenix**   a long-lived bird that was supposed
to be reborn from its ashes

³**antique**   old, but also disfiguring
⁴**untainted**   untouched, but also unhit in the run-
ning course of jousting

XXX

When to the sessions¹ of sweet silent thought
I summon up remembrance of things past,
I sigh the lack of many a thing I sought,
And with old woes new wail my dear time's waste.
Then can I drown an eye, unused to flow,
For precious friends hid in death's dateless² night,
And weep afresh love's long since cancelled³ woe,
And moan th' expense of many a vanished sight.
Then can I grieve at grievances foregone,
10   And heavily from woe to woe tell o'er
The sad account of fore-bemoanèd moan,
Which I new pay as if not paid before.
    But if the while I think on thee, dear friend,
    All losses are restored, and sorrows end.

¹**sessions**   as in a court of law
²**dateless**   endless
³ ll. 7–14   The financial metaphor, as in a court

case, continues through "cancelled," "ex-
pense" (loss), "tell" (count), "account,"
"pay," "losses," etc.

XXXV

No more be grieved at that which thou hast done.
Roses have thorns, and silver fountains mud,
Clouds and eclipses stain[1] both moon and sun,
And loathsome canker lives in sweetest bud.
All men make faults, and even I in this,
Authorizing thy trespass with compare,[2]
Myself corrupting, salving thy amiss,[3]
Excusing thy sins more than thy sins are.[4]
For to thy sensual fault I bring in sense—[5]
10   Thy adverse party is thy advocate—
And 'gainst myself a lawful plea commence.
Such civil war is in my love and hate
        That I an accessary needs must be
        To that sweet thief which sourly robs from me.

[1] **stain**   dim
[2] ll. 6   justifying your sins with the above comparisons
[3] l. 7   corrupting myself by extenuating your sins

[4] l. 8   working harder to excuse your sins than you did to commit them
[5] **sense**   reason

LIV

O, how much more doth beauty beauteous seem
By that sweet ornament which truth doth give![1]
The rose looks fair, but fairer we it deem
For that sweet odor which doth in it live.
The canker-blooms[2] have full as deep a dye
As the perfumèd tincture of the roses,
Hang on such thorns, and play as wantonly
When summer's breath their masked buds discloses.
But, for their virtue[3] only is their show,
10   They live unwooed and unrespected fade,
Die to themselves. Sweet roses do not so;
Of their sweet deaths are sweetest odors made.
        And so of you, beauteous and lovely youth,
        When that shall vade,[4] by verse distills your truth.

[1] **which truth doth give**   keeping faith, probity
[2] **canker-blooms**   dog roses, not as sweetly scented as the real ones
[3] **virtue**   characteristic excellence

[4] **vade**   depart. When your beauty fades, the essence of your truth will be preserved in the poem (like the odor of roses in rose water).

LV

Not marble, nor the gilded monuments[1]
Of princes, shall outlive this pow'rful rhyme,
But you shall shine more bright in these contents
Than unswept stone besmeared with sluttish time.

[1] See Spenser's *Ruins of Rome* XXXII (p. 150), from which this sonnet is partly derived.

When wasteful war shall statues overturn,
And broils² root out the work of masonry,
Nor Mars his sword nor war's quick fire shall burn
The living record of your memory.
'Gainst death and all-oblivious enmity
10   Shall you pace forth; your praise shall still find room³
Even in the eyes of all posterity
That wear this world out to the ending doom.
    So, till the judgment that yourself arise,
    You live in this, and dwell in lovers' eyes.

² **broils** uprisings
³ **room** Shakespeare often puns on "room" and "Rome" (pronounced "rheum" as in Brit. "room" then). The idea that the beloved's praise makes Rome even with himself in the reading eyes of posterity appears to recall Spenser's *Ruins of Rome*.

LXIV

When I have seen by Time's fell¹ hand defaced
The rich proud cost of outworn buried age;²
When sometime lofty towers I see down-razed
And brass eternal slave to mortal rage;³
When I have seen the hungry ocean gain
Advantage on the kingdom of the shore,
And the firm soil win of the wat'ry main
Increasing store with loss and loss with store;
When I have seen such interchange of state,⁴
10   Or state⁵ itself confounded to decay,
Ruin hath taught me thus to ruminate
That Time will come and take my love away.
    This thought is as a death, which cannot choose
    But weep to have that which it fears to lose.

¹ **fell** cruel
² l. 2 monuments built at prideful expense in bygone, forgotten time
³ l. 4 seemingly eternal brass (in burial monuments, etc.) subdued by mortality or deathly warfare
⁴ **state** condition
⁵ **state** here, pomp, stateliness

LXXIII

That time of year thou mayst in me behold
When yellow leaves, or none, or few, do hang
Upon those boughs which shake against the cold,
Bare ruined choirs,¹ where late the sweet birds sang.
In me thou see'st the twilight of such day
As after sunset fadeth in the west,
Which by and by black night doth take away,
Death's second self, that seals up all in rest.
In me thou see'st the glowing of such fire

¹ **Bare ruined choirs** arched parts of churches where service was sung, now ruined and denuded, like boughs of trees in winter

10 That on the ashes of his youth doth lie,
As the death-bed whereon it must expire,
Consumed with that which it was nourished by.
　　This thou perceiv'st, which makes thy love more strong,
　　To love that well which thou must leave ere long.

XCIV

They that have power to hurt and will do none,
That do not do the thing they most do show,[1]
Who, moving others, are themselves as stone,
Unmovèd, cold, and to temptation slow,
They rightly do inherit heaven's graces
And husband[2] nature's riches from expense;
They are the lords and owners of their faces,
Others but stewards[3] of their excellence.
The summer's flower is to the summer sweet,
10 Though to itself it only[4] live and die,
But if that flower with base infection meet,
The basest weed outbraves[5] his dignity.
　　For sweetest things turn sourest by their deeds;
　　Lilies that fester smell far worse than weeds.

[1] **show** seem to do
[2] **husband** preserve
[3] **stewards** keepers, dispensers, not owners
[4] **only** alone
[5] **outbraves** outfaces

CXVI

Let me not to the marriage of true minds
Admit impediments. Love is not love
Which alters when it alteration finds,
Or bends with the remover to remove.[1]
O, no, it is an ever-fixèd mark[2]
That looks on tempests and is never shaken;
It is the star to every wand'ring bark,
Whose worth's unknown, although his height be taken.[3]
Love's not Time's fool,[4] though rosy lips and cheeks
10 Within his bending sickle's compass come;
Love alters not with his brief hours and weeks,
But bears it out even to the edge of doom.[5]
　　If this be error and upon me proved,
　　I never writ, nor no man ever loved.

[1] l. 4 responds to inconstancy with inconstancy
[2] **ever-fixed mark** fixed, distinguishable object
to aid navigation
[3] l. 8 of inestimable worth, although its height
above the horizon can be measured for navigation
[4] **fool** plaything
[5] **doom** Day of Judgment

CXXVIII

How oft, when thou, my music, music play'st
Upon that blessed wood[1] whose motion sounds
With thy sweet fingers, when thou gently sway'st
The wiry concord that mine ear confounds,[2]
Do I envy those jacks[3] that nimble leap
To kiss the tender inward of thy hand,
Whilst my poor lips, which should that harvest reap,
At the wood's boldness by thee blushing stand!
To be so tickled, they would change their state
10   And situation with those dancing chips,
O'er whom thy fingers walk with gentle gait,
Making dead wood more blest than living lips.
    Since saucy jacks[4] so happy are in this,
    Give them thy fingers, me thy lips to kiss.

[1] **wood** keys of spinet or virginal
[2] **confounds** overwhelms
[3] **jacks** here, keys
[4] **jacks** punning on alternative meaning of "fellows"

CXXIX

Th' expense of spirit in a waste of shame
Is lust in action; and, till action, lust
Is perjured, murd'rous, bloody, full of blame,
Savage, extreme, rude, cruel, not to trust,
Enjoyed no sooner but despisèd straight,
Past reason hunted, and no sooner had
Past reason hated, as a swallowed bait
On purpose laid to make the taker mad;
Mad in pursuit and in possession so;
10   Had, having, and in quest to have, extreme;
A bliss in proof,[1] and proved, a very woe;
Before, a joy proposed; behind, a dream.
    All this the world well knows; yet none knows well
    To shun the heaven that leads men to this hell.

[1] **in proof** while experiencing it

CXXX

My mistress' eyes are nothing like the sun;
Coral is far more red than her lips' red;
If snow be white, why then her breasts are dun;[1]
If hairs be wires, black wires grow on her head.
I have seen roses damasked,[2] red and white,
But no such roses see I in her cheeks;

[1] **dun** grayish-brown
[2] **damasked** of the color of damask roses, pink

And in some perfumes is there more delight
Than in the breath that from my mistress reeks.³
I love to hear her speak, yet well I know
10   That music hath a far more pleasing sound.
I grant I never saw a goddess go;⁴
My mistress, when she walks, treads on the ground.
    And yet, by heaven, I think my love as rare
    As any she belied with false compare.

³ **reeks** emanates
⁴ **go** walk

CXLVI

Poor soul, the center of my sinful earth,¹
Thrall to these rebel powers that thee array,²
Why dost thou pine within and suffer dearth,
Painting thy outward walls³ so costly gay?
Why so large cost, having so short a lease,
Dost thou upon thy fading mansion spend?
Shall worms, inheritors of this excess,
Eat up thy charge?⁴ Is this thy body's end?
Then, soul, live thou upon thy servant's⁵ loss,
10   And let that pine to aggravate⁶ thy store;
Buy terms divine in selling hours of dross;⁷
Within be fed, without be rich no more.
    So shalt thou feed on Death, that feeds on men,
    And, Death once dead, there's no more dying then.

¹ **my . . . earth** the body
² **rebel . . . array** the flesh and its desires, which clothe, and are arrayed against, the soul
³ **Painting . . . walls** adorning the body
⁴ **charge** expense
⁵ **thy servant's** the body's
⁶ **aggravate** increase
⁷ l. 11 Make a (divine) contract, i.e., purchase immortality, through selling (giving up) worthless material pleasure.

CLI

Love¹ is too young to know what conscience is;
Yet who knows not conscience is born of love?
Then, gentle cheater, urge not my amiss,²
Lest guilty of my faults thy sweet self prove.³
For, thou betraying me, I do betray
My nobler part to my gross body's treason;
My soul doth tell my body that he may
Triumph in love; flesh stays no farther reason,
But, rising⁴ at thy name, doth point out thee

¹ **Love** young Cupid
² **amiss** sin
³ l. 4 lest in causing my sin you become sinful
like me
⁴ **rising** with bawdy suggestion, as below

10   As his triumphant prize. Proud of this pride,
He is contented thy poor drudge to be,
To stand in thy affairs, fall by thy side.
    No want of conscience hold it that I call
    Her "love" for whose dear love I rise and fall.

1609

Song: O Mistress Mine[1]

O mistress mine, where are you roaming?
O, stay and hear; your true love's coming,
    That can sing both high and low.
Trip no further, pretty sweeting;
Journeys end in lovers meeting,
    Every wise man's son doth know.

What is love? 'tis not hereafter;
Present mirth hath present laughter;
    What's to come is still unsure.
10   In delay there lies no plenty;
Then come kiss me, sweet and twenty,
    Youth's a stuff will not endure.

c. 1601   1623

[1] sung by the clown to Sir Toby Belch and Sir Andrew Aguecheek in the romantic comedy *Twelfth Night* (II.iii)

Song: Fear No More[1]

Fear no more the heat o' th' sun,
    Nor the furious winter's rages;
Thou thy worldly task hast done,
    Home art gone, and ta'en thy wages.
Golden lads and girls all must,
As chimney-sweepers, come to dust.

Fear no more the frown o' th' great;
    Thou art past the tyrant's stroke.
Care no more to clothe and eat;
10   To thee the reed is as the oak.
The scepter, learning, physic, must
All follow this, and come to dust.

[1] In the late romance *Cymbeline* (IV.ii) two brothers sing this over the body of their unknown sister, disguised as a boy, and apparently dead. One brother recites the first stanza, the other the second. In the third and fourth stanzas, the brothers alternate in the first four lines and speak the last two together.

Fear no more the lightning-flash,
　　Nor th' all-dreaded thunder-stone.
Fear not slander, censure rash;
　　Thou hast finish'd joy and moan.
All lovers young, all lovers must
Consign to thee, and come to dust.

No exorciser harm thee!
20　　Nor no witchcraft charm thee!
Ghost unlaid forbear thee!
　　Nothing ill come near thee!
Quiet consummation have,
And renownèd be thy grave!

1609   1623

Song: Full Fathom Five[1]

Full fathom five thy father lies;
　　Of his bones are coral made;
Those are pearls that were his eyes.
　　Nothing of him that doth fade
But doth suffer a sea-change
Into something rich and strange.
Sea-nymphs hourly ring his knell:
　　　　Burden [within]. Ding-Dong.[2]
Hark, now I hear them—Ding-dong, bell.

1611   1623

[1] sung by the spirit Ariel to Ferdinand, who believes his father has drowned, in the late romance *The Tempest* (I.ii)
[2] refrain, from off-stage

From The Tragedy of King Richard III

From Act I, scene i

Now is the winter of our discontent
Made glorious summer by this sun of York;[1]
And all the clouds that low'r'd upon our house
In the deep bosom of the ocean buried.
Now are our brows bound with victorious wreaths,
Our bruised arms hung up for monuments,
Our stern alarums chang'd to merry meetings,
Our dreadful marches to delightful measures.[2]

[1] ll. 1–2　At the beginning of this history play, the house of York is temporarily victorious over the house of Lancaster. The villainous, humpbacked Richard of Gloucester (speaking), the future Richard III, and his brother Edward, now king, are both sons (note "sun") of the house of York. Edward's badge displayed three suns.
[2] **measures**　dances

Grim-visag'd war hath smooth'd his wrinkled front;[3]
10 And now, instead of mounting barbed[4] steeds
To fright the souls of fearful[5] adversaries,
He capers nimbly in a lady's chamber
To the lascivious pleasing of a lute.
But I, that am not shap'd for sportive[6] tricks,
Nor made to court an amorous looking-glass;
I, that am rudely stamp'd, and want love's majesty
To strut before a wanton ambling nymph;
I, that am curtail'd of this fair proportion,
Cheated of feature by dissembling nature,
20 Deform'd, unfinish'd, sent before my time
Into this breathing world, scarce half made up,
And that so lamely and unfashionable
That dogs bark at me as I halt[7] by them—
Why, I, in this weak piping time of peace,[8]
Have no delight to pass away the time,
Unless to see my shadow in the sun
And descant[9] on mine own deformity.
And therefore, since I cannot prove a lover
To entertain these fair well-spoken days,
30 I am determined to prove a villain
And hate the idle pleasures of these days.

c. 1592   1597, 1623

[3] **front** forehead
[4] **barbed** armored
[5] **fearful** frightened
[6] **sportive** amorous
[7] **halt** limp

[8] **piping time of peace** time for music of pipes, not drums
[9] **descant** compose musical variations—comment

From The Winter's Tale

From Act IV, scene iv[1]

POLIXENES   Shepherdess—
A fair one are you—well you fit our ages
With flow'rs of winter.
PERDITA   Sir, the year growing ancient,[2]
80   Not yet on summer's death, nor on the birth
Of trembling winter, the fairest flow'rs o' th' season
Are our carnations and streak'd gillyvors,[3]
Which some call nature's bastards.[4] Of that kind
Our rustic garden's barren, and I care not
To get slips of them.

[1] King Polixenes has come in disguise to catch his son secretly wooing Perdita, supposed to be the daughter of a shepherd. Polixenes will shortly separate the couple.
[2] **the year growing ancient** i.e., in autumn

[3] **gillyvors** a kind of carnation
[4] **bastards** results of artificial breeding. The frequent theme of art and nature is worked out again below.

POLIXENES   Wherefore, gentle maiden,
   Do you neglect them?
PERDITA   For I have heard it said
   There is an art which in their piedness shares
   With great creating nature.
POLIXENES   Say there be;
   Yet nature is made better by no mean[5]
90   But nature makes that mean. So, over that art
   Which you say adds to nature, is an art
   That nature makes. You see, sweet maid, we marry
   A gentler scion to the wildest stock,
   And make conceive a bark of baser kind
   By bud of nobler race. This is an art
   Which does mend nature, change it rather, but
   The art itself is nature.[6]

     c. 1610   1623

[5] **mean** means
[6] **The art itself is nature** But note his attitude
toward his son's projected marriage.

THOMAS CAMPION
1567–1620

Campion composed both words and music for these love songs for one voice, which were to be accompanied (or not) by the lute. Their exquisite purity and perfection, and their classicism, suggest an affinity with Ben Jonson, but Campion's metrical experiments (see "Rose cheeked Laura" and its notes, below) continue Sidney's interest in quantitative verse (see p. 138 above).

Campion has such a purely melodic beat that we don't hear an identifiable speaking voice. That is one reason why this law student, medical doctor, poet, composer, and writer of literary criticism has been unduly neglected.

My Sweetest Lesbia[1]

My sweetest Lesbia, let us live and love;
And, though the sager sort our deeds reprove,
Let us not weigh them. Heaven's great lamps do dive
Into their west, and straight again revive.
But soon as once set is our little light,
Then must we sleep one ever-during night.

If all would lead their lives in love like me,
Then bloody swords and armour should not be;
No drum nor trumpet peaceful sleeps should move,

[1] based on Catullus V. Cf. Ben Jonson, "Song: To Celia (I)," p. 213 below.

10   Unless alarm came from the camp of Love.
But fools do live and waste their little light,
And seek with pain their ever-during night.

When timely death my life and fortune ends,
Let not my hearse be vexed with mourning friends,
But let all lovers, rich in triumph, come
And with sweet pastimes grace my happy tomb.
And, Lesbia, close up thou my little light,
And crown with love my ever-during night.

                           1601

I Care Not for These Ladies

I care not for these ladies that must be wooed and prayed:
Give me kind Amaryllis, the wanton country maid.
Nature Art[1] disdaineth; her beauty is her own.
Her when we court and kiss, she cries: "Forsooth, let go!"
But when we come where comfort is, she never will say no.

If I love Amaryllis, she gives me fruit and flowers;
But if we love these ladies, we must give golden showers.[2]
Give them gold that sell love, give me the nut-brown lass,
Who when we court and kiss, she cries: "Forsooth, let go!"
10   But when we come where comfort is, she never will say no.

These ladies must have pillows and beds by strangers[3] wrought.
Give me a bower of willows, of moss and leaves unbought,
And fresh Amaryllis with milk and honey fed,
Who when we court and kiss, she cries: "Forsooth, let go!"
But when we come where comfort is, she never will say no.

                           1601

[1] **Art** in the sense of something added by man to what is given by nature—a familiar theme, applied here to cosmetics
[2] **golden showers** an allusion to the golden shower descending upon Danae, who was sequestered in a tower
[3] **strangers** foreigners

When to Her Lute Corinna Sings

When to her lute Corinna sings,
Her voice revives the leaden[1] strings,
And doth in highest notes appear,
As any challenged echo clear.
But when she doth of mourning speak,
E'en with her sighs the strings do break.

[1] **leaden** heavy

And as her lute doth live or die,
Led by her passion, so must I.
For when of pleasure she doth sing,
10   My thoughts enjoy a sudden spring;
But if she doth of sorrow speak,
E'en from my heart the strings do break.

1601

Follow Your Saint

Follow your saint, follow with accents sweet;
Haste you, sad notes, fall at her flying feet.[1]
There, wrapped in cloud of sorrow, pity move,
And tell the ravisher of my soul I perish for her love.
But if she scorns my never-ceasing pain,
Then burst with sighing in her sight, and ne'er return again.

All that I sung still[2] to her praise did tend.
Still she was first, still she my songs did end.
Yet she my love and music both doth fly,
10   The music that her echo is, and beauty's sympathy.[3]
Then let my notes pursue her scornful flight;
It shall suffice that they were breathed, and died for her delight.

1601

[1] ll. 1–2   The notes of the singer's song are to
follow the object of their (and his) devotion and
fall, both musically and devotionally, before her.

[2] **still**   always
[3] ll. 9–10   His music is created by her beauty
and concordant with it.

There Is a Garden in Her Face

There is a garden in her face,
    Where roses and white lilies grow;
A heavenly paradise is that place,
    Wherein all pleasant fruits do flow.[1]
There cherries grow which none may buy,
Till "Cherry-ripe"[2] themselves do cry.

Those cherries fairly do enclose
    Of orient[3] pearl a double row,
Which when her lovely laughter shows,
10   They look like rosebuds filled with snow.
Yet them nor peer nor prince can buy,
Till "Cherry-ripe" themselves do cry.

[1] **flow**   abound
[2] **"Cherry-ripe"**   the cry of London fruit-sellers;

no one kisses them until she is ready.
[3] **orient**   gleaming

Her eyes like angels watch[4] them still;
  Her brows like bended bows do stand,
Threatening with piercing frowns to kill
  All that attempt with eye or hand
Those sacred cherries to come nigh,
Till "Cherry-ripe" themselves do cry.

[4]**watch** guard

1617

Rose-cheeked Laura, Come[1]

Rose-cheeked Laura, come;
Sing thou smoothly with thy beauty's
Silent music, either other
    Sweetly gracing.

Lovely forms do flow
From concent[2] divinely framed;
Heaven is music, and thy beauty's
    Birth is heavenly.

    These dull notes we sing
10 Discords need for helps to grace them;
Only beauty purely loving
    Knows no discord;

But still[3] moves delight,
Like clear springs renewed by flowing,
Ever perfect, ever in them-
    selves eternal.

1602

[1] an example of Campion's imitation of classical prosody. Rhyme is avoided. The meter is best described as trochaic with an extra stress at the end of the first line of each stanza.
[2] **concent** musical concord
[3] **still** continually

BEN JONSON
1572–1637

Passionate, quick-tempered, but large-hearted, Jonson was a soldier, an actor, a playwright, and a poet. His love lyrics and the songs for his many fine plays and masques for the court of James I are typically Elizabethan in their splendid use of figurative language. Through imitation, which he describes in his critical writings, he adopted the conventions of Latin love poetry, which formed his poetic personality while he was transforming them to suit his own needs.

This son of a bricklayer, in fact, established a poetic decorum in classical moderation and responsible statement that influenced younger, seventeenth-century Cavalier poets in contact with him (see next section) and created, indirectly, a poetic norm for the eighteenth century. His satirical epigrams and affecting epitaphs are classically spare and apt. His longer poems in heroic couplets reveal a weight of grave authority that is implicit in much of his other work. Although his measured rhetorical patterns are those of public pronouncement, they retain their sensitivity.

Jonson's poetry is far removed from the self-communing, private world of Donne's Metaphysical poetry that modern readers find so congenial (see next section), but it is equally genuine and great. "Her Triumph," for instance, from his "Celebration of Charis," is equal in sensuous lyricism to anything by any other English poet.

To the Reader

Pray thee take care, that tak'st my book in hand,
To read it well; that is, to understand.

1616

On Something That Walks Somewhere

At court I met it, in clothes brave enough
   To be a courtier, and looks grave enough
To seem a statesman. As I near it came,
   It made me a great face; I asked the name;
"A lord, it cried, buried in flesh and blood,
   And such from whom let no man hope least good,
For I will do none; and as little ill,
   For I will dare none." Good Lord, walk dead still.

1616

On My First Daughter

Here lies, to each her parents' ruth,
Mary, the daughter of their youth;
Yet, all heaven's gifts being heaven's due,
It makes the father less to rue.
At six months' end she parted hence
With safety of her innocence;
Whose soul heaven's Queen (whose name she bears),
In comfort of her mother's tears,
Hath placed amongst her virgin train;
10   Where, while that severed doth remain,
This grave partakes the fleshly birth;[1]
Which cover lightly, gentle earth.[2]

1616

[1] l. 11 The grave retains the body until it is reunited with the soul at the resurrection.
[2] l. 12 Cf. Martial, *Epigram* V.xxxiv.9–10:

"And let not hard clods cover her tender bones, nor be you heavy upon her, O earth; she was not so to you."

On My First Son

Farewell, thou child of my right hand, and joy;
    My sin was too much hope of thee, loved boy.
Seven years thou wert lent to me, and I thee pay,
    Exacted by thy fate, on the just day.
Oh, could I lose all father now! For why
    Will man lament the state he should envy?
To have so soon 'scaped world's and flesh's rage,
    And, if no other misery, yet age?
Rest in soft peace, and, asked, say here doth lie
10   Ben Jonson his best piece of poetry;
For whose sake, henceforth, all his vows be such,
    As what he loves may never like too much.[1]

1616

[1] l. 12   Jonson prays that he may never love in
the sense of wanting permanent possession.

Epitaph on Elizabeth, L.H.

Wouldst thou hear what man can say
    In a little? Reader, stay.
Underneath this stone doth lie
    As much beauty as could die;
Which in life did harbor give
    To more virtue than doth live.
If at all she had a fault,
    Leave it buried in this vault.
One name was Elizabeth,
10   The other let it sleep with death:
Fitter where it died to tell,
    Than that it lived at all. Farewell.[1]

1616

[1] ll. 11–12   Puzzling, but perhaps the husband
whose name she bore suffered disgrace.

To Penshurst[1]

Thou art not, Penshurst, built to envious show
    Of touch[2] or marble, nor canst boast a row
Of polished pillars, or a roof of gold;
    Thou hast no lantern[3] whereof tales are told,

[1] **Penshurst**   home of the Sidney family in Kent,
whose lord at this time was Robert Sidney,
Viscount Lisle, younger brother of Sir Philip
Sidney

[2] **touch**   black marble
[3] **lantern**   glass-sided tower on a dome or roof,
to admit light

Or stair, or courts; but stand'st an ancient pile,
    And these grudged at, art reverenced the while.
Thou joy'st in better marks, of soil, of air,
    Of wood, of water; therein thou art fair.
Thou hast thy walks for health as well as sport:
10   Thy Mount,[4] to which the dryads do resort,
Where Pan and Bacchus their high feasts have made,
    Beneath the broad beech and the chestnut shade;
That taller tree,[5] which of a nut was set
    At his great birth, where all the muses met.
There, in the writhed bark, are cut the names
    Of many a sylvan[6] taken with his flames;[7]
And thence the ruddy satyrs oft provoke
    The lighter fauns to reach thy lady's oak.[8]
Thy copse, too, named of Gamage, thou hast there,
20   That never fails to serve thee seasoned deer
When thou wouldst feast or exercise thy friends.
    The lower land, that to the river bends,
Thy sheep, thy bullocks, kine and calves do feed;
    The middle grounds thy mares and horses breed.
Each bank doth yield thee conies,[9] and the tops,
    Fertile of wood, Ashour and Sidney's copse,
To crown thy open table, doth provide
    The purpled pheasant with the speckled side;
The painted partridge[10] lies in every field,
30   And for thy mess is willing to be killed.
And if the high-swoll'n Medway[11] fail thy dish,
    Thou hast thy ponds that pay thee tribute fish:
Fat, aged carps, that run into thy net;
    And pikes, now weary their own kind to eat,
As loath the second draught or cast to stay,
    Officiously,[12] at first, themselves betray;
Bright eels, that emulate them, and leap on land
    Before the fisher, or into his hand.
Then hath thy orchard fruit, thy garden flowers,
40   Fresh as the air and new as are the hours:[13]
The early cherry, with the later plum,
    Fig, grape and quince, each in his time doth come;
The blushing apricot and woolly peach
    Hang on thy walls, that every child may reach.
And though thy walls be of the country stone,

[4]**Mount** a piece of high ground in the park
[5]**That taller tree** An oak still stands, supposed
to have been planted at Sir Philip Sidney's birth.
[6]**sylvan** wood-dweller
[7]**taken with his flames** taken with his passion
or possibly by the love that Sidney felt
[8]**lady's oak** Barbara Gamage became Robert
Sidney's wife. She is said to have fed deer
here. "My lady's oak" is said to be named

after her because the onset of labor came to her
there.
[9]**conies** rabbits
[10]**painted** ornately colorful
[11]**Medway** the nearby river, difficult to fish
[12]**Officiously** obligingly
[13]**the hours** the Horae, female divinities, one
for each season, bringing all good things

They're reared with no man's ruin, no man's groan;
There's none that dwell about them wish them down,
    But all come in, the farmer and the clown,[14]
And no one empty-handed, to salute
50   Thy lord and lady, though they have no suit.[15]
Some bring a capon, some a rural cake,
    Some nuts, some apples; some that think they make
The better cheeses, bring 'em; or else send
    By their ripe daughters, whom they would commend
This way to husbands; and whose baskets bear
    An emblem of themselves, in plum or pear.
But what can this (more than express their love)
    Add to thy free provisions, far above
The need of such? whose liberal board doth flow
60   With all that hospitality doth know!
Where comes no guest but is allowed to eat
    Without his fear, and of thy lord's own meat;
Where the same beer and bread and self-same wine
    That is his lordship's shall be also mine;
And I not fain to sit, as some this day
    At great men's tables, and yet dine away.[16]
Here no man tells[17] my cups, nor, standing by,
    A waiter, doth my gluttony envy,
But gives me what I call, and lets me eat;
70   He knows below he shall find plenty of meat;
Thy tables hoard not up for the next day.[18]
    Nor, when I take my lodging, need I pray
For fire or lights or livery:[19] all is there,
    As if thou then wert mine, or I reigned here;
There's nothing I can wish, for which I stay.
    That found King James, when, hunting late this way
With his brave son, the Prince, they saw thy fires
    Shine bright on every hearth as the desires
Of thy Penates[20] had been set on flame
80   To entertain them; or the country came
With all their zeal to warm their welcome here.
    What (great, I will not say, but) sudden cheer
Didst thou then make 'em! and what praise was heaped
    On thy good lady then! who therein reaped

[14]**clown** countryman
[15]**suit** plea, request
[16]**dine away** receiving poorer food than at the head table
[17]**tells** counts
[18]ll. 70–71 With this and preceding, cf. Martial, *Epigram* III.lviii.33–44: "Nor does the country visitor come empty-handed: that one brings pale honey in its comb, and a pyramid of cheese from Sassina's woodland; that one offers sleepy dormice; this one the bleating offspring of a shaggy mother; another capons debarred from love. And the strapping daughters of honest farmers offer in a wicker basket their mothers' gifts. When work is done, a cheerful neighbor is asked to dine; no niggard table reserves a feast for the morrow; all take the meal, and the full-fed attendant need not envy the well-drunken guest."
[19]**livery** provisions
[20]**Penates** household gods

The just reward of her high housewifery:
     To have her linen, plate, and all things nigh
When she was far; and not a room but dressed
     As if it had expected such a guest!
These, Penshurst, are thy praise, and yet not all.
90   Thy lady's noble, fruitful, chaste withal;
His children thy great lord may call his own,
     A fortune in this age but rarely known.
They are and have been taught religion; thence
     Their gentler spirits have sucked innocence.
Each morn and even they are taught to pray
     With the whole household, and may every day
Read in their virtuous parents' noble parts
     The mysteries[21] of manners, arms, and arts.
Now, Penshurst, they that will proportion[22] thee
100   With other edifices, when they see
Those proud, ambitious heaps, and nothing else,
     May say, their lords have built, but thy lord dwells.

                                        1616

[21]**mysteries** skills
[22]**proportion** compare

Song: To Celia (I)[1]

Come, my Celia, let us prove,[2]
While we may, the sports of love;
Time will not be ours for ever;
He at length our good will sever.
Spend not then his gifts in vain.
Suns that set may rise again,
But if once we lose this light,
'Tis with us perpetual night.
Why should we defer our joys?
10 Fame and rumour are but toys.
Cannot we delude the eyes
Of a few poor household spies?
Or his easier ears beguile,
So removed by our wile?
'Tis no sin love's fruit to steal,
But the sweet theft to reveal:
To be taken, to be seen,
These have crimes accounted been.

                                        1606

[1] appears originally in Jonson's play *Volpone*. The
old but virile title-character and villain sings to

Celia, whose husband has been tricked away.
[2] **prove** experience

Song: To Celia (II)[1]

Drink to me only with thine eyes,
    And I will pledge with mine;
Or leave a kiss but in the cup,
    And I'll not look for wine.
The thirst that from the soul doth rise
    Doth ask a drink divine;
But might I of Jove's nectar sup,
    I would not change for thine.
I sent thee late a rosy wreath,
10   Not so much honouring thee
As giving it a hope that there
    It could not withered be.
But thou thereon didst only breathe,
    And sent'st it back to me;
Since when it grows, and smells, I swear,
    Not of itself, but thee.

1616

[1] As occurs repeatedly in Jonson's poetry, this lyric is lovingly developed from a classical model (passages from the *Epistles* of Philostratus), in accordance with Jonson's idea of right imitation.

From A Celebration of Charis: 2.iv

Her Triumph[1]

See the chariot at hand here of Love,
    Wherein my lady rideth!
Each that draws is a swan or a dove,[2]
    And well the car Love guideth.
As she goes, all hearts do duty
        Unto her beauty;
And enamoured, do wish, so they might
        But enjoy such a sight,
That they still were to run by her side,
10   Through swords, through seas, whither she would ride.

Do but look on her eyes, they do light
    All that Love's world compriseth!
Do but look on her hair, it is bright
    As Love's star[3] when it riseth!
Do but mark, her forehead's smoother
        Than words that soothe her!
And from her arched brows, such a grace
        Sheds itself through the face,
As alone there triumphs to the life
20   All the gain, all the good, of the elements' strife.

[1] **Triumph** victory procession
[2] **dove** a bird sacred to Venus
[3] **Love's star** the planet Venus

Have you seen but a bright lily grow,
　　Before rude hands have touched it?
Have you marked but the fall o' the snow,
　　Before the soil hath smutched it?
Have you felt the wool o' the beaver?
　　　　Or swan's down ever?
Or have smelled o' the bud o' the briar?
　　　　Or the nard[4] i' the fire?
Or have tasted the bag o' the bee?
30　　O so white! O so soft! O so sweet is she!

1640

[4] **nard**　an aromatic ointment

To the Memory of My Beloved, the Author, Mr. William Shakespeare, and What He Hath Left Us[1]

To draw no envy, Shakespeare, on thy name,
　　Am I thus ample[2] to thy book and fame;
While I confess thy writings to be such
　　As neither man nor muse can praise too much:
'Tis true, and all men's suffrage.[3] But these ways
　　Were not the paths I meant unto thy praise:
For silliest ignorance on these may light,
　　Which, when it sounds at best, but echoes right;
Or blind affection,[4] which doth ne'er advance
10　　The truth, but gropes, and urgeth all by chance;
Or crafty malice might pretend this praise,
　　And think to ruin where it seemed to raise.
These are as some infamous bawd or whore
　　Should praise a matron: what could hurt her more?
But thou art proof against them, and indeed
　　Above the ill fortune of them, or the need.
I therefore will begin. Soul of the age!
　　The applause, delight, the wonder of our stage!
My Shakespeare, rise: I will not lodge thee by
20　　Chaucer or Spenser, or bid Beaumont lie
A little further, to make thee a room;[5]
　　Thou art a monument without a tomb,
And art alive still while thy book doth live,
　　And we have wits to read, and praise to give.

[1] published in the first complete edition of Shakespeare's plays, 1623
[2] **ample** liberal
[3] **suffrage** consensus
[4] **affection** feeling
[5] **I will not . . . a room** implicit criticism of another elegy on Shakespeare (by William Basse), which had done what Jonson refuses to do. Chaucer, Spenser, and Beaumont were buried in Westminster Abbey, Shakespeare in Stratford.

That I not mix thee so, my brain excuses:
    I mean with great, but disproportioned,[6] muses;
For if I thought my judgement were of years[7]
    I should commit thee surely with thy peers:
And tell how far thou didst our Lyly outshine,
30   Or sporting Kyd, or Marlowe's mighty line.[8]
And though thou hadst small Latin, and less Greek,
    From thence to honour thee I would not seek
For names, but call forth thundering Aeschylus,
    Euripides, and Sophocles to us,
Pacuvius, Accius, him[9] of Cordova dead,
    To life again, to hear thy buskin[10] tread
And shake a stage; or, when thy socks were on,
    Leave thee alone for the comparison
Of all that insolent Greece or haughty Rome
40   Sent forth, or since did from their ashes come.
Triumph, my Britain, thou hast one to show
    To whom all scenes[11] of Europe homage owe.
He was not of an age, but for all time!
    And all the muses still were in their prime
When like Apollo he came forth to warm
    Our ears, or like a Mercury to charm![12]
Nature herself was proud of his designs,
    And joyed to wear the dressing of his lines,
Which were so richly spun and woven so fit
50   As, since, she will vouchsafe no other wit.
The merry Greek, tart Aristophanes,
    Neat Terence, witty Plautus, now not please,[13]
But antiquated and deserted lie
    As they were not of nature's family.
Yet must I not give nature all: thy art,[14]
    My gentle Shakespeare, must enjoy a part.
For though the poet's matter nature be,
    His art doth give the fashion. And that he
Who casts to write a living line must sweat
60   (Such as thine are) and strike the second heat
Upon the muses' anvil: turn the same
    (And himself with it) that he thinks to frame;
Or for the laurel[15] he may gain a scorn:
    For a good poet's made, as well as born;
And such wert thou. Look how the father's face

[6]**disproportioned**   not fitly to be compared with Shakespeare
[7]**of years**   historically mature, many years later
[8]ll. 29–30   **[John] Lyly . . . [Thomas] Kyd** Elizabethan dramatists; **sporting**   a play on the exuberance of a young goat, a kid. See headnote on Marlowe.
[9]**him**   Seneca. He and those preceding were classical tragedians.
[10]**buskin**   boot worn by ancient tragic actor. The comic actor wore the sock (l. 37).
[11]**scenes**   stages
[12]ll. 45–46   Apollo and Mercury were gods of poetry and eloquence.
[13]ll. 51–52   Aristophanes, Terence, and Plautus were writers of classicial comedy. "Merry Greek" refers to Aristophanes.
[14]l. 55   The relation of nature and art was a standard theme.
[15]**laurel**   as a wreath, traditional prize of poetry

Lives in his issue: even so, the race
Of Shakespeare's mind and manners brightly shines
In his well-turned and true-filed lines:
In each of which he seems to shake a lance,[16]
70   As brandished at the eyes of ignorance.
Sweet swan[17] of Avon! What a sight it were
    To see thee in our waters yet appear,
And make those flights upon the banks of Thames
    That so did take Eliza, and our James![18]
But stay, I see thee in the hemisphere
    Advanced, and made a constellation there![19]
Shine forth, thou star of poets, and with rage[20]
    Or influence[21] chide or cheer the drooping stage;
Which, since thy flight from hence, hath mourned like night,
80   And despairs day, but for thy volume's light.

1623

[16]**shake a lance** play on "Shakespeare," as in
l. 37
[17]**swan** a bird associated with Apollo and poetry
[18]**Eliza . . . James** Elizabeth I, James I, at
whose courts some of Shakespeare's plays were
given

[19]**I see thee . . . there** The gods thus honored
humans.
[20]**rage** poetic or prophetic rapture
[21]**influence** astrological influence

Hymn to Cynthia[1]

Queen and huntress, chaste and fair,
Now the sun is laid to sleep,
Seated in thy silver chair,
State in wonted manner keep:
    Hesperus[2] entreats thy light,
    Goddess excellently bright.

Earth, let not thy envious shade
Dare itself to interpose;
Cynthia's shining orb was made
10   Heaven to clear,[3] when day did close:
    Bless us then with wished sight,
    Goddess excellently bright.

Lay thy bow of pearl apart,
And thy crystal-shining quiver;
Give unto the flying hart
Space to breathe, how short soever:
    Thou that mak'st a day of night,
    Goddess excellently bright.

1600

[1] from Jonson's play *Cynthia's Revels*. Cynthia is
Diana, goddess of the moon, chastity, and hunt-
ing. She was constantly associated, as here, with
Elizabeth I.
[2] **Hesperus** Venus as an evening star
[3] **clear** illuminate

Clerimont's Song[1]

Still[2] to be neat, still to be dressed,
As you were going to a feast;
Still to be powdered, still perfumed:
Lady, it is to be presumed,
Though art's hid causes are not found,
All is not sweet, all is not sound.

Give me a look, give me a face,
That makes simplicity a grace;
Robes loosely flowing, hair as free:
10   Such sweet neglect more taketh me
Than all the adulteries of art:
They strike mine eyes, but not my heart.

1609

[1] from Jonson's play *The Silent Woman*
[2] **Still** continually

The Seventeenth Century

JOHN DONNE
1572–1631

John Donne's poetry is often passionately and stylistically knotty—the work of an adult, sophisticated, and frank intelligence. We have the sense of a dazzling mind piercing to the heart of love, suffering, religious faith, and death, often by uncovering the falsity or fatuity of what is usually said or sung about them. The honesty is convincing. The speakers in his lyrics seldom succumb to what is a danger in such crisis-laden material: indulgent self-dramatizing. His poetry comes to us most frequently as introspective probing at and questioning of the character of experience, in contrast to the "public voice" of most Jonsonian poetry.

The terms found for Donne's most striking expressive means are "Metaphysical wit" and the "Metaphysical conceit". The mental reach of his metaphorical patterns (conceits) often seems to escape from the physical world of many Petrarchan comparisons (fire, ice, roses, ivory, etc.) into a nonphysical one of ideas. This explains the initial choice of the word "Metaphysical" ("beyond" or "after the physical"): these comparisons depend sometimes on abstruse and learned data from scholastic philosophy, alchemy, geography, or astronomy. For instance, when the speaker in "A Nocturnal upon St. Lucy's Day" (the day being the winter solstice, when all seasonal life seems at its lowest point) mourns the death of his beloved, he does not say simply that his life is deprived of meaning. In the second stanza he borrows an idea from alchemy: the alchemist by his art tried to distill from material objects in nature the final essence, or quintessence, of which only the heavenly bodies were supposed to be purely composed. The speaker here turns this idea around so as to say that love has made him a quintessence derived not from something but from nothing, and the conceit is elaborated through the rest of the poem. The vast mental leap entailed in bringing together so unexpectedly the data of disparate experiences—alchemy and human loss here, elsewhere the drawing-compass and sexual love, physical rape and God's conquest of the human soul—is what Donne's contemporaries (but not the eighteenth century) thought of as "wit." Another term often used in discussing him today—*discordia concors* (the discordant made into a harmony)—refers to the same combinatory metaphorical power.

The other qualities of his poetry most often singled out—its metrical roughness, or radical sacrifice of standard alternating patterns of poetic feet, and its unexpected enjambments—are always intentional, frequently in order to project a sense of passionately genuine exclamation, although this apparent disdain for the mellifluous also bespeaks the intellectual straightforwardness of his poetic voice. Reading all the stanzas of "A Nocturnal," for instance, allows us to intuit a regular metrical pattern behind it that is constantly being violated. This regular pattern behind a spoken reading is simply iambic pentameter in all but the third, fourth, and fifth lines of each stanza. The theoretical pattern in the third and fourth lines is iambic tetrameter, in the fifth line iambic trimeter. But in the stanza mentioned above, straight on from the stark imperative of the first line an urgent speaking voice often overturns that pattern more drastically than any other contemporary poet ever did unless he was an imitator of Donne. The clash is part of the music.

The singularity of that voice and the originality of Donne's Metaphysical wit concentrated much critical discussion on his poetry in the nineteenth and twentieth centuries. T.S. Eliot and others have seen him as an important forerunner because of his colloquial immediacy, worldliness, and concrete, often paradoxical, imagery. For a time he was seen as having made an absolute break with the English poetic past, as though his fusion of thought and feeling were utterly new. In this view the supposed loss of that fusion in later centuries—"the dissociation of sensibility" in Eliot's phrase—had led to a poetic crisis from which only a new kind of modern poetry could save us. For most critics Donne's separation from his past and future no longer seems so drastic, although he remains one of the greatest and most intriguing poets in the English tradition. Similarly the vogue that Donne created for Metaphysical expression and "strong lines" no longer seems to account significantly for certain other seventeenth-century poets of serious commitment and intellectually striking expression—Herbert and Vaughan, for instance—who used sometimes to be thought of as constituting a school with Donne.

Born a Catholic in a Protestant, Anglican country, Donne suffered like the rest of his family from a degree of repression. He could not, for instance, take a degree from either Oxford or Cambridge after he had studied there. He studied further in the Inns of Court in London (where he is supposed to have led an adventurous amatory life), traveled abroad, shared in two naval expeditions, and finally gained in Sir Thomas Egerton a powerful patron. A passion that does not enter his poetry is his strong worldly ambition, but he sacrificed that passion and lost a patron by his secret marriage to Egerton's niece, Ann More. He escaped from nearly a decade of financial stringency only after his entirely sincere conversion to Anglicanism, which finally brought him, through the power of his sermons as an Anglican divine, to the deanship of St. Paul's in London. All his love lyrics and most of his religious poetry were written before his ordination in 1615. (His beloved wife died in 1617). His religious prose is as famous, and just as passionately immediate, as his poetry. The notorious contrast between the writer of licentious lyrics and the celebrated clergyman speaks for other dramatic if not theatrical antitheses in his life and poetry.

The Good-Morrow

I wonder, by my troth, what thou and I
Did, till we loved? were we not weaned till then?
But sucked on country pleasures,[1] childishly?
Or snorted[2] we in the Seven Sleepers' den?
'Twas so; but[3] this, all pleasures fancies be.
If ever any beauty I did see,
Which I desired, and got, 'twas but a dream of thee.

And now good-morrow to our waking souls,
Which watch not one another out of fear;
10   For love, all love of other sights controls,
And makes one little room an everywhere.
Let sea-discoverers to new worlds have gone,
Let maps[4] to others, worlds on worlds have shown,
Let us possess our world, each hath one, and is one.

[1] **country pleasures** rustic pleasures, perhaps with sexual overtone, as in "country matters"
[2] **snorted** snored. According to legend, seven Christians of Ephesus, under the persecution of Decius (A.D. 250), were walled up in a cave and slept until the fifth century.
[3] **but** except for
[4] **maps** maps of the heavens

My face in thine eye, thine in mine appears,
And true plain hearts do in the faces rest;
Where can we find two better hemispheres,[5]
Without sharp north, without declining west?
Whatever dies was not mixed equally;[6]
20　If our two loves be one, or, thou and I
Love so alike that none do slacken, none can die.

　　　　　　　　　　　　　　　　　　1633

[5] **hemispheres**　visible parts of the eyeballs
[6] l. 19　Generation and corruption were thought to arise from mixing contraries. The absence of contraries would produce a constant state.

Song: Go and Catch a Falling Star

Go and catch a falling star,
　Get with child a mandrake root,[1]
Tell me where all past years are,
　Or who cleft the Devil's foot,
Teach me to hear mermaids singing,
　Or to keep off envy's stinging,
　　　And find
　　　What wind
Serves to advance an honest mind.

10　If thou be'st born to strange sights,
　Things invisible to see,
Ride ten thousand days and nights,
　Till age snow white hairs on thee:
Thou, when thou return'st, wilt tell me
　All strange wonders that befell thee,
　　　And swear
　　　Nowhere
Lives a woman true, and fair.

If thou findst one, let me know,
20　Such a pilgrimage were sweet.
Yet do not; I would not go,
　Though at next door we might meet;
Though she were true when you met her,
　And last till you write your letter,
　　　Yet she
　　　Will be
False, ere I come, to two, or three.

　　　　　　　　　　　　　　　1630, 1633

[1] **mandrake root**　In this list of impossibilities (ll. 1–9) the reader is challenged to impregnate this forked root, thought to have human shape. It was also thought to be an aphrodisiac.

/

The Sun Rising

    Busy old fool, unruly sun,
    Why dost thou thus,
Through windows and through curtains, call on us?
Must to thy motions lovers' seasons run?
    Saucy pedantic wretch, go chide
    Late schoolboys, and sour prentices;[1]
Go tell court-huntsmen that the King will ride,[2]
Call country ants to harvest offices;[3]
Love, all alike, no season knows, nor clime,
10 Nor hours, days, months, which are the rags of time.[4]

    Thy beams, so reverend and strong
    Why shouldst thou think?
I could eclipse and cloud them with a wink,
But that I would not lose her sight so long:
    If her eyes have not blinded thine,
    Look, and tomorrow late, tell me
Whether both the Indias of spice and mine[5]
Be where thou leftst them, or lie here with me.
Ask for those kings whom thou saw'st yesterday,
20 And thou shalt hear, All here in one bed lay.

    She's all states, and all princes, I,
    Nothing else is.
Princes do but play us;[6] compared to this,
All honor's mimic, all wealth alchemy.[7]
    Thou, sun, art half as happy as we,[8]
    In that the world's contracted thus;
Thine age asks[9] ease, and since thy duties be
To warm the world, that's done in warming us.
Shine here to us, and thou art everywhere;
30 This bed thy center is, these walls thy sphere.[10]

            1633

[1]**prentices** apprentices
[2]l. 7 King James I forced his courtiers to rise early in order to hunt.
[3]**offices** duties
[4]l. 10 I.e., time is torn into fragments; but love is like eternity, unified and whole.
[5]l. 17 the East Indies for spices, the West Indies for gold
[6]**Princes do but play us** We are the models for kings' behaviour.
[7]**all wealth alchemy** fake gold, produced by alchemy
[8]l. 25 The sun can shine on only half the globe at one time.
[9]**asks** requires
[10]l. 30 The earth was thought to lie at the center of the universe, and the sun to revolve around it.

The Canonization

For God's sake hold your tongue, and let me love,
   Or chide my palsy, or my gout,
My five gray hairs, or ruined fortune flout,
   With wealth your state, your mind with arts improve,
      Take you a course, get you a place,[1]
      Observe his honor, or his grace,
And the King's real, or his stamped face
   Contèmplate;[2] what you will, approve,[3]
   So you will let me love.

10   Alas, alas, who's injured by my love?
   What merchant's ships have my sighs drowned?
Who says my tears have overflowed his ground?
   When did my colds a forward spring remove?
      When did the heats which my veins fill
      Add one more to the plaguy bill?[4]
Soldiers find wars, and lawyers find out still
   Litigious men, which quarrels move,
   Though she and I do love.

Call us what you will, we are made such by love;
20   Call her one, me another fly;[5]
We're tapers[6] too, and at our own cost die,
   And we in us find the Eagle and the dove.[7]
      The phoenix riddle hath more wit
      By us: we two being one, are it.[8]
So, to one neutral thing both sexes fit.
   We die and rise the same, and prove
   Mysterious by this love.[9]

We can die by it, if not live by love,
   And if unfit for tombs or hearse
30   Our legend[10] be, it will be fit for verse;
   And if no piece of chronicle[11] we prove,
      We'll build in sonnets pretty rooms,[12]
      As well a well-wrought urn becomes
The greatest ashes, as half-acre tombs,
   And by these hymns, all shall approve
   Us *canonized* for Love.

[1] l. 5 make a career, get a position
[2] **Observe . . . Contèmplate** Worship anything you like—a lord, a bishop, or the king, or even money (with the king's face stamped on it).
[3] **What . . . approve** Try whatever you like.
[4] **plaguy bill** list of plague victims
[5] **fly** insect attracted and killed by flame
[6] **tapers** candles
[7] **Eagle and the dove** emblems of masculine strength and feminine gentleness

[8] ll. 23–24 The mythical phoenix was a unique bird that destroyed itself by fire, and then rose anew from the ashes. Being neither male nor female, it was a self-sufficient, "neutral" being.
[9] l. 27 comprehensible only to faith; like the mysteries of religion
[10] **legend** written record of a saint's life
[11] **chronicle** prose record of major historical events
[12] **rooms** "Room" in Italian is *stanza*.

And thus invoke us: "You, whom reverend love
　　Made one another's hermitage;
　　You, to whom love was peace, that now is rage;[13]
40　　　Who did the whole world's soul extract, and drove
　　　　Into the glasses of your eyes[14]
　　　　(So made such mirrors, and such spies,
　　That they did all to you epitomize)—
　　　Countries, towns, courts: beg from above
　　　A pattern of your love!"

1633

[13]l. 39　The canonized lovers found, as in heavenly love, a peaceful haven; other love is fruitless passion.
[14]ll. 40–41　Like an alchemical transformation, the lovers distilled all the world's significance into each other's reflections in their own eyes, imagined as glass vessels and mirrors.

Twickenham Garden[1]

Blasted with sighs, and surrounded with tears,
　　Hither I come to seek the spring,[2]
　　And at mine eyes, and at mine ears,
　　Receive such balms as else cure everything;
　　But oh, self-traitor, I do bring
　　The spider[3] love, which transubstantiates all,
　　　And can convert manna[4] to gall;
　　And that this place may thoroughly be thought
　　　True Paradise, I have the serpent[5] brought.

10　'Twere wholesomer for me, that winter did
　　　Benight the glory of this place,
　　　And that a grave frost did forbid
　　These trees to laugh, and mock me to my face;
　　　But that I may not this disgrace
　　Endure, nor leave this garden, Love, let me
　　　Some senseless piece of this place be;[6]
　　Make me a mandrake,[7] so I may groan here,
　　　Or a stone fountain weeping out my year.

　　Hither with crystal vials, lovers, come,
20　　And take my tears, which are love's wine,
　　　And try your mistress' tears at home,

[1] In a letter to a patron, Lady Bedford, Donne says that she showed him certain of her verses here, but this title fails to appear in a number of manuscript copies of the poem.
[2] ll. 1–2　The contrast between the joy of spring and misery of the lover is traditional.
[3] spider　Spiders were thought to turn everything they touched into filth and poison.
[4] manna　food sent from heaven to the Israelites in the desert
[5] serpent　The serpent is associated with envy as well as with the Fall.
[6] ll. 14–16　So that I won't have to feel the scorn of the garden, or leave it (i.e., stop loving), let me be a non-feeling object here.
[7] mandrake　a plant whose root was said to have human shape and to scream when uprooted.

For all are false, that taste not just like mine;
   Alas, hearts do not in eyes shine,
Nor can you more judge woman's thoughts by tears,
   Than by her shadow, what she wears.
O perverse sex, where none is true but she,
   Who's therefore true, because her truth kills me.

1633

A Valediction: Of Weeping[1]

        Let me pour forth
My tears before thy face, whilst I stay here,
For thy face coins them, and thy stamp they bear,[2]
And by this mintage they are something worth,
        For thus they be
        Pregnant of thee;
Fruits of much grief they are, emblems of more;
When a tear falls, that thou falls which it bore,
So thou and I are nothing then, when on a diverse shore.[3]

10   On a round ball
A workman that hath copies by, can lay
An Europe, Afric, and an Asia,
And quickly make that, which was nothing, All;[4]
        So doth each tear
        Which thee doth wear,[5]
A globe, yea world, by that impression grow,
Till thy tears mixed with mine do overflow
This world, by waters sent from thee, my heaven dissolved so.

        O more than Moon,
20 Draw not up seas to drown me in thy sphere,[6]
Weep me not dead, in thine arms, but forbear
To teach the sea what it may do too soon;
        Let not the wind
        Example find
To do me more harm than it purposeth;
Since thou and I sigh one another's breath,
Whoe'er sighs most is cruellest, and hastes the other's death.[7]

1633

---

[1] **Valediction** farewell
[2] l. 3 The reflection of your face in a tear is like the king's face on a coin.
[3] **that thou . . . shore** As your image ("that thou") disappears when the tear has struck the ground, so we are dead to each other when we are in different parts of the world.
[4] ll. 10–13 The artisan glues map-sections on a formerly featureless globe, making the whole world from "nothing."

[5] ll. 14–15 each tear, which wears your image
[6] ll. 19–20 You are superior to the moon, which can draw the tides, so do not raise a tide (of tears) that will drown me.
[7] ll. 26–27 The loss of breath, as the principle of vitality and life, was imagined to hasten death; because the lovers breathe as one, the sighs of each endanger the other.

Love's Alchemy

Some that have deeper digged love's mine than I,
Say, where his centric happiness doth lie:
    I have loved, and got, and told,
But should I love, get, tell, till I were old,
I should not find that hidden mystery;
        Oh, 'tis imposture all:
And as no chemic yet the elixir got
        But glorifies his pregnant pot,
        If by the way to him befall
10   Some odoriferous thing, or medicinal,[1]
        So, lovers dream a rich and long delight,
        But get a winter-seeming[2] summer's night.

Our ease, our thrift, our honor, and our day,
Shall we for this vain bubble's shadow pay?
    Ends love in this, that my man[3]
Can be as happy as I can, if he can
Endure the short scorn of a bridegroom's play?
        That loving wretch that swears
        'Tis not the bodies marry, but the minds,
20   Which he in her angelic finds,[4]
        Would swear as justly that he hears,
In that day's rude hoarse minstrelsy, the spheres.[5]
        Hope not for mind in women; at their best
        Sweetness and wit, they're but *Mummy*, possessed.[6]

                                                1633

[1] ll. 7–10 The alchemist never finds the philosopher's stone, but praises his equipment if it accidentally produces some perfume or medicine.
[2] **winter-seeming** cold and short
[3] **man** servant
[4] ll. 18–20 that love-sick fellow who claims that his love is spiritual, not carnal, and that he adores his lover for her spirituality alone
[5] ll. 21–22 would also swear that in the crude music of a contemporary bridal day he hears the ineffable music of the heavens
[6] **at their . . . possessed** Sweet and witty at their best, women turn out to be nothing but well-preserved flesh inhabited by demons, once they are yours ("possessed").

The Flea

Mark but this flea, and mark in this
How little that which thou deny'st me is;
Me it sucked first, and now sucks thee,
And in this flea our two bloods mingled be;
Thou know'st that this cannot be said
A sin, nor shame, nor loss of maidenhead,
        Yet this enjoys before it woo,
        And pampered swells with one blood made of two,
        And this, alas, is more than we would do.[1]

[1] ll. 8–9 Coition was thought to entail mingling blood.

10　Oh stay, three lives in one flea spare,
　　Where we almost, yea more than married are.
　　This flea is you and I, and this
　　Our marriage bed, and marriage temple is;
　　Though parents grudge, and you, we're met
　　And cloistered in these living walls of jet.
　　　　Though use[2] make you apt to kill me,
　　　　Let not to that, self-murder added be,
　　　　And sacrilege, three sins in killing three.

　　Cruel and sudden, hast thou since
20　Purpled thy nail in blood of innocence?
　　Wherein could this flea guilty be,
　　Except in that drop which it sucked from thee?
　　Yet thou triumph'st, and say'st that thou
　　Find'st not thyself, nor me, the weaker now;
　　　　'Tis true; then learn how false, fears be;
　　　　Just so much honor, when thou yield'st to me,
　　　　Will waste, as this flea's death took life from thee.

[2] **use**　habit　　　　　　　　　　　　　　　　　　　　1633

A Nocturnal upon St. Lucy's Day, Being the Shortest Day

　　'Tis the year's midnight, and it is the day's,
　　Lucy's, who scarce seven hours herself unmasks;[1]
　　　　The sun is spent, and now his flasks[2]
　　　　Send forth light squibs, no constant rays;
　　　　　　The world's whole sap is sunk;
　　The general balm the hydroptic earth hath drunk,[3]
　　Whither, as to the bed's-feet, life is shrunk,
　　Dead and interred; yet all these seem to laugh,
　　Compared with me, who am their epitaph.

10　Study me then, you who shall lovers be
　　At the next world, that is, at the next spring:
　　　　For I am every dead thing,
　　　　In whom love wrought new alchemy.
　　　　　　For his art did express[4]
　　A quintessence even from nothingness,
　　From dull privations, and lean emptiness;
　　He ruined me, and I am re-begot
　　Of absence, darkness, death: things which are not.

[1] ll. 1–2　December 13, St. Lucy's Day, was held to be (and sometimes was) the shortest day in the older Julian calendar. In London the sun appeared for only seven or eight hours.
[2] Flasks held mixtures for fireworks ("squibs"); here, they signify the stars (thought to store up light from the sun), which give only flashes of light.
[3] l. 6　Hydroptic patients suffer from raging thirst: the earth has drunk up the source of all vitality.
[4] **express**　squeeze out, extract (an alchemical term)

All others, from all things, draw all that's good,
20 Life, soul, form, spirit, whence they being have;
   I, by love's limbeck,[5] am the grave
   Of all that's nothing. Oft a flood
     Have we two wept, and so
Drowned the whole world, us two; oft did we grow
To be two chaoses, when we did show
Care to aught else; and often absences
Withdrew our souls, and made us carcasses.

But I am by her death (which word wrongs her)
Of the first nothing the elixir grown;[6]
30 Were I a man, that I were one
   I needs must know; I should prefer,
     If I were any beast,
Some ends, some means; yea plants, yea stones detest,
And love; all, all some properties invest;
If I an ordinary nothing were,
As shadow, a light and body must be here.[7]

But I am none; nor will my Sun renew.
You lovers, for whose sake the lesser sun
   At this time to the Goat is run
40   To fetch new lust,[8] and give it you,
     Enjoy your summer all;
Since she enjoys her long night's festival,
Let me prepare towards her, and let me call
This hour her Vigil, and her Eve, since this
Both the year's, and the day's deep midnight is.

1633

---

[5] **limbeck** a still, or alembic
[6] l. 29 Whereas alchemists tried to produce a life-prolonging elixir, the speaker claims to have become the elixir of the non-being that precedes life.
[7] ll. 30–37 In the chain of being, man is conscious of his role, animals and plants show motives of desire and repulsion by movement or direction of growth, and stones love to fall down to their proper, earthly sphere and are raised only by external force. Ordinary absence is caused by a countervailing presence. The lover's nothingness is absolute.
[8] **sun . . . lust** The sun is about to enter the sign of Capricorn, the goat, which is also associated with lust.

The Apparition

When by thy scorn, O murd'ress, I am dead,
   And that thou thinkst thee free
From all solicitation from me,
Then shall my ghost come to thy bed,
And thee, fained vestal,[1] in worse arms shall see;

---

[1] **fained vestal** only pretending to be as chaste as the Roman vestal virgins who guarded the sacred flame

Then thy sick taper will begin to wink,[2]
And he, whose thou art then, being tired before,
Will, if thou stir, or pinch to wake him, think
    Thou call'st for more,
10   And in false sleep will from thee shrink,
And then, poor aspen[3] wretch, neglected thou
Bathed in a cold quicksilver sweat wilt lie,
    A verier ghost than I;
What I will say, I will not tell thee now,
Lest that preserve thee; and since my love is spent,
I had rather thou shouldst painfully repent,
Than by my threat'nings rest still innocent.

1633

[2] l. 5 Her candle, under ghostly influence, will
begin to go out.

[3] **aspen** quivering, like this tree's leaves

A Valediction: Forbidding Mourning

As virtuous men pass mildly away,
    And whisper to their souls to go,
Whilst some of their sad friends do say
    The breath goes now, and some say no,

So let us melt, and make no noise,
    No tear-floods, nor sigh-tempests move;
'Twere profanation of our joys
    To tell the laity our love.

Moving of the earth[1] brings harms and fears,
10   Men reckon what it did and meant;
But trepidation of the spheres,[2]
    Though greater far, is innocent.[3]

Dull sublunary[4] lovers' love
    (Whose soul is sense) cannot admit
Absence, because it doth remove
    Those things which elemented it.[5]

But we, by a love so much refined
    That our selves know not what it is,
Inter-assured of the mind.
20   Care less, eyes, lips and hands to miss.

[1] **Moving of the earth** earthquakes
[2] **trepidation of the spheres** oscillation of the great, concentric spheres carrying the planets and fixed stars, according to the Ptolemaic system
[3] **innocent** harmless
[4] **sublunary** beneath the moon, whose sphere was closest to earth. The sublunary region was the one of physical corruption and change; the heavenly spheres were incorruptible.
[5] ll. 13–16 This love is composed of, and depends upon, the sublunary, sensuous, physical four elements. Without physical contact it ceases to exist.

Our two souls therefore, which are one,
　Though I must go, endure not yet
A breach, but an expansion,
　Like gold to airy thinness beat.

If they be two, they are two so
　As stiff twin compasses are two:
Thy soul, the fixed foot, makes no show
　To move, but doth, if the other do;

And though it in the center sit,
30　Yet when the other far doth roam,
It leans, and hearkens after it,
　And grows erect, as that comes home.

Such wilt thou be to me, who must,
　Like the other foot, obliquely run;
Thy firmness makes my circle just,
　And makes me end where I begun.

1633

The Ecstasy

Where, like a pillow on a bed,
　A pregnant bank swelled up, to rest
The violet's reclining head,
　Sat we two, one another's best.

Our hands were firmly cemented
　With a fast[1] balm, which thence did spring;
Our eye-beams twisted, and did thread
　Our eyes, upon one double string;[2]

So to intergraft our hands, as yet
10　Was all the means to make us one,
And pictures on our eyes to get[3]
　Was all our propagation.

As, 'twixt two equal armies, Fate
　Suspends uncertain victory,
Our souls (which to advance their state[4]
　Were gone out) hung 'twixt her and me.

And whilst our souls negotiate there,
　We like sepulchral statues lay;

[1]**fast** steadfast
[2]ll. 7–8 Eyes were thought to see by sending out beams.
[3]ll. 11–12 **get** beget. Lovers were said pun-ningly to look like babies because a small reflection of one appeared on the other's "pupil."
[4]**state** dignity

All day, the same our postures were,
20   And we said nothing, all the day.

If any, so by love refined
        That he souls' language understood,
And by good love were grown all mind,
        Within convenient distance stood,

He (though he knew not which soul spake,
        Because both meant, both spake the same)
Might thence a new concoction[5] take,
        And part far purer than he came.

This ecstasy[6] doth unperplex,
30   We said, and tell us what we love;
We see by this it was not sex;
        We see we saw not what did move:[7]

But as all several[8] souls contain
        Mixture of things, they know not what,
Love these mixed souls doth mix again,
        And makes both one, each this and that.[9]

A single violet transplant,
        The strength, the color, and the size,
(All which before was poor, and scant)
40   Redoubles still, and multiplies.

When love, with one another so
        Interinanimates two souls,
That abler soul, which thence doth flow,
        Defects of loneliness controls.[10]

We then, who are this new soul, know
        Of what we are composed, and made,
For the atomies[11] of which we grow
        Are souls, whom no change can invade.

But O, alas, so long, so far
50   Our bodies why do we forbear?
They're ours, though they're not we, we are
        The intelligences, they the sphere.[12]

---

[5]**concoction**   purification (as of metals by heat)
[6]**ecstasy**   freeing of soul from body in order to see love directly, apart from bodily senses
[7]**move**   impel us
[8]**several**   individual
[9]ll. 33–36   Since each soul contains an equal part of its own and the other's soul, the two souls are the same, hence one.
[10]l. 44   defects caused by the lack of a necessary ingredient in the separate soul
[11]**atomies**   building-blocks of matter
[12]ll. 51–52   Like the heavenly, crystalline spheres, each body is animated by a spiritual "intelligence."

We owe them thanks because they thus
    Did us to us at first convey,
Yielded their forces, sense, to us,
    Nor are dross to us, but allay.[13]

On man heaven's influence works not so,
    But that it first imprints the air;
So soul into the soul may flow,
60   Though it to body first repair.[14]

As our blood labors to beget
    Spirits as like souls as it can,
Because such fingers need to knit
    That subtle knot which makes us man:[15]

So much pure lovers' souls descend
    To affections, and to faculties,
That sense may reach and apprehend,
    Else a great Prince in prison lies.

To our bodies turn we then, that so
70   Weak men on love revealed may look;
Love's mysteries in souls do grow,
    But yet the body is his book.

And if some lover, such as we,
    Have heard this dialogue of one,
Let him still mark us: he shall see
    Small change, when we're to bodies gone.

1633

[13]**allay** alloy. Bodies are not excess material ("dross"), but unite beneficially with souls to facilitate the lovers' physical meeting.
[14]ll. 57-60 As the stars' influence on us must work through an intervening medium ("air"), so our souls were first united through our bodies (hands, eyes, stanza 2).
[15]ll. 61-64 The soul and the body were thought to affect each other through these spirits produced by the blood.

The Relic

    When my grave is broke up again
    Some second guest to entertain[1]
    (For graves have learned that woman-head,[2]
    To be to more than one a bed)
        And he that digs it spies
A bracelet of bright hair about the bone,
        Will he not let us alone,
And think that there a loving couple lies,

[1]ll. 1-2 Graves were often re-used because of limited burial space.

[2]**woman-head** female behavior

Who thought that this device might be some way
10   To make their souls, at the last busy day,[3]
Meet at this grave, and make a little stay?

    If this fall in a time, or land,
    Where mis-devotion[4] doth command,
    Then he that digs us up will bring
    Us to the Bishop and the King
        To make us relics; then
Thou shalt be a Mary Magdalen, and I
    A something else thereby;[5]
All women shall adore us, and some men;
20   And since at such time miracles are sought,[6]
I would that age were by this paper taught
What miracles we harmless lovers wrought.

    First, we loved well and faithfully,
    Yet knew not what we loved, nor why;[7]
    Difference of sex no more we knew,
    Than our guardian angels do;
        Coming and going, we
Perchance might kiss,[8] but not between those meals;
    Our hands ne'er touched the seals
30   Which nature, injured by late law, sets free.[9]
These miracles we did; but now, alas,
All measure, and all language, I should pass,
Should I tell what a miracle she was.

1633

[3] **last busy day** Judgment Day
[4] **mis-devotion** Protestant reference to Catholic veneration of relics of saints
[5] ll. 17–18 St. Mary Magdalene, cured of evil spirits by Christ, and her lover
[6] l. 20 to authenticate the relic's holiness
[7] l. 24 In a Platonic sense their love was a divine mystery, beyond human understanding.
[8] **kiss** innocent kisses of greeting and leave-taking
[9] ll. 29–30 Although sexual contact is limited by human law but not by nature, the lovers never availed themselves of it.

Elegy XIX. To His Mistress Going to Bed

Come, madam,[1] come, all rest my powers defy,
Until I labor, I in labor lie.
The foe oft-times, having the foe in sight,
Is tired with standing though they never fight.
Off with that girdle, like heaven's zone[2] glistering,
But a far fairer world encompassing.
Unpin that spangled breastplate which you wear,

[1] **madam** Title and attire (below) suggest a woman of some standing.
[2] **zone** a girdle encircling the heavens, probably the Zodiac

That the eyes of busy fools may be stopped there.
Unlace yourself, for that harmonious chime[3]
10 Tells me from you that now 'tis your bed time.
Off with that happy busk, which I envy,
That still can be, and still can stand so nigh.
Your gown's going off such beauteous state reveals,
As when from flowry meads the hill's shadow steals.
Off with that wiry coronet and show
The hairy diadem which on you doth grow:
Off with those shoes, and then safely tread
In this love's hallowed temple, this soft bed.
In such white robes heaven's angels used to be
20 Received by men; thou, Angel, bring'st with thee
A heaven like Mahomet's Paradise; and though
Ill spirits walk in white, we easily know
By this these angels from an evil sprite:
Those set our hairs, but these our flesh upright.
   License my roving hands, and let them go
Behind, before, between, above, below.
O my America! my new found land,
My kingdom, safeliest when with one man manned,
My mine of precious stones, my empery,[4]
30 How blest am I in this discovering thee.
To enter in these bonds is to be free;
Then where my hand is set, my seal shall be.
   Full nakedness, all joys are due to thee.
As souls unbodied, bodies unclothed must be
To taste whole joys.[5] Gems which you women use
Are like Atalanta's balls,[6] cast in men's views,
That when a fool's eye lighteth on a gem,
His earthly soul may covet theirs, not them.
Like pictures, or like books' gay coverings made
40 For laymen, are all women thus arrayed;
Themselves are mystic books, which only we
Whom their imputed grace will dignify[7]
Must see revealed. Then, since I may know,
As liberally as to a midwife, show
Thyself: cast all, yea, this white linen hence,
Here is no penance, much less innocence.[8]
   To teach thee, I am naked first; why than,[9]
What needst thou have more covering than a man?

1654, 1669

[3] **harmonious chime** chiming watch
[4] **empery** empire
[5] **As souls . . . joys** As souls must shed bodies to enjoy heaven, so bodies must shed clothes for full enjoyment.
[6] **Atalanta's balls** Donne alters the story of Atalanta. She agreed to marry only someone who could defeat her in a race; her suitor suc-

ceeded by dropping golden balls in her path to distract her.
[7] l. 42 Protestants held that Christ only imputed merit to us by grace: it really belonged to him. So women only impute their grace to men.
[8] **white . . . innocence** White would imply innocence or an act of penitence to restore it.
[9] **than** then

Satire III. Of Religion

Kind pity chokes my spleen;[1] brave scorn forbids
Those tears to issue which swell my eyelids;
I must not laugh, nor weep sins, and be wise,
Can railing then cure these worn maladies?
Is not our mistress, fair Religion,
As worthy of all our soul's devotion,
As virtue was to the first blinded age?[2]
Are not heaven's joys as valiant to assuage
Lusts, as earth's honor was to them? Alas,
10 As we do them in means, shall they surpass
Us in the end, and shall thy father's spirit
Meet blind philosophers in heaven, whose merit
Of strict life may be imputed faith, and hear
Thee, whom he taught so easy ways and near
To follow, damned?[3] O if thou dar'st, fear this;
This fear great courage and high valor is.
Dar'st thou aid mutinous Dutch,[4] and dar'st thou lay
Thee in ships, wooden sepulchers, a prey
To leaders' rage, to storms, to shot, to dearth?
20 Dar'st thou dive seas and dungeons of the earth?
Hast thou courageous fire to thaw the ice
Of frozen North discoveries? And thrice
Colder than salamanders, like divine
Children in the oven, fires of Spain, and the line,
Whose countries limbecks to our bodies be,[5]
Canst thou for gain bear? And must every he
Which cries not "Goddess!" to thy mistress, draw,
Or eat thy poisonous words?[6] Courage of straw!
O desperate coward, wilt thou seem bold, and
30 To thy foes and His (Who made thee to stand
Sentinel in His world's garrison) thus yield,
And for forbidden wars, leave the appointed field?[7]

[1] ll. 1–4 The spleen was thought to be the seat of laughter and melancholy. Laughing and weeping are no help; ranting will be better.

[2] ll. 5–7 Not knowing Christ, the ancients living before his time could not see the truth as we can; but they were devoted to virtue and honor as we should be to Christian teaching.

[3] Alas . . . damned Those ancient philosophers, blind as they were, may have the saving faith imputed to them by Christ because they lived so virtuously; but we, having the benefit of Christ's clear and easy-to-follow commands, may be damned for taking other paths (about to be described).

[4] mutinous Dutch Englishmen fought against the Spanish overlords in the Netherlands in Donne's time.

[5] And thrice . . . bodies be For personal profit, do you endure (as though you were ever-cold, fire-proof salamanders, or Shadrach, Meshach, and Abednego, surviving the fiery furnace of Daniel 1 and 3) the heat of southern climes and the equator, which desiccates our bodies as stills evaporate fluids? The question defines one of the false courses condemned as false courage in l. 28.

[6] draw . . . words Draw his sword or accept your insults?

[7] ll. 30–32 The progressive, historical degeneration of the world was a familiar notion (see "decrepit wane," l. 38). As a soldier of Christ will you leave the field of battle appointed by him for the sake of the wrong wars?

Know thy foes: the foul Devil, whom thou
Strivest to please, for hate, not love, would allow
Thee fain his whole realm to be quit,[8] and as
The world's all parts wither away and pass,
So the world's self, thy other loved foe, is
In her decrepit wane, and thou, loving this,
Dost love a withered and worn strumpet; last,
40 Flesh (itself's death) and joys which flesh can taste,
Thou lovest; and thy fair goodly soul, which doth[9]
Give this flesh power to taste joy, thou dost loathe.
    Seek true religion. O where? Mirreus,[10]
Thinking her unhoused here, and fled from us,
Seeks her at Rome; there, because he doth know
That she was there a thousand years ago,
He loves her rags so, as we here obey
The statecloth[11] where the Prince sat yesterday.
Crants to such brave[12] Loves will not be enthralled,
50 But loves her only, who at Geneva's called
Religion, plain, simple, sullen, young,
Contemptuous, yet unhandsome; as among
Lecherous humors, there is one that judges
No wenches wholesome but coarse country drudges.
Graius stays still at home here, and because
Some preachers, vile ambitious bawds, and laws,
Still new like fashions, bid him think that she
Which dwells with us is only perfect, he
Embraceth her whom his godfathers will
60 Tender to him, being tender, as wards still
Take such wives as their guardians offer, or
Pay values.[13] Careless Phrygius doth abhor
All, because all cannot be good, as one,
Knowing some women whores, dares marry none.
Gracchus loves all as one, and thinks that so
As women do in diverse countries go
In divers habits, yet are still one kind,
So doth, so is Religion; and this blind-
ness too much light breeds;[14] but unmoved thou
70 Of force must one, and forced but one allow;

[8]ll. 33–35 **the foul Devil . . . quit** The Devil
would like to award (quit) his kingdom to us
(as Christ would), but for hate, not love.

[9]ll. 33–41 **Know thy foes: . . . Devil . . .
world's self . . . Flesh . . . Thou lovest** Man
loves his three enemies: the Devil, the World,
and the Flesh.

[10]**Mirreus** the first of a series of typical figures
(ll. 43–69) who make religious decisions for
superficial reasons. Mirreus loves Catholicism
for its outward show; Dutch Crants loves Cal-
vinism because it lacks show; Graius loves
Anglicanism because it is the local religion;

Phrygius thinks all religions are bad because
some are; Gracchus loves all religions indif-
ferently.

[11]**statecloth** canopy of the monarch's chair of
state, reverenced even in his absence

[12]**brave** sumptuous

[13]**wards . . . Pay values** Wards had to accept
wives appointed by their guardians, or pay a
fine, as did the Anglican who did not attend his
parish church.

[14]**blindness . . . breeds** Finding too much light
everywhere, Gracchus is blinded to the true
religion.

And the right;[15] ask thy father which is she,
Let him ask his;[16] though truth and falsehood be
Near twins, yet truth a little elder is;
Be busy to seek her; believe me this,
He's not of none, nor worst, that seeks the best.
To adore, or scorn an image, or protest,[17]
May all be bad; doubt wisely; in strange way[18]
To stand inquiring right is not to stray;
To sleep, or run wrong is. On a huge hill,
80   Cragged and steep, Truth stands, and he that will
Reach her, about must, and about must go;
And what the hill's suddenness resists, win so;[19]
Yet strive so, that before age, death's twilight,
Thy soul rest, for none can work in that night.
To will implies delay, therefore now do.
Hard deeds, the body's pains; hard knowledge too
The mind's endeavors reach,[20] and mysteries
Are like the sun, dazzling, yet plain to all eyes.
Keep the truth which thou hast found; men do not stand
90   In so ill case here that God hath with His hand
Signed kings blank charters[21] to kill whom they hate,
Nor are they vicars, but hangmen to fate.
Fool and wretch, wilt thou let thy soul be tied
To man's laws, by which she shall not be tried
At the last day? Oh, wilt it then boot[22] thee
To say a Philip, or a Gregory,
A Harry, or a Martin[23] taught thee this?
Is not this excuse for mere contraries
Equally strong? Cannot both sides say so?
100   That thou mayest rightly obey power, her bounds know;
Those passed, her nature, and name's changed; to be
Then humble to her is idolatry.
As streams are, power is; those blest flowers that dwell
At the rough stream's calm head, thrive and prove well,
But having left their roots, and themselves given
To the stream's tyrannous rage, alas, are driven
Through mills, and rocks, and woods, and at last, almost
Consumed in going, in the sea are lost:
So perish souls, which more choose men's unjust
110   Power from God claimed, than God Himself to trust.

1593–98   1633

[15]**the right** the right religion
[16]**ask thy father . . . ask his** Inquire into the historical record until you find true Christianity.
[17]l. 76 to be Protestant; images (of saints, for example) were honored by Catholics, scorned by Protestants.
[18]**in strange way** by an unfamiliar path
[19]ll. 81–82 must circle around the hill in a spiral to overcome its steepness
[20]**Hard deeds . . . reach** The body achieves hard deeds; the mind achieves hard knowledge.
[21]**blank charters** with the name left blank, so the king could fill it in as he wished
[22]**boot** profit
[23]**Philip . . . Gregory . . . Harry . . . Martin** King Philip of Spain; either Gregory VII (pope 1073–85), claimant of infallibility, or Gregory XIV (pope 1590–91); Henry VIII; Martin Luther

Holy Sonnets

VII

At the round earth's imagined corners,[1] blow
Your trumpets, angels, and arise, arise
From death, you numberless infinities
Of souls, and to your scattered bodies go,
All whom the flood did, and fire shall o'erthrow,
All whom war, dearth, age, agues, tyrannies,
Despair, law, chance, hath slain, and you whose eyes
Shall behold God and never taste death's woe.[2]
But let them sleep, Lord, and me mourn a space,
10   For if above all these my sins abound,
'Tis late to ask abundance of Thy grace
When we are there; here on this lowly ground,
Teach me how to repent; for that's as good
As if Thou hadst sealed my pardon with Thy blood.

[1] **At the round . . . trumpets** At Judgment Day four angels stand "on the four corners of the earth" (Revelation 7:1).

[2] **you whose eyes . . . woe** those raised at the Last Judgment. See 1 Corinthians 15:51–52.

X

Death be not proud, though some have called thee
Mighty and dreadful, for thou art not so;
For those whom thou think'st thou dost overthrow
Die not, poor Death, nor yet canst thou kill me.
From rest and sleep, which but thy pictures be,
Much pleasure; then from thee much more must flow,
And soonest our best men with thee do go,
Rest of their bones, and soul's delivery.
Thou art slave to fate, chance, kings, and desperate men,
10   And dost with poison, war, and sickness dwell;
And poppy or charms can make us sleep as well,
And better than thy stroke; why swell'st[1] thou then?
One short sleep past, we wake eternally,
And death shall be no more; Death, thou shalt die.

[1] **swell'st** vauntest

XII

Why are we by all creatures waited on?
Why do the prodigal elements supply
Life and food to me, being more pure than I,
Simple, and further from corruption?[1]

[1] ll. 2–4 A mixture of different, or unequal, things was thought to be subject to corruption; thus man, a mixture of the four elements, is less pure than they.

Why brook'st thou, ignorant horse, subjection?
Why dost thou, bull and boar, so sillily
Dissemble weakness, and by one man's stroke die,
Whose whole kind you might swallow and feed upon?
Weaker I am, woe's me, and worse than you,
You have not sinned, nor need be timorous.
But wonder at a greater wonder, for to us
Created nature doth these things subdue,
But their Creator, whom sin nor nature tied,
For us, His creatures, and his foes, hath died.

XIII

What if this present were the world's last night?
Mark in my heart, O soul, where thou dost dwell,
The picture of Christ crucified, and tell
Whether that countenance can thee affright.
Tears in His eyes quench the amazing light,
Blood fills His frowns, which from His pierced head fell,
And can that tongue adjudge thee unto hell,
Which prayed forgiveness for His foes' fierce spite?
No, no; but as in my idolatry
I said to all my profane mistresses,
Beauty, of pity, foulness only is
A sign of rigor:[1] so I say to thee,
To wicked spirits are horrid shapes assigned,
This beauteous form assures a piteous mind.

[1] **Beauty . . . rigor** Beauty is a sign of pity;
only ugliness is unforgiving.

XIV

Batter my heart, three-personed God; for You
As yet but knock, breathe, shine, and seek to mend;
That I may rise and stand, o'erthrow me, and bend
Your force to break, blow, burn, and make me new.
I, like an usurped town, to another due,
Labor to admit You, but Oh, to no end.
Reason, Your viceroy in me, me should defend,
But is captived, and proves weak or untrue.
Yet dearly I love You, and would be loved fain,
But am betrothed unto Your enemy:
Divorce me, untie or break that knot again,
Take me to You, imprison me, for I,
Except You enthrall me, never shall be free,
Nor ever chaste, except You ravish me.

1633

(ADDED IN 1635)

V

I am a little world made cunningly
Of elements and an angelic sprite,
But black sin hath betrayed to endless night
My world's both parts, and, oh, both parts must die.
You which beyond that heaven which was most high
Have found new spheres, and of new lands can write,
Pour new seas in mine eyes, that so I might[1]
Drown my world with my weeping earnestly,
Or wash it if it must be drowned no more.
10   But oh it must be burnt![2] Alas, the fire
Of lust and envy have burnt it heretofore,
And made it fouler; let their flames retire,
And burn me, O Lord, with a fiery zeal
Of Thee and Thy house, which doth in eating heal.[3]

1635

[1] ll. 5–7 Those who have invented new heavenly spheres beyond the supposed outermost one of the universe (the macrocosm) or have discovered new earthly regions are invited to pour new seas into the microcosm, or little world, of the speaker.

[2] **Drown . . . be burnt** God had promised that no new flood would cover the earth. Traditionally it should finally be destroyed by fire.
[3] ll. 13–14 "The zeal of thy house hath eaten me up" (Psalm 69:9). Unlike the fire of lust and envy, this one heals as it consumes.

From Westmoreland Manuscript

XVIII

Show me, dear Christ, Thy spouse, so bright and clear.
What, is it she which on the other shore
Goes richly painted?[1] or which robbed and tore
Laments and mourns in Germany and here?
Sleeps she a thousand, then peeps up one year?
Is she self-truth and errs? now new, now outwore?
Doth she, and did she, and shall she evermore
On one, on seven, or on no hill appear?[2]
Dwells she with us, or like adventuring knights
10   First travail we to seek, and then make love?
Betray, kind husband, Thy spouse to our sights,
And let mine amorous soul court Thy mild Dove,[3]
Who is most true and pleasing to Thee then
When she is embraced and open to most men.

from ms., 1899

[1] **richly painted** like the whorish woman of Revelation (a Protestant allusion to the ceremony of the Catholic church). In following lines the Protestant church seems just as unlikely a spouse. Calvin's doctrine that the Church "slept" from the time of its primitive purity until the Reformation makes the Visible Church an unlikely bride; so does the Catholic doctrine that

the church is truth, when successive popes change that "truth."
[2] l.8 Solomon built the Temple on one hill; Rome is on seven hills; Geneva is on no hill.
[3] **Dove** a symbol of the Holy Spirit. See Song of Solomon 2: "Open to me, my sister, my love, my dove, my undefiled."

Good Friday, 1613. Riding Westward

Let man's soul be a sphere, and then, in this,
The intelligence that moves, devotion is;[1]
And as the other spheres, by being grown
Subject to foreign motions, lose their own,
And being by others hurried every day,
Scarce in a year their natural form obey:
Pleasure or business, so our souls admit
For their first mover, and are whirled by it.
Hence is 't that I am carried toward the West
10 This day, when my soul's form bends toward the East.
There I should see a Sun, by rising, set,
And by that setting endless day beget;
But that Christ on this cross did rise and fall,
Sin had eternally benighted all.
Yet dare I almost be glad I do not see
That spectacle of too much weight for me.
Who sees God's face, that is self life, must die;[2]
What a death were it then to see God die?
It made His own Lieutenant Nature, shrink;
20 It made His footstool crack, and the sun wink.[3]
Could I behold those hands which span the poles,
And tune all spheres[4] at once, pierced with those holes?
Could I behold that endless height which is
Zenith to us, and to our antipodes,
Humbled below us? or that blood which is
The seat of all our souls, if not of His,
Make dirt of dust, or that flesh which was worn
By God, for His apparel, ragg'd and torn?
If on these things I durst not look, durst I
30 Upon his miserable mother cast mine eye,
Who was God's partner here, and furnished thus
Half of that sacrifice which ransomed us?
Though these things, as I ride, be from mine eye,
They're present yet unto my memory,
For that looks towards them; and Thou look'st towards me,
O Savior, as Thou hang'st upon the tree;
I turn my back to Thee but to receive

---

[1] ll. 1–10 The concentric spheres of the Ptolemaic universe, carrying planets and the fixed stars in their different motions, are each guided by an intelligence or angel; so man's soul, here imagined as a sphere, ought to be guided by devotion to God. Though each inner, planetary sphere has its own orbiting motion from west to east, this motion is almost overcome by the daily east-to-west revolution of the outermost sphere, or first mover, so that the sun (a planet in the Ptolemaic system), for instance, completes its west-to-east orbit only after 365 days of rising in the east and setting in the west. Man's devotion is also likely to be overcome by worldly interests; here it moves the speaker westward on the day of Christ's crucifixion in the east. Donne himself had traveled westward in England and was in the west on Good Friday, 1613.

[2] l. 17 Exodus 33:20: "for there shall no man see me and live."

[3] l. 20 God's footstool, the earth, was said to have quaked and the sun to have been eclipsed at the crucifixion.

[4] **tune all spheres** The various turnings of the spheres were imagined to produce musical tones. We are too used to them to hear them.

Corrections, till Thy mercies bid Thee leave.[5]
O think me worth Thine anger, punish me,
40 Burn off my rusts and my deformity,
Restore Thine image so much, by Thy grace,
That Thou may'st know me, and I'll turn my face.

1613   1633

[5] **leave** stop

Hymn to God My God, in My Sickness[1]

Since I am coming to that holy room
    Where, with Thy choir of saints forevermore,
I shall be made Thy Music, as I come
    I tune the instrument here at the door,
    And what I must do then, think now before.

Whilst my physicians by their love are grown
    Cosmographers, and I their map, who lie
Flat on this bed, that by them may be shown
    That this is my South-west discovery[2]
10   *Per fretum febris*, by these straits to die,[3]

I joy, that in these straits, I can see my West;
    For, though their currents yield return to none,
What shall my West hurt me? As West and East
    In all flat maps[4] (and I am one) are one,
    So death doth touch the resurrection.

Is the Pacific Sea my Home? Or are
    The Eastern riches? Is Jerusalem?[5]
Anyan and Magellan,[6] and Gibràltar,
    All straits, and none but straits, are ways to them,
20   Whether where Japhet dwelt, or Cham, or Shem.[7]

We think that Paradise and Calvary,
    Christ's Cross, and Adam's tree, stood in one place;
Look, Lord, and find both Adams met in me;
    As the first Adam's sweat surrounds my face,
    May the last Adam's blood my soul embrace.[8]

[1] written with reference to Donne's illness in 1623, or possibly on his deathbed
[2] ll. 6–9 Studying the flat world-map (the speaker as a little world, flat on his bed), the doctors foresee death, (west, where the sun declines) by fever (hot south).
[3] l. 10 by heat, but also by the strait, of fever
[4] **in all flat maps** on maps of the world
[5] **Jerusalem . . . Anyan . . . Magellan . . .**

Gibraltar all fabled better places. Jerusalem = vision of peace.
[6] **Magellan** imagined narrow strait, in early maps, between America and Asia
[7] **Japhet . . . Cham . . . Shem** Noah's sons to whom, respectively, Europe, Africa, and Asia were given
[8] ll. 24–25 Christ is the last Adam. The first Adam earned his bread by the sweat of his brow.

So, in His purple[9] wrapped, receive me, Lord,
    By these His thorns give me His other crown;
And as to others' souls I preached Thy word,
    Be this my text, my sermon to mine own,
30   Therefore that He may raise, the Lord throws down.

    1623?   1635

[9] **purple** blood, but also the color reserved for emperors, and of the attire put on Christ in mockery before the Crucifixion.

ROBERT HERRICK
1591–1674

Herrick has to be classed with Cavalier poets like Carew, Lovelace, and Suckling because like them he wrote melodious, formally enchanting lyrics marked by classical restraint, not Renaissance exuberance, and because he also idolized and imitated Ben Jonson. Like Jonson, however, he was no cavalier. The son of one goldsmith and apprenticed to another, he did not reach Cambridge until he was twenty-two. His ordination as an Anglican clergyman was followed by some years of association with Jonson's circle in London. Then, however, he found a safe niche as the rector of a country parish (Dean Prior) far to the southwest, in Devonshire, where during eighteen years he wrote most of his very numerous poems and pined for urban delights.

The urbanity that goes with Jonsonian verse is qualified in Herrick's case by a pleasure in real nature and tiny things and in his feeling for his servant and his dog. Unlike the mistresses of the Cavaliers, his may be only poetic creations. His two most famous poems have for their theme *carpe diem* (seize the day — the short day given to us for love; see below). In the light of his whole work his devotion to Christian doctrine is not in doubt, but his imagination often dwelt and worked in the sensual, classical Latin lyricism of Horace and Catullus. During the Puritan interregnum he lost his post and moved to London, but he returned to Dean Prior at the Restoration.

The Argument of His Book

I sing of brooks, of blossoms, birds and bowers,
Of April, May, of June and Jùly-flowers;
I sing of May-poles, hock-carts,[1] wassails, wakes,[2]
Of bridegrooms, brides and of their bridal cakes;
I write of youth, of love, and have access
By these to sing of cleanly wantonness;
I sing of dews, of rains, and piece by piece
Of balm, of oil, of spice and ambergris;[3]
I sing of times trans-shifting, and I write
10 How roses first came red and lilies white;
I write of groves, of twilights, and I sing
The Court of Mab,[4] and of the Fairy King;
I write of hell; I sing (and ever shall)
Of heaven, and hope to have it after all.

                                                    1648

[1] **hock-carts** carts carrying the last load of harvest, on which Herrick wrote one poem, as on other subjects mentioned here
[2] **wakes** here, church festivals
[3] **ambergris** secretion of sperm whale, main ingredient of a precious perfume
[4] **Mab** queen of fairies

Upon the Loss of His Mistresses

I have lost, and lately, these
Many dainty mistresses:
Stately Julia, prime of all;
Sappho next, a principal;
Smooth Anthea for a skin
White, and heaven-like crystalline;
Sweet Electra, and the choice
Myrrha for the lute and voice;
Next Corinna, for her wit,
10   And the graceful use of it;
With Perilla: all are gone;
Only Herrick's left alone,
For to number sorrow by
Their departures hence, and die.

1648

To Robin Redbreast

Laid out for death, let thy last kindness be
With leaves and moss-work for to cover me:
And while the wood-nymphs my cold corpse inter,
Sing thou my dirge, sweet-warbling chorister!
For epitaph, in foliage, next write this:
    Here, here the tomb of Robin Herrick is.

1648

Delight in Disorder

A sweet disorder in the dress
Kindles in clothes a wantonness;[1]
A lawn[2] about the shoulders thrown
Into a fine distraction;[3]
An erring lace which here and there
Enthralls the crimson stomacher;[4]
A cuff neglectful, and thereby
Ribbons to flow confusedly;
A winning wave, deserving note,
10   In the tempestuous petticoat;
A careless shoe-string, in whose tie
I see a wild civility:[5]
Do more bewitch me than when art
Is too precise in every part.

1648

[1] **wantonness** merriness
[2] **lawn** light scarf
[3] **fine distraction** carefully arranged appearance of disorder
[4] **stomacher** ornamental bosom-to-waist cloth-piece, held in place by lacing of bodice.
[5] **civility** order

Corinna's Going A-Maying

Get up, get up, for shame, the blooming morn
Upon her wings presents the god unshorn.[1]
    See how Aurora[2] throws her fair
    Fresh-quilted[3] colors through the air:
    Get up, sweet slug-a-bed, and see
    The dew bespangling herb and tree.
Each flower has wept and bowèd toward the east
Above an hour since; yet you not dress'd;
    Nay! not so much as out of bed?
10   When all the birds have matins said,
    And sung their thankful hymns: 'tis sin,
    Nay, profanation to keep in,
Whenas[4] a thousand virgins on this day
Spring, sooner than the lark, to fetch in may.[5]

Rise and put on your foliage, and be seen
To come forth, like the spring-time, fresh and green,
    And sweet as Flora. Take no care
    For jewels for your gown, or hair:
    Fear not, the leaves will strew
20   Gems in abundance upon you;
Besides, the childhood of the day has kept,
Against[6] you come, some orient[7] pearls unwept;
    Come and receive them while the light
    Hangs on the dew-locks of the night:
    And Titan[8] on the eastern hill
    Retires himself, or else stands still
Till you come forth. Wash, dress, be brief in praying:
Few beads are best when once we go a-maying.

Come, my Corinna, come; and, coming, mark
30 How each field turns a street, each street a park
    Made green and trimm'd with trees; see how
    Devotion gives each house a bough
    Or branch; each porch, each door ere this
    An ark, a tabernacle is,
Made up of white-thorn neatly interwove;
As if here were those cooler shades of love.
    Can such delights be in the street,
    And open fields, and we not see't?
    Come, we'll abroad; and let's obey
40   The proclamation made for May:
And sin no more, as we have done, by staying;
But, my Corinna, come, let's go a-maying.

[1] **god unshorn** the long-haired sun god, Apollo.
[2] **Aurora** goddess of dawn
[3] **Fresh-quilted** intermixed as in a new quilt of various colors
[4] **whenas** when
[5] **may** white hawthorn blossoms
[6] **against** until
[7] **orient** shining
[8] **Titan** the sun

There's not a budding boy or girl this day
But is got up, and gone to bring in may.
    A deal of youth, ere this, is come
    Back, and with white-thorn laden home.
    Some have despatch'd their cakes and cream
    Before that we have left to dream;[9]
And some have wept, and woo'd, and plighted troth,
50   And chose their priest, ere we can cast off sloth.
    Many a green-gown[10] has been given;
    Many a kiss, both odd and even:
    Many a glance too has been sent
    From out the eye, love's firmament;
Many a jest told of the keys betraying
This night, and locks pick'd, yet we're not a-maying.

Come let us go, while we are in our prime,
And take the harmless folly of the time.
60   We shall grow old apace and die
    Before we know our liberty.
    Our life is short, and our days run
    As fast away as does the sun;
And, as a vapor, or a drop of rain,
Once lost, can ne'er be found again:
    So when or you or I are made
    A fable, song, or fleeting shade,
    All love, all liking, all delight
    Lies drowned with us in endless night.
70   Then while time serves, and we are but decaying,
Come, my Corinna, come, let's go a-maying.

1648

[9]**left to dream** stopped dreaming   [10]**green-gown** from rolling in the grass

To the Virgins, to Make Much of Time

Gather ye rosebuds while ye may,
  Old time is still a-flying;
And this same flower that smiles to-day
  To-morrow will be dying.

The glorious lamp of heaven, the sun,
  The higher he's a-getting,
The sooner will his race be run,
  And nearer he's to setting.

That age is best which is the first,
10 When youth and blood are warmer;
But being spent, the worse, and worst
  Times still succeed the former.

Then be not coy, but use your time,
    And while ye may go marry:
For having lost but once your prime,
    You may for ever tarry.

1648

Upon Her Feet

Her pretty feet
    Like snails did creep
    A little out, and then,
As if they started at bo-peep,[1]
    Did soon draw in again.

1648

[1] **bo-peep** peekaboo

The Night-Piece, to Julia

Her eyes the glow-worm lend thee;
The shooting stars attend thee;
    And the elves also,
    Whose little eyes glow
Like the sparks of fire, befriend thee.

No will-o'-th'-wisp mislight thee,
Nor snake or slow-worm[1] bite thee;
    But on, on thy way,
    Not making a stay,
10 Since ghost there's none to affright thee.

Let not the dark thee cumber;[2]
What though the moon does slumber?
    The stars of the night
    Will lend thee their light
Like tapers clear without number.

Then, Julia, let me woo thee,
Thus, thus to come unto me;
    And when I shall meet
    Thy silv'ry feet
20 My soul I'll pour into thee.

1648

[1] **slow-worm** small snake or lizard
[2] **cumber** disturb

Upon Julia's Clothes

Whenas[1] in silks my Julia goes,
Then, then, methinks how sweetly flows
That liquefaction of her clothes.

Next, when I cast mine eyes and see
That brave[2] vibration each way free,
O how that glittering taketh me!

1648

[1] **Whenas** when   [2] **brave** handsome

Grace for a Child

Here a little child I stand
Heaving up my either hand;
Cold as paddocks[1] though they be,
Here I lift them up to Thee,
For a benison to fall
On our meat and on us all. Amen.

1648

[1] **paddocks** frogs, toads

GEORGE HERBERT
1593–1633

George Herbert was the greatest of the Anglican devotional poets who sought a suitable outward expression of inner, spiritual truth. He was caught in a poetically productive way between conflicting drives. His worldly ambitions, supported by the distinction of his family and by his own abilities, struggled with his genuine vision of Christian charity in the world and of God's final transcendence of the worldly. This struggle afflicted him with an acute sense of the thorniness of the path to God. Hence such poems as "The Collar" and "The Pilgrimage."

Herbert was caught also in another, more purely poetic conflict. He was certain that the direct and simple expression of truth far surpassed Petrarchan adornment and Metaphysical wit (as he says in Jordan [I]), but he possessed an unexcelled ability to find fresh prosodic, metaphorical, and allegorical clothing for his thoughts. The directness and simplicity of his poetry is really an effect of the highest art. Yet honesty finally radiates from the integrity of his craftsmanship. Nearly every poem stands as an elegantly generated organism utterly different from all the others. Each of its constituents contributes to one total effect. Almost no word could be subtracted from it without grave harm to that effect.

In his last three years he turned his back on his dignities at Cambridge and in Parliament to become the rector of the minor parish of Bemerton near Salisbury. Most of his poetry was written there and arranged in the posthumously published *The Temple* as though corresponding to the features and tasks of an Anglican church. His influence as a devotional poet on Crashaw, Vaughan, Traherne, and others has been central. His poetry owes less to his contemporaries than it does to Sidney's directness and his injunction in *Astrophel and Stella* to "look in thy heart and write." Herbert is indeed a Metaphysical poet because of his intellectually probing imagery—so far from the graceful postures of Cavalier hedonism. At the same time, his verse has little in common with Donne's. Ultimately, Donne's jagged multiplicity and complexity of images must have seemed to Herbert self-indulgent and self-defeating, although in "Church Monuments" Herbert comes close to Donne's multifariousness.

"Easter Wings" is more typical of Herbert's Anglican impulse to find a consistent, simple, outward image for inward truth. It is shaped symbolically. The visual design of each stanza suggests the wings of a bird flying upward, and the poem itself develops this symbolism as a prayer to be allowed to rise toward God.

Easter Wings[1]

Lord, who createdst man in wealth and store,[2]
Though foolishly he lost the same,
Decaying more and more
Till he became
Most poor:
With thee
O let me rise
As larks harmoniously,
And sing this day thy victories:
Then shall the fall[3] further the flight in me.

My tender age in sorrow did begin:
And still with sickness and shame
Thou didst so punish sin,
That I became
Most thin.
With thee
Let me combine,
And feel this day thy victory:
For, if I imp my wing on thine,[4]
Affliction shall advance the flight in me.

1633

[1] The vertical arrangement of the two stanzas (originally printed on facing pages) was meant to suggest two birds, or angels, flying upward side by side, their wings outspread.
[2] **store** abundance
[3] **the fall** The fall of Man, causing Christ to sacrifice his life and then, resurrected, to fly to heaven, now gives man a companion to help him to fly there too.
[4] **imp my wing on thine** to mend the injured wing of one bird with feathers from another

Prayer (I)

Prayer, the church's banquet, angel's age,
God's breath in man returning to his birth,
The soul in paraphrase, heart in pilgrimage,
The Christian plummet sounding heav'n and earth;
Engine[1] against th' Almighty, sinners' tower,
Reversèd thunder, Christ-side-piercing spear,
The six-days' world[2] transposing in an hour,
A kind of tune, which all things hear and fear;
Softness, and peace, and joy, and love, and bliss,
Exalted manna, gladness of the best,
Heaven in ordinary,[3] man well dressed,
The Milky Way, the bird of Paradise,
Church-bells beyond the stars heard, the soul's blood,
The land of spices: something understood.

1633

[1] **Engine** weapon of warfare, e.g. a battering-ram
[2] **The six-days' world** the secular world, exclud-ing Sunday; also, the six days of the lower world's creation
[3] **in ordinary** as a daily, fixed ration

Jordan (I)[1]

Who says that fictions only and false hair
Become a verse? Is there in truth no beauty?
Is all good structure in a winding stair?
May no lines pass, except they do their duty
Not to a true, but painted chair?[2]

Is it no verse, except enchanted groves
And sudden arbors shadow coarse-spun lines?[3]
Must purling streams refresh a lover's loves?
Must all be veiled, while he that reads, divines,
Catching the sense at two removes?

Shepherds are honest people, let them sing:
Riddle who list, for me, and pull for Prime:[4]
I envy no man's nightingale or spring
Nor let them punish me with loss of rime
Who plainly say, *My God, My King.*

1633

[1] significance of the title unclear: crossing of the Hebrews into the Promised Land? its waters as a cure for sickness (unlike the rivers of the unbelievers)? its windings like the kind of verse condemned here?
[2] ll. 4–5 Must poetry conform to an artful picture of reality, not to reality itself?
[3] ll. 6–7 Are ornamental clichés (as in artificial landscape architecture) needed in poetry?
[4] ll. 11–12 As far as I am concerned, let others put puzzles in their verse if they wish ("list") and draw for a winning hand at cards (try for the most contrived poetry).

Church Monuments

While that my soul repairs to her devotion,
Here I entomb my flesh, that it betimes
May take acquaintance of this heap of dust,
To which the blast of death's incessant motion,
Fed with exhalation of our crimes,
Drives all at last. Therefore I gladly trust

My body to this school, that it may learn
To spell his elements, and find his birth
Written in dusty heraldry and lines;[1]
10   Which dissolution sure doth best discern,
Comparing dust with dust, and earth with earth.
These laugh at jet and marble, put for signs

To sever the good fellowship of dust,
And spoil the meeting. What shall point out them,
When they shall bow, and kneel, and fall down flat
To kiss those heaps, which now they have in trust?
Dear flesh, while I do pray, learn here thy stem
And true descent: that when thou shalt grow fat

And wanton in thy cravings, thou mayst know
20   That flesh is but the glass[2] which holds the dust
That measures all our time; which also shall
Be crumbled into dust. Mark here below
How tame these ashes are, how free from lust,
That thou mayst fit thy self against thy fall.

1633

[1] l. 9   English parish churches are often crowded with elaborate tombs ("monuments" of the title) displaying family arms and lines of verse.   [2] **glass**   hourglass

The Windows

Lord, how can man preach Thy eternal word?
  He is a brittle, crazy[1] glass;
Yet in Thy temple Thou dost him afford
   This glorious and transcendent place,
   To be a window, through Thy grace.

But when thou dost anneal[2] in glass Thy story,
  Making Thy life to shine within
The holy Preacher's;[3] then the light and glory
   More rev'rend grows, and more doth win:
10   Which else shows wat'rish, bleak, and thin.

[1] **crazy**   filled with cracks
[2] **anneal**   strengthen by heating
[3] **But . . . Preacher's**   God puts his way of life —not simply his teaching—into the preacher.

Doctrine and life, colours and light, in one
      When they combine and mingle, bring
A strong regard and awe: but speech alone
      Doth vanish like a flaring thing,
      And in the ear, not conscience, ring.

                1633

Redemption

Having been tenant long to a rich Lord,
      Not thriving, I resolvèd to be bold,
      And make a suit unto him, to afford
A new small-rented lease, and cancel th'old.[1]
In heaven at his manor I him sought:
      They told me there, that he was lately gone
      About some land, which he had dearly bought
Long since on earth, to take possession.
I straight returned, and knowing his great birth,
10   Sought him accordingly in great resorts,
      In cities, theatres, gardens, parks, and courts:
At length I heard a ragged noise and mirth
      Of thieves and murderers: there I him espied
      Who straight, *Your suit is granted*, said, and died.

                1633

[1] l. 4 a new agreement with the deity granting
Christ's love and forgiveness, not the unforgiv-
ing Law of the Old Testament

Virtue

Sweet day, so cool, so calm, so bright,
The bridal of the earth and sky:
The dew shall weep thy fall tonight,
      For thou must die.

Sweet rose, whose hue, angry[1] and brave,[2]
Bids the rash gazer wipe his eye:
Thy root is ever in its grave,
      And thou must die.

Sweet spring, full of sweet days and roses,
10 A box where sweets compacted lie:
My music shows ye have your closes,[3]
      And all must die.

[1] **angry** red
[2] **brave** bright

[3] **closes** a close is the conclusion of a phrase in
music.

Only a sweet and virtuous soul,
Like seasoned timber, never gives;
But though the whole world turn to coal,[4]
$\qquad$ Then chiefly lives.

$\qquad$ 1633

[4]**coal** a burned, glowing coal at the Last Judgment

The Pilgrimage

I travelled on, seeing the hill, where lay
$\qquad$ My expectation.
$\qquad$ A long it was and weary way.
The gloomy Cave of Desperation
I left on th' one, and on the other side
$\qquad$ The Rock of Pride.

And so I came to Fancy's Meadow, strowed
$\qquad$ With many a flower;
$\qquad$ Fain would I here have made abode,
10 $\qquad$ But I was quickened by my hour.
So to Care's Copse[1] I came, and there got through
$\qquad$ With much ado.

That led me to the Wild of Passion, which
$\qquad$ Some call the Wold;[2]
$\qquad$ A wasted place, but sometimes rich.
Here I was robbed of all my gold,
Save one good angel,[3] which a friend had tied
$\qquad$ Close to my side.

At length I got unto the Gladsome Hill,
20 $\qquad$ Where lay my hope,
$\qquad$ Where lay my heart; and climbing still,
When I had gained the brow and top,
A lake of brackish[4] waters on the ground
$\qquad$ Was all I found.

With that abashed, and struck with many a sting
$\qquad$ Of swarming fears,
$\qquad$ I fell, and cried, "Alas my King,
$\qquad$ Can both the way and end be tears?"
Yet taking heart I rose, and then perceived
30 $\qquad$ I was deceived:

[1]**Copse** thicket
[2]**Wold** barren upland plain

[3]**angel** a gold coin, as well as the heavenly being
[4]**brackish** salty, like tears

My hill was further: so I flung away,
                    Yet heard a cry
          Just as I went, *None goes that way*
          And lives: "If that be all," said I,
"After so foul a journey death is fair,
                    And but a chair."⁵

                    1633

⁵**chair** a place to rest

The Collar¹

          I struck the board,² and cried, "No more.
                    I will abroad.
What? shall I ever sigh and pine?
My lines and life are free; free as the road,
          Loose as the wind, as large as store.³
                    Shall I be still in suit?⁴
          Have I no harvest but a thorn
          To let me blood, and not restore
What I have lost with cordial⁵ fruit?
10   Sure there was wine
          Before my sighs did dry it; there was corn
                    Before my tears did drown it.
          Is the year only lost to me?
                    Have I no bays⁶ to crown it?
No flowers, no garlands gay? all blasted?
                    All wasted?
          Not so, my heart; but there is fruit,
                    And thou hast hands.
          Recover all thy sigh-blown age
20   On double pleasures: leave thy cold dispute
Of what is fit and not. Forsake thy cage,
                    Thy rope of sands,
Which petty thoughts have made, and made to thee
          Good cable, to enforce and draw,
                    And be thy law,
While thou didst wink and wouldst not see.
                    Away! take heed;
                    I will abroad.
Call in thy death's head⁷ there; tie up thy fears.
30   He that forbears
          To suit and serve his need,
                    Deserves his load."

¹ the close-fitting clerical collar
² **board** table
³ **store** abundance
⁴ **in suit** attending as a suitor for preferment

⁵ **cordial** heart-restoring
⁶ **bays** laurel wreath, given for poetic fame
⁷ **death's head** skull, reminder of mortality

But as I raved and grew more fierce and wild
At every word,
Methoughts I heard one calling, *Child!*
And I replied, *My Lord.*

1633

Love (III)

Love bade me welcome, yet my soul drew back
Guilty of dust and sin.
But quick-eyed Love, observing me grow slack
From my first entrance in,
Drew nearer to me, sweetly questioning,
If I lacked any thing.

"A guest," I answered, "worthy to be here."
Love said, "You shall be he."
"I the unkind, ungrateful? Ah my dear,
10   I cannot look on Thee."
Love took my hand, and smiling did reply,
"Who made the eyes but I?"

"Truth, Lord, but I have marred them: let my shame
Go where it doth deserve."
"And know you not," says Love, "who bore the blame?"
"My dear, then I will serve."
"You must sit down," says Love, "and taste my meat."[1]
So I did sit and eat.

1633

[1] **meat** repast, i.e., the communion meal

THOMAS CAREW
1594?–1640

This artistically most impressive and wide-ranging of the Cavalier poets enjoyed diplomatic and court posts under Charles I. His love poetry is certainly characteristic of the Cavaliers, but there is more to his work than this may suggest. In the metrically elegant, classically exquisite, in fact tidy, character of even his most erotic poetry one hears, as with Ben Jonson, the rounded, perfected, formal celebration of an event.

The mental probing of the Metaphysicals was far from Carew's style, yet in his elegy for Donne he produced the most discerning pre-twentieth-century description of that poet's work — using many of Donne's own devices. Carew's idea in "Upon a Ribbon" surely relates to Donne's "The Relic" (and more closely to another poem of Donne's, "The Funeral"). Donne made a profound impression on Carew, then, but the conversion in "Upon a Ribbon" of Donne's idea into a skillfully managed set of tuneful contrasts (the outward symbol of the lady's beauty and the beauty itself, correlative to the outward observance and the inner faith of religion) suggests how firmly Carew adhered to the School of Ben. In "The Spring" the device of the spring opening (a poet's complaint at the inattention of his beloved in the face of the joy produced in the rest of creation as the season revives) is a polished, delightful set of opposed gestures at seasonal contrasts in which attention to the behavior of the lady is classically restrained to little more than five lines. The celebratory, formal decorum initiated by the solemn back-vowels of the first two lines of "Ask me no more where Jove bestows" (p. 260 below) is an effect hardly ever equaled by Jonson himself.

The Spring

Now that the winter's gone, the earth hath lost
Her snow-white robes; and now no more the frost
Candies the grass, or casts an icy cream
Upon the silver lake or crystal stream:
But the warm sun thaws the benumbèd earth,
And makes it tender; gives a sacred[1] birth
To the dead swallow;[2] wakes in hollow tree
The drowsy cuckoo and the humblebee.
Now do a choir of chirping minstrels bring,
10 In triumph to the world, the youthful spring.
The valleys, hills, and woods in rich array
Welcome the coming of the longed-for May.
Now all things smile; only my love doth lower;
Nor hath the scalding noonday sun the power
To melt that marble ice, which still doth hold
Her heart congealed, and makes her pity cold.
The ox, which lately did for shelter fly
Into the stall, doth now securely lie
In open fields; and love no more is made
20 By the fireside; but in the cooler shade
Amyntas now doth with his Chloris sleep
Under a sycamore, and all things keep
Time with the season: only she doth carry
June in her eyes, in her heart January.

1640

[1] **sacred** sacred because non-sexual
[2] **gives . . . swallow** Swallows were supposed to lose all signs of life in winter and to revive in the spring.

Upon a Ribbon

This silken wreath, which circles in mine arm,
Is but an emblem of that mystic charm
Wherewith the magic of your beauties binds
My captive soul, and round about it winds

Fetters of lasting love. This[1] hath entwined
My flesh alone; that hath empaled[2] my mind.
Time may wear out these soft weak bands, but those
Strong chains of brass Fate shall not discompose.
This holy relic may preserve my wrist,
10   But my whole frame doth by that power subsist;
To that my prayers and sacrifice, to this
I only pay a superstitious kiss.
This but the idol, that's the deity;
Religion there is due; here, ceremony;
That I receive by faith, this but in trust;
Here I may tender duty, there I must;
This order as a layman I may bear,
But I become Love's priest when that I wear;
This moves like air; that as the center stands;
20   That knot your virtue tied, this but your hands;
That, nature framed; but this was made by art;
This makes my arm your prisoner; that, my heart.

1640

[1] "This" and "these" in the poem refer to the physical ribbon; "that" and "those," to the immaterial charm exercised by the beloved's beauty (see headnote, and Donne's "The Relic," p. 233 above).
[2] **empaled** fenced in

An Elegy upon the Death of Doctor Donne, Dean of Paul's[1]

Can we not force from widowed poetry,
Now thou art dead, great Donne, one elegy
To crown thy hearse? Why yet did we not trust,
Though with unkneaded dough-baked prose, thy dust,
Such as the unscissored lect'rer from the flower
Of fading rhet'ric, short-lived as his hour,
Dry as the sand that measures it, might lay
Upon the ashes, on the funeral day?[2]
Have we nor tune nor voice? Didst thou dispense
10   Through all our language both the words and sense?
'Tis a sad truth. The pulpit may her plain
And sober Christian precepts still retain;
Doctrines it may, and wholesome uses, frame;
Grave homilies and lectures, but the flame
Of thy brave soul, that shot such heat and light,
As burnt our earth and made our darkness bright,
Committed holy rapes upon the will,
Did through the eye the melting heart distill,
And the deep knowledge of dark truths so teach

[1] first published in the edition of Donne's poetry of 1633
[2] **Why yet . . . funeral day?** Why did we not, as does the lowly officiant at a funeral (measuring his time with an hourglass), entrust your remains to the ashes at least accompanied by short-lived prose?

20 As sense might judge where fancy could not reach,
    Must be desired forever. So the fire
    That fills with spirit and heat the Delphic choir,[3]
    Which, kindled first by thy Promethean breath,[4]
    Glowed here a while, lies quenched now in thy death.
    The Muses' garden, with pedantic weeds
    O'erspread, was purged by thee; the lazy seeds
    Of servile imitation thrown away,
    And fresh invention planted; thou didst pay
    The debt of our penurious bankrupt age:
30 Licentious thefts, that make poetic rage[5]
    A mimic fury, when our souls must be
    Possessed, or[6] with Anacreon's[7] ecstasy
    Or Pindar's,[8] not their own; the subtle cheat
    Of sly exchanges, and the juggling feat
    Of two-edged words, or whatsoever wrong
    By ours was done the Greek or Latin tongue,
    Thou hast redeemed, and opened us a mine
    Of rich and pregnant fancy; drawn a line
    Of masculine[9] expression, which had good
40 Old Orpheus[10] seen, or all the ancient brood
    Our superstitious fools admire, and hold
    Their lead more precious than thy burnished gold,
    Thou hadst been their exchequer,[11] and no more
    They in each other's dung had searched for ore.
    Thou shalt yield no precèdence, but of time
    And the blind fate of language, whose tuned chime
    More charms the outward sense;[12] yet thou mayst claim
    From so great disadvantage greater fame,
    Since to the awe of thy imperious wit
50 Our troublesome language bends, made only fit
    With her tough thick-ribbed hoops to gird about
    Thy giant fancy, which had proved too stout
    For their[13] soft melting phrases. As in time
    They had the start, so did they cull the prime
    Buds of invention many a hundred year,
    And left the rifled fields, besides the fear
    To touch their harvest; yet from those bare lands
    Of what was only thine, thy only hands,
    And that their smallest work, have gleanèd more
60 Than all those times and tongues could reap before.
        But thou art gone, and thy strict laws will be

[3]**Delphic choir** the muses
[4]**Promethean breath** like the fire brought down by Prometheus from heaven
[5]**rage** inspiration
[6]**or** either
[7]**Anacreon** Greek poet to whom were ascribed delicate love lyrics much imitated by the Cavalier poets
[8]**Pindar** another ancient Greek poet

[9]**masculine** virile, in sense of "powerful"
[10]**Orpheus** the legendary original poet in Greek myth
[11]**exchequer** treasury
[12]**Thou shalt . . . sense** You shall yield first place to none, except in being later and not having the superficial musicality of these earlier poets.
[13]**their** referring to these earlier English poets

Too hard for libertines in poetry;
They will recall the goodly exiled train
Of gods and goddesses, which in thy just reign
Was banished nobler poems; now with these,
The silenced tales i' th' *Metamorphoses*
Shall stuff their lines, and swell the windy page,[14]
Till verse, refined by thee in this last age,
Turn ballad-rhyme, or those old idols be
70   Adored again with new apostasy.[15]
    O pardon me, that break with untuned verse
The reverend silence that attends thy hearse,
Whose solemn awful murmurs were to thee,
More than these rude lines, a loud elegy,
That did proclaim in a dumb eloquence,
The death of all the arts; whose influence,
Grown feeble, in these panting numbers[16] lies,
Gasping short-winded accents, and so dies.
So doth the swiftly turning wheel not stand
80   In the instant we withdraw the moving hand,
But some short time retain a faint weak course,
By virtue of the first impulsive force;
And so, whilst I cast on thy funeral pile
The crown of bays,[17] oh, let it crack awhile,
And spit disdain, till the devouring flashes
Suck all the moisture up, then turn to ashes.
    I will not draw thee envy to engross[18]
All thy perfections, or weep all the loss;
Those are too numerous for one elegy,
90   And this too great to be expressed by me.
Let others carve the rest; it shall suffice
I on thy grave this epitaph incise:
    Here lies a king that ruled as he thought fit
    The universal monarchy of wit;
    Here lies two flamens,[19] and both those the best,
    Apollo's[20] first, at last the true God's priest.

1633

[14]**now with these . . . windy page** Poets will bring back the clichés of Greek mythology, recorded in Ovid's work.
[15]**apostasy** abandonment of the true faith
[16]**numbers** verses

[17]**bays** laurel
[18]**engross** copy out
[19]**flamens** priests
[20]**Apollo's** of the pagan god of poetry (an allusion to Donne's love lyrics)

A Song

Ask me no more where Jove bestows,
When June is past, the fading rose;
For in your beauty's orient[1] deep
These flowers, as in their causes,[2] sleep.

[1]**orient** lustrous
[2]**causes** The matter of which something was made was the Aristotelian "material cause."

Ask me no more whither doth stray
The golden atoms of the day;
For in pure love heaven did prepare
Those powders to enrich your hair.

10   Ask me no more whither doth haste
The nightingale, when May is past;
For in your sweet dividing³ throat
She winters, and keeps warms her note.

Ask me no more where those stars light
That downwards fall in dead of night;
For in your eyes they sit, and there
Fixèd become, as in their sphere.⁴

Ask me no more if east or west
The phoenix⁵ builds her spicy nest;
For unto you at last she flies,
20   And in your fragrant bosom dies.

1640

---

³ **dividing** singing a rapid musical passage broken up into many short notes (as a nightingale does)
⁴ l. 16 Heavenly bodies were supposed to occupy concentric crystalline spheres surrounding the earth.

⁵ **phoenix** legendary unique bird that lived 1,000 years, then built a nest of spicy branches, set fire to them, was burned up, and was reborn from the ashes

---

EDMUND WALLER
1606–1687

We tend to associate Waller with such Cavalier poets as Carew, Lovelace, and Suckling because his poetry shows the same Jonsonian virtues and themes as theirs. Today, however, it does not seem to possess their strength, although it is often quite subtle. He lived to write much their kind of poetry far after the Cavalier heyday. Nevertheless for the eighteenth century Waller and Sir John Denham seemed the chief progenitors of the great Jonsonian line of development that reached its climax in that later time. Poems like "Go, Lovely Rose" and "On a Girdle" seem to sum up elegantly and succinctly the hedonistic message of *carpe diem* (see introduction to Herrick, above). In "Of English Verse" pragmatic skepticism gives the Renaissance dream of the eternity of poetry its quietus. It is hard to say which is more interesting in "To a Fair Lady, Playing with a Snake"—the delicate sexual innuendo or the rapid resignifications of the image. The snake in turn guards against lovers, enjoys their wished privilege, and turns into the tempter of the Garden of Eden.

Waller himself came of a rich family, and became richer by marriage. Finding it expedient to leave for France after participating in an unsuccessful plot to take London for the king during the Civil War, he returned to write a panegyric on Cromwell (the opposing Puritan leader), wrote an address of welcome to Charles II at the Restoration, and was held in esteem as a member of Parliament thereafter.

Go, Lovely Rose

Go, lovely rose,
Tell her that wastes her time and me[1]
  That now she knows,
When I resemble[2] her to thee,
  How sweet and fair she seems to be.

Tell her that's young,
And shuns to have her graces spied,
  That hadst thou sprung
In deserts, where no men abide,
10   Thou must have uncommended died.

Small is the worth
Of beauty from the light retired;
  Bid her come forth,
Suffer herseif to be desired,
  And not blush so to be admired.

Then die, that she
The common fate of all things rare
  May read in thee:
How small a part of time they share,
  That are so wondrous sweet and fair.

1645

[1] l. 2 who wastes the short time for love and lays me waste   [2] **resemble** compare

On a Girdle

That which her slender waist confined
Shall now my joyful temples bind;
No monarch but would give his crown,
His arms might do what this has done.[1]

It was my heaven's extremest[2] sphere,
The pale[3] which held that lovely deer;
My joy, my grief, my hope, my love,
Did all within this circle move.

A narrow compass, and yet there
10 Dwelt all that's good and all that's fair;
Give me but what this riband bound,
Take all the rest the sun goes round!

1645

[1] ll. 3–4 Any king would give the circle of his crown if his arms might clasp what this girdle has encircled.   [2] **extremest** outermost [3] **pale** enclosure

To a Fair Lady, Playing with a Snake

Strange! that such horror and such grace
Should dwell together in one place;
A fury's arm, an angel's face!

'Tis innocence, and youth, which makes
In Chloris' fancy such mistakes,
To start[1] at love, and play with snakes.

By this and by her coldness barred,
Her servants[2] have a task too hard;
The tyrant has a double guard!

10   Thrice happy snake! that in her sleeve
May boldly creep; we dare not give
Our thoughts so unconfined a leave.[3]

Contented in that nest of snow
He lies, as he his bliss did know,
And to the wood no more would go.

Take heed, fair Eve! you do not make
Another tempter of this snake;
A marble one so warmed would speak.[4]

1668

[1] **start** be startled
[2] **servants** lovers
[3] **we dare not . . . leave** We must not let even our thoughts travel to where the snake freely goes.
[4] l. 18 Even a statue of a snake would come to life and, like Satan in the serpent of Eden, begin to speak.

Of English Verse

Poets may boast, as safely vain,
Their works shall with the world remain;
Both, bound together, live or die,
The verses and the prophecy.

But who can hope his lines should long
Last in a daily changing tongue?
While they are new, envy prevails;
And as that dies, our language fails.

10   When architects have done their part,
The matter may betray their art:
Time, if we use ill-chosen stone,
Soon brings a well-built palace down.

Poets that lasting marble seek
Must carve in Latin or in Greek;
We write in sand, our language grows,
And, like the tide, our work o'erflows.

Chaucer his sense[1] can only boast,
The glory of his numbers[2] lost!
Years have defaced his matchless strain,
20   And yet he did not sing in vain:

The beauties which adorned that age,
The shining subjects of his rage,[3]
Hoping they should immortal prove,
Rewarded with success his love.

This was the generous poet's scope,
And all an English pen can hope,
To make the fair approve his flame,
That can so far extend their fame.

Verse, thus designed, has no ill fate
30   If it arrive but at the date
Of fading beauty;[4] if it prove
But as long-lived as present love.

1686

[1] **sense** meaning
[2] **numbers** poetry
[3] **rage** inspiration

[4] **If it . . . beauty** if it lasts only as long as the beauty it celebrates

JOHN MILTON
1608–1674

Milton's *Paradise Lost* fulfills the Renaissance ideal of great poetry that powerfully serves the cause of virtue and justice. The genius of this epic poem is closely related to the circumstances of its writing. It is the end-product of an almost infinite series of perilous choices, made in the face of religious and political upheavals in which Milton participated and to the accompaniment of his at first partial and then complete blindness.

Paradise Lost lays aside the glorification of military prowess that had preoccupied heroic poetry from Homer through Virgil

to Spenser. Instead, it accomplishes a "Copernican Revolution" in epic by glorifying humble obedience to the right in the inner theater of the human soul. That is why, in one selection here, the abandoned self-centeredness of Satan, the purity of Adam's attachment to God's law, and the graduation of Eve from narcissistic self-centeredness to respect and love for another are played out largely in terms of an account of inner feelings. Milton chose as well to reject the conspicuously masterful stanza patterns of all the highly regarded heroic poems of his day in favor of what he considered the most natural English form: blank verse (in which he had a precursor in Surrey's translations from the *Aeneid*). The exquisiteness, strength, and complex rhythmic variations with which he handled his lines surpassed the achievement of Surrey's translations and can be ranked with similarly complex elements in the blank verse of Shakespeare's late plays.

In *Paradise Lost*, too, Milton made another revolutionary choice in turning his back (with a few ifs and buts) on the Renaissance effort to clothe the Good in the glories of the pagan gods and pagan mythology. For him, all those gods properly belonged to the devil's party. He turned his back with similar scorn on whatever seemed to him licentious or merely graceful in the love poetry of the Cavaliers. In each case, however, his rejections were selective. Thus, he invokes the beautiful classical Gardens of the Hesperides, but as an image for the biblically relevant truth of Eden: "Hesperian fables true, / If true, here only." The astounding sensuousness of his descriptions applies always to faultless objects such as the abundant, natural riches of Eden and the love of Adam and Eve, whose sexuality is not concealed (another revolutionary choice) but is praised in its primal faultlessness. The learned evocation of far-off or ancient names —"Sabaean odors from the spicy shore / Of Araby the blest," or "Not that fair field of Enna, where Proserpin gath'ring flow'rs / Herself a fairer Flow'r by gloomy Dis was gather'd"—is another aspect of that caressing magic of sound that he manages best, but almost never (another decision) with the obvious artfulness of the Metaphysical conceit.

Milton was probably the most learned of all great poets. From early childhood he was intensively tutored and schooled, and after being graduated from Cambridge he devoted six years to further study. The notes to the two quotations above, when the reader encounters them, will give some intimation of the vast scholarly literature that has grown up to explain the breadth of reference and fastidious justice of his allusions, as well as their frequent linking together of narrative or lyric themes. But Milton's most important gift in exploiting his learning and experience goes beyond poetic allusion to mythopoeia, the making of myths or stories that imaginatively stamp our own lives.

L'Allegro and *Il Penseroso* are early examples of this power, formulating two aspects of personality in what the Middle Ages called a *divisio*—an examination of opposed principles. Our most obvious reward from this power is *Paradise Lost*, but Milton is strikingly mythopoeic even on the subject of himself, in his early sense of poetic vocation and high destiny and in some of his later sonnets, which he characteristically chose to compose in the difficult, choice Italian rhyme scheme (the first eight lines rhyming abbaabba, the last six rhyming in various ways, often cde cde). Even Sidney had compromised by using what, leaving aside Wyatt's experiments, was in English the previously almost universal concluding couplet. Milton's image of himself as a blind, prophetic bard or priest, inspired by a more heavenly muse than other poets could hear, is reinforced by his professed humility about his gift and by his having accomplished every last jot of what he claimed for himself.

His most astonishing early mythopoeic feat is *Lycidas*, a pastoral elegy for a friend. It unites the most discrete classical and Christian myths of death and resurrection in a daringly original way.

Milton's father was a well-to-do Protestant notary and moneylender who had rebelled against his father's Catholicism. He passed on his taste for music to his son and subsidized Milton's prolonged studies and an intellectually profitable and enjoyable visit to Italy. Milton's moral and religious commitment is suggested by his claim that he returned from there only to participate in the coming struggle to purify his country's political and religious life. The Civil War, marked by the beheading of Charles I, the imposition of the Cromwellian, so-called Puritan, regime, and the final defeat of Milton's side, through the restoration of the monarchy, absorbed Milton's intellectual energies as a combative essay writer for the Puritan and other causes and as the regime's official "Latin secretary." Physically defeated, he re-emerged from "the cool element of prose," below, into the heavenly "high region of his fancies," above, to write *Paradise Lost*. His brief epic *Paradise Regained* and his classical drama *Samson Agonistes* are also likely to belong to this

period. All his other poetry here, except for the sonnets, was written before the Puritan interregnum. About his personal life we know that he received students into his home and that his first wife was for a time estranged from him but then returned to bear him children. His austerity was tempered by some conviviality and a number of friendships.

On Shakespeare

What needs my Shakespeare for his honoured bones
The labour of an age in piled stones,
Or that his hallowed relics should be hid
Under a star-ypointing[1] pyramid?
Dear son of memory, great heir of fame,[2]
What need'st thou such weak witness of thy name?
Thou in our wonder and astonishment
Hast built thyself a live-long monument.[3]
For whilst to th' shame of slow-endeavouring art,
10 Thy easy numbers[4] flow, and that each heart
Hath from the leaves of thy unvalued[5] book
Those Delphic[6] lines with deep impression took;
Then thou, our fancy of itself bereaving,
Dost make us marble with too much conceiving;[7]
And so sepùlchered in such pomp dost lie,
That kings for such a tomb would wish to die.

1630   1632

[1] **ypointing** The archaic (and consequently "poetic") y- to prefix a participle imitates Spenser.
[2] l. 5 The muses were daughters of Memory; here Shakespeare becomes their brother.
[3] ll. 7–8 Your works create, in our admiration of them, a monument to you.

[4] **numbers** rhythmical verses
[5] **unvalued** invaluable
[6] **Delphic** associated with the Delphic oracle of Apollo, god of poetry
[7] ll. 13–14 You transfix us with a wealth of thought (cf. "our wonder and astonishment," above).

L'Allegro[1]

Hence, loathèd Melancholy,
    Of Cerberus[2] and blackest Midnight born
In Stygian[3] cave forlorn
    'Mongst horrid shapes, and shrieks, and sights unholy!
Find out some uncouth[4] cell,
    Where brooding Darkness spreads his jealous wings,

[1] the happy man
[2] **Cerberus** dog guarding hell's gate

[3] **Stygian** pertaining to river Styx in hell
[4] **uncouth** unknown, dreadful

And the night-raven sings;
 There, under ebon shades and low-browed rocks,
 As ragged as thy locks,
10 In dark Cimmerian[5] desert ever dwell.
But come, thou Goddess fair and free,
In heaven yclept[6] Euphrosyne,
And by men heart-easing Mirth;
Whom lovely Venus, at a birth,
With two sister Graces more,
To ivy-crowned Bacchus[7] bore:
Or whether (as some sager sing)
The frolic wind that breathes the spring,
Zephyr, with Aurora[8] playing,
20 As he met her once a-Maying,
There, on beds of violet blue,
And fresh-blown[9] roses washed in dew,
Filled her with thee, a daughter fair,
So buxom, blithe, and debonair.[10]
 Haste thee, Nymph, and bring with thee
Jest, and youthful jollity,
Quips and cranks and wanton wiles,
Nods and becks and wreathed smiles,
Such as hang on Hebe's[11] cheek,
30 And love to live in dimple sleek;
Sport that wrinkled Care derides,[12]
And Laughter holding both his sides.
Come, and trip it, as you go,
On the light fantastic toe;
And in thy right hand lead with thee
The mountain-nymph, sweet Liberty;
And, if I give thee honour due,
Mirth, admit me of thy crew,
To live with her, and live with thee,
40 In unreproved pleasures free;
To hear the lark begin his flight,
And, singing, startle the dull night,
From his watch-tower in the skies,
Till the dappled dawn doth rise;
Then to come, in spite[13] of sorrow,
And at my window bid good morrow,
Through the sweet-briar or the vine,
Or the twisted eglantine;
While the cock, with lively din,

[5]**Cimmerian** Cimmeria was imagined as a cloudy, dark, far land.
[6]**yclept** called. Euphrosyne (Mirth) was one of the three graces.
[7]**Bacchus** the wine god
[8]**Zephyr . . . Aurora** the gentle west wind; the dawn

[9]**fresh-blown** just bloomed
[10]**buxom . . . debonair** fetching, cheerful, and pleasant
[11]**Hebe** goddess of youth. She poured nectar for Zeus.
[12]**wrinkled Care derides** derides wrinkled Care
[13]**spite** contempt

50 Scatters the rear of darkness thin;
    And to the stack, or the barn door,
    Stoutly struts his dames before:
    Oft list'ning how the hounds and horn
    Cheerly rouse the slumbering morn,
    From the side of some hoar[14] hill.
    Through the high wood echoing shrill:
    Sometime walking, not unseen,
    By hedgerow elms, on hillocks green,
    Right against the eastern gate[15]
60 Where the great Sun begins his state,[16]
    Robed in flames and amber light,
    The clouds in thousand liveries dight;[17]
    While the ploughman, near at hand,
    Whistles o'er the furrowed land,
    And the milkmaid singeth blithe,
    And the mower whets his scythe,
    And every shepherd tells his tale[18]
    Under the hawthorn in the dale.
    Straight mine eye hath caught new pleasures,
70 Whilst the landskip round it measures:
    Russet lawns, and fallows grey,
    Where the nibbling flocks do stray;
    Mountains on whose barren breast
    The labouring clouds do often rest;
    Meadows trim with daisies pied;[19]
    Shallow brooks, and rivers wide;
    Towers and battlements it sees
    Bosomed high in tufted trees,
    Where perhaps some beauty lies,
80 The cynosure[20] of neighbouring eyes.
    Hard by, a cottage chimney smokes
    From betwixt two aged oaks,
    Where Corydon and Thyrsis met[21]
    Are at their savoury dinner set
    Of herbs and other country messes,[22]
    Which the neat-handed Phillis dresses;
    And then in haste her bower she leaves,
    With Thestylis to bind the sheaves;
    Or, if the earlier season lead,
90 To the tanned haycock in the mead.
    Sometimes, with secure[23] delight,
    The upland hamlets will invite,

[14]**hoar** gray
[15]**eastern gate** the horizon
[16]**state** pomp
[17]**dight** dressed
[18]**tells his tale** tells his story
[19]**pied** variegated
[20]**cynosure** center of attention (literally, con-
stellation containing North Star)
[21]**Corydon and Thyrsis** These, and names
below, are traditional literary ones from pas-
toral.
[22]**messes** portions of food, usually semiliquid,
like a stew
[23]**secure** free from care

When the merry bells ring round,
And the jocund rebecks[24] sound
To many a youth and many a maid
Dancing in the chequered shade,
And young and old come forth to play
On a sunshine holiday,
Till the livelong daylight fail:
100 Then to the spicy nut-brown ale,
With stories told of many a feat,
How Faëry Mab the junkets eat.[25]
She was pinched and pulled, she said;
And by the Friars' lantern[26] led,
Tells how the drudging goblin[27] sweat
To earn his cream-bowl duly set,
When in one night, ere glimpse of morn,
His shadowy flail hath threshed the corn
That ten day-labourers could not end;
110 Then lies him down the lubber fiend,[28]
And, stretched out all the chimney's[29] length,
Basks at the fire his hairy strength,
And crop-full out of doors he flings,
Ere the first cock his matin rings.
Thus done the tales, to bed they creep,
By whispering winds soon lulled asleep.
Towered cities please us then,
And the busy hum of men,
Where throngs of knights and barons bold,
120 In weeds[30] of peace, high triumphs[31] hold,
With store of ladies, whose bright eyes
Rain influence,[32] and judge the prize
Of wit or arms, while both contend
To win her grace whom all commend.
There let Hymen[33] oft appear
In saffron robe, with taper[34] clear,
And pomp, and feast, and revelry,
With mask[35] and antique pageantry:
Such sights as youthful poets dream
130 On summer eves by haunted stream.
Then to the well-trod stage anon,
If Jonson's learned sock[36] be on,
Or sweetest Shakespeare, Fancy's child,

[24]**rebecks** country fiddles
[25]**eat** ate
[26]**Friar's lantern** will-o'-the-wisp
[27]**goblin** Hobgoblin or Robin Goodfellow, a traditional figure
[28]**lubber fiend** a household spirit supposed to do chores
[29]**chimney** fireplace
[30]**weeds** clothes
[31]**triumphs** festivals
[32]**influence** astrological influence, as though the eyes were stars
[33]**Hymen** marriage god
[34]**taper** torch
[35]**mask** drama or entertainment for the aristocracy, with lavish costumes, music, dancing
[36]**sock** reference to Ben Jonson's comedies. The sock, or slipper, was worn by actors in Classical comedy.

Warble his native wood-notes wild.
   And ever, against eating cares,
Lap me in soft Lydian airs,[37]
Married to immortal verse,
Such as the meeting soul may pierce,
In notes with many a winding bout
140 Of linked sweetness long drawn out
With wanton heed and giddy cunning,
The melting voice through mazes running,
Untwisting all the chains that tie
The hidden soul of harmony;
That Orpheus'[38] self may heave his head
From golden slumber on a bed
Of heaped Elysian flowers, and hear
Such strains as would have won the ear
Of Pluto to have quite set free
150 His half-regained Eurydice.
   These delights if thou canst give,
Mirth, with thee I mean to live.

1631–32?   1645

[37]**Lydian airs** traditionally, relaxing, voluptuous music
[38]**Orpheus** This Thracian poet, whose music moved even inanimate things, now hears music that would have moved the god of the underworld to free Orpheus' wife, even though Orpheus himself had failed in his own attempt at the last moment.

Il Penseroso[1]

Hence, vain deluding Joys,
   The brood of Folly without father bred!
How little you bestèd,[2]
   Or fill the fixed mind with all your toys!
Dwell in some idle brain,
   And fancies fond[3] with gaudy shapes possess,
As thick and numberless
   As the gay motes that people the sunbeams,
Or likest hovering dreams,
10   The fickle pensioners[4] of Morpheus' train.
But, hail! thou Goddess sage and holy,
Hail, divinest Melancholy![5]
Whose saintly visage is too bright
To hit[6] the sense of human sight,
And therefore to our weaker view

[1]the pensive man
[2]**bestèd** profit
[3]**fond** foolish
[4]**pensioners** bodyguards
[5]**Melancholy** Unlike mirth, melancholy was diagnosed as a condition arising from too much black bile, one of the four humors (bodily fluids). Intellectual sharpness and study, as well as the modern meaning, were associated with melancholy.
[6]**hit** be borne by

O'erlaid with black, staid Wisdom's hue;
Black, but such as in esteem
Prince Memnon's sister[7] might beseem,
Or that starred Ethiop queen[8] that strove
20   To set her beauty's praise above
The Sea-Nymphs, and their powers offended.
Yet thou art higher far descended:
Thee bright-haired Vesta long of yore
To solitary Saturn bore;[9]
His daughter she; in Saturn's reign
Such mixture was not held a stain.[10]
Oft in glimmering bowers and glades
He met her, and in secret shades
Of woody Ida's inmost grove,
30   Whilst yet there was no fear of Jove.[11]
Come, pensive Nun, devout and pure,
Sober, steadfast, and demure,
All in a robe of darkest grain,[12]
Flowing with majestic train,
And sable stole of cypress lawn[13]
Over thy decent shoulders drawn.
Come, but keep thy wonted state,
With even step, and musing gait,
And looks commercing with the skies,
40   Thy rapt soul sitting in thine eyes:
There, held in holy passion[14] still,
Forget thyself to marble,[15] till
With a sad[16] leaden downward cast
Thou fix them on the earth as fast.[17]
And join with thee calm Peace and Quiet,
Spare Fast, that oft with gods doth diet,
And hears the Muses in a ring
Ay[18] round about Jove's altar sing;
And add to these retired Leisure,
50   That in trim gardens takes his pleasure;
But, first and chiefest, with thee bring
Him that yon soars on golden wing,
Guiding the fiery-wheeled throne,

[7]**Prince Memnon's sister** The Ethiopian (hence black) Prince Memnon had a sister Hemera, in one tradition.

[8]**starred Ethiop queen** Cassiopeia, punished by being made a constellation

[9]**Vesta . . . Saturn bore** Milton invents this parentage because Saturn (cf. "saturnine") is associated with melancholy, and perhaps because the hearth-goddess Vesta was enthroned in heaven and was the sober goddess of the Vestal flame and Virgins.

[10]**in Saturn's reign . . . stain** In Saturn's

Golden Age sex was free and innocent.

[11]**Jove** Saturn's son, master of the less blissful age succeeding the Golden one

[12]**grain** color

[13]**lawn** fine, black gauzy material

[14]**passion** ecstasy

[15]**Forget . . . marble** See note 5 to "On Shakespeare," p. 266 above.

[16]**sad** sober

[17]**fast** intently

[18]**Ay** forever

The Cherub Contemplation;[19]
And the mute Silence hist[20] along,
'Less Philomel[21] will deign a song,
In her sweetest, saddest plight,
Smoothing the rugged brow of Night,
While Cynthia[22] checks her dragon yoke
60   Gently o'er th' accustomed oak.
Sweet bird, that shunn'st the noise of folly,
Most musical, most melancholy!
Thee, chauntress, oft the woods among
I woo, to hear thy even-song;
And, missing thee, I walk unseen
On the dry smooth-shaven green,
To behold the wand'ring moon,
Riding near her highest noon,
Like one that had been led astray
70   Through the heaven's wide pathless way,
And oft, as if her head she bowed,
Stooping through a fleecy cloud.
Oft, on a plat of rising ground,
I hear the far-off curfew[23] sound,
Over some wide-watered shore,
Swinging slow with sullen roar;
Or, if the air will not permit,
Some still removed place will fit,
Where glowing embers through the room
80   Teach light to counterfeit a gloom,
Far from all resort of mirth,
Save the cricket on the hearth,
Or the bellman's[24] drowsy charm
To bless the doors from nightly harm.
Or let my lamp, at midnight hour,
Be seen in some high lonely tower,
Where I may oft outwatch the Bear,[25]
With thrice great Hermes,[26] or unsphere[27]
The spirit of Plato, to unfold
90   What worlds or what vast regions hold
The immortal mind that hath forsook
Her mansion in this fleshly nook;
And of those demons[28] that are found

[19] l. 54   See Ezekiel 1:5–16, where four cheru-
bim (higher angels) stand at four fiery wheels
of the Lord's throne.
[20] hist   summon whisperingly
[21] Philomel   the nightingale, into which chaste
but violated Philomel was transformed
[22] Cynthia   moon goddess, with a team of dra-
gons to draw the moon
[23] curfew   curfew-bell
[24] bellman's   night-watchman's

[25] the Bear   a never-setting constellation in
northern latitudes: stay up all night
[26] thrice great Hermes   Hermes Trismegis-
tus, identified with the Egyptian god Thoth
and with Hermes and the supposed author of
books of arcane knowledge
[27] unsphere   bring down from his heavenly
sphere
[28] demons   supernatural beings of the four ele-
ments, allegedly written about by Hermes

Whose power hath a true consent[29]
With planet or with element.
Sometime let gorgeous Tragedy
In sceptred pall come sweeping by,
In fire, air, flood, or underground,
Presenting Thebes, or Pelop's line,
100 Or the tale of Troy divine,[30]
Or what (though rare) of later age
Ennobled hath the buskined[31] stage.
    But, O sad Virgin! that thy power
Might raise Musaeus[32] from his bower;
Or bid the soul of Orpheus sing
Such notes as, warbled to the string,
Drew iron tears down Pluto's cheek
And made Hell grant what love did seek;[33]
Or call up him that left half-told
110 The story of Cambùscan bold,[34]
Of Camball, and of Algarsife,
And who had Canacé to wife,
That owned the virtuous ring and glass,
And of the wondrous horse of brass
On which the Tartar king did ride;
And if aught else great bards beside
In sage and solemn tunes have sung,
Of tourneys, and of trophies hung,
Of forests, and enchantments drear,
120 Where more is meant than meets the ear.[35]
    Thus, Night, oft see me in thy pale career,
Till civil-suited Morn[36] appear,
Not tricked and frounced,[37] as she was wont
With the Attic boy to hunt,
But kerchieft in a comely cloud,
While rocking winds are piping loud,
Or ushered with a shower still,
When the gust hath blown his fill,
Ending on the rustling leaves,
130 With minute-drops from off the eaves.
And, when the sun begins to fling
His flaring beams, me, Goddess, bring
To arched walks of twilight groves,
And shadows brown, that Sylvan[38] loves,

[29]**consent** correspondence
[30]ll. 99–100 main subjects of Greek tragedy
[31]**buskined** tragic—characterized by the buskin
(boot) of the ancient tragic actor
[32]**Musaeus** legendary Greek poet, contemporary with Orpheus
[33]l. 108 Orpheus' songs made Pluto liberate Orpheus' dead wife, Eurydice.
[34]l. 110 an allusion to Chaucer's unfinished Squire's Tale

[35]ll. 109–120 Spenser's allegorical *The Faerie Queene* best fits this description (and Spenser completed a version of the Squire's Tale).
[36]**civil-suited Morn** Aurora the dawn-goddess, but dressed in decorous (civil) gray sky. She loved the Attic boy Cephalus.
[37]**tricked and frounced** decked out and with curled hair
[38]**Sylvan** forest-god

Of pine, or monumental oak,
Where the rude axe with heaved stroke
Was never heard the nymphs to daunt,
Or fright them from their hallowed haunt.
There, in close covert, by some brook,
140 Where no profaner eye may look,
Hide me from day's garish eye,
While the bee with honied thigh,
That at her flowery work doth sing,
And the waters murmuring,
With such consort³⁹ as they keep,
Entice the dewy-feathered Sleep.
And let some strange mysterious dream
Wave at his wings, in airy stream
Of lively portraiture displayed,
150 Softly on my eyelids laid;
And, as I wake, sweet music breathe
Above, about, or underneath,
Sent by some Spirit to mortals good,
Or th' unseen Genius⁴⁰ of the wood.
    But let my due feet never fail
To walk the studious cloister's pale,⁴¹
And love the high embowed⁴² roof,
With antique pillars' massy-proof,⁴³
And storied windows⁴⁴ richly dight,⁴⁵
160 Casting a dim religious light.
There let the pealing organ blow,
To the full-voice quire below,
In service high and anthems clear,
As may with sweetness, through mine ear,
Dissolve me into ecstasies,
And bring Heaven before mine eyes.
And may at last my weary age
Find out the peaceful hermitage,
The hairy gown and mossy cell,
170 Where I may sit and rightly spell⁴⁶
Of every star that heaven doth shew,
And every herb that sips the dew,
Till old experience do attain
To something like prophetic strain.
    These pleasures, Melancholy, give;
And I with thee will choose to live.

1631–32?   1645

---

³⁹**consort** harmony
⁴⁰**Genius** guardian spirit
⁴¹**pale** enclosure
⁴²**embowed** arched
⁴³**massy-proof** massive strength

⁴⁴**storied windows** stained glass windows
    showing biblical stories
⁴⁵**dight** ornamented
⁴⁶**spell** find out about

How Soon Hath Time

How soon hath Time, the subtle thief of youth,
    Stolen on his wing my three-and-twentieth year!
    My hasting days fly on with full career,
    But my late spring no bud or blossom show'th.
Perhaps my semblance[1] might deceive the truth
    That I to manhood am arrived so near;
    And inward ripeness doth much less appear,
    That some more timely-happy spirits indu'th.[2]
Yet, be it less or more, or soon or slow,
10   It shall be still in strictest measure even[3]
    To that same lot, however mean or high,
Toward which Time leads me, and the will of Heaven.
    All is, if I have grace to use it so,
    As ever in my great Task-Master's eye.

1631   1645

[1] **semblance** appearance
[2] **indu'th** endoweth
[3] **even** corresponding

Lycidas

In this Monody[1] the Author bewails a learned Friend,
unfortunately drowned in his passage from Chester on the
Irish Seas, 1637; and, by occasion, foretells the ruin of our
corrupted Clergy, then in their height.

Yet once more, O ye laurels, and once more,
Ye myrtles brown, with ivy never sere,[2]
I come to pluck your berries harsh and crude,[3]
And with forced fingers rude
Shatter your leaves before the mellowing year.
Bitter constraint and sad occasion dear[4]
Compels me to disturb your season due;
For Lycidas is dead, dead ere his prime,
Young Lycidas, and hath not left his peer.
10 Who would not sing for Lycidas? he knew
Himself to sing, and build the lofty rhyme.
He must not float upon his watery bier
Unwept, and welter[5] to the parching wind,
Without the meed[6] of some melodious tear.[7]
    Begin, then, Sisters of the sacred well[8]

[1] **Monody** a composition, often a dirge, sung by a single voice. "Lycidas" was first published in a volume of commemorative verse for Edward King. He and Milton had been students in the same Cambridge college.
[2] ll. 1–2 Evergreen laurel, myrtle, and ivy are used for the crown of the laureate poet. **brown** dark; **sere** withered
[3] **crude** unripe
[4] **dear** heartfelt, dire
[5] **welter** tumble, writhe
[6] **meed** tribute
[7] **tear** Collections of elegiac verse were often called *lachrymae*, "tears."
[8] **Sisters . . . well** The muses traditionally danced around the altar of Jove at their sacred well, Aganippe, on Mt. Helicon.

That from beneath the seat of Jove doth spring;
Begin, and somewhat loudly sweep the string.
Hence with denial vain and coy excuse:
So may some gentle Muse⁹
20   With lucky¹⁰ words favour my destined urn,
And as he passes turn,
And bid fair peace be to my sable shroud!
For we were nursed upon the self-same hill,
Fed the same flock, by fountain, shade, and rill;
Together both, ere the high lawns¹¹ appeared
Under the opening eyelids of the Morn,
We drove a-field, and both together heard
What time the grey-fly winds her sultry horn,
Batt'ning¹² our flocks with the fresh dews of night,
30   Oft till the star that rose at evening bright
Toward heaven's descent had sloped his westering wheel.
Meanwhile the rural ditties were not mute,
Tempered to th' oaten flute;
Rough Satyrs danced, and Fauns with cloven heel
From the glad sound would not be absent long;
And old Damaetas¹³ loved to hear our song.
   But, oh! the heavy change, now thou art gone,
Now thou art gone, and never must return!
Thee, Shepherd, thee the woods, and desert caves,
40   With wild thyme and the gadding¹⁴ vine o'ergrown,
And all their echoes, mourn.
The willows, and the hazel copses green,
Shall now no more be seen,
Fanning their joyous leaves to thy soft lays.
As killing as the canker to the rose,
Or taint-worm to the weanling herds that graze,
Or frost to flowers, that their gay wardrobe wear,
When first the white-thorn blows;¹⁵
Such, Lycidas, thy loss to shepherd's ear.
50   Where were ye, Nymphs, when the remorseless deep
Closed o'er the head of your loved Lycidas?
For neither were ye playing on the steep,
Where your old bards, the famous Druids, lie,
Nor on the shaggy top of Mona¹⁶ high,
Nor yet where Deva¹⁷ spreads her wizard stream.
Ay me! I fondly¹⁸ dream

---

⁹**Muse** of another poet
¹⁰**lucky** felicitous
¹¹**lawns** glades
¹²**Batt'ning** fattening
¹³**Damaetas** conventional pastoral name, refer-
ring probably to a Cambridge tutor
¹⁴**gadding** wandering
¹⁵**blows** blooms
¹⁶**Mona** probably the slopes ("steep") and the

peak ("top") of Mona, or Anglesey, island off
the northwest coast of Wales that was a resort
of the Druids. King's ship apparently went
down nearby.
¹⁷**Deva** River Dee, east of Anglesey. Changes
in the places where it could be forded were re-
garded as omens for the future: hence "wizard."
¹⁸**fondly** foolishly

Had ye been there, . . . for what could that have done?
What could the Muse herself that Orpheus bore,
The Muse herself, for her enchanting son,
60   Whom universal nature did lament,
When, by the rout that made the hideous roar,
His gory visage down the stream was sent,
Down the swift Hebrus to the Lesbian shore?[19]
    Alas! what boots[20] it with incessant care
To tend the homely, slighted, shepherd's trade,
And strictly meditate the thankless Muse?
Were it not better done, as others use,
To sport with Amaryllis[21] in the shade,
Or with the tangles of Neaera's hair?
70   Fame is the spur that the clear spirit doth raise
(That last infirmity of noble mind)
To scorn delights, and live laborious days;
But the fair guerdon[22] when we hope to find,
And think to burst out into sudden blaze,
Comes the blind Fury with th' abhorred shears,[23]
And slits the thin-spun life. "But not the praise,"
Phoebus[24] replied, and touched my trembling ears:
"Fame is no plant that grows on mortal soil,
Nor in the glistering foil[25]
80   Set off to the world, nor in broad rumour lies,
But lives and spreads aloft by those pure eyes
And perfect witness of all-judging Jove;
As he pronounces lastly on each deed,
Of so much fame in heaven expect thy meed."
    O fountain Arethuse,[26] and thou honoured flood,
Smooth-sliding Mincius, crowned with vocal reeds,
That strain I heard was of a higher mood.
But now my oat[27] proceeds,
And listens to the Herald of the Sea
90   That came in Neptune's plea.[28]
He asked the waves, and asked the felon[29] winds,
What hard mishap hath doomed this gentle swain?
And questioned every gust of rugged wings
That blows from off each beaked promontory.

[19] ll. 58–63 What could the muse Calliope, mother of the original poet Orpheus, have done when maddened female votaries of Dionysus tore him to pieces? His head floated down the river Hebrus and across the sea to the island of Lesbos.

[20] boots profits

[21] Amaryllis conventional pastoral name for a girl, like "Neaera"

[22] guerdon reward

[23] l. 75 Atropos, third of the Fates, cuts the thread of life which is spun and measured by the other two.

[24] Phoebus Apollo, god of poetry

[25] foil placed behind a gem to increase its brilliance

[26] Arethuse fountain in Sicily, emblematic of early pastoral of Theocritus. The river Mincius, on which Virgil was born, suggests Roman pastoral.

[27] oat oaten pipe

[28] ll. 89–90 Triton, blowing his shell trumpet, comes to defend Neptune from responsibility for Lycidas's death.

[29] felon savage

They knew not of his story;
And sage Hippotades[30] their answer brings,
That not a blast was from his dungeon strayed;
The air was calm, and on the level brine
Sleek Panope[31] with all her sisters played.
100   It was that fatal and perfidious bark,
Built in th' eclipse,[32] and rigged with curses dark,
That sunk so low that sacred head of thine.
    Next, Camus,[33] reverend sire, went footing slow,
His mantle hairy, and his bonnet sedge,[34]
Inwrought with figures dim, and on the edge
Like to that sanguine flower inscribed with woe.[35]
"Ah! who hath reft," quoth he, "my dearest pledge?"[36]
Last came, and last did go,
The Pilot of the Galilean Lake;[37]
110   Two massy keys he bore of metals twain
(The golden opes, the iron shuts amain).
He shook his mitred locks, and stern bespake: —
"How well could I have spared for thee, young swain,
Enow[38] of such as, for their bellies' sake,
Creep, and intrude, and climb into the fold![39]
Of other care they little reck'ning make
Than how to scramble at the shearers' feast,
And shove away the worthy bidden guest.
Blind mouths! that scarce themselves know how to hold
120   A sheep-hook, or have learned aught else the least
That to the faithful herdman's art belongs!
What recks it them?[40] What need they? They are sped;[41]
And, when they list,[42] their lean and flashy[43] songs
Grate on their scrannel[44] pipes of wretched straw;
The hungry sheep look up, and are not fed,
But, swoln with wind and the rank mist they draw,
Rot inwardly, and foul contagion spread:
Besides what the grim wolf[45] with privy paw
Daily devours apace, and nothing said.
130   But that two-handed engine[46] at the door

[30]**Hippotades** god of winds
[31]**Panope** one of the Nereids or sea-nymphs
[32]**eclipse** Eclipses were evil omens.
[33]**Camus** Cambridge, in fur-trimmed ("hairy") academic gown
[34]**sedge** made of water plants — iris or rush
[35]**sanguine . . . woe** The hyacinth was said to grow from the blood of a youth accidentally killed by Apollo. Its markings spelled AI AI ("alas, alas").
[36]**my dearest pledge** child (as a token of its parents' love)
[37]l. 109 St. Peter was a fisherman on Lake Galilee; Christ promised him the keys of heaven; as first head of the Church he wears the bishop's miter and denounces false teachers (as here) in 2 Peter 2.

[38]**Enow** enough
[39]ll. 114–15 See parable of the shepherd in John 10:1–28 for this and following.
[40]**What recks it them?** What do they care about it?
[41]**They are sped** They have got what they wanted.
[42]**list** choose
[43]**flashy** trifling
[44]**scrannel** meager
[45]**grim wolf** the Roman Catholic church, or perhaps the anti-Protestant bishops in England
[46]**two-handed engine** variously interpreted — an instrument of retribution against evil clergy; perhaps the two-edged sword of Revelation 1:16, representing the forces of the Reformation.

Stands ready to smite once, and smite no more."
   Return, Alpheus,[47] the dread voice is past
That shrunk thy streams; return, Sicilian Muse,[48]
And call the vales, and bid them hither cast
Their bells and flowrets of a thousand hues.
Ye valleys low, where the mild whispers use[49]
Of shades, and wanton winds, and gushing brooks,
On whose fresh lap the swart star sparely looks,[50]
Throw hither all your quaint enamelled eyes,
140   That on the green turf suck the honied showers,
And purple all the ground with vernal flowers.
Bring the rathe[51] primrose that forsaken dies,
The tufted crow-toe, and pale jessamine,[52]
The white pink, and the pansy freaked[53] with jet,
The glowing violet,
The musk-rose, and the well-attired woodbine,
With cowslips wan that hang the pensive head,
And every flower that sad embroidery wears:
Bid amaranthus[54] all his beauty shed,
150   And daffadillies fill their cups with tears,
To strew the laureate hearse where Lycid lies.
For so, to interpose a little ease,
Let our frail thoughts dally with false surmise.[55]
Ay me! whilst thee the shores and sounding seas
Wash far away, where'er thy bones are hurled;
Whether beyond the stormy Hebrides,
Where thou perhaps under the whelming tide
Visit'st the bottom of the monstrous[56] world;
Or whether thou, to our moist vows[57] denied,
160   Sleep'st by the fable of Bellerus[58] old,
Where the great Vision of the guarded mount
Looks toward Namancos, and Bayona's hold;[59]
Look homeward, Angel, now, and melt with ruth:[60]
And, O ye dolphins, waft the hapless youth.[61]
   Weep no more, woeful shepherds, weep no more,
For Lycidas, your sorrow, is not dead,

[47]**Alpheus** Greek river god in love with Arethusa (l. 85); when she fled to Sicily, he dived under the sea and came up there. She became a fountain and his waters mingled with hers.

[48]**Sicilian muse** of Theocritian pastoral poetry. See note 26.

[49]**use** go frequently

[50]l. 138 The "swart star" is Sirius, the Dog Star, whose days are hot. **swart** darkened by heat; **sparely** seldom

[51]**rathe** early

[52]l. 143 wild hyacinth and jasmine

[53]**freaked** capriciously flecked or streaked

[54]**amaranthus** imaginary unfading flower, ancient symbol of immortality

[55]**false surmise** false because the lost body of Lycidas cannot be strewn with flowers, and because flowers and nature in reality are not saddened for us

[56]**monstrous** inhabited by sea-monsters

[57]**moist vows** tearful prayers

[58]**Bellerus** invented by Milton as founder of Bellerium, Latin name for Land's End in Cornwall, south of King's shipwreck in the Irish Sea

[59]l. 162 St. Michael, the warlike guardian angel, here looks from St. Michael's Mount, off the south shore of Cornwall, toward northwestern Spain, haven of Catholicism.

[60]**ruth** pity

[61]l. 164 i.e., like the poet Arion, thrown overboard and then carried to land by a dolphin

Sunk though he be beneath the wat'ry floor.
So sinks the day-star[62] in the ocean bed,
And yet anon repairs his drooping head,
170 And tricks[63] his beams, and with new-spangled ore
Flames in the forehead of the morning sky:
So Lycidas sunk low, but mounted high,
Through the dear might of Him that walked the waves;
Where,[64] other groves and other streams along,
With nectar pure his oozy locks he laves,
And hears the unexpressive[65] nuptial song,[66]
In the blest kingdoms meek of joy and love.
There entertain him all the Saints above,
In solemn troops, and sweet societies,
180 That sing, and singing in their glory move,
And wipe the tears for ever from his eyes.[67]
Now, Lycidas, the shepherds weep no more;
Henceforth thou art the Genius[68] of the shore,
In thy large recompense, and shalt be good
To all that wander in that perilous flood.
　　Thus sang the uncouth[69] swain to th' oaks and rills,
While the still morn went out with sandals grey:
He touched the tender stops[70] of various quills,[71]
With eager thought warbling his Doric[72] lay:
190 And now the sun had stretched out all the hills,
And now was dropped into the western bay;
At last he rose, and twitched his mantle blue:
To-morrow to fresh woods, and pastures new.

1637　　　　　　　　　　　　　　　　　1645

[62]**day-star** sun
[63]**tricks** trims
[64]**Where** Heaven, the New Jerusalem. See Revelation 22:1-2.
[65]**unexpressive** inexpressible
[66]**nuptial song** the marriage of the Lamb. See Revelation 19:7.

[67]l. 181 See Revelation 7:17, 21:4.
[68]**Genius** guardian spirit
[69]**uncouth** unknown
[70]**stops** finger-holes
[71]**quills** the hollow reeds of the pipe
[72]**Doric** Greek dialect of the pastoral poets Theocritus, Moschus, and Bion

A Book Was Writ of Late

A book was writ of late[1] called *Tetrachordon*,
　And wov'n close, both matter, form, and style;
　The subject new: it walked the town awhile,
　Numb'ring good intellects; now seldom pored on.
Cries the stall-reader,[2] "Bless us! what a word on

[1]**of late** recently; *Tetrachordon*, the title of Milton's pamphlet, means "four-stringed," referring to four biblical passages treating marriage and divorce.

[2]**stall-reader** reader inspecting the work at a book-seller's stall

A title-page is this!''; and some in file
Stand spelling false,[3] while one might walk to Mile-
End Green.[4] Why is it harder, sirs, than *Gordon*,
Colkitto, or *Macdonnel*, or *Galasp*?[5]
10   Those rugged names to our like mouths grow sleek[6]
That would have made Quintilian[7] stare and gasp.
Thy age, like ours, O soul of Sir John Cheke,[8]
Hated not learning worse than toad or asp,[9]
When thou taught'st Cambridge and King Edward Greek.

1647?   1673

[3] **spelling false** misinterpreting
[4] **walk to Mile-End Green** walk all the way to the outskirts of the city
[5] *Gordon . . . Galasp* names of Scottish supporters of King Charles I, and enemies of Milton's party
[6] l. 10 Since our English mouths are rough-hewn and barbarous, these barbarous names are easily accepted (unlike "Tetrachordon").

[7] **Quintilian** Latin rhetorician who condemned the use of foreign words
[8] **Sir John Cheke** famous, learned humanist (1514–1557), who spread the love of classical Latin and Greek; tutor of Edward VI
[9] ll. 12–13 Your age did not loathe learning, as ours does.

When I Consider How My Light Is Spent

When I consider how my light is spent,[1]
Ere half my days in this dark world and wide,
And that one talent[2] which is death to hide
Lodged with me useless, though my soul more bent
To serve therewith my Maker, and present
My true account, lest He returning chide;
"Doth God exact day-labour, light denied?"
I fondly[3] ask: but Patience, to prevent
That murmur, soon replies, "God doth not need
10   Either man's work or his own gifts. Who best
Bear his mild yoke, they serve him best: his state
Is kingly: thousands at his bidding speed,
And post o'er land and ocean without rest;
They also serve who only stand and wait."

1652?   1673

[1] l. 1 Milton became totally blind in 1651.
[2] **talent** Milton plays on two meanings. In the parable of the talents (Matthew 25:14-30) a servant given a talent (large sum of money) by his master buries it instead of using it to earn more. All the servant has is taken away; he is cast "into outer darkness."
[3] **fondly** foolishly

To Mr. Lawrence

Lawrence, of virtuous father virtuous son,[1]
  Now that the fields are dank, and ways are mire,
  Where shall we sometimes meet, and by the fire
  Help waste a sullen day, what may be won
From the hard season gaining? Time will run
  On smoother, till Favonius[2] reinspire
  The frozen earth, and clothe in fresh attire
  The lily and rose, that neither sowed nor spun.[3]
What neat repast shall feast us, light and choice,
10 Of Attic[4] taste, with wine, whence we may rise
  To hear the lute well touched, or artful voice
Warble immortal notes and Tuscan air?
  He who of those delights can judge, and spare
  To interpose them oft,[5] is not unwise.

c. 1653   1673

[1] l. 1 Edward Lawrence (1633–1657), son of the
chairman of Cromwell's Council, often visited
Milton. This line and others are reminiscent of
Horace's cultivated festal cheer in the *Odes*.
[2] **Favonius** the west wind, favorable to vegeta-
tion

[3] l. 8 See Matthew 6:28.
[4] **Attic** elegant, discriminating — characteristic
of Athens
[5] **spare . . . oft** often spare the time to insert
these occasions into life

On His Deceased Wife

Methought I saw my late espoused saint
  Brought to me like Alcestis[1] from the grave,
  Whom Jove's great son to her glad husband gave,
  Rescued from Death by force, though pale and faint.
Mine, as whom washed from spot of childbed taint
  Purification in the Old Law did save,[2]
  And such as yet once more I trust to have
  Full sight of her in Heaven without restraint,
Came vested all in white, pure as her mind.
10 Her face was veiled; yet to my fancied sight
  Love, sweetness, goodness, in her person shined
So clear as in no face with more delight.
  But, O! as to embrace me she inclined,
  I waked, she fled, and day brought back my night.[3]

1658?   1673

[1] **Alcestis** After giving her life for her husband,
she was rescued from the underworld by Her-
cules, son of Jove.
[2] ll. 5–9 The Old Law of the Old Testament
provided a period of bodily purification after
childbirth. Milton's first wife, Mary, died be-
fore the end of this period. His second wife,
Katherine, died after the period was completed.
Perhaps "pure as her mind" (l. 9) refers to

the contrasting inner, spiritual reality of the
New Testament.
[3] l. 14 The disappointed sonneteering lover's
standard complaint — that his day turns to
night and that he sees or has his lady only in
dreams — acquires greater pathos here: having
gone blind, Milton never saw his second wife's
face ("veiled") and could not see the light of
day.

From Paradise Lost

From Book I: The Induction[1]

Of man's first disobedience, and the fruit[2]
Of that forbidden tree, whose mortal taste
Brought death into the world, and all our woe,
With loss of Eden, till one greater Man[3]
Restore us, and regain the blissful seat,[4]
Sing, heavenly Muse,[5] that on the secret top
Of Oreb, or of Sinai,[6] didst inspire
That shepherd who first taught the chosen seed
In the beginning how the heavens and earth
10 Rose out of Chaos; or if Sion hill
Delight thee more, and Siloa's brook[7] that flowed
Fast by the oracle of God, I thence
Invoke thy aid to my adventurous song,
That with no middle flight intends to soar
Above the Aonian mount,[8] while it pursues
Things unattempted yet in prose or rhyme.
And chiefly thou, O Spirit,[9] that dost prefer
Before all temples the upright heart and pure,
Instruct me, for thou knowest; thou from the first
20 Wast present, and with mighty wings outspread
Dove-like sat'st brooding on the vast abyss
And mad'st it pregnant: what in me is dark
Illumine, what is low raise and support;
That to the highth of this great argument
I may assert eternal providence,
And justify the ways of God to men.

. . .

1658?–65?   1667

---

[1] Milton subtly follows but transforms here the traditional openings of previous heroic poems, or epics (cf. the openings of Homer's *Iliad* and Virgil's *Aeneid*). The transcendent importance of his subject will allow him to transcend those poems.
[2] **fruit** the apple, but also the ultimate results of eating it
[3] **Man** Christ, the "second Adam"
[4] **Seat** home, residence
[5] **Muse** Urania, highest of the nine muses, imagined here as having inspired Moses, teacher of Israel, with the knowledge of creation recorded in Genesis
[6] **Sinai** where Moses received the Law from God
[7] **brook** site of the Temple in Jerusalem. Siloa is nearby.

[8] **Aonian mount** home of the muses of classical poetry. *Paradise Lost* will treat matters far higher, in altitude and significance. L. 16 translates a line from the second stanza of Ludovico Ariosto's sixteenth-century heroic poem *Orlando Furioso*, but Milton means that his use of the words is more fundamentally literal.
[9] **Spirit** the Holy Ghost, third person of the Trinity, dwelling within the human soul in preference to man-made temples like Zion's, above. In ll. 20–22 this spirit is the one moving "upon the face of the waters" in Genesis 1:2. Compare Gerard Manley Hopkins's evocation of it as a bird in the concluding couplet of "God's Grandeur" (p. 747 below).

From Book IV

". . . Me miserable! which way shall I fly
Infinite wrath and infinite despair?
Which way I fly is Hell; myself am Hell;
And, in the lowest deep, a lower deep
Still threat'ning to devour me opens wide,
To which the Hell I suffer seems a Heaven.
O, then, at last relent! is there no place
80 Left for repentance, none for pardon left?
None left but by submission; and that word
Disdain forbids me, and my dread of shame
Among the Spirits beneath, whom I seduced
With other promises and other vaunts
Than to submit, boasting I could subdue
Th' Omnipotent. Ay me! they little know
How dearly I abide that boast so vain,
Under what torments inwardly I groan:
While they adore me on the throne of Hell,
90 With diadem and sceptre high advanced,
The lower still I fall, only supreme
In misery: such joy ambition finds!
But say I could repent, and could obtain,
By act of grace, my former state; how soon
Would height recall high thoughts, how soon unsay
What feigned submission swore! Ease would recant[1]
Vows made in pain, as violent and void;
For never can true reconcilement grow
Where wounds of deadly hate have pierced so deep:
100 Which would but lead me to a worse relapse
And heavier fall; so should I purchase dear
Short intermission, bought with double smart.
This knows my Punisher; therefore as far
From granting he, as I from begging, peace.
All hope excluded thus, behold, instead
Of us, outcast, exiled, his new delight,
Mankind, created, and for him this World!
So farewell hope, and with hope, farewell fear,
Farewell remorse! All good to me is lost;
110 Evil, be thou my Good: by thee at least
Divided empire with Heaven's King I hold,
By thee, and more than half perhaps will reign;
As Man ere long, and this new World, shall know."
    Thus while he spake, each passion dimmed his face,
Thrice changed with pale, ire, envy, and despair;[2]
Which marred his borrowed visage, and betrayed
Him counterfeit, if any eye beheld:

[1]**recant** renounce, withdraw
[2]**each passion . . . despair** the successive passions of the deadly sins ire, envy, and despair

changed the ruddy complexion of a young cherub (Satan's disguise) three times to paleness.

For Heavenly minds from such distempers foul
Are ever clear. Whereof he soon aware
120 Each perturbation smoothed with outward calm,
Artificer of fraud; and was the first
That practised falsehood under saintly show,
Deep malice to conceal, couched[3] with revenge:
Yet not enough had practised to deceive
Uriel, once warned; whose eye pursued him down
The way he went, and on th' Assyrian[4] mount
Saw him disfigured, more than could befall
Spirit of happy sort: his gestures fierce
He marked and mad demeanour, then alone,
130 As he supposed, all unobserved, unseen.
So on he fares, and to the border comes
Of Eden,[5] where delicious Paradise,
Now nearer, crowns with her enclosure green,
As with a rural mound, the champaign[6] head
Of a steep wilderness, whose hairy sides
With thicket overgrown, grotesque and wild,
Access denied; and overhead up-grew
Insuperable height of loftiest shade,
Cedar, and pine, and fir, and branching palm,
140 A sylvan scene, and, as the ranks ascend
Shade above shade, a woody theatre[7]
Of stateliest view. Yet higher than their tops
The verdurous wall of Paradise up-sprung;
Which to our general sire gave prospect large
Into his nether empire neighbouring round.
And higher than that wall a circling row
Of goodliest trees, loaden with fairest fruit,
Blossoms and fruits at once[8] of golden hue,
Appeared, with gay enamelled[9] colours mixed;
150 On which the sun more glad impressed his beams
Than in fair evening cloud, or humid bow,[10]
When God hath showered the earth: so lovely seemed
That landscape; and of pure, now purer air
Meets his approach, and to the heart inspires
Vernal[11] delight and joy, able to drive
All sadness but despair. Now gentle gales,
Fanning their odoriferous wings, dispense
Native perfumes, and whisper whence they stole
Those balmy spoils. As when to them who sail
160 Beyond the Cape of Hope, and now are past

---

[3] **couched** hidden
[4] **th' Assyrian** Niphates, named at end of Bk. III
[5] **border . . . Eden** The Garden of Eden is thought of as in the land of Eden.
[6] **champaign** open, level
[7] **ranks . . . theatre** like the ascending, ranked seat-rows of an ancient theater

[8] **at once** at the same time. The Garden has the good things of all seasons at once: successive seasons came after the Fall, when the earth's axis was tipped or the sun's course was changed.
[9] **enamelled** bright
[10] **humid bow** rainbow
[11] **Vernal** springlike

Mozambic, off at sea north-east winds blow
Sabean odours from the spicy shore
Of Araby the Blest, with such delay
Well pleased they slack their course, and many a league
Cheered with the grateful smell old Ocean smiles;[12]
So entertained those odorous sweets the Fiend
Who came their bane, though with them better pleased
Than Asmodëus with the fishy fume
That drove him, though enamoured, from the spouse
170   Of Tobit's son, and with a vengeance sent
From Media post to Egypt, there fast bound.[13]
    Now to th' ascent of that steep savage hill
Satan had journeyed on, pensive and slow;
But further way found none; so thick entwined,
As one continued brake,[14] the undergrowth
Of shrubs and tangling bushes had perplexed[15]
All path of man or beast that passed that way.
One gate there only was, and that looked east
On th' other side: which when th' Arch-felon saw,
180   Due entrance he disdained, and, in contempt,
At one slight bound high overleaped all bound
Of hill or highest wall, and sheer within
Lights on his feet. As when a prowling wolf,
Whom hunger drives to seek new haunt for prey,
Watching where shepherds pen their flocks at eve,
In hurdled cotes[16] amid the field secure,
Leaps o'er the fence with ease into the fold;
Or as a thief, bent to unhoard the cash
Of some rich burgher, whose substantial doors,
190   Cross-barred and bolted fast, fear no assault,
In at the window climbs, or o'er the tiles;[17]
So clomb this first grand Thief into God's fold:
So since into his Church lewd hirelings climb.
Thence up he flew, and on the Tree of Life,[18]
The middle tree and highest there that grew,
Sat like a cormorant;[19] yet not true life
Thereby regained, but say devising death
To them who lived; nor on the virtue[20] thought
Of that life-giving plant, but only used

---

[12]**north-east winds . . . Ocean smiles:** Sailing northeast, the mariners are delayed by winds from that direction. Odors from Saba (Sheba, Yemen) or generally southern Arabia (Arabia felix — "blest") please them.

[13]ll. 166–71 In the apocryphal book of Tobit the demon Asmodeus jealously killed men who had wished to marry Sara. Advised by the angel Raphael, Tobias burned the heart and liver of a fish and the smoke drove Asmodeus far away to Egypt, where he was bound by the angel. Satan lacks the excuse of infatuated jealousy, yet is met by pleasant odors. He will be bound by Christ, the second Adam.

[14]**brake** thicket

[15]**had perplexed** would have made difficult

[16]**hurdled cotes** shelters with hurdles — twig-enlaced frames used for temporary fencing

[17]**tiles** roof-tiles

[18]**Tree of Life** The tree of life and the tree of knowledge were in the middle of the Garden of Eden (see Genesis 2:9).

[19]**cormorant** a rapacious bird, to whom greedy clergy were sometimes compared

[20]**virtue** specific power

200   For prospect what, well used, had been the pledge
     Of immortality. So little knows
     Any, but God alone, to value right
     The good before him, but perverts best things
     To worst abuse, or to their meanest use.
     Beneath him, with new wonder, now he views,
     To all delight of human sense exposed,
     In narrow room Nature's whole wealth; yea, more! —
     A Heaven on Earth: for blissful Paradise
     Of God the garden was, by him in the east
210   Of Eden planted; Eden stretched her line
     From Auran eastward to the royal towers
     Of great Seleucia, built by Grecian kings,
     Or where the sons of Eden long before
     Dwelt in Telassar.[21] In this pleasant soil
     His far more pleasant garden God ordained.
     Out of the fertile ground he caused to grow
     All trees of noblest kind for sight, smell, taste;
     And all amid them stood the Tree of Life,
     High eminent, blooming ambrosial fruit
220   Of vegetable gold; and, next to life,
     Our death, the Tree of Knowledge, grew fast by—
     Knowledge of good, bought dear by knowing ill.[22]
     Southward through Eden went a river large,
     Nor changed his course, but through the shaggy hill
     Passed underneath ingulfed; for God had thrown
     That mountain, as his garden-mould, high raised
     Upon the rapid current, which through veins
     Of porous earth with kindly[23] thirst updrawn
     Rose a fresh fountain, and with many a rill
230   Watered the garden; thence united fell
     Down the steep glade, and met the nether flood,
     Which from his darksome passage now appears,
     And now, divided into four main streams,[24]
     Runs diverse, wandering many a famous realm
     And country whereof here needs no account;
     But rather to tell how, if Art could tell
     How, from that sapphire fount the crispèd[25] brooks,
     Rolling on orient[26] pearl and sands of gold,
     With mazy error under pendent shades
240   Ran nectar, visiting each plant, and fed
     Flowers worthy of Paradise, which not nice Art
     In beds and curious knots, but Nature boon[27]

[21] **Auran . . . Telassar** locations near the junction of the Tigris and Euphrates rivers, at the head of the Persian Gulf, where many believed Eden to have been

[22] l. 222 Milton says in his *Areopagitica*: "And perhaps this is that doom which Adam fell into of knowing good and evil, that is to say of knowing good by evil."

[23] **kindly** natural

[24] l. 233 See Genesis 2:10–14.

[25] **crispèd** rippling

[26] **orient** lustrous

[27] ll. 241–42 not the artifice of intricate flower-beds but the plenty of bounteous, benign ("boon") nature

Poured forth profuse on hill, and dale, and plain,
Both where the morning sun first warmly smote
The open field, and where the unpierc'd shade
Embrowned[28] the noontide bowers. Thus was this place,
A happy rural seat of various view:
Groves whose rich trees wept odorous gums and balm;
Others whose fruit, burnished with golden rind,
250 Hung amiable — Hesperian fables true,
If true, here only — and of delicious taste.[29]
Betwixt them lawns, or level downs, and flocks
Gracing the tender herb, were interposed,
Or palmy hillock; or the flowery lap
Of some irriguous[30] valley spread her store,
Flowers of all hue, and without thorn the rose.[31]
Another side, umbrageous[32] grots and caves
Of cool recess, o'er which the mantling vine
Lays forth her purple grape, and gently creeps
260 Luxuriant; meanwhile murmuring waters fall
Down the slope hills, dispersed, or in a lake,
That to the fringed bank with myrtle crowned
Her crystal mirror holds, unite their streams.
The birds their quire apply;[33] airs, vernal airs,
Breathing the smell of field and grove, attune
The trembling leaves,[34] while universal Pan,
Knit with the Graces and the Hours in dance,
Led on th' eternal Spring.[35] Not that fair field
Of Enna, where Proserpin gathering flowers,
270 Herself a fairer flower, by gloomy Dis
Was gathered—which cost Ceres all that pain
To seek her through the world[36]—nor that sweet grove[37]
Of Daphne, by Orontes and th' inspired

[28]**Embrowned** made dusky
[29]**Thus was . . . delicious taste** Golden fruit (gathered by Hercules in spite of the dragon-guard) hung in the Gardens of the Hesperides. Milton contrasts fabulous mythology with the truth of Eden.
[30]**irriguous** well-watered
[31]**without thorn the rose** Roses grew thorns after the Fall.
[32]**umbrageous** shady
[33]**their quire apply** practice their singing
[34]**airs . . . leaves** "Airs" (both winds and songs) impel the leaves to harmony.
[35]**universal Pan . . . Spring** The pastoral god Pan ("all") was thought of as animating all nature. The Graces, attendants on Venus, brought all gracious things; the Hours, goddesses of the Seasons, brought each season's good things (but spring is unchanging here). The association with Venus and love is common in imagined paradisal gardens, and this garden manifests God's blameless love and that of Adam and Eve.

[36]**Proserpin . . . the world** Proserpina, carried off by Dis (Pluto), was rescued by her mother Ceres, goddess of fruitfulness, but had to return to Dis for half of each year because she had eaten fruit in the underworld. Thus we have winter. The parallel to Eve and to Christ's redemption of man is clear.
[37]ll. 272–85 On the Orontes near Antioch was a grove of Daphne (beloved of Apollo), with such a spring (named after the one on Parnassus); it had an "inspired" oracle of Apollo. On the Isle of Nysa, near Tunis, Ammon (equated with Jupiter and with Noah's son Ham, or Cham) hid his beloved Amalthea and their son Bacchus from his wife, Rhea. On the paradisal Mt. Amara, a day's journey high up smooth rock, Abyssinian emperors educated and delighted their sons; being near the equator, Amara had eternal spring, like the true paradise of Eden in Assyria.

Castalian spring, might with this Paradise
Of Eden strive; nor that Nyseian isle,
Girt with the river Triton, where old Cham,
Whom Gentiles Ammon call, and Libyan Jove,
Hid Amalthea, and her florid[38] son,
Young Bacchus, from his stepdame Rhea's eye;
280 Nor, where Abassin kings their issue guard,
Mount Amara (though this by some supposed
True Paradise) under the Ethiop line
By Nilus' head, enclosed with shining rock,
A whole day's journey high, but wide remote
From this Assyrian garden, where the Fiend
Saw undelighted all delight, all kind
Of living creatures, new to sight and strange:
Two of far nobler shape, erect and tall,
God-like erect, with native honour[39] clad
290 In naked majesty, seemed lords of all,
And worthy seemed; for in their looks divine
The image of their glorious Maker shone,[40]
Truth, wisdom, sanctitude severe and pure—
Severe, but in true filial freedom placed;
Whence true authority in men: though both
Not equal, as their sex not equal seemed;
For contemplation he and valour formed,
For softness she and sweet attractive grace;
He for God only, she for God in him.[41]
300 His fair large front[42] and eye sublime[43] declared
Absolute rule; and hyacinthine[44] locks
Round from his parted forelock manly hung
Clustering, but not beneath his shoulders broad:
She, as a veil down to the slender waist,
Her unadornèd golden tresses wore
Dishevelled, but in wanton[45] ringlets waved
As the vine curls her tendrils, which implied
Subjection, but required with gentle sway,
And by her yielded, by him best received,
310 Yielded with coy[46] submission, modest pride,
And sweet, reluctant, amorous delay.
Nor those mysterious parts were then concealed;
Then was not guilty shame: dishonest Shame
Of Nature's works, Honour dishonourable,
Sin-bred, how have ye troubled all mankind
With shows instead, mere shows of seeming pure,

[38]**florid** ruddy
[39]**native honour** inborn, "primitive" honor, unlike vain honor after the Fall
[40]l. 292 "God created man in his own image" (Genesis 1:27).
[41]l. 299 See 1 Corinthians 11:3.
[42]**front** forehead
[43]**sublime** uplifted
[44]**hyacinthine** like the hair of the beautiful, doomed Hyacinthus, beloved of Apollo; or, impressionistically, flowing with a beauty like the hyacinth's—a standard classical allusion
[45]**wanton** luxuriant
[46]**coy** modest

And banished from man's life his happiest life,
Simplicity and spotless innocence!
So passed they naked on, nor shunned the sight
320   Of God or Angel; for they thought no ill;
So hand in hand they passed, the loveliest pair
That ever since in love's embraces met—
Adam, the goodliest man of men since born
His sons; the fairest of her daughters Eve.
Under a tuft of shade that on a green
Stood whispering soft, by a fresh fountain-side,
They sat them down; and, after no more toil
Of their sweet gard'ning labour than sufficed
To recommend cool Zephyr,[47] and made ease
330   More easy, wholesome thirst and appetite
More grateful, to their supper-fruits they fell—
Nectarine[48] fruits, which the compliant boughs
Yielded them, sidelong as they sat recline[49]
On the soft downy bank damasked[50] with flowers.
The savoury pulp they chew, and in the rind,
Still as they thirsted, scoop the brimming stream;
Nor gentle purpose,[51] nor endearing smiles
Wanted,[52] nor youthful dalliance, as beseems
Fair couple linked in happy nuptial league,
340   Alone as they. About them frisking played
All beasts of th' earth, since wild, and of all chase
In wood or wilderness, forest or den;
Sporting the lion ramped, and in his paw
Dandled the kid; bears, tigers, ounces,[53] pards,
Gambolled before them; th' unwieldy elephant,
To make them mirth, used all his might, and wreathed
His lithe proboscis; close the serpent sly,
Insinuating,[54] wove with Gordian twine[55]
His braided train, and of his fatal guile
350   Gave proof unheeded. Others on the grass
Couched, and, now filled with pasture, gazing sat,
Or bedward ruminating; for the sun,
Declined, was hasting now with prone career
To th' Ocean Isles, and in th' ascending scale
Of Heaven the stars that usher evening rose;
When Satan still in gaze, as first he stood,
Scarce thus at length failed speech recovered sad:—
   "O Hell! what do mine eyes with grief behold?
Into our room[56] of bliss thus high advanced
360   Creatures of other mould—Earth-born perhaps,

---

[47]**Zephyr** breeze
[48]**Nectarine** sweet as the god's drink, nectar
[49]**recline** reclining
[50]**damasked** patterned
[51]**purpose** conversation
[52]**wanted** lacked

[53]**ounces** any large cat-like animals
[54]**insinuating** penetrating sinuously
[55]**Gordian twine** The Gordian knot was so complicated that it was finally unloosed only when Alexander cut it with his sword.
[56]**room** emptied space

Not Spirits, yet to Heavenly Spirits bright
Little inferior—whom my thoughts pursue
With wonder, and could love; so lively shines
In them divine resemblance, and such grace
The hand that formed them on their shape hath poured.
Ah! gentle pair, ye little think how nigh
Your change approaches, when all these delights
Will vanish, and deliver ye to woe—
More woe, the more your taste is now of joy:
370 Happy, but for so happy ill secured
Long to continue,[57] and this high seat, your Heaven,
Ill fenced for Heaven to keep out such a foe
As now is entered; yet no purposed foe
To you, whom I could pity thus forlorn,
Though I unpitied.[58] League with you I seek,
And mutual amity, so strait,[59] so close,
That I with you must dwell, or you with me,[60]
Henceforth. My dwelling, haply, may not please,
Like this fair Paradise, your sense; yet such
380 Accept your Maker's work; he gave it me,
Which I as freely give.[61] Hell shall unfold,
To entertain you two, her widest gates,
And send forth all her kings; there will be room,
Not like these narrow limits, to receive
Your numerous offspring; if no better place,
Thank him who puts me, loath, to this revenge
On you, who wrong me not, for him who wronged.
And, should I at your harmless innocence
Melt, as I do, yet public reason just,
390 Honour and empire with revenge enlarged
By conquering this new world, compels me now
To do what else, though damned, I should abhor.''[62]
    So spake the Fiend, and with necessity,
The tyrant's plea, excused his devilish deeds.
Then from his lofty stand on that high tree
Down he alights among the sportful herd
Of those four-footed kinds, himself now one,
Now other, as their shape served best his end
Nearer to view his prey, and, unespied,
400 To mark what of their state he more might learn
By word or action marked. About them round
A lion now he stalks with fiery glare;
Then as a tiger, who by chance hath spied

[57]**Happy. . . continue** not so well secured as such happy ones ought to be, in order to continue so
[58]**yet no purposed . . . unpitied** I am not a foe to you on purpose, because I could pity you, although God does not pity me. (The irony becomes villainous in what follows.)
[59]**strait** tightened

[60]l. 377 i.e., in sin on earth, or in damnation in hell
[61]**he gave it . . . give** Satan's words here are a travesty of God's freely giving heaven and his son to mankind.
[62]l. 392 Satan uses a tyrant's political excuse, that he performs abhorrent acts for the good of the state.

In some purlieu[63] two gentle fawns at play,
Straight[64] couches close; then, rising, changes oft
His couchant watch, as one who chose his ground,
Whence rushing he might surest seize them both
Gripped in each paw: when Adam, first of men,
To first of women, Eve, thus moving[65] speech,
410   Turned him all ear to hear[66] new utterance flow:—
    "Sole partner and sole part of all these joys,[67]
Dearer thyself than all, needs must the Power
That made us, and for us this ample World,
Be infinitely good, and of his good
As liberal and free[68] as infinite;
That raised us from the dust,[69] and placed us here
In all this happiness, who at his hand
Have nothing merited, nor can perform
Aught whereof he hath need; he who requires
420   From us no other service than to keep
This one, this easy charge, of all the trees
In Paradise that bear delicious fruit
So various, not to taste that only Tree
Of Knowledge, planted by the Tree cf Life;
So near grows Death to Life, whate'er Death is—
Some dreadful thing no doubt; for well thou know'st
God hath pronounced it Death to taste that Tree:
The only sign of our obedience left
Among so many signs of power and rule
430   Conferred upon us, and dominion given
Over all other creatures that possess
Earth, Air, and Sea. Then let us not think hard[70]
One easy prohibition, who enjoy
Free leave so large[71] to all things else, and choice
Unlimited of manifold delights;
But let us ever praise him, and extol
His bounty, following our delightful task,
To prune these growing plants, and tend these flowers;
Which, were it toilsome, yet with thee were sweet."
440   To whom thus Eve replied:—"O thou for whom
And from whom I was formed flesh of thy flesh,
And without whom am to no end, my guide
And head! what thou hast said is just and right.
For we to him, indeed, all praises owe,
And daily thanks—I chiefly, who enjoy
So far the happier lot, enjoying thee
Pre-eminent by so much odds,[72] while thou

---

[63] **purlieu** bordering a forest
[64] **Straight** at once
[65] **moving** initiating
[66] **Turned . . . hear** Satan turned to hear.
[67] l. 411 only partner and unrivaled part of my joys (also, perhaps, only part of Adam that had been removed from him to delight him: Eve was created from Adam's rib)

[68] **free** generous
[69] **dust** Adam had been created from earth; in Hebrew his name means "earth."
[70] **hard** to be hard
[71] **large** general
[72] **Pre-eminent . . . odds** superior to me by so great an advantage

Like consort to thyself canst nowhere find.
That day I oft remember, when from sleep
450 I first awaked, and found myself reposed,
Under a shade, on flowers, much wondering where
And what I was, whence thither brought, and how.
Not distant far from thence a murmuring sound
Of waters issued from a cave, and spread
Into a liquid plain; then stood unmoved,
Pure as th' expanse of Heaven. I thither went
With unexperienced[73] thought, and laid me down
On the green bank, to look into the clear
Smooth lake, that to me seemed another sky.
460 As I bent down to look, just opposite,
A shape within the wat'ry gleam appeared,
Bending to look on me. I started back,
It started back; but pleased I soon returned,
Pleased it returned as soon with answering looks
Of sympathy and love. There I had[74] fixed
Mine eyes till now, and pined with vain desire,
Had not a voice thus warned me: 'What thou seest,
What there thou seest, fair creature, is thyself;
With thee it came and goes: but follow me,
470 And I will bring thee where no shadow stays
Thy coming, and thy soft embraces[75]—he
Whose image thou art; him thou shalt enjoy
Inseparably thine; to him shalt bear
Multitudes like thyself, and thence be called
Mother of human race.' What could I do,
But follow straight, invisibly thus led?
Till I espied thee, fair, indeed, and tall,
Under a platan;[76] yet methought less fair,
Less winning soft, less amiably mild,
480 Than that smooth wat'ry image. Back I turned;
Thou, following, cried'st aloud, 'Return, fair Eve;
Whom fliest thou? Whom thou fliest, of him thou art,
His flesh, his bone; to give thee being I lent
Out of my side to thee, nearest my heart,
Substantial life, to have thee by my side
Henceforth an individual[77] solace dear:
Part of my soul I seek thee, and thee claim
My other half.'[78] With that thy gentle hand
Seized mine: I yielded, and from that time see

[73]**unexperienced** inexperienced
[74]**had** would have
[75]**where no shadow . . . embraces** where no
mere reflection awaits your coming and your
embraces (Narcissus had fallen in love with
his own reflection in a pool, and had died.
Later Satan will tempt Eve to self-pride, by
which she falls.)

[76]**platan** a plane-tree, like a sycamore—a
symbol of Christ but also of erotic love
[77]**individual** inseparable
[78]**Part of . . . half** In Plato's *Symposium*
Aristophanes tells comically how originally
spherical human beings were each cut in half
by the gods and now seek their corresponding
halves in love.

And wisdom, which alone is truly fair.''
　　So spake our general mother, and, with eyes
490　How beauty is excelled by manly grace
Of conjugal attraction unreproved,[79]
And meek surrender, half-embracing leaned
On our first father; half her swelling breast
Naked met his, under the flowing gold
Of her loose tresses hid. He, in delight
Both of her beauty and submissive charms,
Smiled with superior love, as Jupiter
500　On Juno smiles when he impregns the clouds[80]
That shed May flowers, and pressed her matron lip
With kisses pure. Aside the Devil turned
For envy; yet with jealous leer malign
Eyed them askance,[81] and to himself thus plained:—[82]
　　''Sight hateful, sight tormenting! Thus these two,
Imparadised in one another's arms,
The happier Eden, shall enjoy their fill
Of bliss on bliss; while I to Hell am thrust,
Where neither joy nor love, but fierce desire,
510　Among our other torments not the le‿st,
Still[83] unfulfilled, with pain of longing pines!
Yet let me not forget what I have gained
From their own mouths. All is not theirs, it seems;
One fatal tree there stands, of Knowledge called,
Forbidden them to taste. Knowledge forbidden?
Suspicious, reasonless! Why should their Lord
Envy them that? Can it be sin to know?
Can it be death? And do they only stand[84]
By ignorance? Is that their happy state,
520　The proof of their obedience and their faith?
O fair foundation laid whereon to build
Their ruin! Hence I will excite their minds
With more desire to know, and to reject
Envious commands, invented with design
To keep them low, whom knowledge might exalt
Equal with gods. Aspiring to be such,
They taste and die: what likelier can ensue?
But first with narrow search I must walk round
This garden, and no corner leave unspied;
530　A chance but chance may lead[85] where I may meet
Some wandering Spirit of Heaven, by fountain-side
Or in thick shade retired, from him to draw

---

[79]**unreproved** irreproachable
[80]ll. 499–500 Jupiter is often air and Juno earth, or Jupiter is *aether* impregnating Juno, air, and clouds. ''Superior'' thus implies higher physical position. **impregns** impregnates
[81]**askance** sideways, maliciously

[82]**plained** lamented
[83]**Still** continually
[84]**stand** keep from falling
[85]**A chance . . . may lead** There is only a chance, but chance *may* lead.

What further would be learned. Live while ye may,
Yet happy pair; enjoy, till I return,
Short pleasures; for long woes are to succeed!"
1658?–65?   1667

SIR JOHN SUCKLING
1609–1642

The most skeptical and libertine of the Cavaliers (see especially Carew and Lovelace), Suckling wrote unillusioned love lyrics that look back to Donne, although his Cavalier art is typically Jonsonian. Inconstancy in love, as in the first composition below, is a Cavalier pose, but one that Suckling's amiable carnality may have found easy to sustain. The alternating longer and shorter lines of the following lyric and song from a play project a blunt pithiness that is characteristic of his appeal.

Out Upon It! I Have Loved

Out upon it! I have loved
    Three whole days together;
And am like to love three more,
    If it prove fair weather.

Time shall moult away his wings,
    Ere he shall discover
In the whole wide world again
    Such a constant lover.

But the spite on't is, no praise
10   Is due at all to me:
Love with me had made no stays
    Had it any been but she.

Had it any been but she,
    And that very face,
There had been at least ere this
    A dozen dozen in her place.

1659

A Soldier

I am a man of war and might,
And know thus much, that I can fight,
Whether I am in the wrong or right,
        Devoutly.

No woman under heaven I fear,
New oaths I can exactly swear,
And forty healths my brain will bear
        Most stoutly.

10   I cannot speak, but I can do
      As much as any of our crew,
      And, if you doubt it, some of you
           May prove me.

      I dare be bold thus much to say,
      If that my bullets do but play,
      You would be hurt so night and day,
           Yet love me.

                         1659

Song[1]

      Why so pale and wan, fond lover?
         Prithee, why so pale?
      Will, when looking well can't move her,
         Looking ill prevail?
         Prithee, why so pale?

      Why so dull and mute, young sinner'.
         Prithee, why so mute?
      Will, when speaking well can't win her,
         Saying nothing do't?
10   Prithee, why so mute?

      Quit, quit, for shame; this will not move,
         This cannot take her.
      If of herself she will not love,
         Nothing can make her:
         The devil take her!

                     1646

[1] from Suckling's play *Aglaura* (1646)

RICHARD CRASHAW
1612?–1649

Crashaw rebelled against the Protestantism of his clergyman father, adhered to religiously ceremonious High Church Anglicanism at Cambridge, was forced to give up his fellowship there at the time of the Puritan triumph, became a Catholic convert in France, and died in an ecclesiastical post in Italy. Although much of his poetry was written before his official conversion, he is recognized as the outstanding British Catholic poet of his century. His art is strongly related to that of southern Europeans: the Italian poetry of Giambattista Marino and the Latin poetry of Continental Jesuits. Like them, he seeks paradoxically to evoke, by a great rush of highly sensuous, often voluptuous imagery, the purest and most spiritual mysteries and saintly sufferings. Such poetry avoids all restraint. It seeks to amaze and shock readers into a sense of a spiritual truth far from their own slothful human limitations. It is very far, then, from the moderation of Herbert, even though Crashaw admired him.

Again paradoxically, the largely unsensuous, anti-Petrarchan *discordia concors* of Donne's and others' Metaphysical poetry had helped to prepare Crashaw to use the dramatically sensual imagery he deploys so well. Mario Praz, the Italian critic of English literature, claimed that Crashaw's abundant treasury of wit, which poured forth in a kind of ceaseless expressive flood, made him a better poet than his Italian contemporaries who wrote in the same vein. Like theirs, his verse is rightly described as baroque because of its dynamic, uninhibited movement, its drastic contrasts, and its magnificent, theatrical gestures. The baroque sculpture of St. Teresa in ecstasy by Gianlorenzo Bernini (1598–1660) is often compared with Crashaw's hymn to her.

A Hymn to the Name and Honor of the Admirable Saint Teresa

Foundress of the Reformation of the Discalced[1] Carmelites, both men and women. A woman for angelical height of speculation, for masculine courage of performance, more than a woman; who yet a child outran maturity, and durst plot a martydrom.

Love, thou art absolute sole lord
Of Life and Death. To prove the word,
We'll now appeal to none of all
Those thy old soldiers, great and tall,
Ripe men of martyrdom, that could reach down
With strong arms their triumphant crown;
Such as could with lusty breath
Speak loud into the face of death
Their great Lord's glorious name; to none
10 Of those whose spacious bosoms spread a throne
For Love at large to fill. Spare blood and sweat,
And see him take a private seat,
Making his mansion in the mild
And milky soul of a soft child.
      Scarce has she learnt to lisp the name
Of martyr, yet she thinks it shame
Life should so long play with that breath
Which spent can buy so brave a death.
She never undertook to know
20 What death with love should have to do;
Nor has she e'er yet understood
Why to show love, she should shed blood.
Yet though she cannot tell you why,
She can Love, and she can Die.

[1] **discalced** barefoot

Scarce has she blood enough to make
A guilty sword blush for her sake;
Yet has she a heart dares hope to prove
How much less strong is Death than Love.
Be Love but there, let poor six years
30   Be posèd with maturest fears
Man trembles at, you straight shall find
Love knows no nonage,[2] nor the mind.
'Tis Love, not years or limbs that can
Make the martyr or the man.
Love touched her heart, and lo it beats
High, and burns with such brave heats,
Such thirsts to die, as dares drink up
A thousand cold deaths in one cup.
Good reason, for she breathes all fire.
40   Her weak breast heaves with strong desire
Of what she may with fruitless wishes
Seek for amongst her mother's kisses.
Since 'tis not to be had at home
She'll travel to a martyrdom.
No home for hers confesses she
But where she may a martyr be.
She'll to the Moors and trade with them,
For this unvalued[3] diadem.
She'll offer them her dearest breath,
50   With Christ's Name in't, in change for death.
She'll bargain with them, and will give
Them God, teach them how to live
In Him: or, if they this deny,
For him she'll teach them how to die.
So shall she leave amongst them sown
Her Lord's blood, or at least her own.
Farewell then, all the world, Adieu!
Teresa is no more for you.
Farewell, all pleasures, sports, and joys,
60   (Never till now esteemed toys)
Farewell whatever dear may be,
Mother's arms or father's knee;
Farewell house, and farewell home!
She's for the Moors, and Martyrdom!
Sweet, not so fast! lo, thy fair Spouse
Whom thou seek'st with so swift vows
Calls thee back, and bids thee come
T'embrace a milder martyrdom.
Blest powers forbid thy tender life
70   Should bleed upon a barbarous knife;
Or some base hand have power to rase[4]

---

[2] **nonage** youthful incapacity
[3] **unvalued** invaluable

[4] **rase** destroy

Thy breast's chaste cabinet, and uncase
A soul kept there so sweet, oh, no;
Wise heav'n will never have it so.
Thou art Love's victim, and must die
A death more mystical and high;
Into Love's arms thou shalt let fall
A still-surviving funeral.
His is the Dart must make the Death
80   Whose stroke shall taste thy hallowed breath:
A dart thrice dipped in that rich flame
Which writes thy spouse's radiant name
Upon the roof of Heav'n; where aye
It shines, and with a sovereign ray
Beats bright upon the burning faces
Of souls which in that name's sweet graces
Find everlasting smiles. So rare,
So spiritual, pure, and fair
Must be th'immortal instrument
90   Upon whose choice point shall be sent
A life so loved; and that there be
Fit executioners for thee,
The fair'st and first-born sons of fire,
Blest seraphim,[5] shall leave their choir
And turn Love's soldiers, upon thee
To exercise their archery.
        Oh, how oft shalt thou complain
Of a sweet and subtle pain.
Of intolerable joys;
100   Of a death in which who dies
Loves his death, and dies again,
And would for ever so be slain,
And lives, and dies; and knows not why
To live, but that he thus may never leave to die!
        How kindly will thy gentle heart
Kiss the sweetly-killing dart!
And close in his embraces keep
Those delicious wounds, that weep
Balsam to heal themselves with. Thus
110   When these thy deaths, so numerous,
Shall all at last die into one,
And melt thy soul's sweet mansion;
Like a soft lump of incense, hasted
By too hot a fire, and wasted
Into perfuming clouds, so fast
Shalt thou exhale to Heav'n at last
In a resolving Sigh; and then,
Oh, what? Ask not the tongues of men;
Angels cannot tell: suffice,

[5] **seraphim**   angels of the highest order

120   Thy self shall feel thine own full joys
    And hold them fast forever. There
    As soon as thou shalt first appear,
    The moon of maiden stars, thy white
    Mistress,[6] attended by such bright
    Souls as thy shining self, shall come
    And in her first ranks make thee room;
    Where 'mongst her snowy family
    Immortal welcomes wait for thee.
        Oh, what delight, when rèvealed Life shall stand
130   And teach thy lips heav'n with his hand,
    On which thou now may'st to thy wishes
    Heap up thy consecrated kisses.
    What joys shall seize thy soul, when she,
    Bending her blessed eyes on thee,
    (Those second smiles of heaven) shall dart
    Her mild rays through thy melting heart!
        Angels, thy old friends, there shall greet thee,
    Glad at their own home now to meet thee.
        All thy good works which went before
140   And waited for thee, at the door,
    Shall own thee there; and all in one
    Weave a constellation
    Of crowns, with which the King, thy Spouse,
    Shall build up thy triumphant brows.
        All thy old woes shall now smile on thee,
    And thy pains sit bright upon thee;
    All thy sorrows here shall shine,
    All thy Suff'rings be divine.
    Tears shall take comfort and turn gems,
150   And wrongs repent to diadems.
    Ev'n thy deaths shall live; and new
    Dress the soul that erst they slew.
    Thy wounds shall blush to such bright scars
    As keep account of the Lamb's wars.
        Those rare works where thou shalt leave writ
    Love's noble history, with wit
    Taught thee by none but Him, while here
    They feed our souls, shall clothe thine there.
    Each heav'nly word by whose hid flame
160   Our hard hearts shall strike fire, the same
    Shall flourish on thy brows, and be
    Both fire to us and flame to thee;
    Whose light shall live bright in thy face
    By glory, in our hearts by grace.
        Thou shalt look around about, and see
    Thousands of crowned souls throng to be
    Themselves thy crown; sons of thy vows,

[6] **Mistress** the Virgin Mary

The virgin-births with which thy sovereign Spouse
Made fruitful thy fair soul, go now
170 And, with them, all about thee bow
To Him. "Put on," He'll say, "put on,
My rosy love, that thy rich zone,[7]
Sparkling with the sacred flames
Of thousand souls whose happy names
Heav'n keeps upon thy score. Thy bright
Life brought them first to kiss the light
That kindled them to stars." And so
Thou with the Lamb, thy Lord, shalt go;[8]
And wheresoe'er He sets His white
180 Steps, walk with Him those ways of light,
Which who in death would live to see,
Must learn in life to die like thee.

1652

[7] zone   girdle
[8] l. 178   in the procession of the Lamb (Revelation 14:1-5)

ANNE BRADSTREET

1612–1672

Anne Bradstreet was the first true poet, as well as the first female poet, of English-speaking North America. She was not a revolutionary figure like her contemporary Anne Hutchinson in Massachusetts. Her affirmation of a usual female role is evident in "To My Dear and Loving Husband." Nevertheless, her "Prologue" defines, with only partly justified humility, the situation of any woman who turned out to write good poetry in the man's world of the seventeenth century. She was steeped in English poetry of the late sixteenth century and her part of the seventeenth. The jocular satire of "The Author to Her Book" begins with lines worthy of Milton's satirical sonnets, and rather better-humored.

Under the leadership of John Winthrop she sailed from England to Massachusetts with her father, Thomas Dudley, a former estate-steward who became a governor of the Massachusetts Bay Colony, and with her husband of two years, Simon Bradstreet, who filled the same office after his wife's death. Her family was cultured and pros-

perous, and she (probably like the rest of them) underwent some culture-shock in the face of the living and social conditions of the New World. She suffered much from sickness (God's judgment and correction, as she saw it), but she bore eight children and carried on, much praised, the life of a devout, prominent Puritan woman in Cambridge, Ipswich, and finally Andover.

Apparently without her knowledge, her brother-in-law carried to England a copy of her poems that she had made for family use and in 1650 saw to its publication there as *The Tenth Muse* (i.e., Bradstreet, the tenth female muse after the nine other female ones). Although "The Author to Her Book" suggests her resentment, she was probably as much gratified in fact as other sixteenth- and seventeenth-century poets who expressed similar apparent chagrin at being published. Her corrected edition, from which these poems are taken, was brought out in Boston in 1678. Her mature poems have much delicacy and power.

The Author to Her Book

Thou ill-formed offspring of my feeble brain,
Who after birth didst by my side remain,
Till snatched from thence by friends, less wise than true,
Who thee abroad exposed to public view,
Made thee in rags,[1] halting[2] to th' press to trudge,
Where errors were not lessened (all may judge).
At thy return my blushing was not small,
My rambling brat (in print) should mother call;
10   I cast thee by as one unfit for light,
Thy visage was so irksome in my sight;
Yet being mine own, at length affection would
Thy blemishes amend, if so I could:
I washed thy face, but more defects I saw,
And rubbing off a spot still made a flaw.
I stretched thy joints to make thee even feet,[3]
Yet still thou run'st more hobbling than is meet;
In better dress to trim thee was my mind,
But nought save homespun cloth i' th' house I find.
20   In this array 'mongst vulgars may'st thou roam;
In critic's hands beware thou dost not come,
And take thy way where yet thou are not known;
If for thy father asked, say thou hadst none;
And for thy mother, she alas is poor,
Which caused her thus to send thee out of door.

1678

[1] **rags** Paper used to be made out of worn-out rags.
[2] **halting** limping
[3] **feet** in the punning sense of metrical feet.

Bradstreet describes herself as working on the first edition of her book, revising for a second edition, which was in fact published after her death.

The Prologue

To sing of wars, of captains, and of kings,
Of cities founded, commonwealths begun,
For my mean pen are too superior things;[1]
Or how they all, or each, their dates[2] have run
Let poets and historians set these forth;
My obscure lines shall not so dim their worth.

But when my wond'ring eyes and envious heart
10   Great Bartas'[3] sugared lines do but read o'er,
Fool, I do grudge the Muses did not part

[1] ll. 1–3 For my poor poetic ability the subjects of the highest, epic poetry are too lofty.
[2] **dates** endings
[3] **Bartas** Guillaume du Bartas (1544–1590),

French poet, whose epic poems of creation, *The Weeks*, Bradstreet knew in English translation. Their Protestant spirit appealed to her Puritanism.

'Twixt him and me that overfluent store;[4]
A Bartas can do what a Bartas will
But simple I according to my skill.

From schoolboy's tongue no rhet'ric[5] we expect,
Nor yet a sweet consort from broken strings,
Nor perfect beauty where's a main defect:
My foolish, broken, blemished Muse so sings,
And this to mend, alas, no art is able,
20   'Cause nature made it so irreparàble.

Nor can I, like that fluent sweet tongued Greek[6]
Who lisped at first, in future times speak plain.
By art he gladly found what he did seek,
A full requital of his striving pain.
Art can do much, but this maxim's most sure:
A weak or wounded brain admits no cure.

I am obnoxious to each carping tongue
Who says my hand a needle better fits,
A poet's pen all scorn I should thus wrong,
30   For such despite they cast on female wits,[7]
If what I do prove well, it won't advance,[8]
They'll say it's stol'n, or else it was by chance.

But sure the antique Greeks were far more mild;
Else of our sex, why feignèd they those nine
And poesy made Calliope's own child;[9]
So 'mongst the rest they placed the arts divine:
But this weak knot they[10] will full soon untie,
The Greeks did nought, but play the fools and lie.

Let Greeks be Greeks, and women what they are;
40   Men have precedency and still[11] excel,
It is but vain unjustly to wage war;
Men can do best, and women know it well.
Preeminence in all and each is yours;
Yet grant some small acknowledgement of ours.

---

[4] ll. 9–12 I grudge that the muses, patrons of the arts, did not share out poetic skill to me as well as to Du Bartas.
[5] **rhet'ric** expressive skill
[6] **fluent . . . Greek** The Greek orator Demosthenes is said to have cured his natural stammer by the device ("art") of putting pebbles in his mouth at the seashore and speaking loudly and distinctly enough to overcome this obstruction as well as the noise of the surf.

[7] ll. 27–29 All scorn the idea that I should thus wrong the role of a poet.
[8] **advance** succeed
[9] ll. 33–35 Otherwise, why would they have invented the fiction of the nine female muses as patrons of the arts, and of the female muse Calliope as the mother of poetry?
[10] **they** refers to "each carping tongue" above
[11] **still** always

And oh ye high flown quills[12] that soar the skies,
And ever with your prey still catch your praise,
If e'er you deign these lowly lines your eyes,[13]
Give thyme or parsley wreath, I ask no bays;[14]
This mean and unrefined ore of mine
50   Will make your glist'ring gold but more to shine.

1650, 1678

[12]**high flown quills**   exalted pens of poets
[13]l. 47   deign to direct your eyes at these lowly
lines

[14]**bays**   the laurel crown, prize of the successful
poet

To My Dear and Loving Husband

If ever two were one, then surely we.
If ever man were loved by wife, then thee;[1]
If ever wife was happy in a man,
Compare[2] with me, ye women, if you can.
I prize thy love more than whole mines of gold
Or all the riches that the East doth hold.
My love is such that rivers cannot quench,
Nor aught but love from thee, give recompense.
10   Thy love is such I can no way repay;
The heavens reward thee manifold, I pray.
Then while we live, in love let's so persever
That when we live no more, we may live ever.

1650, 1678

[1]**then thee**   then you are
[2]**Compare**   match

SIR JOHN DENHAM
1615–1669

The heroic couplets, sententiousness, and skillfully deployed parallels and contrasts of Denham's "Cooper's Hill" sound to our ears much like those of Alexander Pope. Hence it is easier for us to understand the eighteenth century's veneration of Denham than its admiration of the more lyrical Waller (above, p. 261). Topographical poems like this one have a long Latin and vernacular tradition in the Middle Ages and the Renaissance. Bestowing a suitable decorum on the details of a loved locality is common to all such sententious verse. Nevertheless, only Augustan poetry was likely to rise to the elaborately balanced fluvial simile of tyranny and popular rule in the conclusion here. Our selection follows in the original poem an evocation of the Thames ("Though deep, yet clear, though gentle, yet not dull") and of Cooper's Hill, separated from the Thames by a plain, "between the mountain and the stream embraced,/Which shade and shelter from the hill derives,/While the kind river wealth and beauty gives."

From Cooper's Hill

Here have I seen the king, when great affairs
Give leave to slacken and unbend his cares,
Attended to the chase by all the flower
Of youth, whose hopes a nobler prey devour.
Pleasure with praise and danger they would buy,
And wish a foe that would not only fly.
The stag now conscious of his fatal growth,
At once indulgent to his fear and sloth,
To some dark covert his retreat had made,
250 Where no man's eye, nor heaven's, should invade
His soft repose; when the unexpected sound
Of dogs and men his wakeful ear doth wound.
Roused with the noise, he scarce believes his ear,
Willing to think the illusions of his fear
Had given this alarm; but straight his view
Confirms that more than all he fears is true.
Betrayed in all his strengths, the wood beset,
All instruments, all arts of ruin met,
He calls to mind his strength and then his speed,
260 His winged heels, and then his armed head;
With these to avoid, with that his fate to meet;
But fear prevails and bids him thrust his feet.
So fast he flies that his reviewing eye
Has lost the chasers, and his ear the cry;
Exulting, till he finds their nobler sense
Their disproportioned speed does recompense.
Then curses his conspiring feet, whose scent
Betrays that safety which their swiftness lent.
Then tries his friends: among the baser herd,
270 Where he so lately was obeyed and feared,
His safety seeks; the herd, unkindly[1] wise,
Or chases him from thence, or from him flies.
Like a declining statesman left forlorn
To his friends' pity and pursuers' scorn,
With shame remembers, while himself was one
Of the same herd, himself the same had done.
Thence to the coverts and the conscious[2] groves,
The scenes of his past triumphs and his loves,
Sadly surveying where he ranged alone,
280 Prince of the soil and all the herd his own,
And like a bold knight errant did proclaim
Combat to all, and bore away the dame,
And taught the woods to echo to the stream
His dreadful challenge and his clashing beam;
Yet faintly now declines the fatal strife,

[1] **unkindly** conflicting with the natural alliance
of their kind or species
[2] **conscious** Following a Latin poetic use of this

word, the intensity of the pathos is heightened
by supposing that even unconscious trees feel
it.

So much his love was dearer than his life.[3]
Now every leaf and every moving breath
Presents a foe, and every foe a death.
Wearied, forsaken, and pursued, at last
290   All safety in despair of safety placed,
Courage he thence resumes, resolved to bear
All their assaults, since 'tis in vain to fear.
And now too late he wishes for the fight
That strength he wasted in ignoble flight.
But when he sees the eager chase renewed,
Himself by dogs, the dogs by men pursued,
He straight revokes his bold resolve, and more
Repents his courage than his fear before;
Finds that uncertain ways unsafest are,
300   And doubt a greater mischief than despair.
Then to the stream, when neither friends, nor force,
Nor speed, nor art avail, he shapes this course;
Thinks not their rage so desperate to assay
An element more merciless than they.
But fearless they pursue, nor can the flood
Quench their dire thirst; alas, they thirst for blood.
So toward a ship the oarfinn'd galleys ply,[4]
Which wanting sea to ride, or wind to fly,
Stands but to fall revenged on those that dare
310   Tempt the last fury of extreme despair.
So fares the stag among the enraged hounds,
Repels their force, and wounds returns for wounds.
And as a hero, whom his baser foes
In troops surround, now these assails, now those,
Though prodigal of life, disdains to die,
By common hands; but if he can descry
Some nobler foe's approach, to him he calls
And begs his fate, and then contented falls:
So when the king a mortal shaft lets fly
320   From his unerring hand, then glad to die,
Proud of the wound, to it resigns his blood
And stains the crystal with a purple flood.
This a more innocent and happy chase
Than when of old, but in the self-same place,[5]
Fair liberty pursued, and meant a prey
To lawless power, here turned and stood at bay,
When in that remedy all hope was placed
Which was, or should have been at least, the last.
Here was that Charter sealed wherein the crown

---

[3] l. 286   The stag will not fight for his life as he had fought for his love.
[4] l. 307   Mediterranean pirates used galleys with oars for speed.

[5] **the self-same place**   Runnymede, where traditional English rights were gained from King John and recorded in Magna Carta

330   All marks of arbitrary power lays down.
Tyrant and slave, those names of hate and fear,
The happier style of king and subject bear:
Happy when both to the same center move
When kings give liberty, and subjects love.
Therefore not long in force this Charter stood;
Wanting that seal, it must be sealed in blood.
The subjects armed, the more the princes gave,
The advantage only took the more to crave.
Till kings by giving, give themselves away,
340   And even that power that should deny, betray.
"Who gives constrained, but his own fear reviles,
Not thanked, but scorned; nor are they gifts, but spoils."
Thus kings, by grasping more than they could hold,
First made their subjects by oppression bold;
And popular sway, by forcing kings to give
More than was fit for subjects to receive,
Ran to the same extremes; and one excess
Made both, by striving to be greater, less.
When a calm river, raised with sudden rains,
350   Or snows dissolved, o'erflows the adjoining plains,
The husbandmen with high-raised banks secure
Their greedy hopes, and this he can endure.
But if with bays and dams they strive to force
His channel to a new or narrow course,
No longer then within his banks he dwells;
First to a torrent, then a deluge swells;
Stronger and fiercer by restraint he roars,
And knows no bound, but makes his power his shores.

1642, 1665

RICHARD LOVELACE
1618–1657

We link Lovelace with another Cavalier poet, Suckling, but the idealism of an aristocratic elite is much more transparently delivered in Lovelace's lyrics: honor and personal integrity find exemplary definition in "To Lucasta" and "To Althea." Also, Lovelace's fate was much darker than Suckling's. Inclined to the quiet life that his gifts and birth seemed to promise him, he was imprisoned twice by the Puritans for his efforts on behalf of the king, fought on the Continent, and died in obscurity. Even his sensuality has a note of melancholy, in the conclusion of "Song: To Amarantha," which sounds like the Cavalier version of Marvell's fear of time in "To His Coy Mistress."

Song: To Lucasta, Going to the Wars

Tell me not, sweet, I am unkind,
  That from the nunnery
Of thy chaste breast and quiet mind
  To war and arms I fly.

True, a new mistress now I chase,
  The first foe in the field;
And with a stronger faith embrace
  A sword, a horse, a shield.

Yet this inconstancy is such
10 As you too shall adore;
I could not love thee, dear, so much,
  Loved I not honor more.

                1649

Song: To Amarantha, That She Would Dishevel Her Hair

Amarantha sweet and fair,
Ah, braid no more that shining hair!
  As my curious hand or eye,
Hovering round thee, let it fly.

Let it fly as unconfined
As its calm ravisher, the wind,
  Who hath left his darling, th' East,
To wanton o'er that spicy nest.

Ev'ry tress must be confessed
10 But neatly tangled at the best,
  Like a clue[1] of golden thread,
Most excellently ravelèd.

Do not then wind up that light
In ribands, and o'ercloud in night;
  Like the sun in's early ray,
But shake your head and scatter day.

See, 'tis broke! Within this grove,
The bower, and the walks of love,
  Weary lie we down and rest,
20 And fan each other's panting breast.

Here we'll strip and cool our fire
In cream below, in milk-baths higher;
  And when all wells are drawen dry,
I'll drink a tear out of thine eye.

---

[1] clue ball

Which our very joys shall leave,
That sorrows thus we can deceive;
Or our very sorrows weep,
That joys so ripe, so little keep.

1649

To Althea. From Prison

SONG

When Love with unconfinèd wings
   Hovers within my gates,
And my divine Althea brings
   To whisper at the grates;
When I lie tangled in her hair
   And fettered to her eye,
The gods that wanton in the air
   Know no such liberty.

When flowing cups run swiftly round,
10   With no allaying Thames,[1]
Our careless heads with roses bound,
   Our hearts with loyal flames;
When thirsty grief in wine we steep,
   When healths and draughts go free,
Fishes that tipple in the deep
   Know no such liberty.

When, like committed[2] linnets, I
   With shriller throat shall sing
The sweetness, mercy, majesty,
20   And glories of my King;
When I shall voice aloud how good
   He is, how great should be,
Enlargèd[3] winds that curl the flood
   Know no such liberty.

Stone walls do not a prison make,
   Nor iron bars a cage:
Minds innocent and quiet take
   That for an hermitage.
If I have freedom in my love,
30   And in my soul am free,
Angels alone, that soar above,
   Enjoy such liberty.

1649

---

[1] l. 10 i.e., undiluted with water
[2] **committed** caged
[3] **Enlargèd** freed

ANDREW MARVELL
1621–1678

In one important way Marvell is the crown of seventeeth-century poetry, because he masterfully unites Cavalier lyric grace with Metaphysical seriousness and intellectual surprise. He embodies swift imaginative complexity in lines of a chiseled, marmoreal perfection.

He remains a most appealing poet, of strong interest to modern critics. His small body of lyric verse treats many familiar themes: the relationships of the material world to the transcendent one and of the lower to the higher powers of the psyche ("A Dialogue Between the Soul and the Body"), the intellectual vanity and powerlessness of art, even when it tries to serve God and not just the world ("The Coronet"), sexual love and desire in the male imagination ("The Gallery"), the significance of unspoiled nature and of nature transformed by man's art in gardens ("The Mower Against Gardens" and "The Garden"), and the theme *carpe diem*—seizing the brief day given us for love ("To His Coy Mistress").

He transforms each of these bewitchingly. In those lyrics that have drawn most critical attention he serenely leaves us with a puzzle about his ultimate position, yet he clarifies startlingly the grounds for any attitude that we ourselves are likely to take toward his subject.

He seems to have written almost all his chief lyrics in contact with the country and garden surroundings of the Nunappleton estate, where he was tutor to the daughter of a general on the Puritan side in the Civil War. Despite this position and another one as a colleague of Milton in the Latin secretaryship, this son of a Calvinist clergyman had flirted with Catholicism at Cambridge and may have had leanings toward the opposed, royalist side. From just before the Restoration of the monarchy until his death he was Member of Parliament for Hull in Yorkshire. In these later days he wrote much satirical verse but no meditative lyrics. He is supposed to have saved Milton from persecution at the Restoration.

Bermudas[1]

Where the remote Bermudas ride
In th' ocean's bosom unespied,
From a small boat, that rowed along,
The list'ning winds received this song.
   "What should we do but sing His praise
That led us through the wat'ry maze,
Unto an isle so long unknown,
And yet far kinder than our own?
Where he the huge sea-monsters wracks,[2]
10 That lift the deep upon their backs.
He lands us on a grassy stage,
Safe from the storms' and prelates' rage;
He gave us this eternal Spring
Which here enamels every thing,
And sends the fowls to us in care,
On daily visits through the air;

[1] Religious exiles from England, colonizing the Bermudas, sing the song imagined here.

[2] **wracks** wrecks

He hangs in shades the orange bright,
Like golden lamps in a green night,
And does in the pomegranates close
20   Jewels more rich than Ormus³ shows;
He makes the figs our mouths to meet,
And throws the melons at our feet,
But apples⁴ plants of such a price,
No tree could ever bear them twice;
With cedars, chosen by his hand,
From Lebanon, he stores the land;
And makes the hollow seas, that roar,
Proclaim the ambergris on shore;
He cast (of which we rather⁵ boast)
30   The Gospel's pearl upon our coast,
And in these rocks for us did frame
A temple, where to sound His name.
Oh, let our voice his praise exalt
Till it arrive at Heaven's vault,
Which thence (perhaps) rebounding, may
Echo beyond the Mexique Bay."
      Thus sung they, in the English boat,
An holy and a cheerful note,
And all the way, to guide their chime,
40   With falling oars they kept the time.

1681

³ **Ormus** island, proverbially wealthy dia-
mond market in the Persian Gulf

⁴ **apples** pineapples
⁵ **rather** sooner

The Coronet

When, for the thorns with which I long, too long,
      With many a piercing wound,
      My Saviour's head have crowned,
I seek with garlands to redress that wrong;¹
      Through every garden, every mead,
I gather flowers (my fruits are only flowers),
      Dismantling all the fragrant towers²
That once adorned my shepherdess's head.
And now when I have summed up all my store,
10   Thinking (so I myself deceive)
      So rich a chaplet³ thence to weave
As never yet the king of glory wore;
      Alas I find the Serpent old
      That, twining in his speckled breast,

¹ ll. 1–4 when I seek by making garlands (the
"coronet" of the title, figuratively poems) to
replace the thorns with which I, a sinner, have
long crowned Christ's head

² **fragrant towers** elaborate headdresses (for a
beloved woman)
³ **chaplet** wreath for head

About the flowers disguised does fold,
With wreaths of fame and interest.[4]
Ah, foolish Man, that wouldst debase with them,
And mortal glory, Heaven's diadem!
But Thou who only could'st the Serpent tame,
20   Either his slipp'ry knots at once untie,
And disentangle all his winding snare;
Or shatter too with him my curious frame,[5]
And let these wither, so that he may die,
Though set with skill and chosen out with care.
That they, while Thou on both their spoils dost tread,
May crown Thy feet, that could not crown thy head.

1681

[4] ll. 15–16 Even poems praising Christ are written to gain fame and advantage for the poet.

[5] **curious frame** ingenious headdress of flowers, figuratively poems

A Dialogue Between the Soul and Body[1]

SOUL   Oh, who shall from this dungeon raise
A soul enslaved so many ways?
With bolts of bones, that fettered stands
In feet, and manacled in hands.
Here blinded with an eye, and there
Deaf with the drumming of an ear.
A soul hung up, as 'twere, in chains
Of nerves, and arteries, and veins.
Tortured, besides each other part,
10   In a vain head, and double[2] heart.

BODY   Oh, who shall me deliver whole,
From bonds of this tyrannic soul?
Which, stretched upright, impales[3] me so,
That mine own precipice I go;[4]
And warms and moves this needless frame[5]
(A fever could but do the same).
And, wanting[6] where its spite to try,
Has made me live to let me die:
A body that could never rest,
20   Since this ill spirit it possessed.

[1] Dialogues between soul and body stretch back into the early Middle Ages. Here the soul is the animating, conscious principle, anxious to escape from the material body and its material ills. The body sees no need to be animated and to suffer emotion; it would not suffer and sin at all if it were inanimate matter or a lower, more "natural" form of life.

[2] **double** false
[3] **impales** fences in
[4] l. 14 Animated to walk upright instead of remaining low like unliving matter, the body is in constant danger of falling from its height.
[5] l. 15 The frame of the body has no need to be animated; it would be untroubled if inanimate.
[6] **wanting** lacking

SOUL   What magic could me thus confine
Within another's grief to pine?
Where whatsoever it complain,
I feel, that cannot feel, the pain.[7]
And all my care itself employs,
That to preserve, which me destroys:
Constrained not only to endure
Diseases, but, what's worse, the cure;
And ready oft the port to gain,
30   Am shipwrecked into health again.

BODY   But physic[8] yet could never reach
The maladies thou me dost teach:
Whom first the cramp of hope does tear,
And then the palsy shakes of fear.
The pestilence of love does heat,
Or hatred's hidden ulcer eat.
Joy's cheerful madness does perplex,
Or sorrow's other madness vex:
Which knowledge forces me to know,
40   And memory will not forego.
What but a soul could have the wit
To build me up for sin so fit?
So architects do square and hew,
Green trees that in the forest grew.

1681

[7] ll. 23–24 Being immaterial, the soul does not suffer material hurts, but its being tied to the body makes it conscious of them.   [8] **physic** medical art

To His Coy Mistress

Had we but world enough, and time,
This coyness, Lady, were no crime.
We would sit down, and think which way
To walk, and pass our long love's day.
Thou by the Indian Ganges' side
Shouldst rubies find; I by the tide
Of Humber[1] would complain. I would
Love you ten years before the Flood;
And you should, if you please, refuse
10   Till the Conversion of the Jews.[2]
My vegetable[3] love should grow
Vaster than empires, and more slow.
An hundred years should go to praise

[1] **Humber** Marvell lived in Hull, on this river
[2] **Conversion of the Jews** supposed never to occur
[3] **vegetable** growing like plant-life

Thine eyes, and on thy forehead gaze;
Two hundred to adore each breast,
But thirty thousand to the rest.
An age at least to every part,
And the last age should show your heart.
For, Lady, you deserve this state,[4]
20   Nor would I love at lower rate.
    But at my back I always hear
Time's winged chariot hurrying near;
And yonder all before us lie
Deserts of vast eternity.
Thy beauty shall no more be found,
Nor, in thy marble vault, shall sound
My echoing song: then worms shall try
That long preserved virginity:
And your quaint[5] honor turn to dust,
30   And into ashes all my lust:
The grave's a fine and private place,
But none, I think, do there embrace.
    Now, therefore, while the youthful hue
Sits on thy skin like morning lew,[6]
And while thy willing soul transpires[7]
At every pore with instant fires,
Now let us sport us while we may;
And now, like amorous birds of prey,
Rather at once our time devour,
40   Than languish in his slow-chapped[8] power.
Let us roll all our strength, and all
Our sweetness, up into one ball:
And tear our pleasures with rough strife
Thorough[9] the iron gates of life.
Thus, though we cannot make our sun
Stand still, yet we will make him run.[10]

1681

4**state** dignity
5**quaint** fastidious
6**lew** warmth
7**transpires** breathes out
8**slow chapped** Chaps = jaws. Time was

often depicted devouring his children.
9**Thorough** through
10ll. 45–46 We cannot stop time (as the sun was once stopped by a miracle), but we can speed it up interestingly.

The Gallery

Clora, come view my soul and tell
Whether I have contrived it well:
Now all its several lodgings lie
Composed into one gallery,

And the great arras-hangings,[1] made
Of various facings, by are laid,
That, for all furniture,[2] you'll find
Only your picture in my mind.

Here thou art painted in the dress
10 Of an inhuman murderess;
Examining[3] upon our hearts
Thy fertile shop of cruel arts:
Engines more keen than ever yet
Adornèd tyrant's cabinet,
Of which the most tormenting are
Black eyes, red lips, and curlèd hair.

But, on the other side, thou'rt drawn
Like to Aurora[4] in the dawn;
When in the East she slumbering lies,
20 And stretches out her milky thighs;
While all the morning choir does sing,
And manna[5] falls, and roses spring;
And, at thy feet, the wooing doves
Sit pérfecting their harmless loves.

Like an enchantress here thou show'st,
Vexing thy restless lover's ghost;
And, by a light obscure, dost rave
Over his entrails, in the cave;[6]
Divining thence, with horrid care,
30 How long thou shalt continue fair;
And (when informed) them throw'st away,
To be the greedy vulture's prey.

But, against that, thou sitt'st afloat
Like Venus in her pearly boat:
The halcyons,[7] calming all that's nigh,
Betwixt the air and water fly;
Or, if some rolling wave appears,
A mass of ambergris[8] it bears.
Nor blows more wind than what may well
40 Convoy the perfume to the smell.

These pictures, and a thousand more,
Of thee my gallery do store
In all the forms thou canst invent

[1] **arras-hangings** tapestries
[2] **furniture** furnishings
[3] **Examining** testing
[4] **Aurora** dawn-goddess
[5] **manna** the divinely provided food of the Is-
raelites in the desert, falling from heaven
[6] ll. 27–28 Etruscan and Roman soothsayers
predicted the will of the gods by inspecting the
entrails of sacrificial animals.
[7] **halcyons** aquatic birds (kingfishers) whose
incubation period was supposed to calm the
waves
[8] **ambergris** secretion of sperm whale, used
to make perfume

Either to please me, or torment:
For thou alone, to people me,
Art grown a numerous colony,
And a collection choicer far
Than or Whitehall's or Mantua's⁹ were.

But, of these pictures and the rest,
50   That at the entrance likes me best,
Where the same posture, and the look
Remains with which I first was took:
A tender shepherdess, whose hair
Hangs loosely playing in the air,
Transplanting flowers from the green hill,
To crown her head, and bosom fill.

1681

⁹ **Whitehall's or Mantua's** art galleries

The Picture of Little T.C.¹
In a Prospect of Flowers

See with what simplicity
This nymph begins her golden days!
In the green grass she loves to lie,
And there with her fair aspect tames
The wilder flowers, and gives them names;²
But only with the roses plays,
    And them does tell
What colour best becomes them, and what smell.

Who can foretell for what high cause
10   This darling of the gods³ was born?
Yet this is she whose chaster laws
The wanton Love shall one day fear,
And under her command severe
See his bow broke and ensigns torn.
    Happy, who can
Appease this virtuous enemy of man!

Oh then let me in time compound,
And parley with those conquering eyes,
Ere they have tried their force to wound;
20   Ere with their glancing wheels they drive
In triumph over hearts that strive,
And them that yield but⁴ more despise.
    Let me be laid
Where I may see thy glories from some shade.

¹ probably Theophila Cornewall, born 1644.
² **gives . . . names** as God had caused Adam to
name all animals in Eden.

³ **darling of the gods** Theophila means ''dear
to God.''
⁴ **but** only

Meantime, whilst every verdant thing
Itself does at thy beauty charm,
Reform the errors of the spring:
Make that the tulips may have share
Of sweetness, seeing they are fair;
30   And roses of their thorns disarm;
        But most procure
That violets may a longer age endure.

But, O young beauty of the woods,
Whom nature courts with fruits and flowers,
Gather the flowers, but spare the buds,
Lest Flora, angry at thy crime,
To kill her infants in their prime,
Do quickly make the example yours;
        And ere we see,
40   Nip in the blossom all our hopes and thee.

1681

The Mower Against Gardens

Luxurious[1] Man, to bring his vice in use,
    Did after him the world seduce;
And from the field the flowers and plants allure,
    Where Nature was most plain and pure.
He first enclosèd within the garden's square
    A dead and standing pool of air,
And a more luscious earth for them did knead,
    Which stupefied them while it fed.
The pink grew then as double his mind;
10   The nutriment did change the kind.
With strange perfumes he did the roses taint,
    And flow'rs themselves were taught to paint.[2]
The tulip, white, did for complexion seek,
    And learned to interline its cheek:
Its onion root they then so high did hold,
    That one was for a meadow sold.[3]
Another world was searched, through oceans new,
    To find the Marvel of Peru.[4]
And yet these rarities might be allowed,
20   To Man, that sovereign thing and proud,
Had he not dealt between the bark and tree,
    Forbidden mixtures there to see.
No plant now knew the stock from which it came;

[1] **Luxurious** lecherous
[2] **paint** use cosmetics
[3] ll. 15–16 In Marvell's time tulip bulbs brought
extraordinary prices in the Netherlands.
[4] **Marvel of Peru** an actual species

He grafts upon the wild the tame:
That the uncertain and adulterate fruit
   Might put the palate in dispute.
His green Seraglio[5] has its eunuchs too,
   Lest any tyrant him outdo;
And in the cherry he does Nature vex,
30   To procreate without a sex.[6]
'Tis all enforced, the fountain and the grot,[7]
   While the sweet fields do lie forgot:
Where willing Nature does to all dispense
   A wild and fragrant innocence;
And fauns and fairies do the meadows till,
   More by their presence than their skill.
Their statues,[8] polished by some ancient hand,
   May to adorn the gardens stand,
But howsoe'er the figures do excel,
40   The gods themselves with us do dwell.

1681

[5] **Seraglio** harem
[6] l. 30 i.e., by grafting
[7] **grot** artificial grotto

[8] **statues** ornamental statues of fauns and ancient gods. See last line.

The Garden

How vainly men themselves amaze[1]
To win the palm, the oak, or bays,[2]
And their incessant labors see
Crowned from some single herb or tree,
Whose short and narrow-verged[3] shade
Does prudently their toils upbraid;
While all flow'rs and all trees do close[4]
To weave the garlands of repose.

10   Fair Quiet, have I found thee here,
And Innocence, thy sister dear?
Mistaken long, I sought you then
In busy companies of men,
Your sacred plants, if here below,
Only among the plants will grow.
Society is all but rude,
To[5] this delicious solitude.

[1] **amaze** perplex
[2] ll. 1–2 Leaves of laurel, palm, and oak provided wreaths denoting fame among men.
[3] **narrow-verged** narrowly bordered, suggest-

ing modesty by the smallness of the enclosed area
[4] **close** unite
[5] **To** compared to

No white nor red[6] was ever seen,
So am'rous[7] as this lovely green
Fond lovers, cruel as their flame,
20   Cut in these trees their mistress' name:
Little, alas, they know, or heed,
How far these beauties hers exceed!
Fair trees, wheresoe'er your barks I wound,
No names shall but your own be found.

When we have run our passions' heat,
Love hither makes his best retreat.
The gods, that mortal beauty chase,
Still[8] in a tree did end their race.
Apollo hunted Daphne so,
30   Only that she might laurel grow,[9]
And Pan did after Syrinx speed,
Not as a nymph, but for a reed.[10]

What wondrous life in this I lead!
Ripe apples drop about my head;
The luscious clusters of the vine
Upon my mouth do crush their wine;
The nectarine, and curious[11] peach
Into my hands themselves do reach;
Stumbling on melons, as I pass,
40   Ensnared with flowers, I fall on grass.

Meanwhile the mind, from pleasure less,
Withdraws into its happiness:[12]
The mind, that ocean where each kind
Does straight its own resemblance find;
Yet it creates, transcending these,
Far other worlds, and other seas;
Annihilating all that's made
To a green thought in a green shade.

Here at the fountain's sliding foot,
50   Or at some fruit-tree's mossy root,
Casting the body's vest[13] aside,
My soul into the boughs does glide:
There, like a bird it sits, and sings,

[6]**No white nor red** i.e., of some beloved
woman's complexion
[7]**am'rous** mad
[8]**Still** always
[9]ll. 29–30 The story of Daphne's being turn-
ed into a laurel to save her from the amorously
pursuing Apollo is amusingly reinterpreted
here to serve the truth of the poem.
[10]ll. 31–32 Chased by Pan, Syrinx was simi-

larly transformed into a reed (from which Pan
made his pipes). The myth is modified as
above.
[11]**curious** exquisite
[12]ll. 41–42 Experiencing less outward plea-
sure in its solitude, the mind withdraws into
true happiness.
[13]**the body's vest** the body considered as
clothing of the soul

Then whets,[14] and combs its silver wings;
And, till prepared for longer flight,
Waves in its plumes the various light.

Such was that happy Garden-state,
While Man there walked without a mate:
After a place so pure and sweet,
60   What other help could yet be meet![15]
But 'twas beyond a mortal's share
To wander solitary there:
Two paradises 'twere in one
To live in Paradise alone.

How well the skillful gard'ner drew
Of flowers and herbs this dial[16] new;
Where from above the milder sun
Does through a fragrant zodiac run;
And, as it works, the industrious bee
70   Computes its time as well as we.
How could such sweet and wholesome hours
Be reckoned but with herbs and flow'rs?

1681

[14]**whets** preens
[15]**meet** punning on "helpmeet"
[16]**dial** sundial

HENRY VAUGHAN
1621–1695

Vaughan was a doctor, with much feeling for his native Wales. He served on the royalist side in the Civil War. The deeply felt loss of his brother led him to some of his best poetry.

He was among the last of the Metaphysically inclined poets of the century. Herbert's devotional verse was very important to him. "Regeneration," below, is an expansion of Herbert's idea in "The Pilgrimage," although in very different terms. Vaughan was not capable of, or perhaps interested in, Herbert's integral workmanship; his concern was the message more than the medium, although his imagery is fascinating and his stanzaic structures repay attention.

Only in such a simple work as "Peace" (both martial and hymn-like, like "Onward Christian Soldiers") does he rise to the poem as a felt whole. More important, the symbolic center in his poems lies not in the churchly and formally devotional images of Herbert but in the alchemical and mystical symbols learned from his brother Thomas and, remarkably, in other symbols in nature. In "The Bird" every smallest natural entity's song of praise to the Creator at dawn (the "Day spring" of the Anglican Book of Common Prayer) looks forward to Romanticism. So does the doctrine of childhood innocence, corrupted with age, which he shares with Thomas Traherne.

Regeneration

A ward,[1] and still in bonds, one day
        I stole abroad;
It was high spring, and all the way
        Primrosed, and hung with shade;
          Yet was it frost within,
            And surly winds
Blasted my infant buds, and sin
        Like clouds eclipsed my mind.

Stormed thus, I straight perceived my spring
10   Mere stage, and show,
My walk a monstrous, mountained thing
        Rough-cast with rocks and snow;
          And as a pilgrim's eye,
            Far from relief,
Measures the melancholy sky,
        Then drops, and rains for grief,

So sighed I upwards still; at last
        'Twixt steps and falls
I reached the pinnacle, where placed
20   I found a pair of scales;
          I took them up and laid
            In th' one, late pains;
The other smoke[2] and pleasures weighed
        But proved the heavier grains;

With that some cried, "Away!" Straight I
        Obeyed, and, led
Full east, a fair, fresh field could spy;
        Some called it Jacob's Bed,[3]
          A virgin soil, which no
30   Rude feet e'er trod,
Where (since he stepped there) only go
        Prophets, and friends of God.

Here I reposed; but scarce well set,
        A grove descried
Of stately height, whose branches met
        And mixed on every side;
          I entered, and once in
            (Amazed to see't)
Found all was changed, and a new spring
40   Did all my senses greet;

---

[1] **ward** a minor, still under guardianship
[2] **smoke** inconsequential, insignificant things
[3] **Jacob's Bed** where Jacob saw angels ascending and descending a ladder between earth and heaven (Genesis 28:11–22)

The unthrift[4] sun shot vital gold,
      A thousand pieces,
And heaven its azure did unfold
        Checkered with snowy fleeces;
        The air was all in spice,
          And every bush
A garland wore; Thus fed my eyes,
      But all the ear lay hush.

Only a little fountain lent
50   Some use for ears,
And on the dumb shades language spent,
        The music of her tears;
        I drew her near, and found
          The cistern full
Of divers stones, some bright, and round,
      Others ill-shaped and dull.

The first (pray mark) as quick as light
        Danced through the flood,
But, the last, more heavy than the night,
60   Nailed to the center stood;
        I wondered much, but tired
          At last with thought,
My restless eye that still desired
      As strange an object brought;

It was a bank of flowers, where I descried
        (Though 'twas midday,)
Some fast asleep, others broad-eyed
        And taking in the ray;
        Here musing long, I heard
70   A rushing wind
Which still increased, but whence it stirred
      No where I could not find;

I turned me round, and to each shade
        Dispatched an eye
To see if any leaf had made
        Least motion or reply,
        But while I list'ning sought
          My mind to ease
By knowing, where 'twas, or where not,
80   It whispered, "Where I please."[5]

"Lord," then said I, "on me one breath,
        And let me die before my death."

1650

[4] **unthrift** spendthrift
[5] ll. 70–72, 77–80 Cf. John 3:7–8: "Ye must be born again. The wind bloweth where it listeth [pleases], and thou hearest the sound thereof, but canst not tell whence it cometh, and whither it goeth: so is every one that is born of the Spirit." "Spirit" is etymologically related to words for "breath" and "wind."

The Retreat

Happy those early days, when I
Shined in my angel infancy;
Before I understood this place
Appointed for my second race,[1]
Or taught my soul to fancy aught
But a white, celestial thought;
When yet I had not walked above
A mile or two from my first Love,
And looking back, at that short space
10   Could see a glimpse of His bright face;
When on some gilded cloud, or flower,
My gazing soul would dwell an hour,
And in those weaker glories spy
Some shadows of eternity;
Before I taught my tongue to wound
My conscience with a sinful sound,
Or had the black art to dispense
A several[2] sin to every sense,
But felt through all this fleshly dress
20   Bright shoots of everlastingness.
      Oh, how I long to travel back,
And tread again that ancient track!
That I might once more reach that plain,
Where first I left my glorious train,[3]
From whence the enlightened spirit sees
That shady city of palm trees;
But, ah! my soul with too much stay
Is drunk, and staggers in the way.
Some men a forward motion love,
30   But I by backward steps would move,
And when this dust falls to the urn,
In that state I came return.

1650

[1] **second race** the race of life, after a heavenly
state before birth
[2] **several** separate
[3] **train** procession

Peace

My soul, there is a country
      Far beyond the stars,
Where stands a winged sentry
      All skillful in the wars.[1]
There, above noise and danger,
      Sweet Peace sits crowned with smiles,
And One born in a manger

[1] ll. 1–8 The warlike angelic sentry introduces
the split between the war of earthly existence
and the resting in peace of the afterlife pro-
vided and securely protected by a God of love.

Commands the beauteous files.
He is thy gracious friend,
10   And (Oh, my Soul awake!)
Did in pure love descend
      To die here for thy sake.
If thou canst get but thither,
      There grows the flower of peace,
The rose that cannot wither,
      Thy fortress and thy ease;
Leave then thy foolish ranges;[2]
      For none can thee secure
But One who never changes,
20   Thy God, thy life, thy cure.

1650

[2] **ranges** strayings

The Bird

Hither thou com'st: the busy wind all night
Blew through thy lodging, where thy own warm wing
Thy pillow was. Many a sullen storm
(For which coarse man seems much the fitter born)
      Rained on thy bed
      And harmless head.

And now, as fresh and cheerful as the light,
Thy little heart in early hymns doth sing
Unto that Providence, whose unseen arm
10 Curbed them, and clothed thee well and warm.
      All things that be, praise him, and had
      Their lesson taught them when first made.

So hills and valleys into singing break;
And though poor stones have neither speech nor tongue,
While active winds and streams both run and speak,
Yet stones are deep in admiration.
Thus praise and prayer here beneath the Sun
Make lesser mornings when the great are done.

For each inclosed spirit is a star
20   Enlightening his own little sphere,
Whose light, though fetched and borrowed from far,
      Both mornings makes and evenings there.

But as these birds of light make a land glad,
Chirping their solemn matins[1] on each tree:
So in the shades of night some dark fowls be,
Whose heavy notes make all that hear them sad.

[1] **matins** morning prayer

The turtle[2] then in palm trees mourns
    While owls and satyrs howl;
The pleasant land to brimstone turns,
30   And all her streams grow foul.

Brightness and mirth, and love and faith, all fly,
Till the day-spring breaks forth again from high.

1655

[2] **turtle** turtledove

THOMAS TRAHERNE
1637–1674

"Wonder," from the latest-born of the Metaphysicals, sounds like a poem by Vaughan, but the idea of childhood innocence spoiled by contact with the world is coupled with a poetically formulated social theory of the corrupting selfishness inherent in individual ownership of property. It is hard to believe that the Wordsworth of the "Intimations" ode did not read this poem, but no manuscript of Traherne's works was discovered until 1897. The prose poetry on the same subject in Traherne's *Centuries of Meditation* ("Third Century," 3) is similarly moving: "The corn was orient and immortal wheat, which never should be reaped, nor was ever sown. I thought it stood from everlasting to everlasting. . . . I knew no churlish proprieties . . . with much ado I was corrupted, and made to learn the dirty devices of this world. Which now I unlearn."

Like Vaughan, Traherne functions more on the level of the stanza than the entire poem. The exclamatory, felt richness of his lines sometimes escapes from his complicated stanzaic pattern of longer and shorter lines (pentameters, tetrameters, trimeters, and one dimeter). This easy freedom of Traherne's original version of "Wonder" has been chosen here in preference to the one edited by his brother Philip, who tried heavy-handedly to make all the lines come out right.

Wonder

How like an angel came I down!
    How bright are all things here!
When first among his works I did appear
    Oh, how their glory did me crown!
The world resembled his eternity,
      In which my soul did walk;
    And everything that I did see
      Did with me talk.

The skies in their magnificence,
10   The lively, lovely air,
Oh how divine, how soft, how sweet, how fair!
    The stars did entertain my sense,
And all the works of God so bright and pure,
     So rich and great did seem,
     As if they must endure
        In my esteem.

A native health and innocence
     Within my bones did grow,
And while my God did all his glories show,
20   I felt a vigor in my sense
That was all spirit. I within did flow
     With seas of life, like wine;
    I nothing in the world did know
        But 'twas divine.

Harsh ragged objects were concealed,
     Oppressions, tears and cries,
Sins, griefs, complaints, dissensions, veeping eyes
    Were hid: and only things revealed
Which heavenly spirits and the angels prize.
30   The state of innocence
    And bliss, not trades and poverties,
        Did fill my sense.

The streets were paved with golden stones;
     The boys and girls were mine,
Oh, how did all their lovely faces shine!
    The sons of men were holy ones,
In joy and beauty they appeared to me,
     And everything which here I found,
     While like an angel I did see,
40   Adorned the ground.

Rich diamond and pearl and gold
     In every place was seen;
Rare splendors, yellow, blue, red, white, and green,
    Mine eyes did everywhere behold.
Great wonders clothed with glory did appear,
     Amazement was my bliss.
    That and my wealth was everywhere:
       No joy to this![1]

---

[1] **No joy to this** No joy equalled this.

Cursed and devised proprieties,[2]
50   With envy, avarice,
And fraud, those fiends that spoil even Paradise,
Flew from the splendor of mine eyes;
And so did hedges, ditches, limits, bounds:
I dreamed not aught of those,
But wandered over all men's grounds,
And found repose.

Proprieties themselves were mine,
And hedges ornaments;[3]
Walls, boxes, coffers, and their rich contents
60   Did not divide my joys, but all combine.
Clothes, ribbons, jewels, laces, I esteemed
My joys by others worn;
For me they all to wear them seemed[4]
When I was born.

from ms., 1903

[2] l. 49 things separately owned
[3] **hedges ornaments** Hedges, which delimit separate properties, were no more than ornaments.

[4] ll. 61–63 All wearers of ribbons, jewels, laces seemed to wear them for me.

The Restoration and
Eighteenth Century

JOHN WILMOT,
EARL OF ROCHESTER
1647–1680

Under the protection and guidance of Charles II, the fatherless, seventeen-year-old Earl of Rochester entered and dominated the world of courtly elegance, dissipation, and clever, often brutal, wit that followed the restoration of the monarchy in 1660. Rochester soon joined the escapades of the older court wits and earned a reputation for being a self-destructive rake.

Rochester's verse is worldly but less polished than eighteenth-century verse. Colloquial and with many enjambments, it sometimes breaks into half-lines and employs apparent obscenities whose artistic function surpasses their shock value. He lacked confidence in himself, woman, monarch, and God in so skeptical an age, and therefore mocks the complacent who assert beliefs he cannot share, as in the *Satire Against Reason and Mankind* (1679). Rochester also uses many of the devices of Restoration comedy. *Artemisia to Chloe* (1679) adopts the familiar stage conflicts between town and country, court and commerce, man and woman, adultery and fidelity, wit and pretentious dullard. But Rochester adds his own notes of anger and sadness about a world empty of values, in which "whore is scarce a more reproachful name / Than poetess" and love, the "most generous passion of the mind," has been reduced to fashionable and unpleasing affairs. In the poem's brilliantly grim world, the "fine lady" has "turned o'er / As many books as men" and cares for none of them. Rochester's compelling descriptions of his inner and outer worlds establish him as second only to Dryden as a Restoration poet.

A Letter from Artemisia in the Town to Chloe in the Country[1]

Chloe,
       In verse by your command I write.
Shortly you'll bid me ride astride, and fight:
These talents better with our sex agree
Than lofty flights of dangerous poetry.
Amongst the men, I mean the men of wit
(At least they passed for such before they writ),
How many bold adventurers for the bays,[2]
Proudly designing large returns of praise,
Who durst that stormy, pathless world explore,
10   Were soon dashed back, and wrecked on the dull shore,
Broke of that little stock they had before!
How would a woman's tottering bark be tossed
Where stoutest ships, the men of wit, are lost?

[1]**Artemisia** Artemis, twin sister of Apollo, and the Roman Diana, virgin goddess of the hunt who presided over childbirth and symbolized the productive forces of nature. Like Chloe, the name provides an ironic backdrop for the present unchaste sterile world. **Chloe** a lover of Daphnis in a Greek third-century B.C. pastoral, and a name for Demeter, goddess of the young green crops. Both Chloe and Corinna in l. 189 were often used for women's names in poetry of the period.

[2]**bays** laurel wreath of honor bestowed on a poet

When I reflect on this, I straight grow wise,
And my own self thus gravely I advise:
   Dear Artemisia, poetry's a snare;
Bedlam has many mansions;[3] have a care.
Your muse diverts you, makes the reader sad:
You fancy you're inspired; he thinks you mad.
20   Consider, too, 'twill be discreetly done
To make yourself the fiddle[4] of the town,
To find th'ill-humored pleasure at their need,
Cursed if you fail, and scorned though you succeed!
Thus, like an arrant[5] woman as I am,
No sooner well convinced writing's a shame,
That whore is scarce a more reproachful name
Than poetess—
Like men that marry, or like maids that woo,
'Cause 'tis the very worst thing they can do,
30   Pleased with the contradiction and the sin,
Methinks I stand on thorns till I begin.
    Y'expect at least to hear what loves have passed
In this lewd town, since you and I met last;
What change has happened of intrigues, and whether
The old ones last, and who and who's together.
But how, my dearest Chloe, shall I set
My pen to write what I would fain forget?
Or name that lost thing, love, without a tear,
Since so debauched by ill-bred customs here?
40   Love, the most generous passion of the mind,
The softest refuge innocence can find,
The safe director of unguided youth,
Fraught with kind wishes, and secured by truth;
That cordial drop heaven in our cup has thrown
To make the nauseous draught of life go down;
On which one only blessing, God might raise
In lands of atheists, subsidies of praise,
For none did e'er so dull and stupid prove
But felt a god, and blessed his power in love—
50   This only joy for which poor we were made
Is grown, like play, to be an arrant trade.
The rooks[6] creep in, and it has got of late
As many little cheats and tricks as that.
    But what yet more a woman's heart would vex,
'Tis chiefly carried on by our own sex;
Our silly[7] sex! who, born like monarchs free,
Turn gypsies for a meaner[8] liberty,

[3] **Bedlam . . . mansions** The madhouse has many rooms.
[4] **fiddle** jester, but implying prostitution
[5] **arrant** wandering, as in l. 121, with the connotation of "preeminently bad," as in l. 51

[6] **rooks** cheats, especially in "play" or card games
[7] **silly** witless, foolish
[8] **meaner** baser, ignoble

And hate restraint, though but from infamy.
They call whatever is not common, nice,[9]
60 And deaf to nature's rule, or love's advice,
Forsake the pleasure to pursue the vice.
To an exact perfection they have wrought
The action, love; the passion is forgot.
'Tis below wit, they tell you, to admire,[10]
And ev'n without approving, they desire.
Their private wish obeys the public voice;
'Twixt good and bad, whimsey decides, not choice.
Fashions grow up for taste; at forms they strike;
They know what they would have, not what they like.
70 Bovey's[11] a beauty, if some few agree
To call him so; the rest to that degree
Affected are, that with their ears they see.
    Where I was visiting the other night
Comes a fine lady, with her humble knight,
Who had prevailed on her, through her own skill,
At his request, though much against his will,
To come to London.
As the coach stopped, we hear her voice, more loud
Than a great-bellied woman's in a crowd,
80 Telling the knight that her affairs require
He, for some hours, obsequiously retire.
I think she was ashamed to have him seen:
Hard fate of husbands! The gallant had been,
Though a diseased, ill-favored fool, brought in.
"Dispatch," says she, "that business you pretend,[12]
Your beastly visit to your drunken friend!
A bottle ever makes you look so fine;
Methinks I long to smell you stink of wine!
Your country drinking breath's enough to kill:
90 Sour ale corrected with a lemon peel.
Prithee, farewell! We'll meet again anon."
The necessary thing bows, and is gone.
    She flies upstairs, and all the haste does show
That fifty antic[13] postures will allow,
And then bursts out: "Dear madam, am not I
The altered'st creature breathing? Let me die,
I find myself ridiculously grown,
Embarrassée with being out of town,
Rude and untaught like any Indian queen:
100 My country nakedness is strangely seen.
    "How is love governed, love that rules the state,
And pray, who are the men most worn of late?
When I was married, fools were *à la mode*.

---

[9]**nice** fastidious, prudish
[10]**admire** to regard with wonder, here with love.
    See also ll. 107 and 124.
[11]**Bovey** Sir Ralph Bovey
[12]**pretend** claim, profess
[13]**antic** odd, grotesque

The men of wit were then held *incommode*,[14]
Slow of belief, and fickle in desire,
Who, ere they'll be persuaded, must inquire
As if they came to spy, not to admire.
With searching wisdom, fatal to their ease,
They still find out why what may, should not please;
110 Nay, take themselves for injured when we dare
Make 'em think better of us than we are,
And if we hide our frailties from their sights,
Call us deceitful jilts and hypocrites.
They little guess, who at our arts are grieved,
The perfect joy of being well deceived;
Inquisitive as jealous cuckolds grow:
Rather than not be knowing, they will know
What, being known, creates their certain woe.
Women should these, of all mankind, avoid,
120 For wonder by clear knowledge is destroyed.
Woman, who is an arrant bird of night,
Bold in the dusk before a fool's dull sight,
Should fly when reason brings the glaring light.
    "But the kind, easy fool, apt to admire
Himself, trusts us; his follies all conspire
To flatter his, and favor our desire.
Vain of his proper merit, he with ease
Believes we love him best who best can please.
On him our gross, dull, common flatteries pass,
130 Ever most joyful when most made an ass.
Heavy to apprehend, though all mankind
Perceive us false, the fop concerned is blind,
Who, doting on himself,
Thinks everyone that sees him of his mind.
These are true women's men."
                              Here forced to cease
Through want of breath, not will to hold her peace,
She to the window runs, where she had spied
Her much esteemed dear friend, the monkey,[15] tied.
With forty smiles, as many antic bows,
140 As if 't had been the lady of the house,
The dirty, chattering monster she embraced,
And made it this fine, tender speech at last:
"Kiss me, thou curious miniature of man!
How odd thou art! how pretty! how japan![16]
Oh, I could live and die with thee!" Then on
For half an hour in compliment she run.
    I took this time to think what nature meant

---

[14]*incommode* troublesome
[15]**monkey** the "*cher* dear Pug" of l. 169, and a popular upper-class pet; here with satiric emphasis on "curious miniature of man" in

l. 143
[16]**japan** Fashionable Eastern imports often were lacquered in glossy black.

When this mixed thing into the world she sent,
So very wise, yet so impertinent:[17]
150 One who knew everything; who, God thought fit,
Should be an ass through choice, not want of wit;
Whose foppery, without the help of sense,
Could ne'er have rose to such an excellence.
Nature's as lame in making a true fop
As a philosopher; the very top
And dignity of folly we attain
By studious search, and labor of the brain,
By observation, counsel, and deep thought:
God never made a coxcomb[18] worth a groat.
160 We owe that name to industry and arts:
An eminent fool must be a fool of parts.
And such a one was she, who had turned o'er
As many books as men; loved much, read more;
Had a discerning wit; to her was known
Everyone's fault and merit, but her own.
All the good qualities that ever blessed
A woman so distinguished from the rest,
Except discretion only, she possessed.
But now, *"Mon cher* dear Pug," she cries, *"adieu!"*
170 And the discourse broke off does thus renew:
"You smile to see me, whom the world perchance
Mistakes to have some wit, so far advance
The interest of fools, that I approve
Their merit, more than men's of wit, in love.
But, in our sex, too many proofs there are
Of such whom wits undo, and fools repair.
This, in my time, was so observed a rule
Hardly a wench in town but had her fool.
The meanest common slut, who long was grown
180 The jest and scorn of every pit[19] buffoon,
Had yet left charms enough to have subdued
Some fop or other, fond to be thought lewd.
Foster[20] could make an Irish lord a Nokes,[21]
And Betty Morris[22] had her City[23] cokes.[24]
A woman's ne'er so ruined but she can
Be still revenged on her undoer, man;
How lost soe'er, she'll find some lover, more
A lewd, abandoned fool than she a whore.

---

[17]**impertinent**   trifling, foolish. See also l. 257.
[18]**coxcomb**   a conceited fool
[19]**pit**   the ground level of the theater; often a place in which young men and prostitutes would negotiate, observed by the more fashionable patrons in the boxes, and the less fashionable in the gallery
[20]**Foster**   probably a lower-class woman of dubious virtue
[21]**Nokes**   James Nokes, an actor who played pompous fools
[22]**Betty Morris**   a celebrated prostitute
[23]**City**   the unfashionable commercial district, as opposed to the fashionable court in the City of Westminster
[24]**cokes**   proverbial name for a fool

"That wretched thing Corinna, who had run
190 Through all the several ways of being undone,
Cozened at first by love, and living then
By turning the too dear-bought trick on men—
Gay were the hours, and winged with joys they flew,
When first the town her early beauties knew;
Courted, admired, and loved, with presents fed;
Youth in her looks, and pleasure in her bed;
Till fate, or her ill angel, thought it fit
To make her dote upon a man of wit,
Who found 'twas dull to love above a day;
200 Made his ill-natured jest, and went away.
Now scorned by all, forsaken, and oppressed,
She's a *memento mori*[25] to the rest;
Diseased, decayed, to take up half a crown[26]
Must mortgage her long scarf and manteau gown.
Poor creature! who, unheard of as a fly,
In some dark hole must all the winter lie,
And want and dirt endure a whole half year
That for one month she tawdry may appear.
    "In Easter Term she gets her a new gown,
210 When my young master's worship comes to town,
From pedagogue and mother just set free,
The heir and hopes of a great family;
Which, with strong ale and beef, the country rules,
And ever since the Conquest[27] have been fools.
And now, with careful prospect to maintain
This character, lest crossing of the strain
Should mend the booby breed, his friends provide
A cousin of his own to be his bride.
And thus set out
220 With an estate, no wit, and a young wife
(The solid comforts of a coxcomb's life),
Dunghill and pease forsook, he comes to town,
Turns spark,[28] learns to be lewd, and is undone.
Nothing suits worse with vice than want of sense:
Fools are still wicked at their own expense.
    "This o'ergrown schoolboy lost Corinna wins,
And at first dash to make an ass begins:
Pretends to like a man who has not known
The vanities nor vices of the town;
230 Fresh in his youth, and faithful in his love;
Eager of joys which he does seldom prove;[29]
Healthful and strong, he does no pains endure

---

[25]*memento mori* a reminder of death; commonly a skull

[26]**half a crown** a silver coin worth a modest two shillings six pence, and often a prostitute's fee

[27]**Conquest** of England by William of Normandy in 1066

[28]**spark** flirtatious, foppish suitor

[29]**prove** experience

But what the fair one he adores can cure;
Grateful for favors, does the sex esteem,
And libels none for being kind to him;
Then of the lewdness of the times complains:
Rails at the wits and atheists, and maintains
'Tis better than good sense, than power or wealth,
To have a love untainted, youth, and health.
240   "The unbred puppy, who had never seen
A creature look so gay, or talk so fine,
Believes, then falls in love, and then in debt;
Mortgages all, ev'n to the ancient seat,
To buy this mistress a new house for life;
To give her plate and jewels, robs his wife.
And when t' th' height of fondness he is grown,
'Tis time to poison him, and all's her own.
Thus meeting in her common arms his fate,
He leaves her bastard heir to his estate,
250 And, as the race of such an owl[30] deserves,
His own dull lawful progeny he starves.
    "Nature, who never made a thing in vain,
But does each insect to some end ordain,
Wisely contrived kind keeping fools, no doubt,
To patch up vices men of wit wear out."
Thus she ran on two hours, some grains of sense
Still mixed with volleys of impertinence.
    But now 'tis time I should some pity show
To Chloe, since I cannot choose but know
260 Readers must reap the dullness writers sow.
By the next post such stories I will tell
As, joined with these, shall to a volume swell,
As true as heaven, more infamous than hell.
But you are tired, and so am I.

                    Farewell.

1675?   1679

[30]**owl** metaphorically, a dunce

JOHN DRYDEN
1631–1700

Dryden, the first of fourteen children, attended Westminster School and Trinity College, Cambridge. He served briefly as a minor civil servant in Oliver Cromwell's government, though he was one of the many who welcomed the restoration of Charles II in 1660. Two years later he was elected an original fellow of the scientific Royal Society and soon established himself as the later seventeenth century's leading man of letters. He was appointed poet laureate in 1669 and historiographer royal in 1670. Dryden was secure in these positions under Charles and under Charles's Catholic brother, James II, especially since Dryden himself had converted to Catholicism. He was dismissed, however, when the unpopular James was forced to flee in 1688 and Parliament invited the Dutch Protestant, William of Orange, to be king, as William III.

Given such turbulence it is not surprising that much of Dryden's poetry concerns continuity and change. He used the concept of a timeless general human nature to exploit apparent parallels between the past and present. Judaeo-Christian and Graeco-Roman history provided standards against which the Restoration period could judge itself, as well as repeated patterns that served as guides—or warnings, for Dryden was well aware of history's darker side and of England's need to find her own modern political and literary voice. Since the restoration of Charles seemed to herald a new age, in *Absalom and Achitophel* (1681) Dryden alludes to Virgil's *Aeneid* and its praise of the supposed benevolent new, ultimately Augustan, age emerging with the founding of the Roman Empire. The end of Dryden's poem echoes the ninth book of the *Aeneid*—where Jove agrees to protect the ships of Aeneas, beloved son of Venus—and implies that the greater Christian God will protect

His anointed Charles II. Charles appears in this poem as "The Godlike David," a phrase denoting both the king's divine right, and the biblical contexts Dryden thought relevant for his own age. Nonetheless, Dryden knows that his king rules a limited constitutional monarchy, and lacks the power of an Old Testament patriarch or a Roman emperor. These allusions helped the English to locate analogous circumstances; as backdrop they also made plain that Charles must adapt himself to the special character of his nation—just as in the literary world Dryden must adapt English drama and poetry to the needs of his own audience.

Dryden makes clever use of at least two other devices. The first is a couplet form more fluid and less epigrammatic than Pope's, in which arguments can be made dramatically compelling. In *Absalom and Achitophel*, for example, the exchange between the title characters suggests, respectively, a mind debating with itself and a mind using rhetorical ploys to seduce the weak, while the royal intelligence of David finally is stirred to refute opposing arguments. The second device is Dryden's use of genre and conventions drawn from biblical narrative, farce, drama, and political controversy. In *Mac Flecknoe* (1682), Shadwell is diminished by contrast with the genuine heirs of great fathers in the Bible or in epics; and Flecknoe appears comically as John the Baptist leading the way of Shadwell as Jesus. Similarly, Achitophel seems more ominous because of Dryden's comparison with Satan's temptation of Eve, while the king's final speech in *Absalom* gains immediacy by being modeled on a pamphlet Charles wrote to justify his actions. A man of his time, Dryden includes and evaluates the past for the benefit of the present and the future.

From Absalom and Achitophel[1]

In pious times, e'r Priest-craft did begin,
Before Polygamy was made a sin;
When man, on many, multipli'd his kind,[2]
E'r one to one was, cursedly, confin'd:
When Nature prompted, and no law deny'd
Promiscuous use of Concubine and Bride;
Then, Israel's Monarch, after Heaven's own heart,[3]
His vigorous warmth did, variously, impart
To Wives and Slaves: And, wide as his Command,
10   Scatter'd his Maker's Image through the Land.
Michal,[4] of Royal blood, the Crown did wear,
A Soil ungrateful to the Tiller's care:
Not so the rest; for several Mothers bore
To Godlike David, several Sons before.
But since like slaves his bed they did ascend,
No True Succession could their seed attend.
Of all this Numerous Progeny was none
So Beautiful, so brave as Absalom:[5]
Whether, inspir'd by some diviner Lust,
20   His Father got him with a greater Gust;[6]
Or that his Conscious destiny made way
By manly beauty to Imperial sway.

[1] See 2 Samuel 14–18 and 19:1–15. Absalom, King David's favorite son, is encouraged by Achitophel to rebel against his father. After a temporary retreat and renewed confidence in God's favor, David and his army return to Israel, where the frightened Achitophel hangs himself; Absalom flees, but his long beautiful hair catches in the boughs of an oak tree, and there, against David's orders and to his great grief, Absalom is slain.

This political satire was part of the "exclusion crisis." The Tories wished to preserve the right of succession of the Catholic James, Duke of York, to the throne of his brother, Charles II. The Earl of Shaftesbury and the Whigs wished to exclude James in favor of the king's illegitimate son, the popular and Protestant Duke of Monmouth. The tension came to a head in 1678 when the unsavory Titus Oates claimed to have evidence of a Jesuit plot to kill the king and leading Protestants and, with the help of a Franco-Irish army, to establish Catholicism. The Exclusion Bill, managed by Shaftesbury and backed by the non-Anglican Protestant dissenters of the London merchant classes, twice passed in the House of Commons in the fall of 1680, but failed in the House of Lords. Charles dissolved Parliament but reconvened it on 21 March 1681 in the friendly city of Oxford. Since the treasury was bare, the Whigs expected Charles to capitulate and to exclude his brother in order to gain the funds necessary to run the government. Meanwhile, however, Louis XIV of France had secretly promised Charles £400,000 within the next three years. Thus armed, Charles briefly reconvened Parliament, only to dissolve it again and demoralize his adversaries.

[2] **multipli'd . . . kind**   adapted from Genesis 1: 21–22

[3] **Israel's Monarch … own heart**   David, King Charles II. And see 1 Samuel 13:14, with its ominous "now thy kingdom shall not continue."

[4] **Michal**   Catherine of Braganza (1638–1705), daughter of King John IV of Portugal, married Charles in 1662. Like David's wife Michal, she was childless.

[5] **Absalom**   James Scott (1649–1685), created Duke of Monmouth and then Duke of Buccleugh in 1663, was the acknowledged son of Charles's first known mistress, the humbly born Lucy Walter (c. 1630–1658). Monmouth had already performed well in the fields of love and war.

[6] **got . . . Gust**   begat him with extra relish or vigor (contrast to l. 171 and Achitophel's son)

Early in Foreign fields[7] he won Renown,
With Kings and States alli'd to Israel's[8] Crown:
In Peace the thoughts of War he could remove,
And seem'd as he were only born for love.
What e'r he did was done with so much ease,
In him alone, 'twas Natural to please.
His motions all accompanied with grace;
30   And Paradise was open'd in his face.
With secret Joy, indulgent David view'd
His Youthful Image in his Son renew'd:
To all his wishes Nothing he deni'd,
And made the Charming Annabel[9] his Bride.
What faults he had (for who from faults is free?)
His Father could not, or he would not see.
Some warm excesses, which the Law forbore,
Were constru'd Youth that purg'd by boiling o'r:
And Amnon's Murder,[10] by a specious Name,
40   Was call'd a Just Revenge for injur'd Fame.
Thus Prais'd, and Lov'd, the Noble Youth remain'd,
While David, undisturb'd, in Sion[11] reign'd.
But Life can never be sincerely[12] blest:
Heaven punishes the bad, and proves[13] the best.
The Jews, a Headstrong, Moody, Murmuring race,[14]
As ever tri'd th' extent and stretch of grace;
God's pamper'd people whom, debauch'd with ease,
No King could govern, nor no God could please;
(Gods they had tri'd[15] of every shape and size
50   That God-smiths could produce, or Priests devise:)
These Adam-wits,[16] too fortunately free,
Began to dream they wanted[17] liberty;
And when no rule, no precedent was found
Of men, by Laws less circumscrib'd and bound,
They led their wild desires to Woods and Caves,[18]
And thought that all but Savages were Slaves.
They who when Saul was dead, without a blow,

---

[7] **Foreign fields** in support of the French against the Dutch in 1673, and in support of the Dutch against the French in 1678

[8] **Israel's** England's

[9] **Annabel** Anne, Countess of Buccleugh (1651–1732), known as a rich and clever woman

[10] **Amnon's Murder** See 2 Samuel 13:1-29, where Absalom's servants kill Amnon for assaulting his half-sister Tamar. The parallel is obscure, but may allude to the attack by Monmouth's horse-guards upon Sir John Coventry; they slit his nose for insulting Charles about his sexual promiscuity with actresses.

[11] **Sion** London

[12] **sincerely** purely, wholly

[13] **proves** tests

[14] **Jews . . . race** the English, particularly Protestants

[15] **Gods . . . tri'd** the many Protestant sects

[16] **Adam-wits** misguided desires for freedom, like Adam's

[17] **wanted** lacked

[18] **Woods and Caves** where dissenters from the Church of England sometimes were forced to worship. Lines 53–56 allude to Thomas Hobbes's view that the state of nature, from which man must emerge, is a state of chaos and war.

Made foolish Ishbosheth[19] the Crown forgo;
Who banish'd David did from Hebron[20] bring,
60 And, with a General Shout, proclaim'd him King:
Those very Jews, who, at their very best,
Their Humour[21] more than Loyalty express'd,
Now, wonder'd why, so long, they had obey'd
An Idol Monarch which their hands had made:
Thought they might ruin him they could create;
Or melt him to that Golden Calf, a State.[22]
But these were random bolts: No form'd Design,
Nor Interest made the Factious Crowd to join:
The sober part of Israel, free from stain,
70 Well knew the value of a peaceful reign:
And, looking backward with a wise afright,
Saw Seams of wounds, dishonest[23] to the sight;
In contemplation of whose ugly Scars,
They curs'd the memory of Civil Wars.
The moderate sort of Men, thus qualifi'd,
Inclin'd the Balance to the better side:
And David's mildness manag'd it so well,
The Bad found no occasion to Rebel.
But, when to Sin our bias'd Nature leans,
80 The careful Devil is still at hand with means;
And providently Pimps for ill desires:
The Good old Cause[24] reviv'd, a Plot requires.
Plots, true or false, are necessary things,
To raise up Commonwealths, and ruin Kings.

. . .

150 Of these [plotters] the false Achitophel[25] was first:
A Name to all succeeding Ages Curs'd:
For close Designs, and crooked Counsels fit;
Sagacious, Bold, and Turbulent of wit:[26]

---

[19]**Saul . . . Ishbosheth** Oliver Cromwell (1599–1658) and his ineffectual son Richard (1626–1712). Saul ruled Israel before David; Ishbosheth was slain shortly after Saul's death; see 2 Samuel 4:6–7.

[20]**Hebron** Scotland. Charles actually was brought from Brussels, but as a Stuart was crowned king of Scotland in 1651. David was king of Judah before he was king of Israel.

[21]**Humour** whim

[22]**Calf, a State** In Exodus 32:4; the golden calf replaces the true God; here, a secular republic to replace the divinely appointed king.

[23]**dishonest** shameful, disgraceful

[24]**Good old Cause** of a commonwealth, as in Oliver Cromwell's republic (1649–53)

[25]**Achitophel** 2 Samuel 15:12, 31, 34; 16:15–23; 17:1–23; Anthony Ashley Cooper (1621–1683), created first Earl of Shaftesbury in 1672. He supported Charles I during the early years of the Civil War, joined Oliver Cromwell in January 1644, was prominent in his administration, but opposed his son Richard. One of twelve commissioners to invite Charles II to return, he was created Baron Ashley and appointed chancellor of the exchequer in 1661 and served as lord chancellor 1672–73, after which he was dismissed and went into opposition. He was stridently anti-Catholic and, when it seemed that the Catholic James, the king's brother, would succeed Charles II, anti-monarchic as well. He hoped to install Monmouth because of the weakness of his claim, and thus secure his dependence upon the "people" and his Whig benefactors; see ll. 224–27. Arrested for treason in 1681, Shaftesbury was awaiting trial in the Tower of London when this poem appeared.

[26]**Turbulent of wit** unstable imagination or concepts

Restless, unfix'd in Principles and Place;
In Power unpleas'd, impatient of Disgrace:
A fiery Soul, which working out its way,
Fretted the Pigmy Body to decay:
And o'er-inform'd the Tenement of Clay.[27]
A daring Pilot in extremity;
160   Pleas'd with the Danger, when the Waves went high
He sought the Storms; but for a Calm unfit,
Would Steer too nigh the Sands, to boast his Wit.
Great Wits are sure to Madness near alli'd;
And thin Partitions do their Bounds divide:[28]
Else, why should he, with Wealth and Honour bless'd,
Refuse his Age the needful hours of Rest?
Punish a Body which he could not please;
Bankrupt of Life, yet Prodigal of Ease?
And all to leave, what with his Toil he won,
170   To that unfeather'd, two-Legg'd thing,[29] a Son:
Got, while his Soul did huddled[30] Notions try;
And born a shapeless Lump, like Anarchy.
In Friendship False, Implacable in Hate:
Resolv'd to Ruin or to Rule the State.
To Compass this the Triple Bond he broke;
The Pillars of the public Safety shook:[31]
And fitted Israel for a Foreign Yoke.[32]
Then, seiz'd with Fear, yet still affecting Fame,
Usurp'd a Patriot's[33] All-atoning Name.
180   So easy still it proves in Factious Times,
With public Zeal to cancel private Crimes:
How safe is Treason, and how sacred ill,
Where none can sin against the People's Will:
Where Crowds can wink; and no offence be known,
Since in another's guilt they find their own.
Yet, Fame deserv'd, no Enemy can grudge;
The Statesman we abhor, but praise the Judge.
In Israel's Courts ne'r sat an Abbethdin[34]
With more discerning Eyes, or Hands more clean:

[27]**Fretted . . . Clay** eroded his small, crippled body and overflowed it, like a river overflowing its eroded banks

[28]**thin . . . divide** the slight difference between genius and madness

[29]**unfeathered . . . thing** the definition of man ascribed to Plato by Diogenes Laertius

[30]**huddled** disguised or confusedly thrown together

[31]**Triple Bond . . . shook** between Protestant England, Holland, and Sweden, against Catholic France in 1668. These alliances quickly changed—with Charles's connivance—and within four years England was at war with Holland and allied with France. As in other

places, Dryden either takes liberties with the facts or, like almost all of his countrymen, was ignorant of the king's role in these negotiations. See also the parallel use of "pillars" (l. 953) and "column" (l. 956) which Absalom breaks.

[32]**Foreign Yoke** of France

[33]**Patriot's** referring to those in opposition to the king and the court, specifically the Whigs, who urged the exclusion of James from the throne. See also ll. 965–68, 973.

[34]**Abbethdin** Jewish chief justice of the civil court, comparable to Shaftesbury as lord chancellor

190 Unbrib'd, unsought, the Wretched to redress;
  Swift of Dispatch, and easy of Access.
  Oh, had he been content to serve the Crown,
  With virtues only proper to the Gown;[35]
  Or, had the rankness of the Soil been freed
  From Cockle,[36] that oppress'd the Noble seed:
  David, for him his tuneful Harp had strung,
  And Heaven had wanted one Immortal song.[37]
  But wild Ambition loves to slide, not stand;
  And Fortune's Ice prefers to Virtue's Land:
200 Achitophel, grown weary to possess
  A lawful Fame, and lazy Happiness;
  Disdain'd the Golden fruit to gather free,
  And lent the Crowd his Arm to shake the Tree.

    . . .

220 Achitophel still wants a Chief, and none
  Was found so fit as Warlike Absalom:
  Not, that he wish'd his Greatness to create,
  (For Politicians neither love nor hate:)
  But, for he knew, his Title not allow'd,
  Would keep him still depending on the Crowd:
  That Kingly power, thus ebbing out, might be
  Drawn to the dregs of a Democracy.[38]
  Him he attempts, with studied Arts to please,
  And sheds his Venom,[39] in such words as these.
230 "Auspicious Prince! at whose Nativity
  Some Royal Planet[40] rul'd the Southern sky;
  Thy longing Country's Darling and Desire;
  Their cloudy Pillar, and their guardian Fire:[41]
  Their second Moses, whose extended Wand
  Divides the Seas, and shows the promis'd Land:
  Whose dawning Day, in every distant age,
  Has exercis'd the Sacred Prophets' rage:
  The People's Prayer, the glad Diviners' Theme,
  The Young men's Vision, and the Old men's Dream![42]
240 Thee, Saviour, Thee, the Nation's Vows confess;
  And, never satisfi'd with seeing, bless:
  Swift, unbespoken Pomps,[43] thy steps proclaim,
  And stammering Babes are taught to lisp thy Name.

---

[35]**Gown** of a judge
[36]**rankness . . . Cockle** luxuriant growth freed from weeds
[37]**Heaven . . . song** David would have written one psalm for Achitophel rather than God, who thus would lack it.
[38]**Democracy** popular and therefore unstable government
[39]**sheds . . . Venom** Here and at other places, Achitophel is like the serpent tempting Eve in *Paradise Lost*, Bk. IX.
[40]**Royal Planet** either the sun or Jupiter, each of which predicts royal destiny
[41]**Pillar . . . Fire** See Exodus 13:21, where God guides the Israelites with a pillar of cloud and a pillar of fire.
[42]**Vision . . . Dream** paraphrased from Joel 2:28
[43]**unbespoken Pomps** spontaneous celebrations

How long wilt thou the general Joy detain;
Starve, and defraud the People of thy Reign?
Content ingloriously to pass thy days
Like one of Virtue's Fools that feeds on Praise;
Till thy fresh Glories, which now shine so bright,
Grow Stale and Tarnish with our daily sight.
250 Believe me, Royal Youth, thy Fruit must be,
Or gather'd Ripe, or[44] rot upon the Tree.
Heav'n, has to all allotted, soon or late,
Some lucky Revolution of their Fate:
Whose Motions, if we watch and guide with Skill,
(For human Good depends on human Will,)
Our Fortune rolls, as from a smooth Descent,
And, from the first Impression, takes the Bent:
But, if unseiz'd, she glides away like wind;
And leaves repenting Folly far behind.
260 Now, now she meets you, with a glorious prize,
And spreads her Locks before her as she flies.[45]
Had thus Old David, from whose Loins you spring,
Not dar'd, when Fortune call'd him, to be King,
At Gath[46] an Exile he might still remain,
And heaven's Anointing Oil had been in vain.
Let his successful Youth your hopes engage,
But shun th' example of Declining Age:
Behold him setting in his Western Skies,
The Shadows length'ning as the Vapours rise.
270 He is not now, as when on Jordan's Sand[47]
The Joyful People throng'd to see him Land,
Cov'ring the Beach, and black'ning all the Strand:
But, like the Prince of Angels[48] from his height,
Comes tumbling downward with diminish'd light;
Betray'd by one poor Plot to public Scorn,
(Our only blessing since his Curs'd Return:)
Those heaps of People which one Sheaf did bind,
Blown off and scatter'd by a puff of Wind.
What strength can he to your Designs oppose,
280 Naked of Friends, and round beset with Foes?

If you as Champion of the public Good,
Add to their Arms a Chief of Royal Blood;
What may not Israel hope, and what Applause
Might such a General gain by such a Cause?
Not barren Praise alone, that Gaudy Flower,

[44]**Or . . . or** either . . . or
[45]**spreads . . . she flies** Fortune's flying hair must be seized from the front, for there is nothing to seize when she is beyond you.
[46]**Gath** where David fled from Saul, and Brussels, whence Charles returned to England. See

1 Samuel 27:1–7.
[47]**Jordan's Sand** Dover Beach, where Charles was greeted upon his return. See 2 Samuel 19:15.
[48]**Prince of Angels** Satan

Fair only to the sight, but solid Power:
And Nobler is a limited Command,
300   Giv'n by the Love of all your Native Land,
Than a Successive Title,[49] Long, and Dark,
Drawn from the Mouldy Rolls of Noah's Ark."

What cannot Praise 'effect in Mighty Minds,
When Flattery Sooths, and when Ambition Blinds!
Desire of Power, on Earth a Vicious Weed,
Yet, sprung from High, is of Celestial Seed:
In God 'tis Glory: And when men Aspire,
'Tis but a Spark too much[50] of Heavenly Fire.
Th'Ambitious Youth, too Covetous of Fame,
310   Too full of Angel's Metal[51] in his Frame;
Unwarily was led from Virtue's ways;
Made Drunk with Honour, and Debauch'd with Praise.
Half loath, and half consenting to the Ill,
(For Royal Blood within him struggled still)
He thus repli'd — "And what Pretence have I
To take up Arms for Public Liberty?
My Father Governs with unquestion'd Right;
The Faith's Defender, and Mankind's Delight:
Good, Gracious, Just, observant of the Laws;
320   And Heav'n by Wonders[52] has Espous'd his Cause.
Whom has he Wrong'd in all his Peaceful Reign?
Who sues for Justice to his Throne in Vain?
What Millions has he Pardon'd of his Foes,
Whom Just Revenge did to his Wrath expose!
Mild, Easy, Humble, Studious of our Good;
Inclin'd to Mercy, and averse from Blood.
If Mildness Ill with Stubborn Israel Suit,
His Crime is God's beloved Attribute.
What could he gain, his People to Betray,
330   Or change his Right, for Arbitrary Sway?
Let Haughty Pharaoh Curse with such a Reign,
His Fruitful Nile, and Yoke a Servile Train.
If David's Rule Jerusalem Displease,
The Dog-star[53] heats their Brains to this Disease.
Why then should I, Encouraging the Bad,
Turn Rebel, and run Popularly Mad?
Were he a Tyrant who, by Lawless Might,
Oppress'd the Jews, and Rais'd the Jebusite,[54]
Well might I Mourn; but Nature's Holy Bands

---

[49]**Successive Title** one based on legitimate succession; here, that of James versus that of Monmouth
[50]**Vicious Weed . . . Spark too much** Compare this with Absalom as "cockle" in l. 195, and his overflowing fire in l. 158.
[51]**Metal** mettle
[52]**Wonders** divine portents
[53]**Dog-star** Sirius, a late-summer star thought by the Romans to induce madness
[54]**Jebusite** Catholics

340   Would Curb my Spirits, and Restrain my Hands:
      The People might assert their Liberty;
      But what was Right in them, were Crime in me.
      His Favour leaves me nothing to require;
      Prevents[55] my Wishes, and outruns Desire.
      What more can I expect while David lives?
      All but his Kingly Diadem he gives;
      And that," But there he Paus'd, then Sighing, said,
      "Is Justly Destin'd for a Worthier Head.[56]
      For when my Father from his Toils shall Rest,
350   And late Augment the Number of the Bless'd:
      His Lawful Issue shall the Throne ascend,
      Or the Collateral Line where that shall end.
      His Brother, though Oppress'd with Vulgar Spite,[57]
      Yet Dauntless and Secure of Native Right,
      Of every Royal Virtue stands possess'd;
      Still Dear to all the Bravest, and the Best.
      His Courage Foes, his Friends his Truth Proclaim;
      His Loyalty the King, the World his Fame.
      His Mercy even th' Offending Crowd will find,
360   For sure he comes of a Forgiving Kind.
      Why should I then Repine at Heaven's Decree;
      Which gives me no Pretence to Royalty?
      Yet oh that Fate Propitiously Inclin'd,
      Had rais'd my Birth, or had debas'd my Mind;[58]
      To my large Soul, not all her Treasure lent,
      And then Betray'd it to a mean Descent.
      I find, I find my mounting Spirits Bold,
      And David's Part disdains my Mother's Mold.
      Why am I Scanted by a Niggard Birth?
370   My Soul Disclaims the Kindred of her Earth:
      And made for Empire, Whispers me within;
      Desire of Greatness is a Godlike Sin."

      Him Staggering so when Hell's dire Agent found,
      While fainting Virtue scarce maintain'd her Ground,
      He pours fresh Forces in, and thus Replies:

      "Th' Eternal God Supremely Good and Wise,
      Imparts not these Prodigious Gifts in vain;
      What Wonders are Reserv'd to bless your Reign?
      Against your will your Arguments have shown,
380   Such Virtue's only given to guide a Throne.
      Not that your Father's Mildness I condemn;

[55]**Prevents** anticipates
[56]**Worthier Head** Charles's brother James, the "Collateral Line" (l. 352) because Charles lacked legitimate issue
[57]**Vulgar Spite** because of his Catholicism
[58]**debas'd my Mind** The turning point in Ab-

salom's speech appropriately recalls Satan's words in *Paradise Lost* IV.58–61, as he assumes Achitophel's diabolical role. Dryden accentuates the Miltonic parallels through Achitophel's inversions in l. 373.

But Manly Force becomes the Diadem.
'Tis true, he grants the People all they crave;
And more perhaps than Subjects ought to have:
For Lavish grants suppose a Monarch tame,
And more his Goodness than his Wit[59] proclaim.
But when should People strive their Bonds to break,
If not when Kings are Negligent or Weak?
Let him give on till he can give no more,
390   The Thrifty Sanhedrin[60] shall keep him poor:
And every Shekel[61] which he can receive,
Shall cost a Limb of his Prerogative.[62]
To ply him with new Plots, shall be my care,
Or plunge him deep in some Expensive War;
Which when his Treasure can no more Supply,
He must, with the Remains of Kingship, buy.
His faithful Friends, our Jealousies and Fears,
Call Jebusites; and Pharaoh's Pensioners:
Whom, when our Fury from his Aid has torn,
400   He shall be Naked left to public Scorn.
The next Successor, whom I fear and hate,
My Arts have made Obnoxious to the State;
Turn'd all his Virtues to his Overthrow,
And gain'd our Elders[63] to pronounce a Foe.
His Right, for Sums of necessary Gold,
Shall first be Pawn'd, and afterwards be Sold:
Till time shall Ever-wanting David draw,
To pass your doubtful Title into Law:
If not, the People have a Right Supreme
410   To make their Kings; for Kings are made for them.
All Empire is no more than Pow'r in Trust,
Which when resum'd,[64] can be no longer Just.
Succession, for the general Good design'd,
In its own wrong a Nation cannot bind:
If altering that, the People can relieve,
Better one Suffer, than a Nation grieve.
The Jews well know their power: e're Saul[65] they Chose,
God was their King, and God they durst Depose.
Urge now your Piety, your Filial Name,
420   A Father's Right, and fear of future Fame;
The public Good, that Universal Call,
To which even Heav'n Submitted, answers all.

[59]**Wit**   shrewdness
[60]**Sanhedrin**   the ancient Jewish high court and supreme council; here, the British Parliament
[61]**Shekel**   Hebrew coin; here, probably British pound
[62]**Prerogative**   the king's powers curtailed by Parliament's control of revenues
[63]**Elders**   here, the House of Commons, which passed a bill excluding James from the succession. The bill failed in the House of Lords.
[64]**Empire . . . resum'd**   All royal power is held in trust for the people, who may reclaim it.
[65]**Saul**   The Jews were governed by a council of divinely inspired judges until the people demanded their first king, Saul. The English commonwealth acknowledged only God as king, until Cromwell officially became lord protector in 1653.

Nor let his Love Enchant your generous Mind;
'Tis Nature's trick to Propagate her Kind.
Our fond Begetters, who would never die,
Love but themselves in their Posterity.
Or let his Kindness by th' Effects be tri'd,
Or let him lay his vain Pretence aside.
God said he lov'd your Father; could he bring
430   A better Proof, than to Anoint him King?

. . .

Your Case no tame Expedients will afford;
Resolve on Death, or Conquest by the Sword,
Which for no less a Stake than Life, you Draw;
And Self-defence is Nature's Eldest Law.
Leave the warm People no Considering time;
460   For then Rebellion may be thought a Crime.
Prevail yourself of what Occasion gives,
But try your Title while your Father lives:
And that your Arms may have a fair Pretence,
Proclaim, you take them in the King's Defence:
Whose Sacred Life each minute would Expose
To Plots, from seeming Friends, and secret Foes.
And who can sound the depth of David's Soul?
Perhaps his fear, his kindness may Control.
He fears his Brother, though he loves his Son,
470   For plighted Vows too late to be undone.
If so, by Force he wishes to be gain'd.
Like women's Lechery, to seem Constrain'd:
Doubt not, but when he most affects the Frown,
Commit a pleasing Rape upon the Crown.
Secure his Person to secure your Cause;
They who possess the Prince, possess the Laws."

He said, And this Advice above the rest,
With Absalom's Mild nature suited best;
Unblam'd of Life (Ambition set aside,)
480   Not stain'd with Cruelty, nor puff'd with Pride;
How happy had he been, if Destiny
Had higher plac'd his Birth, or not so high!
His Kingly Virtues might have claim'd a Throne,
And bless'd all other Countries but his own:
But charming Greatness, since so few refuse;
'Tis Juster to Lament him, than Accuse.

. . .

With all these loads of Injuries oppress'd,
And long revolving, in his careful[66] Breast,
Th' event of things; at last his patience tir'd,

[66]**careful** anxious, full of cares

Thus from his Royal Throne by Heav'n inspir'd,
The God-like David[67] spoke: with awful fear
His Train their Maker in their Master hear.

"Thus long have I, by native mercy sway'd,
940 My wrongs dissembl'd, my revenge delay'd:
So willing to forgive th' Offending Age,
So much the Father did the King assuage.
But now so far my Clemency they slight,
Th' Offenders question my Forgiving Right.[68]
That one was made for many, they contend:
But 'tis to Rule, for that's a Monarch's End.
They call my tenderness of Blood, my Fear:
Though Manly tempers can the longest bear.
Yet, since they will divert my Native course,
950 'Tis time to show I am not Good by Force.
Those heap'd Affronts that haughty Subjects bring,
Are burdens for a Camel, not a King;
Kings are the public Pillars of the State,
Born to sustain and prop the Nation's weight:
If my Young Samson[69] will pretend a Call[70]
To shake the Column, let him share the Fall:
But oh that yet he would repent and live!
How easy 'tis for Parents to forgive!
With how few Tears a Pardon might be won
960 From Nature, pleading for a Darling Son!
Poor pitied Youth, by my Paternal care,
Rais'd up to all the Height his Frame could bear:
Had God ordain'd his fate for Empire born,
He would have given his Soul another turn:
Gull'd[71] with a Patriot's name, whose Modern sense
Is one that would by Law supplant his Prince:
The People's Brave,[72] the Politician's Tool;
Never was Patriot yet, but was a Fool.
Whence comes it that Religion and the Laws
970 Should more be Absalom's than David's Cause?
His old Instructor,[73] e're he lost his Place,
Was never thought indu'd with so much Grace.
Good Heav'ns, how Faction can a Patriot Paint!
My Rebel ever proves my People's Saint:
Would They impose an Heir upon the Throne?

[67]**God-like David** This speech inspires awe in its auditors and marks Charles's restoration to his proper role as king now forced to exercise justice rather than misguided mercy. It is based in part on Charles's pamphlet of April 1681, *His Majesties Declaration To all His Loving Subjects*, in which he explains why he dissolved the Oxford Parliament. The restoration of the true king also is the restoration of order.

[68]**Forgiving Right** Whigs questioned Charles's right to pardon their enemies.
[69]**Samson** In Judges 16:25–31 Samson pulls down the pillars of the Philistine temple and dies with his enemies.
[70]**Call** the Puritans' word for divine summons
[71]**Gull'd** duped
[72]**Brave** a man excessively daring
[73]**Instructor** Achitophel / Shaftesbury

Let Sanhedrins be taught to give their Own.[74]
A King's at least a part of Government,
And mine as requisite as their Consent:
Without my Leave a future King to choose,
980 Infers a Right the Present to Depose:
True, they Petition me t' approve their Choice,
But Esau's Hands suit ill with Jacob's Voice.[75]
My Pious Subjects for my Safety pray,
Which to Secure they take my Power away.
From Plots and Treasons Heaven preserve my years,
But Save me most from my Petitioners.[76]
Unsatiate as the barren Womb or Grave;
God cannot Grant so much as they can Crave.
What then is left but with a Jealous Eye
990 To guard the Small remains of Royalty?
The Law shall still direct my peaceful Sway,
And the same Law teach Rebels to Obey:
Votes shall no more Establish'd Pow'r control,
Such Votes as make a Part exceed the Whole:
No groundless Clamours shall my Friends remove,
Nor Crowds have power to Punish e're they Prove:
For Gods, and Godlike Kings their Care express,
Still to Defend their Servants in distress.
Oh that my Power to Saving were confin'd:
1000 Why am I forc'd, like Heaven, against my mind,
To make Examples of another Kind?
Must I at length the Sword of Justice draw?
Oh curs'd Effects of necessary Law!
How ill my Fear they by my Mercy scan.
Beware the Fury of a Patient Man.
Law they require, let Law then show her Face;
They could not be content to look on Grace,
Her hinder parts, but with a daring Eye
To tempt the terror of her Front, and Die.[77]
1010 By their own arts 'tis Righteously decreed,
Those dire Artificers of Death shall bleed.
Against themselves their Witnesses will Swear,[78]
Till Viper-like their Mother Plot[79] they tear:
And suck for Nutriment that bloody gore
Which was their Principle of Life before.

---

[74]**their Own** what they have authority to give
[75]**Jacob's Voice** Genesis 27:22. Jacob disguises himself as his elder brother Esau in order to receive his blind father's blessing and estate. Charles can see and rejects the improper heir.
[76]**Petitioners** The Whigs frequently petitioned for the recall of Parliament—source of their political power.
[77]**Grace . . . Die** In Exodus 33:20-23, Moses sees only the "back parts," or the mercy, of

God; sight of his face, law, brings death.
[78]**will Swear** as some of the presumed anti-Catholics did against the Whigs. As Charles's authority solidifies, that of his enemies collapses.
[79]**Mother Plot** The Popish Plot evaporates. This also alludes to Error in Spenser's *The Faerie Queene* I.i.25 and *Paradise Lost* II.795-802, and is another sign of disruption in the Whigs' "family" as Charles's family coheres.

Their Belial with their Belzebub[80] will fight;
Thus on my Foes, my Foes shall do me Right:
Nor doubt th' event:[81] for Factious crowds engage
In their first Onset, all their Brutal Rage;
1020 Then, let 'em take an unresisted Course,
Retire and Traverse, and Delude their Force:
But when they stand all Breathless, urge the fight,
And rise upon 'em with redoubled might:
For Lawful Pow'r is still Superior found,
When long driven back, at length it stands the ground.''
He said. Th' Almighty, nodding, gave Consent;
And Peals of Thunder shook the Firmament.[82]
Henceforth a Series of new time began,
The mighty Years in long Procession ran:[83]
1030 Once more the Godlike David was Restor'd,
And willing Nations knew their Lawful Lord.

1681

[80]**Belial . . . Belzebub** In *Paradise Lost* Beelzebub is the chief devil after Satan, and a Philistine god, with which Absalom and Achitophel are associated in l. 955. Belial in *Paradise Lost* is a leader of the devils; in the Bible he is the personification of evil, and in Hebrew his name means "worthless."
[81]**event** result
[82]**Th' Almighty . . . Firmament** from Virgil's *Aeneid* IX.104–6, in which Jove nods assent to

Aeneas' mother's request that her son's ships be immune from the attack of Turnus
[83]**new time . . . ran** From Virgil's *Eclogues* IV.5, 12, in which new time begins in a benevolent Saturnian age—for Virgil, the golden reign of Augustus. The allusions change from the ominously Miltonic to the brightly Virgilian. God, nation, and man are in harmony by the end of the poem.

Mac Flecknoe[1]

All human things are subject to decay,
And, when Fate summons, Monarchs must obey:
This Flecknoe found, who, like Augustus,[2] young
Was call'd to Empire, and had govern'd long:
In Prose and Verse, was own'd, without dispute
Through all the Realms of Nonsense, absolute.

[1]The occasion of this literary satire against Thomas Shadwell (1640-1692) remains obscure, though it is the result of long-standing differences and may stem from Shadwell's praise of the Duke of Buckingham's *The Rehearsal* (1671), a parody of Dryden and his heroic plays. Shadwell regarded himself as the heir of Ben Jonson's comedy-of-humor characters—amiable eccentrics with a dominant trait or "humor"—whereas Dryden, who favored the Restoration comedy of wit, thought Shadwell devoid of any true Jonsonian connection. The 1682 unauthorized edition of the poem included the subtitle "Or, A Satire upon the True-Blue-Protestant Poet T.S." In the 1684 edition and all others over which Dryden had control, this

political and religious attack disappears; it has no function in the poem. Dryden likens Shadwell to the son of (Mac) Flecknoe, an inept dramatist, poet, and Catholic priest who may have died in 1678, the year in which the poem began to circulate in manuscript. Shadwell does not quite deserve Dryden's harsh treatment of him; though as a Protestant and Whig, he in fact succeeded the Catholic Tory Dryden as poet laureate in 1688, Dryden's poem has made him an object of laughter in literary history.
[2]**Augustus** Octavian, nephew of Julius Caesar, at the age of thirty-three first emperor of Rome, and in 27 B.C. recipient of the title "Augustus" from his compliant senate. He reigned alone from 30 B.C. to A.D. 14.

This aged Prince now flourishing in Peace,
And blest with issue of a large increase,
Worn out with business, did at length debate
10 To settle the succession of the State:[3]
And pond'ring which of all his Sons was fit
To Reign, and wage immortal War with Wit;
Cried " 'Tis resolv'd; for Nature pleads that He
Should only rule, who most resembles me:
Sh——[4] alone my perfect image bears,
Mature in dullness from his tender years.
Sh—— alone, of all my Sons, is he
Who stands confirm'd in full stupidity.
The rest to some faint meaning make pretence,
20 But Sh—— never deviates into sense.
Some Beams of Wit on other souls may fall,
Strike through and make a lucid interval;
But Sh——'s genuine night admits no ray,
His rising Fogs prevail upon the Day:
Besides his goodly Fabric[5] fills the eye,
And seems design'd for thoughtless Majesty:
Thoughtless as Monarch Oaks, that shade the plain,
And, spread in solemn state, supinely reign.
Heywood and Shirley[6] were but Types of thee,
30 Thou last great Prophet of Tautology:[7]
Even I, a dunce of more renown than they,
Was sent before but to prepare thy way;[8]
And coarsely clad in Norwich Drugget[9] came
To teach the Nations in thy greater name.
My warbling Lute, the Lute I whilom[10] strung
When to King John of Portugal[11] I sung,
Was but the prelude to that glorious day,
When thou on silver Thames did'st cut thy way,
With well tim'd Oars before the Royal Barge,[12]
40 Swell'd with the Pride of thy Celestial charge;
And big with Hymn, Commander of an Host,
The like was ne'er in Epsom Blankets[13] tost
Methinks I see the new Arion[14] Sail,

[3]**succession of the State** a comic version of the serious issue of who would rule England after Charles II's death
[4]**Sh——** Shadwell, the subject of the poem
[5]**goodly Fabric** Shadwell was rotund.
[6]**Heywood and Shirley** Thomas Heywood (c. 1574-1641) and James Shirley (1596-1666) were prolific and poorly regarded dramatists and thus types, or precursors of Shadwell.
[7]**Tautology** repetition of the same idea in different words
[8]**prepare thy way** Dryden mischievously likens Shadwell to John the Baptist preparing the way for Jesus in Matthew 3:3.
[9]**Norwich Drugget** coarse wool that comes,

like Shadwell, from Norwich. John the Baptist was humbly clothed in camel's hair.
[10]**whilom** formerly; a self-conscious archaism
[11]**King John of Portugal** reigned 1640-56, and visited by Flecknoe, who claimed him as a patron
[12]**Thames . . . Royal Barge** a royal pageant on the River Thames
[13]**Epsom Blankets** alludes to Shadwell's *Epsom Wells* (1673) and the false wit Sir Samuel Hearty who was tossed in a blanket in *The Virtuoso* (1676)
[14]**Arion** Greek musician-poet (c. 625 B.C.), who was thrown overboard by pirates and saved by dolphins enthralled by his music

The Lute still trembling underneath thy nail.
At thy well sharpen'd thumb from Shore to Shore
The Treble squeaks for fear, the Bases roar:
Echoes from Pissing-Ally, Sh—— call,
And Sh—— they resound from A—— Hall.[15]
About thy boat the little Fishes throng,
50 As at the Morning Toast,[16] that Floats along.
Sometimes as Prince of thy Harmonious band
Thou wield'st thy Papers in thy threshing[17] hand.
St. Andre's[18] feet ne'er kept more equal time,
Not ev'n the feet of thy own *Psyche*'s rhime:
Though they in number as in sense excel;
So just, so like tautology they fell,
That, pale with envy, Singleton[19] foreswore
The Lute and Sword which he in Triumph bore,
And vow'd he ne'er would act Villerius[20] more.''
60 Here stopp'd the good old Sire; and wept for joy
In silent raptures of the hopeful boy.
All arguments, but most his Plays, persuade,
That for anointed dullness he was made.
    Close to the Walls which fair Augusta[21] bind,
(The fair Augusta much to fears inclin'd)
An ancient fabric,[22] rais'd t' inform the sight,
There stood of yore, and Barbican it hight:[23]
A watch Tower once; but now, so Fate ordains,
Of all the Pile an empty name remains.
70 From its old Ruins Brothel-houses rise,
Scenes of lewd loves, and of polluted joys;
Where their vast Courts the Mother-Strumpets keep,
And, undisturb'd by Watch,[24] in silence sleep.
Near these a Nursery[25] erects its head,
Where Queens are form'd, and future Heroes bred;
Where unfledg'd Actors learn to laugh and cry,
Where infant Punks[26] their tender Voices try,
And little Maximins[27] the Gods defy.
Great Fletcher never treads in Buskins here,

---

[15]**Pissing-Ally . . . A[ston] Hall** an aptly named passageway on the north side of the Thames, and a building so labeled in the first edition, presumably chosen in part for its scatological implications. Its place remains unidentified.
[16]**Morning Toast** excrement thrown in the Thames
[17]**threshing** flailing
[18]**St. Andre** a French dancing master who choreographed Shadwell's mechanically rhymed opera *Psyche* (1675)
[19]**Singleton** John Singleton, a leading musician to Charles II
[20]**Villerius** a character in Sir William D'Avenant's opera *The Siege of Rhodes* (1656),

in which battles were presented in recitative, requiring the actor to use both lute and sword
[21]**Augusta** old Roman name for London, the city now troubled by the Popish Plot. See note 1 to *Absalom and Achitophel* (p. 338 above).
[22]**fabric** building
[23]**Barbican . . . hight** It is called a watch tower or outer defense.
[24]**Watch** the police
[25]**Nursery** a theater-school for young actors and actresses
[26]**infant Punks** fledgling prostitutes
[27]**Maximin** the ranting Roman hero of Dryden's own *Tyrannic Love* (1670)

80 Nor greater Jonson[28] dares in Socks appear.
But gentle Simkin[29] just reception finds
Amidst this Monument of vanish'd minds:
Pure Clinches, the suburbian Muse[30] affords;
And Panton waging harmless War with words.
Here Flecknoe, as a place to fame well known,
Ambitiously design'd his Sh———'s Throne.
For ancient Dekker[31] prophesi'd long since,
That in this Pile should Reign a mighty Prince,
Born for a scourge of Wit, and flail of Sense:
90 To whom true dullness should some *Psyches* owe,
But Worlds of *Misers* from his pen should flow;
Humorists and *Hypocrites*[32] it should produce
Whole Raymond families, and Tribes of Bruce.[33]
      Now Empress Fame had publish'd the renown,
Of Sh———'s Coronation through the Town.
Rows'd by report of Fame, the Nations meet,
From near Bun-Hill, and distant Watling-street.[34]
No *Persian* Carpets spread th' Imperial way,
But scatter'd Limbs of mangled Poets lay:
100 From dusty shops neglected Authors come,
Martyrs of Pies, and Relics of the Bum.[35]
Much Heywood, Shirley, Ogleby[36] there lay,
But loads of Sh——— almost choak'd the way.
Bilk'd Stationers for Yeomen stood prepar'd,[37]
And H———[38] was Captain of the Guard.
The hoary Prince in Majesty appear'd,
High on a Throne of his own Labours rear'd.
At his right hand our young Ascanius[39] sat,
Rome's other hope, and pillar of the State.
110 His Brows thick fogs, instead of glories, grace,
And lambent[40] dullness play'd around his face.
As Hannibal did to the Altars come,

[28]**Fletcher . . . Jonson** John Fletcher (1579-1625) and Ben Jonson (1572-1637?) were popular dramatists admired in the late seventeenth century. Greek and Roman tragic actors wore thick-soled half-boots ("buskins") in tragedy, and light shoes ("socks") in comedy.
[29]**Simkin** a stock character in farce, and a familiar name for a fool
[30]**Clinches . . . suburbian Muse** puns, by a muse from the licentious, unlettered suburbs
[31]**Dekker** Thomas Dekker (c. 1572-1632), prolific dramatist, regarded as inept by Jonson and others, and here a prophet of dullness
[32]*Misers . . . Hypocrites* three of Shadwell's plays
[33]**Raymond . . . Bruce** characters in *The Humorists* (1670) and *The Virtuoso*, respectively

[34]**Bun-hill . . . Watling-street** a field in which victims of the plague of 1665-66 were buried and a street in the unfashionable commercial City of London—hence the narrow range of Shadwell's fame
[35]**Authors . . . Bum** books used to line pie-pans or as toilet paper
[36]**Ogleby** John Ogleby or Ogilby (1600-1676), Scottish hack writer and translator of Aesop, Homer, and Virgil
[37]**Bilk'd . . . prepar'd** cheated publishers willing to be guards, presumably to protect what remains of their interests
[38]**H———** Herringman: Shadwell's and Dryden's publisher until 1678
[39]**Ascanius** Aeneas' son and another mock type of Shadwell
[40]**lambent** flickering; perhaps subtly radiant

Sworn by his Sire a mortal Foe to Rome;[41]
So Sh—— swore, nor should his Vow be vain,
That he till Death true dullness would maintain;
And in his father's Right and Realms defence,
Ne'er to have peace with Wit, nor truce with Sense.
The King himself the sacred Unction[42] made,
As King by Office, and as Priest by Trade:
120   In his sinister hand, instead of Ball,[43]
He plac'd a mighty Mug of potent Ale;
Love's Kingdom[44] to his right he did convey,
At once his Sceptre and his rule of Sway;
Whose righteous Lore the Prince had practis'd young,
And from whose Loins recorded *Psyche* sprung.
His Temples last with Poppies[45] were o'erspread,
That nodding seem'd to consecrate his head:
Just at that point of time, if Fame not lie,
On his left hand twelve reverend Owls[46] did fly.
130   So Romulus, 'tis sung, by Tiber's Brook,[47]
Presage of Sway from twice six Vultures took.
Th' admiring throng loud acclamations make,
And Omens of his future Empire take.
The Sire then shook the honours of his head,[48]
And from his brows damps of oblivion shed
Full on the filial dullness: long he stood,
Repelling from his Breast the raging God;
At length burst out in this prophetic mood:
    "Heavens bless my Son, from Ireland let him reign
140   To far Barbadoes[49] on the Western main;
Of his Dominion may no end be known,
And greater than his Father's be his Throne.
Beyond *Love's Kingdom* let him stretch his Pen."
He paus'd, and all the people cry'd Amen.
Then thus, continu'd he, "My Son advance
Still in new Impudence, new Ignorance.
Success let others teach, learn thou from me
Pangs without birth, and fruitless Industry.
Let *Virtuosos* in five years be Writ;

[41]**Hannibal . . . Rome** Hannibal's father made him swear enmity to Rome when he was nine years old.

[42]**sacred Unction** sacramental oil to anoint the king at his coronation

[43]**sinister . . . Ball** During the coronation the king holds a globe in his left (sinister) hand, and a scepter in his right. The globe, an emblem of the world, is here replaced by Shadwell's world of ale.

[44]*Love's Kingdom* a play by Flecknoe (1664) from which Shadwell's *Psyche* stems

[45]**Poppies** suggests sleep and Shadwell's opium addiction

[46]**Owls** symbols of dullness

[47]**Romulus . . . Brook** presumed founder of Rome, on the river Tiber, as sung in Plutarch's *Life of Romulus*

[48]**honours . . . head** hair. Ll. 134–38 are a parodic fusion of two devices from epic poetry—the father influencing his son, and the Sibyl receiving the god who speaks through her (see Virgil's *Aeneid* VI. 46-51).

[49]**Ireland . . . Barbadoes** both nations then considered homes of dullness, with a long expanse of water—and vacuity—between them

150 Yet not one thought accuse thy toil of wit.
    Let gentle George in triumph tread the Stage,
    Make Dorimant betray, and Loveit rage;
    Let Cully, Cockwood, Fopling, charm the Pit[50]
    And in their folly show the Writer's wit.
    Yet still thy fools shall stand in thy defence,
    And justify their Author's want of sense.
    Let 'em be all by thy own model made
    Of dullness, and desire no foreign aid:
    That they to future ages may be known,
160 Not Copies drawn, but Issue of thy own.
    Nay let thy men of wit too be the same,
    All full of thee, and differing but in name;
    But let no alien S–dl–y[51] interpose
    To lard with wit thy hungry *Epsom* prose.
    And when false flowers of Rhetoric thou would'st cull,
    Trust Nature, do not labour to be dull;
    But write thy best, and top; and in each line,
    Sir Formal's oratory[52] will be thine.
    Sir Formal, though unsought, attends thy quill,
170 And does thy Northern Dedications[53] fill
    Nor let false friends seduce thy mind to fame,
    By arrogating Jonson's Hostile name.
    Let Father Flecknoe fire thy mind with praise,
    And Uncle Ogleby thy envy raise.
    Thou art my blood, where Jonson has no part;[54]
    What share have we in Nature or in Art?
    Where did his wit on learning fix a brand,
    And rail at Arts he did not understand?
    Where made he love in Prince Nicander's[55] vein,
180 Or swept the dust in *Psyche*'s humble strain?
    Where sold he Bargains?[56] Whip-stitch, kiss my Arse,
    Promis'd a Play[57] and dwindled to a Farce?
    When did his Muse from Fletcher scenes purloin,
    As thou whole Eth'rege dost transfuse to thine?
    But so transfus'd as Oil on Waters flow,

[50]**gentle George . . . Pit** Sir George Etherege (c. 1635-1691), respected writer of comedies, especially *The Man of Mode* (1676), from which Dorimant, Loveit, and Fopling come. Colly and Cockwood appeared in *Love in a Tub* (1664). The pit, or ground level of the Restoration theater, was less fashionable than the boxes, and more fashionable than the gallery.

[51]**S–dl–y** Sir Charles Sedley (c.1638-1701), court wit thought to have written the prologue and several lines of Shadwell's *Epsom Wells*

[52]**Sir Formal's oratory** the Ciceronian rhetoric of Sir Formal Trifle in Shadwell's *The Virtuoso*

[53]**Northern Dedications** Shadwell dedicated plays to the Duke and Duchess of Newcastle and their son, in the north of England; the term may also suggest the "gothic," intellectually frozen quality of the plays themselves.

[54]**Nor let . . . part** Dryden, convinced that Shadwell did not understand Jonson, whose "humor" characters he tried to adopt, urges him to imitate Flecknoe and Ogleby instead.

[55]**Nicander** the character who pursues Psyche in Shadwell's play

[56]**sold he Bargains** wrote unexpected obscene replies to innocent questions; quoted from the words of Sir Samuel Hearty in *The Virtuoso*

[57]**Promis'd a Play** as Shadwell did in the dedication to *The Virtuoso*

His always floats above, thine sinks below.
This is thy Province, this thy wondrous way,
New Humours to invent for each new Play:
This is that boasted Bias of thy mind,[58]
190 By which one way, to dullness, 'tis inclin'd;
Which makes thy writings lean on one side still,
And in all changes that way bends thy will.
Nor let thy mountain belly make pretence
Of likeness;[59] thine's a tympany of sense.[60]
A Tun[61] of Man in thy Large bulk is writ,
But sure thou'rt but a Kilderkin[62] of wit.
Like mine thy gentle numbers[63] feebly creep,
Thy Tragic Muse gives smiles, thy Comic sleep.
With whate'er gall thou sett'st thyself to write,
200 Thy inoffensive Satires never bite.
In thy fellonious heart, though Venom lies,
It does but touch thy Irish[64] pen, and dies.
Thy Genius calls thee not to purchase fame
In keen Iambics,[65] but mild Anagram:[66]
Leave writing Plays, and chuse for thy command
Some peaceful Province in Acrostic[67] Land.
There thou may'st wings display and Altars[68] raise,
And torture one poor word Ten thousand ways.
Or it thou would'st thy diff'rent talents suit,
210 Set thy own Songs, and sing them to thy lute."
He said,[69] but his last words were scarcely heard,
For Bruce and Longvil[70] had a Trap prepar'd,
And down they sent the yet declaiming Bard.
Sinking he left his Drugget robe behind,
Born upwards by a subterranean wind.
The Mantle fell to the young Prophet's part,[71]
With double portion of his Father's Art.

1678   1682, 1684

---

[58]**Bias . . . mind** a parody of words from the Epilogue to *The Humorist*. "Bias" is drawn from the twist or "English" one puts on a bowling ball to make it curve.
[59]**likeness** Like Ben Jonson, Shadwell was obese.
[60]**tympany** a tumor or swelling caused by wind; metaphorically, emptiness, as in a drum
[61]**Tun** a wine cask, holding 252 gallons
[62]**Kilderkin** a cask holding 16-18 gallons
[63]**numbers** verses
[64]**Irish** Shadwell was English, but inherits the traits of his spiritual father Flecknoe, whom Dryden arbitrarily treats as Irish.
[65]**keen Iambics** harsh satire, iambics being the original meter of Greek satire
[66]**Anagram** rearrangement of the letters in a word or words to form new words

[67]**Acrostic** a poem in which the first letters of each line form the name of the person or thing written about
[68]**wings . . . Altars** poems in these shapes. Dryden and his later contemporaries regarded all the flashy forms mentioned in ll. 204-08 as "false wit."
[69]**He said** a typical English epic tag, here parodic
[70]**Bruce and Longvil** characters in *The Virtuoso* who drop Sir Formal through a trap door
[71]**Mantle . . . part** as in 2 Kings 2:9-13, where Elisha receives the mantle of Elijah. Elijah ascends to Heaven through a divine whirlwind; Flecknoe's robe stays in this world, presumably borne upwards by his own flatulence or "subterranean wind."

To the Memory of Mr. Oldham[1]

Farewell, too little and too lately known,
Whom I began to think and call my own;
For sure our Souls were near alli'd; and thine
Cast in the same Poetic mould with mine.
One common Note on either Lyre did strike,
And Knaves and Fools we both abhorr'd alike:
To the same Goal did both our Studies drive,
The last set out the soonest did arrive.
Thus Nisus fell upon the slippery place,
10   While his young Friend perform'd and won the Race.[2]
O early ripe! to thy abundant store
What could advancing Age have added more?
It might (what Nature never gives the young)
Have taught the numbers of thy native Tongue.
But Satire needs not those, and Wit will shine
Through the harsh cadence of a rugged line:[3]
A noble Error, and but seldom made,
When Poets are by too much force betray'd.
Thy generous[4] fruits, though gather'd ere their prime
20   Still show'd a quickness;[5] and maturing time
But mellows what we write to the dull sweets of Rime.
Once more, hail and farewell;[6] farewell thou young,
But ah too short, Marcellus[7] of our Tongue;
Thy Brows with Ivy, and with Laurels[8] bound;
But Fate and gloomy Night encompass thee around.

1684

[1] John Oldham (1653-1683) was a young school-teacher whose poetry attracted the attention of Rochester and Dryden. He was best known for his virulent *Satyrs upon the Jesuits* (1679) and several imitations—modernized adaptations—of classical poems. Dryden, at fifty-two, regards his dead junior colleague as both a precursor in satire and a lost potential literary heir. The poem was prefixed to a posthumous volume of Oldham's works.

[2] **Nisus . . . Race** Nisus and the young Euryalus entered a footrace in the funeral games for Anchises (*Aeneid* V.315-38). Nisus slipped on sacrificial blood and rolled into the path of the front-runner Salius, thus enabling his friend to win the race—here, to die first with literary achievements behind him.

[3] **numbers . . . line** polish for his rough verse. Oldham wrote in the rough, darkly satiric mode of Persius and Juvenal which, Dryden says, is not necessarily a fault in satire.

[4] **generous** strong, vigorous

[5] **quickness** energy, sharpness

[6] **hail and farewell** part of the poem's context of Roman allusions, a translation of the Latin *ave atque vale*, often used in funeral inscriptions

[7] **Marcellus** the nephew and presumed heir of the Emperor Augustus (reigned 30 B.C.-A.D. 14). Marcellus died at the age of twenty and was celebrated in Virgil's *Aeneid* VI.860-886.

[8] **Ivy . . . Laurels** wreaths of honor bestowed on a poet

Secular Masque[1]

Enter Janus

JANUS	Chronos,[2] Chronos, mend thy Pace,
	An hundred times the rolling Sun
	Around the Radiant Belt[3] has run
	In his revolving Race.
	Behold, behold, the Goal in sight,
	Spread thy Fans,[4] and wing thy flight.

Enter Chronos, *with a Scythe in his hand, and a great Globe on his Back, which he sets down at his entrance.*

CHRONOS	Weary, weary of my weight,
	Let me, let me drop my Freight,
	And leave the World behind.
10	I could not bear
	Another Year
	The Load of Human-Kind.

Enter Momus[5] *Laughing*

MOMUS	Ha! ha! ha! Ha! ha! ha! well hast thou done,
	To lay down thy Pack,
	And lighten thy Back,
	The World was a Fool e'er since it begun,
	And since neither Janus, nor Chronos, nor I,
	Can hinder the Crimes,
	Or mend the Bad Times,
20	'Tis better to Laugh than to Cry.
CHO. OF ALL 3	*'Tis better to Laugh than to Cry.*
JANUS	Since Momus comes to laugh below,
	Old Time begin the Show,
	That he may see, in every Scene,
	What Changes in this Age have been.
CHRONOS	Then Goddess of the Silver Bow begin.

Horns, or Hunting Music within.
Enter Diana.[6]

DIANA	With Horns and with Hounds I waken the Day,
	And hie to my Woodland walks away;
	I tuck up my Robe, and am buskin'd[7] soon,

[1] Written as an afterpiece for Sir John Vanbrugh's revision of Fletcher's *The Pilgrim*, it was probably first performed at a benefit for Dryden on 29 April 1700, two days before he died. "Secular" is from the Latin *saeculum*, both age and century. "Masque" is a dramatic performance freed from the rules of probability, often including song, dance, and characters wearing masks to indicate their roles; the Roman god Janus, for example, who was associated with gates and doors, and thus with beginnings and ends, had two faces, one looking back and one forward in time.

[2] **Chronos**   god of time

[3] **Radiant Belt**   the skies, or zodiac

[4] **Fans**   wings

[5] **Momus**   god of ridicule

[6] **Diana**   chaste goddess of the moon, the hunt, and of women in childbirth; here, England before the Civil War, 1642-49

[7] **buskin'd**   in boots

30   And tie to my Forehead a waxing Moon.
    I course the fleet Stag, unkennel the Fox,
    And chase the wild Goats o'er summets of Rocks,
    With shouting and hooting we pierce thro' the Sky;
    And Echo turns Hunter, and doubles the Cry.

CHO. OF ALL   *With shouting and hooting, we pierce through the Sky,*
    And Echo turns Hunter, and doubles the Cry.

JANUS   Then our Age was in its Prime,
CHRONOS   Free from Rage.
DIANA   ———— And free from Crime.
MOMUS   A very Merry, Dancing, Drinking,
40   Laughing, Quaffing, and unthinking Time.
CHO. OF ALL   *Then our Age was in its Prime,*
    Free from Rage, and free from Crime,
    A very Merry, Dancing, Drinking,
    Laughing, Quaffing, and unthinking Time.
Dance of Diana's *Attendants.*
Enter Mars[8]

MARS   Inspire the Vocal Brass, Inspire;[9]
    The World is past its Infant Age:
      Arms and Honour,
      Arms and Honour,
    Set the Martial Mind on Fire,
50   And kindle Manly Rage.
    Mars has look'd the Sky to Red;
    And Peace, the Lazy Good, is fled.
    Plenty, Peace, and Pleasure fly;
      The Sprightly Green
    In Woodland-Walks, no more is seen;
    The Sprightly Green, has drunk the Tyrian Dye.[10]
CHO. OF ALL   *Plenty, Peace, &c.*
MARS   Sound the Trumpet, Beat the Drum,
    Through all the World around;
60   Sound a Reveille, Sound, Sound,
      The Warrior God is come.
CHO. OF ALL   *Sound the Trumpet, &c.*
MOMUS   Thy Sword within the Scabbard keep,
      And let Mankind agree;
    Better the World were fast asleep,
      Than kept awake by Thee.
    The Fools are only thinner,
      With all our Cost and Care;
    But neither side a winner,
70   For Things are as they were.

[8]**Mars** god of war, here England from the bloody Civil War through the Cromwells' Commonwealth, 1641-60

[9]**Inspire** breathe, blow into
[10]**Tyrian Dye** purple, hence bloody

CHO. OF ALL   *The Fools are only, &c.*
Enter Venus[11]

VENUS   Calms appear, when Storms are past;
             Love will have his Hour at last:
             Nature is my kindly Care;
             Mars destroys, and I repair;
             Take me, take me, while you may,
             Venus comes not ev'ry Day.

CHO. OF ALL   *Take her, take her, &c.*

CHRONOS   The World was then so light,
80   I scarcely felt the Weight;
             Joy rul'd the Day, and Love the Night.
             But since the Queen of Pleasure left the Ground,
                 I faint, I lag,
                 And feebly drag
             The pond'rous Orb around.

MOMUS   All, all, of a piece throughout;
Pointing
to Diana   Thy Chase had a Beast in View;
to Mars   Thy Wars brought nothing about;
to Venus   Thy Lovers were all untrue.
90 JANUS   'Tis well an Old Age is out,
CHRONOS   And time to begin a New.

CHO. OF ALL   *All, all, of a piece throughout;*
             Thy Chase had a Beast in View;
             Thy Wars brought nothing about;
             Thy Lovers were all untrue.
             'Tis well an Old Age is out,
             And time to begin a New.

Dance of Huntsmen, Nymphs, Warriors *and* Lovers.

1713

[11]**Venus**   goddess of love: the Restoration period, especially the reigns of Charles II (1660–85) and James II (1685–88). Dryden, who lost his posts as poet laureate and historiographer royal under William III (1688-1702), avoids celebrating his reign.

ANNE FINCH, COUNTESS OF WINCHILSEA

1661–1720

Anne Kingsmill was an attendant at the court of the Duchess of York when she met and married the studious young soldier and gentleman Heneage Finch. Their marital happiness, apparently uncharacteristic of their age, included his active encouragement of her poetry. The couple lived in London and were active in court circles until the end of 1688, when they refused to swear allegiance to the new and, in their judgment, usurping monarch, William III. By 1690 they had retired to the family's handsome estate of Eastwell, Kent, where in 1712 her husband inherited the title Earl of Winchilsea.

Many of Anne Finch's poems were published in 1713 and reissued in 1714; they were known to Swift and Pope and a century later praised by Wordsworth. She wrote in several Restoration and eighteenth-century styles and genres, including drama, the pindaric ode, parody, and gentle satire, and used heroic and tetrameter couplets as well as blank verse. In her poems she often considers friendship with women, the power and beauty of nature, and melancholy—what we would call depression. "A Song of the Cannibals" demonstrates an almost metaphysical wit that yokes the worlds of man and jungle when a "Lovely viper" provides the pattern of "a bracelet, for my Love." "A Nocturnal Reverie" blends psychology, meditation, and direct observation of the external world. For example, she sensitively details how "freshen'd Grass now bears itself upright," and chronicles the relationship among varied kinds of light and the beauties they evoke—all in language relatively free of the classical, self-conscious poetic diction her successors would find attractive.

Enquiry after Peace. A Fragment[1]

Peace! where art thou to be found?
Where, in all the spacious Round,
May thy Footsteps be pursu'd?
Where may thy calm Seats be view'd?
On some Mountain dost thou lie,
Serenely near the ambient Sky,
Smiling at the Clouds below,
Where rough Storms and Tempests grow?
Or, in some retired Plain,
10   Undisturb'd dost thou remain?
Where no angry Whirlwinds pass,
Where no Floods oppress the Grass.
High above, or deep below,
Fain I thy Retreat wou'd know.
Fain I thee alone wou'd find,
Balm to my o'er-weary'd Mind.
Since what here the World enjoys,
Or our Passions most employs,
Peace opposes, or destroys.
20   Pleasure's a tumultuous thing,
Busy still, and still on Wing;
Flying swift, from place to place,
Darting from each beauteous Face;
From each strongly mingled Bowl
Through th'inflam'd and restless Soul.
Sov'reign Pow'r who fondly craves,
But himself to Pomp enslaves;
Stands the Envy of Mankind,
Peace, in vain, attempts to find.
30   Thirst of Wealth no Quiet knows,

---

[1] This poem was written to Catherine Cavendish, Countess Thanet, and is in the tradition of Milton's "Il Penseroso."

But near the Death-bed fiercer grows;
Wounding Men with secret Stings,
For Evils it on Others brings.
War who not discreetly shuns,
Through Life the Gauntlet runs.
Swords, and Pikes, and Waves, and Flames,
Each their Stroke against him aims.
Love (if such a thing there be)
Is all Despair, or Extasie.
40   Poetry's the feav'rish Fit,
Th'o'erflowing of unbounded Wit. &c.

1713

A Song of the Cannibals[1]

Lovely viper, haste not on,
Nor curl, in various folds along,
Till from that figur'd coat of thine,
Which ev'ry motion, makes more fin`.
I take, as near as art can do,
A draught, of what I wond'ring view;
Which, in a bracelet, for my Love
Shall be with careful mixtures wove.
So, may'st thou find thy beauties last,
10   As thou doest not, retard thy haste.
So, may'st thou, above all the snakes,
That harbour, in the neigh'bring brakes,[2]
Be honour'd; and where thou do'st pass
The shades be close, and fresh the grass.

c. 1689

[1] a poetic version of Montaigne's prose in "Of
Cannibals," *Essays*, I, 31 (1580)
[2] **brakes** thickets

A Nocturnal Reverie[1]

In such a Night, when every louder Wind
Is to its distant Cavern safe confin'd;
And only gentle Zephyr[2] fans his Wings,
And lonely Philomel,[3] still waking, sings;
Or from some Tree, fam'd for the Owl's delight,
She, hollowing clear, directs the Wand'rer right:

[1] The poem anticipates both mid-eighteenth-
century solemn, subjective, "night-thoughts"
meditations, and later romantic self-conscious-
ness.
[2] **Zephyr** the west wind
[3] **Philomel** the nightingale

In such a Night, when passing Clouds give place,
Or thinly vail the Heav'ns mysterious Face;
When in some River, overhung with Green;
10 The waving Moon and trembling Leaves are seen;
When freshen'd Grass now bears itself upright,
And makes cool Banks to pleasing Rest invite,
Whence springs the Woodbind, and the Bramble-Rose,
And where the sleepy Cowslip shelter'd grows;
Whilst now a paler Hue the Foxglove takes,
Yet checquers still with Red the dusky brakes:
When scatter'd Glow-worms, but in Twilight fine,
Show trivial Beauties watch their Hour to shine;
Whilst Salisb'ry⁴ stands the Test of every Light,
20 In perfect Charms, and perfect Virtue bright:
When Odours, which declin'd repelling Day,
Thro' temp'rate Air uninterrupted stray;
When darken'd Groves their softest Shadows wear,
And falling Waters we distinctly hear;
When thro' the Gloom more venerable shows
Some ancient Fabric,⁵ awful in Repose,
While Sunburnt Hills their Swarthy Looks conceal,
And swelling Haycocks thicken up the Vale:
When the loos'd Horse now, as his Pasture leads,
30 Comes slowly grazing thro' th'adjoining Meads,
Whose stealing Pace, and lengthen'd Shade we fear,
Till torn up Forage in his Teeth we hear:
When nibbling Sheep at large pursue their Food,
And unmolested Kine rechew the Cud;
When Curlews cry beneath the Village-walls,
And to her straggling Brood the Partridge calls;
Their shortliv'd Jubilee the Creatures keep,
Which but endures, whilst Tyrant-Man do's sleep:
When a sedate Content the Spirit feels,
40 And no fierce Light disturbs, whilst it reveals;
But silent Musings urge the Mind to seek
Something, too high for Syllables to speak;
Till the free Soul to a compos'dness charm'd,
Finding the Elements of Rage disarm'd,
O'er all below a solemn Quiet grown,
Joys in th'inferiour⁶ World, and thinks it like her Own:
In such a Night let Me abroad remain,
Till Morning breaks, and All's confus'd again;
Our Cares, our Toils, our Clamours are renew'd,
50 Or Pleasures, seldom reach'd, again pursu'd.

1713

⁴ **Salisb'ry** Anne Tufton, Countess of Salisbury
⁵ **Fabric** building
⁶ **inferiour** lower

JONATHAN SWIFT
1677–1745

Born in Dublin of English parents, Swift received his bachelor's degree from Trinity College but gained much of his real education while secretary to the Whig aristocrat Sir William Temple in England. Here, between 1689 and 1699, he was schooled in some of the most important religious, intellectual, and political quarrels of his day. He took Anglican orders in Ireland in 1694 and in 1713 was made dean of St. Patrick's, where he fought to help the Irish in their dealings with the English. Journeys to England allowed him to visit his friends Pope and Gay, to participate in the opposition to the government of British Prime Minister Sir Robert Walpole, and to enjoy his reputation as author of *Tale of a Tub* (1704) and *Gulliver's Travels* (1726).

Swift's satirical poetry, normally written in tetrameter couplets, strips away falsity and pretensions. In "A Description of a City Shower" (1710), he pictures a chaotic London awash in its own filth, and inverts the Virgilian georgic, which celebrates a prospering nation with strong roots in the country. This description suggests how altered literary form can emphasize the disparity between the real and the ideal, as is also seen in his mockery of the great Duke of Marlborough, subject of "A Satirical Elegy on the Death of a Late Famous General" (1722). Somewhat later Swift used the "progress" piece to show a sequence of decline rather than its conventional sequence of improvement. "Phyllis, or, the Progress of Love" (1728) thus reveals a marriage made not in heaven, but by ambitious parents on behalf of a hypocritical, lustful, and disobedient daughter. But Swift's poetry has a positive side as well. His birthday poem to "Stella" (1727), for example, makes an appeal to virtue and rational behavior. It is as positive about relations between man and woman as "Phyllis" is negative; and although the speaker in "Stella" seeks to correct his ailing friend, his method is to make her think better of herself and of the aging man who loves her.

A Description of a City Shower[1]

Careful Observers may fortell the Hour
(By sure Prognostics) when to dread a Show'r:
While Rain depends,[2] the pensive Cat gives o'er
Her Frolics, and pursues her Tail no more.
Returning Home at Night, you'll find the Sink[3]
Strike your offended Sense with double Stink.
If you be wise, then go not far to Dine,
You'll spend in Coach-hire more than save in Wine.
A coming Show'r your shooting[4] Corns presage,

[1]The poem inverts the serious praise of the country and the nation found in Virgil's *Georgics* (c. 30 B.C.) and its modern imitations.

[2]**depends** impends
[3]**Sink** sewer
[4]**shooting** shooting pains

10   Old Aches throb, your hollow Tooth will rage.
Saunt'ring in Coffee-house is Dulman seen;
He damns the Climate, and complains of Spleen.[5]

    Meanwhile the South rising with dabbled Wings,[6]
A Sable[7] Cloud athwart the Welkin[8] flings,
That swill'd more Liquor than it could contain,
And like a Drunkard gives it up again.
Brisk Susan whips her Linen from the Rope,[9]
While the first drizzling Show'r is born aslope,[10]
Such is that Sprinkling which some careless Queen[11]

20   Flirts[12] on you from her Mop, but not so clean.
You fly, invoke the Gods; then turning, stop
To rail; she singing, still whirls on her Mop.
Not yet, the Dust had shun'd the unequal Strife,
But aided by the Wind, fought still for Life;
And wafted with its Foe by violent Gust,
'Twas doubtful which was Rain, and which was Dust.
Ah! where must needy Poet seek for Aid,
When Dust and Rain at once his Coat invade;
His only Coat, where Dust confus'd with Rain,

30   Roughen the Nap, and leave a mingled Stain.

    Now in contiguous Drops the Flood comes down,
Threat'ning with Deluge this Devoted[13] Town.
To Shops in Crowds the daggled[14] Females fly,
Pretend to cheapen[15] Goods, but nothing buy.
The Templar[16] spruce, while ev'ry Spout's a-broach[17],
Stays till 'tis fair, yet seems to call a Coach.
The tuck'd-up Sempstress walks with hasty Strides,
While Streams run down her oil'd Umbrella's Sides.
Here various Kinds by various Fortunes led,

40   Commence Acquaintance underneath a Shed.
Triumphant Tories, and desponding Whigs,[18]
Forget their Feuds, and join to save their Wigs
Box'd in a Chair[19] the Beau impatient sits,
While Spouts run clatt'ring o'er the Roof by Fits;
And ever and anon with frightful Din
The Leather sounds, he trembles from within.
So when Troy Chair-men bore the Wooden Steed,

[5]**Spleen** fashionable melancholia
[6]**South . . . Wings** the south wind personified, with slightly wet wings
[7]**Sable** black
[8]**Welkin** the sky, in a mock exalted sense of the heavens
[9]**Linen . . . Rope** The servant removes her laundry from the clothesline.
[10]**born aslope** falls at an angle
[11]**Queen** brazen wench, often a prostitute
[12]**Flirts** darts, flits

[13]**Devoted** cursed, doomed
[14]**daggled** with muddied skirts
[15]**cheapen** bargain for
[16]**Templar** a lawyer or student from the Inner or Middle Temple, the Inns of Court;
[17]**Spout's a-broach** Drain pipes pour out water.
[18]**Tories . . . Whigs** A Tory administration had recently replaced the Whigs.
[19]**Chair** a sedan chair with a leather roof, in which a fashionable man would be carried

Pregnant with Greeks, impatient to be freed,
(Those Bully Greeks, who, as the Moderns do,
50 Instead of paying Chair-men, run them thro')
Laoco'n struck the Outside with his Spear,
And each imprison'd Hero quak'd for Fear.[20]

Now from all Parts the swelling Kennels[21] flow,
And bear their Trophies with them as they go:
Filth of all Hues and Odours seem to tell
What Street they sail'd from, by their Sight and Smell.
They, as each Torrent drives, with rapid Force
From Smithfield,[22] or St. Pulchre's[23] shape their Course,
And in huge Confluent join at Snow-Hill Ridge,
60 Fall from the Conduit prone to Holborn-Bridge.[24]
Sweepings from Butchers' Stalls, Dung, Guts, and Blood,
Drown'd Puppies, stinking Sprats[25] all drench'd in Mud,
Dead Cats and Turnip-Tops come tumbling down the Flood.[26]

1710

[20]**Troy . . . Fear** Laocoön hurled his spear at the Trojan Horse, believing it a ruse and filled with Greek soldiers; Virgil's *Aeneid* II.50–52.
[21]**Kennels** the gutters
[22]**Smithfield** the market for livestock, and a street that runs into Snow Hill
[23]**St. Pulchre** St. Sepulchre's Church on Snow Hill
[24]**Confluent . . . Bridge** Snow Hill and Smithfield join at Cock Lane, like the confluence of two rivers, and run downward (prone) from Holborn Conduit into the open sewer Fleet Ditch, then spanned by Holborn Bridge.
[25]**Sprats** herring-like fish
[26]**Flood** Swift adds a note saying that this triplet was a parody of Dryden's hasty and licentious versifying.

Phyllis, or, the Progress of Love[1]

Desponding Phyllis was endu'd
With ev'ry Talent of a Prude,
She trembled when a Man drew near;
Salute[2] her, and she turn'd her Ear:
If o'er against her you were plac'd
She durst not look above your Waist;
She'd rather take you to her Bed
Than let you see her dress her Head;
In Church you heard her through the Crowd
10 Repeat the Absolution loud;
In Church, secure behind her Fan
She durst behold that Monster, Man:

[1]The poem was one of those collected by Swift's young friend Stella (Esther Johnson) and sent to Alexander Pope, who edited them for publication in the third volume of their *Miscellanies* (1727). It is an ironic inversion of the "progress" genre, which assumes the improvement or advancement of the subject discussed.
[2]**Salute** kiss

There practic'd how to place her Head,
And bit her Lips to make them red:
Or on the Mat devoutly kneeling
Would lift her Eyes up to the Ceiling,
And heave her Bosom unaware
For neighb'ring Beaux to see it bare.
   At length a lucky Lover came,
20 And found Admittance from the Dame.
Suppose all Parties now agreed,
The Writings drawn, the Lawyer fee'd,[3]
The Vicar and the Ring bespoke:
Guess how could such a Match be broke.
See then what Mortals place their Bliss in!
Next morn betimes the Bride was missing,
The Mother scream'd, the Father chid,
Where can this idle Wench be hid?
No news of Phyl. The Bridegroom came,
30 And thought his Bride had sculk'd for shame,
Because her Father us'd to say
The Girl had such a Bashful way.
   Now, John the Butler must be sent
To learn the Way that Phyllis went;
The Groom was wish'd to saddle Crop,
For John must neither light nor stop;
But find her where so'er she fled,
And bring her back, alive or dead.
See here again the Dev'l to do;
For truly John was missing too:
40 The Horse and Pillion[4] both were gone
Phyllis, it seems, was fled with John.
Old Madam who went up to find
What Papers Phyl had left behind,
A Letter on the Toilet[5] sees
To my much honor'd Father; These:
('Tis always done, Romances tell us,
When Daughters run away with Fellows)
Fill'd with the choicest common-places,
50 By others us'd in the like Cases.
That, long ago a Fortune-teller
Exactly said what now befell her,
And in a Glass had made her see
A serving-Man of low Degree:
It was her Fate; must be forgiven;
For Marriages are made in Heaven:
His Pardon begg'd, but to be plain,
She'd do't if 'twere to do again.

---

[3]**Writings . . . fee'd** the lawyer paid for draw-
ing up the marriage contract
[4]**Pillion** a soft, light saddle set behind the rider,
normally for a woman
[5]**Toilet** dressing table

Thank God, 'twas neither Shame nor Sin,
60   For John was come of honest Kin:
Love never thinks of Rich and Poor,
She'd beg with John from Door to Door:
Forgive her, if it be a Crime,
She'll never do't another Time,
She ne'er before in all her Life
Once disobey'd him, Maid nor Wife.
One Argument she summ'd up all in,
The Thing was done and past recalling:
And therefore hop'd she would recover
70   His Favor, when his Passion's over.
She valued not what others thought her;
And was—His most obedient Daughter.
    Fair Maidens all attend the Muse
Who now the wand'ring Pair pursues:
Away they rode in homely⁶ Sort
Their Journey long, their Money short;
The loving Couple well bemir'd,
The Horse and both the Riders tir'd:
Their Vittels bad, their Lodging worse,
80   Phyl cri'd, and John began to curse;
Phyl wish'd, that she had strain'd a Limb
When first she ventur'd out with him.
John wish'd, that he had broke a Leg.
When first for her he quitted Peg.
    But what Adventures more befell 'em
The Muse has now not time to tell 'em.
How Jonny wheadled, threaten'd, fawn'd,
Till Phyllis all her Trinkets pawn'd:
How oft she broke her marriage Vows
90   In kindness to maintain her Spouse;
Till Swains unwholesome⁷ spoil'd the Trade,
For now the Surgeon⁸ must be paid;
To whom those Perquisites⁹ are gone
In Christian Justice due to John.
    When Food and Raiment now grew scarce
Fate put a Period to the Farce;¹⁰
And with exact Poetic Justice:
For John is Landlord, Phyllis Hostess;
They keep at Stains the old Blue Boar,¹¹
100   Are Cat and Dog, and Rogue and Whore.

1719   1727

---

⁶**homely** plain, unpretentious
⁷**Swains unwholesome** venereally diseased
country lovers
⁸**Surgeon** doctor
⁹**Perquisites** money given by her lovers goes
to the doctor, not her husband
¹⁰**Period . . . Farce** an end to the absurd comedy
¹¹**old Blue Boar** the inn or public house they
manage

A Satirical Elegy on the Death of a Late Famous General[1]

His Grace! impossible! what dead!
Of old age too, and in his bed!
And could that Mighty Warrior fall?
And so inglorious, after all!
Well, since he's gone, no matter how,
The last loud trump must wake him now:
And, trust me, as the noise grows stronger,
He'd wish to sleep a little longer.
And could he be indeed so old
10   As by the news-papers we're told?
Threescore,[2] I think, is pretty high;
'Twas time in conscience he should die.
This world he cumber'd long enough;
He burn'd his candle to the snuff;
And that's the reason, some folks think,
He left behind so great a s---k.[3]
Behold his funeral appears,
Nor widow's sighs, nor orphan's tears,
Wont[4] at such times each heart to pierce,
20   Attend the progress of his hearse.
But what of that, his friends may say,
He had those honours in his day.
True to his profit and his pride,
He made them weep before he di'd.

Come hither, all ye empty things,
Ye bubbles[5] rais'd by breath of Kings;
Who float upon the tide of state,
Come hither, and behold your fate.
Let pride be taught by this rebuke,
30   How very mean[6] a thing's a Duke;
From all his ill-got honours flung,
Turn'd to that dirt from whence he sprung.

1722   1764

---

[1] John Churchill, Duke of Marlborough (1650–1722), was the most famous general of his age and the architect of British victories, most notably Blenheim (1704), in the War of the Spanish Succession (1702–13). As time went on, however, Swift and the Tories charged Marlborough with prolonging the war for his own profit and glory.

[2] **Threescore** He was seventy-two.
[3] **s---k** stink
[4] **Wont** accustomed
[5] **bubbles** dupes
[6] **mean** contemptible, insignificant

Stella's Birthday. March 13. 1727[1]

This Day, whate'er the Fates decree,
Shall still be kept with Joy by me:
This Day then, let us not be told,
That you are sick, and I grown old,
Nor think on our approaching Ills,
And talk of Spectacles and Pills;
Tomorrow will be Time enough
To hear such mortifying[2] Stuff.
Yet, since from Reason may be brought
10 A better and more pleasing Thought,
Which can in spite of all Decays,
Support a few remaining Days:
From not the gravest of Divines,
Accept for once some serious Lines.

    Although we now can form no more
Long Schemes of Life, as heretofore;
Yet you, while Time is running fast,
Can look with Joy on what is past.

    Were future Happiness and Pain,
20 A mere Contrivance of the Brain,
As Atheists argue, to entice,
And fit their Proselytes for Vice;
(The only Comfort they propose,
To have Companions in their Woes,)
Grant this the Case, yet sure 'tis hard,
That Virtue, stil'd its own Reward,
And by all Sages understood
To be the chief of human Good,
Should acting, die, nor leave behind
30 Some lasting Pleasure in the Mind,
Which by Remembrance will assuage,
Grief, Sickness, Poverty, and Age;
And strongly shoot a radiant Dart,
To shine through Life's declining Part.

    Say, Stella, feel you no Content,
Reflecting on a Life well spent?
Your skilful Hand employ'd to save
Despairing Wretches from the Grave;
And then supporting with your Store,
40 Those whom you dragg'd from Death before:
(So Providence on Mortals waits,
Preserving what it first creates)

    Your gen'rous Boldness to defend
An innocent and absent Friend;

[1] This is the last of a series of birthday verses that Swift wrote every year for his beloved younger friend Stella (Esther Johnson) from 1719 until her death in 1728.

[2] **mortifying** humiliating, but here with implications of death

That Courage which can make you just,
To Merit humbled in the Dust:
The Detestation you express
For Vice in all its glitt'ring Dress:
That Patience under tort'ring Pain,
50 Where stubborn Stoics would complain.

Must these like empty Shadows pass,
Or Forms reflected from a Glass?
Or mere Chimaera's in the Mind,
That fly and leave no Marks behind?
Does not the Body thrive and grow
By Food of twenty Years ago?
And, had it not been still suppli'd,
It must a thousand Times have di'd.
Then, who with Reason can maintain,
60 That no Effects of Food remain?
And, is not Virtue in Mankind
The Nutriment that feeds the Mind?
Upheld by each good Action past,
And still continued by the last:
Then, who with Reason can pretend,
That all Effects of Virtue end?

Believe me Stella, when you show
That true Contempt for Things below,
Nor prize your Life for other Ends
70 Than merely to oblige your Friends;
Your former Actions claim their Part,
And join to fortify your Heart.
For Virtue in her daily Race,
Like Janus³ bears a double Face;
Looks back with Joy where she has gone,
And therefore goes with Courage on.
She at your sickly Couch will wait,
And guide you to a better State.

O then, whatever Heav'n intends,
80 Take Pity on your pitying Friends;
Nor let your Ills affect your Mind,
To fancy they can be unkind.
Me, surely me, you ought to spare,
Who gladly would your Suff'rings share;
Or give my Scrap of Life to you,
And think it far beneath your Due;
You, to whose Care so oft I owe,
That I'm alive to tell you so.

1727

³ **Janus** the Roman god of doorways, beginnings, and the rising and setting sun, whose two faces looked both forward and backward, to the east and the west. Each role is appropriate for the earthly and heavenly state suggested here.

The Character of Sir Robert Walpole[1]

With favour and fortune fastidiously blest,
He's loud in his laugh and he's coarse in his Jest;
Of favour and fortune unmerited vain,
A sharper[2] in trifles, a dupe in the main.[3]
Achieving of nothing, still promising wonders,
By dint of experience improving in Blunders;
Oppressing true merit, exalting the base,[4]
And selling his Country to purchase his peace.[5]
A Jobber of Stocks[6] by retailing false news,
10 A prater at Court in the Stile of the Stews;[7]
Of Virtue and worth by profession a giber,[8]
Of Juries and senates the bully and briber.
Tho' I name not the wretch you know who I mean,
T'is the Cur dog of Britain and spaniel of Spain.

1731   1789

[1] Swift sent this imitation of a French satire on
Cardinal Fleury to the Countess of Suffolk with
an accompanying letter in 1731. Swift was one of
the leaders of the literary opposition to Walpole,
whose political power, bribery, and policy of
peace with Spain he and his colleagues regarded
as a danger to the nation. The poem, a mock
sonnet, uses anapestic instead of Swift's usual
iambic tetrameter.
[2] **sharper** a cheat
[3] **main** in important matters, but perhaps a pun
on "ocean," where the Spanish were boarding
British ships and restricting their trade with

apparent impunity
[4] **oppressing . . . base** The opposition com-
plained that Walpole offered advancement only
to those whom he could bribe.
[5] **peace** both his personal ease and the peace
with Spain. See l. 14.
[6] **Stocks** alluding to Walpole's role in the South
Sea Bubble of 1721, in which vast fortunes were
made and lost as the company's stock rose and
collapsed, with government collusion
[7] **Stews** whore houses
[8] **giber** sneerer, scoffer

ALEXANDER POPE
1688–1744

Roman Catholic, perennially ill, hunch-backed, and four feet six inches in height, Alexander Pope knew more than his share of prejudice and pain. Nonetheless, he became the foremost poet of his time and achieved financial independence through his translations (1715–26) of Homer. Pope's early poetry includes much that is gently satiric and lyrical. In the "Elegy to the Memory of an Unfortunate Lady" (1717), he assumes the role of a suitor grieving over his beloved's suicide; in The Rape of the Lock (1712, 1714, 1717) he uses the mock-heroic to parody both epic grandeur and modern superficiality, while assuring us that his own guiding voice provides successful

values. By 1728, however, personal and literary attacks on Pope had become so frequent and intense that he responded with the first version of the Dunciad, which singles out his enemies and arraigns the decay in modern culture. Predictably, this poem increased hostility against him, especially after he became prominent in the literary opposition to Sir Robert Walpole's government. His career then took a decisive turn toward satire, and the form he normally used was sharp, self-contained pentameter couplets.

Pope's art always was that of the synthesist who adapted the best of the past, criticized the worst, and made both part of his modern vision. This blending is especially deft in his satire, which uses the poetic devices of his three classical Roman predecessors whose ancient art he transmuted for his own purposes. From Horace he learned the conversational polished tone that characterizes the *Epistles to Several Persons* (1731–35). The *Epistle to Burlington* (1731) thus reflects the confidence of someone attacking not vice but folly because he knows that a benevolent God is active on his, the nation's, and man's behalf. Like Horace, Pope prefers the quiet country life and dialogue with an opponent whom the satirist must try to persuade. In the *Epilogue to the Satires* (1738), directed largely against George II and his prime minister, Sir Robert Walpole, Pope speaks in a troubled voice similar to that of the post-Horatian Roman satirist Persius, who complained that Nero's vile example set a tone for the whole nation, and who showed that dialogue in such a world was useless. Somber tones of lament for the nation's decline also fill Pope's *apologia*, a defense of satire or satirists, the *Epistle to Dr. Arbuthnot* (1735), where the doctor urges Pope not to name his adversaries because Walpole or his followers may harm him. A still darker voice in Pope's later works recalls the satires of the last great Roman satirist, Juvenal, who saw collapse everywhere in Nero's and Domitian's imperial Rome. Pope's special genius is, in part, to borrow, modulate, vary, and supersede these several voices within the couplet form.

Unlike Horace, however, Pope does not often find his satiric norm, or objects of praise, in contemporaries; and unlike Persius he does not withdraw into the self, for he always remains a public poet. Even in *Arbuthnot* he looks to his dead or dying parents or to the previous generation for the models of a just, flourishing culture, which seemed less and less likely under his present rulers. By the final version of the *Dunciad* in 1743, those norms are more distant still, and even less achievable. In this epic of decay, he inverts the Christian themes of Milton's *Paradise Lost* and replaces light by darkness, the divine by the diabolical, creation by uncreation, and order by chaos. With Pope's triumph of the dunces, the gentle protected world of *The Rape of the Lock*, and even the threatening but controlled world of Pope's earlier satires, have become faded dreams.

The Rape of the Lock. An Heroi-Comical Poem[1]

CANTO I

What dire Offence from am'rous Causes[2] springs,
What mighty Contests rise from trivial Things,
I sing—This Verse to Caryll, Muse! is due;
This, ev'n Belinda may vouchsafe to view:

[1] At the request of his friend John Caryll, Pope agreed to mediate a squabble that had arisen in 1711 between two prominent neighboring Roman Catholic families when Robert, Baron Petre, cut off a lock of Arabella Fermor's hair. Pope's response to the request was a two-canto 334–line poem. By 1714, the poem had outgrown its occasion and evolved into the larger version, whose mock-epic "machinery" deflates pretensions through contrast with ancient epic grandeur. Pope also makes plain, however, that such epic warfare is unacceptable in his day. His final addition came in 1717, with Clarissa's speech, overtly presenting the female norm.

The *Rape* was prefaced by a letter to Arabella Fermor praising her and discussing the poem's background and its machinery. There is a Latin epigraph from Martial, *Epigrams* 12:34, "Belinda, I did not want to profane your locks, but it pleases me to have granted this to your prayers."

[2] **am'rous Causes** The mock heroic recalls the genuine heroic: Paris and Helen (the Trojan War), Agamemnon and Briseis (the withdrawal of Achilles from combat), Aeneas and Dido (the suicide of Dido and enmity between Carthage and Rome), and Adam and Eve.

Slight is the Subject, but not so the Praise,
If She inspire, and He approve my Lays.
　　Say what strange Motive, Goddess! cou'd compel
A well-bred Lord t'assault a gentle Belle?
Oh say what stranger Cause, yet unexplor'd,
10　Cou'd make a gentle Belle reject a Lord?
In Tasks so bold, can Little Men engage,
And in soft Bosoms dwells such mighty Rage?
　　Sol thro' white Curtains shot a tim'rous Ray,
And op'd those Eyes that must eclipse the Day;
Now Lapdogs give themselves the rowsing Shake,
And sleepless Lovers, just at Twelve, awake:
Thrice rung the Bell, the Slipper knock'd the Ground,[3]
And the press'd Watch return'd a silver Sound.[4]
Belinda still her downy Pillow press'd
20　Her Guardian Sylph[5] prolong'd the balmy Rest.
'Twas he had summon'd to her silent Bed
The Morning-Dream[6] that hover'd o'er her Head.
A Youth more glitt'ring than a Birth-night Beau,[7]
(That ev'n in Slumber caus'd her Cheek to glow)
Seem'd to her Ear his winning Lips to lay,
And thus in Whispers said, or seem'd to say
　　"Fairest of Mortals, thou distinguish'd Care
Of thousand bright Inhabitants of Air!
If e'er one Vision touch'd thy infant Thought,
30　Of all the Nurse and all the Priest have taught,
Of airy Elves by Moonlight Shadows seen,
The silver Token, and the circled Green,[8]
Or Virgins visited by Angel-Pow'rs,
With Golden Crowns and Wreaths of heav'nly Flow'rs,
Hear and believe! thy own Importance know,
Nor bound thy narrow Views to Things below.[9]
Some secret Truths from Learned Pride conceal'd,
To Maids alone and Children are reveal'd:
What tho' no Credit doubting Wits may give?
40　The Fair and Innocent shall still believe.
Know then, unnumber'd Spirits round thee fly,
The light Militia of the lower Sky;
These, tho' unseen, are ever on the Wing,
Hang o'er the Box, and hover round the Ring.[10]
　　Think what an Equipage[11] thou hast in Air,

---

[3]**Slipper . . . Ground** Belinda calls her maid by knocking on the floor with her shoe.

[4]**Sound** of the quarter-hour or hour when a pin on the watch was pressed

[5]**Sylph** one of the spirits inhabiting the air

[6]**Dream** a mock version of Satan at the ear of Eve in *Paradise Lost* IV.800

[7]**Birth-night Beau** a courtier elegantly dressed for the king's birthday

[8]**silver Token . . . circled Green** the coin left by fairies as a reward for good servants, and the burnt circles in the grass where fairies were supposed to have danced

[9]**Nor bound . . . below** comic version of Satan's advice to Eve in *Paradise Lost* IX. 684–732

[10]**Box . . . Ring** the best seats in the theater and the fashionable circular path in Hyde Park, each a place of real and mock courtship

[11]**Equipage** coach, horses, and liveried footmen

And view with scorn Two Pages and a Chair,[12]
As now your own, our Beings were of old,
And once inclos'd in Woman's beauteous Mold;
Thence, by a soft Transition, we repair
50   From earthly Vehicles to these of Air.
Think not, when Woman's transient Breath is fled,
That all her Vanities at once are dead:
Succeeding Vanities she still regards,
And tho' she plays no more, o'erlooks the Cards.
Her Joy in gilded Chariots,[13] when alive,
And Love of Ombre,[14] after Death survive.
For when the Fair in all their Pride expire,
To their first Elements[15] their Souls retire:
The Sprites of fiery Termagants in Flame
60   Mount up, and take a Salamander's[16] Name.
Soft yielding Minds to Water glide away,
And sip with Nymphs, their Elemental Tea.
The graver Prude sinks downward to a Gnome,
In search of Mischief still on Earth to roam.
The light Coquettes in Sylphs aloft repair,
And sport and flutter in the Fields of Air.
   "Know farther yet; Whoever fair and chaste
Rejects Mankind, is by some Sylph embrac'd:[17]
For Spirits, freed from mortal Laws, with ease
70   Assume what Sexes and what Shapes[18] they please.
What guards the Purity of melting Maids,
In Courtly Balls, and Midnight Masquerades,
Safe from the treach'rous Friend, the daring Spark,[19]
The Glance by Day, the Whisper in the Dark;
When kind Occasion prompts their warm Desires,
When Music softens, and when Dancing fires?
'Tis but their Sylph, the wise Celestials know,
Tho' Honour is the Word with Men below.
   "Some Nymphs there are, too conscious of their Face,
80   For Life predestin'd to the Gnomes' Embrace.
These swell their Prospects and exalt their Pride,
When Offers are disdain'd, and Love deni'd.
Then gay ideas crowd the vacant Brain;
While Peers and Dukes, and all their sweeping Train,
And Garters, Stars, and Coronets[20] appear,
And in soft Sounds, *Your Grace*[21] salutes their Ear.

[12]**Chair** a sedan chair, in which one is carried by servants
[13]**Chariots** coaches
[14]**Ombre** fashionable card game, after the Spanish "hombre" or man. See note 4 to Canto 3, below.
[15]**first Elements** The following eight lines outline the theory that the four elements—earth, water, air, fire—were balanced by the "humors" of the body—melancholy, phlegm, blood, choler—and determined one's personality.
[16]**Salamander** believed able to live in fire
[17]**embrac'd** in the sexual sense
[18]**Sexes . . . Shapes** a comic version of the angels in *Paradise Lost* VII. 620-29
[19]**Spark** a showy, flirtatious young man
[20]**Garters . . . Coronets** The first two are emblems of knighthood, the latter of the peerage.
[21]*Your Grace* proper address to a duchess

'Tis these that early taint the Female Soul,
Instruct the Eyes of young Coquettes to roll,
Teach Infant-Cheeks a bidden Blush to know,
90   And little Hearts to flutter at a Beau.
    "Oft when the World imagine Women stray,
The Sylphs thro' mystic Mazes guide their Way,
Thro' all the giddy Circle they pursue,
And old Impertinence expel by new.
What tender Maid but must a Victim fall
To one Man's Treat,²² but for another's Ball?
When Florio speaks, what Virgin could withstand,
If gentle Damon did not squeeze her Hand?
With varying Vanities, from ev'ry Part,
100   They shift the moving Toyshop of their Heart;
Where Wigs with Wigs, with Sword-knots Sword-knots²³ strive
Beaus banish Beaus, and Coaches Coaches drive.
This erring Mortals Levity may call,
Oh blind to Truth! the Sylphs contrive it all.
    "Of these am I, who thy Protection claim,
A watchful Sprite, and Ariel is my Name.
Late, as I rang'd the Crystal Wilds of Air,
In the clear Mirror of thy ruling Star
I saw, alas! some dread Event impend,
110   Ere to the Main this Morning Sun descend.
But Heav'n reveals not what, or how, or where:
Warn'd by thy Sylph, oh Pious Maid beware!
This to disclose is all thy Guardian can.
Beware of all, but most beware of Man!"
    He said; when Shock,²⁴ who thought she slept too long,
Leap'd up, and wak'd his Mistress with his Tongue.
'Twas then Belinda! if Report say true,
Thy Eyes first open'd on a Billet-doux;²⁵
Wounds, Charms, and *Ardors*, were no sooner read,
120   But all the Vision vanish'd from thy Head.
    And now, unveil'd, the Toilet²⁶ stands display'd,
Each Silver Vase in mystic Order laid.
First, rob'd in White, the Nymph intent adores
With Head uncover'd, the Cosmetic Pow'rs.
A heav'nly Image in the Glass appears,
To that she bends, to that her Eyes she rears;
Th'inferior Priestess,²⁷ at her Altar's side,
Trembling, begins she sacred Rites of Pride.
Unnumber'd Treasures ope at once, and here
130   The various Off'rings of the World appear;

---

²²**Treat** an elaborate entertainment
²³**Wigs . . . knots** The beaus are reduced to
their external marks, an elaborate wig or the
ornamental ribbons tied to the hilt of their
unused sword.
²⁴**Shock** a fashionable breed of long-haired
lapdog
²⁵**Billet-doux** a love letter that includes the
traditional Petrarchan language of l. 119
²⁶**Toilet** dressing table
²⁷**inferior Priestess** Belinda's maid Betty

From each she nicely[28] culls with curious [29] Toil,
And decks the Goddess with the glitt'ring Spoil.
This Casket India's glowing Gems unlocks,
And all Arabia[30] breathes from yonder Box.
The Tortoise here and Elephant unite,
Transform'd to Combs, the speckled and the white.
Here Files of Pins extend their shining Rows,
Puffs, Powders, Patches,[31] Bibles, Billet-doux.
Now awful[32] Beauty puts on all its Arms;
140 The Fair each moment rises in her Charms,
Repairs her Smiles, awakens ev'ry Grace,
And calls forth all the Wonders of her Face;
Sees by Degrees a purer Blush[33] arise,
And keener Lightnings[34] quicken in her Eyes.
The busy Sylphs surround their darling Care;
These set the Head, and those divide the Hair,
Some fold the Sleeve, while others plait the Gown;
And Betty's prais'd for Labours not her own.

[28]**nicely** precisely
[29]**curious** careful
[30]**Arabia** Arabian perfumes
[31]**Patches** small pieces of black silk, worn to draw attention to strengths and away from weaknesses
[32]**awful** awe-inspiring
[33]**purer Blush** application of rouge
[34]**keener lightnings** probably eye shadow

CANTO II

Not with more Glories, in th' Etherial Plain,[1]
The Sun first rises o'er the purpled Main,[2]
Than issuing forth, the Rival of his Beams
Launch'd on the Bosom of the Silver Thames.[3]
Fair Nymphs, and well-dress'd Youths around her shone,
But ev'ry Eye was fix'd on her alone.
On her white Breast a sparkling Cross she wore,
Which Jews might kiss, and Infidels adore.[4]
Her lively Looks a sprightly Mind disclose,
10 Quick as her Eyes, and as unfix'd as those:
Favours to none, to all she Smiles extends,
Oft she rejects, but never once offends.
Bright as the Sun, her Eyes the Gazers strike,
And, like the Sun, they shine on all alike.
Yet graceful Ease, and Sweetness void of Pride,
Might hide her Faults, if Belles had Faults to hide:
If to her share some Female Errors fall,
Look on her Face, and you'll forget 'em all.
    This Nymph, to the Destruction of Mankind,
20 Nourish'd two Locks, which graceful hung behind

[1]**Etherial Plain** the sky
[2]**purpled Main** the ocean red at dawn
[3]**Launch'd . . . Thames** Belinda takes a boat from London to Hampton Court Palace, about twelve miles away.
[4]**Cross . . . adore** apparently as a sign of conversion, actually because the cross ends near the seductive cleavage of her bosom

In equal Curls, and well conspir'd to deck
With shining Ringlets her smooth Iv'ry Neck.
Love in these Labyrinths his Slaves detains,
And mighty Hearts are held in slender Chains.
With hairy Sprindges[5] we the Birds betray,
Slight Lines of Hair Surprize the Finny Prey,
Fair Tresses Man's Imperial Race insnare,
And Beauty draws us with a single Hair.
Th' Advent'rous Baron the bright Locks admir'd,
30   He saw, he wish'd, and to the Prize aspir'd:
Resolv'd to win, he meditates the way,
By Force to ravish, or by Fraud betray;
For when Success a Lover's Toil attends,
Few ask, if Fraud or Force attain'd his Ends.
For this, ere Phoebus rose,[6] he had implor'd
Propitious Heav'n, and ev'ry Pow'r ador'd,
But chiefly Love—to Love an Altar built,
Of twelve vast French Romances[7] neatly gilt.
There lay three Garters, half a Pair of Gloves;
40   And all the Trophies of his former Loves.
With tender Billet-doux he lights the Pyre,
And breathes three am'rous Sighs to raise the Fire.
Then prostrate falls, and begs with ardent Eyes
Soon to obtain, and long possess the Prize:
The Pow'rs gave Ear, and granted half his Pray'r,
The rest, the Winds dispers'd in empty Air.[8]
But now secure the painted Vessel[9] glides,
The Sun-beams trembling on the floating Tides,
While melting Music steals upon the Sky,
50   And soften'd Sounds along the Waters die.
Smooth flow the Waves, the Zephyrs[10] gently play,
Belinda smil'd, and all the World was gay.
All but the Sylph—With careful Thoughts opprest,
Th'impending Woe sate heavy on his Breast.
He summons strait his Denizens of Air;
The lucid Squadrons round the Sails repair:
Soft o'er the Shrouds[11] Aerial Whispers breathe,
That seem'd but Zephyrs to the Train beneath.
Some to the Sun their Insect-Wings unfold,
60   Waft on the Breeze, or sink in Clouds of Gold.
Transparent Forms, too fine for mortal Sight,
Their fluid Bodies half dissolv'd in Light.
Loose to the Wind their airy Garments flew,
Thin glitt'ring Textures of the filmy Dew;
Dip in the richest Tincture of the Skies,

---

[5]**Sprindges** snares
[6]**ere Phoebus rose** Phoebus Apollo was god of the sun; hence, before dawn
[7]**French Romances** long, often licentious and stylized love stories

[8]**Pow'rs . . . Air** a frequent response to prayer in epics, where only part of the wish is granted
[9]**painted Vessel** both Belinda and the boat
[10]**Zephyrs** gentle west winds
[11]**Shrouds** rigging, ropes

Where Light disports in ever-mingling Dies,
While ev'ry Beam new transient Colours flings,
Colours that change whene'er they wave their Wings.
Amid the Circle, on the gilded Mast,
70　Superior by the Head,[12] was Ariel plac'd;
His Purple Pinions opening to the Sun,
He rais'd his Azure Wand, and thus begun.
　　"Ye Sylphs and Sylphids, to your Chief give Ear,
Fays, Fairies, Genii, Elves, and Daemons hear![13]
Ye know the Spheres and various Tasks assign'd,[14]
By Laws Eternal, to th'Aerial Kind.
Some in the Fields of purest Aether[15] play,
And bask and whiten in the Blaze of Day.
Some guide the Course of wand'ring Orbs[16] on high,
80　Or roll the Planets thro' the boundless Sky.
Some less refin'd, beneath the Moon's pale Light
Pursue the Stars that shoot athwart the Night,
Or suck the Mists in grosser Air below,
Or dip their Pinions in the painted Bow,[17]
Or brew fierce Tempests on the wintry Main,
Or o'er the Glebe[18] distill the kindly Rain.
Others on Earth o'er human Race preside,
Watch all their Ways, and all their Actions guide:
Of these the Chief the Care of Nations own,
90　And guard with Arms Divine the British Throne.
　　"Our humbler Province is to tend the Fair,
Not a less pleasing, tho' less glorious Care.
To save the Powder from too rude a Gale,[19]
Nor let th' imprison'd Essences exhale,[20]
To draw fresh Colours from the vernal Flow'rs,
To steal from Rainbows ere they drop in Show'rs
A brighter Wash;[21] to curl their waving Hairs,
Assist their Blushes, and inspire their Airs;
Nay oft, in Dreams, Invention we bestow,
100　To change a Flounce, or add a Furbelo.[22]
　　"This Day, black Omens threat the brightest Fair
That e'er deserv'd a watchful Spirit's Care;
Some dire Disaster, or by Force, or Slight,
But what, or where, the Fates have wrapp'd in Night.
Whether the Nymph shall break Diana's Law,[23]

---

[12]**Superior . . . Head** a head taller than his soldiers
[13]**Sylphs . . . hear** a comic version of *Paradise Lost* II.11, and V.600–01. A fay is a kind of fairy; genii and daemons are guardian spirits.
[14]**Spheres . . . assign'd** Each of the nine orders of angels was assigned to one of the nine heavenly spheres.
[15]**Aether** air above the moon, in contrast to the "less refin'd" air below the moon, as in l. 81

[16]**wand'ring Orbs** comets
[17]**painted Bow** rainbow
[18]**Glebe** cultivated fields
[19]**too rude a Gale** too strong a breeze
[20]**Essences exhale** Perfumes escape from the bottle.
[21]**Wash** cosmetic rinse
[22]**Furbelo** a ruffle, normally for a dress or a petticoat
[23]**Diana's Law** chastity

Or some frail China Jar receive a Flaw,
Or stain her Honour, or her new Brocade,
Forget her Pray'rs, or miss a Masquerade,
Or lose her Heart, or Necklace, at a Ball;
110   Or whether Heav'n has doom'd that Shock must fall.
Haste then ye Spirits! to your Charge repair;
The flutt'ring Fan be Zephyretta's Care;
The Drops[24] to thee, Brillante, we consign;
And, Momentilla, let the Watch be thine;
Do thou, Crispissa,[25] tend her fav'rite Lock;
Ariel himself shall be the Guard of Shock.
    "To Fifty chosen Sylphs, of special Note,
We trust th' important Charge, the Petticoat:[26]
Oft have we known that sev'nfold Fence to fail,
120   Tho' stiff with Hoops, and arm'd with Ribs of Whale.
Form a strong Line about the Silver Bound,
And guard the wide Circumference around.
    "Whatever Spirit, careless of his Charge,
His Post neglects, or leaves the Fair at large,
Shall feel sharp Vengeance soon o'ertake his Sins,
Be stopp'd in Vials, or transfix'd with Pins;
Or plung'd in Lakes of bitter Washes lie,
Or wedg'd whole Ages in a Bodkin's[27] Eye:
Gums and Pomatums shall his Flight restrain,
130   While clogg'd he beats his silken Wings in vain;
Or Alum-Styptics,[28] with contracting Power
Shrink his thin Essence like a rivell'd[29] Flower.
Or as Ixion[30] fix'd, the Wretch shall feel
The giddy Motion of the whirling Mill,[31]
In Fumes of burning Chocolate shall glow
And tremble at the Sea that froths below!"
    He spoke; the Spirits from the Sails descend;
Some, Orb in Orb, around the Nymph extend,
Some thrid the mazy Ringlets of her Hair,
140   Some hang upon the Pendants of her Ear;
With beating Hearts the dire Event they wait;
Anxious, and trembling for the Birth of Fate.

---

[24]**Drops** diamond earrings
[25]**Crispissa** from the Latin *crispere,* to curl
[26]**Petticoat** a comic version of the epic hero's shield
[27]**Bodkin** a needle or hairpin
[28]**Alum-Styptics** astringents

[29]**rivell'd** wrinkled
[30]**Ixion** king of Thessaly who tried to seduce Juno, and was punished by being tied to a perpetually revolving wheel in hell
[31]**whirling Mill** instrument for mixing chocolate with milk or water to make hot chocolate

CANTO III

Close by those Meads for ever crown'd with Flow'rs,
Where Thames with Pride surveys his rising Tow'rs,
There stands a Structure[1] of Majestic Frame,

---

[1]**Structure** Hampton Court

Which from the neighb'ring Hampton takes its Name.
Here Britain's Statesmen oft the Fall foredoom
Of Foreign Tyrants, and of Nymphs at home;
Here Thou, Great Anna! whom three Realms obey,[2]
Dost sometimes Counsel take—and sometimes Tea.
    Hither the Heroes and the Nymphs resort,
10   To taste awhile the Pleasures of a Court;
In various Talk th' instructive hours they pass'd
Who gave the Ball, or paid the Visit last:
One speaks the Glory of the British Queen,
And one describes a charming Indian Screen;
A third interprets Motions, Looks, and Eyes;
At ev'ry Word a Reputation dies.
Snuff, or the Fan, supply each Pause of Chat,
With singing, laughing, ogling, and all that.
    Meanwhile declining from the Noon of Day,
20   The Sun obliquely shoots his burning Ray;
The hungry Judges soon the Sentence sign,
And Wretches hang that Jury-men may Dine;
The Merchant from th' Exchange[3] returns in Peace,
And the long Labours of the Toilette cease—
Belinda now, whom Thirst of Fame invites,
Burns to encounter two advent'rous Knights,
At Ombre[4] singly to decide their Doom;
And swells her Breast with Conquests yet to come.
Straight the three Bands prepare in Arms to join,
30   Each Band the number of the Sacred Nine.[5]
Soon as she spreads her Hand, th' Aerial Guard
Descend, and sit on each important Card:
First Ariel perch'd upon a Matadore,[6]
Then each, according to the Rank they bore;
For Sylphs, yet mindful of their ancient Race,
Are, as when Women, wond'rous fond of Place.
    Behold, four Kings in Majesty rever'd,
With hoary Whiskers and a forky Beard;
And four fair Queens whose hands sustain a Flow'r,
40   Th' expressive Emblem of their softer Pow'r;
Four Knaves in Garbs succinct,[7] a trusty Band,
Caps on their heads, and Halberds[8] in their hand;
And Particolour'd[9] Troops, a shining Train,

[2]**Anna . . . obey** Queen Anne reigned over England, Scotland, and Wales from 1702 to 1714; alternatively the three kingdoms are Britain, Ireland, and France, the latter an antiquated claim.
[3]**Exchange** Royal Exchange, marketplace for brokers and bankers as well as merchants
[4]**Ombre** The game (pronounced "omber") is played by three persons holding nine cards, each drawn from a forty-card deck (the 8s, 9s, and 10s have been removed); thirteen are placed in the common pile. The player who seeks to win by taking the most tricks is called the ombre—the man—and names the trumps, as the aggressor Belinda does here.
[5]**Each Band . . . Nine** the nine cards
[6]**Matadore** one of the three highest cards, the highest determined by the choice of trumps
[7]**succinct** close fitting
[8]**Halberds** combination of a spear and a battle-ax on a long handle
[9]**Particolour'd** multi-colored

Draw forth to Combat on the Velvet Plain.[10]
   The skilful Nymph reviews her Force with Care;
"Let Spades be Trumps!" she said, and Trumps they were.[11]
   Now move to War her Sable Matadores,
In Show like Leaders of the swarthy Moors.
Spadillio[12] first, unconquerable Lord!
50   Led off two captive Trumps, and swept the Board.
As many more Manillio[13] forc'd to yield,
And march'd a Victor from the verdant Field.
Him Basto[14] follow'd, but his Fate more hard
Gain'd but one Trump and one Plebeian Card.
With his broad Sabre next, a Chief in Years,
The hoary Majesty of Spades appears;
Puts forth one manly Leg, to sight reveal'd;
The rest his many-colour'd Robe conceal'd.
The Rebel-Knave,[15] who dares his Prince engage,
60   Proves the just Victim of his Royal Rage.
Ev'n mighty Pam[16] that Kings and Queens o'erthrew,
And mow'd down Armies in the Fights of Lu,
Sad Chance of War! now, destitute of Aid,
Falls undistinguished by the Victor Spade!
   Thus far both Armies to Belinda yield;
Now to the Baron Fate inclines the Field.
His warlike Amazon[17] her Host invades,
Th' Imperial Consort of the Crown of Spades.
The Club's black Tyrant first her Victim di'd,
70   Spite of his haughty Mien, and barb'rous Pride:
What boots the Regal Circle on his Head,
His Giant Limbs in State unwieldy spread?
That long behind he trails his pompous Robe,
And of all Monarchs only grasps the Globe?[18]
   The Baron now his Diamonds pours apace;
Th' embroider'd King who shows but half his Face,
And his refulgent Queen, with Pow'rs combin'd,
Of broken Troops an easie Conquest find.
Clubs, Diamonds, Hearts, in wild Disorder seen,
80   With Throngs promiscuous strow the level Green.
Thus when dispers'd a routed Army runs,
Of Asia's Troops, and Afric's Sable Sons,
With like Confusion different Nations fly,
Of various Habit and of various Dye,
The pierc'd Battalions disunited fall,

[10]**Velvet Plain** the green velvet card table. The entire scene is both a sublimated sexual and a mock-epic battle.

[11]**Let Spades . . . were** a parody of Genesis 1:3, "And God said, Let there be light: and there was light"

[12]**Spadillio** ace of spades, here ace of trumps

[13]**Manillio** deuce of spades

[14]**Basto** ace of clubs

[15]**Rebel-Knave** of spades

[16]**Pam** knave of clubs, highest card in the game of Loo

[17]**Amazon** the queen of spades, who allows the Baron to win the next four tricks, and a foreshadowing of Thalestris. See below 4:89–120, and 5:36, 57–66.

[18]**Globe** In English decks only the king of clubs carries the ball as an emblem of his power.

In Heaps on Heaps; one Fate o'erwhelms them all.
   The Knave of Diamonds tries his wily Arts,
And wins (oh shameful Chance!) the Queen of Hearts.
At this, the Blood the Virgin's Cheek forsook,
90 A livid Paleness spreads o'er all her Look;
She sees, and trembles at th' approaching Ill,
Just in the Jaws of Ruin, and Codille.[19]
And now, (as oft in some distemper'd State)
On one nice Trick[20] depends the gen'ral Fate.
An Ace of Hearts steps forth: The King unseen
Lurk'd in her Hand, and mourn'd his captive Queen.
He springs to Vengeance with an eager pace,
And falls like Thunder on the prostrate Ace.[21]
The Nymph exulting fills with Shouts the Sky,
100 The Walls, the Woods, and long Canals reply.
   Oh thoughtless Mortals! ever blind to Fate,
Too soon dejected, and too soon elate!
Sudden these Honours shall be snatch'd away,
And curs'd for ever this Victorious Day.
   For lo! the Board with Cups and Spoons is crown'd,
The Berries crackle, and the Mill turns round.[22]
On shining Altars of Japan[23] they raise
The silver Lamp; the fiery Spirits[24] blaze,
From silver Spouts the grateful[25] Liquors glide,
110 While China's Earth[26] receives the smoking Tide.
At once they gratify their Scent and Taste,
And frequent Cups prolong the rich Repast.
Strait hover round the Fair her Airy Band;
Some, as she sipp'd, the fuming Liquor fann'd,
Some o'er her Lap their careful Plumes display'd,
Trembling, and conscious of the rich Brocade.
Coffee, (which makes the Politician wise,
And see thro' all things with his half-shut Eyes)
Sent up in Vapours to the Baron's Brain
120 New Stratagems, the radiant Lock to gain.
Ah cease rash Youth! desist ere 'tis too late,
Fear the just Gods, and think of Scylla's Fate!
Chang'd to a Bird, and sent to flit in Air,
She dearly pays for Nisus' injur'd Hair![27]

[19]**Codille** The Baron and Belinda are tied at four tricks each; if she loses, she is given "codille," and must pay a stake to the winner.
[20]**nice Trick** skillful play
[21]Since spades are trumps, the red cards' ranking is king, queen, knave, ace; Belinda's trump-king thus takes the Baron's ace of hearts, and wins the game, 5–4.
[22]**Berries . . . round** Coffee beans are roasted and ground in a mill.
[23]**Altars . . . Japan** highly laquered tables
[24]**fiery Spirits** in the base of the lamp heating the coffee

[25]**grateful** delicious
[26]**China's Earth** China tea cups
[27]**Scylla's . . . Hair** Pope cites Ovid, *Metamorphoses* VIII.1–151. Scylla, daughter of King Nysus of Megara, fell in love with King Minos of Crete when he was besieging her father's city. To win his favor, she pulled out her father's lock of purple or golden hair on which his life and power depended, and presented it to Minos, thus killing her father and allowing Minos to take the city. Shocked by her treason, Minos refused the lock and spurned her, whereupon she soon was metamorphosed into a seabird.

But when to Mischief Mortals bend their Will,
How soon they find fit Instruments of Ill!
Just then, Clarissa drew with tempting Grace
A two-edg'd Weapon[28] from her shining Case;
So Ladies in Romance assist their Knight,
130   Present the Spear, and arm him for the Fight.
He takes the Gift with rev'rence, and extends
The little Engine on his Fingers' Ends,
This just behind Belinda's Neck he spread,
As o'er the fragrant Steams she bends her Head:
Swift to the Lock a thousand Sprights repair,
A thousand Wings, by turns, blow back the Hair,
And thrice they twitch'd the Diamond in her Ear,
Thrice she look'd back, and thrice the Foe drew near.
Just in that instant, anxious Ariel sought
140   The close Recesses of the Virgin's Thought;
As on the Nosegay in her Breast reclin'd,
He watch'd th' Ideas rising in her Mind,
Sudden he view'd, in spite of all her Art,
An Earthly Lover lurking at her Heart.
Amaz'd, confus'd, he found his Pow'r expir'd,
Resign'd to Fate, and with a Sigh retir'd.
    The Peer now spreads the glitt'ring Forfex wide,
T'inclose the Lock; now joins it, to divide.
Ev'n then, before the fatal Engine clos'd,
150   A wretched Sylph too fondly interpos'd;
Fate urg'd the Sheers, and cut the Sylph in twain,
(But Airy Substance soon unites[29] again)
The meeting Points the sacred Hairs dissever
From the fair Head, for ever and for ever!
    Then flash'd the living Lightning from her Eyes,
And Screams of Horror rend th' affrighted Skies.
Not louder Shrieks to pitying Heav'n are cast,
When Husbands or when Lap-dogs breathe their last,
Or when rich China Vessels, fall'n from high,
160   In glitt'ring Dust and painted Fragments lie!
    Let Wreaths of Triumph now my Temples twine,
(The Victor cri'd) the glorious Prize is mine!
While Fish in Streams, or Birds delight in Air,
Or in a Coach and Six the British Fair,
As long as Atalantis[30] shall be read,
Or the small Pillow grace a Lady's Bed,
While Visits shall be paid on solemn Days,
When numerous Wax-lights in bright Order blaze,
While Nymphs take Treats, or Assignations give,
170   So long my Honour, Name, and praise shall live!

[28]**two-edg'd Weapon** scissors, the "glitt'ring Forfex" of l. 147
[29]**soon unites** a parody of *Paradise Lost* VI. 330–31, where Satan is wounded by Michael and quickly mends
[30]**Atalantis** fashionable and licentious book by Mary de La Rivière Manly (1672–1724)

What Time wou'd spare, from Steel receives its date,[31]
And Monuments, like Men, submit to Fate!
Steel cou'd the Labour of the Gods destroy,
And strike to Dust th' Imperial Tow'rs of Troy;
Steel cou'd the Works of mortal Pride confound,
And hew Triumphal Arches to the Ground.
What Wonder then, fair Nymph! thy Hairs shou'd feel
The conqu'ring Force of unresisted Steel?

[31]**date** end

CANTO IV

But anxious Cares the pensive Nymph oppress'd
And secret Passions labour'd in her Breast.
Not youthful Kings in Battle seiz'd alive,
Not scornful Virgins who their Charms survive,
Not ardent Lovers robb'd of all their Bliss,
No ancient Ladies when refus'd a Kiss,
Not Tyrants fierce that unrepenting die,
Not Cynthia when her Manteau's[1] pinn'd awry,
E'er felt such Rage, Resentment, and Despair,
10 As Thou, sad Virgin! for thy ravish'd Hair.
    For, that sad moment, when the Sylphs withdrew,
And Ariel weeping from Belinda flew,
Umbriel,[2] a dusky melancholy Spright,
As ever sully'd the fair face of Light,
Down to the Central Earth, his proper Scene,
Repair'd to search the gloomy Cave of Spleen.[3]
    Swift on his sooty Pinions flits the Gnome,
And in a Vapour reach'd the dismal Dome.[4]
No cheerful Breeze this sullen Region knows,
20 The dreaded East is all the Wind that blows.
Here, in a Grotto, shelt'red close from Air,
And screen'd in Shades from Day's detested Glare,
She sighs for ever on her pensive Bed,
Pain at her Side, and Megrim[5] at her Head.
    Two Handmaids wait the Throne: Alike in Place,
But diff'ring far in Figure and in Face.
Here stood Ill-nature like an ancient Maid,
Her wrinkled Form in Black and White array'd;
With store of Pray'rs, for Mornings, Nights, and Noons,
30 Her Hand is fill'd; her Bosom with Lampoons.
    There Affectation with a sickly Mien
Shows in her Cheek the Roses of Eighteen,
Practic'd to Lisp, and hang the Head aside,

[1]**Manteau** a loose, robe-like garment
[2]**Umbriel** from Latin *umbra*, shadow
[3]**Spleen** the modish melancholy experienced by the rich or idle, and thought to be evoked, in part, by the east wind (l. 20)
[4]**Dome** the cave itself. "Vapour(s)" was another term for spleen. See ll. 39 and 59 below.
[5]**Megrim** migraine headache

Faints into Airs, and languishes with Pride;
On the rich Quilt sinks with becoming Woe,
Wrapp'd in a Gown, for Sickness, and for Show.
The Fair-ones feel such Maladies as these,
When each new Night-Dress gives a new Disease.
 A constant Vapour o'er the Palace flies;
40 Strange Phantoms[6] rising as the Mists arise;
Dreadful, as Hermit's Dreams in haunted Shades,
Or bright as Visions of expiring Maids.
Now glaring Fiends and Snakes on rolling Spires,
Pale Spectres, gaping Tombs, and Purple Fires:
Now Lakes of liquid Gold, Elysian[7] Scenes,
And Crystal Domes, and Angels in Machines.[8]
 Unnumber'd Throngs on ev'ry side are seen
Of Bodies chang'd to various forms by Spleen.
Here living Teapots stand, one Arm held out,
50 One bent; the Handle this, and that the Spout:
A Pipkin[9] there like Homer's Tripod walks;
Here sighs a Jar, and there a Goose-pie[10] talks;
Men prove with Child, as pow'rful Fancy works,
And Maids turn'd Bottles, call aloud for Corks.
 Safe pass'd the Gnome thro' this fantastic Band,
A Branch of healing Spleenwort[11] in his hand.
Then thus address'd the Pow'r—Hail wayward Queen!
Who rule the Sex to Fifty from Fifteen,
Parent of Vapours and of Female Wit,
60 Who give th' Hysteric or Poetic Fit,
On various Tempers act by various ways,
Make some take Physic,[12] others scribble Plays;
Who cause the Proud their Visits to delay,
And sent the Godly in a Pett, to pray.
A Nymph there is, that all thy Pow'r disdains,
And thousands more in equal Mirth maintains.
But oh! if e'er thy Gnome could spoil a Grace,
Or raise a Pimple on a beauteous Face,
Like Citron-Waters[13] Matrons' Cheeks inflame,
70 Or change Complexions at a losing Game;
If e'er with airy Horns[14] I planted Heads,
Or rumpled Petticoats, or tumbled Beds,
Or caus'd Suspicion when no Soul was rude,
Or discompos'd the Head-dress of a Prude,
Or e'er to costive[15] Lap-Dog gave Disease,

[6]**Phantoms** hallucinations induced by the Spleen
[7]**Elysian** pleasant, blissful, from the Greek Elysium, home of the blessed after death
[8]**Machines** both a stage device and the role played by the angel in a play or poem
[9]**Pipkin** small earthenware boiler, here walking like the tripods in Pope's source, *Iliad* XVIII.439 ff.

[10]**Goose-pie** Pope says that "a lady of distinction imagined herself in this condition."
[11]**Spleenwort** an herb thought to alleviate the spleen, and a comic version of Aeneas' protective golden bough in *Aeneid* VI
[12]**Physic** medication
[13]**Citron-Waters** lemon-flavored brandy
[14]**airy Horns** imagined horns of a cuckold
[15]**costive** constipated

Which not the Tears of brightest Eyes could ease:
Hear me, and touch Belinda with Chagrin;
That single Act gives half the World the Spleen.''
  The Goddess with a discontented Air
80 Seems to reject him, tho' she grants his Pray'r
A wondrous Bag with both her Hands she binds,
Like that where once Ulysses held the Winds;[16]
There she collects the Force of Female Lungs,
Sighs, Sobs, and Passions, and the War of Tongues.
A Vial next she fills with fainting Fears,
Soft Sorrows, melting Griefs, and flowing Tears.
The Gnome rejoicing bears her Gifts away,
Spreads his black Wings, and slowly mounts to Day.
  Sunk in Thalestris'[17] Arms the Nymph he found,
90 Her Eyes dejected and her Hair unbound.
Full o'er their Heads the swelling Bag he rent,
And all the Furies issued at the Vent.
Belinda burns with more than mortal Ire,
And fierce Thalestris fans the rising Fire.
"O wretched Maid!" she spread her Hands, and cri'd,
(While Hampton's Echoes, "wretched Maid!" repli'd)
"Was it for this you took such constant Care
The Bodkin, Comb, and Essence[18] to prepare;
For this your Locks in Paper-Durance[19] bound,
100 For this with tort'ring Irons[20] wreath'd around?
For this with Fillets[21] strain'd your tender Head,
And bravely bore the double Loads of Lead?
Gods! shall the Ravisher display your Hair
While the Fops envy, and the Ladies stare![22]
Honour forbid! at whose unrival'd Shrine
Ease, Pleasure, Virtue, All, our Sex resign.
Methinks already I your Tears survey,
Already hear the horrid things they say,
Already see you a degraded Toast,
110 And all your Honour in a Whisper lost!
How shall I, then, your helpless Fame defend?
'Twill then be Infamy to seem your Friend!
And shall this Prize, th' inestimable Prize,
Expos'd thro' Crystal to the gazing Eyes,
And heighten'd by the Diamond's circling Rays,
On that Rapacious Hand for ever blaze?

---

[16]**Ulysses . . . Winds** given by Aeolus in *Odyssey* X.19 ff.
[17]**Thalestris** Queen of the Amazons, who were thought (1) to cut off the right breast in order to strengthen the right arm and improve their archery, and (2) to mangle one leg of infant male offspring. Contrast Thalestris' advice with Clarissa's in 5:9–34.
[18]**Essence** perfume

[19]**Paper-Durance** hair-curling paper, fastened with thin strips of lead
[20]**Irons** curling irons
[21]**Fillets** headbands
[22]**display . . . stare** Here, as in ll. 114–16, Thalestris fears that the Baron will mount the hair in a ring, show it as a sexual trophy, and sully Belinda's reputation (ll. 109–110).

Sooner shall Grass in Hyde-Park Circus[23] grow,
And Wits take Lodgings in the Sound of Bow;[24]
Sooner let Earth, Air, Sea, to Chaos fall,
120 Men, Monkies, Lap-dogs, Parrots, perish all!"
      She said; then raging to Sir Plume repairs,
And bids her Beau demand the precious Hairs:
(Sir Plume, of Amber Snuff-box justly vain,
And the nice Conduct of a clouded Cane)[25]
With earnest Eyes, and round unthinking Face,
He first the Snuff-box open'd, then the Case,
And thus broke out—"My Lord, why, what the Devil?
Z—ds![26] damn the Lock! 'fore Gad, you must be civil!
Plague on 't! 'tis past a Jest—nay prithee, Pox!
130 Give her the Hair"—he spoke, and rapp'd his Box.
"It grieves me much" (repli'd the Peer again)
"Who speaks so well shou'd ever speak in vain.
But by this Lock, this sacred Lock I swear,[27]
(Which never more shall join its parted Hair,
Which never more its Honours shall renew,
Clipp'd from the lovely Head where late it grew)
That while my Nostrils draw the vital Air,
This Hand, which won it, shall for ever wear."
He spoke, and speaking in proud Triumph spread
140 The long-contended Honours of her Head.[28]
      But Umbriel, hateful Gnome! forbears not so;
He breaks the Vial whence the Sorrows flow.
Then see! the Nymph in beauteous Grief appears,
Her Eyes half-languishing, half-drown'd in Tears;
On her heav'd Bosom hung her drooping Head,
Which, with a Sigh, she rais'd; and thus she said.
      "For ever curs'd be this detested Day,[29]
Which snatch'd my best, my fav'rite Curl away!
Happy! ah ten times happy, had I been,
150 If Hampton-Court these Eyes had never seen!
Yet am not I the first mistaken Maid,
By Love of Courts to num'rous Ills betray'd.
Oh had I rather un-admir'd remain'd
In some lone Isle, or distant Northern Land;
Where the gilt Chariot[30] never marks the Way,
Where none learn Ombre, none e'er taste Bohea![31]
There kept my Charms conceal'd from mortal Eye,
Like Roses that in Deserts bloom and die.

---

[23]**Hyde-Park Circus** The Ring of I:44, so busy that grass would not grow on it

[24]**in . . . Bow** within the sound of St. Mary-le-Bow Church, in the commercial City of London, as opposed to the "polite" area of St. James's

[25]**nice . . . Cane** skillful management of his fashionably veined cane

[26]**Z---ds!** zounds, from "God's wounds," a tepid blasphemy

[27]**Lock . . . swear** Pope cites Achilles' oath in the *Iliad* I.309–10.

[28]**Honours of her Head** her beautiful hair

[29]**For ever . . . Day** her version of Achilles' lament for his dead friend Patroclus in the *Iliad* XVIII.107 ff.

[30]**Chariot** coach

[31]**Bohea** an astringent tea

What mov'd my Mind with youthful Lords to roam?
160 O had I stay'd, and said my Pray'rs at home!
'Twas this, the Morning Omens seem'd to tell;
Thrice from my trembling hand the Patch-box fell;
The tott'ring China shook without a Wind,
Nay, Poll[32] sate mute, and Shock was most Unkind!
A Sylph too warn'd me of the Threats of Fate,
In mystic Visions, now believ'd too late!
See the poor Remnants of these slighted Hairs!
My hands shall rend what ev'n thy Rapine spares:
These, in two sable Ringlets taught to break,
170 Once gave new Beauties to the snowy Neck.
The Sister-Lock now sits uncouth, alone,
And in its Fellow's Fate foresees its own;
Uncurl'd it hangs, the fatal Shears demands;
And tempts once more thy sacrilegious Hands.
Oh hadst thou, Cruel! been content to seize
Hairs less in sight, or any Hairs but these!

[32] **Poll** her parrot, a fashionable pet, as in IV:120

CANTO V

She said: the pitying Audience melt in Tears,
But Fate and Jove had stopp'd the Baron's Ears.
In vain Thalestris with Reproach assails,
For who can move when fair Belinda fails?
Not half so fix'd, the Trojan cou'd remain,
While Anna begg'd and Dido rag'd in vain.[1]
Then grave Clarissa graceful wav'd her Fan;
Silence ensu'd, and thus the Nymph began.[2]
   "Say, why are Beauties prais'd and honour'd most,
10 The wise Man's Passion, and the vain Man's Toast?
Why deck'd with all that Land and Sea afford,
Why Angels call'd, and Angel-like ador'd?
Why round our Coaches crowd the white-glov'd Beaus,
Why bows the Side-box from its inmost Rows?
How vain are all these Glories, all our Pains,
Unless good Sense preserve what Beauty gains:
That Men may say, when we the Front-box grace,
Behold the first in Virtue, as in Face!
Oh! if to dance all Night, and dress all Day,
20 Charm'd the Small-pox, or chas'd old Age away;
Who would not scorn what Housewife's Cares produce,
Or who would learn one earthly Thing of Use?

[1] **Trojan . . . vain** In *Aeneid* IV.296–449, Anna and her sister Dido urge Aeneas to stay in Carthage. When he leaves, Dido kills herself.
[2] Clarissa's speech (ll. 9–34) was added in 1717; according to a note by Pope or his first editor, William Warburton, it was intended "to open more clearly the moral of the poem in a parody of the speech of Sarpedon to Glaucus in Homer," *Iliad* XII.27–52. Pope replaces Sarpedon's counsel of noble death with Clarissa's of productive life.

To patch, nay ogle, might become a Saint,
Nor could it sure be such a Sin to paint.
But since, alas! frail Beauty must decay,
Curl'd or uncurl'd, since Locks will turn to grey,
Since painted, or not painted, all shall fade,
And she who scorns a Man, must die a Maid;
What then remains, but well our Pow'r to use,
30   And keep good Humour still whate'er we lose?
And trust me, Dear! good Humour can prevail,
When Airs, and Flights, and Screams, and Scolding fail.
Beauties in vain their pretty Eyes may roll;
Charms strike the Sight, but Merit wins the Soul."
    So spoke the Dame, but no Applause ensu'd;
Belinda frown'd, Thalestris call'd her Prude.
"To Arms, to Arms!" the fierce Virago[3] cries,
And swift as Lightning to the Combat flies.
All side in Parties, and begin th' Attack;
40   Fans clap, Silks russle, and tough Whalebones crack;
Heroes' and Heroines' Shouts confus'dly rise,
And base, and treble Voices strike the Skies.
No common Weapons in their Hands are found,
Like Gods they fight, nor dread a mortal Wound.
    So when bold Homer makes the Gods engage,
And heav'nly Breasts with human Passions rage;
'Gainst Pallas, Mars; Latona, Hermes[4] Arms;
And all Olympus rings with loud Alarms.
Jove's Thunder roars, Heav'n trembles all around;
50   Blue Neptune storms, the bellowing Deeps resound;
Earth shakes her nodding Tow'rs, the Ground gives way;
And the pale Ghosts start at the Flash of Day!
    Triumphant Umbriel on a Sconce's Height
Clapp'd his glad Wings, and sat to view the Fight:
Propp'd on their Bodkin Spears, the Sprites survey
The growing Combat, or assist the Fray.
    While thro' the Press enrag'd Thalestris flies,
And scatters Deaths[5] around from both her Eyes,
A Beau and Witling perish'd in the Throng,
60   One di'd in Metaphor, and one in Song.
"O cruel Nymph! a living Death I bear,"
Cri'd Dapperwit, and sunk beside his Chair.
A mournful Glance Sir Fopling upwards cast,
"Those Eyes are made so killing"—was his last:
Thus on Meander's flow'ry Margin lies
Th' expiring Swan,[6] and as he sings he dies.

[3]**Virago** amazon; with negative connotations
[4]**Pallas . . . Hermes** Pallas=Athena, goddess of wisdom; Latona=mother of Apollo and Diana; Hermes=Mercury, messenger of the gods
[5]**Deaths** Here, as in several other places in this scene, "death" and "die" suggest the older meaning of sexual climax. The battle contrasts with the more civilized repression of the card game.
[6]**Meander's . . . Swan** The dying swan sings sweetly on the banks of the winding Meander River in Phrygia.

When bold Sir Plume had drawn Clarissa down,
Chloe stepp'd in, and kill'd him with a Frown;
She smil'd to see the doughty Hero slain,
70 But at her Smile, the Beau reviv'd again.
Now Jove suspends his golden Scales in Air,
Weighs the Men's Wits against the Lady's Hair;
The doubtful Beam long nods from side to side;
At length the Wits mount up, the Hairs subside.[7]
See fierce Belinda on the Baron flies,
With more than usual Lightning in her Eyes;
Nor fear'd the Chief th'unequal Fight to try,
Who sought no more than on his Foe to die.
But this bold Lord, with manly Strength indu'd,
80 She with one Finger and a Thumb subdu'd:
Just where the Breath of Life his Nostrils drew,
A charge of Snuff the wily Virgin threw;
The Gnomes direct, to ev'ry Atom just,
The pungent Grains of titillating Dust.
Sudden, with starting Tears each Eye o'erflows,
And the high Dome re-echoes to his Nose.[8]
Now meet thy Fate, incens'd Belinda cri'd,
And drew a deadly Bodkin from her Side.
(The same, his ancient Personage to deck,
90 Her great great Grandsire wore about his Neck
In three Seal-Rings; which after, melted down,
Form'd a vast Buckle for his Widow's Gown:
Her infant Grandame's Whistle next it grew,
The Bells she jingled, and the Whistle blew;
Then in a Bodkin grac'd her Mother's Hairs,
Which long she wore, and now Belinda wears.)[9]
"Boast not my Fall (he cri'd) insulting Foe!
Thou by some other shalt be laid as low.
Nor think, to die dejects my lofty Mind;
100 All that I dread, is leaving you behind!
Rather than so, ah let me still survive,
And burn in Cupid's Flames,—but burn alive."
"Restore the Lock!" she cries; and all around
"Restore the Lock!" the vaulted Roofs rebound.
Not fierce Othello in so loud a Strain
Roar'd for the Handkerchief that caus'd his Pain.
But see how oft Ambitious Aims are cross'd,
And Chiefs contend 'till all the Prize is lost!
The Lock, obtain'd with Guilt, and kept with Pain,
110 In ev'ry place is sought, but sought in vain:
With such a Prize no Mortal must be blest,
So Heav'n decrees! with Heav'n who can contest?

[7]**Wits . . . subside** The scale, a familiar epic device, shows that Belinda's lock is weightier than the beaus' brains.
[8]**high Dome . . . Nose** The snuff causes him to sneeze.
[9]**The same . . . wears** a comic version of Agamemnon's scepter in *Iliad* II.129 ff., and the descent of the helmet in *Iliad* X.312 ff.

Some thought it mounted to the Lunar Sphere,[10]
Since all things lost on Earth, are treasur'd there.
There Heroes' Wits are kept in pond'rous Vases,
And Beaus' in Snuff-boxes and Tweezer-Cases.
There broken Vows, and Death-bed Alms are found,
And Lovers' Hearts with Ends of Riband bound;
The Courtier's Promises, and Sick Man's Pray'rs,
120 The Smiles of Harlots, and the Tears of Heirs,
Cages for Gnats, and Chains to Yoak a Flea;
Dri'd Butterflies, and Tomes of Casuistry.[11]
But trust the Muse—she saw it upward rise,
Tho' mark'd by none but quick Poetic Eyes:
(So Rome's great Founder[12] to the Heav'ns withdrew,
To Proculus alone confess'd in view.)
A sudden Star, it shot thro' liquid[13] Air,
And drew behind a radiant Trail[14] of Hair.
Not Berenice's[15] Locks first rose so bright,
130 The Heav'ns bespangling with dishevell'd Light.
The Sylphs behold it kindling as it flies,
And pleas'd pursue its Progress thro' the Skies.
This the Beau-monde shall from the Mall survey,[16]
And hail with Music its propitious Ray.
This, the bless'd Lover shall for Venus take,
And send up Vows from Rosamonda's Lake.
This Partridge[17] soon shall view in cloudless Skies,
When next he looks thro' Galileo's Eyes;[18]
And hence th' Egregious Wizard shall foredoom
140 The Fate of Louis, and the Fall of Rome.
Then cease, bright Nymph! to mourn thy ravish'd Hair
Which adds new Glory to the shining Sphere!
Not all the Tresses that fair Head can boast
Shall draw such Envy as the Lock you lost.
For, after all the Murders of your Eye,
When, after Millions slain, your self shall die;
When those fair Suns shall set, as set they must,
And all those Tresses shall be laid in Dust;
This Lock,[19] the Muse shall consecrate to Fame,
150 And mid'st the Stars inscribe Belinda's Name!

1712, 1714, 1717

[10]**Lunar Sphere** In Ariosto's *Orlando Furioso* XXXIV.68 ff., Orlando's lost wits, together with other odds and ends, are found on the moon.
[11]**Casuistry** here, self-serving reasoning about ethical conduct
[12]**Founder** Romulus, whose apparent translation to heaven was witnessed only by the Roman senator Julius Proculus
[13]**liquid** clear
[14]**Trail** like a comet
[15]**Berenice** Her locks, offered to Aphrodite should Berenice's husband return safely from

the wars, disappear from the temple and become a constellation.
[16]**Beau-monde . . . survey** The people of fashion shall see it from their smart walk in St. James's Park, which also contained Rosamonda's Lake (l. 136), associated with mournful lovers.
[17]**Partridge** absurd astrologer who predicted events like the fall of the Pope, as in l. 140
[18]**Galileo's Eyes** telescope
[19]**This Lock** both Belinda's and Pope's poem which, unlike life, is the proper sphere of permanence

From Epistles to Several Persons, To Richard Boyle, Earl of Burlington: Of the Use of Riches

Timon's Villa[1]

At Timon's Villa let us pass a day,
100 Where all cry out, "What sums are thrown away!"
So proud, so grand, of that stupendous air,
Soft and Agreeable come never there.
Greatness, with Timon, dwells in such a draught
As brings all Brobdignag[2] before your thought.
To compass this, his building is a Town,
His pond an Ocean, his parterre a Down:[3]
Who but must laugh, the Master when he sees,
A puny insect, shiv'ring at a breeze!
Lo, what huge heaps of littleness around!
110 The whole, a labour'd Quarry above ground.
Two Cupids squirt before: a Lake behind
Improves the keenness of the Northern wind.
His Gardens next your admiration call,
On ev'ry side you look, behold the Wall!
No pleasing Intricacies intervene,
No artful wildness to perplex the scene;
Grove nods at grove, each Alley has a brother,[4]
And half the platform[5] just reflects the other.
The suff'ring eye inverted Nature sees,
120 Trees cut to Statues,[6] Statues thick as trees,
With here a Fountain, never to be play'd,
And there a Summer-house, that knows no shade;
Here Amphitrite[7] sails thro' myrtle bowers;
There Gladiators fight, or die, in flow'rs;
Un-water'd see the drooping sea-horse mourn,
And swallows roost in Nilus'[8] dusty Urn.

[1]The title of the poem's first edition was *An Epistle to the Right Honourable Earl of Burlington. Occasion'd by his Publishing Palladio's Designs of the Baths, Arches, Theatres, &c of Ancient Rome.* Burlington (1695–1753) was an amateur architect and a patron of English Palladianism. Pope shared Burlington's interest and was at the forefront of the English movement from the formal to the natural garden. The poem is in the tradition of the Horatian epistle, in which the poet respectfully but confidently writes to a distinguished aristocrat. Timon's Villa is a paradigm of the tasteless use of riches, which nature herself must repair. Pope's enemies wrongly claimed that this was an ungenerous attack upon Cannons, the grandiose estate of James Brydges, Duke of Chandos (1673–1744). The portrait probably is a composite.

[2]**Brobdignag** the land in Bk. II of Swift's *Gulliver's Travels* (1726), in which everything is twelve times the normal size
[3]**his parterre a Down** His ornamental arrangement of flower plots is as large as an open tract of upland
[4]**Grove . . . brother** an attack upon the formal garden, which already was antiquated
[5]**platform** a walk or terrace on top of a building or a wall
[6]**Trees . . . Statues** trees or hedges cut into the shapes of statues
[7]**Amphitrite** a sea nymph, Poseidon's wife and Triton's mother
[8]**Nilus** god of the Nile, whose urn should pour water

My Lord advances with majestic mien,
Smit with the mighty pleasure, to be seen:
But soft—by regular approach—not yet—
130 First thro' the length of yon hot Terrace sweat,
And when up ten steep slopes you've dragg'd your thighs,
Just at his Study-door he'll bless your eyes.
    His Study! with what Authors is it stor'd?
In Books, not Authors, curious is my Lord;
To all their dated Backs[9] he turns you round,
These Aldus printed, those Du Suëil[10] has bound.
Lo some are Vellum, and the rest as good
For all his Lordship knows, but they are Wood.
For Locke or Milton 'tis in vain to look,
140 These shelves admit not any modern book.
    And now the Chapel's silver bell you hear,
That summons you to all the Pride of Pray'r.
Light quirks of Music, broken and uneven,
Make the soul dance upon a Jig to Heaven.
On painted Ceilings you devoutly stare,
Where sprawl the Saints of Verrio or Laguerre,[11]
On gilded clouds in fair expansion lie,
And bring all Paradise before your eye.
To rest, the Cushion and soft Dean invite,
150 Who never mentions Hell to ears polite.
    But hark! the chiming Clocks to dinner call;
A hundred footsteps scrape[12] the marble Hall:
The rich Buffet well-colour'd Serpents grace,
And gaping Tritons spew to wash your face.
Is this a dinner? this a Genial[13] room?
No, 'tis a Temple, and a Hecatomb.[14]
A solemn Sacrifice, perform'd in state,
You drink by measure, and to minutes eat.
So quick retires each flying course, you'd swear
160 Sancho's dread Doctor and his Wand[15] were there.
Between each Act the trembling salvers ring,
From soup to sweet-wine, and God bless the King.[16]
In plenty starving, tantaliz'd in state,
And complaisantly help'd to all I hate,

[9]**dated Backs**   the dates of rare editions stamped in gold on their spines
[10]**Aldus . . . Du Suëil**   Aldus Manutius (1450–1515), distinguished Venetian printer of Aldine Press books; Augustin Desuil (1673–1746), an eminent Paris bookbinder. Timon collects things, not thoughts.
[11]**Verrio . . . Laguerre**   fashionable foreign artists, Antonio Verrio (1639–1707) at, among other places, Windsor Castle and Hampton Court; Louis Laguerre (1663–1721) at the Duke of Marlborough's seat, Blenheim
[12]**scrape**   because the floor is so highly polished.

Pope again emphasizes the villa's lack of concern for humanity.
[13]**Genial**   cheerful or comforting, but also in the Latin sense of what is appropriate to a place—as a gaping Triton is not in a dining hall
[14]**Hecatomb**   an ancient Greek sacrifice of 100 or more cattle
[15]**Sancho's . . . Wand**   In *Don Quixote* (1605–15), II.47, a doctor orders food removed before the eager Sancho Panza can eat it.
[16]**God . . . King**   the final toast with port at the end of the meal

Treated, caress'd, and tir'd, I take my leave,
Sick of his civil Pride from Morn to Eve;
I curse such lavish cost, and little skill,
And swear no Day was ever past so ill.
    Yet hence the Poor are cloath'd, the Hungry fed;[17]
170 Health to himself, and to his Infants bread
The Lab'rer bears: What his hard Heart denies,
His charitable Vanity supplies.
    Another age shall see the golden Ear[18]
Imbrown the Slope, and nod on the Parterre,
Deep Harvests bury all his pride has plann'd,
And laughing Ceres[19] re-assume the land.
    Who then shall grace, or who improve the Soil?
Who plants like Bathurst, or who builds like Boyle.[20]
'Tis Use alone that sanctifies Expence,
180 And Splendour borrows all her rays from Sense.

1731

171. 169 From here to the end of the passage, Pope asserts the triumph of nature over disruptive art.
18golden Ear of wheat
19Ceres the waving field, personified as the Roman goddess of agriculture happy in her triumph

20Bathurst . . . Boyle Allen, Lord Bathurst (1684–1775), to whom another epistle was addressed (1733), was a landscape architect; Boyle is the Earl of Burlington. Each man has the "Sense" and understanding of his natural environment that Timon lacks.

An Epistle from Mr. Pope, to Dr. Arbuthnot[1]

P. Shut, shut the door, good John![2] fatigu'd I said,
Tie up the knocker, say I'm sick, I'm dead,
The Dog-star[3] rages! nay 'tis past a doubt,
All Bedlam, or Parnassus,[4] is let out:
Fire in each eye, and Papers in each hand,
They rave, recite, and madden round the land.
    What Walls can guard me, or what Shades can hide?
They pierce my Thickets, thro' my Grot[5] they glide,

1Dr. John Arbuthnot (1667–1735), a literary colleague of Swift, Pope, and Gay in the Scriblerus Club, was physician to Queen Anne in the previous reign. Though one of Pope's dearest friends, he also had a fine public reputation, and thus served as an able "adversarius"; by implication, if this man is persuaded to approve of Pope's satiric mode, the impartial reader should do so as well. The poem uses and plays upon two Horatian traditions—the epistle to a distinguished correspondent, and the satiric *apologia*, here made necessary because of written and spoken attacks on Pope, his deformity, and his family and friends by many critics, chiefly John, Lord Hervey, and Lady Mary Wortley Montagu, each a representative of the court of George II and Sir Robert Walpole. The poem was prefaced by an Advertisement outlining Pope's reasons for writing this "Bill of Complaint."
2John John Serle, Pope's gardener and servant
3Dog-star The constellation Sirius appears in August and was thought by the Romans to induce madness. Roman poetry recitals also were held in August.
4Bedlam . . . Parnassus the madhouse of St. Mary of Bethlehem; the Greek mountain sacred to Apollo and home of the muses, here a symbol of poetry
5Grot Pope built a grotto that went under the London road and allowed a view of his garden at one end and the River Thames at the other.

By land, by water, they renew the charge,
10   They stop the Chariot, and they board the Barge.[6]
No place is sacred, not the Church is free,
Ev'n Sunday shines no Sabbath-day to me:
Then from the Mint[7] walks forth the Man of Rhyme,
Happy! to catch me, just at Dinner-time.
    Is there a Parson, much be-mus'd in Beer,
A maudlin Poetess, a rhyming Peer,
A Clerk, foredoom'd his Father's soul to cross,
Who pens a Stanza when he should engross?[8]
Is there, who lock'd from Ink and Paper, scrawls
20   With desp'rate Charcoal round his darken'd walls?
All fly to Twit'nam[9] and in humble strain
Apply to me, to keep them mad or vain.
Arthur,[10] whose giddy Son neglects the Laws,
Imputes to me and my damn'd works the cause:
Poor Cornus[11] sees his frantic Wife elope,
And curses Wit, and Poetry, and Pope.
    Friend to my Life, (which did not you prolong,
The World had wanted many an idle Song)
What Drop or Nostrum[12] can this Plague remove?
30   Or which must end me, a Fool's Wrath or Love?
A dire Dilemma! either way I'm sped,[13]
If Foes, they write, if Friends, they read me dead.
Seiz'd and tied down to judge, how wretched I!
Who can't be silent, and who will not lie;
To laugh, were want of Goodness and of Grace,
And to be grave, exceeds all Pow'r of Face.
I sit with sad Civility, I read
With honest anguish, and an aching head;
And drop at last, but in unwilling ears,
40   This saving counsel, "Keep your Piece nine years."[14]
    Nine years! cries he, who high in Drury lane[15]
Lull'd by soft Zephyrs thro' the broken Pane,
Rhymes e're he wakes, and prints before Term[16] ends,
Oblig'd by hunger and Request of friends:[17]
"The Piece you think is incorrect: why take it,
I'm all submission, what you'd have it, make it."

[6] l. 10 They invade his coach or barge if he should travel by water.
[7] **Sunday . . . Mint** Debtors were immune from arrest on Sunday, and always were safe in an area of Southwark, in south London, called the Mint.
[8] **engross** to copy a document in a large hand
[9] **Twit'nam** Twickenham, Pope's home on the Thames, about 12 miles from London
[10] **Arthur** Arthur Moore (1660–1730), member of Parliament, whose son James Moore Smythe (1702–1734) plagiarized some of Pope's lines and attacked others. See also ll. 49, 98, 373, 385.

[11] **Cornus** a cuckold, from the Latin *cornu,* horn
[12] **Drop . . . Nostrum** medicine in drops, and patent medicine, the latter often implying quackery
[13] **sped** killed
[14] l. 40 Horace's advice in *Ars poetica,* 386–89
[15] **high . . . Lane** in a garret in the disreputable street associated with the theater
[16] **Term** the legal and publishing terms coincided
[17] **Request of friends** a traditional, and spurious, reason for unknowns to publish

      Three things another's modest wishes bound,
My Friendship, and a Prologue, and ten Pound.
      Pitholeon[18] sends to me: "You know his Grace,
50   I want a Patron; ask him for a Place."[19]
Pitholeon libell'd me—"but here's a Letter
Informs you Sir, 'twas when he knew no better.
Dare you refuse him? Curll[20] invites to dine,
He'll write a Journal, or he'll turn Divine."[21]
      Bless me! a Packet—"'Tis a stranger sues,
A Virgin Tragedy, an Orphan Muse."
If I dislike it, "Furies, death and rage!"
If I approve, "Commend it to the Stage."
There (thank my Stars) my whole Commission ends,
60   The Play'rs and I are, luckily, no friends.
Fir'd that the House reject him, "'Sdeath I'll print it
And shame the Fools—your Int'rest, Sir, with Lintot."[22]
Lintot, dull rogue! will think your price too much.
"Not Sir, if you revise it, and retouch."
All my demurs but double his attacks,
At last he whispers "Do, and we go snacks."[23]
Glad of a quarrel, straight I clap the door,
Sir, let me see your works and you no more.
      'Tis sung, when Midas' Ears began to spring,
70   (Midas, a sacred Person and a King)[24]
His very Minister who spied them first,
(Some say his Queen) was forc'd to speak, or burst.
And is not mine, my Friend, a sorer case.
When ev'ry Coxcomb perks them in my face?
      A. "Good friend forbear! you deal in dang'rous things,
I'd never name Queens, Ministers, or Kings;
Keep close to Ears, and those let Asses prick,
Tis nothing"—P. Nothing? if they bite and kick?
Out with it, Dunciad![25] let the secret pass,
80   That Secret to each Fool, that he's an Ass:
The truth once told, (and wherefore should we lie?)
The Queen of Midas slept, and so may I.
      You think this cruel? take it for a rule,
No creature smarts so little as a Fool.

---

[18] **Pitholeon** "a foolish poet at Rhodes who pretended much to Greek" (Pope's note)
[19] **You know ... Place** A duke ("His Grace") could secure a patronage position, usually in the government; see also l. 238.
[20] **Curll** Edmund Curll (1675–1747), unethical publisher who often printed forged or unauthorized correspondence. See also ll. 113, 380.
[21] **write ... Divine** attack Pope in the newspapers or religious tracts
[22] **Lintot** Bernard Lintot (1675–1736), one of Pope's publishers

[23] **snacks** shares
[24] l. 70 an attack on George II and by implication on his prime minister, Sir Robert Walpole. King Midas of Phrygia receives his asses' ears for wrongly judging that Pan was a better poet than Apollo. He hides his shame under his hat, but tells his wife (or barber) who, then sleepless, whispers the secret to the reeds, which whisper it to the wind. Pope also must tell his "secret."
[25] **Dunciad** the title of Pope's poem (1728) attacking modern poets

Let Peals of Laughter, Codrus![26] round thee break,
Thou unconcern'd canst hear the mighty Crack.
Pit, Box and Gall'ry[27] in convulsions hurl'd,
Thou stand'st unshook amidst a bursting World.
Who shames a Scribbler? break one cobweb thro',
90   He spins the slight, self-pleasing thread anew;
Destroy his Fib, or Sophistry; in vain,
The Creature's at his dirty work again;
Thron'd in the Center of his thin designs;
Proud of a vast Extent of flimsy lines.
Whom have I hurt? has Poet yet, or Peer,
Lost the arch'd eye-brow, or Parnassian sneer?
And has not Colly still his Lord,[28] and Whore?
His Butchers Henley, his Free-masons Moor?[29]
Does not one Table Bavius[30] still admit?
100   Still to one Bishop Philips[31] seem a Wit?
Still Sappho[32]—A. "Hold! for God-sake—you'll offend:
No Names—be calm—learn Prudence of a Friend:
I too could write, and I am twice as tall,[33]
But Foes like these!"—P. One Flatt'rer's worse than all;
Of all mad Creatures, if the Learn'd are right,
It is the Slaver[34] kills, and not the Bite.
A Fool quite angry is quite innocent;
Alas! 'tis ten times worse when they repent.

One dedicates, in high Heroic prose,
110   And ridicules beyond a hundred foes;
One from all Grubstreet[35] will my fame defend,
And, more abusive, calls himself my friend.
This prints my Letters, that expects a Bribe,
And others roar aloud, "Subscribe, subscribe."[36]
There are, who to my Person pay their court,
I cough like Horace, and tho' lean, am short,
Ammon's[37] great Son one shoulder had too high,
Such Ovid's[38] nose, and "Sir! you have an Eye—"

---

[26] **Codrus** name for a bad poet in Virgil (70–19 B.C.) and Juvenal (c. 55–127)

[27] **Pit . . . Gall'ry** the orchestra (or stalls), boxes, and upper balcony of the theater. Pope cites Horace, *Odes* III.3, 7–9 as his source for ll. 86–88.

[28] **Colly . . . Lord** Colley Cibber (1671–1757), actor, dramatist, and poet laureate from 1730, one of Pope's pet hates and an emblem of tasteless royal patronage; (see also l. 373); **Lord** patron

[29] **Henley . . . Moor** John "Orator" Henley (1692–1756), London preacher and teacher of oratory, once praised the butcher's trade; James Moore Smythe was a Freemason

[30] **Bavius** the type of stupid poet and critic who attacked Horace and Virgil. See also l. 250.

[31] **Philips** Ambrose Philips (1670–1749),

minor poet, especially of pastorals, and secretary to the bishop of Armagh, Dr. Hugh Boulter

[32] **Sappho** Lady Mary Wortley Montagu, one of Pope's detractors

[33] **tall** Pope measured about four feet six inches tall.

[34] **Slaver** both saliva and fawning

[35] **Grubstreet** often the London home of hungry and inept hack writers

[36] **subscribe** Prepublication subscriptions were sold for books that sometimes did not appear.

[37] **Ammon** Alexander the Great who, like Pope, was hunchbacked, claimed descent from Jupiter Ammon.

[38] **Ovid** Roman poet (43–18 B.C.) whose works include the *Metamorphoses*

Go on, obliging Creatures, make me see
120   All that disgrac'd my Betters, met in me:
Say for my comfort, languishing in bed,
"Just so immortal Maro[39] held his head:"
And when I die, be sure you let me know
Great Homer died three thousand years ago.

Why did I write? what sin to me unknown
Dipp'd me in Ink, my Parents', or my own?
As yet a Child, nor yet a Fool to Fame,
I lisp'd in Numbers, for the Numbers came.
I left no Calling for this idle trade,
130   No Duty broke, no Father disobey'd.
The Muse but serv'd to ease some Friend, not Wife,
To help me thro' this long Disease, my Life,
To second, ARBUTHNOT! thy Art and Care,
And teach, the Being you preserv'd, to bear.

But why then publish? Granville[40] the polite,
And knowing Walsh,[41] would tell me I could write;
Well-natur'd Garth[42] inflam'd with early praise,
And Congreve lov'd, and Swift[43] endur'd my Lays;
The Courtly Talbot, Somers, Sheffield[44] read,
140   Ev'n mitred Rochester[45] would nod the head,
And St. John's[46] self (great Dryden's friends before)
With open arms receiv'd one Poet more.
Happy my Studies, when by these approv'd!
Happier their Author, when by these belov'd!
From these the world will judge of Men and Books,
Not from the Burnets, Oldmixons, and Cooks.[47]
Soft were my Numbers, who could take offence
While pure Description held the place of Sense?[48]

---

[39] **Maro** Virgil (Publius Virgilius Maro)

[40] **Granville** George Granville, Baron Lansdowne (1666–1735), to whom Pope dedicated *Windsor Forest* (1713). All of the following (ll. 135-41) were early encouragers of Pope.

[41] **Walsh** William Walsh (1663–1708)

[42] **Garth** Sir Samuel Garth (1661–1719), physician and minor poet

[43] **Congreve . . . Swift** William Congreve (1670–1729), the dramatist; Jonathan Swift (1667–1745)

[44] **Talbot . . . Sheffield** Charles Talbot, Duke of Shrewsbury (1660–1718), statesman under William III, Queen Anne, and George I; John, Baron Somers (1651–1716), William III's lord chancellor, to whom Swift dedicated *A Tale of a Tub*; John Sheffield, Duke of Buckingham and Normanby (1648–1721), statesman, poet, and patron of Dryden. Pope edited Sheffield's works.

[45] **mitred Rochester** Francis Atterbury (1662–1732), bishop of Rochester, a writer of distinction, friend of Swift and Pope, and a convicted Jacobite—a supporter of James II and his son—who was banished in 1723

[46] **St. John's** Henry St. John, Viscount Bolingbroke (1678–1751), first minister of Queen Anne and political theorist, was impeached in 1714 and had his name struck from the roll of peers. He fled to France but was pardoned in 1723; he returned to England, becoming a leader of the opposition to Sir Robert Walpole.

[47] **Burnets . . . Cooks** Thomas Burnet (1694–1753), John Oldmixon (1673–1742), and Thomas Cooke (1703–1756) were minor writers who criticized Pope. These and the following authors contrast with Pope's distinguished friends, above.

[48] **Soft . . . Sense** alluding to Pope's early poems, including his *Pastorals* (1709) and *Windsor Forest* (1713)

Like gentle Fanny's[49] was my flow'ry Theme,
150   A painted Mistress, or a purling Stream.
Yet then did Gildon[50] draw his venal quill;
I wish'd the man a dinner, and sat still:
Yet then did Dennis[51] rave in furious fret;
I never answer'd, I was not in debt:
If want provok'd, or madness made them print,
I wag'd no war with Bedlam or the Mint.
    Did some more sober Critic come abroad?
If wrong, I smil'd; if right, I kiss'd the rod.
Pains, reading, study, are their just pretence,
160   And all they want is spirit, taste, and sense.
Commas and points[52] they set exactly right,
And 'twere a sin to rob them of their Mite.
Yet ne'r one sprig of Laurel grac'd these ribalds,[53]
From slashing Bentley down to piddling Tibalds.[54]
Each Wight[55] who reads not, and but scans and spells,
Each Word-catcher that lives on syllables,
Ev'n such small Critics some regard may claim,
Preserv'd in Milton's or in Shakespeare's name.
Pretty! in Amber[56] to observe the forms
170   Of hairs, or straws, or dirt, or grubs, or worms;
The things, we know, are neither rich nor rare,
But wonder how the Devil they got there?
    Were others angry? I excus'd them too;
Well might they rage; I gave them but their due.
A man's true merit 'tis not hard to find,
But each man's secret standard in his mind,
That Casting-weight[57] Pride adds to Emptiness,
This, who can gratify? for who can guess?
The Bard[58] whom pilf'red Pastorals renown,
180   Who turns a Persian Tale for half a crown,[59]
Just writes to make his barrenness appear,
And strains from hard-bound brains eight lines a-year:
He, who still wanting tho' he lives on theft,
Steals much, spends little, yet has nothing left:
And he, who now to sense, now nonsense leaning,

[49] **Fanny** a vain, inept poet in Horace's *Satires* I.iv.21 and I.x.80, and also John, Baron Hervey, attacked as Sporus below; also slang for the female genitals
[50] **Gildon** Charles Gildon (1665–1724), critic and controversialist, perhaps paid to attack Pope in print
[51] **Dennis** John Dennis (1657–1734), dramatist and harsh critic who abused Pope in print. See also ll. 270, 370.
[52] **points** periods
[53] **Ne'er . . . ribalds** The bay-leaf crown of the true poet is not given to this rabble.
[54] **Bentley . . . Tibalds** Richard Bentley (1662–1742), classical scholar who also edited *Paradise Lost*, and used brackets ("slashing") for passages he thought Milton did not write; Lewis Theobald (1688–1744), who criticized Pope's edition of Shakespeare (1725) while, Pope thought, being pedantic in his own. Theobald was the king of the Dunces in the first version of the *Dunciad*. See also l. 372.
[55] **Wight** creature (derogatory)
[56] **Amber** like those dead items in l. 170, preserved as curiosities
[57] **Casting-weight** on a scale
[58] **Bard** Ambrose Philips. See note 31 above.
[59] **half a crown** often a prostitute's fee

Means not, but blunders round about a meaning:
And he, whose Fustian's[60] so sublimely bad,
It is not Poetry, but Prose run mad:
All these, my modest Satire bade translate,[61]
190 And own'd, that nine such Poets made a Tate.[62]
How did they fume, and stamp, and roar, and chafe?
And swear, not Addison himself was safe.
    Peace to all such! but were there One[63] whose fires
True Genius kindles, and fair Flame inspires,
Blest with each Talent and each Art to please,
And born to write, converse, and live with ease:
Shou'd such a man, too fond to rule alone,
Bear, like the Turk,[64] no brother near the throne,
View him with scornful, yet with jealous eyes,
200 And hate for Arts that caus'd himself to rise;
Damn with faint praise, assent with civil leer,
And without sneering, teach the rest to sneer;
Willing to wound, and yet afraid to strike,
Just hint a fault, and hesitate dislike;
Alike reserv'd to blame, or to commend,
A tim'rous foe, and a suspicious friend,
Dreading ev'n fools, by Flatterers besieg'd,
And so obliging that he ne'er oblig'd;
Like Cato, give his little Senate laws,
210 And sit attentive to his own applause;
While Wits and Templars[65] ev'ry sentence raise,
And wonder with a foolish face of praise.
Who but must laugh, if such a man there be?
Who would not weep, if Atticus[66] were he!
    What tho' my Name stood rubric[67] on the walls?
Or plaister'd posts, with Claps[68] in capitals?
Or smoaking forth, a hundred Hawkers load,
On Wings of Winds came flying all abroad?
I sought no homage from the Race that write;
220 I kept, like Asian Monarchs, from their sight:
Poems I heeded (now be-rhym'd so long)
No more than Thou, great GEORGE! a Birth-day Song.[69]
I ne'r with Wits or Witlings pass'd my days,
To spread about the Itch of Verse and Praise;

[60]**Fustian** bombast, claptrap
[61]**translate** both become hack interpreters and transform themselves, as in l.190
[62]**Tate** Nahum Tate (1652–1715), minor poet and dramatist, poet laureate from 1692
[63]**One** Joseph Addison (1672–1719), poet, writer, with Steele, of *The Spectator*, and author of the tragedy *Cato* (1713; see l. 209). In 1715 he apparently attempted to discredit Pope's *Iliad* and evoked an early, then unpublished, version of this portrait. Addison relented.

[64]**Turk** Turkish rulers often executed close relatives and potential rivals.
[65]**Templars** lawyers and law students in the Inner or Middle Temples, their residence halls
[66]**Atticus** Pomponeius Atticus (109–32 B.C.), philosopher, man of letters, friend of Cicero, and exquisite prose stylist
[67]**rubric** in red letters
[68]**Claps** posters
[69]**Birth-day Song** the poet laureate's annual birthday ode for the king

Nor like a Puppy daggled[70] thro' the Town,
To fetch and carry Sing-song up and down;
Nor at Rehearsals sweat, and mouth'd, and cried,
With Handkerchief and Orange[71] at my side:
But sick of Fops, and Poetry, and Prate,
230   To Bufo[72] left the whole Castalian State.[73]
          Proud, as Apollo on his forked hill,
Sat full-blown Bufo, puff'd by ev'ry quill;
Fed with soft Dedication all day long,
Horace and he went hand in hand in song.
His Library, (where Busts of Poets dead
And a true Pindar[74] stood without a head)
Receiv'd of Wits an undistinguish'd race,
Who first his Judgment ask'd, and then a Place:
Much they extoll'd his Pictures, much his Seat,[75]
240   And flatter'd ev'ry day, and some days eat:
Till grown more frugal in his riper days,
He paid some Bards with Port, and some with Praise,
To some a dry Rehearsal[76] was assign'd,
And others (harder still) he paid in kind.[77]
Dryden alone (what wonder?) came not nigh,
Dryden alone escap'd this judging eye:
But still the Great have kindness in reserve,
He help'd to bury whom he help'd to starve.[78]
          May some choice Patron bless each gray goose quill!
250   May ev'ry Bavius have his Bufo still!
So, when a Statesman wants a Day's defence,
Or Envy holds a whole Week's war with Sense,
Or simple Pride for Flatt'ry makes demands;
May Dunce by Dunce be whistled off my hands!
Blest be the Great! for those they take away,
And those they left me—For they left me GAY,[79]
Left me to see neglected Genius bloom,
Neglected die! and tell it on his Tomb;
Of all thy blameless Life the sole Return
260   My Verse, and QUEENSB'RY weeping o'er thy Urn!
Oh let me live my own! and die so too!
("To live and die is all I have to do:")[80]
Maintain a Poet's Dignity and Ease,

---

[70] **daggled** splashed through mud
[71] **Orange** a refreshment sold in the theaters, normally by "orange girls"
[72] **Bufo** Latin for "toad"; a bad patron
[73] **Castalian State** Castalia is a spring sacred to the Muses beneath the peaks ("forked hill," l. 231) of Mt. Parnassus; hence, the world of poetry.
[74] **Pindar** Greek poet of lofty odes, 518–438 B.C.
[75] **Seat** country estate
[76] **dry Rehearsal** poetry or performance pre-sented without wine
[77] **in kind** by reading his own poems
[78] **starve** Dryden died poor but was given an elegant funeral.
[79] **GAY** John Gay (1685–1732), poet, author of *The Beggar's Opera* (1728), and a valued member of the Scriblerus Club, was protected by the Duke of Queensberry (1689–1778) and his wife (l. 260).
[80] l. 262 quoted from John Denham's *Of Prudence* (l. 94)

And see what friends, and read what books I please.
Above a Patron, tho' I condescend
Sometimes to call a Minister my Friend:
I was not born for Courts or great Affairs,
I pay my Debts, believe, and say my Pray'rs,
Can sleep without a Poem in my head,
270 Nor know, if Dennis be alive or dead.
    Why am I ask'd, what next shall see the light?
Heav'ns! was I born for nothing but to write?
Has Life no Joys for me? or (to be grave)
Have I no Friend to serve, no Soul to save?
"I found him close with Swift"—"Indeed? no doubt"
(Cries prating Balbus[81]) "something will come out."
'Tis all in vain, deny it as I will.
"No, such a Genius never can lie still,"
And then for mine obligingly mistakes
280 The first Lampoon Sir Will. or Bubo[82] makes.
Poor guiltless I! and can I chuse but smile,
When ev'ry Coxcomb knows me by my Style?
    Curst be the Verse, how well soe'er it flow,
That tends to make one worthy Man my foe,
Give Virtue scandal, Innocence a fear,
Or from the soft-ey'd Virgin steal a tear!
But he, who hurts a harmless neighbour's peace,
Insults fall'n Worth, or Beauty in distress,
Who loves a Lie, lame slander helps about,
290 Who writes a Libel, or who copies out:
That Fop whose pride affects a Patron's name,
Yet absent, wounds an Author's honest fame:
Who can your Merit selfishly approve,
And show the Sense of it, without the Love;
Who has the Vanity to call you Friend,
Yet wants the Honour injur'd to defend;
Who tells whate'er you think, whate'er you say,
And, if he lie not, must at least betray:
Who to the Dean and silver Bell can swear,
300 And sees at Cannons what was never there:[83]
Who reads but with a Lust to mis-apply,
Make Satire a Lampoon, and Fiction, Lie.
A Lash like mine no honest man shall dread,
But all such babbling blockheads in his stead.
    Let Sporus[84] tremble—A. "What? that Thing of silk,

[81] **Balbus** Latin for "stutterer"
[82] **Sir Will. or Bubo** Sir William Yonge (d. 1755), member of Parliament, ally of Walpole, and a blatherer. *Bubo* is Latin for "owl," a symbol of stupidity, and suggests George Bubb Dodington (1691-1762), a wealthy Whig patron.
[83] **Dean . . . there** charges that Pope's *Epistle to Burlington* (1731) had attacked the taste of

the Duke of Chandos's house and gardens at his estate, Cannons
[84] **Sporus** historically, the castrated boy whom Nero "married"; here, John, Baron Hervey, close confidant of Walpole and Queen Caroline, and a bisexual whom Pope treats as an emblem of Walpole's court and a diabolical threat both to the nation and to himself

Sporus, that mere white Curd of Ass's milk?[85]
Satire or Sense alas! can Sporus feel?
Who breaks a Butterfly upon a Wheel?''[86]
P. Yet let me flap this Bug with gilded wings,
310   This painted[87] Child of Dirt that stinks and stings;
Whose Buzz the Witty and the Fair annoys.
Yet Wit ne'er tastes, and Beauty ne'er enjoys,
So well-bred Spaniels civilly delight
In mumbling of the Game they dare not bite.
Eternal Smiles his Emptiness[88] betray,
As shallow streams run dimpling all the way.
Whether in florid Impotence he speaks,
And, as the Prompter breathes, the Puppet squeaks;[89]
Or at the ear of Eve,[90] familiar Toad,
320   Half Froth, half Venom, spits himself abroad,
In Puns, or Politics, or Tales, or Lies,
Or Spite, or Smut, or Rhymes, or Blasphemies.
His Wit all see-saw between that and this,
Now high, now low, now Master up, now Miss,
And he himself, one vile Antithesis.[91]
Amphibious Thing! that acting either Part,
The trifling Head, or the corrupted Heart!
Fop at the Toilet, Flatt'rer at the Board,
Now trips a Lady, and now struts a Lord.
330   Eve's Tempter thus the Rabbins[92] have express'd,
A Cherub's face, a Reptile all the rest;
Beauty that shocks you, Parts that none will trust,
Wit that can creep, and Pride that licks the dust.
   Not Fortune's Worshipper, nor Fashion's Fool,
Not Lucre's Madman, nor Ambition's Tool,
Not proud, nor servile, be one Poet's praise
That, if he pleas'd, he pleas'd by manly ways;
That Flatt'ry, ev'n to Kings, he held a shame,
And thought a Lie in Verse or Prose the same:
340   That not in Fancy's Maze[93] he wander'd long,
But stoop'd[94] to Truth, and moraliz'd his song:
That not for Fame, but Virtue's better end,
He stood the furious Foe, the timid Friend,
The damning Critic, half-approving Wit,
The Coxcomb hit, or fearing to be hit;
Laugh'd at the loss of Friends he never had,

---

[85] **Ass's milk** food for invalids and the frail
[86] **Wheel** the torture wheel or rack on which a prisoner was stretched taut and either beaten to death or disjointed
[87] **painted** Lord Hervey's make-up
[88] **Emptiness** Lord Hervey's teeth were falling out.
[89] l. 318 Walpole pulls Lord Hervey's strings and speaks through him.

[90] **Eve** Lord Hervey is at Queen Caroline's ear as Satan was at the sleeping Eve's ear in *Paradise Lost* IV.800.
[91] **Antithesis** Here as elsewhere, Pope alludes to Lord Hervey's bisexuality, in contrast to l. 337 and Pope's own "manly ways."
[92] **Rabbins** rabbis
[93] **Fancy's Maze** as in ll. 147–50
[94] **stoop'd** like a hawk swooping on its prey

The dull, the proud, the wicked, and the mad;
The distant Threats of Vengeance on his head,
The Blow unfelt, the Tear he never shed;[95]
350 The Tale reviv'd, the Lie so oft o'erthrown;
Th' imputed Trash[96] and Dullness not his own;
The Morals blacken'd when the Writings 'scape;
The libel'd Person, and the pictur'd Shape;[97]
Abuse on all he lov'd,[98] or lov'd him, spread,
A Friend in Exile,[99] or a Father, dead;
The Whisper[100] that to Greatness still too near,
Perhaps, yet vibrates on his SOVEREIGN'S Ear—
Welcome for thee, fair Virtue! all the past:
For thee, fair Virtue! welcome ev'n the last!
360   A. "But why insult the Poor, affront the Great?"
P. A Knave's a Knave, to me, in ev'ry State,
Alike my scorn, if he succeed or fail,
Sporus at Court, or Japhet[101] in a Jail,
A hireling Scribbler, or a hireling Peer,
Knight of the Post corrupt, or of the Shire,[102]
If on a Pillory, or near a Throne,
He gains his Prince's Ear, or lose his own.[103]
    Yet soft by Nature, more a Dupe than Wit,
Sappho can tell you how this Man was bit:[104]
370 This dreaded Sat'rist Dennis[105] will confess
Foe to his Pride, but Friend to his Distress:
So humble, he has knock'd at Tibald's door,
Has drunk with Cibber, nay has rhym'd for Moor.
Full ten years slander'd, did he once reply?
Three thousand Suns went down on Welsted's[106] Lie:
To please a Mistress, One aspers'd his life;
He lash'd him not, but let her be his Wife:
Let Budgel[107] charge low Grubstreet on his quill,
And write whate'er he pleas'd, except his Will;
380 Let the Two Curlls[108] of Town and Court, abuse
His Father, Mother, Body, Soul, and Muse.
Yet why? that Father held it for a rule

[95] **Blow ... shed** alluding to the rumor that Pope had been whipped for his satires
[96] **Trash** bad works published by Curll
[97] **Shape** of Pope as a hunchbacked ape
[98] **all he lov'd** his family and friends
[99] **Friend in Exile** Bishop Atterbury. See l. 140.
[100] **Whisper** by Lord Hervey
[101] **Japhet** Japhet Crook (1662–1734), a forger and fraud punished with exposure on the pillory, loss of ears, and a slit nose
[102] **Knight ... Shire** a professional false witness; a member of Parliament for his country
[103] **Pillory ... own** These punishments for Japhet are, by implication, deserved by Lord Hervey.

[104] **Sappho ... bit** Lady Mary Wortley Montagu can tell you how she fooled him.
[105] **Dennis** Pope helped to organize a benefit for Dennis.
[106] **Welsted** Leonard Welsted (1698–1747), minor writer who libelled Pope and his friends. See also l. 354.
[107] **Budgel** Eustace Budgell (1686–1737), minor writer who claimed that Pope abused him in *The Grub-Street Journal.* Budgell was thought by some to have benefitted himself by forging the will of the controversial deist Dr. Matthew Tindal (1657–1733).
[108] **Two Curlls** the publisher Edmund and Lord Hervey

It was a Sin to call our Neighbour Fool,
That harmless Mother thought no Wife a Whore,—
Hear this! and spare his Family, James More!
Unspotted Names! and memorable long,
If there be Force in Virtue, or in Song.
    Of gentle Blood[109] (part shed in Honour's Cause,
While yet in Britain Honour had Applause)
Each Parent sprung—A. "What Fortune, pray?"—
390   P. Their own,
And better got than Bestia's[110] from the Throne.
Born to no Pride, inheriting no Strife,
Nor marrying Discord in a Noble Wife,
Stranger to Civil and Religious Rage,
The good Man walk'd innoxious thro' his Age.
No Courts he saw, no Suits would ever try,
Nor dar'd an Oath, nor hazarded a Lie:[111]
Un-learn'd, he knew no Schoolman's subtle Art,[112]
No Language, but the Language of the Heart.
400   By Nature honest, by Experience wise,
Healthy by Temp'rance and by Exercise:
His Life, tho' long, to sickness past unknown,
His Death was instant, and without a groan.
Oh grant me thus to live, and thus to die!
Who sprung from Kings shall know less joy than I.
    O Friend! may each Domestic Bliss be thine!
Be no unpleasing Melancholy mine:
Me, let the tender Office long engage
To rock the Cradle of reposing Age,
410   With lenient[113] Arts extend a Mother's breath,
Make Languor smile, and smooth the Bed of Death,
Explore the Thought, explain the asking Eye,
And keep a while one Parent from the Sky!
On Cares like these if Length of days attend,
May Heav'n, to bless those days, preserve my Friend,[114]
Preserve him social, chearful, and serene,
And just as rich as when he serv'd a QUEEN!
A. Whether that Blessing be denied, or giv'n,
Thus far was right, the rest belongs to Heav'n.[115]

1735

---

[109] **gentle Blood** Pope wrongly thought himself related to the Earls of Down.

[110] **Bestia** a corrupt Roman consul (111 B.C.) bribed by Jugurtha to make a shameful peace, which Rome later disavowed. Pope may be alluding to the Duke of Marlborough, generously rewarded by Queen Anne, or Walpole himself, whose peace policy with Spain Pope and the opposition considered dishonorable.

[111] **Oath . . . Lie** Punitive laws against English Roman Catholics included exclusion from some rights and offices if they did not swear oaths to the Church of England and against the Pope.

[112] **Schoolman's . . . Art** the casuistical reasoning that would negate l. 397

[113] **lenient** soothing

[114] **Friend** Dr. Arbuthnot

[115] **Whether . . . Heav'n** The speaker of these lines is in dispute, but it seems probable that the persuaded Arbuthnot, rather than Pope, would give the final judgment that "Thus far was right."

From The Dunciad

From Book I[1]

The Mighty Mother, and her Son[2] who brings
The Smithfield Muses[3] to the ear of Kings,
I sing. Say you, her instruments the Great![4]
Call'd to this work by Dullness, Jove, and Fate;
You by whose care, in vain decri'd and curs'd,
Still Dunce the second[5] reigns like Dunce the first;
Say how the Goddess bade Britannia sleep,
And pour'd her Spirit[6] o'er the land and deep.
In eldest time, e'er mortals writ or read,
E'er Pallas issu'd from the Thund'rer's head,[7]
Dullness o'er all possess'd her ancient right,
Daughter of Chaos and eternal Night:
Fate in their dotage this fair Idiot gave,
Gross as her sire, and as her mother grave,
Laborious, heavy, busy, bold, and blind,
She rul'd, in native Anarchy, the mind.
Still her old Empire to restore she tries,[8]
For, born a Goddess, Dullness never dies.
O Thou![9] whatever title please thine ear,

10

---

[1] *The Dunciad* in three books appeared in 1728, with Lewis Theobald as its hero of dullness; the poem reappeared in 1729 as *The Dunciad Variorum*, with parodic notes and mock-scholarly apparatus. Pope issued a separate, fourth book in 1742 as *The New Dunciad* and the complete *Dunciad in Four Books* in 1743, with the hero now changed from Theobald to Poet Laureate Colley Cibber (1671–1757), whose politics, patronage by the court, and dubious talents exemplified all that Pope found wrong with modern Britain under George II and Walpole. As Pope says, the "one, great, and remarkable Action" of the poem is "the restoration of the reign of Chaos and Night by the ministry of Dullness their daughter, in the removal of her imperial seat from the [unfashionable, commercial] City, to the polite World, as the Action of the *Aeneid* is the restoration of the empire of Troy by the removal of the race from thence to Latium." Much of the poem suggests the replacement of good with bad values, poets, and cultures, as the epic of the Dunces replaces the epic of Aeneas, and uncreation replaces creation in the ordering of the world.
[2] **Mother . . . Son** the goddess Dullness and her son, Colley Cibber
[3] **Smithfield Muses** Smithfield was the home of Bartholomew Fair, with its carnival booths and trivial entertainments like farce, juggling, and tightrope walking which, under George I

and George II, had been brought to London's fashionable theaters.
[4] **the Great** the king and the aristocrats, especially the court
[5] **Dunce the second** (1) Colley Cibber received the Dunce's mantle from Lewis Theobald of the 1728 version; (2) Cibber received the poet laureateship from Lawrence Eusden; (3) George II received the crown from George I.
[6] **pour'd her Spirit** like l. 28, a parody of the propagating Holy Spirit, as in *Paradise Lost* I. 20–22
[7] **Pallas . . . head** Pallas Athene, goddess of wisdom, issued full grown from the head of Jove.
[8] **Empire . . . tries** In *Paradise Lost* Satan promises Chaos and Night that he will restore their empire in return for directions to the world; see II.894–1009.
[9] **Thou** Jonathan Swift (1667–1745), dean of St. Patrick's in Dublin, author of the Bickerstaff papers (1708), the *Drapier's Letters* (1724), and *Gulliver's Travels* (1726). The *Drapier's Letters* successfully stopped the English from sending a debased copper coin (l. 24) to Ireland ("Boeotia," l. 25); *Gulliver's Travels* "magnifies mankind" in Bk. II, where the people are twelve times normal size. As a leader of the opposition to Sir Robert Walpole, Swift did not "praise the Court" (l. 23), as Pope, writing ironically, knew.

20 Dean, Drapier, Bickerstaff, or Gulliver!
Whether thou choose Cervantes' serious air,
Or laugh and shake in Rab'lais' easy chair,
Or praise the Court, or magnify Mankind,
Or thy griev'd Country's copper chains unbind;
From thy Boeotia tho' her Pow'r retires,
Mourn not, my SWIFT, at ought our Realm acquires,
Here pleas'd behold her mighty wings out-spread
To hatch a new Saturnian age[10] of Lead.
      Close to those walls where Folly holds her throne,
30 And laughs to think Monroe would take her down,[11]
Where o'er the gates, by his fam'd father's hand[12]
Great Cibber's brazen, brainless brothers stand;
One Cell there is, conceal'd from vulgar eye,
The Cave of Poverty and Poetry.
Keen, hollow winds howl thro' the bleak recess,
Emblem of Music caus'd by Emptiness.
Hence Bards, like Proteus[13] long in vain ti'd down,
Escape in Monsters[14] and amaze the town.
Hence Miscellanies[15] spring, the weekly boast
40 Of Curll's chaste press, and Lintot's rubric post:[16]
Hence hymning Tyburn's elegiac lines,[17]
Hence Journals, Medleys, Merc'ries, Magazines:[18]
Sepulchral Lies,[19] our holy walls to grace,
And New-year Odes,[20] and all the Grub-street race.
      In clouded Majesty here Dullness shone . . .

1728

1743

[10]**Saturnian age**   golden age in antiquity, but in alchemy Saturn means lead—hence, a leaden age in Georgian England.

[11]**walls . . . down**   St. Mary of Bethlehem (Bedlam) to which Dr. James Monro (1680–1752) was physician

[12]l. 31   Colley Cibber's father, Caius-Gabriel, executed two stone (not brass) statues for Bedlam's gates—Raving Madness and Melancholy Madness.

[13]**Proteus**   prophetic sea god who could avoid prophesying by changing his shape when seized

[14]**Monsters**   monstrous writing

[15]**Miscellanies**   collections of poetry

[16]**Curll's . . . post**   Edmund Curll (1675–1742),

unethical publisher who was fined for publishing obscene books; Bernard Lintot (1675–1736), one of Pope's publishers who, Pope says, "usually adorned his shop with titles in red [rubric] letters"

[17]**hymning . . . lines**   Prisoners at Tyburn would sing a psalm before being executed; publishers would print elegies about them.

[18]**Journals . . . Magazines**   words in the titles of magazines and newspapers

[19]**Sepulchral Lies**   false epitaphs

[20]**New-year Odes**   The poet laureate was required to write odes for the king's birthday and for the new year.

JAMES THOMSON

1700–1748

Thomson was educated at the College of Edinburgh and began preparation for the Presbyterian ministry (his father's calling); but he abandoned these studies and left for London early in 1725. He became a tutor at Watts's Academy, where he was exposed to Newtonian science and began to write *Winter* (1726). This poem was followed by *Summer*

(1727), *Spring* (1728), and *Autumn* in the first collected edition of *The Seasons* (1730). The much-revised final text (5,541 lines) did not appear until 1746; it remained a popular and important visionary long poem.

In *The Seasons* Thomson explores the worlds of nature, man, and God, and the relationships among them. Paying close attention to natural phenomena, he discovers that apparently random associations actually suggest universal order. *Spring*, for example, considers the transient "love" between birds and moves to the complex and "Matchless joys of virtuous love" among man, woman, and offspring, and thence to the love of God—the realm of "bliss immortal." Thomson draws on varied poetic and intel-lectual contexts, including the Virgilian georgic, a poem in which the rural country-side and its inhabitants are seen as contrib-uting to national greatness, the latinate diction and blank verse associated with Mil-ton's *Paradise Lost*, and Newtonian obser-vation, which indicates laws of regularity. He also makes frequent use of periphrases in which short phrases become longer ones with moral or philosophical implications; bees thus become "busy nations" (l. 510) and suggest a trait of activity that is approp-riate in energetic Britain. Wordsworth called *The Seasons* "a work of inspiration; much of it is written . . . nobly from himself." But it is also a work enriched by Thomson's own and previous eras.

From The Seasons[1]

From Spring

> Behold yon breathing prospect[2] bids the Muse
> Throw all her beauty forth. But who can paint
> Like Nature? Can imagination boast,
> 470 Amid its gay creation, hues like hers?
> Or can it mix them with that matchless skill,
> And lose them in each other, as appears
> In every bud that blows?[3] If fancy[4] then
> Unequal fails beneath the pleasing task,
> Ah, what shall language do? ah, where find words
> Tinged with so many colours and whose power,
> To life approaching, may perfume my lays
> With that fine oil, those aromatic gales
> That inexhaustive flow continual round?
> 480   Yet, though successless, will the toil delight.
> Come then, ye virgins and ye youths,[5] whose hearts
> Have felt the raptures of refining love;
> And thou, Amanda,[6] come, pride of my song!
> Formed by the Graces,[7] loveliness itself!
> Come with those downcast eyes, sedate and sweet,

---

[1]Thomson begins the collected edition with *Spring*, the third part of *The Seasons*, written to emphasize the creative power he shares with the natural world.

[2]**breathing prospect** a living picture of an extended view

[3]**blows** blooms

[4]**fancy** imagination, especially the ability to form images

[5]**virgins . . . youths** unmarried young women and men

[6]**Amanda** Elizabeth Young, whom Thomson courted unsuccessfully. Her poetic name means "worthy to be loved."

[7]**Graces** in Greek mythology, three sisters who confer charm, grace, and beauty upon mortals and nature

Those looks demure that deeply pierce the soul,
Where, with the light of thoughtful reason mixed,
Shines lively fancy and the feeling heart:
Oh come! and, while the rosy-footed May
490   Steals blushing on, together let us tread
The morning dews, and gather in their prime
Fresh-blooming flowers to grace thy braided hair
And thy loved bosom, that improves their sweets.
    See where the winding vale[8] its lavish stores,
Irriguous,[9] spreads. See how the lily drinks
The latent rill, scarce oozing through the grass
Of growth luxuriant, or the humid bank
In fair profusion decks. Long let us walk
Where the breeze blows from yon extended field
500   Of blossomed beans. Arabia cannot boast
A fuller gale of joy than liberal thence
Breathes through the sense, and takes the ravished soul.
Nor is the mead[10] unworthy of thy foot,
Full of fresh verdure[11] and unnumbered flowers,
The negligence[12] of Nature wide and wild,
Where, undisguised by mimic art, she spreads
Unbounded beauty to the roving eye.
Here their delicious task the fervent bees
In swarming millions tend. Around, athwart,
510   Through the soft air, the busy nations[13] fly,
Cling to the bud, and with inserted tube
Suck its pure essence, its ethereal soul.[14]
And oft with bolder wing they soaring dare
The purple heath, or where the wild thyme grows,
And yellow load them with the luscious spoil.[15]
    At length the finished garden to the view
Its vistas opens and its alleys green.
Snatched through the verdant maze, the hurried eye
Distracted wanders; now the bowery[16] walk
520   Of covert[17] close, where scarce a speck of day
Falls on the lengthened gloom, protracted sweeps;
Now meets the bending sky, the river now
Dimpling[18] along, the breezy ruffled lake,
The forest darkening round, the glittering spire,
The ethereal[19] mountain, and the distant main.[20]
But why so far excursive?[21] when at hand,

---

[8]**winding vale** meandering channel
[9]**Irriguous** irrigating
[10]**mead** meadow
[11]**fresh verdure** the green of growing vegetation
[12]**negligence** freedom from restraint or artificiality; "natural" abundance, and not "mimic art"
[13]**busy nations** the bees, so elevated in the georgic tradition
[14]**ethereal soul** formed from an element more

refined than air; hence celestial, heavenly
[15]**spoil** booty
[16]**bowery** full of bowers, arbors
[17]**covert** a thicket
[18]**dimpling** rippling
[19]**ethereal** here, extending into the highest regions, hence into the realms of ether
[20]**main** ocean
[21]**excursive** wandering

Along these blushing borders bright with dew,
And in yon mingled wilderness of flowers,
Fair-handed Spring unbosoms every grace—[22]
530 Throws out the snow-drop and the crocus first,
The daisy, primrose, violet darkly blue,
And polyanthus of unnumbered dyes;
The yellow wall-flower, stained with iron brown,
And lavish[23] stock, that scents the garden round:
From the soft wing of vernal[24] breezes shed,
Anemones, auriculas, enriched
With shining meal[25] o'er all their velvet leaves;
And full ranunculus of glowing red.
Then comes the tulip-race, where beauty plays
540 Her idle freaks:[26] from family diffused
To family, as flies the father-dust,[27]
The varied colours run; and, while they break[28]
On the charmed eye, the exulting florist marks
With secret pride the wonders of his hand.
No gradual bloom is wanting—from the bud
First-born of Spring to Summer's musky tribes;[29]
Nor hyacinths, of purest virgin white,
Low bent and blushing inward; nor jonquils,
Of potent fragrance; nor narcissus fair,
550 As o'er the fabled fountain[30] hanging still;
Nor broad carnations, nor gay-spotted pinks;
Nor, showered from every bush, the damask-rose:
Infinite numbers, delicacies, smells,
With hues on hues expression cannot paint,
The breath of Nature, and her endless bloom.
  Hail, Source of Being! Universal Soul
Of heaven and earth! Essential Presence,[31] hail!
To thee I bend the knee; to thee my thoughts
Continual climb, who with a master-hand
560 Hast the great whole into perfection touched.
By thee the various vegetative tribes,[32]
Wrapt in a filmy net[33] and clad with leaves,
Draw the live ether[34] and imbibe the dew.
By thee disposed into congenial soils,
Stands each attractive[35] plant, and sucks, and swells
The juicy tide, a twining mass of tubes.[36]

[22]**unbosoms . . . grace** brings every beautiful flower from beneath the earth
[23]**lavish** highly perfumed
[24]**vernal** from the Spring
[25]**meal** powder, as in ground grain or nuts
[26]**idle freaks** either frivolous tricks, or the whimsical streaking of the flower
[27]**father-dust** pollen
[28]**break** burst into color
[29]**musky tribes** fragrant flowers
[30]**fabled fountain** The Greek youth Narcissus fell in love with his own image reflected in a pool and was turned into the flower that bears his name.
[31]**Essential Presence** God as creator, in contrast to l. 512, which is created life. Thomson is led to the worship of God rather than his manifestations in nature.
[32]**vegetative tribes** growing plants
[33]**filmy net** network of sap-carrying vessels
[34]**ether** the fluid, airy substance that supports plant life
[35]**attractive** attracting moisture from soil
[36]**tubes** roots

At thy command the vernal sun awakes
The torpid sap, detruded[37] to the root
By wintry winds, that now in fluent[38] dance
570 And lively fermentation[39] mounting spreads
All this innumerous-coloured scene of things.
       As rising from the vegetable world
My theme ascends, with equal wing ascend,
My panting Muse; and hark, how loud the woods
Invite you forth in all your gayest trim.
Lend me your song, ye nightingales! oh, pour
The mazy-running soul of melody
Into my varied verse! while I deduce,
From the first note the hollow cuckoo sings,
580 The symphony of Spring, and touch a theme
Unknown to fame—the passion of the groves.
                . . .
       Connubial leagues agreed, to the deep woods
They haste away, all as their fancy leads,
Pleasure, or food, or secret safety prompts;
That Nature's great command may be obeyed,
Nor all the sweet sensations they perceive
Indulged in vain. Some to the holly-hedge
Nestling repair, and to the thicket some;
Some to the rude protection of the thorn
Commit their feeble offspring. The cleft tree
640 Offers its kind concealment to a few,
Their food its insects, and its moss their nests.
Others apart far in the grassy dale,
Or roughening waste, their humble texture weave
But most in woodland solitudes delight,
In unfrequented glooms, or shaggy banks,
Steep, and divided by a babbling brook
Whose murmurs soothe them all the live-long day
When by kind duty fixed. Among the roots
Of hazel, pendent[40] o'er the plaintive stream,
650 They frame the first foundation of their domes—[41]
Dry sprigs of trees, in artful fabric laid,
And bound with clay together. Now 'tis nought
But restless hurry through the busy air,
Beat by unnumbered wings. The swallow sweeps
The slimy pool, to build his hanging house
Intent. And often, from the careless back
Of herds and flocks, a thousand tugging bills
Pluck hair and wool; and oft, when unobserved,
Steal from the barn a straw—till soft and warm,
660 Clean and complete, their habitation grows.

---

[37]**detruded** thrust down
[38]**fluent** both liquid and in flux
[39]**fermentation** agitation and transformation, all

caused by the sun acting at God's command
[40]**pendent** hanging
[41]**domes** houses

As thus the patient dam assiduous sits,
Not to be tempted from her tender task
Or by sharp hunger or by smooth delight,
Though the whole loosened Spring around her blows,
Her sympathizing lover takes his stand
High on the opponent bank, and ceaseless sings
The tedious time away; or else supplies
Her place a moment, while she sudden flits
To pick the scanty meal. The appointed time
670   With pious toil[42] fulfilled, the callow young,
Warmed and expanded into perfect life,
Their brittle bondage break, and come to light,
A helpless family demanding food
With constant clamour. Oh, what passions then,
What melting sentiments of kindly care,
On the new parents seize! Away they fly
Affectionate, and undesiring bear
The most delicious morsel to their young;
Which equally distributed, again
680   The search begins. Even so a gentle pair,
By fortune sunk, but formed of generous mould,
And charmed with cares[43] beyond the vulgar breast,
In some lone cot amid the distant woods,
Sustain'd alone by providential Heaven,
Oft, as they weeping eye their infant train,
Check their own appetites, and give them all.

. . .

But now the feathered youth their former bounds,
730   Ardent, disdain; and, weighing oft their wings,[44]
Demand the free possession of the sky.
This one glad office more, and then dissolves
Parental love at once, now needless grown:
Unlavish Wisdom never works in vain.
'Tis on some evening, sunny, grateful, mild,
When nought but balm[45] is breathing through the woods
With yellow lustre bright, that the new tribes
Visit the spacious heavens, and look abroad
On Nature's common, far as they can see
740   Or wing, their range and pasture. O'er the boughs
Dancing about, still at the giddy verge
Their resolution fails; their pinions still,
In loose libration stretched, to trust the void
Trembling refuse—till down before them fly
The parent-guides, and chide, exhort, command,
Or push them off. The surging air receives

---

[42]**pious toil** duty to both God and family
[43]**charmed with cares** enchanted with their objects of love and concern. Here and below Thomson invites us to contrast the families of human beings and birds.

[44]**weighing . . . wings** both balancing themselves, and raising their wings, as in "weighing anchor"
[45]**balm** the pleasant aroma of garden herbs, including mint, with implications of soothing

The plumy burden; and their self-taught wings
Winnow the waving element. On ground
Alighted, bolder up again they lead,
750 Farther and farther on, the lengthening flight;
Till, vanished every fear, and every power
Roused into life and action, light in air
The acquitted[46] parents see their soaring race,
And, once rejoicing, never know them more.
　　High from the summit of a craggy cliff,
Hung o'er the deep, such as amazing frowns
On utmost Kilda's[47] shore, whose lonely race
Resign the setting sun to Indian worlds,[48]
The royal eagle draws his vigorous young,
760 Strong-pounced, and ardent with paternal fire,
Now fit to raise a kingdom of their own,
He drives them from his fort, the towering seat
For ages of his empire—which in peace
Unstained he holds, while many a league to sea
He wings his course, and preys in distant isles.

1728　　　　　　　　　　　　　　1746

[46]**acquitted**　both freed and cleared from further obligation
[47]**Kilda**　St. Kilda, the westernmost island of the Scottish Outer Hebrides
[48]**Indian worlds**　probably the West Indies and eastern coast of North America

SAMUEL JOHNSON
1709–1784

Scarred from young boyhood by scrofula, nearly blind in his left eye, and deaf in his left ear, Johnson was a brilliant if moody and melancholic student who read widely in his father's bookshop in Lichfield. Poverty forced him to leave Pembroke College, Oxford, after one year, but he was later awarded honorary doctorates from Trinity College, Dublin, and Oxford. His works include moral essays called *The Rambler* (1750–52), the great *Dictionary of the English Language* (1755), the philosophical tale *Rasselas* (1759), his edition of Shakespeare with its important preface (1765), and some of the best biography and literary criticism in English, the *Lives of the Poets* (1779–81). He also was recognized as a poet of distinction, and was honored by burial in Westminster Abbey; the word "POETA" was carved on his statue in St. Paul's Cathedral.

Johnson's poetry features intense, compact imagery, psychological insight, and a sympathy with human suffering based on personal experience. His pentameter couplet satire *The Vanity of Human Wishes* (1749) urges us to view the unhappy world realistically but not to be defeated by it; hostility, he shows us, can be transmuted into kindness, and hope and fear channeled into useful paths. He seeks a partnership of responsibility—a moral narrator to guide and respect his reader, and a reader willing to learn from the experienced guide. Such an agreement brings the benevolent, though solemn, results of poems like *The Vanity* and the moving elegy to Dr. Levet (1783); violation of it brings the death and disruption of the "Short Song of Congratulation" (1780). For Johnson, the effort of working to unify the moral and the social life is nearly as important as the goal.

The Vanity of Human Wishes[1]

Let observation with extensive view,
Survey mankind, from China to Peru;
Remark each anxious toil, each eager strife,
And watch the busy scenes of crowded life;
Then say how hope and fear, desire and hate,
O'erspread with snares the clouded maze of fate,
Where wav'ring man, betray'd by vent'rous pride,
To tread the dreary paths without a guide,
As treach'rous phantoms in the mist delude,
10   Shuns fancied ills, or chases airy good;
How rarely reason guides the stubborn choice,
Rules the bold hand, or prompts the suppliant voice;
How nations sink, by darling[2] schemes oppress'd,
When vengeance listens to the fool's request.[3]
Fate wings with ev'ry wish th' afflictive dart,[4]
Each gift of nature, and each grace of art,
With fatal heat impetuous courage glows,
With fatal sweetness elocution flows,
Impeachment stops the speaker's[5] pow'rful breath,
20   And restless fire precipitates on[6] death.
   But scarce observ'd, the knowing and the bold
Fall in the gen'ral massacre of gold;
Wide-wasting pest![7] that rages unconfin'd,
And crowds with crimes the records of mankind;
For gold his sword the hireling ruffian draws,
For gold the hireling judge distorts the laws;
Wealth heap'd on wealth, nor truth nor safety buys,
The dangers gather as the treasures rise.
   Let hist'ry tell where rival kings command,
30   And dubious title shakes the madded land,
When statutes glean the refuse of the sword,[8]
How much more safe the vassal than the lord;
Low skulks the hind[9] beneath the rage of pow'r,
And leaves the wealthy traitor in the Tow'r,[10]
Untouch'd his cottage, and his slumbers sound,
Tho' confiscation's vultures hover round.
   The needy traveller, secure and gay,
Walks the wild heath, and sings his toil away.

[1] The poem is an imitation—modernized free adaptation—of Juvenal's tenth satire; Johnson makes significant changes of focus, especially in the conclusion, which turns Roman stoicism into a search for Christian acceptance.
[2] **darling** favorite
[3] **vengeance . . . request** Vengeance punishes the fool by granting his request.
[4] **Fate . . . dart** In the nature of things, a vain human wish flies back to hurt one, like a feath- ered arrow.
[5] **speaker** in Parliament
[6] **precipitates on** falls headlong to
[7] **pest** epidemic, plague
[8] **statutes . . . sword** In rebellious times new laws destroy those spared in combat.
[9] **hind** a peasant farmer or servant
[10] **Tow'r** the Tower of London, in which aristo- cratic "traitors" were imprisoned while await- ing trial

Does envy seize thee? crush th' upbraiding joy,
40   Increase his riches and his peace destroy;
Now fears in dire vicissitude invade,
The rustling brake[11] alarms, and quiv'ring shade,
Nor light nor[12] darkness bring his pain relief,
One shows the plunder, and one hides the thief.
  Yet still one gen'ral cry the skies assails,
And gain and grandeur load the tainted gales;[13]
Few know the toiling statesman's fear or care,
Th' insidious rival and the gaping heir.
  Once more, Democritus,[14] arise on earth,
50   With cheerful wisdom and instructive mirth,
See motley life in modern trappings dress'd,
And feed with varied fools[15] th' eternal jest:
Thou who couldst laugh where want enchain'd caprice,
Toil crush'd conceit, and man was of a piece;
Where wealth unlov'd without a mourner di'd,
And scarce a sycophant was fed by pride;
Where ne'er was known the form of mock debate,
Or seen a new-made mayor's unwieldy state;
Where change of fav'rites made no change of laws,
60   And senates heard before they judg'd a cause;
How wouldst thou shake at Britain's modish tribe,
Dart the quick taunt, and edge the piercing gibe?[16]
Attentive truth and nature to descry,
And pierce each scene with philosophic eye.
To thee were solemn toys or empty show,
The robes of pleasure and the veils of woe:
All aid the farce, and all thy mirth maintain,
Whose joys are causeless, or whose griefs are vain.
  Such was the scorn that fill'd the sage's mind,
70   Renew'd at ev'ry glance on humankind;
How just that scorn ere yet thy voice declare,
Search every state, and canvass ev'ry pray'r.
  Unnumber'd suppliants crowd Preferment's gate,[17]
Athirst for wealth, and burning to be great;
Delusive Fortune hears th' incessant call,
They mount, they shine, evaporate, and fall.
On ev'ry stage the foes of peace attend,
Hate dogs their flight, and insult mocks their end.
Love ends with hope, the sinking statesman's door
80   Pours in the morning worshipper[18] no more;

---

[11] **brake** a thorny thicket

[12] **Nor . . . nor** neither . . . nor

[13] **gain . . . gales** A hunting image: our prayers for gain and grandeur scent the winds, thus allowing us to be hunted by the vengeance (l. 14) or fate (ll. 15–18) of our own creation.

[14] **Democritus** Greek philosopher (c. 460–370 B.C.) called the laughing philosopher because of his contempt for man's weaknesses. Note Johnson's reservations regarding such a view in ll. 69–72.

[15] **motley . . . varied fools** a multi-colored or "varied" garment once worn by fools or court jesters. Contrast this with "man . . . of a piece" in l. 54.

[16] **edge . . . gibe** sharpen insults

[17] **Preferment's gate** the gate or door of a powerful man with jobs to bestow

[18] **morning worshipper** Petitioners were often received in the morning.

For growing names the weekly scribbler lies,
To growing wealth the dedicator flies,
From every room descends the painted face,
That hung the bright Palladium[19] of the place,
And smoak'd in kitchens, or in auctions sold,
To better features yields the frame of gold;
For now no more we trace in ev'ry line
Heroic worth, benevolence divine:
The form distorted justifies the fall,
90   And detestation rids th' indignant wall.
    But will not Britain hear the last appeal,
Sign her foes' doom, or guard her fav'rites' zeal?
Through Freedom's sons no more remonstrance[20] rings,
Degrading nobles and controlling kings;
Our supple tribes repress their patriot throats,
And ask no questions but the price of votes;
With weekly libels and septennial ale,[21]
Their wish is full to riot and to rail.
    In full blown dignity, see Wolsey[22] stand,
100   Law in his voice, and fortune in his hand:
To him the church, the realm, their pow'rs consign,
Thro' him the rays of regal bounty shine,
Turn'd by his nod the stream of honour flows,
His smile alone security bestows:
Still to new heights his restless wishes tow'r,
Claim leads to claim, and pow'r advances pow'r;
Till conquest unresisted ceas'd to please,
And rights submitted, left him none to seize.
At length his sov'reign frowns[23]—the train of state
110   Mark the keen glance, and watch the sign to hate.
Where'er he turns he meets a stranger's eye,
His suppliants scorn him, and his followers fly;
At once is lost the pride of aweful state,
The golden canopy, the glitt'ring plate,
The regal palace, the luxurious board,
The liv'ried army, and the menial lord.
With age, with cares, with maladies oppress'd,
He seeks the refuge of monastic rest.
Grief aids disease, remember'd folly stings,
120   And his last sighs reproach the faith of kings.

[19] **Palladium** The statue of Pallas Athena, a symbol of divine protection, that was preserved in Troy and was stolen by the Greek Diomedes so that Troy would fall. The great man's portrait is removed from a place of power and put in the kitchen, leaving its gold frame ready for a new face.

[20] **remonstrance** The Grand Remonstrance of 1641 insisted that Charles I choose his council from men approved by and accountable to Parliament.

[21] **weekly . . . ale** political attacks in the weekly journals, and the ale given as a bribe for parliamentary elections held every seven years

[22] **full blown . . . Wolsey** Thomas, Cardinal Wolsey (c. 1475–1530). Wolsey's meteoric rise from chaplain to lord chancellor puts him in full bloom, like a mature flower.

[23] **his sov'reign frowns** Henry dismissed Wolsey from office in 1529 and indicted him for high treason in 1530.

Speak thou, whose thoughts at humble peace repine,
Shall Wolsey's wealth, with Wolsey's end be thine?
Or liv'st thou now, with safer pride content,
The wisest justice on the banks of Trent?
For why did Wolsey near the steeps of fate,
On weak foundations raise th' enormous weight?
Why but to sink beneath misfortune's blow,
With louder ruin to the gulphs below?
    What gave great Villiers[24] to th' assassin's knife,
130 And fixed disease on Harley's[25] closing life?
What murder'd Wentworth, and what exil'd Hyde,[26]
By kings protected, and to kings ally'd?
What but their wish indulg'd in courts to shine,
And pow'r too great to keep, or to resign?
    When first the college rolls receive his name,
The young enthusiast quits his ease for fame;
Through all his veins the fever of renown
Burns from the strong contagion of the gown;[27]
O'er Bodley's dome his future labours spread,
140 And Bacon's mansion[28] trembles o'er his head.
Are these thy views? proceed, illustrious youth,
And virtue guard thee to the throne of Truth!
Yet should thy soul indulge the gen'rous[29] heat,
Till captive Science[30] yields her last retreat;
Should Reason guide thee with her brightest ray,
And pour on misty Doubt resistless day;
Should no false Kindness lure to loose delight,
Nor Praise relax, nor Difficulty fright;
Should tempting Novelty thy cell[31] refrain,
150 And Sloth effuse her opiate fumes in vain;
Should Beauty blunt on fops her fatal dart,
Nor claim the triumph of a letter'd heart;
Should no disease thy torpid veins invade,
Nor Melancholy's phantoms haunt thy shade;
Yet hope not life from grief or danger free,
Nor think the doom of man revers'd for thee:

[24]**Villiers** George Villiers, 1st Duke of Buckingham (1592–1628), favorite of James I and Charles I, and assassinated by a jealous officer

[25]**Harley** Robert Harley, 1st Earl of Oxford (1661–1724), prime minister under Queen Anne, imprisoned in 1715, and impeached in 1717 under the new monarch

[26]**Wentworth . . . Hyde** Sir Thomas Wentworth, 1st Earl of Strafford (1593–1641), adviser to Charles I, and impeached and executed by a hostile Parliament; Edward Hyde, 1st Earl of Clarendon (1609–1674), lord chancellor for Charles II, impeached and exiled in 1667. He was James II's father-in-law and the grandfather of Queen Mary and Queen Anne.

[27]**contagion . . . gown** Hercules killed the centaur Nessus, and then put on his bloody, poisoned shirt which was so painful that Hercules tore his own flesh in removing it.

[28]**Bodley's dome . . . Bacon's mansion** the Bodleian Library, Oxford; the study of Friar Roger Bacon (c. 1214–1294) at Oxford. (Built on an arch over a bridge, it was supposed to collapse when a greater man than Bacon passed under it.)

[29]**gen'rous** fruitful, fertilizing

[30]**Science** learning, knowledge

[31]**cell** a small room, here probably a cubicle for study

Deign on the passing world to turn thine eyes,
And pause awhile from letters, to be wise;
There mark what ills the scholar's life assail,
160 Toil, envy, want, the patron, and the jail.
See nations slowly wise, and meanly just,
To buried merit raise the tardy bust.[32]
If dreams yet flatter, once again attend,
Hear Lydiat's life, and Galileo's end.[33]
    Nor deem, when learning her last prize bestows,
The glitt'ring eminence exempt from foes;
See when the vulgar 'scape, despis'd or aw'd,
Rebellion's vengeful talons seize on Laud.[34]
From meaner minds, tho' smaller fines content,
170 The plunder'd palace or sequester'd rent;
Mark'd out by dangerous parts[35] he meets the shock,
And fatal Learning leads him to the block:
Around his tomb let Art and Genius weep,
But hear his death, ye blockheads, hear and sleep.
    The festal blazes, the triumphal show,
The ravish'd standard, and the captive foe,
The senate's thanks, the Gazette's[36] pompous tale,
With force resistless o'er the brave prevail.
Such bribes the rapid Greek[37] o'er Asia whirl'd,
180 For such the steady Romans shook the world;
For such in distant lands the Britons shine,
And stain with blood the Danube or the Rhine;[38]
This pow'r has praise, that virtue scarce can warm,
Till fame supplies the universal charm.
Yet Reason frowns on War's unequal game,
Where wasted nations raise a single name,
And mortgag'd states their grandsires' wreaths regret,
From age to age in everlasting debt;
Wreaths which at last the dear-bought right convey
190 To rust on medals, or on stones decay.
    On what foundation stands the warrior's pride,
How just his hopes let Swedish Charles[39] decide;

---

[32]**tardy bust** monuments to Shakespeare, Milton, Butler, and Dryden long after their deaths

[33]**Lydiat's . . . Galileo's end** Thomas Lydiat (1572–1646), eminent Oxford mathematician who died in obscure poverty; Galileo (1564–1642), forced by the inquisition to deny the Copernican theory that the sun was the center of the universe. He was imprisoned and died blind.

[34]**Laud** William Laud (1573–1645), Charles I's archbishop of Canterbury, impeached and executed by Parliament in 1645

[35]**parts** talents, endowments of mind

[36]**Gazette** the official court newspaper, but by extension any newspaper

[37]**rapid Greek** Alexander the Great

[38]**Britons . . . Rhine** alluding to the victories of John Churchill, Duke of Marlborough (1650–1722), in Austria and Bavaria, especially Blenheim (1704), and perhaps the British campaigns in the War of the Austrian Succession (1740–48)

[39]**Swedish Charles** Charles XII (1682–1718), King of Sweden, a brilliant and ambitious general who conquered Denmark, Saxony in central Germany, and Poland, and was also noted for his indifference to women

A frame of adamant, a soul of fire,
No dangers fright him, and no labours tire;
O'er love, o'er fear, extends his wide domain,
Unconquer'd lord of pleasure and of pain;
No joys to him pacific scepters yield,
War sounds the trump, he rushes to the field;
Behold surrounding kings their pow'r combine,
200   And one capitulate, and one resign;[40]
Peace courts his hand, but spreads her charms in vain;
"Think nothing gain'd," he cries, "till nought remain,
On Moscow's walls till Gothic[41] standards fly,
And all be mine beneath the polar sky."
The march begins in military state,
And nations on his eye suspended wait;
Stern Famine guards the solitary coast,
And Winter barricades the realms of Frost;
He comes, not want and cold his course delay;—
210   Hide, blushing Glory, hide Pultowa's[42] day:
The vanquish'd hero leaves his broken bands,
And shows his miseries in distant lands;
Condemn'd a needy supplicant to wait,
While ladies interpose, and slaves debate.
But did not Chance at length her error mend?
Did no subverted empire mark his end?
Did rival monarchs give the fatal wound?
Or hostile millions press him to the ground?
His fall was destin'd to a barren strand,
220   A petty fortress, and a dubious hand:[43]
He left the name, at which the world grew pale,
To point a moral, or adorn a tale.
   All times their scenes of pompous woes afford,
From Persia's tyrant to Bavaria's lord.
In gay hostility, and barb'rous pride,
With half mankind embattled at his side,
Great Xerxes[44] comes to seize the certain prey,
And starves exhausted regions in his way;
Attendant Flatt'ry counts his myriads o'er,
230   Till counted myriads soothe his pride no more;
Fresh praise is tri'd till madness fires his mind,
The waves he lashes, and enchains the wind;[45]

---

[40]**one capitulate . . . resign** Frederick IV of Denmark capitulated in 1700, and Augustus II of Poland was deposed in favor of Charles's candidate in 1704.

[41]**Gothic** Swedish, but with the implication of "barbaric"

[42]**Pultowa** Site of Charles's defeat by Peter the Great in Russia in 1709. He then fled to Turkey.

[43]ll. 219-20 As Charles besieged Frederikshald in Norway in 1718, he was killed by a mysterious wound inflicted either by his own or by the opposing side.

• [44]**Xerxes** Persia's tyrant of l. 224 (c. 519–465 B.C.), who invaded Greece and was crushed at Salamis in 480 B.C.

[45]**waves . . . wind** Xerxes' bridge of boats across the Hellespont was destroyed by winds and sea. In retaliation, he ordered chains to be thrown into the sea as shackles, and the wind to be whipped.

New pow'rs are claim'd, new pow'rs are still bestow'd,
Till rude resistance lops the spreading god;
The daring Greeks deride the martial show,
And heap their vallies with the gaudy foe;
Th' insulted sea with humbler thoughts he gains,
A single skiff to speed his flight remains;
Th' incumber'd oar scarce leaves the dreaded coast
240 Through purple billows and a floating host.
    The bold Bavarian,[46] in a luckless hour,
Tries the dread summits of Cesarean pow'r,
With unexpected legions bursts away,
And sees defenceless realms receive his sway;
Short sway! fair Austria spreads her mournful charms,
The queen, the beauty, sets the world in arms;
From hill to hill the beacon's rousing blaze
Spreads wide the hope of plunder and of praise;
The fierce Croatian, and the wild Hussar,[47]
250 And all the sons of ravage crowd the war;
The baffled prince in honour's flatt'ring bloom
Of hasty greatness finds the fatal doom,
His foes' derision, and his subjects' blame,
And steals to death from anguish and from shame.
    Enlarge my life with multitude of days,
In health, in sickness, thus the suppliant prays;
Hides from himself his state, and shuns to know,
That life protracted is protracted woe.
Time hovers o'er, impatient to destroy,
260 And shuts up all the passages of joy:
In vain their gifts the bounteous seasons pour,
The fruit autumnal, and the vernal flow'r,
With listless eyes the dotard views the store,
He views, and wonders that they please no more;
Now pall the tasteless meats, and joyless wines,
And Luxury with sighs her slave resigns.
Approach, ye minstrals, try the soothing strain,
Diffuse the tuneful lenitives[48] of pain:
No sounds alas would touch th' impervious ear,
270 Though dancing mountains witness'd Orpheus[49] near;
Nor lute nor lyre his feeble pow'rs attend,
Nor sweeter music of a virtuous friend,
But everlasting dictates crowd his tongue,
Perversely grave, or positively wrong.
The still returning tale, and ling'ring jest,

---

[46]**bold Bavarian** Charles Albert (1697–1745),
elector of Bavaria, who fought Archduchess
Maria Theresa (1717–1780), "fair Austria"
(l. 245), and unsuccessfully sought control of
the Holy Roman Empire
[47]**Croatian . . . Hussar** Austrian colonists in
northwest Yugoslavia (the "Croatian") and the
Hungarian light cavalry (the "Hussar") were
both enlisted on the Austrian side.
[48]**lenitives** medicinal pain relievers
[49]**Orpheus** musician and son of the muse
Calliope, said to be able to enchant and to move
the stones and Thracian mountains in which he
lived

Perplex the fawning niece and pamper'd guest,
While growing hopes scarce awe the gath'ring sneer,
And scarce a legacy can bribe to hear;
The watchful guests still hint the last[50] offence,
280 The daughter's petulance, the son's expence,
Improve[51] his heady rage with treach'rous skill,
And mould his passions[52] till they make his will.
Unnumber'd maladies his joints invade,
Lay siege to life and press the dire blockade;
But unextinguish'd Avarice still remains,
And dreaded losses aggravate his pains;
He turns, with anxious heart and crippled hands,
His bonds of debt, and mortgages of lands;
Or views his coffers with suspicious eyes,
290 Unlocks his gold, and counts it till he dies.
But grant, the virtues of a temp'rate prime
Bless with an age exempt from scorn or crime;
An age that melts with unperceiv'd decay,
And glides in modest innocence away;
Whose peaceful day Benevolence endears,
Whose night congratulating Conscience cheers;
The gen'ral fav'rite as the gen'ral friend:
Such age there is, and who shall wish its end?
Yet ev'n on this her load Misfortune flings,
300 To press the weary minutes' flagging wings:
New sorrow rises as the day returns,
A sister sickens, or a daughter mourns.
Now kindred Merit fills the sable bier,
Now lacerated Friendship claims a tear.
Year chases year, decay pursues decay,
Still drops some joy from with'ring life away;
New forms arise, and diff'rent views engage,
Superfluous lags the vet'ran on the stage,
Till pitying Nature signs the last release,
310 And bids afflicted worth retire to peace.
But few there are whom hours like these await,
Who set unclouded in the gulphs of fate.
From Lydia's monarch[53] should the search descend,
By Solon caution'd to regard his end,
In life's last scene what prodigies surprise,
Fears of the brave, and follies of the wise?
From Marlb'rough's[54] eyes the streams of dotage flow,

[50]**last**   most recent
[51]**Improve**   increase
[52]**passions**   psychological traits acted upon by external actions
[53]**Lydia's monarch**   Croesus (c. 550 B.C.), king of Lydia, warned by the Athenian legisla-tor Solon to consider no man happy who was still alive
[54]**Marlb'rough**   John Churchill, Duke of Marlborough, victor in the War of the Spanish Succession (1701–13; see l. 182), was paralyzed by strokes during the final six years of his life.

And Swift[55] expires a driv'ler and a show.
   The teeming mother, anxious for her race,
320 Begs for each birth the fortune of a face:
Yet Vane[56] could tell what ills from beauty spring;
And Sedley[57] curs'd the form that pleas'd a king.
Ye nymphs of rosy lips and radiant eyes,
Whom Pleasure keeps too busy to be wise,
Whom Joys with soft varieties invite,
By day the frolic, and the dance by night,
Who frown with vanity, who smile with art,
And ask the latest fashion of the heart,
What care, what rules your heedless charms shall save,
330 Each nymph your rival, and each youth your slave?
Against your fame with fondness hate combines,
The rival batters, and the lover mines.[58]
With distant voice neglected Virtue calls,
Less heard and less, the faint remonstrance falls;
Tir'd with contempt, she quits the slipp'ry reign,
And Pride and Prudence take her seat in vain.
In crowd at once, where none the pass defend,
The harmless Freedom, and the private Friend.
The guardians yield, by force superior pli'd;
340 By Int'rest, Prudence; and by Flatt'ry, Pride.
Now beauty falls betray'd, despis'd, distress'd,
And hissing Infamy proclaims the rest.
   Where then shall Hope and Fear their objects find?
Must dull Suspence[59] corrupt the stagnant mind?
Must helpless man, in ignorance sedate,[60]
Roll darkling down the torrent of his fate?
Must no dislike alarm, no wishes rise,
No cries attempt the mercies of the skies?
Enquirer, cease,[61] petitions yet remain,
350 Which heav'n may hear, nor deem religion vain.
Still raise for good the supplicating voice,
But leave to heav'n the measure and the choice,
Safe in his pow'r, whose eyes discern afar
The secret ambush of a specious pray'r.
Implore his aid, in his decisions rest,
Secure whate'er he gives, he gives the best.

---

[55]**Swift** Jonathan Swift (1667–1745), senile in his final years, was wrongly thought to have been exhibited for a fee by his avaricious servants. Though Swift and Marlborough were political enemies, their fates were similar.
[56]**Vane** Anne Vane (1705–1736), mistress of the son of George II—Frederick, Prince of Wales—who abandoned her
[57]**Sedley** Catherine Sedley (1657–1717), mistress of the Duke of York, who abandoned her after becoming James II, but made her a countess in 1686

[58]**batters . . . mines** as elsewhere in this passage, martial siege imagery. In this hostile world, the woman's defenses and reputation are battered at one point and undercut (and filled with explosives) at another.
[59]**Suspence** psychological and moral inactivity
[60]**sedate** calm, passive
[61]**Enquirer, cease** This passage begins the resolution of the poem, which re-examines many of the same wishes, putting them in a spiritual or divine light, instead of a vain human one.

Yet when the sense of sacred presence fires,
And strong devotion to the skies aspires,
Pour forth thy fervours for a healthful mind,
360 Obedient passions, and a will resign'd;
For love, which scarce collective man can fill;
For patience sov'reign o'er transmuted[62] ill;
For faith, that panting for a happier seat,
Counts death kind Nature's signal of retreat:[63]
These goods for man the laws of heav'n ordain,
These goods he grants, who grants the pow'r to gain;
With these celestial wisdom calms the mind,
And makes the happiness she does not find.

1749

[62]**transmuted** Ills are not erased but become goads to faith and patience.
[63]**retreat** the trumpet or drum recalling soldiers at the end of a battle, or withdrawal from battle in general; also a religious retirement. Note the contrast with other destructive martial images in the poem.

A Short Song of Congratulation[1]

Long-expected one and twenty
Ling'ring year at last is flown,
Pomp and pleasure, Pride and Plenty
Great Sir John, are all your own.

Loosen'd from the Minor's tether,[2]
Free to mortgage or to sell,
Wild as wind, and light as feather
Bid the slaves of thrift farewell.

Call the Bettys, Kates, and Jennys[3]
10 Ev'ry name that laughs at Care,
Lavish of your grandsire's guineas,
Show the Spirit of an heir.

All that prey on vice and folly
Joy to see their quarry fly,
Here the Gamester[4] light and jolly
There the lender grave and sly.

[1] Sir John Lade, the nephew and ward of Johnson's friend Henry Thrale, was a ne'er-do-well who married badly and squandered the fortune he inherited on his twenty-first birthday. The manuscript poem was sent with a letter to Mrs. Thrale in 1780.
[2] **tether** literally, a cord used to constrain a child or animal; figuratively, the limits on his finances, authority, and range
[3] **Bettys . . . Jennys** traditional names for servants and other women below Sir John's social class
[4] **Gamester** gambler, especially at cards or dice

Wealth, Sir John, was made to wander,
Let it wander[5] as it will;
See the Jockey, see the Pander,[6]
20   Bid them come, and take their fill.

When the bonny blade carouses,
Pockets full, and spirits high,
What are acres? What are houses?
Only dirt, or wet or dry.

If the Guardian or the Mother
Tell the woes of wilful waste,
Scorn their counsel and their pother,
You can hang or drown at last.

1780   1794

[5] **wander . . . wander** to stray morally, without direction
[6] **Pander** a go-between or pimp

On the Death of Dr. Robert Levet[1]

Condemn'd to hope's delusive mine,[2]
    As on we toil from day to day,
By sudden blasts, or slow decline,
    Our social comforts drop away.

Well tried through many a varying year,
    See Levet to the grave descend;
Officious,[3] innocent, sincere,
    Of ev'ry friendless name the friend.

Yet still he fills affection's eye,
10   Obscurely wise, and coarsely kind;[4]
Nor, letter'd arrogance,[5] deny
    Thy praise to merit unrefin'd.

When fainting nature call'd for aid,
    And hov'ring death prepar'd the blow,
His vig'rous remedy display'd
    The power of art without the show.

[1] Levet (1705–1782), a solemn, humble medical man who never took a medical degree, walked several miles daily to visit his poor patients for little or no reward. He met Johnson in about 1746, and from some years later until his death was one of the unfortunates whom Johnson supported in his own home.
[2] **mine** Roman prisoners in antiquity were con-demned to lead mines; there were comparable penalties in modern Europe and Latin America.
[3] **Officious** doing good offices or deeds
[4] **Obscurely . . . kind** wise though out of public sight, and kind though neither polished nor elegant
[5] **letter'd arrogance** the educated proud

In misery's darkest caverns known,
  His useful care was ever nigh,
Where hopeless anguish pour'd his groan,
20   And lonely want retir'd to die.

No summons mock'd by chill delay,
  No petty gain disdain'd by pride,
The modest wants of ev'ry day
  The toil of ev'ry day supplied.

His virtues walk'd their narrow round,[6]
  Nor made a pause, nor left a void;
And sure th' Eternal Master found,
  The single talent well employ'd.[7]

The busy day, the peaceful night,
30   Unfelt, uncounted, glided by;
His frame was firm, his powers were bright,
  Tho' now his eightieth year was nigh.

Then with no throbbing fiery pain,
  No cold gradation of decay,
Death broke at once the vital chain,[8]
  And freed his soul the nearest way.

1783

[6] **narrow round**   the medical rounds, or the walk
of a guard to survey his area
[7] **Eternal Master . . . employ'd**   an inversion
of Matthew 25:14–30, in which a servant fails

to use his single talent and is punished by God
[8] **vital chain**   the chain to life and the prison
chain implied in l. 1

THOMAS GRAY

1716–1771

Thomas Gray was the only survivor of twelve children. Of modest social standing, he nevertheless went to Eton, where his friends included Horace Walpole, son of the prime minister. Gray was so reclusive that during his nine years of study at Cambridge he left only for holidays, visits to relatives, and further research at the British Museum in London. Gray received his degree in 1743, and in 1768 he was made Regius Professor of Modern History; at his death, however, he left only copious notes for his proposed history of English literature.

He also left only a few poetic fragments and the thirteen poems he grudgingly allowed to appear in his lifetime.

Though capable of whimsy, Gray often portrays a solemn figure—the living poet mourning the dead friend, the adult watching the happily ignorant children at Eton College, the discontented man of ambition among the resigned poor in the *Elegy*. His work also reflects the mid-century shift from classical to native sources and subjects for poetry. In the 1740s he used mock-heroic conventions to eulogize a drowned cat, and gave classical symmetry to his grim "Eton College" ode by dividing its 100 lines evenly between descriptions of the joys of youth and the pains of maturity. By the 1750s, however, after extensive reading in Anglo-Saxon, English, Welsh, and Norse literature and history, Gray introduced sublime and native traditions: he revised lines 57, 59, and 60 of the *Elegy*, changing the

Romans Cato, Cicero, and Caesar to the English Hampden, Milton, and Cromwell. The setting for "The Bard" (1757) is the craggy Mt. Snowdon and the Conway River of medieval Wales, and its subject is drawn from Anglo-Welsh mythology. Gray here takes the form of the elevated Greek Pindaric ode and thoroughly domesticates it.

Sonnet. On the Death of Mr. Richard West[1]

In vain to me the smiling Mornings shine,
And redd'ning Phoebus[2] lifts his golden Fire:
The Birds in vain their amorous Descant[3] join;
Or cheerful Fields resume their green Attire:
These Ears, alas! for other Notes repine,
A different Object do these Eyes require.
My lonely Anguish melts no Heart, but mine;
And in my Breast the imperfect Joys expire.
Yet Morning smiles the busy Race to cheer,
10 And new-born Pleasure brings to happier Men:
The Fields to all their wonted Tribute bear:
To warm their little Loves the Birds complain:
I fruitless mourn to him, that cannot hear,
And weep the more, because I weep in vain.

1742   1775

[1] West, one of Gray's close friends from Eton College, died of tuberculosis at the age of twenty-five. The loss evoked some of Gray's earliest and darkest poems, but this one was so personal that it was not published until after Gray's death. The speaker is isolated in a world whose com-

forts, natural rhythms, and classical poetic conventions are all in vain.
[2] **Phoebus** from Phoebus Apollo, the sun personified at dawn
[3] **Descant** a song in parts

Ode on a Distant Prospect of Eton College[1]

Ye distant spires, ye antique towers,
That crown the wat'ry glade,
Where grateful Science[2] still adores
Her Henry's holy Shade:[3]

[1] The poem mingles the tradition of the reflective Horatian ode with the English tradition of the "prospect" poem in which a view of house, garden, or landscape evokes the speaker's speculations and associations. The word "College" is used in the older sense of a collection of young men set apart for learning; Eton prepared

such students for the university. The title originally was followed by a Greek tag from Menander reading: "I am a man, reason enough for being unhappy."
[2] **Science** learning
[3] **Her . . . shade** the spririt or ghost of Henry VI (1421–1471), who founded Eton in 1440

And ye, that from the stately brow
Of Windsor's heights[4] th' expanse below
Of grove, of lawn, of mead[5] survey,
Whose turf, whose shade, whose flowers among
Wanders the hoary Thames along
10   His silver-winding way.

    Ah happy hills, ah pleasing shade,
Ah fields belov'd in vain,
Where once my careless childhood stray'd,
A stranger yet to pain!
I feel the gales,[6] that from ye blow,
A momentary bliss bestow,
As waving fresh their gladsome wing,
My weary soul they seem to soothe,
And, redolent[7] of joy and youth,
20   To breathe a second spring.

    Say, Father Thames,[8] for thou hast seen
Full many a sprightly race[9]
Disporting on thy margent green
The paths of pleasure trace,
Who foremost now delight to cleave
With pliant arm thy glassy wave?[10]
The captive linnet which enthrall?
What idle progeny succeed
To chase the rolling circle's[11] speed,
30   Or urge the flying ball?

    While some on earnest business bent
Their murm'ring labours[12] ply
'Gainst graver hours, that bring constraint
To sweeten liberty:
Some bold adventurers disdain
The limits of their little reign,
And unknown regions dare descry:
Still as they run they look behind,
They hear a voice in every wind,[13]
40   And snatch a fearful joy.

    Gay hope is theirs by fancy fed,
Less pleasing when possess'd,
The tear forgot as soon as shed,

---

[4]**Windsor's heights** The River Thames runs
between the towers of Windsor Castle and
Eton College.
[5]**mead** meadow
[6]**gales** strong breezes
[7]**redolent** fragrant, here recalling the sweet
pleasures of childhood
[8]**Father Thames** the local deity of the river,
appropriate for a schoolboy mythology

[9]**race** generations of students
[10]**cleave . . . wave** mock-heroic language for
"swim"
[11]**rolling circle** a hoop
[12]**murm'ring labours** both mumbling home-
work aloud, and grumbling about it
[13]**voice . . . wind** the real or imagined voice of
the schoolmaster or other authority

The sunshine of the breast:
Theirs buxom[14] health of rosy hue,
Wild wit, invention ever-new,
And lively cheer of vigour born;
The thoughtless day, the easy night,
The spirits pure, the slumbers light,
50   That fly th' approach of morn.

    Alas, regardless[15] of their doom,
The little victims play!
No sense have they of ills to come,
Nor care beyond to-day:
Yet see how all around 'em wait
The Ministers of human fate,
And black Misfortune's baleful train!
Ah, show them where in ambush stand
To seize their prey the murd'rous band!
60   Ah, tell them, they are men!

    These shall the fury Passions[16] tear,
The vultures of the mind,
Disdainful Anger, pallid Fear,
And Shame that sculks behind;
Or pineing Love shall waste their youth,
Or[17] Jealousy with rankling tooth,
That inly gnaws the secret heart,
And Envy wan, and faded Care,
Grim-visag'd comfortless Despair,
70   And Sorrow's piercing dart.

    Ambition this shall tempt to rise,
Then whirl the wretch from high,
To bitter Scorn a sacrifice,
And grinning Infamy.
The stings of Falshood those shall try,
And hard Unkindness' alter'd eye,
That mocks the tear it forc'd to flow;
And keen Remorse with blood defil'd,
And moody Madness laughing wild
80   Amid severest woe.

    Lo, in the vale of years beneath
A grisly troop are seen,
The painful family of Death,
More hideous than their Queen:
This racks the joints, this fires the veins,
That every labouring sinew strains,

[14]**buxom** lively, brisk
[15]**regardless** heedless
[16]**Passions** the emotions described in the suc-

ceeding lines
[17]**Or . . . Or** either . . . or

Those in the deeper vitals rage:
Lo, Poverty, to fill the band,
That numbs the soul with icy hand,
90 And slow-consuming Age.

　　To each his suff'rings: all are men,
Condemn'd alike to groan,
The tender for another's pain;
Th' unfeeling for his own.
Yet ah! why should they know their fate?
Since sorrow never comes too late,
And happiness too swiftly flies.
Thought would destroy their paradise.
No more; where ignorance is bliss,
100 'Tis folly to be wise.[18]

1742   1747

[18]**ignorance . . . wise** These famous lines indi-
cate what the speaker has learned during the
course of the poem.

Ode on the Death of a Favourite Cat, Drowned in a Tub of Gold Fishes[1]

'Twas on a lofty vase's side,
Where China's gayest art had dy'd
　　The azure flowers, that blow;[2]
Demurest of the tabby kind,
The pensive Selima reclin'd,
　　Gazed on the lake below.

Her conscious tail her joy declar'd;
The fair round face, the snowy beard,
　　The velvet of her paws,
10 Her coat, that with the tortoise vies,
Her ears of jet, and emerald eyes,
　　She saw; and purr'd applause.

Still had she gaz'd; but 'midst the tide
Two angel forms were seen to glide,
　　The Genii[3] of the stream:
Their scaly armour's Tyrian hue[4]
Thro' richest purple to the view
　　Betray'd a golden gleam.

[1] The poem was written at the request of Horace
Walpole to memorialize the death of his cat
Selima. It is one version of the "mock-form,"
in which the disparity between manner, an appar-
ently serious elegy which alludes to classical
mythology, and matter, the death of a cat, pro-
vides much of the fun.

[2] **blow** bloom
[3] **Genii** the ruling deities; here, the gold fish
whose sacred pool is being invaded, to the
intruder's cost
[4] **Tyrian hue** purple dye once obtained from
the bodies of certain shellfish in Tyre, Phœnicia

The hapless Nymph with wonder saw:
20 A whisker first and then a claw,
   With many an ardent wish,
She stretch'd in vain to reach the prize.
What female heart can gold despise?
   What Cat's averse to fish?

Presumptuous Maid! with looks intent
Again she stretch'd, again she bent,
   Nor knew the gulf between.
(Malignant Fate sat by, and smil'd)
The slipp'ry verge her feet beguil'd,
30   She tumbled headlong in.

Eight times emerging from the flood
She mew'd to ev'ry wat'ry God,
   Some speedy aid to send.
No Dolphin came, no Nereid⁵ stirr'd:
Nor cruel Tom, nor Susan⁶ heard.
   A Fav'rite has no friend!

From hence, ye Beauties, undeceiv'd,
Know, one false step is ne'er retriev'd,
   And be with caution bold.
40 Not all that tempts your wand'ring eyes
And heedless hearts, is lawful prize;
   Nor all, that glisters, gold.

1747   1748

⁵ **Dolphin . . . Nereid** A dolphin, charmed by
Arion's music, carried him safely to shore when
he was thrown overboard. Nereids were sea

daughters of Nereus, a sea god.
⁶ **Tom . . . Susan** names for servants

Elegy Written in a Country Churchyard¹

The Curfew tolls the knell of parting day,
The lowing herd wind slowly o'er the lea,²
The plowman homeward plods his weary way,
And leaves the world to darkness and to me.

Now fades the glimmering landscape on the sight,
And all the air a solemn stillness holds,
Save where the beetle wheels his droning flight,
And drowsy tinklings lull the distant folds;

¹ The term "elegy" refers both to the present
poem and to the epitaph from l. 117. Gray wrote

the poem between 1742 and 1750.
² **lea** pasture

Save that from yonder ivy-mantled tow'r
The mopeing owl does to the moon complain
Of such, as wand'ring near her secret bow'r,
Molest her ancient solitary reign.

Beneath those rugged elms, that yew-tree's shade,
Where heaves the turf in many a mould'ring heap,
Each in his narrow cell for ever laid,
The rude[3] Forefathers of the hamlet sleep.

The breezy call of incense-breathing Morn,
The swallow twitt'ring from the straw-built shed,
The cock's shrill clarion, or the ecchoing horn,[4]
No more shall rouse them from their lowly bed.

For them no more the blazing hearth shall burn,
Or busy housewife ply her evening care:
No children run to lisp their sire's return,
Or climb his knees the envied kiss to share.

Oft did the harvest to their sickle yield,
Their furrow oft the stubborn glebe[5] has broke;
How jocund did they drive their team afield!
How bow'd the woods beneath their sturdy stroke!

Let not Ambition mock their useful toil,
Their homely joys, and destiny obscure;
Nor Grandeur hear with a disdainful smile,
The short and simple annals[6] of the poor.

The boast of heraldry, the pomp of pow'r,
And all that beauty, all that wealth e'er gave,
Awaits alike th' inevitable hour.
The paths of glory lead but to the grave.

Nor you, ye Proud, impute to These the fault,
If Mem'ry o'er their Tomb no Trophies[7] raise,
Where thro' the long-drawn isle and fretted[8] vault
The pealing anthem swells the note of praise.

Can storied urn or animated bust[9]
Back to its mansion call the fleeting breath?
Can Honour's voice provoke[10] the silent dust,
Or Flatt'ry soothe the dull cold ear of Death?

Perhaps in this neglected spot is laid
Some heart once pregnant with celestial fire,

10

20

30

40

---

[3]**rude** uneducated
[4]**horn** of the early rising hunter
[5]**glebe** ground, soil
[6]**annals** histories recorded year by year
[7]**Trophies** carved figures emblematic of the

great men's victories — by extension, over death
[8]**fretted** decorated with elaborate relief work
[9]**storied . . . bust** a funeral urn with a story or
epitaph on it; lifelike portrait sculpture
[10]**provoke** move, rouse to action

Hands, that the rod of empire might have sway'd,
Or wak'd to extasy the living lyre.[11]

But Knowledge to their eyes her ample page
50   Rich with the spoils of time did ne'er unroll;
Chill Penury repress'd their noble rage,[12]
And froze the genial current[13] of the soul.

Full many a gem of purest ray serene,[14]
The dark unfathom'd caves of ocean bear:
Full many a flower is born to blush unseen,
And waste its sweetness on the desert air.

Some village-Hampden,[15] that with dauntless breast
The little Tyrant of his fields withstood;
Some mute inglorious Milton here may rest,
60   Some Cromwell[16] guiltless of his country's blood.

Th' applause of list'ning senates to command,
The threats of pain and ruin to despise,
To scatter plenty o'er a smiling land,
And read their hist'ry in a nation's eyes

Their lot forbad: nor circumscrib'd alone
Their growing virtues, but their crimes confin'd;
Forbad to wade through slaughter to a throne,
And shut the gates of mercy on mankind,

The struggling pangs of conscious truth to hide,
70   To quench the blushes of ingenuous[17] shame,
Or heap the shrine of Luxury and Pride
With incense kindled at the Muse's flame.

Far from the madding crowd's ignoble strife,
Their sober[18] wishes never learn'd to stray;
Along the cool sequester'd vale of life
They kept the noiseless tenor of their way.

Yet ev'n these bones from insult to protect
Some frail memorial still erected nigh,
With uncouth rhimes and shapeless sculpture deck'd,[19]
80   Implores the passing tribute of a sigh.

---

[11]**lyre** harp, a symbol of poetry
[12]**rage** eagerness, rapture
[13]**genial current** creative course or progress
[14]**serene** latinism for bright
[15]**Hampden** John Hampden (1594–1643) resisted both Charles I's taxes and autocracy.
[16]**Cromwell** Oliver Cromwell (1599–1658), prime mover of the English Civil Wars (1642–49) and the consequent beheading of Charles I in 1649. The allusion is important as an evoca-

tion of ll. 65-68, where the speaker begins to see the dangers in public life.
[17]**ingenuous** generous, noble
[18]**sober** temperate
[19]**memorial . . . deck'd** By implication, the speaker contrasts the modest tombstones of the poor buried in the churchyard with the elaborate "storied" tombstones of the wealthy buried within the church itself.

Their name, their years, spelt by th' unletter'd muse,
The place of fame and elegy supply:
And many a holy text around she strews,
That teach the rustic moralist to die.

For who to dumb Forgetfulness a prey,
This pleasing anxious being e'er resign'd,
Left the warm precincts of the cheerful day,
Nor cast one longing ling'ring look behind?

90   On some fond breast the parting soul relies,
Some pious drops the closing eye requires;
Ev'n from the tomb the voice of Nature cries,
Ev'n in our Ashes live their wonted Fires.[20]

For thee,[21] who mindful of th' unhonour'd Dead
Dost in these lines their artless tale relate;
If chance, by lonely contemplation led,
Some kindred Spirit shall inquire thy fate,

Haply some hoary-headed Swain[22] may say,
"Oft have we seen him at the peep of dawn
Brushing with hasty steps the dews away
100 To meet the sun upon the upland lawn.

"There at the foot of yonder nodding beech
That wreathes its old fantastic roots so high,
His listless length at noontide wou'd he stretch,
And pore upon the brook that babbles by.

"Hard by yon wood, now smiling as in scorn,
Mutt'ring his wayward fancies he wou'd rove,
Now drooping, woeful wan, like one forlorn,
Or craz'd with care, or cross'd in hopeless love.

"One morn I miss'd him on the custom'd hill,
110 Along the heath and near his fav'rite tree;
Another came; nor yet beside the rill,
Nor up the lawn, nor at the wood was he,

"The next with dirges due in sad array
Slow thro' the church-way path we saw him borne.
Approach and read (for thou can'st read) the lay,
Grav'd on the stone beneath yon aged thorn.''

---

[20]Gray settled on this version of ll. 91–92 only
in the poem's eighth edition of 1753. The
inversion of normal expectations, in which the
dead would be the ash and the living the fire,
signals a major change in the speaker's attitude
towards the villagers, and allows him to "earn"
the kindred spirit (l. 96) who will care about
him as he cares about those around him.
[21]**thee** the objectified poet
[22]**Swain** a country farm laborer

THE EPITAPH

Here rests his head upon the lap of Earth
A Youth to Fortune and to Fame unknown,
Fair Science[23] *frown'd not on his humble birth,*
120 *And Melancholy mark'd him for her own.*

Large was his bounty, and his soul sincere,
Heav'n did a recompence as largely send:
He gave to Mis'ry all he had, a tear,
He gain'd from Heav'n ('twas all he wish'd) a friend.

No farther seek his merits to disclose,
Or draw his frailties from their dread abode,
(There they alike in trembling hope repose)
The bosom of his Father and his God.

1751

[23]*Science*   learning, knowledge

WILLIAM COLLINS
1721–1759

Collins, the son of a hatter, received his degree from Magdalen College, Oxford. Soon after, he went to London to increase his modest literary fame; there, various distractions—ranging from the conversation of Samuel Johnson and James Thomson to the horse races in rural Guildford—slowed his progress. Nevertheless, by December 1746 he had produced a slender but important volume, *Odes on Several Descriptive and Allegoric Subjects* (1747). Unfortunately he was increasingly disabled by physical and mental illness and in 1754 was temporarily placed in MacDonald's madhouse in Chelsea; his sister Anne removed him to Chichester, where he died in 1759.

His poetry is concerned with the role of imagination, individual response to rural external nature and internal emotion, and the speaker's own place in literary traditions. Sometimes it soars into sublime, even religi-ous, mystery. Evening, a favorite time of day, becomes an adored goddess, and Collins becomes as much nature's pilgrim as her poet. The "Ode on the Poetical Character" exalts that character and process of poetic creation through analogies with God as creator and through allusions to Milton as the transcendent poet. Indeed, like other mid-century men of letters, Collins turns to native sources and subjects, including poetry itself, and regards folklore as a richer soil for poetry than book learning. His odes include individual, imagistic descriptions, and allegories of British myths, poets, and achievements, whether in arts or arms. Collins is not, however, a "pre-Romantic," for like Dryden and Pope he deals with public events and authors of national importance and with the poet's relation to the life of the community.

Ode on the Poetical Character[1]

I

As once, if not with light Regard,[2]
I read aright that gifted Bard,[3]
(Him whose School[4] above the rest
His Loveliest Elfin Queen has blest.)
One, only One, unrival'd Fair,
Might hope the magic Girdle wear,[5]
At solemn Tourney hung on high,
The Wish of each love-darting Eye;
Lo! to each other Nymph in turn applied,
As if, in Air unseen, some hov'ring Hand,
Some chaste and Angel-Friend to Virgin-Fame,
   With whisper'd Spell had burst the starting Band,[6]
If left unblest her loath'd dishonour'd Side;
     Happier hopeless Fair, if never
     Her baffled[7] Hand with vain Endeavour
Had touch'd that fatal Zone to her denied!
Young Fancy[8] thus, to me Divinest Name,
     To whom, prepar'd and bath'd in Heav'n,
     The Cest of amplest Pow'r is giv'n:
     To few the God-like[9] Gift assigns,
     To gird their blest prophetic Loins,
And gaze her Visions wild, and feel unmix'd her Flame!

II

The Band, as Fairy Legends say,
Was wove on that creating Day,[10]
When He, who call'd with Thought to Birth
Yon tented[11] Sky, this laughing[12] Earth,
And dress'd[13] with Springs, and Forests tall,
And pour'd the Main engirting all,
Long by the lov'd Enthusiast[14] woo'd,

---

[1] The mark of the noblest poet is a sublime power similar to divine creation. The poem considers several literary traditions and Collins's role in them.

[2] **Regard** both attention and respect

[3] **Bard** Edmund Spenser, whose *Faerie Queene*, the "Elfin Queen" of l. 4, provides the initial mythology of the ode

[4] **School** Spenser's followers are superior to others; the school included Milton himself, who surpassed his model.

[5] **One . . . wear** See *The Faerie Queene* IV.v.3. Venus' "Girdle," or belt (also the "Band" of ll. 12 and 23, the "Zone" of 1, 16, and the "Cest" of l. 19), of chaste love, in Florimel's possession, and won by her at a tourney, will not stay fastened on her unworthy "middle" and should fit only the virtuous Amoret.

[6] **burst . . . Band** unfastened the girdle

[7] **baffled** defeated

[8] **Fancy** imagination, Collins's parallel in poetry to the true chaste Florimel in virtue

[9] **God-like** Like God, imagination has creative power. The analogy between God and poet is implicit in much of the rest of the poem.

[10] **creating Day** the fourth day of creation, as in Genesis 1:14–19, and *Paradise Lost* VII. 339–86

[11] **tented** like a tent, but with implications of tabernacled or enshrined

[12] **laughing** pleasing, fertile

[13] **dress'd** both clothed and embellished

[14] **Enthusiast** Fancy, from l. 17, but with the connotation of "inspiration," as in the Greek meaning of "enthusiasm"

30   Himself in some Diviner[15] Mood,
      Retiring, sate with her alone,
      And plac'd her on his Saphire Throne,
      The whiles, the vaulted Shrine around,
      Seraphic Wires[16] were heard to sound,
      Now sublimest Triumph swelling,
      Now on Love and Mercy dwelling;
      And she, from out the veiling Cloud,[17]
      Breath'd her magic Notes aloud:
      And Thou, Thou rich-hair'd Youth of Morn,[18]
40   And all thy subject Life was born!
      The dang'rous Passions[19] kept aloof,
      Far from the sainted growing Woof:[20]
      But near it sate Ecstatic Wonder,[21]
      List'ning the deep applauding Thunder:
      And Truth, in sunny Vest array'd,
      By whose the Tarsel's[22] Eyes were made;
      All the shad'wy Tribes of Mind,
      In braided Dance their Murmurs join'd,
      And all the bright uncounted Pow'rs,
50   Who feed on Heav'n's ambrosial Flow'rs.
      Where is the Bard, whose Soul can now
      Its[23] high presuming Hopes avow?
      Where He who thinks, with Rapture blind,[24]
      This hallow'd Work for Him design'd?

          III
      High on some Cliff, to Heav'n up-pil'd,[25]
      Of rude Access, of Prospect Wild,
      Where, tangled round the jealous Steep,[26]
      Strange Shades o'erbrow the Valleys deep,
      And holy Genii guard the Rock,[27]
60   Its Glooms embrown, its Springs unlock,
      While on its rich ambitious[28] Head,
      An Eden, like his[29] own, lies spread.

[15]**Diviner** here synonymous with creating

[16]**Seraphic Wires** music of one of the highest orders of angels, the seraphim, coming from harp-like instruments or lyres

[17]**she . . . Cloud** Fancy or inspiration is hidden in the cloud, as the sun was before being unveiled on the fourth day of creation.

[18]**Morn** the sun, but also Phoebus Apollo, god of poetry, often pictured with shaking or flame-like hair. Poetry, the offspring of God and Fancy, controls life in its world as the sun does in the real world.

[19]**Passions** Angry emotions have no place in the created world before the fall.

[20]**sainted . . . Woof** The holy band is being woven in the creating day. The image continues in "braided," l. 48.

[21]**Wonder** admiration

[22]**Tarsel** the male hawk, whose eyes, like Truth's, see well from afar

[23]**It** either the soul, or the girdle, as in "Work" in l. 54

[24]**Rapture blind** blinded by enthusiasm, but suggesting the blindness of Milton, below

[25]**High . . . up-pil'd** Collins suggests Milton's vision of Eden in *Paradise Lost* IV.132-42.

[26]**jealous Steep** steep sides watchfully protected, either by their own danger, or by the "holy Genii," angels, of l. 59

[27]**Rock** suggestive of Mt. Parnassus, the Greek home of the muses, here conflated with a poetic Eden

[28]**ambitious** elevated

[29]**his** Milton's

I view that Oak,[30] the fancied Glades among,
By which as Milton lay, His Ev'ning Ear,
From many a Cloud that dropp'd Ethereal Dew,[31]
Nigh spher'd in Heav'n its native Strains could hear:
On which that ancient Trump[32] he reach'd was hung;
    Thither oft his Glory greeting,
    From Waller's Myrtle Shades retreating,
70 With many a Vow from Hope's aspiring Tongue,
My trembling Feet his guiding Steps pursue;
    In vain—Such Bliss to One alone,
    Of all the Sons of Soul was known,
And Heav'n, and Fancy, kindred Pow'rs,
Have now o'erturn'd th' inspiring Bow'rs,
Or curtain'd close such Scene from ev'ry future View.

1747

[30]**Oak** in "Il Penseroso," ll. 59-60, where Milton's speaker listens to the nightingale's evening song next to an oak
[31]**dropp'd . . . Dew** dripped heavenly dew or gentle rain
[32]**ancient Trump** Milton reaches for the trumpet of prophecy and epic poetry hanging on the oak tree, as the woman reaches for the girdle "hung on high" (l. 7).

Ode to Evening[1]

If aught of Oaten Stop,[2] or Pastoral Song,
May hope, chaste Eve,[3] to soothe thy modest Ear,
    Like thy own solemn Springs,
    Thy Springs, and dying Gales,[4]
O Nymph reserv'd, while now the bright-hair'd Sun
Sits in yon western Tent, whose cloudy Skirts,[5]
    With Brede ethereal[6] wove,
    O'erhang his wavy Bed:
Now Air is hush'd, save where the weak-ey'd Bat,
10 With short shrill Shriek flits by on leathern Wing,
    Or where the Beetle winds[7]
    His small but sullen[8] Horn,
As oft he rises 'midst the twilight Path,
Against the Pilgrim[9] borne in heedless Hum:
    Now teach me, Maid compos'd,
    To breathe some soften'd Strain,
Whose Numbers stealing[10] thro' thy dark'ning Vale,

[1]The unrhymed ode is in the tradition of Milton's translation of Horace's *Odes* I.5, and the comparable practice by Collins's friends Thomas and Joseph Warton.
[2]**Oaten Stop** the hole on a shepherd's reed flute
[3]**chaste Eve** the evening as a pure woman
[4]**dying Gales** breezes dying down
[5]**Skirts** the outer edges of the clouds around the "tent" or temporary resting place of the setting sun
[6]**Brede ethereal** the clouds braided together
[7]**winds** blows
[8]**sullen** mournful
[9]**Pilgrim** probably, a man out for a walk, humming and indifferent to the noisy beetle. But the term includes religious implications.
[10]**Numbers stealing** gentle verses appropriate for the evening

May not unseemly with its Stillness suit,
    As musing[11] slow, I hail
20   Thy genial[12] lov'd Return!
For when thy folding Star[13] arising shows
His paly Circlet, at his warning Lamp
    The fragrant Hours,[14] and Elves
    Who slept in Flow'rs the Day,
And many a Nymph who wreaths her Brows with Sedge,
And sheds the fresh'ning Dew, and lovelier still,
    The Pensive Pleasures[15] sweet
    Prepare thy shadowy Car.[16]
Then lead, calm Vot'ress,[17] where some sheety Lake
30   Cheers the lone Heath, or some time-hallow'd Pile,[18]
    Or up-land Fallows grey
    Reflect its last cool Gleam.
But when chill blust'ring Winds, or driving Rain,
Forbid my willing Feet, be mine the Hut,
    That from the Mountain's Side,
    Views Wilds, and swelling Floods,[19]
And Hamlets brown, and dim-discover'd Spires,
And hears their simple Bell, and marks o'er all
    Thy Dewy Fingers draw
40   The gradual dusky Veil.

While Spring shall pour his Show'rs, as oft he wont,
And bathe thy breathing Tresses,[20] meekest Eve!
    While Summer loves to sport,
    Beneath thy ling'ring Light:
While sallow Autumn fills thy Lap with Leaves,
Or Winter yelling thro' the troublous Air,
    Affrights thy shrinking Train,[21]
    And rudely rends thy Robes,
So long, sure-found beneath the Sylvan Shed,
50   Shall Fancy, Friendship, Science,[22] rose-lipp'd Health,
    Thy gentlest Influence own,
    And hymn thy fav'rite Name!

1747

[11]**musing** silently thoughtful, here appropriate for the poetry he writes inspired by Evening as a "muse"

[12]**genial** cheering, productive, and congenial, suited to his temperament

[13]**folding Star** the evening star Hesperus, at whose appearance the shepherd drives his sheep to their fold

[14]**Hours** goddesses supposed to preside over the change of seasons, here used for the change from day to evening

[15]**Pensive Pleasures** goddesses of enjoyment, here thoughtful and virtuous

[16]**Car** chariot

[17]**Vot'ress** votaress, a woman devoted to worship

[18]**Pile** a building

[19]**Floods** rivers

[20]**breathing Tresses** sweet-smelling hair

[21]**shrinking Train** Evening's attendants from ll. 23–27, who shrink from yelling Winter; also, fewer in winter

[22]**Science** learning

Ode, Written in the Beginning of the Year 1746[1]

I

How sleep the Brave, who sink to Rest,
By all their Country's Wishes blest!
When Spring, with dewy Fingers cold,
Returns to deck their hallow'd Mold,[2]
She there shall dress a sweeter Sod,
Than Fancy's[3] Feet have ever trod.

II

By Fairy Hands[4] their Knell is rung,
By Forms unseen their Dirge is sung;
There Honour comes, a Pilgrim grey,
10   To bless the Turf that wraps their Clay,
And Freedom shall a-while repair,[5]
To dwell a weeping Hermit there!

1747

[1] The poem probably commemorates the British dead in three losing battles; at Fontenoy, Belgium, during the war of the Austrian Succession (1740–48), and at Prestonpans and Falkirk, Scotland, in the battles against Bonnie Prince Charlie during the Jacobite rebellion on his behalf (1745–46). The ode mingles religious and patriotic imagery.
[2] **Mold**   grave
[3] **Fancy**   imagination
[4] **Fairy Hands**   the local British deities praying for fallen heroes
[5] **repair**   both return and restore herself

Ode Occasioned by the Death of Mr. Thomson[1]

I

In yonder Grave a Druid[2] lies
   Where slowly winds the Stealing[3] Wave!
The Year's[4] best Sweets shall duteous rise
   To deck its Poet's sylvan Grave!

II

In yon deep Bed of whisp'ring Reeds
   His airy Harp[5] shall now be laid,

[1] Thomson lived in the Thames village of Richmond, near London, from 1736 until his death in 1748. His good friend Collins had moved there by 1747 and knew the surrounding countryside well. Collins's watery journey carries us through time and space, both towards and away from Thomson's grave and the mourning process. The poem was dedicated to George, later Baron Lyttelton (1709–1773), poet, patron, politician, and friend of Thomson, and included a Greek epigraph from Virgil's *Eclogues* V. 74–75: "These rites shall be thine for ever, both when we pay our yearly vows to the Nymphs, and when we purify our fields"; and 52, "me, too, Daphnis loved."
[2] **Druid**   ancient Celtic priest, magician, or soothsayer, associated with nature and with British liberty, two of Thomson's own subjects
[3] **Stealing**   moving furtively
[4] **Year's**   because Thomson wrote *The Seasons*. Collins uses the familiar convention of nature in mourning.
[5] **airy Harp**   the Aeolian harp, a stringed instrument named after Aeolus, Greek god of the winds, that produces musical sounds when exposed to air currents

That He, whose Heart in Sorrow bleeds[6]
May love thro' Life the soothing Shade.[7]

III

Then Maids and Youths shall linger here,
10 And while its Sounds[8] at distance swell,
Shall sadly seem in Pity's Ear
To hear the Woodland Pilgrim's Knell.[9]

IV

Remembrance oft shall haunt the Shore
When Thames in Summer-wreaths is drest,
And oft suspend the dashing Oar
To bid his gentle Spirit rest!

V

And oft as Ease and Health retire
To breezy Lawn, or Forest deep,
The Friend shall view yon whit'ning Spire,[10]
20 And 'mid the varied Landscape weep.

VI

But Thou, who own'st that Earthy Bed,
Ah! what will ev'ry Dirge avail?
Or Tears, which Love and Pity shed
That mourn beneath the gliding Sail!

VII

Yet lives there one, whose heedless Eye
Shall scorn thy pale Shrine glimm'ring near?
With Him, Sweet Bard, may Fancy die,
And Joy desert the blooming Year.

VIII

But thou, lorn[11] Stream, whose sullen[12] Tide
30 No sedge-crown'd Sisters[13] now attend,
Now waft me from the green Hill's Side
Whose cold Turf hides the buried Friend!

IX

And see, the Fairy Vallies fade,
Dun Night has veil'd the solemn View!
—Yet once again, Dear parted Shade
Meek Nature's Child again adieu!

[6]**He . . . bleeds** a sympathetic mourner, like the speaker
[7]**Shade** the spirit of Thomson, as in l. 35
[8]**its sounds** the sounds of the Aeolian harp (see l. 6), as the wind rises
[9]**Then Maids . . . Knell** Apparently, the young mourners hearing the distant harp, and affected by pity, imagine it to be the death knell of Thomson, the woodland pilgrim.
[10]**Spire** of Richmond's Church of St. Mary Magdalene, in which Thomson was buried
[11]**lorn** forlorn, lonely
[12]**sullen** slow, sluggish
[13]**sedge-crown'd Sisters** the Naiads or local river goddesses who left Richmond's shores upon Thomson's death

X

The genial Meads[14] assign'd to bless
    Thy Life, shall mourn thy early Doom,
Their Hinds,[15] and Shepherd-Girls shall dress
40   With simple Hands thy rural Tomb.

XI

Long, long, thy Stone and pointed Clay[16]
    Shall melt the musing[17] Briton's Eyes,
O! Vales, and Wild Woods, shall He say
    In yonder Grave Your Druid lies!

1749

[14]**genial Meads** productive, life-giving meadows, associated with Thomson's assigned "genius"—from the Latin *genialis*, one's guardian or tutelary deity—for dealing with nature
[15]**Hinds** peasants
[16]**Stone . . . Clay** either his headstone and grave pointed out by a visitor, perhaps pointed to by the stone itself, or the bricks of Thomson's tomb properly "pointed" or filled with mortar. In either case, Collins contrasts the solidity of the stone with the frailty of human clay.
[17]**musing** silently thoughtful, but also suggesting that Thomson has become the muse of the sympathetic Briton

CHRISTOPHER SMART

1722–1771

Smart was educated at Cambridge, where he was made a fellow in 1745. His convivial but eccentric behavior led Thomas Gray to quip that Smart would find himself either in jail or in a madhouse—a sadly prophetic remark. Smart's intense love of God soon developed into a zeal, perhaps a mania, for vocal public prayer that disrupted his career as a hack writer in London. He became unable to deal with daily life, and was confined in madhouses from 1757 to 1758, and again from 1759 to 1763, the period in which both *Jubilate Agno* and *A Song to David* were written. After his release, he resumed translating and writing, but he was arrested for debt in April 1770 and died in King's Bench Prison the following year.

Smart's greatest achievements are his religious poems, remarkable for their splendid diction and often innovative form. *Jubilate Agno*, for example, borrows its basic structure from Hebrew responsive poetry and the Anglican Book of Common Prayer, and is separated into two "Let" and "For" sections with striking parallels and oppositions. One of Smart's ablest adaptations of literary tradition is his use of the "impression" he perceived in Horace's odes — namely, the way a poet can "throw an emphasis on a word or sentence." The brilliant *Song to David*, which uses the familiar aabccb rhyme scheme of the eighteenth-century Horatian ode, thus repeats and varies such words as "ADORATION," "Sweet," and "strong," giving an emphasis that expands their meaning. The poem's progression by means of an association of ideas that touch on all of creation had been exemplified by Thomson; but its organization of stanzas into units of the sacred numbers three and seven and their multiples is Smart's own principle of form, one that contributes to the poem's sense of exalted prayer coming from a poet who associated himself with David the poet of God. The *Song to David* often is considered the best additive, incantatory long lyric poem of the eighteenth century, and ranks among the best in the English language. Largely unknown or coolly received in his lifetime, Smart's major poems are now admired as works of personal vision and revelation that remain anchored in their age.

From A Song to David[1]

I

O thou, that sit'st upon a throne,
With harp of high majestic tone,
  To praise the King of kings;
And voice of heav'n-ascending swell,
Which, while its deeper notes excell,
  Clear, as a clarion, rings:

II

To bless each valley, grove and coast,
And charm the cherubs to the post
  Of gratitude in throngs;
10 To *keep* the days on Zion's mount,[2]
And send the year to his account,
  With dances and with songs:

III

O Servant of God's holiest charge,
The minister of praise at large,
  Which thou may'st now receive;
From thy blest mansion[3] hail and hear,
From topmost eminence appear
  To this the wreath I weave.

. . .

LXIV

For ADORATION, DAVID's psalms
380 Lift up the heart to deeds of alms;
  And he, who kneels and chants,
Prevails his passions to controul,
Finds meat and med'cine to the soul,
  Which for translation[4] pants.

LXV

For ADORATION, beyond match,
The scholar bulfinch aims to catch
  The soft flute's iv'ry touch;[5]
And, careless[6] on the hazel spray,
The daring redbreast keeps at bay
390 The damsel's greedy clutch.

[1] Probably written when Smart was in Bedlam in 1759-60, the poem culminates Smart's long interest in the poetry of adoration and in the complex figure of David, with whom he associated himself. The *Song* was prefaced by an elaborate analytical Contents, and a quotation from 2 Samuel 23:1-2, in which David is called "the sweet psalmist of Israel," who said, "The Spirit of the Lord spake by me, and His word was in my tongue."
[2] *keep . . . mount* observe holy days at the temple
[3] **mansion** heaven
[4] **translation** conveyance from earth to heaven
[5] **scholar . . . touch** The bird imitates the sounds of the flute.
[6] **careless** without cares

LXVI

For ADORATION, in the skies,
The Lord's philosopher[7] espies
   The Dog, the Ram, and Rose;[8]
The planet's ring, Orion's sword;
Nor is his greatness less ador'd
   In the vile worm that glows.[9]

LXVII

For ADORATION on the strings
The western breezes work their wings,[10]
   The captive ear to sooth.—
400   Hark! 'tis a voice[11]—how still, and small—
That makes the cataracts to fall,
   Or bids the sea be smooth.

LXVIII

For ADORATION, incense comes
From bezoar, and Arabian gums;[12]
   And on the civet's[13] fur.
But as for prayer, or ere it faints,[14]
Far better is the breath of saints
   Than galbanum and myrrh.[15]

LXIX

For ADORATION from the down,
410   Of dam'sins to th' anana's[16] crown,
   God sends to tempt the taste;
And while the luscious zest invites,
The sense, that in the scene delights,
   Commands desire be chaste.

LXX

For ADORATION, all the paths
Of grace are open, all the baths
   Of purity refresh;
And all the rays of glory beam
To deck the man of God's esteem,
420   Who triumphs o'er the flesh.

---

[7]**philosopher** astronomer
[8]**Dog . . . Rose** constellations
[9]**vile . . . glows** lowly glowing beetle or firefly
[10]**strings . . . wings** The wind produces sound from an Aeolian harp placed in a tree.
[11]**voice** of God
[12]**bezoar . . . gums** a substance, once thought medicinal, found in the stomachs of ruminants, or cud-chewing animals; resin-like substances extracted from plants

[13]**civet** African civet cat, which secretes a musk-like substance used for perfume
[14]**faints** fades away
[15]**galbanum . . . myrrh** a bitter gum resin obtained from herbs and used in medicine and incense; aromatic gum resin used for incense, perfumes, and medicine
[16]**dam'sins . . . anana** damson plums; pineapple

LXXI

For ADORATION, in the dome
Of Christ the sparrows[17] find an home;
   And on his olives perch:
The swallow also dwells with thee,
O man of God's humility,
   Within his Saviour CHURCH.[18]

LXXII

Sweet is the dew that falls betimes,
And drops upon the leafy limes;
   Sweet Hermon's[19] fragrant air:
430   Sweet is the lilly's silver bell,
And sweet the wakeful tapers smell
   That watch for early pray'r.

LXXIII

Sweet the young nurse with love intense,
Which smiles o'er sleeping innocence;
   Sweet when the lost arrive:
Sweet the musician's ardour beats,
While his vague mind's in quest of sweets,
   The choicest flow'rs to hive.

LXXIV

Sweeter in all the strains of love,
440   The language of thy turtle dove,
   Pair'd to thy swelling chord;
Sweeter with ev'ry grace endu'd,
The glory of thy gratitude,
   Respir'd[20] unto the Lord.

LXXV

Strong is the horse upon his speed;
Strong in pursuit the rapid glede,[21]
   Which makes at once his game:
Strong the tall ostrich on the ground;
Strong thro' the turbulent profound
450   Shoots xiphias[22] to his aim.

LXXVI

Strong is the lion—like a coal
His eye-ball—like a bastion's mole[23]
   His chest against the foes:

---

[17]**sparrows** alluding to Matthew 10:29, and Psalm 84:3
[18]CHURCH alluding to Psalm 84:3
[19]**Hermon** Syrian mountain in Psalm 133
[20]**Respir'd** breathed (spoken) in prayer

[21]**glede** hawk
[22]**xiphias** swordfish
[23]**mole** a large masonry breakwater, sometimes fortified

Strong, the gier-eagle[24] on his sail,
Strong against tide, th' enormous whale
   Emerges as he goes.

LXXVII

But stronger still, in earth and air,
And in the sea, the man of pray'r;
   And far beneath the tide;
460 And in the seat to faith assign'd,
Where ask is have, where seek is find,
   Where knock is open wide.

LXXVIII

Beauteous the fleet before the gale;
Beauteous the multitudes in mail,
   Rank'd arms and crested heads:
Beauteous the garden's umbrage[25] mild,
Walk, water, meditated wild,[26]
   And all the bloomy beds.

LXXIX

Beauteous the moon full on the lawn;
470 And beauteous, when the veil's withdrawn,
   The virgin to her spouse:
Beauteous the temple deck'd and fill'd,
When to the heav'n of heav'ns they build
   Their heart-directed vows.

LXXX

Beauteous, yea beauteous more than these,
The shepherd king upon his knees,
   For his momentous trust;
With wish of infinite conceit,[27]
For man, beast, mute,[28] the small and great,
480   And prostrate dust to dust.

LXXXI

Precious the bounteous widow's mite;[29]
And precious, for extreme delight,
   The largess from the churl:[30]
Precious the ruby's blushing blaze,

---

[24]**gier-eagle** vulture, alluding to Leviticus 11:18
[25]**umbrage** shade
[26]**meditated wild** the consciously made but
irregular English garden
[27]**conceit** conception
[28]**mute** fish

[29]**mite** In Mark 12:42-44, Jesus respects the
widow's small gift of all that she had more than
larger gifts by the wealthy.
[30]**churl** In 1 Samuel 25:18-35, Abigail, wife of
the churl Nabel, gives food and wine to David.

And alba's[31] blest imperial rays,
And pure cerulean[32] pearl.

LXXXII

Precious the penitential tear;
And precious is the sigh sincere,
   Acceptable to God:
490 And precious are the winning flow'rs,
In gladsome Israel's feast[33] of bow'rs,
   Bound on the hallow'd sod.

LXXXIII

More precious that diviner part
Of David, ev'n the Lord's own heart,
   Great, beautiful, and new:
In all things where it was intent,
In all extremes, in each event,
   Proof[34]—answ'ring true to true.

LXXXIV

Glorious the sun in mid career;
500 Glorious th' assembled fires appear;
   Glorious the comet's train:
Glorious the trumpet and alarm;
Glorious th' almighty stretch'd-out arm;
   Glorious th' enraptur'd main:

LXXXV

Glorious the northern lights astream;
Glorious the song, when God's the theme;
   Glorious the thunder's roar:
Glorious hosanna from the den;[35]
Glorious the catholic[36] amen;
510 Glorious the martyr's gore:

LXXXVI

Glorious—more glorious is the crown
Of Him that brought salvation down
   By meekness, call'd thy Son;
Thou at stupendous truth believ'd,
And now the matchless deed's atchiev'd,
   DETERMINED, DARED, and DONE.

1763

[31]**alba** the white stone of Revelation 2:17, associated with Jesus
[32]**cerulean** blue
[33]**feast** from Leviticus 23:34–44, Sukkoth, or the Feast of the Tabernacles and its harvest bower
[34]**Proof** firm, hardened
[35]**den** from Daniel 6:22–23, in which Daniel's faith preserves him in the lion's den
[36]**catholic** universal

From Jubilate Agno (Rejoice in the Lamb)[1]

From Fragment A, Rejoice in God

Rejoice in God, O ye Tongues; give the glory to the Lord, and the Lamb.
Nations, and languages, and every Creature, in which is the breath of Life.
Let man and beast appear before him, and magnify his name together.
Let Noah and his company approach the throne of Grace, and do homage to
    the Ark of their Salvation.
Let Abraham present a Ram,[2] and worship the God of his Redemption.
Let Isaac,[3] the Bridegroom, kneel with his Camels, and bless the hope of
    his pilgrimage.
Let Jacob, and his speckled Drove[4] adore the good Shepherd[5] of Israel.
Let Esau offer a scape Goat for his seed, and rejoice in the blessing of God
    his father.[6]
Let Nimrod,[7] the mighty hunter, bind a Leopard to the altar, and consecrate
    his spear to the Lord.
Let Ishmael[8] dedicate a Tyger, and give praise for the liberty, in which the
10   Lord has let him at large.
Let Balaam appear with an Ass,[9] and bless the Lord his people and his
    creatures for a reward eternal.

[1] Written while Smart was institutionalized between 1759 and 1763, but not published until 1939, the poem is organized around the counterpoint of lines beginning with "Let," which are relatively objective, and "For," which are more personal. Its title means "Rejoice in the Lamb."

[2] **Ram** In Genesis 22:13 God allowed Abraham to sacrifice a ram instead of his son Isaac.

[3] **Isaac** In Genesis 24:12–67 Rebekah gave water to Abraham's servants and camels and was therefore chosen to be Isaac's bride.

[4] **speckled Drove** In Genesis 30:32 Jacob received "speckled and spotted cattle" from Laban.

[5] **good Shepherd** God

[6] **blessing . . . father** In Genesis 27 Jacob disguised himself as Esau in order to receive his blind father's blessing and estate; Esau then had to seek God's blessing.

[7] **Nimrod** from Genesis 10:9

[8] **Ishmael** son of Abraham and Hagar, who was cast out of Israel

[9] **Balaam . . . Ass** from Numbers 22–24: the prophet who sought to curse Israel, was rebuked by the ass he rode, and accepted God's wisdom

From Fragment B, My Cat Jeoffry

For I will consider my cat Jeoffry.
For he is the servant of the Living God duly and daily serving him.
For at the first glance of the glory of God in the East he worships in his way.
For is this done by wreathing his body seven times round with elegant
    quickness.
For then he leaps up to catch the musk,[1] which is the blessing of God upon
    his prayer.
700   For he rolls upon prank to work it in.[2]
For having done duty and received blessing he begins to consider himself.

[1] **musk** probably a catnip treat, perhaps in the shape of a mouse, *musculus* being Latin for "a little mouse"

[2] **rolls . . . in** probably, rolls the musk into his skin, to get the benefit of the treat's scent

For this he performs in ten degrees.
For first he looks upon his fore-paws to see if they are clean.
For secondly he kicks up behind to clear away there.
For thirdly he works it upon stretch with the fore paws extended.
For fourthly he sharpens his paws by wood.
For fifthly he washes himself.
For sixthly he rolls upon wash.
For seventhly he fleas himself, that he may not be interrupted upon the beat.[3]
710   For eighthly he rubs himself against a post.
For ninthly he looks up for his instructions.
For tenthly he goes in quest of food.
For having consider'd God and himself he will consider his neighbour.
For if he meets another cat he will kiss her in kindness.
For when he takes his prey he plays with it to give it a chance.
For one mouse in seven escapes by his dallying.
For when his day's work is done his business more properly begins.
For he keeps the Lord's watch in the night against the adversary.[4]
For he counteracts the powers of darkness by his electrical skin and glaring eyes.
720   For he counteracts the Devil, who is death, by brisking about the life.
For in his morning orisons[5] he loves the sun and the sun loves him.
For he is of the tribe of Tiger.
For the Cherub Cat is a term of the Angel Tiger.[6]
For he has the subtlety and hissing of a serpent, which in goodness he suppresses.
For he will not do destruction, if he is well-fed, neither will he spit without provocation.
For he purrs in thankfulness, when God tells him he's a good cat.
For he is an instrument for the children to learn benevolence upon.
For every house is incomplete without him and a blessing is lacking in the spirit.
For the Lord commanded[7] Moses concerning the cats at the departure of the Children of Israel from Egypt.
730   For every family had one cat at least in the bag.
For the English cats are the best in Europe.
For he is the cleanest in the use of his fore-paws of any quadrupede.
For the dexterity of his defence is an instance of the love of God to him exceedingly.
For he is the quickest to his mark of any creature.
For he is tenacious of his point.
For he is a mixture of gravity and waggery.
For he knows that God is his Saviour.
For there is nothing sweeter than his peace when at rest.
For there is nothing brisker than his life when in motion.
For he is of the Lord's poor and so indeed is he called by benevolence
740   perpetually—Poor Jeoffry! poor Jeoffry! the rat has bit thy throat.

[3] **that . . . beat** so that his routine will not be interrupted to scratch
[4] **adversary** the devil
[5] **orisons** prayers
[6] **Cherub Cat . . . Tiger** He is to the tiger as the cherubim are to a higher order of angels.
[7] **Lord commanded** apparently fanciful

For I bless the name of the Lord Jesus that Jeoffry is better.
For the divine spirit comes about his body to sustain it in complete cat.
For his tongue is exceeding pure so that it has in purity what it wants in
    music.
For he is docile and can learn certain things.
For he can set up with gravity which is patience upon approbation.
For he can fetch and carry, which is patience in employment.
For he can jump over a stick which is patience upon proof positive.
For he can spraggle upon waggle[8] at the word of command.
For he can jump from an eminence into his master's bosom.
750   For he can catch the cork and toss it again.
For he is hated by the hypocrite and miser.
For the former is afraid of detection.
For the latter refuses the charge.
For he camels his back to bear the first notion of business.
For he is good to think on, if a man would express himself neatly.
For he made a great figure in Egypt for his signal services.
For he killed the Ichneumon-rat[9] very pernicious by land.
For his ears are so acute that they sting again.
For from this proceeds the passing quickness of his attention.
760   For by stroaking of him I have found out electricity.
For I perceived God's light about him both wax and fire.
For the Electrical fire is the spiritual substance, which God sends from
    heaven to sustain the bodies both of man and beast.
For God has blessed him in the variety of his movements.
For, tho he cannot fly, he is an excellent clamberer.
For his motions upon the face of the earth are more than any other quadru-
    pede.
For he can tread to all the measures upon the music.
For he can swim for life.
For he can creep.

1759–63   1939

[8] **spraggle . . . waggle**   probably, clamber side-
ways
[9] **Ichneumon-rat**   mongoose

OLIVER GOLDSMITH
1730?–1774

Goldsmith spent his childhood in Lissoy, Kilkenny West, Ireland, where his father was an Anglican curate. After studying at Trinity College, Dublin, he spent the next few years trying—and failing—to become a clergyman, to go to America, to study law, and to complete a medical degree at Edinburgh and Leyden. Though impoverished, he traveled widely in Europe and later turned his experiences to good use in the poem *The Traveller* (1764) and the novel *The Vicar of Wakefield* (1766).

A talented man of letters and a friend of Samuel Johnson, Goldsmith nevertheless remained on the fringes of greatness. He was mocked for his extravagant dress and relative dullness as a speaker. The suspicion and prejudice he experienced as an

Irishman in England are perhaps reflected by the rootless isolated speaker in his poetry, who says of Auburn, "These were thy charms—But all these charms are fled." In *The Deserted Village*, Goldsmith rejects the fashionable blank verse, complex odes, and archaic language, in favor of couplets and plain diction. Filled with contrast between then and now, the poem laments the decline of rural and village life and the loss of honest country folk to the cities. There, urban acts of luxury "thin mankind" and banish the sources of British literary and national greatness to an uncongenial American continent in which old village values cannot be transplanted. Goldsmith uses individual characters like the clergyman and the schoolmaster to illustrate his nostalgic vision of lost innocence, and calls on now debased "sweet Poetry" to teach his contemporaries not to exchange human values for commercial gain. The personification of poetry as "thou loveliest maid" is consistent with the varied and essential portraits of women in the poem. *The Deserted Village* went into five editions in its first year and solidified Goldsmith's reputation as a poet.

The Deserted Village[1]

Sweet Auburn,[2] loveliest village of the plain,
Where health and plenty cheared the labouring swain,
Where smiling spring its earliest visit paid,
And parting summer's lingering blooms delayed,
Dear lovely bowers of innocence and ease,
Seats of my youth, when every sport could please,
How often have I loitered o'er thy green,
Where humble happiness endeared each scene;
How often have I paused on every charm,
10 The sheltered cot,[3] the cultivated farm,
The never failing brook, the busy mill,
The decent[4] church that topped the neighbouring hill,
The hawthorn bush, with seats beneath the shade,
For talking age and whispering lovers made.
How often have I blessed the coming day,[5]
When toil remitting lent its turn to play,
And all the village train[6] from labour free,
Led up[7] their sports beneath the spreading tree,
While many a pastime circled in the shade,
20 The young contending as the old surveyed;
And many a gambol frolicked o'er the ground,

---

[1] The poem concerns the conversion of common lands on which several farmers might graze their cattle into privately owned and often fenced or "enclosed" fields. Goldsmith does not object when these measures are used to increase efficiency and crop-yield, but he does object when the uncomprehending urban rich turn productive farmland into unproductive parkland that forces emigration and, in several senses, desertion of the village. The poem was prefaced by a dedication to the eminent painter Sir Joshua Reynolds (1723–1792), and by a statement of the realities of depopulation and luxury as threats to the nation.

[2] **Auburn** thought by some to be Lissoy, and by others to suggest a town of that name in Wiltshire; probably a composite of idealized places

[3] **cot** cottage, as in l. 380

[4] **decent** suitable, not ostentatious

[5] **day** a summer holiday, possibly Sunday

[6] **train** attendants

[7] **Led up** began

And slights of art and feats of strength went round.
And still as each repeated pleasure tired,
Succeeding sports the mirthful band inspired;
The dancing pair that simply sought renown
By holding out to tire each other down,
The swain[8] mistrustless of his smutted face,
While secret laughter tittered round the place,
The bashful virgin's side-long looks of love,
30   The matron's glance that would those looks reprove.
These were thy charms, sweet village; sports like these,
With sweet succession, taught even toil to please;
These round thy bowers their cheerful influence shed,
These were thy charms—But all these charms are fled.

     Sweet smiling village, loveliest of the lawn,[9]
Thy sports are fled, and all thy charms withdrawn;
Amidst thy bowers the tyrant's[10] hand is seen,
And desolation saddens all thy green:
One only master grasps the whole domain,
40   And half a tillage[11] stints thy smiling plain;
No more thy glassy brook reflects the day,
But choked with sedges, works its weedy way.
Along thy glades, a solitary guest,
The hollow sounding bittern guards its nest;
Amidst thy desert walks the lapwing flies,
And tires their echoes with unvaried cries.
Sunk are thy bowers in shapeless ruin all,
And the long grass o'ertops the mouldering wall,
And trembling, shrinking from the spoiler's hand,
50   Far, far away thy children leave the land.

     Ill fares the land, to hastening ills a prey,
Where wealth accumulates, and men decay;
Princes and lords may flourish, or may fade;
A breath can make them, as a breath has made.
But a bold peasantry, their country's pride,
When once destroyed, can never be supplied.

     A time there was, ere England's griefs began,
When every rood[12] of ground maintained its man;
For him light labour spread her wholesome store,
60   Just gave what life required, but gave no more.
His best companions, innocence and health;
And his best riches, ignorance of wealth.

---

[8]**swain** young country farmer and suitor, but in ll. 64 and 90 just the farmer
[9]**lawn** grassy, open, flat space
[10]**tyrant** the landowner whose wealth, based on commerce, allows him to buy and destroy the neighboring farms and fields, forcing emigration of the farmers. See also ll. 63–76.
[11]**tillage** plowed land
[12]**rood** quarter-acre

But times are altered; trade's unfeeling train
Usurp the land and dispossess the swain;
Along the lawn, where scattered hamlets rose,
Unwieldy wealth, and cumbrous pomp repose;
And every want to opulence allied,
And every pang that folly pays to pride.
These gentle hours that plenty bade to bloom,
70   Those calm desires that asked but little room,
Those healthful sports that graced the peaceful scene,
Lived in each look, and brightened all the green;
These far departing seek a kinder shore,
And rural mirth and manners[13] are no more.

Sweet Auburn! parent of the blissful hour,
Thy glades forlorn confess the tyrant's power.
Here as I take my solitary rounds,
Amidst thy tangling walks, and ruined grounds,
And, many a year elapsed, return to view
80   Where once the cottage stood, the hawthorn grew,
Remembrance wakes with all her busy train,
Swells at my breast, and turns the past to pain.

In all my wanderings round this world of care,
In all my griefs—and God has given my share—
I still had hopes my latest hours to crown,
Amidst these humble bowers to lay me down;
To husband[14] out life's taper at the close,
And keep the flame from wasting by repose.
I still had hopes, for pride attends us still,
90   Amidst the swains to show my book-learned skill,

Around my fire an evening group to draw,
And tell of all I felt, and all I saw;
And, as an hare whom hounds and horns pursue,
Pants to the place from whence at first she flew,
I still had hopes, my long vexations past,
Here to return—and die at home at last.

O blessed retirement, friend to life's decline,
Retreats from care that never must be mine,
How happy he who crowns in shades like these,
100   A youth of labour with an age of ease;
Who quits a world where strong temptations try,
And, since 'tis hard to combat, learns to fly.
For him no wretches, born to work and weep,
Explore the mine, or tempt[15] the dangerous deep;
No surly porter stands in guilty state
To spurn imploring famine from the gate,

[13]**manners** customs, way of life
[14]**husband** to manage prudently
[15]**tempt** try

But on he moves to meet his latter end,
Angels around befriending virtue's friend;
Bends to the grave with unperceived decay,
110 While resignation gently slopes the way;
And all his prospects brightening to the last,
His Heaven commences ere the world be past!

Sweet was the sound when oft at evening's close,
Up yonder hill the village murmur rose;
There as I passed with careless[16] steps and slow,
The mingling notes came softened from below;
The swain responsive as the milk-maid sung,
The sober herd that lowed to meet their young;
The noisy geese that gabbled o'er the pool,
120 The playful children just let loose from school;
The watch-dog's voice that bayed the whispering wind,
And the loud laugh that spoke the vacant[17] mind,
These all in sweet confusion[18] sought the shade,
And filled each pause the nightingale had made.
But now the sounds of population fail,
No cheerful murmurs fluctuate in the gale,[19]
No busy steps the grass-grown foot-way tread,
For all the bloomy flush of life is fled.
All but yon widowed, solitary thing
130 That feebly bends beside the plashy[20] spring;
She, wretched matron, forced, in age, for bread,
To strip the brook with mantling[21] cresses spread,
To pick her wintry faggot from the thorn,
To seek her nightly shed, and weep till morn;
She only left of all the harmless train,
The sad historian of the pensive plain.

Near yonder copse,[22] where once the garden smiled
And still where many a garden flower grows wild;
There, where a few torn shrubs the place disclose,
140 The village preacher's modest mansion[23] rose
A man he was, to all the country dear,
And passing[24] rich with forty pounds a year,
Remote from towns he ran his godly race,
Nor ere had changed, nor wished to change his place;[25]
Unpractised he to fawn, or seek for power,
By doctrines fashioned to the varying hour;
Far other aims his heart had learned to prize,
More skilled to raise the wretched than to rise.

[16]**careless** unconcerned
[17]**vacant** untroubled, as in l. 257
[18]**confusion** irregular mixture
[19]**gale** a strong breeze
[20]**plashy** lightly splashing
[21]**mantling** covering

[22]**copse** coppice, a grove of small trees
[23]**mansion** house. See also ll. 195 and 238.
[24]**passing** abundantly
[25]**place** both the place in which he lived, and
his church "place" or appointment

His house was known to all the vagrant train,
150 He chid their wanderings, but relieved their pain;
The long remembered beggar was his guest,
Whose beard descending swept his aged breast;
The ruined spendthrift, now no longer proud,
Claimed kindred there, and had his claims allowed;
The broken[26] soldier, kindly bade to stay,
Sat by his fire, and talked the night away;
Wept o'er his wounds, or tales of sorrow done,
Shouldered his crutch, and showed how fields were won.
Pleased with his guests, the good man learned to glow,
160 And quite forgot their vices in their woe;
Careless their merits, or their faults to scan,
His pity gave ere charity began.

Thus to relieve the wretched was his pride,
And even his failings leaned to Virtue's side;
But in his duty prompt at every call,
He watched and wept, he prayed and felt, for all.
And, as a bird each fond endearment tries,
To tempt its new fledged offspring to the skies;
He tried each art, reproved each dull delay,
170 Allured to brighter worlds, and led the way.

Beside the bed where parting life was laid,
And sorrow, guilt, and pain, by turns dismayed,
The reverend champion stood. At his control,
Despair and anguish fled the struggling soul;
Comfort came down the trembling wretch to raise,
And his last faultering accents whispered praise.

At church, with meek and unaffected grace,
His looks adorned the venerable place;
Truth from his lips prevailed with double sway,
180 And fools, who came to scoff, remained to pray.
The service past, around the pious man,
With steady zeal each honest rustic ran;
Even children followed with endearing wile,
And plucked his gown, to share the good man's smile.
His ready smile a parent's warmth expressed,
Their welfare pleased him, and their cares distressed;
To them his heart, his love, his griefs were given,
But all his serious thoughts had rest in Heaven.
As some tall cliff that lifts its awful form
190 Swells from the vale, and midway leaves the storm,
Tho' round its breast the rolling clouds are spread,
Eternal sunshine settles on its head.

---

[26]**broken** disabled and discharged from the army

Beside yon straggling fence that skirts the way,
With blossomed furze unprofitably gay,
There, in his noisy mansion, skilled to rule,
The village master taught his little school;
A man severe he was, and stern to view,
I knew him well, and every truant knew;
Well had the boding tremblers learned to trace
200   The day's disasters in his morning face;
Full well they laughed with counterfeited glee,
At all his jokes, for many a joke had he;
Full well the busy whisper circling round,
Conveyed the dismal tidings when he frowned;
Yet he was kind, or if severe in aught,
The love he bore to learning was in fault,
The village all declared how much he knew;
'Twas certain he could write, and cipher[27] too;
Lands he could measure, terms and tides[28] presage,
210   And even the story ran that he could gauge.[29]
In arguing too, the parson owned his skill,
For even tho' vanquished, he could argue still;
While words of learned length, and thundering sound,
Amazed the gazing rustics ranged around,
And still they gazed, and still the wonder grew,
That one small head could carry all he knew.

But past is all his fame. The very spot
Where many a time he triumphed, is forgot.
Near yonder thorn, that lifts its head on high,
220   Where once the sign-post caught the passing eye,
Low lies that house where nut-brown draughts[30] inspired,
Where grey-beard mirth and smiling toil retired,
Where village statesmen talked with looks profound,
And news much older than their ale went round.
Imagination fondly stoops to trace
The parlour splendours of that festive place;
The white-washed wall, the nicely sanded floor,
The varnished clock that clicked behind the door;
The chest contrived a double debt to pay,
230   A bed by night, a chest of drawers by day;
The pictures placed for ornament and use,
The twelve good rules,[31] the royal game of goose;[32]

---

[27]**cipher** do arithmetic
[28]**terms and tides** the four quarter days on which rents, interest, wages and the like were due, and the ecclesiastical feast days or seasons, which changed each year
[29]**gauge** measure the contents of a vessel
[30]**draughts** of the ale in l. 224
[31]**twelve good rules** those appearing beneath a woodcut of Charles I's execution, and including "Pick no quarrells" and "Maintain no ill opinions"
[32]**goose** a game played on a board, the aim of which was to reach the sixty-third and final space by advancing through the throw of dice. Landing on the goose depicted in different spaces doubled the number on the dice.

The hearth, except when winter chilled the day,
With aspen boughs, and flowers, and fennel gay,
While broken tea-cups, wisely kept for show,
Ranged o'er the chimney, glistened in a row.

Vain transitory splendours! Could not all
Reprieve the tottering mansion from its fall!
Obscure it sinks, nor shall it more impart
240   An hour's importance to the poor man's heart;
Thither no more the peasant shall repair
To sweet oblivion of his daily care;
No more the farmer's news, the barber's tale,
No more the wood-man's ballad shall prevail;
No more the smith his dusky brow shall clear,
Relax his ponderous strength, and lean to hear;
The host himself no longer shall be found
Careful to see the mantling bliss[33] go round;
Nor the coy maid, half willing to be pressed,
250   Shall kiss the cup[34] to pass it to the rest.

Yes! let the rich deride, the proud disdain,
These simple blessings of the lowly train,
To me more dear, congenial to my heart,
One native charm, than all the gloss of art;[35]
Spontaneous joys, where Nature has its play,
The soul adopts, and owns their first born sway,
Lightly they frolic o'er the vacant mind,
Unenvied, unmolested, unconfined.
But the long pomp, the midnight masquerade,
260   With all the freaks of wanton wealth arrayed,
In these, ere triflers half their wish obtain,
The toiling pleasure sickens into pain;
And, even while fashion's brightest arts decoy,
The heart distrusting asks, if this be joy.

Ye friends to truth, ye statesmen who survey
The rich man's joys increase, the poor's decay,
'Tis yours to judge, how wide the limits stand
Between a splendid and an happy land.
Proud swells the tide with loads of freighted ore,
270   And shouting Folly hails them from her shore;
Hoards, even beyond the miser's wish abound,
And rich men flock from all the world around.
Yet count our gains. This wealth is but a name
That leaves our useful products still the same.
Not so the loss. The man of wealth and pride,
Takes up a space that many poor supplied;

---

[33]**mantling bliss** the frothing mug watched by the host of the public house in l. 247

[34]**kiss the cup** take a sip
[35]**art** artifice

Space for his lake, his park's extended bounds,
Space for his horses, equipage, and hounds;
The robe that wraps his limbs in silken sloth,
280 Has robbed the neighbouring fields of half their growth;
His seat, where solitary sports are seen,
Indignant spurns the cottage from the green;
Around the world each needful product flies,
For all the luxuries the world supplies.
While thus the land adorned for pleasure all
In barren splendour feebly waits the fall.

   As some fair female unadorned and plain,
Secure to please while youth confirms her reign,
Slights every borrowed charm that dress supplies,
290 Nor shares with art the triumph of her eyes;
But when those charms are past, for charms are frail,
When time advances, and when lovers fail,
She then shines forth solicitous to bless,
In all the glaring impotence of dress.
Thus fares the land, by luxury betrayed,
In nature's simplest charms at first arrayed,
But verging to decline, its splendours rise,
Its vistas[36] strike, its palaces surprise;
While scourged by famine from the smiling land,
300 The mournful peasant leads his humble band;
And while he sinks without one arm to save,
The country blooms—a garden, and a grave.

   Where then, ah, where shall poverty reside,
To scape the pressure of contiguous pride;[37]
If to some common's[38] fenceless limits strayed,
He drives his flock to pick the scanty blade,
Those fenceless fields the sons of wealth divide,
And even the bare-worn common is denied.

   If to the city sped—What waits him there?
310 To see profusion that he must not share;
To see ten thousand baneful arts combined
To pamper luxury, and thin mankind;
To see those joys the sons of pleasure know,
Extorted from his fellow-creature's woe.
Here, while the courtier glitters in brocade,
There the pale artist[39] plies the sickly trade;
Here, while the proud their long drawn pomps display,
There the black gibbet glooms[40] beside the way.

---

[36]**vistas** artificially made views through an
avenue of trees
[37]**contiguous pride** the new luxury invading the
country

[38]**common** unenclosed ground used for grazing
by the village farmers' cattle
[39]**artist** artisan, craftsman
[40]**gibbet glooms** gallows frowns

The dome[41] where pleasure holds her midnight reign,
320 Here richly decked admits the gorgeous train,
Tumultuous grandeur crowds the blazing square,
The rattling chariots clash, the torches glare;
Sure scenes like these no troubles ere annoy!
Sure these denote one universal joy!
Are these thy serious thoughts—Ah, turn thine eyes
Where the poor houseless shivering female lies.
She once, perhaps, in village plenty blessed,
Has wept at tales of innocence distressed;
Her modest looks the cottage might adorn,
330 Sweet as the primrose peeps beneath the thorn;
Now lost to all; her friends, her virtue fled,
Near her betrayer's door she lays her head,
And pinched with cold, and shrinking from the shower,
With heavy heart deplores that luckless hour,
When idly first, ambitious of the town,
She left her wheel[42] and robes of country brown.

Do thine, sweet Auburn, thine, the loveliest train,
Do thy fair tribes participate her pain?
Even now, perhaps, by cold and hunger led,
340 At proud men's doors they ask a little bread!
Ah, no. To distant climes, a dreary scene,
Where half the convex world intrudes between,
Through torrid tracts with fainting steps they go,
Where wild Altama[43] murmurs to their woe.
Far different there from all that charmed before,
The various terrors of that horrid shore.
Those blazing suns that dart a downward ray,
And fiercely shed intolerable day;
Those matted woods where birds forget to sing,
350 But silent bats in drowsy clusters cling,
Those poisonous fields with rank luxuriance crowned
Where the dark scorpion gathers death around;
Where at each step the stranger fears to wake
The rattling terrors of the vengeful snake;
Where crouching tigers[44] wait their helpless prey,
And savage men more murderous still than they;
While oft in whirls the mad tornado flies,
Mingling the ravaged landscape with the skies.
Far different these from every former scene,
360 The cooling brook, the grassy vested green,
The breezy covert of the warbling grove,
That only sheltered thefts of harmless love.

---

[41]**dome** building
[42]**wheel** spinning wheel
[43]**Altama** the Altamaha River in Georgia, a colony founded in part to be settled by the poor.

Eighteenth-century reports stressed its heat, poor soil, neighboring hostile Indians, and nearly mute birds.
[44]**tigers** cougars or "American tigers"

Good Heaven! what sorrows gloomed that parting day,
That called them from their native walks away;
When the poor exiles, every pleasure past,
Hung round their bowers, and fondly looked their last,
And took a long farewell, and wished in vain
For seats like these beyond the western main;
And shuddering still to face the distant deep,
370   Returned and wept, and still returned to weep.
The good old sire, the first prepared to go
To new found worlds, and wept for others' woe.
But for himself, in conscious virtue brave,
He only wished for worlds beyond the grave.
His lovely daughter, lovelier in her tears,
The fond companion of his helpless years,
Silent went next, neglectful of her charms,
And left a lover's for a father's arms.
With louder plaints the mother spoke her woes,
380   And blessed the cot where every pleasure rose;
And kissed her thoughtless babes with many a tear,
And clasped them close in sorrow doubly dear;
Whilst her fond husband strove to lend relief
In all the silent manliness of grief.

O luxury! Thou cursed by heaven's decree,
How ill exchanged are things like these for thee!
How do thy potions with insidious joy,
Diffuse their pleasures only to destroy!
Kingdoms by thee, to sickly greatness grown,
390   Boast of a florid vigour not their own.
At every draught more large and large they grow,
A bloated mass of rank unwieldy woe;
Till sapped their strength, and every part unsound,
Down, down they sink, and spread a ruin round.

Even now the devastation is begun,
And half the business of destruction done;
Even now, methinks, as pondering here I stand,
I see the rural virtues leave the land.
Down where yon anchoring vessel spreads the sail
400   That idly waiting flaps with every gale,
Downward they[45] move a melancholy band,
Pass from the shore, and darken all the strand.
Contented toil, and hospitable care,
And kind connubial tenderness, are there;
And piety with wishes placed above,
And steady loyalty, and faithful love.
And thou, sweet Poetry, thou loveliest maid,

---

[45]**they**   the rural virtues (l. 398) specified in ll.
    403–07, including Poetry

Still first to fly where sensual joys invade;
Unfit in these degenerate times of shame,
410 To catch[46] the heart, or strike for honest fame;
Dear charming nymph, neglected and decried,
My shame in crowds, my solitary pride.
Thou source of all my bliss, and all my woe,
That found'st me poor at first, and keep'st me so;
Thou guide by which the nobler arts excell,
Thou nurse of every virtue, fare thee well.
Farewell, and O where'er thy voice be tried,
On Torno's[47] cliffs, or Pambamarca's[48] side,
Whether where equinoctial fervours[49] glow,
420 Or winter wraps the polar world in snow,
Still let thy voice prevailing over time,
Redress the rigours of the inclement clime;
Aid slighted truth, with thy persuasive strain
Teach erring man to spurn the rage of gain;
Teach him that states of native strength possessed,
Tho' very poor, may still be very blessed;
That trade's proud empire hastes to swift decay,
As ocean sweeps the laboured mole[50] away;
While self dependent power can time defy,
430 As rocks resist the billows and the sky.[51]

1770

[46]**catch**   please, charm, as well as fasten upon
[47]**Torno**   Tornea or Torne, the river, lake, and
town in northern Sweden
[48]**Pambamarca**   an Ecuadorian (then Peruvian)
mountain near Quito

[49]**equinoctial fervours**   heat at the equator
[50]**mole**   a large masonry dike or breakwater
[51]Samuel Johnson wrote ll. 427–30 for Goldsmith.

WILLIAM COWPER

1731–1800

Educated at Westminster School and the Middle Temple, Cowper was called to the bar in 1754. In 1763 he agreed to stand as clerk to the House of Lords, but he attempted suicide three times when faced with the required oral examination. Guilt and a fear of damnation increased his melancholy and led to the first of four attacks of insanity. By 1764 he had undergone a conversion to Calvinistic evangelicalism, and in the following year he shared a country home with the Reverend and Mrs. Morley Unwin. Upon Unwin's death Cowper, Mrs. Unwin, with whom he maintained a close but chaste

friendship, and her children moved to Olney and the Reverend Mr. John Newton's evangelical ministry. Here Cowper and Newton collaborated on the *Olney Hymns* (1779), and here he met Lady Anna Austen, who encouraged his work and initiated *The Task* by pleasantly telling him to write about a sofa. Cowper spent his final years tending his garden and pets, writing poetry, translating Homer (1791) and, especially after Mary Unwin's death in 1796, trying to cope with the mental instability sadly characterized in "The Castaway."

Cowper's long blank-verse poem *The Task*

(1785) stems loosely from the georgic tradition and, like Thomson's *Seasons*, proceeds by means of association of ideas. But Cowper lacks both Virgil's and Thomson's optimism, and uses a plain unmiltonic style that hoped to be clear without being prosaic. Less confident than Thomson of humanity's ability to find God, Cowper contrasts the city and country and emphasizes nature's role in healing the isolated speaker. He conceives of "nature" on a small scale, replaces the prospect with the garden as an emblem of order, and often is personal, meditative, and introspectively pensive. Though Cowper's career as a poet did not begin until he was nearly fifty, *The Task* was so popular that it brought him an offer, unaccepted, of the poet laureateship, and in ways was useful for Wordsworth in *The Prelude*.

From The Task

From Book III, The Garden[1]

The morning finds the self-sequester'd man
Fresh for his task, intend what task he may.
Whether inclement seasons recommend
His warm but simple home, where he enjoys,
390   With her[2] who shares his pleasures and his heart,
Sweet converse, sipping calm the fragrant lymph[3]
Which neatly she prepares; then to his book,
Well chosen, and not sullenly perus'd
In selfish silence, but imparted oft
As aught occurs that she may smile to hear,
Or turn to nourishment, digested well.
Or, if the garden with its many cares,
All well repaid, demand him, he attends
The welcome call, conscious how much the hand
400   Of lubbard[4] labour needs his watchful eye,
Oft loit'ring lazily, if not o'erseen,
Or misapplying his unskilful strength.
Nor does he govern only or direct,
But much performs himself. No works indeed
That ask robust tough sinews, bred to toil,
Servile employ; but such as may amuse,
Not tire, demanding rather skill than force.
Proud of his well-spread walls, he views his trees
That meet (no barren interval between)
410   With pleasure more than ev'n their fruits afford,
Which, save himself who trains them, none can feel:
These, therefore, are his own peculiar[5] charge;

---

[1] The poem, in six books, springs from Lady Anna Austen's suggestion that Cowper write about a sofa. That is his "task" at the beginning of the poem, which soon becomes more discursive; it is loosely unified by the narrator's discursive voice, and by dislike of the city and praise for the retired country life as an aid to piety and virtue.
[2] **her** Mary Unwin, widow of the clergyman Morley Unwin
[3] **fragrant lymph** tea
[4] **lubbard** strong but lazy
[5] **peculiar** specific

No meaner hand may discipline the shoots,
None but his steel approach them. What is weak,
Distemper'd, or has lost prolific pow'rs,
Impair'd by age, his unrelenting hand
Dooms to the knife: nor does he spare the soft
And succulent, that feeds its giant growth,
But barren, at th' expence of neighb'ring twigs
420   Less ostentatious, and yet studded thick
With hopeful gems.[6] The rest, no portion left
That may disgrace his art, or disappoint
Large expectation, he disposes neat
At measur'd distances, that air and sun,
Admitted freely, may afford their aid,
And ventilate and warm the swelling buds.
Hence summer has her riches, autumn hence,
And hence ev'n winter fills his wither'd hand
With blushing[7] fruits, and plenty, not his own.
430   Fair recompense of labour well bestow'd,
And wise precaution; which a clime so rude[8]
Makes needful still, whose spring is but the child
Of churlish winter, in her froward[9] moods
Discov'ring much the temper of her sire.
For oft, as if in her the stream of mild
Maternal nature had revers'd its course,
She brings her infants forth with many smiles;
But, once deliver'd, kills them with a frown.
He, therefore, timely warn'd, himself supplies
440   Her want of care, screening and keeping warm
The plenteous bloom, that no rough blast may sweep
His garlands from the boughs. Again, as oft
As the sun peeps and vernal airs breathe mild,
The fence withdrawn, he gives them ev'ry beam,
And spreads his hopes before the blaze of day.

           . . .

    Ambition, av'rice, penury incurr'd
By endless riot, vanity, the lust
Of pleasure and variety, dispatch,
As duly as the swallows disappear,
The world of wand'ring knights and squires to town.
London ingulphs them all! The shark is there,
And the shark's prey; the spendthrift, and the leech
That sucks him. There the sycophant, and he
Who, with bare-headed and obsequious bows,
820   Begs a warm office,[10] doom'd to a cold jail
And groat[11] per diem, if his patron frown.

---

[6]**gems** from gemma, a bud
[7]**blushing** ruddy
[8]**rude** inclement, harsh
[9]**froward** perverse, angry
[10]**warm office** financially secure position
[11]**groat** silver coin worth fourpence

The levee[12] swarms, as if, in golden pomp,
Were character'd on ev'ry statesman's door,
"BATTER'D AND BANKRUPT FORTUNES MENDED HERE."
These are the charms that sully and eclipse
The charms of nature. 'Tis the cruel gripe
That lean hard-handed poverty inflicts,
The hope of better things, the chance to win,
The wish to shine, the thirst to be amus'd,
830   That at the sound of winter's hoary wing
Unpeople all our counties of such herds
Of flutt'ring, loit'ring, cringing, begging, loose
And wanton vagrants, as make London, vast
And boundless as it is, a crowded coop.
    Oh thou, resort and mart of all the earth,
Chequer'd with all complexions of mankind,
And spotted with all crimes; in whom I see
Much that I love, and more that I admire,
And all that I abhor; thou freckled fair,
840   That pleasest and yet shock'st me, I can laugh
And I can weep, can hope, and can despond,
Feel wrath and pity, when I think on thee!
Ten righteous would have sav'd a city once,
And thou hast many righteous.—Well for thee!
That salt preserves thee; more corrupted else,
And therefore more obnoxious at this hour
Than Sodom[13] in her day had pow'r to be,
For whom God heard his Abr'am plead in vain.

1785

[12]**levee** guests at a morning reception by a powerful person

[13]**Sodom** See Genesis 18–19.

The Castaway[1]

Obscurest night involv'd the sky,
  Th' Atlantic billows roar'd,
When such a destin'd wretch as I,
  Wash'd headlong from on board,
Of friends, of hope, of all bereft,
His floating home for ever left.

No braver chief could Albion[2] boast
  Than he with whom he went,
10 Nor ever ship left Albion's coast,

[1] Cowper's final poem, it is based on an incident in Richard Walter's *A New Voyage round the World by George Anson* (1748), in which a sailor swept overboard cannot be helped by his colleagues who "conceived from the [strong] manner in which he swam, that he might continue sensible . . . of the horror attending his irretrievable situation." The last two stanzas apply the situation to Cowper.

[2] **Albion** England

With warmer wishes sent.
He lov'd them both, but both in vain,
Nor him beheld, nor her again.

Not long beneath the whelming brine,
    Expert to swim, he lay;
Nor soon he felt his strength decline,
    Or courage die away;
But wag'd with death a lasting strife,
Supported by despair of life.

He shouted: nor his friends had fail'd
20   To check the vessel's course,
But so the furious blast prevail'd,
    That, pitiless perforce,
They left their outcast mate behind,
And scudded still before the wind.

Some succour yet they could afford;
    And, such as storms allow,
The cask, the coop,³ the floated cord,
    Delay'd not to bestow.
But he (they knew) nor ship, nor shore,
30 Whate'er they gave, should visit more.

Nor, cruel as it seem'd could he
    Their haste himself condemn,
Aware that flight, in such a sea,
    Alone could rescue them;
Yet bitter felt it still to die
Deserted, and his friends so nigh.

He long survives, who lives an hour
    In ocean, self-upheld;
And so long he, with unspent pow'r,
40   His destiny repell'd:
And ever, as the minutes flew,
Entreated help, or cried—"Adieu!"

At length, his transient respite past,
    His comrades, who before
Had heard his voice in ev'ry blast,
    Could catch the sound no more.
For then, by toil subdued, he drank
The stifling wave, and then he sank.

³ **coop** a large basket for catching fish or, here, castaways

No poet wept him: but the page
50   Of narrative sincere,
That tells his name, his worth, his age,
       Is wet with Anson's tear.
And tears by bards or heroes shed
Alike immortalize the dead.

I therefore purpose not, or dream,
       Descanting on his fate,
To give the melancholy theme
       A more enduring date:
But misery still delights to trace
60   Its 'semblance in another's case.

No voice divine the storm allay'd,
       No light propitious shone;
When, snatch'd from all effectual aid,
       We perish'd, each alone:
But I beneath a rougher sea,
And whelm'd in deeper gulphs than he.

1799   1803

GEORGE CRABBE
1754–1832

Born in Aldeburgh, a poor fishing and smuggling village in Suffolk, Crabbe was oppressed by the country life of his impoverished family and the painful uncertainties of trying to escape—as apprentice doctor, apothecary, and laborer on the local piers. His early literary career in London was equally unsatisfying until, with the combined help of Samuel Johnson, the statesman Edmund Burke, and the painter Sir Joshua Reynolds, he revised and published *The Village* in 1783. Having been ordained into the Church of England, he returned as a curate to Aldeburgh. He later became the Duke of Rutland's domestic chaplain in Belvoir Castle but felt as uneasy there as he had in his childhood home. After leaving the duke's service in 1785, he was cleric in rural parishes and wrote numerous poems.

In his most important works—*The Village*, *The Parish Register* (1807), and *The Borough* (1810)—Crabbe uses a fluid, less rhetorical, heroic couplet than that of Pope. Unlike some of his contemporaries, he had no illusions about country life, and his poems are less sentimental about its benevolent force than Goldsmith's. He subjects several rural persons and classes to severe scrutiny, using virtually novelistic techniques of characterization, realistic portrayal, dialogue, and setting in narrative couplets. Crabbe relied on sense perception rather than poetic conventions for his view of reality, and refused to hide "real ills" behind the "tinsel trappings of poetic pride." In *The Village* his speaker declares, "I paint the cot, / As truth will paint it, and as Bards will not," and in "Peter Grimes" he dramatizes the brutalizing effects of country poverty. Both in verse form and in content Crabbe appeals to what he called the "plain sense and sober judgment" of readers, an approach that led to Byron's accurate assessment that he was "nature's sternest painter."

From The Village[1]

From Book I

The village life, and every care that reigns
O'er youthful peasants and declining swains;[2]
What labour yields, and what, that labour past,
Age, in its hour of languor, finds at last;
What form the real picture of the poor,
Demand a song—the Muse can give no more.
   Fled are those times, when, in harmonious strains,
The rustic poet praised his native plains:
No shepherds now, in smooth alternate verse,
10 Their country's beauty or their nymphs'[3] rehearse;
Yet still for these we frame the tender strain,
Still in our lays fond Corydons[4] complain,
And shepherds' boys their amorous pains reveal,
The only pains, alas! they never feel.
   On Mincio's[5] banks, in Caesar's bounteous reign,
If Tityrus[6] found the Golden Age again,
Must sleepy bards the flattering dream prolong,
Mechanic echoes of the Mantuan[7] song?
From Truth and Nature shall we widely stray,
20 Where Virgil, not where Fancy, leads the way?
   Yes, thus the Muses sing of happy swains,
Because the Muses never knew their pains:
They boast their peasants' pipes;[8] but peasants now
Resign their pipes and plod behind the plough;
And few, amid the rural-tribe, have time
To number syllables, and play with rhyme;
Save honest Duck,[9] what son of verse could share
The poet's rapture and the peasant's care?
Or the great labours of the field degrade,
30 With the new peril of a poorer trade?
   From this chief cause these idle praises spring,
That themes so easy few forbear to sing;
For no deep thought the trifling subjects ask;
To sing of shepherds is an easy task:
The happy youth assumes the common strain,
A nymph his mistress, and himself a swain;[10]
With no sad scenes he clouds his tuneful prayer,

[1]At Crabbe's request, Sir Joshua Reynolds showed Samuel Johnson the manuscript of the poem and elicited Johnson's help; Johnson praised it as "original, vigorous, and elegant."
[2]swains country farm laborers. See also l. 36.
[3]nymphs girlfriends
[4]Corydon a familiar name in pastoral, as in the Eclogues (c. 42–37 B.C.) of Virgil (70–19 B.C.)
[5]Mincio the river running through Mantua in northern Italy, thought to be Virgil's birthplace

[6]Tityrus name of a shepherd in Virgil's Eclogues I
[7]Mantuan Virgilian. Ll. 15-18 and 20 were written by Samuel Johnson.
[8]pipes the shepherd's musical reed
[9]Duck Stephen Duck (1705–1756), a farmer and self-taught poet known as the "thresher poet" and a favorite of Queen Caroline in the previous reign. The line is ironic.
[10]swain a country lover

But all, to look like her, is painted fair.
   I grant indeed that fields and flocks have charms
40   For him that grazes or for him that farms;
But when amid such pleasing scenes I trace
The poor laborious natives of the place,
And see the mid-day sun, with fervid ray,
On their bare heads and dewy temples play;
While some, with feebler heads and fainter hearts,
Deplore their fortune, yet sustain their parts:
Then shall I dare these real ills to hide
In tinsel trappings of poetic pride?
   No; cast by Fortune on a frowning coast,
50   Which neither groves nor happy valleys boast;
Where other cares than those the Muse relates,
And other shepherds dwell with other mates;
By such examples taught, I paint the Cot,[11]
As truth will paint it, and as bards will not:
Nor you, ye poor, of letter'd scorn complain,
To you the smoothest song is smooth in vain;
O'ercome by labour, and bow'd down by time,
Feel you the barren flattery of a rhyme?
Can poets soothe you, when you pine for bread,
60   By winding myrtles round your ruin'd shed?
Can their light tales your weighty griefs o'erpower,
Or glad with airy mirth the toilsome hour?

1783

[11] **paint the Cot**   depict real cottage life

From The Borough, Letter XXII

From The Poor of the Borough: Peter Grimes[1]

The priest attending, found he spoke at times
As one alluding to his fears and crimes:
270   "It was the fall," he mutter'd, "I can show
The manner how—I never struck a blow:"—
And then aloud—"Unhand me, free my chain;
On oath, he fell—it struck him to the brain:—
Why ask my father?—that old man will swear
Against my life; besides, he wasn't there:—

[1] The poem includes twenty-four such letters sent to a presumed correspondent who has asked about the different people and professions of the speaker's country region. The unfilial, sadistic Peter Grimes, seeking to bully an inferior, acquires a series of workhouse boys: "He'd now the power he ever loved to show, / A feeling Being subject to his Blow" (ll. 87–88). After three boys die or are killed in his service, Peter is denied further aid, is ostracized, and falls spiritually and physically ill as the final scene of retribution begins.

What, all agreed?—Am I to die to-day?—
My Lord, in mercy, give me time to pray.''
Then as they watch'd him, calmer he became,
And grew so weak he couldn't move his frame,
280   But murmuring spake,—while they could see and hear
The start of terror and the groan of fear;
See the large dew-beads on his forehead rise,
And the cold death-drop glaze his sunken eyes;
Nor yet he died, but with unwonted force
Seem'd with some fancied being to discourse:
He knew not us, or with accustom'd art
He hid the knowledge, yet exposed his heart;
'Twas part confession and the rest defence,
A madman's tale, with gleams of waking sense.

290   "I'll tell you all," he said, "the very day
When the old man first placed them in my way:
My father's spirit—he who always tried
To give me trouble, when he lived and died—
When he was gone, he could not be content
To see my days in painful labour spent.
But would appoint his meetings, and he made
Me watch at these, and so neglect my trade.

      "'Twas one hot noon, all silent, still, serene,
No living being had I lately seen;
300   I paddled up and down and dipp'd my net,
But (such his pleasure) I could nothing get,—
A father's pleasure, when his toil was done,
To plague and torture thus an only son!
And so I sat and look'd upon the stream,
How it ran on, and felt as in a dream:
But dream it was not; no!—I fix'd my eyes
On the mid stream and saw the spirits rise;
I saw my father on the water stand,
And hold a thin pale boy in either hand;
310   And there they glided ghastly on the top
Of the salt flood, and never touch'd a drop:
I would have struck them, but they knew th' intent,
And smiled upon the oar, and down they went.

      "Now, from that day, whenever I began
To dip my net, there stood the hard old man—
He and those boys: I humbled me and pray'd
They would be gone;—they heeded not, but stay'd:
Nor could I turn, nor would the boat go by,
But gazing on the spirits, there was I:
320   They bade me leap to death, but I was loth to die:
And every day, as sure as day arose,
Would these three spirits meet me ere the close;

To hear and mark them daily was my doom,
And 'Come,' they said, with weak, sad voices, 'come.'
To row away with all my strength I try'd,
But there were they, hard by me in the tide,
The three unbodied forms—and 'Come,' still 'come,' they cried.

"Fathers should pity—but this old man shook
His hoary locks, and froze me by a look:
330   Thrice, when I struck them, through the water came
A hollow groan, that weaken'd all my frame:
'Father!' said I, 'have mercy:'—He replied,
I know not what—the angry spirit lied,—
'Didst thou not draw thy knife?' said he:—'Twas true,
But I had pity and my arm withdrew:
He cried for mercy which I kindly gave,
But he has no compassion in his grave.

"There were three places, where they ever rose,—
The whole long river has not such as those,—
340   Places accursed, where, if a man remain,
He'll see the things which strike him to the brain;
And there they made me on my paddle lean,
And look at them for hours;—accursed scene!
When they would glide to that smooth eddy-space,
Then bid me leap and join them in the place;
And at my groans each little villain sprite
Enjoy'd my pains and vanish'd in delight.

"In one fierce summer-day, when my poor brain
Was burning hot and cruel was my pain,
350   Then came this father-foe, and there he stood
With his two boys again upon the flood;
There was more mischief in their eyes, more glee
In their pale faces when they glared at me:
Still did they force me on the oar to rest,
And when they saw me fainting and oppress'd,
He, with his hand, the old man, scoop'd the flood,
And there came flame about him mix'd with blood;
He bade me stoop and look upon the place,
Then flung the hot-red liquor in my face;
360   Burning it blazed, and then I roar'd for pain,
I thought the demons would have turn'd my brain.

"Still there they stood, and forced me to behold
A place of horrors—they cannot be told—
Where the flood open'd, there I heard the shriek
Of tortured guilt—no earthly tongue can speak:
'All days alike! for ever!' did they say,
'And unremitted torments every day'—

Yes, so they said:''—But here he ceased and gazed
On all around, affrighten'd and amazed;
370 And still he tried to speak, and look'd in dread
Of frighten'd females gathering round his bed;
Then dropp'd exhausted and appear'd at rest,
Till the strong foe the vital powers possess'd;
Then with an inward, broken voice he cried,
''Again they come,'' and mutter'd as he died.

1810

The Nineteenth Century

ROBERT BURNS
1759–1796

Robert Burns's gift for witty satire and his penchant for generalized moral reflection mark him as an eighteenth-century writer. But he is characteristically Romantic in his democratic instincts, sensuous zest, and passionate feelings, his skepticism toward traditions, rules, and institutions, and above all his lyrical spontaneity.

Born into a family of Scottish farmers, Burns spent most of his life in relative rural poverty, except for a brief period of celebrity after publishing *Poems, Chiefly in the Scottish Dialect* (1786). He gained a reputation as an untaught genius, drawing his poetic powers from nature and the soul of the common people. Educated at home, Burns was far from untaught, but he was not averse to promoting this reputation, and his drinking bouts, radical political opinions, and constant sexual affairs enforced the image of a poet too naturally wild to be tamed by rules. His poetic distinction resides in his poems and songs in the Scots dialect—unsurpassed in their high spirits, vigor, and variety of expression. Of the hundreds of verses he set to old Scottish tunes, many display lyric grace and poignant depth of feeling.

Holy Willie's Prayer[1]

O thou that in the heavens does dwell!
Wha, as it pleases best thysel,
Sends ane to heaven and ten to hell,
    A' for thy glory!
And no for ony gude or ill
    They've done before thee.—[2]

I bless and praise thy matchless might,
When thousands thou has left in night,
That I am here before thy sight,
10   For gifts and grace,
A burning and a shining light
    To a' this place.—

What was I, or my generation,
That I should get such exaltation?
I, wha deserv'd most just damnation,
    For broken laws
Sax thousand years ere my creation,
    Thro' Adam's cause!

When from my mother's womb I fell,
20 Thou might hae plunged me deep in hell,

[1] The speaker of this satiric poem is modeled on William Fisher, an old, hypocritical Presbyterian elder of the parish where Burns had his farm.
[2] 11. 3–6 As a good Calvinist, Holy Willie believes in the doctrine of predestination, which holds that God has ordained since the beginning of time the salvation (election) or damnation of each individual soul. Willie smugly assumes that he is one of the elect.

To gnash my gooms, and weep, and wail,
        In burning lakes,
Where damned devils roar and yell
        Chain'd to their stakes.—

Yet I am here, a chosen sample,
To shew thy grace is great and ample:
I'm here, a pillar o' thy temple
        Strong as a rock,
A guide, a ruler and example
30   To a' thy flock.—

O Lord thou kens[3] what zeal I bear,
When drinkers drink, and swearers swear,
And singin' there, and dancin' here,
        Wi' great an' sma';
For I am keepet by thy fear,
        Free frae them a'.—

But yet—O Lord—confess I must—
At times I'm fash'd[4] wi' fleshly lust;
And sometimes too, in warldly trust
40   Vile Self gets in;
But thou remembers we are dust,
        —Defil'd wi' sin.—

O Lord—yestreen[5] —thou kens—wi' Meg—
Thy pardon I sincerely beg!
O may 't ne'er be a living plague,
        To my dishonor!
And I'll ne'er lift a lawless leg
        Again upon her.—

Besides, I farther maun avow,
50 Wi' Leezie's lass, three times—I trow—
But Lord, that friday I was fou[6]
        When I cam near her;
Or else, thou kens, thy servant true
        Wad never steer[7] her.—

Maybe thou lets this fleshy thorn
Buffet thy servant e'en and morn,
Lest he o'er proud and high should turn,
        That he's sae gifted;
If sae, thy hand maun e'en be borne
60   Untill thou lift it.—

[3]**kens** knows
[4]**fash'd** afflicted
[5]**yestreen** last night

[6]**fou** drunk
[7]**steer** bother

Lord bless thy Chosen in this place,
For here thou has a chosen race:
But God, confound their stubborn face,
      And blast their name,
Wha bring thy rulers to disgrace
      And open shame.—

Lord mind Gaun Hamilton's[8] deserts!
He drinks, and swears, and plays at cartes,[9]
Yet has sae mony[10] taking arts
70   Wi' Great and Sma',
Frae God's ain priest the people's hearts
      He steals awa.—

And when we chasten'd him therefore,
Thou kens how he bred sic a splore,[11]
And set the warld in a roar
      O' laughin at us:
Curse thou his basket and his store,
      Kail[12] and potatoes.—

Lord hear my earnest cry and prayer
80 Against that Presbytry of Ayr!
Thy strong right hand, Lord, make it bare
      Upon their heads!
Lord visit them, and dinna spare,
      For their misdeeds!

O Lord my God, that glib-tongu'd Aiken![13]
My very heart and flesh are quaking
To think how I sat, sweating, shaking,
      And piss'd wi' dread,
While Auld[14] wi' hingin[15] lip gaed sneaking
90   And hid his head!

Lord, in thy day o' vengeance try him!
Lord visit him that did employ him!
And pass not in thy mercy by them,
      Nor hear their prayer;
But for thy people's sake destroy them,
      And dinna spare!

[8]**Gaun Hamilton** Gavin Hamilton, a lawyer friend of Burns. Fisher accused Hamilton of loose living before the Presbytery of Ayr (1. 80), an ecclesiastical court, but lost the case.
[9]**cartes** cards
[10]**mony** many
[11]**bred sic a splore** raised such an uproar
[12]**Kail** cabbage
[13]**Aiken** Robert Aiken, Gavin Hamilton's successful defense counsel
[14]**Auld** a minister of the parish, allied with Holy Willie
[15]**hingin** hanging

But Lord, remember me and mine
Wi' mercies temporal and divine!
That I for grace and gear[16] may shine,
100   Excell'd by nane!
And a' the glory shall be thine!
            AMEN! AMEN!

1785   1799

[16]**gear** wealth

To a Mouse

ON TURNING HER UP IN HER NEST, WITH
THE PLOUGH, NOVEMBER, 1785.

Wee, sleeket, cowran,[1] tim'rous *beastie*,
O, what a panic's in thy breastie!
Thou need na start awa sae hasty,
            Wi' bickering brattle![2]
I wad be laith[3] to rin an' chase thee,
            Wi' murd'ring *pattle*![4]

I'm truly sorry Man's dominion
Has broken Nature's social union,
An' justifies that ill opinion,
10   Which makes thee startle,
At me, thy poor, earth-born companion,
            An' *fellow-mortal*!

I doubt na, whyles,[5] but thou may *thieve*;
What then? poor beastie, thou maun[6] live!
A *daimen-icker* in a *thrave*[7]
            'S a sma' request:
I'll get a blessin wi' the lave,[8]
            An' never miss 't!

Thy wee-bit *housie*, too, in ruin!
20   It's silly[9] wa's the win's are strewin!
An' naething, now, to big a new ane,
            O' foggage[10] green!
An' bleak *December's winds* ensuin,
            Baith snell[11] an' keen!

[1]**sleeket, cowran** sleek, cowering
[2]l. 4 with a quick scamper
[3]**laith** loath
[4]*pattle* plowstaff
[5]**whyles** sometimes
[6]**maun** must

[7]l. 15 an occasional ear of corn in a bundle of sheaves
[8]**lave** rest
[9]**silly** frail
[10]**foggage** moss
[11]**snell** harsh

Thou saw the fields laid bare an' wast,
An' weary *Winter* comin fast,
An' cozie here, beneath the blast,
    Thou thought to dwell,
Till crash! the cruel *coulter*[12] past
30   Out thro' thy cell.

That wee-bit heap o' leaves an' stibble,
Has cost thee monie a weary nibble!
Now thou's turn'd out, for a' thy trouble,
    But[13] house or hald,[14]
To thole[15] the Winter's *sleety dribble*,
    An' *cranreuch*[16] cauld!

But Mousie, thou art no thy-lane,[17]
In proving *foresight* may be vain:
The best laid schemes o' *Mice* an' *Men*,
40   Gang aft agley,[18]
An' lea'e us nought but grief an' pain,
    For promis'd joy!

Still, thou art blest, compar'd wi' *me*!
The *present* only toucheth thee:
But Och! I *backward* cast my e'e,
    On prospects drear!
An' *forward*, tho' I canna *see*,
    I *guess* an' *fear*!

1785   1786

[12]*coulter* plowshare
[13]**But** without
[14]**hald** home
[15]**thole** endure

[16]*cranreuch* hoarfrost
[17]**thy-lane** alone
[18]l. 40 go oft astray

From The Jolly Beggars[1]

I AM A BARD of no regard,
    Wi' gentle folks an' a' that;
210   But HOMER LIKE the glowran byke,[2]
    Frae town to town I draw that.

[1]Subtitled "A Cantata" (a story told in song through solos and chorus), "The Jolly Beggars" renders an evening spent among the penniless drinkers and pleasure-seekers at Poosie Nansie's tavern in Mauchline, Ayrshire. In the conclud-ing section presented here, the poet himself sings his part, after the other patrons have had their turn.
[2]**glowran byke** gazing crowd

Chorus—
For a' that an' a' that,
    An' twice as muckle's[3] a' that,
I've lost but ANE,[4] I've TWA behin',
    I've WIFE ENEUGH for a' that.

I never drank the Muses' STANK,[5]
    Castalia's burn[6] an' a' that,
But there it streams an' richly reams,
    My HELICON[7] I ca' that.
        For a' that &c.

220 Great love I bear to all the FAIR,
    Their humble slave an' a' that;
But lordly WILL,[8] I hold it still
    A mortal sin to thraw[9] that.
        For a' that &c.

In raptures sweet this hour we meet,
    Wi' mutual love an' a' that;
But for how lang the FLIE MAY STANG,[10]
    Let INCLINATION law[11] that.
        For a' that &c.

Their tricks an' craft hae put me daft,
    They've ta'en me in, an' a' that,
230 But clear your decks an' here 's the SEX!
    I like the jads[12] for a' that.
        For a' that an' a' that
            An' twice as muckle's a' that,
        My DEAREST BLUID to do them guid,
           They're welcome till 't[13] for a' that.

Recitativo—[14]
So sung the BARD—and Nansie's waws[15]
Shook with a thunder of applause
    Re-echo'd from each mouth!
They toom'd their pocks,[16] they pawn'd their duds,
240 They scarcely left to coor their fuds[17]
    To quench their lowan drouth:[18]

---

[3]**muckle 's** much as
[4]ANE one
[5]STANK stagnant pond
[6]**burn** brook. Castalia was a spring on Mt. Parnassus in Greece, seen as a source of poetic inspiration.
[7]HELICON a mountain in Greece, supposedly the home of the poetic Muses
[8]WILL sexual desire
[9]**thraw** frustrate
[10]STANG bite

[11]**law** rule
[12]**jads** wenches
[13]**till 't** to it
[14]**Recitativo** a musical term for the vocal rendering of purely narrative passages, as opposed to set-pieces, such as songs and arias
[15]**waws** walls
[16]**toom'd their pocks** emptied their pockets
[17]**fuds** backsides
[18]**lowan drouth** raging thirst

Then owre[19] again the jovial thrang
  The Poet did request
To lowse[20] his PACK an' wale[21] a sang,
    A BALLAD o' the best.
      He, rising, rejoicing,
        Between his TWA DEBORAHS,[22]
    Looks round him an' found them
      Impatient for the Chorus.

  Air

250   SEE the smoking bowl before us,
    Mark our jovial, ragged ring!
Round and round take up the Chorus,
    And in raptures let us sing—

          Chorus—
   A fig for those by law protected!
    LIBERTY's a glorious feast!
Courts for Cowards were erected,
    Churches built to please the PRIEST.

What is TITLE, what is TREASURE,
    What is REPUTATION's care?
260   If we lead a life of pleasure,
    'Tis no matter HOW or WHERE.
        A fig, &c.

With the ready trick and fable
    Round we wander all the day;
And at night, in barn or stable,
    Hug our doxies[23] on the hay.
        A fig for &c.

Does the train-attended CARRIAGE
    Thro' the country lighter rove?
Does the sober bed of MARRIAGE
    Witness brighter scenes of love?
        A fig for &c.

---

[19]**owre** over
[20]**lowse** open
[21]**wale** choose
[22]1. 247   a humorous reference to his wenches.

Deborah was a Hebrew prophetess and leader
famed for her victory song after an Israelite
battle triumph; see Judges 4–5.
[23]**doxies** wenches

270   Life is all a VARIORUM,[24]
        We regard not how it goes;
      Let them cant about DECORUM,
        Who have character to lose.
             A fig for &c.

      Here's to BUDGETS, BAGS and WALLETS!
        Here's to all the wandering train!
      Here's our ragged BRATS and CALLETS[25]
        One and all cry out, AMEN!
        A fig for those by LAW protected,
          LIBERTY's a glorious feast!
280   COURTS for Cowards were erected,
         CHURCHES built to please the Priest.

     1785   1801

[24]VARIORUM an entity made up of variety and
differences
[25]CALLETS hussies

John Anderson My Jo

John Anderson my jo,[1] John,
    When we were first acquent;
Your locks were like the raven,
    Your bony brow was brent;[2]
But now your brow is beld, John,
    Your locks are like the snaw;
But blessings on your frosty pow,[3]
    John Anderson my Jo.

John Anderson my jo, John,
10   We clamb the hill the gither;[4]
And mony a canty[5] day, John,
    We've had wi' ane anither:
Now we maun totter down, John,
    And hand in hand we'll go;
And sleep the gither at the foot,
    John Anderson my Jo.

                1790

[1] jo darling   [3] pow head
[2] 1. 4 Your bonny forehead rose high and straight   [4] the gither together
(because of a thick head of hair).   [5] canty merry

WILLIAM BLAKE
1757–1827

Poet, painter, and original visionary thinker, William Blake lived for the most part in uneventful obscurity, working in London as an engraver and print maker. Eventually he combined his poetry and art work through his own technique of "illuminated printing," etching his poems and their surrounding pictorial designs on copper plates and producing his books himself. From 1789 to 1795, in a burst of creative energy partly aroused by the ferment of revolution in France, Blake produced a remarkable set of these illuminated works, which include *Songs of Innocence and of Experience* (represented extensively in this anthology). In this period he tended increasingly to express his ideas in elaborately symbolic mythic narratives known as the Prophetic Books. They are too long to represent here except in brief excerpts, but many critics consider them his most significant writings.

"The Nature of my Work," Blake wrote, "is Visionary or Imaginative. It is my Endeavour to Restore what the Ancients called the Golden Age." This Golden Age is a paradise of fully realized human potential. Man's fall from that state and his prophesied return comprise the grand themes working through all of Blake's poetry. In his poetry of the early 1790s they take the form of a celebration of human energy and a call to revolution. He insists that, in order to restore a paradise of freedom for the body, the will, and the imagination, we need to overthrow three forms of authority: orthodox religion, with its rigid sexual morality; political establishments, whose laws are often designed to keep the poor in their place; and a dominant "common-sense" view of reality based only on what we can learn from the five senses. Blake never ceases to challenge repressive forces or to advocate uninhibited desire, but his later work shifts its emphasis from revo-

lutionary energy toward something like Christian love and forgiveness—though he is never an orthodox Christian. The paradise he encourages us to reclaim is not a heaven in the sky but a world of liberated imagination dwelling within us, however hidden, at all times. Our true saviors, therefore, are the poets and artists who hold the keys to its treasures.

We need to keep this perspective in mind when we read Blake. All of his poetry uses relatively simple diction, concise phrasing, and straightforward syntax, but at the same time carries symbolic overtones that greatly expand or complicate the meaning. In some lines of verse, striking combinations of dissimilar images occur, creating an effect of multiple meanings compressed together, as in "London," where "the hapless Soldiers sigh / Runs in blood down Palace walls" and the "Harlots curse . . . blights with plagues the Marriage hearse." In the Prophetic Books, mythic figures, unique to Blake's symbolic system, operate in a world where normal laws of time, space, cause, and effect seem suspended. With these difficult techniques Blake aims to stimulate the reader's mental powers; he considered "what is not too Explicit as the fittest for Instruction because it rouzes the faculties to act."

Blake's punctuation is highly unorthodox and erratic. To capture the flavor of the original, the selections below follow the text of the *Complete Poetry and Prose of William Blake*, ed. David V. Erdman (Garden City, N.Y., 1982), which adheres faithfully to Blake's own punctuation. In a few instances of the present text, certain full stops (periods and semi-colons) have been silently removed where they would otherwise seriously interrupt the flow of the sense for the reader.

From Poetical Sketches[1]

To the Evening Star

Thou fair-hair'd angel of the evening,
Now, while the sun rests on the mountains, light
Thy bright torch of love; thy radiant crown
Put on, and smile upon our evening bed!
Smile on our loves; and, while thou drawest the
Blue curtains of the sky, scatter thy silver dew
One every flower that shuts its sweet eyes
In timely sleep. Let thy west wind sleep on
The lake; speak silence with thy glimmering eyes,
10   And wash the dusk with silver. Soon, full soon,
Dost thou withdraw; then the wolf rages wide,
And the lion glares thro' the dun[2] forest:
The fleeces of our flocks are cover'd with
Thy sacred dew: protect them with thine influence.

1783

[1] *Poetical Sketches* was Blake's first volume of verse and the only one to be printed in conventional type. Written in the poet's adolescence, these poems often show the influence of Elizabe-

than verse and of such mid-eighteenth-century poets of "sensibility" as Collins and Gray.
[2] **dun** dark

Mad Song

The wild winds weep,
    And the night is a-cold;
Come hither, Sleep,
    And my griefs infold:
But lo! the morning peeps
    Over the eastern steeps,
And the rustling birds of dawn
    The earth do scorn.

Lo! to the vault
10   Of paved heaven,
With sorrow fraught
    My notes are driven:
They strike the ear of night,
    Make weep the eyes of day;
They make mad the roaring winds,
    And with tempests play.

Like a fiend in a cloud
    With howling woe,
After night I do croud,
20   And with night will go;
I turn my back to the east,

From whence comforts have increas'd;
For light doth seize my brain
With frantic pain.

1783

From Songs of Innocence[1]

Introduction

Piping down the valleys wild
Piping songs of pleasant glee
On a cloud I saw a child.
And he laughing said to me

Pipe a song about a Lamb;
So I piped with merry chear,
Piper pipe that song again—
So I piped, he wept to hear

Drop thy pipe thy happy pipe
10 Sing songs of happy chear,
So I sung the same again
While he wept with joy to hear

Piper sit thee down and write
In a book that all may read—
So he vanish'd from my sight.
And I pluck'd a hollow reed.

And I made a rural pen,
And I stain'd[2] the water clear,
And I wrote my happy songs
20 Every child may joy to hear

1789

[1] One of the first of Blake's books in "illuminated printing," *Songs of Innocence* (1789) presents a vision of life as seen through natural, trusting, childlike eyes.

[2] **stain'd** colored, but with a possible overtone of "sullied"

The Ecchoing Green

The Sun does arise,
And make happy the skies.
The merry bells ring
To welcome the Spring.
The sky-lark and thrush,
The birds of the bush,
Sing louder around,
To the bells chearful sound.
While our sports shall be seen
10 On the Ecchoing Green.

Old John with white hair
Does laugh away care,
Sitting under the oak,
Among the old folk,
They laugh at our play,
And soon they all say,
Such such were the joys
When we all girls & boys,
In our youth-time were seen,
20　On the Ecchoing Green.

Till the little ones weary
No more can be merry
The sun does descend,
And our sports have an end:
Round the laps of their mothers,
Many sisters and brothers,
Like birds in their nest,
Are ready for rest;
And sport no more seen,
30　On the darkening Green.

1789

The Lamb

Little Lamb who made thee
　Dost thou know who made thee
Gave thee life & bid thee feed
By the stream & o'er the mead;
Gave thee clothing of delight,
Softest clothing wooly bright;
Gave thee such a tender voice,
Making all the vales rejoice!
　Little Lamb who made thee
10　Dost thou know who made thee

　Little Lamb I'll tell thee,
　Little Lamb I'll tell thee!
He is called by thy name,
For he calls himself a Lamb:
He is meek & he is mild,
He became a little child:
I a child & thou a lamb,
We are called by his name.
　Little Lamb God bless thee.
20　Little Lamb God bless thee.

1789

The Little Black Boy

My mother bore me in the southern wild,
And I am black, but O! my soul is white;
White as an angel is the English child:
But I am black as if bereav'd of light.

My mother taught me underneath a tree
And sitting down before the heat of day,
She took me on her lap and kissed me,
And pointing to the east began to say.

Look on the rising sun: there God does live
10   And gives his light, and gives his heat away.
And flowers and trees and beasts and men recieve
Comfort in morning joy in the noon day.

And we are put on earth a little space,
That we may learn to bear the beams of love,
And these black bodies and this sun-burnt face
Is but a cloud, and like a shady grove.

For when our souls have learn'd the heat to bear
The cloud will vanish we shall hear his voice
Saying: come out from the grove my love & care,
20   And round my golden tent like lambs rejoice.

Thus did my mother say and kissed me,
And thus I say to little English boy
When I from black and he from white cloud free,
And round the tent of God like lambs we joy:

I'll shade him from the heat till he can bear
To lean in joy upon our fathers knee.
And then I'll stand and stroke his silver hair,
And be like him and he will then love me.

                                                  1789

The Chimney Sweeper

When my mother died I was very young,
And my father sold me while yet my tongue
Could scarcely cry weep weep weep weep.[1]
So your chimneys I sweep & in soot I sleep.

Theres little Tom Dacre, who cried when his head
That curl'd like a lambs back, was shav'd, so I said
Hush Tom never mind it, for when your head's bare,
You know that the soot cannot spoil your white hair.

---

[1] **weep . . . weep** the little boy's lisping pronunciation of his street cry, "sweep, sweep"

And so he was quiet, & that very night,
As Tom was a sleeping he had such a sight,
That thousands of sweepers Dick, Joe Ned & Jack
Were all of them lock'd up in coffins of black[2]

And by came an Angel who had a bright key,
And he open'd the coffins & set them all free.
Then down a green plain leaping laughing they run
And wash in a river and shine in the Sun.

Then naked & white, all their bags left behind,
They rise upon clouds, and sport in the wind.
And the Angel told Tom if he'd be a good boy,
He'd have God for his father & never want joy.

And so Tom awoke and we rose in the dark
And got with our bags & our brushes to work.
Tho' the morning was cold, Tom was happy & warm,
So if all do their duty, they need not fear harm.

1789

[2] **coffins of black**   Many chimney sweepers,
contracting lung diseases from the soot of their
trade, died before reaching adolescence.

The Divine Image

To Mercy Pity Peace and Love,
All pray in their distress:
And to these virtues of delight
Return their thankfulness.

For Mercy Pity Peace and Love,
Is God our father dear:
And Mercy Pity Peace and Love,
Is Man his child and care.

For Mercy has a human heart
Pity, a human face:
And Love, the human form divine,
And Peace, the human dress.

Then every man of every clime,
That prays in his distress,
Prays to the human form divine
Love Mercy Pity Peace.

And all must love the human form,
In heathen, turk or jew.
Where Mercy, Love & Pity dwell
There God is dwelling too.

1789

Holy Thursday[1]

Twas on a Holy Thursday their innocent faces clean
The children walking two & two in red & blue & green
Grey headed beadles[2] walkd before with wands as white as snow
Till into the high dome of Pauls they like Thames waters flow

O what a multitude they seemd these flowers of London town
Seated in companies they sit with radiance all their own
The hum of multitudes was there but multitudes of lambs
Thousands of little boys & girls raising their innocent hands

Now like a mighty wind they raise to heaven the voice of song
10 Or like harmonious thunderings the seats of heaven among
Beneath them sit the aged men wise guardians of the poor
Then cherish pity, lest you drive an angel from your door[3]

1784   1789

[1] the Day of Christ's Ascension, forty days after Easter. In London it was customary to march the children of charity schools and orphanages into St. Paul's Cathedral for a special religious service.

[2] **beadles** minor church officials employed to keep order
[3] **lest . . . door** See Hebrews 13:2 ("Be not forgetful to entertain strangers: for thereby some have entertained angels unawares").

From Songs of Experience[1]

Introduction

Hear the voice of the Bard![2]
Who Present, Past, & Future sees
Whose ears have heard
The Holy Word,[3]
That walk'd among the ancient trees.[4]

Calling the lapsed Soul
And weeping in the evening dew;
That might controll
The starry pole;
10 And fallen fallen light renew!

[1] In 1794 Blake combined this set of poems with the earlier *Songs of Innocence* to make up the collection *Songs of Innocence and Experience Shewing the Two Contrary States of the Human Soul.* As the latter phrase indicates, the perspective of Experience expressed in these poems counterbalances the tenets of Innocence, stressing instead the oppressiveness of institutional and spiritual authority, disharmony between man and his environment, and self-interest as the universal force.

[2] **Bard** a singer of heroic tales, an oral poet, sometimes thought to possess prophetic powers
[3] **Holy Word** Cf. John 1:1 ("In the beginning was the Word, and the Word was with God, and the Word was God . . .").
[4] 1. 5 Cf. Genesis 3:8 ("And they heard the voice of the Lord God walking in the garden in the cool of the day: and Adam and his wife hid themselves from the presence of the Lord God amongst the trees of the Garden"); see also Milton, *Paradise Lost* X.92–101.

O Earth O Earth return!
Arise from out the dewy grass;
Night is worn,
And the morn
Rises from the slumberous mass.

Turn away no more:
Why wilt thou turn away
The starry floor
The watry shore
20 Is giv'n thee till the break of day.

1794

Earth's Answer

Earth rais'd up her head,
From the darkness dread & drear.
Her light fled:
Stony dread!
And her locks cover'd with grey despair.

Prison'd on watry shore
Starry Jealousy[1] does keep my den
Cold and hoar
Weeping o'er
10 I hear the Father of the ancient men

Selfish father of men
Cruel jealous selfish fear
Can delight
Chain'd in night
The virgins of youth and morning bear.

Does spring hide its joy
When buds and blossoms grow?
Does the sower
Sow by night?
20 Or the plowman in darkness plow?

Break this heavy chain,
That does freeze my bones around
Selfish! vain,
Eternal bane!
That free Love with bondage bound.

1794

[1] **Starry Jealousy** the jealousy of a sky-dwelling Being, or, possibly, the stars conceived as guards established by such a Being to keep Earth away from heaven's pleasures

490 | William Blake

The Clod & the Pebble

Love seeketh not Itself to please,
Nor for itself hath any care;
But for another gives its ease,
And builds a Heaven in Hells despair.

    So sang a little Clod of Clay,
    Trodden with the cattles feet:
    But a Pebble of the brook
    Warbled out these metres meet.[1]

Love seeketh only Self to please,
10   To bind another to its delight;
Joys in anothers loss of ease,
And builds a Hell in Heavens despite.

                1794

[1] **meet** appropriate

The Sick Rose

O Rose thou art sick.
The invisible worm,
That flies in the night
In the howling storm:

Has found out thy bed
Of crimson joy:
And his dark secret love
Does thy life destroy.

                1794

The Tyger

Tyger Tyger, burning bright,
In the forests of the night;
What immortal hand or eye,
Could frame thy fearful symmetry?

In what distant deeps or skies
Burnt the fire of thine eyes!
On what wings dare he aspire?
What the hand dare sieze the fire?[1]

[1] ll. 7–8 The speaker emphasizes the daring of the Tyger's maker, hinting that he is akin to both Icarus, the disobedient Greek youth who soared with artificial wings too near the sun, and Prometheus, the Titan who stole fire from the gods.

And what shoulder, & what art,
10 Could twist the sinews of thy heart?
And when thy heart began to beat,
What dread hand? & what dread feet?

What the hammer? what the chain,
In what furnace was thy brain?
What the anvil? what dread grasp,
Dare its deadly terrors clasp?

When the stars threw down their spears
And water'd heaven with their tears:[2]
Did he smile his work to see?
20 Did he who made the Lamb make thee?

Tyger, Tyger burning bright,
In the forests of the night:
What immortal hand or eye,
Dare frame thy fearful symmetry?

1794

[2] 11. 17–18 Several allusions are suggested: beams of starlight ("spears") giving way to dewdrops ("tears"), hence, dawn; the stars as agents of repressive reason (see "Earth's Answer," above, 1. 7); the stars as Satan's warrior angels in the war in Heaven (see Revelation 12:4), who drop their weapons in defeat (see Milton, *Paradise Lost* VI. 838–39).

Ah Sun-flower

Ah Sun-flower! weary of time,
Who countest the steps of the Sun:
Seeking after that sweet golden clime
Where the travellers journey is done.

Where the Youth pined away with desire,
And the pale Virgin shrouded in snow
Arise from their graves and aspire,
Where my Sun-flower wishes to go.

1794

The Garden of Love

I went to the Garden of Love,
And saw what I never had seen:
A Chapel was built in the midst,
Where I used to play on the green.

And the gates of this Chapel were shut,
And Thou shalt not. writ over the door;
So I turn'd to the Garden of Love,
That so many sweet flowers bore,

And I saw it was filled with graves,
10   And tomb-stones where flowers should be:
And Priests in black gowns were walking their rounds,
And binding with briars my joys & desires.

1794

London

I wander thro' each charter'd[1] street,
Near where the charter'd Thames does flow.
And mark in every face I meet
Marks of weakness, marks of woe.

In every cry of every Man,
In every Infants cry of fear,
In every voice: in every ban,[2]
The mind-forg'd manacles I hear

How the Chimney-sweepers cry
10   Every blackning Church appalls,
And the hapless Soldiers sigh
Runs in blood down Palace walls

But most thro' midnight streets I hear
How the youthful Harlots curse[3]
Blasts the new-born Infants tear
And blights with plagues the Marriage hearse

1794

[1] **charter'd** To charter is to grant a privilege or entitlement; "charter'd" thus indicates guaranteed liberties, as in "the chartered rights of Englishmen," but also "granted or hired for exclusive use."

[2] **ban** prohibition or curse, but also a marriage announcement (usually spelled "bann")
[3] **Harlots curse** both a spoken utterance and a reference to venereal disease

The Human Abstract[1]

Pity would be no more,
If we did not make somebody Poor:
And Mercy no more could be,
If all were as happy as we;

And mutual fear brings peace;
Till the selfish loves increase.

[1] the contrary poem to "The Divine Image" in *Songs of Innocence*. "Abstract" here means a summary of essential characteristics; hence, a thumbnail sketch of human nature.

Then Cruelty knits a snare,
And spreads his baits with care.

He sits down with holy fears,
10   And waters the ground with tears:
Then Humility takes its root
Underneath his foot.

Soon spreads the dismal shade
Of Mystery² over his head;
And the Catterpiller and Fly
Feed on the Mystery.

And it bears the fruit of Deceit,
Ruddy and sweet to eat;
And the Raven his nest has made
20   In its thickest shade.

The Gods of the earth and sea
Sought thro' Nature to find this Tree³
But their search was all in vain:
There grows one in the Human Brain

1794

² **Mystery**   religious dogma used to hide selfish
or exploitative aims

³ **Gods . . . Tree**   In Norse mythology, the gods
sought a world tree whose roots and branches
bound together heaven, earth, and hell.

The Book of Thel¹

THEL'S MOTTO,

Does the Eagle know what is in the pit?
Or wilt thou go ask the Mole:
Can Wisdom be put in a silver rod?
Or Love in a golden bowl?²

I

The daughters of Mne Seraphim³ led round their sunny flocks,
All but the youngest, she in paleness sought the secret air.
To fade away like morning beauty from her mortal day:
Down by the river of Adona⁴ her soft voice is heard:
And thus her gentle lamentation falls like morning dew.

¹ In this mythological narrative, the first of Blake's
so-called Prophetic Books, the heroine's quest
for self-fulfillment is certainly symbolic, but
the reader need not assume that the poem con-
tains a single predetermined set of meanings.
The Book of Thel displays the long seven-beat
line characteristic of Blake's extended narrative
works.
² **golden bowl**   In Ecclesiastes 12:6 the golden
bowl is a metaphor for mortal life; here it may

also have sexual connotations.
³ **Seraphim**   in the Bible, the highest order of
angels
⁴ **Adona**   This name is perhaps intended to sug-
gest both "Adonai," one of the Hebrew names
of God, and "Adonis," Greek god of the vege-
tation cycle; the undying Garden of Adonis in
Spenser's *The Faerie Queene* III.vi somewhat
resembles Thel's world.

O life of this our spring! why fades the lotus of the water?
Why fade these children of the spring? born but to smile & fall.
Ah! Thel is like a watry bow, and like a parting cloud,
Like a reflection in a glass. like shadows in the water.
10   Like dreams of infants. like a smile upon an infants face,
Like the doves voice, like transient day, like music in the air;
Ah! gentle may I lay me down, and gentle rest my head.
And gentle sleep the sleep of death and gentle hear the voice
Of him that walketh in the garden in the evening time.[5]

The Lilly of the valley breathing in the humble grass
Answer'd the lovely maid and said; I am a watry weed,
And I am very small, and love to dwell in lowly vales;
So weak, the gilded butterfly scarce perches on my head
Yet I am visited from heaven and he that smiles on all
20   Walks in the valley and each morn over me spreads his hand
Saying, rejoice thou humble grass, thou new-born lilly flower,
Thou gentle maid of silent valleys and of modest brooks;
For thou shalt be clothed in light, and fed with morning manna:
Till summers heat melts thee beside the fountains and the springs
To flourish in eternal vales: then why should Thel complain,

Why should the mistress of the vales of Har,[6] utter a sigh.

She ceasd & smild in tears, then sat down in her silver shrine.

Thel answerd. O thou little virgin of the peaceful valley
Giving to those that cannot crave, the voiceless, the o'ertired.
30   Thy breath doth nourish the innocent lamb, he smells thy milky garments,
He crops thy flowers while thou sittest smiling in his face,
Wiping his mild and meekin[7] mouth from all contagious taints.
Thy wine doth purify the golden honey, thy perfume,
Which thou dost scatter on every little blade of grass that springs
Revives the milked cow, & tames the fire-breathing steed.
But Thel is like a faint cloud kindled at the rising sun:
I vanish from my pearly throne, and who shall find my place.
Queen of the vales the Lilly answered, ask the tender cloud,
And it shall tell thee why it glitters in the morning sky,
40   And why it scatters its bright beauty thro' the humid air.
Descend O little cloud & hover before the eyes of Thel.

The Cloud descended, and the Lilly bowd her modest head:
And went to mind her numerous charge among the verdant grass.

      II
O little Cloud the virgin said, I charge thee tell to me,
Why thou complainest not when in one hour thou fade away:
Then we shall seek thee but not find; ah Thel is like to Thee.
I pass away yet I complain, and no one hears my voice.

[5] l. 14 See Genesis 3:8.
[6] **Har** In Blake's earlier poem *Tiriel*, Har is presented as an equivalent of Adam; his "vales" may thus represent a version of the Garden of Eden, the earthly paradise.
[7] **meekin** humble

The Cloud then shew'd his golden head & his bright form emerg'd,
Hovering and glittering on the air before the face of Thel.

50 O virgin know'st thou not our steeds drink of the golden springs
Where Luvah[8] doth renew his horses: look'st thou on my youth,
And fearest thou because I vanish and am seen no more.
Nothing remains; O maid I tell thee, when I pass away,
It is to tenfold life, to love, to peace, and raptures holy:
Unseen descending, weigh my light wings upon balmy flowers;
And court the fair eyed dew to take me to her shining tent;
The weeping virgin, trembling kneels before the risen sun,
Till we arise link'd in a golden band, and never part;
But walk united, bearing food to all our tender flowers

60 Dost thou O little Cloud? I fear that I am not like thee;
For I walk through the vales of Har and smell the sweetest flowers;
But I feed not the little flowers: I hear the warbling birds,
But I feed not the warbling birds. they fly and seek their food;
But Thel delights in these no more because I fade away,
And all shall say, without a use this shining woman liv'd,
Or did she only live to be at death the food of worms.

The Cloud reclind upon his airy throne and answer'd thus.

Then if thou art the food of worms O virgin of the skies,
How great thy use how great thy blessing; every thing that lives,
70 Lives not alone, nor for itself: fear not and I will call
The weak worm from its lowly bed, and thou shalt hear its voice.
Come forth worm of the silent valley, to thy pensive queen.

The helpless worm arose, and sat upon the Lillys leaf,
And the bright Cloud saild on, to find his partner in the vale.

III
Then Thel astonish'd view'd the Worm upon its dewy bed.

Art thou a Worm? image of weakness art thou but a Worm?
I see thee like an infant wrapped in the Lillys leaf:
Ah weep not little voice, thou can'st not speak. but thou can'st weep;
Is this a Worm? I see thee lay helpless & naked: weeping,
80 And none to answer, none to cherish thee with mothers smiles.

The Clod of Clay heard the Worms voice, & raised her pitying head;
She bow'd over the weeping infant, and her life exhal'd
In milky fondness, then on Thel she fix'd her humble eyes.

O beauty of the vales of Har we live not for ourselves,
Thou seest me the meanest thing, and so I am indeed;
My bosom of itself is cold and of itself is dark,

---

[8] **Luvah** here a personification of the sun, but eventually one of the most important figures in Blake's later mythic poems, representing human passion

But he that loves the lowly, pours his oil upon my head
And kisses me, and binds his nuptial bands around my breast,
And says; Thou mother of my children, I have loved thee.
90   And I have given thee a crown that none can take away
But how this is sweet maid, I know not, and I cannot know,
I ponder, and I cannot ponder, yet I live and love.

The daughter of beauty wip'd her pitying tears with her white veil,
And said Alas! I knew not this, and therefore did I weep:
That God would love a Worm I knew, and punish the evil foot
That wilful, bruis'd its helpless form: but that he cherish'd it
With milk and oil I never knew; and therefore did I weep,
And I complained in the mild air, because I fade away,
And lay me down in thy cold bed, and leave my shining lot.

100   Queen of the vales, the matron Clay answerd; I heard thy sighs.
And all thy moans flew o'er my roof but I have call'd them down:
Wilt thou O Queen enter my house. 'tis given thee to enter,
And to return; fear nothing. enter with thy virgin feet.

       IV
The eternal gates terrific porter lifted the northern bar:
Thel enter'd in & saw the secrets of the land unknown;
She saw the couches of the dead, & where the fibrous roots
Of every heart on earth infixes deep its restless twists:
A land of sorrows & of tears where never smile was seen.

She wanderd in the land of clouds thro' valleys dark, listning
110   Dolours & lamentations: waiting oft beside a dewy grave
She stood in silence listning to the voices of the ground,
Till to her own grave plot she came, & there she sat down
And heard this voice of sorrow breathed from the hollow pit.

Why cannot the Ear be closed to its own destruction?
Or the glistning Eye to the poison of a smile!
Why are Eyelids stord with arrows ready drawn,
Where a thousand fighting men in ambush lie?[9]
Or an Eye of gifts & graces, show'ring fruits & coined gold!
Why a Tongue impress'd with honey from every wind?
120   Why an Ear, a whirlpool fierce to draw creations in?
Why a Nostril wide inhaling terror trembling & affright
Why a tender curb upon the youthful burning boy!
Why a little curtain of flesh on the bed of our desire?

The Virgin started from her seat, & with a shriek
Fled back unhindered till she came into the vales of Har
      The End

                    1789

[9] ll. 116–17 The imagery is from courtly love
poetry, where the mistress's eyes are often said
to "slay" her lover with their beams.

From Blake's Notebook

I Askèd a Thief

I askèd a thief to steal me a peach
He turned up his eyes
I ask'd a lithe lady to lie her down
Holy & meek she cries—

As soon as I went
An angel came.
He wink'd at the thief
And smild at the dame—

And without one word said
10 Had a peach from the tree
And still as a maid
Enjoy'd the lady.

1796   1863

Never Pain to Tell Thy Love

Never pain to tell thy love
Love that never told can be
For the gentle wind does move
Silently invisibly

I told my love I told my love
I told her all my heart
Trembling cold in ghastly fears
Ah she doth depart

Soon as she was gone from me
10 A traveller came by
Silently invisibly
O was no deny

1863

Mock on Mock on Voltaire Rousseau[1]

Mock on Mock on Voltaire Rousseau
Mock on Mock on tis all in vain
You throw the sand against the wind
And the wind blows it back again

[1] **Voltaire [and] Rousseau** eighteenth-century
French men of letters, who wished to make reli-
gion conform to reason

And every sand becomes a Gem
Reflected in the beams divine
Blown back they blind the mocking Eye
But still in Israels paths they shine

The Atoms of Democritus[2]
10   And Newtons Particles of light[3]
Are sands upon the Red sea shore
Where Israels tents do shine so bright

1800–08?   1863

[2] **Democritus** Greek philosopher (460–362 B.C.), the first proponent of atoms as the foundation of all things

[3] **Newtons . . . light** The English scientist Sir Isaac Newton (1642–1727) believed that light was composed of a stream of discrete material particles.

The Mental Traveller

I traveld thro' a Land of Men
A Land of Men & Women too
And heard & saw such dreadful things
As cold Earth wanderers never knew

For there the Babe is born in joy
That was begotten in dire woe
Just as we Reap in joy the fruit
Which we in bitter tears did sow

And if the Babe is born a Boy
10   He's given to a Woman Old
Who nails him down upon a rock
Catches his shrieks in cups of gold

She binds iron thorns around his head
She pierces both his hands & feet
She cuts his heart out at his side
To make it feel both cold & heat

Her fingers number every Nerve
Just as a Miser counts his gold
She lives upon his shrieks & cries
20   And she grows young as he grows old

Till he becomes a bleeding youth
And she become a Virgin bright
Then he rends up his Manacles
And binds her down for his delight

He plants himself in all her Nerves
Just as a Husbandman[1] his mould
And she becomes his dwelling place
And Garden fruitful seventy fold

30   An aged Shadow soon he fades
      Wandring round an Earthly Cot[2]
      Full filled all with gems & gold
      Which he by industry had got

And these are the gems of the Human Soul
The rubies & pearls of a lovesick eye
The countless gold of the akeing heart
The martyrs groan & the lovers sigh

They are his meat they are his drink
He feeds the Beggar & the Poor
And the wayfaring Traveller
40   For ever open is his door

His grief is their eternal joy
They make the roofs & walls to ring
Till from the fire on the hearth
A little Female Babe does spring

And she is all of solid fire
And gems & gold that none his hand
Dares stretch to touch her Baby form
Or wrap her in his swaddling-band

But She comes to the Man she loves
50   If young or old or rich or poor
      They soon drive out the aged Host
      A Beggar at anothers door

He wanders weeping far away
Untill some other take him in
Oft blind & age-bent sore distrest
Untill he can a Maiden win

And to allay his freezing Age
The Poor Man takes her in his arms
The Cottage fades before his sight
60   The Garden & its lovely Charms

The Guests are scatterd thro' the land
For the Eye altering alters all
The Senses roll themselves in fear
And the flat Earth becomes a Ball

[1] **Husbandman** farmer   [2] **Cot** cottage

The Stars Sun Moon all shrink away
A desart vast without a bound
And nothing left to eat or drink
And a dark desart all around

The honey of her Infant lips
70 The bread & wine of her sweet smile
The wild game of her roving Eye
Does him to Infancy beguile

For as he eats & drinks he grows
Younger & younger every day
And on the desart wild they both
Wander in terror & dismay

Like the wild Stag she flees away
Her fear plants many a thicket wild
While he pursues her night & day
80 By various arts of Love beguild

By various arts of Love & Hate
Till the wide desart planted oer
With Labyrinths of wayward Love
Where roams the Lion Wolf & Boar

Till he becomes a wayward Babe
And she a weeping Woman Old
Then many a Lover wanders here
The Sun & Stars are nearer rolld

The trees bring forth sweet Extacy
90 To all who in the desart roam
Till many a City there is Built
And many a pleasant Shepherds home

But when they find the frowning Babe
Terror strikes thro the region wide
They cry the Babe the Babe is Born
And flee away on Every side

For who dare touch the frowning form
His arm is witherd to its root
Lions Boars Wolves all howling flee
100 And every Tree does shed its fruit

And none can touch that frowning form
Except it be a Woman Old
She nails him down upon the Rock
And all is done as I have told

1803?   1863

From The Four Zoas[1]

From Night II [*Enion's Lament*]

I am made to sow the thistle for wheat; the nettle for a nourishing dainty
I have planted a false oath in the earth, it has brought forth a poison tree
I have chosen the serpent for a councellor & the dog
390   For a schoolmaster to my children
I have blotted out from light & living the dove & nightingale
And I have caused the earth worm to beg from door to door
I have taught the thief a secret path into the house of the just
I have taught pale artifice to spread his nets upon the morning
My heavens are brass my earth is iron my moon a clod of clay[2]
My sun a pestilence burning at noon & a vapour of death in night

What is the price of Experience do men buy it for a song
Or wisdom for a dance in the street? No it is bought with the price[3]
Of all that a man hath his house his wife his children
400   Wisdom is sold in the desolate market where none come to buy
And in the witherd field where the farmer plows for bread in vain

It is an easy thing to triumph in the summers sun
And in the vintage & to sing on the waggon loaded with corn
It is an easy thing to talk of patience to the afflicted
To speak the laws of prudence to the houseless wanderer

To listen to the hungry ravens cry in wintry season
When the red blood is filld with wine & with the marrow of lambs
It is an easy thing to laugh at wrathful elements
To hear the dog howl at the wintry door, the ox in the slaughter house moan
410   To see a god on every wind & a blessing on every blast
To hear sounds of love in the thunder storm that destroys our enemies house
To rejoice in the blight that covers his field, & the sickness that cuts off his
    children
While our olive & vine sing & laugh round our door & our children bring
    fruits & flowers

Then the groan & the dolor are quite forgotten & the slave grinding at the mill
And the captive in chains & the poor in the prison, & the soldier in the field
When the shatterd bone hath laid him groaning among the happier dead

[1] Blake described his long epic poem *The Four Zoas* (left unprinted during his lifetime) as "A Dream of Nine Nights." This dream-narrative attempts to represent nothing less than the entire spiritual history of Man, from his fall into division, with consequent warfare among the fallen components of his own divided being, to his final reintegration and the restoration of the edenic state. The two passages presented here articulate, respectively, a bitter knowledge of fallen experience and a visionary faith in the possible reunification of divided Man. The speaker of each is Enion, a kind of earth-mother figure, whose haunting speeches are among the most eloquent in the poem.

[2] **brass . . . iron . . . clay** See Daniel 2:33, where these minerals constitute the image of earthly power, doomed to perish.

[3] **No . . . price** See Job 28:12–13 ("But where shall wisdom be found? And where is the place of understanding? Man knoweth not the price thereof").

It is an easy thing to rejoice in the tents of prosperity
Thus could I sing & thus rejoice, but it is not so with me!

From Night VIII [*The Eternal Man*[1]]

As the seed waits Eagerly watching for its flower & fruit
Anxious its little soul looks out into the clear expanse
560 To see if hungry winds are abroad with their invisible army
So Man looks out in tree & herb & fish & bird & beast
Collecting up the scatterd portions of his immortal body
Into the Elemental forms of every thing that grows
He tries the sullen north wind riding on its angry furrows
The sultry south when the sun rises & the angry east
When the sun sets when the clods harden & the cattle stand
Drooping & the birds hide in their silent nests. he stores his thoughts
As in a store house in his memory he regulates the forms
Of all beneath & all above & in the gentle West
570 Reposes where the Suns heat dwells he rises to the Sun
And to the Planets of the Night & to the stars that gild
The Zodiac & the stars that sullen stand to north & south
He touches the remotest pole & in the Center weeps
That Man should Labour & sorrow & learn & forget & return
To the dark valley whence he came to begin his labours anew
In pain he sighs in pain he labours in his universe
Screaming in birds over the deep & howling in the Wolf
Over the slain & moaning in the cattle & in the winds
And weeping over Orc & Urizen[2] in clouds & flaming fires
580 And in the cries of birth & in the groans of death his voice
Is heard throughout the Universe whereever a grass grows
Or a leaf buds The Eternal Man is seen is heard is felt
And all his Sorrows till he reassumes his ancient bliss

c. 1797–1808   1893

[1] Blake's mythology in *The Four Zoas* borrows from medieval Jewish mysticism the notion that every separate thing in the universe was once contained in the body of a single Primal or Eternal Man, who fell and became divided into a world of objects. But portions of the primordial humanity linger on in these objects and struggle to reintegrate, as Enion recognizes in this majestic and moving exposition.

[2] **Orc . . . Urizen** Orc is a spirit of rebellion and passion in Blake's mythology, and Urizen a spirit of orthodox authority and repressive rationality.

From Milton[1]

And did those feet in ancient time
Walk upon Englands mountains green:

[1] These prefatory verses introduce the long prophetic poem *Milton*, which deals with Blake's own recognition and assumption of his mission as a spiritual prophet. Set to music, the verses have become a famous English hymn.

And was the holy Lamb of God
On Englands pleasant pastures seen!

And did the Countenance Divine
Shine forth upon our clouded hills?
And was Jerusalem builded here,
Among these dark Satanic Mills?[2]

Bring me my Bow of burning gold:
10 Bring me my Arrows of desire:
Bring me my Spear: O clouds unfold!
Bring me my Chariot of fire!

I will not cease from Mental Fight,
Nor shall my Sword sleep in my hand:
Till we have built Jerusalem,
In Englands green & pleasant Land.

1804–09

[2] **dark Satanic Mills** any grinding, repetitive,
soulless system of things, including, though not
exclusively limited to, industrial factories

From For the Sexes the Gates of Paradise

[Epilogue]

To The Accuser who is
The God of This World[1]

Truly My Satan thou art but a Dunce
And dost not know the Garment from the Man
Every Harlot was a Virgin once
Nor canst thou ever change Kate into Nan

Tho thou art Worshipd by the Names Divine
Of Jesus & Jehovah thou art still
The Son of Morn in weary Nights decline[2]
The lost Travellers Dream under the Hill

1818?

[1] See Job 1:6–22, 2:1–8. "Satan" means "accuser" or "adversary" in Hebrew. For Blake the role of Satan in the Book of Job as an accuser and punisher of sin conforms to the conventional, orthodox notion of God's own behavior. (see 11. 6–7).
[2] 1. 7 See Isaiah 14:12 ("How art thou fallen from heaven, O Lucifer, son of the morning!").

WILLIAM WORDSWORTH
1770–1850

Wordsworth was the first English poet to base much of his work directly on his own life. His autobiographical poem *The Prelude* vividly recollects his childhood among the mountains, lakes, and valleys of the English Lake District. He lived for a year in France (1791–92), at the height of the French Revolution and fathered there an illegitimate daughter. These circumstances led to an emotional and intellectual crisis that left its mark on most of his major works. But his return to England and the landscape he had loved as a child began his spiritual recovery. In 1797 he began a deep friendship with the younger poet Coleridge, who provided a philosophical framework for Wordsworth's intuitive powers. The friendship led to literary collaboration and the publication of *Lyrical Ballads* (1798), a small volume of poems whose relatively natural style and often humble subjects eventually helped to usher in a new era in English poetry. With the completion of *The Prelude* in 1805, Wordsworth's greatest poetic achievements were behind him, though he received wide public acclaim in his declining years and was appointed poet laureate in 1843.

Generations of readers have revered Wordsworth as a "worshiper" or "prophet" of Nature (his own terms) and have learned from him how to regard Nature as a source of comfort and guidance. But the term "nature poet," frequently applied to him, fails to reflect his many-sided accomplishment. Wordsworth's poetry influenced our modern interest in children and the psychology of childhood, in the stages of growth of the inner self, and in the workings of memory on present feelings. In many ways he is a traditional moralist, stressing the virtues of the simple life and the bonds of love and duty. But he also shows a more modern religious sensibility in his fascination with solitude, with haunting encounters in lonely places, and with states of mind in which his imagination mysteriously overpowers his ordinary sense of things. Wordsworth reshapes the great religious themes of Spenser and Milton—spiritual breakdown and redemption—into a form appropriate to modern experience and belief. In *The Prelude* and other poems of the same period he removes the mythological trappings and framework of traditional religious doctrine and "by words which speak of nothing more than what we are" attempts to rediscover Paradise as "a simple produce of the common day." This aim is reflected in poetry that is sometimes childlike in its diction and rhythms, sometimes elevated, solemn, and complex, but always sensitive to shades of human feeling.

Lines

COMPOSED A FEW MILES ABOVE TINTERN ABBEY, ON
REVISITING THE BANKS OF THE WYE DURING A TOUR.
JULY 13, 1798[1]

Five years have past; five summers, with the length
Of five long winters! and again I hear
These waters, rolling from their mountain-springs
With a soft inland murmur.—Once again

[1] This poem, commonly known by the shortened form of its title, "Tintern Abbey," was given the final and climactic position in the volume *Lyrical Ballads*. Near Tintern, in the valley of the river Wye in the west of England, lie the ruins of a medieval abbey. Wordsworth first visited the area in August 1793, less than a year after his return from his turbulent experiences in France.

Do I behold these steep and lofty cliffs,
That on a wild secluded scene impress
Thoughts of more deep seclusion; and connect
The landscape with the quiet of the sky.
The day is come when I again repose
10   Here, under this dark sycamore, and view
These plots of cottage-ground, these orchard-tufts,
Which at this season, with their unripe fruits,
Are clad in one green hue, and lose themselves
'Mid groves and copses. Once again I see
These hedge-rows, hardly hedge-rows, little lines
Of sportive wood run wild: these pastoral farms,
Green to the very door; and wreaths of smoke
Sent up, in silence, from among the trees!
With some uncertain notice, as might seem
20   Of vagrant dwellers in the houseless woods,
Or of some Hermit's cave, where by his fire
The Hermit sits alone.

                These beauteous forms,
Through a long absence, have not been to me
As is a landscape to a blind man's eye:
But oft, in lonely rooms, and 'mid the din
Of towns and cities, I have owed to them
In hours of weariness, sensations sweet,
Felt in the blood, and felt along the heart;
And passing even into my purer mind,
30   With tranquil restoration:—feelings too
Of unremembered pleasure: such, perhaps,
As have no slight or trivial influence
On that best portion of a good man's life,
His little, nameless, unremembered, acts
Of kindness and of love. Nor less, I trust,
To them I may have owed another gift,
Of aspect more sublime; that blessed mood,
In which the burthen of the mystery,
In which the heavy and the weary weight
40   Of all this unintelligible world,
Is lightened:—that serene and blessed mood,
In which the affections gently lead us on,—
Until, the breath of this corporeal frame
And even the motion of our human blood
Almost suspended, we are laid asleep
In body, and become a living soul:
While with an eye made quiet by the power
Of harmony, and the deep power of joy,
We see into the life of things.

                                    If this
50   Be but a vain belief, yet, oh! how oft—
      In darkness and amid the many shapes
      Of joyless daylight; when the fretful stir
      Unprofitable, and the fever of the world,
      Have hung upon the beatings of my heart—
      How oft, in spirit, have I turned to thee,
      O sylvan Wye! thou wanderer thro' the woods,
      How often has my spirit turned to thee!

      And now, with gleams of half-extinguished thought,
      With many recognitions dim and faint,
60   And somewhat of a sad perplexity,
      The picture of the mind revives again:
      While here I stand, not only with the sense
      Of present pleasure, but with pleasing thoughts
      That in this moment there is life and food
      For future years. And so I dare to hope,
      Though changed, no doubt, from what I was when first
      I came among these hills; when like a roe
      I bounded o'er the mountains, by the sides
      Of the deep rivers, and the lonely streams,
70   Wherever nature led: more like a man
      Flying from something that he dreads than one
      Who sought the thing he loved. For nature then
      (The coarser pleasures of my boyish days,
      And their glad animal movements all gone by)
      To me was all in all.—I cannot paint
      What then I was. The sounding cataract
      Haunted me like a passion: the tall rock,
      The mountain, and the deep and gloomy wood,
      Their colours and their forms, were then to me
80   An appetite;[2] a feeling and a love,
      That had no need of a remoter charm,
      By thought supplied nor any interest
      Unborrowed from the eye.—That time is past,
      And all its aching joys[3] are now no more,
      And all its dizzy raptures. Not for this
      Faint[4] I, nor mourn nor murmur; other gifts
      Have followed; for such loss, I would believe,
      Abundant recompense. For I have learned
      To look on nature, not as in the hour
90   Of thoughtless youth; but hearing oftentimes
      The still, sad music of humanity,
      Nor harsh nor grating, though of ample power
      To chasten and subdue. And I have felt
      A presence that disturbs me with the joy
      Of elevated thoughts; a sense sublime

[2] **appetite** craving   [4] **Faint** become disheartened
[3] **aching joys** pleasures so intense as to be painful

Of something far more deeply interfused,
Whose dwelling is the light of setting suns,
And the round ocean and the living air,
And the blue sky, and in the mind of man:
100 A motion and a spirit, that impels
All thinking things, all objects of all thought,
And rolls through all things. Therefore am I still
A lover of the meadows and the woods,
And mountains; and of all that we behold
From this green earth; of all the mighty world.
Of eye, and ear,—both what they half create,[5]
And what perceive; well pleased to recognise
In nature and the language of the sense[6]
The anchor of my purest thoughts, the nurse,
110 The guide, the guardian of my heart, and soul
Of all my moral being.

                              Nor perchance,
If I were not thus taught, should I the more
Suffer my genial spirits[7] to decay:
For thou[8] art with me here upon the banks
Of this fair river; thou my dearest Friend,
My dear, dear Friend; and in thy voice I catch
The language of my former heart, and read
My former pleasures in the shooting lights
Of thy wild eyes. Oh! yet a little while
120 May I behold in thee what I was once,
My dear, dear Sister! and this prayer I make,
Knowing that Nature never did betray
The heart that loved her; 'tis her privilege,
Through all the years of this our life, to lead
From joy to joy: for she can so inform
The mind that is within us, so impress
With quietness and beauty, and so feed
With lofty thoughts, that neither evil tongues,
Rash judgments, nor the sneers of selfish men,
130 Nor greetings where no kindness is, nor all
The dreary intercourse of daily life,
Shall e'er prevail against us, or disturb
Our cheerful faith, that all which we behold
Is full of blessings. Therefore let the moon
Shine on thee in thy solitary walk;
And let the misty mountain-winds be free
To blow against thee: and, in after years,
When these wild ecstasies shall be matured

[5] **half create** to project back on nature impressions derived from the senses but modified by imagination, memory, and feelings
[6] **language of the sense** outward sense impressions
[7] **genial spirits** innate powers
[8] **thou** Dorothy Wordsworth, the poet's younger sister and close companion

Into a sober pleasure; when thy mind
140 Shall be a mansion for all lovely forms,
Thy memory be as a dwelling-place
For all sweet sounds and harmonies; oh! then,
If solitude, or fear, or pain, or grief,
Should be thy portion, with what healing thoughts
Of tender joy wilt thou remember me
And these my exhortations! Nor, perchance—
If I should be where I no more can hear
Thy voice, nor catch from thy wild eyes these gleams
Of past existence—wilt thou then forget
150 That on the banks of this delightful stream
We stood together; and that I, so long
A worshipper of Nature, hither came
Unwearied in that service: rather say
With warmer love—oh! with far deeper zeal
Of holier love. Nor wilt thou then forget,
That after many wanderings, many years
Of absence, these steep woods and lofty cliffs,
And this green pastoral landscape, were to me
More dear, both for themselves and for thy sake!

1798   1798

Prospectus to *The Recluse*[1]

On Man, on Nature, and on Human Life,
Musing in solitude, I oft perceive
Fair trains of imagery before me rise,
Accompanied by feelings of delight
Pure, or with no unpleasing sadness mixed;
And I am conscious of affecting thoughts
And dear remembrances, whose presence soothes
Or elevates the Mind, intent to weigh
The good and evil of our mortal state.
10 —To these emotions, whencesoe'er they come,
Whether from breath of outward circumstance,
Or from the Soul—an impulse to herself—
I would give utterance in numerous verse.
Of Truth, of Grandeur, Beauty, Love, and Hope,
And melancholy Fear subdued by Faith;
Of blessèd consolations in distress;
Of moral strength, and intellectual Power;

[1] *The Recluse* was Wordsworth's most ambitious poetic project, a major philosophical poem of intended great length. *The Prelude* was written as an introductory poem, but of *The Recluse* itself Wordsworth completed only *The Excursion* (the second of a planned three parts) and a few hundred lines of an unfinished Part I. The poet published some of these latter lines in the Preface to *The Excursion* (1814), calling them "a kind of *Prospectus* of the design and scope of the whole Poem," that is, all of *The Recluse*. The "Prospectus" is the most concise and eloquent statement of Wordsworth's high ambitions as a poet.

Of joy in widest commonalty spread;
Of the individual Mind that keeps her own
20 Inviolate retirement, subject there
To Conscience only, and the law supreme
Of that Intelligence which governs all—
I sing:—"fit audience let me find though few!"[2]

So prayed, more gaining than he asked, the Bard—
In holiest mood. Urania,[3] I shall need
Thy guidance, or a greater Muse, if such
Descend to earth or dwell in highest heaven!
For I must tread on shadowy ground, must sink
Deep—and, aloft ascending, breathe in worlds
30 To which the heaven of heavens is but a veil.
All strength—all terror, single or in bands,
That ever was put forth in personal form—
Jehovah—with his thunder, and the choir
Of shouting Angels, and the empyreal thrones—
I pass them unalarmed. Not Chaos,[4] not
The darkest pit of lowest Erebus,[5]
Nor aught of blinder vacancy, scooped out
By help of dreams—can breed such fear and awe
As fall upon us often when we look
40 Into our Minds, into the Mind of Man—
My haunt, and the main region of my song.
—Beauty—a living Presence of the earth,
Surpassing the most fair ideal Forms
Which craft of delicate Spirits hath composed
From earth's materials—waits upon my steps;
Pitches her tents before me as I move,
An hourly neighbour. Paradise, and groves
Elysian, Fortunate Fields—like those of old
Sought in the Atlantic Main[6]—why should they be
50 A history only of departed things,
Or a mere fiction of what never was?
For the discerning intellect of Man,
When wedded to this goodly universe
In love and holy passion, shall find these
A simple produce of the common day.
—I, long before the blissful hour arrives,
Would chant, in lonely peace, the spousal verse[7]

[2]**fit . . . few** Milton, *Paradise Lost* VII.31.
The "Prospectus" is filled with allusions to
Paradise Lost, designed to impart Wordsworth's
sense of his poetic mission as rivaling or sur-
passing Milton's.
[3]**Urania** the heavenly Muse invoked by Milton
in *Paradise Lost* VII.1–39
[4]**Chaos** a region of uncreated matter—neither
heaven, nor hell, nor the natural creation—
described in *Paradise Lost* Bk. II

[5]**Erebus** in classical myth, the underworld or
hell
[6]**Elysian . . . Main** In Greek myth the Elysian
Fields were the dwelling-place of virtuous souls
in the afterlife; Elysium was sometimes identified
with the Happy Isles ("Fortunate Fields"), lo-
cated, according to legend, somewhere in the
Atlantic Ocean.
[7]**spousal verse** marriage song or epithalamion

Of this great consummation:—and, by words
Which speak of nothing more than what we are,
60 Would I arouse the sensual from their sleep
Of Death, and win the vacant and the vain
To noble raptures; while my voice proclaims
How exquisitely the individual Mind
(And the progressive powers perhaps no less
Of the whole species) to the external World
Is fitted:—and how exquisitely, too—
Theme this but little heard of among men—
The external World is fitted to the Mind;
And the creation (by no lower name
70 Can it be called) which they with blended might
Accomplish:—this is our high argument.[8]
—Such grateful haunts foregoing, if I oft
Must turn elsewhere—to travel near the tribes
And fellowships of men, and see ill sights
Of madding passions mutually inflamed;
Must hear Humanity in fields and groves
Pipe solitary anguish; or must hang
Brooding above the fierce confederate storm
Of sorrow, barricadoed evermore
80 Within the walls of cities—may these sounds
Have their authentic comment; that even these
Hearing, I be not downcast or forlorn!—
Descend, prophetic Spirit! that inspir'st
The human Soul of universal earth,
Dreaming on things to come;[9] and dost possess
A metropolitan[10] temple in the hearts
Of mighty Poets: upon me bestow
A gift of genuine insight; that my Song
With star-like virtue in its place may shine,
90 Shedding benignant influence, and secure,
Itself, from all malevolent effect
Of those mutations that extend their sway
Throughout the nether sphere![11]—And if with this
I mix more lowly matter; with the thing
Contemplated, describe the Mind and Man
Contemplating; and who, and what he was—
The transitory Being that beheld
This Vision; when and where, and how he lived;—
Be not this labour useless. If such theme
100 May sort with highest objects, then—dread Power!
Whose gracious favour is the primal source
Of all illumination,—may my Life

---

[8]**high argument** lofty theme; cf. *Paradise Lost* I.24 ("the height of this great Argument").
[9]**Soul . . . come** Cf. Shakespeare, Sonnet 117 ("the prophetic soul / of the wide world dreaming on things to come").
[10]**metropolitan** foremost or central
[11]**nether sphere** Earth, the material world below the heavens

Express the image of a better time,
More wise desires, and simpler manners;—nurse
My Heart in genuine freedom:—all pure thoughts
Be with me;—so shall thy unfailing love
Guide, and support, and cheer me to the end!

c. 1798–1800   1814

Strange Fits of Passion Have I Known[1]

Strange fits of passion have I known:
And I will dare to tell,
But in the Lover's ear alone,
What once to me befell.

When she I loved looked every day
Fresh as a rose in June,
I to her cottage bent my way,
Beneath an evening-moon.

Upon the moon I fixed my eye,
10   All over the wide lea;
With quickening pace my horse drew nigh
Those paths so dear to me.

And now we reached the orchard-plot;
And, as we climbed the hill,
The sinking moon to Lucy's cot
Came near, and nearer still.

In one of those sweet dreams I slept,
Kind Nature's gentlest boon!
And all the while my eyes I kept
20   On the descending moon.

My horse moved on; hoof after hoof
He raised, and never stopped:
When down behind the cottage roof,
At once, the bright moon dropped.

What fond and wayward thoughts will slide
Into a Lover's head!
"O mercy!" to myself I cried,
"If Lucy should be dead!"

1799   1800

[1] This and the next three poems belong to small groups of lyrics traditionally known as the Lucy Poems. Despite much conjecture, Wordsworth's biographers have not successfully identified Lucy with any known person or located the source of the poet's obvious intensity of feeling.

She Dwelt Among the Untrodden Ways

She dwelt among the untrodden ways
  Beside the springs of Dove,[1]
A Maid whom there were none to praise
  And very few to love:

A violet by a mossy stone
  Half hidden from the eye!
—Fair as a star, when only one
  Is shining in the sky.

She lived unknown, and few could know
10   When Lucy ceased to be;
But she is in her grave, and, oh,
  The difference to me!

1799   1800

[1] **Dove** one of several streams in England with
this name

Three Years She Grew

Three years she grew in sun and shower,
Then Nature said, "A lovelier flower
On earth was never sown;
This Child I to myself will take;
She shall be mine, and I will make
A Lady of my own.

"Myself will to my darling be
Both law and impulse: and with me
The Girl, in rock and plain,
10 In earth and heaven, in glade and bower,
Shall feel an overseeing power
To kindle or restrain.

"She shall be sportive as the fawn
That wild with glee across the lawn
Or up the mountain springs;
And hers shall be the breathing balm,
And hers the silence and the calm
Of mute insensate things.

"The floating clouds their state shall lend
20 To her; for her the willow bend;
Nor shall she fail to see
Even in the motions of the Storm
Grace that shall mould the Maiden's form
By silent sympathy.

"The stars of midnight shall be dear
To her; and she shall lean her ear
In many a secret place
Where rivulets dance their wayward round,
And beauty born of murmuring sound
30 Shall pass into her face.

"And vital feelings of delight
Shall rear her form to stately height,
Her virgin bosom swell;
Such thoughts to Lucy I will give
While she and I together live
Here in this happy dell."

Thus Nature spake—The work was done—
How soon my Lucy's race was run!
She died, and left to me
40 This heath, this calm, and quiet scene;
This memory of what has been,
And never more will be.

1799   1800

A Slumber Did My Spirit Seal

A slumber did my spirit seal;
    I had no human fears:
She seemed a thing that could not feel
    The touch of earthly years.

No motion has she now, no force;
    She neither hears nor sees;
Rolled round in earth's diurnal[1] course,
    With rocks, and stones, and trees.

1799   1800

[1] **diurnal** daily

Resolution and Independence

I

There was a roaring in the wind all night;
The rain came heavily and fell in floods;
But now the sun is rising calm and bright;
The birds are singing in the distant woods;
Over his own sweet voice the Stock-dove broods;
The Jay makes answer as the Magpie chatters;
And all the air is filled with pleasant noise of waters.

II

All things that love the sun are out of doors;
The sky rejoices in the morning's birth;
10   The grass is bright with rain-drops;—on the moors
The hare is running races in her mirth;
And with her feet she from the plashy earth
Raises a mist; that, glittering in the sun,
Runs with her all the way, wherever she doth run.

III

I was a Traveller then upon the moor;
I saw the hare that raced about with joy;
I heard the woods and distant waters roar;
Or heard them not, as happy as a boy;
The pleasant season did my heart employ;
20   My old remembrances went from me wholly;
And all the ways of men, so vain and melancholy.

IV

But, as it sometimes chanceth, from the might
Of joy in minds that can no further go,
As high as we have mounted in delight
In our dejection do we sink as low;
To me that morning did it happen so;
And fears and fancies thick upon me came;
Dim sadness — and blind thoughts, I knew not, nor could name.

V

I heard the sky-lark warbling in the sky;
30   And I bethought me of the playful hare:
Even such a happy Child of earth am I;
Even as these blissful creatures do I fare;
Far from the world I walk, and from all care;
But there may come another day to me—
Solitude, pain of heart, distress, and poverty.

VI

My whole life I have lived in pleasant thought,
As if life's business were a summer mood;
As if all needful things would come unsought
To genial faith, still rich in genial good;
40   But how can He expect that others should
Build for him, sow for him, and at his call
Love him, who for himself will take no heed at all?

VII

I thought of Chatterton,[1] the marvellous Boy,
The sleepless Soul that perished in his pride;

---

[1] **Chatterton** Thomas Chatterton (1752–1770), a precociously gifted poet, who committed sui-   cide at age seventeen in despair over lack of recognition

Of Him[2] who walked in glory and in joy
Following his plough, along the mountain-side:
By our own spirits are we deified;
We Poets in our youth begin in gladness;
But thereof come in the end despondency and madness.

VIII

50 Now, whether it were by peculiar grace,
A leading from above, a something given,
Yet it befell that, in this lonely place,
When I with these untoward thoughts had striven,
Beside a pool bare to the eye of heaven
I saw a Man before me unawares:
The oldest man he seemed that ever wore grey hairs.

IX

As a huge stone is sometimes seen to lie
Couched on the bald top of an eminence;
Wonder to all who do the same espy,
60 By what means it could thither come, and whence;
So that it seems a thing endued with sense:
Like a sea-beast crawled forth, that on a shelf
Of rock or sand reposeth, there to sun itself;

X

Such seemed this Man, not all alive nor dead,
Nor all asleep—in his extreme old age:
His body was bent double, feet and head
Coming together in life's pilgrimage;
As if some dire constraint of pain, or rage
Of sickness felt by him in times long past,
70 A more than human weight upon his frame had cast.

XI

Himself he propped, limbs, body, and pale face,
Upon a long grey staff of shaven wood:
And, still as I drew near with gentle pace,
Upon the margin of that moorish flood[3]
Motionless as a cloud the old Man stood,
That heareth not the loud winds when they call;
And moveth all together, if it move at all.

XII

At length, himself unsettling, he the pond
Stirred with his staff, and fixedly did look
80 Upon the muddy water, which he conned,
As if he had been reading in a book:

---

[2] **Him** Robert Burns, the great Scottish poet, who died in poverty at the age of thirty-seven

[3] **moorish flood** stretch of water on the moors

And now a stranger's privilege I took;
And, drawing to his side, to him did say,
"This morning gives us promise of a glorious day."

XIII

A gentle answer did the old Man make,
In courteous speech which forth he slowly drew:
And him with further words I thus bespake,
"What occupation do you there pursue?
This is a lonesome place for one like you."
90   Ere he replied, a flash of mild surprise
Broke from the sable orbs of his yet-vivid eyes.

XIV

His words came feebly, from a feeble chest,
But each in solemn order followed each,
With something of a lofty utterance drest—
Choice word and measured phrase, above the reach
Of ordinary men; a stately speech;
Such as grave Livers[4] do in Scotland use,
Religious men, who give to God and man their dues.

XV

He told, that to these waters he had come
100   To gather leeches,[5] being old and poor:
Employment hazardous and wearisome!
And he had many hardships to endure:
From pond to pond he roamed, from moor to moor;
Housing, with God's good help, by choice or chance;
And in this way he gained an honest maintenance.

XVI

The old Man still stood talking by my side;
But now his voice to me was like a stream
Scarce heard; nor word from word could I divide;
And the whole body of the Man did seem
110   Like one whom I had met with in a dream;
Or like a man from some far region sent,
To give me human strength, by apt admonishment.

XVII

My former thoughts returned: the fear that kills;
And hope that is unwilling to be fed;
Cold, pain, and labour, and all fleshly ills;
And mighty Poets in their misery dead.
—Perplexed, and longing to be comforted,
My question eagerly did I renew,
"How is it that you live, and what is it you do?"

---

[4] **grave Livers** men of serious moral principle
[5] **leeches** worm used to suck blood for medical purposes. Leech-gatherers would wade in shal-low ponds, picking off the leeches that adhered to their bare legs.

XVIII

120 He with a smile did then his words repeat;
And said that, gathering leeches, far and wide
He travelled; stirring thus about his feet
The waters of the pools were they abide.
"Once I could meet with them on every side;
But they have dwindled long by slow decay;
Yet still I persevere, and find them where I may."

XIX

While he was talking thus, the lonely place,
The old Man's shape, and speech—all troubled me:
In my mind's eye I seemed to see him pace
130 About the weary moors continually,
Wandering about alone and silently.
While I these thoughts within myself pursued,
He, having made a pause, the same discourse renewed.

XX

And soon with this he other matter blended,
Cheerfully uttered, with demeanour kind,
But stately in the main; and when he ended,
I could have laughed myself to scorn to find
In that decrepit Man so firm a mind.
"God," said I, "be my help and stay⁶ secure;
140 I'll think of the Leech-gatherer on the lonely moor!"

1802   1807

⁶ **stay** support

Composed upon Westminster Bridge,¹ September 3, 1802

Earth has not anything to show more fair:
Dull would he be of soul who could pass by
A sight so touching in its majesty:
This City now doth, like a garment, wear
The beauty of the morning; silent, bare,
Ships, towers, domes, theatres, and temples lie
Open unto the fields, and to the sky;
All bright and glittering in the smokeless air.
Never did sun more beautifully steep
10 In his first splendour, valley, rock, or hill;
Ne'er saw I, never felt, a calm so deep!
The river glideth at his own sweet will:
Dear God! the very houses seem asleep;
And all that mighty heart is lying still!

1802   1807

¹ bridge over the Thames near the Houses of
Parliament in London

The World Is Too Much With Us

The world is too much with us; late and soon,
Getting and spending, we lay waste our powers:
Little we see in nature that is ours;
We have given our hearts away, a sordid boon!
This Sea that bares her bosom to the moon;
The winds that will be howling at all hours,
And are up-gathered now like sleeping flowers;
For this, for everything, we are out of tune;
It moves us not.—Great God! I'd rather be
10   A Pagan suckled in a creed outworn;
So might I, standing on this pleasant lea,
Have glimpses that would make me less forlorn;
Have sight of Proteus rising from the sea;
Or hear old Triton[1] blow his wreathèd horn.

                                                  1807

[1] **Proteus . . . Triton** sea-gods in Greek myth-
ology. Triton's horn is a conch shell.

Ode: Intimations of Immortality from Recollections of Early Childhood

The Child is father of the Man;
And I could wish my days to be
Bound each to each by natural piety.[1]

        I
There was a time when meadow, grove, and stream,
The earth, and every common sight,
        To me did seem
        Apparelled in celestial light,
The glory and the freshness of a dream.
It is not now as it hath been of yore;—
        Turn wheresoe'er I may,
        By night or day,
The things which I have seen I now can see no more.

        II
10   The Rainbow comes and goes,
        And lovely is the Rose,
        The Moon doth with delight
Look round her when the heavens are bare;
        Waters on a starry night
        Are beautiful and fair;
    The sunshine is a glorious birth;
    But yet I know, where'er I go,
That there hath past away a glory from the earth.

[1] final lines of Wordsworth's poem "My Heart
Leaps Up"

III

Now, while the birds thus sing a joyous song,
20 And while the young lambs bound
        As to the tabor's sound,[2]
To me alone there came a thought of grief:
A timely utterance gave that thought relief,
        And I again am strong:
The cataracts blow their trumpets from the steep;
No more shall grief of mine the season wrong;
I hear the Echoes through the mountains throng,
The Winds come to me from the fields of sleep,[3]
        And all the earth is gay;
30   Land and sea
    Give themselves up to jollity,
        And with the heart of May
    Doth every Beast keep holiday;—
        Thou Child of Joy,
Shout round me, let me hear thy shouts, thou happy
        Shepherd-boy!

IV

Ye blessèd Creatures, I have heard the call
    Ye to each other make; I see
The heavens laugh with you in your jubilee;
    My heart is at your festival,
40   My head hath its coronal,[4]
The fulness of your bliss, I feel—I feel it all.
        Oh evil day! if I were sullen
        While Earth herself is adorning,
            This sweet May-morning,
        And the Children are culling
            On every side,
        In a thousand valleys far and wide,
        Fresh flowers; while the sun shines warm,
And the Babe leaps up on his Mother's arm:—
50   I hear, I hear, with joy I hear!
        —But there's a Tree, of many, one,
A single Field which I have looked upon,
Both of them speak of something that is gone:
        The Pansy at my feet
        Doth the same tale repeat:
Whither is fled the visionary gleam?
Where is it now, the glory and the dream?

V

Our birth is but a sleep and a forgetting:
The Soul that rises with us, our life's Star,

---

[2] **tabor's sound** beat of a small drum
[3] l. 28 This enigmatic line may refer to morn-ing breezes coming from the west.
[4] **coronal** garland of flowers

60   Hath had elsewhere its setting,
                And cometh from afar:
            Not in entire forgetfulness,
            And not in utter nakedness,
        But trailing clouds of glory do we come
                From God, who is our home:
        Heaven lies about us in our infancy!
        Shades of the prison-house begin to close
                Upon the growing Boy,
                    But He
70   Beholds the light, and whence it flows,
                He sees it in his joy;
        The Youth, who daily farther from the east
                Must travel, still is Nature's Priest,
                And by the vision splendid
                Is on his way attended;
        At length the Man perceives it die away,
        And fade into the light of common day.

                    VI
        Earth fills her lap with pleasures of her own;
        Yearnings she hath in her own natural kind,
80   And, even with something of a Mother's mind,
                And no unworthy aim,
                The homely⁵ Nurse doth all she can
        To make her Foster-child, her Inmate Man,
                Forget the glories he hath known,
        And that imperial palace whence he came.

                    VII
        Behold the Child among his new-born blisses,
        A six years' Darling of a pigmy size!
        See, where 'mid work of his own hand he lies,
        Fretted by sallies of his mother's kisses,
90   With light upon him from his father's eyes!
        See, at his feet, some little plan or chart,
        Some fragment from his dream of human life,
        Shaped by himself with newly-learned art;
                A wedding or a festival,
                A mourning or a funeral;
                And this hath now his heart,
            And unto this he frames his song:
                Then will he fit his tongue
        To dialogues of business, love, or strife;
100   But it will not be long
                Ere this be thrown aside,
                And with new joy and pride
        The little Actor cons another part;

⁵ **homely** simple, homey

Filling from time to time his "humorous stage"[6]
With all the Persons, down to palsied Age,
That Life brings with her in her equipage;
    As if his whole vocation
    Were endless imitation.

      VIII
Thou, whose exterior semblance doth belie
110   Thy Soul's immensity;
Thou best Philosopher, who yet dost keep
They heritage, thou Eye among the blind,
That, deaf and silent, read'st the eternal deep,
Haunted for ever by the eternal mind,—
    Mighty Prophet! Seer blest!
    On whom those truths do rest,
Which we are toiling all our lives to find,
In darkness lost, the darkness of the grave;
Thou, over whom thy Immortality
120 Broods like the Day, a Master o'er a Slave,
A Presence which is not to be put by;
Thou little Child, yet glorious in the might
Of heaven-born freedom on thy being's height,
Why with such earnest pains dost thou provoke
The years to bring the inevitable yoke,
Thus blindly with thy blessedness at strife?
Full soon thy Soul shall have her earthly freight,
And custom lie upon thee with a weight,
Heavy as frost, and deep almost as life!

      IX
130   O joy! that in our embers
      Is something that doth live,
      That nature yet remembers
      What was so fugitive!
The thought of our past years in me doth breed
Perpetual benediction: not indeed
For that which is most worthy to be blest;
Delight and liberty, the simple creed
Of Childhood, whether busy or at rest,
With new-fledged hope still fluttering in his breast:—
140   Not for these I raise
      The song of thanks and praise;
    But for those obstinate questionings
    Of sense and outward things,
    Fallings from us, vanishings;
    Blank misgivings of a Creature

[6] **"humorous stage"** allusion to the comedy of humors, popular among Elizabethan and Jacobean playwrights, which was designed to exhibit different human temperament types and their interaction

Moving about in worlds not realised,[7]
High instincts before which our mortal Nature
Did tremble like a guilty Thing surprised:
    But for those first affections,
150   Those shadowy recollections,
    Which, be they what they may,
Are yet the fountain light of all our day,
Are yet a master light of all our seeing;
    Uphold us, cherish, and have power to make
Our noisy years seem moments in the being
Of the eternal Silence: truths that wake,
    To perish never;
Which neither listlessness, nor mad endeavour,
    Nor Man nor Boy,
160 Nor all that is at enmity with joy,
Can utterly abolish or destroy!
    Hence in a season of calm weather
    Though inland far we be,
Our Souls have sight of that immortal sea
    Which brought us hither,
    Can in a moment travel thither,
And see the Children sport upon the shore,
And hear the mighty waters rolling evermore.

    X
Then sing, ye Birds, sing, sing a joyous song!
170   And let the young Lambs bound
    As to the tabor's sound!
We in thought will join your throng,
    Ye that pipe and ye that play,
    Ye that through your hearts to-day
    Feel the gladness of the May!
What though the radiance which was once so bright
Be now for ever taken from my sight,
    Though nothing can bring back the hour
Of splendour in the grass, of glory in the flower;
180   We will grieve not, rather find
    Strength in what remains behind;
    In the primal sympathy
    Which having been must ever be;
    In the soothing thoughts that spring

---

[7] **Fallings . . . realised** "I was often unable to think of external things as having external existence, and I communed with all that I saw as something not apart from, but inherent in, my own immaterial nature. Many times while going to school have I grasped at a wall or tree to recall myself from this abyss of idealism to the reality. At that time I was afraid of such processes. In later periods of life I have deplored, as we all have reason to do, a subjugation of the opposite character, and have rejoiced over [these] remembrances" (Wordsworth's note). **not realised** not perceived as real

Out of human suffering;
   In the faith that looks through death,
In years that bring the philosophic mind.

    XI
And O, ye Fountains, Meadows, Hills, and Groves,
Forebode not any severing of our loves!
190 Yet in my heart of hearts I feel your might;
I only have relinquished one delight
To live beneath your more habitual sway.
I love the Brooks which down their channels fret,
Even more than when I tripped lightly as they;
The innocent brightness of a new-born Day
       Is lovely yet;
The Clouds that gather round the setting sun
Do take a sober colouring from an eye
That hath kept watch o'er man's mortality;
200 Another race hath been, and other palms[8] are won.
Thanks to the human heart by which we live,
Thanks to its tenderness, its joys, and fears,
To me the meanest flower that blows[9] can give
Thoughts that do often lie too deep for tears.

1802–04   1807

[8] **palms** victory prizes
[9] **meanest . . . blows** smallest flower that
blossoms

From The Prelude[1]

From Book I [*Fair Seed-time*]

Fair seed-time had my soul, and I grew up
Fostered alike by beauty and by fear:
Much favoured in my birth-place, and no less
In that beloved Vale[2] to which erelong
We were transplanted—there were we let loose
For sports of wider range. Ere I had told
Ten birth-days, when among the mountain slopes
Frost, and the breath of frosty wind, had snapped

[1] Wordsworth's greatest poem. Started in 1798 as a preparatory exercise for his projected philosophical poem *The Recluse*, it grew enormously in 1804–05, and by the time of its posthumous publication in 1850 it stood as a fourteen-book epic, tracing the poet's childhood, youth, and young manhood. The title, invented by Wordsworth's widow, alludes to the poem's original function of introducing *The Recluse*: the sub-title, also by Mrs. Wordsworth, more closely accords with the central theme of the work: "The Growth of a Poet's Mind." The selections printed here are taken from the revised version of 1850.
[2] **Vale** the valley of Esthwaite, a lake in the English Lake District. Wordsworth attended school in the nearby village of Hawkshead.

The last autumnal crocus, 'twas my joy
310 With store of springes³ o'er my shoulder hung
To range the open heights where woodcocks run
Along the smooth green turf. Through half the night,
Scudding away from snare to snare, I plied
That anxious visitation;—moon and stars
Were shining o'er my head. I was alone,
And seemed to be a trouble to the peace
That dwelt among them. Sometimes it befel
In these night wanderings, that a strong desire
O'erpowered my better reason, and the bird
320 Which was the captive of another's toil
Became my prey; and when the deed was done
I heard among the solitary hills
Low breathings coming after me, and sounds
Of undistinguishable motion, steps
Almost as silent as the turf they trod.

Nor less when spring had warmed the cultured⁴ Vale,
Moved we as plunderers where the mother-bird
Had in high places built her lodge; though mean
Our object and inglorious, yet the end
330 Was not ignoble. Oh! when I have hung
Above the raven's nest, by knots of grass
And half-inch fissures in the slippery rock
But ill sustained, and almost (so it seemed)
Suspended by the blast that blew amain,
Shouldering the naked crag, oh, at that time
While on the perilous ridge I hung alone,
With what strange utterance did the loud dry wind
Blow through my ear! the sky seemed not a sky
Of earth—and with what motion moved the clouds!

340 Dust as we are, the immortal spirit grows
Like harmony in music; there is a dark
Inscrutable workmanship that reconciles
Discordant elements, makes them cling together
In one society. How strange that all
The terrors, pains, and early miseries,
Regrets, vexations, lassitudes interfused
Within my mind, should e'er have borne a part,
And that a needful part, in making up
The calm existence that is mine when I
350 Am worthy of myself! Praise to the end!
Thanks to the means which Nature deigned to employ;
Whether her fearless⁵ visitings, or those
That came with soft alarm, like hurtless light

³ **springes** bird traps
⁴ **cultured** cultivated
⁵ **fearless** causing no fear

Opening the peaceful clouds; or she may use
Severer interventions, ministry
More palpable, as best might suit her aim.

One summer evening (led by her) I found
A little boat tied to a willow tree
Within a rocky cave, its usual home.
360 Straight I unloosed her chain, and stepping in
Pushed from the shore. It was an act of stealth
And troubled pleasure, nor without the voice
Of mountain-echoes did my boat move on;
Leaving behind her still, on either side,
Small circles glittering idly in the moon,
Until they melted all into one track
Of sparkling light. But now, like one who rows,
Proud of his skill, to reach a chosen point
With an unswerving line, I fixed my view
370 Upon the summit of a craggy ridge,
The horizon's utmost boundary; far above
Was nothing but the stars and the grey sky.
She was an elfin pinnace;[6] lustily
I dipped my oars into the silent lake,
And, as I rose upon the stroke, my boat
Went heaving through the water like a swan;
When, from behind that craggy steep till then
The horizon's bound, a huge peak, black and huge,
As if with voluntary power instinct
380 Upreared its head. I struck and struck again,
And growing still in stature the grim shape
Towered up between me and the stars, and still,
For so it seemed, with purpose of its own
And measured motion like a living thing,
Strode after me. With trembling oars I turned,
And through the silent water stole my way
Back to the covert of the willow tree;
There in her mooring-place I left my bark,—
And through the meadows homeward went, in grave
390 And serious mood; but after I had seen
That spectacle, for many days, my brain
Worked with a dim and undetermined sense
Of unknown modes of being; o'er my thoughts
There hung a darkness, call it solitude
Or blank desertion. No familiar shapes
Remained, no pleasant images of trees,
Of sea or sky, no colours of green fields;
But huge and mighty forms, that do not live
Like living men, moved slowly through the mind
400 By day and were a trouble to my dreams.

[6] **pinnace** small boat

From Book V [*The Boy of Winander*]

There was a Boy: ye knew him well, ye cliffs
And islands of Winander![1]—many a time
At evening, when the earliest stars began
To move along the edges of the hills,
Rising or setting, would he stand alone
Beneath the trees or by the glimmering lake,
370   And there, with fingers interwoven, both hands
Pressed closely palm to palm, and to his mouth
Uplifted, he, as through an instrument,
Blew mimic hootings to the silent owls,
That they might answer him; and they would shout
Across the watery vale, and shout again,
Responsive to his call, with quivering peals,
And long halloos and screams, and echoes loud,
Redoubled and redoubled, concourse wild
Of jocund din; and, when a lengthened pause
380   Of silence came and baffled his best skill,
Then sometimes, in that silence while he hung
Listening, a gentle shock of mild surprise
Has carried far into his heart the voice
Of mountain torrents; or the visible scene
Would enter unawares into his mind,
With all its solemn imagery, its rocks,
Its woods, and that uncertain heaven, received
Into the bosom of the steady lake.

[1] **Winander**   another name for Windermere, the
largest lake in the Lake District

From Book XII [*Spots of Time*]

There are in our existence spots of time,
That with distinct pre-eminence retain
210   A renovating virtue, whence, depressed
By false opinion and contentious thought,
Or aught of heavier or more deadly weight,
In trivial occupations, and the round
Of ordinary intercourse, our minds
Are nourished and invisibly repaired;
A virtue, by which pleasure is enhanced,
That penetrates, enables us to mount,
When high, more high, and lifts us up when fallen.
This efficacious spirit chiefly lurks
220   Among those passages of life that give
Profoundest knowledge to what point, and how,
The mind is lord and master—outward sense

The obedient servant of her will. Such moments
Are scattered everywhere, taking their date
From our first childhood. I remember well,
That once, while yet my inexperienced hand
Could scarcely hold a bridle, with proud hopes
I mounted, and we journeyed towards the hills:
An ancient servant of my father's house
230   Was with me, my encourager and guide:
We had not travelled long, ere some mischance
Disjoined me from my comrade; and, through fear
Dismounting, down the rough and stony moor
I led my horse, and, stumbling on, at length
Came to a bottom, where in former times
A murderer had been hung in iron chains.
The gibbet-mast had mouldered down, the bones
And iron case were gone; but on the turf,
Hard by, soon after that fell deed was wrought,
240   Some unknown hand had carved the murderer's name.
The monumental letters were inscribed
In times long past; but still, from year to year,
By superstition of the neighbourhood,
The grass is cleared away, and to this hour
The characters are fresh and visible:
A casual glance had shown them, and I fled,
Faltering and faint, and ignorant of the road:
Then, reascending the bare common, saw
A naked pool that lay beneath the hills,
250   The beacon on the summit, and, more near,
A girl, who bore a pitcher on her head,
And seemed with difficult steps to force her way
Against the blowing wind. It was, in truth,
An ordinary sight; but I should need
Colours and words that are unknown to man,
To paint the visionary dreariness
Which, while I looked all round for my lost guide,
Invested moorland waste, and naked pool,
The beacon crowning the lone eminence,
260   The female and her garments vexed and tossed
By the strong wind. When, in the blessed hours
Of early love, the loved one[1] at my side,
I roamed, in daily presence of this scene,
Upon the naked pool and dreary crags,
And on the melancholy beacon fell
A spirit of pleasure and youth's golden gleam;
And think ye not with radiance more sublime
For these remembrances, and for the power
They had left behind? So feeling comes in aid

[1] **loved one** Wordsworth's future wife, Mary
Hutchinson

270   Of feeling, and diversity of strength
       Attends us, if but once we have been strong.
       Oh! mystery of man, from what a depth
       Proceed thy honours. I am lost, but see
       In simple childhood something of the base
       On which thy greatness stands; but this I feel,
       That from thyself it comes, that thou must give,
       Else never canst receive. The days gone by
       Return upon me almost from the dawn
       Of life; the hiding-places of man's power
280   Open; I would approach them, but they close.
       I see by glimpses now; when age comes on,
       May scarcely see at all; and I would give,
       While yet we may, as far as words can give,
       Substance and life to what I feel, enshrining,
       Such is my hope, the spirit of the Past
       For future restoration. . . .

1798–1805   1850

Elegiac Stanzas

SUGGESTED BY A PICTURE OF PEELE CASTLE, IN A STORM,
PAINTED BY SIR GEORGE BEAUMONT[1]

I was thy neighbour once, thou rugged Pile!
Four summer weeks I dwelt in sight of thee:
I saw thee every day; and all the while
Thy Form was sleeping on a glassy sea.

So pure the sky, so quiet was the air!
So like, so very like, was day to day!
Whene'er I looked, thy Image still was there;
It trembled, but it never passed away.

How perfect was the calm! it seemed no sleep;
10 No mood, which season takes away, or brings:
I could have fancied that the mighty Deep
Was even the gentlest of all gentle Things.

Ah! THEN, if mine had been the Painter's hand,
To express what then I saw; and add the gleam,
The light that never was, on sea or land,
The consecration, and the Poet's dream;

[1] Wordsworth had visited Peele Castle in northern England many years before he saw his friend Beaumont's stormy-looking painting of the place. The gloom and turbulence of the painting became linked in the poet's mind with his grief over the drowning of his brother, Captain John Wordsworth, in February 1805.

I would have planted thee, thou hoary Pile[2]
Amid a world how different from this!
Beside a sea that could not cease to smile;
20 On tranquil land, beneath a sky of bliss.

Thou shouldst have seemed a treasure-house divine
Of peaceful years; a chronicle of heaven;—
Of all the sunbeams that did ever shine
The very sweetest had to thee been given.

A Picture had it been of lasting ease,
Elysian[3] quiet, without toil or strife;
No motion but the moving tide, a breeze,
Or merely silent Nature's breathing life.

Such, in the fond illusion of my heart,
30 Such Picture would I at that time have made:
And seen the soul of truth in every part,
A stedfast peace that might not be betrayed.

So once it would have been,—'tis so no more;
I have submitted to a new control:
A power is gone, which nothing can restore;
A deep distress[4] hath humanised my Soul.

Not for a moment could I now behold
A smiling sea, and be what I have been:
The feeling of my loss will ne'er be old;
40 This, which I know, I speak with mind serene.

Then, Beaumont, Friend! who would have been the Friend,
If he had lived, of Him whom I deplore,[5]
This work of thine I blame not, but commend;
This sea in anger, and that dismal shore.

O 'tis a passionate Work!—yet wise and well,
Well chosen is the spirit that is here;
That Hulk which labours in the deadly swell,
This rueful sky, this pageantry of fear!

And this huge Castle, standing here sublime,
50 I love to see the look with which it braves,
Cased in the unfeeling armour of old time,
The lightning, the fierce wind, and trampling waves.

[2] **Pile** large structure
[3] **Elysian** In classical mythology virtuous people after death were allowed to dwell in the Elysian Fields, a kind of paradise.
[4] **distress** over the death of John Wordsworth
[5] **deplore** mourn

Farewell, farewell the heart that lives alone,
Housed in a dream, at distance from the Kind![6]
Such happiness, wherever it be known,
Is to be pitied; for 'tis surely blind.

But welcome fortitude, and patient cheer,
And frequent sights of what is to be borne!
Such sights, or worse, as are before me here.—
60   Not without hope we suffer and we mourn.

1805   1807

[6] **Kind**   human race

Surprised by Joy

Surprised by joy—impatient as the Wind
I turned to share the transport—Oh! with whom
But Thee,[1] deep buried in the silent tomb,
That spot which no vicissitude can find?
Love, faithful love, recalled thee to my mind—
But how could I forget thee? Through what power,
Even for the least division of an hour,
Have I been so beguiled as to be blind
To my most grievous loss!—That thought's return
10   Was the worst pang that sorrow ever bore,
Save one, one only, when I stood forlorn,
Knowing my heart's best treasure was no more;
That neither present time, nor years unborn
Could to my sight that heavenly face restore.

1815

[1] **Thee**   Wordsworth's daughter Catherine, who
died in June 1812 at the age of four

SAMUEL TAYLOR COLERIDGE
1772–1834

The immensely gifted Coleridge spent much of his life battling problems—his neuroses, drug addiction, and unhappy marriage—that blocked his creativity. As a result, many of his most promising pieces remain in fragmentary form. The high point of his life as a poet came through his friendship with William Wordsworth. In 1797–98 the two poets collaborated on their groundbreaking volume *Lyrical Ballads*, which included as its longest selection Coleridge's masterpiece "The Rime of the Ancient Mariner." His best-known poems date largely from the same brief period.

Although Coleridge produced relatively few major poems, he was a great poetic innovator. In the "Ancient Mariner" he adapted the medieval folk ballad, introducing a dream-like psychology and a sophisticated use of symbolism. In the pieces commonly known as his "conversation poems," such as "Frost at Midnight," he worked by an associative process evolved from fleeting, ordinary moments in his own life. In these instances, as well as in other poems such as "Kubla Khan," he created new influential poetic modes, notable at once for their vivid imagery and for their richly suggestive psychological density. Coleridge particularly excels at conveying the pain of despair, anxiety, and mental sterility. But he also suggests in such poems as "This Lime Tree

Bower My Prison" and, implicitly, in "Dejection: An Ode" that by turning away from self-preoccupation we can unlock the healing powers of the imagination and spontaneous love and become part of the "One Life" of the world. That Coleridge often expresses his inability to complete this process makes him a tragic figure within his own poetry, but the poems themselves succeed. In their eloquence and wisdom they endure, not as documents of personal failure, but as products of sure creative mastery.

This Lime-Tree Bower My Prison[1]

[ADDRESSED TO CHARLES LAMB, OF THE INDIA HOUSE, LONDON]

Well, they are gone, and here must I remain,
This lime-tree bower my prison! I have lost
Beauties and feelings, such as would have been
Most sweet to my remembrance even when age
Had dimm'd mine eyes to blindness! They, meanwhile,
Friends, whom I never more may meet again,
On springy heath, along the hill-top edge,
Wander in gladness, and wind down, perchance,
To that still roaring dell, of which I told;
10 The roaring dell, o'erwooded, narrow, deep,
And only speckled by the mid-day sun;
Where its slim trunk the ash from rock to rock
Flings arching like a bridge;—that branchless ash,
Unsunn'd and damp, whose few poor yellow leaves
Ne'er tremble in the gale, yet tremble still,
Fann'd by the water-fall! and there my friends
Behold the dark green file of long lank weeds,
That all at once (a most fantastic sight!)
Still nod and drip beneath the dripping edge
Of the blue clay-stone.

20   Now, my friends emerge
Beneath the wide wide Heaven—and view again
The many-steepled tract magnificent
Of hilly fields and meadows, and the sea,

[1] "In June of 1797 some long-expected friends paid a visit to the author's cottage; and on the morning of their arrival, he met with an accident, which disabled him from walking during the whole time of their stay. One evening, when they had left him for a few hours, he composed the following lines in the garden bower" (Coleridge's note); the friends mentioned here were the poet Wordsworth, his sister Dorothy, and the essayist Charles Lamb, who is addressed by name at several points in the poem.

With some fair bark,[2] perhaps, whose sails light up
The slip of smooth clear blue betwixt two Isles
Of purple shadow! Yes! they wander on
In gladness all; but thou, methinks, most glad,
My gentle-hearted Charles! for thou hast pined
And hunger'd after Nature, many a year,
30   In the great City pent, winning thy way
With sad yet patient soul, through evil and pain
And strange calamity! Ah! slowly sink
Behind the western ridge, thou glorious Sun!
Ye purple heath-flowers! richlier burn, ye clouds!
Live in the yellow light, ye distant groves!
And kindle, thou blue Ocean! So my friend
Struck with deep joy may stand, as I have stood,
Silent with swimming sense; yea, gazing round
40   On the wide landscape, gaze till all doth seem
Less gross than bodily; and of such hues
As veil the Almighty Spirit, when yet he makes
Spirits perceive his presence.

                    A delight
Comes sudden on my heart, and I am glad
As I myself were there! Nor in this bower,
This little lime-tree bower, have I not mark'd
Much that has sooth'd me. Pale beneath the blaze
Hung the transparent foliage; and I watch'd
Some broad and sunny leaf, and lov'd to see
50   The shadow of the leaf and stem above
Dappling its sunshine! And that walnut-tree
Was richly ting'd, and a deep radiance lay
Full on the ancient ivy, which usurps
Those fronting elms, and now, with blackest mass
Makes their dark branches gleam a lighter hue
Through the late twilight: and though now the bat
Wheels silent by, and not a swallow twitters,
Yet still the solitary humble-bee
Sings in the bean-flower! Henceforth I shall know
60   That Nature ne'er deserts the wise and pure;
No plot so narrow, be but Nature there,
No waste so vacant, but may well employ
Each faculty of sense, and keep the heart
Awake to Love and Beauty! and sometimes
'Tis well to be bereft of promis'd good,
That we may lift the soul, and contemplate
With lively joy the joys we cannot share.
My gentle-hearted Charles! when the last rook
Beat its straight path along the dusky air

[2] **bark**   boat

70   Homewards, I blest it! deeming its black wing
     (Now a dim speck, now vanishing in light)
     Had cross'd the mighty Orb's dilated glory,
     While thou stood'st gazing; or, when all was still,
     Flew creeking o'er thy head, and had a charm
     For thee, my gentle-hearted Charles, to whom
     No sound is dissonant which tells of Life.

1797   1800

The Rime of the Ancient Mariner[1]

IN SEVEN PARTS

*Facile credo, plures esse Naturas invisibiles quam visibiles
in rerum universitate. Sed horum omnium familiam quis
nobis enarrabit? et gradus et cognationes et discrimina et
singulorum munera? Quid agunt? quae loca habitant? Harum
rerum notitiam semper ambivit ingenium humanum, nun-
quam attigit. Juvat, interea, non diffiteor, quandoque in
animo, tanquam in tabula, majoris et melioris mundi imag-
inem contemplari: ne mens assuefacta hodiernae vitae minutiis
se contrahat nimis, et tota subsidat in pusillas cogitationes.
Sed veritati interea invigilandum est, modusque servandus,
ut certa ab incertis, diem a nocte, distinguamus.* —T. BUR-
NET, *Archaeol. Phil.* p. 68.[2]

ARGUMENT

*How a Ship having passed the Line was driven by storms to
the cold Country towards the South Pole; and how from
thence she made her course to the tropical Latitude of the
Great Pacific Ocean; and of the strange things that befell;
and in what manner the Ancyent Marinere came back to his
own Country.*

---

[1] the first and longest poem in Wordsworth and Coleridge's collection *Lyrical Ballads.* Imitating the medieval ballad form for the verses, Coleridge added the deliberately archaic-sounding marginal glosses in the revised version of 1816 (printed here).

[2] The Latin epigraph is taken from the English theologian Thomas Burnet's *Archaeologiae philosophicae* (1692): "I easily believe that in the universe there are more invisible Natures than visible ones. But who shall explain to us the families of all these? And the ranks, relations, distinctions, and functions of each? How do they act? What places do they inhabit? The human intellect has always skirted about the knowledge of these matters but has never attained it. I do not deny that sometimes it is gratifying to contemplate in one's mind, as in a picture, the image of a greater and better world: for otherwise the mind, accustomed to the minute details of daily life, may become excessively narrow and sink totally into petty thoughts. But meanwhile one must be vigilant for the truth and keep a sense of measure, so as to distinguish the certain from the uncertain, day from night" (editor's translation).

PART I

An ancient Mariner meet- eth three Gallants bidden to a wedding-feast, and detaineth one.	It is an ancient Mariner, And he stoppeth one of three. "By thy long grey beard and glittering eye, Now wherefore stopp'st thou me?

The Bridegroom's doors are opened wide,
And I am next of kin;
The guests are met, the feast is set:
May'st hear the merry din."

10

He holds him with his skinny hand,
"There was a ship," quoth he.
"Hold off! unhand me, grey-beard loon!"
Eftsoons³ his hand dropt he.

The Wedding- Guest is spell- bound by the eye of the old seafaring man, and con- strained to hear his tale.	He holds him with his glittering eye— The Wedding-Guest stood still, And listens like a three years' child: The Mariner hath his will.

The Wedding-Guest sat on a stone:
He cannot choose but hear;
And thus spake on that ancient man,

20

The bright-eyed Mariner.

"The ship was cheered, the harbour cleared,

The Mariner tells how the ship sailed southward with a good wind and fair weather, till it reached the Line.	Merrily did we drop Below the kirk,⁴ below the hill, Below the lighthouse top. The Sun came up upon the left, Out of the sea came he! And he shone bright, and on the right Went down into the sea.

Higher and higher every day,

30

Till over the mast at noon—"
The Wedding-Guest here beat his breast,
For he heard the loud bassoon.

The Wedding- Guest heareth the bridal music; but the Mariner continueth his tale.	The bride hath paced into the hall, Red as a rose is she; Nodding their heads before her goes The merry minstrelsy.

The Wedding-Guest he beat his breast,
Yet he cannot choose but hear;

³**Eftsoons** immediately
⁴**kirk** church

40 And thus spake on that ancient man,
The bright-eyed Mariner.

The ship
driven by a
storm toward
the south pole.

"And now the STORM-BLAST came, and he
Was tyrannous and strong;
He struck with his o'ertaking wings,
And chased us south along.

With sloping masts and dipping prow,
As who pursued with yell and blow
Still treads the shadow of his foe,
And forward bends his head,
The ship drove fast, loud reared the blast,
50 And southward aye we fled.

And now there came both mist and snow,
And it grew wondrous cold:
And ice, mast-high, came floating by,
As green as emerald.

The land of
ice, and of
fearful sounds
where no
living thing
was to be seen.

And through the drifts the snowy clifts
Did send a dismal sheen:
Nor shapes of men nor beasts we ken—
The ice was all between.

The ice was here, the ice was there,
60 The ice was all around:
It cracked and growled, and roared and howled,
Like noises in a swound![5]

Till a great
seabird, called
the Albatross,
came through
the snow-fog,
and was
received with
great joy and
hospitality.

At length did cross an Albatross,
Thorough the fog it came;
As if it had been a Christian soul,
We hailed it in God's name.

It ate the food it ne'er had eat,
And round and round it flew,
The ice did split with a thunder-fit;
70 The helmsman steered us through!

And lo! the
Albatross prov-
eth a bird of
good omen,
and followeth
the ship as
it returned
northward
through fog
and floating
ice.

And a good south wind sprung up behind;
The Albatross did follow,
And every day, for food or play,
Came to the mariners' hollo!

In mist or cloud, on mast or shroud,[6]
It perched for vespers[7] nine;
Whiles all the night, through fog-smoke white,
Glimmered the white Moon-shine."

[5]**swound** swoon
[6]**shroud** a set of ropes supporting the mast
[7]**vespers** evening prayers

The ancient
Mariner in-
hospitably
killeth the
pious bird of
good omen.

80

"God save thee, ancient Mariner!
From the fiends, that plague thee thus!—
Why look'st thou so?"—"With my cross-bow
I shot the ALBATROSS.

PART II

The Sun now rose upon the right:
Out of the sea came he,
Still hid in mist, and on the left
Went down into the sea.

And the good south wind still blew behind,
But no sweet bird did follow,
Nor any day for food or play
Came to the mariners' hollo!

90

His shipmates
cry out against
the ancient
Mariner, for
killing the bird
of good luck.

And I had done a hellish thing,
And it would work 'em woe:
For all averred, I had killed the bird
That made the breeze to blow.
Ah wretch! said they, the bird to slay,
That made the breeze to blow!

But when the
fog cleared
off, they jus-
tify the same,
and thus make
themselves
accomplices to
the crime.

100

Nor dim nor red, like God's own head,
The glorious Sun uprist:
Then all averred, I had killed the bird
That brought the fog and mist.
'Twas right, said they, such birds to slay,
That bring the fog and mist.

The fair breeze
continues; the
ship enters the
Pacific Ocean,
and sails north-
ward, even till
it reaches the
Line.

The fair breeze blew, the white foam flew,
The furrow followed free;
We were the first that ever burst
Into that silent sea.

The ship hath
been suddenly
becalmed.

Down dropt the breeze, the sails dropt down,
'Twas sad as sad could be;
And we did speak only to break
The silence of the sea!

110

All in a hot and copper sky,
The bloody Sun, at noon,
Right up above the mast did stand,
No bigger than the Moon.

Day after day; day after day,
We stuck, nor breath nor motion;
As idle as a painted ship
Upon a painted ocean.

<table>
<tr><td>120</td><td>And the Alba-
tross begins to
be avenged.</td><td>Water, water, every where,
And all the boards did shrink;
Water, water, every where
Nor any drop to drink.</td></tr>
</table>

And the Alba-
120   tross begins to
be avenged.

Water, water, every where,
And all the boards did shrink;
Water, water, every where
Nor any drop to drink.

The very deep did rot: O Christ!
That ever this should be!
Yea, slimy things did crawl with legs
Upon the slimy sea.

About, about, in reel and rout
The death-fires[8] danced at night;
The water, like a witch's oils,
130   Burnt green, and blue and white.

And some in dreams assurèd were

A Spirit had   Of the Spirit that plagued us so;
followed   Nine fathom deep he had followed us
them; one of   From the land of mist and snow.
the invisible
inhabitants of this planet, neither departed souls nor angels; concerning
whom the learned Jew, Josephus, and the Platonic Constantinopolitan,
Michael Psellus, may be consulted. They are very numerous, and there
is no climate or element without one or more.

And every tongue, through utter drought,
Was withered at the root;
We could not speak, no more than if
We had been choked with soot.

The ship-   Ah! well a-day! what evil looks
140   mates, in their   Had I from old and young!
sore distress,   Instead of the cross, the Albatross
would fain   About my neck was hung.
throw the
whole guilt on the ancient Mariner: in sign whereof they hang the dead
sea-bird round his neck.

PART III

There passed a weary time. Each throat
Was parched, and glazed each eye.
A weary time! a weary time!
How glazed each weary eye,

The ancient   When looking westward, I beheld
Mariner be-   A something in the sky.
holdeth a sign
in the element
afar off.

---

[8] **death-fires** St. Elmo's fire, a form of atmos-
pheric electricity sometimes visible about a
ship's rigging and mast

150
At first it seemed a little speck,
And then it seemed a mist;
It moved and moved, and took at last
A certain shape, I wist.[9]

A speck, a mist, a shape, I wist!
And still it neared and neared:
As if it dodged a water-sprite,
It plunged and tacked and veered.

At its nearer approach, it seemeth him to be a ship; and at a dear ransom he freeth his speech from the bonds of thirst.

160
With throats unslaked, with black lips baked,
We could nor laugh nor wail;
Through utter drought all dumb we stood!
I bit my arm, I sucked the blood,
And cried, A sail! a sail!

A flash of joy;

With throats unslaked, with black lips baked,
Agape they heard me call:
Gramercy![10] they for joy did grin,
And all at once their breath drew in,
As they were drinking all.

And horror follows. For can it be a ship that comes onward without wind or tide?

170
See! see! (I cried) she tacks no more!
Hither to work us weal;[11]
Without a breeze, without a tide,
She steadies with upright keel!

The western wave was all a-flame.
The day was well nigh done!
Almost upon the western wave
Rested the broad bright Sun;
When that strange shape drove suddenly
Betwixt us and the Sun.

It seemeth him but the skeleton of a ship.

180
And straight the Sun was flecked with bars,
(Heaven's Mother send us grace!)
As if through a dungeon-grate he peered
With broad and burning face.

And its ribs are seen as bars on the face of the setting Sun.

Alas! (thought I, and my heart beat loud)
How fast she nears and nears!
Are those *her* sails that glance in the Sun,
Like restless gossameres?

---

[9]**wist** knew
[10]**Gramercy** an exclamation of thanks (French,

grand-merci, "great thanks")
[11]**weal** good

The Spectre-
Woman and
her Death-
mate, and no
other on board
the skeleton
ship. Like
190   vessel, like
crew!

Are those *her* ribs through which the Sun
Did peer, as through a grate?
And is that Woman all her crew?
Is that a DEATH? and are there two?
Is DEATH that woman's mate?

Her lips were red, *her* looks were free,
Her looks were yellow as gold:
Her skin was as white as leprosy,
The Night-mare LIFE-IN-DEATH was she,
Who thicks man's blood with cold.

Death and
Life-in-Death
have diced for
the ship's
crew, and she
(the latter)
winneth the
ancient
Mariner.

The naked hulk alongside came,
And the twain were casting dice;
'The game is done! I've won! I've won!'
Quoth she, and whistles thrice.

No twilight
200   within the
courts of the
Sun

The Sun's rim dips; the stars rush out:
At one stride comes the dark;
With far-heard whisper, o'er the sea,
Off shot the spectre-bark.

At the rising
of the Moon,

We listened and looked sideways up!
Fear at my heart, as at a cup,
My life-blood seemed to sip!
The stars were dim, and thick the night,
The steerman's face by his lamp gleamed white;
From the sails the dew did drip—
Till clomb above the eastern bar
210   The hornèd[12] Moon, with one bright star
Within the nether tip.

One after
another,

One after one, by the star-dogged Moon,
Too quick for groan or sigh,
Each turned his face with ghastly pang,
And cursed me with his eye.

His shipmates
drop down
dead.

Four times fifty living men,
(And I heard nor sigh nor groan)
With heavy thump, a lifeless lump,
They dropped down one by one.

220   But Life-in-
Death begins
her work on
the ancient
Mariner.

The souls did from their bodies fly,—
They fled to bliss or woe!
And every soul, it passed me by,
Like the whizz of my cross-bow!''

[12]**hornèd** crescent

PART IV

The Wedding-
Guest feareth
that a Spirit is
talking to him;
"I fear thee, ancient Mariner!
I fear thy skinny hand!
And thou art long, and lank, and brown.
As is the ribbed sea-sand.

I fear thee and thy glittering eye.
And thy skinny hand, so brown."—

230 But the ancient
Mariner as-
sureth him of
his bodily
life, and pro-
ceedeth to
relate his hor-
rible penance.
"Fear not, fear not, thou Wedding-Guest!
This body dropt not down.

Alone, alone, all, all alone,
Alone on a wide wide sea!
And never a saint took pity on
My soul in agony.

He despiseth
the creatures
of the calm,
The many men, so beautiful!
And they all dead did lie:
And a thousand thousand slimy things
Lived on; and so did I.

240 And envieth
that they
should live,
and so many
lie dead.
I looked upon the rotting sea,
And drew my eyes away;
I looked upon the rotting deck,
And there the dead men lay.

I looked to heaven, and tried to pray;
But or ever a prayer had gusht,
A wicked whisper came, and made
My heart as dry as dust.

I closed my lids, and kept them close,
And the balls like pulses beat;
250 For the sky and the sea, and the sea and the sky
Lay like a load on my weary eye,
And the dead were at my feet.

But the curse
liveth for him
in the eye of
the dead men.
The cold sweat melted from their limbs,
Nor rot nor reek did they:
The look with which they looked on me
Had never passed away.

An orphan's curse would drag to hell
A spirit from on high;
But oh! more horrible than that
260 Is the curse in a dead man's eye!
Seven days, seven nights, I saw that curse,
And yet I could not die.

In his loneli-
ness and fixed-
ness he yearn-
eth towards
the journeying
Moon, and the
stars that still
sojourn, yet
still move
onward; and
270 everywhere
the blue sky
belongs to
them, and is their appointed rest, and their native country and their own
natural homes, which they enter unannounced, as lords that are certainly
expected and yet there is a silent joy at their arrival.

The moving Moon went up the sky,
And no where did abide:
Softly she was going up,
And a star or two beside—

Her beams bemocked the sultry main,
Like April hoar-frost spread;
But where the ship's huge shadow lay,
The charmèd water burnt alway
A still and awful red.

By the light
of the Moon
he beholdeth
God's crea-
tures of the
great calm.

Beyond the shadow of the ship,
I watched the water-snakes:
They moved in tracks of shining white,
And when they reared, the elfish light
Fell off in hoary[13] flakes.

Within the shadow of the ship
I watched their rich attire:
Blue, glossy green, and velvet black,
280   They coiled and swam; and every track
Was a flash of golden fire.

Their beauty
and their
happiness.

O happy living things! no tongue
Their beauty might declare:
A spring of love gushed from my heart.

He blesseth
them in his
heart.

And I blessed them unaware:
Sure my kind saint took pity on me,
And I blessed them unaware.

The spell be-
gins to break.

The self-same moment I could pray;
And from my neck so free
290   The Albatross fell off, and sank
Like lead into the sea.

PART V

Oh sleep! it is a gentle thing,
Beloved from pole to pole!
To Mary Queen the praise be given!
She sent the gentle sleep from Heaven,
That slid into my soul.

By grace of
the holy
Mother, the

The silly[14] buckets on the deck,
That had so long remained,

[13]**hoary**   white, like frost
[14]**silly**   simple

300 *ancient Mari-*
ner is refreshed
with rain.

I dreamt that they were filled with dew;
And when I awoke, it rained.

My lips were wet, my throat was cold,
My garments all were dank;
Sure I nad drunken in my dreams,
And still my body drank.

I moved, and could not feel my limbs:
I was so light—almost
I thought that I had died in sleep,
And was a blessèd ghost.

310 *He heareth*
sounds and
seeth strange
sights and
commotions in
the sky and the
element.

And soon I heard a roaring wind.
It did not come anear;
But with its sound it shook the sails,
That were so thin and sere.

The upper air burst into life!
And a hundred fire-flags sheen,[15]
To and fro they were hurried about!
And to and fro, and in and out,
The wan stars danced between.

And the coming wind did roar more loud,
And the sails did sigh like sedge;[16]
320
And the rain poured down from one black cloud;
The Moon was at its edge.

The thick black cloud was cleft, and still
The Moon was at its side:
Like waters shot from some high crag,
The lightning fell with never a jag,
A river steep and wide.

330 *The bodies of*
the ship's
crew are
inspirited, and
the ship moves
on;

The loud wind never reached the ship,
Yet now the ship moved on!
Beneath the lightning and the Moon
The dead men gave a groan.

They groaned, they stirred, they all uprose,
Nor spake, nor moved their eyes;
It had been strange, even in a dream,
To have seen those dead men rise.

The helmsman steered, the ship moved on;
Yet never a breeze up-blew;
The mariners all 'gan work the ropes,
Where they were wont to do;
They raised their limbs like lifeless tools—
340
We were a ghastly crew.

[15]**sheen** shone—a reference to the Southern   [16]**sedge** like wind-blown marsh grass
Lights or Aurora Australis

The body of my brother's son
Stood by me, knee to knee;
The body and I pulled at one rope,
But he said nought to me.''

"I fear thee, ancient Mariner!"
"Be calm, thou Wedding-Guest!
'Twas not those souls that fled in pain,
Which to their corses[17] came again,
But a troop of spirits blest:

For when it dawned—they dropped their arms,
And clustered round the mast;
Sweet sounds rose slowly through their mouths,
And from their bodies passed.

Around, around, flew each sweet sound,
Then darted to the Sun;
Slowly the sounds came back again,
Now mixed, now one by one.

Sometimes a-dropping from the sky
I heard the sky-lark sing;
Sometimes all little birds that are,
How they seemed to fill the sea and air
With their sweet jargoning![18]

And now 'twas like all instruments,
Now like a lonely flute;
And now it is an angel's song,
That makes the heavens be mute.

It ceased; yet still the sails made on
A pleasant noise till noon,
A noise like of a hidden brook
In the leafy month of June,
That to the sleeping woods all night
Singeth a quiet tune.

Till noon we quietly sailed on,
Yet never a breeze did breathe:
Slowly and smoothly went the ship,
Moved onward from beneath.

Under the keel nine fathom deep,
From the land of mist and snow,
The spirit slid, and it was he
That made the ship to go.
The sails at noon left off their tune,
And the ship stood still also.

Marginal glosses:

But not by the souls of the men, nor by daemons of earth or middle air, but by a blessed troop of angelic spirits, sent down by the invocation of the guardian saint. *(line 350)*

The lonesome Spirit from the south-pole carries on the ship as far as the Line, in obedience to *(line 380)*

---

[17]**corses** corpses
[18]**jargoning** in its older sense of "warbling"

the angelic
troop, but still
requireth ven-
geance.

The Sun, right up above the mast,
Had fixed her to the ocean:
But in a minute she 'gan stir,
With a short uneasy motion—
Backwards and forwards half her length
With a short uneasy motion.

390

Then like a pawing horse let go,
She made a sudden bound:
It flung the blood into my head,
And I fell down in a swound.

The Polar
Spirit's fellow-
daemons, the
invisible in-
habitants of
the element,
take part in his
wrong; and
two of them
relate, one to
the other, that
penance long
and heavy for
the ancient
Mariner hath
been accorded
to the Polar
Spirit, who
returneth
southward.

How long in that same fit I lay,
I have not to declare,[19]
But ere my living life returned,
I heard and in my soul discerned
Two voices in the air.

'Is it he?' quoth one, 'Is this the man?
By him who died on cross,
With his cruel bow he laid full low
The harmless Albatross.

400

The spirit who bideth by himself
In the land of mist and snow,
He loved the bird that loved the man
Who shot him with his bow.'
The other was a softer voice
As soft as honey-dew:
Quoth he, 'The man hath penance done,
And penance more will do.'

PART VI

FIRST VOICE

410

'But tell me, tell me! speak again,
Thy soft response renewing—
What makes that ship drive on so fast?
What is the ocean doing?'

SECOND VOICE

'Still as a slave before his lord,
The ocean hath no blast;
His great bright eye most silently
Up to the Moon is cast—

If he may know which way to go;
For she guides him smooth or grim.
See, brother, see! how graciously
She looketh down on him.'

420

[19] l. 394 I cannot tell.

FIRST VOICE

The Mariner
hath been cast
into a trance;
for the angelic
power causeth
the vessel to
drive north-
ward faster
than human
life could
endure.

'But why drives on that ship so fast,
Without or wave or wind?'

SECOND VOICE

'The air is cut away before,
And closes from behind.

Fly, brother, fly! more high, more high!
Or we shall be belated:
For slow and slow that ship will go,
When the Mariner's trance is abated.'

430

The super-
natural motion
is retarded;
the Mariner
awakes, and
his penance
begins anew.

I woke, and we were sailing on
As in a gentle weather:
'Twas night, calm night, the moon was high;
The dead men stood together.

All stood together on the deck,
For a charnel-dungeon[20] fitter:
All fixed on me their stony eyes,
That in the Moon did glitter.

The pang, the curse, with which they died,
Had never passed away:
440
I could not draw my eyes from theirs,
Nor turn them up to pray.

The curse is
finally
expiated.

And now this spell was snapt: once more
I viewed the ocean green,
And looked far forth, yet little saw
Of what had else been seen—

Like one, that on a lonesome road
Doth walk in fear and dread,
And having once turned round walks on,
And turns no more his head;
450
Because he knows, a frightful fiend
Doth close behind him tread.

But soon there breathed a wind on me,
Nor sound nor motion made:
Its path was not upon the sea,
In ripple or in shade.

It raised my hair, it fanned my cheek
Like a meadow-gale of spring—
It mingled strangely with my fears,
Yet it felt like a welcoming.

[20]**charnel-dungeon**   vault for corpses

460

Swiftly, swiftly flew the ship,
Yet she sailed softly too:
Sweetly, sweetly blew the breeze—
On me alone it blew.

And the
ancient Mari-
ner beholdeth
his native
country.

Oh! dream of joy! is this indeed
The light-house top I see?
Is this the hill? is this the kirk?
Is this mine own countree?

We drifted o'er the harbour-bar,
And I with sobs did pray—
470
O let me be awake, my God!
Or let me sleep alway.

The harbour-bay was clear as glass,
So smoothly it was strewn!
And on the bay the moonlight lay,
And the shadow of the Moon.

The rock shone bright, the kirk no less,
That stands above the rock:
The moonlight steeped in silentness
The steady weathercock.

480

And the bay was white with silent light,

The angelic
spirits leave
the dead
bodies,

Till rising from the same,
Full many shapes, that shadows were,
In crimson colours came.

A little distance from the prow

And appear in
their own
forms of light.

Those crimson shadows were:
I turned my eyes upon the deck—
Oh, Christ! what saw I there!

Each corse lay flat, lifeless and flat,
And, by the holy rood![21]
490
A man all light, a seraph-man,[22]
On every corse there stood.

This seraph-band, each waved his hand:
It was a heavenly sight!
They stood as signals to the land,
Each one a lovely light;

This seraph-band, each waved his hand,
No voice did they impart—
No voice; but oh! the silence sank
Like music on my heart.

[21]**rood** cross
[22]**seraph-man** an angel

500
But soon I heard the dash of oars,
I heard the Pilot's cheer;
My head was turned perforce away
And I saw a boat appear.

The Pilot and the Pilot's boy,
I heard them coming fast:
Dear Lord in Heaven! it was a joy
The dead men could not blast.

I saw a third—I heard his voice:
It is the Hermit good!
510
He singeth loud his godly hymns
That he makes in the wood.
He'll shrieve²³ my soul, he'll wash away
The Albatross's blood.

PART VII

The Hermit
of the Wood,
This Hermit good lives in that wood
Which slopes down to the sea.
How loudly his sweet voice he rears!
He loves to talk with marineres
That come from a far countree.

He kneels at morn, and noon, and eve—
520
He hath a cushion plump:
It is the moss that wholly hides
The rotted old oak-stump.

The skiff-boat neared: I heard them talk,
'Why, this is strange, I trow!
Where are those lights so many and fair,
That signal made but now?'

Approacheth
the ship with
wonder.
'Strange, by my faith!' the Hermit said—
'And they answered not our cheer!
The planks looked warped! and see those sails,
530
How thin they are and sere!
I never saw aught like to them,
Unless perchance it were

Brown skeletons of leaves that lag
My forest-brook along;
When the ivy-tod²⁴ is heavy with snow,
And the owlet whoops to the wolf below,
That eats the she-wolf's young.'

²³**shrieve** cleanse of sin
²⁴**ivy-tod** shrub

'Dear Lord! it hath a fiendish look—
(The Pilot made reply)
540   I am a-feared'—'Push on, push on!'
Said the Hermit cheerily.

The boat came closer to the ship,
But I nor spake nor stirred;
The boat came close beneath the ship,
And straight a sound was heard.

The ship sud-
denly sinketh.   Under the water it rumbled on,
Still louder and more dread:
It reached the ship, it split the bay;
The ship went down like lead.

550   *The ancient*   Stunned by that loud and dreadful sound,
Mariner is   Which sky and ocean smote,
saved in the   Like one that hath been seven days drowned
Pilot's boat.   My body lay afloat;
But swift as dreams, myself I found
Within the Pilot's boat·

Upon the whirl, where sank the ship,
The boat spun round and round;
And all was still, save that the hill
Was telling of the sound.

560   I moved my lips—the Pilot shrieked
And fell down in a fit;
The holy Hermit raised his eyes,
And prayed where he did sit.

I took the oars: the Pilot's boy,
Who now doth crazy go,
Laughed loud and long, and all the while
His eyes went to and fro.
'Ha! ha!' quoth he, 'full plain I see,
The Devil knows how to row.'

570   And now, all in my own countree,
I stood on the firm land!
The Hermit stepped forth from the boat,
And scarcely he could stand.

The ancient   'O shrieve me, shrieve me, holy man!'
Mariner earn-   The Hermit crossed his brow.[25]
estly entreat-
eth the Hermit   'Say quick,' quoth he, 'I bid thee say—
to shrieve   What manner of man art thou?'
him; and the
penance of life
falls on him.

[25]**crossed his brow** made the sign of the cross
on his forehead

Forthwith this frame of mine was wrenched
With a woful agony,
580 Which forced me to begin my tale;
And then it left me free.

And ever and anon through-out his future life an agony constraineth him to travel from land to land;

Since then, at an uncertain hour,
That agony returns;
And till my ghastly tale is told,
This heart within me burns.

I pass, like night, from land to land;
I have strange power of speech;
That moment that his face I see,
I know the man that must hear me:
590 To him my tale I teach.

What loud uproar bursts from that door!
The wedding-guests are there:
But in the garden-bower the bride
And bride-maids singing are.
And hark the little vesper bell,
Which biddeth me to prayer!

O Wedding-Guest! this soul hath been
Alone on a wide wide sea:
So lonely 'twas, that God himself
600 Scarce seemèd there to be.

O sweeter than the marriage-feast,
'Tis sweeter far to me,
To walk together to the kirk
With a goodly company!—

To walk together to the kirk,
And all together pray,
While each to his great Father bends,
Old men, and babes, and loving friends
And youths and maidens gay!

And to teach, by his own example, love and reverence to all things that God made and loveth.

610 Farewell, farewell! but this I tell
To thee, thou Wedding-Guest!
He prayeth well, who loveth well
Both man and bird and beast.

He prayeth best, who loveth best
All things both great and small;
For the dear God who loveth us,
He made and loveth all."

The Mariner, whose eye is bright,
Whose beard with age is hoar,
620   Is gone: and now the Wedding-Guest
Turned from the bridegroom's door.

He went like one that hath been stunned,
And is of sense forlorn:[26]
A sadder and a wiser man,
He rose the morrow morn.

1797–98   1798, *1817*

[26]**forlorn** deprived

Kubla Khan[1]

OR, A VISION IN A DREAM. A FRAGMENT

In Xanadu did Kubla Khan
A stately pleasure-dome decree:
Where Alph,[2] the sacred river, ran
Through caverns measureless to man
    Down to a sunless sea.
So twice five miles of fertile ground

[1] "In the summer of the year 1797, the Author, then in ill health, had retired to a lonely farmhouse between Porlock and Linton, on the Exmoor confines of Somerset and Devonshire. In consequence of a slight indisposition, an anodyne had been prescribed, from the effects of which he fell asleep in his chair at the moment that he was reading the following sentence, or words of the same substance, in 'Purchas's Pilgrimage': 'Here the Khan Kubla commanded a palace to be built, and a stately garden thereunto. And thus ten miles of fertile ground were inclosed with a wall.' The Author continued for about three hours in a profound sleep, at least of the external senses, during which time he has the most vivid confidence, that he could not have composed less than from two to three hundred lines; if that indeed can be called composition in which all the images rose up before him as *things*, with a parallel production of the correspondent expressions, without any sensation or consciousness of effort. On awaking he appeared to himself to have a distinct recollection of the whole, and taking his pen, ink, and paper, instantly and eagerly wrote down the lines that are here preserved. At this moment he was unfortunately called out by a person on business from Porlock, and detained by him above an hour, and on his return to his room, found, to his no small surprise and mortification, that though he still retained some vague and dim recollection of the general purport of the vision, yet, with the exception of some eight or ten scattered lines and images, all the rest had passed away like the images on the surface of a stream into which a stone has been cast, but, alas! without the after restoration of the latter!'' (Coleridge's note).

The historical Kublai Khan ruled China in the thirteenth century. His palace and gardens were described by Samuel Purchas in *Purchas His Pilgrimage* (1613), from which Coleridge quotes inexactly. Except for Xanadu, or Xamdu, which derives from Purchas, the names and the particulars of description in the poem are largely imaginative blends of associations drawn from the poet's wide reading.

[2] **Alph** a probable blend of alpha, the first letter of the Greek alphabet, and Alpheus, an ancient river in Greece, said to flow in a channel beneath the sea

With walls and towers were girdled round:
And there were gardens bright with sinuous rills,
Where blossomed many an incense-bearing tree;
10 And here were forests ancient as the hills,
Enfolding sunny spots of greenery.

But oh! that deep romantic chasm which slanted
Down the green hill athwart a cedarn cover!
A savage place! as holy and enchanted
As e'er beneath a waning moon was haunted
By woman wailing for her demon-lover!
And from this chasm, with ceaseless turmoil seething,
As if this earth in fast thick pants were breathing,
A mighty fountain momently³ was forced:
20 Amid whose swift half-intermitted burst
Huge fragments vaulted like rebounding hail,
Or chaffy grain beneath the thresher's flail:
And 'mid these dancing rocks at once and ever
It flung up momently the sacred river.
Five miles meandering with a mazy motion
Through wood and dale the sacred river ran,
Then reached the caverns measureless to man,
And sank in tumult to a lifeless ocean:
And 'mid this tumult Kubla heard from far
30 Ancestral voices prophesying war!
    The shadow of the dome of pleasure
    Floated midway on the waves;
    Where was heard the mingled measure
    From the fountain and the caves.
It was a miracle of rare device,
A sunny pleasure-dome with caves of ice!

A damsel with a dulcimer⁴
In a vision once I saw:
It was an Abyssinian maid,
40 And on her dulcimer she played,
Singing of Mount Abora.⁵
Could I revive within me
Her symphony and song,
To such a deep delight 'twould win me,
That with music loud and long,
I would build that dome in air,
That sunny dome! those caves of ice!
And all who heard should see them there,
And all should cry, Beware! Beware!

³ **momently** moment by moment
⁴ **dulcimer** a stringed musical instrument
⁵ **Mount Abora** probably an echo of Mt. Amara,
  a supposed location of the original earthly para-

dise. See Milton, *Paradise Lost* IV.280–82:
"where Abassin kings their issue guard, / Mount
Amara, though this by some supposed / True
Paradise . . .".

50 His flashing eyes, his floating hair!
Weave a circle round him thrice,
And close your eyes with holy dread,
For he on honey-dew hath fed,
And drunk the milk of Paradise.

1798   1816

Frost at Midnight

The Frost performs its secret ministry,
Unhelped by any wind. The owlet's cry
Came loud—and hark, again! loud as before.
The inmates of my cottage, all at rest,
Have left me to that solitude, which suits
Abstruser musings: save that at my side
My cradled infant[1] slumbers peacefully.
'Tis calm indeed! so calm, that it disturbs
And vexes meditation with its strange
10 And extreme silentness. Sea, hill, and wood,
This populous village! Sea, and hill, and wood,
With all the numberless goings-on of life,
Inaudible as dreams! the thin blue flame
Lies on my low-burnt fire, and quivers not;
Only that film,[2] which fluttered on the grate,
Still flutters there, the sole unquiet thing.
Methinks, its motion in this hush of nature
Gives it dim sympathies with me who live,
Making it a companionable form,
20 Whose puny flaps and freaks the idling Spirit[3]
By its own moods interprets, every where
Echo or mirror seeking of itself.
And makes a toy of Thought.

                                        But O! how oft,
How oft, at school, with most believing mind,
Presageful, have I gazed upon the bars,
To watch that fluttering *stranger*![4] and as oft
With unclosed lids, already had I dreamt
Of my sweet birth-place, and the old church-tower,
Whose bells, the poor man's only music, rang
30 From morn to evening, all the hot Fair-day,
So sweetly, that they stirred and haunted me
With a wild pleasure, falling on mine ear
Most like articulate sounds of things to come!
So gazed I, till the soothing things, I dreamt,

---

[1] **infant** Coleridge's son Hartley
[2] **film** ash or ember
[3] **Spirit** the poet's own consciousness
[4] *stranger* "In all parts of the kingdom these

films are called *strangers* and supposed to portend the arrival of some absent friend" (Coleridge's note).

Lulled me to sleep, and sleep prolonged my dreams!
And so I brooded all the following morn,
Awed by the stern preceptor's face, mine eye
Fixed with mock study on my swimming book:
Save if the door half opened, and I snatched
40   A hasty glance, and still my heart leaped up,
For still I hoped to see the *stranger's* face,
Townsman, or aunt, or sister more beloved,
My play-mate when we both were clothed alike!

Dear Babe, that sleepest cradled by my side,
Whose gentle breathings, heard in this deep calm,
Fill up the interspersèd vacancies
And momentary pauses of the thought!
My babe so beautiful! it thrills my heart
With tender gladness, thus to look at thee,
50   And think that thou shalt learn far other lore,
And in far other scenes! For I was reared
In the great city, pent 'mid cloisters dim,⁵
And saw nought lovely but the sky and stars.
But *thou*, my babe! shalt wander like a breeze
By lakes and sandy shores, beneath the crags
Of ancient mountain, and beneath the clouds,
Which image in their bulk both lakes and shores
And mountain crags: so shalt thou see and hear
The lovely shapes and sounds intelligible
60   Of that eternal language, which thy God
Utters, who from eternity doth teach
Himself in all, and all things in himself.
Great universal Teacher! he shall mould
Thy spirit, and by giving make it ask.

Therefore all seasons shall be sweet to thee,
Whether the summer clothe the general earth
With greenness, or the redbreast sit and sing
Betwixt the tufts of snow on the bare branch
Of mossy apple-tree, while the nigh thatch
70   Smokes in the sun-thaw; whether the eave-drops fall
Heard only in the trances of the blast,⁶
Or if the secret ministry of frost
Shall hang them up in silent icicles,
Quietly shining to the quiet Moon.

1798   1798

---

⁵**cloisters dim** Christ's Hospital, London, where Coleridge attended school

⁶**trances of the blast** a lull in the sound of the wind

Dejection: An Ode[1]

Late, late yestreen I saw the new Moon,
With the old Moon in her arms;
And I fear, I fear, my Master dear!
We shall have a deadly storm.
—BALLAD OF SIR PATRICK SPENCE[2]

I

Well! If the Bard was weather-wise, who made
    The grand old ballad of Sir Patrick Spence,
    This night, so tranquil now, will not go hence
Unroused by winds, that ply a busier trade
Than those which mould yon cloud in lazy flakes,
Or the dull sobbing draft, that moans and rakes
Upon the strings of this Aeolian lute,[3]
        Which better far were mute.
    For lo! the New-moon winter-bright!
10   And overspread with phantom light,
    (With swimming phantom light o'erspread
    But rimmed and circled by a silver thread)
I see the old Moon in her lap,[4] foretelling
    The coming-on of rain and squally blast.
And oh! that even now the gust were swelling,
    And the slant night-shower driving loud and fast!
Those sounds which oft have raised me, whilst they awed,
        And sent my soul abroad,
Might now perhaps their wonted impulse give,
20 Might startle this dull pain, and make it move and live!

II

A grief without a pang, void, dark, and drear,
    A stifled, drowsy, unimpassioned grief,
    Which finds no natural outlet, no relief,
        In word, or sigh, or tear—
O Lady![5] in this wan and heartless mood
To other thoughts by yonder throstle[6] woo'd,
    All this long eve, so balmy and serene,
Have I been gazing on the western sky,
    And its peculiar tint of yellow green:

[1] This much-revised poem, drafted a few days after Coleridge heard the newly written opening stanzas of Wordsworth's "Ode: Intimations of Immortality" in April 1802, bears a close relation to the themes of the "Immortality" Ode and may have influenced Wordsworth's completion of it.

[2] For the full ballad see p. 24 above.

[3] **Aeolian lute** an instrument producing music-like sounds when its strings vibrate in the wind. Named after Aeolus, god of the winds, it is variously designated a lute, lyre, or harp and is an image often used in Romantic poetry.

[4] **old . . . lap** the faint image of the dark side of the moon (caused by reflected light from the earth), sometimes visible within the bright crescent of the new moon

[5] **Lady** "Sara" in the first draft of the poem, signifying Sara Hutchinson, Wordsworth's sister-in-law, with whom Coleridge was in love

[6] **throstle** thrush

30　And still I gaze—and with how blank an eye!
　　And those thin clouds above, in flakes and bars,
　　That give away their motion to the stars;
　　Those stars, that glide behind them or between,
　　Now sparkling, now bedimmed, but always seen:
　　Yon crescent Moon, as fixed as if it grew
　　In its own cloudless, starless lake of blue;
　　I see them all so excellently fair,
　　I see, not feel, how beautiful they are!

　　　　　　　III
　　　　　My genial spirits[7] fail;
40　And what can these avail
　　To lift the smothering weight from off my breast?
　　　　It were a vain endeavour,
　　　　Though I should gaze for ever
　　On that green light that lingers in the west:
　　I may not hope from outward forms to win
　　The passion and the life, whose fountains are within.

　　　　　　　IV
　　O Lady! we receive but what we give,
　　And in our life alone does Nature live:
　　Ours is her wedding garment, ours her shroud!
50　　　And would we aught behold, of higher worth,
　　Than that inanimate cold world allowed
　　To the poor loveless ever-anxious crowd,
　　　Ah! from the soul itself must issue forth
　　A light, a glory, a fair luminous cloud
　　　　Enveloping the Earth—
　　And from the soul itself must there be sent
　　　A sweet and potent voice, of its own birth,
　　Of all sweet sounds the life and element!

　　　　　　　V
　　O pure of heart! thou need'st not ask of me
60　What this strong music in the soul may be!
　　What, and wherein it doth exist,
　　This light, this glory, this fair luminous mist,
　　This beautiful and beauty-making power.
　　　Joy, virtuous Lady! Joy that ne'er was given,
　　Save to the pure, and in their purest hour,
　　Life, and Life's effluence, cloud at once and shower,
　　Joy, Lady! is the spirit and the power,
　　Which wedding Nature to us gives in dower
　　　A new Earth and new Heaven,
70　Undreamt of by the sensual and the proud—
　　Joy is the sweet voice, Joy the luminous cloud—

[7]**genial spirits** innate powers

We in ourselves rejoice!
And thence flows all that charms or ear or sight,
    All melodies the echoes of that voice,
All colours a suffusion from that light.

VI

There was a time when, though my path was rough,
    This joy within me dallied with distress,
And all misfortunes were but as the stuff
    Whence Fancy made me dreams of happiness:
80 For hope grew round me, like the twining vine,
And fruits, and foliage, not my own, seemed mine.
But now afflictions bow me down to earth:
Nor care I that they rob me of my mirth;
    But oh! each visitation
Suspends what nature gave me at my birth,
    My shaping spirit of Imagination.
For not to think of what I needs must feel,
    But to be still and patient, all I can;
And haply by abstruse research to steal
90 From my own nature all the natural man—
This was my sole resource, my only plan:
Till that which suits a part infects the whole,
And now is almost grown the habit of my soul.

VII

Hence, viper thoughts, that coil around my mind,
    Reality's dark dream!
I turn from you, and listen to the wind,
    Which long has raved unnoticed. What a scream
Of agony by torture lengthened out
That lute sent forth! Thou Wind, that rav'st without,
100 Bare crag, or mountain-tairn,[8] or blasted tree,
Or pine-grove whither woodman never clomb,
Or lonely house, long held the witches' home,
    Methinks were fitter instruments for thee,
Mad Lutanist! who in this month of showers,
Of dark-brown gardens, and of peeping flowers,
Mak'st Devils' yule,[9] with worse than wintry song,
The blossoms, buds, and timorous leaves among.
    Thou Actor, perfect in all tragic sounds!
Thou mighty Poet, e'en to frenzy bold!
110   What tell'st thou now about?
        'Tis of the rushing of an host in rout,
With groans, of trampled men, with smarting wounds—
At once they groan with pain, and shudder with the cold!
But hush! there is a pause of deepest silence!
    And all that noise, as of a rushing crowd,

[8]**tairn** pond
[9]**yule** winter festival

With groans, and tremulous shudderings—all is over—
  It tells another tale, with sounds less deep and loud!
    A tale of less affright,
    And tempered with delight,
120 As Otway's[10] self had framed the tender lay,—
    'Tis of a little child
    Upon a lonesome wild,
  Not far from home, but she hath lost her way:
  And now moans low in bitter grief and fear,
  And now screams loud, and hopes to make her mother hear.

VIII

  'Tis midnight, but small thoughts have I of sleep:
  Full seldom may my friend such vigils keep!
  Visit her, gentle Sleep! with wings of healing,
    And may this storm be but a mountain-birth,
130 May all the stars hang bright above her dwelling,
    Silent as though they watched the sleeping Earth!
    With light heart may she rise,
    Gay fancy, cheerful eyes,
  Joy lift her spirit, joy attune her voice;
  To her may all things live, from pole to pole,
  Their life the eddying of her living soul!
    O simple spirit, guided from above,
    Dear Lady! friend devoutest of my choice,
  Thus mayest thou ever, evermore rejoice.

1802   1802, *1817*

[10]**Otway** Thomas Otway (1652–1685), author
of tragic dramas; a substitution for "William"
in the original draft (the tale of the "little child"

in ll. 121–25 resembles Wordsworth's poem
"Lucy Gray")

GEORGE GORDON,
LORD BYRON
1788–1824

Lord Byron, the most famous English poet of his time, was celebrated as much for his life and personality as for his poetry. In his short life, this complex aristocrat was an adventurer, an exile from English society (the result of his scandalous marriage breakup), and a hero of the struggle for freedom. He died of fever in Greece while organizing forces fighting against the Turks for Greek independence. This legendary career gave rise to a character type that long captured the imagination of European writers—the so-called Byronic hero. Handsome and brilliant, but solitary, misanthropic, defiant of convention, and cursed with a dark past and guilty secrets (probably sexual), this figure often appears in Byron's poetry and was sometimes identified by the public with Byron himself.

But there is another, anti-Romantic side to Byron, a man proud of his place in society, attracted to wit and common sense, to the literature of the eighteenth century, especially Pope's poetry, and scornful of what he considered to be the affectations of leading poets in his own age, particularly Wordsworth and Coleridge. Byron is consistent, however, in his hatred of all forms of hypocrisy and self-delusion: prudery masquerading as virtue, abstract philosophical theory as fact, or tyranny and greed as a just social order. He admires sincerity and the natural spontaneity of the heart, though he has few illusions that possessing such qualities can prevent folly or guarantee happiness.

Byron's shorter lyrics are notable for their clear, graceful language and freedom from affectation. Often there is a strong immediacy of feeling, as in "On This Day I Complete My Thirty-Sixth Year." Byron's best work, however, maintains a stance of ironic, detached nonchalance. In *Don Juan* in particular, he uses conversational diction and phrasing, a leisurely, rambling narrative line, wonderfully absurd rhymes, and unexpected shifts in tone to create a richly comic, yet altogether serious vision of life. Byron's work in this mode makes him unique among his contemporaries.

She Walks in Beauty

I

She walks in Beauty, like the night
   Of cloudless climes and starry skies;
And all that's best of dark and bright
   Meet in her aspect and her eyes:
Thus mellowed to that tender light
   Which Heaven to gaudy day denies.

II

One shade the more, one ray the less,
   Had half impaired the nameless grace
Which waves in every raven tress,
10   Or softly lightens o'er her face;
Where thoughts serenely sweet express,
   How pure, how dear their dwelling-place.

III

And on that cheek, and o'er that brow,
   So soft, so calm, yet eloquent,
The smiles that win, the tints that glow,
   But tell of days in goodness spent,
A mind at peace with all below,
   A heart whose love is innocent!

1814   1815

Darkness

I had a dream, which was not all a dream.
The bright sun was extinguished, and the stars
Did wander darkling[1] in the eternal space,
Rayless, and pathless, and the icy Earth
Swung blind and blackening in the moonless air;
Morn came and went—and came, and brought no day,
And men forgot their passions in the dread
Of this their desolation; and all hearts
Were chilled into a selfish prayer for light:
10   And they did live by watchfires—and the thrones,
The palaces of crownèd kings—the huts,
The habitations of all things which dwell,
Were burnt for beacons; cities were consumed,
And men were gathered round their blazing homes
To look once more into each other's face;
Happy were those who dwelt within the eye
Of the volcanoes, and their mountain-torch:
A fearful hope was all the World contained;
Forests were set on fire—but hour by hour
20   They fell and faded—and the crackling trunks
Extinguished with a crash—and all was black.
The brows of men by the despairing light
Wore an unearthly aspect, as by fits
The flashes fell upon them; some lay down
And hid their eyes and wept; and some did rest
Their chins upon their clenchèd hands, and smiled;
And others hurried to and fro, and fed
Their funeral piles with fuel, and looked up
With mad disquietude on the dull sky,
30   The pall of a past World; and then again
With curses cast them down upon the dust,
And gnashed their teeth and howled: the wild birds shrieked,
And, terrified, did flutter on the ground,
And flap their useless wings; the wildest brutes
Came tame and tremulous; and vipers crawled
And twined themselves among the multitude,
Hissing, but stingless—they were slain for food:
And War, which for a moment was no more,
Did glut himself again:—a meal was bought
40   With blood, and each sate sullenly apart
Gorging himself in gloom: no Love was left;
All earth was but one thought—and that was Death,
Immediate and inglorious; and the pang
Of famine fed upon all entrails—men
Died, and their bones were tombless as their flesh;
The meagre by the meagre were devoured,

---

[1] **darkling** in darkness

Even dogs assailed their masters, all save one,
And he was faithful to a corse, and kept
The birds and beasts and famished men at bay,
50 Till hunger clung² them, or the dropping dead
Lured their lank jaws; himself sought out no food,
But with a piteous and perpetual moan,
And a quick desolate cry, licking the hand
Which answered not with a caress—he died.
The crowd was famished by degrees; but two
Of an enormous city did survive,
And they were enemies: they met beside
The dying embers of an altar-place
Where had been heaped a mass of holy things
60 For an unholy usage; they raked up,
And shivering scraped with their cold skeleton hands
The feeble ashes, and their feeble breath
Blew for a little life, and made a flame
Which was a mockery; then they lifted up
Their eyes as it grew lighter, and beheld
Each other's aspects—saw, and shrieked, and died—
Even of their mutual hideousness they died,
Unknowing who he was upon whose brow
Famine had written Fiend. The World was void,
70 The populous and the powerful was a lump,
Seasonless, herbless, treeless, manless, lifeless—
A lump of death—a chaos of hard clay.
The rivers, lakes, and ocean all stood still,
And nothing stirred within their silent depths;
Ships sailorless lay rotting on the sea,
And their masts fell down piecemeal: as they dropped
They slept on the abyss without a surge—
The waves were dead; the tides were in their grave,
The Moon, their mistress, had expired before;
80 The winds were withered in the stagnant air,
And the clouds perished; Darkness had no need
Of aid from them—She was the Universe.

1816   1816

² **clung** in its archaic sense of "caused to shrink
or draw together"

So We'll Go No More A-Roving

I

So we'll go no more a-roving
  So late into the night,
Though the heart be still as loving,
  And the moon be still as bright.

II

For the sword outwears its sheath,
    And the soul wears out the breast,
And the heart must pause to breathe,
    And Love itself have rest.

III

Though the night was made for loving,
10   And the day returns too soon,
Yet we'll go no more a-roving
    By the light of the moon.

1817   1830

From Don Juan[1]

From Canto the First

I

I want a hero: an uncommon want,
    When every year and month sends forth a new one,
Till, after cloying the gazettes[2] with cant,
    The age discovers he is not the true one;
Of such as these I should not care to vaunt,
    I'll therefore take our ancient friend Don Juan[3]—
We all have seen him, in the pantomime,[4]
Sent to the Devil somewhat ere his time.

. . .

LIV

Young Juan now was sixteen years of age,
    Tall, handsome, slender, but well knit: he seemed
Active, though not so sprightly, as a page;
    And everybody but his mother deemed
Him almost man; but she flew in a rage
430   And bit her lips (for else she might have screamed)
If any said so—for to be precocious
Was in her eyes a thing the most atrocious.

LV

Amongst her numerous acquaintance, all
    Selected for discretion and devotion,
There was the Donna Julia, whom to call

[1]an immense unfinished poem in sixteen cantos and nearly 2,000 stanzas that Byron worked on from 1818 until his death. It is based very loosely on the legend of the infamous Spanish seducer. The selection given here presents the adolescent Juan's first involvement in love.

[2]**gazettes** newspapers

[3]**Juan** pronounced as two syllables rhyming with "new one," and "J" as in the English "John"

[4]**pantomime** The story of Don Juan and his damnation for vice was popular on the English pantomime stage.

Pretty were but to give a feeble notion
  Of many charms in her as natural
    As sweetness to the flower, or salt to Ocean,
Her zone[5] to Venus, or his bow to Cupid,
440 (But this last simile is trite and stupid.)

    . . .

      LXV

Alfonso was the name of Julia's lord,
  A man well looking for his years, and who
Was neither much beloved nor yet abhorred:
  They lived together as most people do,
Suffering each other's foibles by accord,
    And not exactly either *one* or *two*;
Yet he was jealous, though he did not show it,
520 For Jealousy dislikes the world to know it.

      LXVI

Julia was—yet I never could see why—
  With Donna Inez[6] quite a favourite friend;
Between their tastes there was small sympathy,
  For not a line had Julia ever penned:
Some people whisper (but, no doubt, they lie,
    For Malice still imputes some private end)
That Inez had, ere Don Alfonso's marriage,
Forgot with him her very prudent carriage;

      LXVII

And that still keeping up the old connection,
530   Which Time had lately rendered much more chaste,
She took his lady also in affection,
  And certainly this course was much the best:
She flattered Julia with her sage protection,
    And complimented Don Alfonso's taste;
And if she could not (who can?) silence scandal,
At least she left it a more slender handle.

      LXVIII

I can't tell whether Julia saw the affair
  With other people's eyes, or if her own
Discoveries made, but none could be aware
540   Of this, at least no symptom e'er was shown;
Perhaps she did not know, or did not care,
    Indifferent from the first, or callous grown:
I'm really puzzled what to think or say,
She kept her counsel in so close a way.

---

[5]**zone** literally, belt or girdle, but with sexual overtones   [6]**Donna Inez** Don Juan's mother

LXIX

Juan she saw, and, as a pretty child,
　Caressed him often—such a thing might be
Quite innocently done, and harmless styled,
　When she had twenty years, and thirteen he;
But I am not so sure I should have smiled
550　When he was sixteen, Julia twenty-three;
These few short years make wondrous alterations,
Particularly amongst sun-burnt nations.

LXX

Whate'er the cause might be, they had become
　Changed; for the dame grew distant, the youth shy,
Their looks cast down, their greetings almost dumb,
　And much embarrassment in either eye;
There surely will be little doubt with some
　That Donna Julia knew the reason why,
But as for Juan, he had no more notion
560　Than he who never saw the sea of Ocean.

LXXI

Yet Julia's very coldness still was kind,
　And tremulously gentle her small hand
Withdrew itself from his, but left behind
　A little pressure, thrilling, and so bland
And slight, so very slight, that to the mind
　'Twas but a doubt; but ne'er magician's wand
Wrought change with all Armida's[7] fairy art
Like what this light touch left on Juan's heart.

LXXII

And if she met him, though she smiled no more,
570　She looked a sadness sweeter than her smile,
As if her heart had deeper thoughts in store
　She must not own, but cherished more the while
For that compression in its burning core;
　Even Innocence itself has many a wile,
And will not dare to trust itself with truth,
And Love is taught hypocrisy from youth.

LXXIII

But passion most dissembles, yet betrays
　Even by its darkness; as the blackest sky
Fortells the heaviest tempest, it displays
580　Its workings through the vainly guarded eye,
And in whatever aspect it arrays

[7]**Armida**　a seductive enchantress in the Italian
epic poem *Jerusalem Delivered* by Tasso

Itself, 'tis still the same hypocrisy;
  Coldness or Anger, even Disdain or Hate,
Are masks it often wears, and still too late.

LXXIV

Then there were sighs, the deeper for suppression,
  And stolen glances, sweeter for the theft,
And burning blushes, though for no transgression,
  Tremblings when met, and restlessness when left;
All these are little preludes to possession,
590 Of which young Passion cannot be bereft,
And merely tend to show how greatly Love is
Embarrassed at first starting with a novice.

LXXV

Poor Julia's heart was in an awkward state;
  She felt it going, and resolved to make
The noblest efforts for herself and mate,
  For Honour's, Pride's, Religion's, Virtue's sake:
Her resolutions were most truly great,
  And almost might have made a Tarquin[8] quake:
She prayed the Virgin Mary for her grace,
600 As being the best judge of a lady's case.

LXXVI

She vowed she never would see Juan more,
  And next day paid a visit to his mother,
And looked extremely at the opening door,
  Which, by the Virgin's grace, let in another;
Grateful she was, and yet a little sore—
  Again it opens, it can be no other,
'Tis surely Juan now—No! I'm afraid
That night the Virgin was no further prayed.

LXXVII

She now determined that a virtuous woman
610 Should rather face and overcome temptation,
That flight was base and dastardly, and no man
  Should ever give her heart the least sensation,
That is to say, a thought beyond the common
  Preference, that we must feel, upon occasion,
For people who are pleasanter than others,
But then they only seem so many brothers.

LXXVIII

And even if by chance—and who can tell?
  The Devil's so very sly—she should discover

---

[8] **Tarquin** an early Roman king, notorious for
cruelty and rape

That all within was not so very well,
620   And, if still free, that such or such a lover
Might please perhaps, a virtuous wife can quell
   Such thoughts, and be the better when they're over;
And if the man should ask, 'tis but denial:
   I recommend young ladies to make trial.

LXXIX

And, then, there are such things as Love divine,
   Bright and immaculate, unmixed and pure,
Such as the angels think so very fine,
   And matrons, who would be no less secure,
Platonic,[9] perfect, "just such love as mine;"
630   Thus Julia said—and thought so, to be sure;
And so I'd have her think, were *I* the man
   On whom her reveries celestial ran.

LXXX

Such love is innocent, and may exist
   Between young persons without any danger.
A hand may first, and then a lip be kissed;
   For my part, to such doings I'm a stranger,
But *hear* these freedoms form the utmost list
   Of all o'er which such love may be a ranger:
If people go beyond, 'tis quite a crime,
640   But not my fault—I tell them all in time.

LXXXI

Love, then, but Love within its proper limits,
   Was Julia's innocent determination
In young Don Juan's favour, and to him its
   Exertion might be useful on occasion;
And, lighted at too pure a shrine to dim its
   Ethereal lustre, with what sweet persuasion
He might be taught, by Love and her together—
   I really don't know what, nor Julia either.

LXXXII

Fraught with this fine intention, and well fenced
   In mail of proof—her purity of soul—
650 She, for the future, of her strength convinced,
   And that her honour was a rock, or mole,[10]
Exceeding sagely from that hour dispensed
   With any kind of troublesome control;
But whether Julia to the task was equal
   Is that which must be mentioned in the sequel.

---

[9]**Platonic** a variety of passionate love that omits physical fulfillment, popularly attributed to the teachings of the Greek philosopher Plato. See also stanza CXVI below.
[10]**mole** breakwater

LXXXIII

Her plan she deem'd both innocent and feasible,
    And, surely, with a stripling of sixteen
Not scandal's fangs could fix on much that's seizable,
660   Or if they did so, satisfied to mean
Nothing but what was good, her breast was peaceable:
    A quiet conscience makes one so serene!
Christians have burnt each other, quite persuaded
That all the Apostles would have done as they did.

LXXXIV

And if in the mean time her husband died,
    But Heaven forbid that such a thought should cross
Her brain, though in a dream! (and then she sigh'd)
    Never could she survive that common loss;
But just suppose that moment should betide,
670   I only say suppose it—*inter nos*.[11]
(This should be *entre nous*, for Julia thought
In French, but then the rhyme would go for nought.)

LXXXV

I only say, suppose this supposition:
    Juan being then grown up to man's estate
Would fully suit a widow of condition,
    Even seven years hence it would not be too late;
And in the interim (to pursue this vision)
    The mischief, after all, could not be great,
680   For he would learn the rudiments of love,
I mean the seraph way of those above.

LXXXVI

So much for Julia! Now we'll turn to Juan.
    Poor little fellow! he had no idea
Of his own case, and never hit the true one;
    In feelings quick as Ovid's Miss Medea[12]
He puzzled over what he found a new one,
    But not as yet imagined it could be a
Thing quite in course, and not at all alarming,
Which, with a little patience, might grow charming.

LXXXVII

Silent and pensive, idle, restless, slow,
690   His home deserted for the lonely wood,
Tormented with a wound he could not know,
    His, like all deep grief, plunged in solitude:
I'm fond myself of solitude or so,
    But then, I beg it may be understood,

---

[11]*inter nos* among ourselves
[12]**Ovid's Miss Medea** *The Metamorphoses* of the Roman poet Ovid presents the legend of Medea's violent passion for Jason.

By solitude I mean a Sultan's (not
A Hermit's), with a haram for a grot.

. . .

XC

Young Juan wandered by the glassy brooks,
    Thinking unutterable things; he threw
Himself at length within the leafy nooks
    Where the wild branch of the cork forest grew;
There poets find materials for their books,
    And every now and then we read them through,
So that their plan and prosody are eligible,
720   Unless, like Wordsworth, they prove unintelligible.

XCI

He, Juan (and not Wordsworth), so pursued
    His self-communion with his own high soul,
Until his mighty heart, in its great mood,
    Had mitigated part, though not the whole
Of its disease; he did the best he could
    With things not very subject to control,
And turned, without perceiving his condition,
Like Coleridge, into a metaphysician.

XCII

He thought about himself, and the whole earth,
    Of man the wonderful, and of the stars,
730   And how the deuce they ever could have birth;
    And then he thought of earthquakes, and of wars,
How many miles the moon might have in girth,
    Of air-balloons, and of the many bars
To perfect knowledge of the boundless skies;—
And then he thought of Donna Julia's eyes.

XCIII

In thoughts like these true Wisdom may discern
    Longings sublime, and aspirations high,
Which some are born with, but the most part learn
740   To plague themselves withal, they know not why:
'Twas strange that one so young should thus concern
    His brain about the action of the sky;
If *you* think 'twas Philosophy that this did,
I can't help thinking puberty assisted.

XCIV

He poured upon the leaves, and on the flowers,
    And heard a voice in all the winds; and then
He thought of wood-nymphs and immortal bowers,
    And how the goddesses came down to men:
He missed the pathway, he forgot the hours,

750   And when he looked upon his watch again,
        He found how much old Time had been a winner—
        He also found that he had lost his dinner.

            XCV
        Sometimes he turned to gaze upon his book,
            Boscan, or Garcilasso;[13]—by the wind
        Even as the page is rustled while we look,
            So by the poesy of his own mind
        Over the mystic leaf his soul was shook,
            As if 'twere one whereon magicians bind
760   Their spells, and give them to the passing gale,
        According to some good old woman's tale.

            XCVI
        Thus would he while his lonely hours away
            Dissatisfied, not knowing what he wanted;
        Nor glowing reverie, nor poet's lay,
            Could yield his spirit that for which it panted.
        A bosom whereon he his head might lay,
            And hear the heart beat with the love it granted,
        With—several other things, which I forget,
        Or which, at least, I need not mention yet.

            XCVII
        Those lonely walks, and lengthening reveries,
770   Could not escape the gentle Julia's eyes;
        She saw that Juan was not at his ease;
            But that which chiefly may, and must surprise,
        Is, that the Donna Inez did not tease
            Her only son with question or surmise;
        Whether it was she did not see, or would not.
        Or, like all very clever people, could not.

                . . .

            CI
        But Inez was so anxious, and so clear
            Of sight, that I must think, on this occasion,
        She had some other motive much more near
            For leaving Juan to this new temptation,
        But what that motive was, I sha'n't say here;
            Perhaps to finish Juan's education,
        Perhaps to open Don Alfonso's eyes,
        In case he thought his wife too great a prize.

            CII
        It was upon a day, a summer's day;—
810   Summer's indeed a very dangerous season,

[13]**Boscan . . . Garcilasso** sixteenth-century
Spanish poets

And so is spring about the end of May;
    The sun, no doubt, is the prevailing reason;
But whatsoe'er the cause is, one may say,
    And stand convicted of more truth than treason,
That there are months which nature grows more merry in,—
March has its hares, and May must have its heroine.

        CIII

'Twas on a summer's day—the sixth of June:
    I like to be particular in dates,
Not only of the age, and year, but moon;
820   They are a sort of post-house, where the Fates
Change horses, making History change its tune,
    Then spur away o'er empires and o'er states,
Leaving at last not much besides chronology,
Excepting the post-obits[14] of theology.

        CIV

'Twas on the sixth of June, about the hour
    Of half-past six—perhaps still nearer seven—
When Julia sate within as pretty a bower
    As e'er held houri[15] in that heathenish heaven
Described by Mahomet, and Anacreon Moore,[16]
830   To whom the lyre and laurels have been given
With all the trophies of triumphant song—
He won them well, and may he wear them long!

        CV

She sate, but not alone; I know not well
    How this same interview had taken place,
And even if I knew, I should not tell—
    People should hold their tongues in any case;
No matter how or why the thing befell,
    But there were she and Juan, face to face—
When two such faces are so, 'twould be wise,
840   But very difficult, to shut their eyes.

        CVI

How beautiful she looked! her conscious heart
    Glowed in her cheek, and yet she felt no wrong:
Oh Love! how perfect is thy mystic art,
    Strengthening the weak, and trampling on the strong!
How self-deceitful is the sagest part
    Of mortals whom thy lure hath led along!—
The precipice she stood on was immense,
So was her creed in her own innocence.

---

[14]**post-obits** loans repaid from the estate of a deceased; here, figuratively, judgment in the afterlife

[15]**houri** in Muslim belief, a beautiful maiden devoted to the pleasures of souls in Paradise

[16]**Anacreon Moore** Byron's friend Thomas Moore; he translated the *Odes* of the ancient poet Anacreon and presented Muslim lore in his own poem *Lallah Rookh*.

CVII

She thought of her own strength, and Juan's youth,
850   And of the folly of all prudish fears,
Victorious Virtue, and domestic Truth,
    And then of Don Alfonso's fifty years:
I wish these last had not occurred, in sooth,
    Because that number rarely much endears,
And through all climes, the snowy and the sunny,
Sounds ill in love, whate'er it may in money.

CVIII

When people say, "I've told you *fifty* times,"
    They mean to scold, and very often do;
When poets say, "I've written *fifty* rhymes,"
860   They make you dread that they'll recite them too;
In gangs of *fifty*, thieves commit their crimes;
    At *fifty* love for love is rare, 'tis true,
But then, no doubt, it equally as true is,
A good deal may be bought for *fifty* Louis.[17]

CIX

Julia had honour, virtue, truth, and love
    For Don Alfonso; and she inly swore,
By all the vows below to Powers above,
    She never would disgrace the ring she wore,
Nor leave a wish which wisdom might reprove;
870   And while she pondered this, besides much more,
One hand on Juan's carelessly was thrown,
Quite by mistake—she thought it was her own;

CX

Unconsciously she leaned upon the other,
    Which played within the tangles of her hair;
And to contend with thoughts she could not smother
    She seemed by the distraction of her air.
'Twas surely very wrong in Juan's mother
    To leave together this imprudent pair,
She who for many years had watched her son so—
880 I'm very certain *mine* would not have done so.

CXI

The hand which still held Juan's, by degrees
    Gently, but palpably confirmed its grasp,
As if it said, "Detain me, if you please;"
    Yet there's no doubt she only meant to clasp
His fingers with a pure Platonic squeeze;
    She would have shrunk as from a toad, or asp,
Had she imagined such a thing could rouse
A feeling dangerous to a prudent spouse.

[17]**Louis** French gold coin

CXII

I cannot know what Juan thought of this,
890   But what he did, is much what you would do;
His young lip thanked it with a grateful kiss,
    And then, abashed at its own joy, withdrew
In deep despair, lest he had done amiss,—
    Love is so very timid when 'tis new:
She blushed, and frowned not, but she strove to speak,
And held her tongue, her voice was grown so weak.

CXIII

The sun set, and up rose the yellow moon:
    The Devil's in the moon for mischief; they
Who called her CHASTE, methinks, began too soon
900   Their nomenclature; there is not a day,
The longest, not the twenty-first of June,
    Sees half the business in a wicked way,
On which three single hours of moonshine smile—
And then she looks so modest all the while!

CXIV

There is a dangerous silence in that hour,
    A stillness, which leaves room for the full soul
To open all itself, without the power
    Of calling wholly back its self-control;
The silver light which, hallowing tree and tower,
910   Sheds beauty and deep softness o'er the whole,
Breathes also to the heart, and o'er it throws
A loving languor, which is not repose.

CXV

And Julia sate with Juan, half embraced
    And half retiring from the glowing arm,
Which trembled like the bosom where 'twas placed;
    Yet still she must have thought there was no harm,
Or else 'twere easy to withdraw her waist;
    But then the situation had its charm,
And then—God knows what next—I can't go on;
920 I'm almost sorry that I e'er begun.

CXVI

Oh Plato! Plato! you have paved the way,
    With your confounded fantasies, to more
Immoral conduct by the fancied sway
    Your system feigns o'er the controlless core
Of human hearts, than all the long array
    Of poets and romancers:—You're a bore,
A charlatan, a coxcomb—and have been,
At best, no better than a go-between.

CXVII

And Julia's voice was lost, except in sighs,
930   Until too late for useful conversation;
The tears were gushing from her gentle eyes,
    I wish, indeed, they had not had occasion;
But who, alas! can love, and then be wise?
    Not that Remorse did not oppose Temptation;
A little still she strove, and much repented,
And whispering "I will ne'er consent"—consented.

. . .

CXXIV

Sweet is the vintage, when the showering grapes
    In Bacchanal[18] profusion reel to earth,
Purple and gushing: sweet are our escapes
    From civic revelry to rural mirth;
Sweet to the miser are his glittering heaps,
990   Sweet to the father is his first-born's birth,
Sweet is revenge—especially to women—
Pillage to soldiers, prize-money to seamen.

CXXV

Sweet is a legacy, and passing sweet
    The unexpected death of some old lady,
Or gentleman of seventy years complete,
    Who've made "us youth" wait too—too long already,
For an estate, or cash, or country seat,
    Still breaking, but with stamina so steady,
That all the Israelites[19] are fit to mob its
1000 Next owner for their double-damned post-obits.

CXXVI

'Tis sweet to win, no matter how, one's laurels,
    By blood or ink; 'tis sweet to put an end
To strife; 'tis sometimes sweet to have our quarrels,
    Particularly with a tiresome friend:
Sweet is old wine in bottles, ale in barrels;
    Dear is the helpless creature we defend
Against the world; and dear the schoolboy spot
We ne'er forget, though there we are forgot.

CXXVII

But sweeter still than this, than these, than all,
1010 Is first and passionate Love—it stands alone,
Like Adam's recollection of his fall;
    The Tree of Knowledge has been plucked—all's known—
And Life yields nothing further to recall

---

[18]**Bacchanal** drunken, wanton; reminiscent of the Bacchanalia, Roman festival of Bacchus, god of wine

[19]**Israelites** moneylenders

Worthy of this ambrosial sin, so shown,
No doubt in fable, as the unforgiven
Fire which Prometheus[20] filched for us from Heaven.

. . .

CCXIV

No more—no more—Oh! never more on me
　　The freshness of the heart can fall like dew,
Which out of all the lovely things we see
　　Extracts emotions beautiful and new,
Hived in our bosoms like the bag o' the bee.
1710　Think'st thou the honey with those objects grew?
Alas! 'twas not in them, but in thy power
To double even the sweetness of a flower.

CCXV

No more—no more—Oh! never more, my heart,
　　Canst thou be my sole world, my universe!
Once all in all, but now a thing apart,
　　Thou canst not be my blessing or my curse:
The illusion's gone for ever, and thou art
　　Insensible, I trust, but none the worse,
And in thy stead I've got a deal of judgment,
1720　Though Heaven knows how it ever found a lodgment.

1818　　　　　　　　　　　　　　　　　1819

[20]**Prometheus** Titan in Greek mythology who befriended the human race with the gift of fire stolen from the gods

On This Day I Complete My Thirty-Sixth Year[1]

I

'Tis time this heart should be unmoved,
　　Since others it hath ceased to move:
Yet, though I cannot be beloved,
　　　　Still let me love!

II

My days are in the yellow leaf;[2]
　　The flowers and fruits of Love are gone;
The worm, the canker, and the grief
　　　　Are mine alone!

[1] written at Missolonghi in Greece where Byron was organizing forces fighting for Greek independence from Turkish rule. He turned thirty-six on January 22, 1824, and died just three months later.
[2] 1.5 Cf. Shakespeare's sonnet LXXIII (p. 198 above), l. 2, and *Macbeth* V.iii.1.

III

The fire[3] that on my bosom preys
10   Is lone as some Volcanic isle;
No torch is kindled at its blaze—
      A funeral pile.

IV

The hope, the fear, the jealous care,
    The exalted portion of the pain
And power of love, I cannot share,
      But wear the chain.

V

But 'tis not *thus*—and 'tis not *here*—
    Such thoughts should shake my soul, nor *now*
Where Glory decks the hero's bier,
20   Or binds his brow.

VI

The Sword, the Banner, and the Field,
    Glory and Greece, around me see!
The Spartan, borne upon his shield,
      Was not more free.

VII

Awake! (not Greece—she *is* awake!)
    Awake, my spirit! Think through *whom*
Thy life-blood tracks its parent lake,
      And then strike home!

VIII

Tread those reviving passions down,
30   Unworthy manhood!—unto thee
Indifferent should the smile or frown
      Of Beauty be.

IX

If thou regret'st thy youth, *why live*?
    The land of honourable death
Is here:—up to the Field, and give
      Away thy breath!

X

Seek out—less often sought than found—
    A soldier's grave, for thee the best;
Then look around, and choose thy ground,
40   And take thy Rest.

1824   1824

[3] **fire** possibly a reference to his guilty and unre-
quited passion for the Greek boy Loukas, his
page at Missolonghi

PERCY BYSSHE SHELLEY
1792–1822

Shelley's brief life was filled with turmoil, largely as a result of his intensely idealistic and impetuous nature. Born into the English upper class, Shelley adopted radical views on religion and politics, and his sexual nonconformity so offended many people that he spent his last years, with his wife and children, in self-imposed exile in Italy. On July 8, 1822, a month before his thirtieth birthday, he drowned in a boating accident off the Italian coast.

Despite the brevity and turbulence of his career, Shelley accomplished a great deal. During his four years in Italy he produced most of his best-known lyrics and his greatest work, the mythic drama *Prometheus Unbound* (1819). This poetry presents several challenges to the reader. Shelley often uses images of indistinct, shadowy things— airy, liquid, or nebulous forms such as mists, streams, and auras of light. Such images frequently occur in tangled clusters or in rapid-fire succession, which blurs them even further, and the phrasing, syntax, sound-patterns, and rhythm of the verse heighten the sense of speed. Nevertheless, his poems usually show precise, elaborate structures of orderly thought or scientifically verifiable descriptions of real phenomena. The "Ode to the West Wind," swift-paced, highly formal in organization, and accurate in its weather descriptions, is a prime example. Such poetry requires the reader to submit to the flow of sensations and emotions while keeping the intellectual powers alert.

Shelley's poetry stresses an intense union of passion and reason, permanent order and fluid movement. At the core of his ideas is the notion (loosely influenced by the philosophy of Plato) that there is an eternal, rational order, a pattern for all our highest values—beauty, harmony, justice, and love. This ideal, most succinctly described in the "Hymn to Intellectual Beauty," exists in a form that the human mind can sense but not describe. Shelley is wary, however, of any human institution or system of thought that claims the authority to define this ideal truth. Like Blake, he views organized religions, political systems, or moral codes as false orders, potentially tyrannical. All such forms, however, are subject to transformation and potential renovation. Faithful adherence to ideal values, as exemplified in the myth of Prometheus, can transform human society into an earthly paradise. But Shelley never lets us forget that the forces of change can always destroy even our best achievements—see, for example, the final chorus of *Hellas*. One of the most passionately idealistic of English poets, Shelley is also extremely tough-minded.

Hymn to Intellectual Beauty[1]

I

The awful shadow of some unseen Power
   Floats though unseen amongst us,—visiting
   This various world with as inconstant wing
As summer winds that creep from flower to flower.—
Like moonbeams that behind some piny mountain shower,
     It visits with inconstant glance
     Each human heart and countenance;

---

[1] "Intellectual" has its older meaning here of non-material or non-sensory; hence intellectual beauty is a beauty that exists beyond the world of the senses.

Like hues and harmonies of evening,—
    Like clouds in starlight widely spread,—
10   Like memory of music fled,—
       Like aught that for its grace may be
Dear, and yet dearer for its mystery.

II

Spirit of BEAUTY, that dost consecrate
    With thine own hues all thou dost shine upon
    Of human thought or form,—where art thou gone?
Why dost thou pass away and leave our state,
This dim vast vale of tears, vacant and desolate?
    Ask why the sunlight not forever
    Weaves rainbows o'er yon mountain river,
20 Why aught should fail and fade that once is shewn,
    Why fear and dream and death and birth
    Cast on the daylight of this earth
    Such gloom,—why man has such a scope
For love and hate, despondency and hope?

III

No voice from some sublimer world hath ever
    To sage or poet these responses given—
    Therefore the name of God and ghosts and Heaven,
Remain the records of their vain endeavour,
Frail spells—whose uttered charm might not avail to sever,
30   From all we hear and all we see,
       Doubt, chance, and mutability.
Thy light alone—like mist o'er mountains driven,
    Or music by the night wind sent
    Through strings of some still instrument,[2]
    Or moonlight on a midnight stream,
Gives grace and truth to life's unquiet dream.

IV

Love, Hope, and Self-esteem, like clouds depart
    And come, for some uncertain moments lent.
    Man were[3] immortal, and omnipotent,
40 Didst thou, unknown and awful as thou art,
Keep with thy glorious train firm state within his heart.
      Thou messenger of sympathies,
      That wax and wane in lovers' eyes—
    Thou — that to human thought art nourishment,
      Like darkness to a dying flame!
      Depart not as thy shadow came,
      Depart not—lest the grave should be,
Like life and fear, a dark reality.

[2] **still instrument** Aeolian or wind harp
[3] **were** would be

V

While yet a boy I sought for ghosts, and sped
50   Through many a listening chamber, cave and ruin,
    And starlight wood, with fearful steps pursuing
Hopes of high talk with the departed dead.
I called on poisonous names[4] with which our youth is fed;
    I was not heard—I saw them not—
    When musing deeply on the lot
Of life, at that sweet time when winds are wooing
    All vital things that wake to bring
    News of buds and blossoming,—
    Suddenly, thy shadow fell on me;
60   I shrieked, and clasped my hands in extacy!

VI

I vowed that I would dedicate my powers
    To thee and thine—have I not kept the vow?
    With beating heart and streaming eyes, even now
I call the phantoms of a thousand hours
Each from his voiceless grave: they have in visioned bowers
    Of studious zeal or love's delight
    Outwatched with me the envious night—
They know that never joy illumed my brow
    Unlinked with hope that thou wouldst free
70   This world from its dark slavery,
    That thou—O awful LOVELINESS,
Wouldst give whate'er these words cannot express.

VII

The day becomes more solemn and serene
    When noon is past—there is a harmony
    In autumn, and a lustre in its sky,
Which through the summer is not heard or seen,
As if it could not be, as if it had not been!
    Thus let thy power, which like the truth
    Of nature on my passive youth
80   Descended, to my onward life supply
    Its calm—to one who worships thee,[5]
    And every form containing thee,
    Whom, SPIRIT fair, thy spells did bind
To fear[6] himself, and love all human kind.

1816   1817

---

[4] **poisonous names** a reference to "God and ghosts and Heaven" (1. 27) and other religious concepts

[5] ll. 73–81 Cf. Wordsworth, "Ode: Intimations of Immortality (p. 518 above), ll. 197-200.
[6] **fear** revere, respect

Ozymandias[1]

I met a traveller from an antique land,
Who said—"Two vast and trunkless legs of stone
Stand in the desert. . . . Near them, on the sand,
Half sunk a shattered visage lies, whose frown,
And wrinkled lip, and sneer of cold command,
Tell that its sculptor well those passions read
Which yet survive, stamped on these lifeless things,
The hand that mocked[2] them, and the heart that fed;
And on the pedestal, these words appear:
10   My name is Ozymandias, King of Kings,
Look on my Works, ye Mighty, and despair!
Nothing beside remains. Round the decay
Of that colossal Wreck, boundless and bare
The lone and level sands stretch far away."

1817   1818

[1] the Greek name for the Egyptian pharaoh Ramses II (thirteenth century B.C.), who caused a huge statue of himself to be erected as a permanent monument to his glory
[2] l. 8 "The hand that mocked" (meaning "copied" or "derided" or both) belongs to the sculptor; "the heart that fed" is Ozymandias's; both "hand" and "heart" are direct objects of "survive" in l. 7.

From Prometheus Unbound[1]
From Act II, scene iv [*The Transfiguration of Asia*][2]

VOICE (*in the air, singing*)

Life of Life! thy lips enkindle
  With their love the breath between them
50 And thy smiles before they dwindle
  Make the cold air fire; then screen them
In those looks where whoso gazes
Faints, entangled in their mazes.

Child of Light! thy limbs are burning
  Through the vest[3] which seems to hide them
As the radiant lines of morning
  Through the clouds ere they divide them,
And this atmosphere divinest
Shrouds thee wheresoe'er thou shinest.

[1] a lyrical drama prophesying the abolition of evil and oppression through the moral growth of humankind. Using the ancient Greek story of the Titan Prometheus, who was bound and tortured by Jupiter for bestowing the gift of fire on human beings, Shelley goes beyond his sources in imagining not only the release of Prometheus from his torment but also the downfall of the tyrant Jupiter and the subsequent perfection of human life. The excerpts here present, from various perspectives, the moment of liberation and transformation.
[2] In Shelley's myth, Asia is the bride of Prometheus and represents universal love. In the hour of Prometheus's release, she becomes a divine force. Her duet here with the Voice in the Air describes the process of this transformation and her own response to it.
[3] **vest** garment

60 Fair are others;—none beholds thee
    But thy voice sounds low and tender
Like the fairest—for it folds thee
    From the sight, that liquid splendour,
And all feel, yet see thee never
As I feel now, lost forever!

    Lamp of Earth! where'er thou movest
        Its dim shapes are clad with brightness
    And the souls of whom thou lovest
        Walk upon the winds with lightness
70 Till they fail, as I am failing,
    Dizzy, lost . . . yet unbewailing!

    ASIA

        My soul is an enchanted Boat
        Which, like a sleeping swan, doth float
    Upon the silver waves of thy sweet singing,
        And thine doth like an Angel sit
        Beside the helm conducting it
    Whilst all the winds with melody are ringing.
        It seems to float ever—forever—
        Upon that many winding River
80   Between mountains, woods, abysses,
        A Paradise of wildernesses,
    Till like one in slumber bound
    Borne to the Ocean, I float down, around,
    Into a Sea profound, of ever-spreading sound.

        Meanwhile thy Spirit lifts its pinions[4]
        In Music's most serene dominions,
    Catching the winds that fan that happy Heaven.
        And we sail on, away, afar,
        Without a course—without a star—
90 But by the instinct of sweet Music driven
        Till, through Elysian garden islets
        By thee, most beautiful of pilots,
        Where never mortal pinnace[5] glided,
        The boat of my desire is guided—
    Realms where the air we breathe is Love
    Which in the winds and on the waves doth move,
    Harmonizing this Earth with what we feel above.

        We have past Age's icy caves,
        And Manhood's dark and tossing waves
100 And Youth's smooth ocean, smiling to betray;
        Beyond the glassy gulphs we flee
        Of shadow-peopled Infancy,

[4] **pinions** wings
[5] **pinnace** small boat

Through Death and Birth to a diviner day,[6]
A Paradise of vaulted bowers
Lit by downward-gazing flowers
And watery paths that wind between
Wildernesses calm and green,
Peopled by shapes too bright to see,
And rest, having beheld—somewhat like thee,
110   Which walk upon the sea, and chaunt melodiously!

[6] **diviner day** an ideal world of prenatal existence

From Act III, scene iv [*The Renovation of the World*][1]

THE SPIRIT OF THE EARTH

Thou knowest that toads and snakes and loathly worms
And venomous and malicious beasts, and boughs
That bore ill berries in the woods, were ever
An hindrance to my walks o'er the green world,
40   And that, among the haunts of humankind
Hard-featured men, or with proud, angry looks
Or cold, staid gait, or false and hollow smiles
Or the dull sneer of self-loved ignorance
Or other such foul masks with which ill thoughts
Hide that fair being whom we spirits call man;
And women too, ugliest of all things evil,
Though fair, even in a world where thou art fair
When good and kind, free and sincere like thee,
When false or frowning made me sick at heart
50   To pass them, though they slept, and I unseen.
Well—my path lately lay through a great City
Into the woody hills surrounding it.
A sentinel was sleeping at the gate:
When there was heard a sound, so loud, it shook
The towers amid the moonlight, yet more sweet
Than any voice but thine,[2] sweetest of all,
A long long sound, as it would never end:
And all the inhabitants leapt suddenly
Out of their rest, and gathered in the streets,
60   Looking in wonder up to Heaven, while yet
The music pealed along. I hid myself
Within a fountain in the public square
Where I lay like the reflex[3] of the moon
Seen in a wave under green leaves—and soon
Those ugly human shapes and visages
Of which I spoke as having wrought me pain,

[1] In this excerpt we are given a report of the total regeneration of human society and earthly life resulting from the liberation of Prometheus and the fall of Jupiter.
[2] **thine** The Spirit is addressing Asia.
[3] **reflex** reflection

Past floating through the air, and fading still
Into the winds that scattered them, and those
From whom they past seemed mild and lovely forms
After some foul disguise had fallen—and all
70 Were somewhat changed, and after brief surprise
And greetings of delighted wonder, all
Went to their sleep again: and when the dawn
Came—wouldst thou think that toads and snakes and efts⁴
Could e'er be beautiful?—yet so they were
And that with little change of shape or hue:
All things had put their evil nature off.
I cannot tell my joy, when o'er a lake,
Upon a drooping bough with nightshade⁵ twined,
80 I saw the two azure halcyons⁶ clinging downward
And thinning one bright bunch of amber berries
With quick, long beaks, and in the deep there lay
Those lovely forms imaged as in a sky.—
So with my thoughts full of these happy changes
We meet again, the happiest change of all.

1818–19   1820

⁴ **efts** small salamanders or lizards
⁵ **nightshade** a plant with poisonous berries

⁶ **halcyons** kingfishers, normally predatory
birds

Ode to the West Wind¹

I

O wild West Wind, thou breath of Autumn's being,
Thou, from whose unseen presence the leaves dead
Are driven, like ghosts from an enchanter fleeing,

Yellow, and black, and pale, and hectic red,
Pestilence-stricken multitudes. O Thou,
Who chariotest to their dark wintry bed

The winged seeds, where they lie cold and low,
Each like a corpse within its grave, until
Thine azure sister of the Spring shall blow

10 Her clarion² o'er the dreaming earth, and fill
(Driving sweet buds like flocks to feed in air)
With living hues and odours plain and hill:

Wild Spirit, which art moving everywhere;
Destroyer and Preserver, hear, O hear!

¹ "This poem was conceived and chiefly written
in a wood that skirts the Arno, near Florence,
and on a day when that tempestuous wind, whose
temperature is at once mild and animating, was

collecting the vapours which pour down the
autumnal rains" (Shelley's note).
² **clarion** trumpet

II

Thou on whose stream, mid the steep sky's commotion,
Loose clouds like Earth's decaying leaves are shed,
Shook from the tangled boughs of Heaven and Ocean,[3]

Angels[4] of rain and lightning: there are spread
On the blue surface of thine aery surge,
20 Like the bright hair uplifted from the head

Of some fierce Maenad,[5] even from the dim verge
Of the horizon to the zenith's height,
The locks of the approaching storm. Thou Dirge

Of the dying year, to which this closing night
Will be the dome of a vast sepulchre,
Vaulted with all thy congregated might

Of vapours, from whose solid atmosphere
Black rain and fire and hail will burst: O hear!

III

Thou who didst waken from his summer dreams
30 The blue Mediterranean, where he lay,
Lulled by the coil of his chrystalline streams,

Beside a pumice[6] isle in Baiae's bay,[7]
And saw in sleep old palaces and towers
Quivering within the wave's intenser day,

All overgrown with azure moss and flowers
So sweet, the sense faints picturing them! Thou
For whose path the Atlantic's level powers

Cleave themselves into chasms, while far below
The sea-blooms and the oozy woods which wear
40 The sapless foliage of the ocean, know

Thy voice, and suddenly grow grey with fear,
And tremble and despoil themselves:[8] O hear!

---

[3]**tangled . . . Ocean** rising water vapor from the sea intermingled with the air of the upper atmosphere
[4]**Angels** divine messengers
[5]**Maenad** member of a group of female worshipers of Dionysus, god of fertility, noted for their savage and intoxicated frenzies
[6]**pumice** a porous, volcanic stone

[7]**Baiae's bay** west of Naples, once the setting for luxurious villas of Roman aristocrats (the "old palaces and towers" of l. 33)
[8]**Sea-blooms . . . themselves** "The vegetation at the bottom of the sea, of rivers, and of lakes, sympathizes with that of the land in the change of seasons, and is frequently influenced by the winds which announce it" (Shelley's note).

IV

If I were a dead leaf thou mightest bear;
If I were a swift cloud to fly with thee;
A wave to pant beneath thy power, and share

The impulse of thy strength, only less free
Than thou, O Uncontrollable! If even
I were as in my boyhood, and could be

50   The comrade of thy wanderings over Heaven,
As then, when to outstrip thy skiey speed
Scarce seemed a vision; I would ne'er have striven

As thus with thee in prayer in my sore need.
Oh! lift me as a wave, a leaf, a cloud!
I fall upon the thorns of life! I bleed!

A heavy weight of hours has chained and bowed
One too like thee: tameless, and swift, and proud.

V

Make me thy lyre,[9] even as the forest is:
What if my leaves are falling like its own!
The tumult of thy mighty harmonies

60   Will take from both a deep, autumnal tone,
Sweet though in sadness. Be thou, Spirit fierce,
My spirit! Be thou me, impetuous one!

Drive my dead thoughts over the universe
Like withered leaves to quicken a new birth!
And, by the incantation of this verse,

Scatter, as from an unextinguished hearth
Ashes and sparks, my words among mankind!
Be through my lips to unawakened Earth

The trumpet of a prophecy![10] O Wind,
70   If Winter comes, can Spring be far behind?

1819   1820

[9]**lyre** Aeolian or wind harp; cf. Coleridge,
"Dejection: An Ode" (p. 554 above).
[10]**trumpet of a prophecy** possibly an allusion
to the trumpet of the Last Judgment in Revelation
11:15

Adonais[1]

AN ELEGY ON THE DEATH OF JOHN KEATS, AUTHOR OF
ENDYMION, HYPERION, ETC.

'Αστὴρ πρὶν μὲν ἔλαμπες ἐνὶ ζωοῖσιν 'Εῷος·
νῦν δὲ θανὼν λάμπεις "Εσπερος ἐν φθιμένοις. — PLATO [2]

I

I weep for Adonais—he is dead!
O, weep for Adonais! though our tears
Thaw not the frost which binds so dear a head!
And thou, sad Hour, selected from all years
To mourn our loss, rouse thy obscure compeers,
And teach them thine own sorrow, say: "With me
Died Adonais; till the Future dares
Forget the Past, his fate and fame shall be
An echo and a light unto eternity!"

II

10   Where wert thou, mighty Mother,[3] when he lay,
When thy Son lay, pierced by the shaft[4] which flies
In darkness? where was lorn Urania
When Adonais died? With veilèd eyes,
'Mid listening Echoes, in her Paradise
She sate, while one, with soft enamoured breath,
Rekindled all the fading melodies,
With which, like flowers that mock the corse[5] beneath,
He had adorned and hid the coming bulk of Death.

III

Oh, weep for Adonais—he is dead!
20   Wake, melancholy Mother, wake and weep!
Yet wherefore? Quench within their burning bed
Thy fiery tears, and let thy loud heart keep
Like his, a mute and uncomplaining sleep;

[1] Although Shelley and Keats knew one another they were never close friends, and Shelley had only a moderate appreciation of Keats's poetry. Nevertheless when Keats died in Rome in February 1821 at the age of twenty-five, Shelley was deeply moved, in part because he saw Keats as a representative of the poetic genius cut off at an early age by the hostile forces of society (Shelley incorrectly believed that negative reviews of Keats's poetry had been responsible for bringing on his mortal illness). *Adonais*, Shelley's tribute to the genius of Keats, takes the traditional form of the pastoral elegy in which mythological or allegorical figures are substituted for actual persons (compare Milton's *Lycidas*). The name "Adonais"
apparently combines allusions to Adonis, in classical mythology a beautiful youth slain by a wild boar, and "Adonai," a title of the Lord God in Hebrew.

[2] Shelley translated this Greek epigraph (which may not in fact be Plato's) as follows:
Thou wert the morning star among the living,
Ere thy fair light had fled—
Now, having died, thou art as Hesperus, giving
New splendour to the dead.
Hesperus is the evening star.

[3] **mighty Mother** Urania, the classic muse of astronomy and heavenly love

[4] **shaft** a reference to the anonymous hostile reviews of Keats's poetry

[5] **corse** corpse

For he is gone, where all things wise and fair
Descend;—oh, dream not that the amorous Deep
Will yet restore him to the vital air;
Death feeds on his mute voice, and laughs at our despair.

IV

Most musical of mourners, weep again!
Lament anew, Urania!—He[6] died,
30 Who was the Sire of an immortal strain,
Blind, old, and lonely, when his country's pride,
The priest, the slave, and the liberticide,
Trampled and mocked with many a loathèd rite
Of lust and blood; he went, unterrified,
Into the gulf of death; but his clear Sprite
Yet reigns o'er earth; the third among the sons of light.[7]

V

Most musical of mourners, weep anew!
Not all to that bright station dared to climb;[8]
And happier they their happiness who knew,
40 Whose tapers yet burn through that night of time
In which suns perished; others more sublime,
Struck by the envious wrath of man or god,
Have sunk, extinct in their refulgent prime;
And some yet live, treading the thorny road,
Which leads, through toil and hate, to Fame's serene abode.

VI

But now, thy youngest, dearest one, has perished—
The nursling of thy widowhood, who grew,
Like a pale flower by some sad maiden cherished,
And fed with true-love tears, instead of dew;
50 Most musical of mourners, weep anew!
Thy extreme hope, the loveliest and the last,
The bloom, whose petals nipped before they blew
Died on the promise of the fruit, is waste;
The broken lily lies—the storm is overpast.

VII

To that high Capital, where kingly Death
Keeps his pale court in beauty and decay,
He came; and bought, with price of purest breath,
A grave among the eternal.—Come away!
Haste, while the vault of blue Italian day
60 Is yet his fitting charnel-roof! while still

---

[6]**He** the poet Milton
[7]**sons of light** great epic poets of Western literature. The other two are presumably Homer and Dante.

[8]ll. 37–45 This stanza alludes to the varying fortunes of poets and their reputations.

He lies, as if in dewy sleep he lay;
Awake him not! surely he takes his fill
Of deep and liquid rest, forgetful of all ill.

VIII

He will awake no more, oh, never more!—
Within the twilight chamber spreads apace
The shadow of white Death, and at the door
Invisible Corruption waits to trace
His extreme way to her dim dwelling-place;
The eternal Hunger sits, but pity and awe
70   Soothe her pale rage, nor dares she to deface
So fair a prey, till darkness, and the law
Of change, shall o'er his sleep the mortal curtain draw.

IX

Oh, weep for Adonais!—The quick Dreams,
The passion-wingèd Ministers of thought,
Who were his flocks, whom near the living streams
Of his young spirit he fed, and whom he taught
The love which was its music, wander not,—
Wander no more, from kindling brain to brain,
But droop there, whence they sprung; and mourn their lot
80   Round the cold heart, where, after their sweet pain,
They ne'er will gather strength, or find a home again.

X

And one with trembling hands clasps his cold head,
And fans him with her moonlight wings, and cries;
"Our love, our hope, our sorrow, is not dead;
See, on the silken fringe of his faint eyes,
Like dew upon a sleeping flower, there lies
A tear some Dream has loosened from his brain."
Lost Angel of a ruined Paradise!
She knew not 'twas her own; as with no stain
90   She faded, like a cloud which had outwept its rain.

XI

One from a lucid urn of starry dew
Washed his light limbs as if embalming them;
Another clipped her profuse locks, and threw
The wreath upon him, like an anadem,[9]
Which frozen tears instead of pearls begem;
Another in her wilful grief would break
Her bow and wingèd reeds, as if to stem
A greater loss with one which was more weak;
And dull the barbèd fire against his frozen cheek.

[9]**anadem** garland

XII

100   Another Splendour on his mouth alit,
That mouth, whence it was wont to draw the breath
Which gave it strength to pierce the guarded wit,[10]
And pass into the panting heart beneath
With lightning and with music: the damp death
Quenched its caress upon his icy lips;
And, as a dying meteor stains a wreath
Of moonlight vapour, which the cold night clips,[11]
It flushed through his pale limbs, and passed to its eclipse.

XIII

And others came . . . Desires and Adorations,
110   Wingèd Persuasions and veiled Destinies,
Splendours, and Glooms, and glimmering Incarnations
Of hopes and fears, and twilight Phantasies;
And Sorrow, with her family of Sighs,
And Pleasure, blind with tears, led by the gleam
Of her own dying smile instead of eyes,
Came in slow pomp;—the moving pomp might seem
Like pageantry of mist on an autumnal stream.

XIV

All he had loved, and moulded into thought,
From shape, and hue, and odour, and sweet sound,
120   Lamented Adonais. Morning sought
Her eastern watch-tower, and her hair unbound,
Wet with the tears which should adorn the ground,
Dimmed the aëreal eyes that kindle day;
Afar the melancholy thunder moaned,
Pale Ocean in unquiet slumber lay,
And the wild Winds flew round, sobbing in their dismay.

XV

Lost Echo[12] sits amid the voiceless mountains,
And feeds her grief with his remembered lay,
And will no more reply to winds or fountains,
130   Or amorous birds perched on the young green spray,
Or herdsman's horn, or bell at closing day;
Since she can mimic not his lips, more dear
Than those for whose disdain she pined away
Into a shadow of all sounds:—a drear
Murmur, between their songs, is all the woodmen hear.

---

[10]**guarded wit** cautious rationality
[11]**clips** embraces
[12]**Echo** a nymph who faded away out of unre-

quited love for Narcissus, a youth who loved
only his own reflection (see l. 141)

XVI

Grief made the young Spring wild, and she threw down
Her kindling buds, as if she Autumn were,
Or they dead leaves; since her delight is flown,
For whom should she have waked the sullen year?
140   To Phoebus was not Hyacinth so dear[13]
Nor to himself Narcissus, as to both
Thou, Adonais: wan they stand and sere
Amid the faint companions of their youth,
With dew all turned to tears; odour, to sighing ruth.

XVII

Thy spirit's sister, the lorn nightingale[14]
Mourns not her mate with such melodious pain;
Not so the eagle, who like thee could scale
Heaven, and could nourish in the sun's domain
Her mighty youth with morning, doth complain,
150   Soaring and screaming round her empty nest,
As Albion[15] wails for thee: the curse of Cain
Light on his head who pierced thy innocent breast,
And scared the angel soul that was its earthly guest!

XVIII

Ah, woe is me! Winter is come and gone,
But grief returns with the revolving year;
The airs and streams renew their joyous tone;
The ants, the bees, the swallows reappear;
Fresh leaves and flowers deck the dead Seasons' bier;
The amorous birds now pair in every brake,[16]
160   And build their mossy homes in field and brere;[17]
And the green lizard, and the golden snake,
Like unimprisoned flames, out of their trance awake.

XIX

Through wood and stream and field and hill and Ocean
A quickening life from the Earth's heart has burst
As it has ever done, with change and motion,
From the great morning of the world when first
God dawned on Chaos; in its stream immersed,
The lamps of Heaven flash with a softer light;
170   All baser things pant with life's sacred thirst;
Diffuse themselves; and spend in love's delight,
The beauty and the joy of their renewèd might.

[13]l. 140 The god Phoebus Apollo created the hyacinth flower out of the blood of the youth Hyacinthus, whom he had loved and accidentally slain.
[14]**nightingale** perhaps a reference to Keats's famous "Ode to a Nightingale"
[15]**Albion** England
[16]**brake** thicket
[17]**brere** briar

XX

The leprous corpse, touched by this spirit tender,
Exhales itself in flowers of gentle breath;
Like incarnations of the stars, when splendour
Is changed to fragrance, they illumine death
And mock the merry worm that wakes beneath;
Nought we know, dies. Shall that alone which knows
Be as a sword consumed before the sheath
By sightless[18] lightning?—the intense atom glows

180   A moment, then is quenched in a most cold repose.

XXI

Alas! that all we loved of him should be,
But for our grief, as if it had not been,
And grief itself be mortal! Woe is me!
Whence are we, and why are we? of what scene
The actors or spectators? Great and mean
Meet massed in death, who lends what life must borrow.
As long as skies are blue, and fields are green,
Evening must usher night, night urge the morrow,
Month follow month with woe, and year wake year to sorrow.

XXII

190   *He* will awake no more, oh, never more!
"Wake thou," cried Misery, "childless Mother, rise
Out of thy sleep, and slake, in thy heart's core,
A wound more fierce than his, with tears and sighs."
And all the Dreams that watched Urania's eyes,
And all the Echoes whom their sister's song
Had held in holy silence, cried: "Arise!"
Swift as a Thought by the snake Memory stung,
From her ambrosial rest the fading Splendour sprung.

XXIII

She rose like an autumnal Night, that springs
200   Out of the East, and follows wild and drear
The golden Day, which, on eternal wings,
Even as a ghost abandoning a bier,
Had left the Earth a corpse. Sorrow and fear
So struck, so roused, so rapt Urania;
So saddened round her like an atmosphere
Of stormy mist; so swept her on her way
Even to the mournful place where Adonais lay.

XXIV

Out of her secret Paradise she sped,
Through camps and cities rough with stone, and steel,
210   And human hearts, which to her aery tread

[18]**sightless** invisible

Yielding not, wounded the invisible
Palms of her tender feet where'er they fell:
And barbèd tongues, and thoughts more sharp than they,
Rent the soft Form they never could repel,
Whose sacred blood, like the young tears of May,
Paved with eternal flowers that undeserving way.

XXV

In the death-chamber for a moment Death,
Shamed by the presence of that living Might,
Blushed to annihilation, and the breath
220   Revisited those lips, and Life's pale light
Flashed through those limbs, so late her dear delight.
"Leave me not wild and drear and comfortless,
As silent lightning leaves the starless night!
Leave me not!" cried Urania: her distress
Roused Death: Death rose and smiled, and met her vain caress.

XXVI

"Stay yet awhile! speak to me once again;
Kiss me, so long but as a kiss may live;
And in my heartless[19] breast and burning brain
That word, that kiss, shall all thoughts else survive,
230   With food of saddest memory kept alive,
Now thou art dead, as if it were a part
Of thee, my Adonais! I would give
All that I am to be as thou now art!
But I am chained to Time, and cannot thence depart!

XXVII

"O gentle child, beautiful as thou wert,
Why didst thou leave the trodden paths of men
Too soon, and with weak hands though mighty heart
Dare the unpastured dragon in his den?
Defenceless as thou wert, oh, where was then
240   Wisdom the mirrored shield,[20] or scorn the spear?
Or hadst thou waited the full cycle, when
Thy spirit should have filled its crescent sphere,[21]
The monsters of life's waste had fled from thee like deer.

XXVIII

"The herded wolves,[22] bold only to pursue;
The obscene ravens, clamorous o'er the dead;
The vultures to the conqueror's banner true
Who feed where Desolation first has fed,

---

[19]**heartless** disheartened
[20]**mirrored shield** used by Perseus to slay
Medusa, because to look at her directly would
have turned him to stone.

[21]l. 242 like the moon going from crescent
state to full
[22]ll. 244–52 The creatures of prey mentioned
in this stanza represent critics and reviewers.

And whose wings rain contagion;—how they fled,
When, like Apollo, from his golden bow
250 The Pythian of the age[23] one arrow sped
And smiled!—The spoilers tempt no second blow,
They fawn on the proud feet that spurn them lying low.

XXIX

"The sun comes forth, and many reptiles spawn;
He sets, and each ephemeral insect then
Is gathered into death without a dawn,
And the immortal stars awake again;
So is it in the world of living men:
A godlike mind soars forth, in its delight
Making earth bare and veiling heaven, and when
260 It sinks, the swarms that dimmed or shared its light
Leave to its kindred lamps the spirit's awful night."

XXX

Thus ceased she: and the mountain shepherds came,
Their garlands sere, their magic mantles rent;
The Pilgrim of Eternity,[24] whose fame
Over his living head like Heaven is bent,
An early but enduring monument,
Came, veiling all the lightnings of his song
In sorrow; from her wilds Ierne sent
The sweetest lyrist[25] of her saddest wrong,
270 And Love taught Grief to fall like music from his tongue.

XXXI

Midst others of less note, came one frail Form,[26]
A phantom among men; companionless
As the last cloud of an expiring storm
Whose thunder is its knell; he, as I guess,
Had gazed on Nature's naked loveliness,
Actaeon-like, and now he fled astray
With feeble steps o'er the world's wilderness,
And his own thoughts, along that rugged way,
Pursued, like raging hounds, their father and their prey.[27]

XXXII

280 A pardlike[28] Spirit beautiful and swift—
A Love in desolation masked;—a Power

---

[23]**Pythian of the age** Lord Byron, who had effectively satirized the reviewers; "Pythian" refers to the god Apollo, who killed the serpent Python.

[24]**Pilgrim of Eternity** Byron, called a pilgrim because of his celebrated poem *Childe Harold's Pilgrimage*

[25]**sweetest lyrist** the Irish poet Thomas Moore (1779–1852), who had written of suffering and oppression in Ireland ("Ierne").

[26]**one frail Form** a reference to Shelley himself

[27]ll. 276–79 Actaeon, a hunter, encountered the naked Diana, goddess of chastity, while she was bathing; in punishment she turned him into a stag, and his own hunting dogs tore him to pieces.

[28]**pardlike** leopard-like

Girt round with weakness;—it can scarce uplift
The weight of the superincumbent hour;
It is a dying lamp, a falling shower,
A breaking billow;—even whilst we speak
Is it not broken? On the withering flower
The killing sun smiles brightly: on a cheek
The life can burn in blood, even while the heart may break.

XXXIII

His head was bound with pansies overblown,
290   And faded violets, white, and pied, and blue;
And a light spear topped with a cypress[29] cone,
Round whose rude shaft dark ivy-tresses grew
Yet dripping with the forest's noonday dew,
Vibrated, as the ever-beating heart
Shook the weak hand that grasped it; of that crew
He came the last, neglected and apart;
A herd-abandoned deer struck by the hunter's dart.

XXXIV

All stood aloof, and at his partial moan
Smiled through their tears; well knew that gentle band
300   Who in another's fate now wept his own,
As in the accents of an unknown land
He sung new sorrow; sad Urania scanned
The Stranger's mien, and murmured: "Who art thou?"
He answered not, but with a sudden hand
Made bare his branded and ensanguined[30] brow,
Which was like Cain's or Christ's[31]—oh! that it should be so!

XXXV

What softer voice is hushed over the dead?
Athwart what brow is that dark mantle thrown?
What form leans sadly o'er the white death-bed,
310   In mockery[32] of monumental stone,
The heavy heart heaving without a moan?
If it be He,[33] who, gentlest of the wise,
Taught, soothed, loved, honoured the departed one,
Let me not vex, with inharmonious sighs,
The silence of that heart's accepted sacrifice.

XXXVI

Our Adonais has drunk poison—oh!
What deaf and viperous murderer could crown
Life's early cup with such a draught of woe?

[29]**cypress** an emblem of mourning
[30]**ensanguined** bloody
[31]ll. 305–06 Christ's brow was scarred by the crown of thorns, Cain's by a mark identifying him as the murderer of his brother Abel.
[32]**mockery** imitation
[33]**He** Leigh Hunt, a friend of both Keats and Shelley and a promoter of their works

The nameless worm[34] would now itself disown:
320 It felt, yet could escape, the magic tone
Whose prelude held all envy, hate, and wrong,
But what was howling in one breast alone,
Silent with expectation of the song,[35]
Whose master's hand is cold, whose silver lyre unstrung.

XXXVII

Live thou, whose infamy is not thy fame!
Live! fear no heavier chastisement from me,
Thou noteless blot on a remembered name!
But be thyself, and know thyself to be!
And ever at thy season be thou free
330 To spill the venom when thy fangs o'erflow;
Remorse and Self-contempt shall cling to thee;
Hot Shame shall burn upon thy secret brow,
And like a beaten hound tremble thou shalt—as now.

XXXVIII

Nor let us weep that our delight is fled
Far from these carrion kites that scream below;
He wakes or sleeps with the enduring dead;
Thou canst not soar where he is sitting now.—
Dust to the dust! but the pure spirit shall flow
Back to the burning fountain whence it came,
340 A portion of the Eternal,[36] which must glow
Through time and change, unquenchably the same,
Whilst thy cold embers choke the sordid hearth of shame.

XXXIX

Peace, peace! he is not dead, he doth not sleep—
He hath awakened from the dream of life—
'Tis we, who lost in stormy visions, keep
With phantoms an unprofitable strife,
And in mad trance, strike with our spirit's knife
Invulnerable nothings.—*We* decay
Like corpses in a charnel; fear and grief
350 Convulse us and consume us day by day,
And cold hopes swarm like worms within our living clay.

XL

He has outsoared the shadow of our night;
Envy and calumny and hate and pain,
And that unrest which men miscall delight,

[34]**nameless worm** the anonymous reviewer of Keats's *Endymion*

[35]ll. 320–23 The promise of future greatness in Keats's early poetry should have been sufficient to silence all negative criticism; no one but the malicious reviewer could be so insensitive.

[36]**pure spirit . . . Eternal** In Neo-Platonic philosophy all individual forms of spirit in this world are derived from one eternal spirit, to which they eventually return, just as water returns to its source in a fountain.

Can touch him not and torture not again;
From the contagion of the world's slow stain
He is secure, and now can never mourn
A heart grown cold, a head grown gray in vain;
Nor, when the spirit's self has ceased to burn,
360　With sparkless ashes load an unlamented urn.

XLI

He lives, he wakes—'tis Death is dead, not he;
Mourn not for Adonais.—Thou young Dawn,
Turn all thy dew to splendour, for from thee
The spirit thou lamentest is not gone;
Ye caverns and ye forests, cease to moan!
Cease, ye faint flowers and fountains, and thou Air,
Which like a mourning veil thy scarf hadst thrown
O'er the abandoned Earth, now leave it bare
Even to the joyous stars which smile on its despair!

XLII

370　He is made one with Nature: there is heard
His voice in all her music, from the moan
Of thunder, to the song of night's sweet bird;[37]
He is a presence to be felt and known
In darkness and in light, from herb and stone,
Spreading itself where'er that Power may move
Which has withdrawn his being to its own;
Which wields the world with never-wearied love,
Sustains it from beneath, and kindles it above.

XLIII

He is a portion of the loveliness
380　Which once he made more lovely: he doth bear
His part, while the one Spirit's plastic stress
Sweeps through the dull dense world, compelling there,
All new successions to the forms they wear;
Torturing th' unwilling dross that checks its flight
To its own likeness, as each mass may bear;[38]
And bursting in its beauty and its might
From trees and beasts and men into the Heaven's light.

XLIV

The splendours of the firmament of time
May be eclipsed, but are extinguished not;

---

[37]**the song . . . bird** the subject of Keats's
"Ode to a Nightingale"
[38]**the one Spirit's plastic stress . . . may bear**
a concept, loosely based on Plato's philosophy,
that posits an opposition between matter and
pure spirit; materiality in its essence is heavy,
formless, ugly, and resistant ("unwilling") to
penetration or shaping ("plastic stress") by the
one Spirit (see note 36 above), but different
material things permit the influence of the Spirit
in varying degrees ("as each mass may bear").
The one Spirit, imposing its own ideal proper-
ties on the flow of matter, gives to all indi-
vidual material things the beauty, goodness, and
particular form that we perceive in them.

390   Like stars to their appointed height they climb,
And death is a low mist which cannot blot
The brightness it may veil. When lofty thought
Lifts a young heart above its mortal lair,
And love and life contend in it, for what
Shall be its earthly doom, the dead live there[39]
And move like winds of light on dark and stormy air.

XLV

The inheritors of unfulfilled renown
Rose from their thrones, built beyond mortal thought,
Far in the Unapparent. Chatterton[40]
400   Rose pale,—his solemn agony had not
Yet faded from him; Sidney, as he fought
And as he fell and as he lived and loved
Sublimely mild, a Spirit without spot,
Arose; and Lucan, by his death approved:
Oblivion as they rose shrank like a thing reproved.

XLVI

And many more, whose names on Earth are dark,
But whose transmitted effluence cannot die
So long as fire outlives the parent spark,
Rose, robed in dazzling immortality.
410   "Thou art become as one of us," they cry,
"It was for thee yon kingless sphere has long
Swung blind in unascended majesty,
Silent alone amid an Heaven of Song.
Assume thy wingèd throne, thou Vesper[41] of our throng!"

XLVII

Who mourns for Adonais? Oh, come forth,
Fond wretch! and know thyself and him aright.
Clasp with thy panting soul the pendulous[42] Earth;
As from a centre, dart thy spirit's light
Beyond all worlds, until its spacious might
420   Satiate[43] the void circumference: then shrink
Even to a point within our day and night;
And keep thy heart light lest it make thee sink
When hope has kindled hope, and lured thee to the brink.

XLVIII

Or go to Rome, which is the sepulchre,
Oh, not of him, but of our joy: 'tis nought
That ages, empires, and religions there

---

[39]**there** in the "young heart" (l. 393)
[40]**Chatterton** Thomas Chatterton (1752–1770) and the other figures mentioned in this stanza, (Sir Philip) Sidney (1554–1586) and the Roman poet Lucan (A.D. 39–65), were all poets who died young.
[41]**Vesper** the evening star
[42]**pendulous** suspended
[43]**Satiate** fill

Lie buried in the ravage they have wrought;
For such as he can lend,—they borrow not
Glory from those who made the world their prey;
430   And he is gathered to the kings of thought
Who waged contention with their time's decay,
And of the past are all that cannot pass away.

    XLIX

Go thou to Rome,—at once the Paradise,
The grave, the city, and the wilderness;
And where its wrecks like shattered mountains rise,
And flowering weeds, and fragrant copses dress
The bones of Desolation's nakedness
Pass, till the spirit of the spot shall lead
Thy footsteps to a slope of green access[44]
440   Where, like an infant's smile, over the dead
A light of laughing flowers along the grass is spread;

    L

And gray walls moulder round, on which dull Time
Feeds, like slow fire upon a hoary brand;
And one keen pyramid with wedge sublime,[45]
Pavilioning the dust of him who planned
This refuge for his memory, doth stand
Like flame transformed to marble; and beneath,
A field is spread, on which a newer band
Have pitched in Heaven's smile their camp of death,
450   Welcoming him we lose with scarce extinguished breath.

    LI

Here pause: these graves are all too young as yet
To have outgrown the sorrow which consigned
Its charge to each; and if the seal is set,
Here, on one fountain of a mourning mind,[46]
Break it not thou! too surely shalt thou find
Thine own well full, if thou returnest home,
Of tears and gall. From the world's bitter wind
Seek shelter in the shadow of the tomb.
What Adonais is, why fear we to become?

    LII

460   The One remains, the many change and pass;
Heaven's light forever shines, Earth's shadows fly;
Life, like a dome of many-coloured glass,
Stains the white radiance of Eternity,

---

[44]**slope . . . access** the Protestant Cemetery in Rome, where Keats is buried
[45]l. 444   the Roman tomb of Gaius Cestius, which dominates the background beyond Keats's grave

[46]l. 454   Shelley had recently mourned the death of his own son William, also buried in the Protestant Cemetery.

Until Death tramples it to fragments.—Die,
If thou wouldst be with that which thou dost seek!
Follow where all is fled!—Rome's azure sky,
Flowers, ruins, statues, music, words, are weak
The glory they transfuse with fitting truth to speak.

LIII

Why linger, why turn back, why shrink, my Heart?
470   Thy hopes are gone before: from all things here
They have departed; thou shouldst now depart!
A light is passed from the revolving year,
And man, and woman; and what still is dear
Attracts to crush, repels to make thee wither.
The soft sky smiles,—the low wind whispers near:
'Tis Adonais calls! oh, hasten thither,
No more let Life divide what Death can join together.

LIV

That Light whose smile kindles the Universe,
That Beauty in which all things work and move,
480   That Benediction which the eclipsing Curse
Of birth can quench not, that sustaining Love
Which through the web of being blindly wove
By man and beast and earth and air and sea,
Burns bright or dim, as each are mirrors of
The fire for which all thirst;[47] now beams on me,
Consuming the last clouds of cold mortality.

LV

The breath whose might I have invoked in song[48]
Descends on me; my spirit's bark is driven,
Far from the shore, far from the trembling throng
490   Whose sails were never to the tempest given;
The massy earth and spherèd skies are riven!
I am borne darkly, fearfully, afar;
Whilst, burning through the inmost veil of Heaven,
The soul of Adonais, like a star,
Beacons from the abode where the Eternal are.

1821   1821

[47]**as each . . . thirst** as each man, beast, etc.,
reflects the spiritual fire (see the "burning fountain" of stanza XXXVIII), that they all long
("thirst") to rejoin
[48]l. 487 See Shelley's "Ode to the West Wind."

From Hellas[1]

CHORUS

1060 The world's great age begins anew,
     The golden years return,
The earth doth like a snake renew
     Her winter weeds[2] outworn;
Heaven smiles, and faiths and empires gleam
Like wrecks of a dissolving dream.

A brighter Hellas rears its mountains
     From waves serener far,
A new Peneus[3] rolls his fountains
     Against the morning-star,
1070 Where fairer Tempes bloom, there sleep
Young Cyclads[4] on a sunnier deep.

A loftier Argo[5] cleaves the main,
     Fraught with a later prize;
Another Orpheus sings again,
     And loves, and weeps, and dies;[6]
A new Ulysses leaves once more
Calypso[7] for his native shore.

O, write no more the tale of Troy,
     If earth Death's scroll must be!
1080 Nor mix with Laian rage[8] the joy
     Which dawns upon the free;
Although a subtler Sphinx renew
Riddles of death Thebes never knew.

---

[1] The Greek war for independence from the Turks, still in progress as Shelley wrote, is the occasion for this lyrical drama. ("Hellas" was the ancient name for Greece.) The final chorus of the drama goes beyond the contemporary situation and "will remind the reader . . . of Isaiah and Virgil, whose ardent spirits overleaping the actual reign of evil which we endure and bewail, already saw the possible and perhaps probable approaching state of society in which '*the lion shall lie down with the lamb*' " (Shelley's note; see Isaiah 65:25 and the Fourth Eclogue of the Latin poet Virgil, which prophesies the return of the golden age). The twentieth-century poet W.B. Yeats closely modeled his "Two Songs from a Play" on this chorus.

[2] **weeds** garments

[3] **Peneus** a river in northern Greece that flows through the valley of Tempe (1. 1070)

[4] **Cyclads** a chain of islands in the Aegean Sea

[5] **Argo** the ship of the hero Jason in his quest for the Golden Fleece

[6] **Orpheus . . . dies** In Greek legend Orpheus was the finest of singers and musicians. Lamenting his dead wife, Eurydice, whom he had attempted unsuccessfully to liberate from the underworld, he was torn to pieces by Thracian women driven to frenzy by the haunting beauty of his song.

[7] **Calypso** a beautiful nymph who encountered the Greek hero Ulysses on his return journey from the Trojan War and detained him for seven years on her island

[8] **Laian rage** Laius, king of Thebes, was killed by his son, Oedipus, in a fierce quarrel, in which neither man knew who the other was. Soon afterward, Oedipus liberated Thebes from the terrors of a Sphinx, who destroyed anyone incapable of answering her riddle (11. 1082–83).

Another Athens shall arise,
   And to remoter time
Bequeath, like sunset to the skies,
   The splendour of its prime,
And leave, if nought so bright may live,
All earth can take or Heaven can give.

1090 Saturn[9] and Love their long repose
   Shall burst, more bright and good
Than all who fell, than One who rose,
   Than many unsubdued;[10]
Not gold, not blood their altar dowers
But votive tears and symbol flowers.

O cease! must hate and death return?
   Cease! must men kill and die?
Cease! drain not to its dregs the urn
   Of bitter prophecy.
1100 The world is weary of the past,
O might it die or rest at last!

1821   1822

---

[9]**Saturn** the god who reigned during the blissful first age of the world
[10]ll. 1092-93 **all who fell** the ancient gods of Greece and Rome; **One who rose** Jesus Christ; **many unsubdued** pagan deities worshiped in Eastern religions

Lines [When the Lamp Is Shattered]

I

When the lamp is shattered,
   The light in the dust lies dead—
When the cloud is scattered,
   The rainbow's glory is shed.
When the lute is broken,
   Sweet tones are remembered not;
When the lips have spoken,
Loved accents are soon forgot.

II

As music and splendour
10 Survive not the lamp and the lute,
   The heart's echoes render
No song when the spirit is mute:—
   No song but sad dirges,
Like the wind through a ruined cell,
   Or the mournful surges
That ring the dead seaman's knell.

III

When hearts have once mingled,
Love first leaves the well-built nest;[1]
    The weak one is singled
20 To endure what it once possesst.
    O, Love! who bewailest
The frailty of all things here,
    Why choose you the frailest
For your cradle, your home, and your bier?

IV

Its passions will rock thee,
As the storms rock the ravens on high:
    Bright reason will mock thee,
Like the sun from a wintry sky.
    From thy nest every rafter
30 Will rot, and thine eagle home
    Leave thee naked to laughter,
When leaves fall and cold winds come.

                            1824

[1] **the well-built nest** the less vulnerable heart

JOHN CLARE
1793–1864

Son of a farm laborer, John Clare published his first volume of poems in 1820. Their vivid descriptions of English rural life won praise, but three subsequent volumes were largely ignored and Clare's life became a struggle against poverty. In 1836 he began to show signs of insanity. He spent the rest of his days, except for one brief interval, in asylums, where he continued to write poetry. While the unaffected and keenly detailed observations of Clare's rural poems convey both hard realism and charm, his present reputation rests chiefly on the poetry written in asylums. Displaying a compressed power and intensity reminiscent of Blake, these poems offer extraordinary glimpses into inner states of sorrow and elation.

Badger

When midnight comes a host of dogs and men
Go out and track the badger to his den,
And put a sack within the hole, and lie
Till the old grunting badger passes by.
He comes and hears—they let the strongest loose.
The old fox hears the noise and drops the goose.
The poacher shoots and hurries from the cry,

And the old hare half wounded buzzes by.
They get a forkèd stick to bear him down
10 And clap the dogs and take him to the town,
And bait him all the day with many dogs,
And laugh and shout and fright the scampering hogs.
He runs along and bites at all he meets:
They shout and hollo down the noisy streets.

He turns about to face the loud uproar
And drives the rebels to their very door.
The frequent stone is hurled where'er they go;
When badgers fight, then every one's a foe.
The dogs are clapt and urged to join the fray;
20 The badger turns and drives them all away.
Though scarcely half as big, demure and small,
He fights with dogs for hours and beats them all.
The heavy mastiff, savage in the fray,
Lies down and licks his feet and turns away.
The bulldog knows his match and waxes cold,
The badger grins and never leaves his hold.
He drives the crowd and follows at their heels
And bites them through—the drunkard swears and reels.

The frighted women take the boys away,
30 The blackguard laughs and hurries on the fray.
He tries to reach the woods, an awkward race,
But sticks and cudgels quickly stop the chase.
He turns agen and drives the noisy crowd
And beats the many dogs in noises loud.
He drives away and beats them every one,
And then they loose them all and set them on.
He falls as dead and kicked by boys and men,
Then starts and grins and drives the crowd agen;
Till kicked and torn and beaten out he lies
40 And leaves his hold and cackles, groans and dies.

1835–37   1920

Secret Love[1]

I hid my love when young till I
Couldn't bear the buzzing of a fly;
I hid my love to my despite
Till I could not bear to look at light:

---

[1] This poem may be compared with Blake's lyrics
"Mad Song" (p. 483 above) and "Never Pain
to Tell Thy Love" (p. 497).

I dare not gaze upon her face
But left her memory in each place;
Where'er I saw a wild flower lie
I kissed and bade my love good-bye.

I met her in the greenest dells,
10   Where dewdrops pearl the wood bluebells;
The lost breeze kissed her bright blue eye,
The bee kissed and went singing by,
A sunbeam found a passage there,
A gold chain round her neck so fair;
As secret as the wild bee's song
She lay there all the summer long.

I hid my love in field and town
Till e'en the breeze would knock me down;
The bees seemed singing ballads o'er,
20   The fly's bass turned a lion's roar;
And even silence found a tongue,
To haunt me all the summer long;
The riddle nature could not prove
Was nothing else but secret love.

after 1842   1920

A Vision

I lost the love of heaven above,
    I spurned the lust of earth below,
I felt the sweets of fancied love,
    And hell itself my only foe.

I lost earth's joys, but felt the glow
    Of heaven's flame abound in me,
Till loveliness and I did grow
    The bard of immortality.

I loved, but woman fell away;
10   I hid me from her faded flame.
I snatched the sun's eternal ray
    And wrote till earth was but a name.

In every language upon earth,
    On every shore, o'er every sea,
I gave my name immortal birth
    And kept my spirit with the free.

1844   1924

JOHN KEATS
1795–1821

The pathetically short-lived Keats abandoned the practice of medicine at twenty and gave himself entirely to poetry. His rapid poetic development reached a peak in the first eight months of 1819, with a concentrated production of brilliant poems, including *The Eve of St. Agnes* and the famous Odes. Ill with tuberculosis, he traveled to Italy in September 1820, in the frail hope that the climate would improve his condition, but died in Rome on February 23, 1821.

Haunted by premonitions of early death, Keats was keenly preoccupied both with sensuous delight and with the shadow of misfortune. In such poems as "Ode on Melancholy," "La Belle Dame sans Merci," "Ode on a Grecian Urn," and "Ode to a Nightingale" he suggests, with dazzling persuasiveness, that erotic fulfillment, artistic beauty, and flights of imagination offer ways to transcend the pains of the world; but the thought always stimulates the counter-realization of joy's impermanence. The great strength of Keats's poetry lies in its openness to the paradoxes and complexities of human experience, its closely woven strands of pleasure and pain. This openness is what Keats called, in one of his rich, thought-provoking letters to friends, "negative capability"—that is, the poet's ability to accept into his work all the contradictions and uncertainties contained in a full range of experience, without imposing on that experience his own illusions or limiting systems of belief.

Keats is one of the supreme masters in English of the lyric and the romance narrative. Here he shows a Shakespearean gift for expressing his thoughts in vivid, unexpected phrases and dense combinations of bold images. Keats loads his verse with images drawn from all the senses, particularly those of taste and touch, often managing to convey an impression of various—or even opposing—sensory experiences flowing together as one. Intricately beautiful patterns of sound and slow, even rhythms, reminiscent of Spenser's versification, characterize his mature style. Undervalued in Keats's time, his style influenced poetry throughout the nineteenth century, including the work of Tennyson, Arnold, and Hopkins.

On First Looking into Chapman's Homer[1]

Much have I travell'd in the realms of gold,
   And many goodly states and kingdoms seen;
   Round many western islands have I been
Which bards in fealty to Apollo[2] hold.
Oft of one wide expanse had I been told
   That deep-brow'd Homer ruled as his demesne;[3]
   Yet did I never breathe its pure serene[4]
Till I heard Chapman speak out loud and bold:
Then felt I like some watcher of the skies

[1] a translation of Homer's epics by the Elizabethan poet George Chapman. Introduced to Homer's works through reading Chapman, Keats was inspired to write this sonnet, his first major poem.
[2] **fealty to Apollo** loyalty to the god of poetry
[3] **demesne** domain
[4] **pure serene** clear atmosphere

10   When a new planet swims into his ken;
    Or like stout Cortez[5] when with eagle eyes
       He star'd at the Pacific—and all his men
    Look'd at each other with a wild surmise—
       Silent, upon a peak in Darien.

1816   1816

[5] **Cortez** Balboa, not Cortez, was the first Euro-
pean to see the Pacific from Darien in Panama;
Cortez, the conqueror of the Aztec Empire, may
have sprung to Keats's mind in association with
the idea of traveling in "realms of gold."

When I Have Fears That I May Cease To Be

    When I have fears that I may cease to be
       Before my pen has glean'd my teeming brain,
    Before high piled books, in charactry,[1]
       Hold like rich garners the full ripen'd grain;
    When I behold, upon the night's starr'd face,
       Huge cloudy symbols of a high romance,
    And think that I may never live to trace
       Their shadows, with the magic hand of chance;
    And when I feel, fair creature of an hour,
10   That I shall never look upon thee more,
    Never have relish in the fairy[2] power
       Of unreflecting love;—then on the shore
    Of the wide world I stand alone, and think
    Till love and fame to nothingness do sink.

1818   1848

[1] **charactry**   written letters of the alphabet
[2] **fairy**   magic

The Eve of St. Agnes[1]

I

    St. Agnes' Eve—Ah, bitter chill it was!
    The owl, for all his feathers, was a-cold;
    The hare limp'd trembling through the frozen grass,
    And silent was the flock in woolly fold:
    Numb were the Beadsman's[2] fingers, while he told
    His rosary, and while his frosted breath,
    Like pious incense from a censer old,

[1] The feast day of St. Agnes, a fourth-century
martyr and the patron saint of virgins, is Janu-
ary 21. According to legend, any young girl
who performed appropriate rituals on the eve-
ning before this saint's day would be granted a
vision of her future husband. Keats's narrative
romance, woven about this tradition, displays
the most successful use of the Spenserian stanza
form since Spenser's *The Faerie Queene*.
[2] **Beadsman**   Beadsmen were hired by noble
families to say the prayers of the rosary for
them.

Seem'd taking flight for heaven, without a death,
Past the sweet Virgin's picture, while his prayer he saith.

II

10 His prayer he saith, this patient, holy man;
Then takes his lamp, and riseth from his knees,
And back returneth, meagre, barefoot, wan,
Along the chapel aisle by slow degrees:
The sculptur'd dead, on each side, seem to freeze,
Emprison'd in black, purgatorial rails:[3]
Knights, ladies, praying in dumb orat'ries,[4]
He passeth by; and his weak spirit fails
To think how they may ache in icy hoods and mails.

III

Northward he turneth through a little door,
20 And scarce three steps, ere Music's golden tongue
Flatter'd to tears this aged man and poor;
But no—already had his deathbell rung;
The joys of all his life were said and sung:
His was harsh penance on St. Agnes' Eve:
Another way he went, and soon among
Rough ashes sat he for his soul's reprieve,
And all night kept awake, for sinner's sake to grieve.

IV

That ancient Beadsman heard the prelude soft;
And so it chanc'd, for many a door was wide,
30 From hurry to and fro. Soon, up aloft,
The silver, snarling trumpets 'gan to chide:
The level chambers, ready with their pride,
Were glowing to receive a thousand guests:
The carved angels, ever eager-eyed,
Star'd, where upon their heads the cornice rests,
With hair blown back, and wings put cross-wise on their breasts.

V

At length burst in the argent revelry,[5]
With plume, tiara, and all rich array,
Numerous as shadows haunting fairily
40 The brain, new stuff'd, in youth, with triumphs gay
Of old romance. These let us wish away,
And turn, sole-thoughted, to one Lady there,
Whose heart had brooded, all that wintry day,
On love, and wing'd St. Agnes' saintly care,
As she had heard old dames full many times declare.

---

[3]**rails** railings of confinement, as in a place of punishment ("purgatorial")
[4]**orat'ries** chapels

[5]**argent revelry** revelers, figuratively glittering like silver

VI

They told her how, upon St. Agnes' Eve,
Young virgins might have visions of delight,
And soft adorings from their loves receive
Upon the honey'd middle of the night,
50 If ceremonies due they did aright;
As, supperless to bed they must retire,
And couch supine their beauties, lily white;
Nor look behind, nor sideways, but require
Of heavens with upward eyes for all that they desire.

VII

Full of this whim was thoughtful Madeline:
The music, yearning like a god in pain,
She scarcely heard: her maiden eyes divine,
Fix'd on the floor, saw many a sweeping train
Pass by—she heeded not at all: in vain
60 Came many a tiptoe, amorous cavalier,
And back retir'd, not cool'd by high disdain;
But she saw not: her heart was otherwhere:
She sigh'd for Agnes' dreams, the sweetest of the year.

VIII

She danc'd along with vague, regardless eyes,
Anxious her lips, her breathing quick and short:
The hallow'd hour was near at hand: she sighs
Amid the timbrels,[6] and the throng'd resort
Of whisperers in anger, or in sport;
'Mid looks of love, defiance, hate, and scorn,
70 Hoodwink'd with faery fancy; all amort,[7]
Save to St. Agnes and her lambs unshorn,[8]
And all the bliss to be before to-morrow morn.

IX

So, purposing each moment to retire,
She linger'd still. Meantime, across the moors,
Had come young Porphyro, with heart on fire
For Madeline. Beside the portal doors,
Buttress'd[9] from moonlight, stands he, and implores
All saints to give him sight of Madeline,
But for one moment in the tedious hours,
80 That he might gaze and worship all unseen;
Perchance speak, kneel, touch, kiss—in sooth such things have been.

X

He ventures in: let no buzz'd whisper tell:
All eyes be muffled, or a hundred swords

---

[6]**timbrels** drums
[7]**amort** unconscious of everything
[8]**St. Agnes . . . unshorn** Lambs were shorn on
St. Agnes' Day, and the wool was later spun
into cloth by nuns (see ll. 115–17); "lambs
unshorn" is thus a way of alluding to the eve of
the feast day.
[9]**Buttress'd** shaded

Will storm his heart, Love's fev'rous citadel:
For him, those chambers held barbarian hordes,
Hyena foemen, and hot-blooded lords,
Whose very dogs would execrations howl
Against his lineage: not one breast affords
Him any mercy, in that mansion foul,
90   Save one old beldame,[10] weak in body and in soul.

XI

Ah, happy chance! the aged creature came,
Shuffling along with ivory-headed wand,
To where he stood, hid from the torch's flame,
Behind a broad hall-pillar, far beyond
The sound of merriment and chorus bland:
He startled her; but soon she knew his face,
And grasp'd his fingers in her palsied hand,
Saying, "Mercy, Porphyro! hie thee from this place;
They are all here to-night, the whole blood-thirsty race!

XII

100   "Get hence! get hence! there's dwarfish Hildebrand;
He had a fever late, and in the fit
He cursed thee and thine, both house and land:
Then there's that old Lord Maurice, not a whit
More tame for his gray hairs—Alas me! flit!
Flit like a ghost away."—"Ah, Gossip[11] dear,
We're safe enough; here in this arm-chair sit,
And tell me how"—"Good Saints! not here, not here;
Follow me, child, or else these stones will be thy bier."

XIII

He follow'd through a lowly arched way,
110   Brushing the cobwebs with his lofty plume,
And as she mutter'd "Well-a—well-a-day!"
He found him in a little moonlight room,
Pale, lattic'd, chill, and silent as a tomb.
"Now tell me where is Madeline," said he,
"O tell me, Angela, by the holy loom
Which none but secret sisterhood may see,
When they St. Agnes' wool are weaving piously."

XIV

"St. Agnes! Ah! it is St. Agnes' Eve—
Yet men will murder upon holy days:
120   Thou must hold water in a witch's sieve,
And be liege-lord of all the Elves and Fays,
To venture so:[12] it fills me with amaze

---

[10]**beldame** old hag
[11]**Gossip** literally, godmother; used here as an affectionate term of address for an old woman

[12]**Thou must . . . To venture so** Porphyro must think he commands magical powers if he believes he can succeed in his purpose.

To see thee, Porphyro!—St. Agnes' Eve!
God's help! my lady fair the conjuror plays
This very night: good angels her deceive!
But let me laugh awhile, I've mickle[13] time to grieve.''

XV

Feebly she laugheth in the languid moon,
While Porphyro upon her face doth look,
Like puzzled urchin on an aged crone
130 Who keepeth clos'd a wond'rous riddle-book,
As spectacled she sits in chimney nook.
But soon his eyes grew brilliant, when she told
His lady's purpose; and he scarce could brook[14]
Tears, at the thought of those enchantments cold,
And Madeline asleep in lap of legends old.

XVI

Sudden a thought came like a full-blown rose,
Flushing his brow, and in his pained heart
Made purple riot: then doth he propose
A stratagem, that makes the beldame start:
140 "A cruel man and impious thou art:
Sweet lady, let her pray, and sleep, and dream
Alone with her good angels, far apart
From wicked men like thee. Go, go!—I deem
Thou canst not surely be the same that thou didst seem.''

XVII

"I will not harm her, by all saints I swear,''
Quoth Porphyro: "O may I ne'er find grace
When my weak voice shall whisper its last prayer,
If one of her soft ringlets I displace,
Or look with ruffian passion in her face:
150 Good Angela, believe me by these tears;
Or I will, even in a moment's space,
Awake, with horrid shout, my foemen's ears,
And beard them, though they be more fang'd than wolves and bears.''

XVIII

"Ah! why wilt thou affright a feeble soul?
A poor, weak, palsy-stricken, churchyard thing,
Whose passing-bell[15] may ere the midnight toll;
Whose prayers for thee, each morn and evening,
Were never miss'd.''—Thus plaining,[16] doth she bring
A gentler speech from burning Porphyro;
160 So woful, and of such deep sorrowing,

---

[13]**mickle** much
[14]**brook** control

[15]**passing-bell** death knell
[16]**plaining** complaining

That Angela gives promise she will do
Whatever he shall wish, betide her weal or woe.

XIX

Which was, to lead him, in close secrecy,
Even to Madeline's chamber, and there hide
Him in a closet, of such privacy
That he might see her beauty unespied,
And win perhaps that night a peerless bride,
While legion'd fairies pac'd the coverlet,
And pale enchantment held her sleepy-eyed,
170   Never on such a night have lovers met.
Since Merlin paid his Demon all the monstrous debt.[17]

XX

"It shall be as thou wishest," said the Dame:
"All cates[18] and dainties shall be stored there
Quickly on this feast-night: by the tambour frame[19]
Her own lute thou wilt see: no time to spare,
For I am slow and feeble, and scarce dare
On such a catering trust my dizzy head.
Wait here, my child, with patience; kneel in prayer
The while: Ah! thou must needs the lady wed,
180   Or may I never leave my grave among the dead."

XXI

So saying, she hobbled off with busy fear.
The lover's endless minutes slowly pass'd;
The dame return'd, and whisper'd in his ear
To follow her; with aged eyes aghast
From fright of dim espial. Safe at last,
Through many a dusky gallery, they gain
The maiden's chamber, silken, hush'd, and chaste;
Where Porphyro took covert, pleas'd amain.[20]
His poor guide hurried back with agues in her brain.

XXII

190   Her falt'ring hand upon the balustrade,
Old Angela was feeling for the stair,
When Madeline, St. Agnes' charmed maid,
Rose, like a mission'd spirit, unaware:
With silver taper's light and pious care,
She turn'd, and down the aged gossip led
To a safe level matting. Now prepare,
Young Porphyro, for gazing on that bed;
She comes, she comes again, like ring-dove fray'd[21] and fled.

[17]l. 171 an obscure line, possibly alluding to
the Arthurian legend of Merlin the magician,
destroyed by Vivien, the woman he loved,
through spells that he himself had taught her
[18]cates delicacies

[19]tambour frame drum-shaped embroidery
frame
[20]amain greatly
[21]fray'd frightened

XXIII

Out went the taper as she hurried in;
200   Its little smoke, in pallid moonshine, died:
She clos'd the door, she panted, all akin
To spirits of the air, and visions wide:
No uttered syllable, or, woe betide!
But to her heart, her heart was voluble,
Paining with eloquence her balmy side;
As though a tongueless nightingale should swell
Her throat in vain, and die, heart-stifled, in her dell.

XXIV

A casement high and triple-arch'd there was,
All garlanded with carven imag'ries
210   Of fruits, and flowers, and bunches of knot-grass,
And diamonded with panes of quaint device,
Innumerable of stains and splendid dyes,
As are the tiger-moth's deep-damask'd[22] wings;
And in the midst, 'mong thousand heraldries,
And twilight saints, and dim emblazonings,[23]
A shielded scutcheon blush'd with blood of queens and kings.[24]

XXV

Full on this casement shone the wintry moon.
And threw warm gules[25] on Madeline's fair breast,
As down she knelt for heaven's grace and boon;
220   Rose-bloom fell on her hands, together prest,
And on her silver cross soft amethyst,
And on her hair a glory, like a saint:
She seem'd a splendid angel, newly drest,
Save wings, for heaven:—Porphyro grew faint:
She knelt, so pure a thing, so free from mortal taint.

XXVI

Anon his heart revives: her vespers done,
Of all its wreathed pearls her hair she frees;
Unclasps her warmed jewels one by one;
Loosens her fragrant boddice; by degrees
230   Her rich attire creeps rustling to her knees;
Half-hidden, like a mermaid in sea-weed,
Pensive awhile she dreams awake, and sees,
In fancy, fair St. Agnes in her bed,
But dares not look behind, or all the charm is fled.

XXVII

Soon, trembling in her soft and chilly nest,
In sort of wakeful swoon, perplex'd she lay,

---

[22]**deep-damask'd** adorned with wavy markings
[23]**emblazonings** heraldic decorations
[24]**blood . . . kings** royal colors displayed on a
coat of arms ("scutcheon")
[25]**gules** heraldic term for red

Until the poppied warmth of sleep oppress'd
Her soothed limbs, and soul fatigued away;
Flown, like a thought, until the morrow-day;
240   Blissfully haven'd both from joy and pain;
Clasp'd like a missal where swart Paynims[26] pray;
Blinded alike from sunshine and from rain,
As though a rose should shut, and be a bud again.

XXVIII

Stol'n to this paradise, and so entranced,
Porphyro gazed upon her empty dress,
And listen'd to her breathing, if it chanced
To wake into a slumberous tenderness;
Which when he heard, that minute did he bless,
And breath'd himself: then from the closet crept,
250   Noiseless as fear in a wide wilderness,
And over the hush'd carpet, silent, stept,
And 'tween the curtains peep'd, where lo!—how fast she slept.

XXIX

Then by the bed-side, where the faded moon
Made a dim, silver twilight, soft he set
A table, and, half anguish'd, threw thereon
A cloth of woven crimson, gold, and jet:—
O for some drowsy Morphean[27] amulet!
The boisterous, midnight, festive clarion,
The kettle-drum, and far-heard clarionet,
260   Affray his ears, though but in dying tone:—
The hall door shuts again, and all the noise is gone.

XXX

And still she slept an azure-lidded sleep,
In blanched linen, smooth, and lavender'd,
While he from forth the closet brought a heap
Of candied apple, quince, and plum, and gourd;
With jellies soother than the creamy curd,
And lucent syrops, tinct with cinnamon;
Manna and dates, in argosy transferr'd
From Fez; and spiced dainties, every one,
270   From silken Samarcand to cedar'd Lebanon.[28]

---

[26]**swart Paynims** dark pagans—a conscious echo of Spenser's *The Faerie Queene*, where the word "paynim" is common

[27]**Morphean** sleep-producing; from Morpheus, god of sleep

[28] ll. 262–70 In the dream brought by St. Agnes, the husband-to-be provided a feast for his beloved. Keats uses exotic, rich language to describe the delicacies Porphyro actually provides: "soother" (smoother); "lucent" (clear); "tinct" (tinged); "manna" (sweet gum); "argosy" (merchant ship). In the Middle Ages, Europeans regarded Fez, Samarcand, and Lebanon, centers of trade in the Islamic world, as exotic spots of wealth and luxury.

XXXI

These delicates he heap'd with glowing hand
On golden dishes and in baskets bright
Of wreathed silver: sumptuous they stand
In the retired quiet of the night,
Filling the chilly room with perfume light.—
"And now, my love, my seraph fair, awake!
Thou art my heaven, and I thine eremite:[29]
Open thine eyes, for meek St. Agnes' sake,
Or I shall drowse beside thee, so my soul doth ache."

XXXII

280
Thus whispering, his warm, unnerved arm
Sank in her pillow. Shaded was her dream
By the dusk curtains:—'twas a midnight charm
Impossible to melt as iced stream:
The lustrous salvers[30] in the moonlight gleam;
Broad golden fringe upon the carpet lies:
It seem'd he never, never could redeem
From such a stedfast spell his lady's eyes;
So mus'd awhile, entoil'd in woofed phantasies.[31]

XXXIII

290
Awakening up, he took her hollow lute,—
Tumultuous,—and, in chords that tenderest be,
He play'd an ancient ditty, long since mute,
In Provence call'd, "La belle dame sans mercy":[32]
Close to her ear touching the melody;—
Wherewith disturb'd, she utter'd a soft moan:
He ceased—she panted quick—and suddenly
Her blue affrayed eyes wide open shone:
Upon his knees he sank, pale as smooth-sculptured stone.

XXXIV

300
Her eyes were open, but she still beheld,
Now wide awake, the vision of her sleep:
There was a painful change, that nigh expell'd
The blisses of her dream so pure and deep:
At which fair Madeline began to weep,
And moan forth witless words with many a sigh;
While still her gaze on Porphyro would keep;
Who knelt, with joined hands and piteous eye,
Fearing to move or speak, she look'd so dreamingly.

XXXV

"Ah, Porphyro!" said she, "but even now
Thy voice was at sweet tremble in mine ear,

---

[29]**eremite** religious devotee
[30]**salvers** serving dishes
[31]**entoil'd . . . phantasies** entangled in woven
fantasies

[32]**"La belle . . . mercy"** "The lovely lady
without pity," a poem by the medieval French
poet Alain Chartier

Made tuneable with every sweetest vow;
310 And those sad eyes were spiritual and clear:
How chang'd thou art! how pallid, chill, and drear!
Give me that voice again, my Porphyro,
Those looks immortal, those complainings dear!
Oh leave me not in this eternal woe,
For if thou diest, my love, I know not where to go.''

XXXVI

Beyond a mortal man impassion'd far
At these voluptuous accents, he arose,
Ethereal, flush'd, and like a throbbing star
Seen mid the sapphire heaven's deep repose;
320 Into her dream he melted, as the rose
Blendeth its odour with the violet,—
Solution sweet: meantime the frost-wind blows
Like Love's alarum pattering the sharp sleet
Against the window-panes; St. Agnes' moon hath set.

XXXVII

'Tis dark: quick pattereth the flaw-blown[33] sleet:
"This is no dream, my bride, my Madeline!"
'Tis dark: the iced gusts still rave and beat:
"No dream, alas! alas! and woe is mine!
Porphyro will leave me here to fade and pine.—
330 Cruel! what traitor could thee hither bring?
I curse not, for my heart is lost in thine,
Though thou forsakest a deceived thing;—
A dove forlorn and lost with sick unpruned wing.''

XXXVIII

"My Madeline! sweet dreamer! lovely bride!
Say, may I be for aye thy vassal blest?
Thy beauty's shield, heart-shap'd and vermeil[34] dyed?
Ah, silver shrine, here will I take my rest
After so many hours of toil and quest,
A famish'd pilgrim,—saved by miracle.
Though I have found, I will not rob thy nest
340 Saving of thy sweet self; if thou think'st well
To trust, fair Madeline, to no rude infidel.

XXXIX

"Hark! 'tis an elfin-storm from faery land,
Of haggard[35] seeming, but a boon indeed:
Arise—arise! the morning is at hand;—
The bloated wassaillers[36] will never heed:—
Let us away, my love, with happy speed;

---

[33]**flaw-blown** blown in gusts
[34]**vermeil** vermilion

[35]**haggard** unruly, wild
[36]**wassaillers** merry-makers

There are no ears to hear, or eyes to see,—
Drown'd all in Rhenish and the sleepy mead:[37]
350   Awake! arise! my love, and fearless be,
For o'er the southern moors I have a home for thee.''

XL

She hurried at his words, beset with fears,
For there were sleeping dragons all around,
At glaring watch, perhaps, with ready spears—
Down the wide stairs a darkling way they found.—
In all the house was heard no human sound.
A chain-droop'd lamp was flickering by each door;
The arras,[38] rich with horseman, hawk, and hound,
Flutter'd in the besieging wind's uproar;
360   And the long carpets rose along the gusty floor.

XLI

They glide, like phantoms, into the wide hall;
Like phantoms, to the iron porch, they glide;
Where lay the Porter, in uneasy sprawl,
With a huge empty flaggon by his side:
The wakeful bloodhound rose, and shook his hide,
But his sagacious eye an inmate owns:[39]
By one, and one, the bolts full easy slide:—
The chains lie silent on the footworn stones;—
The key turns, and the door upon its hinges groans.

XLII

370   And they are gone; ay, ages long ago
These lovers fled away into the storm.
That night the Baron dreamt of many a woe,
And all his warrior-guests, with shade and form
Of witch, and demon, and large coffin-worm,
Were long be-nightmar'd. Angela the old
Died palsy-twitch'd, with meagre face deform;
The Beadsman, after thousand aves[40] told,
For aye unsought for slept among his ashes cold.

1819   1820

[37]**Rhenish . . . mead** Rhine wine and fermented honey liquor
[38]**arras** tapestry

[39]**an inmate owns** recognizes someone of the household
[40]**aves** Hail Marys (*Ave Maria*)

La Belle Dame sans Merci:[1]
A Ballad

I

O what can ail thee, knight at arms,
   Alone and palely loitering?
The sedge has wither'd from the lake,
   And no birds sing.

II

O what can ail thee, knight at arms,
   So haggard and so woe-begone?
The squirrel's granary is full,
   And the harvest's done.

III

I see a lily on thy brow
10   With anguish moist and fever dew,
And on thy cheeks a fading rose
   Fast withereth too.

IV

I met a lady in the meads,
   Full beautiful, a fairy's child;
Her hair was long, her foot was light,
   And her eyes were wild.

V

I made a garland for her head,
   And bracelets too, and fragrant zone;[2]
She look'd at me as she did love,
20   And made sweet moan.

VI

I set her on my pacing steed,
   And nothing else saw all day long,
For sidelong would she bend, and sing
   A fairy's song.

VII

She found me roots of relish sweet,
   And honey wild, and manna dew,[3]
And sure in language strange she said—
   I love thee true.

[1] from the title of a medieval poem by Alain Chartier, meaning "The Lovely Lady without Pity." Keats's manuscript version of the poem, presented here, is generally preferred to the published version of 1820.

[2] **fragrant zone** belt or girdle of sweet-smelling flowers

[3] **manna dew** a miraculous food, like that supplied to the Israelites in Exodus 16:14–36; this line also echoes Coleridge, "Kubla Khan," 1. 53: "For he on honey-dew hath fed."

VIII

30   She took me to her elfin grot,
            And there she wept, and sigh'd full sore,
        And there I shut her wild wild eyes[4]
            With kisses four.

IX

        And there she lulled me asleep,
            And there I dream'd—Ah! woe betide!
        The latest dream I ever dream'd
            On the cold hill's side.

X

        I saw pale kings, and princes too,
            Pale warriors, death pale were they all;
        They cried—"La belle dame sans merci
40   Hath thee in thrall!"

XI

        I saw their starv'd lips in the gloam
            With horrid warning gaped wide,
        And I awoke and found me here
            On the cold hill's side.

XII

        And this is why I sojourn here,
            Alone and palely loitering,
        Though the sedge is wither'd from the lake,
            And no birds sing.

        1819   1820

[4] l. 31 See Wordsworth, "Tintern Abbey,"
l. 119 (p. 504 above).

Bright Star, Would I Were Stedfast As Thou Art[1]

Bright star, would I were stedfast as thou art—
    Not in lone splendour hung aloft the night,
And watching, with eternal lids apart,
    Like nature's patient, sleepless eremite,[2]
The moving waters at their priestlike task
    Of pure ablution[3] round earth's human shores,
Or gazing on the new soft-fallen mask
    Of snow upon the mountains and the moors;

[1] revised from an earlier version and copied on a
blank page of Shakespeare's poems while Keats
was voyaging to Italy in September 1820

[2] eremite hermit, religious recluse
[3] ablution washing, particularly in a religious
ceremony

No—yet still stedfast, still unchangeable,
10   Pillow'd upon my fair love's ripening breast,
To feel for ever its soft swell and fall,
    Awake for ever in a sweet unrest,
Still, still to hear her tender-taken breath,
And so live ever—or else swoon to death.

1819–20   1838

Ode to Psyche[1]

O Goddess! hear these tuneless numbers, wrung
    By sweet enforcement and remembrance dear,
And pardon that thy secrets should be sung
    Even into thine own soft-conched[2] ear:
Surely I dreamt to-day, or did I see
    The winged Psyche with awaken'd eyes?
I wander'd in a forest thoughtlessly,
    And, on the sudden, fainting with surprise,
Saw two fair creatures, couched side by side
10   In deepest grass, beneath the whisp'ring roof
    Of leaves and trembled blossoms, where there ran
        A brooklet, scarce espied:
'Mid hush'd, cool-rooted flowers, fragrant-eyed,
    Blue, silver-white, and budded Tyrian,
They lay calm-breathing on the bedded grass;
    Their arms embraced, and their pinions[3] too;
    Their lips touch'd not, but had not bade adieu,
As if disjoined by soft-handed slumber,
And ready still past kisses to outnumber
20   At tender eye-dawn of aurorean love:[4]
        The winged boy I knew;
But who wast thou, O happy, happy dove?
        His Psyche true!

O latest born and loveliest vision far
    Of all Olympus' faded hierarchy![5]
Fairer than Phoebe's sapphire-region'd star,[6]

[1] "Psyche" means soul in Greek, and in ancient times was represented as a mortal woman beloved by Cupid (the "winged boy" of 1. 21), son of the goddess Venus (the story is told in *The Golden Ass* of Apuleius, a Roman author of the second century A.D.). After many trials, the lovers were united and Psyche herself became an immortal goddess. In Keats's Ode, Psyche may be interpreted as a personification of the poetic imagination.

[2] **soft-conched** seashell-like, though soft
[3] **pinions** wings
[4] 1. 20 waking (or opening of the eyes) to dawning love
[5] ll. 24 Psyche was not worshiped as a goddess until long after the classical gods of Mt. Olympus had become established, and she thus lacked temples of her own (1. 28).
[6] **sapphire-region'd star** the moon, ruled by the goddess Phoebe

Or Vesper,[7] amorous glow-worm of the sky;
Fairer than these, though temple thou hast none,
    Nor altar heap'd with flowers;
30   Nor virgin-choir to make delicious moan
    Upon the midnight hours;
No voice, no lute, no pipe, no incense sweet
    From chain-swung censer teeming;
No shrine, no grove, no oracle, no heat
    Of pale-mouth'd prophet dreaming.

O brightest! though too late for antique vows,
    Too, too late for the fond believing lyre,
When holy were the haunted forest boughs,
    Holy the air, the water, and the fire;
40   Yet even in these days so far retir'd
    From happy pieties, thy lucent fans,[8]
    Fluttering among the faint Olympians,
I see, and sing, by my own eyes inspired.
So let me be thy choir, and make a moan
    Upon the midnight hours;
Thy voice, thy lute, thy pipe, thy incense sweet
    From swinged censer teeming;
Thy shrine, thy grove, thy oracle, thy heat
    Of pale-mouth'd prophet dreaming.

50   Yes, I will be thy priest, and build a fane[9]
    In some untrodden region of my mind,
Where branched thoughts, new grown with pleasant pain,
    Instead of pines shall murmur in the wind:
Far, far around shall those dark-cluster'd trees
    Fledge[10] the wild-ridged mountains steep by steep;
And there by zephyrs, streams, and birds, and bees,
    The moss-lain Dryads[11] shall be lull'd to sleep;
And in the midst of this wide quietness
A rosy sanctuary will I dress
60   With the wreath'd trellis of a working brain,
    With buds, and bells, and stars without a name,
With all the gardener Fancy e'er could feign,
    Who breeding flowers, will never breed the same;
And there shall be for thee all soft delight
    That shadowy thought can win,
A bright torch, and a casement ope at night,
    To let the warm Love in![12]

1819   1820

---

[7]**Vesper** the evening star
[8]**lucent fans** bright wings
[9]**fane** temple
[10]**Fledge** feather

[11]**Dryads** wood nymphs
[12]ll. 66–67 In Apuleius' story Cupid (Love) used to come to Psyche at night through her casement window.

Ode to a Nightingale

I

My heart aches, and a drowsy numbness pains
  My sense, as though of hemlock[1] I had drunk,
Or emptied some dull opiate to the drains
  One minute past, and Lethe-wards[2] had sunk:
'Tis not through envy of thy happy lot,
  But being too happy in thine happiness,—
    That thou, light-winged Dryad of the trees,
      In some melodious plot
  Of beechen green, and shadows numberless,
10   Singest of summer in full-throated ease.

II

O, for a draught of vintage! that hath been
  Cool'd a long age in the deep-delved earth,
Tasting of Flora[3] and the country green,
  Dance, and Provençal song,[4] and sunburnt mirth!
O for a beaker full of the warm South,
  Full of the true, the blushful Hippocrene,[5]
    With beaded bubbles winking at the brim,
      And purple-stained mouth;
  That I might drink, and leave the world unseen,
20   And with thee fade away into the forest dim:

III

Fade far away, dissolve, and quite forget
  What thou among the leaves hast never known,
The weariness, the fever, and the fret
  Here, where men sit and hear each other groan;
Where palsy shakes a few, sad, last gray hairs,
  Where youth grows pale, and spectre-thin, and dies:
    Where but to think is to be full of sorrow
      And leaden-eyed despairs,
  Where Beauty cannot keep her lustrous eyes,
30   Or new Love pine at them beyond to-morrow.

IV

Away! away! for I will fly to thee,
  Not charioted by Bacchus and his pards,[6]
But on the viewless[7] wings of Poesy,

---

[1]**hemlock** an herb (not to be confused with the North American evergreen tree) and, hence, a poison derived from it, used to put the Greek philosopher Socrates to death
[2]**Lethe-wards** toward Lethe, underworld river of forgetfulness in classical mythology
[3]**Flora** Roman goddess of flowers
[4]**Provençal song** songs of Provence, in south-ern France, famous for its love poets in the Middle Ages
[5]**Hippocrene** fountain of the Muses (goddesses of artistic inspiration) on Mt. Helicon in Greece
[6]**Bacchus and his pards** the god of wine, whose chariot was said to be drawn by leo-pards (pards); hence, alcoholic intoxication
[7]**viewless** invisible

Though the dull brain perplexes and retards:
Already with thee! tender is the night,
And haply the Queen-Moon is on her throne,
    Cluster'd around by all her starry Fays;[8]
        But here there is no light,
Save what from heaven is with the breezes blown
40   Through verdurous glooms and winding mossy ways.

V

I cannot see what flowers are at my feet,
    Nor what soft incense hangs upon the boughs,
But, in embalmed[9] darkness, guess each sweet
    Wherewith the seasonable month endows
The grass, the thicket, and the fruit-tree wild;
    White hawthorn, and the pastoral eglantine;
        Fast fading violets cover'd up in leaves;
            And mid-May's eldest child,
The coming musk-rose, full of dewy wine,
50   The murmurous haunt of flies on summer eves.

VI

Darkling[10] I listen; and, for many a time
    I have been half in love with easeful Death,
Call'd him soft names in many a mused rhyme,
    To take into the air my quiet breath;
Now more than ever seems it rich to die,
    To cease upon the midnight with no pain,
        While thou art pouring forth thy soul abroad
            In such an ecstasy!
Still wouldst thou sing, and I have ears in vain—
60   To thy high requiem become a sod.

VII

Thou was not born for death, immortal Bird!
    No hungry generations tread thee down;
The voice I hear this passing night was heard
    In ancient days by emperor and clown:
Perhaps the self-same song that found a path
    Through the sad heart of Ruth,[11] when, sick for home,
        She stood in tears amid the alien corn;
            The same that oft-times hath
Charm'd magic casements, opening on the foam
70   Of perilous seas, in faery lands forlorn.

---

[8]**Fays** fairies
[9]**embalmed** perfumed
[10]**Darkling** in the dark
[11]**Ruth** Heroine of the Book of Ruth in the Bible,

Ruth is a Moabite woman in the land of Judah,
imagined by Keats as working in Judean grain
fields (hence "the alien corn" of l. 67).

VIII

Forlorn! the very word is like a bell
  To toll me back from thee to my sole self!
Adieu! the fancy cannot cheat so well
  As she is fam'd to do, deceiving elf.[12]
Adieu! adieu! thy plaintive anthem fades
  Past the near meadows, over the still stream,
    Up the hill-side; and now 'tis buried deep
      In the next valley-glades:
  Was it a vision, or a waking dream?
80   Fled is that music:—Do I wake or sleep?

1819   1819

[12]**elf** mischievous spirit

Ode on a Grecian Urn

I

Thou still unravish'd bride of quietness,
  Thou foster-child of silence and slow time,
Sylvan historian, who canst thus express
  A flowery tale more sweetly than our rhyme:
What leaf-fring'd legend haunts about thy shape
  Of deities or mortals, or of both,
    In Tempe or the dales of Arcady?[1]
What men or gods are these? What maidens loth?
What mad pursuit? What struggle to escape?
10   What pipes and timbrels?[2] What wild ecstasy?

II

Heard melodies are sweet, but those unheard
  Are sweeter; therefore, ye soft pipes, play on;
Not to the sensual ear, but, more endear'd,
  Pipe to the spirit ditties of no tone:
Fair youth, beneath the trees, thou canst not leave
  Thy song, nor ever can those trees be bare;
    Bold lover, never, never canst thou kiss,
Though winning near the goal—yet, do not grieve;
  She cannot fade, though thou hast not thy bliss,
20 For ever wilt thou love, and she be fair!

[1]**Tempe . . . Arcady** beautiful spots in ancient Greece, representative of the ideal pastoral state

[2]**timbrels** ancient tambourines

III

Ah, happy, happy boughs! that cannot shed
   Your leaves, nor ever bid the spring adieu;
And, happy melodist, unwearied,
   For ever piping songs for ever new;
More happy love! more happy, happy love!
   For ever warm and still to be enjoy'd,
     For ever panting, and for ever young;
All breathing human passion far above,
   That leaves a heart high-sorrowful and cloy'd,
30   A burning forehead, and a parching tongue.

IV

Who are these coming to the sacrifice?
   To what green altar, O mysterious priest,
Lead'st thou that heifer lowing at the skies,
   And all her silken flanks with garlands drest?
What little town by river or sea shore,
   Or mountain-built with peaceful citadel,
     Is emptied of this folk, this pious morn?
And, little town, thy streets for evermore
   Will silent be; and not a soul to tell
40   Why thou art desolate, can e'er return.

V

O Attic[3] shape! Fair attitude! with brede[4]
   Of marble men and maidens overwrought,[5]
With forest branches and the trodden weed;
   Thou, silent form, dost tease us out of thought
As doth eternity: Cold Pastoral!
   When old age shall this generation waste,
     Thou shalt remain, in midst of other woe
Than ours, a friend to man, to whom thou say'st,
   "Beauty is truth, truth beauty,"—that is all
50   Ye know on earth, and all ye need to know.[6]

1819   1820

[3] **Attic** of Attica, the region of Greece surrounding Athens
[4] **brede** embroidered design
[5] **overwrought** adorned all over

[6] ll. 49–50 Some scholars argue that all the words in the poem's last two lines compose the urn's statement to man and should be enclosed in quotation marks.

Ode on Melancholy

I

No, no, go not to Lethe,[1] neither twist
   Wolf's-bane, tight-rooted, for its poisonous wine;
Nor suffer thy pale forehead to be kiss'd
   By nightshade, ruby grape of Proserpine;[2]
Make not your rosary of yew-berries,[3]
   Nor let the beetle,[4] nor the death-moth be
     Your mournful Psyche,[5] nor the downy owl
A partner in your sorrow's mysteries;
   For shade to shade will come too drowsily,
10   And drown the wakeful anguish of the soul.

II

But when the melancholy fit shall fall
   Sudden from heaven like a weeping cloud,
That fosters the droop-headed flowers all,
   And hides the green hill in an April shroud;
Then glut thy sorrow on a morning rose,
   Or on the rainbow of the salt sand-wave,
     Or on the wealth of globed peonies;
Or if thy mistress some rich anger shows,
   Emprison her soft hand, and let her rave,
20   And feed deep, deep upon her peerless eyes.

III

She[6] dwells with Beauty—Beauty that must die;
   And Joy, whose hand is ever at his lips
Bidding adieu; and aching Pleasure nigh,
   Turning to poison while the bee-mouth sips:
Ay, in the very temple of Delight
   Veil'd Melancholy has her sovran[7] shrine,
     Though seen of none save him whose strenuous tongue
Can burst Joy's grape against his palate fine;[8]
   His soul shall taste the sadness of her might,
30   And be among her cloudy trophies[9] hung.

1819   1820

---

[1] **Lethe** river of forgetfulness in the underworld
[2] ll. 2–4 Wolf's-bane and nightshade are poisonous plants. **Proserpine** mythological queen of the underworld
[3] **yew-berries** Yew trees are associated with cemeteries.
[4] **beetle** Egyptian tomb symbol

[5] **Psyche** (Greek) the soul, often represented as a butterfly
[6] **She** the goddess Melancholy, not the "mistress" of l. 18
[7] **sovran** sovereign, i.e., chief or preeminent
[8] **fine** discriminating
[9] **trophies** memorials of victory or conquest displayed in temples and shrines

To Autumn[1]

I

Season of mists and mellow fruitfulness,
  Close bosom-friend of the maturing sun;
Conspiring with him how to load and bless
  With fruit the vines that round the thatch-eves run;
To bend with apples the moss'd cottage-trees,
  And fill all fruit with ripeness to the core;
    To swell the gourd, and plump the hazel shells
With a sweet kernel; to set budding more,
And still more, later flowers for the bees,
10 Until they think warm days will never cease,
    For summer has o'er-brimm'd their clammy cells.

II

Who hath not seen thee oft amid thy store?
  Sometimes whoever seeks abroad may find
Thee sitting careless on a granary floor,
  Thy hair soft-lifted by the winnowing wind;
Or on a half-reap'd furrow sound asleep,
  Drows'd with the fume of poppies, while thy hook[2]
    Spares the next swath and all its twined flowers:
And sometimes like a gleaner[3] thou dost keep
20 Steady thy laden head across a brook;
  Or by a cyder-press, with patient look,
    Thou watchest the last oozings hours by hours.

III

Where are the songs of spring? Ay, where are they?
  Think not of them, thou hast thy music too,—
While barred clouds bloom the soft-dying day,
  And touch the stubble-plains with rosy hue;
Then in a wailful choir the small gnats mourn
  Among the river sallows,[4] borne aloft
    Or sinking as the light wind lives or dies;
30 And full-grown lambs loud bleat from hilly bourn;[5]
  Hedge-crickets sing; and now with treble soft
  The red-breast whistles from a garden-croft;[6]
    And gathering swallows twitter in the skies.

1819   1820

[1] Two days after composing this poem in September 1819, Keats wrote to his friend Reynolds explaining what inspired it: "I never lik'd stubble fields so much as now—Aye better than the chilly green of the spring. Somehow a stubble plain looks warm—in the same way that some pictures look warm—This struck me so much in my Sunday's walk that I composed upon it."
[2] **hook** sickle
[3] **gleaner** one who collects grain left behind by reapers
[4] **sallows** willows
[5] **bourn** area
[6] **garden-croft** small farm plot, vegetable garden

RALPH WALDO EMERSON
1803–1882

Philosopher, essayist, and lecturer, Emerson spent nearly all his life in and around Boston, the center of American intellectual life at the time. He became a successful Unitarian minister but resigned in 1832. He later broke with the church entirely and turned to transcendentalism, which drew on European philosophical idealism and the teachings of Hinduism. His poem "Brahma" expresses the latter influence in its mystical sense of the oneness of God, nature, and the individual. His three published volumes of poetry combine lofty ideas with concrete images and plain language and, occasionally, as in "Hamatreya," with an almost twentieth-century colloquialism and hard wit. Calling for a new kind of American poetry, he stresses the radical notion that each individual can be his or her own prophet if at one with Nature. This conception had a profound influence, especially on his younger contemporary Walt Whitman and through him on many twentieth-century American poets.

The Rhodora[1]

ON BEING ASKED, WHENCE IS THE FLOWER?

In May, when sea-winds pierced our solitudes,
I found the fresh Rhodora in the woods,
Spreading its leafless blooms in a damp nook,
To please the desert[2] and the sluggish brook.
The purple petals, fallen in the pool,
Made the black water with their beauty gay;
Here might the red-bird come his plumes to cool,
And court the flower that cheapens his array.
Rhodora! if the sages ask thee why
10 This charm is wasted on the earth and sky,
Tell them, dear, that if eyes were made for seeing,
Then Beauty is its own excuse for being:
Why thou wert there, O rival of the rose!
I never thought to ask, I never knew:
But, in my simple ignorance, suppose
The self-same Power that brought me there brought you.

1834   1847

[1] **Rhodora** a species of rhododendron   [2] **desert** wilderness

The Snow-Storm

Announced by all the trumpets of the sky,
Arrives the snow, and, driving o'er the fields,
Seems nowhere to alight: the whited air
Hides hills and woods, the river, and the heaven,
And veils the farm-house at the garden's end.
The sled and traveller stopped, the courier's feet
Delayed, all friends shut out, the housemates sit
Around the radiant fireplace, enclosed
In a tumultuous privacy of storm.

10   Come see the north wind's masonry.
      Out of an unseen quarry evermore
      Furnished with tile, the fierce artificer
      Curves his white bastions with projected roof
      Round every windward stake, or tree, or door.
      Speeding, the myriad-handed, his wild work
      So fanciful, so savage, nought cares he
      For number or proportion. Mockingly,
      On coop or kennel he hangs Parian[1] wreaths;
      A swan-like form invests the hidden thorn;
20   Fills up the farmer's lane from wall to wall,
      Maugre[2] the farmer's sighs; and at the gate
      A tapering turret overtops the work.
      And when his hours are numbered, and the world
      Is all his own, retiring, as he were not,
      Leaves, when the sun appears, astonished Art
      To mimic in slow structures, stone by stone,
      Built in an age, the mad wind's night-work,
      The frolic architecture of the snow.

                                              1841

[1] **Parian** a fine type of marble used by ancient   [2] **maugre** despite
Greek sculptors

Hamatreya[1]

Bulkeley, Lee, Willard, Hosmer, Meriam, Flint,[2]
Possessed the land which rendered to their toil
Hay, corn, roots, hemp, flax, apples, wool, and wood.
Each of those landlords walked amidst his farm,
Saying, " 'Tis mine, my children's, and my name's.
How sweet the west wind sounds in my own trees!
How graceful climb those shadows on my hill!
I fancy these pure waters and the flags
Know me, as does my dog: we sympathize;
10   And, I affirm, my actions smack of the soil."
Where are these men? Asleep beneath their grounds;
And strangers, fond as they, their furrows plough.
Earth laughs in flowers, to see her boastful boys
Earth-proud, proud of the earth which is not theirs;
Who steer the plough, but cannot steer their feet
Clear of the grave.
They added ridge to valley, brook to pond,
And sighed for all that bounded their domain.
"This suits me for a pasture; that's my park;
20   We must have clay, lime, gravel, granite-ledge,
And misty lowland, where to go for peat.
The land is well,—lies fairly to the south.

[1] a variant of the Hindu name Maitreya, a figure   in this poem
in the ancient Sanskrit text the *Vishnu Purana*,   [2] l. 1   first settlers of Concord, Massachusetts,
from which Emerson derives the "Earth-Song"   where Emerson lived

'Tis good, when you have crossed the sea and back,
To find the sitfast acres where you left them.''
Ah! the hot owner sees not Death, who adds
Him to his land, a lump of mould the more.
Hear what the Earth says:—

EARTH-SONG

"Mine and yours;
Mine, not yours.
30   Earth endures;
Stars abide—
Shine down in the old sea;
Old are the shores;
But where are old men?
I who have seen much,
Such have I never seen.

"The lawyer's deed
Ran sure,
In tail,[3]
40   To them, and to their heirs
Who shall succeed,
Without fail,
Forevermore.

"Here is the land,
Shaggy with wood,
With its old valley,
Mound, and flood.
But the heritors?—
Fled like the flood's foam.
50   The lawyer, and the laws,
And the kingdom,
Clean swept herefrom.

"They called me theirs,
Who so controlled me;
Yet every one
Wished to stay, and is gone.
How am I theirs,
If they cannot hold me,
But I hold them?''

60   When I heard the Earth-song,
I was no longer brave;
My avarice cooled
Like lust in the chill of the grave.

1847

[3] **in tail** legally binding ("entailing") the inheri-
tance of an estate to a specific succession of
heirs

Days

Daughters of Time, the hypocritic Days,
Muffled and dumb like barefoot dervishes,[1]
And marching single in an endless file,
Bring diadems and fagots[2] in their hands.
To each they offer gifts after his will,
Bread, kingdoms, stars, and sky that holds them all.

I, in my pleached[3] garden, watching the pomp,
Forgot my morning wishes, hastily
Took a few herbs and apples, and the Day
10   Turned and departed silent. I, too late,
Under her solemn fillet[4] saw the scorn.

1852   1857

[1] **dervishes**   an order of Muslim ascetics, dedicated to poverty
[2] **fagots**   bundles of twigs used as firewood

[3] **pleached**   with branches interlaced
[4] **fillet**   headband

Brahma[1]

If the red slayer think he slays,
    Or if the slain think he is slain,
They know not well the subtle ways
    I keep, and pass, and turn again.

Far or forgot to me is near;
    Shadow and sunlight are the same;
The vanquished gods to me appear;
    And one to me are shame and fame.

They reckon ill who leave me out;
10   When me they fly, I am the wings;
I am the doubter and the doubt
    And I the hymn the Brahmin[2] sings.

The strong gods pine for my abode,
    And pine in vain the sacred Seven,[3]
But thou, meek lover of the good!
    Find me, and turn thy back on heaven.

1856   1857

[1] the supreme divinity of Hinduism, personifying the ultimate reality, of which the universe itself is an illusory appearance
[2] **the Brahmin**   member of the highest order in the Hindu caste system; a Hindu priest
[3] **sacred Seven**   the Maharishis or highest saints of Hindu belief

Two Rivers

Thy summer voice, Musketaquit,[1]
Repeats the music of the rain;
But sweeter rivers pulsing flit
Through thee, as thou through Concord Plain.

Thou in thy narrow banks are pent:
The stream I love unbounded goes
Through flood and sea and firmament;
Through light, through life, it forward flows.

I see the inundation sweet,
10   I hear the spending of the stream
Through years, through men, through nature fleet,
Through passion, thought, through power and dream.

Musketaquit, a goblin strong,
Of shard and flint makes jewels gay;
They lose their grief who hear his song,
And where he winds is the day of day.

So forth and brighter fares my stream,—
Who drink it shall not thirst again;[2]
No darkness stains its equal gleam,
20   And ages drop in it like rain.

1856   1858

[1] **Musketaquit**   a river in eastern Massachusetts
[2] l. 18   See John 4:14.

ELIZABETH BARRETT BROWNING

1806–1861

In her own lifetime Elizabeth Barrett Browning's poetry received greater acclaim than that of her husband, Robert Browning, and her work, deservedly, still has its admirers. She is also vividly remembered, still, as the heroine of a real-life romance, rescued from parental tyranny and poor health by Browning, with whom she eloped in 1846. *Sonnets from the Portuguese* (1850), a sequence detailing her love affair with Browning, shows an attractive intensity, and there is clear, vigorous language in some of her late lyrics.

From Sonnets from the Portuguese[1]

XLIII

How do I love thee? Let me count the ways.
I love thee to the depth and breadth and height
My soul can reach, when feeling out of sight
For the ends of Being and ideal Grace.
I love thee to the level of every day's
Most quiet need; by sun and candlelight.
I love thee freely, as men strive for Right;
I love thee purely, as they turn from Praise.
10   I love thee with the passion put to use
In my old griefs, and with my childhood's faith.
I love thee with a love I seemed to lose
With my lost saints,—I love thee with the breath.
Smiles, tears, of all my life!—and, if God choose,
I shall but love thee better after death.

1845–46   1850

[1] These love poems addressed to Browning are
lightly disguised as translations from a fictitious
Portuguese source.

A Musical Instrument

I
What was he doing, the great god Pan,[1]
    Down in the reeds by the river?
Spreading ruin and scattering ban,[2]
Splashing and paddling with hoofs of a goat,
And breaking the golden lilies afloat
    With the dragon-fly on the river.

II
He tore out a reed, the great god Pan,
    From the deep cool bed of the river:
The limpid water turbidly ran,
10   And the broken lilies a-dying lay,
And the dragon-fly had fled away,
    Ere he brought it out of the river.

III
High on the shore sate the great god Pan,
    While turbidly flowed the river;
And hacked and hewed as a great god can,

[1] In Greek myth, Pan is the god of woodlands and
pastures. Human-formed above the waist and
goat-like below, he is usually depicted playing a
reed flute; he once pursued a mortal woman
who escaped his attentions by turning into a
water reed.
[2] **ban** harm

With his hard bleak steel at the patient reed,
Till there was not a sign of a leaf indeed
  To prove it fresh from the river.

####### IV

He cut it short, did the great god Pan
20   (How tall it stood in the river!).
Then drew the pith, like the heart of a man,
Steadily from the outside ring,
And notched the poor dry empty thing
  In holes, as he sate by the river.

####### V

"This is the way," laughed the great god Pan
  (Laughed while he sate by the river),
"The only way, since gods began
To make sweet music, they could succeed."
Then, dropping his mouth to a hole in the reed,
30   He blew in power by the river.

####### VI

Sweet, sweet, sweet, O Pan!
  Piercing sweet by the river!
Blinding sweet, O great god Pan!
The sun on the hill forgot to die,
And the lilies revived, and the dragon-fly
  Came back to dream on the river.

####### VII

Yet half a beast is the great god Pan,
  To laugh as he sits by the river,
Making a poet out of a man:
40 The true gods sigh for the cost and pain,—
For the reed which grows nevermore again,
  As a reed with the reeds in the river.

1860   1862

HENRY WADSWORTH LONGFELLOW
1807–1882

In his own day Longfellow was the most famous of American poets, and many of his works such as the long narrative poems *Evangeline* (1847) and *The Song of Hiawatha* (1855) are still widely read. A professor of Romance languages at Harvard for nearly twenty years, Longfellow was influential in giving mid-nineteenth-century American readers a deeper awareness of European culture and literature. His sonnets on the great English poets (see, for example, "Chaucer") are successful in communicating not only the significance of these figures but also something of the flavor of their style. Longfellow is most valued by modern readers for his skillfully controlled lyrics of introspection and meditation; of these "Mezzo Cammin" is perhaps the most distinguished.

Mezzo Cammin[1]

WRITTEN AT BOPPARD, ON THE RHINE, AUGUST 25, 1842,
JUST BEFORE LEAVING FOR HOME

Half of my life is gone, and I have let
   The years slip from me and have not fulfilled
   The aspiration of my youth, to build
Some tower of song with lofty parapet.
Not indolence, nor pleasure, nor the fret
   Of restless passions that would not be stilled,
   But sorrow, and a care that almost killed,[2]
Kept me from what I may accomplish yet;
Though, half-way up the hill, I see the Past
10   Lying beneath me with its sounds and sights,—
   A city in the twilight dim and vast,
With smoking roofs, soft bells, and gleaming lights,—
   And hear above me on the autumnal blast
   The cataract of Death far thundering from the heights.

1842   1846

[1] an allusion to the first line of Dante's *Divine Comedy*, ''Nel mezzo del cammin di nostra vita'' (At the midpoint of the course of our life). When he wrote this sonnet, Longfellow was (like Dante at the start of his vision) thirty-five years old, the traditional half-way point in a person's life. [2] l. 7 grief over the death in 1835 of his first wife

From The Song of Hiawatha[1]

INTRODUCTION

Should you ask me, whence these stories?
Whence these legends and traditions,
With the odors of the forest,
With the dew and damp of meadows,
With the curling smoke of wigwams,
With the rushing of great rivers,
With their frequent repetitions,
And their wild reverberations,
As of thunder in the mountains?
10   I should answer, I should tell you,
''From the forests and the prairies,
From the great lakes of the Northland,
From the land of the Ojibways,
From the land of the Dacotahs,

[1] a long narrative poem about a legendary American Indian chieftain. In this work Longfellow applied the form of the European folk epic to native American materials. The poem's distinctive trochaic tetrameter was suggested by the Finnish epic *Kalevala*. Longfellow's major source of material on American Indian life and legends was the work of the ethnologist H.R. Schoolcraft (1793-1864), especially *Algic Researches* (1839).

From the mountains, moors, and fen-lands
Where the heron, the Shuh-shuh-gah,
Feeds among the reeds and rushes.
I repeat them as I heard them
From the lips of Nawadaha,
20 The musician, the sweet singer.''
    Should you ask where Nawadaha
Found these songs so wild and wayward,
Found these legends and traditions,
I should answer, I should tell you,
"In the bird's-nests of the forest,
In the lodges of the beaver,
In the hoof-prints of the bison,
In the eyry of the eagle!
    "All the wild-fowl sang them to him,
30 In the moorlands and the fen-lands,
In the melancholy marshes;
Chetowaik, the plover, sang them,
Mahng, the loon, the wild-goose, Wawa,
The blue heron, the Shuh-shuh-gah,
And the grouse, the Mushkodasa!''
    If still further you should ask me,
Saying, "Who was Nawadaha?
Tell us of this Nawadaha,''
I should answer your inquiries
40 Straightway in such words as follow.
    "In the vale of Tawasentha,
In the green and silent valley,
By the pleasant water-courses,
Dwelt the singer Nawadaha.
Round about the Indian village
Spread the meadows and the corn-fields,
And beyond them stood the forest,
Stood the groves of singing pine-trees,
Green in Summer, white in Winter,
50 Ever sighing, ever singing.
    "And the pleasant water-courses,
You could trace them through the valley,
By the rushing in the Spring-time,
By the alders in the Summer,
By the white fog in the Autumn,
By the black line in the Winter;
And beside them dwelt the singer,
In the vale of Tawasentha,
In the green and silent valley.
60   "There he sang of Hiawatha,
Sang the Song of Hiawatha,
Sang his wondrous birth and being,
How he prayed and how he fasted,
How he lived, and toiled, and suffered,

That the tribes of men might prosper,
That he might advance his people!"
    Ye who love the haunts of nature,
Love the sunshine of the meadow,
Love the shadow of the forest,
70   Love the wind among the branches,
And the rain-shower and the snow-storm,
And the rushing of great rivers
Through their palisades of pine-trees,
And the thunder in the mountains,
Whose innumerable echoes
Flap like eagles in their eyries;—
Listen to these wild traditions,
To this Song of Hiawatha!
    Ye who love a nation's legends,
80   Love the ballads of a people,
That like voices from afar off
Call to us to pause and listen,
Speak in tones so plain and childlike,
Scarcely can the ear distinguish
Whether they are sung or spoken;—
Listen to this Indian Legend,
To this Song of Hiawatha!
    Ye whose hearts are fresh and simple,
Who have faith in God and Nature,
90   Who believe that in all ages
Every human heart is human,
That in even savage bosoms
There are longings, yearnings, strivings
For the good they comprehend not,
That the feeble hands and helpless,
Groping blindly in the darkness,
Touch God's right hand in that darkness
And are lifted up and strengthened;—
Listen to this simple story,
100   To this Song of Hiawatha!
    Ye, who sometimes, in your rambles
Through the green lanes of the country,
Where the tangled barberry-bushes
Hang their tufts of crimson berries
Over stone walls gray with mosses,
Pause by some neglected graveyard,
For a while to muse, and ponder
On a half-effaced inscription
Written with little skill of song-craft,
110   Homely phrases, but each letter
Full of hope and yet of heart-break,
Full of all the tender pathos
Of the Here and the Hereafter;—

Stay and read this rude inscription,
Read this Song of Hiawatha!

1854-55   1855

Chaucer

An old man in a lodge within a park;
   The chamber walls depicted all around
   With portraitures of huntsman, hawk, and hound,
   And the hurt deer. He listeneth to the lark,
Whose song comes with the sunshine through the dark
   Of painted glass in leaden lattice bound;
   He listeneth and he laugheth at the sound,
   Then writeth in a book like any clerk.[1]
He is the poet of the dawn, who wrote
10   The Canterbury Tales, and his old age
Made beautiful with song; and as I read
I hear the crowing cock, I hear the note
   Of lark and linnet, and from every page
   Rise odours of ploughed field or flowery mead.

1873   1875

[1] **clerk** scholar. See the portrait of the Clerk
of Oxenford in the *General Prologue* to *The
Canterbury Tales* (above, p. 57).

The Tide Rises, the Tide Falls

The tide rises, the tide falls,
The twilight darkens, the curlew calls;
Along the sea-sands damp and brown
The traveller hastens toward the town,
   And the tide rises, the tide falls.

Darkness settles on roofs and walls,
But the sea, the sea in the darkness calls;
The little waves, with their soft, white hands,
Efface the footprints in the sands,
10   And the tide rises, the tide falls.

The morning breaks; the steeds in their stalls
Stamp and neigh, as the hostler calls;
The day returns, but nevermore
Returns the traveller to the shore,
   And the tide rises, the tide falls.

1880

EDGAR ALLAN POE
1809–1849

Poe's life seems to personify a stereotype: the neurotic, tormented artistic genius. He was from the start at odds with his foster father, and his adult life was marked by ill health, poverty, unhappy love-relationships, and alcoholism. Yet through his sometimes stormy career as a magazine writer and editor, Poe managed to make himself the most enduringly popular of American story tellers and the first major American theoretician of poetry and poetics. The gist of his poetic theory, elaborated in "The Philosophy of Composition" (1846) and "The Poetic Principle" (1850), is that brevity is essential to good poetry (the "absolute effect of even the best epic under the sun is a nullity"), and that "Beauty is the sole legitimate province of the poem." He considered didacticism (discursive explanation) totally hostile to real poetry.

Poe puts his theory into practice in his own poems, trying to create pure beauty, devoid of any didactic message, through exotic, haunting imagery and carefully contrived patterns of assonance and alliteration. While many of his poems suffer from excessive or crude application of these techniques, his most successful capture the morbid fascination of his famous prose tales, as in "The City in the Sea," or embody his theories of poetic beauty, as in "To Helen," with its exotically resonant images ("perfumed sea," "hyacinth hair"). Poe's poetic ideal affected the work of others later in the century—Swinburne and Rossetti in England, for example—and, through its profound influence on the French symbolist movement, left its mark on much twentieth-century poetry.

To Helen

Helen, thy beauty is to me
  Like those Nicéan[1] barks of yore,
That gently, o'er a perfumed sea,
  The weary, way-worn wanderer bore
  To his own native shore.

On desperate seas long wont to roam,
  Thy hyacinth hair,[2] thy classic face,
Thy Naiad[3] airs have brought me home
  To the glory that was Greece,
10 And the grandeur that was Rome.

Lo! in yon brilliant window-niche
  How statue-like I see thee stand,
The agate[4] lamp within thy hand!
  Ah, Psyche,[5] from the regions which
  Are Holy-Land!

1831, 1845

[1] **Nicéan** Scholars have failed to determine precisely what associations Poe attached to the word, although it enhances the classical atmosphere of the poem. Several ancient cities were named Nicea, or the term may derive from the Greek "Nike" or "Nice," meaning victory.

[2] **hyacinth hair** hair in clustered curls like the petals of the hyacinth flower

[3] **Naiad** a term from classical mythology designating nymphs of lakes, rivers, and springs

[4] **agate** a hard, semiprecious stone

[5] **Psyche** in classical legend, the beloved of Cupid. Psyche is said to have held a torch in her window to glimpse her lover coming to her. Cf. Keats, "Ode to Psyche," ll. 66–67 (p. 618 above).

Israfel

*And the angel Israfel, [whose heart-strings are a lute, and] who
has the sweetest voice of all God's creatures.* —KORAN[1]

In Heaven a spirit doth dwell
  "Whose heart-strings are a lute;"
None sing so wildly well
As the angel Israfel,
And the giddy stars (so legends tell)
Ceasing their hymns, attend the spell
  Of his voice, all mute.

Tottering above
  In her highest noon,
10   The enamoured moon
Blushes with love,
  While, to listen, the red levin[2]
  (With the rapid Pleiads,[3] even,
  Which were seven),
  Pauses in Heaven.

And they say (the starry choir
  And the other listening things)
That Israfeli's fire
Is owing to that lyre
20   By which he sits and sings—
The trembling living wire
  Of those unusual strings.

But the skies that angel trod,
  Where deep thoughts are a duty—
Where Love's a grown-up God—
  Where the Houri[4] glances are
Imbued with all the beauty
  Which we worship in a star.

Therefore, thou are not wrong,
30   Israfeli, who despisest
An unimpassioned song;
To thee the laurels belong,
  Best bard, because the wisest!
Merrily live, and long!

---

[1] a quotation not from the Koran itself but from
George Sale's "Preliminary Discourse" to his
translation of the Koran. The phrase in brackets
is Poe's own addition.
[2] **levin** lightning

[3] **Pleiads** a cluster of stars, the Pleiades (known
to the ancients as the Seven Sisters), in the con-
stellation Taurus
[4] **Houri** a pleasure-nymph of the Muslim para-
dise

The ecstasies above
　　With thy burning measures suit—
Thy grief, thy joy, thy hate, thy love,
　　With the fervour of thy lute—
　　Well may the stars be mute!

40　Yes, Heaven is thine; but this
　　Is a world of sweets and sours;
　　Our flowers are merely—flowers,
And the shadow of thy perfect bliss
　　Is the sunshine of ours.

If I could dwell
Where Israfel
　　Hath dwelt, and he where I,
He might not sing so wildly well
　　A mortal melody,
50　While a bolder note than this might swell
　　From my lyre within the sky.

　　　　　　　　　　1831, *1845*

The City in the Sea

Lo! Death has reared himself a throne
In a strange city lying alone
Far down within the dim West,
Where the good and the bad and the worst and the best
Have gone to their eternal rest.
There shrines and palaces and towers
(Time-eaten towers that tremble not!)
Resemble nothing that is ours.
Around, by lifting winds forgot,
10　Resignedly beneath the sky
The melancholy waters lie.

No rays from the holy heaven come down
On the long night-time of that town;
But light from out the lurid sea
Streams up the turrets silently—
Gleams up the pinnacles far and free
Up domes—up spires—up kingly halls—
Up fanes—up Babylon-like[1] walls—
Up shadowy long-forgotten bowers
20　Of sculptured ivy and stone flowers—
Up many and many a marvellous shrine
Whose wreathèd friezes intertwine
The viol, the violet, and the vine.

[1] **Babylon**　wealthy and powerful walled city of
ancient Mesopotamia

Resignedly beneath the sky
The melancholy waters lie.
So blend the turrets and shadows there
That all seem pendulous in air,
While from a proud tower in the town
Death looks gigantically down.

30   There open fanes and gaping graves
Yawn level with the luminous waves;
But not the riches there that lie
In each idol's diamond eye—
Not the gaily-jewelled dead
Tempt the waters from their bed;
For no ripples curl, alas!
Along that wilderness of glass—
No swellings tell that winds may be
Upon some far-off happier sea—
40   No heavings hint that winds have been
On seas less hideously serene.

But lo, a stir is in the air!
The wave—there is a movement there!
As if the towers had thrust aside,
In slightly sinking, the dull tide—
As if their tops had feebly given
A void within the filmy Heaven.
The waves have now a redder glow—
The hours are breathing faint and low—
50   And when, amid no earthly moans,
Down, down that town shall settle hence,
Hell, rising from a thousand thrones,
Shall do it reverence.

1831, *1845*

ALFRED, LORD TENNYSON
1809–1892

Tennyson was perhaps the last major English poet to achieve wide popularity, wealth, and social prestige solely through his poetry. Poet laureate of England for forty-two years and honored with a peerage in his old age, Tennyson became so popular that at least one volume of his poems was to be found in every genteel Victorian household. His polished verses seemed to express the important cultural, social, and religious concerns of the Victorian public. Yet Tennyson was actually a brooding, intense, very private man, as his best verse amply displays. Throughout his poetry, whether in such early lyrics as "Ulysses," "The Lady of Shalott," and "Tithonus," or in the relatively late "monodrama" *Maud*, runs a drama of conflicting yearnings: for private emotional fulfillments and for attachments to the public world of duty and responsibility. Though in later life he gave increasing weight to public over private and subjective concerns, the conflict remains in his poetry.

The single most powerful influence on Tennyson's life and work was his youthful friendship at Cambridge University with the brilliant, sensitive Arthur Hallam. Hallam's sudden death in 1833 devastated Tennyson emotionally; for most of the following decade he led a withdrawn life, looking for some deeper meaning in the loss. At the same time he devoted himself to the discipline of his poetic craft and learned to give a distanced, impersonal edge to poems born of personal grief or yearning. In 1842 he published a two-volume set of collected poems, which brought him his first substantial recognition. Full popular success came in 1850 with the publication of *In Memoriam*,

a long elegiac sequence of lyrics centered on the death of Hallam, mingling reflections on spiritual issues of the age with passages of intense personal feeling. Among Tennyson's major later works, *Maud* (1855) is an important experiment in dramatizing the workings of a troubled mind, and the epic *Idylls of the King* (1859–85) recasts the legends of King Arthur in psychologically realistic narratives.

Much of Tennyson's success stems from his mastery of sound and rhythm. His melodious patterns, combined with a careful choice of image and direction, are especially effective—as in "The Lady of Shalott" and "Tears, Idle Tears"—in evoking far-off dreamy settings and a nostalgic atmosphere. At his best, he is the natural inheritor of the art of Spenser and Keats.

Mariana

Mariana in the moated grange[1]

—MEASURE FOR MEASURE

With blackest moss the flower-plots
  Were thickly crusted, one and all:
The rusted nails fell from the knots
  That held the pear to the gable-wall.
The broken sheds looked sad and strange:
  Unlifted was the clinking latch;
  Weeded and worn the ancient thatch
Upon the lonely moated grange.
    She only said, "My life is dreary,
10   He cometh not," she said;
    She said, "I am aweary, aweary,
      I would that I were dead!"

Her tears fell with the dews at even;
  Her tears fell ere the dews were dried;
She could not look on the sweet heaven,
  Either at morn or eventide.
After the flitting of the bats,
  When thickest dark did trance[2] the sky,
  She drew her casement-curtain by,
20 And glanced athwart the glooming flats.
    She only said, "The night is dreary,

---

[1] In Shakespeare's *Measure for Measure* (III.i.212 ff.), Mariana, forsaken by her lover, is said to wait for him in solitary dejection "at the moated grange" (farm house).

[2] **trance** throw into a trance

He cometh not," she said;
     She said, "I am aweary, aweary,
       I would that I were dead!"

Upon the middle of the night,
    Waking she heard the night-fowl crow;
The cock sung out an hour ere light:
    From the dark fen the oxen's low
Came to her; without hope of change,
30   In sleep she seemed to walk forlorn,
Till cold winds woke the gray-eyed morn
About the lonely moated grange.
     She only said, "The day is dreary,
      He cometh not," she said;
     She said, "I am aweary, aweary,
       I would that I were dead!"

About a stone-cast from the wall
    A sluice with blackened waters slept,
And o'er it many, round and small,
40   The clustered marish-mosses[3] crept.
Hard by a poplar shook alway,
    All silver-green with gnarlèd bark:
For leagues no other tree did mark
    The level waste, the rounding gray.
     She only said, "My life is dreary,
      He cometh not," she said;
     She said, "I am aweary, aweary,
       I would that I were dead!"

And ever when the moon was low,
50   And the shrill winds were up and away,
In the white curtain, to and fro,
    She saw the gusty shadow sway.
But when the moon was very low,
    And wild winds bound within their cell,[4]
The shadow of the poplar fell
Upon her bed, across her brow.
     She only said, "The night is dreary,
      He cometh not," she said;
     She said, "I am aweary, aweary,
60   I would that I were dead!"

All day within the dreamy house,
    The doors upon their hinges creaked;
The blue fly sung in the pane; the mouse
    Behind the mouldering wainscot shrieked,
Or from the crevice peered about.

[3] **marish-mosses** lumps of floating marsh-moss
[4] **cell** the mythical cave of the winds, kept by
the wind-god Aeolus

Old faces glimmered through the doors,
Old footsteps trod the upper floors,
Old voices called her from without.
    She only said, "My life is dreary,
70   He cometh not," she said;
    She said, "I am aweary, aweary,
       I would that I were dead!"

The sparrow's chirrup on the roof,
    The slow clock ticking, and the sound
Which to the wooing wind aloof
    The poplar made, did all confound
Her sense; but most she loathed the hour
    When the thick-moted sunbeam lay
Athwart the chambers, and the day
80 Was sloping toward his western bower.
    Then, said she, "I am very dreary,
       He will not come," she said;
    She wept, "I am aweary, aweary,
       Oh God, that I were dead!"

                 1830

The Lady of Shalott[1]

PART I

On either side the river lie
Long fields of barley and of rye,
That clothe the wold[2] and meet the sky;
And through the field the road runs by
    To many-towered Camelot;[3]
And up and down the people go,
Gazing where the lilies blow[4]
Round an island there below,
    The island of Shalott.

10 Willows whiten, aspens quiver,
Little breezes dusk[5] and shiver
Through the wave that runs for ever
By the island in the river
    Flowing down to Camelot.
Four gray walls, and four gray towers,
Overlook a space of flowers,
And the silent isle imbowers
    The Lady of Shalott.

[1] a highly fantasized early version of the tale of
Lancelot and Elaine, the maid of Astolat (or, as
here, Shalott), which Tennyson later elaborated
and naturalized in his Arthurian epic, *Idylls of
the King*

[2] **wold** high, rolling plain
[3] **Camelot** the legendary capital of King
Arthur's domain
[4] **blow** blossom
[5] **dusk** make shadows

By the margin, willow-veiled,
20 Slide the heavy barges trailed
By slow horses; and unhailed
The shallop[6] flitteth silken-sailed
　　Skimming down to Camelot;
But who hath seen her wave her hand?
Or at the casement seen her stand?
Or is she known in all the land,
　　The Lady of Shalott?

Only reapers, reaping early
In among the bearded barley,
30 Hear a song that echoes cheerly
From the river winding clearly,
　　Down to towered Camelot:
And by the moon the reaper weary,
Piling sheaves in uplands airy,
Listening, whispers " 'Tis the fairy
　　Lady of Shalott."

PART II

There she weaves by night and day
A magic web[7] with colours gay.
She has heard a whisper say,
40 A curse is on her if she stay
　　To look down to Camelot.
She knows not what the curse may be,
And so she weaveth steadily,
And little other care hath she,
　　The Lady of Shalott.

And moving through a mirror clear
That hangs before her all the year,
Shadows of the world appear.
There she sees the highway near
50 　　Winding down to Camelot;
There the river eddy whirls,
And there the surly village-churls,
And the red cloaks of market girls,
　　Pass onward from Shalott.

Sometimes a troop of damsels glad,
An abbot on an ambling pad,[8]
Sometimes a curly shepherd-lad,
Or long-haired page in crimson clad,
　　Goes by to towered Camelot;

[6]**shallop** little boat
[7]**web** tapestry
[8]**pad** gentle, slow-paced horse

60 And sometimes through the mirror blue
 The knights come riding two and two:
 She hath no loyal knight and true,
  The Lady of Shalott.

 But in her web she still delights
 To weave the mirror's magic sights,
 For often through the silent nights
 A funeral, with plumes and lights
  And music, went to Camelot;
 Or when the moon was overhead,
70 Came two young lovers lately wed:
 "I am half sick of shadows," said
  The Lady of Shalott.

   PART III

 A bow-shot from her bower-eaves,
 He rode between the barley-sheaves,
 The sun came dazzling through the leaves,
 And flamed upon the brazen greaves[9]
  Of bold Sir Lancelot.
 A red-cross knight[10] for ever kneeled
 To a lady in his shield,
80 That sparkled on the yellow field,
  Beside remote Shalott.

 The gemmy bridle glittered free,
 Like to some branch of stars we see
 Hung in the golden Galaxy.
 The bridle bells rang merrily
  As he rode down to Camelot;
 And from his blazoned baldric[11] slung
 A mighty silver bugle hung,
 And as he rode his armour rung,
90 Beside remote Shalott.

 All in the blue unclouded weather
 Thick-jewelled shone the saddle-leather,
 The helmet and the helmet-feather
 Burned like one burning flame together,
  As he rode down to Camelot.
 As often through the purple night,
 Below the starry clusters bright,
 Some bearded meteor, trailing light,
  Moves over still Shalott.

[9]**greaves** armor protecting the shins
[10]**red-cross knight** the hero of Spenser's *The Faerie Queene*, Bk. I, a version of St. George

[11]**baldric** ornamented shoulder belt for the attachment of a bugle or sword

100   His broad clear brow in sunlight glowed;
      On burnished hooves his war-horse trode;
      From underneath his helmet flowed
      His coal-black curls as on he rode,
          As he rode down to Camelot.
      From the bank and from the river
      He flashed into the crystal mirror,
      "Tirra lirra," by the river
          Sang Sir Lancelot.

      She left the web, she left the loom,
110   She made three paces through the room,
      She saw the water-lily bloom,
      She saw the helmet and the plume,
          She looked down to Camelot.
      Out flew the web and floated wide;
      The mirror cracked from side to side;
      "The curse is come upon me," cried
          The Lady of Shalott.

      PART IV

      In the stormy east-wind straining,
      The pale yellow woods were waning,
120   The broad stream in his banks complaining.
      Heavily the low sky raining
          Over towered Camelot;
      Down she came and found a boat
      Beneath a willow left afloat,
      And round about the prow she wrote
          The Lady of Shalott.

      And down the river's dim expanse
      Like some bold seër in a trance,
      Seeing all his own mischance—
130   With a glassy countenance
          Did she look to Camelot.
      And at the closing of the day
      She loosed the chain, and down she lay;
      The broad stream bore her far away,
          The Lady of Shalott.

      Lying, robed in snowy white
      That loosely flew to left and right—
      The leaves upon her falling light—
      Through the noises of the night
140   She floated down to Camelot;
      And as the boat-head wound along
      The willowy hills and fields among,
      They heard her singing her last song,
          The Lady of Shalott.

Heard a carol, mournful, holy,
Chanted loudly, chanted lowly,
Till her blood was frozen slowly,
And her eyes were darkened wholly,
    Turned to towered Camelot.
150 For ere she reached upon the tide
The first house by the water-side,
Singing in her song she died,
    The Lady of Shalott.

Under tower and balcony,
By garden-wall and gallery,
A gleaming shape she floated by,
Dead-pale between the houses high,
    Silent into Camelot.
Out upon the wharfs they came,
160 Knight and burgher, lord and dame,
And round the prow they read her name,
    The Lady of Shalott.

Who is this? and what is here?
And in the lighted palace near
Died the sound of royal cheer;
And they crossed themselves for fear,
    All the knights at Camelot:
But Lancelot mused a little space;
He said, "She has a lovely face;
170 God in his mercy lend her grace,
    The Lady of Shalott."

1832, *1842*

Ulysses[1]

It little profits that an idle king,
By this still hearth, among these barren crags,
Matched with an agèd wife, I mete and dole
Unequal laws[2] unto a savage race,
That hoard, and sleep, and feed, and know not me.

I cannot rest from travel: I will drink
Life to the lees: all times I have enjoyed
Greatly, have suffered greatly, both with those
That loved me, and alone; on shore, and when
10 Through scudding drifts the rainy Hyades[3]

[1] According to Dante, *Inferno* XXVI, the wandering hero of Homer's *Odyssey* made one last journey out beyond the Mediterranean into unknown seas, from which he never returned. This dramatic monologue portrays Ulysses in his home kingdom of Ithaca, sometime after his return from the Trojan War, formulating his decision to make this journey.
[2] **unequal laws** laws appropriate to the primitive society of Ithaca
[3] **Hyades** a cluster of stars in the constellation Taurus, said to herald the start of the rainy season

Vext the dim sea: I am become a name;
For always roaming with a hungry heart
Much have I seen and known; cities of men
And manners, climates, councils, governments,
Myself not least, but honoured of them all;
And drunk delight of battle with my peers,
Far on the ringing plains of windy Troy.
I am a part of all that I have met;
Yet all experience is an arch wherethrough

20 Gleams that untravelled world, whose margin fades
For ever and for ever when I move.
How dull it is to pause, to make an end,
To rust unburnished, not to shine in use!
As though to breathe were life. Life piled on life
Were all too little, and of one to me
Little remains: but every hour is saved
From that eternal silence, something more,
A bringer of new things; and vile it were
For some three suns to store and hoard myself,

30 And this gray spirit yearning in desire
To follow knowledge like a sinking star,
Beyond the utmost bound of human thought.

This is my son, mine own Telemachus,
To whom I leave the sceptre and the isle—
Well-loved of me, discerning to fulfil
This labour, by slow prudence to make mild
A rugged people, and through soft degrees
Subdue them to the useful and the good.
Most blameless is he, centred in the sphere

40 Of common duties, decent not to fail
In offices of tenderness, and pay
Meet adoration to my household gods,
When I am gone. He works his work, I mine.

There lies the port; the vessel puffs her sail:
There gloom the dark broad seas. My mariners,
Souls that have toiled, and wrought, and thought with me—
That ever with a frolic welcome took
The thunder and the sunshine, and opposed
Free hearts, free foreheads—you and I are old;

50 Old age hath yet his honour and his toil;
Death closes all: but something ere the end,
Some work of noble note, may yet be done,
Not unbecoming men that strove with Gods.
The lights begin to twinkle from the rocks:

The long day wanes: the slow moon climbs: the deep
Moans round with many voices. Come, my friends,
'Tis not too late to seek a newer world.

Push off, and sitting well in order smite
The sounding furrows; for my purpose holds
60 To sail beyond the sunset, and the baths
Of all the western stars, until I die.
It may be that the gulfs will wash us down;
It may be we shall touch the Happy Isles,[4]
And see the great Achilles,[5] whom we knew.
Though much is taken, much abides; and though
We are not now that strength which in old days
Moved earth and heaven, that which we are, we are;
One equal temper of heroic hearts,
Made weak by time and fate, but strong in will
70 To strive, to seek, to find, and not to yield.

1833   1842

[4] **Happy Isles** Elysium, or the Isles of the Blessed, where virtuous and heroic souls dwelt after death

[5] **Achilles** the chief of the Greek heroes in the Trojan War

Tithonus[1]

The woods decay, the woods decay and fall,
The vapours weep their burthen to the ground,
Man comes and tills the field and lies beneath,
And after many a summer dies the swan.
Me only cruel immortality
Consumes: I wither slowly in thine arms,
Here at the quiet limit of the world,
A white-haired shadow roaming like a dream
The ever-silent spaces of the East,
10 Far-folded mists, and gleaming halls of morn.

Alas! for this gray shadow, once a man—
So glorious in his beauty and thy choice,
Who madest him thy chosen, that he seemed
To his great heart none other than a God!
I asked thee, "Give me immortality."
Then didst thou grant mine asking with a smile,
Like wealthy men who care not how they give.
But thy strong Hours[2] indignant worked their wills,
And beat me down and marred and wasted me,
20 And though they could not end me, left me maimed
To dwell in presence of immortal youth,
Immortal age beside immortal youth,
And all I was, in ashes. Can thy love,

[1] in Greek legend, a Trojan prince beloved of Aurora, goddess of the dawn. Aurora petitioned the gods successfully to grant Tithonus immortality but forgot to ask them to give him eternal youth. In this address to his beloved, the decrepit Tithonus laments his interminable aging.
[2] **Hours** personified Hours of the day, companions of the dawn goddess

Thy beauty, make amends, though even now,
Close over us, the silver star,[3] thy guide,
Shines in those tremulous eyes that fill with tears
To hear me? Let me go: take back thy gift:
Why should a man desire in any way
To vary from the kindly race of men,
30   Or pass beyond the goal of ordinance
Where all should pause, as is most meet for all?

    A soft air fans the cloud apart; there comes
A glimpse of that dark world where I was born.
Once more the old mysterious glimmer steals
From thy pure brows, and from thy shoulders pure,
And bosom beating with a heart renewed.
Thy cheek begins to redden through the gloom,
Thy sweet eyes brighten slowly close to mine,
Ere yet they blind the stars, and the wild team[4]
40   Which love thee, yearning for thy yoke, arise,
And shake the darkness from their loosened manes,
And beat the twilight into flakes of fire.

    Lo! ever thus thou growest beautiful
In silence, then before thine answer given
Departest, and thy tears are on my cheek.

    Why wilt thou ever scare me with thy tears,
And make me tremble lest a saying learnt,
In days far-off, on that dark earth, be true?
"The Gods themselves cannot recall their gifts."

50   Ay me! ay me! with what another heart
In days far-off, and with what other eyes
I used to watch—if I be he that watched—
The lucid outline forming round thee; saw
The dim curls kindle into sunny rings;
Changed with thy mystic change, and felt my blood
Glow with the glow that slowly crimsoned all
Thy presence and thy portals, while I lay,
Mouth, forehead, eyelids, growing dewy-warm
With kisses balmier than half-opening buds
60   Of April, and could hear the lips that kissed
Whispering I knew not what of wild and sweet,
Like that strange song I heard Apollo sing,
While Ilion like a mist rose into towers.[5]

    Yet hold me not for ever in thine East:
How can my nature longer mix with thine?

[3] **silver star** the morning star
[4] **wild team** horses that draw Aurora's chariot
[5] **Ilion . . . towers** towers and walls of Troy
(Ilion), said to have been built by the music of Apollo

Coldly thy rosy shadows bathe me, cold
Are all thy lights, and cold my wrinkled feet
Upon thy glimmering thresholds, when the steam
Floats up from those dim fields about the homes
70 Of happy men that have the power to die,
And grassy barrows[6] of the happier dead.
Release me, and restore me to the ground;
Thou seëst all things, thou wilt see my grave:
Thou wilt renew thy beauty morn by morn;
I earth in earth forget these empty courts,
And thee returning on thy silver wheels.

1833   1860

[6] **barrows** burial mounds

From The Princess

Tears, Idle Tears[1]

Tears, idle tears, I know not what they mean,
Tears from the depth of some divine despair
Rise in the heart, and gather to the eyes,
In looking on the happy Autumn-fields,
And thinking of the days that are no more.

Fresh as the first beam glittering on a sail,
That brings our friends up from the underworld,
Sad as the last which reddens over one
That sinks with all we love below the verge;
10 So sad, so fresh, the days that are no more.

Ah, sad and strange as in dark summer dawns
The earliest pipe of half-awakened birds
To dying ears, when unto dying eyes
The casement slowly grows a glimmering square;
So sad, so strange, the days that are no more.

Dear as remembered kisses after death,
And sweet as those by hopeless fancy feigned
On lips that are for others; deep as love,
Deep as first love, and wild with all regret;
20 O Death in Life, the days that are no more.

1847

[1] "This song came to me on the yellowing autumn-tide at Tintern Abbey, full for me of its bygone memories" (Tennyson's comment). The memories may include Arthur Hallam, whose grave is nearby, and Wordsworth's "Tintern Abbey," with its somewhat similar theme.

From In Memoriam A.H.H.[1]

I

I held it truth, with him who sings
    To one clear harp in divers tones,[2]
    That men may rise on stepping-stones
Of their dead selves to higher things.

But who shall so forecast the years
    And find in loss a gain to match?
    Or reach a hand through time to catch
The far-off interest of tears?

Let Love clasp Grief lest both be drowned,
10   Let darkness keep her raven gloss:
    Ah, sweeter to be drunk with loss,
To dance with death, to beat the ground,

Than that the victor Hours should scorn
    The long result of love, and boast,
    "Behold the man that loved and lost,
But all he was is overworn."

    . . .

VII

Dark house,[3] by which once more I stand
    Here in the long unlovely street,
    Doors, where my heart was used to beat
So quickly, waiting for a hand,

A hand that can be clasped no more—
    Behold me, for I cannot sleep,
    And like a guilty thing I creep[4]
At earliest morning to the door.

He is not here; but far away
10   The noise of life begins again,
    And ghastly through the drizzling rain
On the bald street breaks the blank day.

    . . .

---

[1] *In Memoriam*, generally considered Tennyson's most important work, is a record of the poet's grief for the death of his friend Arthur Henry Hallam. Composed in brief, loosely connected sections over a period of seventeen years, it won on its publication in 1850 the universal acclaim of Victorian readers, who found in the poem strong grounds for sustaining religious faith despite the doubt and materialism of the age. More recent readers tend to admire the personal intensity of the lyrics. *In Memoriam* is notable for its extensive and exemplary use of abba rhymed stanzas.

[2] **him . . . tones** Tennyson identified this figure as the great German poet Goethe.

[3] **Dark house** Hallam's house on Wimpole Street, in London

[4] **And like . . . I creep** Cf. Wordsworth, "Ode: Intimations of Immortality," 1. 148 (p. 522 above) and Shakespeare, *Hamlet* I.i. 148.

XI

Calm is the morn without a sound,
  Calm as to suit a calmer grief,
  And only through the faded leaf
The chestnut pattering to the ground:

Calm and deep peace on this high wold,[5]
  And on these dews that drench the furze,[6]
  And all the silvery gossamers
That twinkle into green and gold:

Calm and still light on yon great plain
10 That sweeps with all its autumn bowers,
  And crowded farms and lessening towers,
To mingle with the bounding main:

Calm and deep peace in this wide air,
  These leaves that redden to the fall;
  And in my heart, if calm at all,
If any calm, a calm despair:

Calm on the seas, and silver sleep,
  And waves that sway themselves in rest,
  And dead calm in that noble breast
20 Which heaves but with the heaving deep.[7]

      . . .

LIV[8]

Oh yet we trust that somehow good
  Will be the final goal of ill,
  To pangs of nature, sins of will,
Defects of doubt, and taints of blood;

That nothing walks with aimless feet;
  That not one life shall be destroyed,
  Or cast as rubbish to the void,
When God hath made the pile complete;

That not a worm is cloven in vain;
10 That not a moth with vain desire
  Is shrivelled in a fruitless fire,
Or but subserves another's gain.

Behold, we know not anything;
  I can but trust that good shall fall

[5]**wold** rolling plain
[6]**furze** low shrubs with yellow flowers, growing on open land
[7]**Calm on the seas . . . the heaving deep** The poet imagines the body of Hallam, who died in Vienna, being brought back to England by ship.
[8]Sections LIV–LVI deal with the crisis in religious faith brought about by the growing

scientific evidence of biological evolution, as revealed in geological and fossil discoveries. Tennyson's distress, fed by such works as Lyell's *Principles of Geology* (1830–33) and Chambers's *Vestiges of Creation* (1844), anticipates the uproar that greeted Darwin's *Origin of Species* in 1859.

At last—far off—at last, to all,
And every winter change to spring.

So runs my dream: but what am I?
  An infant crying in the night:
  An infant crying for the light:
20 And with no language but a cry.

    LV
The wish, that of the living whole
  No life may fail beyond the grave,
  Derives it not from what we have
The likest God within the soul?

Are God and Nature then at strife,
  That Nature lends such evil dreams?
  So careful of the type[9] she seems,
So careless of the single life;

That I, considering everywhere
10   Her secret meaning in her deeds,
  And finding that of fifty seeds
She often brings but one to bear,

I falter where I firmly trod,
  And falling with my weight of cares
  Upon the great world's altar-stairs
That slope through darkness up to God,

I stretch lame hands of faith, and grope,
  And gather dust and chaff, and call
  To what I feel is Lord of all,
20 And faintly trust the larger hope.

    LVI
"So careful of the type?" but no.
  From scarpèd[10] cliff and quarried stone
  She cries, "A thousand types are gone:
I care for nothing, all shall go.

"Thou makest thine appeal to me:
  I bring to life, I bring to death:
  The spirit does but mean the breath:
I know no more." And he, shall he,

Man, her last work, who seemed so fair,
10   Such splendid purpose in his eyes,
  Who rolled the psalm to wintry skies,
Who built him fanes[11] of fruitless prayer,

[9]**type** species
[10]**scarpèd** cut away steeply, thus exposing the
geological strata

[11]**fanes** temples

Who trusted God was love indeed
And love Creation's final law—
Though Nature, red in tooth and claw
With ravine, shrieked against his creed—

Who loved, who suffered countless ills,
Who battled for the True, the Just,
Be blown about the desert dust,
20 Or sealed within the iron hills?

No more? A monster then, a dream,
A discord. Dragons of the prime,
That tare[12] each other in their slime,
Were mellow music matched with him.

O life as futile, then, as frail!
O for thy voice to soothe and bless!
What hope of answer, or redress?
Behind the veil, behind the veil.

. . .

XCV

By night we lingered on the lawn,
For underfoot the herb was dry;
And genial warmth; and o'er the sky
The silvery haze of summer drawn;

And calm that let the tapers burn
Unwavering: not a cricket chirred:
The brook alone far-off was heard,
And on the board the fluttering urn:[13]

And bats went round in fragrant skies,
10 And wheeled or lit the filmy shapes[14]
That haunt the dusk, with ermine capes
And woolly breasts and beaded eyes;

While now we sang old songs that pealed
From knoll to knoll, where, couched at ease,
The white kine[15] glimmered, and the trees
Laid their dark arms about the field.

But when those others, one by one,
Withdrew themselves from me and night,
And in the house light after light
20 Went out, and I was all alone,

[12]**tare** tore (archaic)
[13]**urn** tea kettle
[14]**filmy shapes** moths
[15]**kine** cattle

A hunger seized my heart; I read
   Of that glad year which once had been,
   In those fallen leaves which kept their green,
The noble letters of the dead:

And strangely on the silence broke
   The silent-speaking words, and strange
   Was love's dumb cry defying change
To test his worth; and strangely spoke

    The faith, the vigour, bold to dwell
30   On doubts that drive the coward back,
    And keen through wordy snares to track
Suggestion to her inmost cell.

So word by word, and line by line,
   The dead man touched me from the past,
   And all at once it seemed at last
The living soul was flashed on mine,

And mine in this was wound, and whirled
   About empyreal[16] heights of thought,
   And came on that which is, and caught
40   The deep pulsations of the world,

Aeonian[17] music measuring out
   The steps of Time—the shocks of Chance—
   The blows of Death. At length my trance
Was cancelled, stricken through with doubt.

Vague words! but ah, how hard to frame
   In matter-moulded forms of speech,
   Or even for intellect to reach
Through memory that which I became:

Till now the doubtful dusk revealed
50   The knolls once more where, couched at ease,
    The white kine glimmered, and the trees
Laid their dark arms about the field:

And sucked from out the distant gloom
   A breeze began to tremble o'er
   The large leaves of the sycamore,
And fluctuate all the still perfume,

And gathering freshlier overhead,
   Rocked the full-foliaged elms, and swung
   The heavy-folded rose, and flung
60   The lilies to and fro, and said

[16]empyreal heavenly
[17]Aeonian eternal

"The dawn, the dawn," and died away;
  And East and West, without a breath,
  Mixt their dim lights, like life and death,
To broaden into boundless day.

. . .

CXIX

Doors, where my heart was used to beat
  So quickly, not as one that weeps
  I come once more; the city sleeps;
I smell the meadow in the street;

I hear a chirp of birds; I see
  Betwixt the black fronts long-withdrawn
  A light-blue lane of early dawn,
And think of early days and thee,

And bless thee, for thy lips are bland,
10   And bright the friendship of thine eye;
  And in my thoughts with scarce a sigh
I take the pressure of thine hand.

. . .

CXXIX

Dear friend, far off, my lost desire,
  So far, so near in woe and weal;
  O loved the most, when most I feel
There is a lower and a higher;

Known and unknown; human, divine;
  Sweet human hand and lips and eye;
  Dear heavenly friend that canst not die,
Mine, mine, for ever, ever mine;

Strange friend, past, present, and to be;
10   Loved deeplier, darklier understood;
  Behold, I dream a dream of good,
And mingle all the world with thee.

CXXX

Thy voice is on the rolling air;
  I hear thee where the waters run;
  Thou standest in the rising sun,[18]
And in the setting thou art fair.

What art thou then? I cannot guess;
  But though I seem in star and flower

[18]**Thou . . . sun** Cf. Revelation 19:17 ("And I
saw an angel standing in the sun").

To feel thee some diffusive power,
I do not therefore love thee less:

My love involves the love before;
10   My love is vaster passion now;
Though mixed with God and Nature thou,
I seem to love thee more and more.

Far off thou art, but ever nigh;
I have thee still, and I rejoice;
I prosper, circled with thy voice;
I shall not lose thee though I die.

1833–50   1850

From Maud, A Monodrama[1]

From Part I: XXII

I
850   Come into the garden, Maud,
For the black bat, night, has flown,
Come into the garden, Maud,
I am here at the gate alone;
And the woodbine spices are wafted abroad,
And the musk of the rose is blown.

II
For a breeze of morning moves,
And the planet of Love[2] is on high,
Beginning to faint in the light that she loves
On a bed of daffodil sky,
860   To faint in the light of the sun she loves,
To faint in his light, and to die.

III
All night have the roses heard
The flute, violin, bassoon;
All night has the casement jessamine stirred
To the dancers dancing in tune;
Till a silence fell with the waking bird,
And a hush with the setting moon.

[1] A monodrama is a narrative poem in which various scenes of dramatic action are presented through the voice of a single speaker, the protagonist. The speaker of *Maud* is an impoverished and extremely high-strung young man, who expresses, in passages of remarkable lyric intensity, his love for the aristocratic Maud, his dismay at its frustrations, and his despair after her death. Two such passages are presented here, the first expressing the speaker's rapture at the height of his love for Maud, the second uttered after her death.
[2] **planet of Love** Venus, the morning star

IV

I said to the lily, "There is but one
With whom she has heart to be gay.
870 When will the dancers leave her alone?
She is weary of dance and play."
Now half to the setting moon are gone,
And half to the rising day;
Low on the sand and loud on the stone
The last wheel echoes away.

V

I said to the rose, "The brief night goes
In babble and revel and wine.
O young lord-lover,[3] what sighs are those,
For one that will never be thine?
880 But mine, but mine," so I sware to the rose,
"For ever and ever, mine."

VI

And the soul of the rose went into my blood,
As the music clashed in the hall;
And long by the garden lake I stood,
For I heard your rivulet fall
From the lake to the meadow and on to the wood,
Our wood, that is dearer than all;

VII

From the meadow your walks have left so sweet
That whenever a March-wind sighs
890 He sets the jewel-print of your feet
In violets blue as your eyes,
To the woody hollows in which we meet
And the valleys of Paradise.

VIII

The slender acacia would not shake
One long milk-bloom on the tree;
The white lake-blossom fell into the lake
As the pimpernel[4] dozed on the lea;
But the rose was awake all night for your sake,
Knowing your promise to me;
900 The lilies and roses were all awake,
They sighed for the dawn and thee.

IX

Queen rose of the rosebud garden of girls,
Come hither, the dances are done,

---

[3] **young lord-lover** a young aristocrat, whom
Maud is supposed to marry

[4] **pimpernel** an herb with scarlet, white, or pur-
plish flowers

In gloss of satin and glimmer of pearls,
    Queen lily and rose in one;
Shine out, little head, sunning over with curls,
    To the flowers, and be their sun.

            X
There has fallen a splendid tear
    From the passion-flower at the gate.
910 She is coming, my dove, my dear;
    She is coming, my life, my fate;
The red rose cries, "She is near, she is near;"
    And the white rose weeps, "She is late;"
The larkspur listens, "I hear, I hear;"
    And the lily whispers, "I wait."

            XI
She is coming, my own, my sweet;
    Were it ever so airy a tread,
My heart would hear her and beat,
    Were it earth in an earthy bed;
920 My dust would hear her and beat,
    Had I lain for a century dead;
Would start and tremble under her feet,
    And blossom in purple and red.

        From Part II: IV[1]

            I
O that 'twere possible
After long grief and pain
To find the arms of my true love
Round me once again![2]

            II
When I was wont to meet her
In the silent woody places
By the home that gave me birth,
We stood tranced in long embraces
150 Mixt with kisses sweeter sweeter
Than anything on earth.

            III
A shadow flits before me,
Not thou, but like to thee:
Ah Christ, that it were possible

[1] This section in its original form dates from the period shortly after Hallam's death, to which it was perhaps related. The completed monodrama, written many years later, may be said to have been inspired by these lines.
[2] stanza I Cf. the famous anonymous medieval lyric "Western Wind," p. 44.

For one short hour to see
The souls we loved, that they might tell us
What and where they be.

IV

It leads me forth at evening,
It lightly winds and steals
160   In a cold white robe before me,
When all my spirit reels
At the shouts, the leagues of lights,
And the roaring of the wheels.

V

Half the night I waste in sighs,
Half in dreams I sorrow after
The delight of early skies;
In a wakeful doze I sorrow
For the hand, the lips, the eyes,
For the meeting of the morrow,
The delight of happy laughter,
170   The delight of low replies.

VI

'Tis a morning pure and sweet,
And a dewy splendour falls
On the little flower that clings
To the turrets and the walls;
'Tis a morning pure and sweet,
And the light and shadow fleet;
She is walking in the meadow,
And the woodland echo rings;
In a moment we shall meet;
180   She is singing in the meadow
And the rivulet at her feet
Ripples on in light and shadow
To the ballad that she sings.

VII

Do I hear her sing as of old,
My bird with the shining head,
My own dove with the tender eye?
But there rings on a sudden a passionate cry,
There is some one dying or dead,
And a sullen thunder is rolled;
190   For a tumult shakes the city,
And I wake, my dream is fled;
In the shuddering dawn, behold,
Without knowledge, without pity,
By the curtains of my bed
That abiding phantom cold.

VIII

Get thee hence, nor come again,
Mix not memory with doubt,
Pass, thou deathlike type of pain,
Pass and cease to move about!
200 'Tis the blot upon the brain
That *will* show itself without.

IX

Then I rise, the eavedrops fall,
And the yellow vapours choke
The great city sounding wide;[3]
The day comes, a dull red ball
Wrapt in drifts of lurid smoke
On the misty river-tide.

X

Through the hubbub of the market
I steal, a wasted frame,
210 It crosses here, it crosses there,
Through all that crowd confused and loud,
The shadow still the same;
And on my heavy eyelids
My anguish hangs like shame.

XI

Alas for her that met me,
That heard me softly call,
Came glimmering through the laurels
At the quiet evenfall,
220 In the garden by the turrets
Of the old manorial hall.

XII

Would the happy spirit descend,
From the realms of light and song,
In the chamber or the street,
As she looks among the blest,
Should I fear to greet my friend
Or to say "Forgive the wrong,"
Or to ask her, "Take me, sweet,
To the regions of thy rest"?

XIII

But the broad light glares and beats,
230 And the shadow flits and fleets
And will not let me be;

[3] ll. 202-204   Cf. T.S. Eliot, "The Love Song of
J. Alfred Prufrock" (below, p. 883), ll. 15–19,
which evidently echoes this stanza.

And I loathe the squares and streets,
And the faces that one meets,[4]
Hearts with no love for me:
Always I long to creep
Into some still cavern deep,
There to weep, and weep, and weep
My whole soul out to thee.

1855

[4] And the faces . . . meets Cf. ibid, 1. 27.

ROBERT BROWNING
1812–1889

Robert Browning received a rich but eccentric education, acquired chiefly by reading widely in his father's enormous library, and he began writing poetry in his youth. His famous love affair with the poet Elizabeth Barrett led to their elopement in 1846 and a fifteen-year residence in Italy. After Mrs. Browning's death in 1861, he returned to England and gradually built a reputation—confirmed with the publication of *The Ring and the Book* in 1868—as one of the foremost poets of the age.

Browning's first major success was *Dramatic Lyrics* (1842), which, along with *Dramatic Romances* (1845) and *Men and Women* (1855), established him as the unrivaled master of the dramatic monologue. Browning's dramatic monologue resembles a play in period setting in which we hear only one character speak. Readers must assess the speaker's personality and dramatic situation from his or her words alone, without the overt guidance of the poet's voice. The many self-absorbed or obsessed characters who parade through Browning's works—

mad, possessive, hating, desperately seeking, twisted in their faith—represent attitudes contradictory to the poet's own ostensible values of trust, love, and simple confident belief. At the same time, clearly, these intense obsessions fascinate Browning and in a sense may reflect aspects of his own complex nature.

Browning's poetry presents a wide variety of voices and tones. Typically his style is dramatically active, image-packed, and explosive. It is filled with unusual words, colloquial speech rhythms, compressed phrasing, and obscure references. He broke the mold of conventional Victorian poetic style and thus became an especially important influence on the great moderns. Pound's *Cantos* and the later poems of Yeats contain echoes of Browning's voice, and such dramatic monologues as "Andrea del Sarto" and " 'Childe Roland to the Dark Tower Came' " are important forerunners of Eliot's "The Love Song of J. Alfred Prufrock" and *The Waste Land*.

My Last Duchess

FERRARA[1]

That's my last Duchess painted on the wall,
Looking as if she were alive. I call
That piece a wonder, now: Frà Pandolf's hands
Worked busily a day, and there she stands.
Will 't please you sit and look at her? I said
"Frà Pandolf" by design, for never read
Strangers like you that pictured countenance,
The depth and passion of its earnest glance,
But to myself they turned (since none puts by

10 The curtain I have drawn for you, but I)
And seemed as they would ask me, if they durst,
How such a glance came there; so, not the first
Are you to turn and ask thus. Sir, 't was not
Her husband's presence only, called that spot
Of joy into the Duchess' cheek: perhaps
Frà Pandolf chanced to say "Her mantle laps
Over my lady's wrist too much," or "Paint
Must never hope to reproduce the faint
Half-flush that dies along her throat:" such stuff

20 Was courtesy, she thought, and cause enough
For calling up that spot of joy. She had
A heart—how shall I say?—too soon made glad,
Too easily impressed; she liked whate'er
She looked on, and her looks went everywhere.
Sir, 't was all one! My favour at her breast,
The dropping of the daylight in the West,
The bough of cherries some officious fool
Broke in the orchard for her, the white mule
She rode with round the terrace—all and each

30 Would draw from her alike the approving speech,
Or blush, at least. She thanked men,—good! but thanked
Somehow—I know not how—as if she ranked
My gift of a nine-hundred-years-old name
With anybody's gift. Who'd stoop to blame
This sort of trifling? Even had you skill
In speech—(which I have not)—to make your will
Quite clear to such an one, and say, "Just this
Or that in you disgusts me; here you miss,
Or there exceed the mark"—and if she let

40 Herself be lessoned so, nor plainly set
Her wits to yours, forsooth, and made excuse,
—E'en then would be some stooping; and I choose
Never to stoop. Oh sir, she smiled, no doubt,

---

[1] The speaker, Alfonso II, Duke of Ferrara, whose young first wife died mysteriously in 1561, is imagined as addressing an agent of the Count of Tyrol, father of the duke's intended second bride. Other figures mentioned in the poem are fictitious.

Whene'er I passed her; but who passed without
Much the same smile? This grew; I gave commands;
Then all smiles stopped together. There she stands
As if alive. Will 't please you rise? We'll meet
The company below, then. I repeat,
The Count your master's known munificence
50 Is ample warrant that no just pretence
Of mine for dowry will be disallowed;
Though his fair daughter's self, as I avowed
At starting, is my object. Nay, we'll go
Together down, sir. Notice Neptune, though,
Taming a sea-horse, thought a rarity,
Which Claus of Innsbruck cast in bronze for me!

1842   1842

The Bishop Orders His Tomb at Saint Praxed's Church[1]

ROME, 15—

Vanity, saith the preacher, vanity![2]
Draw round my bed: is Anselm keeping back?
Nephews—sons mine . . . ah, God, I know not! Well—
She, men would have to be your mother once,
Old Gandolf envied me, so fair she was!
What's done is done, and she is dead beside,
Dead long ago, and I am Bishop since,
And as she died so must we die ourselves,
And thence ye may perceive the world's a dream.
10 Life, how and what is it? As here I lie
In this state-chamber, dying by degrees,
Hours and long hours in the dead night, I ask
"Do I live, am I dead?" Peace, peace seems all.
Saint Praxed's ever was the church for peace;
And so, about this tomb of mine. I fought
With tooth and nail to save my niche, ye know:
—Old Gandolf cozened[3] me, despite my care;
Shrewd was that snatch from out the corner South
He graced his carrion with, God curse the same!
20 Yet still my niche is not so cramped but thence

---

[1] the Roman church of Santa Prassede, a virgin
martyr of the second century A.D., who gave
her wealth to the poor. The bishop, his associ-
ates, and his circumstances are imaginary, but
the poem is intended to convey the atmosphere
of the Italian Renaissance. Regarding this poem,
the great Victorian art critic John Ruskin de-
clared, "I know of no other piece of modern

English, prose or poetry, in which there is so
much told, as in these lines, of the Renaissance
spirit—its worldliness, inconsistency, pride,
hypocrisy, ignorance of itself, love of art,
of luxury, and of good Latin'' (*Modern Painters*,
1856).

[2] l. 1 Cf. Ecclesiastes 1:2.
[3] **cozened** cheated

One sees the pulpit o' the epistle-side,[4]
And somewhat of the choir, those silent seats,
And up into the aery dome where live
The angels, and a sunbeam's sure to lurk:
And I shall fill my slab of basalt there,
And 'neath my tabernacle[5] take my rest,
With those nine columns round me, two and two,
The odd one at my feet where Anselm stands:
Peach-blossom marble all, the rare, the ripe
30 As fresh-poured red wine of a mighty pulse[6]
—Old Gandolf with his paltry onion-stone,[7]
Put me where I may look at him! True peach,
Rosy and flawless: how I earned the prize!
Draw close: that conflagration of my church
— What then? So much was saved if aught were missed!
My sons, ye would not be my death? Go dig
The white-grape vineyard where the oil-press stood,
Drop water gently till the surface sink,
And if ye find . . . Ah God, I know not, I! . . .
40 Bedded in store of rotten fig-leaves soft,
And corded up in a tight olive-frail,[8]
Some lump, ah God, of *lapis lazuli*,[9]
Big as a Jew's head cut off at the nape,
Blue as a vein o'er the Madonna's breast . . .
Sons, all have I bequeathed you, villas, all,
That brave Frascati[10] villa with its bath,
So, let the blue lump poise between my knees,
Like God the Father's globe on both his hands
Ye worship in the Jesu Church so gay,
50 For Gandolf shall not choose but see and burst!
Swift as a weaver's shuttle fleet our years:[11]
Man goeth to the grave, and where is he?
Did I say basalt for my slab, sons? Black—
'T was ever antique-black I meant! How else
Shall ye contrast my frieze to come beneath?
The bas-relief in bronze ye promised me,
Those Pans[12] and Nymphs ye wot[13] of, and perchance
Some tripod,[14] thyrsus,[15] with a vase or so,
The Saviour at his sermon on the mount,
60 Saint Praxed in a glory,[16] and one Pan

[4]**epistle-side** the right side of the church as one faces the altar
[5]**tabernacle** stone canopy over the tomb
[6]**pulse** fermented grape mash
[7]**onion-stone** a cheap, unattractive marble
[8]**olive-frail** olive basket
[9]*lapis lazuli* a semiprecious blue stone
[10]**Frascati** wealthy resort outside Rome
[11]l. 51 See Job 7:6 ("My days are swifter than a weaver's shuttle, and are spent without hope").
[12]**Pans** woodland gods, often depicted with goats' legs, noted for their lustful pursuit of wood-nymphs
[13]**wot** know
[14]**tripod** three-legged stool used by priestesses of Apollo at Delphi
[15]**thyrsus** staff wreathed in vines carried by Bacchus, god of wine, or his followers
[16]**glory** halo

Ready to twitch the Nymph's last garment off,
And Moses with the tables[17] . . . but I know
Ye mark me not! What do they whisper thee,
Child of my bowels, Anselm? Ah, ye hope
To revel down my villas while I gasp
Bricked o'er with beggar's mouldy travertine[18]
Which Gandolf from his tomb-top chuckles at!
Nay, boys, ye love me—all of jasper, then!
'T is jasper ye stand pledged to, lest I grieve
70   My bath must needs be left behind, alas!
One block, pure green as a pistachio-nut,
There's plenty jasper somewhere in the world—
And have I not Saint Praxed's ear to pray
Horses for ye, and brown Greek manuscripts,
And mistresses with great smooth marbly limbs?
—That's if ye carve my epitaph aright,
Choice Latin, picked phrase, Tully's[19] every word,
No gaudy ware like Gandolf's second line—
Tully, my masters? Ulpian[20] serves his need!
80   And then how I shall lie through centuries,
And hear the blessed mutter of the mass,
And see God made and eaten all day long,
And feel the steady candle-flame, and taste
Good strong thick stupefying incense-smoke!
For as I lie here, hours of the dead night,
Dying in state and by such slow degrees,
I fold my arms as if they clasped a crook[21]
And stretch my feet forth straight as stone can point,
And let the bedclothes, for a mortcloth,[22] drop
90   Into great laps and folds of sculptor's-work:
And as yon tapers dwindle, and strange thoughts
Grow, with a certain humming in my ears,
About the life before I lived this life,
And this life too, popes, cardinals and priests,
Saint Praxed at his sermon on the mount,
Your tall pale mother with her talking eyes,
And new-found agate urns as fresh as day,
And marble's language, Latin pure, discreet,
—Aha, ELUCESCEBAT[23] quoth our friend?
100   No Tully, said I, Ulpian at the best!
Evil and brief hath been my pilgrimage[24]
All *lapis*, all, sons! Else I give the Pope
My villas! Will ye ever eat my heart?

---

[17]**tables** the stone tablets on which the Ten Commandments were inscribed

[18]**travertine** a light-colored limestone

[19]**Tully** Marcus Tullius Cicero, the great Latin orator and prose stylist

[20]**Ulpian** a Latin writer of the second to third century A.D., much inferior to Cicero

[21]**crook** bishop's staff, a ceremonial version of a shepherd's crook

[22]**mortcloth** cloth used to cover a coffin, funeral pall

[23]ELUCESCEBAT "he was illustrious," a phrase from Gandolph's epitaph and, in the bishop's opinion, an example of Ulpian's poor Latin diction

[24]1. 101 Cf. Genesis 47:9.

Ever your eyes were as a lizard's quick,
They glitter like your mother's for my soul.
Or ye would heighten my impoverished frieze,
Piece out its starved design, and fill my vase
With grapes, and add a vizor[25] and a Term,[26]
And to the tripod ye would tie a lynx
110 That in his struggle throws the thyrsus down
To comfort me on my entablature
Whereon I am to lie till I must ask
"Do I live, am I dead?" There, leave me, there!
For ye have stabbed me with ingratitude
To death—ye wish it—God, ye wish it! Stone—
Gritstone, a-crumble! Clammy squares which sweat
As if the corpse they keep were oozing through—
And no more *lapis* to delight the world!
Well go! I bless ye. Fewer tapers there,
120 But in a row: and, going, turn your backs
—Ay, like departing altar-ministrants,
And leave me in my church, the church for peace,
That I may watch at leisure if he leers—
Old Gandolf, at me, from his onion-stone,
As still he envied me, so fair she was!

1844   1845

[25]**vizor**   mask of a helmet
[26]**Term**   a pillar merging into a bust of Terminus,   god of boundaries. Both are common emblems
in Renaissance sculpture.

Memorabilia[1]

I
Ah, did you once see Shelley plain,
    And did he stop and speak to you,
And did you speak to him again?
    How strange it seems and new![2]

II
But you were living before that,
    And also you are living after;
And the memory I started at—
    My starting moves your laughter.

III
I crossed a moor, with a name of its own
10   And a certain use in the world no doubt,
    Yet a hand's-breadth of it shines alone
    'Mid the blank miles round about:

[1] memorable things
[2] ll. 1–4   In his youth Browning was a fervent
admirer of Shelley's poetry. These lines drama-   tize an actual exchange that Browning once had
with a stranger who had met Shelley.

IV

For there I picked up on the heather
   And there I put inside my breast
A moulted feather, an eagle-feather!
   Well, I forget the rest.

1851   1855

"Childe Roland to the Dark Tower Came"[1]

(SEE EDGAR'S SONG IN *LEAR*)

I

My first thought was, he lied in every word,
   That hoary cripple, with malicious eye
   Askance to watch the working of his lie
On mine, and mouth scarce able to afford
Suppression of the glee, that pursed and scored
   Its edge, at one more victim gained thereby.

II

What else should he be set for, with his staff?
   What, save to waylay with his lies, ensnare
   All travellers who might find him posted there,
10 And ask the road? I guessed what skull-like laugh
Would break, what crutch 'gin write my epitaph
   For pastime in the dusty thoroughfare,

III

If at his counsel I should turn aside
   Into that ominous tract which, all agree,
   Hides the Dark Tower. Yet acquiescingly
I did turn as he pointed: neither pride
Nor hope rekindling at the end descried,
   So much as gladness that some end might be.

IV

For, what with my whole world-wide wandering,
20   What with my search drawn out thro' years, my hope
   Dwindled into a ghost not fit to cope
With that obstreperous joy success would bring,—
I hardly tried now to rebuke the spring
   My heart made, finding failure in its scope.

[1] Some rhymes sung during a scene of storm and anguish by the pretended madman Edgar in Shakespeare's *King Lear* provide Browning with the title and action of this dark, phantasmagoric poem; see *King Lear* III.iv ("Child Rowland to the dark tower came; / His word was still / 'Fie, foh, and fum! / I smell the blood of a British man.' "). "Childe" here is a title of a young candidate for knighthood. "Rowland" is the name of one of the greatest knightly heroes in medieval tales of chivalry; Browning perhaps intended an irony in associating it with the inglorious hero of his own poem.

V²

As when a sick man very near to death
    Seems dead indeed, and feels begin and end
    The tears and takes the farewell of each friend,
And hears one bid the other go, draw breath
Freelier outside, ("since all is o'er," he saith,
30   "And the blow fallen no grieving can amend;")

VI

While some discuss if near the other graves
    Be room enough for this, and when a day
    Suits best for carrying the corpse away,
With care about the banners, scarves and staves:
35 And still the man hears all, and only craves
    He may not shame such tender love and stay.

VII

Thus, I had so long suffered in this quest,
    Heard failure prophesied so oft; been writ
    So many times among "The Band"—to wit,
40 The knights who to the Dark Tower's search addressed
    Their steps—that just to fail as they, seemed best,
    And all the doubt was now—should I be fit?

VIII

So, quiet as despair, I turned from him,
    That hateful cripple, out of his highway
    Into the path he pointed. All the day
Had been a dreary one at best, and dim
Was settling to its close, yet shot one grim
    Red leer to see the plain catch its estray.³

IX

For mark! no sooner was I fairly found
50 Pledged to the plain, after a pace or two,
    Than, pausing to throw backward a last view
O'er the safe road, 't was gone; grey plain all round:
Nothing but plain to the horizon's bound.
    I might go on; nought else remained to do.

X

So, on I went. I think I never saw
    Such starved ignoble nature; nothing throve:
    For flowers—as well expect a cedar grove!
But cockle, spurge,⁴ according to their law
Might propagate their kind, with none to awe,
60 You'd think; a burr had been a treasure-trove.

---

²stanzas V and VI Cf. with John Donne's "A
Valediction: Forbidding Mourning," ll. 1–4
(p. 230 above).

³estray stray or escaped domestic animal
⁴cockle, spurge unpleasant weeds

XI

No! penury, inertness and grimace,
    In some strange sort, were the land's portion. "See
    Or shut your eyes," said Nature peevishly,
"It nothing skills: I cannot help my case:
'T is the Last Judgment's fire must cure this place,
    Calcine[5] its clods and set my prisoners free."

XII

If there pushed any ragged thistle-stalk
    Above its mates, the head was chopped; the bents[6]
    Were jealous else. What made those holes and rents
70 In the dock's[7] harsh swarth leaves, bruised as to baulk
All hope of greenness? 't is a brute must walk
    Pashing their life out, with a brute's intents.

XIII

As for the grass, it grew as scant as hair
    In leprosy; thin dry blades pricked the mud
    Which underneath looked kneaded up with blood.
One stiff blind horse, his every bone a-stare,
Stood stupefied, however he came there:
    Thrust out past service from the devil's stud!

XIV

Alive? he might be dead for aught I know,
80   With that red gaunt and colloped[8] neck a-strain,
    And shut eyes underneath the rusty mane;
Seldom went such grotesqueness with such woe;
I never saw a brute I hated so;
    He must be wicked to deserve such pain.

XV

I shut my eyes and turned them on my heart.
    As a man calls for wine before he fights,
    I asked one draught of earlier, happier sights,
Ere fitly I could hope to play my part.
Think first, fight afterwards—the soldier's art:
90   One taste of the old time sets all to rights.

XVI

Not it! I fancied Cuthbert's reddening face
    Beneath its garniture of curly gold,
    Dear fellow, till I almost felt him fold
An arm in mine to fix me to the place,
That way he used. Alas, one night's disgrace!
    Out went my heart's new fire and left it cold.

[5]**Calcine** bake to a powder   [7]**dock** a coarse weed
[6]**bents** tough, reedy grasses   [8]**colloped** ridged

XVII

Giles then, the soul of honour—there he stands
   Frank as ten years ago when knighted first.
   What honest men should dare (he said) he durst.
100   Good—but the scene shifts—faugh! what hangman-hands
Pin to his breast a parchment? his own bands
   Read it. Poor traitor, spit upon and curst!

XVIII

Better this present than a past like that;
   Back therefore to my darkening path again!
   No sound, no sight as far as eye could strain.
Will the night send a howlet[9] or a bat?
I asked: when something on the dismal flat
   Came to arrest my thoughts and change their train.

XIX

A sudden little river crossed my path
110   As unexpected as a serpent comes.
   No sluggish tide congenial to the glooms;
This, as it frothed by, might have been a bath
For the fiend's glowing hoof—to see the wrath
   Of its black eddy bespate with flakes and spumes.

XX

So petty yet so spiteful! All along,
   Low scrubby alders kneeled down over it;
   Drenched willows flung them headlong in a fit
Of mute despair, a suicidal throng:
The river which had done them all the wrong,
120   Whate'er that was, rolled by, deterred no whit.

XXI

Which, while I forded,—good saints, how I feared
   To set my foot upon a dead man's cheek,
   Each step, or feel the spear I thrust to seek
For hollows, tangled in his hair or beard!
—It may have been a water-rat I speared,
   But, ugh! it sounded like a baby's shriek.

XXII

Glad was I when I reached the other bank.
   Now for a better country. Vain presage!
   Who were the strugglers, what war did they wage,
130   Whose savage trample thus could pad the dank
Soil to a plash? Toads in a poisoned tank,
   Or wild cats in a red-hot iron cage—

[9]**howlet** owl

XXIII

The fight must so have seemed in that fell cirque.[10]
What penned them there, with all the plain to choose?
No foot-print leading to that horrid mews,[11]
None out of it. Mad brewage set to work
Their brains, no doubt, like galley-slaves the Turk
Pits for his pastime, Christians against Jews.

XXIV

And more than that—a furlong on—why, there!
140   What bad use was that engine for, that wheel,
Or brake,[12] not wheel—that harrow fit to reel
Men's bodies out like silk? with all the air
Of Tophet's[13] tool, on earth left unaware,
Or brought to sharpen its rusty teeth of steel.

XXV

Then came a bit of stubbed ground, once a wood,
Next a marsh, it would seem, and now mere earth
Desperate and done with; (so a fool finds mirth,
Makes a thing and then mars it, till his mood
Changes and off he goes!) within a rood[14]—
150   Bog, clay and rubble, sand and stark black dearth.

XXVI

Now blotches rankling, coloured gay and grim,
Now patches where some leanness of the soil's
Broke into moss or substances like boils;
Then came some palsied oak, a cleft in him
Like a distorted mouth that splits its rim
Gaping at death, and dies while it recoils.

XXVII

And just as far as ever from the end!
Nought in the distance but the evening, nought
To point my footstep further! At the thought,
160   A great black bird, Apollyon's[15] bosom-friend,
Sailed past, nor beat his wide wing dragon-penned[16]
That brushed my cap—perchance the guide I sought.

XXVIII

For, looking up, aware I somehow grew,
'Spite of the dusk, the plain had given place
All round to mountains—with such name to grace
Mere ugly heights and heaps now stolen in view.
How thus they had surprised me,—solve it, you!
How to get from them was no clearer case.

---

[10]**cirque** natural arena or hollow in the land
[11]**mews** literally, a horse-stable enclosure
[12]**brake** a rack or torture wheel
[13]**Tophet's** Hell's
[14]**rood** quarter of an acre
[15]**Apollyon** a dragon-winged devil. See Revelation 9:11.
[16]**dragon-penned** jointed like a dragon's wings

XXIX

Yet half I seemed to recognize some trick
170   Of mischief happened to me, God knows when—
In a bad dream perhaps. Here ended, then,
Progress this way. When, in the very nick
Of giving up, one time more, came a click
    As when a trap shuts—you're inside the den!

XXX

Burningly it came on me all at once,
    This was the place! those two hills on the right,
    Crouched like two bulls locked horn in horn in fight;
While to the left, a tall scalped mountain . . . Dunce,
Dotard, a-dozing at the very nonce,[17]
180   After a life spent training for the sight!

XXXI

What in the midst lay but the Tower itself?
    The round squat turret, blind as the fool's heart,
    Built of brown stone, without a counterpart
In the whole world. The tempest's mocking elf
Points to the shipman thus the unseen shelf
    He strikes on, only when the timbers start.

XXXII

Not see? because of night perhaps?—why, day
    Came back again for that! before it left,
    The dying sunset kindled through a cleft:
190   The hills, like giants at a hunting, lay,
Chin upon hand, to see the game at bay,—
    "Now stab and end the creature—to the heft!"[18]

XXXIII

Not hear? when noise was everywhere! it tolled
    Increasing like a bell. Names in my ears
    Of all the lost adventurers my peers,—
How such a one was strong, and such was bold,
And such was fortunate, yet each of old
    Lost, lost! one moment knelled the woe of years.

XXXIV

There they stood, ranged along the hill-sides, met
200   To view the last of me, a living frame
For one more picture! in a sheet of flame
I saw them and I knew them all. And yet
Dauntless the slug-horn[19] to my lips I set,
    And blew. *"Childe Roland to the Dark Tower came."*

1852   1855

[17]**nonce** occasion   [19]**slug-horn** a kind of trumpet or battle-horn
[18]**heft** hilt of a sword or dagger

Andrea del Sarto[1]

(CALLED "THE FAULTLESS PAINTER")

But do not let us quarrel any more,
No, my Lucrezia; bear with me for once:
Sit down and all shall happen as you wish.
You turn your face, but does it bring your heart?
I'll work then for your friend's friend, never fear,
Treat his own subject after his own way,
Fix his own time, accept too his own price,
And shut the money into this small hand
When next it takes mine. Will it? tenderly?
10   Oh, I'll content him,—but to-morrow, Love!
I often am much wearier than you think,
This evening more than usual, and it seems
As if—forgive now—should you let me sit
Here by the window with your hand in mine
And look a half-hour forth on Fiesole,[2]
Both of one mind, as married people use,
Quietly, quietly the evening through,
I might get up to-morrow to my work
Cheerful and fresh as ever. Let us try.
20   To-morrow, how you shall be glad for this!
Your soft hand is a woman of itself,
And mine the man's bared breast she curls inside.
Don't count the time lost, neither; you must serve
For each of the five pictures we require:
It saves a model. So! keep looking so—
My serpentining beauty, rounds on rounds![3]
—How could you ever prick those perfect ears,
Even to put the pearl there! oh, so sweet—
My face, my moon, my everybody's moon,
30   Which everybody looks on and calls his,
And, I suppose, is looked on by in turn,
While she looks—no one's: very dear, no less.
You smile? why, there's my picture ready made,
There's what we painters call our harmony!
A common greyness silvers everything,—[4]
All in a twilight, you and I alike
—You, at the point of your first pride in me
(That's gone you know),—but I, at every point;

[1] Andrea del Sarto (1486–1531) was a noted
painter of the Italian Renaissance. According
to his biographical sketch in Vasari's *Lives of
the Most Eminent Painters*, Andrea showed "a
certain timidity of mind, a sort of diffidence
and want of force in his nature, which rendered
it impossible that those evidences of ardour and
animation which are proper to the more exalted
character, should ever appear in him"; in par-
ticular, he deferred submissively to his wife
Lucrezia, "an artful woman who made him do
as she pleased in all things." In this brilliant
psychological portrait, Browning enlarges on
these points.

[2] **Fiesole** a hill town overlooking Florence

[3] l. 26 a reference to her long ringlets of hair

[4] l. 35 Andrea's paintings are distinctive for
their abundant use of gray.

My youth, my hope, my art, being all toned down
40 To yonder sober pleasant Fiesole.
There's the bell clinking from the chapel-top;
That length of convent-wall across the way
Holds the trees safer, huddled more inside;
The last monk leaves the garden; days decrease,
And autumn grows, autumn in everything.
Eh? the whole seems to fall into a shape
As if I saw alike my work and self
And all that I was born to be and do,
A twilight-piece. Love, we are in God's hand.
50 How strange now, looks the life he makes us lead;
So free we seem, so fettered fast we are!
I feel he laid the fetter: let it lie!
This chamber for example—turn your head—
All that's behind us! You don't understand
Nor care to understand about my art,
But you can hear at least when people speak:
And that cartoon,[5] the second from the door
—It is the thing, Love! so such things should be—
Behold Madonna!—I am bold to say.
60 I can do with my pencil what I know,
What I see, what at bottom of my heart
I wish for, if I ever wish so deep—
Do easily, too—when I say, perfectly,
I do not boast, perhaps: yourself are judge,
Who listened to the Legate's[6] talk last week,
And just as much they used to say in France.
At any rate 't is easy, all of it!
No sketches first, no studies, that's long past:
I do what many dream of, all their lives,
—Dream? strive to do, and agonize to do,
70 And fail in doing. I could count twenty such
On twice your fingers, and not leave this town,
Who strive—you don't know how the others strive
To paint a little thing like that you smeared
Carelessly passing with your robes afloat,—
Yet do much less, so much less, Someone says,
(I know his name, no matter)—so much less!
Well, less is more, Lucrezia: I am judged.
There burns a truer light of God in them,
80 In their vexed beating stuffed and stopped-up brain,
Heart, or whate'er else, than goes on to prompt
This low-pulsed forthright craftsman's hand of mine.
Their works drop groundward, but themselves, I know,
Reach many a time a heaven that's shut to me,
Enter and take their place there sure enough,

_____

[5]**cartoon** a large drawing, intended for later execution in oil or fresco   [6]**Legate** the pope's representative in Florence

Though they come back and cannot tell the world.
My works are nearer heaven, but I sit here.
The sudden blood of these men! at a word—
Praise them, it boils, or blame them, it boils too.
90   I, painting from myself and to myself,
Know what I do, am unmoved by men's blame
Or their praise either. Somebody remarks
Morello's[7] outline there is wrongly traced,
His hue mistaken; what of that? or else,
Rightly traced and well ordered; what of that?
Speak as they please, what does the mountain care?
Ah, but a man's reach should exceed his grasp,
Or what's a heaven for? All is silver-grey
Placid and perfect with my art: the worse!
100   I know both what I want and what might gain,
And yet how profitless to know, to sigh
"Had I been two, another and myself,
Our head would have o'erlooked the world!" No doubt.
Yonder's a work now, of that famous youth
The Urbinate[8] who died five years ago.
('T is copied, George Vasari[9] sent it me.)
Well, I can fancy how he did it all,
Pouring his soul, with kings and popes to see,
Reaching, that heaven might so replenish him,
110   Above and through his art—for it gives way;
That arm is wrongly put—and there again—
A fault to pardon in the drawing's lines,
Its body, so to speak: its soul is right,
He means right—that, a child may understand.
Still, what an arm! and I could alter it:
But all the play, the insight and the stretch—
Out of me, out of me! And wherefore out?
Had you enjoined them on me, given me soul,
We might have risen to Rafael, I and you!
120   Nay, Love, you did give all I asked, I think—
More than I merit, yes, by many times.
But had you—oh, with the same perfect brow,
And perfect eyes, and more than perfect mouth,
And the low voice my soul hears, as a bird
The fowler's pipe,[10] and follows to the snare—
Had you, with these the same, but brought a mind!
Some women do so. Had the mouth there urged
"God and the glory! never care for gain.
The present by the future, what is that?
130   Live for fame, side by side with Agnolo![11]
Rafael is waiting: up to God, all three!"

---

[7]**Morello**   a mountain near Florence
[8]**the Urbinate**   the great painter Raphael (1483–1520), born at Urbino
[9]**Vasari**   Vasari (1511–1574), the biographer of painters, had studied with Andrea.
[10]**fowler's pipe**   bird-catcher's whistle
[11]**Agnolo**   Michelangelo

I might have done it for you. So it seems:
Perhaps not. All is as God over-rules.
Beside, incentives come from the soul's self;
The rest avail not. Why do I need you?
What wife had Rafael, or has Agnolo?
In this world, who can do a thing, will not;
And who would do it, cannot, I perceive:
Yet the will's somewhat—somewhat, too, the power—
140 And thus we half-men struggle. At the end,
God, I conclude, compensates, punishes.
'T is safer for me, if the award be strict,
That I am something underrated here,
Poor this long while, despised, to speak the truth.
I dared not, do you know, leave home all day,
For fear of chancing on the Paris lords.[12]
The best is when they pass and look aside;
But they speak sometimes; I must bear it all.
Well may they speak! That Francis, that first time,
150 And that long festal year at Fontainebleau!
I surely then could sometimes leave the ground,
Put on the glory, Rafael's daily wear,
In that humane great monarch's golden look,—
One finger in his beard or twisted curl
Over his mouth's good mark that made the smile,
One arm about my shoulder, round my neck,
The jingle of his gold chain in my ear,
I painting proudly with his breath on me,
All his court round him, seeing with his eyes,
160 Such frank French eyes, and such a fire of souls
Profuse, my hand kept plying by those hearts—
And, best of all, this, this, this face beyond,
This in the background, waiting on my work,
To crown the issue with a last reward!
A good time, was it not, my kingly days?
And had you not grown restless . . . but I know—
'T is done and past; 't was right, my instinct said;
Too live the life grew, golden and not grey,
And I'm the weak-eyed bat no sun should tempt
170 Out of the grange[13] whose four walls make his world.
How could it end in any other way?
You called me, and I came home to your heart.
The triumph was—to reach and stay there; since
I reached it ere the triumph, what is lost?
Let my hands frame your face in your hair's gold,
You beautiful Lucrezia that are mine!
"Rafael did this, Andrea painted that;

[12] 1. 146 Andrea, who had once been court painter for King Francis I at Fontainebleau, fears meeting Frenchmen; to satisfy his wife's demands, according to Vasari, Andrea had embezzled money given to him by the French king.
[13] **grange** farm building

The Roman's[14] is the better when you pray,
But still the other's Virgin was his wife—''
180   Men will excuse me. I am glad to judge
Both pictures in your presence; clearer grows
My better fortune, I resolve to think.
For, do you know, Lucrezia, as God lives,
Said one day Agnolo, his very self,
To Rafael . . . I have known it all these years . . .
(When the young man was flaming out his thoughts
Upon a palace-wall for Rome to see,
Too lifted up in heart because of it)
"Friend, there's a certain sorry little scrub
190   Goes up and down our Florence, none cares how,
Who, were he set to plan and execute
As you are, pricked on by your popes and kings,
Would bring the sweat into that brow of yours!''
To Rafael's!—And indeed the arm is wrong.
I hardly dare . . . yet, only you to see,
Give the chalk here—quick, thus the line should go!
Ay, but the soul! he's Rafael! rub it out!
Still, all I care for, if he spoke the truth,
(What he? why, who but Michel Agnolo?
200   Do you forget already words like those?)
If really there was such a chance, so lost,—
Is, whether you're—not grateful—but more pleased.
Well, let me think so. And you smile indeed!
This hour has been an hour! Another smile?
If you would sit thus by me every night
I should work better, do you comprehend?
I mean that I should earn more, give you more.
See, it is settled dusk now; there's a star;
Morello's gone, the watch-lights show the wall,
210   The cue-owls[15] speak the name we call them by.
Come from the window, love,—come in, at last,
Inside the melancholy little house
We built to be so gay with. God is just.
King Francis may forgive me: oft at nights
When I look up from painting, eyes tired out,
The walls become illumined, brick from brick
Distinct, instead of mortar, fierce bright gold,
That gold of his I did cement them with![16]
Let us but love each other. Must you go?
220   That Cousin[17] here again? he waits outside?
Must see you—you, and not with me? Those loans?
More gaming debts to pay? you smiled for that?

[14]**The Roman** Raphael
[15]**cue-owls** The owl's cry sounds like "cue."
[16]l. 218 Andrea built the house with the king's
misappropriated money.
[17]**Cousin** the "friend" of l. 5—presumably not

a cousin at all but Lucrezia's lover—whose debts
Andrea is paying off by selling some paintings
to the friend's creditor at a bargain price (see
ll. 5–10).

Well, let smiles buy me! have you more to spend?
While hand and eye and something of a heart
Are left me, work's my ware, and what's it worth?
I'll pay my fancy. Only let me sit
The grey remainder of the evening out,
Idle, you call it, and muse perfectly
How I could paint, were I but back in France,
230 One picture, just one more—the Virgin's face,
Not yours this time! I want you at my side
To hear them—that is, Michel Agnolo—
Judge all I do and tell you of its worth.
Will you? To-morrow, satisfy your friend.
I take the subjects for his corridor,
Finish the portrait out of hand—there, there,
And throw him in another thing or two
If he demurs; the whole should prove enough
To pay for this same Cousin's freak. Beside,
240 What's better and what's all I care about,
Get you the thirteen scudi[18] for the ruff!
Love, does that please you? Ah, but what does he,
The Cousin! what does he to please you more?

I am grown peaceful as old age to-night.
I regret little, I would change still less.
Since there my past life lies, why alter it?
The very wrong to Francis!—it is true
I took his coin, was tempted and complied,
And built this house and sinned, and all is said.
250 My father and my mother died of want.
Well, had I riches of my own? you see
How one gets rich! Let each one bear his lot.
They were born poor, lived poor, and poor they died:
And I have laboured somewhat in my time
And not been paid profusely. Some good son
Paint my two hundred pictures—let him try!
No doubt, there's something strikes a balance. Yes,
You loved me quite enough, it seems to-night.
This must suffice me here. What would one have?
260 In heaven, perhaps, new chances, one more chance—
Four great walls in the New Jerusalem,[19]
Meted on each side by the angel's reed,
For Leonard,[20] Rafael, Agnolo and me
To cover—the three first without a wife,
While I have mine! So—still they overcome
Because there's still Lucrezia,—as I choose.

Again the Cousin's whistle! Go, my Love.

1853   1855

[18]**scudi** Italian silver coins   in Revelation 21:10–21
[19]**New Jerusalem** the heavenly city described   [20]**Leonard** Leonardo da Vinci (1452–1519)

Two in the Campagna[1]

I

I wonder do you feel to-day
　　As I have felt since, hand in hand,
We sat down on the grass, to stray
　　In spirit better through the land,
This morn of Rome and May?

II

For me, I touched a thought, I know,
　　Has tantalized me many times,
(Like turns of thread the spiders throw
　　Mocking across our path) for rhymes
10　　To catch at and let go.

III

Help me to hold it! First it left
　　The yellowing fennel, run to seed
There, branching from the brickwork's cleft,
　　Some old tomb's ruin: yonder weed
Took up the floating weft,[2]

IV

Where one small orange cup amassed
　　Five beetles,—blind and green they grope
Among the honey-meal: and last,
　　Everywhere on the grassy slope
20　　I traced it. Hold it fast!

V

The champaign[3] with its endless fleece
　　Of feathery grasses everywhere!
Silence and passion, joy and peace,
　　An everlasting wash of air—
Rome's ghost since her decease.[4]

VI

Such life here, through such lengths of hours,
　　Such miracles performed in play,
Such primal naked forms of flowers,
　　Such letting nature have her way
30　　While heaven looks from its towers!

VII

How say you? Let us, O my dove,
　　Let us be unashamed of soul,
As earth lies bare to heaven above!

[1] **Campagna** open countryside around Rome
[2] **floating weft** cloth in the process of being woven
[3] **champaign** flat, open country
[4] l. 25 an allusion to the fall of ancient Rome.

How is it under our control
To love or not to love?

VIII

I would that you were all to me,
   You that are just so much, no more.
Nor yours nor mine, nor slave nor free!
   Where does the fault lie? What the core
40 O' the wound, since wound must be?

IX

I would I could adopt your will,
   See with your eyes, and set my heart
Beating by yours, and drink my fill
   At your soul's springs,—your part my part
In life, for good and ill.

X

No. I yearn upward, touch you close,
   Then stand away. I kiss your cheek,
Catch your soul's warmth,—I pluck the rose
   And love it more than tongue can speak—
50 Then the good minute goes.

XI

Already how am I so far
   Out of that minute? Must I go
Still like the thistle-ball, no bar,
   Onward, whenever light winds blow,
Fixed[5] by no friendly star?

XII

Just when I seemed about to learn!
   Where is the thread now? Off again!
The old trick! Only I discern—
   Infinite passion, and the pain
60 Of finite hearts that yearn.

1854   1855

[5] **Fixed**   set on course

EMILY BRONTË
1818–1848

Emily Brontë's poetry, like her novel *Wuthering Heights* (1847), displays intense preoccupation with the intertwining themes of love and death. Many of her poems grew out of stories concerning the make-believe kingdom of Gondal, which Emily and her sisters had conceived in their lonely Yorkshire childhood. Of these, "Remembrance" is particularly impressive for its powerful expression of stoic control over deep-felt grief and longing.

Long Neglect Has Worn Away

Long neglect has worn away
Half the sweet enchanting smile;
Time has turned the bloom to grey;
Mould and damp the face defile.

But that lock of silky hair,
Still beneath the picture twined,
Tells what once those features were,
Paints their image on the mind.

Fair the hand that traced that line,
10   "Dearest, ever deem me true";
Swiftly flew the fingers fine
When the pen that motto drew.

1837   1923

Remembrance

Cold in the earth, and the deep snow piled above thee!
Far, far removed, cold in the dreary grave!
Have I forgot, my Only Love, to love thee,
Severed at last by Time's all-wearing wave?

Now, when alone, do my thoughts no longer hover
Over the mountains on Angora's shore;
Resting their wings where heath and fern-leaves cover
That noble heart for ever, ever more?

Cold in the earth, and fifteen wild Decembers
10   From those brown hills have melted into spring;
Faithful indeed is the spirit that remembers
After such years of change and suffering!

Sweet Love of youth, forgive if I forget thee
While the World's tide is bearing me along:
Sterner desires and darker hopes beset me,
Hopes which obscure but cannot do thee wrong.

No other Sun has lightened up my heaven;
No other Star has ever shone for me:
All my life's bliss from thy dear life was given—
20   All my life's bliss is in the grave with thee.

But when the days of golden dreams had perished
And even Despair was powerless to destroy,
Then did I learn how existence could be cherished,
Strengthened and fed without the aid of joy;

Then did I check the tears of useless passion,
Weaned my young soul from yearning after thine;
Sternly denied its burning wish to hasten
Down to that tomb already more than mine!

And even yet, I dare not let it languish,
30   Dare not indulge in Memory's rapturous pain;
Once drinking deep of that divinest anguish,
How could I seek the empty world again?

1843   1846

HERMAN MELVILLE
1819–1891

Herman Melville is best known as the author of *Moby-Dick*, one of the classics of American fiction. But increasing attention has been paid to his poetry, which was written mainly in his later years, after his earlier careers as seaman and novelist. Like his contemporary Whitman, he was profoundly stirred by the American Civil War, which he commemorated in *Battle-Pieces* (1866), a volume containing some of his finest poems. Three other volumes of poetry followed at sporadic intervals. Many of Melville's poems express an outlook similar to that of *Moby-Dick*, viewing life as filled with cruelties, both natural and manmade, and determined by forces indifferent to our desires. His poetic style, well suited to this somber vision, avoids pretty effects, often using irregular meter, compressed, knotted syntax, and difficult diction. "The Portent" and "March into Virginia" provide good examples of these effects. Little appreciated by his own contemporaries, his rugged, unpolished style has made Melville's poetry appealing to modern readers.

The Portent[1]

Hanging from the beam,
    Slowly swaying (such the law),
Gaunt the shadow on your green,
    Shenandoah![2]
The cut is on the crown
    (Lo, John Brown),
And the stabs shall heal no more.

Hidden in the cap
    Is the anguish none can draw;
10 So your future veils its face,
    Shenandoah!

[1] John Brown (1800–1859) led an assault against the Federal Arsenal at Harper's Ferry, Virginia (now West Virginia), in an attempt to liberate the southern slaves. He was captured and hanged for treason.
[2] **Shenandoah** the Shenandoah Valley, where Harper's Ferry is located

But the streaming beard is shown
(Weird[3] John Brown),
The meteor[4] of the war.

1866

[3] **Weird** possessed of prophetic power or control of destiny

[4] **meteor** Meteors were once thought to forebode impending cataclysms and upheavals.

The March into Virginia

ENDING IN THE FIRST MANASSAS (JULY 1861)[1]

Did all the lets[2] and bars appear
   To every just or larger end,
Whence should come the trust and cheer?
   Youth must its ignorant impulse lend—
Age finds place in the rear.
   All wars are boyish, and are fought by boys,
   The champions and enthusiasts of the state:
      Turbid ardours and vain joys
        Not barrenly abate—
10   Stimulants to the power mature,
        Preparatives of fate.
Who here forecasteth the event?
What heart but spurns at precedent
   And warnings of the wise,
Contemned foreclosures of surprise?
The banners play, the bugles call,
The air is blue and prodigal.
      No berrying party, pleasure-wooed,
No picnic party in the May,
20   Ever went less loth than they
      Into that leafy neighbourhood.
In Bacchic[3] glee they file toward Fate,
Moloch's[4] uninitiate;
Expectancy, and glad surmise
Of battle's unknown mysteries.
All they feel is this: 'tis glory,
A rapture sharp, though transitory,
Yet lasting in belaurelled story.
   So they gaily go to fight,
30   Chatting left and laughing right.

But some who this blithe mood present,
   As on in lightsome files they fare,
Shall die experienced ere three days are spent—

[1] also known as the Battle of Bull Run, fought at Manassas Junction, Virginia, July 21, 1861; one of the worst defeats for the Northern forces in the Civil War

[2] **lets** hindrances

[3] **Bacchic** pertaining to Bacchus, god of wine and festivity

[4] **Moloch** a Palestinian deity of Old Testament times to whom children were sacrificed

Perish, enlightened by the volleyed glare;
Or shame survive, and, like to adamant,[5]
The throe of Second Manassas[6] share.

1866

[5] **adamant** an extremely hard substance
[6] **Second Manassas** The Northern forces were again defeated at Manassas, August 30, 1862.

Monody[1]

To have known him, to have loved him
    After loneness long;
And then to be estranged in life,
    And neither in the wrong;
And now for death to set his seal—
    Ease me, a little ease, my song!

By wintry hills his hermit-mound
    The sheeted snow-drifts drape,
And houseless there the snow-bird flits
10   Beneath the fir-trees' crape:
Glazed now with ice the cloistral vine
    That hid the shyest grape.

1864?   1891

[1] A monody is a brief elegy or dirge; it is gener-
ally assumed that this poem is addressed to the
memory of the novelist Nathaniel Hawthorne (1804–1864), with whom Melville maintained
an intense but difficult friendship.

The Maldive Shark

About the Shark, phlegmatical one,
Pale sot of the Maldive sea,[1]
The sleek little pilot-fish, azure and slim,
How alert in attendance be.
From his saw-pit of mouth, from his charnel of maw,
They have nothing of harm to dread,
But liquidly glide on his ghastly flank
Or before his Gorgonian head;[2]
Or lurk in the port of serrated teeth
10 In white triple tiers of glittering gates,
And there find a haven when peril's abroad,
An asylum in jaws of the Fates!
They are friends; and friendly they guide him to prey,
Yet never partake of the treat—
Eyes and brains to the dotard lethargic and dull,
Pale ravener of horrible meat.

1888

[1] **Maldive sea** an area of the Indian Ocean,
southwest of India

[2] **Gorgonian head** The Gorgon was a snake-
haired woman, direct sight of whom turned the
viewer to stone.

Art

In placid hours well pleased we dream
Of many a brave unbodied scheme.
But form to lend, pulsed life create,
What unlike things must meet and mate:
A flame to melt—a wind to freeze;
Sad patience—joyous energies;
Humility—yet pride and scorn;
Instinct and study; love and hate;
Audacity—reverence. These must mate
And fuse with Jacob's mystic heart,
To wrestle with the angel[1]—Art.

1891

[1] **angel** In Genesis 32:24-30, Jacob wrestles
with an angel who proves to be the Lord God.

WALT WHITMAN
1819–1892

Walt Whitman, the most influential of American poets, was born in rural Long Island. From his mid-teens to his early thirties he worked as a journalist for several newspapers in and around Manhattan, absorbing the politics, culture, street-life, and vitality of the city. He gave up journalism in the 1850s and emerged in 1855 as the author of *Leaves of Grass*. In content and style, this volume was nineteenth-century America's most daring collection of poems. Although it was virtually ignored—except by Emerson, who praised it highly—Whitman persevered with his self-appointed mission as poetic spokesman for his nation, publishing many subsequent editions of the collection and adding new sections to it. Among the most noteworthy of these are "Calamus" (1860), a remarkably frank evocation of homoerotic affections, and "Drum-Taps" (1865), a collection dealing with the American Civil War, which Whitman experienced while working as a volunteer nurse for the Union forces (1862–65). Disabled by a stroke in 1873, he spent the rest of his life in retirement, at last achieving fame and critical recognition.

Whitman's chief intellectual influence was Emerson's philosophy of magnified individualism and the transcendental unity of nature. Many biographers suggest that Whitman's homosexuality provided a more intimate influence, freeing him from the conventional view of eroticism, but also threatening him psychologically. Such a tension could account for Whitman's habit of dispersing his affections over generalized objects—the common people, the American nation, the sensuous delights of the physical world. But neither intellectual debts nor psychological preconditions account for the outstanding features of Whitman's poetic genius: his eloquence and flashes of humor, his keen eye for small details, and his panoramic knowledge of daily human activities. The range, variety, and objective clarity of his verse embody his desire to merge his personality with the collective experience of his countrymen. Just as the Lincoln elegized in the beautiful "When Lilacs Last in the Dooryard Bloomed" is more than an assassinated president—he is a mythic embodiment of America as a whole—so the "Myself" celebrated in the long lyric sequence "Song of Myself" has more to do with the self of each reader than with Walt Whitman the man. "I am large," the poet says, "I contain multitudes."

The boldness of Whitman's project in *Leaves* extends to his style. The poems are written in free verse, without rhyme or definite meter, and the lines sometimes extend to dozens of syllables. Biblical cadences and rhythms, often mingled with everyday colloquialisms, create an effect that hovers between melodious chanting and common talk. With epic sweep Whitman crowds people, places, and things into lengthy, formless catalogues, but he is also master of delicate nuance and sharply precise, economical description. Of special interest to modern poets is his liberal and adroit use of multi-layered imagery and symbolism. Whitman's development of a new poetic style and his powerful, invigorating vision have had an incalculable effect on modern poetry. Every major American poet of this century has felt his influence, which shows no signs of diminishing.

From Song of Myself

1

I celebrate myself, and sing myself,
And what I assume you shall assume,
For every atom belonging to me as good belongs to you.

I loafe and invite my soul,
I lean and loafe at my ease observing a spear of summer grass.
My tongue, every atom of my blood, form'd from this soil, this air,
Born here of parents born here from parents the same, and their parents the same,
I, now thirty-seven years old in perfect health begin,
Hoping to cease not till death.

10   Creeds and schools in abeyance,
Retiring back a while sufficed at what they are, but never forgotten,
I harbor for good or bad, I permit to speak at every hazard,
Nature without check with original energy.

2

Houses and rooms are full of perfumes, the shelves are crowded with perfumes,
I breathe the fragrance myself and know it and like it,
The distillation would intoxicate me also, but I shall not let it.

The atmosphere is not a perfume, it has no taste of the distillation, it is odorless,
It is for my mouth forever, I am in love with it,
I will go to the bank by the wood and become undisguised and naked,
20   I am mad for it to be in contact with me.
The smoke of my own breath,
Echoes, ripples, buzz'd whispers, love-root, silk-thread, crotch and vine,
My respiration and inspiration, the beating of my heart, the passing of blood and air through my lungs,
The sniff of green leaves and dry leaves, and of the shore and dark-color'd sea-rocks, and of hay in the barn,
The sound of the belch'd words of my voice loos'd to the eddies of the wind,
A few light kisses, a few embraces, a reaching around of arms,

The play of shine and shade on the trees as the supple boughs wag,
The delight alone or in the rush of the streets, or along the fields and hill-sides,
The feeling of health, the full-noon trill, the song of me rising from bed and
    meeting the sun.

30 Have you reckon'd a thousand acres much? have you reckon'd the earth
    much?
Have you practis'd so long to learn to read?
Have you felt so proud to get at the meaning of poems?

Stop this day and night with me and you shall possess the origin of all poems,
You shall possess the good of the earth and sun, (there are millions of suns
    left,)
You shall no longer take things at second or third hand, nor look through the
    eyes of the dead, nor feed on the spectres in books,
You shall not look through my eyes either, nor take things from me,
You shall listen to all sides and filter them from your self.

     5

I believe in you my soul, the other I am must not abase itself to you,
And you must not be abased to the other.

Loafe with me on the grass, loose the stop from your throat,
Not words, not music or rhyme I want, not custom or lecture, not even the
    best,
Only the lull I like, the hum of your valvèd voice.

I mind how once we lay such a transparent summer morning,
How you settled your head athwart my hips and gently turn'd over upon me,
And parted the shirt from my bosom-bone, and plunged your tongue to my
    bare-stript heart,
90 And reach'd till you felt my beard, and reach'd till you held my feet.

Swiftly arose and spread around me the peace and knowledge that pass all the
    argument of the earth,
And I know that the hand of God is the promise of my own,
And I know that the spirit of God is the brother of my own,
And that all the men ever born are also my brothers, and the women my
    sisters and lovers,
And that a kelson[1] of the creation is love,
And limitless are leaves stiff or drooping in the fields,
And brown ants in the little wells beneath them,
And mossy scabs of the worm fence, heap'd stones, elder, mullein[2] and
    poke-weed.[3]

---

[1] **kelson** in shipbuilding, a beam added to give structural strength
[2] **mullein** a tall plant with spikes of flowers
[3] **poke-weed** a common weed with poisonous red-purple berries

11

Twenty-eight young men bathe by the shore,
200   Twenty-eight young men and all so friendly;
Twenty-eight years of womanly life and all so lonesome.

She owns the fine house by the rise of the bank,
She hides handsome and richly drest aft the blinds of the window.

Which of the young men does she like the best?
Ah the homeliest of them is beautiful to her.

Where are you off to, lady? for I see you,
You splash in the water there, yet stay stock still in your room.

Dancing and laughing along the beach came the twenty-ninth bather,
The rest did not see her, but she saw them and loved them.

210   The beards of the young men glisten'd with wet, it ran from their long hair,
Little streams pass'd all over their bodies.

An unseen hand also pass'd over their bodies,
It descended tremblingly from their temples and ribs.

The young men float on their backs, their white bellies bulge to the sun, they
    do not ask who seizes fast to them,
They do not know who puffs and declines with pendant and bending arch,
They do not think whom they souse with spray.

. . .

24

Walt Whitman, a kosmos,[4] of Manhattan the son,
Turbulent, fleshy, sensual, eating, drinking and breeding,
No sentimentalist, no stander above men and women or apart from them,
500   No more modest than immodest.

Unscrew the locks from the doors!
Unscrew the doors themselves from their jambs!

Whoever degrades another degrades me,
And whatever is done or said returns at last to me.

Through me the afflatus[5] surging and surging, through me the current and
index.

I speak the pass-word primeval, I give the sign of democracy,
By God! I will accept nothing which all cannot have their counterpart of on
    the same terms.

---

[4] **kosmos** the universe, considered as an ordered   [5] **afflatus** inspiration
system

Through me many long dumb voices,
Voices of the interminable generations of prisoners and slaves,
510   Voices of the diseas'd and despairing and of thieves and dwarfs,
Voices of cycles of preparation and accretion,
And of the threads that connect the stars, and of wombs and of the father-stuff,
And of the rights of them the others are down upon,
Of the deform'd, trivial, flat, foolish, despised,
Fog in the air, beetles rolling balls of dung.
Through me forbidden voices,
Voices of sexes and lusts, voices veil'd and I remove the veil,
Voices indecent by me clarified and transfigur'd.

I do not press my fingers across my mouth,
520   I keep as delicate around the bowels as around the head and heart,
Copulation is no more rank to me than death is.

I believe in the flesh and the appetites,
Seeing, hearing, feeling, are miracles, and each part and tag of me is a
        miracle.

Divine am I inside and out, and I make holy whatever I touch or am touch'd
        from,
The scent of these arm-pits aroma finer than prayer,
This head more than churches, bibles, and all the creeds.

If I worship one thing more than another it shall be the spread of my own
        body, or any part of it,
Translucent mould of me it shall be you!
Shaded ledges and rests it shall be you!
530   Firm masculine colter⁶ it shall be you!
Whatever goes to the tilth⁷ of me it shall be you!
You my rich blood! your milky stream pale strippings of my life!
Breast that presses against other breasts it shall be you!
My brain it shall be your occult convolutions!
Root of wash'd sweet-flag!⁸ timorous pond-snipe!⁹ nest of guarded duplicate
        eggs! it shall be you!
Mix'd tussled hay of head, beard, brawn, it shall be you!
Trickling sap of maple, fibre of manly wheat, it shall be you!
Sun so generous it shall be you!
Vapors lighting and shading my face it shall be you!
540   You sweaty brooks and dews it shall be you!
Winds whose soft-tickling genitals rub against me it shall be you!
Broad muscular fields, branches of live oak, loving lounger in my winding
        paths, it shall be you!
Hands I have taken, face I have kiss'd, mortal I have ever touch'd, it shall be
        you.

⁶ colter   literally, the ground-breaking blade of   ⁹ pond-snipe   a marsh bird with a long bill used
a plow   for digging grubs. The images in this line are all
⁷ tilth   plowing and cultivation   intended to suggest the male genitals.
⁸ sweet-flag   a tall thin-leaved marsh plant, the
calamus

I dote on myself, there is that lot of me and all so luscious,
Each moment and whatever happens thrills me with joy,
I cannot tell how my ankles bend, nor whence the cause of my faintest wish,
Nor the cause of the friendship I emit, nor the cause of the friendship I take
    again.

That I walk up my stoop, I pause to consider if it really be,
A morning-glory at my window satisfies me more than the metaphysics of
    books.

550   To behold the day-break!
The little light fades the immense and diaphanous shadows,
The air tastes good to my palate.

Hefts of the moving world at innocent gambols silently rising freshly exuding,
Scooting obliquely high and low.

Something I cannot see puts upward libidinous prongs,
Seas of bright juice suffuse heaven.

The earth by the sky staid with, the daily close of their junction,
The heav'd challenge from the east that moment over my head,
The mocking taunt, See then whether you shall be master!

       28
Is this then a touch? quivering me to a new identity,
620   Flames and ether making a rush for my veins,
Treacherous tip of me reaching and crowding to help them,
My flesh and blood playing out lightning to strike what is hardly different
    from myself,
On all sides prurient provokers stiffening my limbs,
Straining the udder of my heart for its withheld drip,
Behaving licentious toward me, taking no denial,
Depriving me of my best as for a purpose,
Unbuttoning my clothes, holding me by the bare waist,
Deluding my confusion with the calm of the sunlight and pasture-fields,
Immodestly sliding the fellow-senses away,
630   They bribed to swap off with touch and go and gaze at the edges of me,
No consideration, no regard for my draining strength or my anger,
Fetching the rest of the herd around to enjoy them a while,
Then all uniting to stand on a headland and worry me.

The sentries desert every other part of me,
They have left me helpless to a red marauder,
They all come to the headland to witness and assist against me.

I am given up by traitors,
I talk wildly, I have lost my wits, I and nobody else am the greatest traitor,
I went myself first to the headland, my own hands carried me there.

640   You villain touch! what are you doing? my breath is tight in its throat,
Unclench your floodgates, you are too much for me.

29

Blind loving wrestling touch, sheath'd hooded sharp-tooth'd touch!
Did it make you ache so, leaving me?

Parting track'd by arriving, perpetual payment of perpetual loan,
Rich showering rain, and recompense richer afterward.

Sprouts take and accumulate, stand by the curb prolific and vital,
Landscapes projected masculine, full-sized and golden.

. . .

52

The spotted hawk swoops by and accuses me, he complains of my gab and
    my loitering.

I too am not a bit tamed, I too am untranslatable,
I sound my barbaric yawp over the roofs of the world.

The last scud of day holds back for me,
It flings my likeness after the rest and true as any on the shadow'd wilds,
It coaxes me to the vapor and the dusk.

I depart as air, I shake my white locks at the runaway sun,
I effuse my flesh in eddies, and drift it in lacy jags.

I bequeath myself to the dirt to grow from the grass I love,
1340   If you want me again look for me under your boot-soles.

You will hardly know who I am or what I mean,
But I shall be good health to you nevertheless,
And filter and fibre your blood.

Failing to fetch me at first keep encouraged,
Missing me one place search another,
I stop somewhere waiting for you.

1855, 1881

Out of the Cradle Endlessly Rocking

Out of the cradle endlessly rocking,
Out of the mocking-bird's throat, the musical shuttle,
Out of the Ninth-month midnight,
Over the sterile sands and the fields beyond, where the child leaving his bed
    wander'd alone, bareheaded, barefoot,
Down from the shower'd halo,
Up from the mystic play of shadows twining and twisting as if they were
    alive,
Out from the patches of briers and blackberries,
From the memories of the bird that chanted to me,
From your memories sad brother, from the fitful risings and fallings I heard,

10   From under that yellow half-moon late-risen and swollen as if with tears,
From those beginning notes of yearning and love there in the mist,
From the thousand responses of my heart never to cease,
From the myriad thence-arous'd words,
From the word stronger and more delicious than any,
From such as now they start the scene revisiting,
As a flock, twittering, rising, or overhead passing,
Borne hither, ere all eludes me, hurriedly,
A man, yet by these tears a little boy again,
Throwing myself on the sand, confronting the waves,
20   I, chanter of pains and joys, uniter of here and hereafter,
Taking all hints to use them, but swiftly leaping beyond them,
A reminiscence sing.

Once Paumanok,[1]
When the lilac-scent was in the air and Fifth-month grass was growing,
Up this seashore in some briers,
Two feather'd guests from Alabama, two together,
And their nest, and four light-green eggs spotted with brown,
And every day the he-bird to and fro near at hand,
And every day the she-bird crouch'd on her nest, silent, with bright eyes,
30   And every day I, a curious boy, never too close, never disturbing them,
Cautiously peering, absorbing, translating.

Shine! shine! shine![2]
Pour down your warmth, great sun!
While we bask, we two together.

Two together!
Winds blow south, or winds blow north,
Day come white, or night come black,
Home, or rivers and mountains from home,
Singing all time, minding no time,
40   *While we two keep together.*

Till of a sudden,
May-be kill'd, unknown to her mate,
One forenoon the she-bird crouch'd not on the nest,
Nor return'd that afternoon, nor the next,
Nor ever appear'd again.

And thenceforward all summer in the sound of the sea,
And at night under the full of the moon in calmer weather,
Over the hoarse surging of the sea,
Or flitting from brier to brier by day,
50   I saw, I heard at intervals the remaining one, the he-bird,
The solitary guest from Alabama.

[1] **Paumanok** Indian name for Long Island
[2] The italicized passages in the poem represent
the bird's song.

Blow! blow! blow!
Blow up sea-winds along Paumanok's shore;
I wait and I wait till you blow my mate to me.

Yes, when the stars glisten'd,
All night long on the prong of a moss-scallop'd stake,
Down almost amid the slapping waves,
Sat the lone singer wonderful causing tears.

He call'd on his mate,
60   He pour'd forth the meanings which I of all men know.

Yes my brother I know,
The rest might not, but I have treasur'd every note,
For more than once dimly down to the beach gliding,
Silent, avoiding the moonbeams, blending myself with the shadows,
Recalling now the obscure shapes, the echoes, the sounds and sights after
        their sorts,
The white arms out in the breakers tirelessly tossing,
I, with bare feet, a child, the wind wafting my hair,
Listen'd long and long.

Listen'd to keep, to sing, now translating the notes,
70   Following you my brother.

Soothe! soothe! soothe!
Close on its wave soothes the wave behind,
And again another behind embracing and lapping, every one close,
But my love soothes not me, not me.

Low hangs the moon, it rose late,
It is lagging—O I think it is heavy with love, with love.

O madly the sea pushes upon the land,
With love, with love.

O night! do I not see my love fluttering out among the breakers?
80   *What is that little black thing I see there in the white?*

Loud! loud! loud!
Loud I call to you, my love!

High and clear I shoot my voice over the waves,
Surely you must know who is here, is here,
You must know who I am, my love.

Low-hanging moon!
What is that dusky spot in your brown yellow?
O it is the shape, the shape of my mate!
O moon do not keep her from me any longer.

90 *Land! land! O land!*
Whichever way I turn, O I think you could give me my mate back again if you
  only would,
For I am almost sure I see her dimly whichever way I look.

O rising stars!
Perhaps the one I want so much will rise, will rise with some of you.

O throat! O trembling throat!
Sound clearer through the atmosphere!
Pierce the woods, the earth,
Somewhere listening to catch you must be the one I want.

Shake out carols!
100 *Solitary here, the night's carols!*
Carols of lonesome love! death's carols!
Carols under that lagging, yellow, waning moon!
O under that moon where she droops almost down into the sea!
O reckless despairing carols.

But soft! sink low!
Soft! let me just murmur,
And do you wait a moment you husky-nois'd sea,
For somewhere I believe I heard my mate responding to me,
So faint, I must be still, be still to listen,
110 *But not altogether still, for then she might not come immediately to me.*

Hither my love!
Here I am! here!
With this just-sustain'd note I announce myself to you,
This gentle call is for you my love, for you.

Do not be decoy'd elsewhere,
That is the whistle of the wind, it is not my voice,
That is the fluttering, the fluttering of the spray,
Those are the shadows of leaves.

O darkness! O in vain!
120 *O I am very sick and sorrowful.*

O brown halo in the sky near the moon, drooping upon the sea!
O troubled reflection in the sea!
O throat! O throbbing heart!
And I singing uselessly, uselessly all the night.

O past! O happy life! O songs of joy!
In the air, in the woods, over fields,
Loved! loved! loved! loved! loved!
But my mate no more, no more with me!
We two together no more.

130 The aria sinking,
All else continuing, the stars shining,
The winds blowing, the notes of the bird continuous echoing,
With angry moans the fierce old mother incessantly moaning,
On the sands of Paumanok's shore gray and rustling,
The yellow half-moon enlarged, sagging down, drooping, the face of the sea
 almost touching,
The boy ecstatic, with his bare feet the waves, with his hair the atmosphere
 dallying,
The love in the heart long pent, now loose, now at last tumultuously bursting,
The aria's meaning, the ears, the soul, swiftly depositing,
The strange tears down the cheeks coursing,
140 The colloquy there, the trio, each uttering,
The undertone, the savage old mother incessantly crying,
To the boy's soul's questions sullenly timing, some drown'd secret hissing,
To the outsetting bard.

Demon or bird! (said the boy's soul,)
Is it indeed toward your mate you sing? or is it really to me?
For I, that was a child, my tongue's use sleeping, now I have heard you,
Now in a moment I know what I am for, I awake,
And already a thousand singers, a thousand songs, clearer, louder and more
 sorrowful than yours,
A thousand warbling echoes have started to life within me, never to die.

150 O you singer solitary, singing by yourself, projecting me,
O solitary me listening, never more shall I cease perpetuating you,
Never more shall I escape, never more the reverberations,
Never more the cries of unsatisfied love be absent from me,
Never again leave me to be the peaceful child I was before what there in the
 night,
By the sea under the yellow and sagging moon,
The messenger there arous'd, the fire, the sweet hell within,
The unknown want, the destiny of me.

O give me the clew! (it lurks in the night here somewhere,)
O if I am to have so much, let me have more!

160 A word then, (for I will conquer it,)
The word final, superior to all,
Subtle, sent up—what is it?—I listen;
Are you whispering it, and have been all the time, you seawaves?
Is that it from your liquid rims and wet sands?

Whereto answering, the sea,
Delaying not, hurrying not,
Whisper'd me through the night, and very plainly before daybreak,
Lisp'd to me the low and delicious word death,
And again death, death, death, death,
170 Hissing melodious, neither like the bird nor like my arous'd child's heart,

But edging near as privately for me rustling at my feet,
Creeping thence steadily up to my ears and laving me softly all over,
Death, death, death, death, death.

Which I do not forget,
But fuse the song of my dusky demon and brother,
That he sang to me in the moonlight on Paumanok's gray beach,
With the thousand responsive songs at random,
My own songs awaked from that hour,
And with them the key, the word up from the waves,
180   The word of the sweetest song and all songs,
That strong and delicious word which, creeping to my feet,
(Or like some old crone rocking the cradle, swathed in sweet garments,
    bending aside,)
The sea whisper'd me.

1859, 1881

When I Heard at the Close of the Day[1]

When I heard at the close of the day how my name had been receiv'd with
    plaudits in the capitol, still it was not a happy night for me that follow'd,
And else when I carous'd, or when my plans were accomplish'd, still I was
    not happy,
But the day when I rose at dawn from the bed of perfect health, refresh'd,
    singing, inhaling the ripe breath of autumn,
When I saw the full moon in the west grow pale and disappear in the morning
    light,
When I wander'd alone over the beach, and undressing bathed, laughing with
    the cool waters, and saw the sun rise,
And when I thought how my dear friend my lover was on his way coming, O
    then I was happy,
O then each breath tasted sweeter, and all that day my food nourish'd me
    more, and the beautiful day pass'd well,
And the next came with equal joy, and with the next at evening came my
    friend,
And that night while all was still I heard the waters roll slowly continually up
    the shores,
10   I heard the hissing rustle of the liquid and sands as directed to me whispering
    to congratulate me,
For the one I love most lay sleeping by me under the same cover in the cool
    night,
In the stillness in the autumn moonbeams his face was inclined toward me,
And his arm lay lightly around my breast—and that night I was happy.

1860

[1] from "Calamus," a series of poems devoted to
what Whitman called "manly love"

Vigil Strange I Kept on the Field One Night[1]

Vigil strange I kept on the field one night;
When you my son and my comrade dropt at my side that day,
One look I but gave which your dear eyes return'd with a look I shall never
    forget,
One touch of your hand to mine O boy, reach'd up as you lay on the ground,
Then onward I sped in the battle, the even-contested battle,
Till late in the night reliev'd to the place at last again I made my way,
Found you in death so cold dear comrade, found your body son of responding
    kisses, (never again on earth responding,)
Bared your face in the starlight, curious the scene, cool blew the moderate
    night-wind,
Long there and then in vigil I stood, dimly around me the battlefield spreading,
10   Vigil wondrous and vigil sweet there in the fragrant silent night,
But not a tear fell, not even a long-drawn sigh, long, long I gazed,
Then on the earth partially reclining sat by your side leaning my chin in my
    hands,
Passing sweet hours, immortal and mystic hours with you dearest comrade—
    not a tear, not a word,
Vigil of silence, love and death, vigil for you my son and my soldier,
As onward silently stars aloft, eastward new ones upward stole,
Vigil final for you brave boy, (I could not save you, swift was your death,
I faithfully loved you and cared for you living, I think we shall surely meet
    again,)
Till at latest lingering of the night, indeed just as the dawn appear'd,
My comrade I wrapt in his blanket, envelop'd well his form,
Folded the blanket well, tucking it carefully over head and carefully under
20   feet,
And there and then and bathed by the rising sun, my son in his grave, in his
    rude-dug grave I deposited,
Ending my vigil strange with that, vigil of night and battle-field dim,
Vigil for boy of responding kisses, (never again on earth responding,)
Vigil for comrade swiftly slain, vigil I never forget, how as day brighten'd,
I rose from the chill ground and folded my soldier well in his blanket,
And buried him where he fell.

1865

[1] from "Drum-Taps," Whitman's collection of
poems on the Civil War. The bereaved speaker
of the poem is fictitious.

By the Bivouac's Fitful Flame

By the bivouac's fitful flame,
A procession winding around me, solemn and sweet and slow—but first I
    note,
The tents of the sleeping army, the fields' and woods' dim outline,
The darkness lit by spots of kindled fire, the silence,
Like a phantom far or near an occasional figure moving,

The shrubs and trees, (as I lift my eyes they seem to be stealthily watching
    me,)
While wind in procession thoughts, O tender and wondrous thoughts,
Of life and death, of home and the past and loved, and of those that are far
    away;
A solemn and slow procession there as I sit on the ground,
10 By the bivouac's fitful flame.

1865

A Sight in Camp in the Daybreak Gray and Dim

A sight in camp in the daybreak gray and dim,
As from my tent I emerge so early sleepless,
As slow I walk in the cool fresh air the path near by the hospital tent,
Three forms I see on stretchers lying, brought out there untended lying,
Over each the blanket spread, ample brownish woolen blanket,
Gray and heavy blanket, folding, covering all.

Curious I halt and silent stand,
Then with light fingers I from the face of the nearest the first just lift the
    blanket;
Who are you elderly man so gaunt and grim, with well-gray'd hair, and flesh
    all sunken about the eyes?
10 Who are you my dear comrade?

Then to the second I step—and who are you my child and darling?
Who are you sweet boy with cheeks yet blooming?

Then to the third—a face nor child nor old, very calm, as of beautiful
    yellow-white ivory;
Young man I think I know you—I think this face is the face of the Christ
    himself,
Dead and divine and brother of all, and here again he lies.

1865   1867

When Lilacs Last in the Dooryard Bloom'd[1]

1

When lilacs last in the dooryard bloom'd,
And the great star[2] early droop'd in the western sky in the night,
I mourn'd, and yet shall mourn with ever-returning spring.

Ever-returning spring, trinity sure to me you bring,
Lilac blooming perennial and drooping star in the west,
And thought of him I love.

[1] an elegy for President Abraham Lincoln, assassinated April 14, 1865. The symbolism and development of this poem may be profitably compared with that of other great poetic elegies such as Milton's "Lycidas" (p. 275 above) and Shelley's "Adonais" (p. 584).
[2] **great star** the evening star, Venus

2

O powerful western fallen star!
O shades of night—O moody, tearful night!
O great star disappear'd—O the black murk that hides the star!
10 O cruel hands that hold me powerless—O helpless soul of me!
O harsh surrounding cloud that will not free my soul.

3

In the dooryard fronting an old farm-house near the white-wash'd palings,
Stands the lilac-bush[3] tall-growing with heart-shaped leaves of rich green,
With many a pointed blossom rising delicate, with the perfume strong I love,
With every leaf a miracle—and from this bush in the dooryard,
With delicate-color'd blossoms and heart-shaped leaves of rich green,
A sprig with its flower I break.

4

In the swamp in secluded recesses,
A shy and hidden bird is warbling a song.

20 Solitary the thrush,
The hermit withdrawn to himself, avoiding the settlements,
Sings by himself a song.

Song of the bleeding throat,
Death's outlet song of life, (for well dear brother I know,
If thou wast not granted to sing thou would'st surely die.)

5

Over the breast of the spring, the land, amid cities,
Amid lanes and through old woods, where lately the violets peep'd
    from the ground, spotting the gray debris,
Amid the grass in the fields each side of the lanes, passing the endless grass,
Passing the yellow-spear'd wheat, every grain from its shroud in
    the dark-brown fields uprisen,
30 Passing the apple-tree blows of white and pink in the orchards,
Carrying a corpse to where it shall rest in the grave,
Night and day journeys a coffin.[4]

6

Coffin that passes through lanes and streets,
Through day and night with the great cloud darkening the land,
With the pomp of the inloop'd flags with the cities draped in black,
With the show of the States themselves as of crape-veil'd women standing,

---

[3] **lilac-bush** Speaking about the day of Lincoln's murder, Whitman said: "I remember where I was stopping at the time, the season being advanced, there were many lilacs in full bloom. By one of those caprices that enter and give tinge to events without being at all part of them, I find myself always reminded of the great trag-edy of that day by the sight and odor of these blossoms."

[4] **journeys a coffin** Lincoln's funeral train passed through many cities and rural areas on its route from Washington, D.C., to Springfield, Illinois, attracting thousands of mourners all along the way.

With processions long and winding and the flambeaus[5] of the night,
With the countless torches lit, with the silent sea of faces and the unbared
heads,
With the waiting depot, the arriving coffin, and the sombre faces,
With dirges through the night, with the thousand voices rising strong and
40   solemn,
With all the mournful voices of the dirges pour'd around the coffin,
The dim-lit churches and the shuddering organs—where amid these you
journey,
With the tolling tolling bells' perpetual clang,
Here, coffin that slowly passes,
I give you my sprig of lilac.

      7
(Nor for you, for one alone,
Blossoms and branches green to coffins all I bring,
For fresh as the morning, thus would I chant a song for you O sane and sacred
death.

All over bouquets of roses,
50 O death, I cover you over with roses and early lilies,
But mostly and now the lilac that blooms the first,
Copious I break, I break the sprigs from the bushes,
With loaded arms I come, pouring for you,
For you and the coffins all of you O death.)

      8
O western orb sailing the heaven,
Now I know what you must have meant as a month since I walk'd,
As I walk'd in silence the transparent shadowy night,
As I saw you had something to tell as you bent to me night after night,
As you droop'd from the sky low down as if to my side, (while the other stars
all look'd on,)
60 As we wander'd together the solemn night, (for something I know not what
kept me from sleep,)
As the night advanced, and I saw on the rim of the west how full you were of
woe,
As I stood on the rising ground in the breeze in the cool transparent night,
As I watch'd where you pass'd and was lost in the netherward black of the
night,
As my soul in its trouble dissatisfied sank, as where you sad orb,
Concluded, dropt in the night, and was gone.

      9
Sing on there in the swamp,
O singer bashful and tender, I hear your notes, I hear your call,
I hear, I come presently, I understand you,
But a moment I linger, for the lustrous star has detain'd me,
70 The star my departing comrade holds and detains me.

[5] **flambeaus** lighted torches

10

O how shall I warble myself for the dead one there I loved?
And how shall I deck my song for the large sweet soul that has gone?
And what shall my perfume be for the grave of him I love?

Sea-winds blown from east and west,
Blown from the Eastern sea and blown from the Western sea, till there on the
    prairies meeting,
These and with these and the breath of my chant,
I'll perfume the grave of him I love.

11

O what shall I hang on the chamber walls?
And what shall the picture be that I hang on the walls,
80 To adorn the burial-house of him I love?

Pictures of growing spring and farms and homes,
With the Fourth-month eve at sundown, and the gray smoke lucid and bright,
With floods of the yellow gold of the gorgeous, indolent, sinking sun, burn-
    ing, expanding the air,
With the fresh sweet herbage under foot, and the pale green leaves of the
    trees prolific,
In the distance the flowing glaze, the breast of the river, with a wind-dapple
    here and there,
With ranging hills on the banks, with many a line against the sky, and
    shadows,
And the city at hand with dwellings so dense, and stacks of chimneys,
And all the scenes of life and the workshops, and the workmen homeward
    returning.

12

Lo, body and soul—this land,
My own Manhattan with spires, and the sparkling and hurrying tides, and the
90 ships,
The varied and ample land, the South and North in the light, Ohio's shores
    and flashing Missouri,
And ever the far-spreading prairies cover'd with grass and corn.

Lo, the most excellent sun so calm and haughty,
The violet and purple morn with just-felt breezes,
The gentle soft-born measureless light,
The miracle spreading bathing all, the fulfill'd noon,
The coming eve delicious, the welcome night and the stars,
Over my cities shining all, enveloping man and land.

13

Sing on, sing on you gray-brown bird,
100 Sing from the swamps, the recesses, pour your chant from the bushes,
Limitless out of the dusk, out of the cedars and pines.

Sing on dearest brother, warble your reedy song,
Loud human song, with voice of uttermost woe.

O liquid and free and tender!
O wild and loose to my soul—O wondrous singer!
You only I hear—yet the star holds me, (but will soon depart,)
Yet the lilac with mastering odor holds me.

14

Now while I sat in the day and look'd forth,
In the close of the day with its light and the fields of spring, and the farmers
    preparing their crops,
110   In the large unconscious scenery of my land with its lakes and forests,
In the heavenly aerial beauty, (after the perturb'd winds and the storms,)
Under the arching heavens of the afternoon swift passing, and the voices of
    children and women,
The many-moving sea-tides, and I saw the ships how they sail'd,
And the summer approaching with richness, and the fields all busy with
    labor,
And the infinite separate houses, how they all went on, each with its meals
    and minutia of daily usages,
And the streets how their throbbings throbb'd, and the cities pent—lo, then
    and there,
Falling upon them all and among them all, enveloping me with the rest,
Appear'd the cloud, appear'd the long black trail,
And I knew death, its thought, and the sacred knowledge of death.

120   Then with the knowledge of death as walking one side of me,
And the thought of death close-walking the other side of me,
And I in the middle as with companions, and as holding the hands of
    companions,
I fled forth to the hiding receiving night that talks not,
Down to the shores of the water, the path by the swamp in the dimness,
To the solemn shadowy cedars and ghostly pines so still.

And the singer so shy to the rest receiv'd me,
The gray-brown bird I know receiv'd us comrades three,
And he sang the carol of death, and a verse for him I love.

From deep secluded recesses,
130   From the fragrant cedars and the ghostly pines so still,
Came the carol of the bird.

And the charm of the carol rapt me,
As I held as if by their hands my comrades in the night,
And the voice of my spirit tallied the song of the bird.

Come lovely and soothing death,
Undulate round the world, serenely arriving, arriving,

In the day, in the night, to all, to each,
Sooner or later delicate death.

Prais'd be the fathomless universe,
140 *For life and joy, and for objects and knowledge curious,*
And for love, sweet love—but praise! praise! praise!
For the sure-enwinding arms of cool-enfolding death.

Dark mother always gliding near with soft feet,
Have none chanted for thee a chant of fullest welcome?
Then I chant it for thee, I glorify thee above all,
I bring thee a song that when thou must indeed come, come unfalteringly.

Approach strong deliveress,
When it is so, when thou hast taken them I joyously sing the dead,
Lost in the loving floating ocean of thee,
150 *Laved in the flood of thy bliss O death.*

From me to thee glad serenades,
Dances for thee I propose saluting thee, adornments and feastings for thee,
And the sights of the open landscape and the high-spread sky are fitting,
And life and the fields, and the huge and thoughtful night.

The night in silence under many a star,
The ocean shore and the husky whispering wave whose voice I know,
And the soul turning to thee O vast and well-veil'd death,
And the body gratefully nestling close to thee.

Over the tree-tops I float thee a song,
Over the rising and sinking waves, over the myriad fields and the prairies
160   *wide,*
Over the dense-pack'd cities all and the teeming wharves and ways,
I float this carol with joy, with joy to thee O death.

15

To the tally of my soul,
Loud and strong kept up the gray-brown bird,
With pure deliberate notes spreading filling the night.

Loud in the pines and cedars dim,
Clear in the freshness moist and the swamp-perfume,
And I with my comrades there in the night.

While my sight that was bound in my eyes unclosed,
170 As to long panoramas of visions.

And I saw askant[6] the armies,
I saw as in noiseless dreams hundreds of battle-flags,

---

[6] **askant** with a sideways glance

Borne through the smoke of the battles and pierc'd with missiles I saw them,
And carried hither and yon through the smoke, and torn and bloody,
And at last but a few shreds left on the staffs, (and all in silence,)
And the staffs all splinter'd and broken.

I saw battle-corpses, myriads of them,
And the white skeletons of young men, I saw them,
I saw the debris and debris of all the slain soldiers of the war,
180   But I saw they were not as was thought,
They themselves were fully at rest, they suffer'd not,
The living remain'd and suffer'd, the mother suffer'd,
And the wife and the child and the musing comrade suffer'd,
And the armies that remain'd suffer'd.

16

Passing the visions, passing the night,
Passing, unloosing the hold of my comrades' hands,
Passing the song of the hermit bird and the tallying song of my soul,
Victorious song, death's outlet song, yet varying ever-altering song,
As low and wailing, yet clear the notes, rising and falling, flooding the night,
Sadly sinking and fainting, as warning and warning, and yet again bursting
190   with joy,
Covering the earth and filling the spread of the heaven,
As that powerful psalm in the night I heard from recesses,
Passing, I leave the lilac with heart-shaped leaves,
I leave thee there in the door-yard, blooming, returning with spring.

I cease from my song for thee,
From my gaze on thee in the west, fronting the west, communing with thee,
O comrade lustrous with silver face in the night.

Yet each to keep and all, retrievements out of the night,
The song, the wondrous chant of the gray-brown bird,
200   And the tallying chant, the echo arous'd in my soul,
With the lustrous and drooping star with the countenance full of woe,
With the holders holding my hand nearing the call of the bird,
Comrades mine and I in the midst, and their memory ever to keep, for the
    dead I loved so well,
For the sweetest, wisest soul of all my days and lands—and this for his dear
    sake,
Lilac and star and bird twined with the chant of my soul,
There in the fragrant pines and the cedars dusk and dim.

1865   1866, *1881*

A Noiseless Patient Spider

A noiseless patient spider,
I mark'd where on a little promontory it stood isolated,
Mark'd how to explore the vacant vast surrounding,
It launch'd forth filament, filament, filament, out of itself,
Ever unreeling them, ever tirelessly speeding them.

And you O my soul where you stand,
Surrounded, detached, in measureless oceans of space,
Ceaselessly musing, venturing, throwing, seeking the spheres to connect them
Till the bridge you will need be form'd, till the ductile anchor hold,
10   Till the gossamer thread you fling catch somewhere, O, my soul.

1868   1881

MATTHEW ARNOLD
1822–1888

A rigorous training in ethics and progressive Protestant thought at Rugby School (where his father, the distinguished educator Thomas Arnold, was headmaster) gave Matthew Arnold a lifelong concern with education and culture. His public career as an inspector of schools gained him first-hand knowledge of educational conditions in England, and extensive travel broadened his cultural background. Elected professor of poetry at Oxford in 1857, Arnold concentrated thereafter primarily on his prose, which established him as the leading English critic of his day.

Arnold stands out among major Victorian poets for articulating the central cultural problems of his age. In poem after poem he laments the loss of a common religious faith, the absence of unified cultural purpose, and the fragility of love, and he deplores the selfish materialism and anxious pursuit of trivialities that characterize what he calls "this strange disease of modern life." Though he himself led a busy and useful life, Arnold adds pathos to the gloomy perspective in his poetry by projecting a melancholic, incapacitated self-image. In "Stanzas from the Grande Chartreuse," for example, he sees himself as part of the problem he describes, as someone "wandering between two worlds, / one dead, the other powerless to be born"—that is, between the lost world of religious faith that belonged to his ancestors, and a future world free of a sense of loss and regret. Seeing no way out of this dilemma, he resorts in his poetry to counseling a general withdrawal or retreat.

Arnold's poems tend toward discursiveness, but he is a master of incisive, memorable phrases and, as in the famous closing stanzas of "The Scholar-Gipsy," is deft in handling extended images and similes (a product of his excellent training in classical poetry). He also describes scenes of natural beauty with a charm that reminds one of Keats and Wordsworth. Above all, he remains the eloquent and urbane spokesman for a sense of cultural crisis, felt not only in his own day, but in ours as well.

To Marguerite—Continued[1]

Yes! in the sea of life enisled,
With echoing straits between us thrown,
Dotting the shoreless watery wild,
We mortal millions live *alone*.
The islands feel the enclasping flow,
And then their endless bounds they know.

But when the moon their hollows lights,
And they are swept by balms of spring,
And in their glens, on starry nights,
10 The nightingales divinely sing;
And lovely notes, from shore to shore,
Across the sounds and channels pour—

Oh! then a longing like despair
Is to their farthest caverns sent;
For surely once, they feel, we were
Parts of a single continent!
Now round us spreads the watery plain—
Oh might our marges meet again!

Who order'd, that their longing's fire
20 Should be, as soon as kindled, cool'd?
Who renders vain their deep desire?—
A God, a God their severance ruled!
And bade betwixt their shores to be
The unplumb'd, salt, estranging sea.

1849   1852

[1] the second of two poems addressed to an un-
known young woman, to whom Arnold was
romantically attached at some time in the 1840s

Dover Beach

The sea is calm to-night.
The tide is full, the moon lies fair
Upon the straits;—on the French coast the light
Gleams and is gone; the cliffs of England stand,
Glimmering and vast, out in the tranquil bay.
Come to the window, sweet is the night-air!
Only, from the long line of spray
Where the sea meets the moon-blanch'd land,
Listen! you hear the grating roar
10 Of pebbles which the waves draw back, and fling,
At their return, up the high strand,
Begin, and cease, and then again begin,
With tremulous cadence slow, and bring
The eternal note of sadness in.

Sophocles[1] long ago
Heard it on the Aegean, and it brought
Into his mind the turbid ebb and flow
Of human misery; we
Find also in the sound a thought,
20   Hearing it by this distant northern sea.

The Sea of Faith
Was once, too, at the full, and round earth's shore
Lay like the folds of a bright girdle furl'd.[2]
But now I only hear
Its melancholy, long, withdrawing roar,
Retreating, to the breath
Of the night-wind, down the vast edges drear
And naked shingles[3] of the world.

Ah, love, let us be true
30   To one another! for the world, which seems
To lie before us like a land of dreams,
So various, so beautiful, so new,
Hath really neither joy, nor love, nor light,
Nor certitude, nor peace, nor help for pain;
And we are here as on a darkling plain
Swept with confused alarms of struggle and flight,
Where ignorant armies clash by night.

c. 1848–61   1867

[1] **Sophocles** Greek tragic dramatist (496?–406 B.C.), whom Arnold supremely admired
[2] **girdle furl'd** belt or band gathered together; perhaps an image for the waves at high tide closely hugging the shore
[3] **shingles** pebble beaches

The Scholar-Gipsy[1]

Go, for they call you, shepherd, from the hill;
  Go, shepherd, and untie the wattled cotes![2]
    No longer leave thy wistful flock unfed,
    Nor let thy bawling fellows rack their throats,

[1] " 'There was very lately a lad in the University of Oxford, who was by his poverty forced to leave his studies there; and at last to join himself to a company of vagabond gypsies. Among these extravagant people, by the insinuating subtility of his carriage, he quickly got so much of their love and esteem as that they discovered to him their mystery. After he had been pretty well exercised in the trade, there chanced to ride by a couple of scholars, who had formerly been of his acquaintance. They quickly spied out their old friend among the gypsies; and he gave them an account of the necessity which drove him to that kind of life, and told them that the people he went with were not such imposters as they were taken for, but that they had a traditional kind of learning among them, and could do wonders by the power of imagination, their fancy binding that of others: that he himself learned much of their art, and when he had compassed the whole secret, he intended, he said, to leave their company, and give the world an account of what he had learned.'— [Joseph] Glanvil's *Vanity of Dogmatizing*, 1661" (Arnold's note).
[2] **wattled cotes** sheepfolds built of woven twigs and branches

Nor the cropp'd herbage shoot another head.
But when the fields are still,
And the tired men and dogs all gone to rest,
And only the white sheep are sometimes seen
Cross and recross the strips of moon-blanch'd green,
10   Come, shepherd, and again begin the quest!

Here, where the reaper was at work of late—
In this high field's dark corner, where he leaves
His coat, his basket, and his earthen cruse,[3]
And in the sun all morning binds the sheaves,
Then here, at noon, comes back his stores to use—
Here will I sit and wait,
While to my ear from uplands far away
The bleating of the folded[4] flocks is borne,
With distant cries of reapers in the corn[5]—
20   All the live murmur of a summer's day.

Screen'd is this nook o'er the high, half-reap'd field,
And here till sun-down, shepherd! will I be.
Through the thick corn the scarlet poppies peep,
And round green roots and yellowing stalks I see
Pale pink convolvulus[6] in tendrils creep;
And air-swept lindens yield
Their scent, and rustle down their perfumed showers
Of bloom on the bent grass where I am laid,
And bower me from the August sun with shade;
30   And the eye travels down to Oxford's towers.

And near me on the grass lies Glanvil's book—
Come, let me read the oft-read tale again!
The story of the Oxford scholar poor,
Of pregnant parts[7] and quick inventive brain,
Who, tired of knocking at preferment's door,
One summer-morn forsook
His friends, and went to learn the gipsy-lore,
And roam'd the world with that wild brotherhood,
And came, as most men deem'd, to little good,
40   But came to Oxford and his friends no more.

But once, years after, in the country-lanes,
Two scholars, whom at college erst he knew,
Met him, and of his way of life enquired;
Whereat he answer'd, that the gipsy-crew,
His mates, had arts to rule as they desired
The workings of men's brains,
And they can bind them to what thoughts they will.

---

[3]**cruse** water jug
[4]**folded** penned in
[5]**corn** grain

[6]**convolvulus** morning glory
[7]**Of pregnant parts** abundant gifts of intelligence

"And I," he said, "the secret of their art,
  When fully learn'd, will to the world impart;
50   But it needs heaven-sent moments for this skill."

This said, he left them, and return'd no more.—
  But rumours hung about the country-side,
    That the lost Scholar long was seen to stray,
  Seen by rare glimpses, pensive and tongue-tied,
    In hat of antique shape, and cloak of grey,
      The same the gipsies wore.
  Shepherds had met him on the Hurst[8] in spring;
    At some lone alehouse in the Berkshire moors,
    On the warm ingle-bench,[9] the smock-frock'd boors[10]
60   Had found him seated at their entering,

But, 'mid their drink and clatter, he would fly.
  And I myself seem half to know thy looks,
    And put the shepherds, wanderer! on thy trace;
  And boys who in lone wheatfields scare the rooks
    I ask if thou hast pass'd their quiet place;
      Or in my boat I lie
  Moor'd to the cool bank in the summer-heats,
    'Mid wide grass meadows which the sunshine fills,
    And watch the warm, green-muffled Cumner hills,
70   And wonder if thou haunt'st their shy retreats.

For most, I know thou lov'st retired ground!
  Thee at the ferry Oxford riders blithe,
    Returning home on summer-night, have met
  Crossing the stripling Thames at Bab-lock-hithe,
    Trailing in the cool stream thy fingers wet,
      As the punt's rope chops round;
  And leaning backward in a pensive dream,
    And fostering in thy lap a heap of flowers
    Pluck'd in shy fields and distant Wychwood bowers,
80   And thine eyes resting on the moonlit stream.

And then they land, and thou art seen no more!—
  Maidens, who from the distant hamlets come
    To dance around the Fyfield elm in May,
  Oft through the darkening fields have seen thee roam,
    Or cross a stile into the public way.
      Oft thou hast given them store
  Of flowers—the frail-leaf'd, white anemony,
    Dark bluebells drench'd with dews of summer eves,[11]
    And purple orchises with spotted leaves—
90   But none hath words she can report of thee.

---

[8]**the Hurst** a hill near Oxford (the general locale of all the place names in the poem, save those of the final two stanzas)
[9]**ingle-bench** a seat by the hearth

[10]**smock-frock'd boors** farm hands wearing smocks
[11]l. 88 Cf. Keats, "Ode to a Nightingale" (p. 619 above), ll. 49–50.

And, above Godstow Bridge, when hay-time's here
  In June, and many a scythe in sunshine flames,
    Men who through those wide fields of breezy grass
    Where black-wing'd swallows haunt the glittering Thames,
      To bathe in the abandon'd lasher[12] pass,
        Have often pass'd thee near
    Sitting upon the river bank o'ergrown;
      Mark'd thine outlandish garb, thy figure spare,
      They dark vague eyes, and soft abstracted air—
100   But, when they came from bathing, thou wast gone!

At some lone homestead in the Cumner hills,
  Where at her open door the housewife darns,
    Thou hast been seen, or hanging on a gate
    To watch the threshers in the mossy barns.
      Children, who early range these slopes and late
        For cresses from the rills,
    Have known thee eying, all an April-day,
      The springing pastures and the feeding kine;
      And mark'd thee, when the stars come out and shine,
110   Through the long dewy grass move slow away.

In autumn, on the skirts of Bagley Wood—
  Where most the gipsies by the turf-edged way
    Pitch their smoked tents, and every bush you see
    With scarlet patches tagg'd and shreds of grey,
      Above the forest-ground called Thessaly—
        The blackbird, picking food,
    Sees thee, nor stops his meal, nor fears at all;
      So often has he known thee past him stray,
      Rapt, twirling in thy hand a wither'd spray,
120   And waiting for the spark from heaven to fall.

And once, in winter, on the causeway chill
  Where home through flooded fields foot-travellers go,
    Have I not pass'd thee on the wooden bridge,
    Wrapt in thy cloak and battling with the snow,
      Thy face tow'rd Hinksey and its wintry ridge?
        And thou hast climb'd the hill,
    And gain'd the white brow of the Cumner range;
      Turn'd once to watch, while thick the snowflakes fall,
      The line of festal light in Christ-Church hall[13]—
130   Then sought thy straw in some sequester'd grange.

But what—I dream! Two hundred years are flown
  Since first thy story ran through Oxford halls,
    And the grave Glanvil did the tale inscribe
    That thou wert wander'd from the studious walls

---

[12]**lasher** pool at the base of a dam or weir   [13]**Christ-Church hall** dining hall of Christ-Church College, Oxford

To learn strange arts, and join a gipsy-tribe;
   And thou from earth art gone
Long since, and in some quiet churchyard laid—
   Some country-nook, where o'er thy unknown grave
   Tall grasses and white flowering nettles wave,
140   Under a dark, red-fruited yew-tree's shade.

—No, no, thou hast not felt the lapse of hours!
   For what wears out the life of mortal men?[14]
   'Tis that from change to change their being rolls;
   'Tis that repeated shocks, again, again,
     Exhaust the energy of strongest souls
     And numb the elastic powers.
Till having used our nerves with bliss and teen,[15]
   And tired upon a thousand schemes our wit,
     To the just-pausing Genius[16] we remit
150   Our worn-out life, and are—what we have been.

Thou hast not lived, why should'st thou perish, so?
   Thou hadst *one* aim, *one* business, *one* desire;
     Else wert thou long since number'd with the dead!
   Else hadst thou spent, like other men, thy fire!
     The generations of thy peers are fled,
     And we ourselves shall go;
But thou possessest an immortal lot,
   And we imagine thee exempt from age
   And living as thou liv'st on Glanvil's page,
160   Because thou hadst—what we, alas! have not.

For early didst thou leave the world, with powers
   Fresh, undiverted to the world without,
     Firm to their mark, not spent on other things;
   Free from the sick fatigue, the languid doubt,
     Which much to have tried, in much been baffled, brings.
     O life unlike to ours!
Who fluctuate idly without term or scope,
   Of whom each strives, nor knows for what he strives,
   And each half lives a hundred different lives;[17]
170   Who wait like thee, but not, like thee, in hope.

Thou waitest for the spark from heaven! and we,
   Light half-believers of our casual creeds,
     Who never deeply felt, nor clearly will'd,
   Whose insight never has borne fruit in deeds,
     Whose vague resolves never have been fulfill'd;
     For whom each year we see
   Breeds new beginnings, disappointments new;

[14]ll. 141–42 Cf. Keats, "Ode to a Nightingale,"
ll. 61 ff.
[15]**teen** grief

[16]**Genius** a universal spirit
[17]**half lives** "Lives" is modified adverbially by
"half"; cf. "half-believers," l. 172.

Who hesitate and falter life away,
And lose to-morrow the ground won to-day—
180   Ah! do not we, wanderer! await it too?

Yes, we await it!—but it still delays,
And then we suffer! and amongst us one,[18]
Who most has suffer'd, takes dejectedly
His seat upon the intellectual throne;
And all his store of sad experience he
Lays bare of wretched days;
Tells us his misery's birth and growth and signs,
And how the dying spark of hope was fed,
And how the breast was soothed, and how the head,
190   And all his hourly varied anodynes.

This for our wisest! and we others pine,
And wish the long unhappy dream would end,
And waive all claim to bliss, and try to bear;
With close-lipp'd patience for our only friend,
Sad patience, too near neighbour to despair—
But none has hope like thine!
Thou through the fields and through the woods dost stray,
Roaming the country-side, a truant boy,
Nursing thy project in unclouded joy,
200   And every doubt long blown by time away.

O born in days when wits were fresh and clear,
And life ran gaily as the sparkling Thames;
Before this strange disease of modern life,
With its sick hurry, its divided aims,
Its heads o'ertax'd, its palsied hearts, was rife—
Fly hence, our contact fear!
Still fly, plunge deeper in the bowering wood!
Averse, as Dido did with gesture stern
From her false friend's approach in Hades turn,[19]
210   Wave us away, and keep thy solitude!

Still nursing the unconquerable hope,
Still clutching the inviolable shade,
With a free, onward impulse brushing through,
By night, the silver'd branches of the glade—
Far on the forest-skirts, where none pursue.
On some mild pastoral slope
Emerge, and resting on the moonlit pales[20]
Freshen thy flowers as in former years

---

[18]**one** perhaps Tennyson, appointed poet laureate in 1850 on publication of *In Memoriam*, a work that loosely answers to the account given in ll. 185–90
[19]**Dido . . . turn** Dido, queen of Carthage, committed suicide after the desertion of her lover, the hero Aeneas. When the latter, visiting the underworld, encountered her ghost, she refused to speak and turned away.
[20]**pales** fences

With dew, or listen with enchanted ears,
220　From the dark dingles,[21] to the nightingales!

But fly our paths, our feverish contact fly!
For strong the infection of our mental strife,
　Which, though it gives no bliss, yet spoils for rest;
And we should win thee from thy own fair life,
　Like us distracted, and like us unblest.
　　Soon, soon thy cheer would die,
Thy hopes grow timorous, and unfix'd thy powers,
　And thy clear aims be cross and shifting made;
　And then thy glad perennial youth would fade,
230　Fade, and grow old at last, and die like ours.

Then fly our greetings, fly our speech and smiles!
　—As some grave Tyrian[22] trader, from the sea,
　Descried at sunrise an emerging prow
Lifting the cool-hair'd creepers[23] stealthily,
　The fringes of a southward-facing brow
　　Among the Aegean isles;
And saw the merry Grecian coaster come,
　Freighted with amber grapes, and Chian[24] wine,
　Green, bursting figs, and tunnies steep'd in brine—
240　And knew the intruders on his ancient home,

The young light-hearted masters of the waves—
　And snatch'd his rudder, and shook out more sail;
　And day and night held on indignantly
O'er the blue Midland[25] waters with the gale,
　Betwixt the Syrtes[26] and soft Sicily,
　　To where the Atlantic raves
Outside the western straits; and unbent sails
　There, where down cloudy cliffs, through sheets of foam,
　Shy traffickers, the dark Iberians[27] come;
250　And on the beach undid his corded bales.

1853

---

[21]**dingles**　valleys
[22]**Tyrian**　native of Tyre in Phoenicia, an ancient Mediterranean trading nation that eventually yielded to the wealth and power of the rising Greek civilization
[23]**creepers**　vines
[24]**Chian**　from the island of Chios in the Aegean Sea

[25]**Midland**　"Mediterranean" anglicized
[26]**Syrtes**　waters off the coast of North Africa
[27]**Iberians**　early inhabitants of what is now Spain and Portugal, who, according to ancient authority, negotiated with foreign traders only indirectly, avoiding all face-to-face contact

Stanzas from the Grande Chartreuse[1]

Through alpine meadows soft-suffused
With rain, where thick the crocus blows,
Past the dark forges long disused,
The mule-track from Saint Laurent goes.
The bridge is cross'd, and slow we ride,
Through forest, up the mountain-side.

The autumnal evening darkens round,
The wind is up, and drives the rain;
While, hark! far down, with strangled sound
10   Doth the Dead Guier's[2] stream complain,
Where that wet smoke, among the woods,
Over his boiling cauldron broods.

Swift rush the spectral vapours white
Past limestone scars[3] with ragged pines,
Showing—then blotting from our sight!—
Halt—through the cloud-drift something shines!
High in the valley, wet and drear,
The huts of Courrerie[4] appear.

Strike leftward! cries our guide; and higher
20   Mounts up the stony forest-way.
At last the encircling trees retire,
Look! through the showery twilight grey
What pointed roofs are these advance?—
A palace of the Kings of France?

Approach, for what we seek is here!
Alight, and sparely sup, and wait
For rest in this outbuilding near;
Then cross the sward and reach that gate.
Knock; pass the wicket! Thou art come
30   To the Carthusians' world-famed home.

The silent courts, where night and day
Into their stone-carved basins cold
The splashing icy fountains play—
The humid corridors behold!
Where, ghostlike in the deepening night,
Cowl'd forms brush by in gleaming white.

[1]a monastery of the Carthusian order located high in the French Alps. The Carthusian monks were noted for their age-old traditions of austerity and religious discipline. Arnold and his bride visited the Grande Chartreuse in September 1851.

[2]**Dead Guier** in French, Guiers mort, a river that joins the Guiers vif ("Live") in the valley below the monastery
[3]**scars** cliffs
[4]**Courrerie** village near the monastery

The chapel, where no organ's peal
Invests the stern and naked prayer—
With penitential cries they kneel
40 And wrestle; rising then, with bare
And white uplifted faces stand,
Passing the Host from hand to hand;[5]

Each takes, and then his visage wan
Is buried in his cowl once more.
The cells!—the suffering Son of Man
Upon the wall—the knee-worn floor—
And where they sleep, that wooden bed,
Which shall their coffin be, when dead![6]

The library, where tract and tome
50 Not to feed priestly pride are there,
To hymn the conquering march of Rome,
Nor yet to amuse, as ours are!
They paint of souls the inner strife,
Their drops of blood, their death in life.

The garden, overgrown—yet mild,
See, fragrant herbs are flowering there!
Strong children of the Alpine wild
Whose culture is the brethren's care;
Of human tasks their only one,
60 And cheerful works beneath the sun.

Those halls, too, destined to contain
Each its own pilgrim-host of old,
From England, Germany, or Spain—
All are before me! I behold
The House, the Brotherhood austere!
—And what am I, that I am here?

For rigorous teachers[7] seized my youth,
And purged its faith, and trimm'd its fire,
Show'd me the high, white star of Truth,
70 There bade me gaze, and there aspire.
Even now their whispers pierce the gloom:
What dost thou in this living tomb?

Forgive me, masters of the mind!
At whose behest I long ago

[5]l. 42 a factual error, since the passing of the communion wafer or Host from the priest into the hand of the communicant was not a part of Catholic ritual in Arnold's time. Arnold may have unconsciously substituted a memory of Anglican practice.
[6]ll. 47–48 a factual error (for the Carthusians do not sleep in their coffins), but imaginatively appropriate
[7]**rigorous teachers** probably a reference to his father, Dr. Thomas Arnold, and other masters at Rugby School, where Arnold studied before going on to Oxford

So much unlearnt, so much resign'd—
I come not here to be your foe!
I seek these anchorites,[8] not in ruth,[9]
To curse and to deny your truth;

80　Not as their friend, or child, I speak!
But as, on some far northern strand,
Thinking of his own Gods, a Greek
In pity and mournful awe might stand
Before some fallen Runic stone[10]—
For both were faiths, and both are gone.

Wandering between two worlds, one dead,
The other powerless to be born,
With nowhere yet to rest my head,
Like these, on earth I wait forlorn.
Their faith, my tears, the world deride—
90　I come to shed them at their side.

Oh, hide me in your gloom profound,
Ye solemn seats of holy pain!
Take me, cowl'd forms, and fence me round,
Till I possess my soul again;
Till free my thoughts before me roll,
Not chafed by hourly false control!

For the world cries your faith is now
But a dead time's exploded dream;
My melancholy, sciolists[11] say,
100　Is a pass'd mode, an outworn theme—
As if the world had ever had
A faith, or sciolists been sad!

Ah, if it *be* pass'd, take away,
At least, the restlessness, the pain;
Be man henceforth no more a prey
To these out-dated stings again!
The nobleness of grief is gone—
Ah, leave us not the fret alone!

But—if you cannot give us ease—
110　Last of the race of them who grieve
Here leave us to die out with these
Last of the people who believe!
Silent, while years engrave the brow;
Silent—the best are silent now.

[8]**anchorites** monks
[9]**ruth** repentance
[10]**Runic stone** a stone or monument dedicated to the Nordic gods, covered with letters (runes)
of an alphabet used by the ancient Germanic tribes
[11]**sciolists** glib but shallow "experts" in various fields of knowledge

Achilles ponders in his tent,[12]
The kings of modern thought[13] are dumb;
Silent they are, though not content,
And wait to see the future come.
They have the grief men had of yore,
120 But they contend and cry no more.

Our fathers[14] water'd with their tears
This sea of time whereon we sail,
Their voices were in all men's ears
Who pass'd within their puissant hail.
Still the same ocean round us raves,
But we stand mute, and watch the waves.

For what avail'd it, all the noise
And outcry of the former men?—
Say, have their sons achieved more joys,
130 Say, is life lighter now than then?
The sufferers died, they left their pain—
The pangs which tortured them remain.

What helps it now, that Byron bore,
With haughty scorn which mock'd the smart,
Through Europe to the Aetolian shore[15]
The pageant of his bleeding heart?
That thousands counted every groan,
And Europe made his woe her own?

What boots it, Shelley! that the breeze
140 Carried thy lovely wail away,
Musical through Italian trees
Which fringe thy soft blue Spezzian bay?[16]
Inheritors of thy distress
Have restless hearts one throb the less?

Or are we easier, to have read,
O Obermann![17] the sad, stern page,
Which tells us how thou hidd'st thy head
From the fierce tempest of thine age
In the lone brakes of Fontainebleau,
150 Or chalets near the Alpine snow?

[12]**Achilles . . . tent** Refusing to take part in
battle after quarreling with his leader, Aga-
memnon, Achilles, the greatest of the Greek
heroes in the Trojan War, brooded in his tent.
Achilles here may represent Arnold's older con-
temporary, the writer Carlyle.
[13]**kings of modern thought** certain unspecified
eminent men of letters of Arnold's time
[14]**our fathers** poets of the Romantic period, such

as Byron and Shelley, whom Arnold discusses
in the stanzas following
[15]**Aetolian shore** region of Greece where Bryon
died
[16]**Spezzian bay** Shelley drowned in the Gulf of
Spezzia, off the western coast of Italy.
[17]**Obermann** hero of a Romantic novel of the
same name (1804) by the French writer Étienne
de Senancour (1770–1846)

Ye slumber in your silent grave!—
The world, which for an idle day
Grace to your mood of sadness gave,
Long since hath flung her weeds[18] away.
The eternal trifler breaks your spell;
But we—we learnt your love too well!

Years hence, perhaps, may dawn an age,
More fortunate, alas! than we,
Which without hardness will be sage,
160   And gay without frivolity.
Sons of the world, oh, speed those years;
But, while we wait, allow our tears!

Allow them! We admire with awe
The exulting thunder of your race;
You give the universe your law,
You triumph over time and space!
Your pride of life, your tireless powers,
We laud them, but they are not ours.

We are like children rear'd in shade
170   Beneath some old-world abbey wall,
Forgotten in a forest-glade,
And secret from the eyes of all.
Deep, deep the greenwood round them waves,
Their abbey, and its close[19] of graves!

But, where the road runs near the stream,
Oft through the trees they catch a glance
Of passing troops in the sun's beam—
Pennon,[20] and plume, and flashing lance!
Forth to the world those soldiers fare,
180   To life, to cities, and to war!

And through the wood, another way,
Faint bugle-notes from far are borne,
Where hunters gather, staghounds bay,
Round some fair forest-lodge at morn.
Gay dames are there, in sylvan green;
Laughter and cries—those notes between!

The banners flashing through the trees
Make their blood dance and chain their eyes;
That bugle-music on the breeze
190   Arrests them with a charm'd surprise.
Banner by turns and bugle woo:
Ye shy recluses, follow too!

---

[18]**weeds** mourning clothes   [20]**Pennon** military banner or pennant
[19]**close** enclosure

O children, what do ye reply?—
"Action and pleasure, will ye roam
Through these secluded dells to cry
And call us?—but too late ye come!
Too late for us your call ye blow,
Whose bent was taken long ago.

"Long since we pace this shadow'd nave;
200 We watch those yellow tapers shine,
Emblems of hope over the grave,
In the high altar's depth divine;
The organ carries to our ear
Its accents of another sphere.

"Fenced early in this cloistral round
Of reverie, of shade, of prayer,
How should we grow in other ground?
How can we flower in foreign air?
—Pass, banners, pass, and bugles, cease;
210 And leave our desert to its peace!"

1855

DANTE GABRIEL ROSSETTI
1828–1882

Like Blake, whose work he revived and strongly promoted, Rossetti was both a poet and a painter. In 1848 he joined several other young painters to form the Pre-Raphaelite Brotherhood, which strove to bring to modern English art the qualities they saw in early Italian painting: a fusion of precise natural detail, rich color, formal simplicity, and spirituality. Rossetti's poems reflect these qualities in rich language that is indebted to Keats and the early Tennyson. They also fuse sensuous eroticism with exalted idealism, especially in their depiction of women. A clear example is his early poem "The Blessed Damozel," which became the virtual prototype of Pre-Raphaelite poetry.

The Blessed Damozel[1]

The blessed damozel leaned out
  From the gold bar of heaven;
Her eyes were deeper than the depth
  Of waters stilled at even;
She had three lilies in her hand,
  And the stars in her hair were seven.[2]

[1] another form of "damsel" or young maiden
[2] stars . . . seven possibly a reference to the seven stars held in the right hand of Christ in Revelation 1:16

Her robe, ungirt from clasp to hem,
    No wrought flowers did adorn,
But a white rose of Mary's gift,
10   For service meetly worn;
Her hair that lay along her back
    Was yellow like ripe corn.[3]

Herseemed she scarce had been a day
    One of God's choristers;
The wonder was not yet quite gone
    From that still look of hers;
Albeit, to them she left, her day
    Had counted as ten years.

(To one, it is ten years of years.
20   . . . Yet now, and in this place,
Surely she leaned o'er me—her hair
    Fell all about my face. . . .
Nothing: the autumn-fall of leaves.
    The whole year sets apace.)

It was the rampart of God's house
    That she was standing on;
By God built over the sheer depth
    The which is Space begun;
So high, that looking downward thence
30   She scarce could see the sun.

It lies in Heaven, across the flood
    Of ether,[4] as a bridge.
Beneath, the tides of day and night
    With flame and darkness ridge
The void, as low as where this earth
    Spins like a fretful midge.

Around her, lovers, newly met
    'Mid deathless love's acclaims
Spoke evermore among themselves
40   Their heart-remembered names;
And the souls mounting up to God
    Went by her like thin flames.

And still she bowed herself and stooped
    Out of the circling charm;
Until her bosom must have made
    The bar she leaned on warm,
And the lilies lay as if asleep
    Along her bended arm.

---

[3] **corn** grain

[4] **ether** a hypothetical substance, regarded in former times as filling all of cosmic space

From the fixed place of Heaven she saw
50   Time like a pulse shake fierce
Through all the worlds. Her gaze still strove
      Within the gulf to pierce
Its path; and now she spoke as when
      The stars sang in their spheres.

The sun was gone now; the curled moon
      Was like a little feather
Fluttering far down the gulf; and now
      She spoke through the still weather.
Her voice was like the voice the stars
60   Had when they sang together.[5]

(Ah sweet! Even now, in that bird's song,
      Strove not her accents there,
Fain to be harkened? When those bells
      Possessed the midday air,
Strove not her steps to reach my side
      Down all the echoing stair?)

"I wish that he were come to me,
      For he will come," she said.
"Have I not prayed in Heaven?—on earth,
70   Lord, Lord, has he not pray'd?
Are not two prayers a perfect strength?
      And shall I feel afraid?

"When round his head the aureole clings,
      And he is clothed in white,
I'll take his hand and go with him
      To the deep wells of light;
We will step down as to a stream,
      And bathe there in God's sight.

"We two will stand beside that shrine,
80   Occult, withheld, untrod,
Whose lamps are stirred continually
      With prayers sent up to God;
And see our old prayers, granted, melt
      Each like a little cloud.

"We two will lie i' the shadow of
      That living mystic tree[6]
Within whose secret growth the Dove[7]
      Is sometimes felt to be,
While every leaf that His plumes touch
90   Saith His Name audibly.

[5] ll. 59–60 See Job 38:6–7 ("when the morning stars sang together, and all the sons of God shouted for joy").

[6] living mystic tree For the mystic "tree of life" see Revelation 22:2.
[7] Dove the Holy Ghost

"And I myself will teach to him,
    I myself, lying so,
The songs I sing here; which his voice
    Shall pause in, hushed and slow,
And find some knowledge at each pause,
    Or some new thing to know."

(Alas! we two, we two, thou say'st!
    Yea, one wast thou with me
That once of old. But shall God lift
100   To endless unity
The soul whose likeness with thy soul
    Was but its love for thee?)

"We two," she said, "will seek the groves
    Where the Lady Mary is,
With her five handmaidens, whose names
    Are five sweet symphonies,
Cecily, Gertrude, Magdalen,
    Margaret, and Rosalys.

"Circlewise sit they, with bound locks
110   And foreheads garlanded;
Into the fine cloth white like flame
    Weaving the golden thread,
To fashion the birth robes for them
    Who are just born, being dead.

"He shall fear, haply, and be dumb:
    Then will I lay my cheek
To his, and tell about our love,
    Not once abashed or weak:
And the dear Mother will approve
120   My pride, and let me speak.

"Herself shall bring us, hand in hand,
    To Him round whom all souls
Kneel, the clear-rangèd unnumbered heads
    Bowed with their aureoles:
And angels meeting us shall sing
    To their citherns and citoles.[8]

"There will I ask of Christ the Lord
    Thus much for him and me—
Only to live as once on earth
    With Love,—only to be,
130   As then awhile, for ever now
    Together, I and he."

[8] **citherns and citoles** stringed instruments of
former centuries similar to guitars

She gazed and listened and then said,
   Less sad of speech than mild,—
"All this is when he comes." She ceased.
   The light thrilled towards her, filled
With angels in strong level flight.
   Her eyes prayed, and she smiled.

   (I saw her smile.) But soon their path
140   Was vague in distant spheres:
And then she cast her arms along
   The golden barriers,
And laid her face between her hands,
   And wept. (I heard her tears.)

1847   1850

GEORGE MEREDITH

1828–1909

Best known for novels such as *The Ordeal of Richard Feverel* and *The Egoist*, George Meredith also earned a secure reputation for his poetry. Deserted by his first wife in 1858, he made marital unhappiness the subject of his chief poetic work, *Modern Love* (1862), a sequence of fifty sixteen-line lyrics. These trace the breakdown of a marriage with biting psychological insight, using compressed imagery and syntax to convey the speaker's complex feelings of bitterness and sorrow. Meredith's later poems occasionally show flashes of the same power, as, for example, in "Lucifer in Starlight" (1883), with its somberly majestic evocation of the material universe ("the army of unalterable law").

From Modern Love

I

By this he knew she wept with waking eyes:
That, at his hand's light quiver by her head,
The strange low sobs that shook their common bed,
Were called into her with a sharp surprise,
And strangled mute, like little gaping snakes,
Dreadfully venomous to him. She lay
Stone-still, and the long darkness flowed away
With muffled pulses. Then, as midnight makes
Her giant heart of Memory and Tears
10 Drink the pale drug of silence, and so beat
Sleep's heavy measure, they from head to feet
Were moveless, looking through their dead black years,
By vain regret scrawled over the blank wall.
Like sculptured effigies they might be seen
Upon their marriage-tomb, the sword between;[1]
Each wishing for the sword that severs all.

[1] **the sword between** In many old tales unmarried lovers are represented as sleeping in the same bed, with an unsheathed sword between them to enforce their chastity.

XVII

At dinner, she is hostess, I am host.
Went the feast ever cheerfuller? She keeps
The Topic over intellectual deeps
In buoyancy afloat. They see no ghost.
With sparkling surface-eyes we ply the ball:
It is in truth a most contagious game:
HIDING THE SKELETON, shall be its name.
Such play as this, the devils might appal!
But here's the greater wonder; in that we
10   Enamoured of an acting nought can tire,
Each other, like true hypocrites, admire;
Warm-lighted looks, Love's ephemerioe,[2]
Shoot gaily o'er the dishes and the wine.
We waken envy of our happy lot.
Fast, sweet, and golden, shows the marriage-knot.
Dear guests, you now have seen Love's corpse-light[3] shine.

L

Thus piteously Love closed[4] what he begat:
The union of this ever-diverse pair!
These two were rapid falcons in a snare,
Condemned to do the flitting of the bat.
Lovers beneath the singing sky of May,
They wandered once; clear as the dew on flowers:
But they fed not on the advancing hours:
Their hearts held cravings for the buried day.
Then each applied to each that fatal knife,
10   Deep questioning, which probes to endless dole.
Ah, what a dusty answer gets the soul
When hot for certainties in this our life!—
In tragic hints here see what evermore
Moves dark as yonder midnight ocean's force,
Thundering like ramping hosts of warrior horse,
To throw that faint thin line upon the shore!

1862

2 **ephemerioe** insects with a very brief lifespan
3 **corpse light** glow caused by decaying matter
  in swamps

4 **closed** The wife has now died, possibly by
  suicide.

Lucifer in Starlight

On a starred night Prince Lucifer uprose.
Tired of his dark dominion swung the fiend
Above the rolling ball in cloud part screened,
Where sinners hugged their spectre of repose.
Poor prey to his hot fit of pride were those.
And now upon his western wing he leaned,
Now his huge bulk o'er Afric's sands careened,

Now the black planet shadowed Arctic snows.
Soaring through wider zones that pricked his scars
10 With memory of the old revolt from Awe,[1]
He reached a middle height, and at the stars,
Which are the brain of heaven, he looked, and sank.
Around the ancient track marched, rank on rank,
The army of unalterable law.

1883

[1] ll. 9–10 Satan or Lucifer's flight through space, the scars of defeat caused by his ancient rebellion against God ("Awe"), and his painful memories of that defeat all deliberately echo Milton's *Paradise Lost*, particularly Books 1–4.

EMILY DICKINSON
1830–1886

Born in Amherst, Massachusetts, Emily Dickinson spent her entire life there within a small circle of family and acquaintances, and in her later years became a virtual recluse, refusing to leave her house or to meet strangers. Her rich inner life was poured out in nearly 1,800 poems, only seven of which appeared in print during her lifetime. After her death a selection of her work, *Poems* (1890), was edited by a friend and a critic who had long been interested in her work. It quickly established her reputation, which was later enhanced by avant-garde critics of the 1920s and has continued to grow. Today Emily Dickinson is ranked securely among the handful of great American poets.

Dickinson's most powerful poems grapple both with personal psychological anguish and with general religious concerns. She explores the narrow borderland between life and death, body and soul, human pain and God's wisdom, relying solely on her own intuition and observation: "I like a look of Agony, / Because I know it's true." Her poems compress intensity and intellectual vitality within brief and apparently simple confines. They usually take their stanza form from the common hymn books of her childhood. Within this constricted form, however, an unorthodox and highly original style flourishes. In their manuscript form (not prepared for publication), the poems feature a curious punctuation composed largely of dashes (perhaps indicating vocal pauses), a large number of slant rhymes ("Rooms" / "comes," "mold" / "world"), unexpected figures of speech (" 'Twas like a Maelstrom, with a notch"), and a vocabulary that mixes everyday terms with abstractions ("The Carriage held but just Ourselves—/ and Immortality"). Most notable are such characteristically startling turns of phrase as "And Zero at the Bone," "This is the Hour of Lead," and "I heard a Fly buzz—when I died."

Dickinson grouped approximately half her poems in small packets, known as fascicles, that she stitched together. Recently critics have observed structural interconnections among the individual poems within these groups. To provide readers with an opportunity to study these interconnections we offer here an entire fascicle (No. 16), as well as a selection of individual poems. The numbers prefixed to each poem in this selection are from the standard *Poems of Emily Dickinson*, ed. Thomas H. Johnson, 3 vol. (Cambridge, Mass., 1955). The arrangement within fascicle versions follows *The Manuscript Books of Emily Dickinson*, ed. R.W. Franklin (Cambridge, Mass., 1981). We have not indicated possible variants noted on the Dickinson manuscripts.

258

There's a certain Slant of light,
Winter Afternoons—
That oppresses, like the Heft
Of Cathedral Tunes—

Heavenly Hurt, it gives us—
We can find no scar,
But internal difference,
Where the Meanings, are—

None may teach it—Any—
10   'Tis the Seal Despair—
An imperial affliction
Sent us of the Air—

When it comes, the Landscape listens—
Shadows—hold their breath—
When it goes, 'tis like the Distance
On the look of Death—

c. 1861   1890

303

The Soul selects her own Society—
Then—shuts the Door—
To her divine Majority—
Present no more—

Unmoved—she notes the Chariots—pausing—
At her low Gate—
Unmoved—an Emperor be kneeling
Upon her Mat—

I've known her—from an ample nation—
10   Choose One—
Then—close the Valves of her attention—
Like Stone—

c. 1862   1890

341

After great pain, a formal feeling comes—
The Nerves sit ceremonious, like Tombs—
The stiff Heart questions was it He, that bore,
And Yesterday, or Centuries before?

The Feet, mechanical, go round—
Of Ground, or Air, or Ought[1]—
A Wooden way
Regardless grown,
A Quartz contentment, like a stone—

10 This is the Hour of Lead—
Remembered, if outlived,
As Freezing persons, recollect the Snow—
First—Chill—then Stupor—then the letting go—

    c. 1862   1929

[1] **Ought** nothingness

465

I heard a Fly buzz—when I died—
The Stillness in the Room
Was like the Stillness in the Air—
Between the Heaves of Storm—

The Eyes around—had wrung them dry—
And Breaths were gathering firm
For that last Onset—when the King
Be witnessed—in the Room—

I willed my Keepsakes—Signed away
10 What portion of me be
Assignable—and then it was
There interposed a Fly—

With Blue—uncertain stumbling Buzz—
Between the light—and me—
And then the Windows failed—and then
I could not see to see—

    c. 1862   1896

712

Because I could not stop for Death—
He kindly stopped for me—
The Carriage held but just Ourselves—
And Immortality.

We slowly drove—He knew no haste
And I had put away
My labor and my leisure too,
For His Civility—

We passed the School, where Children strove
10   At Recess—in the Ring—
We passed the Fields of Gazing Grain—
We passed the Setting Sun—

Or rather—He passed Us—
The Dews drew quivering and chill—
For only Gossamer, my Gown—
My Tippet—only Tulle[1]—

We paused before a House that seemed
A Swelling of the Ground—
The Roof was scarcely visible—
20   The Cornice—in the Ground—

Since then—'tis Centuries—and yet
Feels shorter than the Day
I first surmised the Horses' Heads
Were toward Eternity—

c. 1863   1890

[1] **Tippet . . . tulle** A tulle tippet is a neck and
shoulder scarf made of thin, fine netting.

986

A narrow Fellow in the Grass
Occasionally rides—
You may have met Him—did you not
His notice sudden is—

The Grass divides as with a Comb—
A spotted shaft is seen—
And then it closes at your feet
And opens further on—

He likes a Boggy Acre
10 A Floor too cool for Corn—
Yet when a Boy, and Barefoot—
I more than once at Noon

Have passed, I thought, a Whip lash
Unbraiding in the Sun
When stooping to secure it
It wrinkled, and was gone—

Several of Nature's People
I know, and they know me—
I feel for them a transport
20 Of cordiality—

But never met this Fellow
Attended, or alone
Without a tighter breathing
And Zero at the Bone—

1865   1866

1068

Further in Summer than the Birds
Pathetic from the Grass
A minor Nation celebrates
Its unobtrusive Mass.

No Ordinance be seen
So gradual the Grace
A pensive Custom it becomes
Enlarging Loneliness.

Antiquest felt at Noon
10 When August burning low
Arise this spectral Canticle[1]
Repose to typify

Remit as yet no Grace
No Furrow on the Glow
Yet a Druidic[2] Difference
Enhances Nature now

c. 1866   1891

---

[1] **Canticle** a song or hymn
[2] **Druidic** pertaining to the Druids, priests of

pagan nature worship in ancient northern Europe

1540

As imperceptibly as Grief
The Summer lapsed away—
Too imperceptible at last
To seem like Perfidy—
A Quietness distilled
As Twilight long begun,
Or Nature spending with herself
Sequestered Afternoon—
The Dusk drew earlier in—
10 The Morning foreign shone—
A courteous, yet harrowing Grace,
As Guest, that would be gone—
And thus, without a Wing
Or service of a Keel
Our Summer made her light escape
Into the Beautiful.

c. 1865   1891

From Fascicle 15

[410]

The first Day's Night had come—
And grateful that a thing
So terrible—had been endured—
I told my Soul to sing—

She said her Strings were snapt—
Her Bow—to Atoms blown—
And so to mend her—gave me work
Until another Morn—

And then—a Day as huge
10 As Yesterdays in pairs,
Unrolled its horror in my face—
Until it blocked my eyes—

My Brain—begun to laugh—
I mumbled—like a fool—
And tho''tis Years ago—that Day—
My Brain keeps giggling—still.

And Something's odd—within—
That person that I was—
And this One—do not feel the same—
20 Could it be Madness—this?

c. 1862   1947

[411]

The Color of the Grave is Green—
The Outer Grave—I mean—
You would not know it from the Field—
Except it own a Stone—

To help the fond—to find it—
Too infinite asleep
To stop and tell them where it is—
But just a Daisy—deep—

The Color of the Grave is white—
10 The outer Grave—I mean—
You would not know it from the Drifts—
In Winter—till the Sun—

Has furrowed out the Aisles—
Then—higher than the Land
The little Dwelling Houses rise
Where each—has left a friend—

The Color of the Grave within—
The Duplicate—I mean—
Not all the Snows could make it white—
20 Not all the Summers—Green—

You've seen the Color—maybe—
Upon a Bonnet bound—
When that you met it with before—
The Ferret—cannot find—

c. 1862   1935

[414]

'Twas like a Maelstrom,[1] with a notch,
That nearer, every Day,
Kept narrowing its boiling Wheel
Until the Agony

Toyed coolly with the final inch
Of your delirious Hem—
And you dropt, lost,
When something broke—
And let you from a Dream—

---

[1] **Maelstrom**   a large whirlpool

10 As if a Goblin with a Gauge—
Kept measuring the Hours—
Until you felt your Second
Weigh, helpless, in his Paws—

And not a Sinew—stirred—could help,
And sense was setting numb—
When God—remembered—and the Fiend
Let go, then, Overcome—

As if your Sentence stood—pronounced—
And you were frozen led
20 From Dungeon's luxury of Doubt
To Gibbets, and the Dead—

And when the Film had stitched your eyes
A Creature gasped "Reprieve"!
Which Anguish was the utterest—then—
To perish, or to live?

c. 1862   1945

Fascicle 16

[327]

Before I got my eye put out
I liked as well to see—
As other Creatures, that have Eyes
And know no other way—

But were it told to me—Today—
That I might have the sky
For mine—I tell you that my Heart
Would split, for size of me—

The Meadows—mine—
10 The Mountains—mine—
All Forests—Stintless Stars—
As much of Noon as I could take
Between my finite eyes—

The Motions of the Dipping Birds—
The Morning's Amber Road[1]—
For mine—to look at when I liked—
The News would strike me dead—

So safer—guess—with just my soul
Upon the Window pane—
20 Where other Creatures put their eyes—
Incautious—of the Sun—

c. 1862   1955

[607]

Of nearness to her sundered Things
The Soul has special times—
When Dimness—looks the Oddity—
Distinctness—easy—seems—

The Shapes we buried, dwell about,
Familiar, in the Rooms—
Untarnished by the Sepulchre,
The Mouldering Playmate comes—

In just the Jacket that he wore—
10 Long buttoned in the Mold
Since we—old mornings, Children—played—
Divided—by a world—

The Grave yields back her Robberies—
The Years, our pilfered Things—
Bright Knots of Apparitions
Salute us, with their wings—

As we—it were—that perished—
Themself—had just remained till we rejoin them—
And 'twas they, and not ourself
20 That mourned.

c. 1862   1929

[279]

Tie the Strings to my Life, My Lord,
Then, I am ready to go!
Just a look at the Horses—
Rapid! That will do!

Put me in on the firmest side—
So I shall never fall—
For we must ride to the Judgment—
And it's partly, down Hill—

But never I mind the steepest—
10 And never I mind the Sea—
Held fast in Everlasting Race—
By my own Choice, and Thee—

Goodbye to the Life I used to live—
And the World I used to know—
And kiss the Hills, for me, just once—
Then—I am ready to go!

c. 1861   1896

[241]

I like a look of Agony,
Because I know it's true—
Men do not sham Convulsion,
Nor simulate, a Throe—

The Eyes glaze once—and that is Death—
Impossible to Feign
The Beads upon the Forehead
By homely Anguish strung.

c. 1861   1890

[280]

I felt a Funeral, in my Brain,
And Mourners to and fro
Kept treading—treading—till it seemed
That Sense was breaking through—

And when they all were seated,
A Service, like a Drum—
Kept beating—beating—till I thought
My Mind was going numb—

And then I heard them lift a Box
10 And creak across my Soul
With those same Boots of Lead, again,
Then Space—began to toll,

As all the Heavens were a Bell,
And Being, but an Ear,
And I, and Silence, some strange Race
Wrecked, solitary, here—

And then a Plank in Reason, broke,
And I dropped down, and down—
And hit a World, at every plunge,
20 And Finished knowing—then—

c. 1861   1896

[281]

'Tis so appalling—it exhilirates—
So over Horror, it half Captivates—
The Soul stares after it, secure—
A Sepulchre, fears frost, no more—

To scan a Ghost, is faint—
But grappling, conquers it—
How easy, Torment, now—
Suspense kept sawing so—

The Truth, is Bald, and Cold—
10 But that will hold—
If any are not sure—
We show them—prayer—
But we, who know,
Stop hoping, now—

Looking at Death, is Dying—
Just let go the Breath—
And not the pillow at your Cheek
So Slumbereth—

Others, Can wrestle—
20 Yours, is done—
And so of Woe, bleak dreaded—come,
It sets the Fright at liberty—
And Terror's free—
Gay, Ghastly, Holiday!

c. 1861   1935

[282]

How noteless Men, and Pleiads,[1] stand,
Until a sudden sky
Reveals the fact that One is rapt
Forever from the Eye—

Members of the Invisible,
Existing, while we stare,
In Leagueless Opportunity,
O'ertakeless, as the Air—

Why didn't we detain Them?
10   The Heavens with a smile,
Sweep by our disappointed Heads
Without a syllable—

c. 1861   1929

[1] **Pleiads** a small cluster of stars (Pleiades) in
the constellation Taurus

[242]

When we stand on the tops of Things—
And like the Trees, look down—
The smoke all cleared away from it—
And Mirrors on the scene—

Just laying light—no soul will wink
Except it have the flaw—
The Sound ones, like the Hills—shall stand—
No Lightning, scares away—

The Perfect, nowhere be afraid—
10   They bear their dauntless Heads,
Where others, dare not go at Noon,
Protected by their deeds—

The Stars dare shine occasionally
Upon a spotted World—
And Suns, go surer, for their Proof,
As if an Axle, held—

c. 1861   1945

[445]

'Twas just this time, last year, I died.
I know I heard the Corn,
When I was carried by the Farms—
It had the Tassels on—

I thought how yellow it would look—
When Richard went to mill—
And then, I wanted to get out,
But something held my will.

I thought just how Red—Apples wedged
10   The Stubble's joints between—
And the Carts stooping round the fields
To take the Pumpkins in—

I wondered which would miss me, least,
And when Thanksgiving, came,
If Father'd multiply the plates—
To make an even Sum—

And would it blur the Christmas glee
My Stocking hang too high
For any Santa Claus to reach
20   The Altitude of me—

But this sort, grieved myself,
And so, I thought the other way,
How just this time, some perfect year—
Themself, should come to me—

c. 1862   1896

[608]

Afraid! Of whom am I afraid?
Not Death—for who is He?
The Porter of my Father's Lodge
As much abasheth me!

Of Life? 'Twere odd I fear [a] thing
That comprehendeth me
In one or two existences—
As Deity decree—

Of Resurrection? Is the East
10   Afraid to trust the Morn
With her fastidious forehead?
As soon impeach my Crown!

c. 1862   1890

[446]

He showed me Hights I never saw—
"Would'st Climb"—He said?
I said, "Not so."
"With me"—He said—"With me?"

He showed me secrets—Morning's nest—
The Rope the Nights were put across—
"And now, Would'st have me for a Guest?"
I could not find my "Yes"—

And then—He brake His Life,
And lo
A light for me, did solemn glow—
The steadier, as my face withdrew—
And could I further "no"?

c. 1862   1914

CHRISTINA ROSSETTI
1830–1894

Christina Rossetti, the younger sister of Dante Gabriel Rossetti, devoted her life mostly to poetry and religious reflections, living in personal seclusion like her American contemporary Emily Dickinson. At first glance, much of her poetry appears extremely simple—almost childlike—in its diction and tone ("Spring Quiet" and "Uphill"), but closer reading reveals delicate symbolic and emotional nuances. Certain poems, "A Birthday" for example, display her gift for rich simile and exotic imagery. In general, Rossetti conveys an atmosphere of strange otherworldliness peculiarly well suited to her essentially religious view of life.

Spring Quiet

Gone were but the Winter,
    Come were but the Spring,
I would go to a covert
    Where the birds sing;

Where in the whitethorn
    Singeth a thrush,
And a robin sings
    In the holly-bush.

Full of fresh scents
10   Are the budding boughs
Arching high over
    A cool green house:

Full of sweet scents,
    And whispering air
Which sayeth softly:
    "We spread no snare;

"Here dwell in safety,
    Here dwell alone,
With a clear stream
20   And a mossy stone.

"Here the sun shineth
    Most shadily;
Here is heard an echo
    Of the far sea,
      Tho' far off it be."

1847   1866

Echo

Come to me in the silence of the night;
    Come in the speaking silence of a dream;
Come with soft rounded cheeks and eyes as bright
    As sunlight on a stream;
      Come back in tears,
O memory, hope, love of finished years.

Oh dream how sweet, too sweet, too bitter sweet,
    Whose wakening should have been in Paradise,
Where souls brimfull of love abide and meet;
10   Where thirsting longing eyes
      Watch the slow door
That opening, letting in, lets out no more.

Yet come to me in dreams, that I may live
    My very life again tho' cold in death:
Come back to me in dreams, that I may give
    Pulse for pulse, breath for breath:
      Speak low, lean low,
As long ago, my love, how long ago.

1854   1862

A Birthday

My heart is like a singing bird
   Whose nest is in a watered shoot;
My heart is like an apple tree
   Whose boughs are bent with thickset fruit;
My heart is like a rainbow shell
   That paddles in a halcyon[1] sea;
My heart is gladder than all these
   Because my love is come to me.

Raise me a dais of silk and down;
10   Hang it with vair[2] and purple dyes;
Carve it in doves and pomegranates,
   And peacocks with a hundred eyes;
Work it in gold and silver grapes,
   In leaves and silver fleurs-de-lys;[3]
Because the birthday of my life
   Is come, my love is come to me.

1857   1862

[1] **halcyon** tranquil
[2] **vair** gray squirrel fur
[3] **fleur-de-lys** in heraldry, stylized three-petaled lilies

Up-hill

Does the road wind up-hill all the way?
   Yes, to the very end.
Will the day's journey take the whole long day?
   From morn to night, my friend.

But is there for the night a resting-place?
   A roof for when the slow dark hours begin.
May not the darkness hide it from my face?
   You cannot miss that inn.

Shall I meet other wayfarers at night?
10   Those who have gone before.
Then must I knock, or call when just in sight?
   They will not keep you standing at that door.

Shall I find comfort, travel-sore and weak?
   Of labour you shall find the sum.
Will there be beds for me and all who seek?
   Yea, beds for all who come.

1858   1862

ALGERNON CHARLES SWINBURNE
1837–1909

Swinburne's place in the history of English poetry owes much to his virtuoso style. As a young man he became friends with D.G. Rossetti and other members of the Pre-Raphaelite group and shared their interest in producing poetry with self-consciously beautiful surface effects, evident in his command of meter and of intricate sound patterns. (See, for example, "The Garden of Proserpine.") His knowledge and love of Greek mythology and classical poetry are effectively displayed in his tragedy *Atalanta in Calydon* (1865).

Influenced strongly by Shelley, Swinburne repudiated the attitudes of conventional society and championed unorthodox views in politics, morals, and poetic tastes. He wrote the first major critical study of William Blake and admired Whitman. The stress on unrestrained sexual freedom in these poets was attractive to Swinburne, and much of his own verse contains a strong erotic element.

From Atalanta in Calydon[1]

CHORUS

When the hounds of spring are on winter's traces,
    The mother of months[2] in meadow or plain
Fills the shadows and windy places
    With lisp of leaves and ripple of rain;
And the brown bright nightingale amorous
Is half assuaged for Itylus,
For the Thracian ships and the foreign faces,
    The tongueless vigil, and all the pain.[3]

10   Come with bows bent and with emptying of quivers,
    Maiden most perfect, lady of light,
With a noise of winds and many rivers,
    With a clamour of waters, and with might;
Bind on thy sandals, O thou most fleet,
Over the splendour and speed of thy feet;
For the faint east quickens, the wan west shivers,
    Round the feet of the day and the feet of the night.

Where shall we find her, how shall we sing to her,
    Fold our hands round her knees, and cling?
O that man's heart were as fire and could spring to her,

---

[1] a tragedy in the Greek style centering on a boar hunt led by Atalanta, a maiden devoted to Artemis, goddess of the hunt, of chastity, and of the moon. The play's first chorus, given here, is a hymn to the goddess.

[2] **mother of months** Artemis, in her role as goddess of the monthly lunar cycle

[3] ll. 5–8 an allusion to the legend of Philomela. She was raped by Tereus, king of the Thracians, who cut out her tongue. She was avenged by her sister Procne, wife of Tereus, who fed him with the flesh of their own son, Itylus. Philomela became a nightingale, Procne a swallow.

20   Fire, or the strength of the streams that spring!
For the stars and the winds are unto her
As raiment, as songs of the harp-player;
For the risen stars and the fallen cling to her,
    And the southwest-wind and the west-wind sing.

For winter's rains and ruins are over,
    And all the season of snows and sins;
The days dividing lover and lover,
    The light that loses, the night that wins;
And time remembered is grief forgotten,
30   And frosts are slain and flowers begotten,
And in green underwood and cover
    Blossom by blossom the spring begins.

The full streams feed on flower of rushes,
    Ripe grasses trammel a travelling foot,
The faint fresh flame of the young year flushes
    From leaf to flower and flower to fruit;
And fruit and leaf are as gold and fire,
And the oat[4] is heard above the lyre,
And the hoofèd heel of a satyr crushes
40   The chestnut-husk at the chestnut-root.

And Pan[5] by noon and Bacchus[6] by night,
    Fleeter of foot than the fleet-foot kid,
Follows with dancing and fills with delight
    The Maenad and the Bassarid;[7]
And soft as lips that laugh and hide
The laughing leaves[8] of the trees divide,
And screen from seeing and leave in sight
    The god pursuing, the maiden hid.

50   The ivy falls with the Bacchanal's[9] hair
    Over her eyebrows hiding her eyes;
The wild vine slipping down leaves bare
    Her bright breast shortening into sighs;
The wild vine slips with the weight of its leaves,
But the berried ivy catches and cleaves
To the limbs that glitter, the feet that scare
    The wolf that follows, the fawn that flies.

1865

---

[4] **oat** a musical pipe made of an oat straw, often depicted as played by satyrs
[5] **Pan** god of woodlands and of shepherds
[6] **Bacchus** god of wine, presides over orgiastic revels

[7] **Maenad . . . Bassarid** two names for the frenzied women followers of Bacchus.
[8] **leaves** the subject of the main clause in ll. 47–49.
[9] **Bacchanal** a devotee of Bacchus

The Garden of Proserpine[1]

Here, where the world is quiet;
  Here, where all trouble seems
Dead winds' and spent waves' riot
  In doubtful dreams of dreams;
I watch the green field growing
For reaping folk and sowing,
For harvest-time and mowing,
  A sleepy world of streams.

10 I am tired of tears and laughter,
  And men that laugh and weep;
Of what may come hereafter
  For men that sow to reap:
I am weary of days and hours,
Blown buds of barren flowers,
Desires and dreams and powers
  And everything but sleep.

Here life has death for neighbour,
  And far from eye or ear
Wan waves and wet winds labour,
20   Weak ships and spirits steer;
They drive adrift, and whither
They wot[2] not who make thither;
But no such winds blow hither,
  And no such things grow here.

No growth of moor or coppice,[3]
  No heather-flower or vine,
But bloomless buds of poppies,
  Green grapes of Proserpine,
Pale beds of blowing rushes
30 Where no leaf blooms or blushes
Save this whereout she crushes
  For dead men deadly wine.

Pale, without name or number,
  In fruitless fields of corn,[4]
They bow themselves and slumber
  All night till light is born;
And like a soul belated,
In hell and heaven unmated,
By cloud and mist abated
40   Comes out of darkness morn.

Though one were strong as seven,
  He too with death shall dwell,

---

[1] Proserpine or Proserpina (in Greek, Persephone) was carried off by Pluto to become queen of the underworld and the dead. Cf. the lines on Proserpina in Milton, *Paradise Lost* IV.269–72.

[2] **wot** know
[3] **coppice** a thicket of small trees or shrubs
[4] **corn** grain

Nor wake with wings in heaven,
  Nor weep for pains in hell;
Though one were fair as roses,
His beauty clouds and closes;
And well though love reposes,
  In the end it is not well.

50 Pale, beyond porch and portal,
      Crowned with calm leaves, she stands
  Who gathers all things mortal
      With cold immortal hands;
  Her languid lips are sweeter
  Than love's who fears to greet her
  To men that mix and meet her
      From many times and lands.

  She waits for each and other,
      She waits for all men born;
  Forgets the earth her mother,
60   The life of fruits and corn;
  And spring and seed and swallow
  Take wing for her and follow
  Where summer song rings hollow
      And flowers are put to scorn.

  There go the loves that wither,
      The old loves with wearier wings;
  And all dead years draw thither,
      And all disastrous things;
  Dead dreams of days forsaken,
70 Blind buds that snows have shaken,
  Wild leaves that winds have taken,
      Red strays of ruined springs.

  We are not sure of sorrow,
      And joy was never sure;
  To-day will die to-morrow;
      Time stoops⁵ to no man's lure;⁶
  And love, grown faint and fretful,
  With lips but half regretful
  Sighs, and with eyes forgetful
80 Weeps that no loves endure.

  From too much love of living,
      From hope and fear set free,
  We thank with brief thanksgiving
      Whatever gods may be
  That no life lives for ever;
  That dead men rise up never;

---

⁵ **stoops** dives (as a falcon does)

⁶ **lure** a feathered, baited device used to recall
the falcon to its master

That even the weariest river
  Winds somewhere safe to sea.

Then star nor sun shall waken,
90   Nor any change of light:
  Nor sound of waters shaken,
    Nor any sound or sight:
  Nor wintry leaves nor vernal,
  Nor days nor things diurnal;
  Only the sleep eternal
    In an eternal night.

1866

GERARD MANLEY HOPKINS

1844–1889

Gerard Manley Hopkins belonged to a generation of young English intellectuals in the mid-nineteenth century who were captivated by the ritual and dogma of Roman Catholicism. His conversion in 1866 was the central and determining event of his life. After years of study he became a Jesuit priest in 1877 and performed a series of pastoral and teaching duties, finally serving as a professor of classics at University College, Dublin. Having renounced poetry (as too sensuously attractive), he resumed his writing at the request of his superiors, but published no poems in his lifetime. When they finally appeared in 1918 (edited by his friend, the poet Robert Bridges) his poems made an enormous and lasting impact. Such diverse poets as W.H. Auden, David Jones, and Dylan Thomas clearly reflect his influence.

Hopkins is a poet of paradoxes. Despite daring technique and intense expression of earthly joy and despair, he subordinates his bold spirit to austere Christian humility and conservative religious faith. His poems repeatedly unite opposing attachments—to the permanent things of the spirit and to the passing beauties of the physical world. Each thing in the world, Hopkins believes, contains a similar union of spiritual and physical elements: the distinctive set of characteristics (derived from sense data) that gives each thing its own particularity is at the same time the special mark of its divine origin in God. Hopkins calls this pattern of uniqueness "inscape"; inscape is present not only in people and things, but also in poems.

Hopkins's meter, which he calls "sprung rhythm," uses heavily stressed beats occurring at variable intervals imposed on a regular metrical base. Like Whitman (whom Hopkins resembles in some elements of disposition and outlook), he often allows lines of verse to stretch beyond conventional bounds. An elaborately woven texture of sound results from constant use of alliteration, assonance, internal rhymes and half-rhymes, onomatopoeia, and other echo-effects. Devices borrowed from Anglo-Saxon poetry (the kenning-like "morning's minion, kingdom of daylight's dauphin," for example), both archaic and newly coined words, and a sometimes Germanic-sounding syntax further accentuate the distinctiveness of the style. (See, in "The Windhover," "dapple-dawn-drawn Falcon, in his riding / Of the rolling level underneath him steady air"). Although the thought expressed is rarely difficult, the style can be intimidating. Reading the poems aloud immediately reveals their startling beauty and gives flashes of their sense. Further careful study makes their meanings plain without detracting from the pleasure that Hopkins's intricate art provides.

God's Grandeur

The world is charged with the grandeur of God.
  It will flame out, like shining from shook foil;[1]
  It gathers to a greatness, like the ooze of oil[2]
Crushed. Why do men then now not reck his rod?[3]
Generations have trod, have trod, have trod;
  And all is seared with trade; bleared, smeared with toil;
  And wears man's smudge and shares man's smell: the soil
Is bare now, nor can foot feel, being shod.

And for all this, nature is never spent;
10   There lives the dearest freshness deep down things;
And though the last lights off the black West went
  Oh, morning, at the brown brink eastward, springs—
Because the Holy Ghost over the bent
  World broods with warm breast and with ah! bright wings.[4]

1877   1895

[1] **foil** "I mean foil in its sense of leaf or tinsel . . . Shaken goldfoil gives off broad glares like sheet lightning and also, and this is true of nothing else, owing to its zigzag dints and crossings and network of small cornered facets, a sort of fork lightning too" (Hopkins, in a letter to Robert Bridges, January 4, 1883).

[2] **oil** from pressed olives
[3] **reck his rod** heed his rule
[4] ll. 13–14 a combination of Genesis 1:2 ("and the Spirit of God was moving over the face of the waters") and the traditional representation of the Holy Ghost as a dove

The Starlight Night

Look at the stars! look, look up at the skies!
  O look at all the fire-folk sitting in the air!
  The bright boroughs, the circle-citadels there!
Down in dim woods the diamond delves![1] the elves'-eyes!
The grey lawns cold where gold, where quickgold[2] lies!
  Wind-beat whitebeam![3] airy abeles set on a flare![4]
  Flake-doves sent floating forth at a farmyard scare!—
Ah well! it is all a purchase, all is a prize.

Buy then! bid then!—What?—Prayer, patience, alms, vows.
Look, look: a May-mess,[5] like on orchard boughs!
  Look! March-bloom, like on mealed-with-yellow sallows![6]
These are indeed the barn; withindoors house
The shocks.[7] This piece-bright paling[8] shuts the spouse
  Christ home, Christ and his mother and all his hallows.[9]

1877   1918

[1] **delves** pits or mines
[2] **quickgold** dewdrops
[3] **whitebeam** a small tree notable for leaves with white undersides
[4] **abeles . . . flare** white poplars made to flutter by the breeze

[5] **May-mess** a feast of May blossoms
[6] **sallows** willows
[7] **shocks** sheaves of grain
[8] **piece-bright paling** fencing shiny as a coin (piece)
[9] **hallows** saints

The Windhover:[1]

To Christ our Lord

I caught this morning morning's minion,[2] king-
    dom of daylight's dauphin,[3] dapple-dawn-drawn Falcon, in his riding
    Of the rolling level underneath him steady air, and striding
High there, how he rung[4] upon the rein of a wimpling[5] wing
In his ecstasy! then, off, off forth on swing,
    As a skate's heel sweeps smooth on a bow-bend: the hurl and gliding
    Rebuffed the big wind. My heart in hiding
Stirred for a bird,—the achieve of, the mastery of the thing!

Brute beauty and valour and act, oh, air, pride, plume, here
10   Buckle![6] AND the fire that breaks from thee then, a billion
Times told lovelier, more dangerous, O my chevalier![7]

No wonder of it: shéer plód makes plough down sillion[8]
Shine, and blue-bleak embers, ah my dear,
    Fall, gall themselves, and gash gold-vermilion.

1877   1918

[1] the kestrel, a small falcon that can hover facing the oncoming wind
[2] **minion** darling, favorite of a king
[3] **dauphin** eldest son of the king of France, hence, a princely figure, heir to something magnificent
[4] **rung** circled
[5] **wimpling** rippling

[6] **Buckle** This word incorporates a range of meanings from "join together" to "crumple." The latter sense might describe a sudden swoop of the hovering falcon.
[7] **chevalier** a French knight or noble champion. Cf. "dauphin" in 1. 2.
[8] **sillion** archaic word meaning "furrow" or "ridge between furrows"

Pied Beauty[1]

Glory be to God for dappled things—
    For skies of couple-colour as a brinded[2] cow;
      For rose-moles all in stipple upon trout that swim;
Fresh-firecoal chestnut-falls,[3] finches' wings;
    Landscape plotted and pieced—fold,[4] fallow, and plough;
      And áll trádes, their gear and tackle and trim.

All things counter, original, spare, strange;
    Whatever is fickle, freckled (who knows how?)
10   With swift, slow; sweet, sour; adazzle, dim;
He fathers-forth whose beauty is past change:
                     Praise him.

1877   1918

[1] **Pied** variegated, made up of different-colored patches
[2] **brinded** spotted or streaked

[3] **chestnut-falls** Cf. "Chestnuts as bright as coals or spots of vermilion" (Hopkins, *Journals*).
[4] **fold** enclosed area for sheep

Hurrahing in Harvest

Summer ends now; now, barbarous in beauty, the stooks[1] rise
Around; up above, what wind-walks! what lovely behaviour
Of silk-sack clouds! has wilder, wilful-wavier
Meal-drift[2] moulded ever and melted across skies?

I walk, I lift up, I lift up heart, eyes,
Down all that glory in the heavens to glean our Saviour;
And, éyes, heárt, what looks, what lips yet gave you a
Rapturous love's greeting of realer, of rounder replies?

And the azurous[3] hung hills are his world-wielding shoulder
10   Majestic—as a stallion stalwart, very-violet-sweet!—
These things, these things were here and but the beholder
Wanting; which two when they once meet,
The heart rears wings bold and bolder
And hurls for him, O half hurls earth for him off under his feet.

1877   1918

[1] **stooks**   sheaves of grain stacked upright
[2] **Meal-drift**   finely ground grain heaped up
[3] **azurous**   blue

Felix Randal

Felix Randal the farrier,[1] O is he dead then? my duty all ended,
Who have watched his mould of man, big-boned and hardy-handsome
Pining, pining, till time when reason rambled in it and some
Fatal four disorders, fleshed there, all contended?

Sickness broke him. Impatient, he cursed at first, but mended
Being anointed and all; though a heavenlier heart began some
Months earlier, since I had our sweet reprieve and ransom
Tendered to him.[2] Ah well, God rest him all road[3] ever he offended!

This seeing the sick endears them to us, us too it endears.
10   My tongue had taught thee comfort, touch had quenched thy tears,
Thy tears that touched my heart, child, Felix, poor Felix Randal;

How far from then forethought of, all thy more boisterous years,
When thou at the random[4] grim forge, powerful amidst peers,
Didst fettle[5] for the great grey drayhorse his bright and battering sandal!

1880   1918

[1] **farrier**   blacksmith
[2] **sweet reprieve . . . to him**   granted absolution for his sins
[3] **all road**   in whatever way

[4] **random**   irregularly built
[5] **fettle**   beat into shape (a probable condensation of several dialect meanings of "fettle")

Spring and Fall:

to a young child

Márgarét, áre you gríeving
Over Goldengrove unleaving?
Leáves, líke the things of man, you
With your fresh thoughts care for, can you?
Áh! ás the heart grows older
It will come to such sights colder
By and by, nor spare a sigh
Though worlds of wanwood[1] leafmeal[2] lie;
And yet you *will* weep and know why.
10 Now no matter, child, the name:
Sórrow's spríngs áre the same.
Nor mouth had, no nor mind, expressed
What heart heard of, ghost[3] guessed:
It ís the blight man was born for,
It is Margaret you mourn for.

1880   1893

[1] **wanwood** worn-looking autumn trees, with pale leaves (Hopkins's coinage)
[2] **leafmeal** (also coined) probably an adverb analogous to "piecemeal," from which it also borrows some of its meaning
[3] **ghost** soul

As Kingfishers Catch Fire

As kingfishers catch fire, dragonflies draw[1] flame;
As tumbled over rim in roundy wells
Stones ring; like each tucked[2] string tells, each hung bell's
Bow swung finds tongue to fling out broad its name;
Each mortal thing does one thing and the same:
Deals out that being indoors each one dwells;[3]
Selves[4]—goes itself; *myself* it speaks and spells,
Crying *What I do is me: for that I came.*

Í say more: the just man justices;
10 Keeps gráce: thát keeps all his goings graces;
Acts in God's eye what in God's eye he is—
Chríst. For Christ plays in ten thousand places,
Lovely in limbs, and lovely in eyes not his
To the Father through the features of men's faces.

1882?   1918

[1] **draw** in the sense of "delineate" or "depict"
[2] **tucked** plucked
[3] **Deals . . . dwells** proclaims (deals out) the essence (that being) that inhabits (dwells indoors) each one
[4] **Selves** (a verb) manifests its particular individuality

Carrion Comfort[1]

Not, I'll not, carrion comfort, Despair, not feast on thee;
Not untwist—slack they may be—these last strands of man
In me ór, most weary, cry *I can no more*. I can;
Can something, hope, wish day come, not choose not to be.

But ah, but O thou terrible, why wouldst thou rude on me
Thy wring-world[2] right foot rock? lay a lionlimb against me? scan
With darksome devouring eyes my bruisèd bones? and fan,
O in turns of tempest, me heaped there; me frantic to avoid thee and flee?

Why? That my chaff might fly; my grain lie, sheer and clear.
10 Nay in all that toil, that coil,[3] since (seems) I kissed the rod,[4]
Hand rather, my heart lo! lapped strength, stole joy, would laugh, chéer.
Cheer whom though? The hero whose heaven-handling flung me, fóot tród
Me? or me that fought him? O which one? is it each one? That night, that year
Of now done darkness I wretch lay wrestling with (my God!) my God.

1885   1918

[carrion] dead decaying flesh, food for sca-
vengers
[2] **wring-world** capable of wringing (i.e., apply-
ing distressing pressure on) the world. "Rock"

is a verb, "foot" its direct object.
[3] **coil** turmoil
[4] **kissed the rod** accepted the discipline (of God
or the church)

No Worst, There Is None

No worst, there is none. Pitched past pitch of grief,
More pangs will, schooled at forepangs, wilder wring.[1]
Comforter, where, where is your comforting?
Mary, mother of us, where is your relief?
My cries heave, herds-long; huddle in a main,[2] a chief-
woe, world-sorrow; on an age-old anvil wince and sing—
Then lull, then leave off. Fury had shrieked "No ling-
ering! Let me be fell:[3] force[4] I must be brief."
O the mind, mind has mountains; cliffs of fall
10 Frightful, sheer, no-man-fathomed. Hold them cheap
May who ne'er hung there. Nor does long our small
Durance[5] deal with that steep or deep. Here! creep,
Wretch, under a comfort serves in a whirlwind: all
Life death does end and each day dies with sleep.

1885   1918

[1] **wilder wring** wring wilder pangs
[2] **main** an adjective modifying "woe" in the
next line
[3] **fell** savage

[4] **force** perforce
[5] **Durance** endurance, but with overtones of
imprisonment

I Wake and Feel the Fell of Dark[1]

I wake and feel the fell of dark, not day.
What hours, O what black hoürs we have spent
This night! what sights you, heart, saw; ways you went!
And more must, in yet longer light's delay.

With witness I speak this. But where I say
Hours I mean years, mean life. And my lament
Is cries countless, cries like dead letters sent
To dearest him that lives alas! away.

I am gall, I am heartburn. God's most deep decree
10 Bitter would have me taste: my taste was me;
Bones built in me, flesh filled, blood brimmed the curse.

Selfyeast of spirit a dull dough sours. I see
The lost[2] are like this, and their scourge to be
As I am mine, their sweating selves; but worse.

1885   1918

[1] **fell** both a beast's hide and (in archaic usage)
gall or bitterness
[2] **lost** the damned in Hell

That Nature Is a Heraclitean Fire and of the Comfort of the Resurrection[1]

Cloud-puffball, torn tufts, tossed pillows ˈ flaunt forth, then chevy[2] on an air-
built thoroughfare: heaven-roysterers, in gay-gangs ˈ they throng; they
    glitter in marches.
Down roughcast,[3] down dazzling whitewash, ˈ wherever an elm arches,
Shivelights[4] and shadowtackle[5] in long ˈ lashes lace, lance, and pair.
Delightfully the bright wind boisterous ˈ ropes, wrestles, beats earth bare
Of yestertempest's creases; ˈ in pool and rutpeel parches
Squandering ooze to squeezed ˈ dough, crust, dust; stanches, starches
Squadroned masks[6] and manmarks ˈ treadmire toil there
Footfretted in it. Million-fuelèd, ˈ nature's bonfire burns on.
10 But quench her bonniest, dearest ˈ to her, her clearest-selvèd spark
Man, how fast his firedint,[7] ˈ his mark on mind, is gone!

[1] **Heraclitean Fire** The ancient Greek philo-
sopher Heraclitus taught that the universe is in
a state of perpetual flux; all forms are self-
consuming and mutate constantly into slightly
altered forms; the flow of the change is cyclic,
originating in fire and descending through the
heavier elements of air, water, and earth, then
reversing itself to return to fire.
[2] **chevy** chase like hunters

[3] **roughcast** a coarse plaster used on outer walls
[4] **shivelights** splinters of light
[5] **shadowtackle** shadows of tree branches resem-
bling a ship's rigging
[6] **Squadroned masks** hardened impressions
(like molded casts), organized in groups
[7] **firedint** a coined word meaning the mark of
man's flame or spirit

Both are in an unfathomable, all is in an enormous dark
Drowned. O pity and indig [|] nation! Manshape, that shone
Sheer off, disseveral,[8] a star, [|] death blots black out; nor mark
        Is any of him at all so stark
But vastness blurs and time [|] beats level. Enough! the Resurrection,
A heart's-clarion! Away grief's gasping, [|] joyless days, dejection.
        Across my foundering deck shone
A beacon, an eternal beam. [|] Flesh fade, and mortal trash
20   Fall to the residuary worm; [|] world's wildfire, leave but ash:
        In a flash, at a trumpet crash,
I am all at once what Christ is, [|] since he was what I am, and
This Jack,[9] joke, poor potsherd,[10] [|] patch, matchwood, immortal diamond,
        Is immortal diamond.

1888   1918

[8] **disseveral** another coined word meaning separate and singular

[9] **Jack** colloquial for a common fellow

[10] **potsherd** piece of broken pottery

The Twentieth Century

THOMAS HARDY
1840–1928

The son of a builder and master mason, Hardy was an architectural apprentice for six years and worked for another eleven years as an ecclesiastical architect, first in London and then in his native Dorset, before turning entirely to writing. He specialized in church restoration, and his carefully structured fiction and verse exhibit qualities associated with that profession and with the region to which he was so attached: fascination with difficult materials, nostalgia for lost certainties of the past, and a deep sense of local memory and values.

Hardy is one of the two important modern poets who have also been powerful novelists. (The other is D.H. Lawrence.) His poems, which often present wry stories, scenes, or characterizations, remain, like his fiction, close to the world of Dorset (the "Wessex" of his books), where he spent most of his life. He explored that world with a persistent honesty and an ironic skepticism that kept his compassion for wrecked lives from dwindling into sentimentality. Intellectually, his work reflects the triumph in the modern mind of a rueful perception that impersonal, indifferent forces shape human fortunes. Yet his novels also take the personal destinies of their characters seriously; they are driven by ancient assumptions of the tragic, universal import of these characters' suffering and even by a kind of heroic vision of their struggles. Books like *Tess of the D'Urbervilles* (1891) and *Jude the Obscure* (1896) acutely represent Hardy's involved awareness. Against conventional idyllic, pastoral, or piously Christian views of English life they set sympathetic but realistic observation and the scientific perspectives, socially applied, of Darwinian thought.

These novels, especially *Jude the Obscure*, so shocked squeamish critics with their sexual frankness and unsentimental insights that after 1896 Hardy gave up fiction and turned wholly to poetry. The result was the extraordinary emergence of a major poet, fifty-eight years old, in *Wessex Poems and Other Verses* (1898), which included poems dating back to the mid-1880s when he had written most of his early verse. Later important volumes included *Satires of Circumstance* (1914), *Collected Poems* (1919), and *Late Lyrics and Earlier* (1922). Hardy also wrote *The Dynasts*, an allegorical drama, mostly in verse, about the Napoleonic wars; it appeared in three installments (1903, 1906, 1908).

His most striking group of poems appeared in the 1914 volume: the twenty-seven poem sequence called "Poems of 1912–13," represented here by "The Walk," " 'I Found Her Out There,' " "The Voice," "After a Journey," and "At Castle Boterel." This elegiac sequence concerns Hardy's first wife, Emma, who died in 1912, in the thirty-eighth year of a miserable, incompatible marriage. Written in varied verse-forms, the poems recount the estrangement and seek to undo it by imagining an understanding, loving colloquy. The wife's spirit lures the husband back to her native, beloved Cornwall, where they had first met and loved truly. In the bitterly beautiful "After a Journey" the colloquy reaches its most intense expression of desire to remake the past. The eight-line stanzas, with their tricky rhyming (ababcddc) and complex pattern of meter and line-lengths, masterfully channel the poem's dramatic immediacy, visionary incantation, and tone of painful yearning. An almost pure verbal music arises from the pressures of remorse and desire against the resistance of irreversible time. "Poems of 1912–13" was the first of the great sequences that are major works of this century.

The Darkling Thrush[1]

I leant upon a coppice gate[2]
    When Frost was spectre-gray
And Winter's dregs made desolate
    The weakening eye of day.
The tangled bine-stems scored the sky
    Like strings of broken lyres,
And all mankind that haunted nigh
    Had sought their household fires.

The land's sharp features seemed to be
10   The Century's corpse outleant,
His crypt the cloudy canopy,
    The wind his death-lament.
The ancient pulse of germ and birth
    Was shrunken hard and dry,
And every spirit upon earth
    Seemed fervourless as I.

At once a voice arose among
    The bleak twigs overhead
In a full-hearted evensong
20   Of joy illimited;
An aged thrush, frail, gaunt, and small,
    In blast-beruffled plume,
Had chosen thus to fling his soul
    Upon the growing gloom.

So little cause for carolings
    Of such ecstatic sound
Was written on terrestrial things
    Afar or nigh around,
That I could think there trembled through
30   His happy good-night air
Some blessed Hope, whereof he knew
    And I was unaware.

31 December 1900[3]   1902

---

[1] the thrush singing in the darkness—both literal darkness and the darkness of humanity at the end of the century

[2] **coppice gate** gate at the entrance to a small copse, or woods

[3] The poem was written somewhat earlier but dated December 31, 1900 to stress its character as a lament for the death of the nineteenth century and its optimistic hopes.

Channel Firing[1]

That night your great guns, unawares,
Shook all our coffins as we lay,
And broke the chancel window-squares,
We thought it was the Judgment-day

And sat upright. While drearisome
Arose the howl of wakened hounds:
The mouse let fall the altar-crumb,
The worms drew back into the mounds,

10 The glebe cow[2] drooled. Till God called, "No;
It's gunnery practice out at sea
Just as before you went below;
The world is as it used to be:

"All nations striving strong to make
Red war yet redder. Mad as hatters
They do no more for Christés[3] sake
Than you who are helpless in such matters.

"That this is not the judgment-hour
For some of them's a blessed thing,
For if it were they'd have to scour
20 Hell's floor for so much threatening. . . .

"Ha, ha. It will be warmer when
I blow the trumpet (if indeed
I ever do; for you are men,
And rest eternal sorely need)."

So down we lay again. "I wonder,
Will the world ever saner be,"
Said one, "than when He sent us under
In our indifferent century!"

And many a skeleton shook his head.
30 "Instead of preaching forty year,"
My neighbour Parson Thirdly said,
"I wish I had stuck to pipes and beer."

Again the guns disturbed the hour,
Roaring their readiness to avenge,
As far inland as Stourton Tower,[4]
And Camelot, and starlit Stonehenge.[5]

April 1914   1914

---

[1] gunnery practice by British warships in the
English Channel on the eve of World War I
[2] **glebe cow** cow pastured on church grounds
for the pastor's use
[3] **Christés** Christ's (a medieval usage, appro-
priately archaic for the voice of God)

[4] **Stourton Tower** built in the eighteenth
century to commemorate Alfred the Great's
ninth-century victory over Danish invaders
[5] **Camelot . . . Stonehenge** supposed site of
the legendary King Arthur's court; prehistoric
monoliths on Salisbury Plain

From Poems of 1912–13

The Walk[1]

You did not walk with me
Of late to the hill-top tree
    By the gated ways,
    As in earlier days;
    You were weak and lame,
    So you never came,
And I went alone, and I did not mind,
Not thinking of you as left behind.

I walked up there to-day
10 Just in the former way;
    Surveyed around
    The familiar ground
    By myself again:
    What difference, then?
Only that underlying sense
Of the look of a room on returning thence.

                 1914

[1] See headnote on Hardy for comment concerning this poem and the four that follow, all from "Poems of 1912–13."

"I Found Her Out There"

I found her out there[1]
On a slope few see,
That falls westwardly
To the salt-edged air,
Where the ocean breaks
On the purple strand,
And the hurricane shakes
The solid land.

I brought her here,[2]
10 And have laid her to rest
In a noiseless nest
No sea beats near.
She will never be stirred
In her loamy cell
By the waves long heard
And loved so well.

[1] **out there** Emma Hardy's native Cornwall, where Hardy first met and wooed her

[2] **here** Dorset, where Hardy took Emma to live when they were married

So she does not sleep
By those haunted heights
The Atlantic smites
20   And the blind gales sweep,
Whence she often would gaze
At Dundagel's famed head,[3]
While the dipping blaze
Dyed her face fire-red;

And would sigh at the tale
Of sunk Lyonnesse,[4]
As a wind-tugged tress
Flapped her cheek like a flail;
Or listen at whiles
30   With a thought-bound brow
To the murmuring miles
She is far from now.

Yet her shade, maybe,
Will creep underground
Till it catch the sound
Of that western sea
As it swells and sobs
Where she once domiciled,
40   And joy in its throbs
With the heart of a child.

1914

3 **Dundagel's famed head** Tintagel Head, King
Arthur's supposed birthplace
4 **Lyonnesse** legendary name of the southern

coast of Cornwall; associated with King Arthur,
the region was supposed to have sunk beneath
the sea.

The Voice

Woman much missed, how you call to me, call to me,
Saying that now you are not as you were
When you had changed from the one who was all to me,
But as at first, when our day was fair.

Can it be you that I hear? Let me view you, then,
Standing as when I drew near to the town
Where you would wait for me: yes, as I knew you then,
Even to the original air-blue gown!

Or is it only the breeze, in its listlessness
10   Travelling across the wet mead to me here,
You being ever dissolved to wan wistlessness,
Heard no more again far or near?

Thus I; faltering forward,
    Leaves around me falling,
Wind oozing thin through the thorn from norward,
    And the woman calling.

December 1912   1914

After a Journey

Hereto I come to view a voiceless ghost;
    Whither, O whither will its whim now draw me?
Up the cliff, down, till I'm lonely, lost,
    And the unseen waters' ejaculations awe me.
Where you will next be there's no knowing,
    Facing round about me everywhere,
        With your nut-coloured hair,
And gray eyes, and rose-flush coming and going.

Yes: I have re-entered your olden haunts at last;
10   Through the years, through the dead scenes I have tracked you;
What have you now found to say of our past—
    Scanned across the dark space wherein I have lacked you?
Summer gave us sweets, but autumn wrought division?
    Things were not lastly as firstly well
        With us twain, you tell?
But all's closed now, despite Time's derision.

I see what you are doing: you are leading me on
    To the spots we knew when we haunted here together,
The waterfall, above which the mist-bow shone
20   At the then fair hour in the then fair weather,
And the cave just under, with a voice still so hollow
    That it seems to call out to me from forty years ago,
        When you were all aglow,
And not the thin ghost that I now fraily follow!

Ignorant of what there is flitting here to see,
    The waked birds preen and the seals flop lazily;
Soon you will have, Dear, to vanish from me,
    For the stars close their shutters and the dawn whitens hazily.
Trust me, I mind not, though Life lours,
30   The bringing me here; nay, bring me here again!
        I am just the same as when
Our days were a joy, and our paths through flowers.

Pentargan Bay[1]   1914

[1] **Pentargan Bay** a small bay on the northwest
coast of Cornwall, north of Boscastle Harbour

At Castle Boterel[1]

As I drive to the junction of lane and highway,
  And the drizzle bedrenches the waggonette,
I look behind at the fading byway,
  And see on its slope, now glistening wet,
      Distinctly yet

Myself and a girlish form benighted
  In dry March weather. We climb the road
Beside a chaise. We had just alighted
  To ease the sturdy pony's load
10   When he sighed and slowed.

What we did as we climbed, and what we talked of
  Matters not much, nor to what it led,—
Something that life will not be balked of
  Without rude reason till hope is dead,
      And feeling fled.

It filled but a minute. But was there ever
  A time of such quality, since or before,
In that hill's story? To one mind never,
  Though it has been climbed, foot-swift, foot-sore,
20   By thousands more.

Primaeval rocks form the road's steep border,
  And much have they faced there, first and last,
Of the transitory in Earth's long order;
  But what they record in colour and cast
      Is—that we two passed.

And to me, though Time's unflinching rigour,
  In mindless rote, has ruled from sight
The substance now, one phantom figure
  Remains on the slope, as when that night
30   Saw us alight.

I look and see it there, shrinking, shrinking,
  I look back at it amid the rain
For the very last time; for my sand is sinking,
  And I shall traverse old love's domain
      Never again.

March 1913   1914

[1] Boterel Castle is said to be Hardy's invented
name for the town of Boscastle, situated above
a steep hill to the south of Boscastle Harbour
(Cornwall).

During Wind and Rain

They sing their dearest songs—
He, she, all of them—yea,
Treble and tenor and bass,
    And one to play;
With the candles mooning each face. . . .
    Ah, no; the years O!
How the sick leaves reel down in throngs!

They clear the creeping moss—
Elders and juniors—aye,
10 Making the pathways neat
    And the garden gay;
And they build a shady seat. . . .
    Ah, no; the years, the years;
See, the white storm-birds wing across!

They are blithely breakfasting all—
Men and maidens—yea,
Under the summer tree,
    With a glimpse of the bay,
While pet fowl come to the knee. . . .
20   Ah, no; the years O!
And the rotten rose is ript from the wall.

They change to a high new house,
He, she, all of them—aye,
Clocks and carpets and chairs
    On the lawn all day,
And brightest things that are theirs. . . .
    Ah, no; the years, the years;
Down their carved names the rain-drop ploughs.

1917

A.E. HOUSMAN
1859–1936

Descended from clergymen on both sides, Housman was early praised both as a student and as a promising writer. But the boy was frail and subject to bullying at school, his beloved, protective mother died when he was only twelve, and he was alienated from his inept, depressed father, an undistinguished solicitor who invested heavily in unsuccessful inventions. The somewhat morbid family atmosphere included regular, perfunctory religious worship. At Oxford, Housman was so preoccupied with studying the Latin poet Propertius—whose highly sophisticated, erotically charged works later also influenced Ezra Pound—that he failed his final examinations. The miseries of a frustrated homosexual passion also undoubtedly interfered with his studies.

Housman passed the examinations on second try, but had lost the chance for an immediate academic career. He spent the next ten years in a government clerkship in London, meanwhile pursuing his classical studies so successfully that his contributions to learned journals won him a professorship in Latin at University College, London (1892–1911), and then, for the rest of his life, at Cambridge University. The London appointment seemed to liberate him poetically, and he said that the first five months of 1895 were his "most prolific period." Although *A Shropshire Lad* sold very slowly at first and appeared in small editions, it gradually became one of the most popular volumes of serious poetry ever published.

The reason for this success lies in the surface simplicity of form and theme of a typical Housman poem, and in tonal qualities very close to those of folk songs. The stanzas are often balladlike, or made up of rhyming couplets, and the motifs are elegiac, embittered, or sturdily stoical. Housman's evocatively precise phrasing and severe rhythmic control prevent the book from being a collection of sentimental poems about love, death, and nature, but many readers love the poems regardless of such distinctions. Sheer elegance and charm make many of the poems a delight, though some, like poem XXX ("Others, I am not the first"), hint with grim fortitude at the repressed side of Housman's emotional life. Or, like "Eight O'Clock" in *Last Poems*, they give such desperately accurate closeups of a human being *in extremis* that we hardly believe what we are reading—so effectively does Housman objectify and distance, while intimately capturing, the essence of the situation.

Though a modern poet, Housman is not in any ordinary sense experimental. His prosody is the perfection of the simple lyric poem of tradition—the pure stream that came to him from the "songs" of Shakespeare, Blake, and Tennyson. But the spare purity and discipline of his art, and his vividly introspective, yet unpretentious style, make his work a touchstone of pure lyricism in our age.

From A Shropshire Lad

II

Loveliest of trees, the cherry now
Is hung with bloom along the bough,
And stands about the woodland ride
Wearing white for Eastertide.

Now, of my threescore years and ten,
Twenty will not come again,
And take from seventy springs a score,
It only leaves me fifty more.

And since to look at things in bloom
10   Fifty springs are little room,
About the woodlands I will go
To see the cherry hung with snow.

May 1895   1896

XIII

When I was one-and-twenty
    I heard a wise man say,
"Give crowns and pounds and guineas
    But not your heart away;
Give pearls away and rubies
    But keep your fancy free."
But I was one-and-twenty,
    No use to talk to me.

When I was one-and-twenty
10   I heard him say again,
"The heart out of the bosom
    Was never given in vain;
'Tis paid with sighs a plenty
    And sold for endless rue."
And I am two-and-twenty,
    And oh, 'tis true, 'tis true.

January 1895   1896

XIX

To an Athlete Dying Young

The time you won your town the race
We chaired you through the market-place;
Man and boy stood cheering by,
And home we brought you shoulder-high.

To-day, the road all runners come,
Shoulder-high we bring you home,
And set you at your threshold down,
Townsman of a stiller town.

Smart lad, to slip betimes away
10 From fields where glory does not stay
And early though the laurel[1] grows
It withers quicker than the rose.

Eyes the shady night has shut
Cannot see the record cut,
And silence sounds no worse than cheers
After earth has stopped the ears:

[1] **laurel** The ancient Greeks wove wreaths of laurel leaves to crown the heads of victors in various competitions. Thus "laurel" came to mean not only the tree, but a laurel crown and glory or fame. The large, shiny, aromatic leaves soon wither, and so are natural symbols of both the evanescence of reputation and, more pointedly, the brief life of the young man mourned in the poem.

Now you will not swell the rout
Of lads that wore their honours out,
Runners whom renown outran
20   And the name died before the man.

So set, before its echoes fade,
The fleet foot on the sill of shade,
And hold to the low lintel up
The still-defended challenge-cup.

And round that early-laurelled head
Will flock to gaze the strengthless dead,
And find unwithered on its curls
The garland briefer than a girl's.

March 1895   1896

XXX

Others, I am not the first,
Have willed more mischief than they durst:
If in the breathless night I too
Shiver now, 'tis nothing new.

More than I, if truth were told,
Have stood and sweated hot and cold,
And through their reins[1] in ice and fire
Fear contended with desire.

Agued once like me were they,
10   But I like them shall win my way
Lastly to the bed of mould
Where there's neither heat nor cold.

But from my grave across my brow
Plays no wind of healing now,
And fire and ice within me fight
Beneath the suffocating night.

1896

[1] **reins** the seat of emotions and affections, once
thought to be in the loins

LIV

With rue my heart is laden
    For golden friends I had,
For many a rose-lipt maiden
    And many a lightfoot lad.

By brooks too broad for leaping
    The lightfoot boys are laid;
The rose-lipt girls are sleeping
    In fields where roses fade.

August 1893   1896

Eight O'Clock[1]

He stood, and heard the steeple
    Sprinkle the quarters on the morning town.
One, two, three, four, to market-place and people
    It tossed them down.

Strapped, noosed, nighing his hour,
    He stood and counted them and cursed his luck;
And then the clock collected in the tower
    Its strength, and struck.

1922

[1] The traditional time for a hanging in England was 8 a.m.

WILLIAM BUTLER YEATS
1865–1939

William Butler Yeats has a strong claim to the title of greatest modern poet writing in English. His power lies largely in his gift for projecting basic human feelings in singing language that is at once natural, accurate, and evocative. Obvious examples include the expression of persistent love-feeling long after a relationship has ended, in brief but powerful poems like "Memory" and "A Deep-Sworn Vow"; of the bitter challenge of old age, in "The Tower"; and of tragic dismay in the wake of political idealism that engenders violence, in the great sequences about the Irish civil war, "Meditations in Time of Civil War" and "Nineteen Hundred and Nineteen." Better than any other modern poet, Yeats mastered the art of writing straightforwardly, in traditional verse-forms, while at the same time shifting tone and perspective with dazzling speed and impact

— effects normally associated with the more openly experimental work of Pound and Eliot. But Yeats's directly human emotions and concerns are always in the foreground.

A son and brother of artists, the mystically inclined Yeats studied art before turning to poetry and, like Hardy, was essentially self-educated in literary matters. He saturated his mind with the work of the great nineteenth-century poets, and from Blake especially he learned to combine bold visual images with mythical and religious suggestion. At the start of "Leda and the Swan," for instance, he presents a graphic scene of the ravishing of the nymph Leda by the god Zeus; then, having brought a mythical incident to sensuous life, he stresses its mystery as a symbol of human destiny. Another instance is "The Second Coming," with its terrifying vision of the risen Sphinx "slouching" over the desert — the sign of a new barbaric age.

Yeats is also modern Ireland's greatest poet. As a young writer he collected rural lore and tales and used them in his poems, together with evocations of a magical landscape. It was for such poems that he first became known in England, where he was considered a delicate lyricist, the essence of the Irish romanticism known as the "Celtic Twilight" movement. But even in this early work his sense of visionary idealism as disastrously deceptive troubles the dreams of pure joy and eternal tranquility in poems like "The Lake Isle of Innisfree" and "Who Goes with Fergus?" Later, Ireland's brutal, prolonged civil warfare in the period after World War I filled his mature work with dismay. Yeats's work is seldom narrowly nationalistic, though he did show interest in an Irish political movement that was fascist in character and espoused racist ideas about eugenics—in sharp contrast to the left-revolutionary activities of the woman (Maud Gonne) about whom he wrote his greatest love poetry. She had refused him; and although he exalted her as the modern Helen of Troy, beautiful and destructive, and called her his "phoenix," her rejection of him may have influenced his later political views. But those views were extremely idiosyncratic, and the bulk of his work has won acclaim for its humanism as well as its art.

Ireland's travail, and Yeats's serious desire to raise his country's cultural morale, led him to work with others—especially Lady Augusta Gregory, the playwright who was also his staunch patron—to bring about a literary and dramatic renaissance. Their group founded the Abbey Theatre, which produced their plays and those of John Millington Synge and Sean O'Casey, among others. Yeats saw a modern European sophistication and a heroic, classical sensibility as necessary to his country's new sense of itself. His lifelong contributions were honored by the new republic of Eire in 1922 when he was appointed a permanent member of the Irish Senate—a year before he received the Nobel Prize for Literature.

A remarkable essayist and daring experimental playwright, Yeats dwelt imaginatively in a realm of heroic ideals and struggles. Yet he realized how little practical impact his dreams had on his countrymen—see, for instance, his piercing little poem "The Road at My Door." Nor could he help questioning the value of heroism itself. His "Easter, 1916" begins by exalting the leaders of the abortive Easter Rebellion who were executed by the British; it ends by deploring their intransigent, suicidal politics, while cherishing their "excess of love." And his poems and plays centered on the legendary hero Cuchulain are as full of complex considerations as the soliloquies of Shakespeare's Hamlet.

Many of Yeats's poems can be connected with *A Vision* (1925; revised 1937), which he wrote as a result of experiments that he and his wife conducted in "automatic writing"; yet the poems stand independently after all. *A Vision* presents a symbolic scheme, with charts, outlining the cycles of history by analogy with the moon's monthly phases—phases that also parallel the stages of individual lives and the personality-types dominant in successive historical epochs. All this is seriously presented and makes strangely absorbing reading, especially in its prose reveries and incidental comments, but the spirit "messengers" who provided the information also told Yeats that they had come to give him "metaphors for poetry." And the scheme, which embraces a theory of destiny and creativity, helped him keep conflicting ideas and pressures in clear view while composing his more intricate poems: "Byzantium," for instance, or the group of pieces spoken by "Crazy Jane." Nevertheless, these poems are so alive in their own right that they can never be *explained* by reference to *A Vision*.

The Lake Isle of Innisfree[1]

I will arise and go now, and go to Innisfree,
And a small cabin build there, of clay and wattles made:
Nine bean-rows will I have there, a hive for the honeybee,
And live alone in the bee-loud glade.

And I shall have some peace there, for peace comes dropping slow,
Dropping from the veils of the morning to where the cricket sings;
There midnight's all a glimmer, and noon a purple glow,
And evening full of the linnet's wings.

I will arise and go now, for always night and day
10   I hear lake water lapping with low sounds by the shore;
While I stand on the roadway, or on the pavements grey,
I hear it in the deep heart's core.

1890   1892

[1] Innisfree is a tiny island in County Sligo, Ireland.

Who Goes with Fergus?[1]

Who will go drive with Fergus now,
And pierce the deep wood's woven shade,
And dance upon the level shore?
Young man, lift up your russet brow,
And lift your tender eyelids, maid,
And brood on hopes and fear no more.

And no more turn aside and brood
Upon love's bitter mystery;
For Fergus rules the brazen cars,[2]
10   And rules the shadows of the wood,
And the white breast of the dim sea
And all dishevelled wandering stars.

1891   1892

[1] Fergus, a legendary Irish warrior-king, was tricked into giving up his crown. Here and in other poems, Yeats imagines him as now the ruler of an unworldly realm of dreams and unchanging perfection—and of artistic vision—that seems to offer a state of bliss, yet is presented in language evoking frustration and sorrow ("shadows," "dim sea," "dishevelled wandering stars," etc.).

[2] **brazen cars** Suggesting battle chariots and kingly power, this phrase introduces a series of images that undercut the promises of the preceding lines (possibly an echo of Milton's *Paradise Lost* VI.209 ff.: "Arms on Armour clashing bray'd / Horrible discord, and the madding Wheels / Of brazen Chariots rag'd . . .").

The Magi[1]

Now as at all times I can see in the mind's eye,
In their stiff, painted clothes, the pale unsatisfied ones
Appear and disappear in the blue depth of the sky
With all their ancient faces like rain-beaten stones,
And all their helms of silver hovering side by side,
And all their eyes still fixed, hoping to find once more,
Being by Calvary's turbulence unsatisfied,
The uncontrollable mystery on the bestial floor.

1913   1914

[1] the wise kings who brought gifts to the infant Jesus. Here they appear as iconic mental images, constantly seeking a new revelation because disillusioned after Christ's crucifixion (by implication, disappointed in the failure of Christianity and modern civilization). Cf. T.S. Eliot, "Journey of the Magi" (p. 901 below) and Ramon Guthrie, "The Magi" (p. 931).

The Dolls

A doll in the doll-maker's house
Looks at the cradle and bawls:
"That is an insult to us."
But the oldest of all the dolls,
Who had seen, being kept for show,
Generations of his sort,
Out-screams the whole shelf: "Although
There's not a man can report
Evil of this place,
10   The man and the woman bring
Hither, to our disgrace,
A noisy and filthy thing."
Hearing him groan and stretch
The doll-maker's wife is aware
Her husband has heard the wretch,
And crouched by the arm of his chair,
She murmurs into his ear,
Head upon shoulder leant:
"My dear, my dear, O dear,
20   It was an accident."

1913   1914

Memory

One had a lovely face,
And two or three had charm,
But charm and face were in vain
Because the mountain grass
Cannot but keep the form
Where the mountain hare has lain.

1919

A Deep-Sworn Vow

Others because you did not keep
That deep-sworn vow have been friends of mine;
Yet always when I look death in the face,
When I clamber to the heights of sleep,
Or when I grow excited with wine,
Suddenly I meet your face.

1915   1919

Easter, 1916[1]

I have met them at close of day
Coming with vivid faces
From counter or desk among grey
Eighteenth-century houses.
I have passed with a nod of the head
Or polite meaningless words,
Or have lingered awhile and said
Polite meaningless words,
And thought before I had done
10 Of a mocking tale or a gibe
To please a companion
Around the fire at the club,
Being certain that they and I
But lived where motley is worn:
All changed, changed utterly:
A terrible beauty is born.

That woman's[2] days were spent
In ignorant good-will,
Her nights in argument

[1] The Easter Rising (April 1916) was an abortive armed effort to wrest Ireland's independence from England and set up a republic. Fifteen of its leaders, including all the men referred to in the poem, were executed; the one woman mentioned was not. The rebellion, led by the Irish Republican Brotherhood, took place in Dublin. It was an unpopular action, but the executions united the Irish people and thenceforth the leaders were viewed as martyred patriotic heroes.

[2] **That woman** Constance Gore-Booth Markievicz received a death sentence, which was later commuted to imprisonment.

20   Until her voice grew shrill.
     What voice more sweet than hers
     When, young and beautiful,
     She rode to harriers?
     This man[3] had kept a school
     And rode our wingèd horse;[4]
     This other[5] his helper and friend
     Was coming into his force;
     He might have won fame in the end,
     So sensitive his nature seemed,
30   So daring and sweet his thought.
     This other man[6] I had dreamed
     A drunken, vainglorious lout.
     He had done most bitter wrong
     To some who are near my heart,
     Yet I number him in the song;
     He, too, has resigned his part
     In the casual comedy;
     He, too, has been changed in his turn,
     Transformed utterly:
40   A terrible beauty is born.

     Hearts with one purpose alone
     Through summer and winter seem
     Enchanted to a stone
     To trouble the living stream.
     The horse that comes from the road,
     The rider, the birds that range
     From cloud to tumbling cloud,
     Minute by minute they change;
     A shadow of cloud on the stream
50   Changes minute by minute;
     A horse-hoof slides on the brim,
     And a horse plashes within it;
     The long-legged moor-hens dive,
     And hens to moor-cocks call;
     Minute by minute they live:
     The stone's in the midst of all.

     Too long a sacrifice
     Can make a stone of the heart.
     O when may it suffice?
60   That is Heaven's part, our part
     To murmur name upon name,
     As a mother names her child

---

[3] **This man** Padraic Pearse, commandant-general of the insurrection, founder of a boys' school, and author

[4] **our wingèd horse** Pegasus, traditionally associated with poetry (Greek mythology)

[5] **This other** Thomas MacDonagh, poet

[6] **This other man** Major John MacBride, whose marriage to Maud Gonne, Yeats's great love, ended unhappily

When sleep at last has come
On limbs that had run wild.
What is it but nightfall?
No, no, not night but death;
Was it needless death after all?
For England may keep faith[7]
For all that is done and said.
70   We know their dream; enough
To know they dreamed and are dead;
And what if excess of love
Bewildered them till they died?
I write it out in a verse—
MacDonagh and MacBride
And Connolly[8] and Pearse
Now and in time to be,
Wherever green is worn,
Are changed, changed utterly:
80   A terrible beauty is born.

September 25, 1916   1921

[7] **England may keep faith** The British government had promised to grant home rule to Ireland after the successful prosecution of World War I. Though the poem celebrates the courage of the Rising—not its rightness or wisdom—this line frankly contradicts the spirit of irrational militancy.
[8] **Connolly** James Connolly, Marxist trade union organizer

The Second Coming[1]

Turning and turning in the widening gyre
The falcon cannot hear the falconer;
Things fall apart; the centre cannot hold;
Mere anarchy is loosed upon the world,
The blood-dimmed tide is loosed, and everywhere
The ceremony of innocence is drowned;
The best lack all conviction, while the worst
Are full of passionate intensity.

Surely some revelation is at hand;
10   Surely the Second Coming is at hand.
The Second Coming! Hardly are those words out
When a vast image out of *Spiritus Mundi*[2]
Troubles my sight: somewhere in sands of the desert
A shape with lion body and the head of a man,

[1] The return ("second coming") of Christ is prophesied in the New Testament (Matthew 24). Here the return is not of Jesus but of a terrifying inhuman embodiment of pre-Christian and pre-Grecian barbarism. The poem is a sharply prophetic response to the turmoil of Europe following World War I.
[2] *Spiritus Mundi* (Latin) Spirits of the World —i.e., archetypal images in the "Great Memory" of the human psyche. See Yeats's "The Tower" (p. 775 below), l. 86.

A gaze blank and pitiless as the sun,
Is moving its slow thighs, while all about it
Reel shadows of the indignant desert birds.
The darkness drops again; but now I know
That twenty centuries of stony sleep
20 Were vexed to nightmare by a rocking cradle,
And what rough beast, its hour come round at last,
Slouches towards Bethlehem to be born?

1919   1921

Sailing to Byzantium[1]

I

That[2] is no country for old men. The young
In one another's arms, birds in the trees
—Those dying generations—at their song,
The salmon-falls, the mackerel-crowded seas,
Fish, flesh, or fowl, commend all summer long
Whatever is begotten, born, and dies.
Caught in that sensual music all neglect
Monuments of unageing intellect.

II

An aged man is but a paltry thing,
10 A tattered coat upon a stick, unless
Soul clap its hands and sing, and louder sing
For every tatter in its mortal dress,
Nor is there singing school but studying
Monuments of its[3] own magnificence;
And therefore I have sailed the seas and come
To the holy city of Byzantium.

III

O sages standing in God's holy fire
As in the gold mosaic of a wall,
Come from the holy fire, perne in a gyre,[4]
20 And be the singing-masters of my soul.
Consume my heart away; sick with desire
And fastened to a dying animal
It knows not what it is; and gather me
Into the artifice of eternity.

[1] **Byzantium** ancient name of the capital of the Eastern Roman Empire, later called Constantinople and then Istanbul; here, emblematic of the realm of pure spirit and aesthetic transformation, remote from the predicaments of old age and the physical life

[2] **That** the "country" of youth and sensual existence, especially the sexual entrancement of all natural things in the life-cycle

[3] **its** the soul's

[4] **perne in a gyre** swoop down in a spiraling motion or hawklike movement

IV

Once out of nature I shall never take
My bodily form from any natural thing,
But such a form as Grecian goldsmiths make
Of hammered gold and gold enamelling
To keep a drowsy Emperor awake;
30   Or set upon a golden bough to sing
To lords and ladies of Byzantium
Of what is past, or passing, or to come.[5]

1927   1928

[5] ll. 25–32   "I have read somewhere that in the
Emperor's palace at Byzantium was a tree made
of gold and silver, and artificial birds that sang"
(Yeats's note).

The Tower[1]

I

What shall I do with this absurdity—
O heart, O troubled heart—this caricature,
Decrepit age that has been tied to me
As to a dog's tail?
                    Never had I more
Excited, passionate, fantastical
Imagination, nor an ear and eye
That more expected the impossible—
No, not in boyhood when with rod and fly,
10 Or the humbler worm, I climbed Ben Bulben's back[2]
And had the livelong summer day to spend.
It seems that I must bid the Muse go pack,[3]
Choose Plato and Plotinus[4] for a friend
Until imagination, ear and eye,
Can be content with argument and deal
In abstract things; or be derided by
A sort of battered kettle at the heel.

II

I pace upon the battlements and stare
On the foundations of a house, or where
20 Tree, like a sooty finger, starts from the earth;
And send imagination forth
Under the day's declining beam, and call
Images and memories
From ruin or from ancient trees,
For I would ask a question of them all.

[1] Yeats lived in Thoor Ballylee, an old Norman
tower in Galway that held, for him, deep historic
and aristocratic meaning.
[2] ll. 8–10   In these lines Yeats mimics Words-
worth's slow iambic pentameter line as though
he were lapsing into an old man's rambling
reminiscences. **Ben Bulben** mountain in
County Sligo, where he spent much of his child-
hood with his mother's family
[3] **bid the Muse go pack**   give up poetry
[4] **Plato and Plotinus**   the Greek philosopher
Plato (427?–347? B.C.) and the Roman philo-
sopher Plotinus (205?–270 A.D.), here viewed
as passionless abstract thinkers

Beyond that ridge lived Mrs. French,[5] and once
When every silver candlestick or sconce
Lit up the dark mahogany and the wine,
A serving-man, that could divine
30   That most respected lady's every wish,
Ran and with the garden shears
Clipped an insolent farmer's ears
And brought them in a little covered dish.

Some few remembered still when I was young
A peasant girl commended by a song,
Who'd lived somewhere upon that rocky place,
And praised the colour of her face,
And had the greater joy in praising her,
Remembering that, if walked she there,
40   Farmers jostled at the fair
So great a glory did the song confer.

And certain men, being maddened by those rhymes,
Or else by toasting her a score of times,
Rose from the table and declared it right
To test their fancy by their sight;
But they mistook the brightness of the moon
For the prosaic light of day—
Music had driven their wits astray—
And one was drowned in the great bog of Cloone.

50   Strange, but the man who made the song was blind;[6]
Yet, now I have considered it, I find
That nothing strange; the tragedy began
With Homer that was a blind man,
And Helen[7] has all living hearts betrayed.
O may the moon and sunlight seem
One inextricable beam,
For if I triumph I must make men mad.[8]

And I myself created Hanrahan[9]
And drove him drunk or sober through the dawn
60   From somewhere in the neighbouring cottages.
Caught by an old man's juggleries
He stumbled, tumbled, fumbled to and fro

[5]ll. 25–48 Mrs. French and the other figures are associated by local tradition with the region around Thoor Ballylee.
[6]**blind** poet Anthony Raftery (1784–1834)
[7]**Helen** Helen of Troy's beauty (in Homer's *Iliad*) led to the Trojan War, and the dream of such beauty still leads men astray.
[8]l. 57 If my poetry succeeds (in overcoming my predicament of old age) it will cast the kind

of spell that leads people astray (like that cast by Helen's and the peasant girl's beauty, and by the art of Homer and Blind Raftery).
[9]l. 58 a reference to Yeats's *Stories of Red Hanrahan* (1904), in which Hanrahan—the poet's alter ego—is magically gifted yet comically blundering, and in his frustrated way thoroughly knowledgeable in love matters, physical and spiritual

And had but broken knees for hire
And horrible splendour of desire;
I thought it all out twenty years ago:

Good fellows shuffled cards in an old bawn;[10]
And when that ancient ruffian's turn was on
He so bewitched the cards under his thumb
That all but the one card became
70   A pack of hounds and not a pack of cards,
And that he changed into a hare.
Hanrahan rose in frenzy there
And followed up those baying creatures towards—

O towards I have forgotten what—enough!
I must recall a man that neither love
Nor music nor an enemy's clipped ear
Could, he was so harried, cheer;
A figure that has grown so fabulous
There's not a neighbour left to say
80   When he finished his dog's day:
An ancient bankrupt master of this house.

Before that ruin came, for centuries,
Rough men-at-arms, cross-gartered to the knees
Or shod in iron, climbed the narrow stairs,
And certain men-at-arms there were
Whose images, in the Great Memory[11] stored,
Come with loud cry and panting breast
To break upon a sleeper's rest
While their great wooden dice beat on the board.

90   As I would question all, come all who can;
Come old, necessitous, half-mounted man;
And bring beauty's blind rambling celebrant;
The red man the juggler sent
Through God-forsaken meadows; Mrs. French,
Gifted with so fine an ear;
The man drowned in a bog's mire,
When mocking Muses chose the country wench.

Did all old men and women, rich and poor,
Who trod upon these rocks or passed this door,
100   Whether in public or in secret rage
As I do now against old age?
But I have found an answer in those eyes
That are impatient to be gone;
Go therefore; but leave Hanrahan,
For I need all his mighty memories.

[10]**bawn** a fortified enclosure, doubtless abandoned

[11]**Great Memory** reservoir of archetypal images in the psyche

Old lecher with a love on every wind,
Bring up out of that deep considering mind
All that you have discovered in the grave,
For it is certain that you have
110 Reckoned up every unforeknown, unseeing
Plunge, lured by a softening eye,
Or by a touch or a sigh,
Into the labyrinth of another's being;

Does the imagination dwell the most
Upon a woman won or a woman lost?
If on the lost, admit you turned aside
From a great labyrinth out of pride,
Cowardice, some silly over-subtle thought
Or anything called conscience once;
120 And that if memory recur, the sun's
Under eclipse and the day blotted out.

III

It is time that I wrote my will;
I choose upstanding men
That climb the streams until
The fountain leap, and at dawn
Drop their cast at the side
Of dripping stone; I declare
They shall inherit my pride,
The pride of people that were
130 Bound neither to Cause nor to State,
Neither to slaves that were spat on,
Nor to the tyrants that spat,
The people of Burke and of Grattan[12]
That gave, though free to refuse—
Pride, like that of the morn,
When the headlong light is loose,
Or that of the fabulous horn,
Or that of the sudden shower
When all streams are dry,
140 Or that of the hour
When the swan must fix his eye
Upon a fading gleam,
Float out upon a long
Last reach of glittering stream
And there sing his last song.[13]
And I declare my faith:
I mock Plotinus' thought
And cry in Plato's teeth,
Death and life were not

[12]**Burke and . . . Grattan** Edmund Burke (1729–1797) and Henry Grattan (1746–1820), Anglo-Irish statesmen of high integrity and talent
[13]ll. 128–45 These images of "pride" go beyond the word's ordinary meaning to include conceptions of generosity, courage, nature's force and beauty, and exultant joy in the face of tragic knowledge.

150   Till man made up the whole,
      Made lock, stock and barrel
      Out of his bitter soul,
      Aye, sun and moon and star, all,
      And further add to that
      That, being dead, we rise,
      Dream and so create
      Translunar Paradise.
      I have prepared my peace
      With learned Italian things
160   And the proud stones of Greece,
      Poet's imaginings
      And memories of love,
      Memories of the words of women,
      All those things whereof
      Man makes a superhuman
      Mirror-resembling dream.

      As at the loophole there
      The daws chatter and scream,
      And drop twigs layer upon layer.
170   When they have mounted up,
      The mother bird will rest
      On their hollow top,
      And so warm her wild nest.

      I leave both faith and pride
      To young upstanding men
      Climbing the mountain side,
      That under bursting dawn
      They may drop a fly;
      Being of that metal made
180   Till it was broken by
      This sedentary trade.

      Now shall I make my soul,
      Compelling it to study
      In a learned school
      Till the wreck of body,
      Slow decay of blood,
      Testy delirium
      Or dull decrepitude,
      Or what worse evil come—
190   The death of friends, or death
      Of every brilliant eye
      That made a catch in the breath—
      Seem but the clouds of the sky
      When the horizon fades;
      Or a bird's sleepy cry
      Among the deepening shades.

    1926   1928

From Meditations in Time of Civil War

V. The Road at My Door

An affable Irregular,[1]
A heavily-built Falstaffian[2] man,
Comes cracking jokes of civil war
As though to die by gunshot were
The finest play under the sun.

A brown Lieutenant and his men,[3]
Half dressed in national uniform,
Stand at my door, and I complain
Of the foul weather, hail and rain,
10   A pear tree broken by the storm.

I count those feathered balls of soot
The moor-hen guides upon the stream,
To silence the envy in my thought;
And turn towards my chamber, caught
In the cold snows of a dream.[4]

1922?   1928

[1] **Irregular** member of the Irish Republican Army (I.R.A.), dedicated to full independence and opposed to the treaty with England that set up the Irish Free State in 1921 and to the partition of Ireland. The poem describes events during the Irish Civil War (1922–23).

[2] **Falstaffian** jolly, hearty, and extroverted, like the character Falstaff in Shakespeare's *Henry IV* plays

[3] ll. 6–7 soldiers of the National Army of the Irish Free State

[4] ll. 14–15 The aging poet—hardly meant to be a soldier—realizes his full isolation, despite his dream of helping Ireland develop her noblest possibilities (expressed in earlier poems of this sequence).

From Nineteen Hundred and Nineteen[1]

I

Many ingenious lovely things are gone
That seemed sheer miracle to the multitude,
Protected from the circle of the moon
That pitches common things about. There stood
Amid the ornamental bronze and stone
An ancient image made of olive wood—
And gone are Phidias' famous ivories
And all the golden grasshoppers and bees.

[1] In this year began the Anglo–Irish War (1919–21), with its guerrilla fighting and terrorism, which continued well beyond the war's official end.

We too had many pretty toys when young:
10 A law indifferent to blame or praise,
To bribe or threat; habits that made old wrong
Melt down, as it were wax in the sun's rays;
Public opinion ripening for so long
We thought it would outlive all future days.
O what fine thought we had because we thought
That the worst rogues and rascals had died out.

All teeth were drawn, all ancient tricks unlearned,
And a great army but a showy thing;
What matter that no cannon had been turned
20 Into a ploughshare? Parliament and king
Thought that unless a little powder burned
The trumpeters might burst with trumpeting
And yet it lack all glory; and perchance
The guardsmen's drowsy chargers would not prance.

Now days are dragon-ridden, the nightmare
Rides upon sleep: a drunken soldiery
Can leave the mother, murdered at her door,
To crawl in her own blood, and go scot-free;
The night can sweat with terror as before
30 We pieced our thoughts into philosophy,
And planned to bring the world under a rule,
Who are but weasels fighting in a hole.

He who can read the signs nor sink unmanned
Into the half-deceit of some intoxicant
From shallow wits; who knows no work can stand,
Whether health, wealth or peace of mind were spent
On master-work of intellect or hand,
No honour leave its mighty monument,
Has but one comfort left: all triumph would
40 But break upon his ghostly solitude.

But is there any comfort to be found?
Man is in love and loves what vanishes,
What more is there to say? That country round
None dared admit, if such a thought were his,
Incendiary or bigot could be found
To burn that stump on the Acropolis,
Or break in bits the famous ivories
Or traffic in the grasshoppers or bees.

III[1]

Some moralist or mythological poet[2]
Compares the solitary soul to a swan;
I am satisfied with that,
Satisfied if a troubled mirror show it,
Before that brief gleam of its life be gone,
An image of its state;
The wings half spread for flight,
The breast thrust out in pride
Whether to play, or to ride
10   Those winds that clamour of approaching night.

A man in his own secret meditation
Is lost amid the labyrinth that he has made
In art or politics;
Some Platonist[3] affirms that in the station
Where we should cast off body and trade
The ancient habit sticks,
And that if our works could
But vanish with our breath
That were a lucky death,
20   For triumph can but mar our solitude.

The swan has leaped into the desolate heaven:
That image can bring wildness, bring a rage
To end all things, to end
What my laborious life imagined, even
The half-imagined, the half-written page;
O but we dreamed to mend
Whatever mischief seemed
To afflict mankind, but now
That winds of winter blow
30   Learn that we were crack-pated when we dreamed.

1921   1928

[1] This climactic poem in the "Nineteen Hundred and Nineteen" sequence (and in the double sequence made up of "Meditations in Time of Civil War" and "Nineteen Hundred and Nineteen") presents, amid total disillusionment with past dreams of social progress, a brilliant symbolic image of the isolated soul as a swan prepared to fly directly into its fated stormy desolation.

[2] **Some moralist or mythological poet** likely Yeats himself

[3] **Some Platonist** See preceding note.

Two Songs from a Play[1]

I

I saw a staring virgin stand[2]
Where holy Dionysus died,
And tear the heart out of his side,
And lay the heart upon her hand
And bear that beating heart away;
And then did all the Muses sing
Of Magnus Annus[3] at the spring,
As though God's death were but a play.

10   Another Troy must rise and set,
Another lineage feed the crow,
Another Argo's painted prow
Drive to a flashier bauble yet.[4]
The Roman Empire stood appalled:
It dropped the reins of peace and war
When that fierce virgin and her Star
Out of the fabulous darkness called.

II

In pity for man's darkening thought
He walked that room and issued thence
In Galilean turbulence;
20   The Babylonian starlight brought
A fabulous, formless darkness in;
Odour of blood when Christ was slain
Made all Platonic tolerance vain
And vain all Doric discipline.[5]

Everything that man esteems
Endures a moment or a day.
Love's pleasure drives his love away,
The painter's brush consumes his dreams;
The herald's cry, the soldier's tread
30   Exhaust his glory and his might:
Whatever flames upon the night
Man's own resinous heart has fed.[6]

1923   1928

---

[1] The play is *The Resurrection*.
[2] ll. 1–5 The virgin goddess Athene bore the heart of the god Dionysus, torn apart by enemies, to Zeus, who swallowed it and then re-begot Dionysus upon Semele. These mythical events are presented as an early parallel to Christ's death and resurrection.
[3] **Magnus Annus** (Latin) the Great Year, or Platonic Year—a cyclical cosmic span of 36,000 years, within which the births and deaths of deities (and the civilizations that worship them) are repeated in various forms and with varied significance

[4] ll. 9–12 These lines echo Virgil's *Eclogue IV*, foretelling a golden age, and the Chorus in Shelley's *Hellas* beginning "The world's great age begins anew" (p. 598 above).
[5] ll. 13–24 The birth of Jesus betokened the rise of a new irrational civilization on the heels of the rational, Classical era.
[6] ll. 25–32 This stanza emphasizes the secular and modern. The sacrifice is not of Dionysus or Jesus but of the inflammable ("resinous") human heart in the very process of fulfilling ourselves and our dreams, with no hope of enduring identity, results, or grace.

Leda and the Swan[1]

A sudden blow: the great wings beating still
Above the staggering girl, her thighs caressed
By the dark webs, her nape caught in his bill,
He holds her helpless breast upon his breast.

How can those terrified vague fingers push
The feathered glory from her loosening thighs?
And how can body, laid in that white rush,
But feel the strange heart beating where it lies?

A shudder in the loins engenders there
10 The broken wall, the burning roof and tower
And Agamemnon dead.
                            Being so caught up,
So mastered by the brute blood of the air,
Did she put on his knowledge with his power
Before the indifferent beak could let her drop?

1923   1928

[1] In Greek mythology, the Spartan queen Leda
was ravished by the god Zeus in the form of a
swan. From this mating were born Helen of
Troy, who became queen of Sparta, and Clytem-
nestra, who married King Agamemnon of My-
cenae. Helen's abduction by the Trojan prince
Paris led to the Greek expedition against Troy,
commanded by Agamemnon, who was murdered
by Clytemnestra and her lover when he returned
from his victory. (See Homer's epic poem *The
Iliad* and Aeschylus' tragedy *Agamemnon*.)

Among School Children[1]

I

I walk through the long schoolroom questioning;
A kind old nun in a white hood replies;
The children learn to cipher and to sing,
To study reading-books and history,
To cut and sew, be neat in everything
In the best modern way—the children's eyes
In momentary wonder stare upon
A sixty-year-old smiling public man.

II

I dream of a Ledaean body,[2] bent
10 Above a sinking fire, a tale that she
Told of a harsh reproof, or trivial event

[1] As an appointed member (1922) of the Irish
Senate, Yeats focused on cultural and educational
matters. Here he describes visiting a girls' school
taught by nuns using the Montessori method
"in the best modern way." (Devised in 1907
by Maria Montessori, the system stressed less
rigid control and more attention to children's
levels of understanding and possibilities of self-
education than had been customary in class-
rooms.)

[2] **Ledean body** woman of fabulous beauty, like
Leda or her daughter Helen

That changed some childish day to tragedy—
Told, and it seemed that our two natures blent
Into a sphere from youthful sympathy,
Or else, to alter Plato's parable,
Into the yolk and white of the one shell.[3]

III

And thinking of that fit of grief or rage
I look upon one child or t'other there
And wonder if she stood so at that age—
20   For even daughters of the swan can share
Something of every paddler's heritage—[4]
And had that colour upon cheek or hair,
And thereupon my heart is driven wild:
She stands before me as a living child.

IV

Her present image floats into the mind—
Did Quattrocento finger fashion it
Hollow of cheek as though it drank the wind
And took a mess of shadows for its meat?[5]
And I though never of Ledaean kind
30   Had pretty plumage once—enough of that,
Better to smile on all that smile, and show
There is a comfortable kind of old scarecrow.

V

What youthful mother, a shape upon her lap
Honey of generation[6] had betrayed,
And that must sleep, shriek, struggle to escape
As recollection or the drug decide,
Would think her son, did she but see that shape
With sixty or more winters on its head,
A compensation for the pang of his birth,
40   Or the uncertainty of his setting forth?

VI

Plato thought nature but a spume that plays
Upon a ghostly paradigm of things;
Solider Aristotle played the taws

[3] ll. 15–16 In Plato's *Symposium* the comic playwright Aristophanes explains the origin of sex: male and female were once united in a single egg-shaped body that was cut in half as punishment for humanity's support of the Titans in their war against the gods; the two sexes have run about frantically ever since, seeking to reunite. The egg image is apt because after Zeus in the form of a swan ravished Leda she produced eggs containing her children: in one, Helen and Clytemnestra; in the other, the twins Castor and Pollux.

[4] ll. 20–21 Even girls born to become great beauties and heroines like Helen of Troy are in certain basic ways like other children—as in the story of the ugly duckling.

[5] ll. 25–28 The "Ledean body" mentioned in stanza II is now an old woman, frail and hollow-cheeked like certain figures in fifteenth-century Italian paintings (painted by "Quattrocento finger"—Leonardo da Vinci perhaps).

[6] **Honey of generation** the sweetness of sexual love, which "betrays" mothers into the pain of childbirth and the anxieties of parenthood

Upon the bottom of a king of kings;
World-famous golden-thighed Pythagoras
Fingered upon a fiddle-stick or strings
What a star sang and careless Muses heard:
Old clothes upon old sticks to scare a bird.

VII

Both nuns and mothers worship images,
50   But those the candles light are not as those
That animate a mother's reveries,
But keep a marble or a bronze repose.
And yet they too break hearts—O Presences
That passion, piety or affection knows,
And that all heavenly glory symbolise—
O self-born mockers of man's enterprise;

VIII

Labour is blossoming or dancing where
The body is not bruised to pleasure soul,
Nor beauty born out of its own despair,
60   Nor blear-eyed wisdom out of midnight oil.
O chestnut tree, great rooted blossomer,
Are you the leaf, the blossom or the bole?
O body swayed to music, O brightening glance,
How can we know the dancer from the dance?[7]

1926   1928

[7] ll. 41–64 In stanza VI the sense of life's point-lessness is directed toward three of ancient Greece's greatest thinkers, all of whom eventually became old scarecrows, like the speaker and his beloved—a preparation for the utter sadness of stanza VII and for the final stanza's countering affirmation, which finds triumph and transcendence in the life-process itself and in creative action—like the dancer who loses her own mortal body in the imperishable forms she creates with it as she dances.

A Dialogue of Self and Soul

I

My Soul. I summon to the winding ancient stair;
Set all your mind upon the steep ascent,
Upon the broken, crumbling battlement,
Upon the breathless starlit air,
Upon the star that marks the hidden pole;
Fix every wandering thought upon
That quarter where all thought is done:[1]
Who can distinguish darkness from the soul?

[1] **That quarter where all thought is done** the impenetrable realm beyond death, where, from the Soul's standpoint, true thought occurs, but also where, in another sense, it is ended (two senses of "is done"). A similar technique of implying opposed meanings simultaneously is used in the closing stanza of the poem's first section (ll. 33–40—see note 3).

My Self. The consecrated blade upon my knees
10   Is Sato's ancient blade,[2] still as it was,
      Still razor-keen, still like a looking-glass
      Unspotted by the centuries;
      That flowering, silken, old embroidery, torn
      From some court-lady's dress and round
      The wooden scabbard bound and wound,
      Can, tattered, still protect, faded adorn.

My Soul. Why should the imagination of a man
      Long past his prime remember things that are
      Emblematical of love and war?
20   Think of ancestral night that can,
      If but imagination scorn the earth
      And intellect its wandering
      To this and that and t'other thing,
      Deliver from the crime of death and birth.

My Self. Montashigi, third of his family, fashioned it
      Five hundred years ago, about it lie
      Flowers from I know not what embroidery—
      Heart's purple—and all these I set
      For emblems of the day against the tower
30   Emblematical of the night,
      And claim as by a soldier's right
      A charter to commit the crime once more.

My Soul. Such fullness in that quarter[3] overflows
      And falls into the basin of the mind
      That man is stricken deaf and dumb and blind,
      For intellect no longer knows
      Is from the *Ought*, or *Knower* from the *Known*—
      That is to say, ascends to Heaven;
      Only the dead can be forgiven;
40   But when I think of that my tongue's a stone.

                    II
My Self. A living man is blind and drinks his drop.
      What matter if the ditches are impure?
      What matter if I live it all once more?
      Endure that toil of growing up;
      The ignominy of boyhood; the distress
      Of boyhood changing into man;
      The unfinished man and his pain
      Brought face to face with his own clumsiness;

---

[2] **Sato's ancient blade** a 500-year-old Japanese
sword given the poet by Junzo Sato, a Japanese
admirer of his work
[3] **that quarter** This phrase refers both to the
secular realm of love and war just acclaimed by
the Self, and to the afterlife acclaimed by the
Soul in the first and third stanzas.

The finished man among his enemies?—
50   How in the name of Heaven can he escape
That defiling and disfigured shape
The mirror of malicious eyes
Casts upon his eyes until at last
He thinks that shape must be his shape?
And what's the good of an escape
If honour find him in the wintry blast?

I am content to live it all again
And yet again, if it be life to pitch
Into the frog-spawn of a blind man's ditch,
A blind man battering blind men;
Or into that most fecund ditch of all,
The folly that man does
Or must suffer, if he woos
A proud woman not kindred of his soul.

I am content to follow to its source
Every event in action or in thought;
Measure the lot; forgive myself the lot!
When such as I cast out remorse
So great a sweetness flows into the breast
70   We must laugh and we must sing,
We are blest by everything,
Everything we look upon is blest.

1927   1933

Byzantium[1]

The unpurged images of day recede;
The Emperor's drunken soldiery are abed;
Night resonance recedes, night-walkers' song
After great cathedral[2] gong;
A starlit or a moonlit dome disdains
All that man is,
All mere complexities,
The fury and the mire of human veins.

Before me floats an image, man or shade,
10   Shade more than man, more image than a shade;
For Hades' bobbin[3] bound in mummy-cloth
May unwind the winding path;
A mouth that has no moisture and no breath
Breathless mouths may summon;
I hail the superhuman;
I call it death-in-life and life-in-death.

[1] See note 1 to "Sailing to Byzantium," p. 774.
[2] cathedral Hagia Sophia in Istanbul
[3] Hades' bobbin an imagined reel or spool linking the living and the dead

Miracle, bird or golden handiwork,
More miracle than bird or handiwork,
Planted on the starlit golden bough,[4]
20   Can like the cocks of Hades crow,
Or, by the moon embittered, scorn aloud
In glory of changeless metal
Common bird or petal
And all complexities of mire or blood.

At midnight on the Emperor's pavement flit
Flames that no faggot feeds, nor steel has lit,
Nor storm disturbs, flames begotten of flame,
Where blood-begotten spirits come
And all complexities of fury leave,
30   Dying into a dance,
An agony of trance,
An agony of flame that cannot singe a sleeve.

Astraddle on the dolphin's mire and blood,
Spirit after spirit! The smithies break the flood,[5]
The golden smithies of the Emperor!
Marbles of the dancing floor
Break bitter furies of complexity,
Those images that yet
Fresh images beget,
40   That dolphin-torn, that gong-tormented sea.

1930   1932

---

[4] **starlit golden bough** See note 5 to "Sailing to Byzantium" (p. 775).
[5] ll. 33–34 a reference to the traditional belief that the spirits of the dead were borne to the Isle of the Blest on the backs of dolphins

Crazy Jane Talks with the Bishop

I met the Bishop on the road
And much said he and I.
"Those breasts are flat and fallen now,
Those veins must soon be dry;
Live in a heavenly mansion,
Not in some foul sty."

"Fair and foul are near of kin,
And fair needs foul," I cried.
"My friends are gone, but that's a truth
10   Nor grave nor bed denied,
Learned in bodily lowliness
And in the heart's pride.

"A woman can be proud and stiff
When on love intent;
But Love has pitched his mansion in
The place of excrement;
For nothing can be sole or whole
That has not been rent."

1932

Long-legged Fly

That civilisation may not sink,
Its great battle lost,
Quiet the dog, tether the pony
To a distant post;
Our master Caesar is in the tent
Where the maps are spread,
His eyes fixed upon nothing,
A hand under his head.

Like a long-legged fly upon the stream
10   *His mind moves upon silence.*

That the topless towers be burnt
And men recall that face,
Move most gently if move you must
In this lonely place.
She thinks, part woman, three parts a child,
That nobody looks; her feet
Practise a tinker shuffle
Picked up on the street.[1]

Like a long-legged fly upon the stream
20   *Her mind moves upon silence.*

That girls at puberty may find
The first Adam in their thought,
Shut the door of the Pope's chapel,
Keep those children out.
There on that scaffolding reclines
Michael Angelo.
With no more sound than the mice make
His hand moves to and fro.[2]

Like a long-legged fly upon the stream
30   *His mind moves upon silence.*

1939

[1] ll. 11–18 These lines suggest that even a peasant girl is potentially a Helen of Troy. (In Christopher Marlowe's *Dr. Faustus*, Helen's face is said to have "launch'd a thousand ships / And burnt the topless towers of Ilium.")
[2] ll. 21–30 Among the many painted figures on the ceiling of the Sistine Chapel in the Vatican is one of Adam being awakened by God after his creation. The poem envisions the artist, Michelangelo (1475–1564), still at work, and in deep concentration, as he creates the ideal image of man.

Politics

*"In our time the destiny of man presents
its meanings in political terms."*
　　　　　　—THOMAS MANN

How can I, that girl standing there,
My attention fix
On Roman or on Russian
Or on Spanish politics?
Yet here's a travelled man that knows
What he talks about,
And there's a politician
That has both read and thought,
And maybe what they say is true
10　Of war and war's alarms,
But O that I were young again
And held her in my arms.

1938　　　　　　　　　　　1939

EDGAR LEE MASTERS
1869–1950

Born in Kansas, Masters grew up in the Midwest region out of which his poems speak. He attended college only briefly but read voraciously while working in his father's law office and for various newspapers. After 1891 he built a successful law practice in Chicago and was the partner of the great criminal lawyer Clarence Darrow from 1903 to 1911. His poems aroused savage criticism, but he wrote and published many books, including a debunking biography of Lincoln. Of the poetry, only *Spoon River Anthology* (1915) proved durably popular, and it made its mark on such later poets as Kenneth Fearing and Robert Lowell.

Spoon River Anthology once loomed large on the modern poetic scene. It contains over two hundred poems, mostly hard-bitten, in clear American voices. Like the work of Theodore Dreiser, Sherwood Anderson, and others in that deglamorizing era, it strips away pastoral sentimentality about small-town life in the United States and shows the truths of squalor, exploitation, and suffering as well as the brighter realities. This work made a genuine contribution to a new mode of poetry. Its free-verse cadences, based on intensified speech rhythms modified by echoes of traditional forms and public rhetoric, helped open the way to an uninhibited, frank poetry molded from current spoken idiom. Voices of dead citizens of an Illinois town speak from their graves; the title suggests that Masters's model, thoroughly "Americanized," is the ancient *Greek Anthology* with its elegantly restrained elegiac epigrams. The opening poem, "The Hill," Americanizes another very old poetic convention, the *ubi sunt* poem, so-called because the question "ubi sunt?" (Latin for "where are?") precedes a series of names of dead heroes, legendary beauties, or other great figures of myth or history.

The Hill

Where are Elmer, Herman, Bert, Tom and Charley,
The weak of will, the strong of arm, the clown, the boozer, the fighter?
All, all, are sleeping on the hill.

One passed in a fever,
One was burned in a mine,
One was killed in a brawl,
One died in a jail,
One fell from a bridge toiling for children and wife—
All, all are sleeping, sleeping, sleeping on the hill.

10   Where are Ella, Kate, Mag, Lizzie and Edith,
The tender heart, the simple soul, the loud, the proud, the happy one?—
All, all are sleeping on the hill.

One died in shameful child-birth,
One of a thwarted love,
One at the hands of a brute in a brothel,
One of a broken pride, in the search for heart's desire,
One after life in far-away London and Paris
Was brought to her little space by Ella and Kate and Mag—
All, all are sleeping, sleeping, sleeping on the hill.

20   Where are Uncle Isaac and Aunt Emily,
And old Towny Kincaid and Sevigne Houghton,
And Major Walker who had talked
With venerable men of the revolution?—
All, all, are sleeping on the hill.

They brought them dead sons from the war,
And daughters whom life had crushed,
And their children fatherless, crying—
All, all are sleeping, sleeping, sleeping on the hill.

30   Where is Old Fiddler Jones
Who played with life all his ninety years,
Braving the sleet with bared breast,
Drinking, rioting, thinking neither of wife nor kin,
Nor gold, nor love, nor heaven?
Lo! he babbles of the fish-frys of long ago,
Of the horse-races of long ago at Clary's Grove,
Of what Abe Lincoln said
One time at Springfield.

1915

Daisy Fraser

Did you ever hear of Editor Whedon
Giving to the public treasury any of the money he received
For supporting candidates for office?
Or for writing up the canning factory
To get people to invest?
Or for suppressing the facts about the bank,
When it was rotten and ready to break?
Did you ever hear of the Circuit Judge
Helping anyone except the "Q" railroad,
Or the bankers? Or did Rev. Peet or Rev. Sibley
Give any part of their salary, earned by keeping still,
Or speaking out as the leaders wished them to do,
To the building of the water works?
But I—Daisy Fraser who always passed
Along the streets through rows of nods and smiles,
And coughs and words such as "there she goes,"
Never was taken before Justice Arnett
Without contributing ten dollars and costs
To the school fund of Spoon River!

1915

Editor Whedon

To be able to see every side of every question;
To be on every side, to be everything, to be nothing long;
To pervert truth, to ride it for a purpose,
To use great feelings and passions of the human family
For base designs, for cunning ends,
To wear a mask like the Greek actors—
Your eight-page paper—behind which you huddle,
Bawling through the megaphone of big type:
"This is I, the giant."
Thereby also living the life of a sneak-thief,
Poisoned with the anonymous words
Of your clandestine soul.
To scratch dirt over scandal for money,
And exhume it to the winds for revenge,
Or to sell papers,
Crushing reputations, or bodies, if need be,
To win at any cost, save your own life.
To glory in demoniac power, ditching civilization,
As a paranoiac boy puts a log on the track
And derails the express train.
To be an editor, as I was.
Then to lie here close by the river over the place
Where the sewage flows from the village,
And the empty cans and garbage are dumped,
And abortions are hidden.

1915

EDWIN ARLINGTON ROBINSON
1869–1935

Robinson grew up in Gardiner, Maine—the "Tilbury Town" of "Mr. Flood's Party" and other poems. He attended Harvard as a special student for two years, but then began studying poetry and the craft of writing on his own. In 1898, after his parents' deaths, he moved to New York, where for some years he lived a hand-to-mouth existence but managed to get his work published. By rare luck, President Theodore Roosevelt took an interest in his poems and arranged a job for him in the New York Customs House (1905–09). The job gave him leisure to write and think, and his career slowly flourished. Despite Robinson's tendency to write longish discursive poems and longer verse-narratives based on figures in King Arthur's court, a small body of poems of wry integrity and even a certain splendor endures.

"Eros Turannos" and "Mr. Flood's Par-

ty" represent Robinson at his best. These poems well up out of a sense of nostalgia he shared with many other Americans of his generation—not only for lost ways of the past but also for the fast-disappearing memory of them. This nostalgia was fused with a fatalistic perception of the inevitable defeat of cherished values and gallant, fine-grained persons. "Eros Turannos," among other poems, helped introduce into American poetry an adult sensibility in matters of sexual and marital concern; it reads like a highly concentrated Henry James novel and builds into a savage and tragic ending. "Mr. Flood's Party" is as touching and witty a poem as one is ever likely to read. With his charm and ruefulness, his chivalrous associations, and his love of song and "the jug," Mr. Flood might well be the poet himself.

Eros Turannos[1]

She fears him, and will always ask
    What fated her to choose him;
She meets in his engaging mask
    All reasons to refuse him;
But what she meets and what she fears
Are less than are the downward years,
Drawn slowly to the foamless weirs
    Of age, were she to lose him.

Between a blurred sagacity
10   That once had power to sound him,
And Love, that will not let him be
    The Judas that she found him,
Her pride assuages her almost,
    As if it were alone the cost.—
He sees that he will not be lost,
    And waits and looks around him.

[1] Eros, the Greek god of sexual love, is here presented as a cruel tyrant ("Turannos").

A sense of ocean and old trees
   Envelops and allures him;
Tradition, touching all he sees,
20   Beguiles and reassures him;
And all her doubts of what he says
Are dimmed with what she knows of days—
Till even prejudice delays
   And fades, and she secures him.

The falling leaf inaugurates
   The reign of her confusion;
The pounding wave reverberates
   The dirge of her illusion;
And home, where passion lived and died,
30   Becomes a place where she can hide,
While all the town and harbor side
   Vibrate with her seclusion.

We tell you, tapping on our brows,
   The story as it should be,—
As if the story of a house
   Were told, or ever could be;
We'll have no kindly veil between
Her visions and those we have seen,—
As if we guessed what hers have been,
40   Or what they are or would be.[2]

Meanwhile we do no harm; for they
   That with a god have striven,
Not hearing much of what we say,
   Take what the god has given;
Though like waves breaking it may be,
Or like a changed familiar tree,
Or like a stairway to the sea
   Where down the blind are driven.

1916

[2] ll. 33–40 The supposed speaker, presumably a villager living in the community near the great house the heroine owns, reminds us of the ambiguity of our knowledge about other lives.

Mr. Flood's Party

Old Eben Flood, climbing alone one night
Over the hill between the town below
And the forsaken upland hermitage
That held as much as he should ever know
On earth again of home, paused warily.

The road was his with not a native near;
And Eben, having leisure, said aloud,
For no man else in Tilbury Town to hear:

"Well, Mr. Flood, we have the harvest moon
10   Again, and we may not have many more;
The bird is on the wing, the poet says,[1]
And you and I have said it here before.
Drink to the bird." He raised up to the light
The jug that he had gone so far to fill,
And answered huskily: "Well, Mr. Flood,
Since you propose it, I believe I will."

Alone, as if enduring to the end
A valiant armor of scarred hopes outworn,
He stood there in the middle of the road
20   Like Roland's ghost winding[2] a silent horn.
Below him, in the town among the trees,
Where friends of other days had honored him,
A phantom salutation of the dead
Rang thinly till old Eben's eyes were dim.

Then, as a mother lays her sleeping child
Down tenderly, fearing it may awake,
He set the jug down slowly at his feet
With trembling care, knowing that most things break;
And only when assured that on firm earth
30   It stood, as the uncertain lives of men
Assuredly did not, he paced away,
And with his hand extended paused again:

"Well, Mr. Flood, we have not met like this
In a long time; and many a change has come
To both of us, I fear, since last it was
We had a drop together. Welcome home!"
Convivially returning with himself,
Again he raised the jug up to the light;
And with an acquiescent quaver said:
40   "Well, Mr. Flood, if you insist, I might.

"Only a very little, Mr. Flood—
For auld lang syne. No more, sir; that will do."
So, for the time, apparently it did,
And Eben evidently thought so too;

[1] l. 11 a reference to *The Rubaiyât of Omar Khayyam*, in Edward FitzGerald's translation from the twelfth-century Persian
[2] **winding** blowing, an allusion to the medieval Old French narrative poem *The Song of Roland*, in which the hero unavailingly blows his horn to summon help. Here the horn is "silent" because Mr. Flood—a frail but doughty survivor from a forgotten generation—is being compared with the ghost of Roland.

For soon amid the silver loneliness
Of night he lifted up his voice and sang,
Secure, with only two moons listening,
Until the whole harmonious landscape rang—

"For auld lang syne." The weary throat gave out,
50   The last word wavered, and the song was done.
He raised again the jug regretfully
And shook his head, and was again alone.
There was not much that was ahead of him,
And there was nothing in the town below—
Where strangers would have shut the many doors
That many friends had opened long ago.

1921

ROBERT FROST
1874–1963

Frost was born in San Francisco, the son of two schoolteachers of New England origin. His father died when he was ten, and mother and son moved to Lawrence, Massachusetts, where she resumed teaching. In his youth Frost attended Dartmouth College for a few months, worked in a factory, and, after marrying at twenty-one, studied at Harvard for two years. He then taught English and psychology, worked a farm he had acquired in 1900, and wrote poetry. In 1912, having no luck getting published, he took his wife and five children to England and rented a farm in Hertfordshire—not far from Edward Thomas, who became his friend. The English welcomed his work and published his first two books, *A Boy's Will* (1913) and *North of Boston* (1914). In 1915, after the outbreak of World War I, he returned to the United States—to recognition and an increasingly successful career.

Such poems as "The Pasture," "After Apple-Picking," and (when thoughtlessly read) "Stopping by Woods on a Snowy Evening" have given Frost a reputation for being a fairly cheerful pastoral poet, knowledgeable in country things and sturdily optimistic. But Frost can also be grim. His "The

Lovely Shall Be Choosers" may be set beside Robinson's "Eros Turannos" as a study in the brutality to which women can be subjected. His "Acquainted with the Night" and "Desert Places" confront the impersonal darkness and emptiness of a universe without God or purpose, and the inner "night" and "desert places" of the private self. "Directive" places this bleak realism in the context of memory, guiding us to the site of a childhood world now all but eroded yet still held sacred in the speaker's mind and heart. If we add the harsh poem about old age called "Provide, Provide," the poem of adolescent sexual humiliation called "The Subverted Flower," or the nightmare allegory called "The Draft Horse," the image of Frost as the kindly rural sage quickly fades.

Frost, in short, was very much a modern man, close to the psychologically sophisticated, urban sensibility of the greatest modern poets from Baudelaire to Eliot. His versification, too, is fairly sophisticated despite its deceptively conventional surface: blank verse, sonnets, quatrains, and so on. But his variations of stress and line-length, his grafting of natural speech-rhythms onto the expected meter, and his clever improvisations within a form reveal a virtuoso and master of evocative melody. The swirlings and subtleties of his technique allow a wide range of suggested feeling to play through a poem. Although his poems are sometimes blighted by a wearying sort of near-didactic knowingness, they suggest a world of secret, perhaps inexpressible awareness beneath the easy, anecdotal style.

The Pasture

I'm going out to clean the pasture spring;
I'll only stop to rake the leaves away
(And wait to watch the water clear, I may):
I shan't be gone long.—You come too.

I'm going out to fetch the little calf
That's standing by the mother. It's so young
It totters when she licks it with her tongue.
I shan't be gone long.—You come too.

1914

Mending Wall

Something there is that doesn't love a wall,
That sends the frozen-ground-swell under it
And spills the upper boulders in the sun,
And makes gaps even two can pass abreast.
The work of hunters is another thing:
I have come after them and made repair
Where they have left not one stone on a stone,
But they would have the rabbit out of hiding,
To please the yelping dogs. The gaps I mean,
10 No one has seen them made or heard them made,
But at spring mending-time we find them there.
I let my neighbor know beyond the hill;
And on a day we meet to walk the line
And set the wall between us once again.
We keep the wall between us as we go.
To each the boulders that have fallen to each.
And some are loaves and some so nearly balls
We have to use a spell to make them balance:
"Stay where you are until our backs are turned!"
20 We wear our fingers rough with handling them.
Oh, just another kind of outdoor game,
One on a side. It comes to little more:
There where it is we do not need the wall:
He is all pine and I am apple orchard.
My apple trees will never get across
And eat the cones under his pines, I tell him.

He only says, "Good fences make good neighbors."
Spring is the mischief in me, and I wonder
If I could put a notion in his head:
30   "*Why* do they make good neighbors? Isn't it
Where there are cows? But here there are no cows.
Before I built a wall I'd ask to know
What I was walling in or walling out,
And to whom I was like to give offense.
Something there is that doesn't love a wall,
That wants it down." I could say "Elves" to him,
But it's not elves exactly, and I'd rather
He said it for himself. I see him there,
Bringing a stone grasped firmly by the top
40   In each hand, like an old-stone savage armed.
He moves in darkness as it seems to me,
Not of woods only and the shade of trees.
He will not go behind his father's saying,
And he likes having thought of it so well
He says again, "Good fences make good neighbors."

                              1914

After Apple-Picking

My long two-pointed ladder's sticking through a tree
Toward heaven still,
And there's a barrel that I didn't fill
Beside it, and there may be two or three
Apples I didn't pick upon some bough.
But I am done with apple-picking now.
Essence of winter sleep is on the night,
The scent of apples: I am drowsing off.
I cannot rub the strangeness from my sight
10   I got from looking through a pane of glass
I skimmed this morning from the drinking trough
And held against the world of hoary grass.
It melted, and I let it fall and break.
But I was well
Upon my way to sleep before it fell,
And I could tell
What form my dreaming was about to take.
Magnified apples appear and disappear,
Stem end and blossom end,
20   And every fleck of russet showing clear.
My instep arch not only keeps the ache,
It keeps the pressure of a ladder-round.
I feel the ladder sway as the boughs bend.
And I keep hearing from the cellar bin
The rumbling sound

Of load on load of apples coming in.
For I have had too much
Of apple-picking: I am overtired
Of the great harvest I myself desired.
30   There were ten thousand thousand fruit to touch,
Cherish in hand, lift down, and not let fall.
For all
That struck the earth,
No matter if not bruised or spiked with stubble,
Went surely to the cider-apple heap
As of no worth.
One can see what will trouble
This sleep of mine, whatever sleep it is.
Were he not gone,
40   The woodchuck could say whether it's like his
Long sleep, as I describe its coming on,
Or just some human sleep.

                              1914

The Oven Bird

There is a singer everyone has heard,
Loud, a mid-summer and a mid-wood bird,
Who makes the solid tree trunks sound again.
He says that leaves are old and that for flowers
Mid-summer is to spring as one to ten.
He says the early petal-fall is past,
When pear and cherry bloom went down in showers
On sunny days a moment overcast;
And comes that other fall we name the fall.
10   He says the highway dust is over all.
The bird would cease and be as other birds
But that he knows in singing not to sing.
The question that he frames in all but words
Is what to make of a diminished thing.

                              1916

The Witch of Coös[1]

I stayed the night for shelter at a farm
Behind the mountain, with a mother and son,
Two old-believers.[2] They did all the talking.

---

[1] Coös, pronounced KO-AHSS by Frost in a re-
corded reading, is the northernmost county of
New Hampshire.

[2] **old-believers** practitioners of witchcraft, spiri-
tualism, and devil worship. The mother is a
witch and a medium.

MOTHER. Folks think a witch who has familiar spirits
She could call up to pass a winter evening,
But won't, should be burned at the stake or something.
Summoning spirits isn't "Button, button,
Who's got the button," I would have them know.

SON. Mother can make a common table rear
10   And kick with two legs like an army mule.

MOTHER. And when I've done it, what good have I done?
Rather than tip a table for you, let me
Tell you what Ralle the Sioux Control³ once told me.
He said the dead had souls, but when I asked him
How could that be—I thought the dead were souls—
He broke my trance. Don't that make you suspicious
That there's something the dead are keeping back?
Yes, there's something the dead are keeping back.

SON. You wouldn't want to tell him what we have
Up attic, mother?

20   MOTHER.   Bones—a skeleton.

SON. But the headboard of mother's bed is pushed
Against the attic door: the door is nailed.
It's harmless. Mother hears it in the night,
Halting perplexed behind the barrier
Of door and headboard. Where it wants to get
Is back into the cellar where it came from.

MOTHER. We'll never let them, will we, son? We'll never!

SON. It left the cellar forty years ago
And carried itself like a pile of dishes
30   Up one flight from the cellar to the kitchen,
Another from the kitchen to the bedroom,
Another from the bedroom to the attic,
Right past both father and mother, and neither stopped it.
Father had gone upstairs; mother was downstairs.
I was a baby: I don't know where I was.

MOTHER. The only fault my husband found with me—
I went to sleep before I went to bed,
Especially in winter when the bed
Might just as well be ice and the clothes snow.
40   The night the bones came up the cellar stairs

³ **Ralle the Sioux Control** A control is a spirit
that puts a medium in touch with other spirits
and directs the medium's speech and actions.
"Ralle" is the name of such a spirit, who was a
Sioux Indian when alive.

Toffile[4] had gone to bed alone and left me,
But left an open door to cool the room off
So as to sort of turn me out of it.
I was just coming to myself enough
To wonder where the cold was coming from,
When I heard Toffile upstairs in the bedroom
And thought I heard him downstairs in the cellar.
The board we had laid down to walk dry-shod on
When there was water in the cellar in spring
50 Struck the hard cellar bottom. And then someone
Began the stairs, two footsteps for each step,
The way a man with one leg and a crutch,
Or a little child, comes up. It wasn't Toffile:
It wasn't anyone who could be there.
The bulkhead double doors were double-locked
And swollen tight and buried under snow.
The cellar windows were banked up with sawdust
And swollen tight and buried under snow.
It was the bones. I knew them—and good reason.
60 My first impulse was to get to the knob
And hold the door. But the bones didn't try
The door; they halted helpless on the landing,
Waiting for things to happen in their favor.
The faintest restless rustling ran all through them.
I never could have done the thing I did
If the wish hadn't been too strong in me
To see how they were mounted for this walk.
I had a vision of them put together
Not like a man, but like a chandelier.
70 So suddenly I flung the door wide on him.
A moment he stood balancing with emotion,
And all but lost himself. (A tongue of fire
Flashed out and licked along his upper teeth.
Smoke rolled inside the sockets of his eyes.)
Then he came at me with one hand outstretched,
The way he did in life once; but this time
I struck the hand off brittle on the floor,
And fell back from him on the floor myself.
The finger-pieces slid in all directions.
80 (Where did I see one of those pieces lately?
Hand me my button box—it must be there.)
I sat up on the floor and shouted, "Toffile,
It's coming up to you." It had its choice
Of the door to the cellar or the hall.
It took the hall door for the novelty,
And set off briskly for so slow a thing,
Still going every which way in the joints, though,

[4] **Toffile** pronounced TOFFLE by Frost in a
recorded reading. See note 5, below.

So that it looked like lightning or a scribble,
From the slap I had just now given its hand.
90   I listened till it almost climbed the stairs
From the hall to the only finished bedroom,
Before I got up to do anything;
Then ran and shouted, "Shut the bedroom door,
Toffile, for my sake!" "Company?" he said,
"Don't make me get up; I'm too warm in bed."
So lying forward weakly on the handrail
I pushed myself upstairs, and in the light
(The kitchen had been dark) I had to own
I could see nothing. "Toffile, I don't see it.
100   It's with us in the room, though. It's the bones."
"What bones?" "The cellar bones—out of the grave."
That made him throw his bare legs out of bed
And sit up by me and take hold of me.
I wanted to put out the light and see
If I could see it, or else mow the room,
With our arms at the level of our knees,
And bring the chalk-pile down. "I'll tell you what—
It's looking for another door to try.
The uncommonly deep snow has made him think
110   Of his old song, 'The Wild Colonial Boy,'
He always used to sing along the tote road.
He's after an open door to get outdoors.
Let's trap him with an open door up attic."
Toffile agreed to that, and sure enough,
Almost the moment he was given an opening,
The steps began to climb the attic stairs.
I heard them. Toffile didn't seem to hear them.
"Quick!" I slammed to the door and held the knob.
"Toffile, get nails." I made him nail the door shut
120   And push the headboard of the bed against it.
Then we asked was there anything
Up attic that we'd ever want again.
The attic was less to us than the cellar.
If the bones liked the attic, let them have it.
Let them stay in the attic. When they sometimes
Come down the stairs at night and stand perplexed
Behind the door and headboard of the bed,
Brushing their chalky skull with chalky fingers,
With sounds like the dry rattling of a shutter,
130   That's what I sit up in the dark to say—
To no one anymore since Toffile died.
Let them stay in the attic since they went there.
I promised Toffile to be cruel to them
For helping them be cruel once to him.

SON. We think they had a grave down in the cellar.

MOTHER.   We know they had a grave down in the cellar.

SON.   We never could find out whose bones they were.

MOTHER.   Yes, we could too, son. Tell the truth for once.
They were a man's his father killed for me.
140   I mean a man he killed instead of me.
The least I could do was help dig their grave.
We were about it one night in the cellar.
Son knows the story: but 'twas not for him
To tell the truth, suppose the time had come.
Son looks surprised to see me end a lie
We'd kept up all these years between ourselves
So as to have it ready for outsiders.
But tonight I don't care enough to lie—
I don't remember why I ever cared.
150   Toffile, if he were here, I don't believe
Could tell you why he ever cared himself. . . .

She hadn't found the finger-bone she wanted
Among the buttons poured out in her lap.
I verified the name next morning: Tofıile.
The rural letter box said Toffile Lajway.[5]

1923

[5] **Toffile Lajway**   the full name of the witch's murdered husband. The name is of French- Canadian origin (Théophile Lajoie); Coös is just south of Quebec.

Stopping by Woods on a Snowy Evening

Whose woods these are I think I know.
His house is in the village, though;
He will not see me stopping here
To watch his woods fill up with snow.

My little horse must think it queer
To stop without a farmhouse near
Between the woods and frozen lake
The darkest evening of the year.

He gives his harness bells a shake
10   To ask if there is some mistake.
The only other sound's the sweep
Of easy wind and downy flake.

The woods are lovely, dark, and deep,
But I have promises to keep,
And miles to go before I sleep,
And miles to go before I sleep.

1923

Acquainted with the Night

I have been one acquainted with the night.
I have walked out in rain—and back in rain.
I have outwalked the furthest city light.

I have looked down the saddest city lane.
I have passed by the watchman on his beat
And dropped my eyes, unwilling to explain.

I have stood still and stopped the sound of feet
When far away an interrupted cry
Came over houses from another street,

10 But not to call me back or say good-by;
And further still at an unearthly height
One luminary clock against the sky

Proclaimed the time was neither wrong nor right.
I have been one acquainted with the night.

1928

The Lovely Shall Be Choosers

The Voice said, "Hurl her down!"

The Voices, "How far down?"

"Seven levels of the world."

"How much time have we?"

"Take twenty years.
She *would* refuse love safe with wealth and honor!
The lovely shall be choosers, shall they?
Then let them choose!"

"Then we shall let her choose?"

10 "Yes, let her choose.
Take up the task beyond her choosing."

Invisible hands crowded on her shoulder
In readiness to weigh upon her.
But she stood straight still,
In broad round earrings, gold and jet with pearls,
And broad round suchlike brooch,
Her cheeks high-colored,
Proud and the pride of friends.

The Voice asked, "You can let her choose?"

20   "Yes, we can let her and still triumph."

"Do it by joys, and leave her always blameless.
Be her first joy her wedding,
That though a wedding,
Is yet—well, something they know, he and she.
And after that her next joy
That though she grieves, her grief is secret:
Those friends know nothing of her grief to make it shameful.
Her third joy that though now they cannot help but know,
They move in pleasure too far off
30   To think much or much care.
Give her a child at either knee for fourth joy
To tell once and once only, for them never to forget,
How once she walked in brightness,
And make them see it in the winter firelight.
But give her friends, for then she dare not tell
For their foregone incredulousness.
And be her next joy this:
Her never having deigned to tell them.
Make her among the humblest even
40   Seem to them less than they are.
Hopeless of being known for what she has been,
Failing of being loved for what she is,
Give her the comfort for her sixth of knowing
She fails from strangeness to a way of life
She came to from too high too late to learn.
Then send some *one* with eyes to see
And wonder at her where she is,
And words to wonder in her hearing how she came there,
But without time to linger for her story.
50   Be her last joy her heart's going out to this one
So that she almost speaks.
You know them—seven in all."

"Trust us," the Voices said.

1928

Desert Places

Snow falling and night falling fast, oh, fast
In a field I looked into going past,
And the ground almost covered smooth in snow,
But a few weeds and stubble showing last.

The woods around it have it—it is theirs.
All animals are smothered in their lairs.
I am too absent-spirited to count;
The loneliness includes me unawares.

And lonely as it is, that loneliness
10   Will be more lonely ere it will be less—
A blanker whiteness of benighted snow
With no expression, nothing to express.

They cannot scare me with their empty spaces
Between stars—on stars where no human race is.
I have it in me so much nearer home
To scare myself with my own desert places.

1936

Provide, Provide

The witch that came (the withered hag)
To wash the steps with pail and rag
Was once the beauty Abishag,[1]

The picture pride of Hollywood.
Too many fall from great and good
For you to doubt the likelihood.

Die early and avoid the fate.
Or if predestined to die late,
Make up your mind to die in state.

10   Make the whole stock exchange your own!
If need be occupy a throne,
Where nobody can call *you* crone.

Some have relied on what they knew,
Others on being simply true.
What worked for them might work for you.

No memory of having starred
Atones for later disregard
Or keeps the end from being hard.

Better to go down dignified
20   With boughten friendship at your side
Than none at all. Provide, provide!

1936

---

[1] **Abishag** the beautiful young woman provided
to the aged King David to keep him warm. See
1 Kings 3–4.

The Subverted Flower

She drew back; he was calm:
"It is this that had the power."
And he lashed his open palm
With the tender-headed flower.
He smiled for her to smile,
But she was either blind
Or willfully unkind.
He eyed her for a while
For a woman and a puzzle.
10 He flicked and flung the flower,
And another sort of smile
Caught up like fingertips
The corners of his lips
And cracked his ragged muzzle.
She was standing to the waist
In goldenrod and brake,
Her shining hair displaced.
He stretched her either arm
As if she made it ache
20 To clasp her—not to harm;
As if he could not spare
To touch her neck and hair.
"If this has come to us
And not to me alone——"
So she thought she heard him say;
Though with every word he spoke
His lips were sucked and blown
And the effort made him choke
Like a tiger at a bone.
30 She had to lean away.
She dared not stir a foot,
Lest movement should provoke
The demon of pursuit
That slumbers in a brute.
It was then her mother's call
From inside the garden wall
Made her steal a look of fear
To see if he could hear
And would pounce to end it all
40 Before her mother came.
She looked and saw the shame:
A hand hung like a paw,
An arm worked like a saw
As if to be persuasive,
An ingratiating laugh
That cut the snout in half,
An eye become evasive.
A girl could only see

That a flower had marred a man,
50   But what she could not see
Was that the flower might be
Other than base and fetid:
That the flower had done but part,
And what the flower began
Her own too meager heart
Had terribly completed.
She looked and saw the worst.
And the dog or what it was,
Obeying bestial laws,
60   A coward save at night,
Turned from the place and ran.
She heard him stumble first
And use his hands in flight.
She heard him bark outright.
And oh, for one so young
The bitter words she spit
Like some tenacious bit
That will not leave the tongue.
She plucked her lips for it,
70   And still the horror clung.
Her mother wiped the foam
From her chin, picked up her comb,
And drew her backward home.

1942

Directive

Back out of all this now too much for us,
Back in a time made simple by the loss
Of detail, burned, dissolved, and broken off
Like graveyard marble sculpture in the weather,
There is a house that is no more a house
Upon a farm that is no more a farm
And in a town that is no more a town.
The road there, if you'll let a guide direct you
Who only has at heart your getting lost,
10   May seem as if it should have been a quarry—
Great monolithic knees the former town
Long since gave up pretense of keeping covered.
And there's a story in a book about it:
Besides the wear of iron wagon wheels
The ledges show lines ruled southeast-northwest,
The chisel work of an enormous Glacier
That braced his feet against the Arctic Pole.
You must not mind a certain coolness from him
Still said to haunt this side of Panther Mountain.
20   Nor need you mind the serial ordeal

Of being watched from forty cellar holes
As if by eye pairs out of forty firkins.
As for the woods' excitement over you
That sends light rustle rushes to their leaves,
Charge that to upstart inexperience.
Where were they all not twenty years ago?
They think too much of having shaded out
A few old pecker-fretted apple trees.
Make yourself up a cheering song of how
30   Someone's road home from work this once was,
Who may be just ahead of you on foot
Or creaking with a buggy load of grain.
The height of the adventure is the height
Of country where two village cultures faded
Into each other. Both of them are lost.
And if you're lost enough to find yourself
By now, pull in your ladder road behind you
And put a sign up CLOSED to all but me.
Then make yourself at home. The only field
40   Now left's no bigger than a harness gall.
First there's the children's house of make-believe,
Some shattered dishes underneath a pine,
The playthings in the playhouse of the children.
Weep for what little things could make them glad.
Then for the house that is no more a house,
But only a belilaced cellar hole,
Now slowly closing like a dent in dough.
This was no playhouse but a house in earnest.
Your destination and your destiny's
50   A brook that was the water of the house,
Cold as a spring as yet so near its source,
Too lofty and original to rage.
(We know the valley streams that when aroused
Will leave their tatters hung on barb and thorn.)
I have kept hidden in the instep arch
Of an old cedar at the waterside
A broken drinking goblet like the Grail
Under a spell so the wrong ones can't find it,
So can't get saved, as Saint Mark says they mustn't.[1]
60   (I stole the goblet from the children's playhouse.)
Here are your waters and your watering place.
Drink and be whole again beyond confusion.

1947

[1] l. 59 See Mark 4, in which Jesus explains that salvation is reserved to those whose faith has deep roots, not those who merely pick up the catchwords of faith.

The Draft Horse

With a lantern that wouldn't burn
In too frail a buggy we drove
Behind too heavy a horse
Through a pitch-dark limitless grove.

And a man came out of the trees
And took our horse by the head
And reaching back to his ribs
Deliberately stabbed him dead.

The ponderous beast went down
10 With a crack of a broken shaft.
And the night drew through the trees
In one long invidious draft.

The most unquestioning pair
That ever accepted fate
And the least disposed to ascribe
Any more than we had to to hate,

We assumed that the man himself
Or someone he had to obey
Wanted us to get down
20 And walk the rest of the way.

1962

EDWARD THOMAS
1878–1917

The spirit and tone of Edward Thomas's poetry recall the writing of Robert Frost, who became his close friend just before World War I. Then a hard-working professional book reviewer and nature-writer, specializing in detailed, impressionistic accounts of walking tours throughout Britain, Thomas had a keen ear for regional speech and developed a colloquial yet precise and vivid style of description and characterization. Frost showed him that much of his prose was all but poetry, and Thomas was awakened to his true vocation. Thomas's whole body of poetry is the work of two years, 1914–16. An artillery officer and one of the many gifted English poets to die in action, he was killed in France at the Battle of Arras.

The surface simplicity of Thomas's poetry, like that of Frost's—spontaneous, straightforward diction, concreteness, heartfelt humanity, conventional forms handled with natural ease—makes his work readily accessible. Both poets contributed to the modern development of lyric poetry stripped of artificial "poetic" diction, yet far beyond ordinary discourse or small talk, and capable of elevation and melodic power. One brilliant instance is Thomas's "The Owl," which moves with swift, controlled pacing from a casual-sounding opening to an intense, abruptly depressive realization. Even more finely orchestrated is the brief "It Rains," which begins with rich images of an orchard in the rain, then tightens about phantasmal memories of walking with a loved woman in the rain that hint at an elusive joy within present loneliness. "As the Team's Head-Brass" and "Bob's Lane" are earthily elegiac poems, given beautiful conviction by the gruff understatement that both delays and heightens the painful feelings they contend with.

The Owl

Downhill I came, hungry, and yet not starved;
Cold, yet had heat within me that was proof
Against the North wind; tired, yet so that rest
Had seemed the sweetest thing under a roof.

Then at the inn I had food, fire, and rest,
Knowing how hungry, cold, and tired was I.
All of the night was quite barred out except
An owl's cry, a most melancholy cry

Shaken out long and clear upon the hill,
10 No merry note, nor cause of merriment,
But one telling me plain what I escaped
And others could not, that night, as in I went.

And salted was my food, and my repose,
Salted and sobered, too, by the bird's voice
Speaking for all who lay under the stars,
Soldiers and poor, unable to rejoice.

1915   1917

It Rains

It rains, and nothing stirs within the fence
Anywhere through the orchard's untrodden, dense
Forest of parsley. The great diamonds
Of rain on the grassblades there is none to break,
Or the fallen petals further down to shake.

And I am nearly as happy as possible
To search the wilderness in vain though well,
To think of two walking, kissing there,
Drenched, yet forgetting the kisses of the rain:
10 Sad, too, to think that never, never again,

Unless alone, so happy shall I walk
In the rain. When I turn away, on its fine stalk
Twilight has fined to naught, the parsley flower
Figures, suspended still and ghostly white,
The past hovering as it revisits the light.

1916   1920

As the Team's Head-Brass

As the team's head-brass flashed out on the turn
The lovers disappeared into the wood.
I sat among the boughs of the fallen elm
That strewed the angle of the fallow, and
Watched the plough narrowing a yellow square
Of charlock. Every time the horses turned
Instead of treading me down, the ploughman leaned
Upon the handles to say or ask a word,
About the weather, next about the war.
10   Scraping the share he faced towards the wood,
And screwed along the furrow till the brass flashed
Once more.
                    The blizzard felled the elm whose crest
I sat in, by a woodpecker's round hole,
The ploughman said. "When will they take it away?"
"When the war's over." So the talk began—
One minute and an interval of ten,
A minute more and the same interval.
"Have you been out?" "No." "And don't want to, perhaps?"
20   "If I could only come back again, I should.
I could spare an arm. I shouldn't want to lose
A leg. If I should lose my head, why, so,
I should want nothing more . . . Have many gone
From here?" "Yes." "Many lost?" "Yes, a good few.
Only two teams work on the farm this year.
One of my mates is dead. The second day
In France they killed him. It was back in March,
The very night of the blizzard, too. Now if
He had stayed here we should have moved the tree."
30   "And I should not have sat here. Everything
Would have been different. For it would have been
Another world." "Ay, and a better, though
If we could see all all might seem good." Then
The lovers came out of the wood again:
The horses started and for the last time
I watched the clods crumble and topple over
After the ploughshare and the stumbling team.

May 1916   1920

Bob's Lane

Women he liked, did shovel-bearded Bob,
Old Farmer Hayward of the Heath, but he
Loved horses. He himself was like a cob,
And leather-coloured. Also he loved a tree.

For the life in them he loved most living things,
But a tree chiefly. All along the lane
He planted elms where now the stormcock sings
That travellers hear from the slow-climbing train.

Till then the track had never had a name
10 For all its thicket and the nightingales
That should have earned it. No one was to blame.
To name a thing beloved man sometimes fails.

Many years since, Bob Hayward died, and now
None passes there because the mist and the rain
Out of the elms have turned the lane to slough
And gloom, the name alone survives, Bob's Lane.

1916   1920

CARL SANDBURG
1878–1967

The son of Swedish immigrants (his father was a railroad worker), Sandburg worked at odd jobs and rode the rails until, after a brief enlistment during the Spanish-American War, he attended Lombard College (1898–1902) without being graduated. Afterward, he worked mainly in politics and on newspapers. He was district organizer in Milwaukee for the Social Democratic party for two years and assistant to Milwaukee's mayor for another two years, and was associated with the *Chicago Daily News* from 1917 to 1933. He collected and sang folk songs, accompanying himself on the banjo, and wrote successful children's stories and two monumental biographies: *Abraham Lincoln—The Prairie Years* (1926) and *Abraham Lincoln—The War Years* (1939). Sandburg's exuberant poetry, with its free use of Midwest American populist and working-class lingo, echoes what Whitman called his own "barbaric yawp." Sandburg lacks Whitman's depth and grandeur, and his art is far less developed, but he expresses the surging energies of the flood of new immigrant laborers and their children who so changed American ways during the first half of his life. He catches both their high optimism and their spirited awareness of prejudice and exploitation. Sandburg, who sometimes betrays a touch of Swedish idiom and boisterous humor, often combined with delicate lyric effects, was capable of a unique poetic music in pieces like his macabre, sardonic "The Lawyers Know Too Much," his color-splashed, impressionistic satirical fantasy "Balloon Faces," and his comically dreamy "Whiffs of the Ohio River at Cincinnati."

The Lawyers Know Too Much

The lawyers, Bob, know too much.
They are chums of the books of old John Marshall.[1]
They know it all, what a dead hand wrote,
A stiff dead hand and its knuckles crumbling,
The bones of the fingers a thin white ash.
    The lawyers know
    a dead man's thoughts too well.

In the heels of the higgling lawyers, Bob,
Too many slippery ifs and buts and howevers,
Too much hereinbefore provided whereas,
10   Too many doors to go in and out of.

    When the lawyers are through
    What is there left, Bob?
    Can a mouse nibble at it
    And find enough to fasten a tooth in?

    Why is there always a secret singing
    When a lawyer cashes in?
    Why does a hearse horse snicker
    Hauling a lawyer away?

The work of a bricklayer goes to the blue.
20   The knack of a mason outlasts a moon.
The hands of a plasterer hold a room together.
The land of a farmer wishes him back again.
    Singers of songs and dreamers of plays
    Build a house no wind blows over.
The lawyers—tell me why a hearse horse snickers hauling a lawyer's bones.

1920

[1] **old John Marshall** Chief Justice of the United States Supreme Court, 1801–35; a pillar of conservative American thought, and an impor- tant figure in establishing the authority of the Supreme Court in constitutional interpretation

Balloon Faces

The balloons hang on wires in the Marigold Gardens.
They spot their yellow and gold, they juggle their blue and red, they float their faces on the face of the sky.
Balloon-face eaters sit by hundreds reading the eat cards, asking, "What shall we eat?"—and the waiters, "Have you ordered?" they are sixty balloon faces sifting white over the tuxedoes.
Poets, lawyers, ad men, mason contractors, smart-alecks discussing "edu- cated jackasses," here they put crabs into their balloon faces.

Here sit the heavy balloon-face women lifting crimson lobsters into their crimson faces, lobsters out of Sargossa sea-bottoms.
Here sits a man cross-examining a woman, "Where were you last night? What do you do with all your money? Who's buying your shoes now, anyhow?"
So they sit eating whitefish, two balloon faces swept on God's night wind.
And all the time the balloon spots on the wires, a little mile of festoons, they play their own silence play of film yellow and film gold, bubble blue and bubble red.
The wind crosses the town, the wind from the west side comes to the banks of marigolds boxed in the Marigold Gardens.
Night moths fly and fix their feet in the leaves and eat and are seen by the eaters.
The jazz outfit sweats and the drums and the saxophones reach for the ears of the eaters.
The chorus brought from Broadway works at the fun and the slouch of their shoulders, the kick of their ankles, reach for the eyes of the eaters.
These girls from Kokomo and Peoria, these hungry girls, since they are paid-for, let us look on and listen, let us get their number.

Why do I go again to the balloons on the wires, something for nothing, kin women of the half-moon, dream women?
And the half-moon swinging on the wind crossing the town—these two, the half-moon and the wind—this will be about all, this will be about all.

Eaters, go to it; your mazuma pays for it all; it's a knockout, a classy knock-out—and payday always comes.
The moths in the marigolds will do for me, the half-moon, the wishing wind and the little mile of balloon spots on wires—this will be about all, this will be about all.

1920

From Whiffs of the Ohio River at Cincinnati

2

When I asked for fish in the restaurant facing the Ohio River, with fish signs and fish pictures all over the wooden, crooked frame of the fish shack, the young man said, "Come around next Friday—the fish is all gone today."

So, I took eggs, fried, straight up, one side, and he murmured, humming, looking out at the shining breast of the Ohio river, "And the next is something else; and the next is something else."

The customer next was a hoarse roustabout, handling nail kegs on a steam-boat all day, asking for three eggs, sunny side up, three, nothing less, shake us a mean pan of eggs.

And while we sat eating eggs, looking at the shining breast of the Ohio
river in the evening lights, he had his thoughts and I had mine thinking
how the French who found the Ohio river named it La Belle Riviere
meaning a woman easy to look at.

1928

VACHEL LINDSAY
1879–1931

Like Masters and Sandburg, Lindsay grew
up in Illinois and wrote a poetry affected
by Midwestern populism and other regional
values—in Lindsay's case, evangelical
Christianity and an odd mixture of puri-
tanism and bohemianism. He felt a special
vocation early on that set him apart from his
physician father. After three years at Hiram
College he went to Chicago, where he stud-
ied nights at the Art Institute and worked in
a department store by day. In 1904 he en-
rolled in the New York School of Art; but,
unable to earn money as an artist or on a
newspaper, he set out in 1906 on the first of
his long walking tours. Apart from lecturing
in 1909–10 for the Anti-Saloon League,
he spent the next six years trading poems
for food and lodging. In 1913 he sent
"General William Booth Enters into Hea-
ven" to *Poetry* magazine in Chicago (which
also published Masters and Sandburg), and
with its publication Lindsay's name was
established. His reputation slowly waned,

however; in the late 1920s he became
severely depressed, and he eventually com-
mitted suicide.

Only a small number of Lindsay's poems
remain interesting, but he sometimes
achieved a unique success. His most
famous poem, "The Congo," has become
obnoxious for its blatant though uncon-
scious racism, but as a masterpiece of
syncopated, chanting verse it is matched
only by "General William Booth Enters
into Heaven." A celebratory elegy for the
founder of the Salvation Army, this poem
combines bitter compassion for the down-
trodden and alienated—among whom Lind-
say often found himself—with gusto and
inspirationalism. Like the perfect little "The
Flower-Fed Buffaloes," it was written to be
read and to be recited on stage. Lindsay's
genius for conceiving such poems has never
been rivaled. Though less flamboyant, "The
Leaden-Eyed," another performance poem,
is gravely moving.

The Leaden-Eyed

Let not young souls be smothered out before
They do quaint deeds and fully flaunt their pride.
It is the world's one crime its babes grow dull,
Its poor are ox-like, limp and leaden-eyed.
Not that they starve, but starve so dreamlessly,
Not that they sow, but that they seldom reap,
Not that they serve, but have no gods to serve,
Not that they die but that they die like sheep.

1914

General William Booth Enters into Heaven[1]

(TO BE SUNG TO THE TUNE OF "THE BLOOD OF THE LAMB"
WITH INDICATED INSTRUMENT)

I

(*Bass drum beaten loudly.*)
Booth led boldly with his big bass drum—
(Are you washed in the blood of the Lamb?)
The Saints smiled gravely and they said: "He's come."
(Are you washed in the blood of the Lamb?)
Walking lepers followed, rank on rank,
Lurching bravos from the ditches dank,
Drabs from the alleyways and drug fiends pale—
Minds still passion-ridden, soul-powers frail:—
Vermin-eaten saints with moldy breath,
10 Unwashed legions with the ways of Death—
(Are you washed in the blood of the Lamb?)

(*Banjos.*)
Every slum had sent its half-a-score
The round world over. (Booth had groaned for more.)
Every banner that the wide world flies
Bloomed with glory and transcendent dyes.
Big-voiced lasses made their banjos bang,
Tranced, fanatical they shrieked and sang:—
"Are you washed in the blood of the Lamb?"
Hallelujah! It was queer to see
20 Bull-necked convicts with that land make free.
Loons with trumpets blowed a blare, blare, blare
On, on upward thro' the golden air!
(Are you washed in the blood of the Lamb?)

II

(*Bass drum slower and softer.*)
Booth died blind and still by faith he trod,
Eyes still dazzled by the ways of God.
Booth led boldly, and he looked the chief
Eagle countenance in sharp relief,
Beard a-flying, air of high command
Unabated in that holy land.

[1] See headnote on Lindsay. William Booth (1829–1912) was an English revivalist who founded the Salvation Army in 1865 and became its "General." The Army devoted itself to helping and converting what Lindsay (who had made use of it when down and out) called "the submerged tenth of the population"—the "most notoriously degraded." In Lindsay's time the refrain "Are you washed in the blood of the Lamb?," from the Army's best-known hymn, "The Blood of the Lamb," was heard over and over at meetings. (The "blood" is that of Jesus —the "Lamb" sacrificed at the Crucifixion.) The instruments referred to are those characteristically used by Salvation Army bands.

(Sweet flute music.)

30   Jesus came from out the court-house door,
      Stretched his hands above the passing poor.
      Booth saw not, but led his queer ones there
      Round and round the mighty court-house square.
      Then, in an instant all that blear review
      Marched on spotless, clad in raiment new.
      The lame were straightened, withered limbs uncurled
      And blind eyes opened on a new, sweet world.

(Bass drum louder.)

      Drabs and vixens in a flash made whole!
      Gone was the weasel-head, the snout, the jowl!
40   Sages and sibyls now, and athletes clean,
      Rulers of empires, and of forests green!

(Grand chorus of all instruments. Tambourines to the foreground.)

      The hosts were sandalled, and their wings were fire!
      (Are you washed in the blood of the Lamb?)
      But their noise played havoc with the angel-choir.
      (Are you washed in the blood of the Lamb?)
      Oh, shout Salvation! It was good to see
      Kings and Princes by the Lamb set free.
      The banjos rattled and the tambourines
      Jing-jing-jingled in the hands of Queens.

(Reverently sung, no instruments.)

50   And when Booth halted by the curb for prayer
      He saw his Master thro' the flag-filled air.
      Christ came gently with a robe and crown
      For Booth the soldier, while the throng knelt down.
      He saw King Jesus. They were face to face,
      And he knelt a-weeping in that holy place.
      Are you washed in the blood of the Lamb?

                                              1913

The Flower-Fed Buffaloes

The flower-fed buffaloes of the spring
In the days of long ago,
Ranged where the locomotives sing
And the prairie flowers lie low:—
The tossing, blooming, perfumed grass
Is swept away by the wheat,
Wheels and wheels and wheels spin by
In the spring that still is sweet.

But the flower-fed buffaloes of the spring
10   Left us, long ago.
They gore no more, they bellow no more,
They trundle around the hills no more:—
With the Blackfeet, lying low,
With the Pawnees, lying low,
Lying low.

1925   1926

WALLACE STEVENS
1879–1955

The son of a Reading, Pennsylvania, lawyer, Stevens studied at Harvard and the New York Law School and was admitted to the bar in 1904. He practiced law in New York City until 1916 and began publishing his poetry and mixing in literary circles in 1914. In 1908 he joined an insurance firm, and in 1916 he accepted a position with the Hartford Accident and Indemnity Company. (He became a vice president in 1934 and moved permanently to Hartford, Connecticut.) His first book, *Harmonium* (1923; revised edition, 1931), appeared when he was forty-three.

At its best, Stevens's poetry is a rich mixture of vivid images, magnetic patterns of sound, and varied tones—sensual, meditative, comic, flashily elegant, or darkly brooding. While much of his work has a philosophical element, it is most successful when the play of language and feeling is alive enough to prevent any hint of tedious abstractness. (In his later writing, especially, he tended, like many poets of his generation, to lapse into ponderous discourse—to the delight of ponderous critics, but few others.)

The poems presented here show Stevens's art at its most engaging and moving. "Peter Quince at the Clavier" has the dynamics of a piece of romantic music in four movements: delicate lyrical eroticism in Part I, which turns into a bawdy screech; the intensification of these tones, in language far more physical and sexually suggestive, in Part II; the little ballet-like dance move-

ment, at once sardonic, frivolous, and sad, of Part III; and, in Part IV, a combined rhapsody and elegy that is grave but leavened with wit. Though the poem does philosophize by playing with the thought that the whole range of human feeling is a spiritual "music," what affects us is the constantly shifting emotional tonalities and excited fantasy in its language.

Similarly, "Thirteen Ways of Looking at a Blackbird" contemplates the death principle in the midst of life. Yet its succession of thirteen *haiku*-like units (each could be a separate poem with a blackbird-image at its center) is so bright-spirited and full of surprises, despite its darker and increasingly despairing notes, that it cannot be reduced to something flatly gray and obvious. Again, "The Idea of Order at Key West," which takes up the question of whether or not our sense of purpose or "order" in the universe is purely self-deceptive, is absorbed, moment by moment, in impressions and sensations: a woman singing as she walks along the shore; the sea's noise, turbulence, and apparent mimicry of her movement and song; and, later, the pattern created by the lights of offshore fishing boats as night descends. By the end, the poem has been taken over by an intense yearning for "ghostly demarcations" to satisfy our "rage for order." (The sea's "meaningless plungings" give no such reassurance.)

Stevens is chillingly eloquent when he looks deeply into what the impersonal nothingness of nature would feel like if human feeling were applicable. The imagery of "The Snow Man" is even bleaker than the sea-imagery just discussed. The snow man, normally associated with childhood joy, "mimics" man, but no suffering could touch such a "mind of winter"—that is, a non-mind. It could hear no "misery in the sound of the wind." Despite its sparkling descriptive phrases, the poem's single sentence builds to a tragic, depressed climax. In "The Emperor of Ice-Cream," Stevens faces the same bleakness grotesquely and savagely; a woman's death has routed any pleasure in illusion or surface glamor.

"Sunday Morning," in contrast, presents a succession of richly sensuous effects, combined with wistful, rueful rhetoric and some fanciful myth-making. This rather complex poem resolves itself in the beautiful, simple closing stanza, which copes with the finality of death by listing the sweet gifts of the earth that we must cherish during our brief lifetimes. Stevens comes close to Keats in the spirit and lushness of this poem. In *The Auroras of Autumn*, the magnificent sequence of Stevens's old age, he connects the preoccupation of "The Idea of Order at Key West" (the illusion of design in the universe) with the emphasis on the earth's bounty of "Sunday Morning." "An unhappy people in a happy world," we are victims of our illusions who also glory—as the opening lines of the sequence suggest—in the heights and subtleties that our imaginations lead us into. The work is unusual for Stevens in developing, in parts II and III, intimately personal memories. The scale of imagination is very large, and the image of the aurora borealis, or northern lights, as a huge serpent staring down from the sky sets off a wildly far-reaching, yet powerfully directed, chain of association. *The Auroras of Autumn* (1950) shows that Stevens had grown into new powers of immediacy and scope as he entered his seventies.

Peter Quince at the Clavier[1]

I
Just as my fingers on these keys
Make music, so the selfsame sounds
On my spirit make a music, too.

Music is feeling, then, not sound;
And thus it is that what I feel,
Here in this room, desiring you,

Thinking of your blue-shadowed silk,
Is music. It is like the strain
Waked in the elders by Susanna.[2]

[1] Peter Quince is one of the comic bumpkins in Shakespeare's *A Midsummer Night's Dream*. The title suggests that the sophisticated speaker in the poem is a buffoon underneath it all.

[2] l. 9 The tale of Susanna and the Elders is one of the apocryphal books of the Old Testament. Two lecherous, corrupt Elders watch Susanna bathe, and try to seduce her. When she refuses, they claim they saw her commit adultery with a young man, and she is sentenced to death. But through God's intervention the old men who accused her are put to death instead. The poem's speaker is highly self-ironic but also candid; while the Elders' feelings were reprehensible, they were, like his own, a genuine response to beauty, since all feeling is "music" of one sort or another.

10 Of a green evening, clear and warm,
   She bathed in her still garden, while
   The red-eyed elders watching, felt

   The basses of their beings throb
   In witching chords, and their thin blood
   Pulse pizzicati of Hosanna.

     II
   In the green water, clear and warm,
   Susanna lay.
   She searched
   The touch of springs,
20 And found
   Concealed imaginings.
   She sighed,
   For so much melody.

   Upon the bank, she stood
   In the cool
   Of spent emotions.
   She felt, among the leaves,
   The dew
   Of old devotions.

30 She walked upon the grass,
   Still quavering.
   The winds were like her maids,
   On timid feet,
   Fetching her woven scarves,
   Yet wavering.

   A breath upon her hand
   Muted the night.
   She turned—
   A cymbal crashed,
40 And roaring horns.

     III
   Soon, with a noise like tambourines,
   Came her attendant Byzantines.[3]

   They wondered why Susanna cried
   Against the elders by her side;

   And as they whispered, the refrain
   Was like a willow swept by rain.

[3] **attendant Byzantines** Near Eastern servant-
women

Anon, their lamps' uplifted flame
Revealed Susanna and her shame.

And then, the simpering Byzantines
50 Fled, with a noise like tambourines.

IV

Beauty is momentary in the mind—
The fitful tracing of a portal;
But in the flesh it is immortal.

The body dies; the body's beauty lives.
So evenings die, in their green going,
A wave, interminably flowing.
So gardens die, their meek breath scenting
The cowl of winter, done repenting.
So maidens die, to the auroral
60 Celebration of a maiden's choral.

Susanna's music touched the bawdy strings
Of those white elders; but, escaping,
Left only Death's ironic scraping.
Now, in its immortality, it plays
On the clear viol of her memory,
And makes a constant sacrament of praise.

1915   1923

The Emperor of Ice-Cream

Call the roller of big cigars,
The muscular one, and bid him whip
In kitchen cups concupiscent curds.
Let the wenches dawdle in such dress
As they are used to wear, and let the boys
Bring flowers in last month's newspapers.
Let be be finale of seem.
The only emperor is the emperor of ice-cream.

Take from the dresser of deal,
10 Lacking the three glass knobs, that sheet
On which she embroidered fantails once
And spread it so as to cover her face.
If her horny feet protrude, they come
To show how cold she is, and dumb.
Let the lamp affix its beam.
The only emperor is the emperor of ice-cream.

1922   1923

Sunday Morning

I

Complacencies of the peignoir, and late
Coffee and oranges in a sunny chair,
And the green freedom of a cockatoo
Upon a rug mingle to dissipate
The holy hush of ancient sacrifice.[1]
She dreams a little, and she feels the dark
Encroachment of that old catastrophe,[2]
As a calm darkens among water-lights.
The pungent oranges and bright, green wings
10 Seem things in some procession of the dead,
Winding across wide water, without sound.
The day is like wide water, without sound.
Stilled for the passing of her dreaming feet
Over the seas, to silent Palestine,
Dominion of the blood and sepulchre.

II

Why should she give her bounty to the dead?
What is divinity if it can come
Only in silent shadows and in dreams?
Shall she not find in comforts of the sun,
20 In pungent fruit and bright, green wings, or else
In any balm or beauty of the earth,
Things to be cherished like the thought of heaven?
Divinity must live within herself:
Passions of rain, or moods in falling snow;
Grievings in loneliness, or unsubdued
Elations when the forest blooms; gusty
Emotions on wet roads on autumn nights;
All pleasures and all pains, remembering
The bough of summer and the winter branch.
30 These are the measures destined for her soul.

III

Jove in the clouds had his inhuman birth.
No mother suckled him, no sweet land gave
Large-mannered motions to his mythy mind
He moved among us, as a muttering king,
Magnificent, would move among his hinds,
Until our blood, commingling, virginal,
With heaven, brought such requital to desire
The very hinds discerned it, in a star.
Shall our blood fail? Or shall it come to be
40 The blood of paradise? And shall the earth

---

[1] **ancient sacrifice** Christ's crucifixion in Palestine, which devout Christians solemnly commemorate on Sundays

[2] **that old catastrophe** Christ's crucifixion; also, death

Seem all of paradise that we shall know?
The sky will be much friendlier then than now,
A part of labor and a part of pain,
And next in glory to enduring love,
Not this dividing and indifferent blue.[3]

IV

She says, "I am content when wakened birds,
Before they fly, test the reality
Of misty fields, by their sweet questionings;
But when the birds are gone, and their warm fields
50 Return no more, where, then, is paradise?"
There is not any haunt of prophecy,
Nor any old chimera of the grave,
Neither the golden underground, nor isle
Melodious, where spirits gat them home,[4]
Nor visionary south, nor cloudy palm
Remote on heaven's hill, that has endured
As April's green endures; or will endure
Like her remembrance of awakened birds,
Or her desire for June and evening, tipped
60 By the consummation of the swallow's wings.

V

She says, "But in contentment I still feel
The need of some imperishable bliss."
Death is the mother of beauty; hence from her,
Alone, shall come fulfilment to our dreams
And our desires. Although she strews the leaves
Of sure obliteration on our paths,
The path sick sorrow took, the many paths
Where triumph rang its brassy phrase, or love
Whispered a little out of tenderness,
70 She makes the willow shiver in the sun
For maidens who were wont to sit and gaze
Upon the grass, relinquished to their feet.
She causes boys to pile new plums and pears
On disregarded plate. The maidens taste
And stray impassioned in the littering leaves.

VI

Is there no change of death in paradise?
Does ripe fruit never fall? Or do the boughs
Hang always heavy in that perfect sky,

---

[3] ll. 31–45 The mythical improvisation in ll.
31–38 combines pagan and Christian elements,
alluding to legends about Zeus' ravishing of
various nymphs and women and to the biblical
account of Jesus' conception. Ll. 39–45 suggest
that through these matings of the divine and the
human we have inherited a portion of divinity
and that the world as we know it is the only
Paradise we shall ever have.
[4] gat them home went home. The archaic phras-
ing recalls ancient beliefs no longer quite tena-
ble, and the reluctant, affectionate dismissal of
them shifts the poem toward its secular emphasis.

Unchanging, yet so like our perishing earth,
80 With rivers like our own that seek for seas
They never find, the same receding shores
That never touch with inarticulate pang?
Why set the pear upon those river-banks
Or spice the shores with odors of the plum?
Alas, that they should wear our colors there,
The silken weavings of our afternoons,
And pick the strings of our insipid lutes!
Death is the mother of beauty, mystical,
Within whose burning bosom we devise
90 Our earthly mothers waiting, sleeplessly.[5]

    VII
Supple and turbulent, a ring of men
Shall chant in orgy on a summer morn
Their boisterous devotion to the sun,
Not as a god, but as a god might be,
Naked among them, like a savage source.
Their chant shall be a chant of paradise,
Out of their blood, returning to the sky;
And in their chant shall enter, voice by voice,
The windy lake wherein their lord delights,
100 The trees, like serafin, and echoing hills,
That choir among themselves long afterward.
They shall know well the heavenly fellowship
Of men that perish and of summer morn.
And whence they came and whither they shall go
The dew upon their feet shall manifest.

    VIII
She hears, upon that water without sound,
A voice that cries, "The tomb in Palestine
Is not the porch of spirits lingering.
It is the grave of Jesus, where he lay."
110 We live in an old chaos of the sun,
Or old dependency of day and night,
Or island solitude, unsponsored, free,
Of that wide water, inescapable.
Deer walk upon our mountains, and the quail
Whistle about us their spontaneous cries;
Sweet berries ripen in the wilderness;
And, in the isolation of the sky,
At evening, casual flocks of pigeons make
Ambiguous undulations as they sink,
120 Downward to darkness, on extended wings.

1915   1923

---

[5] ll. 88–90 This suddenly very intense passage
perhaps reflects the fact that Stevens's mother
had died not long before the poem was written.

Thirteen Ways of Looking at a Blackbird

I

Among twenty snowy mountains,
The only moving thing
Was the eye of the blackbird.

II

I was of three minds,
Like a tree
In which there are three blackbirds.

III

The blackbird whirled in the autumn winds.
It was a small part of the pantomime.

IV

10   A man and a woman
Are one.
A man and a woman and a blackbird
Are one.

V

I do not know which to prefer,
The beauty of inflections
Or the beauty of innuendoes,
The blackbird whistling
Or just after.

VI

Icicles filled the long window
With barbaric glass.
20   The shadow of the blackbird
Crossed it, to and fro.
The mood
Traced in the shadow
An indecipherable cause.

VII

O thin men of Haddam,[1]
Why do you imagine golden birds?
Do you not see how the blackbird
Walks around the feet
Of the women about you?

VIII

30   I know noble accents
And lucid, inescapable rhythms;

[1] **Haddam** an industrial town in Connecticut. Its "thin men" are practical New Englanders who are "thin" partly because of undernourished imaginations. Their dreams overlook the richness of ordinary life and love.

But I know, too,
That the blackbird is involved
In what I know.

IX

When the blackbird flew out of sight,
It marked the edge
Of one of many circles.

X

At the sight of blackbirds
Flying in a green light,
40   Even the bawds of euphony[2]
Would cry out sharply.

XI

He rode over Connecticut
In a glass coach.
Once, a fear pierced him,
In that he mistook
The shadow of his equipage
For blackbirds.

XII

The river is moving.
The blackbird must be flying.

XIII

50   It was evening all afternoon.
It was snowing.
And it was going to snow.
The blackbird sat
In the cedar-limbs.

1917   1923

[2] **bawds of euphony**   A bawd is a brothel-keeper or procurer of women for sexual hire. "Bawds of euphony" is a whimsical figure of speech, implying that people who traffic in beautiful sounds—poets and musicians—are blasé about beauty. Yet even they, we are told, would be stirred by blackbirds "flying in a green light" —evoking death's interfusion with life.

The Snow Man

One must have a mind of winter
To regard the frost and the boughs
Of the pine-trees crusted with snow;

And have been cold a long time
To behold the junipers shagged with ice,
The spruces rough in the distant glitter

Of the January sun; and not to think
Of any misery in the sound of the wind,
In the sound of a few leaves,

10 Which is the sound of the land
Full of the same wind
That is blowing in the same bare place

For the listener, who listens in the snow,
And, nothing himself, beholds
Nothing that is not there and the nothing that is.

1921   1923

The Idea of Order at Key West[1]

She sang beyond the genius of the sea.
The water never formed to mind or voice,
Like a body wholly body, fluttering
Its empty sleeves; and yet its mimic motion
Made constant cry, caused constantly a cry,
That was not ours although we understood,
Inhuman, of the veritable ocean.

The sea was not a mask. No more was she.
The song and water were not medleyed sound
10 Even if what she sang was what she heard,
Since what she sang was uttered word by word.
It may be that in all her phrases stirred
The grinding water and the gasping wind;
But it was she and not the sea we heard.

For she was the maker of the song she sang.
The ever-hooded, tragic-gestured sea
Was merely a place by which she walked to sing.
Whose spirit is this? we said, because we knew
It was the spirit that we sought and knew
20 That we should ask this often as she sang.
If it was only the dark voice of the sea
That rose, or even colored by many waves;
If it was only the outer voice of sky
And cloud, of the sunken coral water-walled,
However clear, it would have been deep air,
The heaving speech of air, a summer sound
Repeated in a summer without end
And sound alone. But it was more than that,
More even than her voice, and ours, among

[1] Key West is the westernmost island of the Florida Keys, and the name of its seaport (the "town" in l. 45). The contrast between the sea's "mean-ingless" sounds and movements (see l. 30) and our human urge to find pattern and meaning everywhere is the poem's central preoccupation.

30   The meaningless plungings of water and the wind,
       Theatrical distances, bronze shadows heaped
       On high horizons, mountainous atmospheres
       Of sky and sea.

                    It was her voice that made
       The sky acutest at its vanishing.
       She measured to the hour its solitude.
       She was the single artificer of the world
       In which she sang. And when she sang, the sea,
       Whatever self it had, became the self
40   That was her song, for she was the maker. Then we,
       As we beheld her striding there alone,
       Knew that there never was a world for her
       Except the one she sang and, singing, made.

       Ramon Fernandez,[2] tell me, if you know,
       Why, when the singing ended and we turned
       Toward the town, tell why the glassy lights,
       The lights in the fishing boats at anchor there,
       As the night descended, tilting in the air,
       Mastered the night and portioned out the sea,
50   Fixing emblazoned zones and fiery poles,
       Arranging, deepening, enchanting night.

       Oh! Blessed rage for order, pale Ramon,
       The maker's rage to order words of the sea,
       Words of the fragrant portals, dimly-starred,
       And of ourselves and of our origins,
       In ghostlier demarcations, keener sounds.

              1934   1936

[2] **Ramon Fernandez** French critic and aesthetic thinker (1894–1944). Stevens apparently knew his work but never met him, and said that he had simply put together two Spanish names without thinking of the actual Fernandez or his ideas.

From The Auroras of Autumn[1]

        I[2]

This is where the serpent lives, the bodiless.
His head is air. Beneath his tip at night
Eyes open and fix on us in every sky.

[1] The aurora borealis, or northern lights, are streamers of light occasionally seen in the night skies of the northern hemisphere. In this poem they occur in autumn, a circumstance paralleling the underlying human situation: that of someone in the "autumn" of his life looking back to earlier family life. The title applies to the whole of a ten-part sequence, of which the first three and the tenth are given here. For convenience, lines are numbered consecutively all the way through, although each section can be viewed as a separate poem.
[2] In this section the auroras are seen in the image of a serpent of light flashing in the sky and dominating the night. The serpent image leads rapidly to a succession of related associations, all concerning the illusion of significant cosmic form and the existence of a presiding deity.

Or is this another wriggling out of the egg,
Another image at the end of the cave,
Another bodiless for the body's slough?

This is where the serpent lives. This is his nest,
These fields, these hills, these tinted distances,
And the pines above and along and beside the sea.

10 This is form gulping after formlessness,
Skin flashing to wished-for disappearances
And the serpent body flashing without the skin.

This is the height emerging and its base . . .
These lights may finally attain a pole
In the midmost midnight and find the serpent there,

In another nest, the master of the maze
Of body and air and forms and images,
Relentlessly in possession of happiness.

This is his poison: that we should disbelieve
20 Even that. His meditations in the ferns,
When he moved so slightly to make sure of sun,

Made us no less as sure. We saw in his head,
Black beaded on the rock, the flecked animal,
The moving grass, the Indian in his glade.

II³

Farewell to an idea . . . A cabin stands,
Deserted, on a beach. It is white,
As by a custom or according to

An ancestral theme or as a consequence
Of an infinite course. The flowers against the wall
30 Are white, a little dried, a kind of mark

Reminding, trying to remind, of a white
That was different, something else, last year
Or before, not the white of an aging afternoon,

Whether fresher or duller, whether of winter cloud
Or of winter sky, from horizon to horizon.
The wind is blowing the sand across the floor.

³ This section introduces private memory and a sense of loss. The difficulty of reconstructing one's relationship to one's distant past is ironically weighed against the dazzling but coldly impersonal workings of nature—the "frigid brilliances" of the auroras.

Here, being visible is being white,
Is being of the solid of white, the accomplishment
Of an extremist in an exercise . . .

40 The season changes. A cold wind chills the beach.
The long lines of it grow longer, emptier,
A darkness gathers though it does not fall

And the whiteness grows less vivid on the wall.
The man who is walking turns blankly on the sand.
He observes how the north is always enlarging the change,

With its frigid brilliances, its blue-red sweeps
And gusts of great enkindlings, its polar green,
The color of ice and fire and solitude.

III[4]

Farewell to an idea . . . The mother's face,
50 The purpose of the poem, fills the room.
They are together, here, and it is warm,

With none of the prescience of oncoming dreams.
It is evening. The house is evening, half dissolved.
Only the half they can never possess remains,

Still-starred. It is the mother they possess,
Who gives transparence to their present peace.
She makes that gentler that can gentle be.

And yet she too is dissolved, she is destroyed.
She gives transparence. But she has grown old.
60 The necklace is a carving not a kiss.

The soft hands are a motion not a touch.
The house will crumble and the books will burn.
They are at ease in a shelter of the mind

And the house is of the mind and they and time,
Together, all together. Boreal night
Will look like frost as it approaches them

And to the mother as she falls asleep
And as they say good-night, good-night. Upstairs
The windows will be lighted, not the rooms.

70 A wind will spread its windy grandeurs round
And knock like a rifle-butt against the door.
The wind will command them with invincible sound.

. . .

[4] The sequence grows more intimate in this section with a somewhat Freudian psychological probing and recovery of the childhood world watched over by the mother—a world destroyed by time and now only a house "of the mind." Notice the emotional distance between the tender nostalgia of the opening lines and the harshness of the closing lines.

X[5]

An unhappy people in a happy world—
Read, rabbi, the phases of this difference.
An unhappy people in an unhappy world—

220   Here are too many mirrors for misery.
A happy people in an unhappy world—
It cannot be. There's nothing there to roll

On the expressive tongue, the finding fang.
A happy people in a happy world—
Buffo! A ball, an opera, a bar.

Turn back to where we were when we began:
An unhappy people in a happy world.
Now, solemnize the secretive syllables.

Read to the congregation, for today
230   And for tomorrow, this extremity,
This contrivance of the spectre of the spheres,

Contriving balance to contrive a whole,
The vital, the never-failing genius,
Fulfilling his meditations, great and small.

In these unhappy he meditates a whole,
The full of fortune and the full of fate,
As if he lived all lives, that he might know,

In hall harridan, not hushful paradise,
To a haggling of wind and weather, by these lights
240   Like a blaze of summer straw, in winter's nick.

1947   1950

[5] This concluding poem of the sequence playfully
yet seriously explores the paradox of the human
condition, which is seen as an experimental

"contrivance of the spectre of the spheres": a
way of speaking of God without any real faith.

WILLIAM CARLOS WILLIAMS
1883–1963

Williams took his M.D. degree at the University of Pennsylvania, where his famous friendship with Ezra Pound began. After internship in New York City and a year of graduate study in pediatrics in Germany, Williams returned to Rutherford, New Jersey, his home town, where he set up practice, married, and remained for the rest of his life. Eventually he became head pediatrician at Paterson General Hospital. His many experiences as a pediatrician and obstetrician, treating working-class women and their children, formed the staple of many of his writings. He also wrote plays based directly on his own marriage and life as a doctor, and a series of novels based on his wife's girlhood and her family.

Williams's poetry is the most humanly attractive work by any of the modern American poets. He had a special knack for using natural speech, whether cultivated or uneducated, poetically—that is, with an artistic sense of the weight and tensions of language —and an unusual appreciation of how other people feel and think. (See "The Widow's Lament in Springtime," the study of a crowd in "At the Ball Game," or the close-up of an unfortunate young woman in "To Elsie.") And although he was not a painter, Williams had a painter's eye for selecting and focusing on vivid, animated points of attention and seeing space itself as full of vibrations. Among many examples are his impression of the beginning of a yacht race in lines 6–10 of "The Yachts," the comic, brilliantly colorful scene in "Danse Russe," and the visual panorama unfolded (in time and space) in "Spring and All."

On a very small scale, Williams's "The Red Wheelbarrow" perfectly illustrates both his painterly values and his mastery of speech-rhythms, which create an internal balance that is the essence of poetic technique. It is almost a lesson in how to paint or how to look at a painting: "So much depends" on the relationships of color and form in the barnyard scene; "so much depends" also on our capacity—and its varied suggestiveness—to free ourselves from a merely utilitarian view of the life and objects around us when we are able to see them in artistic perspective. The first line is colloquial and open in its invitation to follow through; and the second line, the simple preposition "upon," then prepares us for the specifics to follow. Each two-line stanza has two stressed syllables in the first line and one in the second, and yet there is lively variation in where the stresses fall. Surprisingly, there is much more that could be said about this tiny poem, but the main point is that it provides a clue to Williams's basic methods.

On a much larger scale, his sequence called *Paterson* is a mighty effort to discover the "common language" shared by the poet and the American people. A "common language" involves many things: chiefly, the local history of a region (here, that of Paterson, New Jersey) and the differing cultural streams out of which the present population has come, but also the communication of subjective awareness. Local history and familial cultural traditions are largely forgotten, while the capacity to share our inner lives openly has never been developed. The barriers to social memory and private communion are deep and complex matters of the isolation of persons from one another and of distrust between the sexes; they are rooted in educational and economic deprivation and a general thwarting of our richest needs—epitomized in the word "divorce." *Paterson* swarms with characters, incidents, impressions, and dramatic passages, bound together by the work's wide-ranging introspective and associative process and its quest for the "rigor of beauty" locked away in unarticulated individual experience. The passage included here, beginning with the poet's vision, on the city streets, of a woman of the people who is his true Muse, demonstrates his humanity, his boldly realistic imagination, and his genius for improvising "free" but highly functional, compelling rhythmic patterns.

Williams's belief in a poetry springing from American speech and American life led him to resent bitterly the emphasis placed by Eliot and Pound, especially the former, on assimilating European culture and poetic tradition into their art, although he acknowledged the genius of both poets. His *In the American Grain* (1925) is an exciting effort to show the key figures, historical events, and documents that reveal the essence of America's myth about itself and its underlying psychological pressures. With D.H. Lawrence's *Studies in Classic American Literature* (1923)—an equally small but dynamic book—it stands as a pioneering effort in critical thinking. Toward the end of his life, Williams found many followers among experimental, anti-traditionalist, and region-oriented younger poets—too few of whom, however, could grasp his demanding and even elegant standards. Hart Crane was influenced very early by *In the American Grain*, but Williams's methods took more deeply with a later generation of such unalike poets as Robert Lowell, Allen Ginsberg, Paul Blackburn, and Denise Levertov.

Danse Russe[1]

If when my wife is sleeping
and the baby and Kathleen
are sleeping
and the sun is a flame-white disc
in silken mists
above shining trees,—
if I in my north room
dance naked, grotesquely
before my mirror
10   waving my shirt round my head
and singing softly to myself:
"I am lonely, lonely.
I was born to be lonely,
I am best so!"
If I admire my arms, my face,
my shoulders, flanks, buttocks
against the yellow drawn shades,—

Who shall say I am not
the happy genius[2] of my household?

1917

[1] Russian dance, an apt name for a ballet movement; here, a comic, self-mocking name for the poet's exuberant early-morning dance
[2] **genius** guardian spirit

The Widow's Lament in Springtime

Sorrow is my own yard
where the new grass
flames as it has flamed
often before but not
with the cold fire
that closes round me this year.
Thirtyfive years
I lived with my husband.
The plumtree is white today
10   with masses of flowers.
Masses of flowers
load the cherry branches
and color some bushes
yellow and some red
but the grief in my heart

is stronger than they
for though they were my joy
formerly, today I notice them
and turned away forgetting.
20   Today my son told me
that in the meadows,
at the edge of the heavy woods
in the distance, he saw
trees of white flowers.
I feel that I would like
to go there
and fall into those flowers
and sink into the marsh near them.

1921

Spring and All

By the road to the contagious hospital[1]
under the surge of the blue
mottled clouds driven from the
northeast—a cold wind. Beyond, the
waste of broad, muddy fields
brown with dried weeds, standing and fallen

patches of standing water
the scattering of tall trees

All along the road the reddish
10   purplish, forked, upstanding, twiggy
stuff of bushes and small trees
with dead, brown leaves under them
leafless vines—

Lifeless in appearance, sluggish
dazed spring approaches—

They enter the new world naked,
cold, uncertain of all
save that they enter. All about them
the cold, familiar wind—

20   Now the grass, tomorrow
the stiff curl of wildcarrot leaf
One by one objects are defined—
It quickens: clarity, outline of leaf

[1] **contagious hospital** a hospital for people with
contagious diseases

But now the stark dignity of
entrance—Still, the profound change
has come upon them: rooted, they
grip down and begin to awaken

1923

To Elsie

The pure products of America
go crazy—
mountain folk from Kentucky

or the ribbed north end of
Jersey
with its isolate lakes and

valleys, its deaf-mutes, thieves
old names
and promiscuity between

10   devil-may-care men who have taken
to railroading
out of sheer lust of adventure—

and young slatterns, bathed
in filth
from Monday to Saturday

to be tricked out that night
with gauds
from imaginations which have no

peasant traditions to give them
20   character
but flutter and flaunt

sheer rags—succumbing without
emotion
save numbed terror

under some hedge of choke-cherry
or viburnum—
which they cannot express—

Unless it be that marriage
perhaps
30   with a dash of Indian blood

will throw up a girl so desolate
so hemmed round
with disease or murder

that she'll be rescued by an
agent—
reared by the state and

sent out at fifteen to work in
some hard-pressed
house in the suburbs—

40   some doctor's family, some Elsie—
voluptuous water
expressing with broken

brain the truth about us—
her great
ungainly hips and flopping breasts

addressed to cheap
jewelry
and rich young men with fine eyes

as if the earth under our feet
50   were
an excrement of some sky

and we degraded prisoners
destined
to hunger until we eat filth

while the imagination strains
after deer
going by fields of goldenrod in

the stifling heat of September
Somehow
60   it seems to destroy us

It is only in isolate flecks that
something
is given off

No one
to witness
and adjust, no one to drive the car

1923

The Red Wheelbarrow

so much depends
upon

a red wheel
barrow

glazed with rain
water

beside the white
chickens.

1923

At the Ball Game[1]

The crowd at the ball game
is moved uniformly

by a spirit of uselessness
which delights them—

all the exciting detail
of the chase

and the escape, the error
the flash of genius—

all to no end save beauty
10   the eternal—

So in detail they, the crowd,
are beautiful

for this
to be warned against

saluted and defied—
It is alive, venomous

it smiles grimly
its words cut—

[1] a "major league" baseball game. Williams, observing both the crowd's capacity for appreciating the game's fine points and its latent mob-character, also sees it as an impersonal force of nature, attuned to abstract cosmic processes—symbolized here by the game's occurrence at the summer solstice.

20 The flashy female with her
    mother, gets it—

    The Jew gets it straight—it
    is deadly, terrifying—

    It is the Inquisition, the
    Revolution

    It is beauty itself
    that lives

    day by day in them
    idly—

    This is
30 the power of their faces

    It is summer, it is the solstice
    the crowd is

    cheering, the crowd is laughing
    in detail

    permanently, seriously
    without thought

                              1923

The Yachts

    contend in a sea which the land partly encloses
    shielding them from the too-heavy blows
    of an ungoverned ocean which when it chooses

    tortures the biggest hulls, the best man knows
    to pit against its beatings, and sinks them pitilessly.
    Mothlike in mists, scintillant in the minute

    brilliance of cloudless days, with broad bellying sails
    they glide to the wind tossing green water
    from their sharp prows while over them the crew crawls

10 ant-like, solicitously grooming them, releasing,
    making fast as they turn, lean far over and having
    caught the wind again, side by side, head for the mark.

In a well guarded arena of open water surrounded by
lesser and greater craft which, sycophant, lumbering
and flittering follow them, they appear youthful, rare

as the light of a happy eye, live with the grace
of all that in the mind is fleckless, free and
naturally to be desired. Now the sea which holds them

is moody, lapping their glossy sides, as if feeling
20   for some slightest flaw but fails completely.
Today no race. Then the wind comes again. The yachts

move, jockeying for a start, the signal is set and they
are off. Now the waves strike at them but they are too
well made, they slip through, though they take in canvas.

Arms with hands grasping seek to clutch at the prows.[1]
Bodies thrown recklessly in the way are cut aside.
It is a sea of faces about them in agony, in despair

until the horror of the race dawns staggering the mind,
the whole sea becomes an entanglement of watery bodies
30   lost to the world bearing what they cannot hold. Broken,

beaten, desolate, reaching from the dead to be taken up
they cry out, failing, failing! their cries rising
in waves still as the skillful yachts pass over.

1935

[1] **Arms with hands grasping** Here the poem shifts from accurate description of a yacht race to allegory, with a vision, reminiscent of Dante's *Inferno*, of multitudes in torment, drowning in life's ruthless competition. Meanwhile, the fortunate few, symbolized by the beautiful yachts, sail triumphantly onward over this sea of agonized failure. Other echoes of Dante in the poem include its three-line stanzas (the first of which follows Dante's rhyme-scheme of aba), precisely detailed descriptions, and tragic allegory.

The Dance

In Breughel's[1] great picture, The Kermess,
the dancers go round, they go round and
around, the squeal and the blare and the
tweedle of bagpipes, a bugle and fiddles
tipping their bellies (round as the thick-
sided glasses whose wash they impound)
their hips and their bellies off balance
to turn them. Kicking and rolling about
the Fair Grounds, swinging their butts, those

[1] Pieter Breughel—also spelled Bruegel or Brueghel (1522?-1569), Flemish painter

shanks must be sound to bear up under such
rollicking measures, prance as they dance
in Breughel's great picture, The Kermess.

1944

From Paterson[1]

From Book V, ii[1]

There is a woman in our town
walks rapidly, flat bellied
in worn slacks upon the street
where I saw her.
            neither short
nor tall, nor old nor young
her
      face would attract no

adolescent. Grey eyes looked
10   straight before her.
               Her
            hair
was gathered simply behind the
ears under a shapeless hat.

Her
      hips were narrow, her
               legs
thin and straight. She stopped

me in my tracks—until I saw
20   her
       disappear in the crowd.

An inconspicuous decoration
made of sombre cloth, meant
I think to be a flower, was
pinned flat to her
             right

breast—any woman might have
done the same to

---

[1] See headnote on Williams for general comment. Paterson is a large industrial city in New Jersey where Williams practiced medicine. The first part of this passage describes a workingclass woman he sees on a Paterson street. She becomes his Muse, although he never sees her again. The second (ll. 57–143) concerns the relationship between the materials and form of art, and the artist's complex awareness of life's crudest aspects and of suffering and tragedy, as well as of careless release and joy.

say she was a woman and warn
30   us of her mood. Otherwise

she was dressed in male attire,
as much as to say to hell
with you. Her
              expression was
serious, her
                feet were small.

And she was gone!

.   if ever I see you again
as I have sought you
40   daily without success

I'll speak to you, alas
too late! ask,
What are you doing on the

streets of Paterson? a
thousand questions:
Are you married? Have you any

children? And, most important,
your NAME! which
of course she may not

50   give me—though
I cannot conceive it
in such a lonely and

intelligent woman

.   have you read anything that I have written?
It is all for you

              or the birds   .
or Mezz Mezzrow[2]

           who wrote   .

Knocking around with Rapp and the Rhythm Kings put the
finishing touches on me and straightened me out. To be with
those guys made me know that any white man. if he thought

---

[2] **Mezz Mezzrow** jazz saxophonist, author of
Really the Blues, who wrote about learning from
black musicians and Bessie Smith's singing—a
parallel to Williams's task in making poetry out
of the lives of people with backgrounds very
unlike his own

straight and studied hard, could sing and dance and play with
the Negro. You didn't have to take the finest and most origi-
nal and honest music in America and mess it up because you
were a white man; you could dig the colored man's real mes-
sage and get in there with him, like Rapp. I felt good all over
after a session with the Rhythm Kings, and I began to miss
that tenor sax.

Man, I was gone with it—inspiration's mammy was with me.
And to top it all, I walked down Madison Street one day and
what I heard made me think my ears were lying. Bessie Smith
was shouting the *Downhearted Blues* from a record in a music
shop. I flew in and bought up every record they had by the
mother of the blues—*Cemetery Blues, Bleedin' Hearted,* and
Midnight Blues— then I ran home and listened to them for
hours on the victrola. I was put in a trance by Bessie's moanful
stories and the patterns of true harmony in the piano back-
ground, full of little runs that crawled up and down my spine
like mice. Every note that woman wailed vibrated on the tight
strings of my nervous system: every word she sang answered a
question I was asking. You couldn't drag me away from that
victrola, not even to eat.

. . or the Satyrs, a
pre-tragic play,
a satyric play!
All plays
were satyric when they were most devout.
Ribald as a Satyr!

Satyrs dance![3]
all the deformities take wing
Centaurs
leading to the rout of the vocables
in the writings
of Gertrude
Stein—but
you cannot be
an artist
by mere ineptitude
The dream
is in pursuit!
The neat figures of
Paul Klee
fill the canvas

[3] ll. 58–64 Satyr plays were a very early form of Greek theater, with a chorus of satyrs (mythical wild and lecherous figures with the heads and bodies of men and the legs of goats). Here the poem leads into the connection between basic physical energies and impulses and the furthest reaches of imagination and art — a connection that demands mature intelligence, an ability to encompass the widest range of feeling and experience, and high artistic discipline.

but that
　　　　is not the work
　　　　　　of a child　.
the cure began, perhaps
　　　　　with the abstraction
　　　　　　　　of Arabic art
Dürer
　　　　with his *Melancholy*
　　　　　　　was aware of it—
the shattered masonry. Leonardo
　　　　saw it,
　　　　　　the obsession,
and ridiculed it
　　　　in *La Gioconda*.
　　　　　　Bosch's
congeries of tortured souls and devils
　　　　　who prey on them
　　　　　　　fish
swallowing
　　　　　their own entrails
Freud
　　　　Picasso
　　　　　　Juan Gris.
a letter from a friend
　　　　saying:
　　　　　　For the last
three nights
　　　　I have slept like a baby
　　　　　　without
liquor or dope of any sort!
　　　　we know
　　　　　　that a stasis
from a chrysalis
　　　　has stretched its wings　.
　　　　　　like a bull
or a Minotaur
　　　　or Beethoven
　　　　　　in the scherzo
from the Fifth Symphony
　　　stomped
　　　　　　his heavy feet
I saw love
　　　　mounted naked on a horse
　　　　　　on a swan
the tail of a fish
　　　　the bloodthirsty conger eel
　　　　　　and laughed
recalling the Jew
　　　　in the pit
　　　　　　among his fellows

```
            when the indifferent chap
               with the machine gun
                    was spraying the heap   .
        he had not yet been hit
               but smiled
        comforting his companions   .
               comforting
                    his companions⁴
        Dreams possess me
               and the dance
                    of my thoughts
        involving animals
               the blameless beasts
```

140

1958

⁴ ll. 128–38   a reference to an anonymous Jewish victim of the Nazis who remained true to his humanity until the end, comforting the other victims. His transcendence of his own predicament poses a challenge to the artist's character and imagination.

D.H. LAWRENCE
1885–1930

Lawrence's father was an uneducated miner, and his mother—the stronger force in his development—had been a schoolteacher. He could not afford a university education and studied instead in a teacher-training college. He then taught school for a number of years. Ford Madox Ford, the novelist who edited *The English Review*, recognized his talent and began publishing his poems in 1909. In 1912 he eloped with the German Baroness Frieda von Richtofen, who left her husband and three children. They were finally able to marry in 1914. Tuberculosis kept Lawrence out of World War I, to which he was opposed in any case, but life in Britain became increasingly uncongenial and in 1919 they left the country for good, living in Australia, Mexico, Sicily, Sardinia, Italy, and finally the United States, until Lawrence died of tuberculosis at age forty-four.

The confidential directness of Lawrence's writing introduced a new tone into English poetry. Lyric verse had always been charged with personal feeling, but Lawrence's poems suggest that he is speaking with his closest friend, explaining the exact quality of an experience—and only incidentally hinting at some further meaning. In many ways his work is close to Wordsworth's confessions in *The Prelude* and to Whitman's and Dickinson's most revealing passages, but he is more open about the sources of his emotional confidences. In his unpretentious "Brooding Grief" the poet has been walking on a city street in the rain, concentrating on the memory of his mother as she lay dying. A yellow autumn leaf, blown in the wind, wrenches his attention to the literal scene around him and he wonders why he has been so startled by the sight. The images—the spectre-like apparition of the "quick leaf" and the "rainy swill" on the lamp-lit street—have reinforced the death-vision in his head. In "Piano," a romantically glamorous moment is suddenly swept away by the memory of another singing woman in a humbler childhood scene that moves him far more powerfully.

The emphasis on psychic moments is

central even in Lawrence's longer pieces such as "Hymn to Priapus" and "Snake," where he feels compelled to add a more general insight. And in poems that are ambiguous and symbolic, he usually suggests a psychological state that cannot be anchored in a single, boldly outlined experience. Mystically sexual in spirit, "The Song of a Man Who Has Come Through" delicately invokes a preparation by the self for the possibly dangerous opening of a world of wonders. It can be seen as addressed to the two sides of one's nature and also to a fearful lover, and its language is appropriate to the love-experience of both sexes. "Bavarian Gentians" invokes another kind of preparing—this time for death—but with a comparable sexual mysticism.

Lawrence's critical and psychological writings, including *Fantasia of the Unconscious* (1922) and *Studies in Classic American Literature* (1923), together with such ground-breaking novels as *The Rainbow* (1915), *Women in Love* (1920), and *Lady Chatterley's Lover* (1928) and his poems and shorter fiction, had a crucial impact on literary modernism. He helped introduce a new sexual candor and a myth-making vision that saw enormous meanings in ordinary life. At odds with genteelly hypocritical and overly intellectual attitudes, he stressed a physicality and an instinctual awareness inseparable from the primal psychic forces he felt were streaming through the cosmos. Lawrence's apparent obsession with sex was an aspect of this insistent vitalism. He believed that modern women were still deeply life-responsive, whereas modern men, in their subservience to dehumanized logicality, technology, and abstract economic and social structures, were becoming mere automatons. The poem "Swan" effectively embodies his way of thinking about these matters.

Brooding Grief

A yellow leaf, from the darkness
Hops like a frog before me;
Why should I start and stand still?

I was watching the woman that bore me
Stretched in the brindled darkness
Of the sick-room, rigid with will
To die: and the quick leaf tore me
Back to this rainy swill
Of leaves and lamps and the city street mingled before me.

1916

Piano

Softly, in the dusk, a woman is singing to me;
Taking me back down the vista of years, till I see
A child sitting under the piano, in the boom of the tingling strings
And pressing the small, poised feet of a mother who smiles as she sings.

In spite of myself, the insidious mastery of song
Betrays me back, till the heart of me weeps to belong
To the old Sunday evenings at home, with winter outside
And hymns in the cosy parlour, the tinkling piano our guide.

10   So now it is vain for the singer to burst into clamour
With the great black piano appassionato. The glamour
Of childish days is upon me, my manhood is cast
Down in the flood of remembrance, I weep like a child for the past.

1918

Hymn to Priapus[1]

My love lies underground
With her face upturned to mine,
And her mouth unclosed in a last long kiss
That ended her life and mine.

I danced at the Christmas party
Under the mistletoe
Along with a ripe, slack country lass
Jostling to and fro.

The big, soft country lass,
10   Like a loose sheaf of wheat
Slipped through my arms on the threshing floor
At my feet.

The warm, soft country lass,
Sweet as an armful of wheat
At threshing-time broken, was broken
For me, and ah, it was sweet!

Now I am going home
Fulfilled and alone,
I see the great Orion[2] standing
20   Looking down.

He's the star of my first beloved
Love-making.
The witness of all that bitter-sweet
Heart-aching.

[1] Priapus, son of the fertility deities Aphrodite
and Dionysus, was the Greek and Roman god of
male sexuality. The poem is a "hymn" to his
power because of the incident described and its
complex emotional implications.

[2] Orion the constellation Orion, or the Hunter.

In Greek mythology Orion, a great hunter, was
the son of the sea god Poseidon. Artemis, god-
dess of the hunt, loved him but was tricked into
killing him. Various Greek and Roman legends
associate him with sexual passion.

Now he sees this as well,
This last commission.
Nor do I get any look
Of admonition.

30 He can add the reckoning up
I suppose, between now and then,
Having walked himself in the thorny, difficult
Ways of men.

He has done as I have done
No doubt:
Remembered and forgotten
Turn and about.

My love lies underground
With her face upturned to mine,
And her mouth unclosed in the last long kiss
40 That ended her life and mine.

She fares in the stark immortal
Fields of death;
I in these goodly, frozen
Fields beneath.

Something in me remembers
And will not forget.
The stream of my life in the darkness
Deathward set!

And something in me has forgotten,
50 Has ceased to care.
Desire comes up, and contentment
Is debonair.

I, who am worn and careful,
How much do I care?
How is it I grin then, and chuckle
Over despair?

Grief, grief, I suppose and sufficient
Grief makes us free
To be faithless and faithful together
60 As we have to be.

1917

The Song of a Man Who Has Come Through[1]

Not I, not I, but the wind that blows through me!
A fine wind is blowing the new direction of Time.
If only I let it bear me, carry me, if only it carry me!
If only I am sensitive, subtle, oh, delicate, a winged gift!
If only, most lovely of all, I yield myself and am borrowed
By the fine, fine wind that takes its course through the chaos of the world
Like a fine, an exquisite chisel, a wedge-blade inserted;
If only I am keen and hard like the sheer tip of a wedge
Driven by invisible blows,
10   The rock will split, we shall come at the wonder, we shall find the Hesperides.[2]

Oh, for the wonder that bubbles into my soul,
I would be a good fountain, a good well-head,
Would blur no whisper, spoil no expression.

What is the knocking?
What is the knocking at the door in the night?
It is somebody wants to do us harm.

No, no, it is the three strange angels.[3]
Admit them, admit them.

1917

[1] The "man" of the title has learned to open himself to the possibilities of mystical revelation and to lay aside fear of the unknown. The emphasis, however, is less religious than experiential and sexual.
[2] the Hesperides nymphs guarding the golden apples of Hera, queen of the gods; also the name of the garden where the apples grew, a place of joy and fulfillment
[3] three strange angels benevolent spirits who should be welcomed, not feared—symbolic of the miraculous rewards of being open and receptive. (They recall the three angels to whom Abraham gives hospitality in Genesis 18.)

Snake

A snake came to my water-trough
On a hot, hot day, and I in pyjamas for the heat,
To drink there.

In the deep, strange-scented shade of the great dark carob-tree
I came down the steps with my pitcher
And must wait, must stand and wait, for there he was at the trough before me.

He reached down from a fissure in the earth-wall in the gloom
And trailed his yellow-brown slackness soft-bellied down, over the edge of
   the stone trough
And rested his throat upon the stone bottom,
10   And where the water had dripped from the tap, in a small clearness,

He sipped with his straight mouth,
Softly drank through his straight gums, into his slack long body,
Silently.

Someone was before me at my water-trough,
And I, like a second comer, waiting.

He lifted his head from his drinking, as cattle do,
And looked at me vaguely, as drinking cattle do,
And flickered his two-forked tongue from his lips, and mused a moment,
And stooped and drank a little more,
20   Being earth-brown, earth-golden from the burning bowels of the earth
On the day of Sicilian July, with Etna smoking.

The voice of my education said to me
He must be killed,
For in Sicily the black, black snakes are innocent, the gold are venomous.

And voices in me said, If you were a man
You would take a stick and break him now, and finish him off.

But must I confess how I liked him,
How glad I was he had come like a guest in quiet, to drink at my water-
    trough
And depart peaceful, pacified, and thankless,
30   Into the burning bowels of this earth?

Was it cowardice, that I dared not kill him?
Was it perversity, that I longed to talk to him?
Was it humility, to feel so honoured?
I felt so honoured.

And yet those voices:
If you were not afraid, you would kill him!

And truly I was afraid, I was most afraid,
But even so, honoured still more
That he should seek my hospitality
40   From out the dark door of the secret earth.

He drank enough
And lifted his head, dreamily, as one who has drunken,
And flickered his tongue like a forked night on the air, so black;
Seeming to lick his lips,
And looked around like a god, unseeing, into the air,
And slowly turned his head,
And slowly, very slowly, as if thrice adream,
Proceeded to draw his slow length curving round
And climb again the broken bank of my wall-face.

50   And as he put his head into that dreadful hole,
And as he slowly drew up, snake-easing his shoulders, and entered farther,
A sort of horror, a sort of protest against his withdrawing into that horrid
    black hole,
Deliberately going into the blackness, and slowly drawing himself after,
Overcame me now his back was turned.

I looked round, I put down my pitcher,
I picked up a clumsy log
And threw it at the water-trough with a clatter.

I think it did not hit him,
But suddenly that part of him that was left behind convulsed in undignified
    haste,
60   Writhed like lightning, and was gone
Into the black hole, the earth-lipped fissure in the wall-front,
At which, in the intense still noon, I stared with fascination.

And immediately I regretted it.
I thought how paltry, how vulgar, what a mean act!
I despised myself and the voices of my accursed human education.

And I thought of the albatross,[1]
And I wished he would come back, my snake.

For he seemed to me again like a king,
Like a king in exile, uncrowned in the underworld,
70   Now due to be crowned again.

And so, I missed my chance with one of the lords
Of life.
And I have something to expiate;
A pettiness.

Taormina   1923

---

[1] **the albatross** See Coleridge, "The Rime of the
Ancient Mariner" (p. 533 above), ll. 63–142,
288–291.

Swan

Far-off
at the core of space
at the quick
of time
beats
and goes still
the great swan upon the waters of all endings
the swan within vast chaos, within the electron.

For us
10 no longer he swims calmly
nor clacks across the forces furrowing a great gay trail
of happy energy,
nor is he nesting passive upon the atoms,
nor flying north desolative icewards
to the sleep of ice,
nor feeding in the marshes,
nor honking horn-like into the twilight.—

But he stoops, now
in the dark
20 upon us;
he is treading our women
and we men are put out
as the vast white bird
furrows our featherless women
with unknown shocks
and stamps his black marsh-feet on their white and marshy flesh.

                                                    1929

Bavarian Gentians

Not every man has gentians in his house
in soft September, at slow, sad Michaelmas.

Bavarian gentians, big and dark, only dark
darkening the day-time, torch-like with the smoking blueness of Pluto's
    gloom,[1]
ribbed and torch-like, with their blaze of darkness spread blue
down flattening into points, flattened under the sweep of white day
torch-flower of the blue-smoking darkness, Pluto's dark-blue daze,
black lamps from the halls of Dis, burning dark blue,
giving off darkness, blue darkness, as Demeter's pale lamps give off light,
10 lead me then, lead the way.

Reach me a gentian, give me a torch!
let me guide myself with the blue, forked torch of this flower
down the darker and darker stairs, where blue is darkened on blueness
even where Persephone goes, just now, from the frosted September
to the sightless realm where a darkness is awake upon the dark
and Persephone herself is but a voice
or a darkness invisible enfolded in the deeper dark
of the arms Plutonic, and pierced with the passion of dense gloom,
among the splendour of torches of darkness, shedding darkness on the lost
    bride and her groom.

                                                    1935

[1] ll. 3–4 These lines introduce the poem's central image: the dark-blue gentians are seen as torches leading the way into the realm of death, ruled over by Dis (Hades or Pluto) and Persephone, whose passionate marriage was symbolized by "torches of darkness."

EZRA POUND
1885–1972

Ezra Pound is the most dynamic and controversial figure among the modern poets. He was born in Hailey, Idaho, and educated at the University of Pennsylvania and Hamilton College. He taught for four months at Wabash College in 1907 (he was dismissed because of his unconventionality) and spent most of the rest of his life abroad, in London (1908–19), Paris (1920–24), and Rapallo on the Italian Riviera. In the wave of reaction against the slaughter of World War I and what many viewed as an outworn system of profiteering and exploitation, he was flung up on the shores of Italian fascism and kindred ideologies, despite his humanistic principles. Arrested by the Americans for broadcasting anti-Allied propaganda for the Italian government, he was detained for some six months in the Disciplinary Training Center near Pisa. Instead of being tried for treason, he was adjudged insane and remanded to St. Elizabeth's Hospital in Washington and held there from 1946 to 1958, when his indictment was dismissed and he returned to Italy.

Pound was a friend of Yeats, Williams, Eliot, Joyce, and many other important writers and artists. Each of his best short poems holds a special significance. Yeats thought that Pound's "The Return," with its visionary repossession of the gods and heroes of the mythical past—their slow, hesitant revival in the mind, their full-blooded ebullience as they gather confidence, and then the slow retreat—conveyed better than any poem of his own the ideas in his own *The Vision.* "The Return" was the first poem in English to use staggered line-breaks as a means of rhythmic notation. "The Coming of War: Actaeon," a comparable repossession in a tragic and prophetic mood, is even more impressive in its dream-strangeness and quick but dignified shifts of tone—from the lovely, eerie opening (an impression of the realm beyond death as the ancient Greeks conceived it) to the stern, disturbing images of high cliffs and a sea "harsher than gra-

nite," to the solemn, elegiac ending that gravely echoes the opening. The well-known imagist couplet "In a Station of the Metro" compresses a world of compassionate feeling, precise observation, and literary association into "an intellectual and emotional complex in an instant of time" (Pound's suggestive and influential definition of the poetic image).

Pound's unique poetic intelligence was strengthened by his energetic studies in the poetry of other languages, past and present, and his attempts to grasp the quality of poems in the original Latin or Greek, Italian, Occitan, or Chinese. During his career Pound helped to found several first-rate little magazines, was foreign correspondent for *Poetry* magazine, and encouraged innumerable writers and artists. He saw far more clearly than most other poets that the history of poetic forms and styles is one of testing the inheritance from the past against the need for a personal expression attuned to the sensibility of one's own age. He recognized the genius of Joyce, Eliot, and others in this sort of accommodation, and understood the wide range of choice available to poets, both in following earlier models and in using them in new ways. His *ABC of Reading* and *Literary Essays* are lively, valuable works on the essence of poetic modernism as he saw it.

His longer works represented here are *Hugh Selwyn Mauberley* and the *Cantos*. *Mauberley*, a post-World War I sequence that in some ways parallels Eliot's *The Waste Land*, is a horrified response to the war, an assault on the burgeoning mass-production culture's destruction of cherished values, and a projection of the poet's own psychological crisis. Pound and Eliot felt obliged to depart from the surface continuity of most earlier poetry in English—that is, from continuous narrative or discussion, or simple dramatic exchange. Their emphasis shifted to images and passages directly evoking a state of feeling or awareness, a kind of poetry the French Symbolists had begun writing in the previous century.

Pound went further in the *Cantos*, which he began during World War I and kept issuing in successive volumes for the rest of his life. The selections here show the many sources he draws on and adapts for his purposes. Canto I is a partial translation from Book XI of Homer's *Odyssey* (Odysseus' visit to the underworld in order to consult the prophet Tiresias), with a most modern turn at the end. Canto XIII is based on the writings of Confucius. Canto XLV presents an incantation against usury derived from medieval and Renaissance Christian doctrine. Canto XLVII picks up the *Odyssey* again, though depending less on Homer's text and moving in a highly associative manner. Cantos LXXIV and LXXXI are from the *Pisan Cantos*, written while Pound was a prisoner of the American army in Italy as World War II was ending. They present the poet's effort to keep his psychological balance under extreme circumstances by falling back on memories, by minute observations of nature, and by contemplation of remembered poems, the Bible, and Confucius' writings. *Mauberley* and the *Cantos* are voyages of exploration of our modern world in relation to the past and to certain cherished ideals—hence the model of Odysseus, Homer's epic voyager, and the attention to the moral and social positions of systems of thought and action unlike our own.

The Return[1]

See, they return; ah, see the tentative
    Movements, and the slow feet,
    The trouble in the pace and the uncertain
    Wavering!

See, they return, one, and by one,
With fear, as half-awakened;
As if the snow should hesitate
And murmur in the wind,
          and half turn back;
10   These were the "Wing'd-with-Awe,"
        Inviolable.

Gods of the wingèd shoe!
With them the silver hounds,
        sniffing the trace of air!

Haie! Haie!
    These were the swift to harry;
    These the keen-scented;
    These were the souls of blood.

    Slow on the leash,
        pallid the leash-men!

1912

[1] See comment in headnote on Pound. The diction in ll. 10–18 is modeled on the poetry of Homer as if (wrote Yeats) Pound had been "translating at sight from an unknown Greek masterpiece."

The Coming of War: Actaeon[1]

An image of Lethe,[2]
    and the fields
      Full of faint light
        but golden,
Gray cliffs,
    and beneath them
A sea
Harsher than granite,
    unstill, never ceasing;
10   High forms
      with the movement of gods,
Perilous aspect;
    And one said:
"This is Actaeon."
    Actaeon of golden greaves![3]
Over fair meadows,
Over the cool face of that field,
Unstill, ever moving
Hosts of an ancient people,
20   The silent cortège.

1916

[1] See comment in headnote on Pound. In Greek mythology the hunter Actaeon blunders into a grove sacred to the goddess Artemis, bathing there. She punishes him by changing him to a stag, whereupon he is torn to pieces by his own hunting dogs. The poem presents Actaeon's arrival among the dead, but its tone suits the title's implied analogy between this mythical

event and the blundering of the nations into World War I.
[2] Lethe a river in the underworld from which the souls of the dead were supposed to drink; it had the power to make them forget their past lives.
[3] Actaeon of golden greaves a typical Homeric epithet. Greaves are leg-armor.

In a Station of the Metro[1]

The apparition of these faces in the crowd;
Petals on a wet, black bough.

1916

[1] The Métro is the Paris subway system. See headnote on Pound.

From Hugh Selwyn Mauberley: Part I[1]

I E. P. ODE POUR L'ELECTION DE SON SEPULCHRE[2]

For three years, out of key with his time;
He strove to resuscitate the dead art
Of poetry; to maintain "the sublime"[3]
In the old sense. Wrong from the start—

No, hardly, but seeing he had been born[4]
In a half savage country, out of date;
Bent resolutely on wringing lilies from the acorn;
Capaneus[5]; trout for factitious bait;

    Ἴδμεν γάρ τοι πάνθ', ὅσ' ἐνὶ Τροίῃ
10 Caught in the unstopped ear;
Giving the rocks small lee-way
The chopped seas held him, therefore, that year.

His true Penelope was Flaubert,
He fished by obstinate isles;
Observed the elegance of Circe's hair
Rather than the mottoes on sun-dials.

Unaffected by "the march of events,"[6]
He passed from men's memory in *l'an trentiesme
De son eage*[7]; the case presents
20 No adjunct to the Muses' diadem.

---

[1] Mauberley is presumably the protagonist of the sequence, although he is never mentioned by name in the poems. He is a young American poet who has come to England to be in touch with the ostensible inheritors of classical poetic tradition—much like "E.P." (Ezra Pound) in the title of Poem I.

[2] an ironic play on the title of a sixteenth-century French poem ("De l'élection de son sépulchre," by Pierre Ronsard), meaning "E.P. Ode on the Choice of His Tombstone"

[3] "the sublime" a reference to "On the Sublime," by Longinus (first century A.D.?)

[4] ll. 4–8 The language here mocks British snobbery toward Americans as "half-savage" provincials and toward E.P. himself as naively bent on the impossible.

[5] Capaneus mythical warrior who defied Zeus and was destroyed. See Aeschylus, *The Seven against Thebes.*

[6] ll. 9–17 Line 9, the Sirens' song to Odysseus, "For we know all the things that happened in Troy," symbolizes the siren-song of British classicism that lured E.P. to the "obstinate" British Isles. L. 13 likens the allure of Odysseus' wife Penelope to that of the nineteenth-century French novelist Flaubert, with his stylistic severity and impatience with cant, as well as his elegant simplicity (like that of the goddess Circe's hair). To live by such values rather than by barren clichés (ll. 16 and 17) requires a heroic discipline modeled on that of Odysseus and Penelope.

[7] *l'an . . . eage* "in the thirtieth year of his age"; the quotation is from *Le Grand Testament*, by the fifteenth-century French poet François Villon.

II

The age demanded an image
Of its accelerated grimace,

Something for the modern stage,
Not, at any rate, an Attic grace;[1]

Not, not certainly, the obscure reveries
Of the inward gaze;
Better mendacities
Than the classics in paraphrase!

The "age demanded" chiefly a mould in plaster,
10   Made with no loss of time,
A prose kinema, not, not assuredly, alabaster
Or the "sculpture" of rhyme.

[1] **Attic grace** classical Athenian aesthetic values,
poetic subjectivity, and precise, hard qualities
of form

IV[1]

These fought in any case,
and some believing,
                pro domo, in any case . . .

Some quick to arm,
some for adventure,
some from fear of weakness,
some from fear of censure,
some for love of slaughter, in imagination,
learning later . . .
10   some in fear, learning love of slaughter;

Died some, pro patria,
        non "dulce" non "et decor" . . .
walked eye-deep in hell
believing in old men's lies, then unbelieving
came home, home to a lie,
home to many deceits,
home to old lies and new infamy;
usury age-old and age-thick
and liars in public places.

20   Daring as never before, wastage as never before.
Young blood and high blood,
        fair cheeks, and fine bodies;

fortitude as never before

frankness as never before,
disillusions as never told in the old days,

[1] Poems IV and V denounce World War I. The
Latin phrase "pro domo" means "in defense of
home"; "pro . . . decor" echoes a line from
an ode by Latin poet Horace: "Dulce et decorum

est pro patria mori" (It is sweet and fitting to
die for one's country). Here the sentiment is
repudiated, much as it is in Wilfred Owen's
"Dulce et Decorum Est" (p. 915 below).

hysterias, trench confessions,
laughter out of dead bellies.

V

There died a myriad,
And of the best, among them,
For an old bitch gone in the teeth,
For a botched civilization,

Charm, smiling at the good mouth,
Quick eyes gone under earth's lid,

For two gross of broken statues,
For a few thousand battered books.

1920

From The Cantos

I[1]

And then went down to the ship,
Set keel to breakers, forth on the godly sea, and
We set up mast and sail on that swart[2] ship,
Bore sheep aboard her, and our bodies also
Heavy with weeping, and winds from sternward
Bore us out onward with bellying canvas,
Circe's this craft, the trim-coifed goddess.
Then sat we amidships, wind jamming the tiller,
Thus with stretched sail, we went over sea till day's end.
10 Sun to his slumber, shadows o'er all the ocean,
Came we then to the bounds of deepest water,
To the Kimmerian lands, and peopled cities
Covered with close-webbed mist, unpierced ever
With glitter of sun-rays
Nor with stars stretched, nor looking back from heaven
Swartest night stretched over wretched men there.
The ocean flowing backward, came we then to the place
Aforesaid by Circe.
Here did they rites, Perimedes and Eurylochus,[3]
20 And drawing sword from my hip
I dug the ell-square pitkin;[4]

[1] Except for the final nine lines, Canto I is a compressed translation from Homer's *Odyssey*, Bk. XI (see headnote on Pound and note 6 to *Hugh Selwyn Mauberley*, p. 857 above). In Bk. XI (*Nekuia* or "Book of the Dead"), Odysseus leaves Circe's island and resumes his return journey from the Trojan War to his kingdom of Ithaca and his faithful wife, Penelope. But he must go first to a place where he can summon up the shades of the dead from Hades, to obtain a prediction of the future from the dead prophet

Tiresias. Here, Tiresias asks why Odysseus has summoned him a *second* time (it happens only once in the original). The closing lines drop the Homeric style and take on quite modern characteristics. In an important sense, Pound presents himself as a poetic reincarnation of Odysseus.
[2] **swart** dark
[3] **Perimedes and Eurylochus** members of Odysseus' crew
[4] **pitkin** small pit

Poured we libations unto each the dead,
First mead and then sweet wine, water mixed with white flour.
Then prayed I many a prayer to the sickly death's-heads;
As set in Ithaca, sterile bulls of the best
For sacrifice, heaping the pyre with goods,
A sheep to Tiresias only, black and a bell-sheep.
Dark blood[5] flowed in the fosse,
Souls out of Erebus,[6] cadaverous dead, of brides
30   Of youths and of the old who had borne much;
Souls stained with recent tears, girls tender,
Men many, mauled with bronze lance heads,
Battle spoil, bearing yet dreory[7] arms,
These many crowded about me; with shouting,
Pallor upon me, cried to my men for more beasts;
Slaughtered the herds, sheep slain of bronze;
Poured ointment, cried to the gods,
To Pluto the strong, and praised Proserpine;[8]
Unsheathed the narrow sword,
40   I sat to keep off the impetuous impotent dead,
Till I should hear Tiresias.
But first Elpenor came, our friend Elpenor,[9]
Unburied, cast on the wide earth,
Limbs that we left in the house of Circe,
Unwept, unwrapped in sepulchre, since toils urged other.
Pitiful spirit. And I cried in hurried speech:
"Elpenor, how art thou come to this dark coast?
"Cam'st thou afoot, outstripping seamen?"
        And he in heavy speech:
50   "Ill fate and abundant wine. I slept in Circe's ingle.[10]
"Going down the long ladder unguarded,
"I fell against the buttress,
"Shattered the nape-nerve, the soul sought Avernus.[11]
"But thou, O King, I bid remember me, unwept, unburied,
"Heap up mine arms, be tomb by sea-bord,[12] and inscribed:
"*A man of no fortune, and with a name to come.*
"And set my oar up, that I swung mid fellows."

And Anticlea[13] came, whom I beat off, and then Tiresias Theban,
Holding his golden wand, knew me, and spoke first:
60   "A second time? why? man of ill star,
"Facing the sunless dead and this joyless region?

---

[5]**blood**   of sacrificed animals
[6]**Erebus**   a dark tunnel-like space through which the shades of the dead pass between earth and Hades
[7]**dreory**   (from Anglo-Saxon *dreorig*): dripping with blood
[8]**Pluto, Proserpine**   Latin names for the king and queen of the realm of the dead, to whom Odysseus wisely prays, since he is invoking their subjects

[9]**Elpenor**, a young member of Odysseus' crew, had been left unburied after his fatal accident because the gods ordered Odysseus to leave at once. Because Elpenor had to be given proper burial, the next leg of the journey was a hasty return to Circe's island.
[10]**Circe's ingle**   Circe's hearth (i.e., her palace)
[11]**Avernus**   entrance to Hades
[12]**sea-bord**   edge of the sea
[13]**Anticlea**   Odysseus' mother.

"Stand from the fosse, leave me my bloody bever[14]
"For soothsay."
    And I stepped back,
And he strong with the blood, said then: "Odysseus
"Shalt return through spiteful Neptune,[15] over dark seas,
"Lose all companions." And then Anticlea came.
Lie quiet Divus. I mean, that is Andreas Divus,
In officina Wecheli, 1538, out of Homer.[16]
70   And he sailed, by Sirens and thence outward and away
And unto Circe.
    Venerandam,
In the Cretan's phrase, with the golden crown, Aphrodite,
Cypri munimenta sortita est, mirthful, oricalchi, with golden
Girdles and breast bands, thou with dark eyelids
Bearing the golden bough of Argicida.[17] So that:[18]

                 1917

[14]**bever** drink

[15]**spiteful Neptune** Neptune, god of the sea, was hostile to Odysseus.

[16]ll. 68–69 Andreas Divus' Latin translation of the *Odyssey* was published in 1538 at Wechel's print-shop ("in officina Wechel"), Paris. Here Pound humorously acknowledges his debt to Divus's translation.

[17]ll. 72–76 These lines quote from the *Homeric Hymns*, translated into Latin by Georgius Dartona Cretensis ("the Cretan"). They urge the veneration ("Venerandam") of Aphrodite, goddess of love and beauty and protectress of Cyprus ("Cypri . . . est": "The citadels of Cyprus were her appointed domain"). She wears golden and copper-golden ("oricalchi") ornaments and a golden crown. Because Aphro-

dite supported the Trojans against the Greeks, she is called "Argicida" ("Greek-slayer"). The golden bough is associated with the ancient myth at the heart of much Mediterranean and Near Eastern mythology, according to Sir James Frazer's *The Golden Bough* (a work that has tremendously influenced modern poets and thinkers).

  This combined prayer and invocation to the goddess establishes Aphrodite as the presiding female deity and muse of the whole sequence, as Dionysus is the presiding male deity. It implies that the poet's symbolic Odyssean journey is deeply related to her sexual power and aesthetic radiance.

[18]**So that** The canto ends by pointing us toward all the cantos that are to follow.

XIII

Kung[1] walked
        by the dynastic temple
and into the cedar grove,
        and then out by the lower river,
And with him Khieu, Tchi
        and Tian the low speaking
And "we are unknown," said Kung,
"You will take up charioteering?
        Then you will become known,
10   "Or perhaps I should take up charioteering, or archery?
"Or the practice of public speaking?"[2]
And Tseu-lou said, "I would put the defences in order,"

[1]**Kung** the Chinese philosopher Kung Fu-tse (551?–479? B.C.), better known as Confucius. He appears here with some of his disciples. The account is taken from the works of Confucius, translated into French by M.E. Pauthier and

published as *Doctrines de Confucius* (1893), though the three closing lines are Pound's improvisation.

[2]ll. 7–11 Kung raises the question of the best way to gain a reputation.

And Khieu said, "If I were lord of a province
I would put it in better order than this is."
And Tchi said, "I would prefer a small mountain temple,
"With order in the observances,
        with a suitable performance of the ritual,"
And Tian said, with his hand on the strings of his lute
The low sounds continuing
20   after his hand left the strings,
And the sound went up like smoke, under the leaves,
And he looked after the sound:
        "The old swimming hole,
"And the boys flopping off the planks,
"Or sitting in the underbrush playing mandolins."[3]
        And Kung smiled upon all of them equally.
And Thseng-sie desired to know:
        "Which had answered correctly?"
And Kung said, "They have all answered correctly,
30   "That is to say, each in his nature."
And Kung raised his cane against Yuan Jang,
        Yuan Jang being his elder,
For Yuan Jang sat by the roadside pretending to
        be receiving wisdom.
And Kung said
        "You old fool, come out of it,
Get up and do something useful."
        And Kung said
"Respect a child's faculties
40   "From the moment it inhales the clear air,
"But a man of fifty who knows nothing
        Is worthy of no respect."
And "When the prince has gathered about him
"All the savants and artists, his riches will be fully employed."
And Kung said, and wrote on the bo leaves:
        If a man have not order within him
He can not spread order about him;
And if a man have not order within him
His family will not act with due order;
50   And if the prince have not order within him
He can not put order in his dominions.
And Kung gave the words "order"
and "brotherly deference"
And said nothing of the "life after death."
And he said
        "Anyone can run to excesses,
It is easy to shoot past the mark,
It is hard to stand firm in the middle."

[3] ll. 18–25 Unlike the other disciples, Tian, the artist (i.e., the musician), thinks of his occupation and of the social order in terms of life's joys and of the resonances of the musical sounds he creates.

And they said: If a man commit murder
60   Should his father protect him, and hide him?
And Kung said:
        He should hide him.

And Kung gave his daughter to Kong-Tch'ang
        Although Kong-Tch'ang was in prison.
And he gave his niece to Nan-Young
        although Nan-Young was out of office.
And Kung said "Wang[4] ruled with moderation,
        In his day the State was well kept,
And even I can remember
70 A day when the historians left blanks in their writings,
I mean for things they didn't know,
But that time seems to be passing."
And Kung said, "Without character you[5] will
        be unable to play on that instrument
Or to execute the music fit for the Odes.
The blossoms of the apricot
        blow from the east to the west,
And I have tried to keep them from falling."

                    1925

[4] **Wang** Wu Wang (1169–1115 B.C.), first em-   [5] **you** Tian
peror (1122–1115) of the Chou dynasty

XLV

With *Usura*[1]

With usura hath no man a house of good stone
each block cut smooth and well fitting
that design might cover their face,
with usura
hath no man a painted paradise on his church wall
harpes et luz
or where virgin receiveth message
and halo projects from incision,
10 with usura
seeth no man Gonzaga his heirs and his concubines
no picture is made to endure nor to live with
but it is made to sell and sell quickly[2]
with usura, sin against nature,

[1] *Usura* usury, defined by Pound in a footnote
to the poem as "a charge for the use of purchasing
power, levied without regard to production; often
without regard to the possibilities of production."
[2] ll. 2–13 Where usury prevails, art loses sup-
port and the pride of craftsmanship diminishes.
The church no longer gives artists the support

implied by medieval and early Renaissance paint-
ings on church walls—e.g., of a Paradise com-
plete with harps and lutes ("*harpes et luz*"—a
quotation from the French poet Villon's *Testa-
ment*), or of the Annunciation ("virgin . . .
message"). Nor do we have portraits of great
personages to match those in the Renaissance.

is thy bread ever more of stale rags
is thy bread dry as paper,
with no mountain wheat, no strong flour
with usura the line grows thick
with usura is no clear demarcation
20   and no man can find site for his dwelling.
Stone cutter is kept from his stone
weaver is kept from his loom
WITH USURA
wool comes not to market
sheep bringeth no gain with usura
Usura is a murrain, usura
blunteth the needle in the maid's hand
and stoppeth the spinner's cunning. Pietro Lombardo
came not by usura
30   Duccio came not by usura
nor Pier della Francesca; Zuan Bellin' not by usura
nor was "La Calunnia" painted.
Came not by usura Angelico; came not Ambrogio Praedis,[3]
Came no church of cut stone signed: *Adamo me fecit*.[4]
Not by usura St. Trophime
Not by usura Saint Hilaire,[5]
Usura rusteth the chisel
It rusteth the craft and the craftsman
It gnaweth the thread in the loom
40   None learneth to weave gold in her pattern;
Azure hath a canker by usura; cramoisi[6] is unbroidered
Emerald findeth no Memling[7]
Usura slayeth the child in the womb
It stayeth the young man's courting
It hath brought palsey to bed, lyeth
between the young bride and her bridegroom
          CONTRA NATURAM
They have brought whores for Eleusis
Corpses are set to banquet
50   at behest of usura.[8]

1937

---

[3] ll. 28–33 The names are of late medieval and Renaissance Italian painters, sculptors, and architects. **La Calunnia** a painting by Botticelli.
[4] *Adamo me fecit* Adam made me, an inscription on a pillar in the Church of San Zeno in Verona, reflecting the artist's or craftsman's pride in his handiwork
[5] ll. 35–36 St. Trophime and Saint Hilaire are admired French medieval churches in Arles and Poitiers respectively.
[6] **cramoisi** crimson cloth made to be embroidered

[7] **Memling** Hans Memling, fifteenth-century Flemish painter
[8] ll. 43–50 "Usura" is most devastating in the sexual life, forcing it to go against nature ("CONTRA NATURAM"). Prostitution, venereal disease, and marrying off young women to wealthy old men violate the essential life-mysteries once celebrated in ancient Greece, in Eleusis.

XLVII[1]

Who even dead, yet hath his mind entire!
This sound came in the dark
First must thou go the road
            to hell
And to the bower of Ceres' daughter Proserpine,
Through overhanging dark, to see Tiresias,
Eyeless that was, a shade, that is in hell
So full of knowing that the beefy men know less than he,
Ere thou come tothy road's end.[2]

10   Knowledge the shade of a shade,
Yet must thou sail after knowledge
Knowing less than drugged beasts. *phtheggometha*
thasson[3]
φθεγγώμεθα θᾶσσον
          The small lamps[4] drift in the bay
And the sea's claw gathers them.
Neptunus[5] drinks after neap-tide.
Tamuz! Tamuz!!
The red flame going seaward.

20   By this gate art thou measured.
From the long boats they have set lights in the water,
The sea's claw gathers them outward.
Scilla's[6] dogs snarl at the cliff's base,
The white teeth gnaw in under the crag,
But in the pale night the small lamps float seaward
                Τυ Διώνα

---

[1] This canto is possibly Pound's highest poetic achievement because of its lyrical control of many diverse elements. The resourcefulness of Odysseus and his men (Bk. X of the *Odyssey*) becomes a symbolic model here for the modern intelligence and imagination. The risk-taking human mind, charged with self-transcending sexual energy—symbolized by the herbal drug Molü (Moly) given by the god Hermes to Odysseus—carries us beyond the level of the beasts. Molü enabled Odysseus to resist being changed into a beast by the goddess Circe, but also to win her love and benevolent behavior toward his crew.

The mystical sense (similar to D.H. Lawrence's) of sexuality as a sacred force linked to cosmic process is strong throughout the *Cantos*. Pound associates it with fertility myths and rituals described in Sir James Frazer's *The Golden Bough* (see Canto I, note 17, p. 861), and with the early practical farming lore given in the Greek poet Hesiod's *Works and Days* (the main source of ll. 48–61).

[2] ll. 1–9 After a year in Circe's palace, Odysseus must now resume the homeward voyage (*Odyssey*, Bk. X). He reports Circe's command that he first go to the entrance to the underworld and summon up the dead so that he can consult the shade of the prophet Tiresias about the future ("Who even dead, yet hath his mind entire").

[3] **phtheggometha / thasson:** "Let's give a shout right now!" (a transliteration of the Greek words in the following line). This cry, made by Polites—leader of the reconnoitering mission sent out by Odysseus on Circe's isle—symbolizes the need to take risks in seeking knowledge, for it was dangerous to attract the attention of unknown, possibly hostile beings. Polites and others risk self-sacrifice for the sake of the whole crew, just as the gods Tamuz (the Babylonian name of Adonis) and Adonis (see ll. 18, 28–30, and 100–107) were sacrificed in mythical accounts and fertility rituals.

[4] **small lamps** lamps set adrift as part of a religious ritual

[5] **Neptunus** Neptune (Poseidon)

[6] **Scilla** (Scylla) a six-headed female monster. Each head barked like a dog and showed triple rows of teeth.

TU DIONA[7]

Καὶ Μοῖραι᾽ Ἄδονιν
Kai MOIRAI' ADONIN[8]

30   The sea is streaked red with Adonis,
The lights flicker red in small jars.
Wheat shoots rise new by the altar,
       flower from the swift seed.
Two span, two span to a woman,
Beyond that she believes not. Nothing is of any importance.
To that is she bent, her intention
To that art thou called ever turning intention,
Whether by night the owl-call, whether by sap in shoot,
Never idle, by no means by no wiles intermittent
40   Moth is called over mountain
The bull runs blind on the sword, *naturans*
To the cave art thou called, Odysseus,
By Molü hast thou respite for a little,
By Molü art thou freed from the one bed
       that thou may'st return to another
The stars are not in her counting,
       To her they are but wandering holes.[9]
Begin thy plowing
When the Pleiades go down to their rest,
50   Begin thy plowing
40 days are they under seabord,
Thus do in fields by seabord
And in valleys winding down toward the sea.
When the cranes fly high
       think of plowing.
By this gate art thou measured
Thy day is between a door and a door
Two oxen are yoked for plowing
Or six in the hill field
60   White bulk under olives, a score for drawing down stone,
Here the mules are gabled with slate on the hill road.[10]
Thus was it in time.

---

[7] TU DIONA Thou, Dione (transliteration of the Greek in l. 26). Dione was the name of Aphrodite's mother and could also be used for Aphrodite herself.

[8] *Kai* MOIRAI' ADONIN (transliteration of Greek words in l. 28) "And the Fates [weep over] Adonis"—an elliptical quotation from Bion's Greek poem "Lament for Adonis"

[9] ll. 34–47 The female sexual principle is seen as devoted to conception and gestation. "Two span to a woman" may refer to the length of a newly born child (two hand-spans). Female absorption in the reproductive cycle is matched by the responsive male force (*natura naturans*:

nature obeying its own laws of being). Odysseus is "called" by this principle "to the cave," suggesting that he is drawn sexually to Circe, and later to his wife, Penelope; but he must also approach the cave through which the shades of the dead come and go—a symbolic but still sexually charged image. Molü, like creative intelligence, permits choices but does not free us from sexual forces.

[10] ll. 48–61 rules for the timing and technique of plowing. Ll. 56–57 associate seasonal rules and methods of farming with the poem's sexual and life-cyclical concerns.

And the small stars now fall from the olive branch,
Forked shadow falls dark on the terrace
More black than the floating martin
      that has no care for your presence,
His wing-print is black on the roof tiles
And the print is gone with his cry.
So light is thy weight on Tellus
70   Thy notch no deeper indented
Thy weight less than the shadow
Yet hast thou gnawed through the mountain,
      Scylla's white teeth less sharp.
Hast thou found a nest softer than cunnus
Or has thou found better rest
Hast'ou a deeper planting, doth thy death year
Bring swifter shoot?
Hast thou entered more deeply the mountain?[11]
The light has entered the cave. Io! Io!
80   The light has gone down into the cave,
Splendour on splendour!
By prong have I entered these hills:
That the grass grow from my body,
That I hear the roots speaking together,
The air is new on my leaf,
The forked boughs shake with the wind.
Is Zephyrus more light on the bough, Apeliota
more light on the almond branch?
By this door I have entered the hill.
90   Falleth,
Adonis falleth.
Fruit cometh after. The small lights drift out with the tide,
sea's claw has gathered them outward,
Four banners to every flower
The sea's claw draws the lamps outward.
Think thus of thy plowing
When the seven stars go down to their rest
Forty days for their rest, by seabord
And in valleys that wind down toward the sea
100   Καὶ Μοῖραι᾽ ῎Αδονιν
        KAI MOIRAI' ADONIN
When the almond bough puts forth its flame,
When the new shoots are brought to the altar,
       Τυ Διώνα, Καὶ Μοῖραι
       TU DIONA, KAI MOIRAI

[11] ll. 62–78 This passage is a purely lyrical rendering of the poem's basic tonalities. The images (Tellus is the earth-goddess) extend the ideas of risk and sacrifice to a sense of the evanescence of all life and the meaninglessness of one's pride of identity. In ll. 72–78 the richness and fruitfulness of sexual process transcend all negative realization; see Ben Jonson's "Her Triumph" (part of "A Celebration of Charis" p. 214 above) for the poetic model of ll. 74–78.

Και Μοῖραι' "Αδονιν
KAI MOIRAI' ADONIN
that hath the gift of healing,
that hath the power over wild beasts.[12]

1937

[12]ll. 79-109 a triumphant reprise that does not deny darker aspects of knowledge but does override them. (Zephyrus and Apeliota are, respectively, the East Wind and the West Wind.) The influence of Walt Whitman—especially *Song of Myself* (p. 687 above)—may be seen in the grass imagery of ll. 83-85.

From LXXIV[1]

Serenely in the crystal jet
    as the bright ball that the fountain tosses
(Verlaine) as diamond clearness[2]
    How soft the wind under Taishan[3]
      where the sea is remembered
    out of hell, the pit
    out of the dust and glare evil
    Zephyrus / Apeliota[4]
This liquid is certainly a
10   property of the mind
nec accidens est[5]   but an element
      in the mind's make-up
est agens[6] and functions   dust to a fountain pan otherwise
    Hast 'ou seen the rose in the steel dust
      (or swansdown ever?)
so light is the urging, so ordered the dark petals of iron
we who have passed over Lethe.[7]

1948

[1] These are the final seventeen lines of Canto LXXIV, which begins Pound's *Pisan Cantos*. Written in 1945 during his confinement in an American prison compound in Italy, this group of cantos is an attempt to put his predicament in perspective, in order to avoid breaking down under the stress of the situation. A certain amount of self-justification on political grounds was also involved. The passage portrays the mind as a fountain that throws up images, memories, and feelings from its deep source, like jets of water balancing a ball overhead. This metaphor, describing an actual "property of the mind" that constantly seeks the implicit forms and connections of varied experience, here encompasses tragic elements of that experience. The suggestion at the end that a kind of spiritual death has taken place—that the speaker has "passed over Lethe," the river of forgetfulness in Hades—emphasizes the importance of memory in his struggle to keep his mental and moral balance.

[2] The fountain, or crystal jet, image is borrowed from "Clair de Lune" by French poet Paul

Verlaine: "The great, slender jets of water among the marble statues" ("*Les grands jets d'eau sveltes parmi les marbres*"). Pound may also have recalled a scene from Yeats's novel *John Sherman* (1891)—"a shop window where a little water-jet balanced a wooden ball upon its point"—which stirs up strong pangs of memory for the viewer.

[3] **Taishan** the sacred Oriental mountain that Pound imagined seeing when he looked at the hills outside the American prison camp in Coltano, near Pisa (Italy)

[4] **Zephyrus / Apeliota** the East Wind and the West Wind

[5] **nec accidens est** (Latin) nor is it merely incidental

[6] **est agens** (Latin) it is an active agent or principle

[7] ll. 14-17 See Canto XLVII, note 11 (p. 867), for Pound's use of Ben Jonson's "Her Triumph." as a poetic model; see also note 1, above, for "Lethe."

From LXXXI

Ed ascoltando al leggier mormorio
    there came new subtlety of eyes into my tent,
whether of spirit or hypostasis,
    but what the blindfold hides
or at carneval
                nor any pair showed anger
    Saw but the eyes and stance between the eyes,
colour, diastasis,
    careless or unaware it had not the
10   whole tent's room
nor was place for the full Ειδώς
interpass, penetrate
    casting but shade beyond the other lights
        sky's clear
        night's sea
        green of the mountain pool
        shone from the unmasked eyes in half-mask's space.[1]
What thou lovest well remains,[2]
             the rest is dross
20   What thou lov'st well shall not be reft from thee
What thou lov'st well is thy true heritage
Whose world, or mine or theirs
           or is it of none?
First came the seen, then thus the palpable
    Elysium,[3] though it were in the halls of hell,
What thou lovest well is thy true heritage,
What thou lov'st well shall not be reft from thee.

The ant's a centaur in his dragon world.[4]
    Pull down thy vanity, it is not man
30   Made courage, or made order, or made grace,
    Pull down thy vanity, I say pull down.
    Learn of the green world what can be thy place

---

[1] ll. 1–17 In this passage the imprisoned poet has a partial vision of a forgiving divine presence. He has been in a reverie, improvising a song in his mind culminating in the image of a beautiful woman's eyes, and here the Italian words (l. 1, "And listening to the light murmuring") present a mystical state. The vision appears of "new subtlety of eyes"—an apparition ("of spirit") or a fixing of inner transport ("hypostasis"). Though "carneval" implies a sense of celebration, its literal meaning derives from the Lenten practice of fasting (in medieval Latin *carne vale* means "flesh, farewell"). Only eyes appear—more than one pair—not a full apparition or *eidos* (l. 11, Greek "form" or "knowing"). The beautiful images in ll. 14–17 add to

a sense of promise whose full nature is not yet revealed.

[2] ll. 18–58 a lyrical affirmation that what is lasting is the vision of beauty and truth arrived at through a deep commitment of affection. While the poet recognizes nature's supremacy over human invention, and that one must "pull down" false pride, it is wrong not to act on the basis of one's most principled commitments (see also Canto XLVII, note 3, p. 865 (above).

[3] **Elysium** in Greek myth, the Isle of the Blessed; here, the state of transcendent awareness presented and developed in this canto

[4] ll. 28 and 32–36 The world of insects, which outstrips our most fabulous human imagination, teaches us humility.

In scaled invention or true artistry,
Pull down thy vanity,
                    Paquin[5] pull down!
The green casque has outdone your elegance.

"Master thyself, then others shall thee beare"[6]
       Pull down thy vanity
Thou art a beaten dog beneath the hail,
40   A swollen magpie in a fitful sun,
Half black half white
Nor knowst'ou wing from tail
Pull down thy vanity
              How mean thy hates
Fostered in falsity,
              Pull down thy vanity,
Rathe[7] to destroy, niggard in charity,
Pull down thy vanity,
              I say pull down.

50   But to have done instead of not doing
              this is not vanity
To have, with decency, knocked
That a Blunt[8] should open
       To have gathered from the air a live tradition
or from a fine old eye the unconquered flame
This is not vanity.
       Here error is all in the not done,
all in the diffidence that faltered . . .

                    1948

[5] ll. 35–36 **Paquin** famous Parisian couturier. His like cannot match nature's designs, such as the "green casque" of the newly born wasp.
[6] l. 37 really Pound's own words, based on a line by Chaucer
[7] **Rathe** from Old English, quick and eager— i.e., rashly inclined

[8] **Blunt** Wilfred Scawen Blunt (1840–1922), British poet and independent anti-imperialist thinker, admired by Pound as "the grandest of old men, the last of the great Victorians." Pound asserts here that, whatever his own errors, he has revered the best in the human spirit and tried to be true to it.

H.D. (Hilda Doolittle)
1886–1961

In 1913 a group of Hilda Doolittle's poems appeared in *Poetry* magazine under the name of "H.D., Imagiste." The pen-name—an improvisation by Ezra Pound, who wished to present her work as a triumph of the Imagist movement—stuck thereafter, and so did Pound's label. She attended Bryn Mawr College when Pound and William Carlos Williams were students at the University of Pennsylvania and was a close friend of both, especially Pound, who encouraged her writing when she met him again in 1911 in London. H.D. married the poet Richard Aldington there in 1913, and they collaborated on translations from Greek and Latin. While he was in service during World War I she took over as editor of the important literary magazine *The Egoist*. After the war they separated, and she settled in Switzerland.

Although H.D. later wrote a series of long, meditative, mystical poems, it was the brief early pieces that established and sustained her reputation. "Heat," "Pear Tree," and "Oread" all show a compressed, rapturous metaphorical physicality. Tangibly dense, alive, and mysteriously varied in its qualities, heat actively presses fruit into ripeness and molds it, yet is plowable as well. A pear tree is a mass of silver dust that germinates "summer and ripe fruits." The "sea" in "Oread" is a forest of evergreen in motion. Such poems, comparable in their brevity, concreteness, and instantaneous suggestiveness to Pound's "In a Station of the Metro," represent an important new orientation early in this century. Each centers not on an abstract idea or familiar sentiment but on a striking individual image, charged with a high level of keyed-up perception.

Heat

O wind, rend open the heat,
cut apart the heat,
rend it to tatters.

Fruit cannot drop
through this thick air—
fruit cannot fall into heat
that presses up and blunts
the points of pears
and rounds the grapes.

10 Cut the heat—
plough through it,
turning it on either side
of your path.

1916

Pear Tree

Silver dust,
lifted from the earth,
higher than my arms reach,
you have mounted,
O, silver,
higher than my arms reach,
you front us with great mass;

no flower ever opened
so staunch a white leaf,
10 no flower ever parted silver
from such rare silver;

O white pear,
your flower-tufts
thick on the branch
bring summer and ripe fruits
in their purple hearts.

1916

Oread[1]

Whirl up sea—
whirl your pointed pines,
splash your great pines
on our rocks,
hurl your green over us,
cover us with your pools of fir.

1924

[1] a mountain-nymph in Greek mythology

SIEGFRIED SASSOON
1886–1967

Though one of British poetry's minor figures, Siegfried Sassoon holds a special place because, with Wilfred Owen, he stands at the beginning of our era of war-disillusionment. Wounded in 1917, Sassoon refused to return to the front and protested by casting his Military Cross ribbon into the Mersey River. As a result, he was sent to a war hospital as a victim of shell-shock. Later he did return to the army and was wounded again. He rose to the rank of captain, but declared himself an active pacifist as soon as the war was over. He published two books, *The Old Huntsman* (1917) and *Counterattack* (1918), containing bitter poems centered on the experience of soldiers. "The General," a typical bit of crushing satire, simple and extroverted, wields its rhymes like well-aimed sledgehammer blows. "Repression

of War Experience" is a subtler, psychologically pained monologue by a soldier on leave that ends in hysteria.

The starkness, realism, and irony of his war verse give it a distinction lacking in Sassoon's many later poems. His autobiographical *Memoirs of an Infantry Officer* (1930) should be read alongside two other prose memoirs: Robert Graves's *Good-bye to All That* (1929) and Edmund Blunden's *Undertones of War* (1928). Sassoon's privileged, artistic family, with its Persian-Jewish origins, was thoroughly assimilated into British upper-class life; no doubt, however, his parents' divorce, his father's early death, and his own sickly childhood and brief, unsatisfactory period of study at Cambridge University heightened his sensitivities and helped him see the war with sardonic clarity.

The General

"Good-morning; good-morning!" the General said
When we met him last week on our way to the line.
Now the soldiers he smiled at are most of 'em dead,
And we're cursing his staff for incompetent swine.
"He's a cheery old card," grunted Harry to Jack
As they slogged up to Arras with rifle and pack.

.   .   .   .

But he did for them both by his plan of attack.

1918

Repression of War Experience

Now light the candles; one; two; there's a moth;
What silly beggars they are to blunder in
And scorch their wings with glory, liquid flame—
No, no, not that—it's bad to think of war,
When thoughts you've gagged all day come back to scare you;
And it's been proved that soldiers don't go mad
Unless they lose control of ugly thoughts
That drive them out to jabber among the trees.

Now light your pipe; look, what a steady hand.
10 Draw a deep breath; stop thinking; count fifteen,
And you're as right as rain . . .
                  Why won't it rain? . . .
I wish there'd be a thunder-storm to-night,
With bucketsful of water to sluice the dark,
And make the roses hang their dripping heads.
Books; what a jolly company they are,
Standing so quiet and patient on their shelves,
Dressed in dim brown, and black, and white, and green,
And every kind of colour. Which you will read?
20 Come on; O *do* read something; they're so wise.
I tell you all the wisdom of the world
Is waiting for you on those shelves; and yet
You sit and gnaw your nails, and let your pipe out,
And listen to the silence: on the ceiling
There's one big, dizzy moth that bumps and flutters;
And in the breathless air outside the house
The garden waits for something that delays.
There must be crowds of ghosts among the trees—
Not people killed in battle—they're in France—
30 But horrible shapes in shrouds—old men who died

Slow, natural deaths—old men with ugly souls,
Who wore their bodies out with nasty sins.

·   ·   ·   ·

You're quiet and peaceful, summering safe at home;
You'd never think there was a bloody war on! . . . .
O yes, you would . . . why, you can hear the guns.
Hark! Thud, thud, thud,—quite soft . . . they never cease—
Those whispering guns—O Christ, I want to go out
And screech at them to stop—I'm going crazy;
I'm going stark, staring mad because of the guns.

1918

EDWIN MUIR
1887–1959

The son of a poor crofter, Muir was born in the Orkney Islands, off the Scottish coast, and for his first thirteen years lived a rural existence that had changed little over the centuries. Then the Muirs were forced to go to Glasgow to seek work, and Muir found the rough slum environment a drop from paradise into hell. Both parents and a brother died soon afterward, but Muir survived illness, cultural shock, and all these losses, and worked in a series of office-boy and clerical jobs. Meanwhile, he read voraciously, attended lectures, became a socialist, and attracted the attention of A.R. Orage, editor of the *New Age*, who printed some of his poems and gave him books to review.

In 1919 Muir married the novelist Willa Anderson, and they moved to London. That same year Orage made him assistant editor. He made his living through literary journalism, and by translating (most notably, the novels of Franz Kafka) in collaboration with his wife. His influence in his native Scotland may be seen in his encouragement of Hugh MacDiarmid and in his important comments on the value of writing poetry in the literary Scots dialect—comments that led to estrangement with MacDiarmid when Muir eventually decided that such writing was a blind alley. The Muirs left London in 1921 and spent most of the next half-dozen years in Czechoslovakia and other European countries, settling in Scotland shortly after their return to Britain. After World War II, Muir was director of the British Institute in Prague until 1948 and in Rome in 1949–50. For the rest of his working days he served as head of a college in Scotland. Despite his income-producing labors, he managed to bring out eleven books of poems, beginning with *First Poems* (1925) and ending with *One Foot in Eden* (1956).

Muir's best poems reflect the damage wreaked on human morale by this century's great wars and violent social changes. They also reflect his preoccupation with dream-symbolism, in the wake of his psychoanalysis at the age of thirty-three. The allegorical poem "Then" is a nightmare-vision of endless fighting and mourning. "The Return of the Greeks" sees the aftermath of the Trojan War through modern rather than classical eyes; the vision is desolate, weary, hopeless. "The Horses" imagines the world after the nuclear holocaust we all dread; the poem's ending is at once beautiful and heartbreaking.

Then[1]

There were no men and women then at all,
But the flesh lying alone,
And angry shadows fighting on a wall
That now and then sent out a groan
Buried in lime and stone,
And sweated now and then like tortured wood
Big drops that looked yet did not look like blood.

And yet as each drop came a shadow faded
And left the wall.
10   There was a lull
Until another in its shadow arrayed it,
Came, fought and left a blood-mark on the wall;
And that was all; the blood was all.

If there had been women there they might have wept
For the poor blood, unowned, unwanted,
Blank as forgotten script.
The wall was haunted
By mute maternal presences whose sighing
Fluttered the fighting shadows and shook the wall
20   As if that fury of death itself were dying.

1943

[1] See comment in headnote on Muir. The arche-
typal nightmare-images of war and lamentation
in this poem are so vivid they seem literal memories of actual experience: something that
happened "then."

The Return of the Greeks[1]

The veteran Greeks came home
Sleepwandering from the war.
We saw the galleys come
Blundering over the bar.
Each soldier with his scar
In rags and tatters came home.

Reading the wall of Troy
Ten years without a change
Was such intense employ
10   (Just out of the arrows' range),
All the world was strange
After ten years of Troy.

[1] See comment in headnote on Muir. Muir rein-
terprets the Homeric events to project the mo-
dern postwar psychological situation.

Their eyes knew every stone
In the huge heartbreaking wall
Year after year grown
Till there was nothing at all
But an alley steep and small,
Tramped earth and towering stone.

Now even the hills seemed low
20   In the boundless sea and land,
Weakened by distance so.
How could they understand
Space empty on every hand
And the hillocks squat and low?

And when they arrived at last
They found a childish scene
Embosomed in the past,
And the war lying between—
A child's preoccupied scene
30   When they came home at last.

But everything trite and strange,
The peace, the parcelled ground,
The vinerows—never a change!
The past and the present bound
In one oblivious round
Past thinking trite and strange.

But for their grey-haired wives
And their sons grown shy and tall
They would have given their lives
40   To raise the battered wall
Again, if this was all
In spite of their sons and wives.

Penelope in her tower
Looked down upon the show
And saw within an hour
Each man to his wife go,
Hesitant, sure and slow:
She, alone in her tower.

1946

The Horses

Barely a twelvemonth after
The seven days war that put the world to sleep,
Late in the evening the strange horses came.
By then we had made our covenant with silence,
But in the first few days it was so still

We listened to our breathing and were afraid.
On the second day
The radios failed; we turned the knobs; no answer.
On the third day a warship passed us, heading north,
10   Dead bodies piled on the deck. On the sixth day
A plane plunged over us into the sea. Thereafter
Nothing. The radios dumb;
And still they stand in corners of our kitchens,
And stand, perhaps, turned on, in a million rooms
All over the world. But now if they should speak,
If on a sudden they should speak again,
If on the stroke of noon a voice should speak,
We would not listen, we would not let it bring
That old bad world that swallowed its children quick
20   At one great gulp. We would not have it again.
Sometimes we think of the nations lying asleep,
Curled blindly in impenetrable sorrow,
And then the thought confounds us with its strangeness.
The tractors lie about our fields; at evening
They look like dank sea-monsters couched and waiting.
We leave them where they are and let them rust:
"They'll moulder away and be like other loam."
We make our oxen drag our rusty ploughs,
Long laid aside. We have gone back
30   Far past our fathers' land.
                    And then, that evening
Late in the summer the strange horses came.
We heard a distant tapping on the road,
A deepening drumming; it stopped, went on again
And the corner changed to hollow thunder.
We saw the heads
Like a wild wave charging and were afraid.
We had sold our horses in our fathers' time
To buy new tractors. Now they were strange to us
As fabulous steeds set on an ancient shield
40   Or illustrations in a book of knights.
We did not dare go near them. Yet they waited,
Stubborn and shy, as if they had been sent
By an old command to find our whereabouts
And that long-lost archaic companionship.
In the first moment we had never a thought
That they were creatures to be owned and used.
Among them were some half-a-dozen colts
Dropped in some wilderness of the broken world,
Yet new as if they had come from our own Eden.
50   Since then they have pulled our ploughs and borne our loads,
But that free servitude still can pierce our hearts.
Our life is changed; their coming our beginning.

1956

MARIANNE MOORE
1887–1972

Marianne Moore grew up in Carlisle, Pennsylvania, and attended Bryn Mawr College. (H.D. was her classmate, but they were only slightly acquainted.) She taught stenography from 1911 to 1915 at the American government's Indian School in Carlisle. Her poems began to appear in the British magazine *Egoist* (in 1911 she had made a brief visit to England and France), and in 1921 H.D. and others printed her first book, *Poems*, without her knowledge. In 1925 she began editing the *Dial*, which with *Poetry* magazine played a crucial role in publishing the best new poetry after World War I. Pound and Williams greatly admired her work, and her later career was crowned with many honors. She directly influenced such younger poets as Elizabeth Bishop, Richard Wilbur, and Charles Tomlinson.

Moore's poetry often suggests someone deep in conversation, trying to close in on just the right way to put a thought:

THE MIND IS AN ENCHANTING THING

is an enchanted thing
like the glaze on a
katydid wing . . .

The process of revision—or of thinking aloud—is frequently out in the open. Moore immediately revises the title (which is also the first line), altering "enchanting" to "enchanted" and adding her striking comparison of our mental responses to the iridescent refraction of light by a katydid's wing. Thus she concretely illustrates the poem's subject and conveys the idea of mind as a sense-organ, "enchanted" by whatever it encounters and absorbs. The fifth stanza, which speaks of the heart's "dejection," describes the mind's workings as painful but impersonal therapy. This may suggest a bitter private experience—an implied confession rare in Moore's work. The poem as a whole shows her command of astringent statement, elegant and dazzling imagery, and the dynamics of feeling and intensity.

Her other work reveals comparable artistry. "Poetry," for example, begins trickily. The poet seems to be having a discussion with some "practical" person who asserts that he "dislikes" poetry. She seems to agree with him, but then quickly shifts to the position that poetry does, "after all," have "a place for the genuine." This shift is reinforced by the ironically exaggerated language ("all this fiddle," "perfect contempt") which she introduces to show her supposed "dislike" of her art. But the witty imagery and high-spirited eloquence that follow reveal her actual feeling for it. "A Grave" begins humorously, with a reproach to a supposed boor blocking a view of the sea. By line 8 the poem has closed in on the sea's deadly reality and sloughed off any whimsy or fancifulness, and by line 14 it has begun introducing notes of exquisite beauty linking the sea with life in many forms. Its rhythms now echo those of Whitman's great poems of death in the midst of life, "Out of the Cradle Endlessly Rocking" and "When Lilacs Last in the Dooryard Bloom'd." Moore's poems often have an emphatic and passionate emotional complexity that is somewhat concealed by superficially dry and ironic wit or almost pedantic abstractness.

Poetry[1]

I, too, dislike it: there are things that are important beyond all this fiddle.
   Reading it, however, with a perfect contempt for it, one discovers in
   it after all, a place for the genuine.
      Hands that can grasp, eyes
      that can dilate, hair that can rise
        if it must, these things are important not because a

high-sounding interpretation can be put upon them but because they are
   useful. When they become so derivative as to become unintelligible,
   the same thing may be said for all of us, that we
10   do not admire what
      we cannot understand: the bat
        holding on upside down or in quest of something to

eat, elephants pushing, a wild horse taking a roll, a tireless wolf under
   a tree, the immovable critic twitching his skin like a horse that feels a flea,
                        the base-
      ball fan, the statistician—
      nor is it valid
        to discriminate against "business documents and

school-books"; all these phenomena are important. One must make a
                        distinction[2]
   however: when dragged into prominence by half poets, the result is not
                             poetry,
20   nor till the poets among us can be
      "literalists of
      the imagination"[3]—above
        insolence and triviality and can present

for inspection, "imaginary gardens with real toads in them,"[4] shall
                          we have

---

[1] See comment in headnote on Moore. The version of this poem that appeared in Moore's *Complete Poems* (1967) was three lines long:

I, too, dislike it.
   Reading it, however, with a perfect
      contempt for it, one discovers in
   it, after all, a place for the genuine.

However, Moore also printed her "original" text in the "Notes" section of the book. Although she continually revised all her work, this is the only such reprinting of a poem's entire earlier version. No doubt she meant to tease her critics by offering the condensed version of her most-discussed poem while holding on to the original, complete with notes (see notes 2 and 3, below).

[2] ll. 16–18 *Diary of Tolstoy*, p. 84: "Where the boundary between prose and poetry lies, I shall never be able to understand. The question is raised in manuals of style, yet the answer to it lies beyond me. Poetry is verse: prose is not verse. Or else poetry is everything with the exception of business documents and school books" (Moore's note).

[3] "**literalists of the imagination**" Yeats, *Ideas of Good and Evil* (A.H. Bullen, 1903), p. 182: "The limitation of his [William Blake's] view was from the very intensity of his vision; he was a too literal realist of imagination, as others are of nature; and because he believed that the figures seen by the mind's eye, when exalted by inspiration, were 'eternal existences,' symbols of divine essences, he hated every grace of style that might obscure their lineaments" (Moore's note).

[4] The expression in quotation marks is Moore's own invention: a counterbalance to the Tolstoy and Yeats quotations.

it. In the meantime, if you demand on the one hand,
the raw material of poetry in
   all its rawness and
   that which is on the other hand
      genuine, you are interested in poetry.

                                        1921

A Grave

Man looking into the sea,
taking the view from those who have as much right to it as you have to it
   yourself,
it is human nature to stand in the middle of a thing,
but you cannot stand in the middle of this;
the sea has nothing to give but a well excavated grave.
The firs stand in a procession, each with an emerald turkey foot at the top,
reserved as their contours, saying nothing;
repression, however, is not the most obvious characteristic of the sea;
the sea is a collector, quick to return a rapacious look.
10 There are others besides you who have worn that look—
whose expression is no longer a protest; the fish no longer investigate them
for their bones have not lasted:
   men lower nets, unconscious of the fact that they are desecrating a grave,
   and row quickly away—the blades of the oars
      moving together like the feet of water spiders as if there were no such thing
      as death.
The wrinkles progress among themselves in a phalanx—beautiful under net-
   works of foam,
and fade breathlessly while the sea rustles in and out of the seaweed;
the birds swim through the air at top speed, emitting catcalls as heretofore—
the tortoise shell scourges about the feet of the cliffs, in motion beneath them;
20   and the ocean, under the pulsation of lighthouses and noise of bell buoys,
advances as usual, looking as if it were not that ocean in which dropped
   things are bound to sink—
in which if they turn and twist, it is neither with volition nor consciousness.

                                        1924

The Mind Is an Enchanting Thing[1]

   is an enchanted thing
      like the glaze on a
   katydid-wing
         subdivided by sun
            till the nettings are legion.

[1] See comment in headnote on Moore.

Like Gieseking playing Scarlatti;²

    like the apteryx-awl
        as a beak, or the
kiwi's rain-shawl
10   of haired feathers, the mind
           feeling its way as though blind,
walks along with its eyes on the ground.³

It has memory's ear
    that can hear without
having to hear.
        Like the gyroscope's fall,
        truly unequivocal
because trued by regnant certainty,

20   it is a power of
        strong enchantment. It
is like the dove-
           neck animated by
           sun; it is memory's eye;
it's conscientious inconsistency.

It tears off the veil; tears
    the temptation, the
mist the heart wears,
        from its eyes—if the heart
        has a face; it takes apart
30   dejection. It's fire in the dove-neck's

iridescence; in the
    inconsistencies
of Scarlatti.
        Unconfusion submits
        its confusion to proof; it's
not a Herod's oath⁴ that cannot change.

1944

---

²**Gieseking . . . Scarlatti:** Walter Wilhelm Gieseking (1895–1956), noted pianist; Domenico Scarlatti (1685–1757), composer
³ll. 7–12 The apteryx (or kiwi), a New Zealand bird, has a long, sharp awl-like beak and hairlike feathers. Because its wings are undeveloped, it seeks its food along the ground. The human mind is imagined as having a similar motion and comparable concentration.
⁴**Herod's oath** Herod Antipas (?–40? A.D.), Roman ruler of Judea, promised his stepdaughter Salome whatever she wished if she would dance for him. She asked to have John the Baptist beheaded, and he unwillingly kept his vow (see Mark 6:17–28).

T.S. ELIOT

1888–1965

T.S. Eliot was the son of a successful St. Louis, Missouri, businessman and the grandson of a distinguished clergyman: William Greenleaf Eliot, who founded the first Unitarian church in Missouri and helped found Washington University. An outstanding philosophy student at Harvard, Eliot took his B.A. and M.A. degrees in 1909 and 1910 and completed his doctoral dissertation in 1916. But having married and settled in London in 1915 and launched a literary career there, he did not return to Harvard for his doctoral examination. He taught school, worked as a clerk for Lloyd's Bank, and became associated, first as an editor and then as a director, with the publishing firm of Faber and Faber. In 1914 in London he had met Pound, who saw to it that "The Love Song of J. Alfred Prufrock" was published in *Poetry* magazine and worked unselfishly to advance Eliot's career. This effort culminated in Pound's invaluable suggestions for revising the early draft of *The Waste Land*. (See the "Facsimile" edition of the poem, edited in 1971 by Valerie Eliot, the poet's second wife.)

Eliot's first wife, Vivien Haigh-Wood, was a talented young woman whose psychological problems led to hospitalization and to the couple's separation. Despite a difficult marriage, Eliot managed during their early years to advance his reputation as a poet and critic. His first book was *Prufrock and Other Observations* (1917). Assistant editor of the *Egoist* from 1917 to 1919, he was also reviewing for the *New Statesman* and other publications. In 1919 he began writing for the *Times Literary Supplement* as well, and in 1920 his first book of criticism, *The Sacred Wood*, appeared. By 1927, when he became a British subject and joined the Church of England, he was the dominant figure in Anglo-American poetry. In 1935 his first play, *Murder in the Cathedral*, was produced, marking the start of his career as a successful playwright. In 1948

he received the Nobel Prize for Literature —the only one ever awarded to a poet born in the United States.

When *The Waste Land* appeared in 1922, it immediately established Eliot as the foremost writer of a new kind of poetry in English. His methods had been anticipated by such French poets as Baudelaire, Rimbaud, Laforgue, and Mallarmé, whose work he knew, and to some extent by his friend Ezra Pound. Rather than telling stories, dramatizing situations, or philosophizing, the new poetry worked more like music, moving from one image or highly suggestive phrase to the next and accumulating a set of related or echoing states of feeling. An entire poem could also consist of just one brief, concentrated effect, as in a typical Imagist piece.

A year before *The Waste Land* appeared, Eliot described this process in his essay "Hamlet and His Problems." "The only way of expressing emotion in the form of art," he wrote, "is by finding an 'objective correlative'; in other words, a set of objects, a situation, a chain of events which shall be the formula of that particular emotion; such that, when the external facts, which must terminate in sensory experience, are given, the emotion is immediately evoked." His main point was that poetry cannot convey an emotion or any other inner state just by mentioning it or trying to describe it. There must be something about the phrasing that transmits it directly, as a nerve-stimulus might. Note, for instance, the succession of images ("objects") in the first verse-unit of "The Love Song of J. Alfred Prufrock." The heavily inert "evening spread out against the sky / Like a patient etherised upon a table," the "half-deserted streets," the "restless nights in one-night cheap hotels," the "sawdust restaurants"—and all the other suggestions of a fearful, furtive, overwhelmingly sordid kind of existence—create a precise emotional atmosphere. No generally descriptive language (such as the adjectives we have just used) could have the same impact.

In like manner, the first four lines of *The Waste Land* evoke complex associations of spring: nostalgia and regret, stirrings of new romantic or erotic excitement, a sense of painful awakening, like being born or giving birth. The next few lines return to the comforts of the unawakened "winter" state, and the rest of the stanza bursts into summer imagery and a world of memories, regrets, stirrings, thrills, and routine comforts expressed through the meeting and conversation with Marie. Such effects make up what Eliot calls "the formula" of the many-sided emotion they evoke. Disturbance, passion, the need to give one's life order, and aroused responsiveness to every sort of stimulus—all are suggested in the poem's first eighteen lines and developed throughout the rest of *The Waste Land*. Underlying this method is the sense that a poem's primary task is to project qualities of feeling and awareness and to discover some sort of balance among them.

"The Love Song of J. Alfred Prufrock" has many elements of the sort of dramatic monologue in which Browning specialized. It seems to have one central speaker, a self-conscious, inhibited person of great sensitivity who, unsure of his own masculinity, both desires and fears women. But it does not unfold a dramatic situation so much as it reveals an elusive psychological state; and the many shifts of tone and imagery, without transitions, show it to be well on its way toward the new kind of poetry we find in *The Waste Land*, which represents the new form completely.

"Rhapsody on a Windy Night," too, anticipates a new mode. It tells a "story"—of a post-midnight stroll through squalid Paris streets—that imparts a grimly ironic, morbid vision of "life." But at the same time, the succession of subtly varied rhythmic echoes and disturbing scenes, images, and incidents makes for an independently improvised tonal structure, as in a musical "rhapsody."

The five parts of *The Waste Land* take us through five major complexes of feeling: the sense of immersion in a chaotic existence as meaningless and hopeless as that of Dante's lost souls in the antechamber of Hell (the *Inferno*); three clusters of imagery and other effects (including dramatic scenes, songs, and monologues) suggesting the horrors of a life without loving sympathy; the inroads made on the spirit by debauchery and mechanical lust, and the need for more than day-by-day satisfactions; and a combined transcendent vision and self-ironic ending. Eliot's emotional range and lyrical virtuosity are more fully displayed in this poem than in anything else he wrote, and so are his humor, his compassion, and his dazzling ability to control the poem's major structural connections while shifting its specific focus and feeling rapidly and often.

In later work Eliot retreated from the purely associative and evocative method of *The Waste Land* but retained an exquisite sense of poetic structure and modulation of tone. The beautifully yearning poem "Marina" (based on Shakespeare's *Pericles*) passionately envisions the soul's movement through all weaknesses and disappointments toward its ideal of purity and love. "Journey of the Magi" presents the dilemma of one who has glimpsed a higher form of faith and existence than he can enter fully in his own person. *Four Quartets*, represented here by "Burnt Norton," moves quasi-mystically through a tortuous and recurring effort to see evidences of immortality in a life bounded by human experience.

The Love Song of J. Alfred Prufrock[1]

S'io credessi che mia risposta fosse
a persona che mai tornasse al mondo,
questa fiamma staria senza più scosse.
Ma per ciò che giammai di questo fondo
non tornò vivo alcun, s'i'odo il vero,
senza tema d'infamia ti rispondo.[2]

Let us go then, you and I,
When the evening is spread out against the sky
Like a patient etherised upon a table;
Let us go, through certain half-deserted streets,
The muttering retreats
Of restless nights in one-night cheap hotels
And sawdust restaurants with oyster-shells:
Streets that follow like a tedious argument
Of insidious intent
10   To lead you to an overwhelming question. . .
Oh, do not ask, "What is it?"
Let us go and make our visit.

In the room the women come and go
Talking of Michelangelo.

The yellow fog that rubs its back upon the window-panes,
The yellow smoke that rubs its muzzle on the window-panes,
Licked its tongue into the corners of the evening,
Lingered upon the pools that stand in drains,
Let fall upon its back the soot that falls from chimneys,
20   Slipped by the terrace, made a sudden leap,
And seeing that it was a soft October night,
Curled once about the house, and fell asleep.

And indeed there will be time
For the yellow smoke that slides along the street
Rubbing its back upon the window-panes;
There will be time, there will be time
To prepare a face to meet the faces that you meet;
There will be time to murder and create,
And time for all the works and days of hands
30   That lift and drop a question on your plate;
Time for you and time for me,

[1] See comment in headnote on Eliot. The title, linking the idea of a "love song" with the stuffy, businesslike "J. Alfred Prufrock," is ironic. The name suggests puns: the sturdy "proof-rock," as though the lover were an insurance company; or the prissy "Prue-frock."
[2] a speech from Dante's *Inferno*, XXVII.61–66, by Guido da Montefeltro, burning in hell. Literally:
  If I thought that my reply would be to anyone who might go back to the world, this flame would cease any longer to tremble. But since never from this deep place did anyone return alive, if I hear truth, without fear of infamy I respond to you. This is an ironic epigraph, since Prufrock's misery at believing himself utterly unheroic and lacking in virility, though pitiful, is hardly sinful or sensationally dramatic.

And time yet for a hundred indecisions,
And for a hundred visions and revisions,
Before the taking of a toast and tea.

In the room the women come and go
Talking of Michelangelo.

And indeed there will be time
To wonder, "Do I dare?" and, "Do I dare?"
Time to turn back and descend the stair,
40 With a bald spot in the middle of my hair—
(They will say: "How his hair is growing thin!")
My morning coat, my collar mounting firmly to the chin,
My necktie rich and modest, but asserted by a simple pin—
(They will say: "But how his arms and legs are thin!")
Do I dare
Disturb the universe?
In a minute there is time
For decisions and revisions which a minute will reverse.

For I have known them all already, known them all—
50 Have known the evenings, mornings, afternoons,
I have measured out my life with coffee spoons;
I know the voices dying with a dying fall
Beneath the music from a farther room.
        So how should I presume?

And I have known the eyes already, known them all—
The eyes that fix you in a formulated phrase,
And when I am formulated, sprawling on a pin,
When I am pinned and wriggling on the wall,
Then how should I begin
60 To spit out all the butt-ends of my days and ways?
        And how should I presume?

And I have known the arms already, known them all—
Arms that are braceleted and white and bare
(But in the lamplight, downed with light brown hair!)
Is it perfume from a dress
That makes me so digress?
Arms that lie along a table, or wrap about a shawl.
        And should I then presume?
        And how should I begin?

                .   .   .   .

70 Shall I say, I have gone at dusk through narrow streets
And watched the smoke that rises from the pipes
Of lonely men in shirt-sleeves, leaning out of windows? . . .

I should have been a pair of ragged claws
Scuttling across the floors of silent seas.
        .   .   .   .

And the afternoon, the evening, sleeps so peacefully!
Smoothed by long fingers,
Asleep . . . tired . . . or it malingers,
Stretched on the floor, here beside you and me.
Should I, after tea and cakes and ices,
80   Have the strength to force the moment to its crisis?
But though I have wept and fasted, wept and prayed,
Though I have seen my head (grown slightly bald) brought in upon a platter,[3]
I am no prophet—and here's no great matter;
I have seen the moment of my greatness flicker,
And I have seen the eternal Footman hold my coat, and snicker,
And in short, I was afraid.

And would it have been worth it, after all,
After the cups, the marmalade, the tea,
Among the porcelain, among some talk of you and me,
90   Would it have been worth while,
To have bitten off the matter with a smile,
To have squeezed the universe into a ball
To roll it towards some overwhelming question,
To say: "I am Lazarus, come from the dead,[4]
Come back to tell you all, I shall tell you all"—
If one, settling a pillow by her head,
    Should say: "That is not what I meant at all.
    That is not it, at all."

And would it have been worth it, after all,
100   Would it have been worth while,
After the sunsets and the dooryards and the sprinkled streets,
After the novels, after the teacups, after the skirts that trail along the floor—
And this, and so much more?—
It is impossible to say just what I mean!
But as if a magic lantern threw the nerves in patterns on a screen:
Would it have been worth while
If one, settling a pillow or throwing off a shawl,
And turning toward the window, should say:
    "That is not it at all,
110   That is not what I meant, at all."

     ·   ·   ·   ·   ·

No! I am not Prince Hamlet, nor was meant to be;
Am an attendant lord, one that will do
To swell a progress, start a scene or two,
Advise the prince; no doubt, an easy tool,
Deferential, glad to be of use,
Politic, cautious, and meticulous;
Full of high sentence, but a bit obtuse;

[3] l. 82 John the Baptist, the prophet who was the forerunner of Jesus and baptized him, was beheaded at Herod's command.
[4] l. 94 One of Jesus' miracles was to raise Lazarus from the dead. Prufrock feels like one of the living dead; by daring to tell the woman he desired how he felt, he might have raised himself from that condition.

At times, indeed, almost ridiculous—
Almost, at times, the Fool.[5]

120 I grow old . . . I grow old . . .
I shall wear the bottoms of my trousers rolled.

Shall I part my hair behind? Do I dare to eat a peach?
I shall wear white flannel trousers, and walk upon the beach.
I have heard the mermaids singing, each to each.

I do not think that they will sing to me.

I have seen them riding seaward on the waves
Combing the white hair of the waves blown back
When the wind blows the water white and black.

We have lingered in the chambers of the sea
130 By sea-girls wreathed with seaweed red and brown
Till human voices wake us, and we drown.[6]

1911   1917

[5] ll. 112–20 Prufrock notes rather bitterly that he hardly has the romantic stature of a Hamlet; the character in Shakespeare's play he most resembles is Polonius.
[6] ll. 125–31 These closing lines offer a purely lyrical song that expresses the dreaming pathos of the whole poem without any reference to the implied "story." Eliot's superb control of rhyme creates different tonalities throughout the poem. These tonalities—of the poem's complex sense of high dreams and low self-esteem, of rich traditions that torment us into self-deprecation—are embodied in the poem's lyric close and are far more essential than the implied "story" and "speaker."

Rhapsody on a Windy Night[1]

Twelve o'clock.
Along the reaches of the street
Held in a lunar synthesis,
Whispering lunar incantations
Dissolve the floors of memory
And all its clear relations
Its divisions and precisions,
Every street lamp that I pass
10 Beats like a fatalistic drum,
And through the spaces of the dark
Midnight shakes the memory
As a madman shakes a dead geranium.

    Half-past one,
The street-lamp sputtered,
The street-lamp muttered,
The street-lamp said, "Regard that woman
Who hesitates toward you in the light of the door
Which opens on her like a grin.
20 You see the border of her dress
Is torn and stained with sand,

[1] See comment in headnote on Eliot.

And you see the corner of her eye
Twists like a crooked pin."

The memory throws up high and dry
A crowd of twisted things;
A twisted branch upon the beach
Eaten smooth, and polished
As if the world gave up
The secret of its skeleton,
30   Stiff and white.
A broken spring in a factory yard,
Rust that clings to the form that the strength has left
Hard and curled and ready to snap.

Half-past two,
The street-lamp said,
"Remark the cat which flattens itself in the gutter,
Slips out its tongue
And devours a morsel of rancid butter."
So the hand of the child, automatic,
Slipped out and pocketed a toy that was running along the quay.
40   I could see nothing behind that child's eye.
I have seen eyes in the street
Trying to peer through lighted shutters,
And a crab one afternoon in a pool,
An old crab with barnacles on his back,
Gripped the end of a stick which I held him.

Half-past three,
The lamp sputtered,
The lamp muttered in the dark.
The lamp hummed:
50   "Regard the moon,
La lune ne garde aucune rancune,[2]
She winks a feeble eye,
She smiles into corners.
She smooths the hair of the grass.
The moon has lost her memory.
A washed-out smallpox cracks her face,
Her hand twists a paper rose,
That smells of dust and eau de Cologne,
She is alone
60   With all the old nocturnal smells
That cross and cross across her brain."
The reminiscence comes
Of sunless dry geraniums
And dust in crevices,
Smells of chestnuts in the streets,
And female smells in shuttered rooms,
And cigarettes in corridors
And cocktail smells in bars.

[2] **"La lune . . . rancune"** (French) The moon holds no grudges.

The lamp said,
70 "Four o'clock,
Here is the number on the door.
Memory!
You have the key,
The little lamp spreads a ring on the stair.
Mount.
The bed is open; the tooth-brush hangs on the wall,
Put your shoes at the door, sleep, prepare for life."

The last twist of the knife.

1911   1917

The Waste Land[1]

"Nam Sibyllam quidem Cumis ego ipse oculis meis vidi
in ampulla pendere, et cum illi pueri dicerent: Σίβυλλα
τί θέλεις; respondebat illa: ἀποθανεῖν θέλω.'[2]

For Ezra Pound
il miglior fabbro.[3]

I. THE BURIAL OF THE DEAD

April is the cruellest month, breeding
Lilacs out of the dead land, mixing
Memory and desire, stirring
Dull roots with spring rain.
Winter kept us warm, covering
Earth in forgetful snow, feeding

[1] See comment in headnote on Eliot. From Eliot's introductory note:

Not only the title, but the plan and a good deal of the incidental symbolism . . . were suggested by Miss Jessie L. Weston's book on the Grail legend: *From Ritual to Romance* (Cambridge). Indeed . . . Miss Weston's book will elucidate the difficulties of the poem much better than my notes . . . To another work of anthropology I am indebted in general, one which has influenced our generation profoundly; I mean *The Golden Bough* [by Sir James Frazer]; I have used especially the two volumes *Adonis, Attis, Osiris.* Anyone who is acquainted with these works will immediately recognize in the poem certain references to vegetation ceremonies.

The poem is also saturated with echoes of the Bible and other past literature, especially poetry, annotated by Eliot in detail.

[2] From the Latin *Satyricon* of Petronius (first century A.D.):

For I myself saw—yes, with my own eyes in Cumae—the Sybil hanging in her cage; and when those boys said, "Sybil, what would you like to have?" [*"Sybilla ti theleis'*], she answered, "I want to die." [*"apothanein thelo'*]

The quotation has to do with the legend of the sybil (prophetess) who was granted her wish to be immortal (hence the mocking question the boys ask) but forgot to ask for eternal youth as well and so grew ever older and wearier of life and shrank until so tiny she had to be kept in a cage. She serves as a symbol here of the shrunken, life-weary state of our civilization. (The dialogue is in Greek, the regular practice of educated Romans.)

[3] "For Ezra Pound, the better [or best] artist"—a recognition of Pound's stature and of his helpful editorial suggestions that echoes the tribute paid the Provençal poet Arnaut Daniel by another poet in Dante's *Purgatorio*, XXVI.117. For Pound's role, see T.S. Eliot, *The Waste Land: A Facsimile and Transcript of the Original Drafts Including the Annotations of Ezra Pound*, ed. Valerie Eliot (1971).

A little life with dried tubers.
Summer surprised us, coming over the Starnbergersee
With a shower of rain; we stopped in the colonnade,
10   And went on in sunlight, into the Hofgarten,[4]
And drank coffee, and talked for an hour.
Bin gar keine Russin, stamm' aus Litauen, echt deutsch.[5]
And when we were children, staying at the arch-duke's,
My cousin's, he took me out on a sled,
And I was frightened. He said, Marie,
Marie, hold on tight. And down we went.
In the mountains, there you feel free.
I read, much of the night, and go south in the winter.

What are the roots that clutch, what branches grow
20   Out of this stony rubbish? Son of man,[6]
You cannot say, or guess, for you know only
A heap of broken images, where the sun beats,
And the dead tree gives no shelter, the cricket no relief,[7]
And the dry stone no sound of water. Only
There is shadow under this red rock,
(Come in under the shadow of this red rock),
And I will show you something different from either
Your shadow at morning striding behind you
Or your shadow at evening rising to meet you;
30   I will show you fear in a handful of dust.
                    Frisch weht der Wind
                    Der Heimat zu
                    Mein Irisch Kind,
                    Wo weilest du?[8]
"You gave me hyacinths first a year ago;
"They called me the hyacinth girl."
—Yet when we came back, late, from the hyacinth garden,
Your arms full, and your hair wet, I could not
Speak, and my eyes failed, I was neither
40   Living nor dead, and I knew nothing,
Looking into the heart of light, the silence.
Oed' und leer das Meer.[9]

Madame Sosostris, famous clairvoyante,
Had a bad cold, nevertheless
Is known to be the wisest woman in Europe,
With a wicked pack of cards. Here, said she,

[4]ll. 8–10 **Starnbergersee** a lake near Munich,
Germany; **Hofgarten** a public park with a café
in Munich
[5]l. 12 (German) "I'm not at all Russian, come
from Lithuania, pure German."
[6]l. 20 "Cf. Ezekiel II, i" (Eliot's note).
[7]l. 23 "Cf. Ecclesiastes XII, v" (Eliot's note).
[8]ll. 31–34 "*Tristan und Isolde*, I, verse 5–8"
(Eliot's note). These German lines are sung by

a homesick sailor longing for his girl:
Fresh blows the wind
Towards my homeland.
My Irish girl [literally, child],
Where are you tarrying?
[9]l. 42 "*Tristan und Isolde*, III, verse 24"
(Eliot's note). The German words mean "empty
and wide the sea."

Is your card, the drowned Phoenician Sailor,
(Those are pearls that were his eyes. Look!)
Here is Belladonna, the Lady of the Rocks,
50   The lady of situations.
Here is the man with three staves, and here the Wheel,
And here is the one-eyed merchant, and this card,
Which is blank, is something he carries on his back,
Which I am forbidden to see. I do not find
The Hanged Man. Fear death by water.[10]
I see crowds of people, walking round in a ring.
Thank you. If you see dear Mrs. Equitone,
Tell her I bring the horoscope myself:
One must be so careful these days.

60   Unreal city,[11]
Under the brown fog of a winter dawn,
A crowd flowed over London Bridge, so many,
I had not thought death had undone so many.
Sighs, short and infrequent, were exhaled,
And each man fixed his eyes before his feet.[12]
Flowed up the hill and down King William Street,
To where Saint Mary Woolnoth kept the hours
With a dead sound on the final stroke of nine.
There I saw one I knew, and stopped him, crying: "Stetson!
70   "You who were with me in the ships at Mylae!
"That corpse you planted last year in your garden,
"Has it begun to sprout? Will it bloom this year?
"Or has the sudden frost disturbed its bed?
"O keep the Dog far hence, that's friend to men,
"Or with his nails he'll dig it up again![13]
"You! hypocrite lecteur!—mon semblable,—mon frère!"[14]

[10]ll. 46–56

I am not familiar with the exact constitution of the Tarot pack of cards, from which I have obviously departed to suit my own convenience. The Hanged Man . . . is associated in my mind with the Hanged God of Frazer, and . . . with the hooded figure in the passage of the disciples to Emmaus in Part V. The Phoenician Sailor and the Merchant appear later; also the "crowds of people," and Death by Water is executed in Part IV. The Man with Three Staves . . . I associate . . . with the Fisher King himself. (Eliot's note)

In one version of the Grail legend, the Fisher King's lands had become infertile; women had grown barren. Only a holy knight, overcoming all obstacles to reach the Chapel Perilous, could redeem the land. He would be given a vision of the Holy Grail (the cup containing Christ's blood), and fruitfulness would be restored. Eliot's poem parallels the legend by exploring the spiritual landscape both of the modern world and of a disturbed private psyche that needs to gather its resources to "shore" the "fragments" "against my ruin" (see lines 426 and 431).

[11]**Unreal city** See Charles Baudelaire, "Les Sept Vieillards" ("The Seven Old Men").

[12]ll. 64–65   "Cf. *Inferno*, III, 55–7" (Eliot's note).

[13]ll. 69–75   "Cf. the Dirge in Webster's *White Devil*" (Eliot's note). Eliot's parody of Webster's "But keep the wolf far thence, that's foe to men" seems to refer to hypocritical benefactors who misuse their power. The grotesque passage just preceding this seems to comment on World War I, recently ended, as a ritual slaying and burial of "that corpse" (i.e., those corpses) in anticipation that resurrection will follow. The grim sadness and sardonic tone of ll. 69–75 define the emotional state with which the whole poem copes.

[14]l. 76   "Baudelaire, Preface to *Fleurs du Mal* [Flowers of Evil]" (Eliot's note).

II. A GAME OF CHESS

The Chair she sat in, like a burnished throne,
Glowed on the marble, where the glass
Held up by standards wrought with fruited vines
80   From which a golden Cupidon peeped out
(Another hid his eyes behind his wing)
Doubled the flames of sevenbranched candelabra
Reflecting light upon the table as
The glitter of her jewels rose to meet it,
From satin cases poured in rich profusion.
In vials of ivory and coloured glass
Unstoppered, lurked her strange synthetic perfumes,
Unguent, powdered, or liquid—troubled, confused
And drowned the sense in odours; stirred by the air[15]
90   That freshened from the window, these ascended
In fattening the prolonged candle-flames,
Flung their smoke into the laquearia,[16]
Stirring the pattern on the coffered ceiling.
Huge sea-wood fed with copper
Burned green and orange, framed by the coloured stone,
In which sad light a carvèd dolphin swam.
Above the antique mantel was displayed
As though a window gave upon the sylvan scene
The change of Philomel, by the barbarous king
100   So rudely forced; yet there the nightingale
Filled all the desert with inviolable voice
And still she cried, and still the world pursues,[17]
"Jug Jug"[18] to dirty ears.
And other withered stumps of time
Were told upon the walls; staring forms
Leaned out, leaning, hushing the room enclosed.
Footsteps shuffled on the stair.
Under the firelight, under the brush, her hair
Spread out in fiery points
110   Glowed into words, then would be savagely still.

"My nerves are bad to-night. Yes, bad. Stay with me.
"Speak to me. Why do you never speak. Speak.
   "What are you thinking of? What thinking? What?
"I never know what you are thinking. Think."

I think we are in rats' alley
Where the dead men lost their bones.

---

[15] ll. 77–89 "Cf. *Antony and Cleopatra*, II, ii, l. 190" (Eliot's note).

[16] **laquearia** paneled ceiling

[17] ll. 97–102 **sylvan scene** "Milton, *Paradise Lost*, IV, 140" (Eliot's note); **Philomel . . . king** "Ovid, *Metamorphoses*, VI, Philomela" (Eliot's note)—references to the intrusion of evil on innocence (Satan's view of Eden, and the rape of Philomela by King Tereus).

[18] **"Jug Jug"** phrase used in Elizabethan poetry to suggest the nightingale's song, depreciating its beauty and the bird's association with the tragic Philomela, who was turned into a nightingale

"What is that noise?"
                    The wind under the door.[19]
"What is that noise now? What is the wind doing?"
120   Nothing again nothing.
                                        "Do
"You know nothing? Do you see nothing? Do you remember
"Nothing?"

        I remember
Those are pearls that were his eyes.[20]
"Are you alive, or not? Is there nothing in your head?"
                                        But
O O O O that Shakespeherian Rag—
It's so elegant
130 So intelligent
"What shall I do now? What shall I do?
"I shall rush out as I am, and walk the street
"With my hair down, so. What shall we do tomorrow?
What shall we ever do?"
                        The hot water at ten.
And if it rains, a closed car at four.
And we shall play a game of chess,
Pressing lidless eyes and waiting for a knock upon the door.[21]

When Lil's husband got demobbed, I said—
140 I didn't mince my words, I said to her myself,
HURRY UP PLEASE ITS TIME
Now Albert's coming back, make yourself a bit smart.
He'll want to know what you done with that money he gave you
To get yourself some teeth. He did, I was there.
You have them all out, Lil, and get a nice set,
He said, I swear, I can't bear to look at you.
And no more can't I, I said, and think of poor Albert,
He's been in the army four years, he wants a good time,
And if you don't give it him, there's others will, I said.
150 Oh is there, she said. Something o' that, I said.
Then I'll know who to thank, she said, and give me a straight look.
HURRY UP PLEASE ITS TIME
If you don't like it you can get on with it, I said.
Others can pick and choose if you can't.
But if Albert makes off, it won't be for lack of telling.
You ought to be ashamed, I said, to look so antique.
(And her only thirty-one.)
I can't help it, she said, pulling a long face,
It's them pills I took, to bring it off, she said.

---

[19]"Cf. Webster: 'Is the Wind in that door still?'"
(Eliot's note). The reference is to *The Devil's
Law Case* III. ii.162.
[20]ll. 125, 128–30 an allusion to Shakespeare's
The Tempest

[21]l. 138 "Cf. the game of chess in Middleton's
Women Beware Women" (Eliot's note).

160　(She's had five already, and nearly died of young George.)
　　　The chemist said it would be all right, but I've never been
　　　　　the same.
　　　You *are* a proper fool, I said.
　　　Well, if Albert won't leave you alone, there it is, I said,
　　　What you get married for if you don't want children?
　　　HURRY UP PLEASE ITS TIME
　　　Well, that Sunday Albert was home, they had a hot gammon,
　　　And they asked me in to dinner, to get the beauty of it hot—
　　　HURRY UP PLEASE ITS TIME
　　　HURRY UP PLEASE ITS TIME
170　Goonight Bill. Goonight Lou. Goonight May. Goonight.
　　　Ta ta. Goonight. Goonight.
　　　Good night, ladies, good night, sweet ladies, good night,
　　　　　good night.[22]

III. THE FIRE SERMON

　　　The river's tent is broken; the last fingers of leaf
　　　Clutch and sink into the wet bank. The wind
　　　Crosses the brown land, unheard. The nymphs are departed.
　　　Sweet Thames, run softly, till I end my song.[23]
　　　The river bears no empty bottles, sandwich papers,
　　　Silk handkerchiefs, cardboard boxes, cigarette ends
　　　Or other testimony of summer nights. The nymphs are departed.
180　And their friends, the loitering heirs of City directors;
　　　Departed, have left no addresses.
　　　By the waters of Leman I sat down and wept . . .[24]
　　　Sweet Thames, run softly till I end my song,
　　　Sweet Thames, run softly, for I speak not loud or long.
　　　But at my back in a cold blast I hear
　　　The rattle of the bones, and chuckle spread from ear to ear.

　　　A rat crept softly through the vegetation
　　　Dragging its slimy belly on the bank
　　　While I was fishing in the dull canal
190　On a winter evening round behind the gashouse
　　　Musing upon the king my brother's wreck
　　　And on the king my father's death before him.[25]
　　　White bodies naked on the low damp ground

[22]ll. 139–72　The characters are working-class people in an English pub. **demobbed** demobilized from the army after the war; HURRY UP PLEASE ITS TIME traditional warning of closing time in a pub; **chemist** druggist. The final line mingles echoes of Ophelia's pathetic farewell in *Hamlet* IV.v.72 and of popular song with the goodbyes of the people leaving the pub.

[23]l. 176　"Spenser, 'Prothalamion'" (Eliot's note)

[24]l. 182　See Psalm 137:1: a reference to the Babylonian captivity of the Jews that begins: "By the rivers of Babylon, there we sat down, yea, we wept, when we remembered Zion." Eliot substitutes "Leman"—a term for Lake Geneva (he wrote much of the poem in a sanatorium there) and a word suggesting sexual love since it also means "mistress"—for "Babylon," a place associated in the Bible with wantonness and with tragic history.

[25]ll. 191–92　"Cf. *The Tempest*, I, ii" (Eliot's note).

And bones cast in a little low dry garret,
Rattled by the rat's foot only, year to year.
But at my back from time to time I hear[26]
The sound of horns and motors, which shall bring[27]
Sweeney to Mrs. Porter in the spring.
O the moon shone bright on Mrs. Porter
200   And on her daughter
They wash their feet in soda water[28]
Et O ces voix d'enfants, chantant dans la coupole![29]

Twit twit twit
Jug jug jug jug jug jug
So rudely forc'd.
Tereu[30]

Unreal City
Under the brown fog of a winter noon
Mr. Eugenides, the Smyrna merchant
210   Unshaven, with a pocket full of currants
C.i.f. London: documents at sight,
Asked me in demotic French
To luncheon at the Cannon Street Hotel
Followed by a weekend at the Metropole.[31]

At the violet hour, when the eyes and back
Turn upward from the desk, when the human engine waits
Like a taxi throbbing waiting,
I Tiresias, though blind, throbbing between two lives,
Old man with wrinkled female breasts, can see
220   At the violet hour, the evening hour that strives
Homeward, and brings the sailor home from sea,
The typist home at teatime, clears her breakfast, lights
Her stove, and lays out food in tins.
Out of the window perilously spread
Her drying combinations touched by the sun's last rays,

---

[26]l. 196 "Cf. Marvell, 'To His Coy Mistress' " (Eliot's note).

[27]l. 197 "Cf. Day, 'Parliament of Bees' "— Eliot's note, which also quotes the following lines:
When of the sudden, listening, you shall hear,
A noise of horns and hunting, which shall bring
Actaeon to Diana in the spring,
Where all shall see her naked skin . . .
See note 1 to Pound's "The Coming of War: Actaeon" (p. 856 above).

[28]ll. 198–201 from a bawdy Australian parody of the American song "Little Redwing"

[29]l. 202 "Verlaine, *Parsifal*" (Eliot's note): "And O those voices of children, singing in the church-choir!" This joyful note of innocence heightens by contrast the many suggestions of uncontrolled lust and its human effects in "The Fire Sermon."

[30]ll. 203–06 Three of these lines indicate bird-sounds, including the nightingale's song. **So rudely forc'd** a reference to the rape of Philomela by Tereus (suggested also by the bird-sound "tereu"). See notes 17 and 18, above.

[31]ll. 209–14 "The currants were quoted at a price 'cost, insurance and freight to London'; and the bill of lading, etc., were to be handed to the buyer upon payment of the sight draft" (Eliot's note, as amended by Valerie Eliot). Mr. Eugenides, the unwholesome-looking Smyrna merchant whose name, ironically, suggests wholesome breeding, makes a probably homosexual approach—comparable in its casual grossness to the heterosexual scene in the succeeding passage.

On the divan are piled (at night her bed)
Stockings, slippers, camisoles, and stays.
I Tiresias, old man with wrinkled dugs
Perceived the scene, and foretold the rest—
230   I too awaited the expected guest.
He, the young man carbuncular, arrives,
A small house agent's clerk, with one bold stare,
One of the low on whom assurance sits
As a silk hat on a Bradford millionaire.
The time is now propitious, as he guesses,
The meal is ended, she is bored and tired,
Endeavours to engage her in caresses
Which still are unreproved, if undesired.
Flushed and decided, he assaults at once;
240   Exploring hands encounter no defence;
His vanity requires no response,
And makes a welcome of indifference.
(And I Tiresias have foresuffered all
Enacted on this same divan or bed;
I who have sat by Thebes below the wall
And walked among the lowest of the dead.)
Bestows one final patronising kiss,
And gropes his way, finding the stairs unlit . . .[32]

She turns and looks a moment in the glass,
250   Hardly aware of her departed lover;
Her brain allows one half-formed thought to pass:
"Well now that's done: and I'm glad it's over."
When lovely woman stoops to folly and
Paces about her room again, alone,
She smoothes her hair with automatic hand,
And puts a record on the gramophone.[33]

[32]ll. 215–48

Tiresias, although a mere spectator and not indeed a 'character,' is yet the most important personage in the poem, uniting all the rest. Just as the one-eyed merchant, seller of currants, melts into the Phoenician sailor, and the latter is not wholly distinct from Ferdinand Prince of Naples, so all the women are one woman, and the two sexes meet in Tiresias. What Tiresias *sees*, in fact, is the substance of the poem. The whole passage from Ovid is of great anthropological interest. . . . (Eliot's note).

Eliot completes this note with a Latin quotation from Ovid's *Metamorphoses* II. 421–43: Jupiter told his wife, Juno, that he thought women took greater pleasure in love than men; she disagreed, and they asked Tiresias to decide, since he knew love both as a man and as a woman. (After seeing two snakes copulating, he had beaten them with his staff, and been

changed into a woman for seven years; he was changed back when he again saw the snakes copulating and once more attacked them.) Because Tiresias agreed with Jupiter, Juno struck him blind; but to compensate, Jupiter gave him the gift of prophecy. At this moment in Eliot's poem, Tiresias embodies the widest range of human awareness and sensibility.

[33]ll. 253–56 "Goldsmith, the song in *The Vicar of Wakefield*" (Eliot's note). Goldsmith's lines are sung by a seduced woman:

When lovely woman stoops to folly,
  And finds too late that men betray,
What charm can sooth her melancholy,
  What art can wash her guilt away?

The only art her guilt to cover,
  To hide her shame from every eye,
To give repentance to her lover,
  And wring his bosom—is to die.

"This music crept by me upon the waters"[34]
And along the Strand, up Queen Victoria Street.
O City city, I can sometimes hear
260 Beside a public bar in Lower Thames Street,
The pleasant whining of a mandoline
And a clatter and a chatter from within
Where fishmen lounge at noon: where the walls
Of Magnus Martyr[35] hold
Inexplicable splendour of Ionian white and gold.

        The river sweats
        Oil and tar
        The barges drift
        With the turning tide
270   Red sails
        Wide
        To leeward, swing on the heavy spar.
        The barges wash
        Drifting logs
        Down Greenwich reach
        Past the Isle of Dogs.
                Weialala leia
                Wallala leialala

        Elizabeth and Leicester
280   Beating oars
        The stern was formed
        A gilded shell
        Red and gold
        The brisk swell
        Rippled both shores
        Southwest wind
        Carried down stream
        The peal of bells
        White towers
290   Weialala leia
            Wallala leialala

"Trams and dusty trees.
Highbury bore me. Richmond and Kew
Undid me. By Richmond I raised my knees
Supine on the floor of a narrow canoe."

"My feet are at Moorgate, and my heart
Under my feet. After the event
He wept. He promised 'a new start.'
I made no comment. What should I resent?"

[34]l. 257 See *The Tempest* I.ii.391.
[35]**Magnus Martyr** the Church of St. Magnus
Martyr in London

300 "On Margate Sands.
I can connect
Nothing with nothing.
The broken fingernails of dirty hands.
My people humble people who expect
Nothing."
   la la[36]

To Carthage then I came

Burning burning burning burning
O Lord Thou pluckest me out
310 O Lord Thou pluckest

burning[37]

IV. DEATH BY WATER

Phlebas the Phoenician, a fortnight dead,[38]
Forgot the cry of gulls, and the deep sea swell
And the profit and loss.
   A current under sea
Picked his bones in whispers. As he rose and fell
He passed the stages of his age and youth
Entering the whirlpool.
   Gentile or Jew
320 O you who turn the wheel and look to windward,
Consider Phlebas, who was once handsome and tall as you.

V. WHAT THE THUNDER SAID[39]

After the torchlight red on sweaty faces
After the frosty silence in the gardens
After the agony in stony places
The shouting and the crying

[36]ll. 266–306 "The Song of the (three) Thames-daughters begins here. From line 292 to 396 inclusive they speak in turn" (Eliot's note, which also refers us to Wagner's *Götterdämmerung* III.i: the song of the Rhine-daughters, quoted in ll. 277–78 and 290–91).

The Isle of Dogs is a peninsula in the Thames opposite Greenwich, where Queen Elizabeth I was born; Moorgate is a slum-section of London; Margate Sands was a resort spot. "Elizabeth and Leicester" alludes to the queen's love-affair with the Earl of Leicester and an outing together on the royal barge on the Thames. In contrast, poor girls tell of loveless seductions, which they are too humble even to resent. "Lines 293–94 echo Dante's *Purgatorio*, V, 133" (Eliot's note). Eliot's note quotes two lines spoken by a Sienese woman seduced in Maremma:

Remember me, who am la Pia;
 Siena made me, Maremma undid me.
[37]ll. 307–311 The lines using the word "burning" are from Buddha's Fire Sermon, which Eliot's note says "corresponds in importance to the Sermon on the Mount." The other lines are from St. Augustine's *Confessions*; Eliot's note quotes part of a sentence: "to Carthage then I came, where a cauldron of unholy loves sang all about mine ears."
[38]**Phlebas the Phoenician** a name apparently invented by Eliot
[39]"In the first part of Part V three themes are employed: the journey to Emmaus, the approach to Chapel Perilous (see Miss Weston's book) and the present decay of eastern Europe" (Eliot's note).

Prison and palace and reverberation
Of thunder of spring over distant mountains
He who was living is now dead
We who were living are now dying
330 With a little patience

Here is no water but only rock
Rock and no water and the sandy road
The road winding above among the mountains
Which are mountains of rock without water
If there were water we should stop and drink
Amongst the rock one cannot stop or think
Sweat is dry and feet are in the sand
If there were only water amongst the rock
Dead mountain mouth of carious teeth that cannot spit
340 Here one can neither stand nor lie nor sit
There is not even silence in the mountains
But dry sterile thunder without rain
There is not even solitude in the mountains
But red sullen faces sneer and snarl
From doors of mudcracked houses
                              If there were water

        And no rock
        If there were rock
        And also water
350   And water
        A spring
        A pool among the rock
        If there were the sound of water only
        Not the cicada
        And dry grass singing
        But sound of water over a rock
        Where the hermit-thrush sings in the pine trees
        Drip drop drip drop drop drop drop[40]
        But there is no water

360 Who is the third who walks always beside you?
When I count, there are only you and I together
But when I look ahead up the white road
There is always another one walking beside you
Gliding wrapt in a brown mantle, hooded
I do not know whether a man or a woman
—But who is that on the other side of you?[41]

---

[40] ll. 357–58 the hermit-thrush Eliot's note quotes from Chapman's *Handbook of Birds of Eastern North America*: "Its notes are not remarkable for variety or volume, but in purity and sweetness of tone and exquisite modulation they are unequalled." Eliot writes: "Its 'water-dripping song' is justly celebrated."

[41] ll. 360–66 These lines "were stimulated by the account of one of the Antarctic expeditions . . .; it was related that . . . at the extremity of their strength [they] had the constant delusion that there was *one more member* than could actually be counted" (Eliot's note).

What is that sound high in the air
Murmur of maternal lamentation
Who are those hooded hordes swarming
370 Over endless plains, stumbling in cracked earth
Ringed by the flat horizon only
What is the city over the mountains
Cracks and reforms and bursts in the violet air
Falling towers
Jerusalem Athens Alexandria
Vienna London
Unreal

A woman drew her long black hair out tight
And fiddled whisper music on those strings
380 And bats with baby faces in the violet light
Whistled, and beat their wings
And crawled head downward down a blackened wall
And upside down in air were towers
Tolling reminiscent bells, that kept the hours
And voices singing out of empty cisterns and exhausted wells

In this decayed hole among the mountains
In the faint moonlight, the grass is singing
Over the tumbled graves, about the chapel
There is the empty chapel, only the wind's home.
390 It has no windows, and the door swings,
Dry bones can harm no one.
Only a cock stood on the rooftree
Co co rico co co rico
In a flash of lightning. Then a damp gust
Bringing rain

Ganga[42] was sunken, and the limp leaves
Waited for rain, while the black clouds
Gathered far distant, over Himavant.
The jungle crouched, humped in silence.
400 Then spoke the thunder
DA
Datta: what have we given?[43]
My friend, blood shaking my heart
The awful daring of a moment's surrender
Which an age of prudence can never retract
By this, and this only, we have existed
Which is not to be found in our obituaries
Or in memories draped by the beneficent spider[44]
Or under seals broken by the lean solicitor

[42]**Ganga** the Ganges River, sacred to Hindus
[43]ll. 402, 412, 419 " 'Datta, dayadhvam, damyata' (Give, sympathise, control). The fable of the meaning of the Thunder is found in the *Brihadaranyaka — Upanishad*" (Eliot's note).
[44]**beneficent spider** "Cf. Webster, The White Devil, V, vi" (Eliot's note).

410   In our empty rooms
        DA
        Dayadhvam: I have heard the key
        Turn in the door once and turn once only
        We think of the key, each in his prison
        Thinking of the key, each confirms a prison[45]
        Only at nightfall, aethereal rumours
        Revive for a moment a broken Coriolanus
        DA
        Damyata: The boat responded
420   Gaily, to the hand expert with sail and oar
        The sea was calm, your heart would have responded
        Gaily, when invited, beating obedient
        To controlling hands

                   I sat upon the shore
        Fishing, with the arid plain behind me[46]
        Shall I at least set my lands in order?
        London Bridge is falling down falling down falling down
        Poi s'ascose nel foco che gli affina[47]
        Quando fiam uti chelidon—O swallow swallow[48]
430   *Le Prince d'Aquitaine à la tour abolie*[49]
        These fragments I have shored against my ruins
        Why then Ile fit you. Hieronymo's mad againe.[50]
        Datta. Dayadhvam. Damyata.
             Shantih   shantih   shantih[51]
    1921   1922

[45]ll. 412–15 "Cf. *Inferno*, XXXIII, 46" (Eliot's note). The reference is to Ugolino's account of his children's starving to death while in prison with him. Eliot's note also quotes a passage from F.H. Bradley's *Appearance and Reality*, p. 346, that connects with Eliot's sense of imprisonment within oneself.

[46]l. 425 "Weston: *From Ritual to Romance*; chapter on the Fisher King" (Eliot's note)

[47]l. 428 "*Purgatorio*: XXVI, 148" (Eliot's note). In this passage the poet Arnaut Daniel has confessed his lusts, then re-entered the purgatorial fire: "Then he hid himself in the fire that refines them."

[48]l. 429 "*Pervigilium Veneris*. Cf. Philomela in Parts II and III" (Eliot's note). The allusion is to an anonymous Latin poem in which the

swallow is substituted for the nightingale in the Philomela myth, and the poet wishes to be able to sing as beautifully: "When shall I be like the swallow?" The words "swallow, swallow" begin a song in Tennyson's *The Princess*.

[49]l. 430 "Gerard de Nerval, Sonnet 'El Desdichado' " (Eliot's note). The French quotation, "The Prince of Aquitaine in the ruined tower," suggests the sense of loss, of isolation, and of a ruined self and civilization that haunts the whole poem.

[50]l. 432 "Kyd's *Spanish Tragedy*" (Eliot's note)

[51]l. 434 "Shantih. Repeated as here, a formal ending to an Upanishad [a sacred Hindu writing]. 'The peace which passeth understanding' is our equivalent to this word" (Eliot's note).

Journey of the Magi[1]

    "A cold coming we had of it,
    Just the worst time of the year
    For a journey, and such a long journey:

[1] See note 1 to W.B. Yeats, "The Magi" (p. 770 above) and headnote on Eliot.

The ways deep and the weather sharp,
The very dead of winter.''[2]
And the camels galled, sore-footed, refractory,
Lying down in the melting snow.
There were times we regretted
The summer palaces on slopes, the terraces,
10   And the silken girls bringing sherbet.
Then the camel men cursing and grumbling
And running away, and wanting their liquor and women,
And the night-fires going out, and the lack of shelters,
And the cities hostile and the towns unfriendly
And the villages dirty and charging high prices:
A hard time we had of it.
At the end we preferred to travel all night,
Sleeping in snatches,
With the voices singing in our ears, saying
20   That this was all folly.

Then at dawn we came down to a temperate valley,
Wet, below the snow line, smelling of vegetation,
With a running stream and a water-mill beating the darkness,
And three trees on the low sky.
And an old white horse galloped away in the meadow.
Then we came to a tavern with vine-leaves over the lintel,
Six hands at an open door dicing for pieces of silver,
And feet kicking the empty wine-skins.
But there was no information, and so we continued
30   And arrived at evening, not a moment too soon
Finding the place; it was (you may say) satisfactory.

All this was a long time ago, I remember,
And I would do it again, but set down
This set down
This: were we led all that way for
Birth or Death? There was a Birth, certainly,
We had evidence and no doubt. I had seen birth and death,
But had thought they were different; this Birth was
Hard and bitter agony for us, like Death, our death.
40   We returned to our places, these Kingdoms,
But no longer at ease here, in the old dispensation,
With an alien people clutching their gods.
I should be glad of another death.[3]

1927

[2] ll. 1–5 The quoted lines are adapted from a sermon by the seventeenth-century Anglican bishop Lancelot Andrewes. One change in the text is from the third to the first person, since one of the Magi is speaking here. See Eliot's "Lancelot Andrewes" in his *Selected Essays*.

[3] l. 43 See the epigraph to *The Waste Land* and note 2 (p. 889 above). The Cumaean Sibyl wanted to die because she had been reduced to a living death; the Magus here has a comparable spiritual experience, but the situation also involves coping with a painfully altered perspective, however valuable. (In 1927, the year he composed this poem, Eliot became a British subject and an Anglican—decisions based on intellectual conviction but entailing serious emotional adjustments.)

Marina[1]

Quis hic locus, quae
regio, quae mundi plaga?[2]

What seas what shores what grey rocks and what islands
What water lapping the bow
And scent of pine and the woodthrush singing through the fog
What images return
O my daughter.

Those who sharpen the tooth of the dog, meaning
Death
Those who glitter with the glory of the hummingbird, meaning
Death
10 Those who sit in the sty of contentment, meaning
Death
Those who suffer the ecstasy of the animals, meaning
Death

Are become unsubstantial, reduced by a wind,
A breath of pine, and the woodsong fog
By this grace dissolved in place

What is this face, less clear and clearer
The pulse in the arm, less strong and stronger—
Given or lent? more distant than stars and nearer than the eye

20 Whispers and small laughter between leaves and hurrying feet
Under sleep, where all the waters meet.

Bowsprit cracked with ice and paint cracked with heat.
I made this, I have forgotten
And remember.
The rigging weak and the canvas rotten
Between one June and another September.
Made this unknowing, half conscious, unknown, my own.
The garboard strake leaks, the seams need caulking.
This form, this face, this life
30 Living to live in a world of time beyond me; let me
Resign my life for this life, my speech for that unspoken,
The awakened, lips parted, the hope, the new ships.

What seas what shores what granite islands towards my timbers
And woodthrush calling through the fog
My daughter.

1930

---

[1] See Shakespeare, *Pericles* V.i—the recognition
scene between Pericles and his daughter Marina;
see comment in headnote on Eliot.

[2] Seneca, *Hercules Furens*: "What place is this,
what / region, what corner of the world?"

From Four Quartets

Burnt Norton[1]

τοῦ λόγου δ'ἐόντος ξυνοῦ ζώουσιν οἱ πολλοί
ὡς ἰδίαν ἔχοντες φρόνησιν.

l. p. 77. Fr. 2

ὁδὸς ἄνω κάτω μία καὶ ὡυτή.

l. p. 89. Fr. 60

Diels: *Die Fragmente der Vorsokratiker* (Herakleitos).[2]

I

Time present and time past
Are both perhaps present in time future,
And time future contained in time past.
If all time is eternally present
All time is unredeemable.
What might have been is an abstraction
Remaining a perpetual possibility
Only in a world of speculation.
What might have been and what has been
10   Point to one end, which is always present.
Footfalls echo in the memory
Down the passage which we did not take
Towards the door we never opened
Into the rose-garden. My words echo
Thus, in your mind.
                    But to what purpose
Disturbing the dust on a bowl of rose-leaves
I do not know.
                    Other echoes
20   Inhabit the garden. Shall we follow?
Quick, said the bird, find them, find them,
Round the corner. Through the first gate,
Into our first world, shall we follow
The deception of the thrush? Into our first world.
There they were, dignified, invisible,
Moving without pressure, over the dead leaves,
In the autumn heat, through the vibrant air,
And the bird called, in response to
The unheard music hidden in the shrubbery,
And the unseen eyebeam crossed, for the roses

---

[1] a Cotswold manor house, now mostly neglected and its history forgotten, with an old rose garden and a now-empty concrete pool. This is the first of a sequence of four poems, following the same overall five-part structure, that appeared separately over several years. The title of each poem is a British or American place-name that evokes for the poet an acute awareness of the continuing presence of past realities and a teasing illusion of epiphany and mystical timelessness.

[2] sayings of the Greek philosopher Heraclitus (sixth century B.C.): "Although a single law governs all things, people live as if everyone existed in a special way." "The way up and the way down are one and the same."

Had the look of flowers that are looked at.
30 There they were as our guests, accepted and accepting.
So we moved, and they, in a formal pattern,
Along the empty alley, into the box circle,
To look down into the drained pool.
Dry the pool, dry concrete, brown edged,
And the pool was filled with water out of sunlight,
And the lotos rose, quietly, quietly,
The surface glittered out of heart of light,
And they were behind us, reflected in the pool.
Then a cloud passed, and the pool was empty.[3]
40 Go, said the bird, for the leaves were full of children,
Hidden excitedly, containing laughter.
Go, go, go, said the bird: human kind
Cannot bear very much reality.
Time past and time future
What might have been and what has been
Point to one end, which is always present.

II

Garlic and sapphires in the mud
Clot the bedded axle-tree.[4]
The trilling wire in the blood
50 Sings below inveterate scars
Appeasing long forgotten wars.
The dance along the artery
The circulation of the lymph
Are figured in the drift of stars
Ascend to summer in the tree
We move above the moving tree
In light upon the figured leaf
And hear upon the sodden floor
Below, the boarhound and the boar
60 Pursue their pattern as before
But reconciled among the stars.

At the still point of the turning world. Neither flesh nor fleshless;
Neither from nor towards; at the still point, there the dance is,
But neither arrest nor movement. And do not call it fixity,
Where past and future are gathered. Neither movement from nor towards,
Neither ascent nor decline. Except for the point, the still point,
There would be no dance, and there is only the dance.

[3] ll. 22–38   These lines project a mystical vision and suggest a revelation of timeless bliss in the image of the lotus, sacred symbolic flower of the Hindu religion.
[4] ll. 47–48   These two lines introduce a hymn of praise (ll. 47–61) for the intricately repeated design that reveals itself throughout the universe. The reconciling of opposites in the very substance of the earth ("garlic and sapphires in the mud") and principle of its turning ("the bedded axle-tree") is a promise of ultimate transcendence ("reconciled among the stars"). An image of Mallarmé's—"thunder and rubies at the axles" ("tonnère et rubis aux moyeux")—in "M'introduire dans ton histoire" is a probable nineteenth-century source of these lines.

I can only say, *there* we have been: but I cannot say where.
And I cannot say, how long, for that is to place it in time.

70 The inner freedom from the practical desire,
The release from action and suffering, release from the inner
And the outer compulsion, yet surrounded
By a grace of sense, a white light still and moving,
Erhebung[5] without motion, concentration
Without elimination, both a new world
And the old made explicit, understood
In the completion of its partial ecstasy,
The resolution of its partial horror.
Yet the enchainment of past and future
80 Woven in the weakness of the changing body,
Protects mankind from heaven and damnation
Which flesh cannot endure.
                                Time past and time future
Allow but a little consciousness.
To be conscious is not to be in time
But only in time can the moment in the rose-garden,
The moment in the arbour where the rain beat,
The moment in the draughty church at smokefall
Be remembered; involved with past and future.
90 Only through time time is conquered.

                III
Here is a place of disaffection[6]
Time before and time after
In a dim light: neither daylight
Investing form with lucid stillness
Turning shadow into transient beauty
With slow rotation suggesting permanence
Nor darkness to purify the soul
Emptying the sensual with deprivation
Cleansing affection from the temporal.
Neither plentitude nor vacancy. Only a flicker
100 Over the strained time-ridden faces
Distracted from distraction by distraction
Filled with fancies and empty of meaning
Tumid apathy with no concentration
Men and bits of paper, whirled by the cold wind
That blows before and after time,
Wind in and out of unwholesome lungs
Time before and time after.

[5] *Erhebung*   (German) elevation or exaltation
[6] ll. 90–113   The "place of disaffection" is lit-
erally the atmosphere of the London underground
system, but it is also the psychological state of
anomie or depressed distancing from spiritual
vitality. See St. John of the Cross, *The Dark of
the Soul* II.vi.4. The place-names are parts of
London or names of underground stations.

Eructation of unhealthy souls
Into the faded air, the torpid
110 Driven on the wind that sweeps the gloomy hills of London,
Hampstead and Clerkenwell, Campden and Putney,
Highgate, Primrose and Ludgate. Not here
Not here the darkness, in this twittering world.

Descend lower, descend only
Into the world of perpetual solitude,
World not world, but that which is not world,
Internal darkness, deprivation
And destitution of all property,
Desiccation of the world of sense,
120 Evacuation of the world of fancy,
Inoperancy of the world of spirit;
This is the one way, and the other
Is the same, not in movement
But abstention from movement; while the world moves
In appetency, on its metalled ways
Of time past and time future.

IV

Time and the bell have buried the day,
The black cloud carries the sun away.
Will the sunflower turn to us, will the clematis
130 Stray down, bend to us; tendril and spray
Clutch and cling?
Chill
Fingers of yew be curled
Down on us? After the kingfisher's wing
Has answered light to light, and is silent, the light is still
At the still point of the turning world.

V

Words move, music moves
Only in time; but that which is only living
Can only die. Words, after speech, reach
140 Into the silence. Only by the form, the pattern,
Can words or music reach
The stillness, as a Chinese jar still
Moves perpetually in its stillness.
Not the stillness of the violin, while the note lasts,
Not that only, but the co-existence,
Or say that the end precedes the beginning,
And the end and the beginning were always there
Before the beginning and after the end.
And all is always now. Words strain,
150 Crack and sometimes break, under the burden,
Under the tension, slip, slide, perish,

Decay with imprecision, will not stay in place,
Will not stay still. Shrieking voices
Scolding, mocking, or merely chattering,
Always assail them. The Word in the desert
Is most attacked by voices of temptation,[7]
The crying shadow in the funeral dance,
The loud lament of the disconsolate chimera.[8]

The detail of the pattern is movement,
160 As in the figure of the ten stairs.[9]
Desire itself is movement
Not in itself desirable;
Love is itself unmoving,
Only the cause and end of movement,
Timeless, and undesiring
Except in the aspect of time
Caught in the form of limitation
Between un-being and being.
Sudden in a shaft of sunlight
170 Even while the dust moves
There rises the hidden laughter
Of children in the foliage
Quick now, here, now, always—
Ridiculous the waste sad time
Stretching before and after.

1936

[7] ll. 155–56 Christ's temptation in the desert. See Luke 4:1–4.

[8] **disconsolate chimera** A chimera is a fabulous monster; here, a creation of depressed fantasy and self-torment militating against sustained faith.

[9] See St. John of the Cross, *The Ascent of Mt. Carmel* II.i.1. The "ten stairs" are on "the ladder of contemplation" leading the soul toward God through darkness or immediate exaltation. ("The way up and the way down are one and the same.")

JOHN CROWE RANSOM
1888–1974

A graduate of Vanderbilt University, Ransom attended Oxford University as a Rhodes Scholar from 1910 to 1913. He taught at Vanderbilt (1914–37) and at Kenyon College (1937–59), where he founded and edited the influential *Kenyon Review*. He is strongly identified with the tendencies in literary theory that he described in *The New Criticism* (1941). The "new critics," much affected by the thinking of Ezra Pound, T.S. Eliot,

and I.A. Richards, turned their attention (in different ways) to the close study of the literary work itself—its structure, texture, tensions, qualities of ambiguity and irony, and patterns of form and emotive suggestion —and away from exclusive concern with literary history, influence, and textual scholarship. In their attempt to objectify the way poems and other literary works create their effects, they also carried criticism away from the prevailing emphasis on private sensitivity of response ("impressionist criticism") and moral judgment.

Ransom remains the most durable poet among the Southern writers who founded the short-lived magazine *Fugitive* (1922–25) and started a movement devoted to regional values and conservative politics. His brief elegies, such as "Bells for John Whiteside's Daughter" and "Dead Boy"—especially the latter—have an acrid edge of psychological realism that sharpens their grieving sweetness. "Janet Waking," though not a pure elegy, mourns the end of a little girl's innocence about death. Ransom had a great gift for combining delicate and tender tones, simple melodic language, colloquial turns, and gaudily chivalric phrasing and knew how to put wit at the service of strong feeling.

Bells for John Whiteside's Daughter

There was such speed in her little body,
And such lightness in her footfall,
It is no wonder her brown study
Astonishes us all.

Her wars were bruited in our high window.
We looked among orchard trees and beyond
Where she took arms against her shadow,
Or harried unto the pond

10 The lazy geese, like a snow cloud
Dripping their snow on the green grass,
Tricking and stopping, sleepy and proud,
Who cried in goose, Alas,

For the tireless heart within the little
Lady with rod that made them rise
From their noon apple-dreams and scuttle
Goose-fashion under the skies!

But now go the bells, and we are ready,
In one house we are sternly stopped
To say we are vexed at her brown study,
20 Lying so primly propped.

      1924

Janet Waking

Beautifully Janet slept
Till it was deeply morning. She woke then
And thought about her dainty-feathered hen,
To see how it had kept.

One kiss she gave her mother.
Only a small one gave she to her daddy
Who would have kissed each curl of his shining baby;
No kiss at all for her brother.

"Old Chucky, old Chucky!" she cried,
10   Running across the world upon the grass
To Chucky's house, and listening. But alas,
Her Chucky had died.

It was a transmogrifying bee
Came droning down on Chucky's old bald head
And sat and put the poison. It scarcely bled,
But how exceedingly

And purply did the knot
Swell with the venom and communicate
Its rigor! Now the poor comb stood up straight
20   But Chucky did not.

So there was Janet
Kneeling on the wet grass, crying her brown hen
(Translated far beyond the daughters of men)
To rise and walk upon it.

And weeping fast as she had breath
Janet implored us, "Wake her from her sleep!"
And would not be instructed in how deep
Was the forgetful kingdom of death.

                  1927

Dead Boy

The little cousin is dead, by foul subtraction,
A green bough from Virginia's aged tree,
And none of the county kin like the transaction,
Nor some of the world of outer dark, like me.

A boy not beautiful, nor good, nor clever,
A black cloud full of storms too hot for keeping,
A sword beneath his mother's heart—yet never
Woman bewept her babe as this is weeping.

A pig with a pasty face, so I had said,
10   Squealing for cookies, kinned by poor pretense
With a noble house. But the little man quite dead,
I see the forbears' antique lineaments.

The elder men have strode by the box of death
To the wide flag porch, and muttering low send round
The bruit of the day. O friendly waste of breath!
Their hearts are hurt with a deep dynastic wound.

He was pale and little, the foolish neighbors say;
The first-fruits, saith the Preacher, the Lord hath taken;
But this was the old tree's late branch wrenched away,
20   Grieving the sapless limbs, the shorn and shaken.

1927

HUGH MacDIARMID
(CHRISTOPHER GRIEVE)
1892-1978

Hugh MacDiarmid was the pen-name of Christopher Grieve, the son of a rural Scottish postman. He took the pseudonym to show that he was writing as a Scot and not as an Englishman. He helped found the Scottish Nationalist party in 1934 and edited the *Voice of Scotland*, the party's quarterly magazine. But over a dozen years earlier he had plunged into the study of Scotland's history and native literary traditions. Few of his countrymen knew anything of the rich achievement of such late medieval Scots poets as Dunbar, Douglas, and Henryson; in MacDiarmid's view, the wide popularity of Robert Burns's poetry was exploited in modern Scotland by sentimental Philistines with no real interest in literature, and he set himself the task of reviving the great Scottish poetic tradition.

Because his greatest lyric poetry is in Scots, MacDiarmid is scarcely known to general readers outside his native land. But he is much admired by poets everywhere, especially for his pioneering poetic sequence, *A Drunk Man Looks at the Thistle* (1926): a grouping of poems in every possible mood —romantic, polemical, politically militant, mystically entranced, bawdy—all built around the events of a single drunken evening. Two of them are given here—the passionately bemused "Love" and the eerie modern ballad "O Wha's the Bride." Along with the energetic, affectionate vignette "Old

Wife in High Spirits," these poems will suggest the quality of MacDiarmid's talent, despite their diction which is as "foreign" as that of an old Scottish ballad. The Braid Scots (Broad Scottish) in which they are written is an English-language dialect. The reader soon grows to recognize its many variants from standard English. (See GLOSSARY, below.)

A gentle person in private life, MacDiarmid was a nationalist, a Communist, and a bank-credit reformist all at once— and thought of himself as a bohemian revolutionary out to shock and overthrow respectably genteel authority. Nevertheless, he was honored in 1950 with a Civil List pension and in 1957 with an honorary LL.D. from Edinburgh University, where he had been a student almost a half-century before. Something of his hard, misfortune-dogged life may be gleaned from the ironically titled autobiography *Lucky Poet* (1943), written after eight miserable years (1933–41) of rugged existence in the Shetland Islands and four years as a factory and shipboard worker during World War II. The name of one of his important works, *First Hymn to Lenin* (1931), will suggest his significant place in the revolutionary poetic movement of that period, which included figures like W.H. Auden in England and Kenneth Fearing in the United States. The power and scope of his best work give him a unique place in modern Scotland and in modern letters, although he wrote far too much in his effort to combine his roles of poet, intransigent activist, and didactic instructor. At once intimately regional and earnestly cosmopolitan, he presents an intellectual personality as individual, contradictory, and controversial as Ezra Pound's.

GLOSSARY

a all; ane owre the eight one (minute) past eight; anither another; auld old; bane bone; bleezin' blazing; blinterin' glittering; breists breasts; cairries carries; cam' came; carline hag; cauld cold; chitterin' shivering; cratur creature; creeshy fattened; dagonit (interjection); deed died; doot doubt; dowie dispirited; dreids guesses; dune weary; endit ended; fleerin' flaring; frae from; gane gone; gie, gi'e give; gied, gi'ed gave; guid good; hae, ha'e have; haud hold; haurdly hardly; hed had; heich high, manically wild; hoo how; ilka every; juist just; ken know; kir wanton; kythed appeared; laneliness loneliness; lauchin' laughing; licht light; lichtnin' lightning; loupit leaped; mair more; muckle much; nae no; naething nothing; nesh nervously alert; nicht night; ocht aught; oot out; or ere, before; owre over, past; plicht plight; raither rather; rickle heap; sae so; sall shall; scunnersome disgusting; shairly surely; sin since; sinnen sinew; skeich spirited; skites skates, streaks by quickly; souple supple; syne then; tashed ruined; thegither together; tipenny tuppenny (old twopence); troot trout; weel well; wha who; whiles at times; wi' with; wrocht wrought; yin one.

Love[1]

A luvin' wumman is a licht
That shows a man his waefu' plicht,
Bleezin' steady on ilka bane,
Wrigglin' sinnen an' twinin' vein,
Or fleerin' quick an' gane again,
And the mair scunnersome the sicht
The mair for love and licht he's fain
Till clear and chitterin' and nesh
Move a' the miseries o' his flesh. . . .

1926

[1] "Suggested by the French of Edmond Rocher" (MacDiarmid's note)

O Wha's the Bride?

O wha's the bride that cairries the bunch
O' thistles blinterin' white?
Her cuckold bridegroom little dreids
What he sall ken this nicht.

For closer than gudeman can come
And closer to'r than hersel',
Wha didna need her maidenheid
Has wrocht his purpose fell.

10   O wha's been here afore me, lass,
    And hoo did he get in?
    —*A man that deed or was I born*
    This evil thing has din.

    And left, as it were on a corpse,
    Your maidenheid to me?
    —*Nae lass, gudeman, sin' Time began*
    'S hed ony mair to gi'e.

    But I can gi'e ye kindness, lad,
    And a pair o' willin' hands,
    And you sall ha'e my breists like stars,
20   *My limbs like willow wands.*

    And on my lips ye'll heed nae mair,
    And in my hair forget,
    The seed o' a' the men that in
    My virgin womb ha'e met. . . .

1926

Old Wife in High Spirits

In an Edinburgh Pub

An auld wumman cam' in, a mere rickle o' banes, in a faded black dress
And a bonnet wi' beads o' jet rattlin' on it;
A puir-lookin' cratur, you'd think she could haurdly ha'e had less
Life left in her and still lived, but dagonit!

He gied her a stiff whisky—she was nervous as a troot
And could haurdly haud the tumbler, puir cratur;
Syne he gied her anither, joked wi' her, and anither, and syne
Wild as the whisky up cam' her nature.

    The rod that struck water frae the rock in the desert
10   Was naething to the life that sprang oot o' her;
    The dowie auld soul was twinklin' and fizzin' wi' fire;
    You never saw ocht sae souple and kir.

Like a sackful o' monkeys she was, and her lauchin'
Loupit up whiles to incredible heights;
Wi' ane owre the eight her temper changed and her tongue
Flew juist as the forkt lichtnin' skites.

    The heich skeich auld cat was fair in her element;
    Wanton as a whirlwind, and shairly better that way
    Than a' crippin thegither wi'laneliness and cauld
20   Like a foretaste o' the graveyaird clay.

Some folk nae doot'll condemn gie'in' a guid spree
To the puir dune body and raither she endit her days
Like some auld tashed copy o' the Bible yin sees
On a street book-barrow's tipenny trays.

A' I ken is weel-fed and weel-put-on though they be
Ninety per cent o' respectable folk never hae
As muckle life in their creeshy carcases frae beginnin' to end
As kythed in that wild auld carline that day!

1962

WILFRED OWEN
1893–1918

Born into a devout, relatively poor family, Owen studied in a technical school, began university work but could not afford to continue, and then made a brief stab at preparing himself for a church career. Having decided he had insufficient faith, he spent several years tutoring in France and perfecting his French. In 1915 he returned to England and enlisted in the army. After training, Owen was commissioned and sent to France in January 1917. The bitter winter, a concussion from a bad fall, and the stress of war experience sent him to a military hospital in Edinburgh. There he met the poet Siegfried Sassoon, who became his mentor. In the thirteen or so months after August 1917, Owen came into his own as a powerful war poet. He returned to action in August 1918 and was killed just a week before the armistice. His volume *Poems*, collected and edited by Sassoon, appeared posthumously in 1920.

The selections included here show the range of Owen's best work. The allegorical "Strange Meeting" recounts a dream-vision of an encounter in hell with an enemy killed in battle, a man whose life was the mirror-image of the speaker's own. Uneven in quality, with obvious echoes of Keats, Tennyson, and other poets, the poem is nevertheless compelling in its surge of remorseful compassion and in its emphatic, off-rhyming couplets. These point up the harsh discrepancies between romantic vision and the shock of war's sheer waste of individual lives and of civilization itself. The tenderly bitter "Arms and the Boy" is almost a perfect antiwar poem in its balance of the gentle, the fierce, and the sardonic. The elegiac sonnet "Anthem for Doomed Youth" moves beautifully from its opening notes of sad indignation, to its deeply tragic center ("Bugles calling for them from sad shires"), to its final quiet concentration of painful, helpless recognition. "Dulce et Decorum Est" details a gas-attack and its ineradicable psychological after-effects, and expresses straightforward scorn for those who manipulate patriotism to lead innocents to their deaths. Owen's characterization of his work—"The Poetry is in the pity"—in his draft of a preface for his first book reveals the source of the pain and toughness of his poems.

Arms and the Boy[1]

Let the boy try along this bayonet-blade
How cold steel is, and keen with hunger of blood;
Blue with all malice, like a madman's flash;
And thinly drawn with famishing for flesh.

Lend him to stroke these blind, blunt bullet-leads
Which long to nuzzle in the hearts of lads,
Or give him cartridges of fine zinc teeth,
Sharp with the sharpness of grief and death.

For his teeth seem for laughing round an apple.
10   There lurk no claws behind his fingers supple;
And God will grow no talons at his heels,
Nor antlers through the thickness of his curls.

1917–18   1920

[1] an ironic echo of the beginning of the Latin poet Virgil's *Aeneid* ("Arma virumque cano": "Arms and the man I sing"): the word "boy" stresses war's victimization of young soldiers, rather than the heroic glamor of a warrior-hero.

Dulce et Decorum Est[1]

Bent double, like old beggars under sacks,
Knock-kneed, coughing like hags, we cursed through sludge,
Till on the haunting flares we turned our backs
And towards our distant rest began to trudge.
Men marched asleep. Many had lost their boots
But limped on, blood-shod. All went lame; all blind;
Drunk with fatigue; deaf even to the hoots
Of tired, outstripped Five-Nines that dropped behind.

Gas! GAS! Quick, boys!—An ecstasy of fumbling,
10   Fitting the clumsy helmets just in time;
But someone still was yelling out and stumbling
And flound'ring like a man in fire or lime . . .
Dim, through the misty panes and thick green light,
As under a green sea, I saw him drowning.

In all my dreams, before my helpless sight,
He plunges at me, guttering, choking, drowning.

[1] an ironic quotation from the Latin poet Horace's serious expression of antique patriotism in a famous line in his *Odes* (given in full in ll. 27–28): "It is sweet and fitting to die for one's country". See, for comparison, Ezra Pound, *Hugh Selwyn Mauberley IV* (and note 1), p. 858 above.

If in some smothering dreams you too could pace
Behind the wagon that we flung him in,
And watch the white eyes writhing in his face,
20   His hanging face, like a devil's sick of sin;
If you could hear, at every jolt, the blood
Come gargling from the froth-corrupted lungs,
Obscene as cancer, bitter as the cud
Of vile, incurable sores on innocent tongues,—
My friend, you would not tell with such high zest
To children ardent for some desperate glory,
The old Lie: Dulce et decorum est
Pro patria mori.

1917–18   1920

Anthem for Doomed Youth

What passing-bells for these who die as cattle?
    Only the monstrous anger of the guns.
    Only the stuttering rifles' rapid rattle
Can patter out their hasty orisons.
No mockeries now for them; no prayers nor bells,
    Nor any voice of mourning save the choirs,—
The shrill, demented choirs of wailing shells;
    And bugles calling for them from sad shires.

What candles may be held to speed them all?
10   Not in the hands of boys, but in their eyes
Shall shine the holy glimmers of good-byes.
    The pallor of girls' brows shall be their pall;
Their flowers the tenderness of patient minds,
And each slow dusk a drawing-down of blinds.

1917–18   1920

Strange Meeting

It seemed that out of battle I escaped
Down some profound dull tunnel, long since scooped
Through granites which titanic wars had groined.
Yet also there encumbered sleepers groaned,
Too fast in thought or death to be bestirred.
Then, as I probed them, one sprang up, and stared
With piteous recognition in fixed eyes,
Lifting distressful hands as if to bless.
And by his smile, I knew that sullen hall,
By his dead smile I knew we stood in Hell.
10   With a thousand pains that vision's face was grained;
Yet no blood reached there from the upper ground,

And no guns thumped, or down the flues made moan.
"Strange friend," I said, "Here is no cause to mourn."
"None," said that other, "save the undone years,
The hopelessness. Whatever hope is yours,
Was my life also; I went hunting wild
After the wildest beauty in the world,
Which lies not calm in eyes, or braided hair,
20   But mocks the steady running of the hour,
And if it grieves, grieves richlier than here.
For of my glee might many men have laughed,
And of my weeping something had been left,
Which must die now. I mean the truth untold,
The pity of war, the pity war distilled.
Now men will go content with what we spoiled,
Or, discontent, boil bloody, and be spilled.
They will be swift with swiftness of the tigress.
None will break ranks, though nations trek from progress.
30   Courage was mine, and I had mystery,
Wisdom was mine, and I had mastery:
To miss the march of this retreating world
Into vain citadels that are not walled.
Then, when much blood had clogged their chariot-wheels,
I would go up and wash them from sweet wells,
Even with truths that lie too deep for taint.
I would have poured my spirit without stint
But not through wounds; not on the cess of war.
Foreheads of men have bled where no wounds were.
40   I am the enemy you killed, my friend.
I knew you in this dark: for so you frowned
Yesterday through me as you jabbed and killed.
I parried; but my hands were loath and cold.
Let us sleep now. . . ."

1917–18   1920

E.E. CUMMINGS
1894–1962

E.E. Cummings grew up as the cherished non-conformist son of a Congregational minister who also taught in Harvard Divinity School. After taking B.A. and M.A. degrees at Harvard, he joined a volunteer ambulance corps in France in 1916. A flippant, critical personal letter, read by French censors, led to his arrest and confinement in a concentration camp—the experience described in his riotous prose account, *The Enormous Room* (1922). His father secured his release and arranged for his return home, but after the war Cummings went back to France as an art student. He then pursued a dual career, as painter and poet. His first book of poems, *Tulips and Chimneys* (1923), confirmed the latter vocation as his primary one. His fame rests on his love-lyrics, his satirical forays, and his clever, typewriter-inspired acrobatics for the eye.

At his best, Cummings wrote a sparkling poetry free of pretentiousness. His work often catches the essence of one tone of the 1920s: romantic gaiety tinged with darker notes—echoes, perhaps, of World War I. The three sonnets reprinted here celebrate love and female beauty in defiance of that inexorable enemy, death. The bittersweet mood of "goodby Betty, don't remember me" is that of post-war Paris; "ladies and gentlemen this little girl" mocks itself, almost, with its circus-barker opening and lover's wit; and "who's most afraid of death? thou" brings the combined ardor, tenderness, and resistance to mortality of all three poems to a level of exalted intensity.

Cummings's boldness and surface surprises divert attention from the sentimentality and underlying conventionality of much of his work. While "who's most afraid of death? thou" is a sonnet, its use of lowercase letters where we would expect capitals, its special spacing and placement of linebreaks, and its energetic deployment of parentheses all conceal the form that is being remodeled and the deeply traditional tragic

eroticism of its movement. Similarly, the wry, mocking "Buffalo Bill's" is in an ancient elegiac mode despite its quick shifts of pace, tone, and attitude; and "ponder, darling, these busted statues," with its mixture of serious diction, slangy irony, and toughly comic sexual imagery, is a modern echo of poems like Marvell's "To His Coy Mistress." Cummings had an unusual feeling for words, punctuation, letters, and spaces as detachable elements in an animated visual-verbal collage of language that could be broken up and reassembled, whether playfully or serious. His "r-p-o-p-h-e-s-s-a-g-r" is a typographical comedy; it acts out a grasshopper's angular distortions as it gathers itself up to leap, does so, then lands and grows still, regaining normal shape at the end with the letters of "grasshopper" all in the right place. His "silence," in contrast, presents a rigorously sculpted image of stasis and anticipation through its placement of phrase and punctuation, including the open parenthesis at the end.

goodby Betty, don't remember me[1]

goodby Betty, don't remember me
pencil your eyes dear and have a good time
with the tall tight boys at Tabari'
s, keep your teeth snowy, stick to beer and lime,
wear dark, and where your meeting breasts are round
have roses darling, it's all i ask of you—
but that when light fails and this sweet profound
Paris moves with lovers, two and two
bound for themselves, when passionately dusk
10   brings softly down the perfume of the world
(and just as smaller stars begin to husk
heaven) you, you exactly paled and curled

with mystic lips take twilight where i know:
proving to Death that Love is so and so.

1923

---

[1] The scene is post-World War I Paris. See comment in headnote on Cummings.

ladies and gentlemen this little girl

ladies and gentlemen this little girl
with the good teeth and small important breasts
(is it the Frolic or the Century whirl?
one's memory indignantly protests)
this little dancer with the tightened eyes
crisp ogling shoulders and the ripe quite too
large lips always clenched faintly, wishes you
with all her fragile might to not surmise
she dreamed one afternoon

10   . . . . or maybe read?

of a time when the beautiful most of her
(this here and This, do you get me?)
will maybe dance and maybe sing and be
absitively posolutely dead,
like Coney Island in winter

1923

who's most afraid of death? thou

who's most afraid of death? thou
                                           art of him
utterly afraid, i love of thee
(beloved) this

                    and truly i would be
near when his scythe takes crisply the whim
of thy smoothness.   and mark the fainting
murdered petals.   with the caving stem.

But of all most would i be one of them

10   round the hurt heart which do so frailly cling . . . .)
i who am but imperfect in my fear

Or with thy mind against my mind, to hear
nearing our hearts' irrevocable play—
through the mysterious high futile day

an enormous stride
                    (and drawing thy mouth toward

my mouth, steer our lost bodies carefully downward)

1925

r-p-o-p-h-e-s-s-a-g-r[1]

         r-p-o-p-h-e-s-s-a-g-r
       who
  a)s w(e loo)k
  upnowgath
      PPEGORHRASS
           eringint(o-
  aThe):l
    eA
     !p:
10   S   a
       (r
  rIvInG   .gRrEaPsPhOs)
                     to
  rea(be)rran(com)gi(e)ngly
  ,grasshopper;

         1935

[1] See comment in headnote on Cummings.

Buffalo Bill's[1]

Buffalo Bill's
defunct
     who used to
     ride a watersmooth-silver
                stallion
and break onetwothreefourfive pigeonsjustlikethat
                        Jesus

he was a handsome man
              and what i want to know is
10   how do you like your blueeyed boy
    Mister Death
                1923

[1] **Buffalo Bill** William Frederick Cody (1846–1917), a famous showman who had been a frontier scout on the Great Plains. See comment in headnote on Cummings.

ponder,darling,these busted statues[1]

(ponder,darling,these busted statues
of yon motheaten forum[2] be aware
notice what hath remained
—the stone cringes
clinging to the stone,how obsolete

lips utter their extant smile . . . .
remark

a few deleted of texture
or meaning monuments and dolls

10   resist Them Greediest Paws of careful
time all of which is extremely
unimportant)whereas Life

matters if or

when the your- and my-
idle vertical worthless
self unite in a peculiarly
momentary

partnership(to instigate
constructive
20   Horizontal
business . . . . even so,let us make haste
—consider well this ruined aqueduct

lady,
which used to lead something into somewhere)

1926

---

[1] See comment in headnote on Cummings.
[2] **forum**   the Forum of ancient Rome, in which broken statues and architectural fragments still remain

plato told

plato told

him:he couldn't
believe it(jesus

told him;he
wouldn't believe
it)lao

tsze[1]
certainly told
him,and general

10   (yes

mam)
sherman;[2]
and even
(believe it
or

not)you
told him:i told
him;we told him
(he didn't believe it,no

20   sir)it took
a nipponized bit of
the old sixth

avenue
el;in the top of his head:to tell

him[3]

1944

[1] ll. 6–7   the Chinese philosopher Lao-tze (sixth century B.C.), thought to be the founder of Taoism
[2] ll. 9–12   General William Tecumseh Sherman, Union hero of the American Civil War, who observed: "War is hell"
[3] ll. 20–25   American scrap iron, sold to Japan (Nippon) before World War II (some of it from the dismantled Third Avenue elevated railway structure in New York City) was used for munitions production ("nipponized"). An American soldier ("him"), killed by such a weapon, was thus "told" what he had not learned from philosophy, religion, and military history: the lesson of pacifism.

silence

silence

.is
a
looking

bird:the

turn
ing;edge,of
life

(inquiry before snow

1958

DAVID JONES
1895–1974

Educated at the Camberwell School of Art, David Jones was a painter and draughtsman before he was a poet. He served in the Welch Fusiliers in World War I and returned to Wales after the war. His 1932 "breakdown," followed by a trip to Palestine, seems to have occasioned the writing of *In Parenthesis*, which T.S. Eliot read for Faber and Faber and published enthusiastically. In 1947, with the recurrence of his mental illness, Jones moved to England for treatment and remained there after his recovery. At first taken up by the English avant-garde, he has gained steadily in stature since his death. *The Sleeping Lord and Other Fragments* (1974) and his posthumous volumes —including *The Dying Gaul and Other Writings* (1978) and *The Roman Quarry and Other Fragments* (1981)—contain brilliant work that will undoubtedly enhance his somewhat delayed recognition as a major figure of this century.

Jones's reputation derives almost exclusively from *In Parenthesis* (1937) and *The Anathémata* (1952), each a long experi-

mental work written several years after a severe mental collapse. *In Parenthesis* grows directly out of Jones's experience as an infantryman in France between December 1915 and July 1916; the section included here is from the climactic, concluding Part 7, which builds up its mood of hysterical and elegiac fatalism with great concreteness and power. Combining prose poetry with verse improvisation, Jones re-creates the world of Cockney and Welsh soldiers: their speech, humor, memories, behavior, and sufferings, together with the history and cultural traditions (mainly unknown to them) from which they came. Much influenced by James Joyce's densely associative and melodic prose style, which also has room for colloquial speech of all kinds, Jones, a Roman Catholic convert, leans heavily on the Mass as well as on Arthurian legend, Biblical reference, mythology, and a loving, detailed knowledge of history and archaeology. He expects readers to pay attention to his careful annotations as an integral part of his poetry.

From In Parenthesis, 7[1]

But why is Father Larkin talking to the dead?

But where's Fatty and Smiler—and this Watcyn boasts he'd seen the open
land beyond the trees, with Jerry coming on in mass—
and they've left Diamond between the beech boles
and old Dawes blaspheming quietly;
and there's John Hales with Wop Castello cross legged under the sallies,
preoccupied with dead lines—gibbering the formulae of their profession—

---

[1]See comment in headnote on Jones. "This writing," Jones's Preface explains, "is called 'In Parenthesis' because I have written it in a kind of space between—I don't know between quite what—but . . . the war itself was a parenthesis—how glad we were to step outside its brackets at the end of '18—and also because our curious type of existence here is altogether in parenthesis."

The named characters are Jones's fellow-soldiers. He calls himself Private Ball. Father

Larkin is obviously a chaplain. "Jerry" is the German soldier (singular or plural; also referred to by soldiers as "he," "him," etc.). The poem mixes free-verse lines with prose-blocks; here, each prose-block of two or more lines is considered a single line. Thus, l. 2 in this text begins "But where's Fatty" and ends with "mass—" because it is a self-contained rhythmic unit that would all run on a single line if the page were wide enough.

Wop defends the D III converted;[2]
and Bates without Coldpepper
digs like a Bunyan muck-raker[3] for his weight of woe.

But it's no good you cant do it with these toy spades, you want axes, heavy
iron for tough anchoring roots, tendoned deep down.
    When someone brought up the Jerry picks it was better, and you did
manage to make some impression. And the next one to you, where he bends
to delve gets it in the middle body. Private Ball is not instructed, and how
could you stay so fast a tide, it would be difficult with him screaming when-
ever you move him ever so little, let alone try with jack-knife to cut clear
the hampering cloth.

10   The First Field Dressing[4] is futile as frantic seaman's shift bunged to stoved
bulwark, so soon the darking flood percolates and he dies in your arms.
    And get back to that digging can't yer—
this aint a bloody Wake
           for these dead, who soon will have their dead
for burials clods heaped over.
Nor time for halsing
nor to clip green wounds
nor weeping Maries bringing anointments[5]
neither any word spoken
nor no decent nor appropriate sowing of this seed
20   nor remembrance of the harvesting
of the renascent cycle
and return
nor shaving of the head nor ritual incising for these *viriles*[6] under each tree.
    No one sings: Lully lully
for the mate whose blood runs down.[7]

Corposant his signal flare
           makes its slow parabola
where acorn hanging cross-trees tangle
and the leafy tops intersect.
30   And white faces lie,
(like china saucers tilted run soiling stains half dry, when the moon shines
on a scullery-rack and Mr. and Mrs. Billington are asleep upstairs and so's
Vi—and any creak frightens you) or any twig moving.[8]

---

[2]ll. 5–6 **and . . . profession** engineers, con-
versing in their special jargon; **the sallies** at-
tacks and bursts of fire; **D III converted** "type
of field telephone" (Jones's note)
[3] **Bunyan muck-raker** an allusion to John Bun-
yan's *The Pilgrim's Progress* and the ordeals of
its hero
[4] **The First Field Dressing** a hospital unit
[5]ll. 15–17 **halsing** supplication and prayer;
weeping Maries Mary Magdalene and other
women at Jesus' tomb

[6]*viriles* (Latin) manly ones (i.e., men who died
giving their utmost)
[7]**Lully, lully . . . runs down** "Cf. poem:
'Lully lulley; lully lulley! / The Falcon hath
borne my mate away!' " (Jones's note).
[8]ll. 26–31 The enemy's ("his") signal-flares
light up the darkness eerily, like St. Elmo's fire
("corposant"), revealing the faces of the dead.
The domestic simile (ll. 30–31) highlights the
surreal grotesqueness of the scene's mixed
beauty and horror.

And it's nearing dark when the trench is digged and they brought forward
R.E.s who methodically spaced their picket-irons and did their work back
and fro, speak low—
cats-cradle tenuous gear.
You can hear their mauls hammering[9]
under the oaks.
    And when they've done the job they file back carrying their implements,
and the covering Lewis team withdraws from out in front and the water-
party is up at last with half the bottles punctured
and travellers' tales.
Stammer a tale stare-eyed of close shaves,
of outside on the open slope:
40 Carrying-parties,
runners who hasten singly,
burdened bearers walk with careful feet
to jolt him as little as possible,
bearers of burdens to and from
stumble oftener, notice the lessening light,
and feel their way with more sensitive feet—
you mustn't spill the precious fragments, for perhaps these raw bones live.
    They can cover him again with skin—in their candid coats, in their
clinical shrines and parade the miraculi.[10]
    The blinded one with the artificial guts—his morbid neurosis retards the
treatment, otherwise he's bonza[11]—and will learn a handicraft.

Nothing is impossible nowadays my dear if only we can get the poor bleeder
through the barrage and they take just as much trouble with the ordinary
soldiers you know and essential-service academicians can match the natural
50 hue and everything extraordinarily well.
    Give them glass eyes to see
and synthetic spare parts to walk in the Triumphs, without anyone feeling
awkward and O, O, O, its a lovely war[12] with poppies on the up-platform
for a perpetual memorial of his body.

Lift gently Dai, gentleness befits his gun-shot wound in the lower bowel—
go easy—easee at the slope—and mind him—wait for this one and
slippy—an' twelve inch an' all—beating up for his counter-attack and—
that packet on the Aid-Post.
    Lower you lower you—some old cows have malhanded little bleeders
for a mother's son.
    LoweryouloweryouprizeMariaHunt,an' gammyfingered upland Gamalin
—down cantcher—low—hands away me ducky—down on hands on hands

---

[9]ll. 32–34 **R.E.'s** Royal Engineers; **picket-irons** "twisted iron stakes used in construction of wire defences"; **mauls** (picket-mauls): "heavy mallets for driving home stakes used in wire entanglements" (Jones's notes)
[10]**miraculi** literally, miraculous men. The Latin word for "miracle" is *miraculum*, of neuter

gender. The sardonic implication is that medical skill turns survivors into objects for display—dehumanized, perhaps neutered.
[11]**bonza** in fine shape (a Cockney adaption of the Australian slang-word "bonzer")
[12]**O, O, O, it's a lovely war.** "Cf. Song: O it's a lovely war" (Jones's note).

down and flattened belly and face pressed and curroodle mother earth[13]
she's kind:
Pray her hide you in her deeps
she's only refuge against
this ferocious pursuer
60   terribly questing.
Maiden of the digged places
          let our cry come unto thee.
Mam, moder,[14] mother of me
Mother of Christ under the tree
reduce our dimensional vulnerability to the minimum—
cover the spines of us
let us creep back dark-bellied where he can't see
don't let it.
There, there, it can't, won't hurt — nothing
70   shall harm my beautiful.
     But on its screaming passage
their numbers writ
and stout canvas tatters drop as if they'd salvoed grape to the mizzen-
sheets and the shaped ash grip[15] rocket-sticks out of the evening sky right
back by Bright Trench
and clots and a twisted clout
on the bowed back of the F.O.O. bent to his instrument.
    . . . theirs . . . H.E. . . . fairly, fifty yards to my front . . .
he's bumping the Quadrangle . . . 2025 hours?—thanks—nicely . . .
X 2 9 b 2 5 . . . 10.5 cm. gun . . . 35 degrees left . . . he's definitely
livening.
    and then the next packet — and Major Knacksbull blames the unrespon-
sive wire.[16]
    And linesmen go out from his presence to seek, and make whole with
adhesive tape, tweezer the copper with deft hands: there's a bad break on
the Bright Trench line—buzz us when you're through.

80   And the storm rises higher
and all who do their business in the valley
do it quickly
and up in the night-shades
where death is closer packed
in the tangled avenues
    fair Balder falleth everywhere
and thunder-besom breakings
bright the wood

---

[13]The Cockney insults in l. 56 (including obscene rhyming slang) emphasize to a stretcher-bearer, under murderous enemy fire, the need to lower the wounded man very gently.

[14]**moder** mother; echoes Chaucer's Middle English in *The Pardoner's Tale*. See note 19 below.

[15]**tatters drop . . . shaped ash grip** "The can-vas fabric of stretcher. The grip of handles of stretcher" (Jones's note).

[16]**F.O.O. . . . unresponsive wire** "Forward Observation Officer. An artillery officer having been sent forward to observe effect of our own or enemy fire is reporting to his battery by Field Telephone" (Jones's note); **H.E.** he (artillery ammunition)

and a Golden Bough for
90 Johnny and Jack
and blasted oaks for Jerry
and shrapnel the swift Jupiter for each expectant tree;
after what hypostases uniting:
withered limbs for the chosen
for the fore-chosen.[17]
Take care the black brush-fall
in the night-rides
where they deploy for the final objective.
    Dark baulks sundered, bear down,
100 beat down, ahurtle through the fractured growings green,
pile high an heaped diversity.
Brast, break, bough-break the backs of them,
every bone of the white wounded who wait patiently—
looking toward that hope:
for the feet of the carriers long coming
bringing palanquins
to spread worshipful beds for heroes.

You can hear him,
suppliant, under his bowery smother
110 but who can you get to lift him away
lift him away
a half-platoon can't.
How many mortal men
to bear the Acorn-Sprite—
She's got long Tom
and Major Lillywhite,[18]
        they're jelly-bags with the weight of it:
        and they'll Carry out Deth[19] tomorrow.

1937

[17]**fair Balder . . . fore-chosen** "Here I have associated in a kind of way, shrapnel with the Thunder God and its effect on the trees of the wood and with the oak-tree as the especial vehicle of the God and with the Balder myth (see *Golden Bough*), and how any chosen thing suffers a kind of piercing and destruction. Cf. Roman Breviary at Sext for the Common of our Lady, Versicle" (Jones's note).
[18]**How many mortal men . . . Major Lillywhite** "I mean that the oak spirit, the *Dryad*, in fact,

took these men to herself in the falling tree" (Jones's note). The name Lillywhite occurs in one of Jones's notes to Part 4: "Cf. song, *Green grow the Rushes-o:* 'Two, two, the lily-white boys clothed all in green-o.' (For Christians, Our Lord and St. John Baptist.)".
[19]**Deth** early spelling of "Death." This verse-unit (ll. 108–18) echoes the prayer—to be allowed to die himself—of the old man who embodies Death in Chaucer's *The Pardoner's Tale.*

ROBERT GRAVES
1895–1985

Son of the Irish poet Alfred Perceval Graves, Robert Graves enlisted in the Royal Welch Fusiliers in 1914 and was sent to France as an officer. His *Goodbye to All That* (1929), an autobiography, in part recounts his terrifying war experience. He and Siegfried Sassoon became friends; when Sassoon publicly spoke out against the war while he was still an officer, Graves helped him avoid being court-martialed. It was arranged that Sassoon should be sent for "neurasthenic" convalescence to a military hospital near Edinburgh. There he and Graves, who had been assigned to escort him, met Wilfred Owen. The psychiatrist in charge, W.H. Rivers, who opened Graves's mind to the "latent" associations and irrational dimensions of poetry, directly influenced several of his early prose works of criticism.

In 1918 Graves married the young feminist painter Nancy Nicholson, and the next year they moved to Oxford, where he began studying at the university while continuing his professional writing. He had published three books of poetry during the war and went on at a prolific pace thereafter. Despite their two children and genuine closeness, the marriage ended in divorce. Meanwhile, Graves maintained a close relationship with the poet Laura Riding, which resulted in—among other things—their books *A Survey of Modernist Criticism* (1927) and *A Pamphlet against Anthologies* (1928). Graves was the author of numerous scholarly and mythological books and historical novels, of which *I, Claudius* is the best known.

Graves's unusually witty, energetic, and accomplished poetry epitomizes the mainstream of British poetry in this century. There is nothing experimental about it; it aims to be impressively articulate—a poetically disciplined form of very intelligent conversation by free, uninhibited, perfectly frank persons. "Down, Wanton, Down" is a fine example of Graves's bawdy humor, in an English tradition of vigorous sexual heartiness that goes back to Chaucer at least. "To Juan at the Winter Solstice" is related to the main thesis of Graves's prose-work *The White Goddess* (1948)—namely, that "the language of poetic myth anciently current in the Mediterranean and Northern Europe was a magical language bound up with popular religious ceremonies in honor of the Moon-goddess, or Muse, some of them dating from the Old Stone Age, and . . . this remains the language of true poetry." All the symbolic lore that is the stuff of myth and religion and the storehouse of poetic imagery takes us ultimately, in his view, back to this Moon-goddess, described in the closing stanza, which at the same time reminds us of how "she" is to be honored. Hers is the "one story and one story only." Graves makes of this essentially discursive poem—almost a lecture on comparative mythology—an exquisitely incantatory song, richly varied in its imagery and in its intricate pattern of meter and line-length in each unrhymed stanza.

Down, Wanton, Down!

Down, wanton, down! Have you no shame
That at the whisper of Love's name,
Or Beauty's, presto! up you raise
Your angry head and stand at gaze?

Poor bombard-captain, sworn to reach
The ravelin and effect a breach—

Indifferent what you storm or why,
So be that in the breach you die!

Love may be blind, but Love at least
10   Knows what is man and what mere beast;
Or Beauty wayward, but requires
More delicacy from her squires.

Tell me, my witless, whose one boast
Could be your staunchness at the post,
When were you made a man of parts
To think fine and profess the arts?

Will many-gifted Beauty come
Bowing to your bald rule of thumb,
Or Love swear loyalty to your crown?
20   Be gone, have done! Down, wanton, down!

                              1933

To Juan at the Winter Solstice[1]

There is one story and one story only
That will prove worth your telling,
Whether as learned bard or gifted child,
To it all lines or lesser gauds belong
That startle with their shining
Such common stories as they stray into.

Is it of trees you tell, their months and virtues,
Or strange beasts that beset you,
Of birds that croak at you the Triple will?
10   Or of the Zodiac and how slow it turns
Below the Boreal Crown,
Prison of all true kings that ever reigned?

Water to water, ark again to ark,
From woman back to woman:
So each new victim treads unfalteringly
The never altered circuit of his fate,
Bringing twelve peers as witness
Both to his starry rise and starry fall.

Or is it of the Virgin's silver beauty,
20   All fish below the thighs?
She in her left hand bears a leafy quince;

---

[1] See comment in headnote on Graves; also, note parallels in Ezra Pound's Canto XLVII and David Jones's In Parenthesis. The poem, addressed to Graves's young son Juan, perhaps also suggests Don Juan, the archetypal lover.

When with her right she crooks a finger, smiling,
How may the King hold back?
Royally then he barters life for love.

Or of the undying snake from chaos hatched,
Whose coils contain the ocean,
Into whose chops with naked sword he springs,
Then in black water, tangled by the reeds,
Battles three days and nights,
30   To be spewed up beside her scalloped shore?[2]

Much snow is falling, winds roar hollowly,
The owl hoots from the elder,
Fear in your heart cries to the loving-cup:
Sorrow to sorrow as the sparks fly upward.
The log groans and confesses:
There is one story and one story only.

Dwell on her graciousness, dwell on her smiling,
Do not forget what flowers
The great boar trampled down in ivy time.[3]
40   Her brow was creamy as the crested wave,
Her sea-blue eyes were wild
But nothing promised that is not performed.

1946

[2] ll. 7–30 These stanzas allude to Celtic and other ancient lore in which the female principle (the White Goddess) speaks through fabulous beasts and prophetic birds. Also associated with the zodiac and cosmic forces, she bends the male principle to her will, at first in joyous, procreative marriage but then toward his death.

[3] l. 39 a reference to Adonis (an example of the Sun-Hero or sacrificed hero-god, as in *The Golden Bough*), who was loved by Aphrodite (an alternative form of the White Goddess) but killed by a wild boar

RAMON GUTHRIE
1896–1973

Ramon Guthrie grew up in poverty. His mother, deserted early on by her husband, earned only the barest living; disciplined and religious, she struggled bravely but committed suicide after a second stroke in 1916. Guthrie joined the American Field Service in France as an ambulance driver the same year. Later he became an observer and formation leader in a bombing squadron, earning a Silver Star. He served again in World War II, doing liaison work with the French Resistance. Essentially self-educated, he eventually matched Pound and Eliot in erudition, but his background and humane sympathies inclined him toward the political left.

The least-known major poet of his generation, Guthrie wrote his most important volumes—*Graffiti* (1959), *Asbestos Phoenix* (1968), and *Maximum Security Ward* (1970) —in his sixties and seventies. Even before his first book, *Trobar Clus*, appeared in 1923, he had played a real if minor role in the expatriate literary scene of postwar

France, publishing both novels and poetry. With the coming of the Depression in 1929, however, he accepted a teaching appointment at Dartmouth College, and for some thirty years dropped into virtual anonymity except for some poems in the *Nation*, an occasional review, and an anthology of French literature. Only his poet friends at Dartmouth, where he remained until retiring in 1963, and a few others knew that he had been writing steadily. When his three final books appeared, each more striking than the one before it, they were briefly acclaimed by reviewers and then disregarded. It is only very recently that he has been brought back into print in *Maximum Security Ward and Other Poems* (1984) and that extended critical attention has begun to be paid to his work.

Some of Guthrie's special qualities can readily be seen in the three poems printed here. His "Homage to Paul Delvaux (1897–)" is a magically sensuous, surrealistic poem that shows not only his affinity for Delvaux's paintings (Guthrie was himself a talented artist) but also his acute psychological insight into the precarious and death-fraught awareness associated with erotic awakening and imaginative arousal. His "The Magi," a facetious half-parody of Eliot's "Journey of the Magi," shows his sophisticated but genial comic sense and his ironic and emphatic disbelief in religion. (Other poems are far more bitter, but none shows Hardy's shocked disillusion or Eliot's yearning for confirmation of his belief— both signs of a closer link with religious faith.) "Today Is Friday," a key poem in the magnificent sequence *Maximum Security Ward*, is a supreme expression of a body and soul in agony. Its images for the kind of relentless pain experienced by, say, a cancer patient *in extremis* come directly out of Guthrie's own multiple, recurrent illnesses in his last years. But the poem's focus is not on the author as someone to be pitied, but rather on the impersonal, unidentified "it" as it imprints its destroying pressure on all its victim's senses.

The Magi[1]

The three wise men looked equivocally
at three different stars.

The one who was fluent in Aramaic[2] asked the shepherds,
"Are there in these place one inn?"

Impious shipwreck.
We had come well supplied
with slippers and sleeping pills
laxatives lighter fluid flea powder
inflatable mattresses and in case of need
10   a month's supply of prophylactics

---

[1] See comment in headnote on Guthrie; see also, for comparison, W.B. Yeats, "The Magi" (p. 770), and T.S. Eliot, "The Journey of the Magi" (p. 901). Guthrie parodies the latter poem to some extent.

[2] **Aramaic** the language of Jesus and his disciples in Palestine; also, the language of the New Testament

Each saying, "I saw this star and
dropping everything, set out,
sur l'éperon du moment, comme disent les Anglais,[3]
quite unprepared, just as I was."

We found three different Kristkinder[4]
in three different mangers
and went home satisfied
leaving three different infants to make what they might
of frankincense and myrrh.

20   We have written three different books
all unpublished
each in his own tongue
telling of the hardships and perils of the voyage.

                                        1968

[3] l. 13   a deliberately unidiomatic literal transla-
tion into French of the English expression "on
the spur of the moment," plus the sophisticated
affectation "as the English say." Guthrie's
comic word-play has a sardonic strain: the poem
satirizes superficial modern reactions—based
on ignorance and tourist-mentality—to signifi-

cant events and situations that might lead to
something like revelation.
[4] **Kristkinder**   (German) Christ-children. Each
of the Magi thinks that *he* has found the true
Christ-child, yet all complacently accept the dif-
ferences of viewpoint.

Homage to Paul Delvaux[1]
(1897–   )

Everywhere about is landscape as far as foot can feel
lamps exude their light on flagstones
there are quaint quiet trains in
corridors of pure perspective

Out of this span of calm I rise
to hear irises unfold   moss grow infallibly
on north bark of larches   Death in temporary form
of Paul Delvaux's discreetly pubic girls
bedmates of gone goddesses walking in gardens of
10   undeflowered music and undeciphered roses
while waiting for their mutual dream to bring about
eclipses of the moon

I walk a long while and wait
I wait a long while and walk
I peer into a well and see a fountain
I peer into a fountain and see
the crystal chrysalis of a chaste nymph
rising toward the sliver of a moon

[1] Belgian surrealist painter. See comment in head-
note on Guthrie.

20   We load our last possessions on a raft
and hoist the makeshift sail
Our awkward innocence defies return
We know this
We feel a deep alarm but do not speak

          Ten deliberate
adjectives too many for one volcanic
somnambulistic mound dormant but
aquiver
         fox in April in the sun

             frisson ou pas frisson
30   frisson   frisson   pas frisson
          frisson en avril[2]

            1968

[2] **frisson** (French) thrill or shudder of feeling or
excitement. Lines 29-31 may be translated:
> *shudder or not a shudder*
>   *shudder   shudder   not a shudder*
> *shudder in April*

Today is Friday

Always it was going on
In the white hollow roar
you could hear it at a hundred paces if you listened closely
and a hemisphere away if you didn't listen at all
if you were paying no attention to it
fixing your mind hard on something else
         I will not hear it
         I will not hear it
         I
10 Screaming it inwardly so hard it seemed
your seminal vesicles must rupture with the strain
you could hear it close at hand
feel it crimping your nerve ends
your brain pan buckling in its grip
see it perform its curious rituals
as pale as ichor
limp as larvae
You could curl up with it and sleep
         Only it was not
20   Only it was not
         Only it

You could taste it being fed intravenously through a
skein of tubes into your most plausible dreams
It was happening   It was going on as suavely
as if it were a rank of drop-forges
smashing diamonds to dust as fast as
they could be fed to them.

Tangible
It is a great protracted
30   totally transparent cube
with sides and angles
perceptibly contracting against
eyeballs and nose and mouth and skin

It is always happening
It is always going on
When it gets tired of going on
maybe it will stop

1970

AUSTIN CLARKE
1896–1974

Austin Clarke was the foremost of a generation of Irish poets who lived under Yeats's shadow. He studied at University College, Dublin, where he was a student of the poet Donagh MacDonagh, who was executed by the British in 1916 after the Easter Rebellion. Clarke took MacDonagh's place at the university in 1917—the year he also published his first book of poems, *The Vengeance of Fionn*, based on Irish myth and much influenced by Yeats's earlier work. In the 1920s, he went to live in London, supporting himself by journalism and a series of novels (all banned in Ireland). He returned to Dublin before the outbreak of World War II, and from 1938 to 1955 gave himself primarily to writing verse plays and organizing the Lyric Theatre Club. He published some of his work under his own imprint (The Bridge Press) until the Dolmen Press, which has been instrumental in providing an outlet for the best modern Irish poets, began to publish him in 1961.

Clarke immersed himself in early Irish poetry in the original Gaelic and—to the degree that poetry in English can mimic Gaelic intricacies of rhyme, consonance, and assonance—absorbed its subject matter, stylistic richness, and prosodic values into his verse. In this sense, and in his frequent closely detailed attention to very local events and concerns, Clarke is a national poet par excellence. While he treats such larger issues as the struggles between the church's influence and free-thinking secularism, the conflicts caused by sexual puritanism and repressive gentility, and the crudity of so much Irish city life, he also takes up such matters as the selling of horse-meat for food or the wearing of modernized habits by nuns. *Mnemosyne Lay in Dust* (1966), his most striking single work and Ireland's outstanding confessional poetic sequence, is a beautifully immediate presentation of a temporary breakdown and amnesia—results of neurotic repression and of a humiliation somehow connected with Ireland's crass new commercialism. This sequence shows how deeply Clarke's Irishness connects with the familiar crises of modern sensibility in the Western world.

From Mnemosyne Lay in Dust[1]

I

Past the house where he was got
In darkness, terrace, provision shop,
Wing-hidden convent opposite
Past public-houses at lighting-up
Time, crowds outside them—Maurice Devane
Watched from the taxi window in vain
National stir and gaiety
Beyond himself: St. Patrick's Day,
The spike-ends of the Blue Coat school,[2]
10 Georgian houses, ribald gloom
Rag-shadowed by gaslight, quiet pavements
    Moon-waiting in Blackhall Place.

For six weeks Maurice had not slept,
Hours pillowed him from right to left side,
Unconsciousness became the pit
Of terror. Void would draw his spirit,
Unself him. Sometimes he fancied that music,
Soft lights in Surrey, Kent,[3] could cure him,
Hypnotic touch, until, one evening,
20 The death-chill seemed to mount from feet
To shin, to thigh. Life burning in groin
And prostate ached for a distant joy.
But nerves need solitary confinement.
    Terror repeals the mind.

Cabs ranked at Kingsbridge Station, Guinness
Tugs[4] moored at their wooden quay, glinting
Of Liffey[5] mudbank; hidden vats
Brewing intoxication, potstill,
Laddering of distilleries
30 Ready to sell their jollities,
Delirium tremens. Dublin swayed,
Drenching, drowning the shamrock:[6] unsaintly
Mirth. The high departments were filed,

[1] See comment in headnote on Clarke. Mnemosyne, Greek goddess of Memory, was the mother of the Muses. The poem's original title, "The Loss of Memory," is too clinical for the protagonist's hysterical amnesia and all its resonances. "Maurice Devane" is the fictional name for Clarke, though not every detail is literal autobiography. Most of the places referred to are in Dublin.

[2] **the Blue Coat school** King's Hospital School, whose students wore blue uniforms

[3] **Surrey, Kent** English counties (dreamt of as places of escape from the pressures at home)

[4] **Guinness / Tugs** tugboats belonging to the Guinness breweries

[5] **Liffey** Irish river

[6] **shamrock** three-leaf clover, emblem of Ireland, here seen as being destroyed ("drowned") by alcoholism

Yard, store, unlit. Whiskey-all-round,
Beyond the wealth of that square mile,
    Was healthing every round.[7]

The eighteenth century hospital
Established by the tears of Madam
Steevens, who gave birth, people said, to
A monster with a pig's snout, pot-head.
40   The Ford turned right, slowed down. Gates opened,
Closed with a clang; acetelyne glow
Of headlights. How could Maurice Devane
Suspect from weeping-stone, porch, vane,
The classical rustle of the harpies,
Hopping in filth among the trees,
The Mansion of Forgetfulness
    Swift gave us for a jest?[8]

[7] **healthing every round** Irish custom of taking turns treating companions to a round of drinks and toasting their health
[8] ll. 37–48 The hospital is St. Patrick's Hospital, founded 1746 by Jonathan Swift. His "jest" in founding this "Mansion of Forgetfulness"

appears in his satirical "Verses on the Death of Dr. Swift":

He gave the little Wealth he had,
To build a House for Fools and mad:
And shew'd by one satyric Touch,
No Nation wanted it so much.

V

Maurice was in an Exhibition Hall
Where crowds of men and fashionable women
In bosoming dresses, embroidered shawl,
    Were moving. But a silent form
Was waiting in a corner. Up marble stairs,
He hurries from mirrored hall to hall, by glimmer
Of statues in niches. The Watcher stares,
    Red tabs upon his uniform.

Again he mounts the steps, alone,
10   Self-followed from mirrors to hall, the crowd
Of visitors waltzing below,
And looking from the bannisters
Upon the billiard tables, playerless,
Green-shaded, saw the Watcher with a frown
Behind a pillar, standing motionless
    Casting the shadow of a policeman.

Once, wandering from a hollow of asphodel,
Still flowering at mid-night, he saw the glint of
Gigantic row of columns beyond the dell,
20   Templed, conical, unbedecked
And knew they were the holy ictyphalli
Curled hair for bushwood, bark or skin
Heavily veined. He worshipped, a tiny satyr,
    Mere prick beneath those vast erections.

Joyously through a gateway, came a running
Of little Jewish boys, their faces pale
As ivory or jasmine, from Lebanon
    To Eden. Garlanded, caressing,
Little girls ran with skip and leap. They hurried,
30   Moon-pointing, beyond the gate. They passed a pale
Of sacred laurel, flowers of the future. Love
    Fathered him with their happiness.

Always in terror of Olympic doom,
He climbed, despite his will, the spiral steps
Outside a building to a cobwebbed top-room.
    There bric-a-brac was in a jumble,
His forehead was distending, ears were drumming
As in the gastric fever of his childhood.
Despite his will, he climbed the steps, stumbling
40   Where Mnemosyne lay in dust.

Dreaming, as sunlight idled, Maurice believed
He darted by with sticks of gelignite,
Unbarracked County Limerick, relieved
    His fellows, fought to the last bullet.
Daring Republican of hillside farm-yards,
Leader of raiding parties, digging at night,
He blew up lorries, captured British arms.
    Rain-hid, he cycled to Belmullet.[1]

Drowsily Maurice was aware
50   Of someone by his bed. A melancholy
Man, sallow, with black moustache, sat there.
    "Where am I?" Voice was hollow.
The other brooded: "Think." His gaze
Was so reproachful, what was his guilt?
Could it be parricide? The stranger
    Still murmured: "Think . . . Think."

1966

[1] ll. 41–48   Maurice has the hallucinatory fantasy that he is a Republican guerrilla fighter in County Limerick during the Anglo-Irish War of 1919– 21, when Clarke was in his early twenties. Belmullet is a town in County Mayo.

HART CRANE
1899–1932

The talented, difficult only child of an unhappy marriage, Hart Crane left the town of Garretsville, Ohio, without finishing high school. He was then eighteen years old, and his talent attracted the interest and support of various literary figures in New York. He combined earthy heartiness with erratic unpredictability (associated with his growing alcoholism and obsessive homosexuality) and an engaging intelligence and sensitivity. In 1932, returning home from Mexico by ship after a year on a Guggenheim Fellowship—

despondent about his work and about the failure of a brief heterosexual relationship — he committed suicide by jumping overboard.

Crane published two volumes of poetry, *White Buildings* (1926) and *The Bridge* (1932), during his brief life. The sheer emotional power of his work and its buoyant promise, even when it does not finally succeed, assure his place in American poetry. His finest achievements are in such image-crowded, inward poems as "Repose of Rivers," "Passage," and a few sections of the six-part sequence "Voyages." His most ambitious work, the sequence *The Bridge*, often loses its way in forced rhetoric, yet it contains poems and passages comparable to those just named.

"Repose of Rivers" is a remarkable repossession of a moment that revived a time of forgotten experience. Its echoing evocativeness resembles the fierce nostalgia of the French Symbolist poet Rimbaud's "The Drunken Boat." Both poems recover a lost childhood world, and both employ what Crane called "the logic of metaphor"— that is, associative leaps from one tonal center, usually a highly suggestive image, to another. The even more densely concentrated "Passage," in which the poet confronts his deepest self-doubts and which ends with an image of the terrifying impersonality of the universe, is rivaled in its stark bleakness only by Poem V of "Voyages," whose cold beauty is one of Crane's great triumphs. A love poem as empty of hope as it is filled with harsh, exciting images, it expresses the erotic magnetism for Crane of his sense of the world as infinitely dangerous and death-fraught. (In this regard, his appeal is much like that of Keats.)

The Bridge is Crane's attempt at an American epic poem—not a long narrative work about gods and heroes, but a sequence suggesting the links between America's present and past, her varied population and geographical sweep, her exalted possibilities and tragic divisions, and the hell of alienation that often troubles her people. The opening poem, "To Brooklyn Bridge," sets up the work's great central symbol, created by human toil yet seemingly divine in its beautiful curve. Its design is seen to embody both freedom and order. "To Brooklyn Bridge" resembles the Rimbaud-like poems already discussed in its development through a series of dazzling metaphors and in its emphasis near the end on the isolated poet standing in the bridge's shadow and praying to it to make his vision a reality. Better than any other part of the sequence, it shows Crane taking his first—and sole—long step toward becoming a twentieth-century Whitman.

Repose of Rivers[1]

The willows carried a slow sound,
A sarabande the wind mowed on the mead.
I could never remember
That seething, steady leveling of the marshes
Till age had brought me to the sea.

Flags,[2] weeds. And remembrance of steep alcoves
Where cypresses shared the noon's
Tyranny; they drew me into hades almost.
And mammoth turtles climbing sulphur dreams
10   Yielded, while sun-silt rippled them
Asunder . . .

---

[1] See comment in headnote on Crane; see also "Passage," ll. 1–10, and notes 2 and 3 (below).

[2] **flags** irises

How much I would have bartered! the black gorge
And all the singular nestings in the hills
Where beavers learn stitch and tooth.
The pond I entered once and quickly fled—
I remember now its singing willow rim.

And finally, in that memory all things nurse;
After the city that I finally passed
With scalding unguents spread and smoking darts
20   The monsoon cut across the delta
At gulf gates . . . There, beyond the dykes

I heard wind flaking sapphire, like this summer,
And willows could not hold more steady sound.

1926

Passage[1]

Where the cedar leaf divides the sky
I heard the sea.
In sapphire arenas of the hills
I was promised an improved infancy.[2]

Sulking, sanctioning the sun,
My memory I left in a ravine,—
Casual louse that tissues the buckwheat,
Aprons rocks, congregates pears
In moonlit bushels
10   And wakens alleys with a hidden cough.[3]

Dangerously the summer burned
(I had joined the entrainments of the wind).
The shadows of boulders lengthened my back:
In the bronze gongs of my cheeks
The rain dried without odour.

"It is not long, it is not long;
See where the red and black
Vine-stanchioned valleys—": but the wind

[1] See comment in headnote on Crane.
[2] ll. 1–4 See "Repose of Rivers," ll. 1–5 and 21–23. The overlapping imagery in these two poems, especially of sea-sounds and "sapphire," is associated with the awakening of memory— felt as miraculous and healing in "Repose of Rivers" and as dismaying in "Passage" because of the adult frustrations and self-deceptions that have prevented a new start ("promised an improved infancy").
[3] ll. 5–10 Memory, instead of healing (see note 2), is smothered in self-contempt, as a "casual louse"—an incidental irritant recalling false dreams and sordid weaknesses.

20 Died speaking through the ages that you know
And hug, chimney-sooted heart of man!
So was I turned about and back, much as your smoke
Compiles a too well-known biography.

The evening was a spear in the ravine
That throve through very oak. And had I walked
The dozen particular decimals of time?[4]
Touching an opening laurel, I found
A thief beneath, my stolen book in hand.

"Why are you back here—smiling an iron coffin?"
"To argue with the laurel," I replied:
"Am justified in transience, fleeing
30 Under the constant wonder of your eyes—."

He closed the book.[5] And from the Ptolemies
Sand troughed us in a glittering abyss.
A serpent swam a vertex to the sun
—On unpaced beaches leaned its tongue and drummed.[6]
What fountains did I hear? what icy speeches?
Memory, committed to the page, had broke.

1926

[4] ll. 11–25 an expansion of the negative perspective of ll. 5–10, stressing the destructive character of time, whether historical, personal, or mechanical ("the dozen particular decimals" of clock-time)

[5] ll. 26–32 The more realistic self strips away the poet-self's pretensions; a bitter, disheartened passage.

[6] the Ptolemies Egypt's rulers, 305?–30 B.C. The imagery in this verse-unit recalls that in W.B. Yeats's "The Second Coming" (p. 773 above).

From Voyages[1]

I

Above the fresh ruffles of the surf
Bright striped urchins flay each other with sand.
They have contrived a conquest for shell shucks,
And their fingers crumble fragments of baked weed
Gaily digging and scattering.

And in answer to their treble interjections
The sun beats lightning on the waves,
The waves fold thunder on the sand;
And could they hear me I would tell them:

[1] Three sections of the six-part "Voyages" are included here. "Voyages I" centers on the irony of the way children play on a beach, completely unaware of the tokens and threat of death all around them; "Voyages II" on the sea's seductive beauty and magisterial destructiveness; and "Voyages V" on the cold impersonality of moonlight that chills the thought of any correspondence between human needs and the impersonal universe. Throughout the poem there is constant tension between the sense of life as demanding passionate intercourse and elements of death and terror.

10   O brilliant kids, frisk with your dog,
      Fondle your shells and sticks, bleached
      By time and the elements; but there is a line
      You must not cross nor ever trust beyond it
      Spry cordage[2] of your bodies to caresses
      Too lichen-faithful from too wide a breast.
      The bottom of the sea is cruel.

[2] **cordage**   the ropes in a ship's rigging

II

      And yet[1] this great wink of eternity,
      Of rimless floods, unfettered leewardings,
      Samite sheeted and processioned where
      Her undinal vast belly moonward bends,
      Laughing the wrapt infections of our love;

      Take this Sea, whose diapason knells
      On scrolls of silver snowy sentences,
      The sceptred terror of whose sessions rends
      As her demeanors motion well or ill,
10   All but the pieties of lovers' hands.

      And onward, as bells off San Salvador
      Salute the crocus lustres of the stars,
      In these poinsettia meadows of her tides,—
      Adagios of islands,[2] O my Prodigal,
      Complete the dark confessions her veins spell.

      Mark how her turning shoulders wind the hours,
      And hasten while her penniless rich palms
      Pass superscription of bent foam and wave,—
      Hasten, while they are true,—sleep, death, desire,
20   Close round one instant in one floating flower.

      Bind us in time, O Seasons clear, and awe.
      O minstrel galleons of Carib fire,
      Bequeath us to no earthly shore until
      Is answered in the vortex of our grave
      The seal's wide spindrift gaze toward paradise.

[1] **And yet**   This phrase shifts emphasis from fear of the sea's powers in "Voyages I" to entrancement of its vast "female" seductiveness.
[2] **Adagios of islands**   "The reference is to the motion of a boat through islands clustered thickly, the rhythm of the motion" (Hart Crane, "General Aims and Theories").

V[1]

Meticulous, past midnight in clear rime,
Infrangible and lonely, smooth as though cast
Together in one merciless white blade—
The bay estuaries fleck the hard sky limits.

—As if too brittle or too clear to touch!
The cables of our sleep so swiftly filed,
Already hang, shred ends from remembered stars.
One frozen trackless smile . . . What words
Can strangle this deaf moonlight? For we

10   Are overtaken. Now no cry, no sword
Can fasten or deflect this tidal wedge,
Slow tyranny of moonlight, moonlight loved
And changed . . . "There's

Nothing like this in the world," you say,
Knowing I cannot touch your hand and look
Too, into that godless cleft of sky
Where nothing turns but dead sands flashing.

"—And never to quite understand!" No,
In all the argosy of your bright hair I dreamed
20   Nothing so flagless as this piracy.

                But now
Draw in your head, alone and too tall here.
Your eyes already in the slant of drifting foam;
Your breath sealed by the ghosts I do not know:
Draw in your head and sleep the long way home.

                    1926

[1] See comment in headnote on Hart Crane and note 1 to this sequence.

From The Bridge

To Brooklyn Bridge[1]

How many dawns, chill from his rippling rest
The seagull's wings shall dip and pivot him,
Shedding white rings of tumult, building high
Over the chained bay waters Liberty—[2]

[1] See comment in headnote on Crane.
[2] ll. 3-4 **building . . . Liberty** The seagull "builds" his flight high above the Statue of Liberty in Upper New York Bay ("the chained bay waters"), and its flight "builds" a vision of Liberty high above the water "chained" below.

Then, with inviolate curve, forsake our eyes
As apparitional as sails that cross
Some page of figures to be filed away;
—Till elevators drop us from our day . . .

10   I think of cinemas, panoramic sleights
With multitudes bent toward some flashing scene
Never disclosed, but hastened to again,
Foretold to other eyes on the same screen;

And Thee,[3] across the harbor, silver-paced
As though the sun took step of thee, yet left
Some motion ever unspent in thy stride,—
Implicitly thy freedom staying thee!

Out of some subway scuttle, cell or loft
A bedlamite speeds to thy parapets,
Tilting there momently, shrill shirt ballooning,
20   A jest falls from the speechless caravan.[4]

Down Wall,[5] from girder into street noon leaks,
A rip-tooth of the sky's acetylene;
All afternoon the cloud-flown derricks turn . . .
Thy cables breathe the North Atlantic still.

And obscure as that heaven of the Jews,
Thy guerdon[6] . . . Accolade thou dost bestow
Of anonymity time cannot raise:
Vibrant reprieve and pardon thou dost show.

O harp and altar, of the fury fused,
30   (How could mere toil align thy choiring strings!)
Terrific threshold of the prophet's pledge,
Prayer of pariah, and the lover's cry,—

[3] **Thee** Brooklyn Bridge, addressed as a deity
[4] ll. 17–20 A crazed person ("bedlamite") may commit suicide by jumping from railings ("parapets") of the bridge—life wasted on the very site of glory ("a jest . . . caravan"). As in the customary invocation to a Muse or presiding deity in the traditional epic, the poet here presents himself humbly (as a "bedlamite"), since he presumes to undertake so mighty an epic task—artistically suicidal and ridiculous (a "jest") in its pathetic failure to match the challenge of the bridge.

[5] **Wall** Wall Street
[6] **guerdon** reward. What the bridge offers its worshipers is as vague as the ancient Jewish conception of heaven. The only sign of approval ("accolade") it proffers is "anonymity": the privilege of losing one's identity in something greater than oneself. This privilege is seen as a "reprieve" and "pardon"—i.e., a release from the prison of the self and the guilt of self-regard.

Again the traffic lights that skim thy swift
Unfractioned idiom, immaculate sigh of stars,
Beading thy path—condense eternity:
And we have seen night lifted in thine arms.

Under thy shadow by the piers I waited;
Only in darkness is thy shadow clear.
The City's fiery parcels[7] all undone,
40   Already snow submerges an iron year . . .

O Sleepless as the river under thee,
Vaulting the sea, the prairies' dreaming sod,
Unto us lowliest sometime sweep, descend
And of the curveship lend a myth to God.[8]

1930

[7] **fiery parcels** lighted windows (now dark) in office buildings   [8] ll. 41–44 a prayer to the bridge, asking it to fulfill the poem's description

BASIL BUNTING
1900–1985

Much influenced by his Quaker mother's ideas, Basil Bunting was jailed as a conscientious objector just as World War I was ending. He briefly attended the London School of Economics in 1920, but dropped out and eventually drifted to Paris. There he met Ezra Pound and Ford Madox Ford, whom he assisted on the *Transatlantic Review* before following Pound to Rapallo, Italy, for a year of discipleship. For fifteen or so years he drifted, working as music critic and editor for a British paper and then living and traveling in various places (including three more years in Rapallo). When World War II broke out, he enlisted in the Royal Air Force but was assigned to vague semi-naval duties. Eventually, Bunting was sent to Persia as an interpreter because he had taught himself medieval Persian. After the war he returned there twice as a foreign correspondent (also serving the British Foreign Office there on occasion); he was expelled in 1951. Thereafter he worked for many years for a provincial Northumbrian newspaper.

Bunting's first major publications were in An *"Objectivists" Anthology* (1932), edited by Louis Zukofsky, another Pound protégé; and in *Active Anthology* (1933), edited by Pound himself. Though his style and attitudes often echo his mentor's too closely, he has his own pure lyricism and a fine gift for suggesting the everyday atmosphere of earlier, semi-rural northern England. The close-ups in Part I of his masterpiece *Briggflatts* (1966)—the work's most successful section, reprinted here—are masterly in their music, precision, and evocation of a Northumbrian pastoral scene and of the stonemason's work and home, as well as of prematurely awakened youthful passion in that setting. In reaching back to Anglo-Saxon memories, and in making fresh use of regional speech, Bunting shares the new tendency of British poets to create a sort of cultural independence movement. Like

David Jones and Geoffrey Hill, he resists London's domination of the spoken language, which drowns out local differences based on long familial traditions and the diverse strains of British history.

Bunting lived in almost total obscurity until sought out in 1963 by poets of a new generation, who wished to establish connections with the surviving writers of the Pound-Williams era.

From Briggflatts: An Autobiography[1]

I

Brag, sweet tenor bull,
descant on Rawthey's[2] madrigal,
each pebble its part
for the fells' late spring.
Dance tiptoe, bull,
black against may.[3]
Ridiculous and lovely
chase hurdling shadows
morning into noon.
10   May on the bull's hide
and through the dale
furrows fill with may,
paving the slowworm's way.

A mason times his mallet
to a lark's twitter,
listening while the marble rests,
lays his rule
at a letter's edge,
fingertips checking,
20   till the stone spells a name
naming none,
a man abolished.
Painful lark, labouring to rise!
The solemn mallet says:
In the grave's slot
he lies. We rot.

Decay thrusts the blade,
wheat stands in excrement
trembling. Rawthey trembles.

---

[1] **Briggflatts** Northumbrian for moorland or fells. Though the poem is subtitled "An Autobiography," Bunting's note tells us that it is "an autobiography, but not a record of fact . . . The truth of the poem is of another kind." Most of the places named in Part I are in Northumber-

land. See also comment in headnote on Bunting. See final six lines for the poem's frame of nostalgic regret.
[2] **Rawthey** a river
[3] **may** "may: the flower, as haw is the fruit, of the thorn" (Bunting's note)

30   Tongue stumbles, ears err
    for fear of spring.
    Rub the stone with sand,
    wet sandstone rending
    roughness away. Fingers
    ache on the rubbing stone.
    The mason says: Rocks
    happen by chance.
    No one here bolts the door,
    love is so sore.

40   Stone smooth as skin,
    cold as the dead they load
    on a low lorry by night.
    The moon sits on the fell
    but it will rain.
    Under sacks on the stone
    two children lie,
    hear the horse stale,
    the mason whistle,
    harness mutter to shaft,
50   felloe to axle squeak,
    rut thud the rim,
    crushed grit.

    Stocking to stocking, jersey to jersey,
    head to a hard arm,
    they kiss under the rain,
    bruised by their marble bed.
    In Garsdale, dawn;
    at Hawes, tea from the can.
60   Rain stops, sacks
    steam in the sun, they sit up.
    Copper-wire moustache,
    sea-reflecting eyes
    and Baltic plainsong speech
    declare: By such rocks
    men killed Bloodaxe.[4]

    Fierce blood throbs in his tongue,
    lean words.
    Skulls cropped for steel caps
    huddle round Stainmore.
70   Their becks[5] ring on limestone,
    whisper to peat.
    The clogged cart pushes the horse downhill.

---

[4] **Bloodaxe** ancient Anglo-Saxon king. "North-umbrians should know Eric *Bloodaxe* but seldom do, because all the school histories are written by or for sothrons [southerners]. Piece his story together from the Anglo-Saxon Chronicle, the Orkneyinga Saga, and Heimskringla, as you fancy" (Bunting's note).
[5] **becks** brooks

In such soft air
they trudge and sing,
laying the tune frankly on the air.
All sounds fall still,
fellside bleat,
hide-and-seek peewit.

Her pulse their pace,
80   palm countering palm,
till a trench is filled,
stone white as cheese
jeers at the dale.
Knotty wood, hard to rive,
smoulders to ash;
smell of October apples.
The road again,
at a trot.
Wetter, warmed, they watch
90   the mason meditate
on name and date.

Rain rinses the road,
the bull streams and laments.
Sour rye porridge from the hob
with cream and black tea,
meat, crust and crumb.
Her parents in bed
the children dry their clothes.
He has untied the tape
100   of her striped flannel drawers
before the range. Naked
on the pricked rag mat
his fingers comb
thatch of his manhood's home.

Gentle generous voices weave
over bare night
words to confirm and delight
till bird dawn.
Rainwater from the butt
110   she fetches and flannel
to wash him inch by inch,
kissing the pebbles,
Shining slowworm[6] part of the marvel.
The mason stirs:
Words!
Pens are too light.
Take a chisel to write.

[6] **slowworm** blindworm, a small legless lizard;
here, an image for the boy's penis

Every birth a crime,
every sentence life.
120 Wiped of mould and mites
would the ball run true?
No hope of going back.
Hounds falter and stray,
shame deflects the pen.
Love murdered neither bleeds nor stifles
but jogs the draftsman's elbow.
What can he, changed, tell
her, changed, perhaps dead?
Delight dwindles. Blame
130 stays the same.

Brief words are hard to find,
shapes to carve and discard:
Bloodaxe, king of York,
king of Dublin, king of Orkney.
Take no notice of tears;
letter the stone to stand
over love laid aside lest
insufferable happiness impede
140 flight to Stainmore,
to trace
lark, mallet,
becks, flocks
and axe knocks.

Dung will not soil the slowworm's
mosaic. Breathless lark
drops to nest in sodden trash;
Rawthey truculent, dingy.
Drudge at the mallet, the may is down,
fog on fells. Guilty of spring
150 and spring's ending
amputated years ache after
the bull is beef, love a convenience.
It is easier to die than to remember.
Name and date
split in soft slate
a few months obliterate.

1968

KENNETH FEARING
1902–1961

Born in Oak Park, Illinois, Fearing attended state universities in Illinois and Wisconsin. After a brief fling at newspaper work and writing for pulp magazines in Chicago (which colored his satirical style), he went to New York, where he became a leading figure of the literary left in the Depression. Although he gave his primary energies to poetry, he did writing of various other sorts, including several novels, for a living. Hardship and two unhappy marriages probably affected his already uncheerful outlook, a result of his sharp understanding of the pity of many lives, with the convergence of the Depression, the advent of World War II, and political disillusionment. His successive volumes, from *Angel Arms* (1929) to *New and Selected Poems* (1956), maintain their bitter irony and compassion and their unsentimental sadness because of what Baudelaire called "the oppression of the city." Fearing's essay "Reading, Writing, and the Rackets," the foreword to his final volume, remains one of our most telling indictments of the age of electronic mass media.

Fearing's sardonic, elegiac, comic genius makes him a special figure. The hilarious streak that rollicks its way through "Cultural Notes," mimicking critical and moral solem-nity, sappy inspirationalism, and political dogmatism, exists alongside a sense of life's grimness. That sense, felt as bleak pointlessness, is also at the center of "Green Light." In a remarkable series of predicates without a subject, the poem speaks of something "bought," "heard," "strange," and so on, but never states what the implied "it" is. Yet the succession of predicates adds up, despite the facetious notes in the third verse-unit, to a feeling of existence as unfocused, disappointing, and pathetic. "Resurrection" sums up what "you" (anyone) "will remember" about life in retrospect. Not as dispirited as "Green Light," it includes the passions and satisfactions; but these are matched by horrors, especially in the mounting ironic catalogue of the second verse-unit. "Memo," the most direct and touching of the poems by Fearing given here, focuses on our helpless loss of moments of tremendous feeling and meaning. The rhythmic precision of Fearing's long, insistently stirring lines owes a debt both to Whitman's *Song of Myself* and to Eliot's *The Waste Land*, but the particular edge he adds—at once rasping, wistful, and cynical—seems to arise from the world of lost souls amid any great city's impersonal streets.

Cultural Notes

Professor Burke's symphony, "Colorado Vistas,"
In four movements,
I Mountains, II Canyons, III Dusk, IV Dawn,
Was played recently by the Philharmonic.
Snapshots of the localities described in music were passed around and the
     audience checked for accuracy.
All O.K.
After the performance Maurice Epstein, 29, tuberculosis, stoker on the
     S.S. Tarboy, rose to his feet and shouted,
"He's crazy, them artists are all crazy,
I can prove it by Max Nordau. They poison the minds of young girls."

10   Otto Svoboda, 500 Avenue A, butcher, Pole, husband, philosopher, argued
        in rebuttal,
"Shut your trap, you.
The question is, does the symphony fit in with Karl Marx?"

At the Friday evening meeting of the Browning Writing League, Mrs.
        Whittamore Ralston-Beckett,
Traveler, lecturer, novelist, critic, poet, playwright, editor, mother, idealist,
Fascinated her audience with a brief talk, whimsical and caustic,
Appealing to the younger generation to take a brighter, happier, more
        sunny and less morbid view of life's eternal fundamentals.
Mrs. Ralston-Beckett quoted Sir Henry Parke-Bennett: "O Beauty," she
        said,
"Take your fingers off my throat, take your elbow out of my eye,
Take your sorrow off my sorrow,
20   Take your hat, take your gloves, take your feet down off the table,
Take your beauty off my beauty, and go."

In the open discussion that followed, Maurice Epstein, 29, tuberculosis,
        stoker on the *S.S. Tarboy*, arose and queried the speaker,
"Is it true, as certain scientists assert, that them artists are all of them
        crazy?"
A Mr. Otto Svoboda present spoke in reply,
"Shut your trap, you. The question is, what about Karl Marx?"

                                      1929

Green Light

Bought at the drug store, very cheap; and later pawned.
After a while, heard on the street; seen in the park.
Familiar, but not quite recognized.
Followed and taken home and slept with.
Traded or sold. Or lost.

Bought again at the corner drug store,
At the green light, at the patient's demand, at nine o'clock.
Re-read and memorized and re-wound.
Found unsuitable.
10   Smashed, put together, and pawned.

Heard on the street, seen in a dream, heard in the park, seen by the light of
        day;
Carefully observed one night by a secret agent of the Greek Hydraulic Min-
        ing Commission, in plain clothes, off duty.
The agent, in broken English, took copious notes. Which he lost.
Strange, and yet not extraordinary.
Sad, but true.

True, or exaggerated, or true;
As it is true that the people laugh and the sparrows fly;
As it is exaggerated that the people change, and the sea stays;
As it is that the people go;
20 As the lights go on and it is night and it is serious, and just the same;
As some one dies and it is serious, and the same;
As a girl knows and it is small, and true;
As the corner hardware clerk might know and it is true, and pointless;
As an old man knows and it is grotesque, but true;
As the people laugh, as the people think, as the people change,
It is serious and the same, exaggerated or true.

Bought at the drug store down the street
Where the wind blows and the motors go by and it is always night, or day;
Bought to use as a last resort,
30 Bought to impress the statuary in the park.
Bought at a cut rate, at the green light, at nine o'clock.
Borrowed or bought. To look well. To ennoble. To prevent disease. To
    entertain. To have.
Broken or sold. Or given away. Or used and forgotten. Or lost.

                                                    1929

Resurrection

You will remember the kisses, real or imagined;
You will remember the faces that were before you, and the words exchanged;
You will remember the minute crowded with meaning, the moment of pain,
    the aimless hour;
You will remember the cities, and the plains, and the mountains, and the
    sea,

And recall the friendly voice of the killer, or the voice of the priest,
    inhumanly sweet;
Recall the triumphant smile of the duped;
You will not forget compassion that glittered in the eyes of the money-
    lender, refusing you, not forget the purpose that lay beneath the
    merchant's warmth;
You will not forget the voice of the bought magistrate quivering in horror
    through the courtroom above prostitute and pimp,
The majesty of the statesman at the microphone, the sober majesty of the
    listening clerk,
10 The face of the fool, radiant on newspaper and screen;

You will remember hope that crawled up the bar-room tap and spoke
    through the confident speech of the lost,
Happiness clearly displayed on the glaring billboards,

Love casually revealed in the magazines and novels, or stated in the trembling limbs of ancient millionaires;
You will remember the triumph easily defined by the rebel messiah, by the breadloaf in the hand of the ghetto wife, by the inscription on the patriot tomb;
You will remember your laughter that rose with the steam from the carcass on the street
In hatred and pity exactly matched.

These are the things that will return to you,
To mingle with the days and nights, with the sound of motors and the sun's warmth,
With fatigue and desire,
20   As you work, and sleep, and talk, and laugh, and die.

                                                                                    1935

Memo

Is there still any shadow there, on the rainwet window of the coffee pot,
Between the haberdasher's and the pinball arcade,
There, where we stood one night in the warm, fine rain, and smoked and laughed and talked.

Is there now any sound at all,
Other than the sound of tires, and motors, and hurrying feet,
Is there on tonight's damp, heelpocked pavement somewhere the mark of a certain toe, an especial nail, or the butt of a particular dropped cigarette?—

(There must be, there has to be, no heart could beat if this were not so,
That was an hour, a glittering hour, an important hour in a tremendous year)

Where we talked for a while of life and love, of logic and the senses, of you and of me, character and fate, pain, revolution, victory and death,

10   Is there tonight any shadow, at all,
Other than the shadows that stop for a moment and then hurry past the windows blurred by the same warm, slow, still rain?

                                                                                    1938

LANGSTON HUGHES
1902–1967

Langston Hughes was the first popular black poet in the United States to add memorably to modern poetry. Born in Missouri, he was the son of a lawyer who became a successful businessman. His grandparents' generation included slaves freed before Emancipation, a follower of John Brown who stood with him at Harper's Ferry, and a great-uncle who was a Congressman. In childhood Hughes shuttled between divorced parents, each concerned to give him a good education. He entered Columbia University in 1921 as an engineering student, but this proved a false start. He soon shipped out for Africa and Europe, knocking about for some three years before joining his mother in Washington, D.C. There he caught the attention of Vachel Lindsay, who praised his writing and helped his career, which flourished even while he was earning a B.A. degree at Lincoln University in Pennsylvania (1929). A prolific writer, Hughes produced fiction, song lyrics, and newspaper columns along with his poetry, and he also edited anthologies. He took a militant interest in politics in the 1930s. When his work began to be published, he quickly became part of the Harlem Renaissance. He also influenced the politicized cultural movement of "Negritude" outside the United States.

Hughes based his main body of verse on black speech, blues, jazz, work-songs, ballads, and a lively feeling for the daily world of black people. His first book, *The Weary Blues* (1926), reflected both these influences and his reading of Vachel Lindsay, Carl Sandburg, and other populist poets who had experimented with free verse and vernacular effects. Intermixed with much rhetoric and other thin material, his purest work is usually close to being a folk or blues lyric. Sometimes it has the shape of a finely caught "found poem," molded from a snatch of conversation or a message scrawled on a postcard. Such work helped make room for a new body of verse enriched by hitherto neglected strains of American speech and song. Later black poets—Gwendolyn Brooks and Michael Harper, for instance—have followed in Hughes's wake. Often, like Imamu Amiri Baraka, they have absorbed his method into more complex and sophisticated structures.

The poems "50-50" and "Down and Out" reveal Hughes's special talent for working musical rhythms and everyday phrasing into a poem. "50-50" begins like the sort of blues song typified by Bessie Smith's "Empty Bed Blues." Lines 2, 3, and 5 are pure blues; only the words "she said" in line 1 set up our expectation of a story with dialogue. The rest of the poem shifts rapidly from the melancholy opening mood to the hard wit of an exploitative lover, and the piece as a whole strikes a balance between these major tonalities. "Down and Out" keeps strictly to the blues form throughout its first verse-unit; then, while continuing to beg and moan, it switches to a ballad stanza and, finally, to a short one-line afterbeat that both leavens and stresses the pathos. The delightful "Letter" seems close to a found poem but is most artful in its gay-spirited realism and rhythmic skill—its suggestion of metrical pattern (lines of from three to five stresses, with syncopated variations) within a free-flowing movement. In such poems Hughes's virtuosity is worn so lightly that it might easily be overlooked.

50-50

I'm all alone in this world, she said,
Ain't got nobody to share my bed,
Ain't got nobody to hold my hand—
The truth of the matter's
I ain't got no man.

Big Boy opened his mouth and said,
Trouble with you is
You ain't got no head!
If you had a head and used your mind
10   You could have *me* with you
All the time.

She answered, Babe, what must I do?

He said, Share your bed—
And your money, too.

1942

Letter

Dear Mama,
*   Time I pay rent and get my food*
and laundry I don't have much left
but here is five dollars for you
to show you I still appreciates you.
My girl-friend send her love and say
she hopes to lay eyes on you sometime in life.
Mama, it has been raining cats and dogs up
10   *here. Well, that is all so I will close.*
*   Your son baby*
*   Respectably as ever,*
*   Joe*

1951

Down and Out

Baby, if you love me
Help me when I'm down and out.
If you love me, baby,
Help me when I'm down and out,
I'm a po' gal
Nobody gives a damn about.

The credit man's done took ma clothes
And rent time's nearly here.
I'd like to buy a straightenin' comb,
10   An' I need a dime fo' beer.

I need a dime fo' beer.

1959

LOUIS ZUKOFSKY
1904-1978

A New Yorker by birth, first native American in an immigrant Jewish family, Zukofsky became a precocious student and earned an M.A. at Columbia University when he was twenty years old. He spent most of his adult life teaching at the Polytechnic Institute of Brooklyn and became one of the varied group of avant-garde poets encouraged by Ezra Pound and William Carlos Williams. He described himself as an "Objectivist"—a term never clearly defined but close to Imagism in its sense that the poem itself must become an independent "object" born of clear understanding of—i.e., experienced participation in—the reality of the world and life around us. Zukofsky was in his fifties before he saw publication of his major books begin with "A" 1-12 (1959). Like Basil Bunting (another Pound protégé), he was "reclaimed" from obscurity by a later generation of poets (Black Mountain and others) who sought living forerunners of their own verse-experimentation. His two collected editions, All: The Collected Shorter Poems 1923-1958 (1965) and All: The Collected Shorter Poems (1966) reveal his intricately and delicately associative, often highly elusive, poetic process.

Zukofsky's work was, at different times, drily intellectual, highly literary—even academic—in its allusiveness, and intimately personal in its familial affection. His earlier writing was strongly leftist, without being primarily political, and expressive of his circumstance as a Jew assimilating an alien, sometimes hostile culture. But his most enduring work resides in the kind of pure, apperceptive impressionism, impeccable in its free verse rhythms, represented by the poems that follow. He did not live to see his long poem "A"—the work of almost a half-century—finally appear as a whole, although sections of it had appeared over the years.

From 29 Poems

2

Not much more than being,
Thoughts of isolate, beautiful
Being at evening, to expect
            at a river-front:

A shaft dims
With a turning wheel;

Men work on a jetty
By a broken wagon;

Leopard, glowing-spotted,
10   The summer river—
Under: The Dragon:

27

Blue light is the night harbor-slip.
If a number are gold they make a crown for the shore.
If three rise vertically, as one nethermost, another
                over that, another topping,
All as if reaching, the vessel is making headway.

The scarf-pins of night-outers are sometimes that way
And, God's sky! if the body of something deploys one
                gold light for'ard,
And, shy, a smile, may it be named? another gold light as trailer,
10 The general "it is after midnight" may be a marriage,
                or a return from the month's ball.

           Masquerade, Mozart,
           Filigree—they used to—

(We had such a nice time)

Red! look out for this island!

Blue! and it hurts the eyes, metallic-glass this
                beacon-light, many-faceted

It is generally safer here because,
           in the white-washed ceiling hulk,
20   not only sparse lights for the deck
           but life-belts

Danger! The general effect of gray light in darkness
           is a man-of-war

Red!

Out far again
Lights—a branch laid on the world—
Their intermittence—

(We look abroad openly)

1966

The Ways

The wakes that boats make
and after they are out of sight
the ways they have made in water:
loops, straight paths,
to do with mirror-like,
tides, the clouds the deep day blue
of the unclouded parts of the sky,
currents, gray sevens or darker shadows
against lighter in and out weaving
10   of mercurial vanishing eights,
or imaginably sights
instantaneously a duration and sun,
and the leaping silver
as of rain-pelted nipples
of the water itself.

After reading, a song

a light snow
a had been fallen

20   the brown most showed
knoll trunk knot treelings' U's

The Sound marsh water

ice clump
sparkling root etc

and so far out.

1967

PATRICK KAVANAGH
1905–1967

Patrick Kavanagh was born and spent his youth in the impoverished world of what he called the "stony grey soil of Monaghan," the Irish county that is the setting for his many poems of rural life. His work is often pastoral, both in its knowledge of country things and occasional pure delight in them and in its local-color accuracy, frequently accompanied by bitterness over the depri-vations of peasant existence. At the age of thirty-four, Kavanagh left Monaghan for Dublin. There he led a contentious, alcoholic, largely uncomfortable life and developed throat cancer. He made a meager living through journalism (including the publishing of his own paper, *Kavanagh's Weekly*) and odd jobs such as house-painting. But his sometimes raucous wit, his fresh, frank cantankerousness, and his clear poetic gifts won him a respected place in Irish letters during his lifetime.

Kavanagh's reputation rests chiefly on a long narrative poem, *The Great Hunger* (1942), which emphasizes not literal hunger but the sexual and psychological hunger caused by a combination of barren circumstances: bondage to the small family farm, domination by a puritanical mother, and a sense of guilt and a fear of adventure that imprison the ill-educated protagonist within the narrowest kind of life. The historical "Great Hunger"—the terrible Irish famine of the 1840s—does not enter the poem directly but lurks, by way of the title, in the poem's whole burden of oppressive emptiness.

"Father Mat"—the poem here—is more typical of his best poetry. If it lacks the other work's uncompromising harshness and realism, it richly balances the emotional pressures embodied in the thoughts and feelings of the country priest who is the poem's center: his pagan mysticism, precariously opposed to Christian asceticism; his earthy but modest oneness with his land and people; and his simple delight—much like Kavanagh's own in some of his earlier poems—in the world's surprising beauty.

Kavanagh's later poetry is often painfully self-conscious in its projection of neglect, failure, self-pity, and general seediness. Still, it retains its sardonic edge, ability to shock, and lyrical originality. Kavanagh remains a bold, unpretentious voice from the common life as he knew it.

Father Mat[1]

I

In a meadow
Beside the chapel three boys were playing football.
At the forge door an old man was leaning
Viewing a hunter-hoe. A man could hear
If he listened to the breeze the fall of wings—
How wistfully the sin-birds come home!

It was Confession Saturday, the first
Saturday in May; the May Devotions
Were spread like leaves to quieten
10   The excited armies of conscience.
The knife of penance fell so like a blade
Of grass that no one was afraid.

Father Mat came slowly walking, stopping to
Stare through gaps at ancient Ireland sweeping
In again with all its unbaptized beauty:
The calm evening,
The whitethorn blossoms,
The smell from ditches that were not Christian.
The dancer that dances in the hearts of men cried:
20   Look! I have shown this to you before—
The rags of living surprised
The joy in things you cannot forget.

[1] Father Mat (named after St. Matthew) is presented as an Irish country priest, presumably in the poet's native County Monaghan.

His heavy hat was square upon his head,
Like a Christian Brother's;[2]
His eyes were an old man's watery eyes,

Out of his flat nose grew spiky hairs.
He was a part of the place,
Natural as a round stone in a grass field;
He could walk through a cattle fair
30   And the people would only notice his odd spirit there.

His curate passed on a bicycle—[3]
He had the haughty intellectual look
Of the man who never reads in brook or book;
A man designed
To wear a mitre,
To sit on committees—
For will grows strongest in the emptiest mind.

The old priest saw him pass
And, seeing, saw
40   Himself a mediaeval ghost.
Ahead of him went Power,
One who was not afraid when the sun opened a flower,
Who was never astonished
At a stick carried down a stream
Or at the undying difference in the corner of a field.

                    II
The Holy Ghost descends
At random like the muse
On wise man and fool,
And why should poet in the twilight choose?

50   Within the dim chapel was the grey
Mumble of prayer
To the Queen of May—
The Virgin Mary with the schoolgirl air.[4]

Two guttering candles on a brass shrine
Raised upon the wall
Monsters of despair
To terrify deep into the soul.

Through the open door the hum of rosaries
Came out and blended with the homing bees.
60   The trees

---

[2] **Christian Brother** member of a Roman Catholic lay order (Brothers of the Christian Schools) dedicated to teaching youth
[3] ll. 31–45 Father Mat's assistant has the qualities that Jesus rebuked in the Gospels: he goes by rote and rule and lacks the sense of awe and wonder that should underlie his vocation—a lack, the poem sardonically suggests, that fits him for the higher circles of ecclesiastical power.
[4] l. 53 See ll. 134–37 and note 8, below.

Heard nothing stranger than the rain or the wind
Or the birds—
But deep in their roots they knew a seed had sinned.

In the graveyard a goat was nibbling at a yew,
The cobbler's chickens with anxious looks
Were straggling home through nettles, over graves.
A young girl down a hill was driving cows
To a corner at the gable-end of a roofless house.

Cows were milked earlier,
70   The supper hurried,
Hens shut in,
Horses unyoked,
And three men shaving before the same mirror.

III

The trip of iron tips on tile
Hesitated up the middle aisle,
Heads that were bowed glanced up to see
Who could this last arrival be.

Murmur of women's voices from the porch,
Memories of relations in the graveyard.
80   On the stem
Of memory imaginations blossom.

               In the dim
Corners in the side seats faces gather,
Lit up now and then by a guttering candle
And the ghost of day at the window.
A secret lover is saying
Three Hail Marys[5] that she who knows
The ways of women will bring
Cathleen O'Hara (he names her) home to him.
90   Ironic fate! Cathleen herself is saying
Three Hail Marys to her who knows
The ways of men to bring
Somebody else home to her—
"O may he love me."
What is the Virgin Mary now to do?

IV
          From a confessional
The voice of Father Mat's absolving
Rises and falls like a briar in the breeze.

[5] **Hail Marys** Hail Mary: first words of a Roman
Catholic prayer to the Virgin Mary. The prayer
is familiarly called a "Hail Mary."

As the sins pour in the old priest is thinking
100 His fields of fresh grass, his horses, his cows,
His earth into the fires of Purgatory.
It cools his mind.
"They confess to the fields," he mused,
"They confess to the fields and the air and the sky,"
And forgiveness was the soft grass of his meadow by the river;
His thoughts were walking through it now.

His human lips talked on:
"My son,
Only the poor in spirit shall wear the crown;
110 Those down
Can creep in the low door
On to Heaven's floor."[6]

The Tempter[7] had another answer ready:
"Ah lad, upon the road of life
Tis best to dance with Chance's wife
And let the rains that come in time
Erase the footprints of the crime."

The dancer that dances in the hearts of men
Tempted him again:
120 "Look! I have shown you this before;
From this mountain top I have tempted Christ
With what you see now
Of beauty—all that's music, poetry, art
In things you can touch every day.
I broke away
And rule all dominions that are rare;
I took with me all the answers to every prayer
That young men and girls pray for: love, happiness, riches—"
O Tempter! O Tempter!

V
130 As Father Mat walked home
Venus was in the western sky
And there were voices in the hedges:
"God the Gay is not the Wise."

"Take your choice, take your choice,"
Called the breeze through the bridge's eye.
"The domestic Virgin and Her Child
Or Venus with her ecstasy."[8]

1947

---

[6] ll. 108–112 See the Sermon on the Mount in Matthew 5—especially 5:3–10.
[7] **The Tempter** Satan, or the Devil. See Matthew 4.

[8] ll. 134–37 Father Mat must choose between the pagan Queen of May and the Virgin Mary. (The more fortunate poet can accept both as merely different phases of the same figure.)

ROBERT PENN WARREN

b. 1905

Born in Guthrie, Kentucky, Warren was edu-
cated in local public schools and at Vander-
bilt University, later doing graduate work
at the University of California and Yale and
then studying at Oxford University as a
Rhodes Scholar. He became known early as
a contributor to *Fugitive*, a magazine stress-
ing Southern verse and traditions, and there-
after as a founder and the managing editor
of the *Southern Review*. Together with the
critic Cleanth Brooks, he gained wider
national attention through their textbook
Understanding Poetry (1938). This book
helped revolutionize the teaching of poetry
by centering on the specific artistry of in-
dividual poems rather than on historical,
biographical, or didactic considerations or
on paraphrasing poems primarily for their
ideas. This approach was the gist of the
then "new" criticism: a term coined by
John Crowe Ransom, another associate of
the *Fugitive* group.

A professor for many years, Warren has

been a prolific writer of fiction, poetry,
criticism, and general essays, winning fame
above all for his novel *All the King's Men*
(1946)—a study of Southern political power
and demagoguery based on the career of
Governor Huey Long of Louisiana but
clearly relevant to more than one particular
region of the country. He has received vir-
tually every award available to American
writers and, in 1986, was appointed the first
Poet Laureate of the United States. He was
married to another gifted writer, the late
Eleanor Clark.

The poems that follow illustrate two main
characteristics of Warren's verse. "Bearded
Oaks" reflects his early absorption of Donne
and the other seventeenth-century Meta-
physical poets, an influence largely trans-
mitted by way of T. S. Eliot (whose idiom
flavors that of "Bearded Oaks"). The other
chief characteristic, seen in "Little Girl
Wakes Early," is Warren's natural bent for
story-telling.

Bearded Oaks

The oaks, how subtle and marine,
Bearded, and all the layered light
Above them swims; and thus the scene,
Recessed, awaits the positive night.

So, waiting, we in the grass now lie
Beneath the languorous tread of light:
The grasses, kelp-like, satisfy
The nameless motions of the air.

Upon the floor of light, and time,
10   Unmurmuring, of polyp made,
We rest; we are, as light withdraws,
Twin atolls on a shelf of shade.

Ages to our construction went,
Dim architecture, hour by hour:
And violence, forgot now, lent
The present stillness all its power.

The storm of noon above us rolled,
Of light the fury, furious gold,
The long drag troubling us, the depth:
20   Dark is unrocking, unrippling, still.

Passion and slaughter, ruth, decay
Descend, minutely whispering down,
Silted down swaying streams, to lay
Foundation for our voicelessness.

All our debate is voiceless here,
As all our rage, the rage of stone;
If hope is hopeless, then fearless is fear,
And history is thus undone.

Our feet once wrought the hollow street
30   With echo when the lamps were dead
At windows, once our headlight glare
Disturbed the doe that, leaping, fled.

I do not love you less that now
The caged heart makes iron stroke,
Or less that all that light once gave
The graduate dark should now revoke.

We live in time so little time
And we learn all so painfully,
That we may spare this hour's term
To practice for eternity.

1935

Little Girl Wakes Early

Remember when you were the first one awake, the first
To stir in the dawn-curdled house, with little bare feet
Cold on boards, every door shut and accurst,
And behind shut doors no breath perhaps drew, no heart beat.

You held your breath and thought how all over town
Houses had doors shut, and no whisper of breath sleeping,
And that meant no swinging, nobody to pump up and down,
No hide-and-go-seek, no serious play at housekeeping.

So you ran outdoors, bare feet from the dew wet,
10   And climbed the fence to the house of your dearest friend,
And opened your lips and twisted your tongue, all set
To call her name—but the sound wouldn't come in the end,

For you thought how awful, if there was no breath there
For answer. Tears start, you run home, where now mother,
Over the stove, is humming some favorite air.
You seize her around the legs, but tears aren't over,

And won't get over, not even when she shakes you—
And shakes you hard—and more when you can't explain.
Your mother's long dead. And you've learned that when loneliness
    takes you
There's nobody ever to explain to—though you try again and again.

1985

WILLIAM EMPSON

b. 1906

Empson, a disciple of the critic and theorist I.A. Richards, studied English and mathematics at Cambridge University. In the 1930s he taught English literature at Tokyo National University and at the National University in Peking. He was Chinese editor for the British Broadcasting Corporation from 1941 to 1946. He later served as professor of English at Sheffield University until his retirement. His critical influence has been stronger than his poetic impact, but both modes of writing express the same highly developed and extremely original sensibility. He combines high wit (including outrageously intellectual punning), Marxist-influenced perspectives, and the playful seriousness of the happiest kind of verbophile in everything he writes.

Empson is represented here by two villanelles (poems of five three-line stanzas and a final four-line stanza, with only two rhymes) and by an unrhymed, rather discursive poem with mostly five-stress lines and an uneven, deliberately jerky rhythmic pattern. The first, called simply "Villanelle," concerns the pain of an enduring love for a woman who no longer feels love herself, although she is "still kind." The theme is common in poetry, the form is old and familiar, and the essential emotion comes through clearly. But the poem challenges us with diction like "your chemic beauty," "pain's secondary phase," and "we miss our cue," and a subtle perspective

and analytical intelligence are superimposed on what would otherwise be a simple lover's complaint. The same principle is seen in the other villanelle, "Missing Dates," which uses an even more intellectualized vocabulary—that of a scientist or some other learned person—combined with more emotional phrasing to lament the inevitable end of life-energy and of life itself, as the poisonous "waste" of existence accumulates in the bloodstream.

The third poem, "Homage to the British Museum," is a heartfelt witticism based on a chart in the London institution that is preeminent among museums, libraries, and research centers. Presenting the world's religions comparatively, this chart is the "Supreme God" of the modern, scientifically oriented mind, and Empson's description suggests that it has an organic life of its own. The poem's movement resembles a mocking sermon that also reflects yearning for a simple faith no longer possible; hence the self-interruptions and qualifications, so different from the rhythm of the villanelles. This wryly light-hearted poem recalls Empson's prose, especially his famous *Seven Types of Ambiguity* (1930), which demonstrates the central role of ambiguity in poetry, and *Some Versions of Pastoral* (1935), a discussion of the ironic and liberating function of the kind of writing called "pastoral."

Villanelle[1]

It is the pain, it is the pain, endures.
Your chemic beauty burned my muscles through.
Poise of my hands reminded me of yours.

What later purge from this deep toxin cures?
What kindness now could the old salve renew?
It is the pain, it is the pain, endures.

The infection slept (custom or change inures)
And when pain's secondary phase was due
Poise of my hands reminded me of yours.

10   How safe I felt, whom memory assures,
Rich that your grace safely by heart I knew.
It is the pain, it is the pain, endures.

My stare drank deep beauty that still allures.
My heart pumps yet the poison draught of you.
Poise of my hands reminded me of yours.

You are still kind whom the same shape immures.
Kind and beyond adieu. We miss our cue.
It is the pain, it is the pain, endures.
Poise of my hands reminded me of yours.

1935

[1] See comment in headnote on Empson. The villanelle is a demanding form whose pattern of repetitions encourages strong emotional effects close to those of music, although it is often used for light verse in English. Notice, in addition to the rhyme scheme, the repetition of the opening line at the ends of the second and fourth tercets and as the third line of the concluding quatrain, and the repetition of the third line at the ends of the third and fifth tercets and of the quatrain. Empson uses the same form in "Missing Dates" (p. 966), as does Dylan Thomas in "Do Not Go Gentle into That Good Night" (p. 985).

Homage to the British Museum[1]

There is a Supreme God in the ethnological section;
A hollow toad shape, faced with a blank shield.
He needs his belly to include the Pantheon,[2]
Which is inserted through a hole behind.
At the navel, at the points formally stressed, at the organs of sense,
Lice glue themselves, dolls, local deities,
His smooth wood creeps with all the creeds of the world.

[1] See comment in headnote on Empson.
[2] **Pantheon** all the gods of a people; in this instance (with atheistic irony), all the gods of all the peoples, as represented in the British Museum's ingenious comparative-religion display

Attending there let us absorb the cultures of nations
And dissolve into our judgement all their codes.
10   Then, being clogged with a natural hesitation
(People are continually asking one the way out),
Let us stand here and admit that we have no road.
Being everything, let us admit that is to be something,
Or give ourselves the benefit of the doubt;
Let us offer our pinch of dust all to this God,
And grant his reign over the entire building.

1935

Missing Dates[1]

Slowly the poison the whole blood stream fills.
It is not the effort nor the failure tires.
The waste remains, the waste remains and kills.

It is not your system or clear sight that mills
Down small to the consequence a life requires;
Slowly the poison the whole blood stream fills.

They bled an old dog dry yet the exchange rills
Of young dog blood gave but a month's desires;
The waste remains, the waste remains and kills.

10   It is the Chinese tombs and the slag hills
Usurp the soil, and not the soil retires.[2]
Slowly the poison the whole blood stream fills.

Not to have fire is to be a skin that shrills.
The complete fire is death. From partial fires
The waste remains, the waste remains and kills.

It is the poems you have lost, the ills
From missing dates, at which the heart expires.
Slowly the poison the whole blood stream fills.
The waste remains, the waste remains and kills.

1940

[1] The title denotes all the lost or neglected possibilities and repressed memories of any life, which accumulates psychic "waste" (ll. 15–17) just as mechanical systems do physical waste. See also comment in headnote on Empson, and note 1 to his "Villanelle" (p. 965 above).

[2] ll. 7–11 "It is true about the old dog, at least I saw it reported somewhere, but the legend that a fifth or some such part of the soil of China is given up to ancestral tombs is (by the way) not true" (Empson's note).

W.H. AUDEN
1907–1973

The son of a physician and professor of public health at the University of Birmingham, Auden specialized in biology at school and won a natural sciences scholarship to Oxford University, intending to become a mining engineer. Instead, he discovered his poetic vocation and became part of the brilliant young group of university poets that included Stephen Spender, Louis MacNeice, and C. Day Lewis. During the 1930s he began traveling widely—to Germany, Iceland, China, and finally the United States, where he took up residence in 1939 and become a naturalized citizen in 1946. He also went to Spain in support of the Loyalist government during the civil war, although he took no part in the military struggle. His sympathies with the victims of the Nazis led the homosexual Auden to marry Erika Mann, Thomas Mann's daughter, in 1935 so that she could get a passport and flee Germany. Deeply interested in opera, he composed libretti for Stravinsky and others. Over the years he shifted from his youthful Communist sympathies and D.H. Lawrence-like psychic mysticism to more conservative and even traditionally Christian positions.

Almost from the start Auden was admired by other poets of his own generation and older. Among the group of writers who came of age at the end of the 1920s, he was outstanding for his ability to catch the new moods produced by worldwide economic and political crisis. His first book was privately printed by Spender, in 1928; and the next two were accepted by T.S. Eliot for Faber and Faber and appeared in 1930 and 1933. (All three were simply called *Poems*; although the 1933 volume was printed as a "second edition," they are not identical.) Thereafter he was generally held to be the foremost British poet born in this century.

Auden's versatility shows the influence of many strains of English verse, and his work is notable for the pure melodic line that is intrinsic to the English lyric tradition. He uses the melodic element so flexibly that it serves ambiguous, ironic, and intellectually complex functions to an unusual degree. "The Decoys," written in 1931, is both a lovely, elegiac song and something of a riddle; while it does not explain its compelling symbols, its tone and imagery suggest the deceptiveness of apparent innocence and goodness in a mad, violent world. Three poems written in 1936 illustrate Auden's range. "O What Is That Sound" echoes old folk ballads like "Edward" and "Lord Randal" in its question-and-answer method of building horror, but its versification is far more complex, and, like "The Decoys," it presents a riddle — an undefined state of gathering political and personal disaster. The poem that was eventually to become the tenth in the "Sonnets from China" sequence reveals, half-humorously and with an ingenious play of images and manipulation of the sonnet form, the poet's preoccupation with Freudian insights and with a dark primitivism under the surface of civilization. "On This Island," perhaps Auden's purest lyrical poem, describes a "view" with sensuous precision, meanwhile unfolding the inner process by which art achieves empathy with the world outside ourselves.

Auden's more mature poetry combines humane, tender feeling with a sophistication that, in "Lullaby," borders on cynicism. In "Musée des Beaux Arts" and "The Shield of Achilles" (his most grimly poignant poem), the overriding irony gives the humane feeling an unsentimental, depressive power. Sometimes his ironic sense forces Auden into a variety of wit or rhetoric that undercuts the depressive power and weakens an otherwise bitterly effective poem. This is true of his famous elegy "In Memory of W.B. Yeats" and the brilliant but only half-successful "September 1, 1939," which remains unforgettable even though he excluded it from his collected work. The less flamboyant "Prime" brims over with magical reverie, punctuated by reminders of hard realities that the waking soul must confront. With this poem, written in 1949, and "The Decoys," written in 1952, Auden achieves exquisite lyrical mastery, while coping directly with worldly awareness and unease. The monumental task of editing Auden's often-revised and chronologically scrambled text was performed by Edward Mendelson in preparing the posthumous *Collected Poems* (1978).

The Decoys[1]

There are some birds in these valleys
Who flutter round the careless
With intimate appeal,
By seeming kindness trained to snaring,
They feel no falseness.

Under the spell completely
They circle can serenely,
And in the tricky light
The masked hill has a purer greenness.
10 Their flight looks fleeter.

But fowlers, O, like foxes,
Lie ambushed in the rushes.
Along the harmless tracks
The madman keeper crawls through brushwood,
Axe under oxter.[2]

Alas, the signal given,
Fingers on trigger tighten.
The real unlucky dove
Must smarting fall away from brightness
20 Its love from living.

May 1931   1932

[1] See comment in headnote on Auden. One implication of the title is that good people such as devoted teachers and clergymen may, with innocent good will, mislead those they seem to help the most; they may, unconsciously, be serving the interests of a destructive system ("the madman keeper").

[2] **oxter** armpit

O What Is That Sound[1]

O what is that sound which so thrills the ear
    Down in the valley drumming, drumming?
Only the scarlet soldiers, dear,
    The soldiers coming.

[1] See comment in headnote on Auden. This is one of several poems in which Auden adapts characteristics of the folk ballad to modern circumstance or sensibility.

O what is that light I see flashing so clear
   Over the distance brightly, brightly?
Only the sun on their weapons, dear,
   As they step lightly.

O what are they doing with all that gear,
10   What are they doing this morning, this morning?
Only their usual manoeuvres, dear,
   Or perhaps a warning.

O why have they left the road down there,
   Why are they suddenly wheeling, wheeling?
Perhaps a change in their orders, dear.
   Why are you kneeling?

O haven't they stopped for the doctor's care,
   Haven't they reined their horses, their horses?
Why, they are none of them wounded, dear,
20   None of these forces.

O is it the parson they want, with white hair,
   Is it the parson, is it, is it?
No, they are passing his gateway, dear,
   Without a visit.

O it must be the farmer who lives so near.
   It must be the farmer so cunning, so cunning?
They have passed the farmyard already, dear,
   And now they are running.

O where are you going? Stay with me here!
30   Were the vows you swore deceiving, deceiving?
No, I promised to love you, dear,
   But I must be leaving.

O it's broken the lock and splintered the door,
   O it's the gate where they're turning, turning;
Their boots are heavy on the floor
   And their eyes are burning.

October 1932   1936

On This Island[1]

Look, stranger, on this island now
The leaping light for your delight discovers,
Stand stable here
And silent be,

[1] See comment in headnote on Auden.

That through the channels of the ear
May wander like a river
The swaying sound of the sea.

Here at the small field's ending pause
When the chalk wall falls to the foam and its tall ledges
10   Oppose the pluck
And knock of the tide,
And the shingle scrambles after the suck-
-ing surf,
And the gull lodges
A moment on its sheer side.

Far off like floating seeds the ships
Diverge on urgent voluntary errands,
And the full view[2]
Indeed may enter
20   And move in memory as now these clouds do,
That pass the harbour mirror
And all the summer through the water saunter.

1935   1936

[2] Eventually, the "full view" may be able to absorb the wider world of human enterprise and assimilate it to the more concentrated empathy of the moment "here" at the sea's edge.

From Sonnets from China[1]

X

So an age ended, and its last deliverer died
In bed, grown idle and unhappy; they were safe:
The sudden shadow of a giant's enormous calf
Would fall no more at dusk across their lawns outside.

They slept in peace: in marshes here and there no doubt
A sterile dragon lingered to a natural death,
But in a year the slot had vanished from the heath;
A kobold's knocking in the mountain petered out.

Only the sculptors and the poets were half-sad,
10   And the pert retinue from the magician's house
Grumbled and went elsewhere. The vanquished powers were glad

[1] This sonnet sequence is based partly on the Sino-Japanese War of the 1930s, but is mostly devoted to an ironic contemplation of humanity's evolution. In Sonnet X, the enlightened mind has brought freedom from ancient fears and superstitions — but the "vanquished powers" have retreated from the external world into our unconscious psychic lives.

To be invisible and free; without remorse
Struck down the silly sons who strayed into their course,
And ravished the daughters, and drove the fathers mad.

1936   1939

Lullaby[1]

Lay your sleeping head, my love,
Human on my faithless arm;
Time and fevers burn away
Individual beauty from
Thoughtful children, and the grave
Proves the child ephemeral:
But in my arms till break of day
Let the living creature lie,
Mortal, guilty, but to me
10   The entirely beautiful.

Soul and body have no bounds:
To lovers as they lie upon
Her tolerant enchanted slope
In their ordinary swoon,
Grave the vision Venus sends
Of supernatural sympathy,
Universal love and hope;
While an abstract insight wakes
Among the glaciers and the rocks
20   The hermit's carnal ecstasy.[2]

Certainty, fidelity
On the stroke of midnight pass
Like vibrations of a bell
And fashionable madmen raise
Their pedantic boring cry:
Every farthing of the cost,
All the dreaded cards foretell,
Shall be paid, but from this night
Not a whisper, not a thought,
30   Not a kiss nor look be lost.[3]

Beauty, midnight, vision dies:
Let the winds of dawn that blow
Softly round your dreaming head

[1] See comment in headnote on Auden.
[2] ll. 11–20 Under the spell of Venus, goddess of love, opposites (ordinary lovers and ascetic hermits) converge, if only while the illusion holds sway. (Auden's perspective and style approach those of Yeats in this poem.)

[3] ll. 21–30 Though prophets ("fashionable madmen") are right about love's sweetest illusions inevitably being dispelled by reality, the vision of a moment of grace truly experienced remains intact.

Such a day of welcome show
Eye and knocking heart may bless,
Find our mortal world enough;
Noons of dryness find you fed
By the involuntary powers,
Nights of insult let you pass
40   Watched by every human love.

January 1937   1940

Musée des Beaux Arts[1]

About suffering they were never wrong,
The Old Masters:[2] how well they understood
Its human position; how it takes place
While someone else is eating or opening a window or just walking
    dully along;
How, when the aged are reverently, passionately waiting
For the miraculous birth, there always must be
Children who did not specially want it to happen, skating
On a pond at the edge of the wood:
They never forgot
10   That even the dreadful martyrdom must run its course
Anyhow in a corner, some untidy spot
Where the dogs go on with their doggy life and the torturer's horse
Scratches its innocent behind on a tree.

In Breughel's *Icarus*,[3] for instance: how everything turns away
Quite leisurely from the disaster; the ploughman may
Have heard the splash, the forsaken cry,
But for him it was not an important failure; the sun shone
As it had to on the white legs disappearing into the green
Water; and the expensive delicate ship that must have seen
20   Something amazing, a boy falling out of the sky,
Had somewhere to get to and sailed calmly on.

December 1938   1940

---

[1] (French) Museum of Fine Arts
[2] **The Old Masters** the great European painters before 1700
[3] **Breughel's *Icarus*** *The Fall of Icarus*, a painting by Flemish artist Pieter Breughel (1522?–1565). In Greek mythology the master craftsman Daedalus fashioned wings of wax and feathers for his son Icarus and himself in order to escape from the Cretan labyrinth. Icarus flew too near the sun, the wax melted, and he fell into the sea and drowned.

In Memory of W.B. Yeats[1]

(D. JAN. 1939)

I

He disappeared in the dead of winter:
The brooks were frozen, the airports almost deserted,
And snow disfigured the public statues;
The mercury sank in the mouth of the dying day.
What instruments we have agree
The day of his death was a dark cold day.

Far from his illness
The wolves ran on through the evergreen forests,
The peasant river was untempted by the fashionable quays;
10   By mourning tongues
The death of the poet was kept from his poems.

But for him it was his last afternoon as himself,
An afternoon of nurses and rumours;
The provinces of his body revolted,
The squares of his mind were empty,
Silence invaded the suburbs,
The current of his feeling failed; he became his admirers.

Now he is scattered among a hundred cities
And wholly given over to unfamiliar affections,
20   To find his happiness in another kind of wood
And be punished under a foreign code of conscience.
The words of a dead man
Are modified in the guts of the living.

But in the importance of noise of to-morrow
When the brokers are roaring like beasts on the floor of the Bourse,[2]
And the poor have the sufferings to which they are fairly accustomed,
And each in the cell of himself is almost convinced of his freedom,
A few thousand will think of this day
As one thinks of a day when one did something slightly unusual.
30   What instruments we have agree
The day of his death was a dark cold day.

II

You were silly like us;[3] your gift survived it all:
The parish of rich women, physical decay,
Yourself. Mad Ireland hurt you into poetry.[4]
Now Ireland has her madness and her weather still,

---

[1] William Butler Yeats (1865–1939), felt by younger contemporaries to have been the quintessential modern poet, because of his genius and his combined tragic sense of the age and artistic integrity
[2] the Bourse the French stock exchange, in Paris
[3] You were silly like us Yeats had human foibles.

[4] ll. 33–34 parish of rich women a reference to Lady Augusta Gregory's patronage of Yeats; possibly also to Mrs. Annie Horniman's support of Dublin's Abbey Theatre. These lines allude to the parochialism and political fanaticism attributed to Ireland in Yeats's poems.

For poetry makes nothing happen: it survives
In the valley of its making where executives
Would never want to tamper, flows on south
From ranches of isolation and the busy griefs,
40   Raw towns that we believe and die in; it survives,
A way of happening, a mouth.

III[5]

Earth, receive an honoured guest:
William Yeats is laid to rest.
Let the Irish vessel lie
Emptied of its poetry.

In the nightmare of the dark
All the dogs of Europe bark,
And the living nations wait,
Each sequestered in its hate;

50   Intellectual disgrace
Stares from every human face,
And the seas of pity lie
Locked and frozen in each eye.

Follow, poet, follow right
To the bottom of the night,
With your unconstraining voice
Still persuade us to rejoice;

With the farming of a verse
Make a vineyard of the curse,
60   Sing of human unsuccess
In a rapture of distress;

In the deserts of the heart
Let the healing fountain start,
In the prison of his days
Teach the free man how to praise.

February 1939   1940

---

[5] Section III Originally this section included three additional stanzas between the present first and second ones:

Time that is intolerant
Of the brave and innocent,
And indifferent in a week
To a beautiful physique,

Worships language and forgives
Everyone by whom it lives;
Pardons cowardice, conceit,
Lays its honours at their feet.

Time that with this strange excuse
Pardoned Kipling and his views,
And will pardon Paul Claudel,
Pardons him for writing well.

These stanzas cited Yeats's contemporaries Rudyard Kipling and French poet Paul Claudel as authors whose artistry made up for their rightist attitudes — an implicit defence of Yeats on similar grounds.

September 1, 1939[1]

I sit in one of the dives[2]
On Fifty-Second Street[3]
Uncertain and afraid
As the clever hopes expire
Of a low dishonest decade:
Waves of anger and fear
Circulate over the bright
And darkened lands of the earth,
Obsessing our private lives;
10   The unmentionable odour of death
Offends the September night.

Accurate scholarship can
Unearth the whole offence
From Luther until now
That has driven a culture mad,[4]
Find what occurred at Linz,[5]
What huge imago made
A psychopathic god:[6]
I and the public know
20   What all schoolchildren learn,
Those to whom evil is done
Do evil in return.

Exiled Thucydides[7] knew
All that a speech can say
About Democracy,
And what dictators do,
The elderly rubbish they talk
To an apathetic grave;
Analysed all in his book,
30   The enlightenment driven away,
The habit-forming pain,
Mismanagement and grief:
We must suffer them all again.

---

[1] date of the German invasion of Poland, the start of World War II (two days later the British and French declared war against Germany). See comment in headnote on Auden. (Although this is one of his best-known poems, Auden rejected it from later collections.)
[2] **dives** tawdry bars or taverns
[3] **Fifty-Second Street** in New York City
[4] ll. 12–15 The "offence" is the history of militant nationalism since the sixteenth century (at first associated with Luther and the Protestant Reformation).

[5] **Linz** Adolf Hitler's Austrian birthplace
[6] ll. 17–18 The "imago" (a psychoanalytic term) is the father image that drove Hitler toward distorted ideals; it also suggests that history, with its past wars, has created a murderous imago for all of us.
[7] **Thucydides** fifth-century B.C. Greek historian, author of *The Peloponnesian Wars* (written when he was exiled from Athens)

Into this neutral air
Where blind skyscrapers use
Their full height to proclaim
The strength of Collective Man,
Each language pours its vain
Competitive excuse:
40   But who can live for long
In an euphoric dream;
Out of the mirror they stare,
Imperialism's face
And the international wrong.

Faces along the bar
Cling to their average day:
The lights must never go out,
The music must always play,
All the conventions conspire
50   To make this fort assume
The furniture of home;
Lest we should see where we are,
Lost in a haunted wood,
Children afraid of the night
Who have never been happy or good.

The windiest militant trash
Important Persons shout
Is not so crude as our wish:
What mad Nijinsky wrote
60   About Diaghilev[8]
Is true of the normal heart;
For the error bred in the bone
Of each woman and each man
Craves what it cannot have,
Not universal love
But to be loved alone.

From the conservative dark
Into the ethical life
The dense commuters come,
70   Repeating their morning vow,
"I *will* be true to the wife,
I'll concentrate more on my work,"
And helpless governors[9] wake
To resume their compulsory game:
Who can release them now,
Who can reach the deaf,
Who can speak for the dumb?

---

[8] ll. 59–60 Vaslav Nijinsky, great early-twentieth-century Russian ballet dancer, and Sergei Pavlovich Diaghilev, his producer and choreographer. Nijinsky wrote that Diaghilev wanted the exclusive love of anyone he had anything to do with.

[9] **helpless governors** unconscious psychological triggering mechanisms

All I have is a voice
To undo the folded lie,
80 The romantic lie in the brain
Of the sensual man-in-the-street
And the lie of Authority
Whose buildings grope the sky:
There is no such thing as the State
And no one exists alone;
Hunger allows no choice
To the citizen or the police;
We must love one another or die.

Defenceless under the night
90 Our world in stupor lies;
Yet, dotted everywhere,
Ironic points of light
Flash out wherever the Just
Exchange their messages:
May I, composed like them
Of Eros[10] and of dust,
Beleaguered by the same
Negation and despair,
Show an affirming flame.

September 1939   1940

[10]**Eros** Greek god of love, usually associated
with sexual love, but closer here to richly
humane affection

From Horae Canonicae[1]

1: Prime

Simultaneously, as soundlessly,
    Spontaneously, suddenly
As, at the vaunt of the dawn, the kind
    Gates of the body fly open
To its world beyond, the gates of the mind,
    The horn gate and the ivory gate
Swing to, swing shut, instantaneously[2]

[1] **Horae Canonicae** (Latin) the canonical hours
—seven periods of the day designated for
Christian prayer and worship. **Prime** (from
Latin *primus*: "first") is the first daylight canon-
ical hour, beginning at sunrise or at 6 a.m. In
this sequence of poems the Christian resonances
are absorbed into psychological states and asso-
ciations of the time of day involved.
[2] ll. 3–7 In Homer's *Odyssey* XIX, dreams are
said to enter the mind either by the gate of horn,
when based on reality, or by the gate of ivory,
when based on fantasy. Both "gates" swing
shut at the moment of waking.

Quell the nocturnal rummage
Of its rebellious fronde,[3] ill-favored,
10   Ill-natured and second-rate,
Disenfranchised, widowed and orphaned
      By an historical mistake:
Recalled from the shades to be a seeing being,
      From absence to be on display,
Without a name or history I wake
Between my body and the day.

Holy this moment, wholly in the right,
      As, in complete obedience
To the light's laconic outcry, next
20   As a sheet, near as a wall,
Out there as a mountain's poise of stone,
      The world is present, about,
And I know that I am, here, not alone
      But with a world and rejoice
Unvexed, for the will has still to claim
      This adjacent arm as my own,
The memory to name me, resume
      Its routine of praise and blame,
And smiling to me is this instant while
30   Still the day is intact, and I
The Adam sinless in our beginning,
      Adam still previous to any act.

I draw breath; that is of course to wish
      No matter what, to be wise,
To be different, to die and the cost,
      No matter how, is Paradise
Lost of course and myself owing a death:
      The eager ridge, the steady sea,
The flat roofs of the fishing village
40   Still asleep in its bunny,
Though as fresh and sunny still, are not friends
      But things to hand, this ready flesh
No honest equal, but my accomplice now,
      My assassin to be, and my name
Stands for my historical share of care
      For a lying self-made city,
Afraid of our living task, the dying
      Which the coming day will ask.[4]

1949   1951

---

[3] **fronde** a rebel party during the minority of Louis XIV of France
[4] ll. 29–48 At the moment of waking, while one is still detached from the daily world of mate-rial existence and from the body, one's existence is like Adam's in Paradise before he sinned; when one is fully awake, that world of innocence is lost.

The Shield of Achilles[1]

She looked over his shoulder
    For vines and olive trees,
Marble well-governed cities
    And ships upon untamed seas,
But there on the shining metal
    His hands had put instead
An artificial wilderness
    And a sky like lead.

A plain without a feature, bare and brown,
10   No blade of grass, no sign of neighborhood,
Nothing to eat and nowhere to sit down,
    Yet, congregated on its blankness, stood
    An unintelligible multitude,
A million eyes, a million boots in line,
Without expression, waiting for a sign.

Out of the air a voice without a face
    Proved by statistics that some cause was just
In tones as dry and level as the place:
    No one was cheered and nothing was discussed;
20   Column by column in a cloud of dust
They marched away enduring a belief
Whose logic brought them, somewhere else, to grief.

She looked over his shoulder
    For ritual pieties,
White flower-garlanded heifers,
    Libation and sacrifice,
But there on the shining metal
    Where the altar should have been,
She saw by his flickering forge-light
30   Quite another scene.

Barbed wire enclosed an arbitrary spot
    Where bored officials lounged (one cracked a joke)
And sentries sweated for the day was hot:
    A crowd of ordinary decent folk
    Watched from without and neither moved nor spoke
As three pale figures were led forth and bound
To three posts driven upright in the ground.[2]

---

[1] In Homer's *Iliad* XVIII, Hephaestos, god of fire and forge, makes a glorious new shield for the sea-nymph Thetis to give her son Achilles. It represents the scenes that, in Auden's poem, Thetis expects to see (stanzas 1, 4, and 7) and many others as well. But in our century, the beautiful scenes of Homeric vision have been replaced by drabber, depressive ones of mass war, cultural barrenness, and totalitarian cruelty.

[2] ll. 36–37 a scene analogous to that of the crucifixion (Christ between two thieves). It also suggests concentration camps and the practices of modern repressive and militaristic governments.

The mass and majesty of this world, all
That carries weight and always weighs the same
40 Lay in the hands of others; they were small
And could not hope for help and no help came:
What their foes liked to do was done, their shame
Was all the worst could wish; they lost their pride
And died as men before their bodies died.

She looked over his shoulder
For athletes at their games,
Men and women in a dance
Moving their sweet limbs
Quick, quick, to music,
50   But there on the shining shield
His hands had set no dancing-floor
But a weed-choked field.

A ragged urchin, aimless and alone,
Loitered about that vacancy; a bird
Flew up to safety from his well-aimed stone:
That girls are raped, that two boys knife a third,
Were axioms to him, who'd never heard
Of any world where promises were kept,
Or one could weep because another wept.

60   The thin-lipped armorer,
Hephaestos, hobbled away,
Thetis of the shining breasts
Cried out in dismay
At what the god had wrought
To please her son, the strong
Iron-hearted man-slaying Achilles
Who would not live long.[3]

1952

[3] ll. 62–68 It was Achilles' fate to be killed toward the end of the Trojan War. Auden's concluding lines give the poem a wrenching turn: the murderous character of the glamorous Homeric hero makes him, and the *Iliad* itself, appropriate forerunners to our own age, despite Homer's glorious art and Thetis' visionary anticipation.

DYLAN THOMAS
1914–1953

Thomas was born in Swansea, Wales, where his father was a schoolteacher. He had his only formal education in Swansea Grammar School and then, from 1931 on, devoted himself to writing. After his first book, *Eighteen Poems* (1934), appeared, he went to live in London and soon was broadcasting for the British Broadcasting Corporation and writing scripts and short stories. In 1937 he married Caitlin Macnamara in London. They had three children, and, to help support the family, he made a number of prolonged tours—so popular that they ushered in a new era of public readings—in the United States after the war. Thomas wrote vividly subjective short stories and two interesting autobiographical books, *Portrait of the Artist as a Young Dog* (1940) and *Adventures in the Skin Trade* (posthumously published in 1955). Shortly before his death he completed his witty, touching, and earthy radio script *Under Milk Wood*. His acute alcoholism (unfortunately a factor in the popular interest he aroused) precipitated his early death.

Thomas's poetry burst on the British scene in the mid-1930s. Though its rhapsodic intensity could not be ignored, it was regarded with a good deal of distrust because the Auden school of lyrical but often coolly ironic poetry was in the ascendancy. Following World War II there was also in Britain a reaction against any emotionalism that might recall the tensions and near-hysteria of the war period. Thomas found American readers and listeners far more receptive to his style of writing.

Thomas's poems all have an incantatory quality; they are self-hypnotized by their obsession with the onrush of death from the moment of conception. "The Force That Through the Green Fuse Drives the Flower" (published when he was nineteen) begins with the stricken realization that the very life-force that explodes organisms into being destroys them in another phase, and it ends with an image that compares the devouring worm after death to the male organ that generates life. On a different level, the wartime elegy "A Refusal to Mourn the Death, by Fire, of a Child in London" rejects discontinuity between life and death; the poem is a celebration of the organic oneness of the physical world, but its cumulative phrasing has more force than its surface assertions. "Fern Hill," despite its lilting whimsy and children's fairy-tale tone of wonder, becomes a song of irreversible doom. "In My Craft or Sullen Art," published in 1945 (like "A Refusal to Mourn" and "Fern Hill", in 1945 (like . . . Hill")), connects the poet's driven labor with the impersonal force of the "raging moon" and the heedless lovers who "lie abed" and embody the whole of fatality. The villanelle "Do Not Go Gentle into That Good Night," written in 1941 as Thomas's father was dying, is the poet's simplest expression of this constant preoccupation of his work. The emotional intensity in all these poems is very high; the verse-forms, often fairly elaborate, almost always include uniform stanzas, refrain-like repetition, and richly emphatic sound-echoing. Anyone who has heard Thomas read, whether in person or in a recording, will realize the importance of the patterned sound for the escalation of feeling in his verse.

The Force That Through the Green Fuse Drives the Flower[1]

The force that through the green fuse drives the flower
Drives my green age; that blasts the roots of trees
Is my destroyer.
And I am dumb to tell[2] the crooked rose
My youth is bent by the same wintry fever.

The force that drives the water through the rocks
Drives my red blood; that dries the mouthing streams
Turns mine to wax.
And I am dumb to mouth unto my veins
10   How at the mountain spring the same mouth sucks.

[1] See comment in headnote on Thomas.
[2] ll. 4, 9, 14, 19, 21 **dumb to tell [mouth]** have no way of explaining to

The hand that whirls the water in the pool
Stirs the quicksand; that ropes the blowing wind
Hauls my shroud sail.
And I am dumb to tell the hanging man
How of my clay is made the hangman's lime.

The lips of time leech to the fountain head;
Love drips and gathers, but the fallen blood
Shall calm her sores.[3]
And I am dumb to tell a weather's wind
20   How time has ticked a heaven round the stars.[4]

And I am dumb to tell the lover's tomb
How at my sheet goes the same crooked worm.

1934

[3] ll. 16–18   a cosmic sexual image of the mortal world's recurrent impregnation by the "fountain head" (God? an eternal life-force?)

[4] l. 20   Mortals have created ("ticked") the idea of timeless heaven out of the very pressures of time itself.

A Refusal to Mourn the Death, by Fire, of a Child in London[1]

Never until the mankind making
Bird beast and flower
Fathering and all humbling darkness
Tells with silence the last light breaking
And the still hour
Is come of the sea tumbling in harness

And I must enter again the round
Zion of the water bead
And the synagogue of the ear of corn[2]
10   Shall I let pray the shadow of a sound
Or sow my salt seed
In the least valley of sackcloth to mourn

The majesty and burning of the child's death.
I shall not murder
The mankind of her going with a grave truth
Nor blaspheme down the stations of the breath
With any further
Elegy of innocence and youth.

[1] See comment in headnote on Thomas.
[2] ll. 7–9   These lines present the whole material cosmos, organic and inorganic, as a holy communion. **Zion**   heaven or the heavenly city;

synagogue   place of communal worship (the Hebrew connotations reflect the importance of the Old Testament in Welsh Low Church religious observance)

Deep with the first dead lies London's daughter,
20   Robed in the long friends,
The grains beyond age, the dark veins of her mother,[3]
Secret by the unmourning water
Of the riding Thames.
After the first death, there is no other.[4]

1946

[3] ll. 19–21 See preceding note. The earth's strata, seen as belonging to the same mystical communion as the water bead and the ear of corn (ll. 8–9), are personified as a protective maternal body.

[4] l. 24 This delphic utterance combines tones of consolation, mystification, and stubborn denial of the continuing power of death; it suggests that the "first dead" (l. 19) established an organic link between humanity and the rest of creation, making all subsequent death meaningless.

Fern Hill[1]

Now as I was young and easy under the apple boughs
About the lilting house and happy as the grass was green,
    The night above the dingle starry,
      Time let me hail and climb
    Golden in the heydays of his eyes,
And honoured among wagons I was prince of the apple towns
And once below a time I lordly had the trees and leaves
    Trail with daisies and barley
    Down the rivers of the windfall light.

10   And as I was green and carefree, famous among the barns
About the happy yard and singing as the farm was home,
    In the sun that is young once only,
      Time let me play and be
    Golden in the mercy of his means,
And green and golden I was huntsman and herdsman, the calves
Sang to my horn, the foxes on the hills barked clear and cold,
    And the sabbath rang slowly
    In the pebbles of the holy streams.

All the sun long it was running, it was lovely, the hay
20   Fields high as the house, the tunes from the chimneys, it was air
    And playing, lovely and watery
      And fire green as grass.
    And nightly under the simple stars
As I rode to sleep the owls were bearing the farm away,
All the moon long I heard, blessed among stables, the nightjars
    Flying with the ricks, and the horses
      Flashing into the dark.

[1] a country house in Wales belonging to an aunt of Dylan Thomas. See comment in headnote on Thomas.

And then to awake, and the farm, like a wanderer white
With the dew, come back, the cock on his shoulder: it was all
   Shining, it was Adam and maiden,
     The sky gathered again
And the sun grew round that very day.
So it must have been after the birth of the simple light
In the first, spinning place, the spellbound horses walking warm
   Out of the whinnying green stable
     On to the fields of praise.

And honoured among foxes and pheasants by the gay house
Under the new made clouds and happy as the heart was long,
   In the sun born over and over,
40   I ran my heedless ways,
My wishes raced through the house high hay
And nothing I cared, at my sky blue trades, that time allows
In all his tuneful turning so few and such morning songs
   Before the children green and golden
     Follow him out of grace,

Nothing I cared, in the lamb white days, that time would take me
Up to the swallow thronged loft by the shadow of my hand,
   In the moon that is always rising,
     Nor that riding to sleep
50   I should hear him fly with the high fields
And wake to the farm forever fled from the childless land.
Oh as I was young and easy in the mercy of his means,
   Time held me green and dying
     Though I sang in my chains like the sea.

                       1946

In My Craft or Sullen Art

In my craft or sullen art
Exercised in the still night
When only the moon rages
And the lovers lie abed
With all their griefs in their arms,
I labour by singing light
Not for ambition or bread
Or the strut and trade of charms
On the ivory stages
10   But for the common wages
Of their most secret heart.

Not for the proud man apart
From the raging moon I write
On these spindrift pages

Nor for the towering dead
With their nightingales and psalms
But for the lovers, their arms
Round the griefs of the ages,
Who pay no praise or wages
20   Nor heed my craft or art.

1946

Do Not Go Gentle into That Good Night[1]

Do not go gentle into that good night,
Old age should burn and rave at close of day;
Rage, rage against the dying of the light.

Though wise men at their end know dark is right,
Because their words had forked no lightning they
Do not go gentle into that good night.

Good men, the last wave by, crying how bright
Their frail deeds might have danced in a green bay,
Rage, rage against the dying of the light.

10   Wild men who caught and sang the sun in flight,
And learn, too late, they grieved it on its way,
Do not go gentle into that good night.

Grave men, near death, who see with blinding sight
Blind eyes could blaze like meteors and be gay,
Rage, rage against the dying of the light.

And you, my father, there on the sad height,
Curse, bless, me now with your fierce tears, I pray.
Do not go gentle into that good night.
Rage, rage against the dying of the light.

1952

[1] See comment in headnote on Thomas. Compare, also, Thomas's use of the villanelle form with William Empson's in "Villanelle" (p. 965; see also note) and in "Missing Dates" (p. 966).

STEVIE SMITH

1902–1971

Stevie Smith was born Florence Margaret Smith but, because of her extraordinary smallness, was called Stevie by her family —after the English jockey Steve Donaghue. Her father, a shipping agent, deserted the family when she was three, and for the rest of her life she lived with an aunt in London. From 1923 to 1953 she worked as a freelance broadcaster for the British Broadcasting Corporation. Though she published her first novel (*Novel on Yellow Paper; or, Work It Out for Yourself*) in 1936, and her first book of poems (*A Good Time Was Had by All*) in 1937, it was not until her *Selected Poems* appeared in 1962 that she became well known in England.

Smith is an eccentric poet, remotely similar to Emily Dickinson in the gnomic quality of her writing, and to Edward Lear in the cultivated naiveté of her style. She combines childlike vision, mature intelligence, and disconcerting humor. Her poems, often adaptations of nursery rhymes, fairy tales, or hymns, appear playful and sometimes zany—an impression supported by the drawings or doodlings that illustrate her books—but their surface facetiousness usually masks a sense of blank loneliness and a terrifying isolation as in "Scorpion," where the poet uses the biblical quotation "This night shall thy soul be required of thee" to pray for death. Smith offers a cold appraisal of the world, particularly of the decaying English gentility that was her childhood milieu. Her strongest tone is elegiac: she uses wry humor to explore an enduring obsession with death and its attendant agonies.

Our Bog is Dood

Our Bog is dood, our Bog is dood,
They lisped in accents mild,
But when I asked them to explain
They grew a little wild.
How do you know your Bog is dood
My darling little child?

We know because we wish it so
That is enough, they cried,
And straight within each infant eye
10   Stood up the flame of pride,
And if you do not think it so
You shall be crucified.

Then tell me, darling little ones,
What's dood, suppose Bog is?
Just what we think, the answer came,
Just what we think it is.
They bowed their heads. Our Bog is ours
And we are wholly his.

But when they raised them up again
20   They had forgotten me
Each one upon each other glared
In pride and misery
For what was dood, and what their Bog
They never could agree.

Oh sweet it was to leave them then,
And sweeter not to see,
And sweetest of all to walk alone
Beside the encroaching sea,
The sea that soon should drown them all,
That never yet drowned me.

1950

Not Waving But Drowning

Nobody heard him, the dead man,
But still he lay moaning:
I was much further out than you thought
And not waving but drowning.

Poor chap, he always loved larking
And now he's dead
It must have been too cold for him his heart gave way,
They said.

10   Oh, no no no, it was too cold always
(Still the dead one lay moaning)
I was much too far out all my life
And not waving but drowning.

1957

Scorpion

"This night shall thy soul be required of thee"[1]
My soul is never required of *me*
It always has to be somebody else of course
Will my soul be required of me tonight perhaps?

(I often wonder what it will be like
To have one's soul required of one
But all I can think of is the Out-Patients' Department—
"Are you Mrs. Briggs, dear?"
No, I am Scorpion.)

[1] l. 1 Luke 12:20

10   I should like my soul to be required of me, so as
     To waft over grass till it comes to the blue sea
     I am very fond of grass, I always have been, but there must
     Be no cow, person or house to be seen.

     Sea and *grass* must be quite empty
     Other souls can find somewhere *else.*

     O Lord God please come
     And require the soul of thy Scorpion

     Scorpion so wishes to be gone.

                 1972

THEODORE ROETHKE

1908–1963

Roethke was born in Saginaw, Michigan, the son of a greenhouse gardener, to whose death by cancer when the boy was fourteen Roethke traced his recurrent mental breakdowns. Educated at the University of Michigan and Harvard Graduate School, he taught at several American universities, most notably the University of Washington, where he encouraged a new generation of West Coast poets.

Roethke's early greenhouse environment provided him with the central images for his poetry. He began to reclaim his childhood world in his "greenhouse" sequence (1942–46), in which he looks with microscopic attention at growing plants struggling into being. Later his images from nature extended to swamps and boglands, always seen as mirrors of the turbulent psyche, and to snails, slugs, snakes, and frogs—"the small shapes, willow-shy"—that in his work represent healing instinctual life alien to the human condition.

Much of Roethke's work draws on the concepts of collective unconscious, rebirth, and psychic integration. In later poems like "In a Dark Time," which are almost neo-Elizabethan in their formal elegance, he is deeply interested in mysticism. Roethke's focus is narrow. There is little of the public, social world in his work. At the age of forty-five he married Beatrice O'Connell, whom his poem "I Knew a Woman" celebrates. Though Roethke was often tormented, the sensibility that emerges in his poetry is nevertheless remarkably gentle.

My Papa's Waltz

The whiskey on your breath
Could make a small boy dizzy;
But I hung on like death:
Such waltzing was not easy.

We romped until the pans
Slid from the kitchen shelf;
My mother's countenance
Could not unfrown itself.

10   The hand that held my wrist
   Was battered on one knuckle;
   At every step you missed
   My right ear scraped a buckle.

You beat time on my head
With a palm caked hard by dirt,
Then waltzed me off to bed
Still clinging to your shirt.

1948

Elegy for Jane

MY STUDENT, THROWN BY A HORSE

I remember the neckcurls, limp and damp as tendrils;
And her quick look, a sidelong pickerel smile;
And how, once startled into talk, the light syllables leaped for her,
And she balanced in the delight of her thought,
A wren, happy, tail into the wind,
Her song trembling the twigs and small branches.
The shade sang with her;
The leaves, their whispers turned to kissing;
And the mold sang in the bleached valleys under the rose.

10   Oh, when she was sad, she cast herself down into such a pure depth,
   Even a father could not find her:
   Scraping her cheek against straw;
   Stirring the clearest water.

My sparrow, you are not here,
Waiting like a fern, making a spiny shadow.
The sides of wet stones cannot console me,
Nor the moss, wound with the last light.

If only I could nudge you from this sleep,
My maimed darling, my skittery pigeon.
20   Over this damp grave I speak the words of my love:
   I, with no rights in this matter,
   Neither father nor lover.

1953

The Visitant

1

A cloud moved close. The bulk of the wind shifted.
A tree swayed over water.
A voice said:
Stay. Stay by the slip-ooze. Stay.

Dearest tree, I said, may I rest here?
A ripple made a soft reply.
I waited, alert as a dog.
The leech clinging to a stone waited;
And the crab, the quiet breather.

2

10 Slow, slow as a fish she came,
Slow as a fish coming forward,
Swaying in a long wave;
Her skirts not touching a leaf,
Her white arms reaching towards me.

She came without sound,
Without brushing the wet stones,
In the soft dark of early evening,
She came,
The wind in her hair,
20 The moon beginning.

3

I woke in the first of morning.
Staring at a tree, I felt the pulse of a stone.

Where's she now, I kept saying.
Where's she now, the mountain's downy girl?

But the bright day had no answer.
A wind stirred in a web of appleworms;
The tree, the close willow, swayed.

1953

I Knew a Woman

I knew a woman, lovely in her bones,
When small birds sighed, she would sigh back at them;
Ah, when she moved, she moved more ways than one:
The shapes a bright container can contain!
Of her choice virtues only gods should speak,
Or English poets who grew up on Greek
(I'd have them sing in chorus, cheek to cheek).

How well her wishes went! She stroked my chin,
She taught me Turn, and Counter-turn, and Stand;
10 She taught me Touch, that undulant white skin;
I nibbled meekly from her proffered hand;
She was the sickle; I, poor I, the rake,
Coming behind her for her pretty sake
(But what prodigious mowing we did make).

Love likes a gander, and adores a goose:
Her full lips pursed, the errant note to seize;
She played it quick, she played it light and loose;
My eyes, they dazzled at her flowing knees;
Her several parts could keep a pure repose,
20 Or one hip quiver with a mobile nose
(She moved in circles, and those circles moved).

Let seed be grass, and grass turn into hay:
I'm martyr to a motion not my own;
What's freedom for? To know eternity.
I swear she cast a shadow white as stone.
But who would count eternity in days?
These old bones live to learn her wanton ways:
(I measure time by how a body sways).

1958

In a Dark Time[1]

In a dark time, the eye begins to see,
I meet my shadow in the deepening shade;
I hear my echo in the echoing wood—
A lord of nature weeping to a tree.
I live between the heron and the wren,
Beasts of the hill and serpents of the den.

What's madness but nobility of soul
At odds with circumstance? The day's on fire!
I know the purity of pure despair,
10 My shadow pinned against a sweating wall.
That place among the rocks—is it a cave,
Or winding path? The edge is what I have.

A steady storm of correspondences!
A night flowing with birds, a ragged moon,
And in broad day the midnight come again!
A man goes far to find out what he is—
Death of the self in a long, tearless night,
All natural shapes blazing unnatural light.

Dark, dark my light, and darker my desire.
20 My soul, like some heat-maddened summer fly,
Keeps buzzing at the sill. Which I is *I*?
A fallen man, I climb out of my fear.
The mind enters itself, and God the mind,
And one is One, free in the tearing wind.

1964

[1] For Roethke's own explanation of this poem see *The Contemporary Poet as Artist and Critic*, ed. Anthony Ostroff (Boston: Little, Brown and Co., 1964).

CHARLES OLSON
1910–1970

Born in Worcester, Massachusetts, where his father was a postman, Olson spent his summers in Gloucester on Cape Ann, the setting of *The Maximus Poems*. He studied at Wesleyan and Harvard Universities, and during the war served as assistant chief of the Foreign Language Division of the Office of War Information. He then became an adviser and strategist with the Democratic Party's National Committee, but abandoned politics to concentrate on poetry. From 1951 to 1959 he taught at Black Mountain College in North Carolina, an experimental college of the arts, where he served as rector. He returned to Gloucester to work on his Maximus series, teaching intermittently at the State University of New York at Buffalo and at the University of Connecticut, until his death from cancer at the age of fifty-nine.

The leading spokesman for the Black Mountain school of poets, which included Robert Creeley and Robert Duncan, Olson is associated, in both his theory and his practice, with post-modernist poetics. His major achievement is *The Maximus Poems*, an epic poem in three volumes that seeks to extend the methods of Ezra Pound's *Cantos* and William Carlos Williams's *Paterson*. The sequence traces the development of a hero—Olson in the persona of Maximus (named after the philosopher Maximus of Tyre, second century A.D.)—and features Gloucester, Massachusetts, as the model "polis" and microcosm of America. Olson

began writing his epic in 1950 as a series of "letters" to himself, Gloucester, and other hypothetical recipients. On completion, it included more than 300 separate but interrelated poems that attempt to represent the post-modern age.

Believing that humanism, with its endorsement of universal values and the ethic of progress, is dead, Olson returns to a celebration of local place (Gloucester, its people, scenes, and history) confident that in the particular, in particularity itself, can be found a force to assert "against the 'loss' of values of the universal." His vision of redemption through knowing the objective and particular demanded a new theory of poetry which he called "projectivism." Rejecting closed forms and "the verse that print bred," Olson described the poem as an object, a unit of energy, passed from writer to reader, which has its own organic laws rooted in the recognition that form and content must be realized simultaneously. (See his 1950 essay "Projective Verse.") *The Maximus Poems* are constructed on the principle of juxtaposition and are rich in allusion and documentary borrowing. While Olson loved using colloquial idiom to recover localism, he also achieved a complex layering of history through documentary references and mythological allusion, from sources as various as Mayan hieroglyphics, the Norse Eddas, and Algonquian tales.

From The Maximus Poems

Maximus, to Himself

I have had to learn the simplest things
last. Which made for difficulties.
Even at sea I was slow, to get the hand out, or to cross
a wet deck.
       The sea was not, finally, my trade.
But even my trade, at it, I stood estranged

from that which was most familiar. Was delayed,
and not content with the man's argument
that such postponement
10 is now the nature of
obedience,

> that we are all late
> in a slow time,
> that we grow up many
> And the single
> is not easily
> known

It could be, though the sharpness (the *achiote*)[1]
I note in others,
20 makes more sense
than my own distances. The agilities

> they show daily
> who do the world's
> businesses
> And who do nature's
> as I have no sense
> I have done either

I have made dialogues,
have discussed ancient texts,
30 have thrown what light I could, offered
what pleasures
doceat[2] allows

> But the known?
This, I have had to be given,
a life, love, and from one man
the world.

> Tokens.
> But sitting here
> I look out as a wind
40 and water man, testing
> And missing
> some proof

I know the quarters
of the weather, where it comes from,
where it goes. But the stem of me,
this I took from their welcome,
or their rejection, of me

[1] *achiote* (Spanish — associated with sharpness of taste)

[2] **doceat** teaching: literally, that he, she, or it teach (present subjunctive of Latin *docere*)

And my arrogance
was neither diminished
50   nor increased,
by the communication

2

It is undone business
I speak of, this morning,
with the sea
stretching out
from my feet

1960

Song 3

This morning of the small snow
I count the blessings, the leak in the faucet
which makes of the sink time, the drop
of the water on water as sweet
as the Seth Thomas[1]
in the old kitchen
my father stood in his drawers to wind (always
he forgot the 30th day, as I don't want to remember
the rent
10   a house these days
so much somebody else's,
especially,
Congoleum's[2]

       Or the plumbing,
that it doesn't work, this I like, have even used paper clips
as well as string to hold the ball up And flush it
with my hand
         But that the car doesn't, that no moving thing moves
without that song I'd void my ear of, the musickracket
20   of all ownership . . .
          Holes
in my shoes, that's all right, my fly
gaping, me out
at the elbows, the blessing
             that difficulties are once more

      "In the midst of plenty, walk
      as close to
      bare
         In the face of sweetness,
30   piss

---

[1] **Seth Thomas** brand name of clock   [2] **Congoleum** trade name for a floor covering, like linoleum

                    In the time of goodness,
          go side, go
          smashing, beat them, go as
          (as near as you can

          tear

          In the land of plenty, have
          nothing to do with it
                              take the way of
          the lowest,
40   including
          your legs, go
          contrary, go

          sing

                              1960

Maximus to Gloucester, Letter 27 [withheld]

          I come back to the geography of it,
          the land falling off to the left
          where my father shot his scabby golf
          and the rest of us played baseball
          into the summer darkness until no flies
          could be seen and we came home
          to our various piazzas where the women
          buzzed

          To the left the land fell to the city,
10   to the right, it fell to the sea

          I was so young my first memory
          is of a tent spread to feed lobsters
          to Rexall[1] conventioneers, and my father,
          a man for kicks, came out of the tent roaring
          with a bread-knife in his teeth to take care of
          a druggist they'd told him had made a pass at
          my mother, she laughing, so sure, as round
          as her face, Hines[2] pink and apple,
          under one of those frame hats women then

20   This, is no bare incoming
          of novel abstract form, this[3]

          is no welter or the forms
          of those events, this,

---

[1] **Rexall** drugstore chain
[2] **Hines** Olson's mother's maiden name

[3] ll. 20–21 quotation from Alfred North White-
head, *Adventures in Ideas* (New York: Mac-
millan, 1961), p. 240

Greeks, is the stopping
of the battle

    It is the imposing
of all those antecedent predecessions, the precessions

of me, the generation of those facts
which are my words, it is coming

30   from all that I no longer am, yet am,
the slow westward motion of

more than I am

There is no strict personal order

for my inheritance.

    No Greek will be able

to discriminate my body.

    An American

is a complex of occasions,

themselves a geometry

40   of spatial nature.

    I have this sense,

that I am one

with my skin

    Plus this—plus this:

that forever the geography

which leans in

on me I compell

backwards I compell Gloucester

to yield, to

50   change

    Polis[4]
is this

                                1968

[4] **Polis** Greek word for city; Olson defined it thus: "Polis . . . the community or body of citizens, not their dwellings, not their houses, not their being as material, but being as group with will, and that will is from the Sanskrit stem to fill or fulfill" (essay, "Definitions of Undoings," 1956).

The Moon Is the Number 18[1]

is a monstrance,
the blue dogs bay,
and the son sits,
grieving

is a grinning god, is
the mouth of, is
the dripping moon

while in the tower the cat
preens
10 and all motion
is a crab

and there is nothing he can do but what they do, watch
the face of waters, and fire

The blue dogs paw,
lick the droppings, dew
or blood, whatever
results are. And night,
the crab, rays round
attentive as the cat to catch
20 human sound

The blue dogs rue,
as he does, as he would howl, confronting
the wind which rocks what was her, while prayers
striate the snow, words blow
as questions cross fast, fast
as flames, as flames form, melt
along any darkness

Birth is an instance as is a host, namely, death

The moon has no air

30 In the red tower
in that tower where she also sat
in that particular tower where watching & moving are,
there,
there where what triumph there is, is: there
is all substance, all creature
all there is against the dirty moon, against
number, image, sortilege—

alone with cat & crab,
and sound is, is, his
40 conjecture

[1] See Tarot Card 18.

1970

ELIZABETH BISHOP
1911–1979

Elizabeth Bishop was born in Worcester, Massachusetts. Her father died when she was eight months old, and she and her mother went to live with her maternal grandparents in Nova Scotia. When Bishop was four years old, her mother was placed in a mental institution. (See her short story, "In the Village," in *Questions of Travel* [New York: Farrar Straus and Giroux, 1965]). Educated at Vassar, she became friends there with Mary McCarthy and met Marianne Moore (to whom she is often compared). After traveling widely she lived in Key West and, for twenty years, in Brazil, becoming well known as a translator of Brazilian poetry. She returned to live in the United States in 1969 and taught at Harvard until her death.

Bishop is respected for the impeccable craftsmanship of her poetry. She writes with a dextrous objectivity and understated wit in a language of unmannered simplicity, as in "The Fish," about which Ernest Hemingway wrote admiringly: "I wish I knew as much about it as she does." She has spoken of "the always more successful surrealism of everyday life," and many of her poems work their way down to the unsettling emotional subtext of any given moment. "In the Waiting Room," for instance, describes an unremarkable scene in which a child reads the *National Geographic* in a dentist's office. But the painful juxtaposition of the familiar office and the exotic foreign world collapses the child's sense of identity in a moment of vertigo. "Sestina," with its rigorous form and its diction from folk tale, records a domestic scene in a family kitchen that becomes suddenly surreal as the environment assumes the pain of its human occupants. In general, her poems are evocations of real scenes and situations, recorded with such careful fidelity that they emerge resonant and luminous. "The Fish" offers a typical description of this kind—in it, the act of watching a hooked fish so intensely leads to a moment of ecstatic release, a moment of "earthly trust" in the natural world. Bishop wrote: "My outlook is pessimistic. I think we are still barbarians. . . . But I think we should be gay in spite of it, sometimes even giddy—to make life endurable and to keep ourselves 'new, tender, quick.'"

The Fish

I caught a tremendous fish
and held him beside the boat
half out of the water, with my hook
fast in a corner of his mouth.
He didn't fight.
He hadn't fought at all.
He hung a grunting weight,
battered and venerable
and homely. Here and there
10   his brown skin hung in strips
like ancient wallpaper,
and its pattern of darker brown
was like wallpaper:
shapes like full-blown roses

stained and lost through age.
He was speckled with barnacles,
fine rosettes of lime,
and infested
with tiny white sea-lice,
20   and underneath two or three
rags of green weed hung down.
While his gills were breathing in
the terrible oxygen
—the frightening gills,
fresh and crisp with blood,
that can cut so badly—
I thought of the coarse white flesh
packed in like feathers,
the big bones and the little bones,
30   the dramatic reds and blacks
of his shiny entrails,
and the pink swim-bladder
like a big peony.
I looked into his eyes
which were far larger than mine
but shallower, and yellowed,
the irises backed and packed
with tarnished tinfoil
seen through the lenses
40   of old scratched isinglass.
They shifted a little, but not
to return my stare.
—It was more like the tipping
of an object toward the light.
I admired his sullen face,
the mechanism of his jaw,
and then I saw
that from his lower lip
—if you could call it a lip—
50   grim, wet, and weaponlike,
hung five old pieces of fish-line,
or four and a wire leader
with the swivel still attached,
with all their five big hooks
grown firmly in his mouth.
A green line, frayed at the end
where he broke it, two heavier lines,
and a fine black thread
still crimped from the strain and snap
60   when it broke and he got away.
Like medals with their ribbons
frayed and wavering,
a five-haired beard of wisdom
trailing from his arching jaw.

I stared and stared
and victory filled up
the little rented boat,
from the pool of bilge
where oil had spread a rainbow
70   around the rusted engine
to the bailer rusted orange,
the sun-cracked thwarts,
the oarlocks on their strings,
the gunnels—until everything
was rainbow, rainbow, rainbow!
And I let the fish go.

1946

Sestina

September rain falls on the house.
In the failing light, the old grandmother
sits in the kitchen with the child
beside the Little Marvel Stove,
reading the jokes from the almanac,
laughing and talking to hide her tears.

She thinks that her equinoctial tears
and the rain that beats on the roof of the house
were both foretold by the almanac,
10 but only known to a grandmother.
The iron kettle sings on the stove.
She cuts some bread and says to the child,

It's time for tea now; but the child
is watching the teakettle's small hard tears
dance like mad on the hot black stove,
the way the rain must dance on the house.
Tidying up, the old grandmother
hangs up the clever almanac

on its string. Birdlike, the almanac
20 hovers half open above the child,
hovers above the old grandmother
and her teacup full of dark brown tears.
She shivers and says she thinks the house
feels chilly, and puts more wood in the stove.

It was to be, says the Marvel Stove.
I know what I know, says the almanac.
With crayons the child draws a rigid house

and a winding pathway. Then the child
puts in a man with buttons like tears
30 and shows it proudly to the grandmother.

But secretly, while the grandmother
busies herself about the stove,
the little moons fall down like tears
from between the pages of the almanac
into the flower bed the child
has carefully placed in the front of the house.

Time to plant tears, says the almanac.
The grandmother sings to the marvellous stove
and the child draws another inscrutable house.

1965

In the Waiting Room

In Worcester, Massachusetts,
I went with Aunt Consuelo
to keep her dentist's appointment
and sat and waited for her
in the dentist's waiting room.
It was winter. It got dark
early. The waiting room
was full of grown-up people,
arctics and overcoats,
10 lamps and magazines.
My aunt was inside
what seemed like a long time
and while I waited I read
the *National Geographic*
(I could read) and carefully
studied the photographs:
the inside of a volcano,
black, and full of ashes;
then it was spilling over
20 in rivulets of fire.

Osa and Martin Johnson
dressed in riding breeches,
laced boots, and pith helmets.
A dead man slung on a pole
—"Long Pig," the caption said.
Babies with pointed heads
wound round and round with string;
black, naked women with necks
wound round and round with wire

30   like the necks of light bulbs.
       Their breasts were horrifying.
       I read it right straight through.
       I was too shy to stop.
       And then I looked at the cover:
       the yellow margins, the date.

       Suddenly, from inside,
       came an *oh!* of pain
       —Aunt Consuelo's voice—
       not very loud or long.
40   I wasn't at all surprised;
       even then I knew she was
       a foolish, timid woman.
       I might have been embarrassed,
       but wasn't. What took me
       completely by surprise
       was that it was *me*:
       my voice, in my mouth.
       Without thinking at all
       I was my foolish aunt,
50   I—we—were falling, falling,
       our eyes glued to the cover
       of the *National Geographic*,
       February, 1918.

       I said to myself: three days
       and you'll be seven years old.
       I was saying it to stop
       the sensation of falling off
       the round, turning world
       into cold, blue-black space.
60   But I felt: you are an *I*,
       you are an *Elizabeth*,
       you are one of *them*.
       Why should you be one, too?
       I scarcely dared to look
       to see what it was I was.
       I gave a sidelong glance
       —I couldn't look any higher—
       at shadowy gray knees,
       trousers and skirts and boots
70   and different pairs of hands
       lying under the lamps.
       I knew that nothing stranger
       had ever happened, that nothing
       stranger could ever happen.
       Why should I be my aunt,
       or me, or anyone?
       What similarities—

boots, hands, the family voice
I felt in my throat, or even
80   the *National Geographic*
and those awful hanging breasts—
held us all together
or made us all just one?
How—I didn't know any
word for it—how "unlikely" . . .
How had I come to be here,
like them, and overhear
a cry of pain that could have
got loud and worse but hadn't?

90   The waiting room was bright
and too hot. It was sliding
beneath a big black wave,
another, and another.

Then I was back in it.
The War was on. Outside,
in Worcester, Massachusetts,
were night and slush and cold,
and it was still the fifth
of February, 1918.

1976

One Art

The art of losing isn't hard to master;
so many things seem filled with the intent
to be lost that their loss is no disaster.

Lose something every day. Accept the fluster
of lost door keys, the hour badly spent.
The art of losing isn't hard to master.

Then practice losing farther, losing faster:
places, and names, and where it was you meant
to travel. None of these will bring disaster.

10   I lost my mother's watch. And look! my last, or
next-to-last, of three loved houses went.
The art of losing isn't hard to master.

I lost two cities, lovely ones. And, vaster,
some realms I owned, two rivers, a continent.
I miss them, but it wasn't a disaster.

—Even losing you (the joking voice, a gesture
I love) I shan't have lied. It's evident
the art of losing's not too hard to master
though it may look like (*Write* it!) like disaster.

1976

ROBERT HAYDEN
b. 1913

Robert Hayden was born in Detroit, Michigan, of a poor black family that supported his literary ambitions. He attended Detroit City College (now Wayne State University), where he was encouraged by the poet Langston Hughes, and later studied with W.H. Auden at the University of Michigan. In the 1930s he worked on a Federal Writers' Project in Detroit, in charge of research into local black history and folk lore, and then worked part time as drama and music critic for a local black newspaper. Hayden became a member of the Baha'i faith, which he said supported his vision that the work of the artist is a form of worship. In 1946 he became professor of English at Fisk University, where he launched the Counterpoise series, a poetry-publishing venture to encourage Afro-American writing, and in 1969 he left to teach at the University of Michigan. From 1976 to 1978 he was the first black consultant in poetry at the Library of Congress.

Hayden's primary subject is his experience as a black American. He insists, however, that the poet must be an artist, concerned with technique, and not a propagandist: "The truly revolutionary poets are always those who are committed to some integrated vision of art and life. Theirs is an essentially spiritual vision." His poems are often narratives that evoke scenes from contemporary life or from the historical past. " ' "Mystery Boy" Looks for Kin in Nashville' " records his search for a "named" past—a characteristic quest. Hayden sifts through wounding memories, particularly the painful legacies of experiences of racial discrimination, while struggling to assert an affirmative vision rooted in a religious confidence.

" 'Mystery Boy' Looks for Kin in Nashville"

Puzzle faces in the dying elms
promise him treats if he will stay.
Sometimes they hiss and spit at him
like varmints caught
in a thicket of butterflies.

A black doll,
one disremembered time,
came floating down to him
through mimosa's fancywork leaves and blooms
to be his hidden bride.

10

From the road beyond the creepered walls
they call to him now and then,
and he'll take off in spite of the angry trees,
hearing like the loudening of his heart
the name he never can he never can repeat.

And when he gets to where the voices were—
Don't cry, his dollbaby wife implores;
I know where they are, don't cry.
We'll go and find them, we'll go
20   and ask them for your name again.

1970

On Lookout Mountain

I listen for the sounds of cannon, cries
vibrating still upon the air,
timeless echoes in echoic time—
imagine how they circle out and out

concentric with Kilroy's cries,
as beyond the tangent calm
of this midcentury morning he burns
or freezes in the warfare of our peace.

I gaze through layered light,
10   think of the death-for-foothold inching climb
of Union soldiers struggling up
the crackling mountainside.

And here where Sunday alpinists
pick views and souvenirs,
here daring choices stained
the clouds with dubious victory.

A world away, yet nearer than our hope
or our belief, the scions of that fighting climb
endless hills of war, amid war's peaks
20   and valleys broken, scattered fall.

Have done, have done. Behold how bright
upon the mountain the gadget feet
of trivia shine.
Oh, hear the stuffed gold eagle sing.

1970

The Whipping

The old woman across the way
  is whipping the boy again
and shouting to the neighborhood
  her goodness and his wrongs.

Wildly he crashes through elephant ears,
  pleads in dusty zinnias,
while she in spite of crippling fat
  pursues and corners him.

She strikes and strikes the shrilly circling
10   boy till the stick breaks
in her hand. His tears are rainy weather
  to woundlike memories:

My head gripped in bony vise
  of knees, the writhing struggle
to wrench free, the blows, the fear
  worse than blows that hateful

Words could bring, the face that I
  no longer knew or loved . . . .
Well, it is over now, it is over,
20   and the boy sobs in his room,

And the woman leans muttering against
  a tree, exhausted, purged—
avenged in part for lifelong hidings
  she has had to bear.

                                        1975

RANDALL JARRELL
1914–1965

Born in Nashville, Tennessee, of parents
who divorced when he was an infant, Jarrell
spent an isolated childhood in which his
only refuge, as he described it, was to read
in the public libraries. He was educated
at Vanderbilt University and taught from
1937 to 1939 at Kenyon College, where he
was a friend of Robert Lowell and John
Crowe Ransom. He enlisted in the Army
Air Corps in 1942, serving as a trainer of
pilots. After the war he taught at Sarah
Lawrence and, from 1947 until his suicide,

at the Women's College of the University
of North Carolina at Greensboro.

Jarrell is an erudite and versatile writer—
poet, novelist, author of children's stories,
and critic—whose verse is marked by pathos
and grace. He uses dreams, folklore, and
fairy tales as sources for poetry, drawing
on the ambiguous world of childhood, at
once innocent and full of terror. His major
form is the dramatic monologue, often with
a female speaker. "The Black Swan" retells,
in images of extraordinary vulnerability, an

ancient fairy tale from a young girl's perspective. Its subject betrays a characteristic brooding over a lost and unresolved childhood, and a fascination with death. Jarrell wrote with empathy about other men's war experiences, and his "Death of the Ball Turret Gunner," in which the aerial gunner is killed in his womb-like ball turret and "born" into death, has often been anthologized. Presenting the event through the extended analogy of an abortion gives the brief poem its unexpected power.

The Death of the Ball Turret Gunner[1]

From my mother's sleep I fell into the State,
And I hunched in its belly till my wet fur froze.
Six miles from earth, loosed from its dream of life,
I woke to black flak and the nightmare fighters.
When I died they washed me out of the turret with a hose.

1945

[1] "A ball turret was a plexiglass sphere set into the belly of a B-17 or B-24, and inhabited by two .50 caliber machine-guns and one man, a short small man. When this gunner tracked with his machine guns a fighter attacking his bomber from below, he revolved with the turret; hunched upside-down in his little sphere, he looked like the foetus in the womb. The fighters which attacked him were armed with cannon firing explosive shells. The hose was a steam hose" (Jarrell's note).

The Black Swan

When the swans turned my sister into a swan
   I would go to the lake, at night, from milking:
The sun would look out through the reeds like a swan,
   A swan's red beak; and the beak would open
And inside there was darkness, the stars and the moon.

Out on the lake a girl would laugh.
   "Sister, here is your porridge, sister,"
I would call; and the reeds would whisper,
   "Go to sleep, go to sleep, little swan."
10 My legs were all hard and webbed, and the silky

Hairs of my wings sank away like stars
   In the ripples that ran in and out of the reeds:
I heard through the lap and hiss of water
   Someone's "Sister . . . sister," far away on the shore,
And then as I opened my beak to answer

I heard my harsh laugh go out to the shore
   And saw—saw at last, swimming up from the green
Low mounds of the lake, the white stone swans:
   The white, named swans . . . "It is all a dream,"
20 I whispered, and reached from the down of the pallet

To the lap and hiss of the floor.
   And "Sleep, little sister," the swans all sang
From the moon and stars and frogs of the floor.
   But the swan my sister called, "Sleep at last, little sister,"
And stroked all night, with a black wing, my wings.

1951

The Orient Express

One looks from the train
Almost as one looked as a child. In the sunlight
What I see still seems to me plain,
I am safe; but at evening
As the lands darken, a questioning
Precariousness comes over everything.

Once after a day of rain
I lay longing to be cold; and after a while
I was cold again, and hunched shivering
10 Under the quilt's many colors, gray
With the dull ending of the winter day.
Outside me there were a few shapes
Of chairs and tables, things from a primer;
Outside the window
There were the chairs and tables of the world. . . . .
I saw that the world
That had seemed to me the plain
Gray mask of all that was strange
Behind it—of all that *was*—was all.

20 But it is beyond belief.
One thinks, "Behind everything
An unforced joy, an unwilling
Sadness (a willing sadness, a forced joy)
Moves changelessly"; one looks from the train
And there is something, the same thing
Behind everything: all these little villages,
A passing woman, a field of grain,
The man who says good-bye to his wife—
A path through a wood full of lives, and the train
30 Passing, after all unchangeable
And not now ever to stop, like a heart—

It is like any other work of art.
It is and never can be changed.
Behind everything there is always
The unknown unwanted life.

1951

The Elementary Scene

Looking back in my mind I can see
The white sun like a tin plate
Over the wooden turning of the weeds;
The street jerking—a wet swing—
To end by the wall the children sang.

The thin grass by the girls' door,
Trodden on, straggling, yellow and rotten,
And the gaunt field with its one tied cow—
The dead land waking sadly to my life—
10   Stir, and curl deeper in the eyes of time.

The rotting pumpkin under the stairs
Bundled with switches and the cold ashes
Still holds for me, in its unwavering eyes,
The stinking shapes of cranes and witches,
Their path slanting down the pumpkin's sky.

Its stars beckon through the frost like cottages
(Homes of the Bear, the Hunter—of that absent star,
The dark where the flushed child struggles into sleep)
Till, leaning a lifetime to the comforter,
20   I float above the small limbs like their dream:

I, I, the future that mends everything.

1960

JOHN BERRYMAN
1914–1972

Born John Smith, Berryman grew up in McAlister, Oklahoma. His father, who killed himself when Berryman was eleven, was a banker and his mother a teacher. When his mother remarried, he took his stepfather's name. He was educated at Columbia University and Clare College, Cambridge. After teaching at various universities he was professor of humanities at the University of Minnesota from 1955 until his death. Berryman, who married three times and was prone to over-drinking and to paranoid depression, converted to Catholicism toward the end of his life, and his last poems reflect his religious speculations. He committed suicide in 1972.

Berryman's first success as a poet was his *Homage to Mistress Bradstreet* (1956). In this long poem, Berryman conceives the Puritan poet as his nurse and imaginary lover. Berryman moves in and out of her consciousness and engages her in dialogue. This early experiment in shifting perspective and counterpointed voices was expanded in the three volumes of *Dream Songs*, where the poems are confessional in the manner of Robert Lowell's *Life Studies*. Denying that these poems were literal autobiography, Berryman explained that the songs should be treated as a single long poem which, "whatever its wide cast of characters, is essentially about an imaginary character (not the poet, not me) named Henry, a white American in early middle age sometimes in black face, who has suffered an irreparable loss." The *Dream Songs* exhibit remarkable variety: syncopated rhythms, idiosyncrasies of syntax, and a repeated pattern in each poem of three six-line stanzas, irregular in both metre and rhyme. Witty and learned, they shift tone from the colloquial to the formal, creating a remarkable pathos—the cranky, bitter humor of

the minstrel show, full of low comedy, coarse jokes, terror, and grief. In "Song 366," Berryman writes: "These Songs are not meant to be understood, you understand / They are only meant to terrify and to comfort." The *Dream Songs* have both the lucidity and the insanity of dreams. They connect less with a public world than Lowell's poems do, but express the familiar anxieties of the modern poet in a world that despairs of values.

From The Dream Songs

1

Huffy Henry hid   the day,
unappeasable Henry sulked.
I see his point, — a trying to put things over.
It was the thought that they thought
they could *do* it made Henry wicked & away.
But he should have come out and talked.

All the world like a woolen lover
once did seem on Henry's side.
Then came a departure.
10   Thereafter nothing fell out as it might or ought.
I don't see how Henry, pried
open for all the world to see, survived.

What he has now to say is a long
wonder the world can bear & be.
Once in a sycamore I was glad
all at the top, and I sang.
Hard on the land wears the strong sea
and empty grows every bed.

1964

29

There sat down, once, a thing on Henry's heart
só heavy, if he had a hundred years
& more, & weeping, sleepless, in all them time
Henry could not make good.
Starts again always in Henry's ears
the little cough somewhere, an odour, a chime.

And there is another thing he has in mind
like a grave Sienese[1] face a thousand years
would fail to blur the still profiled reproach of. Ghastly,
10   with open eyes, he attends, blind.
All the bells say: too late. This is not for tears;
thinking.

But never did Henry, as he thought he did,
end anyone and hacks her body up
and hide the pieces, where they may be found.
He knows: he went over everyone, & nobody's missing.
Often he reckons, in the dawn, them up.
Nobody is ever missing.

1964

[1] **Sienese** style of painting developed in Siena,
Italy, in the late thirteenth and the fourteenth
centuries

53

He lay in the middle of the world, and twitcht.
More Sparine[1] for Pelides,[2]
human (half) & down here as he is,
with probably insulting mail to open
and certainly unworthy words to hear
and his unforgivable memory.

—I seldom *go* to *films*. They are too exciting,
said the Honourable Possum.[3]
—It takes me so long to read the 'paper,
10   said to me one day a novelist[4] hot as a firecracker,
because I have to identify myself with everyone in it,
including the corpses, pal.'

Kierkegaard wanted a society, to refuse to read 'papers,
and that was not, friends, his worst idea.
Tiny Hardy, toward the end, refused to say *anything*,
a programme adopted early on by long Housman,
and Gottfried Benn[5]
said:—We are using our own skins for wallpaper and we cannot win.

1964

[1] **Sparine** a tranquillizer
[2] **Pelides** epithet for Achilles, son of Peleus
[3] **Honourable Possum** T.S. Eliot; reference to
Eliot's *Old Possum's Book of Practical Cats*
(1939)

[4] **novelist** Saul Bellow
[5] **Gottfried Benn** German poet and physician,
(1886–1956)

76

Henry's Confession

Nothin very bad happen to me lately.
How you explain that?—I explain that, Mr. Bones,
terms o' your bafflin odd sobriety.
Sober as man can get, no girls, no telephones,
what could happen bad to Mr. Bones?
—*If* life is a handkerchief sandwich,

in a modesty of death I join my father
who dared so long agone leave me.
A bullet on a concrete stoop
10   close by a smothering southern sea
spreadeagled on an island, by my knee.
—You is from hunger, Mr. Bones,

I offers you this handkerchief, now set
your left foot by my right foot,
shoulder to shoulder, all that jazz,
arm in arm, by the beautiful sea,[1]
hum a little, Mr. Bones.
—I saw nobody coming, so I went instead.

1964

[1] **by the beautiful sea**   a popular song of 1914

Sonnet 7

I've found out why, that day, that suicide
From the Empire State falling on someone's car
Troubled you so; and why we quarrelled. War,
Illness, an accident, I can see (you cried)
But not this: what a bastard, not spring wide!. .
I said a man, life in his teeth, could care
Not much just whom he spat it on. . and far
Beyond my laugh we argued either side.

"One has a right not to be fallen on!. ."
10   (Our second meeting. . yellow you were wearing.)
Voices of our resistance and desire!
Did I divine then I must shortly run
Crazy with need to fall on you, despairing?
Did you bolt so, before it caught, our fire?

1967

Scholars at the Orchid Pavilion[1]

1

Sozzled, Mo-tsu,[2] after a silence, vouchsafed
a word alarming: "We must love them all!"
Affronted, the fathers jumped.
"Yes" he went madly on and waved in quest
of his own dreadful subject "O the fathers"
he cried "must not be all!"
Whereat upon consent we broke up for the day.

2

The bamboo's bending power formed our theme
next dawn, under a splendid wind. The water
10   flapped to our tender gaze.
Girls came & crouched with tea. Great Wu[3] pinched one,
forgetting his later nature. How the wind howled,
tranquil was our pavilion,
watching & reflecting, fingering bamboo.

3

"Wild geese & bamboo" muttered Ch'en Hung-shou[4]
"block out our boundaries of fearful wind.
Neither requires shelter.
I shelter among painters, doing bamboo.
The young shoots unaffected by the wind
20   mock our love for their elders."
Mo-tsu opened his mouth & closed it to again.

4

"The bamboo of the Ten Halls"[5] went on Ch'en
"of my time, are excellently made.
I cannot find so well
ensorcelled those of later or former time.
Let us apply the highest praise, pure wind,
to those surpassing masters;—
having done things, a thing, along that line myself."

1972

---

[1] Berryman described this poem as "a testing-out
of the idea of Heaven"; possibly based on a
painting known as *Scholars of the Northern Chi
Dynasty Collating Classic Texts* (A.D. 673).
[2] **Mo-tsu** Chinese philosopher (479–372 B.C.),
who preached a doctrine of universal love
[3] **Great Wu** Emperor Wu (reigned A.D. 502–
50), first ruler of the Liang Dynasty, who became
an enthusiastic convert to Ch'an Buddhism and
retired to a monastery, giving up his throne
[4] **Ch'en Hung-shou** Chinese painter (1598–
1652)
[5] **"The bamboo of the Ten Halls"** reference to
a painting book, *The Hall of the Ten Bamboos*
(1633)

1014

P.K. PAGE
b. 1916

P.K. Page's family left England for Canada when she was two, and she grew up in Calgary. In 1941 she became part of the group, champions of modernism, centered about the Montreal magazine *Preview*. For a number of years she was a script writer for the National Film Board of Canada, where she met her husband, W. Arthur Irwin. He was later to become his country's ambassador to Brazil and then Mexico, and so she lived in those countries for extended periods. In Brazil, reduced to a kind of silence because she did not yet know Portuguese, she began painting—"as if starting from a pre-verbal state"—and sought expressive release through line and color. Her drawings are reciprocal with the highly visual character of her poetry and the fascination with translucence that can be seen in the title of her volume *The Glass Air: Selected Poems* (1985).

Page is indeed a poet obsessed with "seeing." She delights in sighting an image and watching its exfoliations as it shifts under scrutiny and changes under the eye of imagination: "the eye, altering, alters all." Her aesthetic preoccupation with language and metaphor resembles that of Wallace Stevens. She strives for an order of perception transcending ordinary sensuous vision, so that the eye becomes a symbol and a vehicle for passing over into the visionary.

In this poet's work, Brazil and Mexico represent imaginative antipodes. Brazil embodies the daylight world of endless, dizzying, sensuous detail. Mexico is the mystical night world of proliferating symbols. "Coming as I do from a random or whim-oriented culture, this recurrence or interrelating of symbols into an ordered and significant pattern . . . was curiously illuminating." She shares with Doris Lessing and Robert Graves an interest in Sufism that helps her explore her intuitions outside the assumptions of Christian mysticism.

After Rain

The snails have made a garden of green lace:
broderie anglaise from the cabbages,
chantilly from the choux-fleurs, tiny veils—
I see already that I lift the blind
upon a woman's wardrobe of the mind.

Such female whimsy floats about me like
a kind of tulle, a flimsy mesh,
while feet in gum boots pace the rectangles—
garden abstracted, geometry awash—
10   an unknown theorem argued in green ink,
dropped in the bath.
Euclid in glorious chlorophyl, half drunk.

I none too sober slipping in the mud
where rigged with guys of rain
the clothes-reel gauche
as the rangey skeleton of some

gaunt delicate spidery mute
is pitched as if
listening;
20   while hung from one thin rib
a silver web—
its infant, skeletal, diminutive,
now sagged with sequins, pulled ellipsoid,
glistening.

I suffer shame in all these images.
The garden is primeval, Giovanni
in soggy denim squelches by my hub
over his ruin,
shakes a doleful head.
30   But he so beautiful and diademmed,
his long Italian hands so wrung with rain
I find his ache exists beyond my rim
and almost weep to see a broken man
made subject to my whim.

O choir him, birds, and let him come to rest
within this beauty as one rests in love,
till pears upon the bough
encrusted with
small snails as pale as pearls
40   hang golden in
a heart that knows tears are a part of love.

And choir me too to keep my heart a size
larger than seeing, unseduced by each
bright glimpse of beauty striking like a bell,
so that the whole may toll,
its meaning shine
clear of the myriad images that still—
do what I will—encumber its pure line.

1967

Deaf-Mute in the Pear Tree

His clumsy body is a golden fruit
pendulous in the pear tree

Blunt fingers among the multitudinous buds

Adriatic blue the sky above and through
the forking twigs

Sun ruddying tree's trunk, his trunk
his massive head thick-nobbed with burnished curls
tight-clenched in bud

(Painting by Generalić.[1] Primitive.)

10   I watch him prune with silent secateurs

Boots in the crotch of branches shift their weight
heavily as oxen in a stall

Hear small inarticulate mews from his locked mouth
a kitten in a box

Pear clippings fall
                    soundlessly on the ground
Spring finches sing
                    soundlessly in the leaves

A stone. A stone in ears and on his tongue

20   Through palm and fingertip he knows the tree's
quick springtime pulse

Smells in its sap the sweet incipient pears

Pale sunlight's choppy water glistens on
his mutely snipping blades

And flags and scraps of blue
above him make regatta of the day

But when he sees his wife's foreshortened shape
sudden and silent in the grass below
uptilt its face to him

30   then air is kisses, kisses

stone dissolves

his locked throat finds a little door

and through it feathered joy
flies screaming like a jay

1985

[1] **Generalić:** Ivan Generalić, twentieth-century
Yugoslav painter in the tradition of magic neo-
primitivism

ROBERT LOWELL
1917–1977

Robert Lowell was born in Boston, Massachusetts, of an established New England family that included the literary figures James Russell Lowell and Amy Lowell. He began his studies at Harvard University, but after two years transferred to Kenyon College in Ohio to study under John Crowe Ransom. Perhaps under the influence of his mentor, Allen Tate, Lowell converted to Catholicism in 1940. In 1943 he was jailed for six months as a conscientious objector, an experience recorded in his poem "Memories of West Street and Lepke." In 1949 he suffered the first of many recurrent manic attacks that led to mental breakdown and hospitalization.

Lowell is probably the most influential American poet since World War II. His early poems were Christian in theme and intellectually knotty, but also showed real power of passionate phrasing and rhythm. He came into his own artistically, however, with the publication of *Life Studies* (1959), most of which is confessional—that is, centered on Lowell's and his family's private lives. Such a poem is "Skunk Hour," in which Lowell makes himself unequivocally the speaker of the poem, exploring personal guilt and sexual confusion. However, the poem does not remain a private confession. Personal breakdown mirrors the poet's perception of the intellectual and moral degeneration of his culture. Throughout *Life Studies*, which became the model for the new school of confessional poetry, themes of distorted and embittered love, intensely painful family relationships, the breakdown of marriage, and sojourns in mental hospitals constitute a fierce attack on American society, for its history of puritanical repression and predatory capitalism. Lowell's interest in American history continued to be a central preoccupation in his work. It is the subject of "For the Union Dead," where the legacy of the American Civil War haunts the civil rights struggle and race riots of the 1960s. Lowell's last book, *Day by Day*, is also in the mode of what he called his "verse autobiography." It is an elegiac book, sounding the threats of aging and dying and the despair of blocked love in a poem like "Suicide."

Memories of West Street and Lepke

Only teaching on Tuesdays, book-worming
in pajamas fresh from the washer each morning,
I hog a whole house on Boston's
"hardly passionate Marlborough Street,"
where even the man
scavenging filth in the back alley trash cans,
has two children, a beach wagon, a helpmate,
and is a "young Republican."
I have a nine months' daughter,
10   young enough to be my granddaughter.
Like the sun she rises in her flame-flamingo infants' wear.

These are the tranquillized *Fifties*,
and I am forty. Ought I to regret my seedtime?
I was a fire-breathing Catholic C.O.,[1]

---

[1] **C.O.** Lowell was sentenced to prison in 1943 as a conscientious objector (C.O.). He protested the saturation bombing of Germany by the Allies.

and made my manic statement,
telling off the state and president, and then
sat waiting sentence in the bull pen
beside a Negro boy with curlicues
of marijuana in his hair.

20   Given a year,
I walked on the roof of the West Street Jail, a short
enclosure like my school soccer court,
and saw the Hudson River once a day
through sooty clothesline entanglements
and bleaching khaki tenements.
Strolling, I yammered metaphysics with Abramowitz,
a jaundice-yellow ("it's really tan")
and fly-weight pacifist,
so vegetarian,
30   he wore rope shoes and preferred fallen fruit.
He tried to convert Bioff and Brown,[2]
the Hollywood pimps, to his diet.
Hairy, muscular, suburban,
wearing chocolate double-breasted suits,
they blew their tops and beat him black and blue.

I was so out of things, I'd never heard
of the Jehovah's Witnesses.
"Are you a C.O.?" I asked a fellow jailbird.
"No," he answered, "I'm a J.W."
40   He taught me the "hospital tuck,"
and pointed out the T-shirted back
of *Murder Incorporated*'s Czar Lepke,[3]
there piling towels on a rack,
or dawdling off to his little segregated cell full
of things forbidden the common man:
a portable radio, a dresser, two toy American
flags tied together with a ribbon of Easter palm.
Flabby, bald, lobotomized,
he drifted in a sheepish calm,
50   where no agonizing reappraisal
jarred his concentration on the electric chair—
hanging like an oasis in his air
of lost connections. . . .

1959

---

[2] **Bioff and Brown** William Bioff and George
Browne were extortion racketeers.
[3] **Lepke** Lepke Buchalter, head of Murder, Inc.,
a nationwide Mafia racketeering business, was
convicted of murder and executed at Sing Sing
in 1944.

Skunk Hour

[FOR ELIZABETH BISHOP][1]

Nautilus Island's hermit
heiress still lives through winter in her Spartan cottage;
her sheep still graze above the sea.
Her son's a bishop. Her farmer
is first selectman in our village;
she's in her dotage.

Thirsting for
the hierarchic privacy
of Queen Victoria's century,
she buys up all
the eyesores facing her shore,
and lets them fall.

The season's ill—
we've lost our summer millionaire,
who seemed to leap from an L.L. Bean
catalogue.[2] His nine-knot yawl
was auctioned off to lobstermen.
A red fox stain covers Blue Hill.

And now our fairy
decorator brightens his shop for fall;
his fishnet's filled with orange cork,
orange, his cobbler's bench and awl;
there is no money in his work,
he'd rather marry.

One dark night,
my Tudor Ford climbed the hill's skull;
I watched for love-cars. Lights turned down,
they lay together, hull to hull,
where the graveyard shelves on the town. . . .
My mind's not right.

A car radio bleats,
"Love, O careless Love. . . ." I hear
my ill-spirit sob in each blood cell,
as if my hand were at its throat. . . .
I myself am hell;
nobody's here—

10

20

30

---

[1] The scene is Castine, Maine, where Lowell had
a summer house. For Lowell's commentary on
this poem and, in particular, its indebtedness to
Bishop see *The Contemporary Poet as Artist*

and Critic, ed. Anthony Ostroff (Boston: Little,
Brown and Co., 1964).
[2] **an L.L. Bean catalogue** a mail-order cata-
logue that deals in sporting goods

only skunks, that search
in the moonlight for a bite to eat.
They march on their soles up Main Street:
40   white stripes, moonstruck eyes' red fire
under the chalk-dry and spar spire
of the Trinitarian Church.

I stand on top
of our back steps and breathe the rich air—
a mother skunk with her column of kittens swills the garbage pail.
She jabs her wedge-head in a cup
of sour cream, drops her ostrich tail,
and will not scare.

1959

For the Union Dead

"Relinquunt Omnia Servare Rem Publicam." [1]

The old South Boston Aquarium stands
in a Sahara of snow now. Its broken windows are boarded.
The bronze weathervane cod has lost half its scales.
The airy tanks are dry.

Once my nose crawled like a snail on the glass;
my hand tingled
to burst the bubbles
drifting from the noses of the cowed, compliant fish.

My hand draws back. I often sigh still
10   for the dark downward and vegetating kingdom
of the fish and reptile. One morning last March,
I pressed against the new barbed and galvanized

fence on the Boston Common. Behind their cage,
yellow dinosaur steamshovels were grunting
as they cropped up tons of mush and grass
to gouge their underworld garage.

Parking spaces luxuriate like civic
sandpiles in the heart of Boston.
A girdle of orange, Puritan-pumpkin colored girders
20   braces the tingling Statehouse,

---

[1] "They relinquish all to serve the state"; inscription on a monument by Augustus Saint-Gaudens dedicated to Robert Gould Shaw (1837–1863), commander of the first black regiment in the North, who died in an assault against Fort Wagner, South Carolina. The monument stands on Boston Common opposite the Massachusetts State House.

shaking over the excavations, as it faces Colonel Shaw
and his bell-cheeked Negro infantry
on St. Gaudens' shaking Civil War relief,
propped by a plank splint against the garage's earthquake.

Two months after marching through Boston,
half the regiment was dead;
at the dedication,
William James[2] could almost hear the bronze Negroes breathe.

Their monument sticks like a fishbone
30   in the city's throat.
Its Colonel is as lean
as a compass-needle.

He has an angry wrenlike vigilance,
a greyhound's gentle tautness;
he seems to wince at pleasure,
and suffocate for privacy.

He is out of bounds now. He rejoices in man's lovely,
peculiar power to choose life and die—
when he leads his black soldiers to death,
40   he cannot bend his back.

On a thousand small town New England greens,
the old white churches hold their air
of sparse, sincere rebellion; frayed flags
quilt the graveyards of the Grand Army of the Republic.

The stone statues of the abstract Union Soldier
grow slimmer and younger each year—
wasp-waisted, they doze over muskets
and muse through their sideburns . . .

Shaw's father wanted no monument
50   except the ditch,
where his son's body was thrown
and lost with his "niggers."

The ditch is nearer.
There are no statues for the last war here;
on Boylston Street, a commercial photograph
shows Hiroshima boiling

[2] **William James** (1842–1910) American phil-
osopher, brother of novelist Henry James

over a Mosler Safe, the "Rock of Ages"
that survived the blast. Space is nearer.
When I crouch to my television set,
60   the drained faces of Negro school-children rise like balloons.

Colonel Shaw
is riding on his bubble,
he waits
for the blessèd break.

The Aquarium is gone. Everywhere,
giant finned cars nose forward like fish;
a savage servility
slides by on grease.

1964

Water

It was a Maine lobster town—
each morning boatloads of hands
pushed off for granite
quarries on the islands,

and left dozens of bleak
white frame houses stuck
like oyster shells
on a hill of rock,

and below us, the sea lapped
10   the raw little match-stick
mazes of a weir,
where the fish for bait were trapped.

Remember? We sat on a slab of rock.
From this distance in time,
it seems the color
of iris, rotting and turning purpler,

But it was only
the usual gray rock
turning the usual green
20   when drenched by the sea.

The sea drenched the rock
at our feet all day,
and kept tearing away
flake after flake.

One night you dreamed
you were a mermaid clinging to a wharf-pile,
and trying to pull
off the barnacles with your hands.

We wished our two souls
30   might return like gulls
to the rock. In the end,
the water was too cold for us.

1964

Suicide

You only come in the tormenting
hallucinations of the night,
when my sleeping, prophetic mind
experiences things
that have not happened yet.

Sometimes in dreams
my hair came out in tufts
from my scalp,
I saw it lying there
10   *loose on my pillow like flax.*

Sometimes in dreams
my teeth got loose in my mouth . . .
Tinker, Tailor, Sailor, Sailor—
they were cherrystones,
as I spat them out.

I will not come again to you,
and risk the help I fled—
the doctors and darkness and dogs,
the hide and seek for me—
20   *"Cuckoo, cuckoo. Here I am . . ."*

If I had lived
and could have forgotten
that eventually it had to happen,
even to children—
it would have been otherwise.

One light, two lights, three—
it's day, no light is needed.
Your car I watch for never comes,
you will not see me peeping for you
30   behind my furtively ajar front door.

The trees close branches and redden,
their winter skeletons are hard to find;
a friend seldom seen
is not the same—
how quickly even bad cooking eats up a day.

I go to the window,
and even open it wide—
five floors down, the trees are bushes and weeds,
too contemptible and small
40   to delay a sparrow's fall.

Why haven't you followed me here,
as you followed me everywhere else?
You cannot do it
with vague fatality
or muffled but lethal sighs.

Do I deserve credit
for not having tried suicide—
or am I afraid
the exotic act
50   will make me blunder,

not knowing error
is remedied by practice,
as our first home-photographs,
headless, half-headed, tilting
extinguished by a flashbulb?

                                        1977

GWENDOLYN BROOKS

b. 1917

Born in Topeka, Kansas, Brooks grew up in Chicago. After studying at Wilson Junior College, she married at the age of twenty-two and had two children. During the 1930s she served as publicity director for the NAACP Youth Council in Chicago. She has taught at several universities and has also edited the literary magazine *Black Position*.

Bronzeville—her fictional name for the black ghetto of Chicago, providing the title for her first book, *A Street in Bronzeville* (1945)—is the locus of much of Brooks's best work. She writes a deliberately anec-dotal, colloquial poetry, full of vignettes of ordinary people in street scenes and domes-

tic scenes who suffer poverty and the oppres-sion of racism. Brooks speaks of her cha-racters as "dropouts . . . These are the people who are essentially saying 'Kilroy is here. We *are*.' But they're a little uncertain of their identity. I want to represent their basic uncertainty." Her subject is the ghetto dweller struggling with the poignancy of failure: the poor of "kitchenette building," who haven't time for dreams. Brooks has always been technically innovative, playing with various forms—ballads, sonnets, jazz improvisations—yet her poetry has become increasingly political.

kitchenette building

We are things of dry hours and the involuntary plan,
Grayed in, and gray. "Dream" makes a giddy sound, not strong
Like "rent," "feeding a wife," "satisfying a man."

But could a dream send up through onion fumes
Its white and violet, fight with fried potatoes
And yesterday's garbage ripening in the hall,
Flutter, or sing an aria down these rooms

Even if we were willing to let it in,
Had time to warm it, keep it very clean,
10   Anticipate a message, let it begin?

We wonder. But not well! not for a minute!
Since Number Five is out of the bathroom now,
We think of lukewarm water, hope to get in it.

1945

The Bean Eaters

They eat beans mostly, this old yellow pair.
Dinner is a casual affair.
Plain chipware on a plain and creaking wood,
Tin flatware.

Two who are Mostly Good.
Two who have lived their day,
But keep on putting on their clothes
And putting things away.

And remembering . . .
10   Remembering, with twinklings and twinges,
As they lean over the beans in their rented back room that
       is full of beads and receipts and dolls and cloths,
       tobacco crumbs, vases and fringes.

1960

We Real Cool

             The Pool Players.
        Seven at the Golden Shovel.

We real cool. We
Left school. We

>Lurk late. We
>Strike straight. We
>
>Sing sin. We
>Thin gin. We
>
>Jazz June. We
>Die soon.

>1960

ROBERT DUNCAN
b. 1919

Duncan was born in Oakland, California, and his mother died shortly after his birth. Orphaned because his father, a day laborer, was unable to keep him, he was adopted and raised in Bakersfield, California, where his adoptive father was an architect. He grew up as Robert Edward Symms, reverting to his original surname in 1942. His adoptive parents were orthodox theosophists, and the esoteric doctrines he learned as a child had an enormous influence on his later poetry. Duncan studied at the University of California from 1936 to 1938 and again during the mid-1940s after some years in New York, where he had become part of a literary circle including Anaïs Nin, Kenneth Patchen, and George Barker. Since 1945 he has mainly lived in San Francisco as a leading poetic figure, associated with the Black Mountain or Projectivist movement since its origin in 1952.

Associated with Charles Olson and Robert Creeley as an exponent of projective verse, Duncan combines high lyrical gifts with a tendency toward didacticism by theorizing in his verse. Many of his poems are about poetry itself—its nature and creation. However, as "Ingmar Bergman's *Seventh Seal*" demonstrates, he has a deeply felt social vision.

Ingmar Bergman's *Seventh Seal*[1]

This is the way it is. We see
three ages in one: the child Jesus
innocent of Jerusalem and Rome
—magically at home in joy—
that's the year from which
our inner persistence has its force.

The second, Bergman shows us,
carries forward image after image
of anguish, of the Christ crossd
10   and sends up from open sores of the plague

[1] **Bergman's *Seventh Seal***   film by Swedish director Ingmar Bergman produced in 1956

(shown as wounds upon His corpse)
from lacerations in the course of love
(the crown of whose kingdom tears the flesh)

. . . There is so much suffering!
What possibly protects us
from the emptiness, the forsaken cry,
the utter dependence, the vertigo?
Why do so many come to love's edge
only to be stranded there?

20   The second face of Christ, his
evil, his Other, emaciated, pain and sin.
Christ, what a contagion!
What a stink it spreads round

our age! It's our age!
and the rage of the storm is abroad.
The malignant stupidity of statesmen rules.
The old riders thru the forests race
    shouting: the wind! the wind!
Now the black horror cometh again.

30   And I'll throw myself down
as the clown does in Bergman's *Seventh Seal*
to cower as if asleep with his wife and child,
hid in the caravan under the storm.

Let the Angel of Wrath pass over.
Let the end come.
War, stupidity and fear are powerful.
We are only children. To bed! to bed!
    To play safe!

To throw ourselves down
40   helplessly, into happiness,
    into an age of our own, into
    our own days.
There where the Pestilence roars,
where the empty riders of the horror go.

1960

After a Passage in Baudelaire[1]

Ship, leaving or arriving, of my lover,
my soul, leaving or coming into this harbor,
among your lights and shadows   shelterd,
at home in your bulk, the cunning
regularity and symmetry thruout
of love's design, of will, of your
attractive cells and chambers .

riding forward, darkest of shades
over the shadowd waters .
10   into the light, neat, symmetrically
arranged above your watery reflections
disturbing your own image, moving as you are

. What passenger, what sailor,
looks out into the swirling currents round you
as if into those depths into a mirror?

What lights in what port-holes
raise in my mind again   hunger and impatience?
to make my bed down again, there, beyond me,
as if this room too, my bedroom, my lamp at my side,
20   were among those lights sailing out
                    away from me.

We too, among the others, passengers
in that *charme infini et mystérieux*,[2]
in that suitable symmetry, that precision
everywhere, the shining fittings, the fit
of lights and polisht surfaces to the dark,
to the flickering shadows of them,
we too, unfaithful to me, sailing away,
leaving me.

30   *L'idée poétique*, the idea of a poetry,
that rises from the movement, from the
outswirling curves and imaginary figures
round this ship, this fate, this sure thing,

est l'hypothèse d'un être vaste, immense,

compliqué, mais eurythmique.[3]

1964

[1] The passage occurs in the prose journals
("Rockets," xxiv) of the French poet Charles
Baudelaire (1821–1867), quoted in the original
in lines 23, 30, and 35–6.
[2] *charme infini et mystérieux* infinite and mys-
terious charm
[3] ll. 30, 35–6 *L'idée poétique . . . euryth-*
mique: The poetic idea is the hypothesis of a
vast, immense being, complex yet
harmonious.

Strains of Sight

1

He brought a light so she could see
Adam move nakedly in the lighted room.
It was a window in the tree.
It was a shelter where there was none.

She saw his naked back and thigh
and heard the notes of a melody
where Adam out of his nature came
into four walls, roof and floor.

He turned on the light and turnd back,
10   moving with grace to catch her eye.
She saw his naked loneliness.

Now I shall never rest, she sighd,
until he strips his heart for me.
The body flashes such thoughts of death
so that time leaps up, and a man's hand

seen naked catches upon my breath
the risk we took in Paradise.
The serpent thought before the tomb
laid naked, naked, naked before the eyes,

20   reflects upon itself in a bare room.

2

In the questioning phrase the voice
—he raises his eyes from the page—
follows towards some last
curve of the air, suspended above

its sign, that point, that .
And asks, Who am I then?
Where am I going? There is no time
like now that is not like now.

Who? turns upon some body where
30   the hand striving to tune
curves of the first lute whose strings are nerves
sees in the touch the phrase will

rise . break
as the voice does? above some moving obscurity
ripples out in the disturbd pool,
shadows and showings where we would read
—raising his eyes from the body's lure—

what the question is,
where the heart reflects.

1964

HOWARD NEMEROV
b. 1920

Born in New York, Nemerov received his A.B. degree from Harvard in 1941 and then served in both the Royal Canadian Air Force, flying combat missions against German shipping in the North Sea and, in 1944–45, the U.S. Army Air Corps. He has taught at Bennington College, Brandeis University, and the University of Minnesota, and is currently a professor at Washington University in St. Louis. In 1977 he received the Pulitzer Prize for his *Collected Poems*.

Nemerov is the author of plays, novels, and criticism as well as poems. His work is low-keyed, habitually ironic, and somewhat distanced, despite its humane concerns. He is a satirist of human foibles, particularly people's propensity to take themselves too seriously. "The Goose Fish" is characteristic—a romantic scene in which two people making love on a beach seem mocked by the stare of a dead goose fish. Nemerov's skepticism and bitterness are leavened but not dispelled by his humor. In response to the accusation that his poems are jokes, he replied: "I'm inclined to agree, insisting however they are bad jokes and even terrible jokes, emerging from the nature of things and from the blind side or the dark side, the side everyone concerned with 'values' would just as soon forget."

History of a Literary Movement

After Margrave died, nothing
Seemed worth while. I said as much
To Grumbach, who replied:
"The oscillations of fashion
Do not amuse me. There have been
Great men before, there will be
Other great men. Only man
Is important, man is ultimate."
I can still see him sitting there,
10   Sipping level by level his
Pousse-café. He was a fat man.
Fat men are seldom the best
Creative writers.

                    The rest of us
Slowly dispersed, hardly
Ever saw each other again,
And did not correspond, for
There was little enough to say.
Only Impli and I
20 Hung on, feeling as we did
That the last word had not
Finally been said. Sometimes
I feel, I might say, cheated.
Life here at Bad Grandstein
Is dull, is dull, what with
The eternal rocks and the river;
And Impli, though one of my
Dearest friends, can never,
I have decided, become great.

                    1947

The Goose Fish

On the long shore, lit by the moon
To show them properly alone,
Two lovers suddenly embraced
So that their shadows were as one.
The ordinary night was graced
For them by the swift tide of blood
That silently they took at flood,
And for a little time they prized
        Themselves emparadised.

10 Then, as if shaken by stage-fright
Beneath the hard moon's bony light,
They stood together on the sand
Embarrassed in each other's sight
But still conspiring hand in hand,
Until they saw, there underfoot,
As though the world had found them out,
The goose fish turning up, though dead,
        His hugely grinning head.

There in the china light he lay,
20 Most ancient and corrupt and grey.
They hesitated at his smile,
Wondering what it seemed to say
To lovers who a little while
Before had thought to understand,
By violence upon the sand,
The only way that could be known
        To make a world their own.

It was a wide and moony grin
Together peaceful and obscene;
30 They knew not what he would express,
So finished a comedian
He might mean failure or success,
But took it for an emblem of
Their sudden, new and guilty love
To be observed by, when they kissed,
   That rigid optimist.

So he became their patriarch,
Dreadfully mild in the half-dark.
His throat that the sand seemed to choke,
40 His picket teeth, these left their mark
But never did explain the joke
That so amused him, lying there
While the moon went down to disappear
Along the still and tilted track
   That bears the zodiac.

                  1955

RICHARD WILBUR

b. 1921

The son of a portrait painter, Richard Wilbur was born in New York and grew up in North Caldwell, New Jersey. He graduated from Amherst College in 1942 and served with the U.S. Army in Italy and Germany. After receiving his M.A. from Harvard in 1947, he taught at Harvard, Wellesley College, and finally Wesleyan University (1957–77).

As poet, critic, translator, and editor, Wilbur is a model of the contemporary man of letters. His versatility is reflected in his translations of Molière and his libretto for the comic opera *Candide*, and his poetry is notable for its elegant lyrical grace and formal strictness. His typical method is to work with extended metaphor, as in "Love Calls Us to the Things of This World," where the poet wakes to see the laundry outside his window transformed to angels. He elaborates the conceit with a wonderful whimsy—his astounded soul, delighting in this blessed laundry, momentarily refuses to descend to the waking body. Wilbur revels in his game of wit, and the poem is as brilliantly contrived as any by John Donne. His sheer exuberance is a testament to the pleasure he takes in "the things of the world." As "The Beautiful Changes" also attests, this celebration of the wonder of "things," seen clearly by the eye attentive to metaphor, is Wilbur's signature as a poet.

The Beautiful Changes

One wading a Fall meadow finds on all sides
The Queen Anne's Lace lying like lilies
On water; it glides
So from the walker, it turns
Dry grass to a lake, as the slightest shade of you
Valleys my mind in fabulous blue Lucernes.

The beautiful changes as a forest is changed
By a chameleon's turning his skin to it;
As a mantis, arranged
10   On a green leaf, grows
Into it, makes the leaf leafier, and proves
Any greenness is deeper than anyone knows.

Your hands hold roses always in a way that says
They are not only yours; the beautiful changes
In such kind ways,
Wishing ever to sunder
Things and things' selves for a second finding, to lose
For a moment all that it touches back to wonder.

1947

Love Calls Us to the Things of This World[1]

The eyes open to a cry of pulleys,
And spirited from sleep, the astounded soul
Hangs for a moment bodiless and simple
As false dawn.
               Outside the open window
The morning air is all awash with angels.

Some are in bed-sheets, some are in blouses,
Some are in smocks: but truly there they are.
Now they are rising together in calm swells
10   Of halcyon feeling, filling whatever they wear
With the deep joy of their impersonal breathing;

Now they are flying in place, conveying
The terrible speed of their omnipresence, moving
And staying like white water; and now of a sudden
They swoon down into so rapt a quiet
That nobody seems to be there.
              The soul shrinks

From all that it is about to remember,
From the punctual rape of every blessèd day,
20   And cries,
      "Oh, let there be nothing on earth but laundry,
Nothing but rosy hands in the rising steam
And clear dances done in the sight of heaven."

---

[1] "The title comes from St. Augustine"; Wilbur
in *The Contemporary Poet as Artist and Critic*,
ed. A. Ostroff (Boston: Little, Brown and Co.,
1964).

Yet, as the sun acknowledges
With a warm look the world's hunks and colours,
The soul descends once more in bitter love
To accept the waking body, saying now
In a changed voice as the man yawns and rises,

"Bring them down from their ruddy gallows;
30   Let there be clean linen for the backs of thieves;
Let lovers go fresh and sweet to be undone,
And the heaviest nuns walk in a pure floating
Or dark habits,
          keeping their difficult balance."

                   1956

Advice to a Prophet

When you come, as you soon must, to the streets of our city,
Mad-eyed from stating the obvious,
Not proclaiming our fall but begging us
In God's name to have self-pity,

Spare us all word of the weapons, their force and range,
The long numbers that rocket the mind;
Our slow, unreckoning hearts will be left behind,
Unable to fear what is too strange.

Nor shall you scare us with talk of the death of the race.
10   How should we dream of this place without us?—
The sun mere fire, the leaves untroubled about us,
A stone look on the stone's face?

Speak of the world's own change. Though we cannot conceive
Of an undreamt thing, we know to our cost
How the dreamt cloud crumbles, the vines are blackened by frost,
How the view alters. We could believe,

If you told us so, that the white-tailed deer will slip
Into perfect shade, grown perfectly shy,
The lark avoid the reaches of our eye,
20   The jack-pine lose its knuckled grip

On the cold ledge, and every torrent burn
As Xanthus[1] once, its gliding trout
Stunned in a twinkling. What should we be without
The dolphin's arc, the dove's return,

These things in which we have seen ourselves and spoken?
Ask us, prophet, how we shall call
Our natures forth when that live tongue is all
Dispelled, that glass obscured or broken

In which we have said the rose of our love and the clean
30   Horse of our courage, in which beheld
The singing locust of the soul unshelled,
And all we mean or wish to mean.

Ask us, ask us whether with the worldless rose
Our hearts shall fail us; come demanding
Whether there shall be lofty or long standing
When the bronze annals of the oak-tree close.

                                1961

¹ **Xanthus**   a river in Asia Minor

PHILIP LARKIN

1922–1985
:

Born in Warwickshire, Larkin was educated at Oxford during World War II, and his experiences there provided the basis for *Jill* (1946), the first of his two novels. He later worked as a librarian, mostly at the University of Hull, and was also jazz-feature writer for the London *Daily Telegraph* from 1961 to 1971.

In his early work Larkin was associated with a group of poets at Oxford called "The Movement," whose anthology *New Lines* (editor Robert Conquest, 1956) was offered to counter the poetics of modernism. Rejecting the rhetorical style of Dylan Thomas and the metaphysical portentousness of T.S. Eliot, the group sought a conversational idiom for poetry, candid and faithful to ordinary experience. Larkin openly expressed his contempt for modernism (because, he claimed, it offers obscurity without profundity), preferring the forthright virtues of Thomas Hardy, whom he acknowledged as his most important influence.

Larkin's poetry, conventional in formal technique, is tough-minded, skeptical, and reserved, recording human foibles with wit and a certain affection. He adapts his traditional style to modern subjects, particularly the spiritually blank ordinary lives of provincial or suburban people. He has a novelist's power of characterization and can create a complete personality in a poem as brief as "Mr. Bleaney," in which the minimal life of a lonely man is movingly portrayed. His viewpoint is often that of a solitary, cautious bachelor, aware of his limitations, of something "toad-like" squatting on his soul that ties him to habit and to a fear of change. Larkin's pervasive melancholic tone is perhaps redeemed by his wry stoicism—that of a reluctant agnostic, confronting change, diminution, and death with sardonic resignation.

Toads

Why should I let the toad *work*
    Squat on my life?
Can't I use my wit as a pitchfork
    And drive the brute off?

Six days of the week it soils
    With its sickening poison—
Just for paying a few bills!
    That's out of proportion.

Lots of folk live on their wits:
10   Lecturers, lispers,
Losels, loblolly-men, louts—
    They don't end as paupers;

Lots of folk live up lanes
    With fires in a bucket,
Eat windfalls and tinned sardines—
    They seem to like it.

Their nippers have got bare feet,
    Their unspeakable wives
Are skinny as whippets—and yet
20   No one actually *starves*.

Ah, were I courageous enough
    To shout *Stuff your pension!*
But I know, all too well, that's the stuff
    That dreams are made on:

For something sufficiently toad-like
    Squats in me, too;
Its hunkers are heavy as hard luck,
    And cold as snow,

And will never allow me to blarney
30   My way to getting
The fame and the girl and the money
    All at one sitting.

I don't say, one bodies the other
    One's spiritual truth;
But I do say it's hard to lose either,
    When you have both.

1955

Poetry of Departures

Sometimes you hear, fifth-hand,
As epitaph:
He chucked up everything
And just cleared off,
And always the voice will sound
Certain you approve
This audacious, purifying
Elemental move.

And they are right, I think.
10 We all hate home
And having to be there:
I detest my room,
Its specially-chosen junk,
The good books, the good bed,
And my life, in perfect order:
So to hear it said

He walked out on the whole crowd
Leaves me flushed and stirred,
Like *Then she undid her dress*
20 Or *Take that you bastard*;
Surely I can, if he did?
And that helps me stay
Sober and industrious.
But I'd go today,

Yes, swagger the nut-strewn roads,
Crouch in the fo'c'sle
Stubbly with goodness, if
It weren't so artificial,
Such a deliberate step backwards
30 To create an object:
Books; china; a life
Reprehensibly perfect.

1955

Here

Swerving east, from rich industrial shadows
And traffic all night north; swerving through fields
Too thin and thistled to be called meadows,
And now and then a harsh-named halt, that shields
Workmen at dawn; swerving to solitude
Of skies and scarecrows, haystacks, hares and pheasants,
And the widening river's slow presence,
The piled gold clouds, the shining gull-marked mud,

Gathers to the surprise of a large town:
10   Here domes and statues, spires and cranes cluster
Beside grain-scattered streets, barge-crowded water,
And residents from raw estates, brought down
The dead straight miles by stealing flat-faced trolleys,
Push through plate-glass swing doors to their desires—
Cheap suits, red kitchen-ware, sharp shoes, iced lollies,
Electric mixers, toasters, washers, driers—

A cut-price crowd, urban yet simple, dwelling
Where only salesmen and relations come
Within a terminate and fishy-smelling
20   Pastoral of ships up streets, the slave museum,
Tattoo-shops, consulates, grim head-scarfed wives;
And out beyond its mortgaged half-built edges
Fast-shadowed wheat-fields, running high as hedges,
Isolate villages, where removed lives

Loneliness clarifies. Here silence stands
Like heat. Here leaves unnoticed thicken,
Hidden weeds flower, neglected waters quicken,
Luminously-peopled air ascends;
And past the poppies bluish neutral distance
30   Ends the land suddenly beyond a beach
Of shapes and shingle. Here is unfenced existence:
Facing the sun, untalkative, out of reach.

1964

Mr. Bleaney

"This was Mr. Bleaney's room. He stayed
The whole time he was at the Bodies,[1] till
They moved him." Flowered curtains, thin and frayed,
Fall to within five inches of the sill,

Whose window shows a strip of building land,
Tussocky, littered. "Mr. Bleaney took
My bit of garden properly in hand."
Bed, upright chair, sixty-watt bulb, no hook

Behind the door, no room for books or bags—
10   "I'll take it." So it happens that I lie
Where Mr. Bleaney lay, and stub my fags
On the same saucer-souvenir, and try

Stuffing my ears with cotton-wool, to drown
The jabbering set he egged her on to buy.
I know his habits—what time he came down,
His preference for sauce to gravy, why

[1] the Bodies the Car Bodies plant, where Mr.
Bleaney worked

He kept on plugging at the four aways—[2]
Likewise their yearly frame: the Frinton folk
Who put him up for summer holidays,
20 And Christmas at his sister's house in Stoke.

But if he stood and watched the frigid wind
Tousling the clouds, lay on the fusty bed
Telling himself that this was home, and grinned,
And shivered, without shaking off the dread

That how we live measures our own nature,
And at his age having no more to show
Than one hired box should make him pretty sure
He warranted no better, I don't know.

1964

[2] plugging at the four aways continually placing
bets on football matches played away from the
teams' home cities.

JAMES DICKEY
b. 1923

Born in Atlanta, Georgia, Dickey began undergraduate study at Clemson College in South Carolina, but after a year enlisted as a fighter-bomber pilot in World War II. He then studied at Vanderbilt University, receiving his M.A. in 1950, but was recalled to active service as a training officer in the Korean War. Afterward, he left a teaching position at the University of Florida to work for a time in advertising in New York. He has taught in several universities since then, most recently the University of South Carolina. He was poetry consultant to the Library of Congress 1966–68. Although primarily a poet, he has also written literary criticism and fiction. His novel *Deliverance* (1970) was made into a popular film in 1973.

Dickey has certain affinities with a kind of emotional extremism evident in Dylan Thomas and Theodore Roethke. In his autobiographical *Self-Interviews*, he describes the poet as a totally responsive, intensified man, with an aggressive hold on reality. Heroic self-affirmation is a recurring theme in his poetry. In "The Performance," a prisoner about to be executed must set himself a redeeming task (a gymnastic trick) to reassert his identity and dignity. Most of

Dickey's poems are narratives, and he often explores the monstrous and grotesque within ordinary life: a voyeur contemplating rape, a man engaged in bestiality. "There's a razor's edge between sublimity and absurdity. And that's the edge I try to walk."

A sophisticated craftsman, he is noted for the rhetorical clamor and exuberance of his poems. He describes them as often emerging from precognitive rhythms from which the words follow: "Now and then I began to hear lines of verse, lines without words to them, that had what was to me a very compelling sound: an unusual sound of urgency and passion, of grave conviction, or inevitability, of the same kind of drive and excitement that one hears in a good passage of slow jazz." Describing himself as one of the "empathizers," he seeks in his poetry to achieve a mystical unity with nature, as in "The Heaven of Animals," that re-enacts the fearless, passionate encounter of hunter and animal engaged in an endlessly repeated ritual sacrifice. Dickey is one of the most popular American poets, and the power of his work comes from his willingness to explore extremes of feeling and from a visceral erotic energy.

The Performance

The last time I saw Donald Armstrong
He was staggering oddly off into the sun,
Going down, of the Philippine Islands.
I let my shovel fall, and put that hand
Above my eyes, and moved some way to one side
That his body might pass through the sun,

And I saw how well he was not
Standing there on his hands,
On his spindle-shanked forearms balanced,
10   Unbalanced, with his big feet looming and waving
In the great, untrustworthy air
He flew in each night, when it darkened.

Dust fanned in scraped puffs from the earth
Between his arms, and blood turned his face inside out,
To demonstrate its suppleness
Of veins, as he perfected his role.
Next day, he toppled his head off
On an island beach to the south,

And the enemy's two-handed sword
20   Did not fall from anyone's hands
At that miraculous sight,
As the head rolled over upon
Its wide-eyed face, and fell
Into the inadequate grave

He had dug for himself, under pressure.
Yet I put my flat hand to my eyebrows
Months later, to see him again
In the sun, when I learned how he died,
And imagined him, there,
30   Come, judged, before his small captors,

Doing all his lean tricks to amaze them—
The back somersault, the kip-up—
And at last, the stand on his hands,
Perfect, with his feet together,
His head down, evenly breathing,
As the sun poured up from the sea

And the headsman broke down
In a blaze of tears, in that light
Of the thin, long human frame
40   Upside down in its own strange joy,
And, if some other one had not told him,
Would have cut off the feet

Instead of the head,
And if Armstrong had not presently risen
In kingly, round-shouldered attendance,
And then knelt down in himself
Beside his hacked, glittering grave, having done
All things in this life that he could.

1957

The Heaven of Animals

Here they are. The soft eyes open.
If they have lived in a wood
It is a wood.
If they have lived on plains
It is grass rolling
Under their feet forever.

Having no souls, they have come,
Anyway, beyond their knowing.
Their instincts wholly bloom
10   And they rise.
The soft eyes open.

To match them, the landscape flowers,
Outdoing, desperately
Outdoing what is required:
The richest wood,
The deepest field.

For some of these,
It could not be the place
It is, without blood.
20   These hunt, as they have done,
But with claws and teeth grown perfect,

More deadly than they can believe.
They stalk more silently,
And crouch on the limbs of trees,
And their descent
Upon the bright backs of their prey

May take years
In a sovereign floating of joy.
And those that are hunted
30   Know this as their life,
Their reward: to walk

Under such trees in full knowledge
Of what is in glory above them,
And to feel no fear,
But acceptance, compliance.
Fulfilling themselves without pain

At the cycle's center,
They tremble, they walk
Under the tree,
40   They fall, they are torn,
They rise, they walk again.

1962

DENISE LEVERTOV
b. 1923

Levertov, now considered an American poet, was born in England. Her father, a Russian Jew, converted to Christianity and became an Anglican minister whose lifelong ambition was to unite the Christian and Jewish religions. Her parents had been prisoners of war under house arrest in Leipzig in World War I; when Levertov was a child, their English home became a center for receiving and relocating Jewish refugees from Nazism. Educated at home by her parents, Levertov had no formal schooling except for ballet and painting classes. She worked as a civilian nurse at St. Luke's Hospital in London during World War II and in 1947 married an American soldier, the novelist Mitchell Goodman. In 1948, she moved to New York, where her son was born the following year.

She was poetry editor of the *Nation* for three years and has taught at several American universities.

Despite spending her youth in England, Levertov was deeply influenced by American poetry (particularly William Carlos Williams). Identified with the Black Mountain school, her poetry is intensely focused on the actual and immediate. Her poem "Pleasures," for instance, is a series of roving perceptions recorded in layers of images. Her political activism during the Vietnam War and afterward is reflected in the social concerns and general tone of her volume *The Sorrow Dance* (1966). Yet her characteristic style still involves a search for sensually powerful and organically structured images.

Pleasures

I like to find
what's not found
at once, but lies

within something of another nature,
in repose, distinct.
Gull feathers of glass, hidden

in white pulp: the bones of squid
which I pull out and lay
blade by blade on the draining board—

10   tapered as if for swiftness, to pierce
        the heart, but fragile, substance
        belying design.   Or a fruit, *mamey*,

cased in rough brown peel, the flesh
rose-amber, and the seed:
the seed a stone of wood, carved and

polished, walnut-colored, formed
like a brazilnut, but large,
large enough to fill
the hungry palm of a hand.

20 I like the juicy stem of grass that grows
within the coarser leaf folded round,
and the butteryellow glow
in the narrow flute from which the morning-glory
opens blue and cool on a hot morning.

1959

Terror

Face-down; odor
of dusty carpet. The grip
of anguished stillness.

Then your naked voice, your
head knocking the wall, sideways,
the beating of trapped thoughts against iron.

If I remember, how is it
my face shows
barely a line? Am I
10 a monster, to sing
in the wind on this sunny hill

and not taste the dust always,
and not hear
that rending, that retching?
How did morning come, and the days
that followed, and quiet nights?

1959

Losing Track

Long after you have swung back
away from me
I think you are still with me:

you come in close to the shore
on the tide
and nudge me awake the way

a boat adrift nudges the pier:
am I a pier
half-in half-out of the water?

10   and in the pleasure of that communion
I lose track,
the moon I watch goes down, the

tide swings you away before
I know I'm
alone again long since,

mud sucking at gray and black
timbers of me,
a light growth of green dreams drying.

1964

LOUIS SIMPSON
b. 1923

Born and brought up in Jamaica, Louis Simpson moved to New York at the age of seventeen, as a student in Columbia University. He served as a combat infantryman in World War II, and afterwards completed his studies at Columbia, earning his Ph.D. in 1959 while working in publishing as an editor. He then turned to university teaching and is now professor of English at the State University of New York, Stony Brook.

Simpson began as a realistic poet, writing in standard metrical forms. His first book, *The Arrivists: Poems 1940–1949*, explores the impact of combat on the young soldier. "Carentan O Carentan," a ballad, describes with understated anguish the ambush of an American infantry patrol by German soldiers. He became an increasingly rigorous social critic, finding irony, "the poor man's nerve-tic," the most appropriate tone for dealing with the disease of materialism, which he feels has undermined truer values of democratic society. In "A Story about Chicken Soup," chicken soup becomes a metaphor for the ordinary life as opposed to the simultaneous horrors of the contemporary world: the German child who sits smiling amid the rubble of war, the Jewish dead. His radically uncompromising political message is clear: war is a conspiracy to maintain class barriers, to keep some people permanently poor. In making a narrative of his own life, Simpson tried to emulate the simplicity of proverbs, ballads, and stories. The result is a poetry of genuine humanity —all the more so because of its sardonic edge.

Carentan O Carentan[1]

Trees in the old days used to stand
And shape a shady lane
Where lovers wandered hand in hand
Who came from Carentan.

This was the shining green canal
Where we came two by two
Walking at combat-interval.
Such trees we never knew.

The day was early June, the ground
10   Was soft and bright with dew.
Far away the guns did sound,
But here the sky was blue.

The sky was blue, but there a smoke
Hung still above the sea
Where the ships together spoke
To towns we could not see.

Could you have seen us through a glass
You would have said a walk
Of farmers out to turn the grass,
20   Each with his own hay-fork.

The watchers in their leopard suits
Waited till it was time,
And aimed between the belt and boot
And let the barrel climb.

I must lie down at once, there is
A hammer at my knee.
And call it death or cowardice,
Don't count again on me.

Everything's all right, Mother,
30   Everyone gets the same
At one time or another.
It's all in the game.

I never strolled, nor ever shall,
Down such a leafy lane.
I never drank in a canal,
Nor ever shall again.

[1] **Carentan** town in Normandy, France; during
World War II captured by U.S. troops after a
severe battle June 8–12, 1944

There is a whistling in the leaves
And it is not the wind,
The twigs are falling from the knives
40   That cut men to the ground.

Tell me, Master-Sergeant,
The way to turn and shoot.
But the Sergeant's silent
That taught me how to do it.

O Captain, show us quickly
Our place upon the map.
But the Captain's sickly
And taking a long nap.

Lieutenant, what's my duty,
50   My place in the platoon?
He too's a sleeping beauty,
Charmed by that strange tune.

Carentan O Carentan
Before we met with you
We never yet had lost a man
Or known what death could do.

                    1949

A Story about Chicken Soup

In my grandmother's house there was always chicken soup
And talk of the old country—mud and boards,
Poverty,
The snow falling down the necks of lovers.

Now and then, out of her savings
She sent them a dowry. Imagine
The rice-powdered faces!
And the smell of the bride, like chicken soup.

But the German's killed them.
10   I know it's in bad taste to say it,
But it's true. The Germans killed them all.

                    * * *

In the ruins of Berchtesgaden[1]
A child with yellow hair
Ran out of a doorway.

----

[1] **Berchtesgaden**   a resort town in southern Germany, famous as Hitler's mountain retreat

A German girl-child—
Cuckoo, all skin and bones—
Not even enough to make chicken soup.
She sat by the stream and smiled.

Then as we splashed in the sun
20   She laughed at us.
We had killed her mechanical brothers,
So we forgave her.

* * *

The sun is shining.
The shadows of the lovers have disappeared.
They are all eyes; they have some demand on me—
They want me to be more serious than I want to be.

They want me to stick in their mudhole
Where no one is elegant.
They want me to wear old clothes,
30   They want me to be poor, to sleep in a room with many others—

Not to walk in the painted sunshine
To a summer house,
But to live in the tragic world forever.

1963

FRANK O'HARA
1926–1966

Born in Baltimore, Maryland, O'Hara grew up in Grafton, Massachusetts. He began to study music at an early age and had ambitions to be a concert pianist. In World War II he served on a destroyer in the South Pacific. On his return to the United States he entered Harvard University, where he decided upon writing as a career and helped found the Poet's Theater in Cambridge before going on to graduate work at the University of Michigan. In 1951 he settled in New York, becoming editorial associate and art critic for *Arts News* (his reviews were published as *Art Chronicles* in 1975). He had joined the staff of the Museum of Modern Art and was associate curator of exhibitions of painting and sculpture when, at the age of forty, he was struck by a taxi and fatally injured.

O'Hara, like John Ashbery, was a member of the New York school of poets, which had affinities with the leading abstract expressionist painters in New York City. He often resorted to the techniques of Surrealism and Dadaism—reconceived in a colloquial American idiom, as in the poem "Chez Jane," with its structure dictated by its rapid-fire, discontinuous images. O'Hara also collaborated with other artists on collages, lithographs, comic strips, and musical dialogues. His most famous poem, "Why I Am Not a Painter," is based on a painting, "Oranges," by Grace Hartigan, which, in keeping with the poem's sardonic humor, surfaces only indirectly as a subject. This technique of displacement underscores his insistence that the recalcitrant forces of pain, of the truly "terrible," resist full expression in a poem.

His poetry is casual and spontaneous, and characterized by personable wit and extravagant fantasy. In "Personism: A Manifesto" (1959), he wrote: "I am mainly preoccupied with the world as I experience it . . . What is happening to me, allowing for lies and exaggerations which I try to avoid, goes into my poems." "The Day Lady Died," for example, begins with a defensive preoccupation with irrelevant de-

tails—the day's distractions and transactions—which provides the context for an elegiac protest against the death of the great jazz singer Billie Holiday. Notoriously offhand about his writing, frequently losing poems, O'Hara was a prolific writer. When his posthumous *The Collected Poems* was edited by Donald Allen in 1971, it contained 590 pages and was a mammoth salvaging effort—of poems left in his apartment or sent in letters to friends.

Chez Jane[1]

The white chocolate jar full of petals
swills odds and ends around in a dizzying eye
of four o'clocks now and to come. The tiger,
marvellously striped and irritable, leaps
on the table and without disturbing a hair
of the flowers' breathless attention, pisses
into the pot, right down its delicate spout.
A whisper of steam goes up from that porcelain
urethra. "Saint-Saëns!"[2] it seems to be whispering
10   curling unerringly around the furry nuts
of the terrible puss, who is mentally flexing.
Ah be with me always, spirit of noisy
contemplation in the studio, the Garden
of Zoos, the eternally fixed afternoons!
There, while music scratches its scrofulous
stomach, the brute beast emerges and stands,
clear and careful, knowing always the exact peril
at this moment caressing his fangs with
a tongue given wholly to luxurious usages;
20   which only a moment before dropped aspirin
in this sunset of roses, and now throws a chair
in the air to aggravate the truly menacing.

1957

[1] Jane Freilicher, a New York painter
[2] **Saint-Saëns** French composer Camille Saint-Saëns (1835–1921), who wrote an orchestral suite entitled "The Carnival of the Animals"

The Day Lady Died[1]

It is 12:20 in New York a Friday
three days after Bastille day,[2] yes
it is 1959 and I go get a shoeshine
because I will get off the 4:19 in Easthampton
at 7:15 and then go straight to dinner
and I don't know the people who will feed me

I walk up the muggy street beginning to sun
and have a hamburger and a malted and buy
an ugly NEW WORLD WRITING to see what the poets
10   in Ghana are doing these days
                    I go on to the bank
and Miss Stillwagon (first name Linda I once heard)
doesn't even look up my balance for once in her life
and in the GOLDEN GRIFFIN I get a little Verlaine
for Patsy with drawings by Bonnard although I do
think of Hesiod, trans. Richmond Lattimore or
Brendan Behan's new play or *Le Balcon* or *Les Nègres*
of Genet, but I don't, I stick with Verlaine
after practically going to sleep with quandariness

20   and for Mike I just stroll into the PARK LANE
Liquor Store and ask for a bottle of Strega and
then I go back where I came from to 6th Avenue
and the tobacconist in the Ziegfeld Theatre and
casually ask for a carton of Gauloises and a carton
of Picayunes, and a NEW YORK POST with her face on it

and I am sweating a lot by now and thinking of
leaning on the john door in the 5 SPOT
while she whispered a song along the keyboard
to Mal Waldron[3] and everyone and I stopped breathing

                          1964

[1] The "lady" is blues singer Billie Holiday (1915–1959), known as "Lady Day."
[2] **Bastille day** July 14

[3] **Mal Waldron** jazz pianist who accompanied Billie Holiday

Why I Am Not a Painter

I am not a painter, I am a poet.
Why? I think I would rather be
a painter, but I am not. Well,

for instance, Mike Goldberg
is starting a painting. I drop in.

"Sit down and have a drink" he
says. I drink; we drink. I look
up. "You have SARDINES in it."
"Yes, it needed something there."
10   "Oh." I go and the days go by
and I drop in again. The painting
is going on, and I go, and the days
go by. I drop in. The painting is
finished. "Where's SARDINES?"
All that's left is just
letters, "It was too much," Mike says.

But me? One day I am thinking of
a color: orange. I write a line
about orange. Pretty soon it is a
20   whole page of words, not lines.
Then another page. There should be
so much more, not of orange, of
words, of how terrible orange is
and life. Days go by. It is even in
prose, I am a real poet. My poem
is finished and I haven't mentioned
orange yet. It's twelve poems, I call
it ORANGES. And one day in a gallery
I see Mike's painting, called SARDINES.

1971

A.R. AMMONS
b. 1926

Archie Randolph Ammons was born near Whiteville, North Carolina, and experienced a rural, Protestant childhood. From 1944 to 1946 he served in the U.S. Naval Reserve in the South Pacific. He received his B.S. in 1949 from Wake Forest College and worked as an elementary school principal in North Carolina and, after a year of graduate work at the University of California, Berkeley, as vice president in a biological glass manufacturing firm. He then turned to teaching and is now Goldwin Smith Professor of Poetry at Cornell.

A poet of particulars, Ammons resists cat-egories and abstractions. He often chooses long, loose catalogue forms for his poems, which become meditative rambles over landscapes. "Corsons Inlet" describes a walk along a tidal inlet, celebrating the world that impinges on his consciousness in eddies of meaning. In "He Held Radical Light," where he has trouble rejecting the "hook of metaphysics," he returns, as always, to the concrete—the immanent—appreciating its fleeting designs. Ammons's style is disarmingly casual, colloquial, and good-humored, although his preoccupations are ontological.

Corsons Inlet[1]

I went for a walk over the dunes again this morning
to the sea,
then turned right along
    the surf
            rounded a naked headland
            and returned

    along the inlet shore:

it was muggy sunny, the wind from the sea steady and high,
crisp in the running sand,
10   some breakthroughs of sun
        but after a bit

continuous overcast:

the walk liberating, I was released from forms,
from the perpendiculars,
        straight lines, blocks, boxes, binds
of thought
into the hues, shadings, rises, flowing bends and blends
            of sight:

                    I allow myself eddies of meaning:
20 yield to a direction of significance
running
like a stream through the geography of my work:
you can find
in my sayings
                swerves of action
                like the inlet's cutting edge:
            there are dunes of motion,
organizations of grass, white sandy paths of remembrance
in the overall wandering of mirroring mind:

30 but Overall is beyond me: is the sum of these events
I cannot draw, the ledger I cannot keep, the accounting
beyond the account:

in nature there are few sharp lines: there are areas of
primrose
        more or less dispersed;
disorderly orders of bayberry; between the rows
of dunes,
    irregular swamps of reeds,
        though not reeds alone, but grass, bayberry, yarrow, all . . .
40 predominantly reeds:

[1] located in southeast New Jersey

I have reached no conclusions, have erected no boundaries,
shutting out and shutting in, separating inside
    from outside: I have
    drawn no lines:
    as

manifold events of sand
change the dune's shape that will not be the same shape
tomorrow,

      so I am willing to go along, to accept
50   the becoming
    thought, to stake off no beginnings or ends, establish
        no walls:

by transitions the land falls from grassy dunes to creek
to undercreek: but there are no lines, though
      change in that transition is clear
      as any sharpness: but "sharpness" spread out,
allowed to occur over a wider range
than mental lines can keep:

the moon was full last night: today, low tide was low:
60   black shoals of mussels exposed to the risk
    of air
and, earlier, of sun,
waved in and out with the waterline, waterline inexact,
caught always in the event of change:
      a young mottled gull stood free on the shoals
      and ate
to vomiting: another gull, squawking possession, cracked a crab,
picked out the entrails, swallowed the soft-shelled legs, a ruddy
turnstone running in to snatch leftover bits:

70   risk is full: every living thing in
siege: the demand is life, to keep life: the small
white blacklegged egret, how beautiful, quietly stalks and spears
      the shallows, darts to shore
           to stab—what? I couldn't
    see against the black mudflats—a frightened
    fiddler crab?

        the news to my left over the dunes and
reeds and bayberry clumps was
      fall: thousands of tree swallows
80   gathering for flight:
      an order held
      in constant change: a congregation
rich with entropy: nevertheless, separable, noticeable
      as one event,

              not chaos: preparations for
flight from winter,
cheet, cheet, cheet, cheet, wings rifling the green clumps,
beaks
at the bayberries
90   a perception full of wind, flight, curve,
          sound:
      the possibility of rule as the sum of rulelessness:
the "field" of action
with moving, incalculable center:

in the smaller view, order tight with shape:
blue tiny flowers on a leafless weed: carapace of crab:
snail shell:
              pulsations of order
              in the bellies of minnows: orders swallowed,
100   broken down, transferred through membranes
to strengthen larger orders: but in the large view, no
lines or changeless shapes: the working in and out, together
          and against, of millions of events: this,
                    so that I make
                    no form of
                    formlessness:

orders as summaries, as outcomes of actions override
or in some way result, not predictably (seeing me gain
the top of a dune,
110   the swallows
could take flight—some other fields of bayberry
              could enter fall
              berryless) and there is serenity:

              no arranged terror: no forcing of image, plan,
or thought:
no propaganda, no humbling of reality to precept:

terror pervades but is not arranged, all possibilities
of escape open: no route shut, except in
          the sudden loss of all routes:

120   I see narrow orders, limited tightness, but will
not run to that easy victory:
              still around the looser, wider forces work:
              I will try
          to fasten into order enlarging grasps of disorder, widening
      scope, but enjoying the freedom that
      Scope eludes my grasp, that there is no finality of vision,
      that I have perceived nothing completely,
              that tomorrow a new walk is a new walk.

He Held Radical Light

He held radical light
as music in his skull: music
turned, as
over ridges immanences of evening light
rise, turned
back over the furrows of his brain
into the dark, shuddered,
shot out again
in long swaying swirls of sound:

10 reality had little weight in his transcendence
so he
had trouble keeping
his feet on the ground, was
terrified by that
and liked himself, and others, mostly
under roofs:
nevertheless, when the
light churned and changed

his head to music, nothing could keep him
20 off the mountains, his
head back, mouth working,
wrestling to say, to cut loose
from the high, unimaginable hook:
released, hidden from stars, he ate,
burped, said he was like any one
of us: demanded he
was like any one of us.

1971

ROBERT CREELEY
b. 1926

Born in Arlington, Massachusetts, Robert
Creeley entered Harvard University in 1943
but left after one year to join the American
Field Service as an ambulance driver in
India and Burma. Creeley met the poet
Charles Olson in 1950 and in 1954 joined
him on the faculty of Black Mountain
College, where he founded and edited *Black
Mountain Review*. He received his M.A.
from the University of New Mexico in 1960
and since 1966 has been teaching at the State

University of New York at Buffalo.

Creeley's poems have been described as
"minimal." They are almost invariably
brief and composed of short lines, with
punctuation and line-breaks recording the
hesitant movement of internal thought-
processes. Poetry, for Creeley, seems almost
a kind of stumbling—as if he were groping
for ways to express that elusive process.

His poems, then, are gnomic records of
moments of feeling. In those having to do

with love he achieves delicate intimacy entirely through implication. "Rain" is typically evocative; uneasy, trapped in the fatuousness of self-absorption, he asks that love, like rain, release him, bringing a "decent happiness."

Creeley insists that he has always been embarrassed by the "so-called larger view. I've been given to write about that which has the most intimate presence for me."

The Whip

I spent a night turning in bed,
my love was a feather, a flat

sleeping thing. She was
very white

and quiet, and above us on
the roof, there was another woman I

also loved, had
addressed myself to in

a fit she
10   returned. That

encompasses it. But now I was
lonely, I yelled,

but what is that? Ugh,
she said, beside me, she put

her hand on
my back, for which act

I think to say this
wrongly.

1955

Kore[1]

As I was walking
    I came upon
chance walking
    the same road upon.

[1] **Kore** the Greek corn goddess Persephone, daughter of Demeter

As I sat down
  by chance to move
later
  if and as I might,

light the wood was,
10   light and green,
and what I saw
  before I had not seen.

It was a lady
  accompanied
by goat men
  leading her.

Her hair held earth.
  Her eyes were dark.
A double flute
20   made her move.

"O love,
  where are you
leading
  me now?"

1960

The Rain

All night the sound had
come back again,
and again falls
this quiet, persistent rain.

What am I to myself
that must be remembered,
insisted upon
so often? Is it

that never the ease,
10 even the hardness,
of rain falling
will have for me

something other than this,
something not so insistent—
am I to be locked in this
final uneasiness.

Love, if you love me,
lie next to me.
Be for me, like rain,
20   the getting out

of the tiredness, the fatuousness, the semi-
lust of intentional indifference.
Be wet
with a decent happiness.

1960

ALLEN GINSBERG
b. 1926

Allen Ginsberg was born in Newark, New Jersey, the son of a high-school teacher of English who was himself a poet. His mother, Naomi, a Russian émigré, suffered from mental illness and was institutionalized during the poet's adolescence; her death in 1956 occasioned Ginsberg's famous elegiac poem, *Kaddish*. Ginsberg received his B.A. degree from Columbia University in 1948. In 1949 he was treated briefly in the Columbia Psychiatric Institute. He then returned to New Jersey and began a correspondence with William Carlos Williams, whose work he greatly admired and who later wrote prefaces to his first two books.

In 1954 Ginsberg went to San Francisco and, with Jack Kerouac, Gregory Corso, and Lawrence Ferlinghetti, started what came to be called the Beat Movement. Ferlinghetti's new firm, City Lights Books, published Ginsberg's *Howl & Other Poems*, an immediate popular success in 1956. The book was an astonishing breakthrough for American poetry in the 1950s. Influenced by Blake's revolutionary mysticism, and using a long line and rhythm adapted from Whitman, Ginsberg developed a loose, incantatory style that was most effective in public performance. His was a poetry to be heard, more than read; a poetry of the street

that strove to have an impact on popular culture, breaking with the tradition of academicism and erudition associated with poets like T.S. Eliot and the early Robert Lowell.

In the 1960s Ginsberg began a period of world travel that gained him an international reputation. At poetry readings, peace demonstrations, love-ins, and be-ins, he became a central figure in the anti-Vietnam War protests. In general, the "Beats" spoke for a counter-cultural movement committed to radical transformation of American life, which was felt to be politically and spiritually sick. Ginsberg delighted in political invective. In "America," he makes himself into an *enfant terrible* attacking every American piety from money to sobriety and the work ethic. There is, of course, a great deal of comic buffoonery in the poem, as he imitates the popular parody of the ignorant red man, and especially in his closing reference to his own homosexuality; yet his criticism of popular culture is shrewd. He believes that the prevailing ethos of competition and material success, enshrined in the pages of *Time* magazine and *Reader's Digest*, is driving his generation to the psychiatrist's couch. That Ginsberg can also be compellingly intimate is clear in his gentle, nostalgic portrait of his Aunt Rose.

America

America I've given you all and now I'm nothing.
America two dollars and twentyseven cents January 17, 1956.
I can't stand my own mind.
America when will we end the human war?
Go fuck yourself with your atom bomb.
I don't feel good don't bother me.
I won't write my poem till I'm in my right mind.
America when will you be angelic?
When will you take off your clothes?
10   When will you look at yourself through the grave?
When will you be worthy of your million Trotskyites?
America why are your libraries full of tears?
America when will you send your eggs to India?
I'm sick of your insane demands.
When can I go into the supermarket and buy what I need with my good
        looks?
America after all it is you and I who are perfect not the next world.
Your machinery is too much for me.
You made me want to be a saint.
There must be some other way to settle this argument.
20   Burroughs[1] is in Tangiers I don't think he'll come back it's sinister.
Are you being sinister or is this some form of practical joke?
I'm trying to come to the point.
I refuse to give up my obsession.
America stop pushing I know what I'm doing.
America the plum blossoms are falling.
I haven't read the newspapers for months, everyday somebody goes on trial
        for murder.
America I feel sentimental about the Wobblies.[2]
America I used to be a communist when I was a kid I'm not sorry.
I smoke marijuana every chance I get.
30   I sit in my house for days on end and stare at the roses in the closet.
When I go to Chinatown I get drunk and never get laid.
My mind is made up there's going to be trouble.
You should have seen me reading Marx.
My psychoanalyst thinks I'm perfectly right.
I won't say the Lord's Prayer.
I have mystical visions and cosmic vibrations.
America I still haven't told you what you did to Uncle Max after he came
        over from Russia.

[1] **Burroughs** William S. Burroughs, author of *Junkie* (1953) and *Naked Lunch* (1959)
[2] **Wobblies** Industrial Workers of the World, a revolutionary labor union launched in Chicago in 1905

I'm addressing you.
Are you going to let your emotional life be run by Time Magazine?
40   I'm obsessed by Time Magazine.
I read it every week.
Its cover stares at me every time I slink past the corner candystore.
I read it in the basement of the Berkeley Public Library.
It's always telling me about responsibility. Businessmen are serious. Movie
     producers are serious. Everybody's serious but me.
It occurs to me that I am America.
I am talking to myself again.

Asia is rising against me.
I haven't got a chinaman's chance.
I'd better consider my national resources.
50   My national resources consist of two joints of marijuana millions of genitals
     an unpublishable private literature that goes 1400 miles an hour and
     twentyfive-thousand mental institutions.
I say nothing about my prisons nor the millions of underprivileged who live
     in my flowerpots under the light of five hundred suns.
I have abolished the whorehouses of France, Tangiers is the next to go.
My ambition is to be President despite the fact that I'm a Catholic.

America how can I write a holy litany in your silly mood?
I will continue like Henry Ford my strophes are as individual as his auto-
     mobiles more so they're all different sexes.
America I will sell you strophes $2500 apiece $500 down on your old
     strophe
America free Tom Mooney[3]
America save the Spanish Loyalists
America Sacco & Vanzetti[4] must not die
60   America I am the Scottsboro boys.[5]
America when I was seven momma took me to Communist Cell meetings
     they sold us garbanzos[6] a handful per ticket a ticket costs a nickel and
     the speeches were free everybody was angelic and sentimental about the
     workers it was all so sincere you have no idea what a good thing the
     party was in 1935 Scott Nearing[7] was a grand old man a real mensch
     Mother Bloor[8] made me cry I once saw Israel Amter[9] plain. Everybody
     must have been a spy.

[3] **Tom Mooney**   radical labor leader arrested
on charges of setting a bomb that exploded at a
parade in San Francisco. His trial evoked world-
wide protest. His death sentence was commuted
to life imprisonment by President Woodrow
Wilson.

[4] **Sacco & Vanzetti**   Nicola Sacco and Barto-
lomeo Vanzetti, Italian-born anarchists, were
accused of murdering a paymaster and his guard
in South Braintree, Massachusetts. Although the
evidence was insubstantial, they were executed
in 1927. The case became a cause célèbre, since
many believed they were executed for their
radical views rather than for the crime.

[5] **the Scottsboro boys**   In 1916, nine Scottsboro
blacks were sentenced to death in Alabama on a
charge of raping two white girls. Their case was
taken up by liberal and radical groups.

[6] **garbanzos**   garbanzo beans

[7] **Scott Nearing**   a committed communist and
noted lecturer, author of *The Conscience of a
Radical* (1965)

[8] **Mother Bloor**   Ella Reeve Bloor, well-known
feminist activist of the Socialist Party of America

[9] **Israel Amter**   American radical, one of the
leaders of the underground Communist party
founded in 1921

America you don't really want to go to war.
America it's them bad Russians.
Them Russians them Russians and them Chinamen. And them Russians.
The Russia wants to eat us alive. The Russia's power mad. She wants to take
    our cars from out our garages.
Her wants to grab Chicago. Her needs a Red Readers' Digest. Her wants
    our auto plants in Siberia. Him big bureaucracy running our filling-
    stations.
That no good. Ugh. Him make Indians learn read. Him need big black
    niggers. Hah. Her make us all work sixteen hours a day. Help.
America this is quite serious.
America this is the impression I get from looking in the television set.
70 America is this correct?
I'd better get right down to the job.
It's true I don't want to join the Army or turn lathes in precision parts
    factories, I'm nearsighted and psychopathic anyway.
America I'm putting my queer shoulder to the wheel.

1956

To Aunt Rose

Aunt Rose—now—might I see you
with your thin face and buck tooth smile and pain
        of rheumatism—and a long black heavy shoe
          for your bony left leg
limping down the long hall in Newark on the running carpet
        past the black grand piano
        in the day room
          where the parties were
       and I sang Spanish loyalist songs
10   in a high squeaky voice
        (hysterical) the committee listening
        while you limped around the room
        collected the money—
Aunt Honey, Uncle Sam, a stranger with a cloth arm
        in his pocket
        and huge young bald head
          of Abraham Lincoln Brigade[1]

—your long sad face
        your tears of sexual frustration
20   (what smothered sobs and bony hips
          under the pillows of Osborne Terrace)
     —the time I stood on the toilet seat naked
        and you powdered my thighs with Calomine
        against the poison ivy—my tender
        and shamed first black curled hairs

[1] **Abraham Lincoln Brigade** name of an American brigade. During the Spanish Civil War (1936–39), many international brigades went to Spain to fight for the elected government.

what were you thinking in secret heart then
        knowing me a man already—
and I an ignorant girl of family silence on the thin pedestal
        of my legs in the bathroom—Museum of Newark.

30   Aunt Rose
Hitler is dead, Hitler is in Eternity; Hitler is with
        Tamburlane and Emily Brontë

Though I see you walking still, a ghost on Osborne Terrace
        down the long dark hall to the front door
        limping a little with a pinched smile
        in what must have been a silken
                flower dress
welcoming my father, the Poet, on his visit to Newark
        —see you arriving in the living room
40   dancing on your crippled leg
        and clapping hands his book
        had been accepted by Liveright

Hitler is dead and Liveright's gone out of business
The Attic of the Past and Everlasting Minute are out of print
        Uncle Harry sold his last silk stocking
        Claire quit interpretive dancing school
        Buba sits a wrinkled monument in Old
        Ladies Home blinking at new babies

last time I saw you was the hospital
50   pale skull protruding under ashen skin
        blue veined unconscious girl
        in an oxygen tent
the war in Spain has ended long ago
        Aunt Rose

                    1961

"Back on Times Square, Dreaming of Times Square"

Let some sad trumpeter stand
        on the empty streets at dawn
and blow a silver chorus to the
        buildings of Times Square,
memorial of ten years, at 5 AM, with
        the thin white moon just
                visible
        above the green & grooking McGraw
        Hill offices

10   a cop walks by, but he's invisible
                with his music

        The Globe Hotel, Garver lay in
            grey beds there and hunched his
            back and cleaned his needles—
        where I lay many nights on the nod
            from his leftover bloody cottons
            and dreamed of Blake's voice talking—
                I was lonely,
                Garver's dead in Mexico two years,
20   hotel's vanished into a parking lot
        And I'm back here—sitting on the streets
        again—
                The movies took our language, the
                    great red signs
                A DOUBLE BILL OF GASSERS
                Teen Age Nightmare
                Hooligans of the Moon

        But we were never nightmare
            hooligans but seekers of
30   the blond nose for Truth

        Some old men are still alive, but
                the old Junkies are gone—

        We are a legend, invisible but
                legendary, as prophesied

        NY 1958   1963

JAMES MERRILL
b. 1926

A native New Yorker born into a wealthy family, Merrill spends much of his time in Greece. His first, privately printed collection of poems and short stories, *Jim's Book* (1942), appeared five years before his graduation from Amherst College. Since then he has published thirteen books of poetry and a collection of short stories and has received many awards.

As a young poet, Merrill was often described as fastidious. His poetry, while witty and formally accomplished, was mannered.

Fellow poet Richard Howard described such poems as "The Black Swan" and "Portrait" from *First Poems* (1951) as "painted narcissism." Yet his later poems manage to be at once autobiographical and mythical, as in "Days of 1964," in which he found archetypal ramifications in ordinary experience. Many of his best lyrics focus on personal or domestic scenes, yet the compassion and intensity of his perspective give such private moments a deep resonance. In "Between Us," for instance, the poet describes his own hand reaching to his wife in bed as a phantasmal, shrunken face, and in that image locates a common human loneliness and need. He is fascinated with time as it is lived in the deteriorating body and in the mind struggling to recover memory.

Merrill's poems play with complex syntactic structures and formal rhyme schemes, yet manage to be unselfconscious and paradoxically casual in their formal elegance.

He often writes about love as a complex riddle. Thus in "Days of 1964," the poet's Greek cleaning woman, Kyria Kleo, is seen as a goddess of love, glistening with inseparable love and pain, and love is a climbing to the heights even of illusion. Despite his elegant style, Merrill's poems are not abstract. His poetry is a form of distancing, of translating the simple, ordinary moment into heightened, compassionate perception.

Between Us

A . . . face? There
It lies on the pillow by
Your turned head's tangled graying hair:
Another — like a shrunken head, too small!
My eyes in dread
Shut. Open. It is there,

Waxen, inhuman. Small.
The taut crease of the mouth shifts. It
Seems to smile,
10   Chin up in the wan light. Elsewhere
I have known what it was, this thing, known
The blind eye-slit

And knuckle-sharp cheekbone—
Ah. And again do.
Not a face. A hand, seen queerly. Mine.
Deliver me, I breathe
Watching it unclench with a soft moan
And reach for you.

1966

The Mad Scene

Again last night I dreamed the dream called Laundry.
In it, the sheets and towels of a life we were going to share,
The milk-stiff bibs, the shroud, each rag to be ever
Trampled or soiled, bled on or groped for blindly,
Came swooning out of an enormous willow hamper
Onto moon-marbly boards. We had just met. I watched
From outer darkness. I had dressed myself in clothes
Of a new fiber that never stains or wrinkles, never

Wears thin. The opera house sparkled with tiers
10   And tiers of eyes, like mine enlarged by belladonna,
Trained inward. There I saw the cloud-clot, gust by gust,
Form, and the lightning bite, and the roan mane unloosen.
Fingers were running in panic over the flute's nine gates.
Why did I flinch? I loved you. And in the downpour laughed
To have us wrung white, gnarled together, one
Topmost mordent of wisteria,
As the lean tree burst into grief.

1966

Days of 1964

Houses, an embassy, the hospital,
Our neighborhood sun-cured if trembling still
In pools of the night's rain . . .
Across the street that led to the center of town
A steep hill kept one company part way
Or could be climbed in twenty minutes
For some literally breathtaking views,
Framed by umbrella pines, of city and sea.
Underfoot, cyclamen, autumn crocus grew
10   Spangled as with fine sweat among the relics
Of good times had by all. If not Olympus,
An out-of-earshot, year-round hillside revel.

I brought home flowers from my climbs.
Kyria Kleo who cleaned for us
Put them in water, sighing *Virgin, Virgin.*
Her legs hurt. She wore brown, was fat, past fifty,
And looked like a Palmyra[1] matron
Copied in lard and horsehair. How she loved
You, me, loved us all, the bird, the cat!
20   I think now she *was* love. She sighed and glistened
All day with it, or pain, or both.
(We did not notably communicate.)
She lived nearby with her pious mother
And wastrel son. She called me her real son.

I paid her generously, I dare say.
Love makes one generous. Look at us. We'd known
Each other so briefly that instead of sleeping
We lay whole nights, open, in the lamplight,
And gazed, or traded stories.

---

[1] **Palmyra** Roman name for the ancient city of   for its magnificent ruins and distinctive style of Tadmor, an oasis in the Syrian desert, famous   sculpture

30   One hour comes back—you gasping in my arms
With love, or laughter, or both,
I having just remembered and told you
What I'd looked up to see on my way downtown at noon:
Poor old Kleo, her aching legs,
Trudging into the pines. I called,
Called three times before she turned.
Above a tight, skyblue sweater, her face
Was painted. Yes. Her face was painted
Clown-white, white of the moon by daylight,
40   Lidded with pearl, mouth a poinsettia leaf,
Eat me, pay me—the erotic mask
Worn the world over by illusion
To weddings of itself and simple need.

Startled mute, we had stared—was love illusion?—
And gone our ways. Next, I was crossing a square
In which a moveable outdoor market's
Vegetables, chickens, pottery kept materializing
Through a dream-press of hagglers each at heart
Leery lest he be taken, plucked,
50   The bird, the flower of that November mildness,
Self lost up soft clay paths, or found, foothold,
Where the bud throbs awake
The better to be nipped, self on its knees in mud—
Here I stopped cold, for both our sakes;

And calmer on my way home bought us fruit.

Forgive me if you read this. (And may Kyria Kleo,
Should someone ever put it into Greek
And read it aloud to her, forgive me, too.)
I had gone so long without loving,
60   I hardly knew what I was thinking.

Where I hid my face, your touch, quick, merciful,
Blindfolded me. A god breathed from my lips.
If that was illusion, I wanted it to last long;
To dwell, for its daily pittance, with us there,
Cleaning and watering, sighing with love or pain.
I hoped it would climb when it needed to the heights
Even of degradation, as I for one
Seemed, those days, to be always climbing
Into a world of wild
70   Flowers, feasting, tears—or was I falling, legs
Buckling, heights, depths,
Into a pool of each night's rain?
But you were everywhere beside me, masked,
As who was not, in laughter, pain, and love.

1966

JAMES WRIGHT
1927–1980

Born in Martins Ferry, Ohio, a steel-mill town, Wright grew up on a small farm nearby. After serving with the U.S. Army in Japan in World War II, he attended Kenyon College, receiving his B.A. in 1952, and studied at the University of Vienna on a Fulbright Scholarship in 1953. He received his Ph.D. from the University of Washington in 1959, working under Theodore Roethke. He taught at various universities, and at Hunter College in New York City from 1966 until his death.

Originally identified with a group of poets who cultivated a new simplicity of style combined with personal intensity and anchored in "deep images," Wright drew his subjects from ordinary life and from the experience of the lowly and of social outcasts, embodied in the Judas figure of his second book of poetry, *Saint Judas* (1959). As a man who could find no reprieve from a consuming despair, the apostle seemed to provide the poet with a human archetype. His vision is pessimistic: "I do not have a talent for happiness." In his early, more conventional poetry Wright explored the guilt induced by his sense of the inadequacy of language, and of the poet's craft in particular, in confronting human pain. His later poetry abandons traditional meter and rhyme, taking its structure from a juxtaposition of images and its tone from the casual rhythms of the speaking voice. His pessimism is increasingly balanced in his work by a heightened sense of the restorative powers of nature. He shares with Theodore Roethke a sensitivity to the minutiae of nature and an intuition of blessed presences enduring in the midst of nature's violence. His empathy with the non-human world, powerfully expressed in "A Blessing," and his enduring commitment to the value of love are the most poignant aspects of his work.

A Blessing

Just off the highway to Rochester, Minnesota,
Twilight bounds softly forth on the grass.
And the eyes of those two Indian ponies
Darken with kindness.
They have come gladly out of the willows
To welcome my friend and me.
We step over the barbed wire into the pasture
Where they have been grazing all day, alone.
They ripple tensely, they can hardly contain their happiness
10   That we have come.
They bow shyly as wet swans. They love each other.
There is no loneliness like theirs.
At home once more,
They begin munching the young tufts of spring in the darkness.
I would like to hold the slenderer one in my arms,
For she has walked over to me
And nuzzled my left hand.
She is black and white,
Her mane falls wild on her forehead,

20 And the light breeze moves me to caress her long ear
That is delicate as the skin over a girl's wrist.
Suddenly I realize
That if I stepped out of my body I would break
Into blossom.

                                                1963

Willy Lyons

My uncle, a craftsman of hammers and wood,
Is dead in Ohio.
And my mother cries she is angry.
Willy was buried with nothing except a jacket
Stitched on his shoulder bones.
It is nothing to mourn for.
It is the other world.
She does not know how the roan horses, there,
Dead for a century,
10 Plod slowly.
Maybe they believe Willy's brown coffin, tangled heavily in moss,
Is a horse trough drifted to shore
Along that river under the willows and grass.
Let my mother weep on, she needs to, she knows of cold winds.
The long box is empty.
The horses turn back toward the river.
Willy planes limber trees by the waters,
Fitting his boat together.
We may as well let him go.
20 Nothing is left of Willy on this side
But one cracked ball-peen hammer and one suit,
Including pants, his son inherited,
For a small fee, from Hesslop's funeral home;
And my mother,
Weeping with anger, afraid of winter
For her brothers' sake:
Willy, and John, whose life and art, if any,
I never knew.

                                                1968

The Journey

Anghiari[1] is medieval, a sleeve sloping down
A steep hill, suddenly sweeping out
To the edge of a cliff, and dwindling.
But far up the mountain, behind the town,
We too were swept out, out by the wind,
Alone with the Tuscan grass.

[1] **Anghiari**   village in Tuscany, Italy

Wind had been blowing across the hills
For days, and everything now was graying gold
With dust, everything we saw, even
10   Some small children scampering along a road,
Twittering Italian to a small caged bird.
We sat beside them to rest in some brushwood,
And I leaned down to rinse the dust from my face.

I found the spider web there, whose hinges
Reeled heavily and crazily with the dust,
Whole mounds and cemeteries of it, sagging
And scattering shadows among shells and wings.
And then she stepped into the center of air
Slender and fastidious, the golden hair
20   Of daylight along her shoulders, she poised there,
While ruins crumbled on every side of her.
Free of the dust, as though a moment before
She had stepped inside the earth, to bathe herself.

I gazed, close to her, till at last she stepped
Away in her own good time.

Many men
Have searched all over Tuscany and never found
What I found there, the heart of the light
Itself shelled and leaved, balancing
30   On filaments themselves falling. The secret
Of this journey is to let the wind
Blow its dust all over your body,
To let it go on blowing, to step lightly, lightly
All the way through your ruins, and not to lose
Any sleep over the dead, who surely
Will bury their own, don't worry.

1982

JOHN ASHBERY
b. 1927

John Ashbery was born on a farm near Rochester, New York. He received his B.A. degree from Harvard in 1949 and his M.A. from Columbia University in 1951. He went to Paris as a Fulbright Scholar in 1955 and remained there for ten years, working as an art critic for various journals, including *Arts News* and the European edition of the *New York Herald Tribune*. Associated with the New York school of poets, he was a close friend of Frank O'Hara. He has also written several plays.

Ashbery has identified his literary predecessors as Wallace Stevens and W.H. Auden, and his poetry is somewhat reflective of their influence, though he has neither the formal elegance of Stevens nor the disciplined virtuosity of Auden. He has said that his poetry does not have subjects and resists the notion of art as a "supreme fiction" that tidies reality into heightened moments of artistic order. In "The Painter," he expounds his wish that "nature, not art, might usurp the canvas," a provocative statement that incurs the malicious mirth of others who find the project ridiculous. With a kind of bathos, Ashbery has the distraught painter disappear into the subject of his painting. Wishing to be encyclopedic, to include incoherence and incompletion in order to be faithful to the complexities of selfhood, he writes poems that often have a random quality and an attractive conversational tone, achieving their effects by means of association. They frequently comment on themselves as they are being written, since they seek to record a process of thought — a mind exploring its own ambiguities. "My Erotic Double" is a witty conversation between the poet and his other self, but though they find each other "pleasant," the underlying tone of their dialogue is anguished, conveyed in the image of their dreams like "a barge made of ice." The double seems to be the dreaming, desiring other that rescues the poet with word play, but to what end?

The Painter

Sitting between the sea and the buildings
He enjoyed painting the sea's portrait.
But just as children imagine a prayer
Is merely silence, he expected his subject
To rush up the sand, and, seizing a brush,
Plaster its own portrait on the canvas.

So there was never any paint on his canvas
Until the people who lived in the buildings
Put him to work: "Try using the brush
10 As a means to an end. Select, for a portrait,
Something less angry and large, and more subject
To a painter's moods, or, perhaps, to a prayer."

How could he explain to them his prayer
That nature, not art, might usurp the canvas?
He chose his wife for a new subject,
Making her vast, like ruined buildings,
As if, forgetting itself, the portrait
Had expressed itself without a brush.

Slightly encouraged, he dipped his brush
20 In the sea, murmuring a heartfelt prayer:
"My soul, when I paint this next portrait
Let it be you who wrecks the canvas."
The news spread like wildfire through the buildings:
He had gone back to the sea for his subject.

Imagine a painter crucified by his subject!
Too exhausted even to lift his brush,
He provoked some artists leaning from the buildings
To malicious mirth: "We haven't a prayer
Now, of putting ourselves on canvas,
30   Or getting the sea to sit for a portrait!"

Others declared it a self-portrait.
Finally all indications of a subject
Began to fade, leaving the canvas
Perfectly white. He put down the brush.
At once a howl, that was also a prayer,
Arose from the overcrowded buildings.

They tossed him, the portrait, from the tallest of the
    buildings;
And the sea devoured the canvas and the brush
As though his subject had decided to remain a prayer.

1970

Crazy Weather

It's this crazy weather we've been having:
Falling forward one minute, lying down the next
Among the loose grasses and soft, white, nameless flowers.
People have been making a garment out of it,
Stitching the white of lilacs together with lightning
At some anonymous crossroads. The sky calls
To the deaf earth. The proverbial disarray
Of morning corrects itself as you stand up.
You are wearing a text. The lines
10   Droop to your shoelaces and I shall never want or need
Any other literature than this poetry of mud
And ambitious reminiscences of times when it came easily
Through the then woods and ploughed fields and had
A simple unconscious dignity we can never hope to
Approximate now except in narrow ravines nobody
Will inspect where some late sample of the rare,
Uninteresting specimen might still be putting out shoots, for all we know.

1977

My Erotic Double

He says he doesn't feel like working today.
It's just as well. Here in the shade
Behind the house, protected from street noises,
One can go over all kinds of old feeling,
Throw some away, keep others.
                              The wordplay
Between us gets very intense when there are
Fewer feelings around to confuse things.
Another go-round? No, but the last things
You always find to say are charming, and rescue me
Before the night does. We are afloat
On our dreams as on a barge made of ice,
Shot through with questions and fissures of starlight
That keep us awake, thinking about the dreams
As they are happening. Some occurrence. You said it.

I said it but I can hide it. But I choose not to.
Thank you. You are a very pleasant person.
Thank you. You are too.

                              1979

At North Farm

Somewhere someone is traveling furiously toward you,
At incredible speed, traveling day and night,
Through blizzards and desert heat, across torrents, through narrow passes.
But will he know where to find you,
Recognize you when he sees you,
Give you the thing he has for you?

Hardly anything grows here,
Yet the granaries are bursting with meal,
The sacks of meal piled to the rafters.
The streams run with sweetness, fattening fish;
Birds darken the sky. Is it enough
That the dish of milk is set out at night,
That we think of him sometimes,
Sometimes and always, with mixed feelings?

                              1981

GALWAY KINNELL
b. 1927

Born in Providence, Rhode Island, Kinnell received his A.B. from Princeton in 1948 and his M.A. from the University of Rochester in 1949. He served in the U.S. Navy from 1945 to 1946. From 1951 to 1954, he was administrator of the liberal arts program at the University of Chicago, after which he taught in France and Iran. He has been poet-in-residence at various colleges and universities—most recently at New York University—and in 1984 received a MacArthur Foundation grant.

As the titles of many of his books may suggest—*Black Light* (1966), *Body Rags* (1968), *Poems of Night* (1968), and *The Book of Nightmares* (1971)—Kinnell is obsessed with violence, suffering, and death. His vision is bleak and harsh, and his primary tone is sorrowful. *The Book of Nightmares*, the sequence from which an extract is reproduced here, is typical of his work. It consists of ten long meditative poems, in form like irregular odes, each made up of seven sections of varying length. In each poem, he tries to come to terms with the nightmares that confront us.

The section presented here, "The Dead Shall Be Raised Incorruptible," is a lamentation over war. The poem's seven parts achieve much of their power by juxtaposition. The poem begins with a portrait of the corpse on the eternal battlefield. An insane monologue by a burnt-out Vietnam veteran is followed by phrases from television ads for products that sanitize the bodily functions. Part 4 records the last testament of a Christian man. In an apocalyptic vision of orphic dismemberment, he wills the parts of his body to the earth he has desecrated by his madness, greed, and fear of love. The poem concludes like a prayer, ironically echoing the words of the crucified Christ: "Do not remove this last, poison cup from our lips." The rhetorical energy of the poem comes, in part, from the use of lists. In several sections the poet details, with nightmarish repetition, the parts of the desecrated body. Kinnell has succeeded in writing a powerful threnody against war; his outrage at man's murderousness is profound and moving.

From The Book of Nightmares

VI: The Dead Shall Be Raised Incorruptible[1]

1

A piece of flesh gives off
smoke in the field—

carrion,
caput mortuum,
orts,
pelf,
fenks,
sordes,
gurry dumped from hospital trashcans.

[1] 1 Corinthians 15:22

10 *Lieutenant!*
This corpse will not stop burning!

2

"That you Captain? Sure,
sure I remember—I still hear you
lecturing at me on the intercom, *Keep your guns up, Burnsie!*
and then screaming, *Stop shooting, for crissake, Burnsie,*
those are friendlies! But crissake, Captain,
I'd already started, burst
after burst, little black pajamas jumping
and falling . . . and remember that pilot
20 who'd bailed out over the North,
how I shredded him down to catgut on his strings?
one of his slant eyes, a piece
of his smile, sail past me
every night right after the sleeping pill . . .

"It was only
that I loved the *sound*
of them, I guess I just loved
the *feel* of them sparkin' off my hands . . ."

3
On the television screen:

30 Do you have a body that sweats?
Sweat that has odor?
False teeth clanging into your breakfast?
Case of the dread?
Headache so perpetual it may outlive you?
Armpits sprouting hair?
Piles so huge you don't need a chair to sit at a table?

We shall not all sleep, but we shall be changed . . .

4
In the Twentieth Century of my trespass on earth,
having exterminated one billion heathens,
40 heretics, Jews, Moslems, witches, mystical seekers,
black men, Asians, and Christian brothers,
every one of them for his own good,

a whole continent of red men for living in unnatural community
and at the same time having relations with the land,
one billion species of animals for being sub-human,
and ready to take on the bloodthirsty creatures from the other planets,
I, Christian man, groan out this testament of my last will.

I give my blood fifty parts polystyrene,
twenty-five parts benzene, twenty-five parts good old gasoline,

50 to the last bomber pilot aloft, that there shall be one acre
 in the dull world where the kissing flower may bloom,
 which kisses you so long your bones explode under its lips.

 My tongue goes to the Secretary of the Dead
 to tell the corpses, "I'm sorry, fellows,
 the killing was just one of those things
 difficult to pre-visualize—like a cow,
 say, getting hit by lightning."

 My stomach, which has digested
 four hundred treaties giving the Indians
60 eternal right to their land, I give to the Indians,
 I throw in my lungs which have spent four hundred years
 sucking in good faith on peace pipes.

 My soul I leave to the bee
 that he may sting it and die, my brain
 to the fly, his back the hysterical green color of slime,
 that he may suck on it and die, my flesh to the advertising man,
 the anti-prostitute, who loathes human flesh for money.

 I assign my crooked backbone
 to the dice maker, to chop up into dice,
70 for casting lots as to who shall see his own blood
 on his shirt front and who his brother's,
 for the race isn't to the swift but to the crooked.

 To the last man surviving on earth
 I give my eyelids worn out by fear, to wear
 in his long nights of radiation and silence,
 so that his eyes can't close, for regret
 is like tears seeping through closed eyelids.

 I give the emptiness my hand: the pinkie picks no more noses,
 slag clings to the black stick of the ring finger,
80 a bit of flame jets from the tip of the fuck-you finger,
 the first finger accuses the heart, which has vanished,
 on the thumb stump wisps of smoke ask to ride into the emptiness.

 In the Twentieth Century of my nightmare
 on earth, I swear on my chromium testicles
 to this testament
 and last will
 of my iron will, my fear of love, my itch for money, and my madness.

   5
 In the ditch
 snakes crawl cool paths
90 over the rotted thigh, the toe bones

twitch in the smell of burnt rubber,
the belly
opens like a poison nightflower,
the tongue has evaporated,
the nostril
hairs sprinkle themselves with yellowish-white dust,
the five flames at the end
of each hand have gone out, a mosquito
sips a last meal from this plate of serenity.

100 And the fly,
the last nightmare, hatches himself.

6

I ran
my neck broken I ran
holding my head up with both hands I ran
thinking the flames
the flames may burn the oboe
but listen buddy boy they can't touch the notes!

7

A few bones
lie about in the smoke of bones.

110 Membranes,
effigies pressed into grass,
mummy windings,
desquamations,
sags incinerated mattresses gave back to the world,
memories left in mirrors on whorehouse ceilings,
angel's wings
flagged down into the snows of yesteryear,

kneel
on the scorched earth
120 in the shapes of men and animals:

do not let this last hour pass,
do not remove this last, poison cup from our lips.

And a wind holding
the cries of love-making from all our nights and days
moves among the stones, hunting
for two twined skeletons to blow its last cry across.

Lieutenant!
This corpse will not stop burning!

1971

W.S. MERWIN
b. 1927

The son of a Presbyterian minister, Merwin was born in New York and educated at Princeton University. From 1949 to 1951 he worked as a tutor in France, Portugal, and Majorca, and later did much translation of poetry from Spanish, Portuguese, Latin, and French, in both conventional forms and free verse; an excellent selection is published in *Selected Translations 1948–1968* (New York: Athenaeum, 1975). Particularly beautiful are his translations of the French poet Jean Follain, and the Russian, Osip Mandelstam. He has received numerous awards and fellowships and since 1968 has lived in the United States, primarily in Hawaii.

Influenced by Robert Graves, whose son he tutored in Majorca, he often returns in his own poetry to myth and legend and to meditations on the mysteries of poetic creation. In the early poem "The Bathers," he plays with the ancient conceit of metamorphosis—the bathers, like sea birds reflected against the sea's blue mirror, imagine the sea itself as a bird from which they might learn the secret of flight. The spell is broken with the final metamorpho-

sis of the sea into a serpent swallowing the sun. It is his remarkable linguistic and rhythmic control that permits Merwin to sustain such a magical fantasy for the reader. However, he is also skillful with humorous, colloquial subjects like "The Drunk in the Furnace," a poem that equally displays his technical virtuosity. Luring the young like a pied piper, the dionysian drunk embodies the incorrigible subversive joke that the irrational plays on ordered and conventional mores—here represented by the narrowly religious. Yet Merwin is concerned not only with man's alienation from the irrational and creative in himself, but also with his victimization of his fellow man and of nature. "For a Coming Extinction" is an example of his many poems about animals, which lament man's irresponsible drive to dominate creation and, in so doing, to destroy himself. Merwin's great poetic range, both in subject and style, perhaps stems from his experience as a translator, which has given him access to other cultures and literary traditions. His translations (fifteen books) have made an invaluable contribution to contemporary poetry.

The Bathers

They make in the twining tide the motions of birds.
Such are the cries, also, they exchange
In their nakedness that is soft as a bird's
Held in the hand, and as fragile and strange.

And the blue mirror entertains them till they take
The sea for another bird: the crumbling
Hush-hush where the gentlest of waves break
About their voices would be his bright feathers blowing.

Only the dull shore refrains. But from this patient
10   Bird each, in the plumage of his choice,
Might learn the deep shapes and secret of flight

And the shore be merely a perch to which they might
Return. And the mirror turns serpent
And their only sun is swallowed up like a voice.

1956

The Drunk in the Furnace

For a good decade
The furnace stood in the naked gully, fireless
And vacant as any hat. Then when it was
No more to them than a hulking black fossil
To erode unnoticed with the rest of the junk-hill
By the poisonous creek, and rapidly to be added
      To their ignorance,

They were afterwards astonished
To confirm, one morning, a twist of smoke like a pale
10   Resurrection, staggering out of its chewed hole,
And to remark then other tokens that someone,
Cosily bolted behind the eye-holed iron
Door of the drafty burner, had there established
      His bad castle.

Where he gets his spirits
It's a mystery. But the stuff keeps him musical:
Hammer-and-anvilling with poker and bottle
To his jugged bellowings, till the last groaning clang
As he collapses onto the rioting
20   Springs of a litter of car-seats ranged on the grates,
      To sleep like an iron pig.

In their tar-paper church
On a text about stoke-holes that are sated never
Their Reverend lingers. They nod and hate trespassers.
When the furnace wakes, though, all afternoon
Their witless offspring flock like piped rats to its siren
Crescendo, and agape on the crumbling ridge
      Stand in a row and learn.

1960

For a Coming Extinction

Gray whale
Now that we are sending you to The End
That great god
Tell him
That we who follow you invented forgiveness
And forgive nothing

I write as though you could understand
And I could say it
One must always pretend something
10   Among the dying

When you have left the seas nodding on their stalks
Empty of you
Tell him that we were made
On another day

The bewilderment will diminish like an echo
Winding along your inner mountains
Unheard by us
And find its way out
Leaving behind it the future
20   Dead
And ours

When you will not see again
The whale calves trying the light
Consider what you will find in the black garden
And its court
The sea cows the Great Auks[1] the gorillas
The irreplaceable hosts ranged countless
And fore-ordaining as stars
Our sacrifices
30   Join your word to theirs
Tell him
That it is we who are important

1967

[1] **Great Auks** black and white diving birds of
northern seas

CHARLES TOMLINSON
b. 1927

Born in Stoke-on-Trent, Staffordshire, Tomlinson received his B.A. from Queens' College, Cambridge, in 1948, and his M.A. from the University of London in 1955. Since 1956 he has taught English literature at the University of Bristol but has had periods of U.S. residence and has found the American Southwest particularly absorbing. His interest in French Symbolist and modern American poetry, and his translations from the Spanish, mark him as one of the most cosmopolitan among his English contemporaries.

Tomlinson, who began his career as a painter and whose first attempts at writing were film scripts, is an intensely visual poet. (He has said that translating and painting are accompanying disciplines to his poetry.) His poems are often meticulous descriptions in which the reader is actively conducted through a process of seeing, in minute detail, the color, mass, and shape of particular objects and landscapes. He has written: "My theme is relationship. The hardness of crystals, the fact of cut glass; but also the shifting of light, the energizing weather which is the result of the combination of sun and frost—these are the images for a certain mental climate, components of the moral landscape of my poetry in general."

In "Farewell to Van Gogh," the "relationship" he seeks to establish with nature is a respect for its otherness. Despite the painter's "instructive frenzy," indeed the visionary violence with which he reinvents the natural landscape, nature assumes its own rhythms and disperses the "rhetoric" of the painter in a way that is humbling but also salutary. The marvelously modulated rhythm, achieved by the piling of adjectives, imitates nature's calm independence of our intentions. "On the Hall at Stowey" is a model of Tomlinson's method. With a painter's attention to details of light and shade, he focuses his loving description on the stone walls of the house, crafted with a mason's skill, the true measure of the house's worth. He is angered by our modern capacity to diminish this grandeur with suburban renovation and neglect: "What we had not / Made ugly, we had laid waste." Rather than the house's famous tenant, it is the beauty of the house itself, as crafted artifact five centuries old, that compels the poet.

Paring the Apple

There are portraits and still-lives.

And there is paring the apple.

And then? Paring it slowly,
From under cool-yellow
Cold-white emerging. And . . .?

The spring of concentric peel
Unwinding off white,
The blade hidden, dividing.

There are portraits and still-lives
10   And the first, because "human"
Does not excel the second, and
Neither is less weighted
With a human gesture, than paring the apple
With a human stillness.

The cool blade
Severs between coolness, apple-rind
Compelling a recognition.

1960

Farewell to Van Gogh[1]

The quiet deepens. You will not persuade
    One leaf of the accomplished, steady, darkening
Chestnut-tower to displace itself
    With more of violence than the air supplies
When, gathering dusk, the pond brims evenly
    And we must be content with stillness.

[1] Vincent Van Gogh, Dutch painter (1853–1890)

Unhastening, daylight withdraws from us its shapes
  Into their central calm. Stone by stone
  Your rhetoric is dispersed until the earth
10   Becomes once more the earth, the leaves
  A sharp partition against cooling blue.

Farewell, and for your instructive frenzy
  Gratitude. The world does not end tonight
  And the fruit that we shall pick tomorrow
  Await us, weighing the unstripped bough.

                              1960

On the Hall at Stowey[1]

Walking by map, I chose unwonted ground,
  A crooked, questionable path which led
Beyond the margin, then delivered me
  At a turn. Red marl
Had rutted the aimless track
  That firmly withheld the recompense it hid
Till now, close by its end, the day's discoveries
  Began with the dimming night:

A house. The wall-stones, brown.
10   The doubtful light, more of a mist than light
Floating at hedge-height through the sodden fields
  Had yielded, or a final glare
Burst there, rather, to concentrate
  Sharp saffron, as the ebbing year—
Or so it seemed, for the dye deepened—poured
  All of its yellow strength through the way I went:

Over grass, garden-space, over the grange
  That jutted beyond, lengthening-down
The house line, tall as it was,
20   By tying it to the earth, trying its pride
  (Which submitted) under a nest of barns,
    A walled weight of lesser encumbrances—
Few of which worsened it, and none
  As the iron sheds, sealing my own approach.

[1] Alfoxden, a house near the town of Nether
Stowey, rented by William Wordsworth while
he worked on the *Lyrical Ballads*

All stone. I had passed these last, unwarrantable
  Symbols of—no; let me define, rather
The thing they were not, all that we cannot be,
  By the description, simply of that which merits it:
Stone. Why must (as it does at each turn)
30   Each day, the mean rob us of patience, distract us
Before even its opposite?—before stone, which
  Cut, piled, mortared, is patience's presence.

The land farmed, the house was neglected: but
  Gashed panes (and there were many) still showed
Into the pride of that presence. I had reached
  Unchallenged, within feet of the door
Ill-painted, but at no distant date—the least
  Our prodigal time could grudge it; paused
To measure the love, to assess its object,
40   That trusts for continuance to the mason's hand.

Five centuries—here were (at the least) five—
  In linked love, eager excrescence
Where the door, arched, crowned with acanthus,
  Aimed at a civil elegance, but hit
This sturdier compromise, neither Greek, Gothic
  Nor Strawberry, clumped from the arching-point
And swathing down, like a fist of wheat,
  The unconscious emblem for the house's worth.

Conclusion surrounded it, and the accumulation
50   After Lammas growth. Still coming on
Hart's-tongue by maiden-hair
  Thickened beneath the hedges, the corn levelled
And carried, long-since; but the earth
  (Its tint glowed in the house wall)
Out of the reddish dark still thrust up foison
  Through the browning-back of the exhausted year:

Thrust through the unweeded yard, where earth and house
  Debated the terrain. My eye
Caught in those flags a gravestone's fragment
60   Set by a careful century. The washed inscription
Still keen, showed only a fragile stem
  A stave, a broken circlet, as
(Unintelligibly clear, craft in the sharp decrepitude)
  A pothook grooved its firm memorial.

Within, wet from the failing roof,
  Walls greened. Each hearth refitted
For a suburban whim, each room
  Denied what it was, diminished thus

To a barbarous mean, had comforted (but for a time)
70   Its latest tenant. Angered, I turned to my path
Through the inhuman light, light that a fish might swim
     Stained by the greyness of the smoking fields.

Five centuries. And we? What we had not
     Made ugly, we had laid waste—
Left (I should say) the office to nature
     Whose blind battery, best fitted to perform it
Outdoes us, completes by persistence
     All that our negligence fails in. Saddened,
Yet angered beyond sadness, where the road
80   Doubled upon itself I halted, for a moment
Facing the empty house and its laden barns.

                                    1960

ANNE SEXTON
1928–1974

Born in Newton, Massachusetts, Anne Sexton married at the age of sixteen and worked as a fashion model. After the birth of her first child in 1953, she suffered a mental breakdown, and the experience stimulated a desire to write poetry. She studied briefly with W.D. Snodgrass in 1958 and later at Boston University with Robert Lowell. (Sylvia Plath was a fellow student.) Sexton herself later taught poetry at several universities, high schools, and mental institutions. Continually under psychiatric care, she was hospitalized again in 1962 and 1973. She committed suicide in October 1974.

Sexton is identified with the generation of confessional poets. Her first book, *To Bedlam and Part Way Back* (1960), concerns the experience of mental collapse and partial recovery. Yet Sexton's work is not simply a poetry for therapy. At its best (like the work of all genuine poets suffering from mental illness) it uses language and poetic structures that take it beyond mere case history. "Ringing the Bells" is a portrait of women in a mental hospital. Its deliberate nursery-rhyme rhythms emphasize the pathos of "crazy ladies" reduced to the status of children. "The Starry Night," as the quotation from Van Gogh suggests, is metaphysical in intent. The dramatic night sky, against which a single tree is visible and seemingly rising, to be absorbed by its energy, reminds the poet of the ancient gnostic symbol of the serpent. She would die thus, reabsorbed naturally, with "no cry," into the primal order of the dark universe. Sexton's last book, *45 Mercy Street* (1976), from which "End, Middle, Beginning" is taken, seems to be an effort to locate a kind of existential wounding that begins at the root of life and destroys any belief in love.

Sexton was willing to be unashamedly a woman poet, drawing on the biological and emotional, even metaphysical, world of the female. Her poems about motherhood, daughterhood, and the generational connections between women are among her most eloquent.

Ringing the Bells

And this is the way they ring
the bells in Bedlam[1]
and this is the bell-lady
who comes each Tuesday morning
to give us a music lesson
and because the attendants make you go
and because we mind by instinct,
like bees caught in the wrong hive,
we are the circle of the crazy ladies
10 who sit in the lounge of the mental house
and smile at the smiling woman
who passes us each a bell,
who points at my hand
that holds my bell, E flat,
and this is the gray dress next to me
who grumbles as if it were special
to be old, to be old,
and this is the small hunched squirrel girl
on the other side of me
20 who picks at the hairs over her lip,
who picks at the hairs over her lip all day,
and this is how the bells really sound,
as untroubled and clean
as a workable kitchen,
and this is always my bell responding
to my hand that responds to the lady
who points at me, E flat;
and although we are no better for it,
they tell you to go. And you do.

1960

[1] **Bedlam** popular name for lunatic asylum
after the Hospital of St. Mary at Bethlehem,
southeast London, England

The Starry Night

*That does not keep me from having a terrible
need of—shall I say the word—religion. Then I
go out at night to paint the stars.*
—VINCENT VAN GOGH[1] IN A LETTER TO HIS BROTHER

The town does not exist
except where one black-haired tree slips
up like a drowned woman into the hot sky.
The town is silent. The night boils with eleven stars.

[1] **Vincent Van Gogh** Dutch painter (1853–
1890); letter written September 1888

Oh starry starry night! This is how
I want to die.

It moves. They are all alive.
Even the moon bulges in its orange irons
to push children, like a god, from its eye.
10   The old unseen serpent swallows up the stars.[2]
Oh starry starry night! This is how
I want to die:

into that rushing beast of the night,
sucked up by that great dragon, to split
from my life with no flag,
no belly,
no cry.

1962

[2] **serpent swallows up the stars** The Gnostic symbol of the ouroboros, a dragon or serpent biting its own tail, describes the circumferential movement of the universe — from unity to multiplicity, and the return to unity.

End, Middle, Beginning

There was an unwanted child.
Aborted by three modern methods
she hung on to the womb,
hooked onto it
building her house into it
and it was to no avail,
to black her out.

At her birth
she did not cry,
10   spanked indeed,
but did not yell—
instead snow fell out of her mouth.

As she grew, year by year,
her hair turned like a rose in a vase,
and bled down her face.
Rocks were placed on her to keep
the growing silent,
and though they bruised,
they did not kill,
20   though kill was tangled into her beginning.

They locked her in a football
but she merely curled up
and pretended it was a warm doll's house.

They pushed insects in to bite her off
and she let them crawl into her eyes
pretending they were a puppet show.

Later, later,
grown fully, as they say,
they gave her a ring,
30   and she wore it like a root
and said to herself,
"To be not loved is the human condition,"
and lay like a statue in her bed.

Then once,
by terrible chance,
love took her in his big boat
and she shoveled the ocean
in a scalding joy.

Then,
40   slowly,
love seeped away,
the boat turned into paper
and she knew her fate,
at last.
Turn where you belong,
into a deaf mute
that metal house,
let him drill you into no one.

1976

THOMAS KINSELLA

b. 1928

Born in Dublin, Ireland, Kinsella was educated at University College in that city. He joined the Irish civil service in 1948 and served until 1965, by which time he had become assistant principal officer in the Department of Finance. From 1965 to 1970 he taught at Southern Illinois University in Carbondale, and since 1970 he has been professor of English at Temple University, dividing his time between Philadelphia and Dublin. He has been associated with Dolmen Press and with Cuala Press in Ireland and in 1972 founded Peppercanister Press. His notable translations from the Irish include the great Cuchulain-saga called *The Táin* (1969).

Kinsella's sharply probing poems are what he has called "self-surgeries." His earliest work, strongly influenced by W.H. Auden, uses a monologue technique. In his sequence *Nightwalker* he presents himself as "vagabond / tethered," compelled to understand the responsibilities and loyalties of love, family, and history, both personal and public. While steeped in his Gaelic heritage and local Dublin lore, he seeks to draw on the whole of Western tradition. In *A Technical Supplement*, for instance, he attempts a re-creation of the historical personage of Diderot, the French encyclopedist. In poems like "Ancestor" and "His Father's Hands," Kinsella uses his family history as a route to understanding "the yoke of one's being" and to enter "the heart of the pit" that is poetic memory.

His poems have a concentrated moral gravity in their deeply psychological explorations and sometimes grow so inward as to seem almost purely private. And although he can also look outward—as in his militantly political "Butcher's Dozen," on the thirteen Irish people killed in Derry by British paratroopers in 1972, his most telling work remains that of private sensibility. In his cryptic "First Light," it is clear that love is a heroic battle against the attrition of feeling. This poem demonstrates Kinsella's capacity to condense the problems of intimate communication in a moment of terrible anguish.

First Light

A prone couple still sleeps.
Light ascends like a pale gas
Out of the sea: dawn-
Light, reaching across the hill
To the dark garden. The grass
Emerges, soaking with grey dew.

Inside, in silence, an empty
Kitchen takes form, tidied and swept,
Blank with marriage—where shrill
10   Lover and beloved have kept
Another vigil far
Into the night, and raved and wept.

Upstairs a whimper or sigh
Comes from an open bedroom door
And lengthens to an ugly wail
—A child enduring a dream
That grows, at the first touch of day,
Unendurable.

1961

Ancestor

I was going up to say something,
and stopped. Her profile against the curtains
was old, and dark like a hunting bird's.

It was the way she perched on the high stool,
staring into herself, with one fist
gripping the side of the barrier around her desk
—or her head held by something, from inside.
And not caring for anything around her

10   or anyone there by the shelves.
   I caught a faint smell, musky and queer.

I may have made some sound—she stopped rocking
and pressed her fist in her lap; then she stood up
and shut down the lid of the desk, and turned the key.
She shoved a small bottle under her aprons
and came toward me, darkening the passageway.

Ancestor . . . among sweet- and fruit-boxes.
Her black heart . . .
              Was that a sigh?
—brushing by me in the shadows,
20   with her heaped aprons, through the red hangings
   to the scullery, and down to the back room.

                        1972

His Father's Hands

I drank firmly
and set the glass down between us firmly.
You were saying.

My father
Was saying.

His finger prodded and prodded,
marring his point. Emphas-
emphasemphasis.

I have watched
10   his father's hands before him

    cupped, and tightening the black Plug
between knife and thumb,
carving off little curlicues
to rub them in the dark of his palms,
or cutting into new leather at his bench,
levering a groove open with his thumb,
insinuating wet sprigs for the hammer.

He kept the sprigs in mouthfuls
and brought them out in silvery
20   units between his lips.

I took a pinch out of their hole
and knocked them one by one into the wood,

                  *

bright points among hundreds gone black,
other children's—cousins and others, grown up.

Or his bow hand scarcely moving,
scraping in the dark corner near the fire,
his plump fingers shifting on the strings.

To his deaf, inclined head
he hugged the fiddle's body,
30   whispering with the tune

with breaking heart
whene'er I hear
in privacy, across a blocked void,

the wind that shakes the barley.
The wind. . .
round her grave. . .

on my breast in blood she died. . .
But blood for blood without remorse
I've ta'en. . .

40   Beyond that.

                    *

Your family, Thomas, met with and helped
many of the Croppies in hiding from the Yeos[1]
or on their way home after the defeat
in south Wexford. They sheltered the Laceys
who were later hanged on the Bridge in Ballinglen
between Tinahely and Anacorra.

From hearsay, as far as I can tell
the Men Folk were either Stone Cutters
or masons or probably both.
50   In the 18
and late 1700s even the farmers
had some other trade to make a living.

They lived in Farnese among a Colony
of North of Ireland or Scotch settlers left there
in some of the dispersals or migrations
which occurred in this Area of Wicklow and Wexford
and Carlow. And some years before that time
the Family came from somewhere around Tullow.

Beyond that.

[1] **Croppies . . . Yeos** Irish rebels inspired by
the French Revolution and volunteer "Yeo-
manry" helping to repress them in the 1798
Rebellion.

60   Littered uplands. Dense grass. Rocks everywhere,
wet underneath, retaining memory of the long cold.

First, a prow of land
chosen, and webbed with tracks;
then boulders chosen
and sloped together, stabilized in menace.

I do not like this place.
I do not think the people who lived here
were ever happy. It feels evil.
Terrible things happened.
70   I feel afraid here when I am on my own.

*

Dispersals or migrations.
Through what evolutions or accidents
toward that peace and patience
by the fireside, that blocked gentleness. . .

That serene pause, with the slashing knife,
in kindly mockery,
as I busy myself with my little nails
at the rude block, his bench.

The blood advancing
80   —gorging vessel after vessel—
and altering in them
one by one.

Behold, that gentleness already
modulated twice, in others:
to earnestness and iteration;
to an offhandedness, repressing various impulses.

*

Extraordinary. . . The big block—I found it
years afterward in a corner of the yard
in sunlight after rain
90   and stood it up, wet and black:
it turned under my hands, an axis
of light flashing down its length,
and the wood's soft flesh broke open,
countless little nails
squirming and dropping out of it.

1979

THOM GUNN
b. 1929

Born in Gravesend, Kent, Thom Gunn served in the British army from 1948 to 1950 and then became a student at Cambridge University, where he earned B.A. and M.S. degrees. Later he studied at Stanford University in California, and in the 1950s he shifted back and forth between the two countries until he set up permanent residence in San Francisco and became a member of the faculty at the University of California, Berkeley.

At first identified with "The Movement" poets, whose anthology *New Lines* (1956) was an influential attack on modernism, Gunn has always tried to write a poetry responsive to the realistic, concrete experience of ordinary individuals. He chooses seemingly mundane subjects—the motorcyclists of California (in "On the Move"), criminals, soldiers—and yet his poems are highly intellectual meditations. In "On the Move," the motorcyclists, lacking the hidden purpose that instinct affords the animal, create their own purpose through constant movement, daring "a future." Gunn finds this admirable. In a world without absolutes, they become a symbol of the lust for direction that cannot be satisfied except by a refusal of stasis. The poem's traditional meters are astounding and very satisfying, as if the poet, by a kind of verbal instinct, had found a fluid form to contain chaos.

Gunn moves easily between conventional and experimental styles of prosody and is often linked with Ted Hughes because of his early interest in violence in nature and in everyday human life, but much of his work is subtler in its psychological turns. His experience of the counterculture of his adopted home, San Francisco, in the 1960s led to an interest in the mysticism associated with hallucinatory drugs, often thought to be the subtext of his volume *Moly*. While early poems seem to record a vision of life as a vicious game, with the poet struggling for heroic action or mythic postures, later ones become increasingly introspective. Thus, "For Signs" describes the poet moving in a lunar landscape where he hallucinates a younger, dreaming self, his "dream mentor." The moon pulls him back to earlier pain, as if this cyclical return to past moments were a necessary route to expiation. With its surrealist imagery of doubleness and lunar light, the poem creates a remarkably mysterious atmosphere.

On the Move

The blue jay scuffling in the bushes follows
Some hidden purpose, and the gust of birds
That spurts across the field, the wheeling swallows,
Have nested in the trees and undergrowth.
Seeking their instinct, or their poise, or both,
One moves with an uncertain violence
Under the dust thrown by a baffled sense
Or the dull thunder of approximate words.

On motorcycles, up the road, they come:
10   Small, black, as flies hanging in heat, the Boys,
Until the distance throws them forth, their hum
Bulges to thunder held by calf and thigh.

In goggles, donned impersonality,
In gleaming jackets trophied with the dust,
They strap in doubt—by hiding it, robust—
And almost hear a meaning in their noise.

Exact conclusion of their hardiness
Has no shape yet, but from known whereabouts
They ride, direction where the tires press.
20   They scare a flight of birds across the field:
Much that is natural, to the will must yield.
Men manufacture both machine and soul,
And use what they imperfectly control
To dare a future from the taken routes.

It is a part solution, after all.
One is not necessarily discord
On earth; or damned because, half animal,
One lacks direct instinct, because one wakes
Afloat on movement that divides and breaks.
30   One joins the movement in a valueless world,
Choosing it, till, both hurler and the hurled,
One moves as well, always toward, toward.

A minute holds them, who have come to go:
The self-defined, astride the created will
They burst away; the towns they travel through
Are home for neither bird nor holiness,
For birds and saints complete their purposes.
At worst, one is in motion; and at best,
Reaching no absolute, in which to rest,
40   One is always nearer by not keeping still.

California   1957

In Santa Maria del Popolo[1]

Waiting for when the sun an hour or less
Conveniently oblique makes visible
The painting on one wall of this recess
By Caravaggio,[2] of the Roman School,
I see how shadow in the painting brims
With a real shadow, drowning all shapes out
But a dim horse's haunch and various limbs,
Until the very subject is in doubt.

[1] The poem refers to the painting *The Conversion of St. Paul*, in the church of Santa Maria del Popolo, in Rome.

[2] **Caravaggio** Michelangelo da Caravaggio (1573–1610)

But evening gives the act, beneath the horse
10 And one indifferent groom, I see him sprawl,
Foreshortened from the head, with hidden face,
Where he has fallen, Saul becoming Paul.
O wily painter, limiting the scene
From a cacophony of dusty forms
To the one convulsion, what is it you mean
In that wide gesture of the lifting arms?

No Ananias[3] croons a mystery yet,
Casting the pain out under name of sin.
The painter saw what was, an alternate
20 Candor and secrecy inside the skin.
He painted, elsewhere, that firm insolent
Young whore in Venus' clothes, those pudgy cheats,
Those sharpers; and was strangled, as things went,
For money, by one such picked off the streets.

I turn, hardly enlightened, from the chapel
To the dim interior of the chuch instead,
In which there kneel already several people,
Mostly old women: each head closeted
In tiny fists holds comfort as it can.
30 Their poor arms are too tired for more than this
—For the large gesture of solitary man,
Resisting, by embracing, nothingness.

1961

[3] **Ananias** a disciple at Damascus in the story of
the conversion and baptism of St. Paul (Acts
23:2)

A Map of the City

I stand upon a hill and see
A luminous country under me,
Through which at two the drunk must weave;
The transient's pause, the sailor's leave.

I notice, looking down the hill,
Arms braced upon a windowsill;
And on the web of fire escapes
Move the potential, the gray shapes.

I hold the city here, complete:
10 And every shape defined by light
Is mine, or corresponds to mine,
Some flickering or some steady shine.

This map is ground of my delight.
Between the limits, night by night,
I watch a malady's advance,
I recognize my love of chance.

By the recurrent lights I see
Endless potentiality
The crowded, broken, and unfinished!
20   I would not have the risk diminished.

1961

For Signs

1

In front of me, the palings of a fence
Throw shadows hard as board across the weeds;
The cracked enamel of a chicken bowl
Gleams like another moon; each clump of reeds
Is split with darkness and yet bristles whole.
The field survives, but with a difference.

2

And sleep like moonlight drifts and clings to shape.
My mind, which learns its freedom every day,
Sinks into vacancy but cannot rest.
10   While moonlight floods the pillow where it lay,
It walks among the past, weeping, obsessed,
Trying to master it and learn escape.

I dream: the real is shattered and combined,
Until the moon comes back into that sign
It stood in at my birth hour; and I pass
Back to the field where, statued in the shine,
Someone is gazing upward from the grass
As if toward vaults that honeycomb the mind.

Slight figure in a wide black hat, whose hair
20   Massed and moon-colored almost hides his face.
The thin white lips are dry, the eyes intense
Watching not thing, but lunar orgy, chase,
Trap, and cool fantasy of violence.
I recognize the pale long inward stare.

His tight young flesh is only on the top.
Beneath it is an answering moon, at full,
Pitted with craters and with empty seas.

Dream mentor, I have been inside that skull,
I too have used those cindered passages.

30 But now the moon leaves Scorpio:[1] I look up.

3

No, not inconstant, though it is called so.
For I have always found it waiting there,
Whether reduced to an invisible seed,
Or whether swollen again above the air
To rake the oubliettes of pain and greed
Opened at night in fellowship below.

It goes, and in its going it returns,
Cycle that I in part am governed by
And cannot understand where it is dark.
40 I lean upon the fence and watch the sky,
How light fills blinded socket and chafed mark.
It soars, hard, full, and edged, it coldly burns.

1971

[1] **Scorpio**   eighth sign of the zodiac: the scorpion

JOHN MONTAGUE
b. 1929

John Montague was born in Brooklyn, New York, and educated at St. Patrick's College, Armagh. He received his B.A. in English and History from University College, Dublin, in 1949, and his M.F.A. from the University of Iowa in 1955. He worked for the State Tourist Board, Dublin, from 1956 to 1961, and since then has taught at a variety of universities, including the University of California, Berkeley; University College, Dublin; the University of Vincennes; and the University of Cork. He has published over fifteen books of poetry and is well known as an editor, particularly of *The Faber Book of Irish Verse* (1974).

Despite the "casual displacement" of his Brooklyn birth, Montague is an Irish poet. Obsessed with what he calls his tribal preoccupations, he explains: "I am usually classed as an Irish poet and that is true insofar as I am deeply involved with the landscape and people of Ireland, particularly Ulster. In Gaelic poetry, Ireland appears both as a maiden and a hag, a sort of national muse, and her hold is still strong, especially now that her distinctive culture is being submerged." One can see the allegorical thrust behind "The Wild Dog Rose" as the poet tries to capture his sense of his Irish past. The old hag, who seems almost to grow out of the desolation of the Ulster landscape, becomes synonymous with the dying culture, though without losing any of her individuality. The poet, remembering the ancient awe she inspired in him as a child, sees her now demythologized. The poem becomes a cultural elegy. Montague is distinctive as an Irish poet in that his technique blends the influences of American post-modernism with the lyric tradition of Gaelic poetry.

The Trout

Flat on the bank I parted
Rushes to ease my hands
In the water without a ripple
And tilt them slowly downstream
To where he lay, light as a leaf,
In his fluid sensual dream.

Bodiless lord of creation
I hung briefly above him
Savouring my own absence
10   Senses expanding in the slow
Motion, the photographic calm
That grows before action.

As the curve of my hands
Swung under his body
He surged, with visible pleasure.
I was so preternaturally close
I could count every stipple
But still cast no shadow, until

The two palms crossed in a cage
20   Under the lightly pulsing gills.
Then (entering my own enlarged
Shape, which rode on the water)
I gripped. To this day I can
Taste his terror on my hands.

1966

The Wild Dog Rose

I go to say goodbye to the *Cailleach*[1]
that terrible figure who haunted my childhood
but no longer harsh, a human being
merely, hurt by event.
              The cottage,
circled by trees, weathered to admonitory
shapes of desolation by the mountain winds,
struggles into view. The rank thistles
and leathery bracken of untilled fields
10   stretch behind with—a final outcrop—
the hooped figure by the roadside,
its retinue of dogs

---

[1] *Cailleach* "Irish (and Scots Gaelic) for an old woman, a hag; and also a nun" (Montague's note).

which give tongue
as I approach, with savage, whinging cries
so that she slowly turns, a moving nest
of shawls and rags, to view, to stare
the stranger down.
          And I feel again
that ancient awe, the terror of a child
20 before the great hooked nose, the cheeks
dewlapped with dirt, the staring blue
of the sunken eyes, the mottled claws
clutching a stick
          but now hold

and return her gaze, to greet her,
as she greets me, in friendliness.
Memories have wrought reconciliation
between us, we talk in ease at last,
like old friends, lovers almost,
30 sharing secrets.
          Of neighbours
she quarreled with, who now lie
in Garvaghey graveyard, beyond all hatred;
of my family and hers, how she never married,
though a man came asking in her youth
"You would be loath to leave your own"
she sighs, "and go among strangers"—
his parish ten miles off.
          For sixty years
40 since she has lived alone in one place.
Obscurely honoured by such confidences,
I idle by the summer roadside, listening,
while the monologue falters, continues,
rehearsing the small events of her life.
The only true madness is loneliness,
the monotonous voice in the skull
that never stops
          because never heard.

          II
And there
50 where the dogrose shines in the hedge
she tells me a story so terrible
that I try to push it away,
my bones melting.
          Late at night
a drunk came beating at her door
to break it in, the bolt snapping
from the soft wood, the thin mongrels
rushing to cut, but yelping as
he whirls with his farm boots
60 to crush their skulls.

                    In the darkness
they wrestle, two creatures crazed
with loneliness, the smell of the
decaying cottage in his nostrils
like a drug, his body heavy on hers,
the tasteless trunk of a seventy year
old virgin, which he rummages while
she battles for life
                    bony fingers
70 reaching desperately to push
against his bull neck. "I prayed
to the Blessed Virgin herself
for help and after a time
I broke his grip."
                    He rolls
to the floor, snores asleep,
while she cowers until dawn
and the dogs' whimpering starts
him awake, to lurch back across
80 the wet bog.

    III
                    And still
the dog rose shines in the hedge.
Petals beaten wide by rain, it
sways slightly, at the tip of a
slender, tangled, arching branch
which with her stick, she gathers
into us.
                    "The wild rose
is the only rose without thorns,"
90 she says, holding a wet blossom
for a second, in a hand knotted
as the knob of her stick.
"Whenever I see it, I remember
the Holy Mother of God and
all she suffered."
                    Briefly
the air is strong with the smell
of that weak flower, offering
its crumbled yellow cup
100 and pale bleeding lips
fading to white
                    at the rim
of each bruised and heart-
shaped petal.

                    1971

ADRIENNE RICH
b. 1929

Born in Baltimore, Maryland, Adrienne Rich received her B.A. from Radcliffe College in 1951. In 1953 she married Alfred H. Conrad, an economist at Harvard, with whom she had three sons. In 1966 the family moved to New York, and Rich began teaching at various universities and became deeply involved in the anti-Vietnam War movement. Her husband died in 1970. She was awarded the National Book Award for poetry in 1974, which she rejected for herself but accepted as co-winner with Audre Lord, "in the name of all women."

Rich, a leading feminist poet, has struggled to identify and resolve the problems encountered by women writers. Her poems describe her sense of frustration, guilt, and anger at the "discontinuity of female life" —and the implications of the female role in love, marriage, and parenthood, which imposes an artificial dichotomy between love ("womanly, maternal, altruistic") and egotism ("a force directed by men into creation, ambition, achievement"). Her early poems, such as the well-known "Living in Sin," were conventionally formal, but later, as in her "Ghazals," she worked with more open forms, looser incantatory rhythms, and heavily symbolic imagery. Her poem "Snapshots of a Daughter-in-Law" (1963) was a major breakthrough, and since that time she has become increasingly radical in her search for a new language and new vision in her poetry. *The Will to Change* (1971) is, in her opinion, her first book in which "at last the woman in the poem and the woman writing the poem became the same person."

"The Phenomenology of Anger" is clearly an effort to write a polemical poem that makes an aggressively political point through the juxtaposition of anecdotes, moods, and images. Spoken by a woman, it attempts a description and classification of the causes of feminist anger. The speaker describes her condition as that of a fugitive, exiled from the "real" which offers her only the choices of madness, suicide, or murder. She is also a fugitive from her own self-hatred, rooted in her sense of cooption by a culture that is no longer viable. The woman sees her male partner as the agent of war and ecological disaster and concludes that the male impulse to power has wreaked havoc on the "dogeared earth." Through the power of its invective, the poem would create a new consciousness, involving a return to an original vision of a world of men and women living "gaily / in collusion with green leaves."

In "Your small hands," section 6 of a sequence of love poems to a female partner, it is clear that Rich's anger is revolutionary in implication. Knowing that she is caught in the perennial paradox that to end violence, violence may be "unavoidable," her images of hands compile a catalogue of constructive actions that nurture and repair. Like many modern poets who demand that poetry be a public, political force to make a critique of modern culture, Rich is increasingly pulled toward rhetorical statement. The lyric moment gives way in her poetry to the longer sequence as a vehicle for her social ideas.

Though she is primarily a poet, Rich is also an important critic. In *On Lies, Secrets, & Silence: Selected Prose 1966-1978*, she traces, from a feminist perspective, her personal, literary, and political development.

The Phenomenology of Anger

1. The freedom of the wholly mad
to smear & play with her madness
write with her fingers dipped in it
the length of a room

which is not, of course, the freedom
you have, walking on Broadway
to stop & turn back or go on
10 blocks; 20 blocks

but feels enviable maybe
10   to the compromised

curled in the placenta of the real
which was to feed & which is strangling her.

2. Trying to light a log that's lain in the damp
as long as this house has stood:
even with dry sticks I can't get started
even with thorns.
I twist last year into a knot of old headlines
—this rose won't bloom.

How does a pile of rags the machinist wiped his hands on
20   feel in its cupboard, hour upon hour?
Each day during the heat-wave
they took the temperature of the haymow.
I huddled fugitive
in the warm sweet simmer of the hay

muttering: *Come.*

3. Flat heartland of winter.
The moonmen come back from the moon
the firemen come out of the fire.
Time without a taste: time without decisions.

30   Self-hatred, a monotone in the mind.
The shallowness of a life lived in exile
even in the hot countries.
Cleaver, staring into a window full of knives.

4. White light splits the room.
Table. Window. Lampshade. You.
My hands, sticky in a new way.
Menstrual blood
seeming to leak from your side.

Will the judges try to tell me
40   which was the blood of whom?

5. Madness. Suicide. Murder.
Is there no way out but these?
The enemy, always just out of sight
snowshoeing the next forest, shrouded
in a snowy blur, abominable snowman
—at once the most destructive
and the most elusive being
gunning down the babies at My Lai[1]
vanishing in the face of confrontation.

50   The prince of air and darkness
computing body counts, masturbating
in the factory
of facts.

6. Fantasies of murder: not enough:
to kill is to cut off from pain
but the killer goes on hurting

Not enough. When I dream of meeting
the enemy, this is my dream:

white acetylene
60   ripples from my body
effortlessly released
perfectly trained
on the true enemy

raking his body down to the thread
of existence
burning away his lie
leaving him in a new
world; a changed
man

70   7. I suddenly see the world
as no longer viable:
you are out there burning the crops
with some new sublimate
This morning you left the bed
we still share
and went out to spread impotence
upon the world

[1] In March 1968, a large number of Vietnamese civilians were massacred by U.S. troops at My Lai in South Vietnam. A military jury later convicted Lieutenant William L. Calley Jr. of premeditated murder.

I hate you.
I hate the mask you wear, your eyes
80   assuming a depth
they do not possess, drawing me
into the grotto of your skull
the landscape of bone
I hate your words
they make me think of fake
revolutionary bills
crisp imitation parchment
they sell at battlefields.

Last night, in this room, weeping
90   I asked you: *what are you feeling?*
do you feel anything?

Now in the torsion of your body
as you defoliate the fields we lived from
I have your answer.

8. Dogeared earth. Wormeaten moon.
A pale cross-hatching of silver
lies like a wire screen on the black
water. All these phenomena
are temporary.

100   I would have loved to live in a world
of women and men gaily
in collusion with green leaves, stalks,
building mineral cities, transparent domes,
little huts of woven grass
each with its own pattern—
a conspiracy to coexist
with the Crab Nebula, the exploding
universe, the Mind—

9. *The only real love I have ever felt*
110   *was for children and other women.*
Everything else was lust, pity,
self-hatred, pity, lust.
This is a woman's confession.
Now, look again at the face
of Botticelli's Venus, Kali,[2]
the Judith of Chartres[3]
with her so-called smile.

[2] **Kali** the Black, in Hindu mythology, the hideous and blood-thirsty aspect of the Goddess. She dances on the dead body of Shiva, her husband, and by this act transforms the corpse (*shava* in Sanskrit) into Shiva, the living God.

[3] **Judith of Chartres** relief on the north portal of Chartres Cathedral, France, depicting the biblical Judith who murdered the Assyrian general Holofernes by beheading him while he slept

10. how we are burning up our lives
testimony:

120
                the subway
                hurtling to Brooklyn
                her head on her knees
                asleep or drugged

        la vía del tren subterráneo
        es peligrosa[4]

                many sleep
                the whole way
                others sit
                staring holes of fire into the air
130   others plan rebellion:
                night after night
                awake in prison, my mind
                licked at the mattress like a flame
                till the cellblock went up roaring

        Thoreau setting fire to the woods

        Every act of becoming conscious
        (it says here in this book)
        is an unnatural act

        1972   1973

[4] ll. 124–25 (Spanish)   The route of the under-
ground train is dangerous.

From 21 Love Poems

6

Your small hands, precisely equal to my own—
only the thumb is larger, longer—in these hands
I could trust the world, or in many hands like these,
handling power-tools or steering-wheel
or touching a human face. . . . Such hands could turn
the unborn child rightways in the birth canal
or pilot the exploratory rescue-ship
through icebergs, or piece together
the fine, needle-like sherds of a great krater-cup
10   bearing on its sides
figures of ecstatic women striding

to the sibyl's den or the Eleusinian[1] cave—
such hands might carry out an unavoidable violence
with such restraint, with such a grasp
of the range and limits of violence
that violence ever after would be obsolete.

1978

[1] **Eleusinian** The ancient city of Eleusis in Attica
was famous for the mysteries celebrated in honor
of Demeter and Persephone.

TED HUGHES
b. 1930

Ted Hughes, a Yorkshire man, worked as a ground radio mechanic in the Royal Air Force and later earned B.A. and M.A. degrees at Cambridge University. At Cambridge he met and married the American Sylvia Plath in 1956; they had two children. They separated in 1963, some months before her suicide. His early volumes, *The Hawk in the Rain* (1957) and *Lupercal* (1960), established him as England's foremost younger poet, and his *Crow* (1970) made the most sensational impact of any book by a member of his poetic generation.

In a radio broadcast, Hughes described his early passion for ornithology as his primary route to poetry. His childhood interest in collecting specimens was somehow converted, later, to a hunt for poetic symbols from the animal world. His favorite symbols, perhaps, are birds, both as victims and predators. Hughes sees animal violence primarily as an irrepressible, anarchic form of energy that leads him to an understanding of deep-seated predatory human instincts. In the savagery-obsessed poem "Pike," for example, the violence of the dark psyche surfaces to confront the poet in the image of a vast, unseen pike. Hughes pursues raw sensation and cruelty with a harsh, sardonic honesty.

His *Crow* sequence, deeply rooted in myth and fable, creates a figure, "Crow," at the center of a cosmogony and myth-like history that both echoes and parodies the Bible.

Through this figure, at once grotesque, hideous, and pathetic, Hughes can project a fierce vision of the human predicament as all but hopeless. The sequence of sixty-six poems and songs begins with "Two Legends," recounting the hatching of "Crow" before human creation, and traces his fantastical, solitary journey as he observes the human story, an allegory of devastation and loss. Hughes varies his poetic styles, drawing from the rhythmic subtleties of song and nursery rhyme, and sounding a wide variety of tones. "Littleblood," which ends the sequence, is a model of his method.

As in a legend, he uses a poignant metonymy—the song to "Littleblood" records the human progress from a fearful innocence to a pained and brutalized wisdom. *Crow* offers a world torn by violence and entropy, a dualist vision of a universe caught in a battle between good and evil, where the Serpent is coeval with God, and the negatives of creation—hatred, pain, greed, lust, fear, death itself—are the more powerful forces. Sheer survival, in the knowledge of guilt and the damnation of civilization, is the only possible egress from these poems. While Hughes's vision is dark, brutal, and elemental, he is one of the few poets actually recording the violence and barbarity hidden beneath the veneer of our civilization, and his poems echo a pain and desolation that have been earned by personal experience.

Pike

Pike, three inches long, perfect
Pike in all parts, green tigering the gold.
Killers from the egg: the malevolent aged grin.
They dance on the surface among the flies.

Or move, stunned by their own grandeur
Over a bed of emerald, silhouette
Of submarine delicacy and horror.
A hundred feet long in their world.

In ponds, under the heat-struck lily pads—
10 Gloom of their stillness:
Logged on last year's black leaves, watching upwards.
Or hung in an amber cavern of weeds

The jaws' hooked clamp and fangs
Not to be changed at this date;
A life subdued to its instrument;
The gills kneading quietly, and the pectorals.

Three we kept behind glass,
Jungled in weed: three inches, four,
And four and a half: fed fry to them—
20 Suddenly there were two. Finally one.

With a sag belly and the grin it was born with.
And indeed they spare nobody.
Two, six pounds each, over two feet long,
High and dry and dead in the willow-herb—

One jammed past its gills down the other's gullet:
The outside eye stared: as a vice locks—
The same iron in this eye
Though its film shrank in death.

A pond I fished, fifty yards across,
30 Whose lilies and muscular tench
Had outlasted every visible stone
Of the monastery that planted them—

Stilled legendary depth:
It was as deep as England. It held
Pike too immense to stir, so immense and old
That past nightfall I dared not cast

But silently cast and fished
With the hair frozen on my head
For what might move, for what eye might move.
40 The still splashes on the dark pond,

Owls hushing the floating woods
Frail on my ear against the dream
Darkness beneath night's darkness had freed,
That rose slowly towards me, watching.

1960

From Crow

Two Legends

I

Black was the without eye
Black the within tongue
Black was the heart
Black the liver, black the lungs
Unable to suck in light
Black the blood in its loud tunnel
Black the bowels packed in furnace
Black too the muscles
Striving to pull out into the light
10 Black the nerves, black the brain
With its tombed visions
Black also the soul, the huge stammer
Of the cry that, swelling, could not
Pronounce its sun.

II

Black is the wet otter's head, lifted.
Black is the rock, plunging in foam.
Black is the gall lying on the bed of the blood.

Black is the earth-globe, one inch under,
An egg of blackness
20 Where sun and moon alternate their weathers

To hatch a crow, a black rainbow
Bent in emptiness
                    over emptiness
But flying

1970

That Moment

When the pistol muzzle oozing blue vapour
Was lifted away
Like a cigarette lifted from an ashtray

And the only face left in the world
Lay broken
Between hands that relaxed, being too late

And the trees closed forever
And the streets closed forever

And the body lay on the gravel
10   Of the abandoned world
Among abandoned utilities
Exposed to infinity forever

Crow had to start searching for something to eat.

                                        1970

Dawn's Rose

Is melting an old frost moon.

Agony under agony, the quiet of dust,
And a crow talking to stony skylines.

Desolate is the crow's puckered cry
As an old woman's mouth
When the eyelids have finished
And the hills continue.

A cry
Wordless
10   As the newborn baby's grieving
On the steely scales.

As the dull gunshot and its after-râle
Among conifers, in rainy twilight.

Or the suddenly dropped, heavily dropped
Star of blood on the fat leaf.

                                        1970

Littleblood

O littleblood, hiding from the mountains in the mountains
Wounded by stars and leaking shadow
Eating the medical earth.

O littleblood, little boneless little skinless
Ploughing with a linnet's carcase
Reaping the wind and threshing the stones.

O littleblood, drumming in a cow's skull
Dancing with a gnat's feet
With an elephant's nose with a crocodile's tail.

10   Grown so wise grown so terrible
Sucking death's mouldy tits.

Sit on my finger, sing in my ear, O littleblood.

1970

GARY SNYDER
b. 1930

Gary Snyder is a Westerner born in San Francisco and brought up in Oregon and Washington. He received his B.A. in anthropology from Reed College in 1951, at which time he lived among the Great Basin Indian tribes. He also worked intermittently as a logger, a seaman, and a Forest Service trail crew member in the Pacific Northwest. He studied Oriental languages at the University of California, Berkeley, from 1953 to 1956, and meanwhile came to know Allen Ginsberg and other Beat poets. In 1956, he began studying Zen Buddhism on a scholarship from the First Zen Institute of America, living mainly in Japan from 1956 to 1964. *Earth House Hold* (1969) is a poetic travel journal of his Japanese experiences. He now lives in the United States.

Among the San Francisco poets of the 1950s and 1960s, Snyder is perhaps the most influential after Allen Ginsberg, with whom he shares a countercultural commitment.

But while Ginsberg is essentially urban, Snyder is a primitivist. He brings to his poetry a sophisticated knowledge of Eastern mysticism and sees the world as a network of relationships inaccessible to Western rationality, which is cut off from the world of nature, dream, myth, and dance. Snyder's poetry moves between poles of nature mysticism and pragmatic politics, expounding a program for survival in a time of political and ecological oppression. He writes in a colloquial style, focusing on simple anecdotes or sharp, uncomplicated images as in "Front Lines," which describes the rape of the American wilderness by realty companies. The brutality of his imagery — "they say / To the land, / Spread your legs" — carries his point. Perhaps because of the accessibility of his poetics and revolutionary politics, his poetry has acquired a large popular following.

I Went into the Maverick Bar

I went into the Maverick Bar
In Farmington, New Mexico.
And drank double shots of bourbon
          backed with beer.
My long hair was tucked up under a cap
I'd left the earring in the car.

Two cowboys did horseplay
          by the pool tables,

A waitress asked us

10   where are you from?
a country-and-western band began to play
"We don't smoke Marijuana in Muskokie"
And with the next song,
                  a couple began to dance.

They held each other like in High School dances
               in the fifties;
I recalled when I worked in the woods
               and the bars of Madras, Oregon.
That short-haired joy and roughness—
20   America—your stupidity.
I could almost love you again.

We left—onto the freeway shoulders—
              under the tough old stars—
In the shadow of bluffs
            I came back to myself,
To the real work, to
            "What is to be done."

                    1974

Front Lines

The edge of the cancer
Swells against the hill—we feel
           a foul breeze—
And it sinks back down.
The deer winter here
A chainsaw growls in the gorge.

Ten wet days and the log trucks stop,
The trees breathe.
Sunday the 4-wheel jeep of the
10 Realty Company brings in
Landseekers, lookers, they say
To the land,
Spread your legs.

The jets crack sound overhead, it's OK here;
Every pulse of the rot at the heart
In the sick fat veins of Amerika
Pushes the edge up closer—

A bulldozer grinding and slobbering
Sideslipping and belching on top of
20 The skinned-up bodies of still-live bushes
In the pay of a man
From town.

Behind is a forest that goes to the Arctic
And a desert that still belongs to the Piute[1]
And here we must draw
Our line.

1974

[1] **Piute** American Indians dwelling in California,
Nevada, Utah, and Arizona

Bedrock

for Masa

Snowmelt pond   warm granite
we make camp,
no thought of finding more.
and nap
and leave our minds to the wind.

on the bedrock, gently tilting,
sky and stone,

teach me to be tender.

the touch that nearly misses—
10 brush of glances—
tiny steps—
that finally cover worlds
       of hard terrain.
cloud wisps and mists
gathered into slate blue
bolts of summer rain.

tea together in the purple starry eve;
new moon soon to set,
why does it take so
20 long to learn to
love,
       we laugh
             and grieve.

1974

SYLVIA PLATH
1932–1963

Sylvia Plath was born in Boston. Her father, a professor of biology and German at Boston University, died after a long and painful illness when she was a child, and the trauma of that loss is explored in bitter elegies in *The Colossus* and *Ariel*. By the time she attended Smith College, she had already published poetry and prose in *The Christian Science Monitor* and *Seventeen*. In 1952 she won *Mademoiselle*'s College Board fiction contest. Her autobiographical novel, *The Bell Jar* (published under the pseudonym Victoria Lucas one month before her death), describes her years as a student, including a psychological breakdown and attempted suicide in her junior year. She received her B.A. in 1954 and on a Fulbright Scholarship attended Cambridge University. There she met and married Ted Hughes, with whom she had two children. She returned to teach at Smith College from 1957 to 1959, attending, in 1958, Robert Lowell's graduate writing seminar at Boston University, where she met Anne Sexton. Identified with the confessional school of poetry, Plath said that Lowell and Sexton freed new subjects for poetry—such normally "private and taboo" subjects as nervous breakdown and experiences in mental hospitals. In 1959 she returned to England, where she lived until her suicide in 1963.

The most powerful poetry of recent decades has often engaged in psychological probing that has taken poets to the edge of madness. Sylvia Plath has become the model *par excellence* of this process. She is best known for poems that describe suicidal depression and that are violent, bitter tirades against father, husband, and lover. Consequently her sheer poetic skill and range of subject-matter are often neglected.

"Daddy," her most famous poem, is addressed to the vampire father / husband who holds her in a psychological clamp, a dialectic of love and hate. He is the internal devil with whom she battles. She brings to the poem all the imagery of the archetypal victim of the Holocaust, seeming to care little about the presumption involved in appropriating such experience. It is as if the only route to self-preservation were a savage rebellion against power, embodied in the paternal psyche, which must be destroyed. To create the impression of the childish self crying out in terror and rage, she uses the compelling rhythmic repetitions of nursery rhyme, as well as its primitive imagery—"devil," "vampire," "pretty red heart."

Plath clearly had a suicidal compulsion. "Edge" describes a phantasmal suicide. Mother and children become classical symbols acting out the necessity of self-destruction; a superb control of language imitates the terrifying stasis of a Greek funeral urn as the three living forms seem to return naturally to the alabaster stillness of death. The horror of this moment is displaced: "the garden / Stiffens and odors bleed." "Balloons," however, shows Plath capable of whimsy and maternal gentleness, although even here the world invades with its destructiveness. "Words" expresses the poet's despair at finding a language as precise as axes; words are inevitably dulled by that destiny that undermines everything.

Plath at her darkest is death-ridden and emptied of love; human experience is terrible and ungovernable; relationships are puppet-like and meaningless. Her poetry becomes a weapon of outrage, compelling because of its taut, ruthless imagery, which shocks for reasons of its poetic rightness.

Daddy

You do not do, you do not do
Any more, black shoe
In which I have lived like a foot
For thirty years, poor and white,
Barely daring to breathe or Achoo.

Daddy, I have had to kill you.
You died before I had time——
Marble-heavy, a bag full of God,
Ghastly statue with one gray toe
10   Big as a Frisco seal

And a head in the freakish Atlantic
Where it pours bean green over blue
In the waters off beautiful Nauset.
I used to pray to recover you.
Ach, du.[1]

In the German tongue, in the Polish town
Scraped flat by the roller
Of wars, wars, wars.
But the name of the town is common.
20   My Polack friend

Says there are a dozen or two.
So I never could tell where you
Put your foot, your root,
I never could talk to you.
The tongue stuck in my jaw.

It stuck in a barb wire snare.
Ich, ich, ich, ich,[2]
I could hardly speak.
I thought every German was you.
30   And the language obscene

An engine, an engine
Chuffing me off like a Jew.
A Jew to Dachau, Auschwitz, Belsen.
I began to talk like a Jew.
I think I may well be a Jew.

The snows of the Tyrol, the clear beer of Vienna
Are not very pure or true.
With my gipsy ancestress and my weird luck
And my Taroc pack and my Taroc pack
40   I may be a bit of a Jew.

[1] **Ach, du** (German) Ah, you
[2] **Ich . . .** (German) I, I, I, I

I have always been scared of *you*,
With your Luftwaffe,[3] your gobbledygoo.
And your neat mustache
And your Aryan eye, bright blue.
Panzer-man,[4] panzer-man, O You——

Not God but a swastika
So black no sky could squeak through.
Every woman adores a Fascist,
The boot in the face, the brute
50   Brute heart of a brute like you.

You stand at the blackboard, daddy,
In the picture I have of you,
A cleft in your chin instead of your foot
But no less a devil for that, no not
Any less the black man who

Bit my pretty red heart in two.
I was ten when they buried you.
At twenty I tried to die
And get back, back, back to you.
60   I thought even the bones would do.

But they pulled me out of the sack,
And they stuck me together with glue.
And then I knew what to do.
I made a model of you,
A man in black with a Meinkampf[5] look

And a love of the rack and the screw.
And I said I do, I do.
So daddy, I'm finally through.
The black telephone's off at the root,
70   The voices just can't worm through.

If I've killed one man, I've killed two——
The vampire who said he was you
And drank my blood for a year,
Seven years, if you want to know.
Daddy, you can lie back now.

There's a stake in your fat black heart
And the villagers never liked you.
They are dancing and stamping on you.
They always *knew* it was you.
80   Daddy, daddy, you bastard, I'm through.

12 October 1962   1965

[3] **Luftwaffe** (German) "Air Force"
[4] **Panzer** (German) "armored"

[5] **Meinkampf** *Mein Kampf* (My Battle): Adolf Hitler's autobiography

Ariel[1]

Stasis in darkness.
Then the substanceless blue
Pour of tor and distances.

God's lioness,
How one we grow,
Pivot of heels and knees!—The furrow

Splits and passes, sister to
The brown arc
Of the neck I cannot catch,

10   Nigger-eye
Berries cast dark
Hooks——

Black sweet blood mouthfuls,
Shadows.
Something else

Hauls me through air——
Thighs, hair;
Flakes from my heels.

White
20   Godiva, I unpeel——
Dead hands, dead stringencies.

And now I
Foam to wheat, a glitter of seas.
The child's cry

Melts in the wall.
And I
Am the arrow,

The dew that flies
Suicidal, at one with the drive
30   Into the red

Eye, the cauldron of morning.

27 October 1962   1965

[1] Sylvia Plath's horse, named after the "airy"
spirit in Shakespeare's *The Tempest*

Words

Axes
After whose stroke the wood rings,
And the echoes!
Echoes traveling
Off from the center like horses.

The sap
Wells like tears, like the
Water striving
To re-establish its mirror
10   Over the rock

That drops and turns,
A white skull,
Eaten by weedy greens.
Years later I
Encounter them on the road——

Words dry and riderless,
The indefatigable hoof-taps.
While
From the bottom of the pool, fixed stars
20   Govern a life.

1 February 1963   1965

Balloons

Since Christmas they have lived with us,
Guileless and clear,
Oval soul-animals,
Taking up half the space,
Moving and rubbing on the silk

Invisible air drifts,
Giving a shriek and pop
When attacked, then scooting to rest, barely trembling.
Yellow cathead, blue fish——
10   Such queer moons we live with

Instead of dead furniture!
Straw mats, white walls
And these traveling
Globes of thin air, red, green,
Delighting

The heart like wishes or free
Peacocks blessing

Old ground with a feather
Beaten in starry metals.
20   Your small

Brother is making
His balloon squeak like a cat.
Seeming to see
A funny pink world he might eat on the other side of it,
He bites,

Then sits
Back, fat jug
Contemplating a world clear as water.
A red
30   Shred in his little fist.

   5 February 1963   1965

Edge

The woman is perfected.
Her dead

Body wears the smile of accomplishment,
The illusion of a Greek necessity

Flows in the scrolls of her toga,
Her bare

Feet seem to be saying:
We have come so far, it is over.

Each dead child coiled, a white serpent,
10   One at each little

Pitcher of milk, now empty.
She has folded

Them back into her body as petals
Of a rose close when the garden

Stiffens and odors bleed
From the sweet, deep throats of the night flower.

The moon has nothing to be sad about,
Staring from her hood of bone.

She is used to this sort of thing.
20   Her blacks crackle and drag.

   5 February 1963   1965

GEOFFREY HILL
b. 1932

Born in Worcestershire, Geoffrey Hill was educated at Oxford University. He is professor of English literature at the University of Leeds. He has won many prizes for his work and became a Fellow of the Royal Society of Literature in 1972.

Hill is a hermetic poet, erudite and bookish. He has the modernist's awareness of the texture of history in the living moment and in the manner of T.S. Eliot uses scholarly allusions to create a world that is remarkably contemporary. For instance, *Mercian Hymns* (four sections of which are printed here) is a sequence of thirty prose-poems loosely based on the historical King Offa, who reigned in Mercia and the greater part of southern England from 757 to 796. In the poems, Offa becomes the "presiding genius of the West Midlands"—an archetypal figure roaming in time from the eighth to the twentieth century. These archaeological musings over history and legend, while describing the imagined consciousness of Offa, also include diggings into the poet's own childhood memories, as is clear in Section XXV: "I speak this in memory of my grandmother." For purposes of the poem, Hill invents a poetic language that blends the archaic and the modern—in Section IX he describes cemeteries as "spoil-heaps of chrysanths dead in their plastic macs, eldorado of washstand-marble"—and the mixing of idioms gives the poem its peculiar rhetorical force.

Hill is always impressive as a stylist, particularly in his capacity to use traditional metrical forms (the two sections from "An Apology for the Revival of Christian Architecture in England" are modified Petrarchan sonnets) with fluid grace. In its fierceness, scrupulous precision, and, at moments, visionary energy, his poetry is at once learned and direct.

From Mercian Hymns

VI

The princes of Mercia were badger and raven. Thrall
  to their freedom, I dug and hoarded. Orchards
  fruited above clefts. I drank from honeycombs of
  chill sandstone.

"A boy at odds in the house, lonely among brothers."
  But I, who had none, fostered a strangeness; gave
  myself to unattainable toys.

Candles of gnarled resin, apple-branches, the tacky
  mistletoe. "Look" they said and again "look." But
10 I ran slowly; the landscape flowed away, back to
  its source.

In the schoolyard, in the cloakrooms, the children
  boasted their scars of dried snot; wrists and
  knees garnished with impetigo.

IX

The strange church smelled a bit "high," of censers
and polish. The strange curate was just as ap-
propriate: he took off into the marriage-service.
No-one cared to challenge that gambit.

Then he dismissed you, and the rest of us followed,
sheepish next-of-kin, to the place without the
walls: spoil-heaps of chrysanths dead in their
plastic macs, eldorado of washstand-marble.

Embarrassed, we dismissed ourselves: the three mute
10   great-aunts borne away down St. Chad's Garth in
a stiff-backed Edwardian Rolls.

I unburden the saga of your burial, my dear. You had
lived long enough to see things "nicely settled."

XII

Their spades grafted through the variably-resistant
soil. They clove to the hoard. They ransacked epi-
phanies, vertebrae of the chimera, armour of wild
bees' larvae. They struck the fire-dragon's fac-
eted skin.

The men were paid to caulk water-pipes. They brewed
and pissed amid splendour; their latrine seethed
its estuary through nettles. They are scattered
to your collations, moldywarp.

10   It is autumn. Chestnut-boughs clash their inflamed
leaves. The garden festers for attention: telluric
cultures enriched with shards, corms, nodules, the
sunk solids of gravity. I have accrued a golden
and stinking blaze.

XXV

Brooding on the eightieth letter of *Fors Clavigera*,[1]
I speak this in memory of my grandmother, whose
childhood and prime womanhood were spent in the
nailer's darg:[2]

---

[1] **Fors Clavigera** "See *The Works of John Rus-kin*, London (1903–1912), xxix, pp. 170–180" (Hill's note).

[2] **darg** "a day's work, the task of a day (O.E.D.). Ruskin employs the word, here and elsewhere" (Hill's note).

The nailshop stood back of the cottage, by the fold.
It reeked stale mineral sweat. Sparks had furred
its low roof. In dawn-light the troughed water
floated a damson-bloom of dust—

not to be shaken by posthumous clamour. It is one
10   thing to celebrate the "quick forge,"[3] another
to cradle a face hare-lipped by the searing wire.[4]

Brooding on the eightieth letter of *Fors Clavigera*,
I speak this in memory of my grandmother, whose
childhood and prime womanhood were spent in the
nailer's darg.

1971

[3] **"quick forge"** "See W. Shakespeare, Henry V, V, Chorus, 23. The phrase requires acknowledgement but has no bearing on the poem" (Hill's note).
[4] l. 11 "I seem not to have been strictly accurate. Hand-made nails were forged from rods. Wire was used for the cover, 'French nails' made by machine. But: 'wire' = 'metal wrought into the form of a slender rod or thread' (O.E.D.)" (Hill's note).

From An Apology for The Revival of Christian Architecture in England[1]

The Laurel Axe

Autumn resumes the land, ruffles the woods
with smoky wings, entangles them. Trees shine
out from their leaves, rocks mildew to moss-green;
the avenues are spread with brittle floods.

Platonic England, house of solitudes,
rests in its laurels and its injured stone,
replete with complex fortunes that are gone,
beset by dynasties of moods and clouds.

It stands, as though at ease with its own world,
10   the mannerly extortions, languid praise,
all that devotion long since bought and sold,

[1] a sequence of thirteen sonnets. The two printed here are respectively Nos. 9 and 11.

the rooms of cedar and soft-thudding baize,
tremulous boudoirs where the crystals kissed
in cabinets of amethyst and frost.

1978

Idylls of the King

The pigeon purrs in the wood; the wood has gone;
dark leaves that flick to silver in the gust,
and the marsh-orchids and the heron's nest,
goldgrimy shafts and pillars of the sun.

Weightless magnificence upholds the past.
Cement recesses smell of fur and bone
and berries wrinkle in the badger-run
and wiry heath-fern scatters its fresh rust.

"O clap your hands" so that the dove takes flight,
10   bursts through the leaves with an untidy sound,
plunges its wings into the green twilight

above this long-sought and forsaken ground,
the half-built ruins of the new estate,
warheads of mushrooms round the filter-pond.

1978

PETER REDGROVE
b. 1932

Born in Surrey, Redgrove was educated at Queens' College, Cambridge. He began his career as a scientific journalist and editor and then turned to teaching. He has been a visiting professor at several universities and, since 1966, poet-in-residence at Falmouth School of Art, Cornwall.

Like Robert Graves, but perhaps less scholarly and erudite, Redgrove is interested in exploring poetry's foundations in myth and dream and in searching out the relation between the conscious and unconscious mind. In "Required of You This Night" he describes the dreaming and waking worlds as barely distinguishable. With that exhaus-

tive, almost banal struggle characteristic of certain recurrent nightmares, the poet fights to bring the night sky, with its stars, to his dreams that he may waken. The image of moonlight dominates Redgrove's imagination. It represents the dark forces of the night world with its exuberant yet frightening capacity to effect alchemical transformations. He is interested in all forms of metamorphosis. In "Light Hotel," a child astride a log is both a rider mounted on a "wide green horse," and a green sylvan creature in a foliate dress. Deliberately echoing William Blake, he insists that, to the attentive imagination, the world is engaged in continual metamorphosis—each grain of sand holds "its plate-glass terrace." Redgrove's poems are often rhythmically loose and yet have a contained energy; they depend on a technique of free association and a proliferation of images, and always end with a carefully prepared resolution. In "For No Good Reason," for instance, a mood conjured by imagistic details of the debris of an abandoned house proves the carefully prepared occasion by which to identify the poet's own domestic crisis, belying the disingenuous title.

For No Good Reason

I walk on the waste-ground for no good reason
Except that fallen stones and cracks
Bulging with weed suit my mood
Which is gloomy, irascible, selfish, among the split timbers
Of somebody's home, and the bleached rags of wallpaper.
My trouser-legs pied with water-drops,
I knock a sparkling rain from hemlock-polls,
I crash a puddle up my shin,
Brush a nettle across my hand,
10 And swear—then sweat from what I said:
Indeed, the sun withdraws as if I stung.

Indeed, she withdrew as if I stung,
And I walk up and down among these canted beams, bricks and scraps,
Bitten walls and weed-stuffed gaps
Looking as it would feel now, if I walked back,
Across the carpets of my home, my own home.

1961

Required of You This Night

A smoky sunset. I dab my eyes.
It stinks into the black wick of the wood.

Sparks wriggle, cut. I turn my back.
And night is at my frosty back.

I turn again. All stars!
It's bedtime.

There's no sky in my dreams, I dream none.
I work for sky, I work by sprinting up,
Breathing, sprinting up, and one star appears.

10 I chase it. It enlarges and I wake.
Dawn climbs into the sky like black smoke with white nails.

It's compact with the day's sharpness.
I'll dry my sopping pillow in it.
How long'll that take? I guess till sunset.

And then it sinks
All befrogged into that white glare.
The night is at my back instantly,
Draughty, and no star at all.
I weep again. I weep again frankly.
20 Sleep is nothing when you do it,
And nothing but a prim smile,
Except you're fighting to pull the sun down
That may not come unless you fight
Not for you anyway, Peter.

1966

Light Hotel

The little girl riding the fallen tree like a spindly horse,
Like a queen mounted on a green spider;
The little girl's white flesh is so sacred, so queenly,
I love and fear it so much

Carefully I think only of her dress,
Her foliate dress that falls in dry green pleats,
Or think as I look away from her sunlit face
How the sunlight holds a great conference in a sandgrain
With its plate-glass terraces and vista-windows of gold-tinge,

10 Then how the moon will hold her conference in the same sealed chamber.
In between times the non-staff have no clearing to do, no ashes to empty,
No glasses to polish, the light simply passes, great guest,

The light simply passes from the hotel, it is left untouched,
And above the million sand-grains, the one girl swishing her wide green
horse.

1979

IMAMU AMIRI BARAKA
(LE ROI JONES)
b. 1934

Born Everett Le Roi Jones in Newark, New Jersey, Imamu Amiri Baraka is the son of black professional parents: his father a postal supervisor and his mother a social worker. He was educated at Rutgers and Howard universities, earning his B.A. in English from Howard in 1954. For two years he served in the air force in Puerto Rico as a gunner and aerial climatographer—a radicalizing experience. ("The Air Force made me understand the white sickness.") In 1957 he settled in New York, working as a jazz critic and serving as editor for small magazines and presses associated with the Black Mountain poets.

Baraka's first volume of poems, *Preface to a Twenty Volume Suicide Note*, was published in 1961, and in 1964 his play *Dutchman* was produced off-Broadway. Becoming a militant spokesman for the American black community, he founded the Black Arts Repertory Theater in Harlem in 1965 to teach black nationalism and the arts. He returned to Newark in 1966 to found Spirit House Theater and organized the Committee for United Newark, a community action group.

"Let my poems be a graph of me," Baraka has written. Poems like "An Agony. As Now" and "I Substitute for the Dead Lecturer" are psychologically brutal portraits of the mind alone and brooding. Through their surrealistic riffs of images and masterful use of line breaks, the poems convey a sense of unrelieved anguish—from self-hatred, the aridity of living in a modern urban environment, a sense of inauthenticity. Speaking as a black poet, Baraka holds himself accountable to "the poor (and their minds / turn open like sores)" and struggles continually with a sense of his own inadequacy. "To understand that you are black in a society where black is an extreme liability is one thing, but to understand that it is the *society* that is lacking and impossibly deformed, and not *yourself,* isolates you even more." By his exploration of this isolation as he experiences it in his own pained condition, Baraka has created one of the most eloquent testaments to black experience in America.

The Turncoat

The steel fibrous slant & ribboned glint
of water. The Sea. Even my secret speech is moist
with it. When I am alone & brooding, locked in
with dull memories & self hate, & the terrible disorder
of a young man.

I move slowly. My cape spread stiff & pressing cautiously
in the first night wind off the Hudson. I glide down
onto my own roof, peering in at the pitiful shadow of myself.

How can it mean anything? The stop & spout, the
10 wind's dumb shift. Creak of the house & wet smells
coming in. Night forms on my left. The blind still
up to admit a sun that no longer exists. Sea move.

I dream long bays & towers . . . & soft steps on moist sand.
I become them, sometimes. Pure fight. Pure fantasy. Lean.

1961

I Substitute for the Dead Lecturer

> *What is most precious, because*
> *it is lost. What is lost,*
> *because it is most*
> *precious.*

They have turned, and say that I am dying. That
I have thrown
my life
away. They
have left me alone, where
there is no one, nothing
save who I am. Not a note
nor a word.

     Cold air batters
10 the poor (and their minds
turn open
like sores). What kindness
What wealth
can I offer? Except
what is, for me,
ugliest. What is
for me, shadows, shrieking
phantoms. Except
they have need
20 of life. Flesh
at least,
    should be theirs.

The Lord has saved me
to do this. The Lord
has made me strong. I
am as I must have
myself. Against all
thought, all music, all
my soft loves.

30   For all these wan roads
I am pushed to follow, are
my own conceit. A simple muttering
elegance, slipped in my head

pressed on my soul, is my heart's
worth. And I am frightened
that the flame of my sickness
will burn off my face. And leave
the bones, my stewed black skull,
an empty cage of failure.

1964

An Agony. As Now

I am inside someone
who hates me. I look
out from his eyes. Smell
what fouled tunes come in
to his breath. Love his
wretched women.

Slits in the metal, for sun. Where
my eyes sit turning, at the cool air
the glance of light, or hard flesh
10   rubbed against me, a woman, a man,
without shadow, or voice, or meaning.

This is the enclosure (flesh,
where innocence is a weapon. An
abstraction. Touch. (Not mine,
Or yours, if you are the soul I had
and abandoned when I was blind and had
my enemies carry me as a dead man
(if he is beautiful, or pitied.

It can be pain. (As now, as all his
20   flesh hurts me.) It can be that. Or
pain. As when she ran from me into
that forest.
            Or pain, the mind
silver spiraled whirled against the
sun, higher than even old men thought
God would be. Or pain. And the other. The
yes. (Inside his books, his fingers. They
are withered yellow flowers and were never
beautiful.) The yes. You will, lost soul, say
30   "beauty." Beauty, practiced, as the tree. The
slow river. A white sun in its wet sentences.

Or, the cold men in their gale. Ecstasy. Flesh
or soul. The yes. (Their robes blown. Their bowls
empty. They chant at my heels, not at yours.) Flesh

or soul, as corrupt. Where the answer moves too quickly.
Where the God is a self, after all.)

Cold air blown through narrow blind eyes. Flesh,
white hot metal. Glows as the day with its sun.
It is a human love, I live inside. A bony skeleton
40   you recognize as words or simple feeling.

But it has no feeling. As the metal, is hot, it is not,
given to love.

It burns the thing
inside it. And that thing
screams.

1964

MICHAEL HARPER
b. 1938

Born in Brooklyn, New York, Harper was
educated at U.C.L.A. (B.A. 1961; M.A.
1963) and then earned his master of fine
arts at the Writers Workshop, the University
of Iowa. He has taught at the University of
Illinois, California State University, and
Reed College and is now a professor of
English at Brown University.

Harper's poetry derives as much from
the tradition of black music as from litera-
ture. In describing his first book, *Dear John,
Dear Coltrane* (1970), he said that the
poems are "rhythmic, rather than metric,
the pulse is jazz, the tradition generally oral."

"Poetry is to be spoken or sung." Influenced
by the work of jazz musicians like Billie
Holiday, Charlie Parker, and John Coltrane,
he attempts poetic improvisations that stress
color and mood and use the idiom of black
speech.

His deep interest in the history of black
America as it is chronicled in individual
lives is clear from the title of his second
book, *History Is Your Own Heartbeat* (1971).
Harper's poetry is an eloquent testament to
his cultural tradition, an effort to bring life
to the damaged history of black America.

For Bud[1]

Could it be, Bud
that in slow galvanized
fingers beauty seeped
into *bop* like Bird[2]
weed and Diz[3] clowned —
Sugar waltzing
back into dynamite,
sweetest left hook you

---

[1] **Bud** Bud Powell (1924–1966), pianist and
composer, one of a small group, including
Charlie Parker and Dizzy Gillespie, who created
the jazz movement known as bebop

[2] **Bird** Charlie Parker (1920–1955), saxophone
player and composer

[3] **Diz** Dizzy Gillespie (b. 1917), trumpet player
and composer

10 ever dug, baby;
could it violate violence
Bud, like Leadbelly's[3]
chaingang chuckle,
the candied yam
twelve string clutch
of all blues:
there's no rain
anywhere, soft
enough for you.

1970

[3] **Leadbelly** Huddie Ledbetter (1888–1949),
famous black singer whose songs were often
about his experiences of imprisonment

Reuben, Reuben[1]

I reach from pain
to music great enough
to bring me back,
swollenhead, madness,
lovefruit, a pickle of hate
so sour my mouth twicked
up and would not sing;
there's nothing in the beat
to hold it in
10 melody and turn human skin;
a brown berry gone
to rot just two days on the branch;
we've lost a son,
the music, *jazz*, comes in.

1970

[1] Michael Harper's son, Reuben Masai Harper

Makin' Jump Shots

He waltzes into the lane
'cross the free-throw line,
fakes a drive, pivots,
floats from the asphalt turf
in an arc of black light,
and sinks two into the chains.

One on one he fakes
down the main, passes
into the free lane
and hits the chains.

A sniff in the fallen air—
he stuffs it through the chains
riding high:
"travelling" someone calls—
and he laughs, stepping
to a silent beat, gliding
as he sinks two into the chains.

1973

MARGARET ATWOOD
b. 1939

Born in Ottawa, Margaret Atwood grew up in Toronto. Her father was an entomologist who specialized in forest insects, and she spent much time as a child in the bush country of northern Ontario and Quebec, which provides images for much of her poetry and fiction. She earned a B.A. degree from the University of Toronto in 1961 and her M.A. from Radcliffe College in 1962. For a time she taught in Canadian universities and was a senior editor at the House of Anansi in Toronto. She has also written six novels, which have earned her an international reputation.

Like many other modern poets, Atwood has experimented frequently with the poetic sequence. "Disembarking at Quebec" is the introductory poem to *The Journals of Susanna Moodie*, a sequence of poems based on the life of an English gentlewoman who emigrated in 1832 to Upper Canada (now Ontario). Moodie provides Atwood with a Canadian archetype that enables her to explore the moral and psychological problems of colonialism. With perceptive irony she records the pathetically incongruous conjunction of a Victorian sensibility and its world of porcelain civility with a mysteriously impersonal and hostile wildnerness that makes no accommodation to the human. Atwood is also deeply interested in the "power politics" of sexual relationships. Like Adrienne Rich, she understands that the myths of romantic love often mask a politics of domination of the female, to the point that even language is compromised. In her recent poetry, she has extended her analysis of power to the arena of world politics. In her poem "Torture," based on the grotesque anecdotes that surface in the reports of organizations like Amnesty International, she explores the sadistic phenomenon of political repression, its imagination for violence caught brilliantly in the image of a female face carved to a "mute symbol."

Disembarking at Quebec[1]

Is it my clothes, my way of walking,
the things I carry in my hand
—a book, a bag with knitting—
the incongruous pink of my shawl

[1] introductory poem to *The Journals of Susanna Moodie*, monologues written in the persona of Moodie (1805–1885), English immigrant who wrote *Roughing It in the Bush*, an account of pioneering in Canada

this space cannot hear

or is it my own lack
of conviction which makes
these vistas of desolation,
long hills, the swamps, the barren sand, the glare
10   of sun on the bone-white
driftlogs, omens of winter,
the moon alien in day-
time a thin refusal

The others leap, shout

Freedom!

The moving water will not show me
my reflection.

The rocks ignore.

I am a word
20   in a foreign language.

1970

Torture

What goes on in the pauses
of this conversation?
Which is about free will
and politics and the need for passion.

Just this: I think of the woman
they did not kill.
Instead they sewed her face
shut, closed her mouth
to a hole the size of a straw,
10   and put her back on the streets,
a mute symbol.

It doesn't matter where
this was done or why or whether
by one side or the other;
such things are done as soon
as there are sides

and I don't know if good men
living crisp lives exist
because of this woman or in spite
20 of her.
       But power
like this is not abstract, it's not concerned
with politics and free will, it's beyond slogans

and as for passion, this
is its intricate denial,
the knife that cuts lovers
out of your flesh like tumours,
leaving you breastless
and without a name,
30 flattened, bloodless, even your voice
cauterized by too much pain,

a flayed body untangled
string by string and hung
to the wall, an agonized banner
displayed for the same reason
flags are.

                       1981

Earth

It isn't winter that brings it
out, my cowardice,
but the thickening summer I wallow in
right now, stinking of lilacs, green
with worms & stamens duplicating themselves
each one the same

I squat among rows of seeds & imposters
and snout my hand into the juicy dirt:
charred chicken bones, rusted nails,
10 dogbones, stones, stove ashes.
Down there is another hand, yours, hopeless,
down there is a future

in which you're a white white picture
with a name I forgot to write
underneath, and no date,

in which you're a suit
hanging with its stubs of sleeves
in a cupboard in a house
in a city I've never entered,

20   a missed beat in space
     which nevertheless unrolls itself
     as usual. As usual:
     that's why I don't want to go on with this.

     (I'll want to make a hole in the earth
     the size of an implosion, a leaf, a dwarf
     star, a cave
     in time that opens back & back into
     absolute darkness and at last
     into a small pale moon of light
30   the size of a hand,
     I'll want to call you out of the grave
     in the form of anything at all)

                        1981

SEAMUS HEANEY
b. 1939

Born to a Catholic family in Northern Ireland, Heaney received his B.A. from Queen's University, Belfast, in 1961. He has taught widely in secondary schools and universities since then.

With his first book, *Death of a Naturalist*, Heaney began his work of revealing life in rural Ireland as he experienced it in his boyhood. Steeped in Irish lore and history, he equates language with the rich loam of the Irish bog that continually renews itself, and his poetry is noted for its inventive language and sharp, immediate physical imagery. While he has written often of poetry itself, he is also concerned with the poet's political role; the poet is both helpless witness and accomplice in the fratricidal battles of his country. A Catholic caught in the sectarian violence of his native Belfast, he understands the trap of history.

"Casualty" is an elegy to a friend killed in a bomb blast, and the casual victim of Ireland's sectarian violence. Heaney captures the fisherman for the reader in a few carefully chosen anecdotal details: his gestures ordering a stout in a pub, their conversations about poetry. His death is set against the terrible incident of "Bloody Sunday," January 30, 1972: thirteen men died when British paratroopers fired on Catholic demonstrators. The reader is reminded of W.B. Yeats's poem "Easter, 1916," as if this incident repeated the earlier tragedy Yeats was describing. Heaney is equally moved and repelled by the spectacle of a people united by tragic and possibly futile martyrdom. All the poet can do is hold to his bewilderment and the pain of his loss as he describes his friend the morning of his death in his "proper haunt," the open sea, working with the skill and patience of his trade. The bombed-out pub and the imagined face of his friend before the blast—remorseful and terrified—are set against this moment of communion when "I tasted freedom with him." "Casualty," with its carefully controlled rhyme scheme, is a superb elegy, giving human dignity by the power of its art to the memory of a man so brutally and uselessly murdered.

But Heaney is also a master of gentler moments, as in "The Skunk," a whimsical love poem to his wife. That her presence could be so lovingly conjured by this nocturnal visitor is a testament to his skill. He is one of contemporary Ireland's most versatile poets.

Casualty

I

He would drink by himself
And raise a weathered thumb
Towards the high shelf,
Calling another rum
And blackcurrant, without
Having to raise his voice,
Or order a quick stout
By a lifting of the eyes
And a discreet dumb-show
10   Of pulling off the top;
At closing time would go
In waders and peaked cap
Into the showery dark,
A dole-kept breadwinner
But a natural for work.
I loved his whole manner,
Sure-footed but too sly,
His deadpan sidling tact,
His fisherman's quick eye
20   And turned observant back.

Incomprehensible
To him, my other life.
Sometimes, on his high stool,
Too busy with his knife
At a tobacco plug
And not meeting my eye,
In the pause after a slug
He mentioned poetry.
We would be on our own
30   And, always politic
And shy of condescension,
I would manage by some trick
To switch the talk to eels
Or lore of the horse and cart
Or the Provisionals.[1]

But my tentative art
His turned back watches too:
He was blown to bits
Out drinking in a curfew
40   Others obeyed, three nights
After they shot dead
The thirteen men in Derry.[2]

[1] **Provisionals**   the Provisional Irish Republican
Army (IRA)
[2] ll. 41–42   On Sunday, January 30, 1972, British
paratroopers opened fire on Catholics demon-
strating in Derry; thirteen demonstrators were
killed.

PARAS THIRTEEN, the walls said,
BOGSIDE NIL. That Wednesday[3]
Everybody held
His breath and trembled.

           II
It was a day of cold
Raw silence, wind-blown
Surplice and soutane:
50   Rained-on, flower-laden
Coffin after coffin
Seemed to float from the door
Of the packed cathedral
Like blossoms on slow water.
The common funeral
Unrolled its swaddling band,
Lapping, tightening
Till we were braced and bound
Like brothers in a ring.

60   But he would not be held
At home by his own crowd
Whatever threats were phoned,
Whatever black flags waved.
I see him as he turned
In that bombed offending place.
Remorse fused with terror
In his still knowable face,
His cornered outfaced stare
Blinding in the flash.

70   He had gone miles away
For he drank like a fish
Nightly, naturally
Swimming towards the lure
Of warm lit-up places,
The blurred mesh and murmur
Drifting among glasses
In the gregarious smoke.
How culpable was he
That last night when he broke
80   Our tribe's complicity?
"Now you're supposed to be
An educated man,"
I hear him say. "Puzzle me
The right answer to that one."

---

[3] ll. 43–44   the death toll listed like a football
score: British paramilitary 13; the Bogside, a
poor Catholic district of Derry, 0

III

I missed his funeral,
Those quiet walkers
And sideways talkers
Shoaling out of his lane
To the respectable
90   Purring of the hearse . . .
They move in equal pace
With the habitual
Slow consolation
Of a dawdling engine,
The line lifted, hand
Over fist, cold sunshine
On the water, the land
Banked under fog: that morning
I was taken in his boat,
100   The screw purling, turning
Indolent fathoms white,
I tasted freedom with him.
To get out early, haul
Steadily off the bottom,
Dispraise the catch, and smile
As you find a rhythm
Working you, slow mile by mile,
Into your proper haunt
Somewhere, well out, beyond . . .

110   Dawn-sniffing revenant,
Plodder through midnight rain,
Question me again.

1979

The Skunk

Up, black, striped and damasked like the chasuble
At a funeral mass, the skunk's tail
Paraded the skunk. Night after night
I expected her like a visitor.

The refrigerator whinnied into silence.
My desk light softened beyond the verandah.
Small oranges loomed in the orange tree.
I began to be tense as a voyeur.

After eleven years I was composing
10   Love-letters again, broaching the word "wife"
Like a stored cask, as if its slender vowel
Had mutated into the night earth and air

Of California. The beautiful, useless
Tang of eucalyptus spelt your absence.
The aftermath of a mouthful of wine
Was like inhaling you off a cold pillow.

And there she was, the intent and glamorous,
Ordinary, mysterious skunk,
Mythologized, demythologized,
20   Snuffing the boards five feet beyond me.

It all came back to me last night, stirred
By the sootfall of your things at bedtime,
Your head-down, tail-up hunt in a bottom drawer
For the black plunge-line nightdress.

1979

A Bat on the Road

*A batlike soul waking to consciousness of itself in
darkness and secrecy and loneliness.*

You would hoist an old hat on the tines of a fork
and trawl the mouth of the bridge for the slight
bat-thump and flutter. Skinny downy webs,

babynails clawing the sweatband . . . But don't
bring it down, don't break its flight again,
don't deny it; this time let it go free.

Follow its bat-flap under the stone bridge,
under the Midland and Scottish Railway
and lose it there in the dark.

10   Next thing it shadows moonslicked laurels
or skims the lapped net on a tennis court.
Next thing it's ahead of you in the road.

What are you after? You keep swerving off,
flying blind over ashpits and netting wire;
invited by the brush of a word like *peignoir*,

rustles and glimpses, shot silk, the stealth of floods
So close to me I could hear her breathing
and there by the lighted window behind trees

it hangs in creepers matting the brickwork
20   and now it's a wet leaf blowing in the drive,
now soft-deckled, shadow-convolvulus

by the White Gates. Who would have thought it? At the White Gates
She let them do whatever they liked. Cling there
as long as you want. There is nothing to hide.

1984

Versification

INTRODUCTION

Poetry differs most obviously from prose by being measured out in lines. It resembles all other speech and writing in that its words are arranged in syntactical units—phrases, clauses, sentences, and even paragraphs. In fact, given the great rhythmic variety of poetry as well as the absence of rhyme in many poems, division into lines (lineation) is the simplest, most direct signal—to the eye and, more important, to the ear—that a piece of writing purports to be a poem.

The first of the three sections of this essay, "Poetic Rhythm," thus begins by discussing how the poetic line disciplines and affects the sound of spoken language. Once we understand this connection, we can appreciate the force of meter and rhythm in the shaping of poems. The various meters are discussed next: iambic, trochaic, triple, stress, and syllabic. The section closes with a discussion of free verse and of other key aspects of rhythm, in particular the poet's handling of syllables and pause.

The second section, "Rhyme, Stanza, and the Poem As a Whole," treats the nature of rhyme, rhymed poems not arranged in stanzas, and some of the more familiar stanzas that have been used in the myriad kinds of poems and songs our tradition provides. The section also provides a selected glossary of types of poems—narrative poems, odes, sonnets, villanelles, and so forth.

Section III comprises a metrical supplement, the purpose of which is to delve farther into the nature of meter, to suggest possible ways of marking meter—especially that of metrically puzzling lines—and to provide substantial assistance with special topics such as medieval meters, stress verse, and sprung rhythm. A short bibliography closes the essay.

The index on p. 1180 lists all the terms defined in the essay.

I. POETIC RHYTHM

The Poetic Line

Poetic **rhythm** as used in this essay refers only to sound patterns, not to the patterning of ideas or images or some other aspect of poetic meaning. It is very much what Ezra Pound meant by **prosody**: "The articulation of the total sound of a poem (not bits of certain shapes gummed together)." Prosody, in Pound's usage, refers to the technique of versification; more usually, prosody refers to the study of versification, and of metrical structure in particular, and prosodists are those engaged in such study. Rhythm differs from **meter** in that it takes all aspects of the poem's stream of sound into account, whereas meter refers only to a pronounced and *measurable* rhythmic pulse (to "meter" is to measure). Before turning to meter, let's examine briefly the effect of the line on spoken language.

When we read poetry aloud, we adapt the stream of sound—with varying degrees of skill, depending on our sensitivity and experience—to take line-breaks (**lineation**) into account. First, we speak more resonantly and slowly, taking care that we not shortchange any word or pause—including the pause signaled by the end of the line. Second, because these particular words have been grouped together in a line, to some extent irrespective of syntax, we tend to adjust them to each other within what we see as a patterned unit, setting up a hierarchy of relative importance. Thus, we change the pitch, intensity, and duration of syllables to give certain words greater or lesser emphasis than they would receive if the passage were in prose.

Third, each line-break provides an opportunity for emphasis unavailable in prose, and the word occupying the final position can carry a degree of importance equivalent to the last word in a sentence or other important grammatical unit. (One immediately sees the kind of counterpoint or tension a poet can set up between line-endings and sentence endings.) Further, line length and position can be manipulated freely, or the poet can leave extra space between words in a line to provide visual clues to pause and emphasis. And fourth, because the human mind loves uncovering patterns, we look for words that echo each other —through rhyme, alliteration, consonance, assonance—and perhaps give them extra stress. Or we may give extra weight to a pause or pauses that divide a line symmetrically. Or, most important, we may discover that we are dealing with a line that exhibits the high degree of rhythmical regularity we call meter.

Meter

Lineation in itself is not enough to make a poem; a piece must have the kind of rhythm we recognize as poetic, or it will come perilously close to chopped-up prose, no matter how striking its imagery, vocabulary, thought, or emotion. Among the literary arts, meter belongs uniquely to poetry. At the same time, of course, poetry can be rhythmical without regular meter. Thus "free" verse, which would have struck most readers of an earlier era as too much like prose, sounds quite rhythmical enough to twentieth-century ears.

For example, a modern reader who gave proper attention to each separate line in the following nonmetrical passage (which I have adapted from a famous poem), with normal speech-emphasis on the syllables marked with the stress symbol "+s," would probably hear in it a fairly satisfying rhythm:

> +s +s +s
> So let's melt without noise,
> +s +s +s
> Not moved by floods of tears or sigh-tempests,
> +s +s
> Our joys would be profaned
> +s +s +s
> If we told our love to the laity.

Traditionally, however, poets have turned to greater rhythmic regularity than the foregoing to obtain satisfying effects, and John Donne actually wrote:

> x / x / x / x /
> So let us melt, and make no noise,
> x / x \ x / x /
> No tear-floods, nor sigh-tempests move;
> x \ x / x \ x /
> 'Twere profanation of our joys
> x / x /x\ x /
> To tell the laity our love.

In this scansion of four lines from Donne's "A Valediction: Forbidding Mourning," the slant lines mark metrical accents or beats, with "x" used for unaccented syllables. (**Scansion** is the use of visual symbols to mark meter.) The ordinary slant line—/—is used when the accent is a stressed syllable; the backwards slant line— \ —is used when the accent is an unstressed syllable that can be "promoted" to an accent to fulfill the metrical pattern. (In this essay the term *accent* is reserved for metrical emphasis, and *stress* for linguistic emphasis. Accents are usually, but not always, stressed words or syllables.)

If you compare the two passages for a moment, it is obvious that Donne's lines sound much more like traditional poetry than does my modified version. Of course, they rhyme — and in the seventeenth century the pronunciation of "love" and "move" was still variable enough to yield a much closer if not exact rhyme than it does today. (In the twentieth century, "love" and "move" are an example of "eye" rhyme rather than of exact or perfect rhyme.) Far more important, however, is the lines' rhythmical regularity, considerably greater than that of ordinary speech or prose. Donne's lines are highly metrical; in fact, he is using one of the most popular stanza patterns in English poetry, a four-beat rhyming quatrain.

Each of the four lines has the same number of accents, based mainly on the regular alternation between weaker and stronger (unstressed and stressed) syllables. This regular alternation is obvious in the first line, "SO LET US MELT and MAKE NO NOISE," but not quite as obvious in the other lines. At first glance the compound words in the second line seem to present some difficulties; however, if we follow the normal stress patterns of spoken English—as we must do in assigning metrical accent—we find that "TEAR-floods" and "sigh-TEM-pests" fit the meter perfectly.

With few exceptions meter enhances, rather than overrides, ordinary speech stress. Thus, in the third line, "profanation" has one main stress: on the third syllable. But its first syllable carries a secondary stress, and, if the meter has led us to expect it, this syllable can easily be promoted to the status of an accent. Similarly, "laity" in the fourth line has a secondary stress on its last syllable. In determining the position of accents in a line, we take into account **relative stress**. That is, if a syllable is somewhat stronger than the ones surrounding it, it can be promoted; if it is weaker, it can be demoted.

This leaves only two other accents in Donne's stanza unaccounted for metrically: "nor" in the second line and "of" in the third, neither appreciably stronger than its adjacent syllables. However, once a regular rhythmic swing has been set up, we are very ready to feel a continuing beat, so that, as in these two cases, we tend to promote the second of three unstressed syllables to an accent.

(See "Promotion and Demotion," p. 1163, in the metrical supplement, for the conditions under which unstressed syllables are promoted and stressed ones demoted.)

ACCENTUAL-SYLLABIC VERSE AND FOOT SCANSION

The four lines from Donne's poem, then, have a very regular pattern. Each has eight syllables and four accents, with the accents positioned on the second, fourth, sixth, and eighth syllables. Like the bulk of poetry in English, Donne's poem is **accentual-syllabic** verse (also called **syllable-stress** verse). In accentual-syllabic verse, both the number of syllables and the number of accents in each line are fixed, and the syllables with heaviest emphasis in normal speech alternate in regular patterns with lighter syllables. This is the general principle, although, as we have seen, unstressed syllables can be promoted to accents (and stressed ones demoted). Also, there are exceptions to the strict alternation of stressed and unstressed, and in special circumstances the number of syllables will vary slightly. Neither accentual-syllabic verse nor any other kind operates with absolutely mechanical regularity.

Nonetheless, the relatively high degree of regularity in number and position of stresses in accentual-syllabic verse has led to a descriptive terminology that, despite its drawbacks, is still the most familiar: "foot" or "classical" scansion. Thus, although the metrical supplement depends on the generally more helpful beat-offbeat method of scansion, one still needs to know the following terminology and basic tenets of foot scansion.

Foot scansion has to do with basic units of combined unaccented and accented syllables, called "feet." A description of accentual-syllabic meter includes two terms, one to describe the *number* of feet, the other the *kind* of foot, in a line. According to the number of feet, lines are described as monometer (one foot), dimeter (two feet), trimeter (three feet), tetrameter (four feet), pentameter (five feet), hexameter (six feet), heptameter (seven feet), or octameter (eight feet).

Each foot generally has one stressed syllable, with unstressed syllables varying in number and position. The term *rising* rhythm is used to refer to a foot in which the weak syllables precede the strong; in *falling* rhythm the strong syllable comes first. The most common foot by far is the **iamb** (x/), an unaccented syllable (x) followed by an accented one (/). Next in frequency is the **trochee** (/x), an accented syllable followed by an unaccented one.

Both the iamb and the trochee are *duple* feet, because there are only two syllables in each foot. An iambic poem is in duple rising rhythm; a trochaic, in duple falling rhythm. The equivalent *triple* feet, with three syllables, are the **anapest** (xx/), in triple rising rhythm, and the **dactyl** (/xx), in triple falling rhythm. Poems exclusively in triple meter are quite rare; more usually, a poem with a triple-meter flavor has some duple feet mixed in with the triple ones.

The iamb, trochee, anapest, and dactyl are the only feet recognized by some metrists. However, others admit a foot with no stress, the **pyrrhic** (xx), and its complement with two stresses, the **spondee** (//). Others also find additional three-syllable feet and even some four-syllable feet useful; e.g., the amphibrach (x/x), the cretic (/x/), the ionic *a majore* (//xx), and ionic *a minore* (xx//), and first, second, third, and fourth paeons (/xxx, x/xx, xx/x, and xxx/).

In the following examples a vertical line (|) above the text shows foot boundaries, and a slant line (/) between words shows line-breaks.

Examples of iambic meters

Yeats's poem "Memory" (p. 771) is in **iambic trimeter**: "And two or three had charm."

Donne's "A Valediction: Forbidding Mourning" (p. 230) is in **iambic tetrameter**: "So let us melt, and make no noise." Wordsworth's sonnet "Composed upon Westminster Bridge" (pp. 517 and 1163) is in **iambic pentameter**: "The beauty of the morning; silent, bare." This is the meter used by Shakespeare in his sonnets and plays (pp. 195–201 and 203–05), by Pope in the heroic couplets of *The Rape of the Lock* (p. 373), by Milton in the blank verse of *Paradise Lost* (p. 283), and extensively by Keats in his odes (pp. 617–24); it is, in fact, the most famous English meter.

The other iambic meters are far less frequent than these three-beat, four-beat, and five-beat lines. **Iambic monometer** and **iambic dimeter** crop up as one-beat and two-beat variations in songs. Donne's "Go and Catch a Falling Star" (p. 222) has two rhyming iambic monometer lines in each stanza, e.g.: "And find / What wind." Dryden's metrically varied "Secular Masque" (p. 358) provides iambic dimeter examples: "I faint, I lag."

Sidney's "Loving in truth" (Sonnet I, p. 141) and Auden's "So an age ended" (*Sonnets from China* X, p. 970) are unusual sonnets, in that they are **iambic hexameter** rather than iambic pentameter. (Auden's sonnet is less regular than Sidney's.) Spenser closes each stanza of *The Faerie Queene* (pp. 166–75) with an iambic hexameter line: "And unto Venus' grace the gate doth open right." These six-beat lines, also known as **alexandrines**, are sometimes used as variations in poems in heroic (iambic pentameter) couplets (see

p. 1152)—not always successfully, as Pope points out wittily in his *Essay on Criticism*:

x / |x   / |x   / | x / | x

"A needless Alexandrine ends the Song, / That like a wounded Snake, drags its slow

/ |x /   x / | x   / | x

length along" (ll.356–57). But Pope can write exquisite ones: "Flies o'er th' unbending

/ | x   / |x / | x   /

Corn, and skims along the Main" (l. 373).

Many of the lines in Blake's "Holy Thursday" (p. 488) are strict **iambic heptameter**:

x   / | x /|x / | x   / |x / | x \ | x   /

"Then cherish pity, lest you drive an angel from your door." In practice, the two long lines
—**iambic heptameter** and **iambic octameter**—are fairly rare, since a seven-beat line
tends to divide into four-beat and three-beat lines and an eight-beat one into two four-beat
ones. Blake's poem shows this tendency, as does Sidney's "What Length of Verse?"
(p. 139), which alternates hexameter and heptameter lines (I have added space at the
natural breaking point):

x   / | x / | x / | x   / | x / |x /

What length of verse can serve   brave Mopsa's good to show

x   /| x   / | x / |x / | x / | x   / | x /

Whose virtues strange, and beauties such,   as no man them may know?

(Probably the only familiar example of **octameter** is a trochaic one, Poe's "The Raven"

/ x| / x| / x | / x| / x|/ x | /   x | / x

—e.g., "Once upon a midnight dreary, while I pondered, weak and weary." Although
the meter of "The Raven" is trochaic octameter, such internal rhymes as "*dreary/weary*"
in many of the lines effectively divide them into trochaic tetrameter lines.)

See also the metrical supplement, pp. 1161–66.

Examples of trochaic and triple meters

Metrical poems in noniambic meters are rare enough to provide a special pleasure, simply
by virtue of their unusual meter. The earliest example of strict trochaic verse in the
anthology is Sidney's "Eleventh Song": "Who is it that this dark night" (p. 147). Sidney,
who firmly ensconced trochaic verse in the English tradition, mixes two kinds of **trochaic
tetrameter** lines:

/ x| /   x| / x | /

Who is it that this dark night

\ x| /   x| / x | / x

Underneath my window plaineth?

Both lines are in falling rhythm and have four accents. However, the first line has only
seven syllables, because the last unstressed syllable is missing. It ends, then, the way
iambic lines generally do: with a stressed syllable. Such an ending is called **masculine**.
The second line, which ends with an unstressed syllable, has a **feminine ending**. Trochaic
lines with a masculine ending are "truncated" or "catalectic." Thus many of the lines in

/ x| / x| /   x |

Blake's "The Tyger" (p. 490) are trochaic tetrameter catalectic—"Tyger Tyger, burning

/   / x |/   x| / x|

bright"—as are many in Milton's "L'Allegro" (p. 266): "Meadows trim with daisies

/

pied." In contrast, Shelley's *Prometheus Unbound* (p. 578) retains the feminine endings:

/ x| /   x |/ x | / x

"Life of Life! thy lips enkindle." (Because the feminine ending in trochaic verse is so
much rarer than the masculine, it is sometimes—confusingly—termed "acatalectic"; i.e.,
"not catalectic.")

Trochees are also frequently substituted for iambs in an otherwise iambic poem—particularly in the first foot of a line or after a strong internal pause, as in lines 88 and 91 of
Book IV of *Paradise Lost* (p. 284): "Under what torments inwardly I groan" and "The

/ x |

|/ x |

lower still I fall, only supreme."

See also the metrical supplement, pp. 1166–67.

The **triple verse** forms are rarely strict, since duple feet are frequently substituted for at least one of the line's triple feet. An example is the first foot of this **anapestic tetrameter**

                        x / | x x   / |x x

line from Blake's "The Chimney Sweeper" (p. 486): "And got with our bags & our

/ | x x /

brushes to work." Hardy alternates strict **dactylic tetrameter** lines (with a double feminine ending) and dactylic tetrameter catalectic ones (with a masculine ending) in "The Voice"

    /   x x | /   x   x | / x x | / x x   /   x x | /   x x|

(p. 760): "Woman much missed, how you call to me, call to me, / Saying that now you are

/ x x   /

not as you were." Because triple verse forms use even dactyls and anapests interchangeably, it is not always clear whether to call a poem in triple meter "anapestic" or "dactylic." Nor is the borderline between a poem in duple meter and one in triple meter always technically distinct, because an iambic poem can tolerate some anapestic feet, and a trochaic poem can tolerate some dactylic ones.

See the metrical supplement, pp. 1168–70, for suggestions on how to deal with the anomalies of triple verse.

THE OTHER METERS

Accentual-syllabic verse has dominated poetry in English since the sixteenth century. However, the two ways of counting that form the basis of accentual-syllabic meter—by accent and by syllable—have maintained separate and independent traditions.

Stress verse

In accentual or **stress verse**, only the number of accents in each line is fixed. (To be consistent in our distinction between metrical *accent* and linguistic *stress*, we should no doubt select the name "accentual" verse over "stress" verse, but the latter is more graceful.) Accents may be separated by one or more unaccented syllables or even juxtaposed. The best analogy is with music, in which the same amount of time can be filled by a long note, two shorter notes, or some combination of notes and rests. (A pause, in poetry, is equivalent to a musical rest.) So long as musical and metrical accents come at what we perceive as fairly regular time intervals, what happens in between is highly flexible. It is obvious why stress verse lends itself to songs of all kinds—religious and secular lyrics, ballads, nursery rhymes, lullabies, and so forth.

The first half of each stanza of Blake's "Mad Song" (p. 483) is made up of four **two-stress** lines; the second half, of three three-stress lines and a closing two-stress line. Note the variable number of syllables and placement of accents of the opening lines:

               x   /   x   /
            The wild winds weep,
            x x   /   x x /
            And the night is a-cold;
            x   /   x   /
            Come hither, Sleep,
            x   x /   x /
            And my griefs infold

Yeats's "Easter, 1916" (p. 771) is a splendid showcase for the gamut of possibilities of **three-stress** verse. The first sixteen lines, rather colloquially reminiscent for the most part, have from six to nine syllables, and the placement of accents is varied—including

$$x \quad x / \quad x / \quad / \quad / \quad x \quad x$$

juxtaposed stresses (e.g. "All changed, changed utterly"). When the poem breaks into a more heightened mode of reminiscence, however, much of the tonal contrast is conveyed by the sudden regularity of the iambic trimeter lines. Throughout, the poem's aural and rhythmic textures reinforce and help create the shifting flow of thought, feeling, and awareness that constitutes the poem's "meaning."

The most venerable of the stress meters—and indeed the most venerable meter in English—is the **four-stress** line, which in its alliterative form dates from Anglo-Saxon times. (See the sections on Old English and Medieval alliterative verse in the metrical supplement, pp. 1174–76.) "Ubi Sunt?" (p. 37) mixes four-stress and three-stress lines in the stanza-form known as rime couée (see "six-line stanza," p. 1155). A few of the opening four-stress lines of the stanzas show again the flexibility in placement of accent and number of syllables:

$$/ \quad x \quad / \quad x/ \ x \quad x \quad / \ x$$
Where beeth they biforen us weren . . . .
$$/ \ x \quad x \quad / \quad x \quad x \quad / \ x \quad x \quad /$$
Eten and drunken and maden hem glad . . .
$$x \quad / \ x \ \backslash \quad x \ / \quad x \quad /$$
Here paradis hy nomen here . . .
$$/ \quad x \quad / \quad x \ / \ x \quad /$$
If that feend, that foule thing

For a fine contemporary example of four-stress verse, see Bishop's "Sestina" (p. 1000), in which the lines range from seven to twelve syllables.

See also the metrical supplement, pp. 1171–77.

Syllabic verse

In accentual-syllabic verse, of course, the number of syllables is set; but poems exist in **syllabic verse** in which only the number of syllables in each line is determined, and the number and position of stresses vary. The purest syllabic poems thus lack the regular beat we find in accentual-syllabic and stress verse, so that their rhythms approach more closely those of normal speech. (The line-breaks, as always, modify the rhythms of normal speech.)

The sixteenth-century poet Wyatt, for example, frequently wrote in iambic pentameter; but some of his lines read better as decasyllables (lines with ten syllables). His rhythms in "The Long Love That in My Thought" (p. 130), while heightened, are interestingly closer to normal speech than his contemporary Surrey's strict iambic pentameter translation of the same sonnet by Petrarch, "Love That Doth Reign" (p. 133). Although Surrey allows trochaic substitutions at the beginning of his lines, any flexibility that this variation provides is more than offset by his rigid observance of a strong accent on the fourth syllable. It is always a monosyllable and is frequently followed by a pause. (In this, Surrey is following one of the conventions of French decasyllabic verse.)

Wyatt's rhythms, in contrast, are freer and actually closer to those of the original Italian (p. 130). (Petrarch's poem uses 11-syllable—**hendecasyllabic**—lines, which sometimes look longer; however, adjacent vowels in different syllables are joined together in a process known as elision—see the metrical supplement, pp. 1165–66—to make one syllable.)

```
        x  /    /      x  \ x    /      x    /  x
    The long love that in my thought doth harbour
        x  \  x   /   x    /    x  / x \
    And in mine heart doth keep his residence
    /  x  x /    /  x    x    /      x /
    Into my face presseth with bold pretence
        x  /  x  /   x       /   x  x  /   x
    And therein campeth, spreading his banner.
```

Syllabic poems need not, of course, have lines all the same length; for example, they might alternate nine-syllable and eleven-syllable lines. Or, if they are divided into stanzas, the first stanza provides the pattern of line lengths to be followed in subsequent stanzas. Marianne Moore has pressed the prose–rhythm aspect of syllabic verse so far that, were her stanzas unrhymed, it would be hard to distinguish her verse from speech or the freer forms of free verse. For a discussion of her syllabic verse, and Auden's, see the metrical supplement, pp. 1176–77.

Free Verse

In modern times, both the number of stresses and the number of syllables in the line have been allowed to vary, leading to the aptly named **nonmetrical** or **free verse**. Like poems in free verse, poems in accentual-syllabic and stress meters frequently have several different line lengths, but these are generally gathered into rhymed stanzas that repeat the same pattern throughout the poem. Free-verse poems, in contrast, commonly have very irregular or intermittent rhyme patterns—if indeed rhyme is structurally present—and such great flexibility in stanza length that the term *verse unit* is perhaps more appropriate than *stanza*. A quick look at the latter pages of the anthology reveals numerous examples of free-verse poems mixed in with more traditional ones.

(If the line too is discarded—either entirely or lengthened to include a number of independent syntactic units—but the rhythm still seems more heightened and the language more charged than that of ordinary prose, we have moved into the realm of **prose poetry**. See the selections from Jones's *In Parenthesis* [p. 923] and Hill's *Mercian Hymns* [p. 1116]. At this point, of course, poetry touches certain highly rhythmical works of prose fiction, and short, self-contained passages from a novel like James Joyce's *Ulysses* may be essentially indistinguishable from prose poetry.)

Free verse is most simply defined as verse that is on the one hand not confined by any metrical constraints and on the other hand free to use any metrical or nonmetrical resource available, but on an irregular basis. Because of its eclecticism, it can be very delicately attuned to the ebb and flow of thought and feeling. The only constraint in free verse is lineation, without which a literary work has essentially committed itself to prose—or to prose poetry.

We find numerous poems in free verse that use short lines to establish rhythmical units that to some extent balance each other, although the number of stresses and syllables in them differs. Or a longer line may be divided by a pause; or, as in the case of William Carlos Williams's later poetry (see pp. 842–46), actually broken into three separate units, with line endings and indentation indicating timing and emphasis.

All in all, modern and contemporary poets have exploited the possibilities of space and typography to give considerable visual guidance to the rhythms of their poems; see, for example, selections by Cummings, Eliot, Olson, Pound, and Williams.

At the same time, especially in a poem of considerable length, there may be substantial sections, or at least clusters of lines, that suggest a regular metrical norm. For example, the opening lines of Eliot's poetic sequence *The Waste Land* (p. 889) suggest a four-beat stress verse that bears a striking kinship to a poem written eight centuries earlier: the fragment from "Canute at Ely" (p. 18).

Even when such regular norms are not set up and the number of accents per line varies greatly, accents are generally separated by only one or two unaccented syllables, and so the lines have a comfortably familiar rhythm. The effect of lineation, in nonmetrical as well as metrical poems, is a rhythmic heightening of the language that leads us to perceive the possibility of accents at regular time intervals. That is, if the poem gives us any opportunity, we are eager to find a relatively regular alternation of accented and unaccented syllables, as in the first lines of Walt Whitman's "Song of Myself" (p. 687):

> x / x \ x / x / x /
> I celebrate myself, and sing myself,
> x   x / x /   /   x x /
> And what I assume you shall assume,
> x / xx / x x/ x x / x / x/   x /
> For every atom belonging to me as good belongs to you.

Here, as in metrical verse, a secondarily stressed syllable ("-brate") can be promoted to an accent if the rhythmic context is appropriate. With free verse, though, one should be extremely careful not to promote syllables unless the poem really suggests the possibility — as Whitman's does — or, for that matter, to demote them. In Williams's "The Dance" (p. 841), for example, the triple rhythm is so exuberantly pervasive that we can thump along happily in three- and four-beat triple verse—"rollicking measures" that are perfectly congruent with the poem's subject.

Pound's "In a Station of the Metro" demands different treatment, because this two-line poem does not encourage any easy duple or triple flow:

> x x x / x x   / / x x x   /
> The apparition of these faces in the crowd;
> / x x x /   /   /
> Petals on a wet, black bough.

One could, of course, go against the meaning and the relative weight of "these" and argue that it should not carry an accent. It would then be possible to set up an alternating pattern by promoting "ap-," "of," "in," and "on" (nowhere near as strong as the secondarily stressed "-brate" in the Whitman) and demoting "black"—a word far stronger than any of the syllables being promoted. (See the metrical supplement, p. 1163, on promoting the middle syllable in a run of three unstressed ones and demoting the middle syllable in a series of three stressed ones.) Such mishandling of the poem's flow of sound would seemingly be according to the rules, but any reading that tried to bring out this beat pattern would sound slow and mechanical, because the unstressed syllables are too short and weak to fill such a pattern without artificial lengthening. And it would be disastrous to the meaning.

If, however, we enhance, rather than go counter to, the linguistic rhythm, perhaps hurrying slightly over the run of three unaccented syllables and slowing slightly for the juxtaposed accents, we find how beautifully the rhythm complements the meaning. In the first line "these faces" stand out rhythmically as well as conceptually, and this special stressing relates them to the stressed words in the second line. Thus the sound of the poem alerts us to the correspondence between faces and fallen petals before we even begin to explore all the nuances of such a relationship, which goes far beyond the visual similarity of faces standing out of an undifferentiated mass and fallen petals against a dark bough. Rare beauty, fragility, and mortality are certainly involved, especially given the underground scene, the crowd, and the word "apparition," which suggest a Dantesque, hellish locale. This is complemented by the image of natural process in which the loveliest blossoms fall, beset by the elements (the bough is wet with rain) and time.

See also twentieth-century headnotes.

Other Aspects of Rhythm

To uncover the rhythm of Pound's "In a Station of the Metro," a high degree of attention to the relative weight and timing of syllables is necessary. In metrical verse this same attention should be paid; and pause, so important in nonmetrical verse, must also be taken into account. (So sensitive are some poets—Pound among them—to the quantities of syllables and the degrees of pause that some of their poems, metrical or nonmetrical, can have their rhythm indicated by musical notation.)

THE NATURE OF THE SYLLABLE

Although in reading poetry aloud we may slightly adjust the sound of the words to reflect our sense of the poem's basic meter, we are still dealing with syllables of a certain pitch, intensity, duration, difficulty of articulation, and vowel and consonant quality.

Quantity refers to the relative length of syllables. It was the main metrical component in ancient Greek poetry and played a prominent role as well in Latin poetry. (Some foot prosodists still use the classical symbols [- for long syllables and ⌣ for short] to indicate stressed and unstressed syllables.) In the classical languages, complex patterns of long and short syllables could be set up, but English syllable length is far too variable to provide a satisfactory basis for meter. Yet a poet with an excellent ear for English quantities—Sidney, for example—was able to write some fine quantitative poems. See his "Fortune, Nature, Love" (p. 140), in **elegiac distichs**. The elegiac distich joins classical hexameter and pentameter. Sidney uses a hexameter scanning $--|--|-\smile\smile|-\smile\smile|-\smile\smile|--$ and a pentameter scanning $--|-\smile\smile|-||-\smile\smile|-\smile\smile|-$. (Unlike the English pentameter, the classical one has two equal half-lines of 2½ feet each.)

However, most poems in English modeled on classical meters substitute stressed syllables for long ones and unstressed for short. At least, they make sure the two systems coincide—as they do with only a few exceptions in Campion's beautiful "Rose-cheeked Laura, Come" (p. 208).

Still, the ear readily perceives some syllables as taking more time to say than others. This is a matter not only of vowel length but of the number and kind of consonants in the syllable and the characteristics of adjacent syllables. Notice how much more quickly one says the first three syllables of "apparition" than the last three syllables of Pound's poem: "wet, black bough." The pause signaled by the comma slows these syllables, of course, but by themselves "wet," "black," and "bough" obviously take more time to say than "a," "pa," and "ri." By and large, a polysyllabic word will take a much shorter time to say than an equivalent number of monosyllabic words. The monosyllables are liable to be weightier (notice the longer vowels and more numerous consonants) and articulated more clearly. (We do not pronounce both "p's" in "apparition," whereas we would do so if they were in separate words; e.g., "don't rap pa on the knuckles.")

This is not a hard-and-fast rule, of course, because some polysyllabic words go by far more slowly, and some monosyllables far more quickly. All one can do is be attentive to the sound of the line, weighing the syllables and pauses properly while keeping the meter in mind. Take the following three pairs of lines, all in iambic pentameter, and notice how much slower the rhythm is in each of the second lines.

First, from Pope's *Essay on Criticism*:

> These Equal Syllables alone require,
> Tho' oft the Ear the open Vowels tire

second from Keats's ode "To Autumn" (p. 624):

> Or sinking as the light wind lives or dies;
> And full-grown lambs loud bleat from hilly bourn

and third, from Milton's *Paradise Lost* (p. 286—for the elision of "many a" see the metrical supplement, pp. 1169–70):

> Of Araby the Blest, with such delay
> Well pleased they slack their course, and many a league

Stress and length are not the only important sound qualities of the syllables in these selections; note also the repetition within the line of certain vowels and consonants. Pope humorously uses excessive **assonance** (the repetition of the same vowel sound) in his second line, and Keats sets up a pattern of short and long "i" sounds in his first line. Keats also uses **alliteration** (the repetition of the same initial consonant): "l" in both lines, "b" in the second.

"And full-grown lambs loud bleat from hilly bourn" also exhibits to a marked degree the technique that Kenneth Burke has named **colliteration**: the clustering of similar consonant sounds. Thus *b* not only alliterates in this passage but colliterates with *f* and *m*. (The full series of sounds phonetically related to *b* is *f, v, m, p, b*; another series—*n, d, t, th*—is also represented in the line, but more subtly.) Such repetitions, by calling particular attention to certain syllables, subtly alter the rhythm of a line. Rhyme (taken up in the next section) is the most powerful of such echoes and thus a potent means of controlling rhythm, especially when the rhyme words are close together—either within the same line or at the ends of adjacent lines, as in Pope's rhyming couplets. When rhyme calls such insistent attention to itself, the other words in the line are put in the somewhat subordinate position of leading up to the expected rhyme.

PAUSE

By chance, Milton's sound echoes are fairly subtle in the blank verse lines quoted above—see the "s" alliteration and "o" assonance, not to mention colliteration, in the preceding line, "Sabean odours from the spicy shore"—but his use of **pause** (also called **caesura**) and **enjambment** is absolutely typical. (**Blank verse** is unrhymed iambic pentameter, usually divided not into stanzas but into **verse paragraphs** signaled, as in prose, by indentation.)

The only metrical, as opposed to syntactical, pause in ordinary modern verse in English is the pause at the end of the line. (We are leaving aside the half-lines of medieval alliterative verse—see the metrical supplement, pp. 1174–76—and such special cases as lines broken by regular internal rhyme—see p. 1150.) This pause at the end of the line can be emphasized or deemphasized by the poet's manipulation of the ordinary rhythms of language. For example, when the end of the line coincides with the end of a sentence or clause or phrase, or with a mark of punctuation of any kind, the pause is emphasized. (The term **end-stopped** is sometimes used for lines that end with a punctuation mark—or would end with one if the line were punctuated normally.) When there is no such coincidence, the line is said to be **enjambed** or **run on**, and the pause is deemphasized.

Dependent as it is on meaning, pause is a matter of far more than silences of one length or another. It is bound up with phrasing and intonation, influencing the speed, emphasis, and pitch of surrounding words and phrases, whether it is indicated by punctuation (the prose meaning), metrically by the line break, or by some other visual device (indentations and extra spaces between words, for example).

Milton is famous for placing his strongest pauses within his blank verse lines rather than at their ends. (That is, this is where he chooses to end his important sentences, clauses, or phrases.) In the absence of regular rhyme, Milton's combination of enjambment and frequent caesuras effectively breaks down the pentameter component of iambic pentameter. Although the iambic swing continues, the individual lines lose some of their integrity, for Milton deals with a five-beat, ten-syllable unit only as one possibility among many. The result is some of the most rhythmically flexible and interesting metrical verse in the language.

Internal pauses determined by prose meaning can, of course, be regularized to provide rhythmically repetitive patterns. We have already noted (p. 1144) Surrey's eagerness to observe some degree of pause after the fourth syllable. Pope and other eighteenth-century writers of heroic couplets routinely expected at least one caesura near the middle of the line, thus to some extent countering a ten-syllable unit. Poets writing metrical or nonmetrical verse can draw on repetitive phrasing—and the pauses that set off such phrasing—to create highly regular rhythms. To some extent, Biblical poetry provides the model for such rhythms, especially when the line falls into two complementary units, but any kind of phrasal repetition can create strong rhythms. (See, for example, selections by Christopher Smart [p. 442], Dylan Thomas [p. 980], and Walt Whitman [p. 686].)

But for the most part, poets writing in English use internal pause irregularly as needed to reinforce meaning and to provide rhythmic variety, as in these lines from Shakespeare's Sonnet CXXIX (p. 200):

> Th' expense of spirit in a waste of shame
> Is lust in action; and till action, lust
> Is perjured, murd'rous, bloody, full of blame,
> Savage, extreme, rude, cruel, not to trust

Notice how strongly the enjambment of the first and second lines, the numerous pauses, and the weight of the syllables modify the meter. Compare the savage insistence of these lines to, for example, the gently mellifluous, rockingly regular opening of Shakespeare's Sonnet XVIII (p. 195), with its easy alternation of stressed and unstressed syllables, its lack of caesuras, and its dutifully end-stopped lines:

> Shall I compare thee to a summer's day?
> Thou art more lovely and more temperate.
> Rough winds do shake the darling buds of May,
> And summer's lease hath all too short a date.

When one realizes that both passages are in the same meter, iambic pentameter,[1] it becomes obvious how extraordinarily important to the poem's stream of sound are the nonmetrical aspects of rhythm.

---

[1] The meter is quite regular. The only foot reversal is "Savage" in line 4 of Sonnet CXXIX. In the same line "rude," the middle syllable in a series of three stressed syllables, can be "demoted" so that it does not carry a metrical accent. Several words, as the middle syllables in a run of three unstressed ones, can be promoted to accents: "in" in line 1 and "and" in line 2 of CXXIX; in Sonnet XVIII, "to" in line 1, "and" in line 2, and in the same line the secondarily stressed "-ate" can be promoted. For more on promotion and demotion, see the metrical supplement, p. 1163.

II. RHYME, STANZA, AND THE POEM AS A WHOLE

Rhyme

PERFECT MASCULINE END-RHYME

Rhyme, a wonderfully powerful device for pleasing the ear, shaping rhythm, and organizing poems, is second only to meter in the poet's armament of prosodic techniques. The most important kind of rhyme by far, as a quick inspection of the anthology shows, is **end-rhyme** or **terminal rhyme**, the rhyming of the last words in the lines. In this essay, unless otherwise qualified, "rhyme" refers to end-rhyme. Two frequent kinds of end-rhyme are the rhyming of successive lines—aabbcc, etc.— and **alternate rhyme**: ababcdcd, etc. (A letter is assigned to each rhyme; "x" can be used for lines that do not rhyme.)

Generally, end-rhyme is **perfect** and **masculine**; that is, a rhyme word ends with a stressed syllable that differs from its rhyme-mate only in the sound of its initial consonants: *vain / lain; weep / sleep; acold / infold; require / tire; temperate / short a date* (in an older pronunciation, when "-ate" and "date" would have had essentially identical vowel sounds). Note that **identical rhyme** or **rime riche**, in which the rhyming stressed syllables are exactly the same, is not perfect rhyme. The initial consonants must differ in the perfect form, which is also know as **full** or **exact rhyme**.

OTHER RHYME POSITIONS

Rhyme positions other than end-rhyme are rare in English. **Internal** or **leonine** rhyme refers to the rhyming of the last word in the line with one inside the line, usually at or near the center and before a caesura. Internal rhyme usually involves long lines, like Poe's "Once upon a midnight dreary, while I pondered weak and weary." Some example can be found in the "Proverbs of Alfred" (p. 18) and Layamon's *Brut* (p. 21). Blake switches from end rhyme to internal rhyme in the last lines of "The Garden of Love" (p. 491):

> And Priests in black gowns   were walking their rounds,
> And binding with briars   my joys & desires.

In **interlaced rhyme**, lines not only rhyme their last words but use another set of rhyming words positioned in the middle of the line. See the excerpt from *Noah* (p. 45).

DOUBLE AND TRIPLE RHYME

If a weak syllable follows the rhyming stressed syllable, the rhyme is **feminine** or **double**. The vowels and consonants after the stressed syllable must be identical for two words to rhyme exactly. Double rhymes are rare in verse in rising rhythms, because of the addition of an extra syllable at the end of the line. (A feminine ending is the obvious correlative of a feminine rhyme.) Note how few occur in the selections from Shakespeare's iambic pentameter sonnets (pp. 195–201): LIV: *roses / discloses*; XCIV: *graces / faces*; CXVI: *shaken / taken*.

More frequently, double rhyme is used in a humorous context, as in Swift's iambic tetrameter "Phyllis, or, the Progress of Love" (p. 366). See especially the run of three rhyming couplets (ll. 67–72): *all in / recalling* (where "recalling" is evidently pronounced "recallin' "), *recover / over* (closer in sound than now), *thought her / Daughter.*

In stress verse and accentual-syllabic verse in falling rhythms, lines end somewhat more frequently with a weak syllable, so that double rhymes are relatively more common. The four stanzas in trochaic tetrameter in the excerpt from Shelley's *Prometheus Unbound* (p.

578) provide good examples: *enkindle / dwindle, between them / screen them, gazes / mazes*. Hopkins uses double rhyme brilliantly, as in "The Windhover" (p. 748): *riding / striding / gliding / hiding, billion / sillion / vermilion*, and Skelton's "To Mistress Margaret Hussey" offers fine examples (p. 127): *Coliander / pomander / Cassander*, etc.

Triple Rhyme occurs occasionally—mainly in the full form of dactylic verse—when a stressed syllable is followed by two unstressed ones, as in Hardy's "The Voice" (p. 760): *call to me / all to me; view you, then / knew you then, listlessness / wistlessness;* and in Swinburne's "Atalanta in Calydon" (p. 742): *sing to her / spring to her / cling to her*.

NEAR, SLANT, OR OFF-RHYME

Especially in modern times, poets have explored the possibilities of sound echoes in rhyme position that are not exact but that still have much of the effect of rhyme. Such inexact or imperfect rhymes—generally referred to as **near**, **slant**, or **off-rhymes** (although there are a number of other names, and some prosodists restrict one or another of the familiar names to specific types of inexact rhyme)—take various forms in a continuum from almost exact rhyme to very faint sound echoes. Only a few of the most frequent types are discussed here, and remember that poets use all these inexact rhymes in an irregular fashion within the line as well.

In **consonance** the consonants stay the same but the vowels differ. In the fullest form of consonance, which is very close to the effect of exact rhyme, only the vowel in the stressed syllable changes, and the consonants before the vowel as well as after it are identical. Wilfred Owen's "Strange Meeting" and "Arms and the Boy" (pp. 916 and 915) provide superb examples: *escaped / scooped; groined / groaned; blade / blood; flash / flesh; leads / lads*, etc.

In a less exact form of consonance—some prosodists restrict the term *near rhyme* to this half-consonance—only the final consonants agree, as in "teeth" and "death" in "Arms and the Boy." Here, the colliteration of the initial "t" and "d" adds to the power of the off-rhyme. In the same poem Owen also rhymes "apple" and "supple" and "heels" and "curls." In the first case, there is no initial consonant in "apple," so the rhymes seem quite close. In the second, one of the consonants is "h", which is not generally considered a full consonant. (The rhyme is closer in Standard British English than in American English, where the "r" of "curls" is usually pronounced rather than simply modifying the "u" sound.)

A more unambiguous form of half-consonance would be *tigress / progress* in "Strange Meeting," where "pro-" and "ti-" are far apart in sound. Blake uses half-consonance frequently—see, for example, *dear / care, face / dress,* and *distress / Peace* in "The Divine Image" (p. 487). And Emily Dickinson's work offers many examples of this kind of near rhyme (and of every kind of sound echo, even the faintest): e.g., in #986 (p. 729), *seen / on, Corn / noon, Sun / gone*. **Eye-rhyme**—in which the spelling suggests that words are exact rhymes but the ear tells us otherwise—can be considered a form of half-consonance; e.g., in standard modern pronunciation, Donne's *love / move*, Pope's *gown / own* and *works / corks*, Yeats's *brood / wood, ones / stones,* and *push / rush*.

Rhyme involving **assonance**, in which the vowel stays the same but the consonants differ, is less frequent than consonance. (Assonance is a very popular form of rhyme in the Spanish and French traditions.) One striking early example is the final rhyme of the ballad "Sir Patrick Spens" (p. 24): *deip / feit*, and Blake rhymes *lambs / hands* in "Holy Thursday" (p. 488).

Two other kinds of rhyme should be mentioned. In **weak** or **light rhyme** one of the rhyming syllables is unstressed. Hopkins's "The Windhover" (p. 748) follows the rhyme scheme of a Petrarchan sonnet (abba abba cdcdcd). In addition, the feminine *b* rhymes—

riding / striding / gliding / hiding—are also light rhymes in relationship to the *a* series: *king- / wing / swing / thing.* "King-" is an example of a **broken rhyme,** in which a disyllabic or polysyllabic word is broken at the line-end so that the stressed syllable can serve as half of a rhyme pair. Hopkins uses it in a serious context, and so does Auden — though in a gently witty way—in his *pluck / suck-* rhyme in "On This Island" (p. 969). But it is a technique more typical of humorous verse.

NON-STANZAIC RHYMED VERSE

Poems not broken into stanzas may show a mixed rhyme scheme, as in Frost's "After Apple-Picking" (p. 799). A more regular rhyme scheme is of course also possible, as in Yeats's "The Dolls" (p. 770) and "Easter, 1916" (p. 771) and Heaney's "Casualty" (p. 1130). (These mix exact and inexact rhymes.) These three poems rhyme ababcdcd . . ., which immediately suggests that they could be broken into four-line stanzas. But since neither poet consistently employs a full stop at the end of every fourth line, the poems are truly nonstanzaic.

Ordinarily, **rhyming couplets,** in which lines rhyme in pairs—with an occasional **triplet** (three rhymed lines) thrown in for variety—constitute the bulk of rhyming poetry not organized in stanzas. Iambic pentameter couplets (also known as **heroic couplets** or **decasyllabics**) are the most prevalent, but iambic tetrameter ones (**octosyllabics**)—which actually were in use earlier—are often seen too. (The four-beat meter was familiar from the medieval English alliterative tradition.)

Chaucer, already expert with octosyllabic couplets, introduced rhyming ten-syllable couplets into English. These were based, like the eight-syllable ones, on French models. In most cases they fit even a strict iambic pattern. However, he used other patterns as well, and one should be wary of forcing his verse into the iambic pentameter mold. This is especially true where there is some ambiguity about pronunciation—for example, about whether the final *-e* in some words was pronounced as a separate syllable.

Both the four-beat and five-beat couplets are suited to extended description. Narration is served well by the **open** form that Chaucer used, in which each couplet is not routinely set off syntactically from its neighbor. Jonson's couplets, both tetrameter and pentameter, are metrically more regular. (See his memorial poems for his children and Shakespeare and "To Penshurst," pp. 209–10, 215, 210). See also Donne's and Carew's heroic couplets (pp. 234–38 and 257–60). For later examples of the open form see Browning's dramatic monologue "My Last Duchess" (p. 663).

The **closed couplet,** in contrast—introduced by Denham (see "Cooper's Hill," p. 305) and brought to perfection by Pope (p. 372)—encourages witty antithesis and observation and is superb for didactic, satirical, and philosophical poetry. Some difference in its effect can be gauged by comparing passages from Chaucer's *Canterbury Tales* (p. 48) and Pope's mock-epic *The Rape of the Lock* (p. 373). See other eighteenth-century selections for additional examples of strict iambic pentameter couplets in the closed form.

For an early example of four-stress rhyming couplets, see Mannyng's "The Dancers of Colbek" (p. 31). For regular iambic tetrameter couplets in the open form, see, in addition to Jonson, Milton's *L'Allegro* and *Il Penseroso* (pp. 266 and 270) and Marvell's "The Garden" (p. 318); for closed form , see Swift's "Phyllis" (p. 366), "A Satirical Elegy" (p. 369), and "Stella's Birthday" (p. 370).

Blake's "Holy Thursday" (p. 488) provides a good example of longer, seven-beat rhyming couplets (although here they are grouped in quatrains). He is adapting the once popular fourteener (see p. 1154). Note how easily each couplet breaks after the fourth beat, leading to the $x^4a^3x^4a^3$ ballad measure. Compare "Judas" (p. 39).

With few exceptions, rhyming couplets are made up of lines of the same length, but of course they need not be. **Poulter's measure**, for example, popular in the sixteenth century, alternated six-beat and seven-beat lines (hexameters and heptameters). These long lines showed the usual tendency to break apart into shorter lines, leading to the familiar short meter of the hymnals. The jouncy awkwardness of poulter's measure is put to excellent effect in Sidney's scathing catalogue of Mopsa's charms in "What Length of Verse?" (p. 139). Marvell's "The Mower Against Gardens" (p. 317) provides another example of couplets made up of unequal lines, this time five-stress and four-stress.

Another famous form of rhymed nonstanzaic verse, usually in iambic pentameter, is **terza rima**, the meter of Dante's *Divine Comedy*, which uses a triplet base and rhymes ababcbcdcded . . . *Terza rima* is excellent for maintaining forward momentum and would probably be used more frequently were it as easy to find three rhyme words in English as in Italian. For examples, see Shelley's "Ode to the West Wind" (p. 581) and Frost's "Acquainted with the Night" (p. 805). (Note that these poems are laid out in tercets—three-line stanzas—but these are not invariably self-contained and so are not stanzaic in the ordinary sense.)

The two rhyme schemes just discussed—couplet and *terza rima*—can be used with off-rhymes as well as exact rhymes. See also "Couplet Stanza" and "Tercet," p. 1154.

Stanza Forms

INTRODUCTION

In its strictest sense, a **stanza** is a self-contained grouping of lines, bound together by rhyme, the pattern of which the poem repeats at least once. In the strictest stanzaic poems, the rhyme scheme, meter, and number of lines are repeated exactly, although, naturally, some poets have been more flexible and have varied these elements at need. Poems in free verse may also be said to have stanzas if their separate units each contain the same number of lines, despite the absence of regular meter, a rhyme scheme, or the grammatical independence that ordinary stanzas have. (Handled carefully and if not overused, the enjambed or run-on stanzas of free verse can provide an effective counterpoint of syntax and form like that of enjambed lines.)

Stanzas may be short or long, may have simple or complex rhyme schemes, and may have lines of uniform or varied length. The possibilities are legion—songs tend to be particularly varied—and one will find many poems in the anthology with stanzas that look quite unorthodox. Sometimes it is possible, however, to see from the rhyme scheme that a stanza combines two or three of the forms listed below, perhaps with a couplet or triplet thrown in. (Not all the traditional stanzas can be named here; prosody handbooks and such specialized studies as Lewis Turco's *The New Book of Forms* provide valuable additional information.)

DESCRIPTIVE SYMBOLS

There are various ways of describing the meter and rhyme scheme of a stanza. The one used here assigns a raised numeral to the number of accents in the line and a letter to each rhyme. Thus each four-line stanza of Housman's iambic trimeter "With rue my heart is laden " (*A Shropshire Lad* LIV, p. 766) is designated abab^3; or, if one wishes to designate the feminine endings in the first and third lines, a~ba~b^3. (Note that this symbol system does not indicate whether a line is in rising or falling rhythm or duple or triple; that information must be given separately. The usual assumption would be that the verse is accentual-syllabic and in duple rising rhythm—that is, iambic—unless additional information is provided.)

The very popular ballad stanza alternates four-beat and three-beat lines and rhymes only the second and fourth lines: x⁴a³x⁴a³. A superscript is needed for each line, and "x" designates an unrhymed line. (Some prosodists assign a letter to each line, whether it rhymes or not—a⁴b³c⁴b³—but this practice, when applied to longer stanzas, makes it difficult to recognize the rhyme pattern at a glance.)

Only one other symbol is needed—the prime sign (') for inexact rhyme. Thus the pattern of the first three stanzas of Dickinson's "I heard a Fly buzz" (#465, p. 728), in ballad meter, is x⁴a³x⁴a'³; that of the fourth, x⁴a³x⁴a³.

We can give extended treatment here only to the more traditional rhymed stanzas. It will help to remember that any combination of meter and rhyme scheme is possible for a given stanza-length. For instance, any four-line stanza is a quatrain, and any five-line one a quintet. See also "A Note on Unrhymed Stanzas," pp. 1156–57.

STANZAS

Two-line stanza (couplet stanza)

Rarely used, except as a refrain, the couplet stanza can be seen in the third part of Stevens's "Peter Quince at the Clavier" (p. 821) and in Brooks's "We Real Cool" (p. 1025; and see note, p. 1157).

Three-line stanza (tercet or triplet)

Various rhyme schemes are possible with three-line stanzas: aaa; axa; or the *terza rima* pattern (see p. 1153). For an aaa⁴ tercet see Waller's "To a Fair Lady, Playing with a Snake" (p. 263) and Frost's "Provide, Provide" (p. 807).

Four-line stanza (quatrain)

The so-called **ballad stanza, ballad meter**, or **common meter** just mentioned is the most familiar and most influential of the various ballad forms and one of the most widely used **quatrains** (another name for a four-line stanza). It was preceded by an earlier, long-lined ballad form made up of rhyming couplets with seven-stress lines. The ballad stanza comes from the breaking apart of each of these long lines into two parts, a four-stress line and a three-stress one, retaining the original couplet rhyme at the end of the second and fourth lines. Ballad meter, which is sometimes strict iambic and sometimes verges more toward stress verse, is thus closely linked to the most famous of these long-line forms, the line of seven beats and fourteen syllables known as the **fourteener**. See "Sir Patrick Spens" (p. 24) for the ballad stanza, and "Judas" (p. 39) for erratic examples of the fourteener.

When the syllable count and iambic pattern are regularized, we have the common meter or **common measure** of the hymnals, frequently given as 8-6-8-6, and frequently rhyming a⁴b³a⁴b³. For the fully rhymed form see Lovelace's "Song: To Lucasta, Going to the Wars" (p. 308); for the x⁴a³x⁴a³ form see "Jerusalem, My Happy Home" (p. 136) and many of Dickinson's stanzas (pp. 726 ff.). Other related forms include **short measure**— xa³x⁴a³ (or ab³a⁴b³)—for which see Dickinson's "The first Day's Night had come" (p. 731) and "poulter's measure," p. 1153; and **long measure**—xaxa⁴ (or abab⁴)—as in Collins's ode on Thomson's death (p. 440), Johnson's "On the Death of Dr. Robert Levet" (p. 425), and Hardy's "Channel Firing" (p. 758).

The iambic pentameter **Sicilian quatrain**, abab⁵, is used not only by itself, as in Gray's

"Elegy Written in a Country Churchyard" (p. 431) and Larkin's "Mr. Bleaney" (p. 1038), but as a unit in the English or Shakespearean sonnet. Another pentameter quatrain, abba⁵, known as an **Italian quatrain**, serves a similar role in the Italian sonnet. A stanza using enclosing rhymes, as in the Italian quatrain, is known as an **envelope stanza**. The iambic tetrameter **In Memoriam stanza**, abba⁴, named after Tennyson's poem (see p. 651), is another. The **rubaiyat stanza**, an Arabic form made famous in English by Edward Fitzgerald's translation of *The Rubáiyát of Omar Khayyám* rhymes aaba⁵. Frost uses an interesting variant of this, aaba⁴, in "Stopping by Woods on a Snowy Evening" (p. 804), with the "b" rhyme picked up in the next stanza much as in *terza rima*—except that Frost's stanzas are self-contained.

Five-line stanza (quintet)

Five-line stanzas are fairly rare. One should note, however, the **bob and wheel**, a¹baba³, used in *Sir Gawain and the Green Knight* (p. 111) to separate the alliterative verse units. The "bob" is the one-stress line, the "wheel" the three-stress quatrain. The **English quintet** uses various line lengths and rhymes ababb, as in Waller's "Go, Lovely Rose" (p. 262) and Donne's "Hymn to God My God, in My Sickness" (p. 243). The iambic pentameter **Sicilian quintet** extends the Sicilian quatrain: ababa⁵. A variant of the Sicilian quintet is seen in Herbert's "Jordan (I)" (p. 251): abab⁵a⁴.

Six-line stanza (sestet)

A very simple and popular extension of common meter in either the ballad or hymnal form is a six-line stanza rhyming either x⁴a³x⁴a³x⁴a³ or a⁴b³a⁴b³a⁴b³. For an example of the first, see Yeats's "Crazy Jane Talks with the Bishop" (p. 795).

The **Sicilian sestet** extends the Sicilian quintet, ababab⁵. The **Italian sestet** has the form abcabc⁵, as in Herbert's "Church Monuments" (p. 252). The Italian sestet combines with the Italian octave in the Italian sonnet (the familiar cdecde⁵; see "Eight-line stanza," below). A **heroic sestet**, also iambic pentameter, combines a quatrain and a couplet: ababcc⁵. (As efefgg⁵ this is the familiar ending of a Shakespearean sonnet.) Another combination of quatrain and couplet, abbacc, shows up as the sestet of Wyatt's and Surrey's sonnets (as cddcee⁵).

The **sextilla** is a tetrameter stanza rhyming ababcc⁴ (or aabccb⁴). It is quite common; see, for example, Arnold's "Stanzas from the Grand Chartreuse" (p. 715).

Rime couée or **tail rhyme**, popular in medieval romances, most frequently takes the form aa⁴b³cc⁴b³, although there are other possibilities. See, for example, Dunbar's "The Dance of the Seven Deadly Sins" (p. 121), Gray's "Ode on the Death of a Favourite Cat" (p. 430), and Smart's "A Song to David" (p. 433).

Closely related and also a medieval form is the stanza rhyming aaa⁴b²a⁴b², named the **Burns stanza** after the much later poet. See, for example, "To a Mouse" (p. 477) and "Holy Willie's Prayer" (p. 474).

Seven-line stanza (septet)

By far the most famous of the seven-line stanzas is **rhyme royal**: ababbcc⁵. Other names for this iambic pentameter stanza are the **Chaucerian** or **Troilus stanza**. See the selections from Chaucer's *Troylus and Criseyde* (p. 99), Henryson's "The Testament of Cresseid" (p. 116), Wyatt's less metrically regular "They Flee from Me" (p. 129), and Auden's "The Shield of Achilles" (p. 979).

Eight-line stanza (octave)

The **Italian octave** doubles the Italian quatrain, abbaabba⁵. It is most generally used in the

Italian sonnet's octave-sestet combination, where it may or may not be isolated as a separate stanza. See sonnets by Wyatt, Surrey, and Milton; also "Sonnet," pp. 1160–61. The **Sicilian octave** doubles the Sicilian quatrain: abababab^5. Sidney uses it for his sonnet "Come sleep" (Sonnet XXXIX, p. 144) and Gray for his "Sonnet. On the Death of Mr. Richard West" (p. 427).

Ottava rima, abababcc^5, combines a Sicilian sestet and a heroic couplet. See Yeats's "Sailing to Byzantium" (p. 774), "Nineteen Hundred and Nineteen" (p. 780), and "Among School Children" (p. 784); and, for a famously humorous version, Byron's "Don Juan" (p. 561).

The **ballade stanza**, which like rhyme royal originated in the French ballade tradition, is the rhyme royal stanza plus an added "b" rhyme: ababbcbc^5. For examples, see Chaucer's "To Rosemounde" (p. 106) and the octaves of Spenser's sonnets, where it is not set off separately.

Longer stanzas

The most famous nine-line stanza is the **Spenserian stanza**, which adds an alexandrine to the ballade stanza: ababbcbc^{5}c^6. See *The Faerie Queene* (p. 166) and Keats's *The Eve of St. Agnes* (p. 604).

Longer stanzas are a notable feature of odes. One of the stanzas that Keats uses, a ten-line form combining a Sicilian quatrain and an Italian sestet, ababcdecde^5, is sometimes called the English ode stanza.

See also "Ode," p. 1160.

THE REFRAIN

One other special feature of rhymed stanzaic poetry should be mentioned: the **refrain**, a repeated stanza, line, or smaller unit. Refrains offer a splendid opportunity for providing musical and tonal variety while still maintaining a pattern of repetition, and so they tend to have rhyme schemes and metrical schemes that differ from the poem's basic stanza. Refrains may be totally self-contained or carry on from some element in the preceding stanza.

For one-line refrains and partial refrains see, for example, Chaucer's ballade "To Rosemounde" (p. 106), Wyatt's "Blame Not My Lute" (p. 131), Jonson's "Hymn to Cynthia" (p. 217), Elizabeth Barrett Browning's "A Musical Instrument" (p. 630), Tennyson's "Tears, Idle Tears" (p. 650), Masters's "The Hill" (p. 792), and Frost's "The Pasture" (p. 798).

For longer refrains see the ballad and lyric sections (pp. 23–29 and pp. 36–44), Tennyson's "Mariana" (p. 640), and Yeats's highly evocative refrain in "Long-legged Fly" (p. 790).

A NOTE ON UNRHYMED STANZAS

Before the advent of free verse, unrhymed metrical stanzas tended to be based on classical quantitative meters. The most successful maintain a regular accentual pattern as well as a quantitative one. See, for example, Campion's "Rose-cheeked Laura, Come" (p. 208). One fine unrhymed metrical poem is Tennyson's "Tears, Idle Tears" (p. 650). Because of the numerous repetitions and refrain-like fifth line of each five-line stanza, the lack of rhyme is hardly noticed.

Twentieth-century poets frequently use unrhymed couplets, triplets, quatrains, etc. Lines may be of any length and vary greatly from stanza to stanza; sometimes, too, stanzas are not in the least self-contained. Still, some of the minimal expectations of the form remain, and one should look for tonal shifts and significant development from one stanza to the next.

The Poem as a Whole

GENERAL CONSIDERATIONS

Poems take as their subject matter everything of human concern, in whatever realm: day-to-day reality with its sensuous, emotional, psychological, and intellectual dimensions; or the realm of dream, vision, reverie, and the free-floating imaginative spirit. Love or hate, birth or death, conviviality or alienation, hope or despair, an urge to confess or convert or instruct or prophesy, a walk in the country or in a war zone—anything can give impetus to a poem.

Poems are works of art, expressive of human thought, feeling, and awareness. Their artistic material is language, just as paint, stone, or musical tones are the mediums of other arts. Poems can make use of any mode or level of language—literary or nonliterary; oral or written; standard or substandard; preached, screeched, or sung; stumbling or rhythmically regular; colloquial or formal; jargonized or pure; high, middle, or low.

Whatever their ostensible subject, or the overall tone they project—passionately importunate, bitterly sarcastic, lovingly patient, serenely meditative, rigorously philosophical, didactically informative, evangelically committed, stringently philosophical, or attentively descriptive—poems must be approached word by word, line by line, stanza by stanza, in order to catch the full quality of each poetic unit. For they are dynamic structures, and at every moment one should try to be attentive to the exact quality of the emotionally and sensuously charged awareness that they are projecting.

Versification plays its part in creating these poetic units or tonal centers. The triple meter in Williams's "The Dance" (p. 841), as I pointed out on p. 1146, matters to the poem's projection of the feeling of Brueghel's painting. Think how incongruous the meter would be to Auden's "Musée des Beaux Arts" (p. 972) or to Guthrie's "Homage to Paul Delvaux" (p. 932).

It matters in Brooks's "We Real Cool" (p. 1025) that the line- and stanza-breaks come in the unusual place that they do—not after the rhyme but after what would traditionally be the first word of the next line. With one deft stroke she has changed the lines from two-stress ones (in which "we" would be subordinate) to three-stress ones, effectively syncopating and over-stressing them (three syllables and three accents in all but the first and last lines). This emphasis on the word "we," combined with obsessive repetition, heavy alliteration, insistent rhyme, and over-stressing, projects a magnificently self-admiring and cocky assurance. When the scheme is broken by the omission of "we" in the last line, its sudden absence reinforces the insight "We / die soon."

It matters in Auden's "The Shield of Achilles" (p. 979) that the longer stanzas are in rhyme royal. If we fail to recognize this stanza, used so notably, for example, by Chaucer in *Troylus and Criseyde* (p. 99), we lose one dimension of Auden's comparison of the present war-age with the heroic past. The comparison is not entirely ironic, because the values of that heroic, golden, romantically tinged age—as preserved in literature—were in their own way as suspect as institutionalized twentieth-century cruelties.

It matters in Wordsworth's "Composed upon Westminster Bridge" (p. 517) that two lines pause over small catalogues from the disparate realms of city and country, rhythmically pointing up the similarity of their effect on the poet: "Ships, towers, domes, theatres and temples" and "valley, rock, or hill."

It matters in Yeats's "Memory" (p. 771) that the first lines are end-stopped and succeeding lines not. The difference helps point up the disparity between the realm of relatively commonplace women (at least to the poet) and the wild and wonderful realm that he uses to project the quality of one special woman. It also matters that only the last line of the poem provides an exact rhyme, giving special authority to the hold the loved—and lost—woman has on the poet's imagination.

So it goes in any good poem, and one should always ask what effect, however slight, the rhythmical, metrical, and other formal aspects of a poem have on its meaning. One way of thinking about these matters is to ask oneself what would be lost if the meter of a particular poem were triple rather than duple, or if the poem were a sestina or in couplets or blank verse or free verse rather than in rhyming stanzas, or if this word did not rhyme with (or echo in some other way) that one, or if these syllables were as weighty as those, or if this caesura were moved elsewhere, or if this line were enjambed rather than end-stopped, or if some prosodic or traditional element were missing.

The following glossary of types, brief though it is, may be of some assistance in making such comparisons. Also, one can learn a good bit about individual poets' practice and achievement by comparing their handling of the same or similar forms: blank verse, couplet verse, sestinas, sonnets, or any of the many forms that the English tradition has evolved or adapted from other literatures.

A GLOSSARY OF TYPES

alliterative verse   a special form of unrhymed, four-beat stress verse in which half-lines are joined by alliteration on key syllables. The meter of Old English poetry, it was revived in the fourteenth century. See Langland's *Piers Plowman* (p. 108) and the metrical romance *Sir Gawain and the Green Knight* (p. 111). See also the headnote to *Beowulf* (p. 3) and "Alliterative Stress Verse" in the metrical supplement, pp. 1174–76.

ballade   a French form dominant in the fourteenth and fifteenth centuries and introduced into English by Chaucer. The ballade uses a limited number of rhymes, a refrain, and frequently an envoy. "To Rosemounde" (p. 106) omits the envoy but is otherwise typical; it uses the standard three eight-line stanzas, each with the *same* ababbcbC rhymes (note the "C" refrain). See "Eight-line stanza," pp. 1155–56.

blank verse   unrhymed iambic pentameter, first used in the sixteenth century by Surrey for his translation of two books of Virgil's *Aeneid* and, because of the skill of the poets who have used it, highly influential. It is generally organized in **verse paragraphs**, the length of which is determined by subject matter. Only free verse, where regular rhyme is also missing, can match the rhythmic and tonal flexibility of blank verse, the effects of which range from the most natural and colloquial speech to high rhetoric or lyric intensity. Without the help of end-rhyme in defining the line, the handling of line-breaks (end-stopped or enjambed) and caesuras (number and placement) takes on particular importance in the rhythmic flow of the verse. Note the very different blank-verse rhythms—partly attributable to greater flexibility in the number of syllables and place-ment of stresses in the later examples—of Surrey's *Aeneid* (p. 134), Shakespeare's plays (pp. 203–05), Milton's *Paradise Lost* (p. 283), Cowper's *The Task* (p. 462), Wordsworth's *The Prelude* (p. 523), Browning's "The Bishop Orders His Tomb" (p. 664), Yeats's "The Second Coming" (p. 773), and Stevens's "Sunday Morning" (p. 824).

couplet verse   non-stanzaic verse in which lines rhyme in pairs; popular from Chaucer on. Two types are generally recognized: open, in which there is considerable enjambment from one line and couplet to the next, and closed, in which the couplet forms a syntacti-cal unit. Iambic pentameter couplets in the closed form dominated eighteenth-century poetry. For examples see "Non-stanzaic Verse," p. 1152.

dramatic verse verse conceived as lines spoken by a character in a dramatic scene. In actual drama, of course—e.g., the excerpts from Shakespeare's plays (p. 203)—the verse is meant to be spoken by actors on stage. In literary dramatic verse, however, no actors are involved; instead, an identifiable character presumably addresses other characters (who may be silent) in a dramatic situation. See Browning's dramatic monologues, especially "My Last Duchess" (p. 663) and "Andrea del Sarto" (p. 674).

elegiac verse poetry in which there is a strong element of lament, whether for a specific death or, more generally, for any aspect of existence the poet considers sad or even tragic. Elegies tend to be elevated in diction and meditative in tone and to suggest sources of consolation in the larger rhythms of nature. See, for example, Milton's *Lycidas* (p. 275), Gray's "Elegy Written in a Country Churchyard" (p. 431), Tennyson's "In Memoriam" (p. 651), and Whitman's "When Lilacs Last in the Dooryard Bloom'd" (p. 699). "Elegy" has also been applied to any poem on any subject—e.g., Donne's elegy "To His Mistress Going to Bed" (p. 234)—that could have been treated in elegiac distichs (see p. 1147) by classical poets.

free verse nonmetrical verse dating, in English, from translations of the Bible and—in later development—from Whitman and predominant in contemporary poetry. See "Free Verse," pp. 1145–46, for discussion and examples.

lyric verse originally one of the three great divisions of classical poetry—epic, dramatic, and lyric—from one perspective less a division by literary genre than by art form: heroic narrative poetry, in which words predominate; drama, in which action predominates; and song, in which music predominates. A large proportion of the earlier stanzaic poems in this anthology, including those on the pages devoted to the Renaissance, are lyrics or song texts in the original sense. However, the term *lyric* has broadened to include essentially all poetry in which the most notable element is the projection of personal emotion and awareness—which means nearly all the poems in the anthology. (The eighteenth century, with its predilection for didactic, descriptive, and satiric verse, is an exception.)

modern poetic sequence a grouping of mainly lyric (in the general sense) poems and passages, rarely uniform in pattern, that tend to interact as an organic whole. The modern poetic sequence is the main form that the long poem takes in our time and is characterized by a suggestion of some strong psychological pressure that has brought it into being. A striking modulation toward the form is Dickinson's Fascicle 16 (p. 733). Given the limitations of space, Fascicle 16 and Eliot's *The Waste Land* (p. 889) are the only complete sequences in the anthology. However, there are selections from sequences by Whitman (*Song of Myself*), Hardy (*Poems of 1912–13*), Yeats, Williams, Pound, Lowell, and others.

narrative verse verse that tells a story. The most venerable forms of narrative verse are the **epic** and the **ballad**, originally existing only in the oral tradition. With the introduction of writing, some of these were recorded and served as models for literary forms. For early forms and a discussion of their characteristics, see the selections from *Beowulf* (p. 4) and the ballad section (p. 23), together with their headnotes. See also "ballad meter," p. 1154. Later epic or heroic poems include the metrical romance *Sir Gawain and the Green Knight* (p. 111), Spenser's *The Faerie Queene* (p. 166), and Milton's *Paradise Lost* (p. 283); for a mock-epic see Pope's *The Rape of the Lock* (p. 373). Literary ballads include Drayton's "His Ballad of Agincourt" (p. 182), Coleridge's "The Rime of the Ancient Mariner" (p. 533), and Keats's "La Belle Dame sans Merci" (p. 615). Narrative verse takes other forms as well; see, for example, the selections from Chaucer's *Canterbury Tales* (p. 48), Langland's *Piers Plowman* (p. 108), Marlowe's *Hero and Leander* (p. 185), and Byron's *Don Juan* (p. 561), as well as Keats's

The Eve of St. Agnes (p. 604), which uses the Spenserian stanza.

ode usually an elevated, serious, and metrically complex lyric poem, frequently of considerable length, e.g., Spenser's "Epithalamion" (p. 155). However, odes take many forms, ranging from stanzaic (Horatian) odes, in which a fairly simple stanza form is repeated—e.g., Gray's "Ode on a Distant Prospect of Eton College" (p. 427) or his humorous elegy "Ode on the Death of a Favourite Cat" (p. 430), in *rime couée*; to the more complex lyric-contemplative stanzaic odes of Keats (pp. 617-24); to the irregularities of Wordsworth's (Cowleyan or pseudo-Pindaric) immortality ode (p. 518). A historical reason for the variety can be found in the blending of different classical traditions deriving from Pindar and Horace, but the poetic reason would seem to lie in the classically sanctioned possibilities for irregularity. The assumption of irregularity was to some extent a misunderstanding of the three-part structure of each section of a Pindaric ode: strophe, antistrophe, and epode. No matter how complex, the strophe and antistrophe were metrically identical. The epode differed in structure, however, and this apparent imbalance could be seen as ignoring the rules of exact formal repetition, leaving the poet free to improvise according to the needs of his material and thus to incorporate radical shifts of tone and subject. (From this point of view, odes offered a freedom within the metrical tradition similar to that provided by the modern poetic sequence.) For other examples, see Collins's "Ode to Evening" (p. 438), an unrhymed ode based on Horace's quatrain of two longer lines followed by two shorter ones; Coleridge's "Dejection: An Ode" (p. 554); and Shelley's "Ode to the West Wind" (p. 581), in *terza rima*.

rhyme royal seven-line iambic pentameter stanza rhyming ababbcc originating in the French ballade tradition and introduced by Chaucer. It was the dominant stanza for serious verse in the fifteenth century and is still used in the twentieth. For examples see "Seven-line stanza," p. 1155.

satiric verse verse that ridicules vice or folly from the standpoint of generally accepted norms of behavior. Depending on the object of the satire, the tone may range from gentle raillery to savage invective. (And satire can modulate into sardonic jeering for its own sake.) Satiric verse is akin to **didactic verse**, that is, one of its aims is also to teach (right thought and behavior); however, it instructs through laughter at what is evil or foolish rather than through a sober presentation of needed information. See, for example, Jonson's epigram "On Something That Walks Somewhere" (p. 209), Donne's "Satire III" (p. 236), Dryden's "Mac Flecknoe" (p. 350), Swift's satirical elegy (p. 369), and the selection from Pope's *Dunciad* (p. 407).

sestina thirty-nine-line Provençal form consisting of six sestets and one tercet known as the **envoy** or **envoi**. Each stanza is unrhymed—perhaps one reason for its popularity with twentieth-century poets; however, the six end-words of the first stanza are repeated in subsequent stanzas and in the envoy in a different, but set pattern. For the order see Bishop's "Sestina" (p. 1000) and Ashbery's "The Painter" (p. 1069), both in four-stress meter.

sonnet by far the most popular short poem in English, consisting of fourteen rhymed iambic pentameter lines. The two most familiar forms are the English (or Shakespearean) sonnet, essentially three quatrains and a couplet rhyming abab cdcd efef gg, and the Italian (or Petrarchan) sonnet, an octave and sestet rhyming abbaabba cdecde (or cdcdcd). Originally a Provençal form but used superbly by Petrarch, the sonnet was introduced into English from the Italian by Wyatt (p. 128) and his younger contemporary Surrey (p. 133), but with one crucial change: a closing couplet, where Petrarch had none, so that their rhyme schemes are abbaabba cddcee. (See pp. 129 and 130 for the original Italian of two of Petrarch's sonnets.) The different structures of the two main types of sonnet suggest different dynamics. The form of the Italian sonnet suggests a major shift or "turn" between the octave and sestet, whereas the English form suggests three related sections summarized or counteracted in a pithy closing couplet. Of course there are numerous other possibilities, including keeping the rhyme scheme but ignoring the divisions it suggests. With the exception of the eighteenth century, sonnets have proliferated since the sixteenth century. (Related sonnets are sometimes grouped as **sonnet sequences**.) See in particular the sonnets of Spenser (who gave his name to a sonnet rhyming ababbcbccdcdee), Sidney, Shakespeare, Donne, Milton (who used the Italian rhyme scheme but ignored the shift between octave and sestet), Wordsworth, Keats, Hopkins, and Cummings (who has broken up his sonnets visually).

terza rima non-stanzaic Italian form invented by Dante (*The Divine Comedy*) and introduced into English by Chaucer. Rhyming ababcbcdcded . . ., it has elements of triplet verse, with the middle line of one triplet providing the rhyme sound for the next. For examples see "Non-stanzaic Verse," p. 1153.

villanelle a nineteen-line French form made up of five tercets and one quatrain. It uses two rhymes only and, in addition, repeats the first and third lines of the opening tercet at the end of the other stanzas. For the pattern see Empson's "Villanelle" (p. 965) and "Missing Dates" (p. 966), Bishop's "One Art" (p. 1003), and Dylan Thomas's "Do Not Go Gentle into That Good Night" (p. 985).

III. METRICAL SUPPLEMENT

Iambic Verse

BEAT-OFFBEAT SCANSION: DESCRIPTIVE SYMBOLS

The section on meter in the first section of this essay provided a brief introduction to the accentual-syllabic, stress, and syllabic verse traditions of poetry in English. The purpose of this supplement is to suggest how one may approach the sometimes confusing rhythms of metrical verse with a certain confidence and gaiety of spirit. It builds on a relatively new method of scansion, Derek Attridge's beat-offbeat method as presented in his book *The Rhythms of English Poetry* (London and New York: Longman, 1982).

Once the method of beat-offbeat scansion has become familiar—not a difficult task, since it draws not only on the insights of many other methods but also on our innate sense of rhythm—the principles of other scansions become clear. One can then more effectively draw on the discoveries of traditional foot scansion, or of generative metrics (as practiced on the one hand by Morris Halle and Samuel J. Keyser and on the other by Paul Kiparsky), or of any other method of scansion that shows itself to be truly sensitive to the sound of poetry.

One advantage that beat-offbeat scansion has over foot scansion and some other methods is that it offers a simple visual method of distinguishing metrically accented and unaccented syllables (**beats** and **offbeats**) from linguistically stressed and unstressed syllables. Consider "in" in the first line of Shakespeare's Sonnet CXXIX, "Th' expense of spirit in a waste of shame," and "rude" in the fourth, "Savage, extreme, rude, cruel, not to trust" from the point of view of foot scansion. How should the feet "-it in" and "rude, cru-" be marked?

In the case of the unstressed but accented "in," some foot prosodists dealing with "-it in" would choose not to mark the accent at all, resulting in a pyrrhic: |x x|. Others would assign a secondary accent, \, to "in": |x \|. And still others would mark the foot as a normal iamb: |x /|. In the case of the stressed but unaccented "rude" in "rude, cru-," some prosodists would choose two accents, resulting in a spondee: |/ /|. Others would choose a secondary accent, relying on our recognition of the principles of relative stress to read the foot as an iamb: |\ /|. And still others would mark the foot as a normal iamb: |x /|.

Beat-offbeat scansion solves the problem rather simply, as we shall see below, because the relevant distinctions are built into its symbol system. For the metrical accents or beats, **B** is assigned to a stressed syllable and **B̄** to an unstressed one that has been promoted. For the unaccented syllables or offbeats, o is assigned to an unstressed syllable, and ȯ to a stressed one that has been demoted.

A practical result is that beat-offbeat scansion leads to a performance truer to the rhythms of the poems. One is helped to feel the continuing beat of the poem but is not irresistibly nudged, on the one hand, into overstressing syllables like "in" that actually should be rather unemphatically pronounced; or, on the other hand, into understressing syllables like "rude" that are very emphatic indeed.

One unusual feature of the beat-offbeat system is that unaccented syllables are gathered together symbolically, so that the *offbeat* separating two beats may consist of one (o), two (ŏ), or even (though rarely) three (o̊) unstressed syllables. We have already mentioned the symbol for a stressed syllable that has been demoted, ȯ, and there is another special offbeat: ô, for an implied offbeat. This last case occurs when there are no syllables between beats, so that we have in effect two juxt.posed accents. In the strictest sense this situation is a contradiction in terms, since there must be some degree of separation, however minimal, between beats—even the tiniest moment of silence—for us to recognize them as separate entities. Hence the possibility for an implied offbeat. (See pp. 1163–65).

A *beat* is really a simpler matter than an offbeat. Usually it is attached to a stressed syllable (B) or an unstressed syllable that has been promoted (B̄). Attridge also hypothesizes an unrealized beat, [B]—particularly at the end of three-beat lines and in the context of song. Like the implied offbeat, it is not connected to any syllable at all and is supplied internally by the responsive reader.

Obviously, another crucial difference from foot prosody is that beat-offbeat scansion dispenses with the foot and treats the line as the basic unit. (In this, Attridge's practice is closer to that of the generative metrists, although there are highly significant differences.)

Here, then, are the two lines from Sonnet CXXIX with the symbols of traditional foot scansion above the line and those of beat-offbeat scansion below:

|x x |
|x / |
x / |x /|x \ |x / |x /
Th' expense of spirit in a waste of shame
o B o Bo B̄ o B o B

| / /|
| x /|
/ x |x / | \ /|x /|x /
Savage, extreme, rude, cruel, not to trust
B ŏ B ȯ Bo B o B

For further comparison, here are the lines with word- and phrase-stress marked (+s for stressed syllables, −s for unstressed):

−s +s −s +s−s−s−s +s −s +s
Th' expense of spirit in a waste of shame
o B o Bo B̄ o B o B

+s−s −s +s   +s   +s−s +s −s +s
Savage, extreme, rude, cruel, not to trust
B   ŏ   B   ȯ   Bo B   o   B

PROMOTION AND DEMOTION

Note that "in," promoted to a beat, is the middle syllable in a run of three unstressed syllables, and "rude," demoted to an offbeat, is the middle syllable in a series of three stressed syllables. Such is the built-in tendency of the language toward the alternation of stressed and unstressed syllables—and our physical and psychological readiness to perceive rhythmic regularity—that we feel the rhythmic pulse must continue. (Remember how easily one can sing or play—or listen, stamp, or tap to—a series of consecutive loud or soft notes without for a moment losing one's sense of the music's pulse.)

Besides the case of three unstressed syllables in a row, an unstressed syllable tends to be promoted to a beat if it lies between a line boundary and another unstressed syllable. This is important at the end of an iambic line (and at the beginning of a trochaic one). At the end of the second line of Shakespeare's Sonnet XVIII, (p. 195), we can see both principles of promotion at work:

　　　　　　　　　　−s −s   −s 　　　　−s−s
Thou art more lovely and more temperate
o   B   o   B   o B̄   o   B   o B̄

Conversely, given two stressed syllables at the beginning of an iambic line, it is natural to demote the first, as in the sixth, seventh, and tenth lines of Sonnet CXXIX (p. 200). Note that in the sixth line promotion is also at work:

　　　　　　+s +s
Past reason hunted, and no sooner had
ȯ   B o   B o   B̄   o B o B

The opening four syllables of the sixth line of one of Wordsworth's most famous sonnets, "Composed upon Westminster Bridge" (p. 517), provide a handsome example of both principles of demotion at work:

　　　+s　　+s　　+s　　　+s
Ships, towers, domes, theatres, and temples lie
ȯ   B   ȯ   Bo B̄   o   B   o   B

"Ships" is demoted because it follows a line boundary and is adjacent to a stressed syllable, and "domes" can be demoted for the same reason that "rude" was in the Shakespeare—because it is the middle syllable in a series of three stressed syllables. (Note too that the sixth syllable is promoted and that the second word, here a monosyllable, is one of those metrically handy ones—like "power" and "flower"—that can be one or two syllables as needed.)

It is important to remember, in performing a poem, that stressed syllables that have been demoted ("ships" and "domes") may be given a weight equal to the adjacent stressed syllables ("towers" and "the-"). One should probably be careful, however, not to override the beat by overstressing a demoted syllable. Nor need one pronounce with special strength an unstressed syllable that has been promoted; again, the only adjustment to the meter might be to avoid understressing it in relation to the surrounding unstressed syllables.

IMPLIED AND DOUBLE OFFBEATS

So far we have been considering only lines that maintain an easy offbeat-beat alternation, either naturally or through fairly straightforward principles of promotion and demotion.

There are of course times in accentual-syllabic meters when this regular rhythm is interrupted. The simplest interruption involves switching a stressed with an unstressed syllable at the opening of the line or after a strong internal pause. The fourth line of Sonnet CXXIX provides an example of **initial inversion** and hence of a *double* offbeat (ŏ):

+s−s

Savage, extreme, rude, cruel, not to trust

B   ŏ B   ȯ   Bo B o B

There are numerous examples in Shakespeare's sonnets of initial inversion, including the ninth line of CXXIX ("Mad in pursuit . . ."). In Sonnet XXXV ("No more be grieved," p. 197), for instance, both the second and third lines start with inversions:

+s−s

Roses have thorns, and silver fountains mud,

B   ŏ   B   o Bo B   o   B

+s   −s

Clouds and eclipses stain both moon and sun

B   ŏ Bo B   o   B o B

The seventh line of Shelley's "Ozymandias" (p. 578) provides a simple example of inversion after a strong internal pause:

+s   −s

Which yet survive, stamped on these lifeless things

o   B o B ô B   ŏ   B o B

The symbol "ô" stands for an *implied* offbeat—one not supported by a syllable. In strict accentual-syllabic verse it must be compensated for by a double offbeat—here, by the words "on these." An implied offbeat represents, in essence, our tendency to perceive beats as falling at regular time intervals. Thus in reading Shelley's line aloud we probably elongate "-vive" and pause at the comma to make up somewhat for the missing syllable. Conversely, we may say "on these" slightly faster, in order to approximate the time one unstressed syllable takes. We are dealing here, however, with psychological time, which is not physically measurable.

It is not necessary that an implied offbeat coincide with a grammatical pause. What is necessary, at least in strict accentual-syllabic verse, is a compensating double offbeat. One of the most famous examples of this pairing of an implied offbeat and a double offbeat, because the effect is repeated, is in the second line quoted below, from Marvell's iambic tetrameter "The Garden" (p. 318):

Annihilating all that's made

o B o B̄o B   o   B

To a green thought in a green shade.

ŏ   B ô B   ŏ B ô B

"To a green thought in a green shade" has generated a great deal of comment by foot prosodists, because in this iambic tetrameter poem the most sensible reading, "to a GREEN THOUGHT in a GREEN SHADE," does not contain a single iamb; rather, the sequence would be pyrrhic, spondee, pyrrhic, spondee (top scansion below). Other prosodists, relying on relative stress and the subordination of adjectives to the nouns that they modify, would give the sequence as trochee, iamb, trochee, iamb (second scansion):

x x | /   / | x x | /   /

\ x | x   / | \ x | x   /

To a green thought in a green shade

It is at moments like these that the benefit of using a scansion for strict accentual-syllabic verse that does not involve the foot becomes obvious. All that beat-offbeat scansion demands of an implied offbeat is that it be compensated for *somewhere* in the same line by a double offbeat.

The pattern of "To a green thought in a green shade," with the double offbeats preceding the implied ones, is the usual one. However, line 72 of Marlowe's iambic pentameter *Hero and Leander* (p. 185), offers back-to-back implied offbeats, with the second one followed by a double offbeat. The scansion that a foot prosodist would probably use, also given, reflects the problem of having to indicate a heavier stress on "my" than on "slack" (as in the Marvell "to" and "in" in the second scansion have to be indicated as being more stressed than "green"):

$$x \setminus \ | \ x \quad / \ | \ / \quad x \ | \ x / \ | \ x \quad /$$
That my slack muse sings of Leander's eyes
$$\breve{o} \quad B \ \hat{o} \ B \ \hat{o} \ B \quad \breve{o} \ B \ o \quad B$$

There are also occasions on which the compensating double offbeat is postponed until later in the line, as in line 15 of Yeats's "The Second Coming" (p. 773):

A gaze blank and pitiless as the sun
$$o \ B \ \hat{o} \ B \quad o \quad B \breve{o} \ \overline{B} \ o \ B$$

In sum, most of the metrical problems presented by poems in iambic meter can be solved by the principles that we have just discussed. Within a strict accentual-syllabic framework we expect a **beat** to be realized by a stressed syllable or by promotion—that is, by an unstressed syllable lying between two other unstressed syllables, or between an unstressed syllable and a line boundary. We expect an **offbeat** to be realized by one unstressed syllable or by demotion—that is, by a stressed syllable lying between two other stressed syllables, or between a line boundary and a stressed syllable. We expect a **double offbeat** only in cases of initial inversion or when it compensates for an implied offbeat.

EXTRA SYLLABLES

There are certain conditions under which extra unstressed syllables may appear in a line without upsetting the strict accentual-syllabic meter. An iambic pentameter line, for example, generally has a **masculine ending**; that is, it ends with a stressed syllable. However, an unstressed syllable at the end of the line, creating an eleven-syllable line with a **feminine ending**, is a common variation:

But this is true, so like was one the other,
$$o \ B o \ B \quad o B \quad o \ B \quad o B o$$
As he imagin'd Hero was his mother
$$o \ B o \ B o \quad B o \ B \quad o \ B \ o$$

(These lines—39 and 40—and the following are from Marlowe's *Hero and Leander*, p. 185.)

More rarely, an unstressed syllable is added (l. 4) before a strong internal pause without upsetting the meter:

$$-s$$
The one Abydos, the other Sestos hight
$$o \ B \quad o \ B \quad \breve{o} \ B o \ B \quad o \ B$$

ELISION

Eleven-syllable lines resulting from the addition of a weak syllable either at line-end or before a caesura are routine in strict iambic pentameter. However, additional weak syllables elsewhere in the line are avoided in the strict form. Most such syllables can be made to vanish and the syllable count preserved by a process known as **elision**, in which suitable syllables can be run together, so that two make one. Actually, the last example can be read as a ten-syllable line if one accepts the common elision of "the" and a following vowel:

The one Abydos, the⌢other Sestos hight

o B o B o   B o B o B

Elision commonly occurs in cases where there is an unstressed vowel before a consonant or where one syllable ends with a vowel and the next begins with one ("the oth-"). Frequently the poet or editor helps by removing the elided vowel and marking it with an apostrophe, as in line 57:

(s)   (s)

Would have allur'd the vent'rous youth of Greece

o   B o B o B o B o B

In the sixteenth century the ending "-ed" was pronounced; however, it was commonly elided to fit the meter. Thus words like "allured" could be given either two or three syllables as needed. An unstressed vowel before "r," as in the middle syllable of "venturous," is especially susceptible to elision. (Some words appear in the elided form so frequently that they have the name **poetic contractions**; e.g., "ne'er" for "never," "e'er" for "ever," and "e'en" for "even.")

A good example of a line in which the vowels ending and starting a syllable have coalesced is provided by *Hero and Leander* again (l. 68):

(s)

That heavenly path with many⌢a curⁱ⌢ous dint

o   B o B o B o B o B

Here "many a" and "curious" have been reduced to two syllables (and "heaven" contracted to "heav'n," although it is not so spelled). Examples of elision abound in all periods, and the best and most enjoyable way to find out which syllables are traditionally elided is to read the poetry.

Trochaic Verse

Trochaic verse is treated in essentially the same way as iambic verse; however, there are some slight differences. Also, beat-offbeat scansion is useful for poems that from the perspective of foot scansion would appear to be mixed iambic and trochaic, leading to some descriptive problems (see "Mixed Duple Verse" below). That is, when a poem mixes lines that maintain an offbeat-beat pattern in with lines that use a beat-offbeat pattern, the key question is whether an essentially falling rhythm is maintained throughout. If so, one is justified in calling the poem trochaic.

Falling rhythm is more than a matter of the beat routinely preceding the offbeat, although this is the most effective tool. It is enhanced by two-syllable words stressed on the first syllable ("TYger TYger, BURNing BRIGHT"); however, it can be countered to some extent by monosyllables, polysyllables, and words in rising rhythm. Without this softening effect the meter can be very insistent indeed. (Incidentally, like stress verse, trochaic verse is especially popular for songs, because the opening beat coincides handily with the musical beat.)

The strictest form of trochaic verse demands feminine line endings, as in these lines (48–49) from Shelley's *Prometheus Unbound* (p. 578):

> Life of Life! thy lips enkindle
> B o B o B o B o
> With their love the breath between them
> B̄ o B o B o B o

More typical, however, is a truncated or "catalectic" line—in which the final unstressed syllable is omitted, so that the ending is masculine—as in the first three seven-syllable lines of Blake's "The Tyger" (p. 490). Note that the falling rhythm is not entirely lost in the eight-syllable fourth line, despite its ability to be scanned as a perfect iambic tetrameter:

> Tyger Tyger, burning bright,
> B o B o B o B
> In the forests of the night;
> B̄ o B o B̄ o B
> What immortal hand or eye,
> B o B o B o B
> Could frame thy fearful symmetry?
> o B o B o B oB̄

Initial inversions are permissible in strict trochaic verse, as in iambic. From Donne's "Song: Go and Catch a Falling Star" (p. 222):

> Though she were true when you met her,
> o B o B ô B o B o
> And last till you write your letter
> o B ôB o B o B o

Despite the opening offbeat in each line, the meter remains strict trochaic tetrameter, where Blake's "Could frame thy fearful symmetry" does not. Blake's line fails to pair an opening offbeat with the implied offbeat needed to correct the meter. (Note that the implied offbeat is delayed in the first line of the Donne.)

Mixed Duple Verse

When dealing with poems in falling rhythm, it can be misleading to label individual lines—e.g., "Could frame thy fearful symmetry"—either "iambic" or "trochaic." Blake's four-stanza "London" (p. 492) is a good case in point. All sixteen lines end with a beat. Nine lines, including most of the first stanza and the whole second stanza, start with an offbeat, are eight syllables long, and could be termed "iambic tetrameter." The remaining seven lines, including the whole third stanza, start with a beat, are seven syllables long, and could be termed "trochaic tetrameter catalectic." Yet there is an underlying rhythmic consistency that would be belied by calling the first two stanzas iambic, the third trochaic, and the fourth a mixture of the two.

More accurately, we may say that the poem as a whole is in four-beat accentual-syllabic verse. We may describe it further by saying that it is in strict duple rhythm, that initial offbeats are optional, and that the rhythm is predominantly falling—thanks in large part to the number of two-syllable words with the stress on the first syllable. (Every line in the poem has at least one such word, and ten lines have two.) Having established this falling rhythm, Blake is able to intensify it with superb effect, most notably in the vivid and horrifying third stanza. Part of its powerful, pounding insistence derives from the omission of all initial offbeats:

How the Chimney-sweepers cry
B o B o B o B
Every blackning Church appalls,
B o B o B o B
And the hapless Soldiers sigh
B̄ o B o B o B
Runs in blood down Palace walls
B o B o Bo B

(Notice too that the key word "appalls," which accurately labels Blake's opinion of contemporary social and economic conditions, gains special force by being the only word in the poem in rising rhythm.) In any case, definition is hardly the issue; what matters is our sensitivity to the rhythmic shifts within the poem as a whole, and Blake is adept at using sound effects to help create meaning. (Look, for instance, at the ways in which the last stanza of "London" uses rhythm and rhyme to pick up from all the preceding stanzas and hammer home the poet's anguish at the piteous plight of England's poor.)

Trochaic verse may indeed be relatively unsubtle compared with iambic—the beat-offbeat pattern can so easily be enhanced by the numerous two-syllable words stressed on the first syllable—but in the hands of a master like Blake it is capable of remarkable effects.

Triple Verse

We have been looking so far at poems in fairly strict duple rising and falling rhythm, in which double offbeats are generally present only to compensate for the omission of an unstressed syllable elsewhere in the line. In triple verse, a double offbeat between beats is the norm, and in the strictest triple verse—**anapestic** (triple rising) and **dactylic** (triple falling)—it is required. Much triple verse, however, mixes single and double offbeats to such an extent that the number of syllables varies considerably from line to line, and the presence of an initial offbeat may be optional as well (so that neither a rising nor a falling rhythm is firmly established). In such cases terms from foot prosody like iambic, anapestic, trochaic, and dactylic lose their usefulness, and we do better to think in terms of the number of beats (a four-beat line? a three-beat one?), the handling of offbeats (always double? occasionally single as well? always present or absent at the start of the line?), and whether the rhythm is generally rising or falling.

Still, where the meter is strict, naming it "anapestic trimeter" or "dactylic tetrameter," for example, can save time. One of the earliest poems in English containing lines in regular triple meter, "Her Triumph" from Ben Jonson's "A Celebration of Charis" (p. 214), alternates anapestic trimeter lines with iambic trimeter (feminine ending) ones in the first part of each stanza:

See the chariot at hand here of Love,
˙ŏ B ŏ B ŏ˙ B
Wherein my lady rideth!
o B o Bo Bo
Each that draws is a swan or a dove,
˙ŏ B ŏ B ŏ B
And well the car Love guideth!
o B o B o Bo

"See" and "Each" in lines 1 and 3 are demoted, as the dot above the offbeat symbol indicates, to fit the metrical pattern of the poem as a whole. (They should still be read with the proper speech emphasis. Notice how much stronger they are than "do" and "have," the words that occupy the equivalent position in the next stanzas.) The demotion rules for triple verse, as formulated by Attridge, are more extensive than those for duple: "A stressed syllable, or an unstressed syllable and a stressed syllable (in either order), or two stressed syllables, may realize an offbeat between two stresses, or after a line-boundary and before a stress." (Remember that an offbeat will usually be formed of two unstressed syllables, however.)

The rhythmic pulse in triple verse is powerful enough to override any stresses that are extraneous to the meter. We see this clearly in the last two lines of Blake's "The Chimney Sweeper," (p. 486), where we are not tempted to add an extra beat between "cold" and "hap-" or between "need" and "harm," despite the stressed words "Tom," "not," and "fear":

> And got with our bags & our brushes to work.
> o   B   ŏ   B   ŏ   B   ŏ   B
>
>   +s   +s   −s +s
> Tho' the morning was cold, Tom was happy & warm,
> ŏ   B   ŏ   B   ˙ŏ   B   ŏ   B
>
>   +s +s   +s   +s
> So if all do their duty, they need not fear harm.
> ŏ   B   ŏ   B ŏ   B   ˙ŏ˙   B

Only in the first of the lines just quoted is a single offbeat substituted for a double, and at the point where it has least effect on the rhythm (the first position in the line). However, single offbeats are frequent enough in the first stanza of the "The Chimney Sweeper"— the third line is in duple rhythm, in fact—to limit the usefulness of calling the meter of this stanza "anapestic tetrameter." "Four-beat triple rising" is probably exact enough:

> When my mother died I was very young,
> ŏ   B o B ŏ   B o B
> And my father sold me while yet my tongue
> ŏ   B o B   ŏ   B   o B
> Could scarcely cry weep weep weep weep.
> o   B   o B ȯ   B   ḃȯ   B
> So your chimneys I sweep & in soot I sleep.
> ŏ   B   ŏ B   ȯ B o B

Among the major modern poets, Thomas Hardy is one of the most partial to triple rhythms. His poem "The Voice" (p. 760) is a rhythmically insistent example of **dactylic** verse. For the first three stanzas it is in quite strict dactylic tetrameter, alternating full lines with truncated ones (the technical name for these is "dactylic tetrameter catalectic"):

> Woman much missed, how you call to me, call to me,
> B   ŏ   B   ŏ   B   ŏ   B   ŏ
> Saying that now you are not as you were
> B   ŏ   B   ŏ   B   ŏ   B
> When you had changed from the one who was all to me,
> B   ŏ   B   ŏ   B   ŏ   B ŏ
> But as at first, when our day was fair.
> B ŏ B   ŏ   B o B

In this first stanza Hardy substitutes a single offbeat for a double one only once ("was" in the fourth line), and the second stanza also has one such substitution, in the same position. (This eighth line also has two examples of elision.) Having set up this minimal variation, Hardy skillfully breaks away from strict dactylic tetrameter in the last line of the third stanza—where there is only one double offbeat (also the last offbeat in the stanza)—and radically changes the rhythm for his fourth stanza. This rhythmic shift helps create two distinct tonal centers. The first three stanzas blend momentary exaltation at the repossession of the beloved woman's presence with doubt as to whether the experience has actually occurred. Then the last stanza distances the vision to such an extent that doubt predominates, with all the man's yearning to commune with his dead love still intact:

> Thus I; faltering forward,
> o B̂oB ŏ   B o
> Leaves around me falling,
> B   o B   o B o
> Wind oozing thin through the thorn from norward,
> B   ˙ŏ   B   ŏ   B   o B o
> And the woman calling.
> ŏ   B o   B o

Few poems in triple verse provide this kind of metrical relief. For example, note how difficult it is to vary significantly the insistent swing set up in the first lines of the chorus from Swinburne's "Atalanta in Calydon" (p. 742), which strongly establishes a four-beat triple meter despite the presence of single offbeats:

> When the hounds of spring are on winter's traces,
> ŏ   B   o   B   ŏ   B o   B o
> The mother of months in meadow or plain
> o   B   ŏ   B   o   B   ŏ   B
> Fills the shadows and windy places
> B   o   B   ŏ   B o B o

Note too that line lengths in the first three stanzas vary from eight to twelve syllables. The lines just quoted have eleven, ten, and nine syllables respectively. The opening lines of the third stanza have eleven, eight, and twelve:

> Where shall we find her, how shall we sing to her,
> B   ŏ   B o B   ŏ   B ŏ
> Fold our hands round her knees, and cling?
> B   o B   ŏ   B o   B
> O that man's heart were as fire and could spring to her
> B   ŏ ˙ B   ŏ B   ŏ   B   ŏ

Also, the position of the beats is variable enough so that in these lines, at least, neither a rising nor a falling rhythm is firmly established. (However, the poem switches to duple rising rhythm after the first twenty-four lines.) The only constant, then, is the number of beats per line, and although the overriding triple flavor and the absence of implied offbeats keep these stanzas from being true stress verse, they are moving in that direction.

See also Jarrell's "The Black Swan" (p. 1007), which is predominantly in four-stress triple verse. (Although it is unrhymed, the repetitions and other sound echoes give an effect of off-rhyme.)

Stress Verse

ORDINARY STRESS VERSE

There is no hard and fast line beyond which a poem stops being in accentual-syllabic duple verse or in triple verse and turns into stress verse. In fact, the terms *stress verse* or *accentual verse* have been used to cover a wide range of poems, and criteria other than the ones used here can easily be defended.

The most obvious examples of stress verse are those in which the number of unstressed syllables (and, if they are present, secondarily stressed syllables) in each line varies considerably, while the number of beats stays the same. However, a poem in which the number of syllables as well as the number of beats stays the same, but in which the position of the beats varies greatly—especially if implied and three-syllable offbeats are present— is certainly closer to stress verse than to either accentual-syllabic or triple verse.

In a good bit of stress verse, the beats will be immediately obvious because they are attached to the only stressed syllables in the line. However, many lines, as in accentual-syllabic and triple verse, have more stresses than beats. Frequently these are the stressed syllables of relatively unimportant words, and so there is no doubt where the beats fall, or one of the stressed syllables is an obvious candidate for demotion.

In other cases, alliteration may reinforce the beat-carrying syllables, and sometimes we simply recognize that there is more than one possibility and, if the author has left no clue, make a tentative choice. On rare occasions there are fewer stresses than beats per line, and we choose the unstressed syllable that can be promoted most easily. And we must always be open to the possibility that neither promotion nor demotion is necessary because the poet has changed the metrical pattern for that particular line.

I touched briefly on two-stress, three stress, and four-stress verse on pp. 1143–44. Here it is worth looking at more extensive examples from the work of Skelton, Yeats, Auden, and Blake; at Hopkins's idiosyncratic form of stress verse, sprung rhythm; and at medieval alliterative stress verse.

Skelton's "To Mistress Margaret Hussey" (p. 127) uses two-beat lines of four, five, and six syllables brilliantly in some dozen different patterns (if we count promotions and demotions), such as:

> Merry Margaret
> B o B ŏ
> As midsummer flower,
> o B ŏ B
> Gentle as falcon . . .
> B ŏ B o
> With solace and gladness . . .
> o B ŏ B o
> Far, far passing . . .
> B ó B o
> As patient and as still . . .
> o B ŏ B
> Coliander . . .
> B̄ o B o

The poem's rhythmic virtuosity and playfulness—as when Skelton piles up epithets that have the same pattern ("So joyously, / So maidenly, / So womanly"; "Coliander, / Sweet pomander, / Good Cassander")—help counteract the doggerel effect of the short lines and of rhymes coming so closely together. The result is the most quickly moving and lighthearted tribute to a lady in the whole tradition.

Blake, Yeats, and Auden—the last-named a master at picking up and modifying not only Yeats's meters but practically everyone else's—have some notable poems that employ three-beat rhymed stress verse for extended passages. The following three selections are from, respectively, Blake's "The Human Abstract" (p. 492), Yeats's "Easter, 1916" (p. 771), and Auden's "September 1, 1939" (p. 975):

Pity would be no more,
B ŏ   B̄ o B
If we did not make somebody Poor:
ŏ   B o B ŏ   B
And Mercy no more could be,
o   B ŏ   B o   B
If all were as happy as we
o B   ŏ   B ŏ   B

I have passed with a nod of the head
ŏ   B   ŏ B ŏ   B
Or polite meaningless words,
ŏ B ô B   ŏ   B
Or have lingered awhile and said
ŏ   B   ŏ B o   B
Polite meaningless words
o B ô B   ŏ   B

Waves of anger and fear
B   o B ŏ   B
Circulate over the bright
B ŏ B ŏ   B
And darkened lands of the earth,
o   B o   B   ŏ   B
Obsessing our private lives;
o B   ŏ   B o B
The unmentionable odour of death
ŏ   B ŏ   B ŏ   B
Offends the September night.
o B   ŏ   B o B

The possibility of varying the number of syllables and position of beats in each line—or of keeping them the same over a stretch of lines—is a major expressive resource for poets writing in stress verse. Thus Yeats signals a marked change in tone in "Easter, 1916" when he switches from the thoughtfully slow-moving and varied sixteen lines that compose the opening verse unit to the quick-fire sureness of the regular iambic trimeter in the next nine lines, which recall characteristics of the rebellion's heroes and heroines. Or Auden can give considerable prominence to the remarkable ten-syllable line "The unmentionable odour of death" by sandwiching it between sharper seven-syllable ones. Also, as in free verse—which is most closely allied to stress verse—stress verse can accommodate a word such as "unmentionable" without distorting it, by promotion or elision, to fit one of the other meters. See also Bishop's four-stress sestina (p. 1000).

SPRUNG RHYTHM

Hopkins, it should be remembered, although famous for the form of stress verse he called "sprung rhythm," also wrote in accentual-syllabic verse. The two should not be confused. (In his poems in accentual-syllabic verse, the device he called "counterpointing" depends on inversions and delayed compensation.) Sprung rhythm is an unusual form of stress verse in that it involves extensive demotion. Hopkins not only demotes stressed syllables in ways familiar from accentual-syllabic and triple-verse practice, but cheerfully demotes them in what would ordinarily be considered an unassailable beat position: a stressed syllable lying between two unstressed ones. He gets away with this through his concept of the "outride," essentially an unstressed syllable (or syllables) treated as extrametrical and analogous to the occasional extra weak syllable before an internal pause in accentual-syllabic verse. Thus triple offbeats are a familiar characteristic of his poetry.

In reciting a poem in sprung rhythm, we should be sure that the beats emerge clearly; however, as always, demoted syllables retain a degree of stress. Therefore Hopkins's lines are among the most heavily stressed—and, because of the presence of triple offbeats, among the longest—in English poetry. (His extensive use of compounds with a strong second member—"dawn-drawn," "bow-bend," "blue-bleak"—also contributes to the heavy stressing of his lines.)

Hopkins left notes to help with the scansion of his unorthodox sprung-rhythm poems, and my tentative reading of his five-beat modified Petrarchan sonnet "The Windhover" depends to some extent on his markings of outrides. These are: in line 2, "dau*phin*" and "Fal*con*"; 3, "roll*ing*," "*him*"; 4, "*there*"; 6, "*heel*"; 8, "achieve *of*"; 11, "love*lier*," "dan*gerous*"; 12, "*of it*." Because of his unfamiliar practice, I have marked the stress patterns of the first few lines and of additional selected lines. (I have also placed a dot below the three-syllable offbeat symbol—ŏ—when the middle syllable has been demoted.)

```
 -s +s    -s +s -s   +s -s    +s -s  +s
I caught this morning morning's minion, king-
 o B    o  B o   B o    B o   B

 -s   -s +s -s    +s  -s  +s -s +s   -s   +s-s -s  -s +s-s
dom of daylight's dauphin, dapple-dawn-drawn Falcon, in his riding
 ŏ  B o   B    ŏ   B   o   B   ŏ  Bo

 -s  -s  +s-s  +s-s-s  -s +s   -s  +s -s +s  -s   +s-s
Of the rolling level underneath him steady air, and striding
 ŏ  B   ŏ  B̄ o B    ŏ   B  o   Bo

High there, how he rung upon the rein of a wimpling wing
 B    ŏ    B   ŏ   B  ŏ B o B   o   B

In his ecstasy! then off, off forth on swing,
 ŏ  B  ŏ    B ôB ôB  o   B

As a skate's heel sweeps smooth on a bow-bend: the hurl and gliding
 ŏ  B    ŏ·    B    ŏ B    ŏ  B  o  B o

Rebuffed the big wind. My heart in hiding
 o  B  o  B ô B    o   B  o B o

Stirred for a bird, — the achieve of, the mastery of the thing!
 B    ŏ   B    ŏ  B   ŏ  B    ŏ   B

 +s   +s -s -s   +s -s  -s +s  -s  +s   +s    +s    +s
Brute beauty and valour and act, oh, air, pride, plume, here
 ò  B  ŏ   B   ŏ   B   ŏ·  B   ò   B
```

+s −s   −s   −s +s   −s   +s   −s   +s   +s −s +s −s
Buckle! AND the fire that breaks from thee then, a billion

˘ŏ   B̄   o   B   o   B   ŏ˙   B o B o

Times told lovelier, more dangerous, O my chevalier!

B   ȯ   B   ŏ̆   B   ŏ̆   B   ŏ B

No wonder of it: shéer plód makes plough down sillion

o   B   ŏ̆   B ô B   o   B   o B o

Shine, and blue-bleak embers, ah my dear,

B   o   B   o B o   B   o B

Fall, gall themselves, and gash gold-vermilion.

ȯ   B   o B   o   B ô B   o B o

It is amazing that in a five-beat poem in which, for example, a line can have up to eight stresses (see the thirteen-syllable ninth line), Hopkins should indicate additional beat-carrying stresses. In two cases, however, it looks as if he does. Because of the first outride in the third line ("roll*ing*"), "level" would appear to have offbeat status, and so the first syllable of "underneath," as well as the last, must carry a beat. Then the capitalization of "and" in line 10 suggests that it carries a beat, despite the necessity of demoting the first syllable of the adjacent "buckle" to stay within the limit of five beats per line. (To repeat: these are only conjectured readings for lines 3 and 10; for example, "and" in line 10 might be an extrametrical sixth beat.)

In both cases the unusual emphasis would serve as a guide to meaning as well as performance. The third line's lilt and flow, balancing "ROLLing level" and "-NEATH him steady," does seem to correspond to the graceful, undulating sweep of the falcon's flight. Too, without the special attention given to "and" in line 10, its pivotal character could be missed (and note the subtle reinforcement later in the line by the repeated "n" sound in "then" and "billion"). For it is at this instant that realization dawns of the parallel between the manifest glory of what is after all a mere bird ("*brute* beauty") and the hidden glory of the divine in human form.

ALLITERATIVE STRESS VERSE

Old English poetry

After dealing with the dizzyingly prolific stress patterns of Hopkins's verse, we can approach two special cases of stress verse, those of Old English and fourteenth-century Middle English unrhymed **alliterative verse**, with a certain insouciance. Hopkins's sprung-rhythm poems are highly alliterative; in just the first two lines of "The Windhover" he alliterates heavily on "m" and "d," on "k" ("caught/ king"), and to some extent on "f." However, such alliteration is not necessary to the meter. In both Old English and fourteenth-century alliterative verse it is.

Because the "English" of a thousand years ago is so unfamiliar to the modern speaker, the first selections in the anthology (pp. 3–15)—the epic *Beowulf*, the elegiac "Seafarer" and "Wife's Lament," and the panegyric or praise poem "Brunanburg"—are of necessity given only in translation. However, Old Germanic alliterative meter, of which Old English verse is one example, did not suddenly vanish with the Norman conquest and the rise in importance of French and Latin versification. Because it contributed to the development of English verse as we know it today, we should be aware of its main metrical features.

The typical Old English poem is nonstanzaic and unrhymed (although a "riming" poem has survived, and rhyme does occur occasionally within the line). Most lines are divided in two, and the resulting half-lines or **hemistichs** are syntactically independent, so that sentences and clauses, especially late in the period, end even more frequently in the middle of the line than at its end. Each half-line generally has two main stresses, with a variable number of unstressed (and secondarily stressed) syllables, and half-lines are linked by alliteration of the stressed syllables. Marking only the main accents in the traditional manner (and putting the alliterating letters in boldface), here are lines 14-17 of "Seafarer" (p. 11):

hu ic **earm**cearig   **is**cealdne sae

winter wunade   wraeccan lastum,

winemaegum bidroren,

bihongen **h**rimgicelum;   **h**aegl scurum fleag.

The third line is lacking a half-line, but in the usual pattern, the first stressed syllable of the second half-line alliterates with one or two of the stressed syllables in the first half-line. (Alliteration normally refers to the repetition of identical-sounding initial consonants: "w" in the second line quoted above, "h" in the fourth; however, in alliterative verse, the absence of an initial consonant—"ic," "earm-," "is-"—serves the same purpose, so that in effect any vowel alliterates with any other.)

Ezra Pound's translation of "Seafarer" captures much of the flavor of the Old English original:

List how I, care-wretched, on ice-cold sea,
Weathered the winter, wretched outcast
Deprived of my kinsmen;
Hung with hard ice-flakes, where hail-scur flew

Middle English alliterative verse

Although the alliterative meter went into decline after the Norman Conquest, a Middle English form appeared in the fourteenth century. It is represented in the anthology by substantial selections from *Piers Plowman* (p. 108) and from *Sir Gawain and the Green Knight* (p. 111), where a "bob and wheel" stanza (see p. 1155) separates the long-line alliterative passages.

Here is the opening of *Piers Plowman* with only structural, not optional, alliteration in boldface—and note that the apparent end rhyme "were / here" is fortuitous, not structural:

In a **s**omer **s**eson   whenne **s**ofte was the **s**unne

I **sh**op me into a **shr**oud   as I a **sh**ep were,

In **h**abite as an **h**ermite   un**h**oly of werkes,

Wente **w**ide in this **w**orld   **w**ondres to here.

The bare minimum for a metrical line in Middle English alliterative verse, as in Old English, is two half-lines of two beats each, in which the syllable occupying the first beat position of the second half-line has the same initial sound as one of the syllables in beat position in the first half-line. (There are some rare exceptions.) Most often, the repeating sound will be a consonant or consonant cluster (the usual meaning of "alliteration") —

"s," "sh," "h," "w" in the first four lines of *Piers*. However, as in Old English, the absence of an initial consonant in the stressed syllables in beat position also has metrical significance. Thus on occasion—more rarely than in Old English—any vowel "alliterates" with any other, as in line 94 of *Gawain*, "Of alderes, of armes, of other aventurus." "H" may alliterate with vowels as well, as in line 136, "There hales in at the halle dor an aghlich mayster."

In Middle English alliterative verse it is usual for both stressed syllables in beat position in the first half-line to alliterate with the first stress in the second half-line; and sometimes (as in the first line of *Piers*) the second stress in the second half-line alliterates as well. Whether any additional stresses—these are almost always in the first half-line—alliterate with the main beats is structurally irrelevant. Naturally, such additional alliteration has an aesthetic impact; line 17 of *Piers*, "A fair feeld ful of folk fand I there-betwene," is even more memorable than the first line. Another extrametrical effect is the alliteration of unstressed syllables with the main beats or with each other, and occasionally the alliterating sound will be carried into the next line. (See "d" in lines 15 and 16 of *Piers* and "h" in lines 27 and 28; "sh" in line 2 is not the same sound as "s" in line 1.) Note that extra weak syllables have been added and that the meter has begun to take on a rising iambic-anapestic rhythm that has a very different effect from the more strongly stressed falling rhythm of Old English poetry.

Modern alliterative verse

Twentieth-century poets have also drawn on the effects of Old English and Middle English alliterative verse, without necessarily hewing to the metrical rules. Because it is unrhymed, it can be fitted easily into a free-verse context, where it sounds much more like itself than in Hopkins's verse. An archaic flavor can be imparted to the most modern free verse by the use of heavy alliteration along with obsolete words and, for maximum effect, the sparse syntax and reliance on an opening beat typical of Old English poetry. Pound's Canto I (p. 859) provides a superb example. Auden's *The Age of Anxiety* (not excerpted in the anthology) is the longest twentieth-century alliterative work in English. From its first lines, however, the vocabulary and intimate, selfconsciously questioning tone tell us that we are in modern times:

> My deuce, my double, my dear image
>
> Is it lively there, that land of glass
>
> Where song is a grimace, sound logic
>
> A suite of gestures? You seem amused.

Even when alliterative stress verse is not being consciously mimicked, as here, one finds throughout the centuries techniques related to it used for powerful effects—the mid-line break, heavy alliteration, or juxtaposed strong stresses. In general, in reading the poems in the anthology, and watching how an accentual-syllabic norm gradually asserted itself in the mainstream of English poetry, one should keep in mind that variations from the norm can frequently be seen as representing a return to—or at least a cognate version of—elements present in the earliest English verse.

For example: rhyme prevails in the English tradition. Yet some of the greatest verse, especially Elizabethan blank verse and modern free verse, is—like the Old English—unrhymed. In accentual-syllabic verse, the line tends to be not only metrically but also syntactically autonomous. Yet in Shakespeare and other Elizabethan dramatists, and in Milton, we find something like the flexibility of Old English phrasing.

In accentual-syllabic verse the number of syllables in each line and the number and position of stresses are highly predictable. Yet superb verse has been written through the centuries—from folk ballads to the highly wrought verse of Coleridge, Hopkins, Yeats, and free-verse practitioners—that relies on stress in a way similar to the Old English tradition.

Syllabic Verse

Because English is a stress language, it is natural for poets to base their meters on the perceptible differences in intensity between syllables within the word, or between words within the phrase. However, poets also control other aspects of sound besides stress (it should be noted that stress is not simply a matter of loudness but of pitch and syllable length as well) to create subsidiary rhythms. Most important are the number of syllables, their length, and the way in which internal pauses are handled. (See pp. 1147–49 for a discussion of syllabic weight and pause.)

In accentual-syllabic verse, of course, the number of syllables is set; but poems exist in syllabic verse in which only the number of syllables in each line is determined, and the number and position of stresses vary. In languages that are relatively unstressed, like French and Italian, the syllable can be used as the main metrical component; but in English, especially if the verse is unrhymed, few people can distinguish pure syllabic verse (in which the disposition and number of accents are completely uncontrolled) from free verse. However, when the poet distributes stresses and sound echoes skillfully—as Auden and Moore do—syllabic poems have a pleasingly different rhythm from that of accentual-syllabic or stress verse. Also, the poet can easily regularize the number of stresses and their positions in each line and so provide at will the beat-offbeat pattern of accentual-syllabic verse. (Indeed, especially when such poems rhyme, we hear them as loosened accentual-syllabic verse, this time with the accents rather than the syllables providing the variety.)

Auden's "Prime" (p. 977) is a sophisticated example of syllabic verse. It alternates lines of nine and seven syllables; however, Auden's syllable count is maintained only by the strenuous use of a form of elision in which two syllables are elided into one for purposes of the syllable count, but meant to be pronounced fully, as indicated by the scansion below:

> Simultaneously, as soundlessly,
> ŏ B ŏ B ŏ
> Spontaneously, suddenly
> o B ŏ B ŏ
> As, at the vaunt of the dawn, the kind
> B ŏ B ŏ B o B
> Gates of the body fly open
> B ŏ B ŏ B o
> To its world beyond, the gates of the mind,
> ŏ B oB o B ŏ B
> The horn gate and the ivory gate
> o B ôB ŏ B ŏ B

Obviously the poem is moving constantly toward and away from accentual-syllabic, triple, and stress verse patterns, as free verse does, and it is these rhythmic patterns, not the syllable count, that we notice. (This is especially true because Auden is, whatever the official count, varying the number of syllables we actually hear in each line; his elision is a mental, not a sonal construct.) We need to make a certain effort not to read the poem as being in four-beat stress verse, but it is worthwhile to attend more closely to phrasal stress patterns and less to the relative strength of adjacent syllables and to considerations of which unstressed syllables could be be "promoted"—that is, felt as maintaining a regular beat (e.g., the secondarily stressed syllables of "simultaneously," "soundlessly," "spontaneously," and "suddenly.")

In nonaccentual syllabic verse, as in free verse—and to a lesser extent in stress verse— the rhythm of each line should be considered relatively independently from that of the other lines. This necessity is particularly evident when adjacent lines have even greater differences in their numbers of syllables, as in Marianne Moore's "The Mind Is an Enchanting Thing" (p. 880), an example of stanzaic syllabic verse, which rhymes axabbx. (Each stanza, including the one quoted below, repeats the 6, 5, 4, 6, 7, 9 pattern.) With no predictably smooth alternation of stressed and unstressed syllables to help, and no demand on us to find a certain number of beats in each line, our perception of which syllables constitute beats depends more heavily on phrasing and sonal clues other than stress patterns than it does in accentual-syllabic and triple verse scansion.

Syllabic verse thus allows for considerable flexibility of interpretation, both of meaning and performance. For example, where performance is concerned, "-shawl" in the third line below, because it rhymes with "awl," could be given greater stress; I happen to think that the humorously ungainly quality of the mind as wet, flightless bird is better served if the rhyme is awkward as well. Or from the point of view of meaning, perhaps "along" in the sixth line should receive no stress, so that the emphasis on "walks" will be greater, thus reinforcing the ludicrously poignant image of an earthbound bird:

> like the apteryx-awl
> ŏ B ŏ B
> as a beak, or the
> ŏ B ŏ
> kiwi's rain-shawl
> B o B o
> of haired feathers, the mind
> o B ôB ŏ B
> feeling its way as though blind,
> B ŏ B ŏ B
> walks along with its eyes on the ground.
> B oB ŏ B ŏ B

Taking this stanza in isolation, except for the repeated rhyme-sounds that would traditionally disqualify it from being called free verse, the lines have free verse's flexibility. Stresses are in variable positions and vary from one to four, and the number of syllables varies from four to nine. And like much free verse, the lines move toward and away from standard metrical norms. (Note how the triple verse flavor of the next-to-last line spills over to the last, so that we are tempted to ignore a stress on "walks" and read it as anapestic trimeter.) There are no effects that we have not encountered previously, but the proportions are different, for variation is the norm.

Coda: Other Possible "Meters"

Non-traditional meters other than the syllabic have been less extensively explored. Theoretically, any quality of sound can be metered or measured. One could, for example, set up the same kinds of patterns found in syllabic verse but count words instead of syllables (one could call this technique **isoverbal**), and indeed some poets have experimented with such a word-count prosody. (Note the pattern of Williams's "The Red Wheelbarrow," p. 839.)

Or syllables can be fairly arbitrarily named "long" or "short" and dispersed in some intellectually apprehensible pattern, as poets writing in English have done in attempting to reproduce classical quantitative meters. Or certain sound qualities can be repeated in subtle patterns; for example, so many instances of "f" in a line, or of "f" and cognate sounds (v, m, b, p), or of back vowels, or of front vowels. Or other subtle progressions of pitch and timbre and length and quality can be set up, or the same word repeated at the beginning of every line, or each line given the same number of phrases or clauses, etc. Anything that can be counted can by definition be considered as providing the basis for a metric, but it is intellectually and practically more defensible to relegate sound elements that are unrelated to stress patterns or to syllable count to the nonmetrical aspect of prosody.

FURTHER READING

Numerous books and articles have been written on the theory and history of English prosody, and the following list is only an introduction to a vital and busy field.

The most comprehensive reference book is the *Princeton Encyclopedia of Poetry and Poetics*, enlarged edition (Princeton: Princeton University Press, 1974) edited by Alex Preminger and others. A more specialized reference work, the new *Princeton Handbook of Poetic Terms* (1986), should also be of considerable assistance.

Babette Deutsch's *Poetry Handbook: a Dictionary of Terms*, 4th edition (New York: Harper and Row, 1982) is concise and sensible, with useful examples.

Karl Shapiro's and Robert Beum's *A Prosody Handbook* (New York: Harper and Row, 1965) covers the essential prosodic topics on a chapter-by-chapter basis.

Jakob Schipper's *A History of English Versification* (Folcroft, Pa.: Folcroft Library, 1973; reprint of 1910 Oxford edition) is our most valuable compendium of technical information on meter, rhyme, and stanza. A translated and abridged version of his three-volume *Englische Metrik*, it unfortunately lacks an index but offers an analysed table of contents. It is far superior to George Saintsbury's better-known *Historical Manual of English Prosody* (London: Macmillan, 1910) and three-volume *A History of English Prosody from the Twelfth Century to the Present*, 2nd edition (London: Macmillan, 1923).

An important book on metrics—because particularly responsive to poets' flexible handling of meter—is Derek Attridge's *The Rhythms of English Poetry* (London: Longman, 1982), the source for the beat-offbeat method of scansion discussed in the metrical supplement.

For a complete overview of the field, from Anglo-Saxon times to the present, Terry V.F. Brogan's annotated bibliography, *English Versification, 1570–1980* (Baltimore: Johns Hopkins University Press, 1981), is invaluable.

ALSO:

Attridge, Derek. *Well-Weighed Syllables: Elizabethan Verse in Classical Metres*. Cambridge: Cambridge University Press, 1974.

Gross, Harvey. *Sound and Form in Modern Poetry: A Study of Prosody from Thomas Hardy to Robert Lowell.* Ann Arbor: University of Michigan Press, 1964.

Halle, Morris, and Samuel J. Keyser. *English Stress: Its Form, Its Growth, and Its Role in Verse.* New York: Harper and Row, 1971.

Hartman, Charles O. *Free Verse: An Essay on Prosody.* Princeton: Princeton University Press, 1980.

Kiparsky, Paul. "The Rhythmic Structure of English Verse." *Linguistic Inquiry* 8 (1977): 189–247.

Malof, Joseph. *A Manual of English Meters.* Westport, Conn.: Greenwood Press, 1978 (reprint of 1970 University of Indiana edition).

McAuley, James. *Versification: A Short Introduction.* East Lansing, Mich.: Michigan State University Press, 1966.

Smith, Egerton. *The Principles of English Metre.* Westport, Conn.: Greenwood Press, 1970 (reprint of 1923 Oxford edition).

Thompson, John. *The Founding of English Metre.* London: Routledge and Kegan Paul, 1961.

Turco, Lewis. *The New Book of Forms: A Handbook of Poetics.* Hanover, NH: University Press of New England, 1986.

Wimsatt, W.K., Jr., and Monroe C. Beardsley. "The Concept of Meter: An Exercise in Abstraction." *PMLA* 74 (1959): 585–98.

Wimsatt, W.K., Jr., ed. *Versification: Major Language Types. Sixteen Essays.* New York: New York University Press for MLA, 1970.

Woods, Susanne. *Natural Emphasis: English Versification from Chaucer to Dryden.* San Marino, Calif.: Huntington Library, 1985.

Versification Index

INDEX